# FOCUS ON  MAKING

The textbook introduces an *ethical framework* in Chapter 1 and then asks students to use the framework when addressing a real-world ethical dilemma in each chapter.

| Page | Organization and Topic |
|------|------------------------|
| 19 | **Bausch & Lomb**—Sales tactics and financial reporting |
| 47 | **Merck**—Advertising by drug companies |
| 106 | Temporary labor versus regular employees—Economic and social issues |
| 149 | **State of Arizona**—Public financial support of vehicle purchases and the environment |
| 192 | U.S. government defense contractor—Allocation of underapplied overhead cost between government and commercial contracts |
| 239 | **The Boeing Company**—Deferral of aircraft program costs and value of **McDonnell-Douglas** acquisition |
| 279 | **ABC consultants**—Responsibilities for quality services and client benefits |
| 318 | **Tampa General Hospital**—Estimates and accounting systems for measuring organ acquisition costs |
| 354 | Cement kilns—Disposal of hazardous waste |
| 388 | College and work settings—Individual responsibility for reporting time delays to a work team |
| 438 | Employee responsibility for identifying and reducing workplace inefficiencies |
| 480 | **GlaxoSmithKline** and **World Health Organization**—Charging lower pharmaceutical prices in developing countries than in developed countries |
| 531 | Gasoline stations and rental car companies—Prices following terrorist events of September 11, 2001 |
| 567 | **Bristol-Myers Squibb** and **Harley-Davidson**—Accidental versus intentional overproduction of inventory; company policies to prevent channel stuffing |
| 605 | **New York Stock Exchange**—Board of directors oversight of pay for CEO Richard Grasso |
| 653 | Canadian **Chartered Management Accountants, Multiple Sclerosis Society of Canada, Canadian Society of Association Executives, American Red Cross,** and **Ontario Physical and Health Education Association**—Efficient and effective use of resources in not-for-profit organizations |

## ETHICS ETHICS HOMEWORK PROBLEMS

Each chapter includes at least one homework problem that asks students to apply *ethical decision making*. Each problem contains ambiguities, conflicts of interest, and value judgments.

| Problem | Organization and Topic |
|---------|------------------------|
| 1.25 | Student collaboration on homework and professor policy in a college course |
| 1.26 | Workplace pressure to falsify time report in city government |
| 1.28 | Ethical skills needed by entry level accountants |
| 1.30 | **Wal-Mart** and **Proctor & Gamble** consumer research on RFID technology |
| 2.34 | Timeliness and quality of budget information for a family-owned business |
| 3.35 | Biases in business plan for a travel agency |
| 4.30 | Foreign versus domestic product |
| 4.31 | Conflict of interest in outsourcing decision. |
| 4.35 | **Texas Society of CPAs** and **AICPA**; CPA responsibilities for quality of work and confidentiality for outsourcing of income tax return preparation |
| 5.27 | Accounting for sale of scrap by construction contractor |
| 6.34 | Britain's **Health and Safety Commission** targets and risks; responsibilities and company goals for workplace health and safety |
| 7.38 | Corporate and governmental responsibilities for environmental accounting reports; compare U.S. and Japanese companies such as **Kodak** and **Canon** |
| 8.27 | **Better Business Bureau** guidelines, not-for-profit food organization cost allocations to administration, fund raising, and programs |
| 8.31 | Allocation of administration and public relations costs under professional basketball player contract |
| 8.32 | Consider government audits of **Stanford** and other universities; evaluate accountant responsibility for maximizing cost reimbursements |
| 9.32 | Joint cost decision and company-wide versus division manager interests |
| 9.34 | Mad cow disease and the use of animal by-products in livestock feed |
| 10.21 | Responsibility of new staff accountant in CPA firm to seek help from supervisor |
| 11.30 | Student behavior within college course grading system |
| 12.33 | Use of cost-benefit analysis by **Ford Motor Company** for the Pinto |
| 13.31 | Price collusion between two owners of gasoline stations in a small town |
| 13.34 | Ethics of reverse-engineering by **Caterpillar** and **Komatsu**; social costs and benefits of reducing reliance on manufacturing labor |
| 14.26 | Manager incentives for channel stuffing |
| 15.28 | SEC settlement costs paid by **Xerox** and its insurance companies on behalf of Xerox officers |
| 16.33 | Controversy over working conditions in low-cost international outsource factories by companies such as **Nike** |

# eGrade Plus

## www.wiley.com/college/eldenburg
## Based on the Activities You Do Every Day

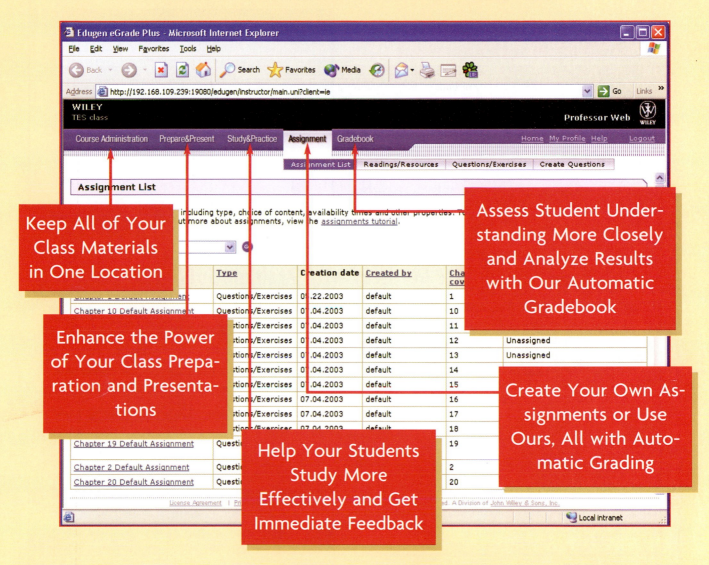

Keep All of Your Class Materials in One Location

Enhance the Power of Your Class Preparation and Presentations

Help Your Students Study More Effectively and Get Immediate Feedback

Assess Student Understanding More Closely and Analyze Results with Our Automatic Gradebook

Create Your Own Assignments or Use Ours, All with Automatic Grading

**All the content and tools you need, all in one location, in an easy-to-use browser format.**

**Choose the resources you need, or rely on the arrangement supplied by us.**

Now, many of Wiley's textbooks are available with eGrade Plus, a powerful online tool that provides a completely integrated suite of teaching and learning resources in one easy-to-use website. eGrade Plus integrates Wiley's world-renowned content with media, including a multimedia version of the text, PowerPoint slides, and more. Upon adoption of eGrade Plus, you can begin to customize your course with the resources shown here.

**See for yourself!**

**Go to www.wiley.com/college/egradeplus for an online demonstration of this powerful new software.**

# Students,
# eGrade Plus Allows You to:

## Study More Effectively

## Get Immediate Feedback When You Practice on Your Own

eGrade Plus problems link directly to relevant sections of the **electronic book content,** so that you can review the text while you study and complete homework online. Additional resources include **student quizzes** and other problem-solving resources.

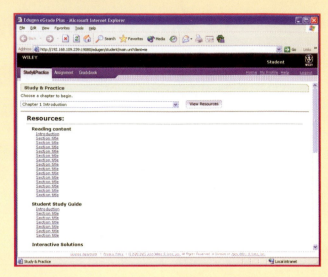

## Complete Assignments / Get Help with Problem Solving

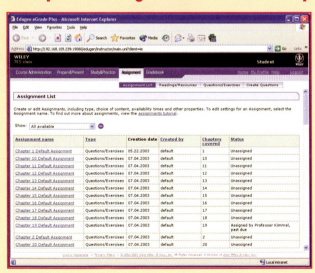

An **"Assignment"** area keeps all your assigned work in one location, making it easy for you to stay on task. In addition, many homework problems contain a **link** to the relevant section of the **electronic book,** providing you with a text explanation to help you conquer problem-solving obstacles as they arise.

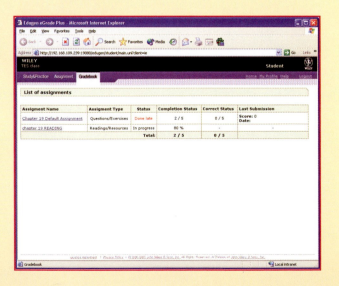

## Keep Track of How You're Doing

A **Personal Gradebook** allows you to view your results from past assignments at any time.

# Cost Management

▶ Measuring,
Monitoring,
and
Motivating
Performance

**Leslie G. Eldenburg, PhD**
*University of Arizona*

**Susan K. Wolcott, PhD, CPA, CMA**
*WolcottLynch Associates*

## A Musical Note

If you think about it, jazz music is a good analogy for cost accounting. Jazz is an enticing mix of *structure, interaction, context,* and *creativity.* These are also the core ingredients of this text.

*Cost Management* has a unifying *structure* to help students approach, understand, and apply accounting information. It analyzes, the *interaction,* or exchange, between accounting information and sound decision making. It shows students the importance of the business *context,* the understanding of which is critical to cost management and high quality business decisions. And it helps students develop the *creativity* needed for good decision-making, stimulating them to think about accounting problems and problem-solving in more complex ways.

**WILEY**

John Wiley & Sons, Inc.

## DEDICATION

**W**e dedicate this textbook to Cindy Lynch, whose ideas stimulated us to write a student-oriented book with the specific objective of using cost accounting content and cognitive development theory to improve critical thinking skills. Cindy introduced Susan to cognitive development research literature, and together they developed and refined the *Steps for Better Thinking* model. Cindy helped us at the beginning of our work on the textbook. We sorely missed her help after her untimely death in early 2001. This textbook memorializes her life and work.

*Publisher* Susan Elbe
*Associate Publisher* Jay O'Callaghan
*Senior Editor* Mark Bonadeo
*Senior Development Editor* Nancy Perry
*Project Editor* Ed Brislin
*Assistant Editor* Brian Kamins
*Marketing Manager* Steven Herdegen
*Media Editor* Allie K. Morris
*Senior Production Editor* Lari Bishop
*Art Director* Dawn L. Stanley
*Senior Illustration Editor* Anna Melhorn
*Senior Photo Editor* Sara Wight
*Art Studio* Electra Graphics
*Text Design* Delgado and Company, Inc.
*Cover Design* Norm Christensen
*Cover Photo* © Markus Amon/Stone/Getty Images

This book was set in 10/12 Times New Roman by Matrix Publishing and was printed by VonHoffmann Corp. The cover was printed by VonHoffmann Corp.

This book is printed on acid free paper. ∞

To order books or for customer service please, call 1-800-CALL WILEY (225-5945).

***Library of Congress Cataloging in Publication Data:***
Eldenburg, Leslie.
    Cost management : measuring, monitoring, and motivating performance / Leslie
Eldenburg, Susan K. Wolcott.
      p.  cm.
    Includes index.
    ISBN 0-471-20549-4 (cloth)
    1. Cost accounting. 2. Managerial accounting. I. Wolcott, Susan K. II. Title.
  HF5686.C8E453 2004
  658.15′52—dc22                             2004042295

Printed in the United States of America

10 9 8 7 6 5 4 3 2 1

# About the Authors

Leslie G. Eldenburg, PhD, is a McCoy-Rogers Fellow at the University of Arizona. She has also taught at California State University–Fresno. She received her MBA and PhD from the University of Washington. She passed the CPA exam in 1985 and has taught review courses for the CMA exam. Leslie has served as faculty advisor for an IMA student chapter and for the Multicultural Business Student Association. She received a number of awards recognizing her activities in teaching, student support, and as faculty advisor for student organizations. She is an active member of the American Accounting Association (AAA), the Management Section of the AAA, the IMA, and the Healthcare Financial Management Association. She has served on and chaired numerous committees within these organizations and currently is the Management Section's Secretary-Treasurer and co-chairs its Doctoral Consortium Committee. Before becoming an academic, she worked in hospital finance at Virginia Mason Hospital in Seattle, Washington. Her research interests include issues in healthcare and hospital accounting, and she has published in *The Accounting Review, The Journal of Accounting and Economics, The Journal of Medical Decision Making, The Journal of Corporate Finance, The International Journal of Accounting, Information Systems Research, Healthcare Financial Management,* and *Controller's Quarterly.* In addition, she currently serves on several editorial boards. Leslie has also co-authored chapters in *Health Care Administration, The Encyclopedia of Accounting,* and the forthcoming *Handbook of Management Accounting Research,* and *Handbook of Cost Accounting.*

Susan K. Wolcott, PhD, CPA, CMA, is an educational consultant with WolcottLynch Associates. Her consulting practice takes her to conferences and campuses around the world where she works with faculty and programs to support critical thinking development, competency assessment, and curriculum innovation. Her publications include *Developing Critical Thinking Skills: The Key to Professional Competencies,* an American Accounting Association Academic Partners Toolkit. She chaired the AICPA Core Competency Framework Curriculum Evaluation Task Force, developed the Taxonomy of AICPA Core Competencies, and authored numerous assessment materials for the AICPA Educational Competency Assessment Web site. Additional publications can be found in *Issues in Accounting Education, Journal of Accounting Education, Assessment Update, IDEA Center Papers,* and other journals. She is a member of the AAA, IMA, IIA, and Washington Society of CPAs, where she participates on the Consulting Services Committee. She previously served on the board of directors, as President of the Educational Foundation, and as Chair of the Education Committee of the Colorado Society of CPAs. She also served as Vice President of Membership for the Portland-Columbia Chapter of the IMA and was a program committee member and presenter for the AACSB Outcomes Assessment Seminar. She was previously on the accounting faculty at the University of Denver, where she received the MBA Core Diamond Award for teaching. She regularly teaches CPA and CMA review courses, and she has also taught courses at the University of Washington, Helsinki School of Economics—Mikkeli, Instituto de Empresa in Madrid, and J. L. Kellogg Graduate School of Management at Northwestern University. She worked in public accounting for ten years, including three years with Coopers & Lybrand (Portland, Oregon). She holds PhD and MS degrees in Accounting and Information Systems from Northwestern University and a BBA in Accounting from the University of Portland.

# Preface

*Cost Management: Measuring, Monitoring, and Motivating Performance* was written to help students learn to appropriately apply cost accounting methods in a variety of organizational settings. To achieve this goal, students must also develop professional competencies, such as strategic/critical thinking, risk analysis, decision making, ethical reasoning, and communication. Most textbooks focus on content knowledge and then expect students to "magically" demonstrate professional competencies. As an author team, we bring to this textbook extensive knowledge about cost accounting as well as about the best approaches for teaching and learning professional competencies. This textbook bridges the gap between typical student performance and what we would like students to be able to do by

- Maintaining a central focus on business decision making.
- Explicitly addressing uncertainties and biases.
- Adopting a writing style that is accessible and interesting to students.
- Concentrating on all types of organizations.
- Focusing on ethical reasoning.
- Simultaneously challenging and guiding students to learn.
- Helping instructors assess student competencies.

**Maintaining a Central Focus on Business Decision Making** A decision-making model, *Steps for Better Thinking,* is introduced in Chapter 1, and the focus on decision making continues throughout the remainder of the textbook and its supplements, including homework, assessment material, and online practice. This approach helps students understand that *memorizing the material is not good enough.* Specifically, it helps students

- Recognize the role of cost accounting in providing information used by managers and other decision makers.
- Learn content knowledge more deeply and apply it more readily when learned in the context of real business problems.
- Go beyond mechanical applications and analyze and adapt cost accounting methods to their organization's situation.
- Learn to evaluate the usefulness of new accounting methods and business practices that will arise in the future.

**Explicitly Addressing Uncertainties and Biases** Many students fail to recognize that cost accounting information is subject to uncertainties and biases. This failure causes them to place undue reliance on computational results and inhibits their ability to evaluate the assumptions, limitations, behavioral implications, and qualitative factors that influence business decisions. These types of weaknesses inhibit student development of professional competencies such as the IMA's Knowledge, Skills, and Abilities (KSAs). To overcome these weaknesses, *Cost Management* explicitly addresses uncertainties and biases in the content and homework problems in every chapter.

**Adopting a Writing Style that Is Accessible and Interesting to Students** *Cost Management* is written in a style that students can easily understand, and it incorporates interesting scenarios that pique student interest. The goal is to help students learn the basic cost accounting knowledge on their own before they come to class so that class discussions can be used to further develop their accounting expertise and to focus on more complex issues such as qualitative factors that influence information and decisions, and the effects of uncertainty and bias.

**Concentrating on All Types of Organizations** Manufacturing is now a small part of U.S. business, while service and not-for-profit organizations are increasingly important. Our students need to apply cost accounting techniques in a variety of settings. Accordingly, we focus throughout the textbook on a wide range of business organizations, including large and small, public and private, U.S. and international, manufacturing, retail, service, and not-for-profit. Real organizations include **Motorola, Reichhold, Hyperion,** and **Charleston County Council.** Hypothetical organizations include Small Animal Clinic, Die Gefleckte Kuh Eis (The Spotted Cow Creamery), Nighthawk Law Firm, Aluminum Benders, and Middletown Children's Clinic. Students learn to apply cost accounting in different settings, and they also learn about the types of decisions and factors that are important to different types of organizations.

**Focusing on Ethical Reasoning** The accounting profession currently faces negative media attention and increased governmental regulation, largely because a number of accountants and managers have behaved unethically. To develop better ethical reasoning skills, students need greater exposure to realistic ethical issues. *Cost Management* avoids scenarios that have simplistic, "correct" solutions. Instead, the ethical dilemmas contain ambiguities, conflicts of interest, and value judgments. The textbook presents a framework for ethical decision making in Chapter 1. Students will use this framework when addressing ethical dilemmas in every chapter. With this continual practice, students are likely to develop their own process for ethical decision making to use within other classes and over their careers.

**Simultaneously Challenging and Guiding Students to Learn** Educational research indicates that students need repeated practice with *appropriately designed* learning activities to develop professional competencies such as strategic/critical thinking. Students must be challenged to develop new skills, but at the same time they need guidance so that they do not falter and become discouraged.

A significant and innovative feature of this textbook is the use of a decision-making model, *Steps for Better Thinking,* as a pedagogical tool to foster students' analytical and critical thinking skills. The model is used to analyze chapter-opening vignettes, help students tackle ethical scenarios, and structure the end-of-chapter problem material. The model helps instructors build a better syllabus by identifying the complexity of homework problems and helping them anticipate potential student difficulties. It also reduces student confusion about what they are expected to do and encourages them to think about accounting problems more complexly. *Steps for Better Thinking* is used to identify levels of competency in the AICPA Core Competency Framework, so it is tied directly to the competencies students need for entry to the accounting profession.*

*Steps for Better Thinking* also helped us increase the connection of chapter content with end-of-chapter material. Instead of expecting students to "magically" apply content knowledge to complex business problems, the homework problems guide students through the thinking process. Longer problems are broken down into a series of questions that first address cost accounting material and then apply the material to more complex questions involving uncertainties, biases, behavioral issues, analytical reasoning, and judgment.

**Helping Instructors Assess Student Competencies** Instructors and programs are increasingly called on to assess student learning outcomes. However, they often struggle in their efforts to assess competencies such as decision making, risk analysis, and strategic/critical thinking. A unique and value-added feature of *Cost Management* is that it incorporates a pre-course problem (available in the Instructor's Manual), plus one or two problems in each chapter of the textbook (identified by a ☆ icon) that are designed for assessment of such competencies. A detailed assessment rubric, student examples, and a discussion of typical student approaches for each of these problems are available on the Instructor's Web site. The assessment methodology corresponds with materials on the *AICPA Educational Competency Assessment Web site.*

Use of the assessment problems and resources is optional. Some instructors may elect to use one or more assessment problems to learn more about their students' strengths and weaknesses as they teach the cost accounting course. Others may use these resources as part of a program assessment plan.

## ORGANIZATION OF COST ACCOUNTING CONTENT

*Cost Management* includes traditional as well as the most current practices in cost accounting. The focus is on methods that will be useful to students in their professional careers. First we introduce the students to relevant costs and their use in decision making, including cost functions and cost behavior. Then, once students understand cost behavior, they are better able to under-

---

*Available online at eca.aicpaservices.org.

stand the uses and limitations of cost allocations. Because performance measurement and evaluation relies on a thorough understanding of both decision making and allocation information, the last section of the book considers a variety of performance measurement and evaluation techniques and issues. Following is a more detailed description of each of these three sections. We view some topics, such as **quality** and **international practices,** as pervasive. Therefore, we include these topics throughout the textbook rather than as stand-alone chapters.

## ■ Part I. Measuring and Using Costs for Management Decisions

The chapters in Part I focus on identifying and using relevant information for management decisions. Chapter 1 introduces a decision-making framework that is used throughout the textbook. This framework helps students describe management decisions, identify relevant costs, evaluate the quality of information used in decisions, and develop ethical decision-making skills. Chapters 2, 3, and 4 address ways to categorize costs, analyze cost behavior, and use costs to make decisions. This approach motivates student interest in course material by immediately involving them in realistic business problems. Focusing on decisions also allows students to relate cost accounting material to their own personal lives, increasing their perceptions of course relevance.

## ■ Part II. Measuring and Assigning Costs for Internal and External Reporting

The chapters in Part II explore the assignment of costs to products and other activities of an organization. Chapter 5 begins with the relatively simple assignment of costs to customized products and services. Chapter 6 introduces the more complex cost assignment methods used in process costing. Chapter 7 explores the development and use of activity-based costing and activity-based management. Chapters 8 and 9 present the more specialized practices for assigning costs for support departments, joint products, and byproducts. This section helps students move beyond a purely mechanical application toward a deeper understanding of the reasons behind and limitations of cost assignment techniques. We also introduce basic concepts related to standard costs and overapplied and underapplied overhead beginning with Chapter 5. This approach more closely ties chapter content to contemporary business practice.

## ■ Part III. Planning, Monitoring, and Motivating

The chapters in Part III use budgets and benchmarks to plan and monitor financial and nonfinancial performance. These chapters also examine the use of incentives and compensation, combined with benchmarks, to motivate performance. Chapters 10 and 11 focus on the development and use of budgets and benchmarks. Chapter 12 addresses long-term, strategic investment decisions. Chapter 13 introduces contemporary issues related to pricing and cost management. Chapter 14 examines various ways to measure and report costs for internal and external income statements. Chapter 15 provides an overview of financial performance measures and introduces the challenges that accountants and managers face when motivating performance inside organizations. In Chapter 16, the balanced scorecard is presented as a method for using both financial and nonfinancial information to help achieve an organization's strategic goals. Although students are asked to consider the behavioral influences of accounting practices throughout the textbook, Part III focuses more specifically on the motivational uses of accounting information. Students are asked to recognize both intended and unintended behavioral consequences of performance metrics.

## ■ Sequencing

We have written the chapters so that they can be taught in any sequence, although we recommend that the first two chapters be taught sequentially at the beginning of the course. The instructor's resources provide several examples of syllabi using the chapters in different sequences. Margin notes are used to refer students to more detailed information about a topic that is addressed in another chapter.

## CHAPTER FOCUS

### ■ Chapter 1: The Role of Accounting Information in Management Decision Making

Chapter 1 provides an overview of organizational decision making and introduces students to the use of cost accounting information in decision making. Techniques for identifying and using relevant information are reviewed. A model for developing higher quality decisions *(Steps for Better Thinking)* is introduced. Finally, this model is applied to ethical decision making. We do not introduce basic accounting terms in this chapter but give students a general overview of the importance of cost accounting information.

### ■ Chapter 2: The Cost Function

We first review accounting terms that relate to cost behavior and explain the cost function. At this point we also discuss limitations of the information produced by cost functions and problems with uncertainties and bias in developing cost functions. This focus allows students to consider the quality of information as they learn cost accounting methods. We present and illustrate techniques that are used to describe cost behavior (engineered estimates, analysis at the account level, two-point method, and regression analysis). Scatterplots are introduced as a way to provide additional information about cost behavior. Linear and nonlinear (e.g., learning curves) cost functions are presented. Although this chapter is longer than our other chapters, the first part is primarily a review of relevant cost terms that students know from introductory managerial accounting.

### ■ Chapter 3: Cost-Volume-Profit Analysis

Single and multiple product examples are used to explore the development and use of CVP information, before and after taxes. Examples of spreadsheets with input sections and cell referencing are introduced so that students can easily perform sensitivity analysis. Because of the early focus on bias and uncertainties, students better understand the need for sensitivity analysis. Qualitative factors are explored, as are problems with uncertainty and bias. The margin of safety and operating leverage are introduced and then used to analyze risk of operations. Examples show the use of CVP information for both decision making and monitoring purposes. One of the homework problems asks students to develop a spreadsheet that can later be altered to calculate information needed to answer questions presented in the San Jose Chips Case that may be used with this chapter.

### ■ Chapter 4: Relevant Costs for Nonroutine Operating Decisions

Nonroutine decisions such as special order, make or buy, keep or drop, product emphasis, and maximizing constrained resources are covered in Chapter 4. This chapter is placed early in the text to allow students additional practice in developing and using cost function information. We find that students better understand the relevancy of their cost accounting course when they immediately use skills that are taught early in the course. In addition, relatively simple decision-making scenarios allow greater discussion of qualitative factors that potentially override quantitative results. Linear programming software is used to solve for optimal sales mixes when resources are constrained. As in all of our chapters, the effects of uncertainty and bias on decision making are also explored.

### ■ Chapter 5: Job Costing

Chapter 5 introduces job costing and accounting for spoilage under job costing. The first part of the chapter reviews job-costing basics in a manufacturing setting and then extends this method to the service sector. Actual versus normal job costing methods are compared, and calculations for over- and under-applied overhead are explained. An example in this chapter highlights potential problems that arise if allocated costs are part of the information used to choose between two different jobs when there are capacity constraints. We also include a discussion of the costs of spoilage, rework, and scrap in job costing, describing opportunity costs that arise from poor quality. Behavioral implications of the accounting methods used to record spoilage are explored.

## ▪ Chapter 6: Process Costing

Chapter 6 presents process-costing methods using FIFO, weighted average, and standard costs. We developed a single format that is used to calculate equivalent units for both the FIFO and weighted average methods. This format also helps students understand the difference between the two methods. In this chapter's examples, an accountant makes a decision about the best process costing method for her organization, comparing and contrasting information from FIFO and weighted average methods. In addition, accounting methods for the spoilage, rework, and scrap that arise in mass production are illustrated.

## ▪ Chapter 7: Activity-Based Costing and Management

A team of employees implements an ABC system in this chapter, and information from the ABC system is compared to that from a traditional job costing system. ABM is described using a specific example for customer-related costs. In another ABM example, an accountant develops quality cost information aimed at reducing costs while improving quality. The benefits, costs, and limitations of ABC systems are discussed, as well as recent academic research results.

## ▪ Chapter 8: Measuring and Assigning Support Department Costs

The direct, step-down, and reciprocal methods are described and illustrated in this chapter. Excel Solver is used to develop costs for the reciprocal method. Allocations are illustrated using a not-for-profit children's clinic. Information from single- versus dual-rate allocation methods is compared. The quality of support cost allocation information is discussed, with emphasis on its limitations, including behavior implications.

## ▪ Chapter 9: Joint Product and By-Product Costing

Physical volume, sales at the split-off point, net realizable value, and constant gross margin NRV methods are compared and contrasted in this chapter. Appropriate use of relevant cost information for decisions about further processing is discussed. Main products and by-products are defined, and methods for accounting for by-products are compared and contrasted.

## ▪ Chapter 10: Static and Flexible Budgets

After illustrating the development of a static budget, adjustments are made to develop a flexible budget reflecting activity levels, price changes, and elimination of costs over which managers have no control. This treatment of static and flexible budgeting reflects the actual sequence of events used by most businesses. Students better understand that forecasts are made, developed into a budget, and then adjusted to develop a benchmark as actual operations unfold. For instructors who want students to have more in-depth knowledge of static budgets, the Appendix includes an example of a detailed cash budget. We also introduce participative, zero-based, rolling, ABC, and kaizen budgets. Behavioral aspects of budgeting are explored, as are the effects of uncertainties and bias in budget information.

## ▪ Chapter 11: Standard Costs and Variance Analysis

The development and use of direct and overhead cost standards and variances are presented in this chapter. Behavioral effects arising from the use of this information are explored through an example in which a purchasing department buys cheaper materials that require more labor time and effort. In the Appendix, profit-related variances (revenue and contribution margin-related variances) are described and calculated.

## ▪ Chapter 12: Strategic Investment Decisions

Net present value analysis and other capital budgeting techniques are described, and then compared and contrasted in this chapter. Examples with increasing complexity develop capital budgeting with income taxes. Inflation effects are considered in the Appendix using both the real rate and nominal rate methods. Uncertainties and bias in capital budget information is emphasized in this chapter. A case developed for this chapter requires that students use their own judgment to choose an appropriate MACRs schedule, the life of the project, and discount rates (including a risk premium specific to this decision), among others.

### ■ Chapter 13: Joint Management of Revenues and Costs

Students learn to develop and implement Target, kaizen, and life cycle costing systems. Product pricing techniques (cost and market based) are also introduced, with emphasis on current pricing practices that are based on demand. An economic model is introduced to calculate a profit-maximizing price.

### ■ Chapter 14: Measuring and Assigning Costs for Income Statements

Absorption, variable, and throughput income statements are compared and contrasted. Factors that affect the choice of fixed overhead allocation rate volume measures (theoretical, practical, normal, and budgeted) are explored. The uses and limitations of information produced by these three income statements are discussed. Several examples and homework problems address the incentives under absorption costing of inventory buildup to improve this period's income.

### ■ Chapter 15: Performance Evaluation and Compensation

Agency theory and responsibility accounting are introduced to explore the assignment of decision-making authority and responsibility. Performance evaluation measures (ROI, residual income, and EVA) are compared and contrasted. Transfer pricing approaches are illustrated. Incentives that give rise to sub-optimal decision making are described for each type of performance measure and transfer price policy.

### ■ Chapter 16: Strategic Performance Measurement

This chapter emphasizes the strategic decision-making model introduced in Chapter 1, highlighting the role of long-term strategic decision making. The balanced scorecard is then introduced as a method that can be used to combine financial and non-financial performance measures to gauge progress and motivate employees. The strengths and weaknesses of the balanced scorecard are discussed, including uncertainties about the best choice of measures, mistakes in implementation, and the effects of bias on performance measure choices.

## TARGET AUDIENCE

*Cost Management* was written primarily for a junior or senior-level undergraduate cost accounting course. However, the focus on decision making and the real-world emphasis also makes the textbook appropriate for a master's level or graduate course.

## QUALITY CONTROL

We have made every effort to eliminate errors and create high-quality materials. We each reviewed and checked the details in final drafts of all chapters and solutions, and we obtained the usual reviews from cost accounting instructors and proofreaders. *To ensure further accuracy and to evaluate the connection of the assignment materials with the chapter content,* faculty reviewers, in several passes, checked the wording of end-of-chapter material, ensured that all concepts within the chapter are practiced in homework material, and verified that the solutions provide adequate explanation and use the same terminology and formats as illustrated in the textbook. To ensure that all resources are tightly connected to the chapter content, we assumed responsibility for preparation of the Solution Manual, Instructor's Manual, and assessment materials. In addition, we co-authored the Test Bank and worked closely with the author of the study guide. We personally made sure that all terminology and methods are consistent with the chapters *and that the test bank includes questions requiring students to demonstrate analysis and strategic/critical thinking, in addition to the typical questions involving cost accounting content.*

# CHAPTER FEATURES

*Cost Management* uses a number of pedagogical features in each chapter to enhance teaching and learning.

## ■ Learning Objectives

At the beginning of each chapter, several questions are posed to provide a structure for student learning. These questions also appear in the margins where the material is first presented, organize the chapter summary, and identify homework material and test bank problems.

### This Chapter Addresses the Following Questions:

**Q1** How is activity-based costing (ABC) different from traditional costing?

**Q2** What are activities, and how are they identified?

**Q3** What process is used to assign costs in an ABC system?

**Q4** How are cost drivers selected for activities?

**Q5** What is activity-based management (ABM)?

**Q6** What are the benefits, costs, and limitations of ABC and ABM?

## ■ Chapter Opener and Analysis

The chapter-opening example motivates students by presenting an interesting, real-world application of chapter material. It is followed by an analysis of the business decision-making process demonstrated in the vignette, using the framework of *Steps for Better Thinking*.

Here is an example from Chapter 1. Please turn to Chapter 1 to see the discussion that follows.

### MOTOROLA'S IRIDIUM PROJECT: LOOK BEFORE YOU LEAP

In 1985, while vacationing in the Caribbean, the wife of a **Motorola** executive became frustrated because she could not call clients using her cell phone. Over time, her frustration led to the creation of a research team, including the executive, to address the problem. The team envisioned a 77-satellite network orbiting the earth so that cellular phones could be used for international calls without interruption (Finkelstein and Sanford, 2000; Smolowitz, 1999). In 1991, Motorola formed a separate company, **Iridium,** to share the risk and cost of the project with a global consortium of firms. Iridium became a public company in 1997.

In late 1998, the first phones were sold. The company charged $3,000 for each phone, and calls cost $4 to $9 per minute. Fewer customers signed up for service than predicted—only 20,000 during the first 10 months. Motorola had predicted two million users by 2002 (Smolowitz, 1999). After spending $5 billion on development, Iridium defaulted on $1.5 billion in bonds and declared bankruptcy in August 1999. It was one of the 20 largest bankruptcies in U.S. history (Finkelstein and Sanford, 2000).

What went wrong? The cell phones were bulky and could not be used inside buildings. During the 11 years of Iridium's development, land-based cellular service expanded faster than expected, and customer expectations changed. With the high costs, customers required more sophisticated technology in the phone sets. In addition, Iridium's partners failed to provide adequate sales teams and marketing plans (Finkelstein and Sanford, 2000).

Marketing professors Jagdish Sheth of Emory University and Rajendra Sisodia of Bentley College argued that Iridium's technology and marketing were flawed and that managers apparently fell into a "sunk cost fallacy." Managers continued to invest in the project after it should have been abandoned (Sheth and Sisodia, 1999). ■

SOURCES: S. Finkelstein and S. H. Sanford, "Learning from Corporate Mistakes: The Rise and Fall of Iridium," *Organizational Dynamics* 29, no. 2 (2000), pp. 138–148; J. N. Sheth and R. Sisodia, "Manager's Journal: Why Cell Phones Succeeded Where Iridium Failed," *The Wall Street Journal,* August 23, 1999, p. A14; I. Smolowitz, "Iridium: Lessons for all Companies," *Business Forum* 24, no. 1/2 (2000), pp. 37–38; and J. Schack, "Iridium Splashes Down," *Institutional Investor,* January 2000, p. 98.

## Realistic Examples

After the presentation of a major cost accounting method, a realistic example of an organizational setting with interactions between accountants and managers demonstrates the method and introduces qualitative factors and relevant decision-making issues. The same setting is often used several different times in a chapter to introduce various aspects of each method. These examples enhance student learning by demonstrating cost accounting methods, clarifying the business context, and raising issues addressed by accountants, managers, and others.

This is a retail sector example from Chapter 3 (Cost-Volume-Profit Analysis).

---

**98 CHAPTER 3 ▸ COST-VOLUME-PROFIT ANALYSIS**

### DIE GEFLECKTE KUH EIS (THE SPOTTED COW CREAMERY) (PART 2)
### THE INFLUENCE OF SALES MIX ON PROFITABILITY

The owner of The Spotted Cow Creamery has several profitable stores. He asked the store managers to provide information about their sales mix, specifically the amount of beverage versus ice cream products sold. Beverages provide a much larger contribution margin than ice cream. After analyzing the data, he found that about half of the revenues in the most profitable stores were for the sale of beverages. In addition, these stores have more stable sales throughout the winter because they sell specialty coffee beverages as well as soft drinks.

The owner shared this information with Holger, the manager of a less profitable store. Holger investigates the contribution margins from beverages and ice cream at his store. He sets up a spreadsheet to examine the influence of the sales mix on profitability, shown in Exhibit 3.5(a). He finds that beverages are about 15% of total revenue ($6,000 ÷ $40,000). The contribution margin ratio for beverages is 93% ($5,600 ÷ $6,000), whereas the contribution margin for ice cream is 42% ($14,400 ÷ $34,000). When he changes the desired sales mix in the spreadsheet from 15% to 50% beverages to match the sales mix of more profitable stores, the after-tax income increases by a sizeable amount from $3,000 to $8,353 as indicated in Exhibit 3.5(b).

Holger realizes that several strategies would increase the percentage of beverages in his current sales mix. First, he could require the sales clerks to suggest a beverage with each sale. In addition, he could emphasize beverages in his advertising. He could also analyze his competitors' beverage prices to be certain that his prices are competitive. A small drop in the price of beverages might increase the volume of beverages sold more than enough to offset the decline in contribution margin ratio. He uses the spreadsheet to perform sensitivity analysis around these factors.

**EXHIBIT 3.5** Spreadsheet for The Spotted Cow Creamery

**(a) Current Sales Mix**

| | A | B | C | D |
|---|---|---|---|---|
| 1 | | | | |
| 2 | Input section | | | |
| 3 | | Beverage | Ice Cream | Total |
| 4 | Revenue | €6,000 | €34,000 | €40,000 |
| 5 | Variable cost | 400 | 19,600 | 20,000 |
| 6 | Current sales mix in revenues | 15% | 85% | 100% |
| 7 | Fixed costs | | | 16,000 |
| 8 | Tax rate | | | 25% |
| 9 | Desired sales mix in revenues | 15% | 85% | 100% |
| 10 | | | | |
| 11 | | | | Weighted Average |
| 12 | Contribution margin ratio | 93% | 42% | 50% |
| 13 | | | | |
| 14 | Income statement | | | |
| 15 | Revenue | €6,000 | €34,000 | €40,000 |
| 16 | Variable cost | 400 | 19,600 | 20,000 |
| 17 | Contribution margin | 5,600 | 14,400 | 20,000 |
| 18 | | | | |
| 19 | Fixed costs | | | 16,000 |
| 20 | Pretax income | | | 4,000 |
| 21 | Taxes | | | 1,000 |
| 22 | After tax income | | | €3,000 |

**(b) Desired Sales Mix**

| | A | B | C | D |
|---|---|---|---|---|
| 1 | | | | |
| 2 | Input section | | | |
| 3 | | Beverage | Ice Cream | Total |
| 4 | Revenue | €6,000 | €34,000 | €40,000 |
| 5 | Variable cost | 400 | 19,600 | 20,000 |
| 6 | Current sales mix in revenues | 15% | 85% | 100% |
| 7 | Fixed costs | | | 16,000 |
| 8 | Tax rate | | | 25% |
| 9 | Desired sales mix in revenues | 50% | 50% | 100% |
| 10 | | | | |
| 11 | | | | Weighted Average |
| 12 | Contribution margin ratio | 93% | 42% | 68% |
| 13 | | | | |
| 14 | Income statement | | | |
| 15 | Revenue | €20,000 | €20,000 | €40,000 |
| 16 | Variable cost | 1,333 | 11,529 | 12,863 |
| 17 | Contribution margin | 18,667 | 8,471 | 27,137 |
| 18 | | | | |
| 19 | Fixed costs | | | 16,000 |
| 20 | Pretax income | | | 11,137 |
| 21 | Taxes | | | 2,784 |
| 22 | After tax income | | | €8,353 |

---

## Guide Your Learning

After major sections in each chapter, *Guide Your Learning* boxes give students the opportunity to confirm their understanding of key terms and concepts and analyze the cost accounting methods introduced in the chapter examples. They are asked to identify problems and uncertainties, explore the pros and cons of alternatives, evaluate behavioral implications, and recognize decision maker values and priorities. Suggested answers to these questions are available to instructors and students online at www.wiley.com/college/eldenburg.

---

### GUIDE YOUR LEARNING 3.3 — The Spotted Cow Creamery (Part 2)

The Spotted Cow Creamery (Part 2) illustrates the influence of sales mix on profitability. For this illustration:

| Compute It | Identify Uncertainties | Explore Uses |
|---|---|---|
| For Exhibit 3.5, manually recalculate:<br>• Sales mix in units<br>• Sales mix in revenues<br>• Weighted average contribution margin ratio | At the end of the illustration, the store manager was considering several strategies for changing his store's sales mix. What uncertainties does the manager face? | How was CVP information used by the owner? How was it used by the manager? |

## ■ Focus on Ethical Decision Making

Each chapter includes an ethical dilemma. As a follow-up, one or more homework problems address ethical issues. To provide students with guidance for addressing these problems, a framework for ethical decision making is introduced in Chapter 1. The framework calls for students to

- Identify ethical problems as they arise.
- Objectively consider the well-being of others and society when exploring alternatives.
- Clarify and apply ethical values when choosing a course of action.
- Work toward ongoing improvement of personal and organizational ethics.

Suggested answers for each dilemma are provided on the instructor and student Web sites.

Shown is our ethical decision-making vignette from Chapter 6 (process costing including spoilage, rework, and scrap).

### FOCUS ON ETHICAL DECISION MAKING
### Cost Overruns at Boeing

During 2002, The Boeing Company settled, without admitting guilt, a securities fraud lawsuit. The lawsuit which was settled for $92.5 million, claimed that the company had improperly failed to report abnormal production losses on its income statement during the first half of 1997. The company's production had been out of control. The company's audit firm, Deloitte & Touche, notified the board of directors' audit committee that the company experienced negative trends during 1996 in "overtime, parts shortages, rework, defective parts, and out-of-sequence work" (Holmes and France, 2002, p. 213).

In most companies, production problems of this nature would have been reflected in inventory and then in cost of goods sold as units were sold. However, Boeing uses a practice called program accounting, a long-term standard costing system. Instead of assigning actual costs to each plane built, the company allocates an expected cost. Actual product costs are accumulated in a cost pool that is recorded as an asset. The asset is reduced for costs allocated to planes built. However, no adjustment is made each period for the amount of cost that has been underapplied or overapplied. Instead, the company depends on the reliability of its long-term cost estimates. Boeing uses this accounting method because it experiences a learning curve when it launches a new type of plane. The company expects higher production costs early in a program and lower production costs later. Thus, program accounting allows the company to allocate an average cost to planes throughout the life of a program.

As production problems grew, Boeing's managers estimated during May 1997 that total production costs would exceed estimates by $1 billion. The lawsuit claimed that the abnormal costs should have been recognized during the second quarter of 1997, similar to the treatment for abnormal spoilage presented in this chapter. However, Boeing's lawyer argued that the costs were typical for periods in which production levels were unusually high and that costs were expected to even out over the life of the project (Holmes and France 2002). The company ultimately announced an abnormal production loss in October 1997, when production on two product lines was temporarily halted.

Why should it matter whether the loss was reported in May versus October of 1997? In August 1997, Boeing completed its acquisition of McDonnell-Douglas and paid through a stock swap. According to Holmes and France (2002), "If investors had understood the scope of the problems, the stock would probably have tumbled and the McDonnell deal—which hinged on Boeing's ability to maintain a lofty share price—would have been jeopardized."

SOURCES: S. Holmes and M. France, "Boeing's Secret: Did the Aircraft Giant Exploit Accounting Rules to Conceal a Huge Factory Snafu?" *Business Week*, May 20, 2002, pp. 110–120; and Boeing Company Annual Report for the year ended December 31, 2002, available under Investor Relations at www.boeing.com.

#### Practice Ethical Decision Making

In Chapter 1, we learned about a process for making ethical decisions (Exhibit 1.11). You can address the following questions for this ethical dilemma to improve your skills for making ethical decisions. Think about your answers to these questions and discuss them with others.

| Ethical Decision-Making Process | Questions to Consider about This Ethical Dilemma |
|---|---|
| Identify ethical problems as they arise. | Was Boeing's delay in recognizing losses for its 777 program an ethical issue? Why or why not? |
| Objectively consider the well-being of others and society when exploring alternatives. | Describe a McDonnell-Douglas shareholder's viewpoint and a Boeing shareholder's viewpoint about whether Boeing should have recognized the losses earlier. What assumptions lie behind each viewpoint? |
| Clarify and apply ethical values when choosing a course of action. | When managers are faced with long-term uncertainties about their costs such as in this situation, what criteria should they use to decide how to report costs publicly? What values did you use to arrive at the solution? |
| Work toward ongoing improvement of personal and organizational ethics. | How might Boeing continuously improve its public reporting of product costs? |

## ■ Margin Notes

Several types of margin notes are used throughout each chapter to briefly present supplemental information and real-world examples. *Current Practice* and *International* notes present interesting examples of cost accounting concepts, methods, or issues for real organizations. *Alternative Terms* acquaint students with terminology they may encounter in the workplace, in other textbooks, or on professional examinations. *Chapter Reference* notes are used to help students locate expanded discussions of a topic that are presented elsewhere in the textbook. *Helpful Hints* provide students with suggestions to help them apply concepts or techniques.

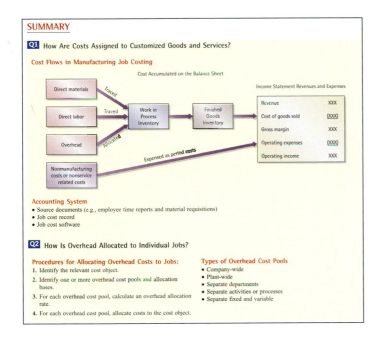

# REVIEW

## ■ Chapter Summary

The chapter Summary is organized using the Learning Objective questions presented at the beginning of the chapter and provides an overview of all key cost accounting methods and concepts. Thus, unlike traditional summaries, *the Summary in this text reviews both quantitative and qualitative content of the chapters*. It is a visual tool for students to use as an overview when they begin a chapter and as a review when they complete it.

## ■ Self-Study Problems

Each chapter provides one or two self-study problems that address the most important content introduced in the chapter and are similar to end-of-chapter Exercises and Problems. Each Self-Study Problem is accompanied by a solution that guides students through the calculations and thinking processes.

# END-OF-CHAPTER ASSIGNMENT MATERIAL

The end-of-chapter material reinforces student learning of cost accounting techniques as well as helps them develop professional competencies such as analytical and decision-making skills.

## ■ Questions

Short-answer Questions provide students with practice using the terminology and cost accounting techniques learned in the chapter.

## ■ Exercises

Exercises focus primarily on ensuring that students learn to properly apply cost accounting methods.

## Problems

Problems give students additional practice using cost accounting techniques, and they also pose open-ended questions requiring judgment (e.g., identify uncertainties, analyze information, explore incentives and biases, evaluate alternatives, and recommend a course of action). The requirements support better performance by guiding students through the steps needed to fully address a problem, from less to more complex aspects. Following is an example from Chapter 3 (Cost-Volume-Profit Analysis). The Q3, Q4, and Q5 icons relate to three different learning objectives. The coding icons ( ⓔ ❶ ❷ ) are explained below.

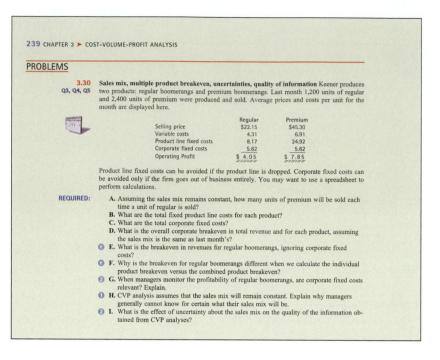

## Exercise and Problem Types, Codes, and Icons

A number of codes and icons are used in the end-of-chapter materials to make it easier for instructors to select homework assignments and to enhance student learning.

**Q3, Q4, Q5, Q6 Learning Objectives.** Each Exercise and Problem is keyed to one or more Learning Objective questions.

ⓔ ❶ ❷ ❸ ❹ **Complexity Coding.** Students often have difficulty answering open-ended questions, and instructors feel frustrated because they do not understand students' inabilities to respond. In this book, icons help instructors choose appropriate Exercises and Problems for their syllabi, and they help students recognize how to approach a particular homework question.

- Individual questions having single correct answers are not labeled.
- Questions having a single answer, but asking students to stretch their knowledge to a new type of situation not addressed in the chapter, are marked with an Extend icon ( ⓔ ).
- Open-ended questions are labeled with an icon for the required skill level in *Steps for Better Thinking* ( ❶ , ❷ , ❸ , ❹ ).

**Communication.** Both the IMA and AICPA emphasize the importance of communication skills. Therefore, several Problems in each chapter require students to prepare a written memorandum or to describe communication for a given setting.

**ETHICS** **Ethics.** The Ethics icon indicates homework Problems that focus on ethical dilemmas, many featuring real-world scenarios. Students explore the uncertainties and multiple perspectives before drawing conclusions. These problems are likely to generate lively class discussions because of differences among students' perceptions and values.

**CMA** **CPA** **CMA/CPA.** The **CMA** icon and the **CPA** icon indicate that an Exercise or Problem is adapted from a previous CMA or CPA examination. Both of these examinations currently include multiple-choice format questions, practice with prior examination problems will help students learn the cost accounting material. Multiple-Choice Questions, some of which are adapted from previous CMA or CPA examinations, are available on the text's Web site at www.wiley.com/college/eldenburg.

**Spreadsheet.** Spreadsheets are introduced in various chapters, with examples of data input areas so that sensitivity analysis can easily be performed. Students replicate or expand these examples in certain homework problems, which require the use of electronic spreadsheet software. For example, students use spreadsheets to develop financial models, perform regression analysis, calculate optimal sales mixes, and perform reciprocal cost allocations (using Excel Solver for the last two activities).

☆ **Assessment.** Identified by a star, one or two problems in each chapter are designed to assess student professional competencies such as decision making, risk analysis, and strategic/critical thinking. A detailed assessment rubric, student examples, and a discussion of typical student approaches are available for each of these problems.

www.wiley.com/ college/eldenburg **Web.** The Web icon indicates that a Problem requires students to access information or conduct research on the Internet. Some of these Problems refer students to the textbook Web site to download an Excel dataset or other information. Other Problems require students to conduct research on the Internet.

**Group.** Certain problems are particularly useful for student **group** activities. These problems would be difficult for most students working alone, and student learning would be enhanced through collaboration with others in the class. Additional guidance for using the problem with groups is available in the Instructor's Manual.

## ■ Build Your Professional Competencies

Each chapter includes two types of Problems that help students focus on their professional development.

- A **Focus on Professional Competency** Problem in each chapter asks students to explore in detail one of the twenty AICPA core competencies. These competencies are similar to the IMA's knowledge, skills, and abilities (KSAs) used by management accountants in the workplace. Students are encouraged to tie the competency to cost accounting content, and reflect on their own competency development.
- One or two **Integrating Across the Curriculum Problems** in each chapter ask students to integrate cost accounting material with the content of other accounting and business core courses, such as auditing, marketing, or finance.

The examples on the left are from Chapter 9, Joint Product and By-Product Costing.

---

### BUILD YOUR PROFESSIONAL COMPETENCIES

**9.33**
**Q4, Q7**  **Focus on Professional Competency: Marketing/Client Focus**  *Internal and external customer relationships, accountant objectivity*  Review the following definition and elements for the Marketing/Client Focus competency.[2]

**DEFINITION:**  Individuals who are marketing- and client-focused are better able to anticipate and meet the changing needs of clients, employers, customers, and markets. This involves both the ability to recognize market needs and the ability to develop new markets.

---

**368** CHAPTER 9 ▶ JOINT PRODUCT AND BY-PRODUCT COSTING

#### ELEMENTS FOR THIS COMPETENCY INCLUDE

| Level 1 | Level 2 | Level 3 | Level 4 |
|---|---|---|---|
| 1. Identifies factors that motivate internal and external customers to enter into relationships or continue doing business with an organization<br><br>2. Articulates uncertainties about relationships with internal and external customers | 3. Recognizes and understands employer/client protocol and expectations | 4. Develops an effective plan for addressing a particular employer/client need | 5. Builds good working relationships over time<br><br>6. Generates new engagements for services over time |

**REQUIRED:**

A. An important goal for internal accountants is to enter into productive working relationships with internal customers—people they work with inside their organizations. Focus on competency elements 1, 2, 3, 4, and 5, which describe skills needed for effectively working with others. Answer the following questions:

❶ 1. Why do accountants need to actively work on their relationships with internal customers? Why is relationship building an open-ended problem?

❶ 2. List factors that might motivate internal customers to enter into productive working relationships with accounting personnel.

❷ 3. What do internal customers typically expect from accounting personnel?

❷ 4. How can accountants recognize whether they are developing good working relationships with internal customers?

❸ 5. In this chapter, we learned that managers sometimes use joint cost accounting information inappropriately in making decisions. How can accountants help managers avoid this misuse of accounting information? Develop a strategy and describe how it could be implemented.

B. An important goal for public accountants is to enter into productive working relationships with their external customers. Consider competency elements 1, 2, 3, 4, and 5, and answer the following questions:

❷ 1. How is working with internal customers the same as working with external customers? How is it different?

❷ 2. Objectivity is a cornerstone of the accounting profession. Discuss the positive and negative aspects of how this affects the ability of auditors to develop good working relationships with their clients.

**9.34**
**Q1**  **Integrating Across the Curriculum: Economics and Governmental Regulation**  *Beef by-products in animal feed, by-product economics, regulator responsibilities*  During early 2004, the U.S. beef industry faced a crisis. A slaughtered dairy cow in Washington State was infected with bovine spongiform encephalopathy, more commonly known as "mad cow disease." Government regulators and consumer groups were alarmed because humans who eat contaminated beef may become ill with a fatal brain-wasting disease. The finding of mad cow disease caused domestic beef prices to drop considerably. It also triggered a potential loss of $3 billion in beef exports, as numerous countries immediately banned the import of U.S. beef. Mad cow disease destroyed the British beef industry during the 1990s, and industry groups wanted to avoid a similar fate in the United States.

The only known cause of mad cow disease was the ingestion of infected animal parts. For many years, cattle had routinely been fed by-products from the beef rendering industry. Before the 1990s, this practice was viewed as an economic and ecological success. Beef by-products from slaughterhouses, packing plants, butcher shops, and restaurants totaled approximately 44,000 tons per week in the United States. In the rendering process the remains were ground up and then cooked, which removed the water. The residue could be turned into fats, oils, or meat and bone meal. U.S. sales of meat and bone meal totaled approximately 3.2 billion tons per year. The rendering process provided beef by-product revenues, reduced the cost of protein in cattle feed, and avoided the need to dispose of the beef by-products.

Following an outbreak of mad cow disease in Britain, scientists determined the manner in which the disease spread. With this new information, regulators throughout the world banned the use of beef by-products in cattle feed. However, the 1997 U.S. ban did not prohibit the use of beef

---

## ■ Additional Problems and Cases

**www.wiley.com/ college/eldenburg**  The Instructor's Web site offers additional problems and cases. The problems may be used to give students additional practice or to replace homework assignments used in previous terms. Cases too long to include in the textbook are also provided. These cases use the content from specific chapters in a setting where students must identify the relevant information and issues. Excel spreadsheet templates are tied to several of the cases so that students can focus more on the appropriate use of the spreadsheet information.

## SUPPLEMENTS: THE TEACHING AND LEARNING PACKAGE

*Cost Management* features a full range of teaching and learning resources. Driven by the same principles of the textbook, these materials provide a consistent and well-integrated set of learning materials. Please turn to the Resource Sampler on page xxii for a quick look at some examples of instructor and student resources.

## INSTRUCTOR RESOURCES

### ■ *Cost Management* Web site

www.wiley.com/
college/eldenburg

On this Web site instructors will find electronic versions of the **Solutions Manual, Guide Your Learning and Ethics solutions, Instructor's Manual, Test Bank, Computerized Test Bank, PowerPoint** presentations, and other resources. In addition, portions of the *Cost Management* Web site are available with eGradePlus, a new online resource that integrates text and media and allows you to customize your course with the following tools:

- *Course Administration* tools help instructors manage their course and integrate Wiley Web site resources with course management systems, thereby helping instructors keep all class materials in one location.
- A *Prepare and Present* tool contains all instructor resources. Instructors can easily adapt, customize, and add to these resources to meet the needs of their particular course.
- An *Assignment* area is one of the most powerful features of the *Cost Management* Web site. It allows instructors to assign online homework and quizzes comprised of end-of-chapter textbook questions. Instructors save time as results are automatically graded and recorded in an instructor gradebook. Students benefit from the option to receive immediate feedback on their work, allowing them to quickly gauge their understanding of course content.
- An *Instructor's Gradebook* will keep track of student progress and allow instructors to analyze individual and overall class understanding of course concepts.

### ■ Instructor's Manual (prepared by the text authors)

Designed to help instructors maximize student learning, the Instructor's Manual offers teaching suggestions for each chapter of the main text, and it explains content presentation in a more collaborative learning environment. The Instructor's Manual provides alternative syllabi and ways to organize course materials, suggestions for teaching each chapter, the authors' teaching philosophy and recommendations, as well as guidance for using the many electronic and print assessment tools available with the text.

### ■ Assessment Methods and Guidance

The textbook is accompanied by several types of assessment materials.

**Pre-Course Test (prepared by the text authors)** Available on the *Cost Management* Web site, the pre-course test includes multiple-choice questions, computational problems, and an open-ended essay problem. Professors can choose to use all or part of the test to evaluate student knowledge and/or strategic/critical thinking at the beginning of the course.

**Online Multiple-Choice Questions (prepared by the text authors)** Fifteen to twenty-five multiple choice questions per chapter are available to instructors and students in computerized format compatible with WebCT, Blackboard, or eGrade Plus, and will also be available on the student Web site. Many of the questions are adapted from prior CPA and CMA professional exams. Instructors can use these questions as graded or ungraded, pre-class or after-class student exercises. Both the CMA and CPA exams currently use a multiple-choice format, so allowing students to practice with computerized multiple-choice questions provides a preview for these exams.

**Test Bank (prepared by Robert Hurt, Cal Poly Pomona, and the text authors)** The Test Bank is a comprehensive testing package that allows instructors to tailor examinations according to chapter objectives, learning skills, and content. It includes traditional types of questions (e.g., true-false, multiple-choice, matching, computational, and short-answer), as well as open-ended problems that are similar to those in the textbook. All questions are cross-referenced to chapter objectives and to level of complexity, using the same coding scheme found in the end-of-chapter assignment material.

**Computerized Test Bank** The Computerized Test Bank allows instructors to create and print multiple versions of the same test by scrambling the order of all the different types of questions found in the Test Bank. It even allows answers to be scrambled within a particular multiple-choice question. Instructors can modify and customize test questions by changing existing problems or adding their own.

**Competency Assessment Problems (prepared by the text authors)** One or two problems in each chapter are designed for assessment of student professional competencies such as decision making, risk analysis, and strategic/critical thinking. These problems are identified with a star ☆ adjacent to the problem number. A detailed assessment rubric, student examples, and a discussion of typical student approaches are available on the *Cost Management* Web site for each of these problems.

## Checklist of Key Figures

Available in the Instructor's Manual and on the Instructor's Web site at www.wiley.com/college/eldenburg, the check figures allow students to verify the accuracy of their answers as they work through assignments.

## Solutions Manual (prepared by the text authors)

The solutions manual contains detailed solutions to end-of-chapter assignment material. The solutions provide more than just answers—they guide students through the required computational and thinking processes.

## PowerPoint Slides (one set prepared by Gail Kaciuba, Midwestern State University, and one set prepared by Leslie Eldenburg, University of Arizona)

These electronic lecture aids allow professors to visually present key concepts found in each chapter of the main text. Intended as a lecture guideline, the PowerPoint slides present material in a concise "bullet" format that enables easy note-taking. Two different sets are available to accommodate differences in individual teaching styles.

## Instructor's Resource CD

The Instructor's Resource CD provides all instructor support material and supplements in an electronic format that is easy to navigate and use.

## WebCT and Blackboard

WebCT and Blackboard offer an integrated set of course management tools that enable instructors to easily design, develop, and manage Web-based and Web-enhanced courses. The Wiley *Cost Management* WebCT and Blackboard courses contain all online resources for students and can be customized to fit individual professor needs.

### ■ The Faculty Resource Network

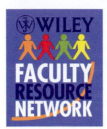

The **Faculty Resource Network** is a group of peers ready to support the use of online course management tools and discipline specific software/ learning systems in the classroom. They will help you apply innovative classroom techniques, implement specific software packages, and tailor the technology experience to the specific needs of each individual class. The Faculty Resource Network also provides you with virtual training sessions led by faculty for faculty. All you need to participate in a virtual seminar is high-speed internet access and a phone line. For more information about the Faculty Resource Network please contact your Wiley representative or go to **www.FacultyResourceNetwork.com**

### ■ Business Extra Select

Wiley's **Business Extra Select** program is a simple, integrated, online custom-publishing process that allows you to combine content from Wiley's leading business publications with copyright-cleared content from such respected sources as *Fortune, The Economist, The Wall Street Journal, Harvard Business School* cases, and much more. In just a few simple steps you can help your students make the connection between the concepts you teach in your class and their real-world applications!

## STUDENT RESOURCES

### ■ *Cost Management* Web Site

 The Eldenburg *Cost Management* Web site provides a wealth of support materials that will help students develop their understanding of course concepts and increase their ability to solve problems. On this Web site students will find **Web Quizzing, Excel templates, Guide Your Learning and ethics solutions,** and other resources. In addition, portions of the student Web site are available with **eGradePlus,** an online study aid where students will find **Interactive Homework Questions** assigned by their instructors, an online gradebook, and much more.

### ■ Problem-Solving Guide (prepared by Gail Kaciuba, Midwestern State University)

This study guide improves students' success rates in solving homework assignments and exam questions. It offers chapter reviews, practice exercises, and accounting tips. Solutions for all questions and problems explain answers and comment on problem-solving techniques. In addition, exercise solutions include a diagnostic to help students locate errors. All content is presented in a manner that allows for mastery of individual concepts before students progress to more difficult concepts.

# Resource Sampler

*Cost Management* features a full range of teaching and learning resources. Driven by the same principles presented in the textbook, these materials provide a consistent and well-integrated set of learning materials. Take a look at a few samples.

SAMPLE RESOURCES
FOR STUDENTS
AND INSTRUCTORS

## ■ PowerPoint Slides: Sets 1 and 2

These electronic lecture aids allow professors to visually present key concepts found in each chapter of the main text. Students can access them for study and review.

**PowerPoint Set 1** provides additional examples of key concepts. The slide set featured below uses PowerPoint special effects to highlight concepts, and uses a step-by-step feature to solve problems so that students can follow the problem-solving sequence. In addition, this set of slides has original problems, leaving all textbook problems available for homework assignments.

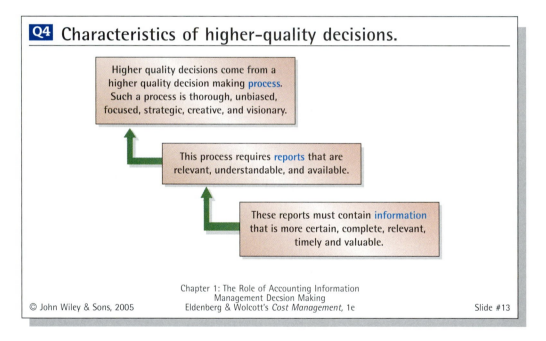

**Q4 Characteristics of higher-quality decisions.**

Higher quality decisions come from a higher quality decision making process. Such a process is thorough, unbiased, focused, strategic, creative, and visionary.

This process requires reports that are relevant, understandable, and available.

These reports must contain information that is more certain, complete, relevant, timely and valuable.

Chapter 1: The Role of Accounting Information
Management Decision Making
Eldenberg & Wolcott's *Cost Management*, 1e

© John Wiley & Sons, 2005

Slide #13

**PowerPoint Set 2** has a more traditional style that can be used in overhead format so that no high-tech presentation hardware is needed. These slides include problems from the textbook to illustrate concepts and content.

### Relevant Information

- Information is relevant if it:
  - *Differs* across the alternatives, and
  - Is about expected *future* costs or revenues
- Relevant information can include:
  - Quantitative data such as revenues and costs
  - Qualitative (non-numerical) factors

## ■ Excel Templates

Following is an example of an **Excel spreadsheet template** for CVP analysis from chapter 3. This spreadsheet accompanies a homework problem that requires sensitivity analysis. It is also a financial model that can be altered slightly for required calculations in the San Jose Chip Case. A number of chapters include spreadsheet templates that are set up with an input section with cells that are referenced in the analysis section. In this textbook, students are asked to produce spreadsheets that can be used by managers who need to easily perform sensitivity analysis. In addition, data sets are available for regression analysis, and students learn to use Excel solver to find optimal sales mixes with constrained resources among other uses.

| | A | B | C | D | E | F |
|---|---|---|---|---|---|---|
| 1 | | | | | | |
| 2 | | *Toddler Toy Company* | | | | |
| 3 | | **Assumptions for Coming Year** | | | | |
| 4 | | | Baby Dolls | Teddy Bears | Toy Cars | Total |
| 5 | | Volume | 200,000 | 125,000 | 225,000 | |
| 6 | | Selling price per unit | $3.50 | $2.75 | $3.15 | |
| 7 | | Fixed costs | $65,000 | $125,000 | $35,000 | |
| 8 | | Variable cost per unit | $2.05 | $1.75 | $2.45 | |
| 9 | | | | | | |
| 10 | | Target pretax profit | | | | $0 |
| 11 | | Investment | | | | $2,000,000 |
| 12 | | Change in values for all products: | | | | |
| 13 | | Increase in volume | | | | 0% |
| 14 | | Increase in price per unit | | | | 0% |
| 15 | | Increase in variable cost per unit | | | | 0% |
| 16 | | Increase in total fixed cost | | | | $0 |
| 17 | | | | | | |
| 18 | | **Profit Calculations:** | | | | |
| 19 | | | | Product | | |
| 20 | | | | | | |
| 21 | | | Baby Dolls | Teddy Bears | Toy Cars | Total |
| 22 | | Actual Sales Volume (units) | 200,000 | 125,000 | 225,000 | 550,000 |
| 23 | | % Weight | 36.36% | 22.73% | 40.91% | 100.00% |
| 24 | | | | | | |
| 25 | | Unit Sales Price | $3.500 | $2.750 | $3.150 | $3.186 |
| 26 | | Variable Cost Per Unit | $2.050 | $1.750 | $2.450 | $2.145 |
| 27 | | Contrib. Margin/Unit | $1.450 | $1.000 | $0.700 | $1.041 |
| 28 | | | | | | |
| 29 | | Total Sales Revenue | $700,000 | $343,750 | $708,750 | $1,752,500 |
| 30 | | Total Variable Costs | $410,000 | $218,750 | $551,250 | $1,180,000 |
| 31 | | Fixed Costs | $65,000 | $125,000 | $35,000 | $225,000 |
| 32 | | Operating Profit | $225,000 | $0 | $122,500 | **$347,500** |
| 33 | | | | | | |
| 34 | | Profit % of Sales | 32.14% | 0.00% | 17.28% | 19.83% |
| 35 | | | | | | |
| 36 | | | | | | |
| 37 | | **Breakeven and Target Profit Analyses:** | | | | |
| 38 | | | | Product | | |
| 39 | | | | | | |
| 40 | | | Baby Dolls | Teddy Bears | Toy Cars | Total |
| 41 | | | | | | |
| 42 | | Sales Volume (units) | 78,603 | 49,127 | 88,428 | 216,157 |
| 43 | | | | | | |
| 44 | | Total Sales Revenue | $275,109 | $135,098 | $278,548 | $688,755 |
| 45 | | Total Variable Costs | $161,135 | $85,972 | $216,648 | $463,755 |
| 46 | | Total Contribution Margin | $113,974 | $49,127 | $61,900 | $225,000 |
| 47 | | Fixed Costs | | | | $225,000 |
| 48 | | Net Profit | | | | $0 |

## SAMPLE RESOURCES FOR INSTRUCTORS

### ■ Instructor's Manual

Designed to help instructors maximize student learning, the **Instructor's Manual** offers teaching suggestions for each chapter of the main text and explains content presentation in a more collaborative learning environment. The Instructors Manual provides alternative syllabi and ways to organize course materials, suggestions for teaching each chapter, the authors' teaching philosophy and recommendations, as well as guidance for using the many electronic and print assessment tools available with the text.

The following sample illustrates **guidance for in-class collaborative activities** for one of the homework problems in Chapter 1. Similar guidance is provided for all homework problems accompanied by this icon 👥.

### Problem 1.26

This problem may be assigned as individual homework or as group homework. Alternatively, it may be used for in-class collaboration. Below are ideas for in-class collaborative-learning activities. Depending on how much class time you would like to devote to this problem, you may wish to use one, several, or all of the following activities.

| Instructions Given to Students | Comments |
|---|---|
| Write a one-sentence answer to Part A: What is the ethical issue here?<br><br>Time Limit: 5 minutes | Ask two groups to read their sentences or to write them on the board. Ask for comments from other students in the class. This activity will help students learn how to articulate an ethical issue. |
| Identify *at least* 4 alternative solutions for this problem (Part B).<br><br>Time Limit: 5 minutes | Ask one group to read its list, and then ask for additional solutions from other groups. Unless prompted, most students tend to identify only a couple of simplistic alternatives. This activity will encourage students think more broadly and creatively about possible solutions. |
| Create a list of information that is relevant to your decision (Part D). Include information that was not explicitly described in the problem.<br><br>Time Limit: 5 minutes | Ask one group to read its list. Ask another group to read items on its list that were not included on the first list. Ask other students for additional relevant items. This activity will help clarify the meaning of relevant information and encourage students to think beyond explicitly-presented information. |
| Reach an agreement about whether the problem is open-ended (Part E), and write "Yes" or "No" in large letters on one side of a piece of paper. On the other side of the paper, list your reasons (not large).<br><br>Time Limit: 5 minutes | Have all groups simultaneously hold up their answers and count the number with "Yes" and with "No." If there are any "No's" in the class, ask one or two of those groups to explain their reasons. Then ask for reasons from two groups that answered "Yes." Ask for additional comments from other students. Be sure to spend enough time discussing this question so that all students ultimately understand why this is an open-ended problem. Many students may believe that this problem has a simple "correct" solution and fail to realize that there are several open-ended dimensions to the solution, including how the entry-level accountant should communicate with the department director and with his/her boss. A more complete discussion of Part B will set the stage for this part. (Also see the solution manual for this problem.) |
| 2 Entry-level accountant groups: Prepare a short script for how you would respond to the department director (Part H). With the guidance of all members, have one member practice the script for presentation to the class.<br><br>Other groups: Write a short paragraph identifying the preferred solution from your point of view (department director, boss, or taxpayers), and explain why (Part F).<br><br>Time Limit: 10–15 minutes | Ask two groups to take the perspective of the entry level accountant. Divide the rest of the groups among the other three perspectives.<br><br>Have each entry-level accountant group present their script. Ask one group from each of the other perspectives read its paragraph.<br><br>As a whole class, discuss the quality of the various solutions. The purpose of this activity is to help students develop solutions to an ethical dilemma in light of multiple perspectives. |

## ■ Test Bank

The **Test Bank** is a comprehensive testing package that allows instructors to tailor examinations according to chapter objectives, learning skills, and content. It includes traditional types of questions (e.g., true-false, multiple-choice, matching, computational, and short-answer), as well as open-ended problems that are similar to those in the textbook. All questions are cross-referenced to chapter objectives and to level of complexity, using the same coding scheme found in the end-of-chapter assignment material.

Here is a sample from the test bank questions for Chapter 5, Job Costing

---

**5.** In an actual costing system, the overhead allocation rate is calculated as *actual overhead cost/actual quantity of the allocation base.* In a normal costing system, the rate is calculated as *estimated overhead cost/estimated quantity of the allocation base.*
   a. Explain why there is no single, "correct" way to allocate overhead (provide at least two reasons).
   b. List at least 2 pros and 2 cons for using actual costing in a job costing system.
   c. List at least 2 pros and 2 cons for using normal costing in a job costing system.

---

The **Test Bank** also provides a summary chart for each chapter that shows the chapter objectives covered by each test question and the question types available in each chapter.

| Chapter 5 Job Costing | | | | | |
|---|---|---|---|---|---|
| **Learning Questions** | **True / False** | **Multiple choice** | **Exercises** | **Short answer** | **Problems** |
| Q1: How are costs assigned to customized goods and services? | 1–5 | 1–19, 25–28, 41–43, 45, 47, 48 | 1–3 | 1–2 | 1 |
| Q2: How is overhead allocated to individual jobs? | 6–10 | 20–24, 29–32, 34–40, 44, 46, 49–51 | 4–6 | 3–4 | 2 |
| Q3: What is the difference between actual costing and normal costing? | 11–15 | 33, 52–60 | 7–8 | 5–6 | 2–3 |
| Q4: What are the uses and limitations of job cost information? | 16–20 | 61–70 | 13–15 | 7–8 | 1–4 |
| Q5: How are spoilage, rework and scrap handled in job costing? | 21–25 | 71–90 | 9–11 | 9–10 | 5–6 |
| Q6: What are the quality and behavioral implications of spoilage? | 26–30 | 91–96 | 16–18 | 11–12 | 5–6 |
| Comprehensive terminology | | | 12 | | |

*(continued)*

| | True/ False | Multiple Choice | Exercises | Short answer | Problems |
|---|---|---|---|---|---|
| Questions With Single Correct Answers | All | All | All | 6 | |
| Open-Ended Questions: | | | | | |
| Step 1: Identify the problem, relevant information, and uncertainties | | | | 1–3, 5, 8–12 | |
| Step 2: Explore interpretations and connections | | | | 3–5, 7, 10 | 1–6 |
| Step 3: Prioritize alternatives and implement conclusions | | | | | 3–6 |
| Step 4: Envision and direct strategic innovation | | | | | 6 |

## SAMPLE RESOURCES FOR STUDENTS

## ■ On-Line Multiple-Choice Questions

Fifteen to twenty five **multiple-choice questions** per chapter are available in computerized format compatible with WebCT, Blackboard, or eGrade Plus. Many of the questions are adapted from prior CPA and CMA professional exams. Both the CMA and CPA exams include multiple-choice format questions; allowing students to practice with computerized multiple-choice questions provides a preview for these exams.

---

**50% (1 out of 2 correct)**

 **1.** A manufacturer operating with excess capacity has been asked to fill a special order at $7.25 per unit. No other use of the currently idle cpacity can be found. The manufacturer's usual variable costs per unit are $3.00 for direct materials, $2.00 for direct labor, $1.00 for variable overhead, and $0.50 for sales commission. No sales commission would be paid on this special order. The average fixed overhead per unit is $0.25. The expected contribution margin per unit for the special order is
   ○ A. $0.00.
   ○ B. $0.25.
   → C. $0.75.
   ○ D. $1.00.

 **2.** In an outsourcing decision, the general rule is for managers to:
   ⊙ A. Choose the option with the lowest relevant costs.
   ○ B. Maximize the use of constrained resources.
   ○ C. Outsource if the supplier's price is lower than the allocated fixed costs plus any relevant variable costs.
   ○ D. Exclude any opportunity costs in an outsourcing decision.

Retake Test

## ■ Problem-Solving Guide

Available in print, the **Problem-Solving Guide** improves students' success rates in solving homework assignments and exam questions. It offers chapter reviews, practice exercises, and accounting tips. Solutions for all questions and problems offer answer explanations and comment on problem-solving techniques. In addition, exercise solutions include a diagnostic to help students locate errors. All content is presented in a manner that allows for mastery of individual concepts before students progress to more difficult concepts. Following is an excerpt from Chapter 4.

**Q7** What limitations and uncertainties should be considered when making nonroutine operating decisions?

In all decision making, the quality of the quantitative and qualitative information available should be considered. This is especially true for nonroutine operating decisions, because a company may have less experience gathering this type of information than it does for routine decisions.

- There are always uncertainties accompanying the information; suppliers may change their prices, future market forces may require a change in the product's price, or competitors may introduce a product that makes the company's product obsolete.
- The quality of the information may be lower if the information is not up-to-date or if the accounting system is not aggregating and summarizing cost and revenue information in an appropriate way.
- The information used in making the decision is only useful input to a quantitative analysis technique if the assumptions of the technique are not violated. Companies need to consider whether linear cost and revenue assumptions hold for any range of activity. If the assumptions do hold for some relevant range of activity, then companies need to make sure that they plan to operate within this relevant range.

The quality of the decision-making process must also be taken into consideration.

- Companies must watch for decision-maker bias. Decision-makers may have a stake in a decision. A product line manager most likely does not want his product discontinued, and a supervisor of a particular business process will not want this activity outsourced. Since these individuals are so close to the necessary information, they frequently cannot be removed from the decision-making process.
- The decision-making process can be improved by performing sensitivity analyses, which show how the decision might change if the input data changes.
- The decision-making process should include the consideration of the company's long-term strategic plans. Even if the analysis shows that a particular business segment should be eliminated, for example, keeping the segment may be more in line with the company's goals.

# Acknowledgments

We gratefully acknowledge the patient support of both of our husbands, John Kovacik and George Taniwaki. Eric Noreen greatly influenced Leslie's ideas about managerial and cost accounting topics and teaching. The team at Wiley provided wonderful help and guidance throughout the publication process. In particular, Mark Bonadeo, Senior Acquisitions Editor, has always been generous in his support of our innovative approach and ideas. Nancy Perry, Senior Development Editor, helped us develop the content and style of the book, and her attention to detail greatly improved the appearance and accuracy of our text. Brian Kamins, Assistant Editor, has been instrumental in providing materials for instructors willing to class-test our materials, and provided assistance continually. Lari Bishop, Senior Production Editor, patiently guided us through the copyediting and page-proof stages. Dawn Stanley, Senior Designer, was instrumental in giving the text its clear and easy-to-use format. Anna Melhorn, Senior Illustration Editor, managed the development process of our exhibits. Sara Wight, Senior Photo Editor, searched diligently for photos to illustrate our examples. Ed Brislin, Project Editor, helped us develop supplements. Allie Morris, Media Editor, worked with us to develop a rich set of online resources for students and instructors. Kristen Babrowski, Development Program Assistant, managed many important details during the development phase. Other Wiley staff who lent us their support as we developed the vision of our text include Steve Herdegen, Marketing Manager; Jay O'Callaghan, Associate Publisher; Susan Elbe, Publisher; and Harry Nolan, Director of Design. We extend particular thanks to Robert Weinstein, who was instrumental in helping us refine our message in a more concise manner, and Shane Moriarity and Carl Allen, who graciously allowed us access to their extensive end-of-chapter materials, compiled from many years of teaching cost accounting at the undergraduate level.

## ◼ Ancillary Authors

We thank Robert Hurt and Gail Kaciuba for developing the following supplemental materials.

> Robert Hurt, *California State Polytechnic University, Pomona, CA:* Test Bank
>
> Gail Kaciuba, *Midwestern State University, TX:* Problem-Solving Guide and PowerPoint author

## ◼ Accuracy Checkers

> James M. Emig, *Villanova University:* Text and Solutions Manual
> Anthony Fontana, *Governor's State University:* Text and Solutions Manual
> A. Anthony Falgiani, *Western Illinois University:* Text, Solutions Manual, and Problem-Solving Guide
> Dick D. Wasson, *Southwestern College:* Text and Solutions Manual

Many people provided excellent reviews and feedback at focus groups and during the class-testing process, all of which were instrumental in content development. These reviewers and focus group participants are listed below; however, we especially praise Gail Kaciuba, Michael Motren, Margaret Shackell-Dowell, Priscilla Reis, Ken Sinclair, and Carol Springer for their attention to detail and critical analysis of our work.

## ◼ Class-Testers

Charles Christianson
*Luther College*

Jane Cote
*Washington State University*

Donald Gribbin
*Southern Illinois University*

David Honodel
*University of Denver*

Gail Kaciuba
*DePaul University*

Bob Picard
*Idaho State University*

Ranjani Krishnan
*Michigan State University*

Priscilla Reis
*Idaho State University*

Suneel Maheshwari
*Marshall University*

Margaret Shackell-Dowell
*University of Notre Dame*

Pam Meyer
*University of Louisiana*

Carol Springer
*Georgia State University*

Tamara Phelan
*Northern Illinois University*

Students: Michael Baron, Sarah Beck, Christopher Berg, Liz Blakemore, Dan Bolles, Jeff Branstad, Stephanie Bulthaup, Britt Cerdena, Adam Cornwell, Vickie Corson, Bryan Crow, James Dosen, Margarita Drachan, Jessica Eide, Nick Fleece, Jonathan Flemming, Kristin Funke, Michelle Gallagher, George Hein, Lucas Hohnstein, Lance Johnson, Joe Kanaval, Kristin Koch, N. Phelps Lane, Brent Lawton, Trevor McClain-Duer, Scott McNeilly, Tim Messenger, Aaron Milberger, Michael Milligan, Saud Nagadan, Jamie Noble, Tamara Potwora, Josh Randall, Heather Rathert, Peter Rogers, Alison Ruddy, Stephanie Sanchez, Justin Scardina, Kristy Surovic, Danai Tobaiwa, Rose Vega, Debra Wolfe, and Brandon Young.

## ■ Focus Group Participants

Ramji Balakrishnan
*University of Iowa*

Joanna Ho
*University of California, Irvine*

Leonard Branson
*University of Illinois, Springfield*

Joel Hodes
*Northeastern Illinois University*

Roberta Cable
*Pace University, White Plains*

Frances Kennedy
*Clemson University*

Martha Chapel
*University of Notre Dame*

David Keys
*Northern Illinois University*

Richard Chaplin
*Farleigh Dickinson University*

Ranjani Krishnan
*Michigan State University*

Alan Czyzewski
*Indiana State University*

Kip R. Krumwiede
*Brigham Young University*

Karl Dahlberg
*Rutgers University*

Ron Kucic
*University of Denver*

Terry Elliott
*Morehead State University*

Maria Leach
*Jackson State University*

Samir Fahmy
*St. John's University*

Margarita Lenk
*Colorado State University*

Nick Fessler
*Abilene Christian University*

Chunyan Li
*Pace University, Pleasantville*

Anthony Fontana
*Governor's State University*

Adam Maiga
*University of Wisconsin Milwaukee*

Harlan Fuller
*Illinois State University*

Maureen Mascha
*Marquette University*

Nashwa E. George
*Montclair State University*

Ann McGowan
*Texas A&M University*

R. Lynn Hannan
*Georgia State University*

Laurie McWhorter
*University of North Carolina, Charlotte*

James Hesford
*Washington University, St. Louis*

Eileen Peacock
*Oakland University*

Mike Peterson
*Arizona State University*

Mina Pizzini
*University of Texas at Dallas*

Marjorie Platt
*Northeastern University*

Barbara Roper
*Chicago State University*

Margaret Shackell-Dowell
*University of Notre Dame*

Kenneth Sinclair
*Lehigh University*

Raj Singhal
*University of Indianapolis*

Charlene Spoede Budd
*Baylor University*

Carol W. Springer
*Georgia State University*

Geoff Sprinkle
*Indiana University at Bloomington*

William Stahlin
*Stevens Institute of Technology*

William Stammerjohan
*Mississippi State University*

Lakshmi Tatikonda
*University of Wisconsin*

Wim van der Stede
*University of Southern California*

Marcia Weidenmier
*Texas Christian University*

Michael Wilson
*Metropolitan State University*

## ■ Reviewers

Penne Ainsworth
*University of Wyoming*

Michael Alles
*Rutgers University*

Felix E. Amenkhienan
*Radford University*

Ranjani Ananthakrishnan
*Michigan State University,
Broad School of Management*

Jack Bailes
*Oregon State University*

Craig Bain
*Northern Arizona University*

Ramji Balakrishnan
*University of Iowa*

Wayne Bremser
*Villanova University*

Stephen A. Butler
*Oklahoma University*

Chiaho Chang
*Montclair State University*

Bea Bih-Horng Chiang
*The College of New Jersey*

Charles Christianson
*Luther College*

B. Douglas Clinton
*Northern Illinois University*

Elizabeth Cole
*Old Dominian University*

Jane Cote
*Washington State University*

Elizabeth Davis
*Baylor University*

Michael Eames
*Santa Clara*

Samir B. Fahmy
*St. John's University*

A. Anthony Falgiani
*Western Illinois University*

Timothy A. Farmer
*University of Missouri-St. Louis*

Bud Fennema
*Florida State University*

Nicholas J. Fessler
*Abilene Christian University*

Ken Fowler
*San Jose State University*

George R. French
*Indiana University Southeast*

Edward S. Goodhart
*Shippensburg University*

Donald W. Gribbin
*Southern Illinois University*

Robert Gruber
*University of Wisconsin-Whitewater*

Sanjay Gupta
*Valdosta State University*

R. Lynn Hannan
*Georgia State University*

David J. Harr
*George Mason University*

James Hesford
*Washington University, St. Louis*

Joanna Ho
*University of California-Irvine*

David R. Honodel
*University of Denver*

Robert L. Hurt
*California State Polytechnic
University Pomona*

Douglas Johnson
*Arizona State University*

Bill Joyce
*Eastern Illinois University*

Gail Kaciuba
*Midwestern State University*

Sanford R. Khan
*University of Cincinnati*

Zafar Khan
*Eastern Michigan University*

Larry N. Killough
*Virginia Tech*

Stacy E. Kovar
*Kansas State University*

Leslie Kren
*University of Wisconsin-Milwaukee*

Kip R. Krumwiede
*Brigham Young University*

Chor T. Lau
*California State University, Los Angeles*

Charles Leflar
*University of Arkansas*

Margarita Lenk
*Colorado State University*

D. Jordan Lowe
*University of Nevada-Las Vegas*

Suneel Maheshwari
*Marshall University*

Ann McGowan
*Texas A&M University*

Kevin McNelis
*New Mexico State University*

Pam Meyer
*University of Louisiana*

Ann Murphy
*Metropolitan State College of Denver*

Khursheed Omer
*University of Houston*

Joyce A. Ostrosky
*Illinois State University*

Diane D. Pattison
*University of San Diego*

Mike Petersen
*Arizona State University*

Tamara Phelan
*Northern Illinois University*

Bob Picard
*Idaho State University*

Mina Pizzini
*University of Texas at Dallas*

Marjorie Platt
*Northeastern University*

Paul Polinski
*Case Western Reserve University*

Priscilla R. Reis
*Idaho State University*

Kimberly A. Richardson
*James Madison University*

Ida Robinson-Backmon
*University of Baltimore*

Patrick Rogan
*Saddleback College and
Orange Coast College*

Harold P. Roth
*University of Tennessee-Knoxville*

George Schmelzle
*Indiana University, Purdue University*

Margaret Shackell-Dowell
*University of Notre Dame*

Erin Sims
*DeVry University*

Alice B. Sineath
*Forsyth Technical Community College*

Naomi S. Soderstrom
*University of Colorado-Boulder*

Charlene Spoede Budd
*Baylor University*

Carol W. Springer
*Georgia State University*

Geoff Sprinkle
*Indiana University at Bloomington*

William Stammerjohan
*Mississippi State University*

Nathan Stuart
*University of Florida*

Lakshmi U. Tatikonda
*University of Wisconsin-Osh Kosh*

Sandra C. Vera-Munoz
*University of Notre Dame,
Mendoza College of Business*

Marcia Weidenmier
*Texas Christian University*

Benson Wier
*Virginia Commonwealth University*

James E. Williamson
*San Diego State University*

# Brief Contents

# Contents

## 2 The Cost Function 36

# PART TWO ■ MEASURING AND ASSIGNING COSTS FOR INTERNAL AND EXTERNAL REPORTING

## 5 Job Costing 174

# 6 Process Costing   214

# 7 Activity-Based Costing and Management 256

# 8 Measuring and Assigning Support Department Costs 296

# 9 Joint Product and By-Product Costing   338

# PART THREE ■ PLANNING, MONITORING, AND MOTIVATING

# 10 Static and Flexible Budgets   370

# 11 Standard Costs and Variance Analysis 414

## 12 Strategic Investment Decisions 464

# 13 Joint Management of Revenues and Costs 508

## 14 Measuring and Assigning Costs for Income Statements 548

# 15 Performance Evaluation and Compensation 588

# 16 Strategic Performance Measurement   628

CHAPTER

# 1

# The Role of Accounting Information in Management Decision Making

## ▶In Brief

Managers use cost accounting information to help them make different types of decisions, which include developing organizational strategies, creating operating plans, and monitoring and motivating organizational performance. Managers achieve higher-quality decisions by using higher-quality relevant information and decision-making practices. Managers also need to recognize ethical dilemmas and consider the well-being of others and society when making decisions.

### This Chapter Addresses the Following Questions:

**Q1** What types of decisions do managers make for an organization?
**Q2** What is the role of accounting information in management decision making?
**Q3** How do uncertainties and biases affect the quality of decisions?
**Q4** How can managers make higher-quality decisions?
**Q5** What information is relevant for decision making?
**Q6** What is ethical decision making, and why is it important?

# MOTOROLA'S IRIDIUM PROJECT: LOOK BEFORE YOU LEAP

In 1985, while vacationing in the Caribbean, the wife of a **Motorola** executive became frustrated because she could not call clients using her cell phone. Over time, her frustration led to the creation of a research team, including the executive, to address the problem. The team envisioned a 77-satellite network orbiting the earth so that cellular phones could be used for international calls without interruption (Finkelstein and Sanford, 2000; Smolowitz, 1999). In 1991, Motorola formed a separate company, **Iridium,** to share the risk and cost of the project with a global consortium of firms. Iridium became a public company in 1997.

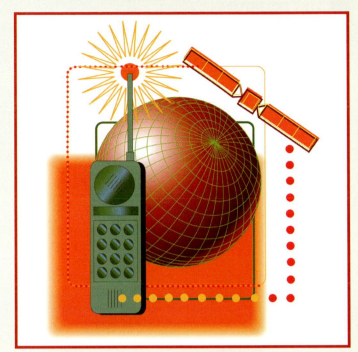

In late 1998, the first phones were sold. The company charged $3,000 for each phone, and calls cost $4 to $9 per minute. Fewer customers signed up for service than predicted—only 20,000 during the first 10 months. Motorola had predicted two million users by 2002 (Smolowitz, 1999). After spending $5 billion on development, Iridium defaulted on $1.5 billion in bonds and declared bankruptcy in August 1999. It was one of the 20 largest bankruptcies in U.S. history (Finkelstein and Sanford, 2000).

What went wrong? The cell phones were bulky and could not be used inside buildings. During the 11 years of Iridium's development, land-based cellular service expanded faster than expected, and customer expectations changed. With the high costs, customers required more sophisticated technology in the phone sets. In addition, Iridium's partners failed to provide adequate sales teams and marketing plans (Finkelstein and Sanford, 2000).

Marketing professors Jagdish Sheth of Emory University and Rajendra Sisodia of Bentley College argued that Iridium's technology and marketing were flawed and that managers apparently fell into a "sunk cost fallacy." Managers continued to invest in the project after it should have been abandoned (Sheth and Sisodia, 1999). ■

SOURCES: S. Finkelstein and S. H. Sanford, "Learning from Corporate Mistakes: The Rise and Fall of Iridium," *Organizational Dynamics* 29, no. 2 (2000), pp. 138–148; J. N. Sheth and R. Sisodia, "Manager's Journal: Why Cell Phones Succeeded Where Iridium Failed," *The Wall Street Journal,* August 23, 1999, p. A14; I. Smolowitz, "Iridium: Lessons for all Companies," *Business Forum* 24, no. 1/2 (2000), pp. 37–38; and J. Schack, "Iridium Splashes Down," *Institutional Investor,* January 2000, p. 98.

## UNCERTAINTIES, BIASES, AND MANAGEMENT DECISION QUALITY

 **Q3** How do uncertainties and biases affect the quality of decisions?

**CHAPTER REFERENCE**

Sometimes decision makers intentionally use biased information because they receive some type of benefit. These types of biases are discussed later in the Colorado Boulders example.

### ■ Uncertainties

A perfect world would have no uncertainties. Managers would be able to perfectly foresee the future and use accounting information to make "correct" decisions. But the world isn't perfect! **Uncertainties** are issues and information about which we have doubt. For example, the exact level of future sales for a product is uncertain.

Managers often face a great deal of uncertainty when they launch a new product. For example, Motorola's Iridium project was subject to many uncertainties related to changing technology, competition, and customer preferences. Over the 11 years it took to develop the Iridium system, land-based cellular service expanded much more rapidly than expected. Widespread availability of less costly and more convenient cellular technology dramatically reduced Iridium's potential market.[1]

### ■ Biases

Managers make poor decisions when they fail to adequately recognize and allow for uncertainties. This type of failure often occurs because of management biases. **Biases** are preconceived notions adopted without careful thought. For example, a manager who dislikes change might automatically reject a proposal that would alter operations and improve efficiency. Similarly, a manager who likes the prestige of leading a large, publicly visible company might promote a merger that reduces shareholder value. Biases cause decision makers to ignore weaknesses in their preferred course of action and prevent them from adequately exploring alternatives.

According to Dartmouth strategy professor Sydney Finkelstein and management consultant Shade Sanford, several factors might have biased managers in favor of continuing the Iridium project.[2]

- Motorola had a history of success with technological innovation.
- Motorola's culture called for managers to support their projects.
- Iridium's CEO had received $1.5 million in Iridium stock options, giving him substantial financial incentives to continue the project.
- Motorola had entered into several contracts with Iridium, providing it with revenue for further development of its own satellite technology.

### ■ Decision Quality

**Decision quality** refers to the characteristics of a decision that affect the likelihood of achieving a positive outcome. Uncertainty and bias reduce decision quality. On average, higher-quality decisions have more positive outcomes because they involve less uncertainty and decision makers are less biased. With lower-quality decisions, the opposite is true. Managers can actively work to reduce or eliminate their biases. Although uncertainties cannot be eliminated, managers can make higher-quality decisions by acknowledging and more thoroughly addressing uncertainties. Later in the chapter we will revisit uncertainties and bias and introduce a process to improve decision making.

## MANAGEMENT DECISION MAKING

 **Q1** What types of decisions do managers make for an organization?

People at different levels within an organization continuously make many different kinds of decisions. They range from broad decisions, such as the markets pursued by the organization, to detailed decisions, such as how to respond to a customer on the telephone. Exhibit 1.1 presents an overview of the decisions that managers make in organizations. It also suggests the role that information systems have in measuring, monitoring, and motivating performance. To better understand the flow of decisions and information, we consider how each part of Exhibit 1.1 relates to a hypothetical small restaurant called Mama's Pizza Outlet.

---

[1]S. Finkelstein and S. H. Sanford, "Learning from Corporate Mistakes: The Rise and Fall of Iridium," *Organizational Dynamics* 29, no. 2 (2000), pp. 138–148.
[2]S. Finkelstein and S. H. Sanford, "Learning from Corporate Mistakes: The Rise and Fall of Iridium," *Organizational Dynamics* 29, no. 2 (2000), pp. 138–148.

**EXHIBIT 1.1**
Overview of Management
Decision Making

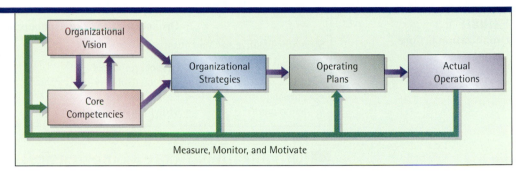

Measure, Monitor, and Motivate

## ■ Organizational Vision

The most far-reaching decision managers make is to identify and shape the organization's vision. The **organizational vision** is the core purpose and ideology of the organization, which guides the organization's overall direction and approaches toward its various stakeholder groups (see Exhibit 1.2). Organizational success increases when employees understand the organizational vision and work collectively to achieve it. To clarify and communicate the vision to employees and other stakeholders, managers sometimes divide the vision into one or more written statements. The definitions of these statements vary from organization to organization. In general, a vision statement is a theoretical description of what the organization should become. A mission statement is a high-level declaration of the organization's purpose. A core values statement is a summary of the beliefs that define the organization's culture. Some managers also publish codes of conduct or statements describing the organization's social or environmental responsibilities.

Suppose that Jason Tuttle, the owner/manager of Mama's Pizza Outlet, believes that the company's purpose is to do the following:

- Financially support his family's lifestyle.
- Ensure the long-term financial well-being of his family.
- Provide a work environment that he enjoys.
- Offer customers enjoyable, moderately-priced eating experiences.
- Enrich the employees' personal lives and careers.

Jason knew that creating value for customers is the key to the company's success. Therefore, he focused on customers when he created the following vision statement, which he posts in the restaurant:

*Mama's Pizza Outlet customers always want to come back because we provide the best eating experience possible.*

**EXHIBIT 1.2**
Organizational Vision

**Organizational Vision**

Core Purpose and Ideology

Create Value for Stakeholders:

- Owners (for-profit)
- Donors (not-for-profit)
- Constituents (governmental)

- Employees
- Customers/clients
- Suppliers

- Community
- Society
- Others

**CURRENT PRACTICE**

### Domino's Pizza Vision

Exceptional people on a mission to be the best pizza delivery company in the world utilizing the company's guiding principles, which are:

At the moment of choice . . .

1. We demand integrity.
2. Our people come first.
3. We take great care of our customers.

4. We make great pizzas every day.
5. We operate with smart hustle and positive energy.

SOURCE: © 2000 Domino's Pizza LLC. www.dominos.com.

**EXHIBIT 1.3**
Organizational Core
Competencies

### Organizational Core Competencies

Strengths Relative to Competitors:

- Productivity
- Skills
- Knowledge
- Technologies
- Physical resources
- Customer/supplier relationships
- Reputation
- Growth opportunities
- Legal rights
- Regulatory advantages
- Financial resources

## ■ Organizational Core Competencies

**Organizational core competencies** are the organization's strengths relative to competitors. The organizational vision and core competencies are closely related. To create value for stakeholders, an organization must have strengths relative to competitors. The vision should build on existing and achievable strengths. Exhibit 1.3 presents many different potential areas of organizational strength.

After giving careful consideration to his vision and to his ability to compete successfully in this type of business, Jason identified the following core competencies for Mama's Pizza Outlet:

- His experience as a manager for a pizza restaurant chain
- Sufficient financial resources to support start-up operations for one year
- High-traffic physical location with bargain rent
- Unique family-owned pizza recipe that customers like

Before proceeding with a plan to launch the restaurant, Jason should analyze how likely it is that the core competencies will result in the achievement of his vision. This analysis relies on estimates and assumptions about the company's ability to compete effectively. He should also monitor over time how well the vision is being met and whether his understanding of the company's strengths relative to competitors undergoes any significant changes. His vision for the company might change over time, leading to a reexamination of core competencies.

## ■ Organizational Strategies

**Organizational strategies** (Exhibit 1.4) are the tactics that managers use to take advantage of core competencies while working toward the organizational vision. Strategies guide long-term decisions such as the proportion of financing through debt and equity, types of goods and services offered, and investments in property, plant, and equipment. Some of these decisions are made and then rarely reconsidered (e.g., form of business organization). Other strategic decisions, such as goods and services offered, should be reevaluated periodically. To monitor strategic progress, managers establish and monitor long-term goals such as market leadership or high-quality customer service.

Jason must make many long-term decisions. Examples include the following:

- Purchase versus lease of restaurant space, pizza ovens, and furnishings
- Type of customer service (e.g., order at counter, table, and delivery)
- Long-term staffing (e.g., contract with a chef)
- Long-term supplier arrangements

**CURRENT PRACTICE**

In 2001, Intel bought Xircom as part of a strategy to provide a more complete line of networking products. Xircom added connectivity from mobile devices to corporate networks.[3]

**EXHIBIT 1.4**
Organizational Strategies

### Organizational Strategies

Long-Term Goals

Organizational Structure

Financial Structure

Long-Term Resource Allocation
- Investments/divestments
- Nature of operations
- Products or services and markets

---

[3]For more information, see J. Radigan, "Intel Extends Its Mobile Strategy," *CFO.com,* January 16, 2001.

**EXHIBIT 1.5**
Operating Plans

> ### Operating Plans
>
> Specific Performance Objectives
>
> Short-Term Financing
>
> Short-Term Resource Allocation
> - Production of goods/services
> - Inbound and outbound logistics
> - Marketing and sales
> - Service
> - Technology
> - Human resources
> - Cash flows

To monitor success of the company's strategies, Jason should also establish long-term goals that he can use to monitor long-term performance.

## Operating Plans

**Operating plans** (Exhibit 1.5) involve specific short-term decisions that shape the organization's day-to-day activities such as drawing cash from a bank line of credit, hiring an employee, or ordering materials. Operating plans often include specific performance objectives, such as budgeted revenues and costs.

Jason must make numerous day-to-day and other short-term decisions. Examples include the following:

- Specific orders and deliveries from vendors
- Advertisements placed in a local newspaper
- Procedures for using cash register and order entry system
- Weekly employee work schedule

## Actual Operations

**Actual operations** are the various actions taken and results achieved over a period of time. Actual operations include customer orders received, revenues earned, number of employees hired, costs incurred, units of goods or services produced, cash received and paid, and so on. Data about actual operations are collected and measured by the organization's information system and then used to monitor and motivate performance.

## Measuring, Monitoring, and Motivating Performance

Managers need information to help them make the types of decisions indicated in Exhibit 1.1. For example, managers need information about costs to help them decide whether to sell a particular product. They also need information to measure actual operations so that they can monitor the success of their decisions and motivate employees to work toward the organizational vision. Decisions are monitored by comparing actual operating results to plans such as budgets and to long-term goals. Desirable employee behavior is often motivated by tying employee performance evaluation and pay to long-term or short-term results. An organization's information system can be designed to measure and report information used for decision making as well as for monitoring and motivating (Exhibit 1.6).

Jason worked with his accountant to ensure that the information system collects the data he needs to measure, monitor, and motivate short-term and long-term performance. He planned to regularly monitor several measures.

- Actual sales compared to short-term and long-term sales targets
- Ratio of cost of ingredients to sales by type of menu item
- Monthly, quarterly, and annual cash flows and profits
- Employee turnover rates

**INTERNATIONAL**

DaimlerChrysler launched a strategy to cut costs by sharing parts across its Mercedes, Chrysler, and Mitsubishi brands. This strategy led to quality deficiencies in Mercedes vehicles, the company's most valuable brand.[4]

 **Q2** What is the role of accounting information in management decision making?

---

[4]See G. Edmondson and K. Kerwin, "Stalled," *Business Week,* September 29, 2003, pp. 54–56.

**EXHIBIT 1.6**
Measure, Monitor, and Motivate

| Measure Performance, Monitor Progress, and Motivate Employees | |
|---|---|
| **Compare Actual Operating Results**<br>• To specific performance objectives<br>• To progress toward long-term goals | **Provide Information for Evaluation**<br>• Of organizational vision<br>• Of organizational core competencies<br>• Of organizational strategies<br>• Of operating plans |
| **Reward Employees**<br>• Performance evaluation<br>• Bonuses or other compensation | |
| **Report to Stakeholders**<br>• Internal reporting<br>• External reporting | |

The information system also generates quarterly financial statements that Jason gives to his bank under the terms of a loan agreement. The bank uses the financial statements to monitor his ability to repay the bank loan.

## COST ACCOUNTING AND DECISION MAKING

**Q2** What is the role of accounting information in management decision making?

**CURRENT PRACTICE**

IMA is an international professional organization devoted to management accounting and financial management. For more information, see the organization's Web site at www.imanet.org.

What is cost accounting, and how does it relate to the idea of measuring, monitoring, and motivating? **Institute of Management Accountants (IMA)** defines **cost accounting** as "a technique or method for determining the cost of a project, process, or thing." Further, IMA suggests that this information is determined through "direct measurement, arbitrary assignment, or systematic and rational allocation."[5]

###  Management Accounting and Financial Accounting

Cost accounting information is used for both management and financial accounting activities. **Management accounting** is the process of gathering, summarizing, and reporting financial and nonfinancial information used internally by managers to make decisions. An example of cost accounting information that is also management accounting information is a breakdown of customer service costs by both product line and average cost per customer service call. **Financial accounting** is the process of preparing and reporting financial information used most frequently by decision makers outside of the organization, such as shareholders and creditors. An example of cost accounting information that is also financial accounting information is the valuation of ending inventory shown on the balance sheet.

### A Brief History of Cost Accounting

Cost accounting techniques were first developed in the early 1800s. As organization size increased, the need for measuring, monitoring, and motivating performance grew. By the mid-1800s, cost accounting practices were well developed. For example, railroad accountants calculated the cost per ton-mile and operating expenses per dollar of revenue. One of the earliest detailed costing systems was developed for Andrew Carnegie's steel mills, for which material and labor cost information was produced on a daily basis. Then in the early 1900s, organizations were required to provide external reports such as financial statements and tax returns. Because the cost to keep two sets of books for separate information requirements was relatively high, cost accounting focused primarily on information for income tax returns and financial statements.

From the early 1900s until the mid-1970s, cost accounting practices changed very little. However, as the business environment became more global, competition increased. In turn,

---

[5]See IMA *Statement on Management Accounting No. 2: Management Accounting Terminology* (Montvale, NJ: NAA, June 1, 1983), p. 25.

demand grew for more sophisticated cost accounting information. Recent technological innovation has enabled cost accountants to develop previously infeasible cost accounting systems. Today, cost accounting information is used for a variety of purposes, including internal decision making, measuring and monitoring performance at all levels, and aligning employee and stakeholder goals. Furthermore, managers now use cost accounting information to analyze the profitability of customers and to coordinate transactions with suppliers—extending traditional cost accounting beyond the walls of the organization.

## ■ Strategic Cost Management

**CHAPTER REFERENCE**

See Chapter 16 for a complete discussion of the balanced scorecard.

Cost accounting is often defined narrowly as relating to the measurement of costs within an organization (demonstrated by the IMA definition). However, cost accounting information is increasingly defined more broadly to include both financial and nonfinancial information, and to include items that do not relate strictly to the measurement of costs. From this trend, a new term has been introduced: **Strategic cost management** refers to a simultaneous focus on reducing costs and strengthening an organization's strategic position.[6] As strategic cost management gains in popularity, organizations also adopt balanced scorecards. The **balanced scorecard** is a formal approach used to help organizations translate their vision into objectives that can be measured and monitored using both financial and nonfinancial performance measures.

The role of cost and managerial accountants is much broader than in the past. In this text, therefore, we not only master techniques for generating cost accounting information, but also learn how to use that information in business decisions. We learn to recognize and work with information that is not perfect. Specifically, we learn how both uncertainties in cost accounting information and decision-maker bias can result in poor decisions.

---

### GUIDE YOUR LEARNING  **1.1**  Key Terms

Stop to confirm that you understand the new terms introduced in the last several pages.

| | |
|---|---|
| *Uncertainties (p. 4) | Actual operations (p. 7) |
| *Biases (p. 4) | Cost accounting (p. 8) |
| Decision quality (p. 4) | Management accounting (p. 8) |
| Organizational vision (p. 5) | Financial accounting (p. 8) |
| *Organizational core competencies (p. 6) | Strategic cost management (p. 9) |
| *Organizational strategies (p. 6) | Balanced scorecard (p. 9) |
| *Operating plans (p. 7) | |

For each of these terms, write a definition in your own words. For starred terms, list at least one example that is different from the ones given in this textbook.

---

### CURRENT PRACTICE

#### Professional Management Accounting Certification

IMA is an international organization of financial management executives and accountants that provides a wide variety of information and activities for its members, including local meetings with informative speakers, continuing professional education, and Web-based and printed information about current management and cost accounting practices.

The **Certified Management Accountant (CMA)** designation is recognized internationally and is offered by IMA. To become a CMA, you must meet educational and work experience requirements and also pass a four-part examination covering the following areas:

1. Business analysis
2. Management accounting and reporting
3. Strategic management
4. Business applications

More information is available from IMA's Web site at www.imanet.org under Certification.

---

[6]See R. Cooper and R. Slagmulder, "The Scope of Strategic Cost Management," in James Edwards (ed.), *Emerging Practices in Cost Management* (Boston, MA: Warren, Gorham & Lamont, 1999).

## INFORMATION SYSTEMS AND MANAGEMENT DECISION MAKING

**Q2** What is the role of accounting information in management decision making?

Managers use many types of information to help them make decisions. Information can be gathered formally or informally. Formal methods include point-of-service optical character readers, such as those used when customers purchase merchandise at retail stores. Such systems track inventory levels, geographic distribution of sales, trends, the relationship between prices and sales, and so on. Informal methods are also important for collecting information from inside or outside the organization. For example, individuals inside a company often gather product pricing information by reading industry trade journals or examining competitor's Web sites.

Most organizations have many databases that contain information collected formally or informally from internal or external sources. Access to database information is often restricted to specific individuals. In addition, much valuable information is not readily accessible because it is held in the minds of employees. This information, called *intellectual capital,* is not formally captured by the information system. Thus, it is difficult for decision makers, even within an organization, to gain access to all of the information they might wish to use. It is easy to argue that managers should obtain more and better information to help them make decisions. However, the benefit must exceed the cost of generating information.

### ■ Internal and External Reports

To facilitate decision making and meet external reporting requirements, accounting departments use software to generate a variety of internal and external reports that summarize or highlight information. An **internal report** is a document that presents information for use only inside an organization. An **external report** is a document that presents information for use outside an organization. Exhibit 1.7 summarizes common types of internal and external reports.

**EXHIBIT 1.7** Examples of Internal and External Reports

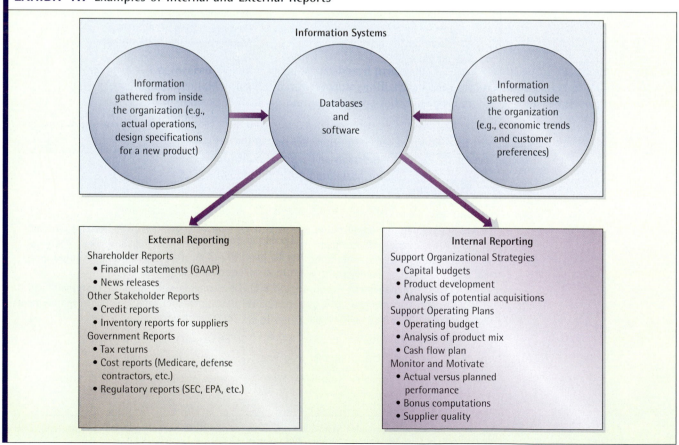

Internal reports are designed to provide information for the types of management decisions introduced in Exhibits 1.1 through 1.6. Some internal reports, such as monthly sales summaries, are issued regularly. Other internal reports, such as the analysis of a potential business acquisition, are generated for onetime use.

External reports can be distributed to different constituencies for many purposes. External reports such as income tax returns are required. Others are discretionary, such as a news release about a joint venture agreement. Some reports, such as financial statements given to a supplier to obtain credit, facilitate business activities.

Although reports are developed for a specific audience, they may be used for other purposes. For example, internal reports such as quarterly sales data can be shared with people outside the organization. Similarly, external reports such as financial statements are sometimes used within the organization. In addition, organizations use reports prepared outside the organization (e.g., by consultants or vendors) for internal decision making.

## Improvements in Information for Management Decision Making

The detail and quality of organizational data have improved in recent years. Historically, organizations used one accounting system that gathered information for financial statements. These data, prepared using Generally Accepted Accounting Principles (GAAP), were used for both external and internal reporting. This type of information was not always ideal for management decision making. As a result, resources were often poorly allocated, leading to operating and investment inefficiencies.

## Business Intelligence Systems

Recent information system developments have focused on business intelligence (BI). The Internet and BI software provide opportunities for managers to save costs and improve profitability in the following ways:

- Integrating systems
  - Throughout an organization
  - Between an organization and its customers and suppliers

- Improving management of
  - Customer relationships
  - Supply chains
  - Work teams within an organization

## IMPROVING INFORMATION AND ITS USE IN DECISION MAKING

**Q3** How do uncertainties and biases affect the quality of decisions?

**Q4** How can managers make higher-quality decisions?

For business decisions, managers use information to form expectations about the future. For example, managers might use past sales information to predict future sales trends. Or they might use past costs to predict future costs. Their expectations help them decide on the best organizational strategies and operating plans.

## Types of Uncertainty

Virtually all business decisions are made under a cloud of uncertainty, as illustrated in Exhibit 1.8. Because the future cannot be seen—and even historical information is imperfect—decision makers cannot perfectly predict future results. Many types of uncertainties cloud management decisions. Managers may be unable to

- **Accurately describe a problem.** For example, managers cannot fully know why sales failed to meet expectations. Was product demand overestimated? Was the selling price too high? Were there problems with product or service quality?

---

[7]See Guyton and Lund, "Transforming the Revenue Cycle," *Healthcare Financial Management,* March 2003, pp. 72–78.
[8]For more information, see J. Kerstetter, "The Info Tech 100: Software," *Business Week Online,* June 24, 2002.

**EXHIBIT 1.8** Making Decisions Under a Cloud of Uncertainty

- **Identify all possible options.** For example, managers may be unable to envision new ways of doing business, even though they are possible.
- **Know the outcomes of various options.** For example, managers cannot exactly anticipate the amount of future costs, even when operating plans are unchanged from the prior period.
- **Anticipate all future conditions.** For example, managers cannot foresee all possible future actions by customers, vendors, or competitors. They also cannot foresee unpredictable natural, governmental, or other externally generated events.

## ■ Path to Higher-Quality Decisions

Higher-quality decisions result from better information as well as from better decision processes. Organizations often use complex and sophisticated information systems to gather and organize information for decision making. Because of this sophistication, some decision makers are mistakenly confident that the information they use is correct, and they ignore uncertainty. Other decision makers, recognizing that uncertainties always cloud decisions, go to the other extreme. Instead of relying on imperfect information, they believe it is sufficient to use only their intuition to make important business decisions. Neither of these approaches is optimal.

Exhibit 1.9 summarizes the path to higher-quality decisions. Higher quality information has fewer uncertainties. It is more complete and directly relevant to the decision. It is timely, helping managers *as* they make decisions, not after the fact. In addition, it has value: The benefits exceed the cost of generating the information. An important role of an accounting or other information system is to capture higher-quality information and report it in a way that improves its usefulness for decision making. Higher-quality reports are more directly relevant to the decision. They are easily understood and readily available to decision makers. In turn, a higher-quality decision-making process is more thorough and unbiased. It is more clearly focused on organizational priorities and encourages strategic, creative, and visionary thinking.

This chapter has already introduced two pervasive issues: ways in which uncertainty can cloud decisions and an approach to higher-quality decisions. Next, we expand upon two additional pervasive issues: information relevance and the decision-making process.

**EXHIBIT 1.9**
Path to Higher-Quality
Management Decisions

# RELEVANT INFORMATION FOR DECISION MAKING

**Q5** What information is relevant for decision making?

As highlighted in Exhibit 1.9, higher-quality decisions make use of higher-quality information. One of the characteristics of higher-quality information is its direct relevance to the decision. **Relevant information** helps the decision maker evaluate and choose among alternative courses of action. Relevant information concerns the future and varies with the action taken. On the other hand, **irrelevant information** does not vary with the action taken and therefore is not useful for decision making. Although the information may be accurate, it simply does not help the decision maker evaluate the alternatives. Managers are less efficient and make lower-quality decisions when they allow irrelevant information to inappropriately influence their choices.

Whether a given type of information is relevant or irrelevant depends on the decision and other factors. Suppose a student is deciding whether to sign up for a particular college course. If the student has selected a degree program and wishes to graduate as quickly as possible, relevant information includes whether the course counts toward graduation. However, if the student's goal is to take courses in a variety of disciplines to explore possible degree programs, then it might be irrelevant whether the course will help meet graduation requirements.

## ■ Relevant and Irrelevant Cash Flows

Cash flows are commonly used as information in management decisions. Thus, managers often need to distinguish between relevant and irrelevant cash flows. **Relevant cash flows** are **incremental cash flows;** that is, they occur under one course of action or decision alternative, but not under another. Such cash flows are also called **avoidable cash flows** because they are avoided if the course of action or decision alternative is not taken. They are relevant because they help managers distinguish among alternatives. Suppose management is deciding between two courses of action: whether to lease or build office space. The costs of constructing the building are avoidable cash flows if management chooses the lease alternative. Therefore, the costs of constructing the building are relevant to the lease-or-build decision.

**Irrelevant cash flows**, also called **unavoidable cash flows,** occur regardless of which course of action or decision alternative is chosen. They are unavoidable, no matter which action is taken. They are irrelevant for a specific decision because they do not help managers choose among alternatives. Whether the organization leases or builds office space, it will still incur electrical costs for lighting. Therefore, electrical costs are an unavoidable cash flow, making them irrelevant to the lease-or-build decision.

---

### GUIDE YOUR LEARNING  1.2  Key Terms

Stop to confirm that you understand the new terms introduced in the last several pages.

| | |
|---|---|
| *Internal report (p. 10) | *Incremental cash flows (p. 13) |
| *External report (p. 10) | *Avoidable cash flows (p. 13) |
| *Relevant information (p. 13) | *Irrelevant cash flows (p. 13) |
| *Irrelevant information (p. 13) | *Unavoidable cash flows (p. 13) |
| *Relevant cash flows (p. 13) | |

For each of these terms, write a definition in your own words. For starred terms, list at least one example that is different from the ones given in this textbook.

---

## ■ Identifying Relevant Cash Flows

To identify relevant cash inflows and outflows, we use an incremental cash flow approach. For example, in the lease-or-build decision, we would identify any additional cash inflows and outflows that would occur if the new facilities were built, and compare them to the inflows and outflows for the lease option.

Consider the arguments that sports teams make when they want a city to build a new sports facility. The following illustration highlights the importance of distinguishing between relevant (avoidable) and irrelevant (unavoidable) cash flows.

## COLORADO BOULDERS
### IDENTIFYING RELEVANT CASH FLOWS

In the summer of 2003, Desert View, a medium-sized city in southern Arizona, faced a major crisis. The owner of the Colorado Boulders baseball club threatened to move spring training to another city unless Desert View built new spring training facilities. Civic leaders and sports fans began to pressure the city government to subsidize the new facilities to keep the team in town and bring in more teams.

One argument made in favor of the new facilities was that tax revenues from the expenditures made by fans totaled more than $2 million per year. Given this argument, the government could afford to build new facilities. Following are the computations used to support this position:

| 2003 Expenditures by Fans (300,000 attendance) | |
|---|---|
| Ticket sales | $ 1,500,000 |
| Concession expenditures | 4,500,000 |
| Travel costs (primarily automobile) | 1,500,000 |
| Food before and after game | 3,000,000 |
| Entertainment | 600,000 |
| Lodging | 9,000,000 |
| Shopping goods | 7,300,000 |
| Total Expenditures by Fans | $27,400,000 |

| Estimated City, County, and State Tax Revenues | |
|---|---|
| City admissions tax (10% of ticket sales) | $ 150,000 |
| Sales tax (7.9% of nonticket fan expenditures) | 2,046,100 |
| Total Tax Revenues | $2,196,100 |

*Note:* About 12% of the fans were from outside the state.

The city planned to tax hotels, recreational vehicle parks, and car rental agencies to raise the funds needed for the new facilities. Owners of these businesses objected, arguing that these revenues were not relevant to the new training facilities. They claimed that they were already fully booked during the spring training months with golfers and tourists unrelated to baseball. Therefore, having new facilities for spring baseball training would not increase their revenues. They expressed concern that the increase in taxes might actually decrease their revenues by driving tourists away.

### Identifying Relevant Cash Flows

Which, if any, cash flows are relevant to the city's decision? Relevant cash flows are those that are avoided if the alternative is not taken. If spring training were not available, tourists would visit other Desert View attractions, such as the Desert Museum (a desert zoo and botanical gardens). They might attend spring training games already being played at the old facilities. Many other activities are available for both local residents and tourists, including golfing, spas, shopping malls, and other tourist attractions. The weather that attracts spring baseball training also attracts a large number of tourists who simply want to spend a few weeks in the sun. All of the listed revenues would likely be generated in Desert View whether or not major league spring training is held in Desert View. Therefore, none of the cash flows are relevant in deciding whether the city should build a new stadium.

The arguments that favor public subsidization of privately owned sports teams are frequently made by team owners and local politicians based on assumptions about increased revenues. Such assumptions have not been supported by research. In fact, research has found no increases in local revenues even during years when an event as big as the Super Bowl is played in the area (see the listed sources).

Will additional revenues be generated from the new spring training facilities? Hotel owners say they have no room for additional baseball fans in their hotels. Although some people attend spring training games, they come to Desert View during February and March for golf and other activities, in addition to spring training. Therefore, none of the revenues listed are incremental. If visitors do not attend baseball games, they will still spend their vacation money in Desert View. Thus, city taxes will be collected either way. Yet, all of the costs will be incurred to build the training facilities. When incremental revenues and costs are compared, it appears that the city and county will build the stadium without collecting any additional tax revenues to pay for the facilities.

The politicians and sports fans in favor of this proposal used biased information in hopes of influencing the decision to build new training facilities.

Sources: J. Ward, "If You Build It, Will They Come?" *The American City and County*, April 2002, pp. 38–44; R. Noll and A. Zimbalist (eds.), *Sports, Jobs and Taxes: The Economic Impact of Sports Teams and Stadiums* (Washington, DC: Brookings Institution Press, 1997); M. S. Rosentraub, "Major League Lo$ers" (New York: Basic Books, 1997); K. Badenhausen and L. Kump, "Cashing In," *Forbes*, September 17, 2001; and M. K. Ozanian, "Football Follies," *Forbes*, September 17, 2001.

---

### GUIDE YOUR LEARNING 1.3 Colorado Boulders

Colorado Boulders illustrates the identification of relevant cash flows. For this illustration:

| Define It | Identify the Problem | Identify Uncertainties | Explore Biases | Prioritize Options |
|---|---|---|---|---|
| In your own words, distinguish between relevant and irrelevant information. | What decision was being addressed? Who was responsible for making the decision? | Why was the amount of relevant cash flows uncertain? | What types of biases were involved in this decision? | Given the uncertainties and biases in situations such as this one, how can a high-quality decision be made? |

## Impact of Biases

The type of bias described in the Colorado Boulders example occurs frequently and may or may not be intentional. Biases cause decision makers to ignore information that is contrary to their preconceived notions. In other words, biases cause decision makers to discard relevant information and inappropriately take into account irrelevant information. Bureaucratic inertia contributes to this type of bias; individuals inside an organization might not be motivated to seek or adequately analyze relevant information.

## Importance of Identifying Relevant Information

As you can see from the Colorado Boulders example, it is important for decision makers to identify the relevant (incremental) cash flows and other information. Failure to do so often leads to poor decisions. When others are promoting a course of action, more objective individuals analyze relevant cash flows to help uncover biased information. Identifying relevant information is a useful skill that requires practice. We will work on developing this skill throughout this textbook.

## STEPS FOR BETTER THINKING: A DECISION-MAKING PROCESS

 **Q4** How can managers make higher-quality decisions?

Few management decisions can be made with absolute certainty. However, managers can improve the quality of uncertain decisions by using a higher-quality decision-making process. Steps for Better Thinking, presented in Exhibit 1.10, is an example of a decision-making process that leads to higher-quality decisions. We introduce Steps for Better Thinking here and then refer to it continuously throughout the textbook.

Steps for Better Thinking is a process for addressing **open-ended problems**—ones with no single "correct" solution due to significant uncertainties. The decision maker's task for open-ended problems is to find the best—not the only—possible solution. Most management decisions are open-ended; Steps for Better Thinking will improve your ability to address them.

Steps for Better Thinking is portrayed as a series of increasingly difficult skills that are needed for higher-quality decisions. Exhibit 1.10 is portrayed as a set of steps because strong performance in the lower-level skills sets the stage for strong performance in the higher-level skills. Conversely, if the lower-level skills are weak, then the entire structure will also be

**EXHIBIT 1.10** Steps for Better Thinking: A Decision-Making Process

| FOUNDATION Knowledge and Skills | STEP 1 Identify the Problem, Relevant Information, and Uncertainties | STEP 2 Explore Interpretations and Connections | STEP 3 Prioritize Alternatives and Implement Conclusions | STEP 4 Envision and Direct Strategic Innovation |
|---|---|---|---|---|
| • Repeat or paraphrase information from textbooks, notes, etc.<br><br>• Reason to single "correct" solution, perform computations, etc. | • Identify problem and acknowledge reasons for enduring uncertainty and absence of single "correct" solution<br><br>• Identify relevant information and uncertainties embedded in the information | • Interpret information: (1) Recognize and control for own biases (2) Articulate assumptions and reasoning associated with alternative points of view (3) Qualitatively interpret evidence from a variety of points of view<br><br>• Organize information in meaningful ways that encompass problem complexities | • After thorough analysis, develop and use reasonable guidelines for prioritizing factors to consider and choosing among solution options<br><br>• Efficiently implement conclusions, involving others as needed | • Acknowledge, explain, and monitor limitations of endorsed solution<br><br>• Integrate skills into ongoing process for generating and using information to guide strategic innovation |

Step 4: Envisioning

Step 3: Prioritizing

Step 2: Exploring

Step 1: Identifying

Foundation: Knowing

weak. To help explain the meaning of each step, we refer to the **Motorola Iridium** case from the beginning of this chapter.

**Knowing.** The foundation of Steps for Better Thinking consists of the knowledge and basic skills needed to deal with a problem. To launch a project such as Iridium, an organization would need to have knowledge in many areas, including:

- Cellular telephones and satellite communications
- Consumer markets and distribution methods
- Research and development methods
- Technical knowledge and expertise for development of new technology
- Production processes and costs
- Sales and marketing strategies

**Step 1—Identifying.** This step involves identifying relevant information and uncertainties. Recognizing uncertainties, as highlighted in Exhibits 1.8 and 1.9, is also an extremely important part of managerial decision making. It usually requires much practice to become adept at this part of the process. There were many uncertainties in the Iridium project, including customer preferences and the size of the customer market. Managers sometimes fail to adequately identify major uncertainties. This failure, in turn, causes them to make decisions without adequate analysis or to be overly confident in their decisions.

**Step 2—Exploring.** This step includes recognizing and controlling biases and more thoroughly considering uncertainties, as emphasized earlier in Exhibits 1.8 and 1.9, and also interpreting information from different viewpoints. For this kind of assessment, we must be adept at recognizing and evaluating assumptions, gauging the quality of information, and putting ourselves "in others' shoes." We can think of Step 2 as analyzing the strengths and weaknesses of different alternatives. Adequate performance of Step 2 is often the most time-consuming and important step when addressing open-ended problems. Too often, decision makers are hasty and fail to thoroughly analyze the information related to a problem; they jump to a conclusion. Careful attention to Step 2 activities increases the probability of making the best decision. As discussed earlier in the chapter, Motorola and Iridium managers were biased toward continuing the Iridium project. Biases caused the managers to discount problematic issues, such as the large size of the Iridium phones, the inability to use the phones indoors, the high cost of the phones and service, competition from land-based cellular systems, and reliance on partner marketing efforts.[9]

**Step 3—Prioritizing.** Step 3 involves making trade-offs and choosing the best possible alternative, then efficiently implementing it. For managers, these activities include ensuring that the organization's values, core competencies, and strategies are adequately considered. Efficient implementation includes motivating performance within the organization. In decisions such as continuation of the Iridium project, any weaknesses at Steps 1 and 2 automatically lead to weaknesses at Step 3. It is not possible to reach a high-quality decision when there are major uncertainties or when managers are biased toward a course of action.

**Step 4—Envisioning.** This step is necessary because open-ended problems cannot be solved with absolute certainty and because the economic environment changes. Management decisions require monitoring and possible revision during implementation and as new events occur over time. The most gifted decision makers act strategically to recognize change and new threats and also to visualize new opportunities. According to Dartmouth strategy professor Sydney Finkelstein and management consultant Shade Sanford, major losses in the Iridium project might have been prevented if the managers had objectively reevaluated the project in 1996 at the end of the development stage. They concluded that the project was probably a good one at the time it was originally launched. However, they argued that changes in competition and Iridium's technological problems should have precluded further investment.[10]

## ETHICAL DECISION MAKING

 **Q6** What is ethical decision making, and why is it important?

We are each responsible for our own behavior. Furthermore, managers and accountants are responsible for the behavior of the organizations they manage. For this reason, ethical behavior is both an individual and an organizational obligation. Steps in **ethical decision making** are presented in Exhibit 1.11.

The unethical behavior of a few accountants and managers has greatly affected investor beliefs and the value of the stock market. When investors lose faith in information produced by organizations, they are unwilling to invest, and market downturns occur. These events happen because accountants and managers fail to use ethical decision making.[11] Ethical behavior is required of every employee within an organization.

[9]S. Finkelstein and S. H. Sanford, "Learning from Corporate Mistakes: The Rise and Fall of Iridium," *Organizational Dynamics* 29, no. 2 (2000), pp. 138–148.

[10]S. Finkelstein and S. H. Sanford, "Learning from Corporate Mistakes: The Rise and Fall of Iridium," *Organizational Dynamics* 29, no. 2 (2000), pp. 138–148.

[11]See I. J. Dugan, "Before Enron, Greed Helped Sink the Respectability of Accounting," *The Wall Street Journal,* March 14, 2002, p. A1; and "High Profiles in Hot Water," *The Wall Street Journal,* June 28, 2002, p. B1.

**EXHIBIT 1.11** Steps in Ethical Decision Making

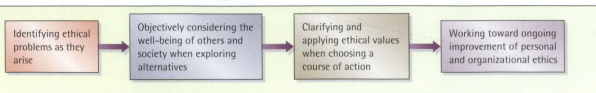

### Enron and the Reputation of Accountants

During the early 2000s, the business world was shaken by numerous cases of financial reporting fraud involving accountants in both private industry and audit firms. Accountants at Enron manipulated financial statements and grossly overstated profits with the complicity of auditors. Exposure of the fraud triggered the largest corporate bankruptcy in U.S. history. Investigations into the role of Enron's auditor led to the demise of Arthur Andersen, one of the world's largest public accounting firms. The incident involving Enron was followed by exposure of numerous other financial fraud cases, causing widespread doubt about the integrity of accountants and auditors. Accountants were no longer viewed as the most trusted professionals; they had fallen to the bottom of Americans' "Who Do You Trust?" polls. The accounting profession responded by launching renewed efforts to ensure integrity and regain public trust. In his inaugural address as chairman of the AICPA, S. Scott Voynich stated, "Integrity is not something you carry with you only when you meet clients or walk through your office door. It's a way of living, 24 hours a day, seven days a week. Integrity also means working collaboratively with any affected parties to create something that leaves the world better off."

SOURCE: D. R. Dwares and M. M. McGuane, "Attorneys Talk About Representing Accountants in the Era of Enron and Other Corporate Scandals," *The CPA Journal*, March 2003; "Voynich Elected AICPA Chairman; Stresses Integrity in Inaugural Speech," news release, American Institute of Certified Public Accountants, October 21, 2003, available on-line at www.aicpa.org/news/index.htm.

## ■ Conflicting Interests

It is common in business situations for the interests of various parties to be at odds. For example, if one division's products compete successfully, another division may lose sales and then receive fewer of the organization's resources. If one person is promoted to the position of chief financial officer, someone else is not promoted, and that person may leave the firm in search of better opportunities elsewhere. If a company invests funds in an environmental protection program, less money is available for shareholder dividends.

## ■ Motive for Ethical Behavior

Do we expect people to resolve conflicts of interest by making choices in their own best interests? If so, this expectation raises another question. What do we mean by "best interests"? Do we necessarily mean greed, selfishness, and insensitivity? Although our society is based on capitalism, we do not believe that anything goes. More is at stake than financial gain or other supposed rewards. Integrity, reputation, self-respect, and social welfare are compelling rewards for ethical behavior.

The following Bausch & Lomb case provides an opportunity to analyze the ethics of decision making.

## FOCUS ON ETHICAL DECISION MAKING
## Bausch & Lomb's Sales Tactics

By 1993, Bausch & Lomb (B&L) had experienced steadily increasing sales for many years. Customers viewed its merchandise, including eye care supplies and Rayban sunglasses, as high quality. Top management at B&L set high targets for future revenue increases and expected division managers to meet the targets. Unfortunately, sales growth in the contact lens division turned sluggish. Despite efforts by sales representatives to promote ever-increasing sales, it became clear that the division would not meet its sales goals (Maremont, 1994 and 1995; SEC 1997).

Top divisional managers made a bold move. According to the SEC, just 11 days before the end of the year, B&L held a meeting with its 32 independent contact lens distributors. The distributors were told that B&L was changing its contact lens distribution activities. The company wanted its distributors to take over its large-volume sales to eye doctors and major retailers. To handle the shift in sales, B&L insisted that distributors take significant deliveries of contact lenses before year-end. The quantities were equivalent to one-to-two years of the distributors' previous purchases, even though many still owned four-to-twelve months' inventory. In addition, prices were 50% higher than in the past. Distributors were told that they would lose their distributorships if they refused (Maremont, 1994; SEC 1997).

To reduce distributors' concerns, B&L told the distributors they would have to pay for inventory as it sold during the next six months, with the balance payable for the remaining inventory due at the end of six months. No interest would be charged. However, B&L insisted that each distributor sign a promissory note. B&L's sales representatives orally promised many of the distributors that they wouldn't have to pay for the shipments until sold and that payment terms could be renegotiated if the new sales program was not successful (Maremont, 1994; SEC 1997).

Contrary to its promises, B&L continued to sell to its high-volume retail accounts—at prices lower than what they charged distributors. Thus, distributors could neither sell their inventories nor make profits. Some distributors then sold products on the gray market, increasing competition for B&L's other customers. By late 1994, many distributors demanded that B&L allow them to return excess inventories (Maremont, 1994).

*Business Week* published an investigation into B&L's practices. The Securities and Exchange Commission (SEC) soon launched its own investigation. During the next year, B&L's CEO retired, and the company restated its earnings to reverse the sales (Maremont, 1995; Norton, 1995). Although an investigation by B&L's board of directors concluded that management did nothing wrong (*The Wall Street Journal*, 1995), the SEC imposed a cease-and-desist order against B&L and three of its contact lens division officers (SEC, 1997).

Mark Maremont, a reporter for *Business Week*, posited that B&L's problems stemmed from problems within its corporate culture. He claimed that the forceful management style and performance-oriented focus of the CEO encouraged B&L's managers to do whatever they could to meet sales targets. The CEO's annual bonus was weighted 30% on sales growth, 30% on earnings growth, 30% on return on equity, and 10% on customer satisfaction. According to Maremont, "Many of Corporate America's most successful companies share similar goals. Good managers attempt to balance that orientation with effective controls and compensation plans that also reward practices that pay off in the longer term. B&L's saga shows what happens when those countervailing forces aren't strong enough" (Maremont, 1995, p. 80).

Sources: M. Maremont, "Blind Ambition: How the Pursuit of Results Got Out of Hand at Bausch & Lomb," *Business Week*, October 23, 1995, pp. 78–92; M. Maremont, "Investigations: Numbers Game at Bausch & Lomb?" *Business Week*, December 19, 1994, pp. 104–110; E. Norton, "CEO Gill to Retire from Bausch & Lomb; Carpenter Is Seen as Possible Successor," *The Wall Street Journal*, December 14, 1995, p. B10; "Panel at Bausch & Lomb Releases Results of Probe," *The Wall Street Journal*, April 24, 1996, p. B5; and Administrative Proceeding File No. 3-9488, U.S. Securities and Exchange Commission (SEC), November 17, 1997, available on-line at www.sec.gov/litigation/admin/3439329.txt.

**CHAPTER REFERENCE**

See Chapter 15 for a complete discussion about compensation and its effects on manager and employee behavior.

## ■ Analyzing the Ethics of a Decision

One way to improve our ethical decision making is to analyze the decision-making process used by others. The steps in Exhibit 1.11 are used in the following analyses of Bausch & Lomb.

**Identifying Ethical Problems As They Arise** The contact lens division managers at Bausch & Lomb should have been aware that their actions were inappropriate. However, in their attempt to achieve sales targets and meet the CEO's demands, the managers apparently failed to consider whether their decision involved an ethical dilemma. When a corporate culture rewards employees for "making the numbers" without appropriate regard to how results are achieved, individuals often begin by taking small steps that are "slightly wrong" and then increase the size of these steps over time. They can avoid ethical missteps through earlier recognition of ethical dilemmas.

**Objectively Considering the Well-Being of Others and Society** Bausch & Lomb's contact lens managers were under extreme pressure to achieve targeted sales growth. In turn, this pressure encouraged the managers to adopt biased assumptions about future sales prospects and to ignore the effects of their actions on others. For example:

- Shareholders made potentially poor investment decisions because they relied on reported financial statement values.
- Distributors incurred additional inventory carrying costs because they were forced to accept shipments they did not need.
- Employees who worked for the managers were pressured to overstate sales.

People are more likely to make ethical decisions when they stop to objectively consider how others might be affected by their actions.

**Clarifying and Applying Ethical Values When Choosing a Course of Action** Perhaps the most telling aspects of the B&L case are the ethical trade-offs the managers apparently made. Their decision suggests that great emphasis was placed on attempting to meet the current year's sales target, with less emphasis on ethical values such as the following:

- Dealing fairly with distributors
- Addressing the company's real sales growth problems
- Establishing and maintaining an honest corporate culture

An analysis of the values in their decision might have helped the managers clarify their priorities and hopefully discouraged them from adopting their course of action.

Although the managers were primarily responsible, many employees were involved in the scheme to overstate sales. For example, individual sales personnel participated in obtaining written contracts from distributors for the additional shipments. Accountants recorded the transactions as sales revenue. These employees might have used rationalizations such as "Everyone else is doing it" or "I'll be fired if I don't do what I'm told." However, these employees adopted the same questionable values as the managers when they agreed to go along.

**Working Toward Ongoing Improvement of Personal and Organizational Ethics** As instances of ethical wrongdoing have mounted over time, it has become increasingly clear that ethical behavior is the responsibility of individuals as well as organizations. In 2002, the U.S. Congress passed the Sarbanes-Oxley Act, which requires public company managers and boards of directors to assume greater legal responsibility. Managers are now required to self-assess internal controls and financial reporting risks. The board of directors and its audit committee are required to increase their oversight of managers and auditors. The process of implementing the new requirements is an opportunity for organizations to reassess their policies and culture. The best organizations actively seek ways to learn from past behaviors and to continuously work toward becoming more ethical.[12] In the following Current Practice is IMA's Code of Ethics.

---

[12]Protiviti, Inc., "Insights on Today's Sarbanes-Oxley and Corporate Governance Challenges: Survey of Chief Financial Officers with 300 Publicly Held U.S. Companies," September 2003.

## IMA Ethical Standards

In today's modern world of business, individuals in management accounting and financial management constantly face ethical dilemmas. For example, if the accountant's immediate superior instructs the accountant to record the physical inventory at its original costs when it is obvious that the inventory has a reduced value due to obsolescence, what should the accountant do? To help make such a decision, here is a brief general discussion of ethics and the "Standards of Ethical Conduct for Members."

Ethics, in its broader sense, deals with human conduct in relation to what is morally good and bad, right and wrong. To determine whether a decision is good or bad, the decision-maker must compare his/her options with some standard of perfection. This standard of perfection is not a statement of static position but requires the decision-maker to assess the situation and the values of the parties affected by the decision. The decision-maker must then estimate the outcome of the decision and be responsible for its results. Two good questions to ask when faced with an ethical dilemma are, "Will my actions be fair and just to all parties affected?" and "Would I be pleased to have my closest friends learn of my actions?"

Individuals in management accounting and financial management have a unique set of circumstances relating to their employment. To help them assess their situation, the Institute of Management Accountants (IMA) has developed the following "Standards of Ethical Conduct for Members."

### Standards of Ethical Conduct for Members

Members of IMA have an obligation to the public, their profession, the organizations they serve, and themselves, to maintain the highest standards of ethical conduct. In recognition of this obligation, the IMA has promulgated the following standards of ethical conduct for its members. Members shall not commit acts contrary to these standards nor shall they condone the commission of such acts by others within their organizations.

Members shall abide by the more stringent code of ethical conduct, whether that is the standards widely practiced in their country or IMA's Standards of Ethical Conduct. In no case will a member conduct herself or himself by any standard that is not at least equivalent to the standards identified for members in IMA's Standards of Ethical Conduct.

The standards of ethical conduct for IMA members are published in SMA 1C (Statement on Management Accounting).

### Competence

Members have a responsibility to:

- Maintain an appropriate level of professional competence by ongoing development of their knowledge and skills.
- Perform their professional duties in accordance with relevant laws, regulations, and technical standards.
- Prepare complete and clear reports and recommendations after appropriate analyses of relevant and reliable information.

### Confidentiality

Members have a responsibility to:

- Refrain from disclosing confidential information acquired in the course of their work except when authorized, unless legally obligated to do so.
- Inform subordinates as appropriate regarding the confidentiality of information acquired in the course of their work and monitor their activities to assure the maintenance of that confidentiality.
- Refrain from using or appearing to use confidential information acquired in the course of their work for unethical or illegal advantage either personally or through third parties.

### Integrity

Members have a responsibility to:

- Avoid actual or apparent conflicts of interest and advise all appropriate parties of any potential conflict.
- Refrain from engaging in any activity that would prejudice their ability to carry out their duties ethically.
- Refuse any gift, favor, or hospitality that would influence or would appear to influence their actions.

*(continued)*

- Refrain from either actively or passively subverting the attainment of the organization's legitimate and ethical objectives.
- Recognize and communicate professional limitations or other constraints that would preclude responsible judgement or successful performance of an activity.
- Communicate unfavorable as well as favorable information and professional judgements or opinions.
- Refrain from engaging in or supporting any activity that would discredit the profession.

### Objectivity

Members have a responsibility to:

- Communicate information fairly and objectively.
- Disclose fully all relevant information that could reasonably be expected to influence an intended user's understanding of the reports, comments, and recommendations presented.

### Resolution of Ethical Conflict

In applying the standards of ethical conduct, members may encounter problems in identifying unethical behavior or in resolving an ethical conflict. When faced with significant ethical issues, members should follow the established policies of the organization bearing on the resolution of such conflict. If these policies do not resolve the ethical conflict, such members should consider the following courses of action.

- Discuss such problems with the immediate superior except when it appears that the superior is involved, in which case the problem should be presented initially to the next higher managerial level. If a satisfactory resolution cannot be achieved when the problem is initially presented, submit the issues to the next higher managerial level. If the immediate superior is the chief executive officer, or equivalent, the acceptable reviewing authority may be a group such as the audit committee, executive committee, board of directors, board of trustees, or owners. Contact with levels above the immediate superior should be initiated only with the superior's knowledge, assuming the superior is not involved. Except where legally prescribed, communication of such problems to authorities or individuals not employed or engaged by the organization is not considered appropriate.
- Clarify relevant ethical issues by confidential discussion with an objective advisor (e.g., IMA Ethics Counseling service) to obtain a better understanding of possible courses of action. Consult your own attorney as to legal obligations and rights concerning the ethical conflict.
- If the ethical conflict still exists after exhausting all levels of internal review, there may be no other recourse on significant matters than to resign from the organization and to submit an informative memorandum to an appropriate representative of the organization. After resignation, depending on the nature of the ethical conflict, it may also be appropriate to notify other parties.

Source: Institute of Management Accountants, Ethical Standards, SMA 1c (Statement on Management Accounting). Adapted with permission. Retrieved from www.imanet.org (from the site map, click on Ethics Center).

---

### GUIDE YOUR LEARNING 1.5 Ethical Decision Making

Stop to confirm that you understand the process for making ethical decisions introduced in the last several pages. For this process:

| Identify Problem | Identify Uncertainties | Explore Alternatives and Values |
|---|---|---|
| Why is it sometimes difficult to recognize an ethical dilemma? | What types of uncertainties are involved in addressing ethical problems? Consider uncertainties about:<br>• The effects of alternatives on the well-being of others and society<br>• Which values are most important in a given setting<br>• How to improve personal and organizational ethics | Discuss how the IMA Ethical Standards help you:<br>• Identify ethical problems as they arise<br>• Objectively consider the well-being of others and society when exploring alternatives<br>• Clarify and apply ethical values when choosing a course of action<br>• Work toward ongoing improvement of personal and organizational ethics |

# BUILDING YOUR PROFESSIONAL COMPETENCIES

Regardless of your career plans, you will be called upon to make a wide range of decisions. These decisions include how you perform your own work, how you supervise the work of others, how you contribute as a team member, and even whether you change jobs. Across professions, individuals with better decision-making skills are valued more highly than individuals with poor decision-making skills. Individuals who recognize and control their own biases, and who more thoroughly address uncertainties, make better decisions. These individuals have greater value to their organizations. Although it may appear easy, effectively considering biases and uncertainties is a difficult skill to develop. Effort and practice are required to develop all of the skills you need for professional success.

College is often seen as a place where students "receive" knowledge. However, higher education and business schools increasingly recognize that merely receiving knowledge is not sufficient for students. College must also be a place where students learn to take greater responsibility for their own development. To help educators and students work toward this goal, many professional organizations now provide guidance about the types of skills needed in the profession (see Current Practice).

---

**CURRENT PRACTICE**

### Accountant Professional Competencies

- **Institute of Management Accountants (IMA)** publishes reports on important professional knowledge, skills, and abilities for management accounting professionals. These reports are accessible through www.imanet.org. (From the home page, click on Resources, and then click on IMA Studies. Select an individual study to see the details.)
- The **American Institute of Certified Public Accountants (AICPA)** publishes a list of core competencies for success as entry-level accountants. See eca.aicpaservices.org/. (You must register to use this Web site, but no fee is charged for access. Once you are registered, click on *Library*, then click on *Core Competency Framework*, and then click on *Core Competency Database*. Choose one of the three competency categories and then select an individual competency to see the details.)

---

## ■ Focus on Professional Competencies in This Textbook

This textbook will help you develop your professional competencies—skills that you need for professional success. Just as an organization's core competencies measure the company's strengths, your own core or professional competencies measure your strengths as an individual in the workplace. Because accounting is the subject matter of this textbook, we understandably focus on skills specifically desired by the accounting profession. However, most of the competencies addressed in this textbook are also important for success in other professions. You can use the tools introduced in this textbook as a guide to your own professional development, regardless of your planned career.

## ■ Steps for Better Thinking: A Tool for Building Professional Competencies

In this chapter, we used Steps for Better Thinking (Exhibit 1.10) as a process for management decision making. Steps for Better Thinking also serves as a tool that helps you build your professional competencies. Skills in the lower steps support skills in the higher steps. Your knowledge base (the foundation) will continue to expand throughout your life. Thus, you can begin your efforts by building your knowledge while also working sequentially through the four steps.

# SUMMARY

### Q1 What Types of Decisions Do Managers Make for an Organization?

**Overview of Management Decision Making**

Measure, Monitor, and Motivate

### Q2 What Is the Role of Accounting Information in Management Decision Making?

**Terminology**
- Cost accounting
- Management accounting
- Financial accounting
- Strategic cost management
- Balanced scorecard

**Uses for Which Accountants Gather Data from Inside and Outside the Organization**

Creating External Reports for
- Government
- Shareholders
- Other stakeholders

Creating Internal Reports for
- Evaluating and updating organizational strategies
- Communicating and monitoring operating plans
- Measuring, monitoring, and motivating performance

### Q3 How Do Uncertainties and Biases Affect the Quality of Decisions?

**Effects of Uncertainties and Biases**

Uncertainties and biases create barriers to high-quality decisions.

**Uncertainties Prevent Managers From**
- Accurately describing a problem
- Identifying all possible options
- Knowing the outcomes of various options
- Anticipating all future conditions

**Biases Inhibit**
- Recognition of uncertainties
- Thorough analyses
- Consideration of alternative viewpoints
- Critical evaluation of priorities
- Continuous improvement

### Q4 How Can Managers Make Higher-Quality Decisions?

**Path to Higher-Quality Decisions**

**Decision-Making Process for Higher-Quality Decisions: Steps for Better Thinking**

Knowing    ❸ Prioritizing

❶ Identifying    ❹ Envisioning

❷ Exploring

---

**Q5** **What Information Is Relevant for Decision Making?**

**Relevant Information**

Helps decision makers evaluate and choose among alternative courses of action by:

  (1) Concerning the future

  (2) Varying with the action taken

Includes incremental (avoidable) cash flows

**Irrelevant Information**

Not useful for decision making

Includes unavoidable cash flows

---

**Q6** **What Is Ethical Decision Making, and Why Is It Important?**

**Components of Ethical Decision Making**

- Identify ethical problems as they arise.
- Objectively consider the well-being of others and society when exploring alternatives.
- Clarify and apply ethical values when choosing a course of action.
- Work toward ongoing improvement of personal and organizational ethics.

**Individual and Organizational Obligation**

**Fraudulent Financial Reporting**

- Decreases organizational market value
- Decreases value of accounting profession

**Rewards of Ethical Behavior**

- Integrity
- Reputation
- Self-respect
- Social welfare

---

## KEY TO SYMBOLS

ⓔ This question requires students to extend knowledge beyond the applications shown in the textbook.

❶ This question requires Step 1 skills (**Identifying**) in Steps for Better Thinking (Exhibit 1.10).

❷ This question requires Step 2 skills (**Exploring**) in Steps for Better Thinking (Exhibit 1.10).

❸ This question requires Step 3 skills (**Prioritizing**) in Steps for Better Thinking (Exhibit 1.10).

❹ This question requires Step 4 skills (**Envisioning**) in Steps for Better Thinking (Exhibit 1.10).

---

## Self-Study Problems

### Self-Study Problem 1   Uncertainties

**Q3**   Top Flight Surveillance Company is developing a very small video camera system that would allow flight officers to monitor and record passenger behavior from the cockpit of any airplane. The research and development costs began to increase at an alarming rate, and managers decided to stop developing the product.

**REQUIRED:**

❶ A. Identify as many uncertainties as you can in evaluating the viability of this new video product.

❶ B. Pick one of the items you identified in part (A) and explain why it is uncertain.

#### Solution to Self-Study Problem 1

A. When answering this question, think about what we are unable to know for sure. Some possible uncertainties for this problem include the following: Will other types of security devices, such as impenetrable doors, reduce the need for the videos? Will airline companies want this type of product? What other possible uses for the camera make development worthwhile? How much more time and money will be needed to develop the product? Will competitors be working on a similar product? Would the product be subject to government regulation?

If it was difficult for you to identify more than two uncertainties, you should practice this skill. Look for questions at the end of each chapter that ask about uncertainties.

B. Knowing why something cannot be known for sure will help you understand the difficulty of making decisions in the business world. Here is an example of an explanation for why we cannot know whether competitors will be working on a similar product. Because product development is so secretive, we often cannot know that other companies are doing similar development until the products are released. Product development may be happening all around the globe. If a small company were to release a similar product in a foreign country, news may not reach Top Flight Surveillance Company.

### Self-Study Problem 2 Decision Bias

**Q3, Q4**

Todd Emeril's sister must decide whether to open a small restaurant near the local university. Todd developed a spreadsheet to estimate the sales volume his sister could expect at the restaurant. Todd believes that his sister's cooking is exceptionally good and that students will flock to the restaurant, particularly for dinner when meal prices are higher. To test his assumption that students would enjoy his sister's recipes, Todd invited a number of his friends to eat dinner at his sister's home. A few of his friends were not that impressed with the food, but Todd assumes they would be in the minority when he estimates the sales volume.

**REQUIRED:**

② A. In what ways does Todd appear to be biased?

② B. How could Todd recognize and control for his biases?

### Solution to Self-Study Problem 2

A. Todd believes that his sister's cooking is good, and he ignores his friends' opinions that the cooking is not that good. If he does not account for this bias, the actual volume of sales at the restaurant will likely be lower than his estimate. In addition, he believes that students will buy dinners more often than lunches, so he could be overestimating cash inflows. He does not seem to know whether lunches or dinners contribute more to profits, on average. He does not explore the effects of competitors' prices and menus. He fails to consider whether students would be the best customers to attract.

B. It is usually easier to recognize someone else's biases than to recognize and control one's own biases! Todd might begin by asking himself whether he has a preference about whether his sister should open the restaurant. If so, then he should carefully watch for bias as he develops the sales estimate. One way to control for bias is to use more formal methods for collecting and analyzing information. For example, Todd could ask potential customers to eat a meal and fill out a survey that has numerical ratings. When Todd tallies these ratings, he will probably be less biased in interpreting the results. Also, he could ask an independent person to interpret the survey findings. He could ask friends to compare the value of the meals his sister cooks with the value of meals from other restaurants, by giving them price information with the free meals. He needs to analyze the contribution of both lunches and dinners and explore the effects of changes in sales mix on both revenues and costs.

---

**REVIEW** Use the exercises in the following boxes in the chapter to review key terms and key techniques, analyze chapter illustrations, improve your learning of new concepts, and practice ethical decision making:

Guide Your Learning 1.1: Key Terms (p. 9)

Guide Your Learning 1.2: Key Terms (p. 13)

Guide Your Learning 1.3: Colorado Boulders (p. 15)

Guide Your Learning 1.4: Key Terms (p. 18)

Guide Your Learning 1.5: Ethical Decision Making (p. 22)

---

## QUESTIONS

**1.1** Explain the importance of the following types of management decisions: organizational vision, organizational core competencies, organizational strategies, and operating plans.

**1.2** Why do managers need to measure, monitor, and motivate performance?

**1.3** List three types of internal reports and explain how each is used. List three types of external reports and explain how each is used.

**1.4** What types of information in addition to cost accounting are needed for management decisions?

**1.5** Explain why avoidable (incremental) cash flows are relevant. Explain why unavoidable cash flows are irrelevant.

**1.6** What are uncertainties, and how do they affect the quality of management decisions?

**1.7** What are biases, and how do they affect the quality of management decisions?

**1.8** In your own words, explain the path to higher-quality decisions.

**1.9** Explain why it is important for both individuals and organizations to behave ethically.

**1.10** Explain why it is important for you to assume responsibility for development of your own professional skills.

## EXERCISES

**1.11** **Q1** **Types of manager decisions** Suppose that each of the following is an activity conducted by **Microsoft Corporation**.

**REQUIRED:** Identify whether each activity is most likely part of (1) organizational strategies, (2) operating plans, (3) actual operations, or (4) measuring, monitoring, and motivating. For each item, explain why.

- **A.** Comparing the timeliness of development steps of a new release of Windows® with the timeline that was laid out to guide development.
- **B.** Developing a timeline for release of new Windows and Microsoft Office® products over the next year.
- **C.** Debugging the next version of Windows.
- **D.** Providing technical support to customers who are having problems with Microsoft Office.
- **E.** Estimating cash expenditures for the next year.
- **F.** Comparing budgeted costs to actual costs and discussing major differences with department managers.
- **G.** Deciding whether to construct a new building on the Microsoft campus.

**1.12** **Q1** **Types of personal decisions** Many of the ideas in this chapter relate not only to what organizations do, but also to your personal life.

**REQUIRED:** ⓔ For each of the following, give an example related to your personal life.

- **A.** Vision
- **B.** Core competencies
- **C.** Long-term strategies
- **D.** Short-term planning
- **E.** Actual results
- **F.** Measuring, monitoring, and motivating

**1.13** **Q5** **Relevant costs** Avery Car Rental charges its customers $26 per day plus $0.20 per mile. Its competition rents cars for $35 per day and $0.08 per mile.

**REQUIRED:** ⓔ How many miles would a customer need to drive on a four-day rental so that the cost of the two alternatives would be the same?

**1.14** **Q5** **Relevant costs** Suppose the current average cost per mile for operating a car is $0.40. Susan is required to drive to a client's office that is 50 miles away (100 miles round-trip). She can use her own car and be reimbursed $0.30 per mile or use a company-owned vehicle.

**REQUIRED:** ⓔ **A.** What costs would be included in the current average cost per mile that might be irrelevant to Susan's decision to drive 100 miles?
**B.** Suppose Susan determined that the cost of gasoline and maintenance for her car is about $0.25 per mile. Which alternative is better?

**1.15** **Q5** **Relevant costs, other relevant factors** **NetFlix** is a service that allows subscribers to rent three DVDs at a time for $21.95 per month. As soon as a customer returns one DVD, Netflix sends another. Customers can return as many movies as they want during a month, and they can keep each DVD for as long as they want.

**REQUIRED:** ⓔ **A.** How many DVDs do you need to rent per month to be indifferent between the cost of renting movies from a **Blockbuster** store at $3.95 each and subscribing to NetFlix?
❶ **B.** What factors other than cost would influence your decision?

**1.16** **Relevant costs, uncertainties** Toys for Boys has 10,000 toy cars painted a gray color that are not
Q3, Q5 selling well. The selling price of the cars could be reduced from the current price of $8.00 to $5.00
each. Alternatively, the cars could be painted red at a cost of $2.00 each and sold for $8.00. Red
cars sell very well.

REQUIRED:  **A.** Should Toys for Boys paint the cars? Show your calculations.
❷ **B.** Which option seems to have less uncertainty? Discuss.

**1.17** **Relevant costs, uncertainties, other relevant factors** This semester, you moved to an apartment
Q3, Q5 eight miles from campus and will commute to classes three times a week. This decision will let
you achieve significant savings. However, you have not yet decided whether to use your car or
ride the bus to get to campus. You estimate the following costs for each alternative:

**Driving Your Car**
Monthly payments on your car of $220.00

Maintenance expenses of $37.00 per month (This cost is an average and reflects oil
changes, car washes, and lubricants.)

University parking fees of $150.00 per semester (four months)

You would spend approximately $60.00 in gasoline per month. You estimate a total of
600 miles driven every month, which includes approximately 200 miles per month for three
trips per week to campus (approximately 12 round trips per month).

**Riding the Bus**
You have two alternatives regarding the purchase of bus tickets:
(1) You may buy a semester ticket with unlimited rides for $225.00 per semester (Bus A).
(2) You may purchase each ticket individually for $2.00 each way (Bus B).

If you decide to buy the semester bus pass, you estimate that you will ride the bus quite
often and replace approximately 200 miles from your car's monthly allowance of
600 miles.

REQUIRED:  **A.** Based only on cost, which alternative would you choose? Show your calculations. Assume that a semester lasts four months and that you will always ride the bus to campus if
you choose one of the bus options.
❶ **B.** Discuss uncertainties about your calculations for part (A).
❶ **C.** List factors that could affect your decision but that cannot be valued in dollars.

# PROBLEMS

**1.18** **Uncertainties** You have been admitted to the College of Business at your university. You decide
Q3 to become an accounting major and are now planning the sequence of classes that you would like
to take over the next two years.

REQUIRED:  ❶ **A.** List several uncertainties about your class sequence. Include in your list uncertainties at
the beginning of your accounting program, as well as uncertainties that might occur as
you register for courses each term.
❶ **B.** Pick one of the items you identified in part (A) and explain why it is uncertain.

**1.19** **Relevant information** Suppose you are responsible for ordering a replacement for your office
Q4, Q5 photocopy machine. Part of your job is to decide whether to buy it or lease it.

REQUIRED:  ❶ **A.** Describe something that could be considered relevant information in this decision and explain why it is relevant.
❶ **B.** Describe something that could be considered irrelevant information in this decision and
explain why it is irrelevant.
❷ **C.** Explain why it was important to distinguish between relevant and irrelevant information
in this problem.

**1.20** **Uncertainties, degree of uncertainty** Community Children's Hospital can invest in one of two
**Q3** different projects. The first project is to purchase and operate a hotel that is located two blocks
from the hospital. The CEO of the hospital has no experience operating a hotel, but the hospital
does provide rooms for in-patients, and so she is familiar with cleaning requirements and managing housekeeping staff. However, the hospital does little advertising and does not have a large
public relations staff. In addition, the hospital and hotel are located in a part of town that is
deteriorating.

The other investment opportunity is to replace the heart monitors in the neonatal intensive care
unit (critical care for newborns and infants). The new monitors would provide a range of functions, including monitoring the body temperature and blood pressure of infants, as well as monitoring heart functions. Each monitor can be used for up to four infants with information about each
infant forwarded to one computer that is monitored by a special technician. The current monitors
are bedside monitors that need to be read every 10 minutes by nursing staff.

**REQUIRED:** ❶ **A.** Prepare a list of uncertainties that the CEO faces if she buys the hotel.
❶ **B.** Prepare a list of uncertainties the CEO faces if she replaces the heart monitors.
❷ **C.** Which scenario appears to have a greater degree of uncertainty? Why?

**1.21** **Decision-maker bias** Gene Horita was choosing a major in his sophomore year. He enjoyed the
**Q3, Q4** accounting classes at his university, but also found the information systems classes to be interesting. Gene's father is a public accountant and has been pressuring Gene to choose an accounting
major. Gene always resented the fact that his father was not home very much during income tax
season and was unable to go to most sporting events in which Gene participated in high school.
Gene is uncertain whether he would want that lifestyle in the future when he has a family. He is
leaning toward information systems as a major because he thinks he can get a job with more regular working hours with this major.

**REQUIRED:** ❷ **A.** In what ways does Gene appear to be biased?
❷ **B.** How could Gene recognize and control for his biases?

**1.22** **Identifying open-ended problems** The textbook defined *open-ended problems* as problems with
**Q3** no single correct solution due to significant uncertainties.

**REQUIRED:** Discuss reasons why each of the following problems is open-ended.

❶ **A.** The managers of Flow Systems, an irrigation equipment manufacturer, are considering
the purchase of new welding equipment that will reduce labor costs. In addition, the
equipment is much safer than the equipment it would replace. The added safety is expected to reduce Flow System's insurance costs by half.
❶ **B.** Amira Salazar needs to choose between two summer internship offers she recently received. If she accepts a summer internship with **IBM** in its finance department, she will
be located in South Carolina and work in the strategic planning department. If she accepts an internship with **Hewlett-Packard**, she will be located in Idaho and work on a
special costing project for a new printer design.

☆ **1.23** **Relevant information, uncertainties, information for decision making** Janet Baker is deciding
**Q3, Q4, Q5** where to live during her second year in college. During her first year, she lived in the residence
 hall. Recently her friend Rachel asked her to share an off-campus apartment for the upcoming
school year. Janet likes the idea of living in an apartment, but she is concerned about how much
it will cost.

To help her decide what to do, Janet collected information about costs. She would pay $400
per month in rent. The minimum lease term on the apartment is six months. Janet estimates that
her share of the utility bills will be $75 per month. She also estimates that groceries will cost $200
per month. Janet spent $350 on a new couch over the summer. If she lives in the residence hall,
she will put the couch in storage at a cost of $35 per month. Janet expects to spend $7,500 on tuition and $450 on books each semester. Room and board at the residence hall would cost Janet
$2,900 per semester (four months). This amount includes a food plan of 20 meals per week. This
cost is nonrefundable if the meals are not eaten.

**REQUIRED:
INFORMATION
ANALYSIS**

The following questions will help you analyze the information for this problem. Do not turn in your answers to these questions unless your professor asks you to do so.

**ⓔ A.** Use ONLY the cost information collected by Janet for the following tasks.
   **1.** List all of the costs for each option. *Note:* Some costs may be listed under both options.
   **2.** Review your lists and cross out the costs that are irrelevant to Janet's decision. Explain why these costs are irrelevant.
   **3.** Calculate and compare the total *relevant* costs of each option.
   **4.** Given the cost comparison, which living arrangement is the better choice for Janet? Explain.

**① B.** Identify uncertainties in the cost information collected by Janet.
   **1.** Determine whether each cost is likely to be (i) known for sure, (ii) estimated with little uncertainty, or (iii) estimated with moderate or high uncertainty.
   **2.** For each cost that is known for sure, explain where Janet would obtain the information.
   **3.** For each cost that must be estimated, explain why the cost cannot be known.

**① C.** List additional information that might be relevant to Janet's decision (list as many items as you can).
   **1.** Costs not identified by Janet.
   **2.** Factors other than costs.

**② D.** Explain why conducting a cost comparison is useful to Janet, even if factors other than costs are important to her decision.

**② E.** Consider your own preferences for this problem. Do you expect Janet's preferences to be the same as yours? How can you control for your biases as you give Janet advice?

**③ F.** Think about what Janet's priorities might be for choosing a housing arrangement. How might different priorities lead to different choices?

**④ G.** Describe how information that Janet gains over this next year might affect her future housing arrangements.

Suppose Janet asks for your advice. Turn in your answers to the following.

**REQUIRED:
WRITTEN
ASSIGNMENT**

**③ H.** Use the information you learned from the preceding analyses to write a memo to Janet with your recommendation and a discussion of its risks. Refer in your memo to the information that would be useful to Janet.

**1.24**
**Q3, Q4, Q5**

**Relevant information, recommendation** Francisco owns a camper and loves to visit national parks with his family. However, the family only takes two one-week trips in the camper each year. Francisco's wife would rather stay in motels than the camper. She presented him with the following itemization of the cost per trip, hoping that he will sell the camper and use motels instead.

|  | Cost per Trip |
|---|---|
| Camper: | |
| Cost: $20,000 | |
| Usable for 10 seasons, 2 camping trips per season | $1,000 |
| Transportation expense: | |
| 1,000 miles @ $0.37 per mile | 370 |
| Includes: | |
| $0.15 per mile for gasoline, oil, tires, and maintenance | |
| $0.22 per mile for depreciation and insurance | |
| Groceries | 250 |
| Beverages | 100 |
| Cost per trip | $1,720 |
| Cost per person ($1,720/5 family members) | $  344 |

**REQUIRED:**

**ⓔ A.** What are the relevant costs for deciding whether the family should go on one more camping trip this year?

**ⓔ B.** What are the relevant costs for deciding whether Francisco should sell the camper? Assume the family will take the same vacations but stay in motels if the camper is sold.

*(continued)*

**❶ C.** What factors other than costs might influence the decision to sell the camper? List as many as you can.

**❷ D.** Consider your own preferences for this problem. Do you expect Francisco's preferences to be the same as yours? How can you control for your biases and consider this problem from Francisco's point of view?

**❸ E.** Francisco asks you to help him decide what to do. Do you think he should sell the camper? Why or why not?

**1.25** **Ethical decision making, relevant information, uncertainties, biases** In two of his classes, Larry's professors said that he could work homework problems with other students as long as he turned in his own answers. In another class, the professor said that students could not work with other students. Each time the professor collected homework, students were required to write a statement at the bottom of their assignment that assured the professor that the homework had been the student's own effort.

Q3, Q4, Q5, Q6

Half an hour before class, Larry's girlfriend Annie asked if he would help her finish the last three homework problems so she could hand them in on time. Larry asked her how she would feel about signing the statement if he helped her.

REQUIRED:

**❶ A.** What is the ethical issue here?

**❶ B.** What alternatives are available to Larry?

**❶ C.** If the professor discovers that Annie and Larry's answers are similar in ways that reflect the fact that they worked together, what might happen? What risks are involved?

**❶ D.** What information is relevant to Larry's decision?

**❶ E.** Is this an open-ended problem? Why or why not?

**❷ F.** Explore this problem from different perspectives:
   **1.** Annie
   **2.** Larry
   **3.** The professor

**❸ G.** How important is it for students to behave ethically?

**❹ H.** By exploring the ethics of this situation, what could Larry and Annie learn about professional ethics?

**1.26** **Ethical decision making, relevant information, uncertainties, biases** You are an entry-level accountant at city hall. You work for the accounting department, but have been loaned out to the department responsible for building and maintaining roads while the managers develop their annual budget. The director of the department is in the middle of a nasty divorce. He asks you to work on a Saturday to finish up details of the budget. When you arrive, he asks you to work on a schedule for his personal financial information for the upcoming divorce court case. When you finish the statements, he tells you to record your hours as overtime and bill them to the city.

Q3, Q4, Q5, Q6

REQUIRED:

**❶ A.** What is the ethical issue here?

**❶ B.** What are your alternatives?

**❶ C.** If you do as the director asks and your boss finds out, what might happen? What risks are involved?

**❶ D.** What information is relevant to your decision?

**❶ E.** Is this an open-ended problem? Why or why not?

**❷ F.** Explore this problem from different perspectives:
   **1.** Your own
   **2.** The department director
   **3.** Your boss
   **4.** The taxpayers

**❸ G.** How important is it for you to behave ethically?

**❸ H.** Based on your analysis of the situation, write a short "script" for how you would respond to the department director.

**❹ I.** Suppose you decide not to do what the director asks. Discuss the issues you would consider as you decide whether to report this incident to your boss.

**1.27**

Q3, Q4

**Quality of decisions** Maria and Tracey became good friends while working at the same company. Two years ago, they both decided to increase their savings so that they could eventually purchase homes. Each began by putting a portion of every paycheck into a savings account. At the end of the first year, they had each accumulated $4,000. Because their savings accounts paid a very small interest rate, they decided to invest the savings to earn a higher rate of return. Maria and Tracey both hoped to save enough money to buy homes within five years.

Maria decided to take an investment course offered through the company. The course taught her about different types of investments and strategies for investing. She then purchased and read an investment book to learn more. She learned that some investments are riskier than others, and that investors must balance risk against desired return. Higher risk leads to higher returns on average; however, higher risk could also lead to low returns or even loss. She also learned that investment advisors recommend diversifying risky investments. One way to diversify is to invest in mutual funds, which invest in many different organizations. Maria decided that she was willing to assume some risk, but was not comfortable with a high level. She decided to invest her $4,000 in a stock market mutual fund. She read *Consumer Reports* to learn about different mutual funds, and selected a fund that invests conservatively in fairly stable companies. However, the stock market did not do well in the first year. The value of her mutual fund at the end of a year was $4,050.

Tracey talked with her boyfriend and other friends about how they invest. Her boyfriend's cousin recommended investing in a start-up company that sells video games. He told her that the games were very hot with teenagers and that the company would probably be acquired, resulting in big gains for investors. This opportunity sounded good to Tracey, so she decided to invest her entire $4,000 in the company's stock. After 10 months, she was excited to learn that the company was being acquired. She received stock in the acquiring company in exchange for her original stock. At the end of the year, the market value of her stock was $8,200.

**REQUIRED:** Evaluate the quality of the investment decisions made by Maria and Tracey. *Hint*: Refer to Exhibit 1.9.

① A. List the information used by Maria in making her investment decision.
① B. List the information used by Tracey in making her investment decision.
② C. Did Maria appear to use high-quality information? Explain.
② D. Did Tracey appear to use high-quality information? Explain.
② E. Describe Maria's decision-making process. What did she do to explore her options? Did she appear to be biased? What were her priorities? How did she reach a conclusion?
② F. Describe Tracey's decision-making process. What did she do to explore her options? Did she appear to be biased? What were her priorities? How did she reach a conclusion?
② G. Did Maria appear to use a high-quality decision-making process? Explain.
② H. Did Tracey appear to use a high-quality decision-making process? Explain.
③ I. Given your analyses of the information and decision-making processes used by Maria and Tracey, which investor made a higher-quality decision? Explain.

# BUILD YOUR PROFESSIONAL COMPETENCIES

**1.28**

Q3, Q4, Q5, Q6

ETHICS

**Focus on Professional Competency: Professional Demeanor**  *Relevance of competency definitions, developing personal and ethical skills*

Review the following definition and elements for the Professional Demeanor competency.[13]

**DEFINITION:**  *The accounting profession is committed to maintaining a public reputation for excellence in the performance of important roles in business and society. Individuals entering the accounting*

---

[13]The definition and elements are reprinted with permission from AICPA; copyright © 1978–2000 & 2003 by American Institute of Certified Public Accountants. The AICPA's Core Competency Framework can be accessed at eca.aicpaservices.org.

*profession should behave in a manner that is consistent with the character and standards of the discipline of accounting, as well as the norms of the environment in which they interact. This competency involves demonstrating objectivity, integrity, and ethical behavior. It also includes a commitment to stable work performance, as well as a commitment to continuously acquire new skills and knowledge.*

## ELEMENTS FOR THIS COMPETENCY INCLUDE

| Level 1 | Level 2 | Level 3 | Level 4 |
|---------|---------|---------|---------|
| 1. Commits to confidentiality, quality, efficiency, growth in personal conduct and capabilities, and ethical behavior<br>2. Accepts professional development as an uncertain and life-long process<br>3. Identifies career and personal goals<br>4. Identifies ethical dilemmas | 5. Evaluates information, including others' professional criticism and evaluation, in a manner free of distortions, personal bias or conflicts of interest<br>6. Relates lessons learned from prior mistakes to new situations<br>7. Considers the impact of alternative solutions on various stakeholders in an ethical dilemma | 8. Conducts oneself with honesty<br>9. Objectively considers others' professional criticism or evaluation when making decisions<br>10. Adheres to a level of personal appearance appropriate to the environment<br>11. Recognizes situations where professional ethical standards apply and behaves accordingly<br>12. Uses appropriate ethical values in making decisions<br>13. Prioritizes career and personal goals | 14. Measures oneself against evolving standards and meets or exceeds those standards<br>15. Manages stress and performs reliably under changing or unusual demands<br>16. Takes appropriate action to gain competencies |

**REQUIRED:**

**1** **A.** In Chapter 1, you learned the importance of identifying relevant information for management decision making. Explain how the AICPA's description of competencies such as professional demeanor is relevant to your development as a professional.

**B.** Focus on competency elements 1, 2, 6, 9, 14, and 16, which relate to continuous improvement. Answer the following questions:

**2**     **1.** Why are these competency elements important for accounting professionals?

**1**     **2.** What does it mean for standards to evolve? Explain why you cannot fully anticipate all of the behaviors and knowledge you will need during your professional career.

**2**     **3.** Identify a mistake you made in the past and explain what you learned from the experience. How have you applied what you learned to new situations?

**4**     **4.** Is it possible to improve personal conduct over time? If so, how? If no, why not?

**3** **C.** Focus on competency elements 3 and 13, which relate to career and personal goals. Why is it necessary to identify and prioritize your career and personal goals?

**D.** Focus on competency elements 5 and 9, which relate to objectivity and bias. Answer the following questions:

**1**     **1.** Which material in Chapter 1 addresses these competency elements? Explain.

**2**     **2.** Think of a situation when you were not objective in making a decision. How did your bias affect the quality of your decision?

**E.** Focus on competency elements 1, 4, 7, 11, and 12, which directly address ethical decision making. Answer the following questions:

**1**     **1.** Which material in Chapter 1 addresses these competency elements? Explain.

**1**     **2.** Is it always easy to identify an ethical dilemma? Why or why not?

**2**     **3.** Why is it important to consider the impact on various stakeholders in an ethical dilemma?

**2**     **4.** Provide examples of values that are (a) ethical and (b) unethical. Explain.

**1.29**

Q1, Q2, Q5

**Integrating Across the Curriculum: Auditing** *Quality of information, relevant information to auditors* Aden, Inc. is a manufacturer of television sets. The company recently revised its production processes and invested in new equipment to reduce labor costs.

REQUIRED:

**A.** Following are possible measures that Aden could use to monitor product defects. Discuss the quality of information provided by each measure. (*Hint:* See Exhibit 1.9)

❷ **1.** Ratio of defective televisions returned to the number of televisions sold (data from customer service department records and sales department records).

❷ **2.** Monthly defective unit warranty costs incurred (data from the general ledger).

❷ **3.** Monthly number of defects discovered during routine tests of televisions at the end of the manufacturing process (data from production records).

❷ **4.** Customer survey responses to the question, "How satisfied are you with the quality of your television set?" on a scale from 1 (very satisfied) to 5 (very unsatisfied). Surveys are mailed to 1 percent of randomly selected repeat customers from sales records.

❷ **B.** List ideas about what Aden's managers might want to learn from monitoring product defects. (*Hint:* Use Exhibit 1.6 to help you generate ideas.)

**C.** The measures used by managers to monitor operations are often used by auditors when auditing financial statements. Explain why information about product defects might be relevant to Aden's auditors when they audit the following:

❷ **1.** Warranty liabilities

❷ **2.** Lower of cost or market adjustment for inventory

❷ **3.** Allowance for doubtful accounts receivable

**1.30**

Q2, Q6

ETHICS

**Integrating Across the Curriculum: Technology and Information Systems** *Internal and external information, internal reports* Managers continuously seek ways to improve productivity and reduce costs. Many manufacturers and retailers incur large costs to track inventory. During 2003, managers began to consider the use of radio frequency identification (RFID) tags to replace bar codes that were currently used to track inventory receipt, movement, and sale. When embedded in individual products, RFID tags allow companies to use radio signals to track every product item. The 2003 cost of RFID tags, at $0.50 to $1.50 per chip, was considered too high for many low-margin products. However, the cost was expected to drop to acceptable levels for widespread use over the next few years.

**Wal-Mart**, known as a leader in the use of technology, notified its top 100 suppliers that they would be required to attach RFID tags to their products by 2005. Technology experts estimated the new systems and software would cost Wal-Mart's suppliers approximately $10 million each. For Wal-Mart, the new technology was expected to not only reduce the cost of tracking inventory, but to also reduce losses from theft.

To further investigate the use of RFID, Wal-Mart and **Procter & Gamble** secretly launched a research project in a suburban Tulsa, Oklahoma, Wal-Mart store. Researchers monitored the movement of a particular lipstick product using RFID tags in the lipstick packaging, electronic readers concealed in the store shelves, and Webcams. A sign on the lipstick display informed customers about the use of closed-circuit television and electronic security at the store.

When news of the testing became publicly known, consumer advocacy groups raised alarms about the potential loss of privacy from RFID tags. They claimed that proliferation of RFID technology could eventually allow retailers to track their products after customers buy them and leave the store. These concerns prompted a California state senate subcommittee to hold public hearings on RFID. Similar actions were likely to be taken in other states.

SOURCES: "Chipping Away at Your Privacy," *Chicago Sun-Times,* November 9, 2003; H. Wolinsky, "P&G, Wal-Mart Store Did Secret Test of RFID," *Chicago Sun-Times,* November 9, 2003; E. Shein, "Radio Flier: Wal-Mart presents its vendors with an offer they can't refuse," *CFO Magazine,* November 5, 2003; and J. Black, "Playing Tag with Shoppers' Anonymity," *Business Week Online,* July 21, 2003.

REQUIRED:

❸ **A.** Would the information from RFID tags be considered internally or externally generated information? (See Exhibit 1.7.) Explain.

*(continued)*

**B.** Information gathered by Wal-Mart from its in-store research on the RFID technology was most likely summarized in one or more internal reports. Were these internal reports most likely used to (1) support organizational strategies, (2) support operating plans, or (3) monitor and motivate? Explain.

**C.** Provide arguments for and against Wal-Mart's decision to conduct research on its customers without explicitly informing them.

# 2

# The Cost Function

## ▶In Brief

Managers need a basic understanding of the organization's costs if they are to react quickly to change and create successful organizational strategies and operating plans. Managers use classifications and estimation techniques to understand and anticipate future cost behavior. They can then estimate relevant costs to help them make decisions and plan future operations.

### This Chapter Addresses the Following Questions:

**Q1** What are different ways to describe cost behavior?

**Q2** What is a learning curve?

**Q3** What process is used to estimate future costs?

**Q4** How are the engineered estimate, account analysis, and two-point methods used to estimate cost functions?

**Q5** How does a scatter plot assist with categorizing a cost?

**Q6** How is regression analysis used to estimate a mixed cost function?

**Q7** What are the uses and limitations of future cost estimates?

# AMERICA WEST AIRLINES: WEATHERING AN ECONOMIC DOWNTURN

The airline industry was hit hard by the terrorist events that occurred September 11, 2001. Flights were canceled for about a week, during which time the airlines continued to incur costs but earned no revenue. Once flight schedules resumed, the airlines experienced a huge drop in demand for services. America West's managers responded by immediately reducing flight schedules and cutting costs.

The U.S. government offered to guarantee loans for airline companies in an attempt to bail out the industry. America West Airlines was already in a precarious financial position prior to these events. Therefore, it was the first airline to use government-backed loans. Airline analysts were skeptical about America West's ability to survive in the long term because of its past history. Many believed it should not be given loans through the government's program because its financial performance had been poor for a long time.

By April and May of 2002, however, the airline began to rehire pilots and other airline personnel and to increase the number of scheduled flights. The company had survived the crisis. Two factors enabled America West to weather this difficult business environment. One was an increase in the quality of operations. For many years it had one of the poorest records for on-time and canceled flights. But by late 2001 and early 2002, it was a leader in on-time flights. America West managers also had a good understanding of the company's cost structure and were able to reduce costs by analyzing the flight schedules and cutting flights with low volumes. This move enabled them to cut other activities for those flights such as baggage handling and aircraft cleaning without affecting the quality of service. In July 2003, America West Holdings Corporation reported its first quarterly profit in three years.

By the end of 2003, America West's managers faced concerns about their ability to maintain low costs. Their pilots had rejected two contract offers. Union representatives argued that the pilots and other employees should receive a higher share of the airline's financial success. ■

SOURCES: "Airline Flight Delays, Service Complaints Declined in April," *The Wall Street Journal*, June 4, 2002, p. D4; "America West Holdings Corp," *The Wall Street Journal*, March 20, 2002; M. Trottman, "America West Faces Discord with Pilots," *The Wall Street Journal*, July 25, 2003, p. B5; and R. Velotta, "America West Plans Growth after Favorable Changes," *Las Vegas SUN*, December 5, 2003.

## USING RELEVANT COSTS TO MAKE DECISIONS ABOUT THE FUTURE

### ■ Key Decision Factors for America West

Managers know that unforeseen events occur, although rarely as extreme as the events of September 11. Managers need to be able to respond quickly to changes in their environment. If they understand the relationship between changes in an organization's activities and changes in the costs of those activities, they can better lead the organization through uncertain times.

Faced with a sudden and severe decline in demand for flight travel, the managers of **America West** quickly made decisions about which flights and other services to cut. How do managers make these types of decisions? The following discussion uses Steps for Better Thinking to summarize key factors that America West's managers needed to consider for this case.

**Knowing.** America West's managers needed considerable knowledge before they could select and implement reasonable cost-cutting alternatives. They needed detailed knowledge about their business environment and America West's operations and costs.

**Identifying.** Identifying relevant issues, costs, and information enabled America West's managers to recognize key threats and opportunities. It was especially important for the managers to engage in the following:

- Creatively identify possible courses of action.
- Isolate relevant information about costs and benefits for those options.
- Recognize uncertainties about various elements such as the business environment, quality of service, and costs.

**Exploring.** Analyzing the pros and cons of alternatives is always a difficult task. America West's managers needed to do the following:

- Remain unbiased while they investigated the costs, benefits, and risks of alternative strategies and operating plans.
- Anticipate the reactions of various stakeholders to any cost-cutting plans. For example, employee morale was probably down following the terrorist attacks. What additional impacts to morale would result from cost-cutting measures?
- Understand quality from the customer's point of view.
- Consider in their analyses the strengths and weaknesses of other major airlines.
- Take into account the expected effects of each alternative on cash flows and quality of service.
- Evaluate the quality of their information about important factors such as the business environment, their quality of service, and costs. They could place greater reliance on higher quality information.

**Prioritizing.** Once America West's managers thoroughly explored the alternatives, they were in a position to choose the best options. This step required the following activities:

- Select strategies and operating plans consistent with the company's vision and core competencies.
- Take quick and decisive action, knowing that the company's cash flows worsened each day management's decision was delayed.

**Envisioning.** America West's managers also had to remain open to future events and opportunities for improvement. The following tasks were important for the managers:

- Consider the future as they made short-term decisions to cut costs.
- Continue the company's efforts toward improved quality.
- Maintain flexibility to respond to future unanticipated changes in the business environment.

### ■ Estimating Relevant Costs

Key parts of America West's decision process required managers to measure the effects of alternative cost-cutting scenarios on cost. Even though this type of evaluation might sound like an obvious and simple thing to do, it is not always easy to identify or calculate relevant costs. Because relevant costs involve the future, we cannot perfectly predict them. The best we can do is to carefully identify and estimate how costs will be affected by a decision.

## IDENTIFYING RELEVANT COSTS FOR A DECISION

 **Q1** What are different ways to describe cost behavior?

**HELPFUL HINT**

In Chapter 1 we learned that relevant information concerns the future and varies with the action taken. Only incremental (avoidable) costs are relevant.

For America West's managers, a first step in evaluating relevant costs was identifying the costs that would be affected by a particular cost-cutting scenario—in other words, the relevant costs. Exhibit 2.1 provides examples of relevant costs for several alternatives that America West's managers might have considered.

### ■ Relevant Costs for a Cost Object

A **cost object** is a thing or activity for which we measure costs. Cost objects include such things as individual products, product lines, projects, customers, departments, and even the entire company. Cost objects also include activities such as putting tires on bike wheels as part of the manufacturing process for bicycles. Managers identify one or more cost objects based on the relevant information they need for a particular decision, for budgeting and planning, or for valuing products or services.

### ■ Identifying Relevant Costs from the Accounting System

One way to identify relevant costs is to search the accounting system for types of costs that might be affected by a decision. However, not all relevant costs appear in the accounting system. For example, to estimate cost savings from layoffs, employee severance pay would not appear in the accounting system until *after* the decision is made. At the same time, some costs from the accounting system are irrelevant. Human resources department costs would not change if only a few employees were laid off, so that cost would be irrelevant. Careful thought and judgment are required to identify relevant costs; however, it helps to know whether costs are direct or indirect.

### ■ Direct and Indirect Costs

**Direct costs** are easily traced to individual cost objects because a clear cause-and-effect relationship generally exists between the cost object and the cost. Suppose managers at Magik Bicycles want to know more about their costs. The costs of parts such as tires, handle bars, and frames can be traced directly not only to the production of individual bicycles, but also to an entire product line.

**Indirect costs** are not easily traced to individual cost objects. Often, these costs relate to more than one cost object, such as multiple products or services. For Magik Bicycles, maintenance and electricity at the manufacturing facility are indirect costs when the cost object is an individual bicycle. Although these costs are needed to produce bicycles, we

**EXHIBIT 2.1** Relevant Costs for Cost-Cutting Alternatives

| Relevant Cost | Alternative Cost-Cutting Measures | | | |
|---|---|---|---|---|
| | Cancel Food Service on a Flight | Reduce Number of Scheduled Flights | Delay Replacement of Ticket Counter Computers | Discontinue All Operations at an Airport |
| Food | ✓ | ✓ | | ✓ |
| Fuel | | ✓ | | ✓ |
| Cost of new computers | | | ✓ | |
| Wages of manager for airport operations | | | | ✓ |

**ALTERNATIVE TERMS**

Some people use the term *factory burden* to refer to *overhead.*

**HELPFUL HINT**

Cost pools are groups of costs accumulated for a particular cost object. Costs are often pooled at the department level. Costs are also sometimes pooled around activities.

**CURRENT PRACTICE**

When the owners of **Starbucks Coffee** opened their first coffee shops, instead of focusing on food, they adopted a strategy of offering a variety of coffee beverages that were relatively unknown to consumers at the time. Their opportunity cost was the potential profit from offering a larger food menu. See Starbucks' Web site at www.starbucks.com for more information on its history.

**CURRENT PRACTICE**

"**Iridium**'s backers seem to have fallen into a classic sunk-cost fallacy. Having already spent billions of dollars and years of effort on the project, they were loath to abandon it. Instead, they redoubled their efforts, and spent more billions."[2]

cannot trace them to each unit. However, these costs are direct costs when the cost object is an entire product line. In some cases, indirect costs are potentially traceable, but gathering information is overly expensive. For example, the cost of inner tube valve caps could be traced to each bike, but the cost of each cap is very small while the cost of tracking would be relatively high.

All production costs except direct materials and direct labor are often combined into groups (cost pools) in the accounting system and referred to as **overhead costs.** These costs are often common costs for many different aspects of operations and cannot be easily related to individual products or services. For Magik Bicycles, it is easy to relate the cost of tires to each bike, but difficult to relate the salary of the production supervisor to each bike. However, the supervisor's cost is related to the production line.

## ■ Opportunity Costs

When we consider alternative courses of action, we can think of each alternative as an opportunity. When one alternative is chosen, the benefits of the other alternatives are no longer available. The benefits we forego when we choose one alternative over the next best alternative are called **opportunity costs.** Suppose you attend a basketball game. You pay cash for a ticket and spend time at the game. You forgo the opportunity to spend that money and time on something else such as studying, going to a movie or concert, or just hanging out with friends or family. The benefits forgone from the next best alternative are the opportunity costs of attending the basketball game.

Opportunity costs are often difficult to measure. As individuals, we informally value opportunity costs each time we choose a particular course of action. However, managers need to formally value opportunity costs to make higher-quality decisions. They need to anticipate and develop estimates for future revenues and costs regardless of whether they will later appear in the accounting system.

## ■ Sunk Costs

**Sunk costs** are expenditures made in the past. When deciding whether to keep already-existing equipment, the original cost of the equipment is not a factor; it is a sunk cost. Because they cannot be changed by any future decisions, sunk costs are unavoidable and therefore not relevant to decision making.

Contrary to good decision-making practices, research indicates that managers tend to include sunk costs in their decisions.[1] Their inclusion might occur because sunk costs are readily visible in the accounting records or because managers become emotionally attached to prior decisions. Accountants promote improved decision making by identifying sunk costs and helping managers understand why these sunk costs should not influence the decision-making process.

| GUIDE YOUR LEARNING **2.1** Key Terms |
|---|

Stop to confirm that you understand the new terms introduced in the last several pages:

| | |
|---|---|
| *Cost object (p. 39) | *Overhead cost (p. 40) |
| *Direct cost (p. 39) | *Opportunity cost (p. 40) |
| *Indirect cost (p. 39) | *Sunk cost (p. 40) |

For each of these terms, write a definition in your own words. For starred terms, list at least one example that is different from the ones given in this textbook.

---

[1]See Hal Arkes and Peter Ayton, "Think Like a Dog," *Psychology Today,* January/February 2000; and Hal Arkes and Peter Ayton, "The Sunk Cost and Concorde Effects: Are Humans Less Rational than Lower Animals?" *Psychological Bulletin,* September 1999.
[2]J. N. Sheth and R. Sisodia, "Why Cell Phones Succeed Where Iridium Failed," *The Wall Street Journal,* August 23, 1999, p. A14.

# COST BEHAVIOR

**Q1** What are different ways to describe cost behavior?

The next step in estimating a relevant cost is to describe how that cost would change under different decision alternatives. **Cost behavior** is the variation in costs relative to the variation in an organization's activities. Accountants need to anticipate changes in costs as decisions are made about activities such as production, merchandise sales, and services. To understand cost behavior, accountants analyze the effects of changes in their organizations' activities on costs.

The ability to analyze cost behavior requires knowledge of an organization's economic environment and operations. For example, some of **America West's** costs, such as beverages, vary with the number of passengers. Some costs, such as fuel and flight attendant wages, vary with the number of flights. Other costs, such as counter space lease and airport management salaries, vary with the number of airports that America West uses. Still other costs do not vary with passenger, flight, or airport-related volumes, including costs such as building costs and salaries for corporate headquarters.

## ■ Variable, Fixed, and Mixed Costs

Total **variable costs** change proportionately with changes in activity levels. For Magik Bicycles, the cost of tires varies with number of bicycles produced. If each tire costs $5, the variable cost per bike is $10 and total variable cost increases by $10 for each bike produced. Exhibit 2.2(a) provides a graph of the variable cost of tires. Another activity in bike production is mounting the tires onto wheels. As the number of bikes produced increases, the labor cost to mount tires onto wheels increases proportionately and is therefore a variable cost.

We assume that variable cost per unit remains constant, but sometimes this assumption is not the case. Suppose Magik's managers are able to negotiate a lower cost for tires as their purchase quantity increases. For purchases up to 120 tires, the variable cost per unit is constant at $10 per bike. However, the variable cost per bike drops to $6 for any additional purchases after the first 120 tires, as illustrated in Exhibit 2.2(b).

Total **fixed costs** do not vary with small changes in activity levels such as production, sales, and services provided. Some fixed costs are easy to classify, such as rent, insurance, and property taxes. Exhibit 2.3(a) illustrates the cost of rent and sales volumes for a Magik Bicycle retail store. Within a specific range of sales ($0 to $30,000), rent cost is $6,000. However, if sales are greater than $30,000, more space will be needed and total fixed cost will increase to $8,000 as shown in Exhibit 2.3(b). Fixed costs such as rent often increase in a stepwise manner.

**ALTERNATIVE TERMS**

Some people use the terms *constant* (in total dollar amount) or *committed* to describe a *fixed cost*.

**EXHIBIT 2.2** Total Variable Cost of Tires for Bicycle Production

(a) Constant Per–Unit Variable Cost

(b) Incremental Price Reduction in Per–Unit Variable Cost

**EXHIBIT 2.3** Fixed Cost of Rent

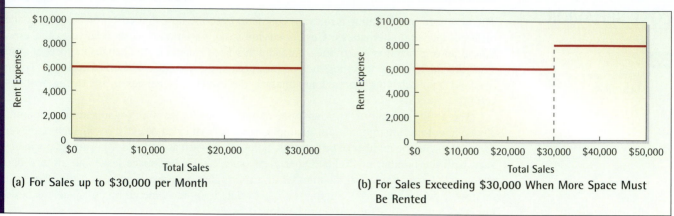

(a) For Sales up to $30,000 per Month

(b) For Sales Exceeding $30,000 When More Space Must Be Rented

Some fixed costs are more difficult to classify. For example, varying levels of bike production do not significantly change the amount of electricity used, assuming no change in hours of operation. Keep in mind that the dollar amount of a fixed cost is not necessarily "fixed" at one value. For Magik Bicycles, the rate for a kilowatt-hour of electricity might change, the cost for heating and cooling depends on weather conditions, and the total electric bill varies from month to month. Nevertheless, electricity is still considered a fixed cost for bike production because the cost of electricity is not significantly affected by changes in the volumes of operating activity (number of bikes produced).

In reality, many costs are **mixed costs;** they are partly fixed and partly variable. Suppose that Magik Bicycles incurs a fixed cost of $10,000 to generate a television advertisement, and then a variable cost of $500 each time the advertisement is aired on television. As shown in Exhibit 2.4, the total television advertising cost is a mixed cost because part is fixed and part varies with the number of times the advertisement is aired on television.

ALTERNATIVE TERMS

These terms are synonymous: *mixed cost* and *semivariable cost.*

## ■ Classifying Costs

To classify costs correctly, we need to identify the cost object and also understand the nature of the business. When **America West** managers want to add a flight to their existing route from San Francisco to New York, the cost object is that flight. The cost of gates at the San Francisco airport is fixed with respect to adding a new flight. If the managers want to add new routes, the cost of gates at new destinations varies with the number of new routes. The cost of baggage handling at each airport is a mixed cost. Part of it is fixed (the depreciation on equipment) and part of it is variable (labor costs for baggage handling).

**EXHIBIT 2.4**
Mixed Cost for Television Advertising

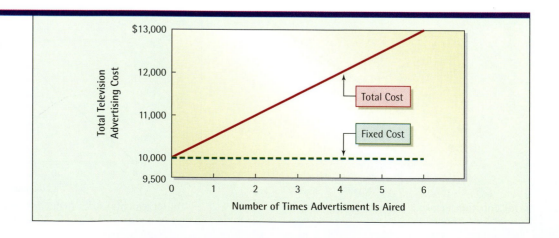

**EXHIBIT 2.5** Cost Classifications When a Bicycle Is the Cost Object

| | Fixed | Variable | Direct | Indirect |
|---|---|---|---|---|
| Rent for manufacturing plant | X | | | X |
| Direct labor (assuming a guaranteed 40-hour week) | X | | X | |
| Direct labor (assuming work hours fluctuate with production volume) | | X | X | |
| Tires | | X | X | |
| Valve caps for tires | | X | | X |
| Lubrication and other supplies for production equipment | | X | | X |
| Utilities | X | | | X |
| Product line supervisor salary | X | | | X |

Because variable costs are easily traceable to the units or services produced, they are often automatically considered direct costs. As a result, many people mistakenly believe that direct costs are always variable and that indirect costs are always fixed. Yet fixed and variable costs can each be either direct or indirect, depending on the cost object. In addition, some direct variable costs (e.g., valve caps for bicycle tires) are very small per unit and are pooled with a variety of indirect costs. Some direct variable costs are difficult to separate from other costs, such as lubrication and other supplies for the equipment used to assemble bikes. The cost to track these costs is more than the benefit, so they are classified as indirect costs. Exhibit 2.5 shows classifications of several costs for Magik Bicycles when each bicycle is the cost object and several different models are manufactured in one plant.

## ■ Relevant Range

A **relevant range** is a span of activity for a given cost object where total fixed costs remain constant and variable costs per unit of activity remain constant. Suppose that America West begins service to a new destination. The number of flights is estimated, gates and aircraft are leased, and employees are hired. Managers may add a few flights, or drop a few flights, and the fixed costs and variable costs per flight (fuel and personnel) remain constant. However, if the new route is successful, managers may decide to add a number of new flights, in which case new gates must be leased and new employees hired. The fixed and variable costs for the original destination are no longer valid because America West is operating within a new relevant range.

Variable cost rates can also change across relevant ranges, as was shown in Exhibit 2.2(b). In that graph, Magik Bicycles paid $10 per bike for 0–60 bikes, and $6 per bike after that. Within a particular relevant range of purchases, the variable cost per tire is constant. However, once purchase volumes move into a different relevant range, a different variable cost per bike applies. In many cases, the variable cost will be lower at a higher relevant range. But in some cases, especially when resources are limited, a higher variable cost might apply. For example, a utility company may charge customers one cost per kilowatt over a range of usage and then a higher amount per kilowatt for a higher level of usage. The purpose would be to encourage conservation and efficient use of utilities.

**Marginal cost** is the incremental cost of an activity, such as producing a unit of goods or services. Marginal cost is often relevant for decision making. Within the relevant range, variable cost approximates marginal cost. Accordingly, accountants often use variable cost as a measure of marginal cost. Although the terms *variable cost* and *marginal cost* may be used interchangeably, they are not always the same, especially when the incremental or marginal unit moves into the next relevant range. For example, in Exhibit 2.4(b), the first $30,000 in sales has a fixed cost of $6,000 for rental of retail space. The next incremental sales (above $30,000) require an expansion of retail space, costing an additional $2,000 in fixed costs. Thus, the marginal (first few) sales would increase fixed costs by $2,000.

## ■ Cost Functions

It is easy to assume that costs behave linearly—in other words, that fixed costs remain fixed and the variable cost per unit remains constant. However, total costs more often resemble a large S-curve, as shown in Exhibit 2.6. Notice that within a relevant range of activity, the change in total cost as volume increases is nearly linear.

A **cost function** is an algebraic representation of the total cost of a cost object over a relevant range of activity. When we create a cost function, we assume that within a relevant range of activity the total fixed costs remain fixed and the variable cost per unit remains constant. Notice in Exhibit 2.6 that when volume is very low or very high, the total cost function is nonlinear. However, when volume is in the relevant range, the cost function is linear or close to linear.

Given the preceding definitions of fixed and variable costs within the relevant range, we can write the cost function algebraically as

$$TC = F + V \times Q$$

where TC is total cost, $F$ is total fixed cost, $V$ is the variable cost per unit of activity, and $Q$ is the volume of activity.

**ALTERNATIVE TERMS**

Some people use the term *semifixed* to describe a *stepwise linear cost.*

When the slope of a variable cost function changes at some point but remains linear after the change, it is called a **piecewise linear cost function.** The variable cost function in Exhibit 2.2(b) is piecewise linear because it involves more than one relevant range. When a fixed cost function changes at some point but remains constant after the change, it is called a **stepwise linear cost function.** The fixed cost function in Exhibit 2.3(b) is stepwise linear because it includes more than one relevant range. Exhibit 2.7 presents the algebraic expressions for the cost functions in Exhibits 2.2, 2.3, and 2.4.

## ■ Cost Driver

A **cost driver** is some input or activity that causes changes in total cost for a cost object. In cost functions, $Q$ represents the quantity of the cost driver. For **America West**, when the

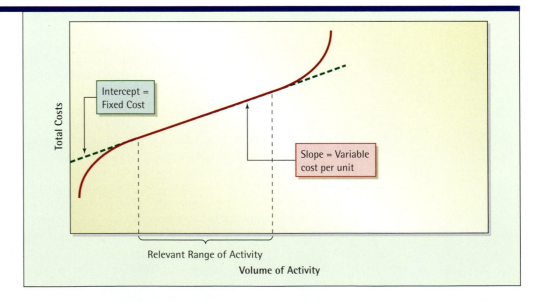

**EXHIBIT 2.6**
Total Costs over a Wide Range of Activity

**EXHIBIT 2.7** Algebraic Expressions for Various Cost Functions

| Type of Cost | Algebraic Function | Relevant Range | Reference |
|---|---|---|---|
| Variable | TC = $10 × Q<br>(TC = Total cost of tires) | Q > 0<br>(Q = Number of bikes produced) | Exhibit 2.2(a) |
| Variable (piecewise linear) | TC = $10 × Q<br>TC = $600 + $3(Q − 60)<br>(TC = Total cost of tires) | Q ≤ 60<br>Q > 60<br>(Q = Number of bikes produced) | Exhibit 2.2(b) |
| Fixed | TC = $6,000<br>(TC = Total cost of rent) | Q ≥ 0<br>(Q = Sales) | Exhibit 2.3(a) |
| Fixed (stepwise linear) | TC = $6,000<br>TC = $8,000<br>(TC = Total cost of rent) | Q ≤ $30,000<br>Q > $30,000<br>(Q = Sales) | Exhibit 2.3(b) |
| Mixed | TC = $10,000 + $500 × Q<br>(TC = Total cost of<br>advertisement) | Q ≥ 0<br>(Q = Number of times<br>advertisement is aired) | Exhibit 2.4 |

cost object is the entire organization, the number of passengers is a cost driver for in-flight beverage costs. The number of flights is a cost driver for fuel and flight attendant wages. The number of airports used by America West is a cost driver for counter space lease and airport management salaries.

For retail organizations such as **Banana Republic**, sales are likely to be a cost driver for many costs. When the cost object is a single Banana Republic store, sales are likely to drive the cost of clothing sold, sales commissions, and shopping bags. However, sales do not drive all types of costs for Banana Republic. For example, when the cost object is the entire organization, the total number of stores is likely to drive company-wide costs such as store manager salaries, electricity, cash registers, and clothing racks.

The same cost object might have different cost drivers in different settings. For example, when electricity is the cost object, in a retail setting the cost driver would be hours the store was open. In a manufacturing setting, the cost driver could be either machine hours or number of units manufactured, assuming that each unit requires the same number of machine hours.

## Identifying Potential Cost Drivers

Identifying potential cost drivers is a process that is specific to the organization. When the cost object is a product or service, people closest to the manufacturing or service delivery process generally have the best information about cost drivers. Spending time in the actual manufacturing or service delivery area and asking questions about operations, we gain insight about both the activities that take place and the potential cost drivers for these activities.

An organization's information system can help identify cost drivers. Large organizations often use enterprise resource programs (ERPs) to track both financial and nonfinancial information. ERP systems help identify potential cost drivers with detailed information such as the organization's interactions with customers and suppliers.

## No Apparent Cost Driver

Some costs cannot easily be associated with any type of cost driver. For example, legal costs at Magik Bicycles include any costs resulting from liability suits, costs for settling contract disputes, and costs to protect the brand name. These costs are not driven by any activity, such as the number of bicycles produced. To estimate these costs, we gather information about the type and expected costs of legal activities for the next period.

## ■ Discretionary Costs

**Discretionary costs** reflect periodic (usually annual) decisions about the maximum amount that will be spent on costs for activities such as advertising, executive travel, or research and development. Discretionary costs are considered managed fixed or managed variable costs, because managers decide the amount to spend on discretionary costs. These expenditures are often based on past profitability and can be altered during the period, depending on cash flow. The past behavior of discretionary costs might not be relevant to their future behavior.

## ■ Economies of Scale

Accountants need to investigate possible economies of scale when estimating a cost function. For example, if we double the size of our human resources department we may be able to handle three times as many employees. This change would cause the slope of the total cost function to flatten over large volumes of employees. Volume discounts are another example of economies of scale.

## ■ Learning Curves

When organizations start a new product line or hire new workers, the **learning curve** is the rate at which labor hours decrease as the volume of production or services increases. Over time, the learning curve leads to greater productivity; goods and services are produced more quickly as workers and supervisors learn more about their jobs and develop more efficient practices. Several different ways can be used to estimate learning curves. All of the approaches use a learning rate. This rate can be determined by analyzing historical data using statistical methods. The following example discusses the cumulative average-time learning curve approach.

Suppose that Magik Bicycles initiates a new production line, and each time the number of bicycles produced doubles, the cumulative average time to produce that number of bicycles is 80% of the time required for the previous production amount. Specifically, the average time to produce two bicycles is 80% of the time required to produce one bicycle. The average time to produce four bicycles is 80% of the average time to produce two bicycles, and so on. We would say that employees at Magik Bicycles have an 80% cumulative learning rate. If it takes three hours to produce the first bicycle, we estimate it will take $0.80 \times 3 = 2.4$ hours per bike, or a total of 4.8 hours to make two bicycles. To make four bicycles, it will take $0.80 \times 2.4 = 1.92$ hours per bike, or a total of 7.68 hours for the four bikes.

To simplify our calculations, we can mathematically represent the cumulative average-time learning curve for repetitive tasks using the following equation:

$$Y = \alpha X^r$$

where $Y$ is the cumulative average labor hours used for $X$ units of product or services produced, $\alpha$ is the time required for the first unit produced, and $r$ is an index for the rate of learning calculated as follows:

$$r = \ln(\text{percent learning})/\ln(2)$$

where ln is the natural logarithm. For the Magik Bicycles example, the index for an 80% learning rate is

$$r = \ln(0.80)/\ln(2) = -0.322$$

In this case, 1.92 hours per bicycle, on average, are required to produce four bicycles, as calculated here:

$$Y = \alpha X^r = 3 \text{ hours for the first bicycle} \times 4 \text{ bicycles}^{-0.322} = 3(0.64) = 1.92 \text{ hours}$$

Exhibit 2.8 shows the learning curve for Magik Bicycles. The learning curve formula is useful when we want to estimate future costs in cases where learning is likely to cause costs to decline.

---

[3]Taken from the introduction to a report on travel and entertainment costs, *CFO.com,* December 1, 2002.
[4]Note 1—Summary of Significant Accounting Policies, The Boeing Company 2002 Annual Report, available at www.boeing.com (click "Investor Relations").

**EXHIBIT 2.8**
Learning Curve for Magik
Bicycles

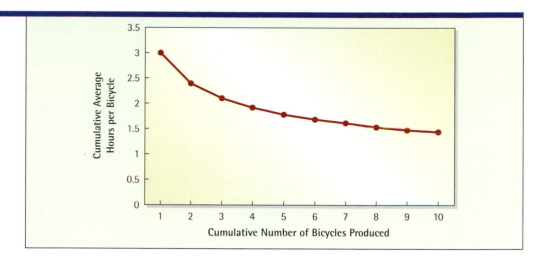

**GUIDE YOUR LEARNING** 2.2 Key Terms

Stop to confirm that you understand the new terms introduced in the last several pages:

Cost behavior (p. 41)
*Variable cost (p. 41)
*Fixed cost (p. 41)
*Mixed cost (p. 42)
Relevant range (p. 43)
Marginal cost (p. 43)

Cost function (p. 44)
Piecewise linear cost function (p. 44)
Stepwise linear cost function (p. 44)
*Cost driver (p. 44)
*Discretionary cost (p. 46)
Learning curve (p. 46)

For each of these terms, write a definition in your own words. For starred terms, list at least one example that is different from the ones given in this textbook.

## FOCUS ON ETHICAL DECISION MAKING
### Discretionary Costs

In the pharmaceutical industry, drug companies are granted patents on new drugs, providing them with up to 17 years of competitive protection for that drug. As patent lives expire, other companies are able to develop comparable (and oftentimes generic) drugs. In turn, the drug companies face decreasing revenues for the drug.

To counteract this loss of revenue, many companies increase their discretionary spending on advertising to consumers. For example, Merck spent $135.4 million in 2001 on direct-to-consumer media advertising for its arthritis drug, Vioxx, and Pharmacia spent $130.4 million on its arthritis drug, Celebrex. These were the two most heavily advertised drugs in 2001 (Bittar, p. SR24).

Yet the former chairman of the Food and Drug Administration's Arthritis Advisory Committee says that all anti-inflammatory drugs are equally effective in relieving arthritis pain. While Vioxx and Celebrex reduce risk for stomach problems, only 4% to 5% of patients are at risk for these types of problems, and both drugs are much more expensive than other anti-inflammatory drugs. Similar arguments have been made about the cost of highly advertised antihistamines that may not be worth the extra money (Bonifazi, p. R8).

Many consumer and medical groups are concerned about whether drug company advertising is ethical. Advertisements are designed to promote use of a particular drug and may not provide sufficient information for patients about the pros and cons of alternatives that could be much less expensive. In addition, "critics say that rapidly increasing drug costs are directly related to the fast growth of drug advertising." (Bittar, p. SR24).

*(continued)*

Drug companies, on the other hand, are likely to view advertising as a normal part of business operations. Their goal is to promote sales of their own products, not necessarily to provide objective information for consumers. Advertising can also serve a legitimate educational purpose by informing consumers about drugs that might be more effective than over-the-counter or prescription medications they are currently using.

SOURCES: W. Bonifazi, "Hard Sell: Drug Makers Are Spending Billions on 'Direct to Consumer' Ads; But Just How Effective Are the Products?" *The Wall Street Journal,* March 25, 2002, p. R8; and C. Bittar, "Special Report: Prescription Drugs," *Adweek,* April 22, 2002, p. SR24.

**Practice Ethical Decision Making**

In Chapter 1, we learned about a process for making ethical decisions (Exhibit 1.11). You can address the following questions for this ethical dilemma to improve your skills for making ethical decisions. Think about your answers to these questions and discuss them with others.

| Ethical Decision-Making Process | Questions to Consider about This Ethical Dilemma |
| --- | --- |
| Identify ethical problems as they arise. | Does advertising create an ethical problem for pharmaceutical companies? Why or why not? |
| Objectively consider the well-being of others and society when exploring alternatives. | Describe the different viewpoints about whether pharmaceutical companies should advertise. What assumptions lie behind each viewpoint? Are differences in ethical values evident in the different viewpoints? |
| Clarify and apply ethical values when choosing a course of action. | What is the best overall solution to this problem for society? What values did you use to arrive at the solution? What ethical values should drug companies use to address the concerns of their critics? |
| Work toward ongoing improvement of personal and organizational ethics. | How might drug companies continuously improve their advertising practices to benefit themselves and society? |

## INFORMATION USED TO ESTIMATE COSTS

**Q3** What process is used to estimate future costs?

Although past costs are not directly relevant to decisions, they are often useful in estimating future cost behavior. For example, past materials and labor costs might be the best estimate of future production costs. Historical costs are generally recorded and coded within the accounting system so that they can be summarized in different ways depending on the cost object of interest. Magik Bicycles' accounting system might be used to create one or more reports of last year's production costs, material usage, and labor hours. The ease with which information can be identified for a particular cost object depends on the design of the accounting system as well as the nature of the information.

Information for some costs cannot be obtained easily from the accounting system. Suppose the managers of Magik Bicycles are estimating next year's production costs. They gather information about changes in direct materials costs from their suppliers' price lists or from other vendors' Web sites.

When estimating a cost function, accountants usually begin with past cost information if it is available. Although past cost information might be accurate and useful, it may at times be unavailable, irrelevant, or outdated. Sometimes a combination of information sources is the best choice. Exhibit 2.9 presents a decision tree for deciding whether to use past costs or other information when estimating a cost function.

**EXHIBIT 2.9** Deciding Whether to Use Past Costs for Estimating a Cost Function

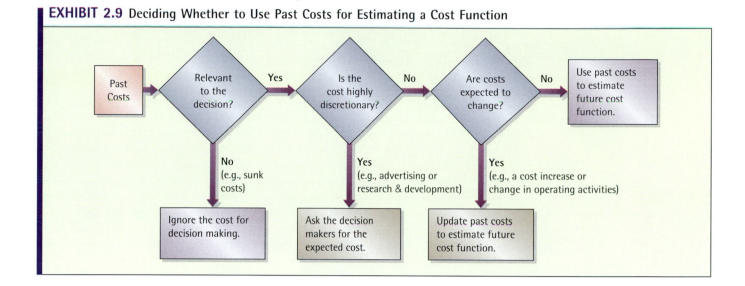

## COST ESTIMATION TECHNIQUES

**Q4** How are the engineered estimate, the account analysis, and two-point methods used to estimate cost functions?

**Q5** How does a scatter plot assist with categorizing a cost?

As we gather relevant information, we may have a general idea of the cost behavior. However, we need to select one or more techniques for estimating the dollar amount of relevant costs. The following techniques are used to estimate a cost function.

- Engineered estimate of cost
- Analysis at the account level
- Two-point method
- High-low method
- Regression analysis

Although each of these methods may be used, the choice is open-ended. No single technique is useful in all circumstances. Although some techniques are generally better than others, the best technique often depends on the circumstances for a particular decision. As we look at each technique, pay particular attention to its assumptions. Poor management decisions can result if the quality of cost estimates is not considered.

### ■ Engineered Estimate of Cost

One method used to estimate a cost function is the **engineered estimate of cost.** Each activity is analyzed according to the amount of labor time, materials, and other resources used. Costs are assigned according to these measurements. Suppose **DaimlerChrysler** begins production of a new automobile model, such as the PT Cruiser. Engineers and accountants use the new model's design specifications to estimate the cost of direct and indirect materials for a production run of Cruisers. In addition, the proposed manufacturing process is analyzed to determine the cost effects of any changes from the existing manufacturing processes. The accountants communicate with purchasing department personnel to determine whether the prices of inputs are likely to change. From this information, a total cost function is developed for the production of Cruisers for the next period.

Although engineers traditionally develop engineered estimates of cost, anyone having sufficient knowledge about activities and costs can develop a cost function using this method. For example, earlier in the chapter we estimated the number of labor hours required when a learning curve is involved. We could use this approach to develop a labor cost function for new products or services.

Suppose Sunghoon, a consultant in an accounting firm, wishes to create a cost budget for a consulting job. Sunghoon begins by identifying the various tasks that must be performed and incidental costs (such as travel and printing) that might be incurred. He then develops a time budget by specifying the professional level (e.g., partner, manager, supervisor, or staff) and number of hours needed to perform each task. While developing the time budget, Sunghoon refers to records from prior consulting jobs and his knowledge about the new job. He then creates a budget for professional labor cost by applying cost rates for each type of staff

**ALTERNATIVE TERMS**

These terms are synonymous: *engineered estimate of cost method*, *industrial engineering method*, and *work-measurement method*.

to the time budget. Next, Sunghoon develops budgets for each incidental cost. Finally, he combines the costs from all budgets to estimate the total cost for the job.

## Analysis at the Account Level

Another way to create a cost function is to use **analysis at the account level.** Using this technique, we review the pattern of a cost over time in the accounting system and use our knowledge of operations to classify the cost as variable, fixed, or mixed. Costs such as managers' salaries are usually fixed; they are often directly associated in the general ledger with a particular department or product. Costs for variable materials used in the production process are usually available in the general ledger or in production records. Costs such as manufacturing overhead are often mixed; they tend to include fixed costs such as insurance and property taxes for the plant and variable costs such as indirect supplies used in manufacturing. For costs we identify as mixed, we must use another cost estimation technique such as the two-point method or regression analysis to determine the fixed and variable components. Sometimes we are uncertain about the nature of the cost function. A scatter plot provides helpful information about the relationship between a cost and potential cost driver.

## Scatter Plots

A **scatter plot** is a graphical technique in which data points for past costs are plotted against a potential cost driver. Scatter plots provide a quick way to learn more about the behavior of a cost and to determine whether a potential cost driver is viable as $Q$ in the cost function. We visually analyze scatter plots to improve our understanding of a cost's behavior and to decide whether the cost might be completely fixed, completely variable, or mixed.

The following data are from one of Magik Bicycles' manufacturing plants. They include weekly costs for packing bikes, together with a possible cost driver, the number of bikes shipped.

| Number of Bikes Shipped | Total Packing Cost |
|:---:|:---:|
| 200 | $729 |
| 270 | 870 |
| 250 | 820 |
| 210 | 720 |
| 300 | 950 |
| 175 | 700 |

Exhibit 2.10a shows a scatter plot of these data. Notice that the data points seem to fall in a general upward linear pattern, suggesting that total packing costs increase with the number of bikes shipped. In addition, if we draw a trend line roughly through the middle of the data points as shown in Exhibit 2.10(b) and continue the line to the vertical axis, the intercept appears to be above zero. Thus, the scatter plot suggests that the cost of packing is a mixed cost with an apparent variable component (the slope) and a fixed component (the intercept).

## Two-Point Method

The **two-point method** uses any two sets of data points for cost and a cost driver to algebraically calculate a mixed cost function. These data points can be drawn from a scatter plot. The line should resemble the general pattern of the data and be drawn using a ruler on a printed scatter plot or using a spreadsheet's line-draw feature. Spreadsheet programs such as Excel create a trend line representing the best fit for the data points.

We create the cost function by selecting and performing calculations with any two points on the line, even if they are not original data points. Variable cost *(V)* is calculated by computing the slope of the line—the change in cost compared to the change in the cost driver *(Q)* between the two points. Given *V*, the fixed cost is calculated by solving for *F* in the formula TC $= F + V \times Q$ for one of the two data points.

The lower trend line in Exhibit 2.10(b) was created using Excel. Two points on the trend line have values for $Q$ of 240 and 190 bicycles on the horizontal axis. These same points have respective values for TC of $800 and $700 on the vertical axis. Using those two points, we calculate variable cost as follows:

**EXHIBIT 2.10** Scatter Plot of Total Packing Costs

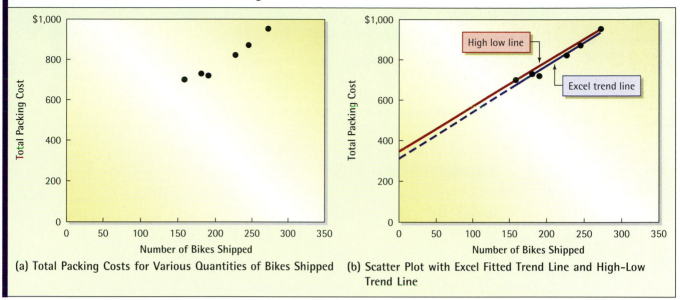

(a) Total Packing Costs for Various Quantities of Bikes Shipped

(b) Scatter Plot with Excel Fitted Trend Line and High-Low Trend Line

$$\text{Change in cost} \div \text{Change in the cost driver}$$
$$= (\$800 - \$700) \div (240 - 190) \text{ bicycles}$$
$$= \$100 \div 50 \text{ bicycles} = \$2 \text{ per bicycle}$$

Thus, $V = \$2$ per bicycle. We can now calculate fixed cost using 190 bikes as follows:

$$\$700 = F + 190 \text{ bicycles} \times \$2 \text{ per bicycle}$$
$$F = \$700 - \$380 = \$320$$

**HELPFUL HINT**

We could have used the total cost for 240 units to solve for fixed costs as follows: $\$800 = F + 240$ bicycles $\times$ \$2 per bicycle, so $F = \$800 - \$480 = \$320$.

The total cost function (per week) for packing bikes is estimated as

$$TC = \$320 + \$2Q$$

## ■ High-Low Method

The **high-low method** is a specific application of the two-point method using the highest and lowest data points of the cost driver. Although this technique is useful for illustration in classroom settings, it is inappropriate when we want to estimate an organization's costs as accurately as possible. The problem with this method is that the highest and lowest cost driver observations are often atypical and might lie outside the normal range of activities. Therefore, this method frequently distorts the cost function. However, sometimes we only have two or three data points, in which case the high-low method may be our only choice.

The top trend line in Exhibit 2.10(b) uses the highest and lowest observations for number of bicycles packed. Notice that this linear function misses most of the data points. Using the high-low method, we calculate the total cost function for Magik Bicycles' packing activities as follows:

$$\text{Change in cost} \div \text{Change in the cost driver}$$
$$= (\$950 - \$700) \div (300 - 175) \text{ bicycles}$$
$$= \$250 \div 125 \text{ bicycles} = \$2 \text{ per bicycle}$$

The variable cost $V$ is \$2 per bicycle. Fixed cost is calculated using 175 bikes as follows:

$$\$700 = F + 175 \text{ bicycles} \times \$2 \text{ per bicycle}$$
$$F = \$700 - \$350$$
$$= \$350$$

The total cost function for packing bikes, then, is

$$TC = \$350 + \$2Q$$

**EXHIBIT 2.11** Estimating Relevant Costs for a Cost Object

| Identify relevant costs for the cost object | Estimate a Cost Function for Each Relevant Cost | | | | Combine all relevant cost estimates for the cost object |
|---|---|---|---|---|---|
| | Obtain information needed for estimation | Categorize costs as fixed, variable, or mixed | Select and apply cost estimation techniques | Specify the cost function and then estimate the future cost | |
| | ◄——— Continuously Evaluate Uncertainties and Quality of Information ———► | | | | |

## ESTIMATING THE COST FUNCTION

Exhibit 2.11 summarizes the activities involved in estimating a cost function for a particular cost object. The following Small Animal Clinic example demonstrates how to create a cost function.

 **Q3** What process is used to estimate future costs?

### SMALL ANIMAL CLINIC (PART 1)
### CREATING A COST FUNCTION

Small Animal Clinic is a nonprofit clinic that provides limited veterinarian services, primarily vaccinations, for the surrounding community. The clinic has been growing each year, and its manager expects this trend to continue. The recent growth has actually been driven by an economic downturn. With rising unemployment, more people are unable to pay regular veterinarian fees. Many have turned to Small Animal Clinic, which charges a lower rate for services. A local foundation has provided Small Animal Clinic a matching grant for its services. For example, if a pet owner pays $30 for an examination and vaccines, the foundation will match the fee with an additional $30. This support has enabled the clinic to keep its rates low.

### Identify Relevant Costs and Obtain Information Needed for Estimation

As part of her operating plans, Leticia Brown, the manager of Small Animal Clinic, would like to create a budget of next year's revenues and costs. Leticia estimates that the clinic will provide services for 3,800 visits next year. The accountant, Josh Hardy, determined that the cost object is the clinic, and the cost driver for the clinic as a whole is the number of animal visits. Then from the accounting records, he identified five relevant costs for the clinic: part-time veterinarians, technicians, treatment supplies, rent, and administration costs. He performed analysis at the account level to obtain the information needed to estimate future costs. The information for the last three years follows. Because Small Animal Clinic is a nonprofit organization, its profit is referred to as surplus.

| | 2003 | 2004 | 2005 |
|---|---|---|---|
| Animal visits | 2,500 | 3,000 | 3,500 |
| Veterinary fees | $ 72,500 | $ 90,000 | $105,000 |
| Foundation matching grant | 72,500 | 90,000 | 105,000 |
| Total Revenue | 145,000 | 180,000 | 210,000 |
| Expenses: | | | |
| Part-time veterinarians | 24,000 | 32,800 | 42,000 |
| Technicians | 71,000 | 78,000 | 78,049 |
| Treatment supplies | 4,000 | 4,600 | 5,200 |
| Rent | 8,000 | 8,500 | 8,750 |
| Administration | 38,000 | 39,600 | 41,200 |
| Total Expenses | 145,000 | 163,500 | 175,199 |
| Surplus | $ 0 | $ 16,500 | $ 34,801 |

## Categorize Costs, Apply Cost Estimation Techniques, and Estimate Future Costs

To create individual cost functions, Josh categorizes each cost as fixed, variable, or mixed, and identifies potential cost drivers for the variable and mixed costs. He then selects the appropriate cost estimation technique for the mixed costs, develops the cost function, and estimates future costs for each relevant cost.

**Part-Time Veterinarians.** Josh studies the payroll records and finds a lot of variation in the cost of veterinarians. Part-time veterinarians are called in as necessary and are paid on an hourly basis. Most of their time is spent with animals, so Josh determines it is a direct cost. Therefore, he thinks that the amount of time the veterinarians spend with each animal might be a cost driver. However, the accounting system does not record the visit time per animal. Instead, records are available for the total number of animal visits. Josh considers other potential cost drivers such as number of veterinarians on-call and the hours the clinic is open, but eliminates them because they seem less likely than number of animal visits to have a cause-and-effect relationship with veterinarian wages. Therefore, he categorizes veterinarian fees as a variable cost and plans to use number of animal visits as the cost driver.

Josh knows that although veterinarian pay is increased periodically, no increase is planned for next year. Because last year's information is the most current, he uses only last year's data to create the cost function. In 2005, this category included no fixed costs, and the variable cost per animal visit was $12.00 ($42,000 total cost ÷ 3,500 animal visits). The cost function for veterinarians, then, is

$$TC = \$0 + \$12.00 \text{ per animal visit} \times Q \text{ animal visits}$$

Josh can now estimate 2006 costs, with $Q = 3,800$ animal visits.

$$TC = \$12.00 \text{ per animal visit} \times 3,800 \text{ animal visits} = \$45,600$$

**Technicians.** Josh learns from payroll records that the technical staff is permanent and paid on a salary basis. The technicians clean examination rooms, prepare supplies, fill out paper work, handle the reception desk, and assist the veterinarians with each visit. Because they work on many different tasks, Josh concludes that this cost is indirect and fixed.

Again, Josh uses the most current information in his cost function. A 2.5% salary increase is expected for 2006. With no variable costs and only the fixed cost of $78,049 for 2005, the updated cost function for technicians is

$$TC = (\$78,049 \times 1.025) + \$0Q = \$80,000$$

Josh estimates the 2006 cost for technicians to be $80,000.

**Treatment Supplies.** Josh believes that treatment supplies is either a variable or mixed cost. He learns from the technicians that treatment supplies include items that vary depending on the services provided, such as vaccination serum and syringes. He also learns that supplies include items such as lab coats for clinic employees that vary by number of employees rather than visits. He concludes that the cost of treatment supplies is a mixed cost, and he believes that number of animal visits has a cause-and-effect relationship for the variable portion.

Josh learns that few significant changes occurred in the cost or use of treatment supplies over the past three years. Therefore, he decides to use all three years' data to estimate the cost function. With only three data points, he uses the high-low method to separate the fixed and variable components of treatment supplies. He first identifies the highest and lowest data points for the cost driver, which is number of animal visits. The lowest number of animal visits was in 2003, and the highest number was in 2005. He calculates the variable cost per unit by dividing the change in cost ($5,200 − $4,000) by the change in volume (3,500 − 2,500) for these two data points:

$$(\$5,200 - \$4,000) \div (3,500 - 2,500) = \$1,200 \div 1,000 = \$1.20 \text{ per animal visit}$$

Next, Josh substitutes the variable cost rate into the cost equation for 2005 and solves for the fixed costs:

$$TC = F + V \times Q$$
$$\$5,200 = F + \$1.20 \text{ per animal visit} \times 3,500 \text{ animal visits}$$
$$\$5,200 = F + \$4,200$$
$$F = \$1,000$$

Josh's cost function for treatment supplies is

$$TC = \$1,000 + \$1.20 \text{ per animal visit} \times Q \text{ animal visits}$$

*(continued)*

He can now estimate costs for treatment supplies in 2006, assuming 3,800 animal visits.

$$TC = \$1,000 + \$1.20 \text{ per animal visit} \times 3,800 \text{ animal visits} = \$5,560$$

**Rent.** Josh knows that rent can change annually when the lease is renewed. However, rent changes depend on local rates rather than on the level of operating activity at the clinic. Accordingly, he categorizes rent as a fixed cost.

Josh uses the most recent rent amount and sets up his cost function.

$$TC = \$8,750 + \$0Q$$
$$TC = \$8,750$$

He does not update this figure because he learns that the property manager is not planning to increase rent for 2006. Therefore, his estimate for rent is also $8,750.

**Administration.** Josh learns that administration includes costs to set up files for new animals and office supplies related to the paperwork for each visit. Josh reviews the general ledger entries and finds that the remainder of the administrative cost is for salaries, general office supplies, and telephone, which Josh concludes are fixed costs. Thus, he concludes that administration is a mixed cost, with animal visits as the cost driver for the variable portion.

Josh performs an account analysis of the administrative costs, separating the cost of supplies such as file folders, tabs, and the forms required for each visit. From his analysis, he calculates the cost of these supplies as $8,000 in 2003, $9,600 in 2004, and $11,200 in 2005, or about $3.20 per animal visit. He bases his estimate of fixed administrative costs on the most recent year's data. During 2005 total administrative costs were $41,200. When he subtracts the variable cost of $11,200, this leaves $30,000 ($41,200 − $11,200) as his estimate of the fixed cost. Therefore, his cost function for administration is

$$TC = \$30,000 + \$3.20 \text{ per animal visit} \times Q \text{ animal visits}$$

Josh now estimates administration cost for 2006.

$$TC = \$30,000 + \$3.20 \text{ per animal visit} \times 3,800 \text{ animal visits} = \$42,160$$

## Combine All Relevant Cost Estimates

Josh creates the following summary of his cost functions and estimated costs for 2006.

| Cost | Category | Fixed Cost | Variable Cost per Animal Visit | 2006 Estimated Cost for 3,800 Animal Visits |
|---|---|---|---|---|
| Part-time veterinarians | Variable | $      0 | $12.00 | $  45,600 |
| Technicians | Fixed | 80,000 | 0.00 | 80,000 |
| Treatment supplies | Mixed | 1,000 | 1.20 | 5,560 |
| Rent | Fixed | 8,750 | 0.00 | 8,750 |
| Administration | Mixed | 30,000 | 3.20 | 42,160 |
| Total | | $119,750 | $16.40 | $182,070 |

The total cost function for Small Animal Clinic is

$$TC = \$119,750 + \$16.40 \text{ per animal visit} \times Q \text{ animal visits}$$

Based on Leticia's estimate of 3,800 animal visits for next year, Josh estimates that total 2006 costs will be:

$$\$119,750 + \$16.40 \text{ per animal visit} \times 3,800 \text{ animal visits} = \$182,070$$

## Estimating Profit

Leticia told Josh that she did not expect any major changes from 2005 to 2006 in the types of services provided, the average fees, or the matching grant. Although Josh does not know last year's average fees, he calculates it from last year's revenue information (which includes the matching grant):

$$\text{Average revenue in 2005} = \text{Total 2005 revenue} \div \text{ Number of animal visits in 2005}$$
$$= \$210,000 \div 3,500 \text{ animal visits}$$
$$= \$60.00 \text{ per animal visit}$$

Given average revenues of $60.00 per animal visit, budgeted revenues for next year (including the matching grant) are:

Budgeted revenues = Estimated 2006 animal visits × Average revenue rate
= 3,800 animal visits × $60.00 per animal visit
= $228,000

Using the budgeted revenues and costs as calculated, Josh tells Leticia that he expects Small Animal Clinic to earn a surplus during 2006 of $45,930 ($228,000 − $182,070).

---

| GUIDE YOUR LEARNING **2.3** Small Animal Clinic (Part 1) | | |
| --- | --- | --- |
| Small Animal Clinic (Part 1) illustrates how to create a cost function when the entire organization is the cost object. For this illustration: | | |
| **Define It** | **Identify Problem** | **Identify Uncertainties** |
| Which definitions, analysis techniques, and computations were used? | No specific decision was being addressed in the illustration. List some possible uses for the budget created in the illustration. | What were the uncertainties? Consider uncertainties about:<br>• Categorizing costs as fixed, variable, or mixed<br>• Cost drivers<br>• Use of past costs to estimate future costs<br>• Choice of estimation techniques<br>• Interpreting computations |

## REGRESSION ANALYSIS

**Q6** How is regression analysis used to estimate a mixed cost function?

**HELPFUL HINT**

In this chapter, we focus only on *linear* or *least-squares* regression analysis. Other nonlinear forms of regression are beyond the scope of this textbook.

**CHAPTER REFERENCE**

Appendix 2A presents additional regression topics including an example of multiple regression analysis, choosing among cost drivers, assumptions for regression analysis, and other data considerations.

**HELPFUL HINT**

The squared error is the square of the distance from each observation to the regression trend line.

In the Small Animal Clinic illustration, Josh used the high-low method to estimate the cost function for treatment supplies. This method is often not sufficiently accurate because it uses the two most extreme data points, which could distort the cost function. An alternative estimation technique is regression analysis, a statistical technique that measures the average change in a dependent variable for every unit change in one or more independent variables. Regression analysis uses all of the available data points and often improves the accuracy of a cost function.

**Simple regression analysis** develops a cost function by calculating values for the statistical relationship between total cost and a single cost driver. **Multiple regression analysis** develops a cost function by calculating values for the statistical relationship between total cost and two or more cost drivers.

### ■ Simple Regression Analysis

In Exhibit 2.10 we created a scatter plot for a cost object, packing costs, and a cost driver, number of bikes. We used Excel to draw a trend line and developed a cost function using that data. Simple regression analysis is a statistical method used to find the trend line that minimizes the distance from every data point to the line. The slope of the line represents the variable cost per unit, and the intercept of the line with the vertical axis represents the fixed cost. The distance between each observation and the line is called the *error term*. In locating a slope that best fits all of the available data, regression analysis minimizes the squared error terms.

Simple regression analysis then estimates the following equation:

$$Y = \alpha + \beta X + \varepsilon$$

where $Y$ is the dependent variable (total cost), $\alpha$ (alpha) is the intercept (fixed cost), $\beta$ (beta) is the slope coefficient (variable cost per unit), $X$ is the independent variable (the cost driver), and $\varepsilon$ (epsilon) is the error term, also called the residual.

**EXHIBIT 2.12**
Questions Addressed
by Simple Regression
Analysis

| Question about the Cost Function | Relevant Simple Regression Statistics |
|---|---|
| How confident can we be that the actual fixed cost is greater than zero (i.e., that there is a fixed component in the cost function)? | *t*-statistic and *p*-value for the alpha coefficient |
| How confident can we be that the actual variable cost per unit of the cost driver is greater than zero (i.e., that there is a variable component in the cost function)? | *t*-statistic and *p*-value for the beta coefficient |
| Overall, how well does the cost driver explain the behavior (i.e., the variation) in the cost? | Adjusted *R*-square, as well as *t*-statistic and *p*-value for both coefficients |

HELPFUL HINT
You can use the Help function to learn how to apply regression in Excel. The Web-based option sends you directly to an Excel tutorial.

We usually use a computer program such as Excel or SAS to perform regression analysis. The ability of computer programs to easily perform regression analyses makes the cost of using this technique low. Thus, the cost of performing regression analysis is not likely to exceed the benefits.

## ◼ Interpreting Simple Regression Results

Regression analysis provides the best estimate of the cost function in cases with a strong positive linear relationship between the cost and the cost driver. However, the data points we use in a regression rarely fit into an absolutely straight line. Deviations from linearity may occur because the true underlying cost function is not strictly linear. Deviations may also occur because the regression data typically come from past costs and activities that might be mismeasured or include unusual events, shifts in cost behavior over time, or random fluctuations. When interpreting regression results, we need to keep in mind that we are using regression analysis *only* because we do not know the actual cost function and must estimate it. Furthermore, we might not be confident that the cost we are trying to estimate is a mixed cost. We use regression to estimate the cost function and to learn more about how the cost behaves. Exhibit 2.12 presents the questions that we address when using simple regression to estimate a cost function.

HELPFUL HINT
The standard error for each coefficient tells us the amount of variation we could expect in our estimates using the value of the coefficient as expected cost.

Exhibit 2.13 shows the output from regressing Magik Bicycles' packing costs on the number of bikes packed. For each coefficient (alpha and beta), the regression output includes both a *t*-statistic and a *p*-value. We examine the *t*-statistic calculated for each coefficient to evaluate whether that coefficient is significantly greater than zero. The *t*-statistic compares the coefficient with its standard error. If the coefficient is small relative to the standard error, we cannot be confident that the coefficient is different from zero. If the *t*-statistic is significantly large (above 2.00), we have more confidence that our estimates for fixed and

**EXHIBIT 2.13**
Regression Analysis Results
for Shipping Costs and
Number of Bikes

```
SUMMARY OUTPUT
          Regression Statistics
Multiple R              0.98203762
R Square               0.96439789
Adjusted R Square      0.95549736
Standard Error         20.9306335
Observations                    6


                                  Standard
              Coefficients         Error        t Stat      P-value
Intercept      314.374297       47.2560438    6.65257335   0.00265124
X Variable 1     2.06601723      0.19847861   10.409269    0.00048107
```

variable costs are different from zero. The *p*-value gives the statistical significance of the *t*-statistic, or the probability that the coefficient is not different from zero. Acceptable *p*-values generally need to be less than 0.10, and preferably less than 0.05.

A low *p*-value for the alpha coefficient gives us confidence that the fixed cost is significantly different from zero. Similarly, a low *p*-value for the beta coefficient gives us confidence that the variable cost is significantly different from zero. If a *p*-value is too high, we conclude that the coefficient should not be used in the cost function. Sometimes only one of the coefficients is statistically greater than zero. In this case, we generally conclude that the cost is not mixed, but instead is variable or fixed (depending on which coefficient is significant).

Interpreting the output from the Magik Bicycles example (Exhibit 2.13), the intercept (fixed cost) is \$314 and the *p*-value for the *t*-statistic is 0.002. This result means that the fixed cost has a probability of being zero about 2 in 1,000 times. We are quite confident that it is different from zero. The beta coefficient (\$2.07) also has a small *p*-value (0.0004). Using this information, our total cost function would be TC = \$314 + \$2.07$Q$, where $Q$ is the number of bikes.

The adjusted *R*-square statistic reflects an estimate of the percent of variation in cost that is explained by the cost driver. In the Magik Bicycles example, the adjusted *R*-square is 0.95. This result means that the variation in number of bikes packed explains about 95% of the variation in packing cost. An advantage of regression analysis when more than one potential cost driver is involved is that we can compare the adjusted *R*-squares from several regressions that have different cost drivers for the same cost. The cost driver that provides the highest adjusted *R*-square explains the largest portion of changes in cost.

We will next illustrate how to use simple regression analysis to estimate a cost function for Small Animal Clinic. The process we will use is summarized in Exhibit 2.14. We will also compare the results for simple regression with the two-point and high-low methods.

**ALTERNATIVE TERMS**

The *adjusted R-square* is also called the *adjusted coefficient of determination*.

---

**EXHIBIT 2.14**
Using Regression Analysis to Estimate a Cost Function

1. **Consider the behavior of the cost.** Decide whether the cost is likely to be a good candidate for regression analysis. The best candidates for regression are costs that appear to be mixed.

2. **Generate a list of possible cost drivers.** The cost drivers must be economically plausible; changes in the cost driver could potentially affect cost.

3. **Gather data.** We need data for both the dependent variable (the cost being estimated) and for one or more independent variables (the cost drivers).

4. **Plot the cost for each potential cost driver.** Scatter plots that have a positive slope or a football-shaped pattern indicate a potential linear relationship between the cost and the cost driver. Eliminate any cost drivers that do not exhibit a positive linear relationship with cost. If no cost drivers remain, the cost should not be estimated using regression analysis.

5. **Perform the regression analysis.** For each remaining potential cost driver, perform simple regression analysis with that driver as the independent variable. If necessary, perform a series of multiple regression analyses with different combinations of cost drivers. Use a spreadsheet program such as Excel to perform the regressions.

6. **Evaluate the appropriateness of each cost driver.** Use the goodness of fit statistic (adjusted *R*-square) to select those cost drivers that explain a high proportion of variability in the cost.

7. **Evaluate the sign and significance of the cost function's components.** Verify that each coefficient is positive. Use the *p*-values for the *t*-statistics to determine whether the intercept coefficient reflecting fixed cost and slope coefficient reflecting variable cost are significantly different from zero.

8. **Write the cost function as TC = $F + V \times Q$.** If significantly different from zero, use the intercept coefficient as the estimated fixed cost and the independent variable coefficient as the estimated variable cost.

## SMALL ANIMAL CLINIC (PART 2)
## TWO-POINT METHOD AND REGRESSION ANALYSIS

When Josh shows Leticia his revenue and cost estimates, she questions him about the cost of treatment supplies. Believing his estimate to be too high, she asks him to investigate this cost further.

### Revised Analysis of the Treatment Supplies Cost

When Josh originally estimated the cost function for treatment supplies, he had only three data points—the cost for each of the past three years. With so few data points, he had used the high-low method to estimate the cost function. Using quarterly data, however, would give him more data points, allowing him to use other estimation techniques that would generate a higher-quality cost function.

Josh is also concerned about the accuracy of the data for the number of animal visits, which are tracked manually at the reception desk, and sometimes not recorded. He considers using the number of bills recorded in the accounting system to count the number of animal visits, but a single pet owner often brings in more than one pet and yet receives a single bill. He considers whether another cost driver would be more accurate.

Josh knows that the veterinarians use different supplies for each visit because the needs of each pet are different. For example, a puppy may get a series of vaccinations at the same time, whereas an adult dog gets only one or two vaccinations. Yet when he uses number of animal visits as the cost driver, he assumes that the same amount of supplies is used for each visit. Josh knows that the bill for each visit includes charges for supplies. Therefore, the revenue per visit varies with the number and type of supplies used. He determines that revenue might be better correlated with treatment supplies than number of animal visits. He also thinks that the data for revenue per visit are more accurate because they are recorded by the accounting system when bills are created.

### Quarterly Data

Although Josh believes that revenue may be better correlated with treatment supplies cost than animal visits, he decides to analyze both drivers to learn more about their behavior. He collects the following quarterly data for his analyses.

| Quarter | Treatment Supplies Cost | Animal Visits | Revenues |
|---|---|---|---|
| 2003–1 | $1,000 | 500 | $18,125 |
| 2003–2 | 920 | 725 | 17,400 |
| 2003–3 | 1,120 | 700 | 20,300 |
| 2003–4 | 960 | 575 | 16,675 |
| 2004–1 | 966 | 750 | 18,900 |
| 2004–2 | 1,058 | 960 | 20,700 |
| 2004–3 | 1,288 | 600 | 24,300 |
| 2004–4 | 1,288 | 690 | 26,100 |
| 2005–1 | 1,404 | 700 | 28,350 |
| 2005–2 | 1,092 | 595 | 23,100 |
| 2005–3 | 1,404 | 910 | 29,400 |
| 2005–4 | 1,300 | 1,295 | 24,150 |

### Scatter Plots

First Josh creates scatter plots of the treatment supplies cost against animal visits and against revenues. When creating the scatter plots, he wants the vertical axes on the two plots to have the same scale so that he can compare them. He visually examines the plots and fits a trend line to each plot. Josh notices that most of the cost points are relatively close to the trend line in the revenue scatter plot shown in Exhibit 2.15(a), whereas many of the data points are further away from the trend line in the animal visit scatter plot in Exhibit 2.15(b). This observation suggests that revenue is likely to provide a more accurate cost function than number of animal visits.

### Two-Point Method

First Josh decides to use the two-point method with revenue as the cost driver. He selects the points when revenues are $20,000 and $25,000, and draws a vertical line from these points on the revenue axis to the trend line, shown in Exhibit 2.15(a). Where each vertical line intersects the trend line, he draws a horizontal line to the cost axis and visually estimates the cost for the two points as $1,000 and $1,233, respectively. Dividing the change in cost ($1,233 − $1,000) by the change in revenues ($25,000 − $20,000), he estimates a variable cost of $0.047 per dollar of revenue, or 4.7% of revenues. He then uses the data point for cost of $1,000 to estimate the fixed cost, using the following formula for the cost function:

**EXHIBIT 2.15** Scatter Plots for Quarterly Treatment Supplies Cost

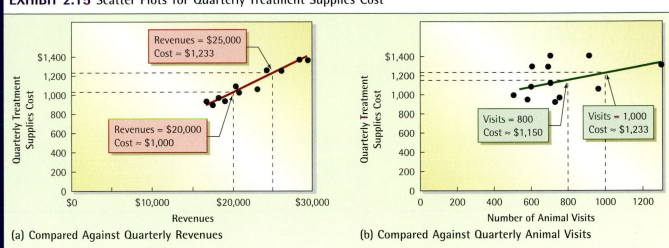

(a) Compared Against Quarterly Revenues

(b) Compared Against Quarterly Animal Visits

$$\$1,000 = F + (4.7\% \times \$20,000)$$
$$F = \$1,000 - \$940 = \$60$$

Given these calculations, he estimates the cost function as TC = $60 + 4.7% × Revenues

Next Josh uses the two-point method with animal visits as the cost driver. He uses the same procedures as previously described to choose two points on the trend line, shown in Exhibit 2.15(b). Given these two points, he estimates the cost function as:

$$TC = \$813 + \$0.42 \times \text{Number of Animal Visits}$$

## Simple Regression Analysis

Josh is concerned that his calculations using the two-point method may not be as accurate as he would like. He decides to perform simple regression analysis. When number of animal visits is the cost driver as in Exhibit 2.16(a), the adjusted $R$-square is 0.035, which is very low. But when revenue is the cost driver as in Exhibit 2.16(b), the adjusted $R$-square is quite high at 0.915, suggesting that changes in revenue explain about 91.5% of the changes in supplies cost. He concludes that revenue is a much better cost driver than animal visits. However, he waits to reach a final conclusion until he analyzes the rest of the regression results.

Focusing on Exhibit 2.16(b), Josh observes that the coefficients for both the intercept (259) and independent variable (0.040) are positive, as required to create a cost function. He notices that the $p$-value for the intercept is 0.01, suggesting only a small probability that the intercept could be zero. The $p$-value for the coefficient on revenue is even smaller at 0.00000068, suggesting a tiny probability that the coefficient could be zero. These results give Josh considerable confidence in the regression results. He creates a new cost function for treatment supplies as follows.

$$TC = \$259 + 4.0\% \times \text{Revenue}$$

## Revised Cost Estimate

Josh's earlier estimate of $228,000 for 2006 revenue includes the matching grant. However, the grant, which accounts for half of all revenues, is not included in the quarterly data used to estimate the new cost function. Therefore, Josh needs to divide estimated revenues in half when using the new cost function: $228,000 ÷ 2 = $114,000. His revised estimate of the treatment supply cost for 2006 is:

$$TC = \$259 + (4.0\% \times \$114,000) = \$4,819$$

Next, he revises his estimate of total 2006 costs. He previously estimated total costs to be $182,070, including $5,560 in treatment supplies. His new estimate for total 2006 costs is $181,329 ($182,070 − $5,560 + $4,819). Finally, he revises his estimate of the 2006 surplus to account for changes in total costs:

$$\text{Estimated surplus} = \$228,000 - \$181,329 = \$46,671$$

*(continued)*

**EXHIBIT 2.16**
Simple Regressions for
Quarterly Treatment
Supplies Cost

### Regression Statistics

| | |
|---|---|
| Multiple R | 0.35044032 |
| R Square | 0.12280842 |
| Adjusted R Square | 0.03508926 |
| Standard Error | 174.643357 |
| Observations | 12 |

| | Coefficients | Standard Error | t Stat | P-value |
|---|---|---|---|---|
| Intercept | 934.164081 | 189.252112 | 4.93608271 | 0.00059059 |
| Animal Visits | 0.28778123 | 0.24321795 | 1.18322365 | 0.2640863 |

(a) Using Animal Visits as the Cost Driver

### Regression Statistics

| | |
|---|---|
| Multiple R | 0.96078362 |
| R Square | 0.92310516 |
| Adjusted R Square | 0.91541568 |
| Standard Error | 51.7074871 |
| Observations | 12 |

| | Coefficients | Standard Error | t Stat | P-value |
|---|---|---|---|---|
| Intercept | 258.579519 | 82.7169413 | 3.12607689 | 0.0107621 |
| Revenue | 0.03998896 | 0.00364975 | 10.9566301 | 6.8389E-07 |

(b) Using Revenues as the Cost Driver

## Review of Methods, Total Cost Function

Josh reviews his results to gain a better understanding of how the various methods compare. A summary of his treatment supply cost estimates for 2006, for both cost drivers and for each estimation technique, follows:

| | | 2006 Estimate |
|---|---|---|
| Number of Animal Visits (3,800 estimated for 2006): | | |
| High-low method | TC = $1,000 + $1.20 per visit × Visits | $5,560 |
| Two-point method | TC = $813 + $0.42 per visit × Visits | $2,409 |
| Simple regression | TC = $934 + $0.29 per visit × Visits | $2,036 |
| Revenues ($114,000 estimated for 2006): | | |
| Two-point method | TC = $60 + 4.7% × Revenues | $5,700 |
| Simple regression | TC = $259 + 4.0% × Revenues | $4,819 |

Josh is glad that he is no longer using his original estimate based on the high-low method and animal visits as a cost driver. He believes that method would significantly overestimate the treatment costs. He is surprised to learn that the other two methods for animal visits as the cost driver might have significantly underestimated the cost. After comparing the two-point and regression results, he concludes that the two-point method is not very accurate. Overall, he decides that he will probably use regression analysis in the future to help with this type of estimate.

Finally, Josh revises the total cost function for the clinic. Even though revenue from pet owners is now being used as the driver for treatment supplies, other parts of the function still use the number of animal visits as the driver. He subtracts the $1.20 per animal visit that had been attributed to treatment supplies, leaving $15.20 for the other relevant variable costs. He also adjusts total fixed costs by subtracting $741 ($1,000 old fixed cost estimate − $259 new fixed cost estimate), leaving $119,009. Thus, the revised cost function is

TC = $119,009 + ($15.20 × Number of animal visits) + (4.0% × Fee revenue)

Josh and Leticia decide to continue budgeting average revenue per animal visit at $60 ($30 in fees plus $30 in matching grant). They can now use this cost function to analyze best-case and worst-case scenarios and will be better prepared for unexpected changes that might occur next year.

| | | |
|---|---|---|
| **GUIDE YOUR LEARNING 2.4** Small Animal Clinic (Part 2) | | |

Small Animal Clinic (Part 2) illustrates the two-point and simple regression methods for estimating a cost function. For this illustration:

| Describe It | Identify Problem and Information | Compare Estimation Methods |
|---|---|---|
| In your own words, explain how the two-point and regression methods were used to estimate a cost function. | Why did Josh need to create a new cost function? Why did Josh need to gather additional information? | Refer to Josh's comparison of the estimated cost using various estimation methods.<br>• Explain why Josh thinks that each of the other cost functions is inferior to the one he decided to use.<br>• Explain in detail why the numerical result for Josh's final choice is different from each of the other cost estimates.<br>• In general, what are the pros and cons of each estimation method? |

# USES AND LIMITATIONS OF COST ESTIMATES

 **Q7** What are the uses and limitations of future cost estimates?

Uncertainties are a fact of life in the business world. Even the best available information and best decision-making processes may lead to poor outcomes. Nevertheless, managers make better decisions and obtain better average results when they use higher-quality information and decision-making processes. Because of uncertainties about future cost behavior, we need to evaluate the quality of both our data and the various estimation techniques.

## ■ Information Quality

One factor that affects the quality of past cost information is whether the accounting system is able to directly trace the costs to individual cost objects. For example, if Magik Bicycles' accounting system traces the cost of handlebars to each bicycle produced, then past handlebar costs are known with high accuracy. This information, in turn, will improve the quality of future handlebar cost estimates.

If the accounting system cannot trace a relevant cost to a cost object, the cost must instead be allocated. For example, costs such as insurance can be traced to the production facility but cannot be traced to any one bicycle. However, a portion of these costs can be allocated to each bicycle produced. Accounting systems often accumulate indirect costs into overhead cost pools that tend to include a mixture of both fixed and variable costs. Appropriate cost drivers for these cost pools are often difficult to identify. Nevertheless, past accounting data might be the best information available for estimating indirect costs.

Recall from Chapter 1 that higher-quality information is more certain, complete, relevant, timely, and valuable. Better accounting systems improve the quantity, relevance, and timeliness of cost information. However, we may be unable to obtain higher-quality information. For example, in the Small Animal Clinic illustration, Josh initially lacked sufficient data to use regression analysis to separate mixed costs into fixed and variable components. This circumstance occurs frequently in the business world. Other common reasons why past cost information might be unavailable or too unreliable to use include the following:

- The organization has operated for only a few periods.
- The organization's operations have changed substantially.
- Inflation, deflation, or other economic changes have altered the behavior of costs.
- The organization operates in an environment where technologies and costs change rapidly.
- The organization's accounting system does not currently capture and report the needed information.

Under these circumstances, cost estimates based on past costs are of lower quality than cost estimates from better data. In addition, the quality of information often deteriorates over time. Accordingly, cost functions are most useful for estimating costs over short time periods, such as for the next year.

## ■ Average Costs

Because financial accounting information is readily available, accountants and managers often want to rely on it for decision making. However, financial accounting measures are usually based on average costs, which are inappropriate for decision making. The **average cost**

**EXHIBIT 2.17** Advantages and Disadvantages of Cost Behavior Analysis Approaches

| Method and Description | Advantages | Disadvantages |
|---|---|---|
| **Engineered Estimate of Cost** Analysis of labor time, materials, and other resources used in each activity<br><br>Cost estimates are based on resources used | • Can use when no past data are available<br>• Provides a benchmark for what future costs should be<br>• Most accurate for estimating costs of repetitive activities<br>• Identifies and measures some nonlinear cost functions (e.g., economies of scale and learning curves) | • Difficult to estimate some types of costs, such as overhead<br>• Time-consuming<br>• May not identify all costs |
| **Analysis at the Account Level** A review of the pattern in past costs recorded in the accounting system<br><br>Knowledge of operations is used to classify cost as variable, fixed, or mixed | • Can be used when only one period of data is available<br>• Best for costs that are fixed or variable<br>• Provides information about types of costs incurred | • Difficult to identify costs that are not strictly fixed or strictly variable<br>• Relies on past costs, which might not represent future costs |
| **Scatter Plot** Plot of past data points for cost against a potential cost driver<br><br>Visual analysis of plot is used to decide whether cost might be completely fixed, completely variable, or mixed | • Provides information about cost behavior in relation to potential cost drivers<br>• Facilitates evaluation of whether a potential cost driver is viable | • Does not compute a cost function<br>• Relies on past costs, which might not represent future costs |
| **Two-Point Method** Algebraic calculation of a linear mixed cost function using any two data points of the cost and cost driver | • Can be used with as few as two data points<br>• Computationally simple | • Difficult to identify most representative data points for estimating future costs<br>• Ignores all but two data points (inefficient use of data)<br>• Mismeasures the cost function if data points come from more than one relevant range<br>• Relies on past costs, which might not represent future costs |
| **High-Low Method** Specific application of the two-point method using the highest and lowest data points of the cost driver | • Same as two-point method<br>• Does not require judgment for selecting data points | • Same as two-point method<br>• Highest and lowest data points are often atypical, distorting the cost function |
| **Regression Analysis** Statistical technique that measures the average change in a dependent variable for every unit change in one or more independent variables<br><br>Creates a linear cost function where variable cost is the slope of the regression line and fixed cost is the intercept | • Increases cost function accuracy by using all available data points<br>• Best for a strong positive linear relationship between the cost and cost driver<br>• Easy to perform with available software<br>• Provides statistics for evaluating the quality of results | • Mismeasures the cost function if data points come from more than one relevant range<br>• Inefficient for estimating a strictly fixed or strictly variable cost function<br>• Relies on past costs, which might not represent future costs |

(AC) is simply computed as total costs (TC) divided by the quantity ($Q$) of activity or production (AC = TC/$Q$).

When average costs are used to estimate the cost function (TC = 0 + AC $\times$ $Q$), fixed costs are assumed to be variable. Therefore, future costs are either overestimated or underestimated unless future production is exactly the quantity used to calculate average cost per unit. Consequently, we usually avoid using financial statement costs—or any other average costs—for decision making.

**HELPFUL HINT**

Cost-benefit analysis is the practice of considering the relevant costs and benefits when making decisions, such as whether to spend resources developing higher quality information.

## ■ Quality of Estimation Techniques

Exhibit 2.17 summarizes the advantages and disadvantages of each cost behavior analysis approach introduced in this chapter. None of the methods is best in all circumstances. For example, regression analysis is a higher-quality technique than the two-point or high-low methods for separating mixed costs into fixed and variable components. However, regression cannot be used when too few observations of past costs are available. In addition, most of the methods in Exhibit 2.17 rely on past costs, which might need updating. The engineered estimate of cost method can be used when no past costs are available, and it also provides a benchmark that can be used to monitor the efficiency of costs in the future. Although we know that higher-quality techniques result in higher-quality information, we do not always use higher-quality techniques. Sometimes the cost exceeds the benefit; at other times we do not have adequate information required by a higher-quality technique.

## ■ Reliance on Cost Estimates

Concerns we have about the quality of cost information affect our reliance on the results. Managers might delay growth opportunities or alter operating decisions to avoid assuming extra risk in cases where they are less sure about their cost estimates. As managers make decisions, the quality of information affects the alternatives that they consider and the weight they place on various pieces of information.

| GUIDE YOUR LEARNING **2.5** Key Terms |
| --- |

Stop to confirm that you understand the new terms introduced in the last several pages.

| | |
| --- | --- |
| Engineered estimate of cost (p. 49) | High-low method (p. 51) |
| Analysis at the account level (p. 50) | Simple regression analysis (p. 55) |
| Scatter plot (p. 50) | Multiple regression analysis (p. 55) |
| Two-point method (p. 50) | Average cost (p. 62) |

For each of these terms, write a definition in your own words.

---

**APPENDIX 2A**

## Regression Analysis—Additional Topics

---

**MULTIPLE REGRESSION ANALYSIS**

Multiple regression is used when more than one cost driver may provide the best estimate of a cost function. We use the same method to estimate the cost function as that illustrated in the chapter. The only difference is that two or more independent variables (cost drivers) are used in the regression analysis.

**Q6** How is regression analysis used to estimate a mixed cost function?

## ■ Choosing Cost Drivers for Multiple Regression

Sometimes several cost drivers appear to be correlated with the cost we are estimating; their scatter plots show a possible linear relationship with the cost object. In these cases, we include all of the potential drivers in a multiple regression to determine the significance of each. Then we drop those drivers that have insignificant $t$-statistics. Remember, however, that each potential cost driver must have economic plausibility—a reason to believe that each one might drive the cost we are trying to estimate.

## PRINT MASTERS PRINT SHOP
## USING MULTIPLE REGRESSION TO ESTIMATE A COST FUNCTION

Print Masters Print Shop incurs overhead costs that are related to its printing machines (maintenance, depreciation, insurance, etc.) and to the amount of paper printed (ink, storage and handling of paper, packing materials, etc.). Exhibit 2A.1 summarizes monthly data for overhead costs, machine hours, and reams of paper used for Print Masters Print Shop.

### Scatter Plots and Simple Regression Results
A scatter plot is presented for machine hours in Exhibit 2A.2(a) and for reams of paper in Exhibit 2A.2(b). Each plot suggests a potential linear relationship with printing overhead costs because it appears to have an upward slope, although the slope does not appear to be very steep in either plot. Thus, based on the scatter plots both cost drivers appear to be viable. Simple regression analysis for each potential cost driver confirms this evidence. Following is a summary of the simple regression results:

|  | Machine Hours | Reams of Paper |
|---|---|---|
| Intercept coefficient | $58,800 | $68,109 |
| $t$-statistic ($p$-value) | 11.43 (<0.0001) | 11.63 (<0.0001) |
| Independent variable coefficient | $19.11 | $0.02 |
| $t$-statistic ($p$-value) | 4.09 (0.0003) | 3.08 (0.005) |
| Adjusted $R$-square | 0.35 | 0.22 |

**EXHIBIT 2A.1**
Data for Print Shop Overhead Costs and Two Potential Cost Drivers

| Month | Overhead Costs | Machine Hours | Reams of Paper |
|---|---|---|---|
| 1 | $68,948 | 959 | 828,000 |
| 2 | 87,171 | 1,227 | 1,246,000 |
| 3 | 84,448 | 1,351 | 874,000 |
| 4 | 89,030 | 1,480 | 958,000 |
| 5 | 83,303 | 952 | 1,356,000 |
| 6 | 82,660 | 986 | 1,332,000 |
| 7 | 78,793 | 931 | 1,170,000 |
| 8 | 82,834 | 1,439 | 958,000 |
| 9 | 77,829 | 945 | 1,238,000 |
| 10 | 72,303 | 869 | 978,000 |
| 11 | 78,804 | 1,171 | 890,000 |
| 12 | 85,850 | 1,228 | 1,162,000 |
| 13 | 70,343 | 928 | 892,000 |
| 14 | 85,991 | 950 | 1,376,000 |
| 15 | 77,626 | 1,016 | 1,160,000 |
| 16 | 70,397 | 902 | 928,000 |
| 17 | 77,189 | 948 | 1,220,000 |
| 18 | 75,443 | 1,130 | 1,064,000 |
| 19 | 79,599 | 1,335 | 830,000 |
| 20 | 72,690 | 1,052 | 1,034,000 |
| 21 | 76,307 | 860 | 1,280,000 |
| 22 | 79,725 | 1,188 | 1,096,000 |
| 23 | 80,492 | 1,254 | 850,000 |
| 24 | 87,697 | 1,187 | 1,390,000 |
| 25 | 76,516 | 948 | 936,000 |
| 26 | 83,055 | 1,015 | 1,320,000 |
| 27 | 75,021 | 971 | 956,000 |
| 28 | 85,210 | 1,111 | 1,304,000 |
| 29 | 84,531 | 1,326 | 1,238,000 |
| 30 | 78,575 | 1,017 | 1,026,000 |

**EXHIBIT 2A.2** Scatter Plot of Print Shop Overhead Costs

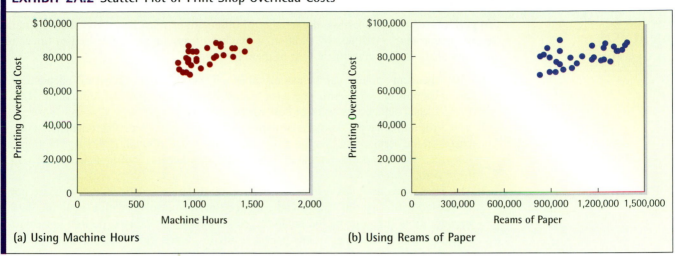

(a) Using Machine Hours      (b) Using Reams of Paper

The intercepts and slope coefficients for both regressions are highly significant. However, the adjusted $R$-square is 0.35 for machine hours and 0.22 for reams of paper. Thus, neither driver appears to be an overall good predictor of the variation in printing overhead cost.

## Multiple Regression Analysis

We can perform multiple regression analysis for printing overhead cost using both machine hours and reams of paper as independent variables. We will then see whether any improvement in overall explanatory ability occurs. The following excerpts come from the Excel printout for this regression:

```
             Regression Statistics
Multiple R                    0.90921678
R Square                      0.82667515
Adjusted R Square             0.81383627
Standard Error                 2371.2674
Observations                          30
```

|              | Coefficients | Standard Error | t Stat | P-value |
|--------------|-------------|----------------|--------|---------|
| Intercept | 30338.7951 | 4371.83243 | 6.93960613 | 1.856E-07 |
| Machine Hours | 24.3711259 | 2.57880204 | 9.45056098 | 4.7054E-10 |
| Reams of Paper | 0.02073146 | 0.00247049 | 8.39163567 | 5.2945E-09 |

The adjusted $R$-square of 0.81 is much higher than for either individual cost driver. Therefore, the two drivers together appear to explain much more of the variation in printing overhead cost.

The intercept term (fixed cost) is $30,339 and is statistically significant. Both potential cost drivers, machine hours and reams of paper, are positive and significant. The total cost function is:

$$TC = \$30{,}339 + (\$24.37 \times \text{machine hours}) + (\$0.02 \times \text{reams of paper})$$

If we expect that next month we will use 1,000 machine hours and 1 million reams, we can predict our total cost to be

$$TC = \$30{,}339 + (\$24.37)(1{,}000) + (0.02)(1{,}000{,}000)$$
$$= \$30{,}339 + \$24{,}370 + \$20{,}000$$
$$= \$74{,}709$$

## REGRESSION ANALYSIS ASSUMPTIONS

To perform regression analysis, the number of observations must be greater than the number of independent variables. In addition, a number of assumptions are used in linear regression analysis. We investigate four of them here.

1. The dependent variable can be calculated as a linear function of a set of independent variables plus an error term. The error term is the distance from the regression trend line for each actual data point of cost versus cost driver.
2. The error terms have a normal distribution with a mean of zero. The *t*-statistics are based on the assumption that the errors are normally distributed. If this assumption is incorrect, we cannot know with any confidence whether the coefficients are different from zero.
3. The error terms have a constant variance for all of the observations, and they are not correlated with each other. Constant variance can be a problem with accounting data because costs from one period could be related to costs in the next period. For example, an accrual that occurs in one period is often reversed in the next period. In addition, variance often increases at higher or lower levels of activity. If error terms are correlated, the standard errors are inaccurate, and therefore the *t*-statistics are not meaningful.
4. Relatively little correlation occurs among the independent variables. If the independent variables are highly correlated (multicollinearity), the coefficients are more likely to be inaccurate, which would create inaccuracies in our estimated cost functions. An example of correlated independent variables could be direct labor hours and machine hours, when labor is used to manage machines.

We test for the linearity assumption by examining a scatter plot to see whether the relationship between cost and the cost driver appears to have a generally linear trend. If this assumption is not met, linear regression analysis is not a useful tool. We test for normal distribution, uniform variance, and uncorrelated error terms using scatter plots or other statistics methods. We plot the error terms against the independent variables. If error terms with small (large) values are associated with independent variables of small (large) values, the error terms are correlated with each other and the results from this model will not accurately reflect the underlying cost function. To determine whether independent variables are correlated, we use the correlation functions in a spreadsheet or statistical program. Independent variables that have a high correlation (above about 70%) may cause problems with regression analysis. The correlated variables can be entered in a regression together and then independently to see whether the coefficient and *t*-statistics are affected by the correlation.

## ADDITIONAL REGRESSION ANALYSIS CONSIDERATIONS

 **Q7** What are the uses and limitations of future cost estimates?

We can use regression analysis when we know that the majority of costs are likely to be only fixed or only variable, but in these cases, other techniques may be just as accurate and require less data-gathering time. Suppose we want to estimate a cost function for handlebars, which vary with production volume at Magik Bicycles. Either we ask purchasing for the current per-unit cost and to check for price updates, or we divide the total cost of a recent purchase by the number of units purchased to develop an estimate of that variable cost. Similarly, to estimate a future fixed cost, we base our estimate on the fixed cost from one or more prior periods in the same manner shown for rent in Small Animal Clinic (Part 1).

### ■ Stepwise Linear Fixed Costs

We learned earlier that the cost function for some fixed costs is stepwise linear. For example, in Exhibit 2.3(b), the cost function for rent, which increases as more space is needed due to high sales revenues, is

$$\text{TC} = \$6,000, \text{ for } Q \leq \$30,000 \text{ in sales}$$
$$\text{TC} = \$8,000, \text{ for } Q > \$30,000 \text{ in sales}$$

What happens if we apply regression analysis to past cost data from this stepwise linear cost function? Consider the following three possibilities:

1. If all the data points occurred when $Q$ was below $30,000, then rent will appear to be a fixed cost at $6,000.
2. If all the data points occurred when $Q$ was above $30,000, then rent will appear to be a fixed cost at $8,000.
3. If some data points occurred when $Q$ was below $30,000 and other data points occurred when $Q$ was above $30,000, then the regression trend line might be similar to the one shown in Exhibit 2A.3. The simple regression results would appear to have both fixed and variable components. However, the cost estimates from the regression will only be accurate at a few points along the regression trend line.

To develop the most accurate cost function, we must define the cost according to its relevant range and reflect the appropriate limits in the cost function.

## ■ Piecewise Linear Variable Costs

We learned earlier that the cost function for some variable costs is piecewise linear; the per-unit cost changes across relevant ranges of activity. For example, in Exhibit 2.2(b), the function for the total cost of bicycle tires based on a volume purchase discount is

$$TC = \$10Q, \text{ for } Q \le \text{ bikes manufactured}$$

$$TC = \$600 + \$6(Q - 60), \text{ for } Q > 60 \text{ bikes manufactured}$$

What happens if we apply regression analysis to past cost data from this piecewise linear cost function? Consider the following three possibilities:

1. If all the data points occurred when $Q$ was below 60, then the cost will appear to be variable at $10 per bike.
2. If all of the data points occurred when $Q$ was above 60, then the cost will appear to be variable at $6 per bike.
3. If some data points occurred when $Q$ was below 60 and other data points occurred when $Q$ was above 60, then the regression trend line might be similar to the one shown in Exhibit 2A.4. The simple regression results would underestimate per unit variable cost when $Q$ is below 60 and overestimate it when $Q$ is above 60.

Once again, it is important to define the cost according to its relevant range and reflect the appropriate limits in the cost function if we wish to develop the most accurate cost function.

**EXHIBIT 2A.3** Regression Trend Line for a Stepwise Linear Fixed Cost

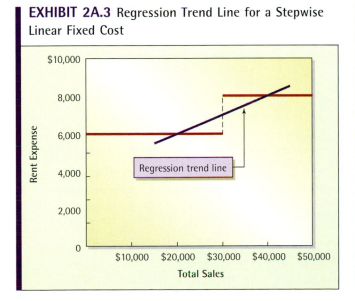

**EXHIBIT 2A.4** Regression Trend Line for a Piecewise Linear Variable Cost

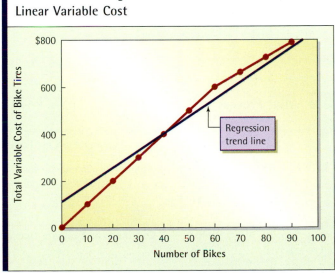

## ■ Data Limitations

The results from regression analysis are only as accurate as the data we use. The following need to be checked before data are used in regression analysis:

- The relationship between the cost and cost driver is economically plausible.
- Cost and cost driver data are matched and recorded in the appropriate period.
- Inflation and deflation have been taken into consideration.
- The relevant range reflects similar technologies across the range.
- No clerical errors occurred in the recorded data.
- Any data from periods with unusual events are eliminated.
- The activity levels for which we are predicting cost are within the relevant range; that is, we are not predicting cost for activity levels that are greater (smaller) than the largest (smallest) in our data set.
- We have removed any outliers, that is, observations that are much larger or much smaller and would unduly influence the regression results.

# SUMMARY

**Q1** **What Are Different Ways to Describe Cost Behavior?**

### Linear Cost Function

$TC = F + V \times Q$

$TC$ = Total cost
$F$ = Total fixed cost
$V$ = Variable cost per unit of activity
$Q$ = Volume of activity (cost driver)

### Assumptions:

Within the relevant range, fixed costs remain fixed and the variable cost per unit remains constant.

### Nonlinear Cost Functions

Economies of scale: Average costs decline with volume of production.

Learning curve: Variable costs decline with experience.

No apparent pattern: No relationship is noted between cost and a potential cost driver.

### Linear Cost Functions Across More Than One Relevant Range

Stepwise linear: Fixed costs change across relevant ranges.

Piecewise linear: Variable costs change across relevant ranges.

**Q2** **What Is a Learning Curve?**

### Description

Rate at which labor hours decrease as the volume of production or services increases

### Formula

Cumulative average-time learning model is measured as

$$Y = \alpha X^r$$

where $Y$ = cumulative average labor hours used for $X$ units
$\alpha$ = time required for the first unit
$r$ = an index for the rate of learning

**Q3** **What Process Is Used to Estimate Future Costs?**

| Identify relevant costs for the cost object | Estimate a Cost Function for Each Relevant Cost | | | | Combine all relevant cost estimates for the cost object |
|---|---|---|---|---|---|
| | Obtain information needed for estimation | Categorize costs as fixed, variable, or mixed | Select and apply cost estimation techniques | Specify the cost function and then estimate the future cost | |

◄———— **Continuously Evaluate Uncertainties and Quality of Information** ————►

## Q4 How Are the Engineered Estimate, Account Analysis, and Two-Point Methods Used to Estimate Cost Functions?

### Engineered Estimate of Cost
Analyze amount of labor time, materials, and other resources used in each activity. Estimate costs based on resources used.

### Analysis at the Account Level
Review pattern in past costs recorded in the accounting system. Use knowledge of operations to classify cost as variable, fixed, or mixed.

### Two-Point Method
Algebraically calculate a linear mixed cost function using any two data points of the cost and a cost driver. Preferably use the most representative data points.

### High-Low Method
Apply the two-point method using the highest and lowest data points of the cost driver.

## Q5 How Does a Scatter Plot Assist with Categorizing a Cost?

Plot past data points for cost against a potential cost driver. Visually analyze plot to decide whether cost might be completely fixed, completely variable, or mixed.

## Q6 How Is Regression Analysis Used to Estimate a Mixed Cost Function?

Statistically measure the average change in a dependent variable for every unit change in one or more independent variables. Create a linear cost function where variable cost is the slope of the regression line and fixed cost is the intercept.

### Simple Regression
One independent variable

### Multiple Regression (Appendix 2A)
Two or more independent variables

## Q7 What Are the Uses and Limitations of Future Cost Estimates?

### Examples of Reasons to Estimate Future Costs
- Budgeting
- Planning future operations, such as setting employee work schedules, financing activities
- Making specific decisions, such as discontinuing a line of business, renting additional retail store space, or hiring new employees

### What Do Managers Need to Consider When Using Estimates of Future Costs?
- Uncertainties
  - Actual future costs are unknown

- Reliability of cost estimates is uncertain because of uncertainties about:
  - ► Cost behavior classification
  - ► Cost drivers
  - ► Changes in cost behavior over time
- Other considerations
  - Quality of cost information
    - ► Appropriateness of past costs for estimating future costs
    - ► Accounting system information
    - ► Information from outside the accounting system
  - Quality of estimation techniques
  - Reasonableness of cost function assumptions

---

## KEY TO SYMBOLS

**ⓔ** This question requires students to extend knowledge beyond the applications shown in the textbook.

**❶** This question requires Step 1 skills (**Identifying**) in Steps for Better Thinking (Exhibit 1.10).

**❷** This question requires Step 2 skills (**Exploring**) in Steps for Better Thinking (Exhibit 1.10).

**❸** This question requires Step 3 skills (**Prioritizing**) in Steps for Better Thinking (Exhibit 1.10).

**❹** This question requires Step 4 skills (**Envisioning**) in Steps for Better Thinking (Exhibit 1.10).

# Self-Study Problems

## Self-Study Problem 1 | Opportunity Costs, Relevant Information

**Q1**

After a severe downturn in the economy, Frank was laid off from his position as sales director for a large resort in New England. While he was working at the resort, he saved enough money to start his own business. He would like to buy a franchise for a sandwich shop and open a new store, but he could also work as a salesperson in his father-in-law's hardware store and put his savings into other investments. He begins to identify all of the relevant cash flows for the decision. First he determines his opportunity costs.

**REQUIRED:**

❶ **A.** If Frank decides to start a sandwich shop, what opportunities does he forgo?

❶ **B.** What are the cost objects about which Frank needs to gather information?

❶ **C.** List the cash flows for which Frank needs information when he evaluates the decision.

❷ **D.** Frank faces the risk that the sandwich shop cash flows will not meet his needs. How does this risk affect Frank's decision?

### Solution to Self-Study Problem 1

**A.** If Frank starts a sandwich shop, he forgoes the opportunity to work at the hardware store and to use his savings for other investments. He also forgoes the opportunity for additional leisure time. Although this alternative is not specifically quantifiable, it is certainly a relevant opportunity cost.

**B.** The first cost object that Frank should consider is the sandwich shop franchise, and the relevant cash flows to open and operate a new store. Then he would consider the opportunity costs, which include two major cost objects: (1) his work at the hardware store; and (2) potential investments.

**C.** He should be able to get estimates of cash flows from the franchise, for costs such as food, labor, and incidentals. He also needs to gather information about the cost for specific locations, and the costs to rent or build the store. He would need cost information about meeting city requirements for licenses and permits, insurance requirements, and local, state and federal taxes. For the opportunity costs, he needs to know the salary and fringe benefits available from working at the hardware store. He also needs to know investment options and potential returns on his investments for the money he has in savings.

**D.** Frank will want to evaluate the likelihood that the cash flows will turn out to be as he predicts. The sandwich shop option might be riskier than either of his other options. In that case, he should consider risk in addition to estimated cash flows when evaluating his opportunities. (*Note:* In Chapter 12 we will learn specific methods for incorporating risk into an investment decision.) In addition, Frank might require a minimum level of cash inflows, perhaps for supporting a family. He needs to consider the consequences of lower cash flows than predicted. If he faces a relatively high probability that the cash flows from the sandwich shop do not meet his needs, then Frank may be unwilling to consider this alternative. Frank's reluctance to invest in the sandwich shop depends on the severity of the consequences and his degree of risk aversion.

## Self-Study Problem 2 | Cost Driver Choice Using Regression

**Q2, Q6**

Nursery Supply manufactures wooden planter tubs for small trees. Each wooden planter requires about the same level of effort in labor and machinery. The managers of Nursery Supply want to improve the quality of their budgets. They are considering three alternative cost drivers for overhead: assembly time, labor hours, and machine hours. The statistics for regressions using last year's monthly data for each of the three possible cost drivers follow:

> Cost driver = Assembly time
> Intercept = $55,000 ($t$-statistic = 2.44, $p$-value = 0.08)
> Slope = $21.00 ($t$-statistic = 2.85, $p$-value = 0.05)
> Adjusted $R$-square = 0.31
>
> Cost driver = Labor hours
> Intercept = $20,000 ($t$-statistic = 2.95, $p$-value = 0.03)
> Slope = $31.00 ($t$-statistic = 3.00, $p$-value = 0.01)
> Adjusted $R$-square = 0.46

Cost driver = Machine hours
    Intercept = $10,000 ($t$-statistic = 1.45, $p$-value = 0.25)
    Slope = $38.00 ($t$-statistic = 3.19, $p$-value = 0.005)
    Adjusted $R$-square = 0.70

A. Write the cost function for each of the cost drivers.

B. Explain the meaning of the adjusted $R$-square for the assembly time analysis.

C. Explain the meaning of the $p$-value for the intercept in the machine hours analysis.

D. Explain the meaning of the $p$-value for the slope in the labor hours analysis.

E. Given only the regression results, which cost driver would you choose for overhead costs? Explain.

F. Why do managers often use models such as a cost function to estimate future costs?

## Solution to Self-Study Problem 2

**REQUIRED:**

A. Each cost function is written using the regression intercept term as the fixed cost and the slope as the variable cost.

Cost driver = Assembly time
    TC = $55,000 + $21.00 × assembly time

Cost driver = Labor hours
    TC = $20,000 + $31.00 × labor hours

Cost driver = Machine hours
    TC = $38.00 × machine hours
    (*Note:* Because the $p$-value for its $t$-statistic is 0.25, the intercept is not statistically different from zero. Therefore, the fixed cost is assumed to be zero.)

B. The adjusted $R$-square indicates that variation in assembly time explains about 31% of the variation in overhead. The remaining 69 percent is unexplained.

C. The $p$-value for the intercept in the regression of overhead cost against machine hours is 0.25. It means a 25% probability that the intercept (fixed cost) is zero instead of $10,000.

D. The $p$-value of the slope in the labor hours regression is 0.01, which means a 1% probability that the variable cost for overhead related to labor hours could be zero instead of $31.00 per labor hour.

E. First we examine the adjusted $R$-square (see Exhibit 2.14, items 6 and 7). At 70%, machine hours appears to be the best cost driver. However, we also need to evaluate whether its coefficients are reasonable. The slope coefficient is positive and has only a small probability of being zero ($p$-value 0.005), so it is likely to be a reasonable estimate. The intercept coefficient is generally reasonable as long as it is not significantly negative. In this case, the intercept has a high $p$-value (0.25), so we can assume the fixed cost is zero.

F. Managers cannot know future costs. Nevertheless, they need to estimate future costs to make decisions. A cost function based on past information helps managers estimate future costs; the function can also be updated to incorporate expected cost information so that predictions are as precise as possible. Using a model such as the cost function also helps managers be more methodical in their approach to cost estimation, improving the quality of cost estimates. Higher-quality estimation methods provide higher-quality information for decision making.

 **REVIEW** Use the exercises in the following boxes in the chapter to review key terms and key techniques, analyze chapter illustrations, improve your learning of new concepts, and practice ethical decision making:

Guide Your Learning 2.1: Key Terms (p. 40)

Guide Your Learning 2.2: Key Terms (p. 47)

Guide Your Learning 2.3: Small Animal Clinic (Part 1) (p. 55)

Guide Your Learning 2.4: Small Animal Clinic (Part 2) (p. 61)

Guide Your Learning 2.5: Key Terms (p. 63)

Focus on Ethical Decision Making: Discretionary Costs (p. 47)

## QUESTIONS

**2.1** "As volume increases, total cost increases and per-unit cost decreases." What type of linear cost function does this describe? Draw a simple graph of this type of cost function.

**2.2** An automobile assembly plant closes every August to retool for the next year's model. How should August's cost data be used in estimating the overhead cost function?

**2.3** You have been asked to provide the president with an approximate cost function for the firm's activities, and it must be done by this afternoon. Some members of the Board of Directors want to understand why performance varies so much across store locations. They have asked for a quick analysis today and want a more detailed analysis next week. Which cost estimation technique(s) should you consider using? Explain.

**2.4** At two levels of activity within the relevant range, average costs are $192 and $188, respectively. Assuming the cost function is linear, what can be said about the existence of fixed and variable costs?

**2.5** List two opportunities you would forgo when you decide to study on a Friday night. List relevant cash flows for those two opportunities. Is it possible to assign a quantitative value to the benefits you receive from either of these two missed opportunities? Explain.

**2.6** Explain how information from a scatter plot helps in categorizing a cost as fixed, variable, or mixed.

**2.7** Explain the analysis at the account level approach to developing a cost function.

**2.8** List two examples of nonlinear cost functions and describe a method of developing a cost function for each one.

**2.9** The director of Meals on Wheels, a service that delivers meals to the elderly, is setting work schedules for a new crew. The director knows that the team will work more slowly in the beginning, but would like to set a schedule that approximates their learning rate so that the volunteers know their scheduled work times will usually reflect the actual time spent. Explain how the cumulative average learning-time approach would help the director estimate time more accurately.

**2.10** The trend line developed using regression analysis provides a more accurate representation of a mixed cost function than the two-point or high-low methods. Explain why.

## EXERCISES

**2.11** **Cost object, cost function estimation, opportunity cost** A computer manufacturer is deciding whether to produce a large monitor with a thin flat screen. One of the managers suggested that the incremental costs for this line of manufacturing will be primarily variable because the company currently has a lot of idle capacity.

Q1, Q4, Q5, Q6

**REQUIRED:**
**A.** What is the cost object in this decision?
**B.** Is the accounting system likely to have the information needed to develop a cost function? Explain.
**C.** What might be an appropriate estimation technique for this cost? Explain.
**①** **D.** What is the opportunity cost for using this idle capacity? Explain.

**2.12** **Direct and indirect costs** Frida's Tax Practice has two departments, tax and audit. The tax department has two product lines, business returns and individual returns. A list of costs and three cost objects from Frida's Tax Practice follow.

Q1

**REQUIRED:** For each cost, identify whether it is direct or indirect for each cost object.

| Cost | Tax Department | Personal Returns | Mr. Gruper's Personal Tax Return |
|---|---|---|---|
| A. Subscription to personal tax law updates publication | | | |
| B. Ink supplies for tax department photocopy machine | | | |
| C. Portion of total rent for tax department office space | | | |
| D. Wages for tax department administrative assistant | | | |
| E. Tax partner's salary | | | |
| F. Charges for long-distance call to Mr. Gruper about personal tax return questions | | | |
| G. Tax partner lunch with Mr. Gruper (the tax partner has lunch with each client at least once per year) | | | |

**2.13** **Linear, stepwise linear, and piecewise linear cost functions**
Q1, Q4

A. Total fixed costs are $10,000 per week and the variable cost per unit is $8.00. Write the algebraic expression for the cost function and graph it. What are the assumptions of the cost function?

ⓔ B. Total fixed costs are $25,000 per week up to 2,000 units a week and then jump up to $35,000 per week. The variable cost per unit is $8.00. Write the algebraic expression for the cost function and graph it.

ⓔ C. The average cost to produce 10,000 units is $45.00 and the average cost to produce 12,000 units is $44.00. Estimate the average cost to produce 15,000 units.

D. The total cost function for Hot Dog Days, a hot dog cart business in Central Park, is TC = $5,000 +45% × total revenues. Estimate the total cost for a month when total revenues are $10,000.

**2.14** **Piecewise linear cost function, regression measurement error** The following is the description
Q4, Q6 of a cost: Total fixed costs are $50,000 per month and the variable cost per unit is $10.00 when production is under 1,000 units. The variable cost drops to $9.00 per unit after the first 1,000 units are produced.

REQUIRED:

A. Write the algebraic expression of the cost function and graph it.

B. Assume that the cost function just described is a reasonable representation of total costs. If the accountant performed regression analysis on weekly observations of this cost and did not realize that there were two relevant ranges, what problems would arise in the cost function that was produced? In other words, how would the cost function be mismeasured?

**2.15** **Learning curve, graphing** The managers of Tax Plus hired three recent accounting graduates.
Q2 When they started preparing simple tax returns, it took six hours to complete the first return. The supervisor believes an 80% learning rate is typical for this type of work.

REQUIRED:

A. Estimate the cumulative average time per return to prepare two returns.

B. Use a spreadsheet to plot four points on the learning curve and then explain in your own words why the cumulative average time drops.

**2.16** **Cost function and assumptions** Bison Sandwiches is a small restaurant that sells a variety of
Q4, Q7 sandwiches and beverages. Total fixed costs are $20,000 per month. Last month total variable costs were $8,000 when total sales were $32,000.

REQUIRED:

A. Write out the algebraic expression for the cost function.

B. What assumptions do we make when we develop this cost function?

**2.17** **Direct and indirect costs; fixed, variable, and mixed costs** Your sister turned her hobby into a
Q1 small business called Glazed Over. She is a potter and manufactures and sells bowls that can be used for decoration or for birdbaths. She has one employee who works 40 hours a week no matter how many bowls are made. She has asked your advice in developing a cost function for the bowls so that she can estimate costs for the next period.

REQUIRED: The following list of costs comes from your sister's general ledger. Assume the cost object is an individual unit (i.e., bowl). Categorize each cost as direct or indirect (D or I), and as fixed, variable, or mixed (F, V, or M).

A. Employee wages
B. Clay used to make bowls
C. Depreciation on the kilns
D. Glaze (the finish painted on the bowls)
E. Brushes for the glaze
ⓔ F. Electricity

G. Business license
ⓔ H. Advertising
I. Pottery studio maintenance (cost of weekly cleaning service)
J. Packing materials for the bowls

**2.18**
**Q1, Q3**

**Cost function, opportunity cost, relevant costs** Yummy Yogurt sells yogurt cones in a variety of natural flavors. Data for a recent month follow:

| | | |
|---|---:|---:|
| Revenue | | $9,000 |
| Cost of ingredients | $4,500 | |
| Rent | 1,000 | |
| Store attendant salary | 2,300 | |
| | | 7,800 |
| Profit | | $1,200 |

REQUIRED:

ⓔ A. Categorize each cost as fixed or variable.

B. Create a cost function.

ⓔ C. What is the opportunity cost when a new flavor of yogurt replaces an old one? (Assume that all yogurts are priced the same, but the variable costs for each flavor are different because different ingredients are used.)

D. Yummy Yogurt's managers are concerned that they sometimes lose business because of long customer lines during peak times. Therefore, they are considering whether to remove one table for customers and add an extra cash register in that space, so that throughput time (customer wait and service time) decreases. Is the cost of store rent relevant to the decision? Why or why not?

**2.19**
**Q1**

**Relevant costs; fixed, variable, and mixed costs** Consider the following two cost objects:

1. Purchasing a pizza shop
2. Investing in a fishing boat

REQUIRED:

For each of the following costs, determine whether the cost is relevant to running a pizza shop (PS), investing in a fishing boat (FB), or both (B). Also, classify each cost as primarily fixed (F), variable (V), or mixed (M).

A. Hourly wages  ⓔ E. Utilities

B. Ingredients  ⓔ F. Advertising

ⓔ C. Employee benefits  ⓔ G. Insurance

D. Fishing equipment

**2.20**
**Q4**

**Engineered estimate of cost, cost-based price** Julie Long, the manager of the Hamburger Haven, has been told that to earn a reasonable profit she should price her hamburgers at 300% of the cost of ingredients. Ms. Long has gathered the following data on the cost of ingredients used to make a hamburger.

1. Preformed frozen hamburger patties are purchased from a distributor. Each pound includes seven patties. The distributor charges $1.69 per pound.
2. Hamburger buns are purchased for $1.29 per dozen.
3. Dill pickle slices are purchased by the gallon jar. A gallon costs $8.95 and contains roughly 2,000 pickle slices. Four slices are placed on each burger.
4. Large, ripe tomatoes currently sell for $0.69 each. One tomato yields eight slices and one slice is placed on each burger.
5. A $0.59 head of lettuce provides enough lettuce for 40 burgers.
6. Mayonnaise is purchased in 16-ounce jars for $1.49. One-quarter ounce of mayonnaise is placed on a burger.
7. A $0.79 jar of mustard provides enough mustard for 150 burgers.
8. A $0.99 jar of catsup is sufficient for 50 burgers.
9. A pound of cheese yields 16 slices. Cheese costs $2.59 per pound and each cheeseburger receives one slice.
10. Onions cost $0.15 each and yield enough chopped onions for 45 hamburgers.

REQUIRED:

A. What is the cost of ingredients for a plain burger (meat and bun only)?

B. What is the cost of materials and suggested selling price for a burger with everything except cheese?

*(continued)*

**C.** People are willing to pay only $0.25 extra for cheese. What price should Ms. Long charge for a hamburger with everything except cheese if she wants the price of a cheeseburger with everything to be 300% of the cost of ingredients?

**D.** Should Ms. Long consider her competitors' prices in addition to her costs? Explain.

**2.21**
**Q1**

**Fixed, variable, and mixed costs** Spencer and Church is a CPA firm engaged in local practice. Some selected items from its chart of accounts are listed here.

REQUIRED:

For each account, indicate whether the account represents a fixed, variable, or mixed cost for the operations of the local practice office. If mixed, indicate whether it is predominantly fixed or variable. Explain your answers.

**A.** Staff wages
**B.** Clerical wages
**C.** Rent
**D.** Licenses
**E.** Insurance
**F.** Office supplies

**G.** Professional dues
**H.** Professional subscriptions
**I.** FICA taxes (Social Security taxes)
**J.** Property taxes
**K.** Advertising

**2.22**
**Q6**

**Cost function using regression, other potential cost drivers** The new cost analyst in your accounting department just received a computer-generated report that contains the results of a simple regression analysis. He was estimating the costs of the marketing department using units sold as the cost driver. The summary results of the report are as follows:

| Variable | Coefficient | $t$-statistic | $p$-value |
|---|---|---|---|
| Intercept | 12.44 | 1.39 | 0.25 |
| Units sold | 222.35 | 2.48 | 0.001 |
| Adjusted $R$-square = 0.61 | | | |

REQUIRED:

**A.** Write an equation for the cost function based on the regression analysis.
**B.** What does the adjusted $R$-square tell you?
**C.** What other cost drivers could potentially explain marketing costs? Explain.

**2.23**
**Q5, Q6, Q7**

www.wiley.com/
college/eldenburg

**Scatter plot, cost function using regression, three potential cost drivers** Maintenance costs covering 15 months of operation for Central Industries are available at the Wiley Web site at www.wiley.com/college/eldenburg. Maintenance consists of regularly scheduled tasks to keep machinery operating efficiently and occasional repairs. The regular tasks include inspecting, cleaning, oiling, and repairing worn parts. The potential cost drivers are units of output, direct labor hours, and number of machine setups. The data are presented in thousands.

REQUIRED:

**A.** For each potential cost driver, prepare a scatter plot versus maintenance cost and then perform a simple regression.
**B.** From analyzing the scatter plots, which cost driver appears to be the best? Explain.
**C.** Which cost driver appears to have the best explanatory ability for maintenance costs? Explain.
**D.** In the regression with the highest adjusted $R$-square, examine the $t$-statistics and $p$-values to determine whether both the intercept and slope coefficients are significant. Does maintenance cost appear to be primarily fixed, primarily variable, or mixed? Write out the cost function for this cost driver.
**E.** Explain why the future cost function might be different from a cost function based on past cost information.

# PROBLEMS

**2.24**
**Q5, Q6, Q7**

**Cost function using high-low and regression, quality of cost estimates** Following are sales and administrative cost data for Big Jack Burgers for the last four months:

| | Sales | Administrative Costs |
|---|---|---|
| September | $ 632,100 | $43,333 |
| October | 842,500 | 57,770 |
| November | 1,087,900 | 62,800 |
| December | 1,132,100 | 68,333 |

Administrative cost is a mixed cost, and sales is a potential cost driver.

**REQUIRED:**

**A.** Using the high-low method, create a cost function for administrative costs.

**B.** In your own words, explain why the high-low method might not be a good method for estimating the cost function.

❷ **C.** Create a scatter plot and add a trend line. After examining the plot, use your judgment to determine whether the cost is fixed, variable, or mixed.

**D.** Perform regression analysis to create a cost function for administrative costs.

❷ **E.** Can we know for certain that the cost function from part (D) provides a good estimate for next month's administrative costs? Why or why not?

❷ **F.** Discuss whether sales are an economically plausible driver for administration costs for Big Jack Burgers.

**2.25**
**Q5, Q6, Q7**

**Scatter plot, cost function using regression** The following scatter plot and simple regression results used revenue as a potential cost driver for research and development costs.

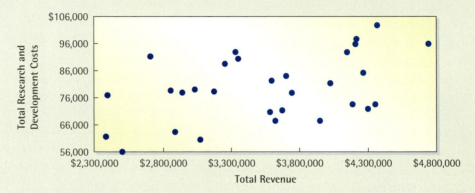

SUMMARY OUTPUT

| Regression Statistics | |
| --- | --- |
| Multiple R | 0.462332038 |
| R Square | 0.213750914 |
| Adjusted R Square | 0.185670589 |
| Standard Error | 10894.44062 |
| Observations | 30 |

| | Coefficients | Standard Error | t Stat | P-value |
| --- | --- | --- | --- | --- |
| Intercept | 50364.97682 | 10834.0628 | 4.648761758 | 7.2426E-05 |
| Revenue | 0.008179276 | 0.002964572 | 2.759007802 | 0.01010244 |

**REQUIRED:**

❶ **A.** Discuss whether the scatter plot suggests that revenue is a cost driver for research and development costs

**B.** Using the regression results, write the cost function for research and development costs.

❶ **C.** Based on the regression results, discuss whether it would be appropriate to use total revenue as a cost driver for research and development costs.

❷ **D.** If you use the cost function from part (B) to estimate next month's research and development costs, what assumptions are you making? Identify at least three assumptions and discuss their reasonableness.

**2.26**
**Q3, Q6, Q7**

**Cost driver, cost categories, appropriateness of regression, relevant information** Susan looked at her long-distance telephone bill with dismay. After leaving her job last year to become a self-employed consultant, her long-distance charges had grown considerably. She had not changed long-distance plans for years, partly because she hated taking the time to review the range of service providers and plans. However, the size of her long-distance bill made it clear that it was time to make a change. She had recently seen numerous ads by telephone companies offering much lower rates than she was currently paying, but she was sure that at least some of those plans offered low rates only for night and weekend calls.

Susan called her current long-distance service provider and asked how she could obtain a lower rate. She mentioned hearing that a competitor was currently offering long distance at 5¢ per minute. In responding to the service representative's questions, Susan verified that most of her long-distance calls are weekday and out of state. She also agreed that her activity over the past two months—approximately 500 minutes of long distance per month—was her best estimate for future calling activity. Given this information, the service representative suggested that Susan buy the following long-distance service plan:

1. Up to 500 minutes of long distance for a flat fee of $20 per month.
2. No refunds would be provided for usage less than 500 minutes per month.
3. Any minutes over 500 per month would be billed at 10¢ per minute.
4. No service change fee or cancellation fee would apply.

**REQUIRED:**

    **A.** What is the cost driver for Susan's long-distance telephone costs, assuming that the cost object is her consulting business?

    **B.** In the proposed service plan, which of the costs are fixed and which are variable? Explain.

**❶ C.** Would regression analysis be an appropriate tool for Susan to use in deciding whether to buy the new service plan? Why or why not?

**❶ D.** Is the cost of Susan's current long-distance service plan relevant to this decision? Why or why not?

**❶ E.** Explain why Susan cannot be certain whether the new service plan will reduce her long-distance costs.

**❶ F.** List additional information that might be relevant to Susan in deciding whether to buy the new service plan.

**❶ G.** Are Susan's long-distance services most likely a discretionary cost? Explain.

**❷ H.** Are Susan's long-distance services most likely a direct or indirect cost, assuming that the cost object is an individual consulting job? Explain.

**❷ I.** Describe the pros and cons of the new service plan.

**2.27**
Q3, Q6, Q7

**Learning curve, uncertainty, regression measurement error** The following learning curve guidelines are based on statistical analyses averaged over various industries and time periods. On average, learning rates are expected to vary depending on the proportion of work performed by workers (hand assembly) versus the proportion performed by machines:

| | Learning Rate |
|---|---|
| 75% hand assembly and 25% machining | 80% |
| 50% hand assembly and 50% machining | 85% |
| 25% hand assembly and 75% machining | 90% |

SOURCE: "Learning Curve Calculator," Johnson Space Center, National Aeronautics and Space Administration (NASA), available at www.jsc.nasa.gov/bu2/learn.html.

The managers of Fancy Furniture decided to start a new product line. When the production line was started, it took 10 hours to make the first batch of six chairs. The learning rate is estimated to be 90%.

**REQUIRED:**

    **A.** Estimate the cumulative average time per batch to make four batches.

**❶ B.** Identify possible reasons why the actual learning curve might be different from the estimate in part (A).

**❷ C.** Explain how you might use the learning rate guidelines in the preceding chart to evaluate the reasonableness of the learning rate for Fancy Furniture.

**ⓔ D.** What problems would arise if information for the first few weeks of production were used in a regression analysis to estimate a cost function for the new product line?

**2.28**
Q1, Q3

**Cost categories, cost function, opportunity cost** The university's Wildcat Lair has been reporting losses in past months. In July, for example, the loss was $5,000.

| | | |
|---|---:|---:|
| Revenue | | $70,000 |
| Expenses | | |
| Purchases of prepared food | $21,000 | |
| Serving personnel | 30,000 | |
| Cashier | 5,500 | |
| Administration | 10,000 | |
| University surcharge | 7,000 | |
| Utilities | 1,500 | 75,000 |
| Loss | | $ (5,000) |

The Lair purchases prepared food directly from University Food Services. This charge varies proportionately with the number and kind of meals served. Personnel who are paid by the Lair serve the food, tend the cash register, bus and clean tables, and wash dishes. The staffing levels in the Lair rarely change; the existing staff can usually handle daily fluctuations in volume. Administrative costs are primarily the salaries of the Lair manager and her office staff. The university charges the Lair a surcharge of 10% of its revenue. Utility costs are the costs of cooling, heating, and lighting the Lair during its normal operating hours.

The university's management is considering shutting the Lair down because it has been operating at a loss.

**REQUIRED:**

**A.** List the fixed expenses of the Wildcat Lair.

**B.** List the variable expenses of the Wildcat Lair and the most likely cost driver for each expense.

**C.** Write out the cost function for running the Wildcat Lair.

**D.** Estimate the profit or loss for August if the revenues of the Lair increase to $80,000.

**e E.** Explain why the original data show a loss but part (D) shows a profit. Be specific.

**e F.** What is the university's opportunity cost if it closes the Wildcat Lair? Describe the opportunity cost and provide calculations for July and August.

**2.29** **Cost behavior, scatter plot** Polar Bear Ski Wear is a shop that sells skiwear at a ski resort. Its
**Q3, Q5** cost accountant developed the following scatter plot for the cost of electricity for lights, heating, and cooling against retail sales revenue.

**REQUIRED:**

**A.** In a business such as retail sales, what usually causes the cost of electricity to vary?

**❶ B.** In what time of year would most skiwear be sold at a ski resort?

**❷ C.** In the scatter plot, the cost of electricity appears to be related to volume of retail sales. If this shop specialized in selling swimwear, would the scatter plot look different? Explain what would change.

**❷ D.** Identify and explain another cost that is similar in nature to the cost of electricity. When you plot the cost against a cost driver, a relationship becomes apparent. However, the cost varies with something other than the cost driver. (Think of other situations where this type of relationship might occur.)

**2.30** **Learning curve, cost-based prices, financial statements** Two competitors each began producing
**Q2** and selling the same product last year. In both cases the cost of the first unit was $300. Firm A's managers were uncertain about the future of the product, so they sold each unit for actual cost plus a 50% markup for profit. Firm B's managers were confident that the product would be a success.

They expected to sell 100 units of the product over its life. The managers set their selling price at the average cost to produce 100 units plus a 50% markup.

The production of this product is mostly labor and subject to an 85% learning rate. Last year firm A sold 5 units of the product, while firm B sold 150 units (more than initially anticipated). This year, firm A's managers decided to match firm B's selling price set last year. Meanwhile, firm B's managers anticipated selling another 150 units. Therefore, they calculated the average cost to produce the second group of 150 units and set their current year price at this year's average cost plus a 50% markup. At the end of this year, firm A sold only 10 units, while firm B sold 150 units.

**REQUIRED:**
**e** Calculate net income for the two firms for this year and last year. (*Hint:* The amount of time it takes to produce a unit is not specified, but you can adapt the learning curve to estimate the average cost to produce a unit by replacing cost for hours.)

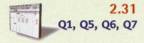

**2.31**
**Q1, Q5, Q6, Q7**

www.wiley.com/
college/eldenburg

**Cost function using regression, scatter plot, discretionary cost** Costs for the marketing department and total sales of Belford's, a British chain of department stores located in the United Kingdom and other European countries, are available on the Web site www.wiley.com/college/eldenburg. You have been asked to develop a cost function for next month's cost. The head of the marketing department believes that the department's costs are related to volume of sales (in British pounds).

**REQUIRED:**
**A.** Create a scatter plot of the data.
**1 B.** From analyzing the plot, do you think sales are a potential cost driver? Explain.
**C.** Perform a regression analysis between marketing department costs and sales. Write the algebraic expression for total cost.
**2 D.** Explain why it is economically plausible for sales to be a cost driver for marketing costs.
**2 E.** When you present the results of the regression analysis to the head of the marketing department, she tells you that the department costs are discretionary costs. If this statement is true, why might a linear relationship appear between the cost and sales?
**1 F.** After your discussion with the head of marketing, you now know that department costs are discretionary. In this situation, explain why regression analysis would not be appropriate for estimating future marketing department costs.

**2.32**
**Q5, Q6**

www.wiley.com/
college/eldenburg

**Cost function using regression, scatter plots, three potential cost drivers** Laura Mills is the controller of Peer Jets International, a manufacturer of small corporate jets. She has undertaken a project to study the behavior of overhead cost. She has assembled factory overhead data for the last 30 months from the company's manufacturing facility. Laura has asked you to develop a model to predict the level of manufacturing overhead.

The following categories of information are available to Laura. Manufacturing overhead includes all of the overhead costs associated with the manufacturing plant. Labor hours are the number of hours manufacturing employees worked. Machine hours are the total hours that machinery was used for the period. Tons of raw materials are all of the raw materials that were used for that particular month. Data for this problem are available at the Wiley Web site www.wiley.com/college/eldenburg.

**REQUIRED:**
**A.** Create a scatter plot of manufacturing overhead for each of the potential cost drivers.
**e B.** Would you eliminate any of the potential cost drivers based on the scatter plots? Why or why not?
**C.** Explain why you create a scatter plot of the data before you perform regression analysis.
**D.** To practice your regression analysis skills, perform a simple regression analysis of manufacturing overhead for each of the three potential cost drivers. Write the cost function from each regression.
**E.** Based on the simple regression results, which cost driver does the best job of explaining manufacturing overhead costs? Explain.
**1 F.** Do your regression results support your answer to part (B)? Explain.

**2.33**
**Q6**

**Cost function using multiple regression (Appendix 2A)** Refer to the data and requirements of Problem 2.32.

**REQUIRED:** A. Perform multiple regression using all three cost drivers. Compare the adjusted *R*-squares and cost functions for the multiple regression with the results of simple regressions for each potential cost driver.

B. Which cost drivers do the best job of explaining manufacturing overhead costs? Explain.

ⓔ C. Select only the cost drivers that do the best job of explaining manufacturing overhead costs. Perform multiple regression analysis for those cost drivers and write the cost function.

❷ D. Explain why more than one cost driver is plausible for manufacturing overhead costs.

**2.34**
**Q3, Q7**
**ETHICS**

**Use of prior year costs, quality of information** Software Solutions is a family-owned business that has been in operation for more than 15 years. The board of directors is comprised of mainly family members, plus a few professionals such as an accountant and lawyer. Regina is a staff accountant who has been working on the budget for the last several weeks. The Director of Finance needs to present the budget at the next board meeting and wants a preliminary copy in two days. Regina is certain that she will not be able to finish the budget within two days. Several department heads have not turned in their preliminary figures, and two departments have budgeted large increases in fixed costs for replacing computer equipment. Regina knows she should have alerted the Director of Finance about these budgeted increases, but she has not had time.

One of her coworkers knows that Regina is behind and suggests that she use last year's budgets for those departments that have not provided information and also for the departments that increased their budgets by large amounts. The coworker says that the budget can be straightened out later because the board does not pay attention to the details.

**REQUIRED:** ❶ A. Is this an ethical dilemma for Regina? Why or why not?

❷ B. Why might it be important for the board of directors to have as much updated information as possible about the budget?

❸ C. What should Regina do, given that not enough time is available to gather high-quality information? Explain your thinking.

**2.35**
**Q5, Q6, Q7**

**Scatter plots, cost function using regression, two potential cost drivers** Suppose we need to predict the cost of maintenance for Brush Prairie High School for the upcoming school year. From the school district records we gather weekly data about costs and volumes for two potential cost drivers: labor hours used in the maintenance department and number of enrolled students.

| | | Potential Cost Drivers | |
| | Total Maintenance | Number of Maintenance | Number of |
| Week | Cost | Hours Worked | Students |
| --- | --- | --- | --- |
| 1 | $16,690 | 238 | 534 |
| 2 | 13,560 | 194 | 532 |
| 3 | 13,540 | 108 | 534 |
| 4 | 16,060 | 229 | 530 |
| 5 | 12,430 | 101 | 533 |
| 6 | 20,860 | 298 | 537 |
| 7 | 18,420 | 244 | 540 |
| 8 | 12,310 | 98 | 540 |
| 9 | 13,770 | 108 | 541 |
| 10 | 16,990 | 225 | 538 |
| 11 | 20,650 | 289 | 540 |
| 12 | 14,770 | 118 | 539 |

**REQUIRED:** ❶ A. Identify and explain two potential cost drivers for total maintenance cost, in addition to number of students and maintenance hours worked.

B. Create a scatter plot, first for maintenance cost against hours worked and then maintenance cost against students.

ⓔ C. Would you eliminate either cost driver based on the plots? Explain.

ⓔ D. Perform regression analysis using each cost driver. Use your judgment to determine the most appropriate cost driver and write out the cost function for maintenance cost.

❶ E. Can we know for certain that the cost driver chosen in part (D) is the best cost driver? Why or why not?

☆ **2.36**
Q1, Q3, Q4, Q7

**Cost function using account analysis and high-low method** The Elder Clinic, a not-for-profit organization, provides limited medical services to low-income elderly patients. The manager's summary report for the past four months of operations is reproduced here.

|  | March | April | May | June | Total |
|---|---|---|---|---|---|
| Number of patient visits | 849 | 821 | 778 | 842 | 3,290 |
| Patient fees | $ 4,230 | $ 4,180 | $ 3,875 | $ 4,260 | $ 16,545 |
| Medical staff salaries | 13,254 | 13,256 | 13,254 | 14,115 | 53,879 |
| Medical supplies used | 3,182 | 3,077 | 2,934 | 3,175 | 12,368 |
| Administrative salaries | 3,197 | 3,198 | 3,197 | 3,412 | 13,004 |
| Rent | 1,000 | 1,000 | 1,000 | 1,100 | 4,100 |
| Utilities | 532 | 378 | 321 | 226 | 1,457 |
| Other expenses | 2,854 | 2,776 | 2,671 | 2,828 | 11,129 |
| Total expenses | 24,019 | 23,685 | 23,377 | 24,856 | 95,937 |
| Operating surplus (loss) | $(19,789) | $(19,505) | $(19,502) | $(20,596) | $(79,392) |

The clinic receives an operating subsidy from the city, but unfortunately, the operating loss that has been incurred through June $(79,392) is larger than anticipated. Part of the problem is the salary increase that went into effect in June, which had been overlooked when the budget was submitted to the city last year. To compound the problem, the warm summer months traditionally bring with them an increase in heat-related health problems. Thus, the clinic is likely to experience an increase in patient visits during July.

The clinic's managers are considering an increase in patient fees to reduce losses. However, they are reluctant to raise fees because the patients have low incomes. They will raise fees only if it is necessary.

**REQUIRED:**
**ANALYZE**
**INFORMATION**

The following questions will help you analyze the information for this problem. Do not turn in your answers to these questions unless your professor asks you to do so.

1 **A.** Use your judgment to classify costs as fixed, variable, or mixed. Explain how you classified each item.

**B.** Create a cost function for the Elder Clinic. Use the high-low method to estimate the function for any mixed costs.

**C.** Use the cost function to estimate July expenses based on a projection of 940 patient visits.

1 **D.** List reasons why management of the Elder Clinic cannot know with certainty what the expenses will be during July. List as many reasons as you can.

2 **E.** Describe the pros and cons of using your cost estimate from part (C) to decide whether to raise patient fees.

**REQUIRED:**
**WRITTEN**
**ASSIGNMENT**

The managers need your July cost estimate to help them decide whether to raise patient fees. Turn in your answer to the following.

3 **F.** Use the information you learned from the preceding analyses to write a memo to the director of the Elder Clinic presenting your estimate of July costs. Provide the director with appropriate information for understanding your methodology and evaluating the reliability of your cost estimate.

**2.37**
Q1, Q3, Q4, Q7

**Cost function judgment and methodology** Suppose you have the responsibility of creating a cost function for the costs of an Internet service provider's help line.

**REQUIRED:**

1 **A.** What is the cost object? Identify where you might obtain information about past costs for the cost object.

1 **B.** Identify at least two potential cost drivers. Explain where you might obtain information about past volumes for each cost driver.

2 **C.** What other information would you like to obtain before estimating the cost function? How might you obtain that information?

2 **D.** Identify the techniques introduced in this chapter that you would be most likely to use in creating the cost function. Explain why.

**2.38**
**Q4, Q5, Q7**

**Personal cost function, information system, two-point and high-low methods** Pick a cost from your personal budget that varies, such as entertainment, education, or automobile operating expenses. For this cost, practice using the estimation techniques you have just learned.

**REQUIRED:**

❸ **A.** Apply engineered estimate of cost to develop a monthly budget for the cost by analyzing what you think the cost should be. Use the following steps:
  • Identify the activities that drive the cost.
  • Plan the monthly level for each activity.
  • Determine a cost per unit for each activity.
  • Combine the activity levels with the costs to create a monthly budget.

**B.** Apply analysis at the account level to your cost. Analyze your checkbook, credit card statements, or other spending information to gather several months' past expenditures for this cost. Study this information to gain an understanding of the types of costs you have incurred in the past. Then address the following questions:

❶ **1.** Can you classify the cost as fixed, variable, or mixed? Why or why not?

❷ **2.** Are you missing information for some parts of the cost (such as for cash expenditures)? In what ways could you change your record-keeping to provide better information about this cost? What would be the costs and benefits of doing so?

❷ **C.** Refer to the cost information you already gathered. If you think that the cost is variable or mixed, select one or more potential cost drivers and collect data for them. Create a scatter plot of the cost against each cost driver. If you do not think the cost is variable or mixed, create a line chart of the cost over time. Examine your chart.

**1.** Do you see any patterns? For example, does the cost seem to increase with a cost driver (or over time)? Does the cost seem to be fixed at a given level?

❷ **2.** How does the graph affect your understanding of this cost's behavior? Explain.

❷ **D.** If you think your cost is variable or mixed, refer to the data you used to create the preceding scatter plot. Choose only one cost driver and use the two-point and high-low methods to estimate the cost function.

**1.** Are the cost functions similar? Why or why not?

❷ **2.** Are the fixed and variable costs about what you would expect them to be? Why or why not?

❷ **3.** How comfortable would you be to use one of these cost functions to create a budget for next month? Explain.

❷ **E.** In what ways is your personal budget estimation problem the same as the cost estimation problem for a business? Explain.

**2.39**
**Q3, Q6, Q7**

**Adjusting data for use with regression, outlier** Smeyer Industries is a large firm with more than 40 departments, each employing 35 to 100 persons. Recent experience suggests that the cost function used to estimate overhead in Department IP-14 is no longer appropriate. The current function was developed three years ago. Since then, a number of changes occurred in the facilities and processes used in Department IP-14. The changes happened one at a time. Each time a change was made, the cost accountant felt the change was not major enough to justify calculating a new overhead cost function. Now it is clear that the cumulative effect of the changes has been large.

You have been assigned the task to develop a new cost function for overhead in Department IP-14. Initial analysis suggests that the number of direct labor hours is an appropriate cost driver. Departmental records are available for nine months. The records reveal the following information.

| Month | Actual Overhead | Direct Labor Hours |
|---|---|---|
| March | $68,200 | 8,812 |
| April | 71,250 | 8,538 |
| May | 68,150 | 8,740 |
| June | 73,500 | 9,176 |
| July | 38,310 | 2,123 |
| August | 70,790 | 9,218 |
| September | 80,350 | 8,943 |
| October | 68,750 | 8,821 |
| November | 68,200 | 8,794 |

An assistant has analyzed the data for March through July and made the appropriate adjustments except for the following items (for which the assistant was unsure of the proper treatment).

1. The semiannual property tax bill for Department IP-14 was paid on June 30. The entire amount, $3,000 was charged to overhead for June.
2. The costs to install a new piece of equipment with a life of 10 years in the department were charged to overhead in April. The installation costs were $4,300.
3. Factory depreciation is allocated to Department IP-14 every month. The department's share, $8,000, is included in overhead.
4. A strike closed the plant for three weeks in July. Several nonunion employees were kept on payroll during the strike. Their duties were general housekeeping and "busy work." These costs were charged to overhead.

You also have the details for the overhead account for the months of August and September. They are presented in the following table. You were hired on October 1 and have been keeping the department accounts since then. Therefore, you know that the data for October and November are correct, except for any adjustments needed for the preceding items.

### Department IP-14
### Overhead Control
### August

| Date | Explanation | Amount |
|---|---|---|
| Aug. 4 | Miscellaneous supplies | $10,450 |
| Aug. 5 | Payroll for indirect labor | 5,500 |
| Aug. 15 | Power costs: Department IP-14 | 12,250 |
| Aug. 19 | Payroll for indirect labor | 6,000 |
| Aug. 19 | Overtime premium | 890 |
| Aug. 24 | Factory depreciation | 8,000 |
| Aug. 26 | Miscellaneous supplies | 27,700 |
| | Total for August | $70,790 |

### Department IP-14
### Overhead Control
### September

| Date | Explanation | Amount |
|---|---|---|
| Sept. 2 | Payroll for indirect labor | $ 6,000 |
| Sept. 7 | Miscellaneous supplies | 12,100 |
| Sept. 15 | Power costs: Department IP-14 | 11,100 |
| Sept. 15 | Power costs: Department IB-4 | 10,850 |
| Sept. 16 | Payroll for indirect labor | 6,500 |
| Sept. 16 | Overtime premium | 950 |
| Sept. 21 | Miscellaneous supplies | 19,350 |
| Sept. 28 | Factory depreciation | 8,000 |
| Sept. 30 | Payroll for indirect labor | 5,500 |
| | Total for September | $80,350 |

August has 31 days and September has 30 days.

**REQUIRED:**

**ⓔ A.** Using the information provided, adjust the monthly cost data to more accurately reflect the overhead costs incurred during each month.

**❷ B.** Discuss whether the data for July should be included in the estimate of future costs. Use a scatter plot to help you answer this question.

**❷ C.** Develop a cost function by regressing overhead costs in Department IP-14 on direct labor hours. Discuss whether your cost function would be reasonable for estimating future overhead costs. Ignore any items you will discuss in part (D).

**❷ D.** Identify and discuss any additional adjustments that might be needed to more accurately measure overhead costs for the regression in part (C).

**E.** Explain why adjustments probably need to be made to information from accounting records when estimating a cost function.

# BUILD YOUR PROFESSIONAL COMPETENCIES

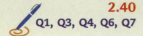

**2.40**

**Q1, Q3, Q4, Q6, Q7**

**Focus on Professional Competency: Measurement** *Identify, evaluate, recommend, and communicate measurement methods* Review the following definition and elements for the Measurement competency.[5]

**DEFINITION:** *Measures used should be both relevant (that is, bear on the decision to be made) and reliable (consistently measure what they purport to measure). Various measurement and disclosure criteria used by accounting professionals—such as GAAP, OCBOA (Other Comprehensive Basis of Accounting) and tax reporting—have been codified to some degree. Other performance measures (such as Economic Value Added) or stated criteria (for example, investment performance) are used for special purposes. Some measurement criteria (such as effectiveness of internal control) are measured qualitatively, rather than quantitatively.*

## ELEMENTS FOR THIS COMPETENCY INCLUDE

| Level 1 | Level 2 | Level 3 | Level 4 |
|---|---|---|---|
| 1. Identifies what needs to be measured<br><br>2. Describes uncertainties about data and how items should be measured<br><br>3. Appropriately applies a given measurement method | 4. Describes the pros and cons of alternative methods of measurement<br><br>5. Describes the implications of ambiguities when estimates are required | 6. Determines an appropriate, relevant, and reliable measure for the intended use<br><br>7. Presents the measurement results objectively using applicable standards of disclosure or reporting | 8. Recognizes changing circumstances and reconsiders measurement methods and estimates as appropriate |

**REQUIRED:**

**❶ A.** Focus on competency element 1, which requires accountants to identify what needs to be measured. Which material in Chapter 2 addresses this competency element? Explain.

**❷ B.** Focus on competency elements 2 and 5, which address uncertainties in accounting measurement. Why is dealing with uncertainties important when making accounting measurements?

**C.** Focus on competency elements 3, 4, 6, and 8, which relate to choosing and appropriately applying measurement methods. Answer the following questions:

    **1.** What different measurement methods were introduced in Chapter 2 for estimating a cost function?

    **2.** Describe the pros and cons of each method.

    **❷ 3.** When estimating a cost function, what does it mean for a measurement to be (a) appropriate, (b) relevant, and (c) reliable?

    **❷ 4.** Explain why it is often difficult to identify an appropriate, relevant, and reliable measure for estimating a cost function.

    **❷ 5.** Explain why it is important to consider changing circumstances when estimating a cost function.

**❷ D.** Focus on competency element 7, which relates to the need for accountants to be objective. When accountants consider standards for disclosure or reporting, they often think about accounting rules, such as GAAP or the income tax code. In cost accounting, many reports are prepared for internal management use and do not follow a standard set of rules. Nevertheless, accountants need to present cost accounting reports in a way that is useful for internal management.

    Suppose you are a cost accountant and have just finished estimating a cost function. The controller asks you to provide a memo describing the cost function and how you estimated it. Why is it important for you to present the measurement results objectively? What are some other characteristics that might be important when preparing this report? (Think about the following types of questions: How should the report be formatted? What information should be included? What else should you consider when designing the report?)

---

[5]The definition and elements are reprinted with permission from AICPA; copyright © 1978–2000 & 2003 by American Institute of Certified Public Accountants. The AICPA's Core Competencies Framework can be accessed at eca. aicpaservices.org.

**2.41**
**Q6, Q7**

**Integrating Across the Curriculum: Statistics** *Cost function using multiple regression, cost inflation, lagged cost driver (Appendix 2A)* Red's Furniture Manufacturing produces a line of tables and chairs from specialty hardwoods. It makes three different styles of chairs, and each chair takes about the same amount of direct labor time to manufacture. Shawn Hargrove was the company's new cost accountant and was preparing a direct labor cost budget for 20X5. The previous cost accountant had always estimated direct labor costs based on a regression of the cost against the number of chairs produced using monthly data from the prior four years. This approach seemed to be economically plausible, so Shawn began his cost estimate by following the method used in prior years. However, Shawn was not pleased with his regression results.

Shawn thought about ways to improve the cost function estimate. He realized that the past cost information did not take into account pay raises. Every January, the company gives its employees a cost of living pay increase. Each of the past four years, the employees had received a 2% raise. He learned from management that a 2% raise is planned for 20X5, too. Shawn thought that prior years' labor costs should be increased to 20X5 pay levels to provide a more accurate prediction of 20X5 costs. He planned to adjust prior year pay using the following formula:

$$\text{Labor cost at 20X5 level} = \text{Labor cost at prior pay level} \times (1.02)^t$$

where
$$t = 1 \text{ for 20X4}$$
$$t = 2 \text{ for 20X3}$$
$$t = 3 \text{ for 20X2}$$
$$t = 4 \text{ for 20X1}$$

Shawn also considered the degree to which direct labor costs vary with production. The company's policy is to increase the number of workers when production volumes increase, and to decrease the number of workers when production volumes decrease. However, it often takes time for the company to hire qualified new workers, and the managers often delay laying employees off when volumes decline. Thus, at least some lag is evident between the time that production volumes change and labor costs change. Shawn thought that an additional cost driver for direct labor costs might be the prior month's volume of chairs produced.

**www.wiley.com/
college/eldenburg**

The data provide monthly direct labor costs and number of chairs produced for the past four years. These data are available at the Web site www.wiley.com/college/eldenburg

**REQUIRED:**

**A.** Estimate the cost function using the same method as in prior years. Explain why Shawn was displeased with the results.

**B.** Explain why the annual pay increases cause a problem with the cost function estimated in part (A). In what way is the cost function mismeasured?

**C.** Use the formula developed by Shawn to adjust the labor cost data for pay increases. Reestimate the cost function. Explain whether you consider it to be a reasonable cost function for estimating 20X5 direct labor costs.

**D.** To the analysis you performed in part (C), add a second independent variable for the number of chairs produced in the preceding month. Reestimate the cost function. Do the statistics suggest that it is a reasonable cost function?

**E.** Explain what the two slope coefficients from part (D) mean in terms of the cost function.

**F.** Do you agree that both independent variables should be used to estimate 20X5 direct labor costs? Why or why not?

# Cost-Volume-Profit Analysis

## ▶In Brief

Managers need to estimate future revenues, costs, and profits to help them plan and monitor operations. They use cost-volume-profit (CVP) analysis to identify the levels of operating activity needed to avoid losses, achieve targeted profits, plan future operations, and monitor organizational performance. Managers also analyze operational risk as they choose an appropriate cost structure.

## This Chapter Addresses the Following Questions:

**Q1** What is cost-volume-profit (CVP) analysis, and how is it used for decision making?

**Q2** How are CVP calculations performed for a single product?

**Q3** How are CVP calculations performed for multiple products?

**Q4** What is the breakeven point?

**Q5** What assumptions and limitations should managers consider when using CVP analysis?

**Q6** How are margin of safety and operating leverage used to assess operational risk?

# COLECO: FAULTY FORECASTS

In the early 1980s, personal computers were still somewhat a novelty. At that time, **Coleco** manufactured a small computer called Adam. In addition, it sold Colecovision games for home computers. Coleco marketed Adam and its computer games heavily, hoping in 1982 for a hot seller during the Christmas and holiday gift season. However, Adam and Colecovision did not sell well. Coleco found itself close to bankruptcy.

Then in 1983 Coleco purchased the license to manufacture Cabbage Patch Dolls. It began production for Christmas 1983. Coleco widely publicized the dolls' arrival at toy stores, but managers anticipated greater sales of Adam in their production schedules. They did not emphasize production of the Cabbage Patch Dolls. These dolls became hot sellers that Christmas, and inventories were depleted rapidly. The scarcity generated so much interest that customers fought

with each other for the dolls and even wrecked some toy stores while trying to purchase Cabbage Patch Dolls for the holidays. Because of the shortage, advertising for the dolls was canceled shortly after their introduction.

Coleco's managers continued to think that the company's reputation would be based on computers. However, Cabbage Patch Dolls became their most successful product for the next several years. After success with Cabbage Patch Dolls and action figure toys called Masters of the Universe, Coleco continued to aim for hot sellers. This strategy involved a great deal of uncertainty, and by 1988 the company was bankrupt. ■

SOURCES: L. Brannon and A. McCabe, "Time-Restricted Sales Appeals," *Cornell Hotel and Restaurant Administration Quarterly,* August/September 2001, pp. 47–53; and K. Fitzgerald, "Toys Face Scrooge-Like Christmas," *Advertising Age,* September 19, 1988, pp. 30–32.

## DETERMINING A PROFITABLE MIX OF PRODUCTS

### ■ Key Decision Factors for Coleco

What went wrong with **Coleco's** decision to emphasize production of Adam instead of Cabbage Patch Dolls? The problems began with uncertainties about which products would be popular at Christmas. Coleco's managers could not know which products would sell best. Nevertheless, it was necessary for them to make decisions about the types and volumes of products to manufacture. They forecast the number and type of products that would sell and then made production decisions accordingly. The following discussion summarizes key issues in Coleco's decision-making process.

**Knowing.** Knowledge about consumer markets, competition, production processes, and costs were critical when Coleco's managers decided which product to emphasize. Coleco needed this knowledge for its potential markets—dolls, computers, and games. Given the company's experience, its knowledge was probably greater for producing Adam than for Cabbage Patch Dolls. However, doll manufacturing was a relatively simple process compared to producing computers.

**Identifying.** Companies commonly face major uncertainties in their product markets, particularly in the toy industry where competition is often fierce and consumer tastes change rapidly. However, Coleco's uncertainties were greater than most because of the relatively new—and competitive—computer market. For example, the managers did not know:

- How quickly consumers would embrace computers
- What would persuade consumers to purchase a first computer
- How quickly computer technology and competition would change
- Exactly how much the computers would cost to produce

**Exploring.** Coleco's managers faced a difficult task in adequately exploring their decision to emphasize Adam over Cabbage Patch Dolls. However, thorough analysis is crucial for this type of decision. For example, the managers needed to do the following:

- Anticipate which product would sell best. Although market research helps managers estimate product demand, they would still have considerable uncertainty about actual product sales.
- Avoid biased forecasts and analyses. Managers often have emotional attachments to sunk costs, such as the large investment already made in Adam, that should not affect decision making.
- Consider risks associated with the cost structure for each product. Compared to Adam, Cabbage Patch dolls probably had lower fixed costs and a greater proportion of variable costs. When more of a product's costs are variable, profit is less risky because the sales volumes needed to cover fixed costs are relatively lower. Cabbage Patch may have carried less operating risk than Adam.

**Prioritizing.** Given limited resources and their analyses of expected profit from the two products, Coleco's managers decided to prioritize production of Adam over Cabbage Patch Dolls. This decision might have been clouded by management biases, as already discussed.

**Envisioning.** Despite previous poor sales of Adam, Coleco's managers continued promoting the product. In hindsight, it is easy to criticize the company for this strategy; however, it would have been difficult for Coleco's managers to adequately estimate product sales. Later, the managers adopted an ongoing strategy of seeking hot-selling toys. This strategy ultimately failed.

### ■ Decision Making Using Information about Revenues and Costs

Because **Coleco's** managers overestimated Adam sales and underestimated Cabbage Patch Doll sales, they not only incurred substantial losses on the Adam line, but also lost the opportunity to gain more profit by selling additional Cabbage Patch Dolls. In Chapter 2, we focused primarily on the estimation of costs. However, managers combine information about revenues and costs to help them decide the mix and volumes of goods or services to produce and sell. They also use this information to monitor operations and evaluate profitability risk. In this chapter, we combine revenues and costs in our analyses.

# COST-VOLUME-PROFIT ANALYSIS

**Q1** What is cost-volume-profit (CVP) analysis, and how is it used for decision making?

**Q2** How are CVP calculations performed for a single product?

**CURRENT PRACTICE**

According to Jon Scheumann, director of the business process consulting firm Gunn Partners, successful organizations need a culture that is attuned to cost management and that pays attention to cost structures.[1]

**Cost-volume-profit (CVP) analysis** is a technique that examines changes in profits in response to changes in sales volumes, costs, and prices. Accountants often perform CVP analysis to plan future levels of operating activity and provide information about:

- Which products or services to emphasize
- The volume of sales needed to achieve a targeted level of profit
- The amount of revenue required to avoid losses
- Whether to increase fixed costs
- How much to budget for discretionary expenditures
- Whether fixed costs expose the organization to an unacceptable level of risk

## ■ Profit Equation and Contribution Margin

CVP analysis begins with the basic profit equation.

$$\text{Profit} = \text{Total revenue} - \text{Total costs}$$

Separating costs into variable and fixed categories, we express profit as:

$$\text{Profit} = \text{Total revenue} - \text{Total variable costs} - \text{Total fixed costs}$$

The **contribution margin** is total revenue minus total variable costs. Similarly, the **contribution margin per unit** is the selling price per unit minus the variable cost per unit. Both contribution margin and contribution margin per unit are valuable tools when considering the effects of volume on profit. Contribution margin per unit tells us how much revenue from each unit sold can be applied toward fixed costs. Once enough units have been sold to cover all fixed costs, then the contribution margin per unit from all remaining sales becomes profit.

If we assume that the selling price and variable cost per unit are constant, then total revenue is equal to price times quantity, and total variable cost is variable cost per unit times quantity. We then rewrite the profit equation in terms of the contribution margin per unit.

$$\text{Profit} = P \times Q - V \times Q - F = (P - V) \times Q - F$$

where

$P$ = Selling price per unit
$V$ = Variable cost per unit
$(P - V)$ = Contribution margin per unit
$Q$ = Quantity of product sold (units of goods or services)
$F$ = Total fixed costs

We use the profit equation to plan for different volumes of operations. CVP analysis can be performed using either:

- Units (quantity) of product sold
- Revenues (in dollars)

## ■ CVP Analysis in Units

We begin with the preceding profit equation. Assuming that fixed costs remain constant, we solve for the expected quantity of goods or services that must be sold to achieve a target level of profit.

**Profit equation:** $\qquad \text{Profit} = (P - V) \times Q - F$

**Solving for Q:** $\qquad Q = \dfrac{F + \text{Profit}}{(P - V)}$ = Quantity (units) required to obtain target profit

Notice that the denominator in this formula, $(P - V)$, is the contribution margin per unit.

---

[1]Editorial, "A Proactive Approach to Cost Cutting," *SmartPros,* June 2002, www.smartpros.com.

Suppose that Magik Bicycles wants to produce a new mountain bike called Magikbike III and has forecast the following information.

> Price per bike = $800
> Variable cost per bike = $300
> Fixed costs related to bike production = $5,500,000
> Target profit = $200,000
> Estimated sales = 12,000 bikes

We determine the quantity of bikes needed for the target profit as follows:

$$\text{Quantity} = (\$5,500,000 + \$200,000) \div (\$800 - \$300) = 11,400 \text{ bikes}$$

## ■ CVP Analysis in Revenues

The **contribution margin ratio (CMR)** is the percent by which the selling price (or revenue) per unit exceeds the variable cost per unit, or contribution margin as a percent of revenue. For a single product, it is

$$\text{CMR} = \frac{P - V}{P}$$

To analyze CVP in terms of total revenue instead of units, we substitute the contribution margin ratio for the contribution margin per unit. We rewrite the equation to solve for the total dollar amount of revenue we need to cover fixed costs and achieve our target profit as

$$\text{Revenue} = \frac{F + \text{Profit}}{(P - V)/P} = \frac{F + \text{Profit}}{\text{CMR}}$$

To solve for the Magikbike III revenues needed for a target profit of $200,000, we first calculate the contribution margin ratio as follows:

$$\text{CMR} = (\$800 - \$300) \div \$800 = 0.625$$

A contribution margin ratio of 0.625 means that 62.5% of the revenue from each bike sold contributes first to fixed costs and then to profit after fixed costs are covered.

$$\text{Revenue} = (\$5,500,000 + \$200,000) \div 0.625 = \$9,120,000$$

We check to see that the two results are identical by multiplying the number of units (11,400) times price ($800) to obtain the revenue amount ($9,120,000).

The contribution margin ratio can also be written in terms of total revenues (TR) and total variable costs (TVC). That is, for a single product, the CMR is the same whether we compute it using per-unit selling price and variable cost or using total revenues and total variable costs. Thus, we can create the following mathematically equivalent version of the CVP formula.

**HELPFUL HINT**

Computing the CVP using total revenues and total variable costs is useful in cases where per-unit variable costs are unknown.

$$\text{Revenues} = \frac{F + \text{Profit}}{(TR - TVC)/TR}$$

For Magikbike III we could use the forecast information about volume (12,000 bikes) to determine the contribution margin ratio.

> Total revenue = $800 × 12,000 bikes = $9,600,000
> Total variable cost = $300 × 12,000 bikes = $3,600,000
> Total contribution margin = $9,600,000 − $3,600,000 = $6,000,000
> Contribution margin ratio = $6,000,000 ÷ $9,600,000 = 0.625

## ■ CVP for Multiple Products

Many organizations sell a combination of different products or services. The **sales mix** is the proportion of different products or services that an organization sells. For example, we learned in the opening vignette that **Coleco** sold both Adam computers and Cabbage Patch dolls. To use CVP in the case of multiple products or services, we assume a constant sales mix in addition to the other CVP assumptions. Assuming a constant sales mix allows CVP computations to be performed using combined unit or revenue data for an organization as a whole. Later in the chapter we will learn how to perform detailed computations for the sales mix.

**EXHIBIT 3.1**
CVP Graph for Magik
Bicycles' Magikbike III.

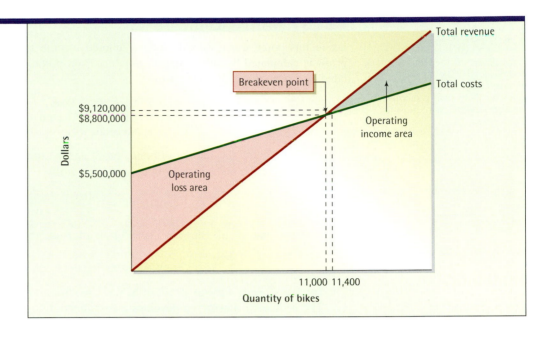

## Breakeven Point

**Q4** What is the breakeven point?

**CURRENT PRACTICE**

The U.S. Small Business Administration Web site recommends the use of breakeven analysis and refers small business owners to a breakeven analysis calculator and CVP graphing tool.[2]

Managers often want to know the level of activity required to break even. A CVP analysis can be used to determine the **breakeven point,** or level of operating activity at which revenues cover all fixed and variable costs, resulting in zero profit. We can calculate the breakeven point from any of the preceding CVP formulas, setting profit to zero. Depending on which formula we use, we calculate the breakeven point in either number of units or in total revenues. For Magikbike III, breakeven points are:

$$\text{Breakeven quantity} = (\$5,500,000 + \$0) \div (\$800 - \$300) = 11,000 \text{ bikes}$$
$$\text{Breakeven revenue} = (\$5,500,000 + \$0) \div 0.625 = \$8,800,000$$

## Cost-Volume-Profit Graph

A **cost-volume-profit graph** (or CVP graph) shows the relationship between total revenues and total costs; it illustrates how an organization's profits are expected to change under different volumes of activity. Exhibit 3.1 presents a CVP graph for Magikbikes III. Notice that when no bikes are sold, fixed costs are $5,500,000, resulting in a loss of $5,500,000. As sales volume increases, the loss decreases by the contribution margin for each bike sold. The cost and revenue lines intersect at the breakeven point of 11,000, which means zero loss and zero profit. Then as sales increase beyond this breakeven point, we see an increase in profit, growing by the $500 contribution margin for each bike sold. Profits achieve the target level of $200,000 when sales volume reaches 11,400.

| GUIDE YOUR LEARNING **3.1** Key Terms |
|---|

Stop to confirm that you understand the new terms introduced in the last several pages.

| | |
|---|---|
| Cost-volume-profit (CVP) analysis (p. 89) | *Sales mix (p. 90) |
| Contribution margin (p. 89) | Breakeven point (p. 91) |
| Contribution margin per unit (p. 89) | Cost-volume-profit graph (p. 91) |
| Contribution margin ratio (CMR) (p. 90) | |

For each of these terms, write a definition in your own words. For the starred term, list at least one example that is different from the ones given in this textbook.

---

[2]Do a search for Breakeven Analysis at the U.S. Small Business Administration Web site, available at www.sba.gov.

## ■ CVP with Income Taxes

**ALTERNATIVE TERMS**

Some people use the terms *operating income (loss)* or *income (loss) before income taxes* instead of *pretax profit (loss)*. Similarly, some people use *net income (loss)* instead of *after-tax profit (loss)*.

Up to this point, our CVP calculations ignored income taxes. An organization's after-tax profit is calculated by subtracting income tax from pretax profit. The tax is usually calculated as a percentage of pretax profit.

$$\text{After-tax profit} = \text{Pretax profit} - \text{Taxes}$$
$$= \text{Pretax profit} - (\text{Tax rate} \times \text{Pretax profit})$$
$$= \text{Pretax profit} \times (1 - \text{Tax rate})$$

If we want to know the amount of pretax profit needed to achieve a target level of after-tax profit, we solve the preceding formula for pretax profit:

$$\text{Pretax profit} = \frac{\text{After-tax profit}}{(1 - \text{Tax rate})}$$

Suppose that Magik Bicycles plans for an after-tax profit of $20,000 and its tax rate is 30%. Then,

$$\text{Pretax profit} = \$20,000 \div (1 - 0.30) = \$28,571$$

The company needs a pretax profit of $28,571 to earn an after-tax profit of $20,000.

The following illustration develops a cost function to calculate the volumes needed to break even and to achieve a target after-tax profit when multiple products are involved.

### DIE GEFLECKTE KUH EIS (THE SPOTTED COW CREAMERY) (PART 1)
### CVP ANALYSIS WITH INCOME TAXES

Die Gefleckte Kuh Eis (The Spotted Cow Creamery) is a popular ice cream emporium near a university in Munich, Germany. Information for the most recent month (amounts in euros) appears here.

| | |
|---|---:|
| Revenue | €40,000 |
| Cost of food and beverages sold | 20,000 |
| Labor | 15,000 |
| Rent | 1,000 |
| Pretax profit | 4,000 |
| Income taxes (25%) | 1,000 |
| After-tax profit | € 3,000 |

The store owner asked the manager, Holger Soderstrom, to estimate results for the next month. This particular outlet has not performed as well as the owner's other three outlets. Holger believes that sales volumes will increase to €48,000 next month because it has been an unusually hot and dry summer.

### Estimating the Cost Function

To perform CVP analysis, Holger first estimates the cost function. Using accounting records, he classifies each cost as fixed or variable and then estimates next month's cost. Of the costs listed in the accounting records, labor (€15,000) and rent (€1,000) are most likely fixed (assuming employees work fixed schedules). Assuming that fixed costs do not change from month to month, Holger's best estimate of next month's fixed costs is €16,000 (€15,000 + €1,000). The remaining item, cost of food and beverages sold (€20,000), is most likely a variable cost. Because The Spotted Cow Creamery's focus is retail sales of ice cream and other food items, Holger can reasonably assume that sales volume drives this variable cost. Thus, he estimates expected variable costs as a percent of revenue:

$$€20,000 \div €40,000 = 0.50, \text{ or } 50\% \text{ of revenue}$$

Holger combines his fixed and variable cost estimates to create the following cost function for next month:

$$TC = €16,000 + (50\% \times \text{Revenues})$$

### Estimating After-Tax Profit

If next month's revenues are €48,000, Holger expects total variable costs to be (50% × €48,000) = €24,000. Therefore, his estimate of pretax profit is

$$\text{Pretax profit} = €48,000 - €16,000 - €24,000 = €8,000$$

Holger estimates income taxes and after-tax profit, assuming that income taxes remain at 25% of pretax profit:

$$\text{After-tax profit} = €8,000(1 - 0.25) = €6,000$$

## Calculating Revenues to Achieve Targeted After-Tax Profit

Holger presents the preceding information to the owner. However, the owner still has concerns about this outlet because the other outlets have achieved after-tax profits of about €8,000 each during the last few months. The owner thinks that sales volume might be the problem. To help analyze this possibility, Holger determines the sales volume necessary to earn after-tax profits of €8,000 per month. He begins by calculating the targeted pretax profit:

$$\text{Pretax profit} = €8,000 \div (1 - 0.25) = €10,667$$

Next, he uses the following CVP formula to solve for targeted revenue:

$$\text{Revenues} = \frac{F + \text{Profit}}{\text{CMR}}$$

Substituting in the preceding information:

$$\text{Revenues} = (€16,000 + €10,667) \div 0.50 = €53,334$$

Notice that Holger uses the contribution margin ratio calculated with the sales revenue and variable costs from his original analysis.

Holger summarizes his target profit calculations for the owner as follows:

| | |
|---|---:|
| Revenue | €53,334 |
| Cost of food and beverages sold (50% of €53,334) | 26,667 |
| Labor (fixed) | 15,000 |
| Rent (fixed) | 1,000 |
| Pretax profit | 10,667 |
| Income taxes (25%) | 2,667 |
| After-tax profit | € 8,000 |

For the outlet to achieve an after-tax profit of €8,000, revenues need to increase by 33% [(€53,334 − €40,000) ÷ €40,000] over last month.

Holger presents this information to the owner and argues that sales will increase to €53,334 because the weather will be hotter next month. However, the owner thinks that Holger may be worried about being replaced, and so his revenue estimates are probably biased upwards. The owner decides to investigate Holger's estimates further by comparing his revenues and costs to those in the other outlets.

| GUIDE YOUR LEARNING  **3.2**  The Spotted Cow Creamery (Part 1) |
|---|

The Spotted Cow Creamery (Part 1) illustrates a multiple-product CVP analysis with income taxes. For this illustration:

| Define It | Identify Problem and Information | Identify Uncertainties | Explore Assumptions | Explore Biases |
|---|---|---|---|---|
| Which definitions, analysis techniques, and computations were used? | What decisions were being addressed? What information was relevant to the decisions? | What types of uncertainties were there? Consider uncertainties about: <br> • Revenue and cost estimates <br> • Interpreting results <br> • Relevant range of operations <br> • Feasibility of activity level | Reread the first part of this chapter and identify the assumptions used in developing the CVP formulas. How reasonable are these assumptions for The Spotted Cow Creamery? | Why and how might the manager's bias influence the computations? Why would the owner be uncertain whether the manager had created biased revenue or cost estimates? |

## PERFORMING CVP ANALYSES WITH A SPREADSHEET

Spreadsheets are often used for CVP computations, particularly when an organization has multiple products. Spreadsheets simplify the basic computations and can be designed to show how changes in volumes, selling prices, costs, or sales mix alter the results.

Q3 How are CVP calculations performed for multiple products?

### ■ CVP Calculations for a Sales Mix

Although The Spotted Cow Creamery sells multiple products, the CVP analysis performed by the store manager did not provide computations for individual products. Instead, the analysis focused on the total amount of revenue needed to achieve a target profit. If the manager wants to use CVP results to plan future operations for individual products, the required revenue for each product needs to be determined. Such computations are performed using the sales mix. The sales mix should be stated as a proportion of units when performing CVP computations in units, and it should be stated as a proportion of revenues when performing CVP computations in revenues. Sales mix computations can become cumbersome if performed manually; it is easiest to use a spreadsheet.

To demonstrate CVP computations using a spreadsheet, suppose that Magik Bicycles developed three different products, a small bike for children and youths, a road bike, and a mountain bike. Total fixed costs for the company are $14,700,000. Forecasted sales volumes are as follows. The sales mix in percentages is calculated from these volumes.

|  | Youth | Road | Mountain | Total |
|---|---|---|---|---|
| Forecasted volume (units) | 10,000 | 18,000 | 12,000 | 40,000 |
| Expected sales mix in units | 25% | 45% | 30% | 100% |

Because of increased competition and an economic downturn, the managers of Magik Bicycles are uncertain about the company's ability to achieve the forecasted level of sales. They would like to know the minimum amount of sales needed for an after-tax profit of $100,000. The company's income tax rate is 30%. The expected unit selling prices, variable costs, and contribution margins for each product are as follows:

|  | Youth | Road | Mountain |
|---|---|---|---|
| Price per unit | $200 | $700 | $800 |
| Variable cost per unit | 75 | 250 | 300 |
| Contribution margin per unit | $125 | $450 | $500 |

Exhibit 3.2 shows a sample CVP spreadsheet for Magik Bicycles. Notice that all of the input data is placed in an area labeled as "Input section" in the spreadsheet. The calculations are performed outside of this area (formulas for this spreadsheet are shown in Appendix 3A). Spreadsheets designed this way allow users to alter the assumptions in the input section without performing any additional programming.

The spreadsheet in Exhibit 3.2 first uses the input data to compute expected revenues, costs, and income. The revenues and variable costs for each product are computed by multiplying the expected sales volume times the selling price and variable cost per unit shown in the input area. The revenues and variable costs for the three products are then combined to determine total revenues and total variable costs for the company. After subtracting expected fixed costs and income taxes (30% of pretax income), the expected after-tax income is $455,000.

When an organization produces and sells a number of different products or services, we use the weighted average contribution margin per unit to determine the breakeven point or target profit in units. Similarly, we use the weighted average contribution margin ratio to determine the breakeven point or target profit in revenues. "Weighted average" here refers to the expected sales mix: 10,000 youth bikes or $2,000,000 in revenues, 18,000 road bikes or

CURRENT PRACTICE

Spreadsheet skills are important professionally. The American Institute of Certified Public Accountants (AICPA) states that an entry-level accountant should be able to "appropriately use electronic spreadsheets and other software to build models and simulations."[3]

---

[3]This skill is an element of the competency "Leverage Technology to Develop and Enhance Functional Competencies," *AICPA Core Competency Framework,* accessed through the Library at eca.aicpaservices.org/.

**EXHIBIT 3.2**

Spreadsheet for Magik Bicycles CVP with Multiple Products

| | A | B | C | D | E |
|---|---|---|---|---|---|
| 1 | | | | | |
| 2 | **Input section** | Youth Bikes | Road Bikes | Mtn. Bikes | |
| 3 | Expected sales volume-units | 10,000 | 18,000 | 12,000 | |
| 4 | Price per unit | $200 | $700 | $800 | |
| 5 | Variable cost per unit | $75 | $250 | $300 | |
| 6 | | | | | |
| 7 | Fixed costs | $14,700,000 | | | |
| 8 | Desired after-tax profit | $100,000 | (enter zero for breakeven) | | |
| 9 | Income tax rate | 30% | | | |
| 10 | | | | | |
| 11 | | | | | |
| 12 | **Contribution Margin** | Youth Bikes | Road Bikes | Mtn. Bikes | Total Bikes |
| 13 | Units | 10,000 | 18,000 | 12,000 | 40,000 |
| 14 | Revenue | $2,000,000 | $12,600,000 | $9,600,000 | $24,200,000 |
| 15 | Variable costs | 750,000 | 4,500,000 | 3,600,000 | 8,850,000 |
| 16 | Contribution margin | $1,250,000 | $8,100,000 | $6,000,000 | $15,350,000 |
| 17 | | | | | |
| 18 | Contrib. margin per unit | $125.00 | $450.00 | $500.00 | $383.75 |
| 19 | Contrib. margin ratio | 62.50% | 64.29% | 62.50% | 63.43% |
| 20 | | | | | |
| 21 | Expected sales mix in units | 25.00% | 45.00% | 30.00% | 100.00% |
| 22 | Expected sales mix in revenues | 8.26% | 52.07% | 39.67% | 100.00% |
| 23 | | | | | |
| 24 | **Expected Income** | | | | |
| 25 | Contribution margin (above) | | | | $15,350,000 |
| 26 | Fixed costs | | | | 14,700,000 |
| 27 | Pretax income | | | | 650,000 |
| 28 | Income taxes | | | | 195,000 |
| 29 | After-tax income | | | | $455,000 |
| 30 | | | | | |
| 31 | **Preliminary CVP Calculations** | | | | |
| 32 | Target pretax profit for CVP analysis | | | | $142,857 |
| 33 | Fixed costs plus target pretax profit | | | | $14,842,857 |
| 34 | | | | | |
| 35 | **CVP analysis in units** | Youth Bikes | Road Bikes | Mtn. Bikes | Total Bikes |
| 36 | CVP calculation in units | 9,669.614 | 17,405.305 | 11,603.537 | 38,678 |
| 37 | Revenue | $1,933,923 | $12,183,713 | $9,282,829 | $23,400,465 |
| 38 | Variable costs | 725,221 | 4,351,326 | 3,481,061 | 8,557,608 |
| 39 | Contribution margin | $1,208,702 | $7,832,387 | $5,801,768 | 14,842,857 |
| 40 | Fixed costs | | | | 14,700,000 |
| 41 | Pretax income | | | | 142,857 |
| 42 | Income taxes | | | | 42,857 |
| 43 | After-tax income | | | | $100,000 |
| 44 | | | | | |
| 45 | **CVP analysis in revenues** | Youth Bikes | Road Bikes | Mtn. Bikes | Total Bikes |
| 46 | CVP calculation in revenues | $1,933,923 | $12,183,713 | $9,282,829 | $23,400,465 |
| 47 | Variable costs | 725,221 | 4,351,326 | 3,481,061 | 8,557,608 |
| 48 | Contribution margin | $1,208,702 | $7,832,387 | $5,801,768 | 14,842,857 |
| 49 | Fixed costs | | | | 14,700,000 |
| 50 | Pretax income | | | | 142,857 |
| 51 | Income taxes | | | | 42,857 |
| 52 | After-tax income | | | | $100,000 |

*Note:* Appendix 3A provides a version of this spreadsheet showing the cell formulas.

$12,600,000 in revenues, and 12,000 mountain bikes or $9,600,000 in revenues. Given the sales mix, the weighted average contribution margin per unit is calculated as the combined contribution margin ($15,350,000) divided by the total number of units expected to be sold (40,000), or $383.75 per unit as computed in Exhibit 3.2.[4] The weighted average contribution margin ratio is the combined contribution margin ($15,350,000) divided by combined revenue ($24,200,000), or 63.43%.[5]

---

[4]Another way to compute the weighted average contribution margin per unit is to sum the contribution margins for the three products, weighted by number of units sold as follows: (10,000 ÷ 40,000)($200 − $75) + (18,000 ÷ 40,000)($700 − $250) + (12,000 ÷ 40,000)($800 − $300) = $383.75.

[5]Another way to compute the weighted average contribution margin ratio is to sum the contribution margin ratios for the three products, weighted by revenues as follows: ($2,000,000 ÷ $24,200,000)[($200 − $75) ÷ $200] + ($12,600,000 ÷ $24,200,000)[($700 − $250) ÷ $700] + ($9,600,000 ÷ $24,200,000)[($800 − $300) ÷ $800] = 63.43%.

The spreadsheet in Exhibit 3.2 performs CVP computations using both units and revenues. To achieve an after-tax target profit of 100,000, the company must earn a pretax profit of $142,857 [$100,000 ÷ (1 − 0.30)]. To compute the total number of units (bikes) that must be sold to achieve the target profit, we divide the fixed costs plus the target profit by the weighted average contribution margin per unit:

$$\text{Units needed for target profit} = Q = \frac{F + \text{Profit}}{(P - V)} = \frac{\$14,700,000 + \$142,857}{\$383.75 \text{ per unit}} = 38,678 \text{ units}$$

Magik needs to sell 38,678 units to achieve an after-tax target profit of $100,000. To determine the number of units for each product that must be sold, we multiply the total number of units (38,678) by each product's expected sales mix in units. For example, the company must sell 38,678 units × (10,000 units ÷ 40,000 units), or 9,670 youth bikes.

To calculate the amount of revenue needed to achieve the target after-tax profit of $100,000, we divide the fixed costs plus the target pretax profit by the weighted average contribution margin ratio:

$$\text{Revenues} = \frac{F + \text{Profit}}{\text{CMR}} = \frac{\$14,700,000 + \$142,857}{63.43\%} = \$23,400,373$$

The difference between the spreadsheet and this hand-calculated amount is due to rounding, as are any differences in the following amounts. To determine the revenues for each product that must be sold, we multiply the total revenues ($23,400,373) by each product's expected sales mix in revenues. For example, the company must achieve $23,400,373 × ($2,000,000 ÷ $24,200,000), or $1,933,914 in revenues from youth bikes. Notice that the required revenue for each product is equal to the required number of units times the expected selling price. For youth bikes, 9,670 units × $200 per unit = $1,934,000.

The results of calculations using units and revenues are always identical. Because information in the example was given in units, it would have been easiest to create the spreadsheet using only the computations for CVP in units. However, in some situations per-unit information is not available. In those cases, it is necessary to perform CVP calculations using revenues. Later in the chapter we revisit the ice cream shop illustration to analyze the influence of sales mix on the total contribution margin.

## ■ CVP Sensitivity Analysis

 **Q5** What assumptions and limitations should managers consider when using CVP analysis?

One of the benefits of creating a spreadsheet with a separate input section is that additional CVP analyses can easily be performed by the changing input data. For example, suppose the managers of Magik Bicycles want to know the number of bikes they must sell to break even. We can return to the spreadsheet in Exhibit 3.2 and change the "Desired after-tax profit" to zero. The resulting spreadsheet, showing only CVP calculations in units, is presented in Exhibit 3.3.

The managers of Magik Bicycles could use the CVP spreadsheet to perform several different types of sensitivity analyses. Suppose sales of the mountain bike are falling behind

**EXHIBIT 3.3**
Spreadsheet Results for Magik Bicycles Breakeven Analysis

| | A | B | C | D | E |
|---|---|---|---|---|---|
| 31 | **Preliminary CVP Calculations** | | | | |
| 32 | Target pretax profit for CVP analysis | | | | $0 |
| 33 | Fixed costs plus target pretax profit | | | | $14,700,000 |
| 34 | | | | | |
| 35 | **CVP analysis in units** | Youth Bikes | Road Bikes | Mtn. Bikes | Total Bikes |
| 36 | CVP calculation in units | 9,576.547 | 17,237.785 | 11,491.857 | 38,306 |
| 37 | Revenue | $1,915,309 | $12,066,450 | $9,193,485 | $23,175,244 |
| 38 | Variable costs | 718,241 | 4,309,446 | 3,447,557 | 8,475,244 |
| 39 | Contribution margin | $1,197,068 | $7,757,003 | $5,745,928 | 14,700,000 |
| 40 | Fixed costs | | | | 14,700,000 |
| 41 | Pretax income | | | | 0 |
| 42 | Income taxes | | | | 0 |
| 43 | After-tax income | | | | $0 |

expectations. They could determine the effects of the change in sales mix on results. Every assumption in the data input box is easily changed to update information. Sensitivity analysis helps managers explore the potential impact of variations in data they consider to be particularly important or uncertain.

## Discretionary Expenditure Decision

**Q1** What is cost-volume-profit (CVP) analysis, and how is it used for decision making?

CVP analysis also helps managers make business decisions such as whether to increase or decrease discretionary expenditures. For example, suppose the managers of Magik Bicycles want to advertise one of their products more heavily. A distributor pointed out that the road bike price was less than a competitor's price for a model with fewer features. The competitor's brand name is quite well known, but the distributor thinks that he could sell at least 10% more road bikes if Magik launched a regional advertising campaign.

The managers of Magik estimate that an additional expenditure of $100,000 in advertising will increase road bike sales by 5%, to 18,900 bikes. To estimate the effects of the proposed expenditure, we return to the spreadsheet in Exhibit 3.2 and make two changes. First, fixed costs would increase by $100,000 to $14,800,000. Second, the expected volume of road bikes sold would increase to 18,900. The resulting spreadsheet in Exhibit 3.4 indicates that after-tax profits are expected to increase by $213,500 from $455,000 to $668,500. Notice on the spreadsheet that the change in sales mix affects the weighted average contribution margin; it changes from 383.75 to $385.21.

**CHAPTER REFERENCE**

Chapter 4 uses CVP analysis for additional types of decisions. We also learn that decisions are often influenced by qualitative information that is not valued in numerical terms.

We could perform the same calculation without the spreadsheet by subtracting the $100,000 investment in fixed costs from the additional contribution margin of $405,000 [900 bikes × ($700 − $250)]. The resulting incremental after-tax profit is $213,500 [($405,000 − $100,000)(1 − 0.30)]. Because profits are expected to increase more than costs for this advertising campaign, the managers would be likely to make the additional investment.

## Planning, Monitoring, and Motivating with CVP

CVP analyses are useful for planning and monitoring operations and for motivating employee performance. If the owner of The Spotted Cow Creamery obtains similar information for the other outlets, results can be compared to identify differences in revenue levels and cost functions. For example, unusually high labor costs might suggest that the low-profit outlet is overstaffed or inefficient. Once the owner analyzes the reasons for differences in profitability, emphasis can be placed on increasing revenues, reducing costs, or both. The owner can also hold managers more accountable for performance, which should motivate their work efforts toward the owner's goals.

**CHAPTER REFERENCE**

In Chapter 10, CVP analysis is used to create flexible budgets for measuring and monitoring performance at different levels of activity.

**EXHIBIT 3.4**
Spreadsheet for Magik Bicycles Advertising Expenditure Decision

| | A | B | C | D | E |
|---|---|---|---|---|---|
| 12 | **Contribution Margin** | Youth Bikes | Road Bikes | Mtn. Bikes | Total Bikes |
| 13 | Units | 10,000 | 18,900 | 12,000 | 40,900 |
| 14 | Revenue | $2,000,000 | $13,230,000 | $9,600,000 | $24,830,000 |
| 15 | Variable costs | 750,000 | 4,725,000 | 3,600,000 | 9,075,000 |
| 16 | Contribution margin | $1,250,000 | $8,505,000 | $6,000,000 | $15,755,000 |
| 17 | | | | | |
| 18 | Contrib. margin per unit | $125.00 | $450.00 | $500.00 | $385.21 |
| 19 | Contrib. margin ratio | 62.50% | 64.29% | 62.50% | 63.45% |
| 20 | | | | | |
| 21 | Expected sales mix in units | 24.45% | 46.21% | 29.34% | 100.00% |
| 22 | Expected sales mix in revenues | 8.05% | 53.28% | 38.66% | 100.00% |
| 23 | | | | | |
| 24 | **Expected Income** | | | | |
| 25 | Contribution margin (above) | | | | $15,755,000 |
| 26 | Fixed costs | | | | 14,800,000 |
| 27 | Pretax income | | | | 955,000 |
| 28 | Income taxes | | | | 286,500 |
| 29 | After-tax income | | | | $668,500 |

## DIE GEFLECKTE KUH EIS (THE SPOTTED COW CREAMERY) (PART 2)
## THE INFLUENCE OF SALES MIX ON PROFITABILITY

The owner of The Spotted Cow Creamery has several profitable stores. He asked the store managers to provide information about their sales mix, specifically the amount of beverage versus ice cream products sold. Beverages provide a much larger contribution margin than ice cream. After analyzing the data, he found that about half of the revenues in the most profitable stores were for the sale of beverages. In addition, these stores have more stable sales throughout the winter because they sell specialty coffee beverages as well as soft drinks.

The owner shared this information with Holger, the manager of a less profitable store. Holger investigates the contribution margins from beverages and ice cream at his store. He sets up a spreadsheet to examine the influence of the sales mix on profitability, shown in Exhibit 3.5(a). He finds that beverages are about 15% of total revenue (€6,000 ÷ €40,000). The contribution margin ratio for beverages is 93% (€5,600 ÷ €6,000), whereas the contribution margin for ice cream is 42% (€14,400 ÷ €34,000). When he changes the desired sales mix in the spreadsheet from 15% to 50% beverages to match the sales mix of more profitable stores, the after-tax income increases by a sizeable amount from €3,000 to €8,353 as indicated in Exhibit 3.5(b).

Holger realizes that several strategies would increase the percentage of beverages in his current sales mix. First, he could require the sales clerks to suggest a beverage with each sale. In addition, he could emphasize beverages in his advertising. He could also analyze his competitors' beverage prices to be certain that his prices are competitive. A small drop in the price of beverages might increase the volume of beverages sold more than enough to offset the decline in contribution margin ratio. He uses the spreadsheet to perform sensitivity analysis around these factors.

**EXHIBIT 3.5** Spreadsheet for The Spotted Cow Creamery

### (a) Current Sales Mix

|   | A | B | C | D |
|---|---|---|---|---|
| 1 | | | | |
| 2 | **Input section** | | | |
| 3 | | Beverage | Ice Cream | Total |
| 4 | Revenue | €6,000 | €34,000 | €40,000 |
| 5 | Variable cost | 400 | 19,600 | 20,000 |
| 6 | Current sales mix in revenues | 15% | 85% | 100% |
| 7 | Fixed costs | | | 16,000 |
| 8 | Tax rate | | | 25% |
| 9 | Desired sales mix in revenues | 15% | 85% | 100% |
| 10 | | | | |
| 11 | | | | Weighted Average |
| 12 | Contribution margin ratio | 93% | 42% | 50% |
| 13 | | | | |
| 14 | Income statement | | | |
| 15 | Revenue | €6,000 | €34,000 | €40,000 |
| 16 | Variable cost | 400 | 19,600 | 20,000 |
| 17 | Contribution margin | 5,600 | 14,400 | 20,000 |
| 18 | | | | |
| 19 | Fixed costs | | | 16,000 |
| 20 | Pretax income | | | 4,000 |
| 21 | Taxes | | | 1,000 |
| 22 | After tax income | | | €3,000 |

### (b) Desired Sales Mix

|   | A | B | C | D |
|---|---|---|---|---|
| 1 | | | | |
| 2 | **Input section** | | | |
| 3 | | Beverage | Ice Cream | Total |
| 4 | Revenue | €6,000 | €34,000 | €40,000 |
| 5 | Variable cost | 400 | 19,600 | 20,000 |
| 6 | Current sales mix in revenues | 15% | 85% | 100% |
| 7 | Fixed costs | | | 16,000 |
| 8 | Tax rate | | | 25% |
| 9 | Desired sales mix in revenues | 50% | 50% | 100% |
| 10 | | | | |
| 11 | | | | Weighted Average |
| 12 | Contribution margin ratio | 93% | 42% | 68% |
| 13 | | | | |
| 14 | Income statement | | | |
| 15 | Revenue | €20,000 | €20,000 | €40,000 |
| 16 | Variable cost | 1,333 | 11,529 | 12,863 |
| 17 | Contribution margin | 18,667 | 8,471 | 27,137 |
| 18 | | | | |
| 19 | Fixed costs | | | 16,000 |
| 20 | Pretax income | | | 11,137 |
| 21 | Taxes | | | 2,784 |
| 22 | After tax income | | | €8,353 |

## GUIDE YOUR LEARNING  3.3  The Spotted Cow Creamery (Part 2)

The Spotted Cow Creamery (Part 2) illustrates the influence of sales mix on profitability. For this illustration:

| Compute It | Identify Uncertainties | Explore Uses |
|---|---|---|
| For Exhibit 3.5, manually recalculate:<br>• Sales mix in units<br>• Sales mix in revenues<br>• Weighted average contribution margin ratio | At the end of the illustration, the store manager was considering several strategies for changing his store's sales mix. What uncertainties does the manager face? | How was CVP information used by the owner? How was it used by the manager? |

# ASSUMPTIONS AND LIMITATIONS OF COST-VOLUME-PROFIT ANALYSIS

**Q5** What assumptions and limitations should managers consider when using CVP analysis?

**CHAPTER REFERENCE**

Chapter 2 explains the importance of the relevant range in measuring the cost function.

Exhibit 3.6 summarizes the input data, assumptions, and uses of CVP analysis. CVP analysis relies on several assumptions. In Chapter 2 we assumed for the linear cost function ($F + V \times Q$) that production volumes are within a relevant range of operations where fixed costs remain fixed and variable costs remain constant. In addition, for CVP analysis, we assume that selling prices remain constant and that the sales mix is constant. Sensitivity analysis can be performed to determine the sensitivity of profits to these assumptions.

## ■ Uncertainties and Quality of Input Data

As indicated in Exhibit 3.6, CVP analysis relies on forecasts of expected revenues and costs. CVP assumptions rule out fluctuations in revenues or costs that might be caused by common business factors such as supplier volume discounts, learning curves, changes in production efficiency, or special customer discounts. In addition, many uncertainties may arise about whether CVP assumptions will be violated, such as the following:

- Can volume of operating activity be achieved?
- Will selling prices increase or decrease?
- Will sales mix remain constant?
- Will fixed or variable costs change as operations move into a new relevant range?
- Will costs change due to unforeseen causes?
- Are revenue and cost estimates biased?

**EXHIBIT 3.6** Input Data, Assumptions, and Uses of CVP Analysis

**Input Data for CVP Analysis**

Expected Revenues (volume and selling price)

Expected Costs (cost function)

Sales Mix (for multiple products)

→

**CVP Analysis and Assumptions**

Calculate number of units or revenues needed for:

- Breakeven
- Target profit

Assumptions:

- Operations within a relevant range
- Linear cost function
  - Fixed costs remain constant
  - Variable cost per unit remains constant
- Linear revenue function
  - Sales mix remains constant
  - Prices remain constant

→

**Use Results to:**

Describe volume, revenues, costs, and profits:

- Values at breakeven or target profit.:
  - Units sold
  - Revenues
  - Variable, fixed, and total costs
- Sensitivity of results to changes in:
  - Levels of activity          – Selling price
  - Cost function               – Sales mix
- Indifference point between alternatives
- Feasibility of planned operations

Assist with plans and decisions such as:

- Budgets
- Product emphasis
- Selling price
- Production or activity levels
- Employee work schedules
- Raw material purchases
- Discretionary expenditures such as advertising
- Proportions of fixed versus variable costs

Monitor operations by comparing expected and actual:

- Volumes, revenues, costs, and profits
- Profitability risk

**EXHIBIT 3.7** Examples of Business Uncertainties

| Ashanti Goldfields Company Ltd. | Bank of Montreal | Coca-Cola FEMSA, S.A. de C.V. | eBay, Inc. | Nokia Corporation | Sony Corporation |
|---|---|---|---|---|---|
| Ghana | Canada | Mexico | United States | Finland | Japan |
| Gold mining and exploration | Credit and non-credit banking services | Production and distribution of Coca-Cola products | Web-based marketplace and payment services | Mobile communications | Electronic equipment design and manufacturing |
| • Gold prices<br>• Anticipated life of mines<br>• Power supply<br>• Labor relations | • Changes in global capital markets<br>• Interest rates<br>• Regulatory changes<br>• Technological changes | • Deterioration in relationships with the Coca-Cola Company<br>• Governmental price controls<br>• More stringent environmental regulations<br>• High inflation | • Retaining active user base<br>• Consumer confidence in Web site security<br>• Management of fraud loss<br>• Retaining key employees | • Global network reliance on large multiyear contracts<br>• Failure of product quality<br>• System or network disruptions<br>• Electromagnetic field-related litigation | • Levels of consumer spending<br>• Speed and nature of technology change<br>• Change in consumer preferences<br>• Ability to reduce workforce |
| Examples adapted from "Forward-Looking Information" in Form 20-F (filed with the SEC). | Examples adapted from "Caution Regarding Forward-Looking Statements" under "Investor Relations" at www4.bmo.com. | Examples adapted from "Cautionary Statements" in presentation to J.P. Morgan, July 2003 | Examples adapted from "Risk Factors That May Affect Results of Operations and Financial Condition" in 2002 annual report. | Examples adapted from "Risk Factors" in 2002 annual report. | Examples adapted from "Cautionary Statement" under Investor Relations at www.sony.net/index.html. |

**CHAPTER REFERENCE**

We address the quality of expected revenue and cost information further in Chapter 10 (budgeting).

All organizations are subject to uncertainties, leading to risk that they will fail to meet expectations. Exhibit 3.7 summarizes major business uncertainties for six companies in a variety of industries around the world. Even though each organization is subject to unique business risks, all face uncertainties related to the economic environment. Some organizations are subject to more uncertainty than others. For example, uncertainties are greater in industries experiencing rapid technological and market change or intense competition.

## ■ Quality of CVP Technique

To help managers make better decisions, accountants evaluate the quality of the techniques they use, given the organizational setting and decisions to be made. This evaluation helps determine when techniques such as CVP analysis are likely to be an appropriate tool and how much reliance to place on the results. The quality of information generated from an analysis technique is higher if the economic setting is consistent with the technique's underlying assumptions.

Strict CVP assumptions are violated in many business settings. The types of uncertainties already discussed can lead to nonlinear behavior in revenues and costs. In addition, it may be difficult to determine the point of operating activity where operations move into a new relevant range.

Nevertheless, in many business settings CVP analysis provides useful information. Accountants and managers use their knowledge of the organization's operations and their judgment to evaluate whether the CVP assumptions are reasonable for their setting. They can rely more on CVP results when the assumptions are less likely to be violated. Also, the data used in CVP calculations must be updated continually to be useful.

## ■ CVP for Nonprofit Organizations

The basic CVP formulas in this chapter are written for typical for-profit businesses such as manufacturers, retailers, or service providers. Nonprofit organizations often receive grants and donations. These revenue sources complicate CVP calculations because they could be affected by quantity of goods or services sold. Grants and donations that are unrelated to the quantity of goods or services sold are offset against fixed costs in the CVP formulas. However, when grants and donations vary with a not-for-profit organization's operating activities, they might be included in revenues or subtracted from variable costs. The treatment depends on the nature of the grant or donation.

The following illustration continues the story of Small Animal Clinic from Chapter 2. Recall that Small Animal Clinic is a not-for-profit organization that treats small animals. It received a foundation grant that matches incoming revenues. For example, if a pet owner pays $30 in fees, the foundation matches with an additional $30 to the clinic. In this case, the grant is included in revenues for CVP calculations.

## SMALL ANIMAL CLINIC
### NOT-FOR-PROFIT ORGANIZATION CVP ANALYSIS WITH TWO RELEVANT RANGES

Leticia Brown, Small Animal Clinic manager, and the accountant, Josh Hardy, are completing the operating budget for 2006. Leticia estimated that the clinic will experience 3,800 animal visits, and Josh estimated the cost function as follows:[6]

$$TC = \$119,009 + \$16.40Q$$

where $Q$ is the number of animal visits. Leticia and Josh budgeted revenue per animal visit at $60 ($30 in fees plus $30 in matching grant). Thus, they estimated that the clinic should achieve a surplus of $46,671 [($60)(3,800) − $119,009 − ($16.40)(3,800)]. The clinic is a not-for-profit organization and pays no income taxes on its surplus.

To complete the planning process for next year, Leticia asks Josh to compute the clinic's breakeven point. As manager of a not-for-profit organization, she is particularly sensitive to financial risk and wants to know how much the clinic's activity levels could drop before a loss would occur.

### Breakeven Compared to Budget

Josh performs the following calculations. With revenue per visit of $60, the contribution margin per animal visit is

$$P - V = \$60.00 - \$16.40 = \$43.60$$

Josh solves for $Q$ with profit equal to $0 to find the breakeven point in number of animal visits:

$$Q = \frac{F + \text{Profit}}{(P - V)} = \frac{(\$119,009 + \$0)}{\$43.60} = 2,730 \text{ visits}$$

Leticia is pleased to see that the budgeted number of animal visits (3,800) is significantly higher than the breakeven number. This result gives her considerable assurance that the clinic is not likely to incur a loss, even if revenues fail to achieve targeted levels or if costs exceed estimated amounts.

### Potential Investment in New Equipment

During the first two months of 2006, Leticia learns that the number of animal visits at Small Animal Clinic is running approximately 10% higher than the budget, and costs seem to be under control. Leticia thinks that the clinic might be on track for a high surplus this year.

For the past two years, Leticia has been interested in purchasing equipment costing $200,000 to provide low-cost neutering services. This year PAWS, a local charity, offered to pay for half of the equipment cost, but only after the clinic raises the other half of the funds. Currently the clinic has no excess cash because surpluses from prior years were invested in other projects. Thus, the

*(continued)*

[6] In the Chapter 2 illustration Small Animal Clinic (Part 2), the cost function was calculated as: TC = $119,009 + ($15.20)(Number of animal visits) + (0.04)(Fee revenue). If average fee revenue is $30 per animal visit, then the last term in the cost function can be rewritten as (0.04)($30)(Number of animal visits), which can be simplified as ($1.20)(Number of animal visits). This substitution allows the cost function to be rewritten as: TC = $119,009 + ($16.40)(Number of animal visits). This version of the cost function is appropriate for estimating total costs for the clinic, but it would not be appropriate for estimating total costs for a single animal visit, where the fees vary depending on the services performed.

clinic needs to raise $100,000 to receive the PAWS grant. Leticia asks Josh to calculate the number of animal visits needed to achieve a surplus of $100,000.

## Calculating and Analyzing Targeted Activity Level

Josh calculates the expected quantity needed to achieve $100,000 surplus as follows:

$$Q = \frac{F + \text{Profit}}{P - V} = \frac{\$119,009 + \$100,000}{\$60.00 - \$16.40} = \frac{\$219,009}{\$43.60} = 5,024 \text{ animal visits}$$

He then calculates the total dollar amount of revenue needed:

$$\text{Revenues} = \frac{F + \text{Profit}}{(P - V)/P} = \frac{\$119,009 + \$100,000}{\$43.60/\$60.00} = \$310,389$$

Josh tells Leticia that the clinic will need to earn $301,389 in revenues or 5,024 visits to achieve a surplus of $100,000.

The budgeted level of activity (3,800 animal visits) is substantially higher than the level of activity needed to break even (2,730 animal visits). If animal visits continue to exceed this year's budget by 10%, Josh estimates that animal visits will reach 4,180 (3,800 × 1.10) by year-end. However, he thinks that it would be very difficult to achieve a targeted surplus of $100,000 (5,024 animal visits).

## CVP Adjusted for Change in Relevant Range

As Josh works on his report, he realizes that the clinic's cost function might change if the number of animal visits gets very high. Leticia told him that she will probably hire another technician and need to rent more space and purchase additional equipment if animal visits exceed 4,000 this year. Therefore, Josh's cost function for 5,024 visits is wrong. He develops a new cost function assuming that an additional technician, space, and equipment will increase fixed costs by about $60,000 per year.

$$TC = (\$119,009 + \$60,000) + \$16.40Q = \$179,009 + \$16.40Q, \text{ for } Q > 4,000$$

Thus, Josh's earlier CVP analysis was incorrect when animal visits exceed 4,000. The level of activity needed for a targeted surplus of $100,000 needs to be recalculated:

$$(\$179,009 + \$100,000) \div \$43.60 = 6,400 \text{ for } Q > 4,000$$

Josh notices that an activity level of 6,400 animal visits is noticeably higher than the 5,024 visits he first calculated. He realizes how important it is to adjust for the relevant range when performing CVP analyses.

When Josh shows Leticia the new results, they agree that the clinic cannot raise the funds for new equipment by increasing the number of visits to 6,400. Leticia may need to cut costs or seek other ways to pay for the neutering equipment. The additional fixed cost would also require the clinic to have a much higher volume of operations to avoid a loss.

---

### GUIDE YOUR LEARNING  3.4  Small Animal Clinic

Small Animal Clinic illustrates a CVP analysis with target profit and two relevant ranges for a not-for-profit organization. For this illustration:

| Define It | Identify Problem and Information | Identify Uncertainties | Explore Assumptions |
|---|---|---|---|
| Describe how the CVP computations change when more than one relevant range is involved. | What decisions were being addressed? Why was CVP information useful for the decisions? | What were the uncertainties? Consider uncertainties about: <br>• Revenue and cost estimates <br>• Interpreting results <br>• Relevant range of operations <br>• Feasibility of activity level | How reasonable are the CVP assumptions for Small Animal Clinic? |

# MARGIN OF SAFETY AND DEGREE OF OPERATING LEVERAGE

In Small Animal Clinic, the manager used CVP information to help her learn how much the volume of business could decline before the clinic would incur a loss. The manager of Spotted Cow Creamery was able to identify the specific products to emphasize for increased profitability. Managers are often interested in these types of questions. In addition, information from CVP analysis can be used to help manage operational risk.

**Q6** How are margin of safety and operating leverage used to assess operational risk?

## Margin of Safety

The **margin of safety** is the excess of an organization's expected future sales (in either revenue or units) above the breakeven point. The margin of safety indicates the amount by which sales could drop before profits reach the breakeven point:

> Margin of safety in units = Actual or estimated units of activity − Units at breakeven point
> Margin of safety in revenues = Actual or estimated revenue − Revenue at breakeven point

The margin of safety is computed using actual or estimated sales values, depending on the purpose. To evaluate future risk when planning, use estimated sales. To evaluate actual risk when monitoring operations, use actual sales. If the margin of safety is small, managers may put more emphasis on reducing costs and increasing sales to avoid potential losses. A larger margin of safety gives managers greater confidence in making plans such as incurring additional fixed costs.

The **margin of safety percentage** is the margin of safety divided by actual or estimated sales, in either units or revenues. This percentage indicates the extent to which sales can decline before profits become zero.

$$\text{Margin of safety percentage in units} = \frac{\text{Margin of safety in units}}{\text{Actual or estimated units}}$$

$$\text{Margin of safety percentage in revenues} = \frac{\text{Margin of safety in revenue}}{\text{Actual or estimated revenue}}$$

When the original budget was created for Small Animal Clinic, the breakeven point was calculated as 2,730 animal visits, or $163,800 in revenues. However, Leticia and Josh expected 3,800 animal visits, for $228,000 in revenue. Their margin of safety in units of animal visits was 1,070 (3,800 − 2,730) and in revenues was $64,200 ($228,000 − $163,800). Their margin of safety percentage was 28.2% (1,070 ÷ 3,800, or $64,200 ÷ $228,000). In other words, their sales volume could drop 28.2% from expected levels before they expected to incur a loss. Exhibit 3.8 provides a CVP graph for this information.

**EXHIBIT 3.8**
CVP Graph and Margin of Safety for Small Animal Clinic

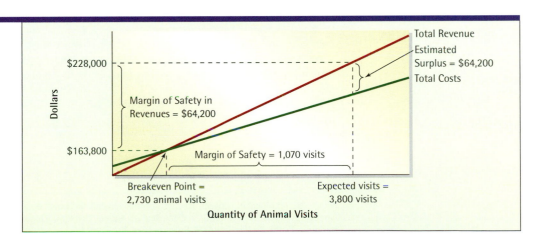

## ■ Degree of Operating Leverage

Managers decide how to structure the cost function for their organizations. Often, potential trade-offs are made between fixed and variable costs. For example, a company could purchase a vehicle (a fixed cost) or it could lease a vehicle under a contract that charges a rate per mile driven (a variable cost). Exhibit 3.9 lists some of the common advantages and disadvantages of fixed costs. One of the major disadvantages of fixed costs is that they may be difficult to reduce quickly if activity levels fail to meet expectations, thereby increasing the organization's risk of incurring losses.

The **degree of operating leverage** is the extent to which the cost function is made up of fixed costs. Organizations with high operating leverage incur more risk of loss when sales decline. Conversely, when operating leverage is high an increase in sales (once fixed costs are covered) contributes quickly to profit. The formula for operating leverage can be written in terms of either contribution margin or fixed costs, as shown here.[7]

$$\text{Degree of operating leverage in terms of contribution margin} = \frac{\text{Contribution margin}}{\text{Profit}} = \frac{TR - TVC}{\text{Profit}} = \frac{(P - V) \times Q}{\text{Profit}}$$

$$\text{Degree of operating leverage in terms of fixed costs} = \frac{F}{\text{Profit}} + 1$$

Managers use the degree of operating leverage to gauge the risk associated with their cost function and to explicitly calculate the sensitivity of profits to changes in sales (units or revenues):

$$\text{\% change in profit} = \text{\% change in sales} \times \text{Degree of operating leverage}$$

For Small Animal Clinic, the variable cost per animal visit was $16.40 and the fixed costs were $119,009. With budgeted animal visits of 3,800, the managers expected to earn a profit of $46,671. The expected degree of operating leverage using the contribution margin formula is then calculated as follows:

$$\text{Degree of operating leverage} = \frac{(\$60 - \$16.40) \times 3,800 \text{ visits}}{\$46,671} = \frac{\$165,680}{\$46,671} = 3.55$$

We arrive at the same answer of 3.55 if we use the fixed cost formula:

$$\text{Degree of operating leverage} = \frac{\$119,009}{\$46,671} + 1 = 2.55 + 1 = 3.55$$

| EXHIBIT 3.9 Advantages and Disadvantages of Fixed Costs | Common Advantages | Common Disadvantages |
|---|---|---|
| | • Fixed costs might cost less in total than variable costs.<br>• Companies might require unique assets (e.g., expert labor or specialized production facilities) that must be acquired through long-term commitments.<br>• Fixed assets such as automation and robotics equipment can significantly improve operating efficiency.<br>• Fixed costs are easier to plan; they do not fluctuate with levels of activity. | • Investing in fixed resources might divert management attention away from the organization's core competencies.<br>• Fixed costs typically require a longer financial commitment; it can be difficult to reduce them quickly.<br>• Underinvestment or overinvestment in fixed costs could affect profits and may not easily be changed in the short term. |

[7]To see the relationship between the two formulas, recall the profit equation: Profit $= (P - V) \times Q - F$, which can be rewritten as $F + \text{Profit} = \text{Contribution margin}$. In turn, Degree of operating leverage $= \text{Contribution margin} \div \text{Profit} = (F + \text{Profit}) \div \text{Profit} = (F \div \text{Profit}) + 1$.

The degree of operating leverage and margin of safety percentage are reciprocals.

$$\text{Margin of safety percentage} = \frac{1}{\text{Degree of operating leverage}}$$

$$\text{Degree of operating leverage} = \frac{1}{\text{Margin of safety percentage}}$$

If the margin of safety percentage is small, then the degree of operating leverage is large. In addition, the margin of safety percentage is smaller as the fixed cost portion of total cost gets larger. As the level of operating activity increases above the breakeven point, the margin of safety increases and the degree of operating leverage decreases. For Small Animal Clinic, the reciprocal of the margin of safety percentage is 3.55 (1 ÷ 0.282). The reciprocal of the degree of operating leverage is 0.282 (1 ÷ 3.55).

## ■ Using the Degree of Operating Leverage to Plan and Monitor Operations

Managers need to consider the degree of operating leverage when they decide whether to incur additional fixed costs, such as purchasing new equipment or hiring new employees. They also need to consider the degree of operating leverage for potential new products and services that could increase an organization's fixed costs relative to variable costs. If additional fixed costs cause the degree of operating leverage to reach what they consider an unacceptably high level, managers often use variable costs—such as temporary labor—rather than additional fixed costs to meet their operating needs.

For example, the technicians at the Small Animal Clinic are paid a salary and work 40-hour weeks. Suppose Leticia could hire part-time technicians at $20.00 per hour instead of hiring full-time technicians at the current salaries of $78,009. If each visit requires about an hour of technician time, the new cost function would be TC = ($119,009 − $78,009) + ($16.40 + $20.00)Q = $41,000 + $36.40Q. The breakeven point decreases considerably to 1,738 animal visits [$41,000 ÷ ($60.00 − $36.40) per animal visit] or $104,280. Profit at Q = 3,800 animal visits is $48,680 [$228,000 − $41,000 − (3,800 animal visits × $36.40 per animal visit)]. Operating leverage at 3,800 animal visits becomes 1.84 [($41,000 ÷ $48,680) + 1], which is much lower than the 3.55 when technicians are a fixed cost. Although operating leverage improved, the cost for technicians increased from $18.75 per hour [$78,009 ÷ (2 technicians × 2,080 hours per technician per year)] to $20.00 per hour.

The advantage of having technicians as hourly workers is that they can be scheduled only for hours when appointments are also scheduled. When business is slow fewer technician hours are needed, which means less risk of incurring losses if the number of visits drops. Exhibit 3.10 provides a CVP graph of the two options. Risk decreases considerably when the breakeven point is so much lower. On the other hand, it may be more difficult to hire qualified and dependable technicians unless work hours and pay can be guaranteed.

An **indifference point** is the level of activity at which equal cost or profit occurs across multiple alternatives. To provide Leticia with additional information as she considers changing the cost structure, Josh calculates the indifference point. Using the budgeted assumptions, Josh sets the two cost functions equal to each other and then solves for Q as follows:

$$\$41,000 + \$36.40Q = \$119,009 + \$16.40Q$$
$$\$20Q = \$78,009, \text{ so } Q = 3,901$$

When visits are fewer than 3,901, the clinic profit will be greater using more variable cost. When visits exceed 3,901, the clinic is better off using more fixed costs, assuming that the fixed costs remain constant up to 4,000 visits. When visits exceed 4,000, we know that additional fixed costs will be incurred, and then a new indifference point will need to be calculated.

---

[8]S. Kallapur and L. Eldenburg, "Uncertainty, Real Options, and Cost Behavior: Evidence from Washington State Hospitals," University of Arizona Working Paper, 2003.

**EXHIBIT 3.10** CVP Graph for Small Animal Clinic with Different Degrees of Operating Leverage

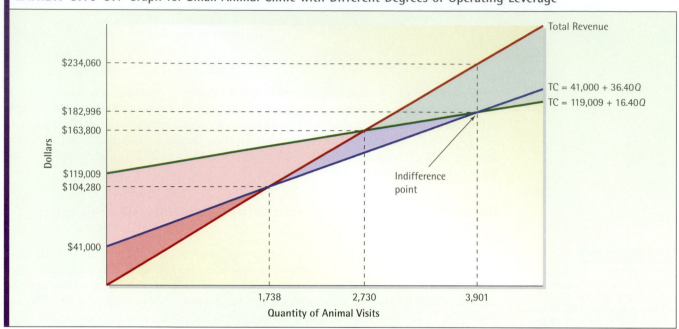

Notice that the indifference point calculation ignores operational risk. At 3,901 animal visits, the clinic is expected to earn the same profit under the two cost function alternatives. However, the clinic's operational risk is greater for the cost function having higher fixed costs. Therefore, the clinic's manager would not necessarily be indifferent between the two cost functions if 3,901 animal visits were expected.

| GUIDE YOUR LEARNING | 3.5 | Key Terms |
| --- | --- | --- |

Stop to confirm that you understand the new terms introduced in the last several pages:

Margin of safety (p. 103)          Degree of operating leverage (p. 104)
Margin of safety percentage (p. 103)   Indifference point (p. 105)

For each of these terms, write a definition in your own words.

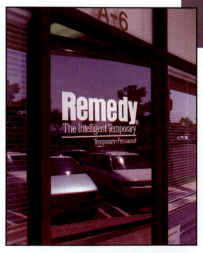

## FOCUS ON ETHICAL DECISION MAKING
### Temporary Labor

In recent years, U.S. companies have increasingly relied on temporary labor (also called contingent or contract workers) to fill positions that in the past would have been filled by regular employees. Temporary jobs span the entire workforce including manufacturing, service, farm, and professional services. Managers gain many benefits including the following:

● Reduce risk of loss by increasing the proportion of variable costs.
● Quickly increase and decrease employment levels in response to economic changes.
● Pay higher wages to skilled workers without inflating the pay scales of regular employees.
● Pay lower wages and avoid making hiring commitments to low-skilled employees.
● Fill positions while recruiting permanent workers during labor shortages.

Many economists and business analysts argue that temporary labor is good for workers and the economy. Temporary work arrangements provide the following economic benefits:

- Reduce overall unemployment levels because employers are less reluctant to hire temporary labor than regular employees.
- Increase employment opportunities for new workforce entrants, workers laid off from jobs, and workers wanting flexible work schedules.
- Improve regular employee morale by reducing their unemployment risk.

On the other hand, labor groups, homeless advocacy groups, and others believe that temporary labor arrangements are socially harmful. They argue that the use of temporary labor contributes to the following issues:

- Unfairly reduces overall pay scales for skilled and unskilled workers.
- Increases unemployment risk for the least-skilled and lowest-paid workers, contributing to poverty and homelessness.
- Reduces worker representation as well as health care and retirement benefits.

SOURCES: J. C. Cooper and K. Madigan, "U.S.: Labor's New Flexibility Cuts Two Ways," *Business Week,* December 24, 2001; and S. N. Houseman, A. L. Kalleberg, and G. A. Erickcek, "The Role of Temporary Help Employment in Tight Labor Markets," Upjohn Institute Staff Working Paper No. 01-73, July 2001. Available at www.upjohninst.org/publications/wp/01-73.pdf.

### Practice Ethical Decision Making

In Chapter 1, we learned about a process for making ethical decisions (Exhibit 1.11). You can address the following questions to improve your skills for making ethical decisions. Think about your answers to these questions and discuss them with others.

| Ethical Decision-Making Process | Questions to Consider about This Ethical Dilemma |
|---|---|
| Identify ethical problems as they arise. | Does the hiring of temporary labor create an ethical problem? Why or why not? |
| Objectively consider the well-being of others and society when exploring alternatives. | Different viewpoints for this problem were described in the preceding example. What assumptions lie behind each viewpoint? |
| Clarify and apply ethical values when choosing a course of action. | Is the hiring of temporary labor a business issue, a social issue, or both? Explain. Identify the values you use to answer the following questions:<br>• Is it fair for employers to pay different wage rates and provide different benefits to temporary and permanent workers who perform the same jobs?<br>• Is it fair for businesses to pass their business risks directly on to the employees? |
| Work toward ongoing improvement of personal and organizational ethics. | How can company managers determine on an ongoing basis whether their hiring practices are ethical? |

## APPENDIX 3A

### Spreadsheet Formulas for Magik Bicycles Spreadsheet

The following formulas were used for the spreadsheet shown in Exhibit 3.2.

| | A | B | C | D | E |
|---|---|---|---|---|---|
| 1 | | | | | |
| 2 | **Input section** | Youth Bikes | Road Bikes | Mtn. Bikes | |
| 3 | Expected sales volume-units | 10,000 | 18,000 | 12,000 | |
| 4 | Price per unit | 200 | 700 | 800 | |
| 5 | Variable cost per unit | 75 | 250 | 300 | |
| 6 | | | | | |
| 7 | Fixed costs | 14,700,000 | | | |
| 8 | Desired after-tax profit | 100,000 | (enter zero for breakeven) | | |
| 9 | Income tax rate | 0.3 | | | |
| 10 | | | | | |
| 11 | | | | | |
| 12 | **Contribution Margin** | Youth Bikes | Road Bikes | Mtn. Bikes | Total Bikes |
| 13 | Units | =B3 | =C3 | =D3 | =SUM(B3:D3) |
| 14 | Revenue | =B3*B4 | =C3*C4 | =D3*D4 | =SUM(B14:D14) |
| 15 | Variable costs | =B5*B3 | =C5*C3 | =D5*D3 | =SUM(B15:D15) |
| 16 | Contribution margin | =B14-B15 | =C14-C15 | =D14-D15 | =SUM(B16:D16) |
| 17 | | | | | |
| 18 |   Contrib. margin per unit | =B16/B13 | =C16/C13 | =D16/D13 | =E16/E13 |
| 19 |   Contrib. margin ratio | =B16/B14 | =C16/C14 | =D16/D14 | =E16/E14 |
| 20 | | | | | |
| 21 | Expected sales mix in units | =B3/$E13 | =C3/$E13 | =D3/$E13 | =SUM(B21:D21) |
| 22 | Expected sales mix in revenues | =B14/$E14 | =C14/$E14 | =D14/$E14 | =SUM(B22:D22) |
| 23 | | | | | |
| 24 | **Expected Income** | | | | |
| 25 | Contribution margin (above) | | | | =E16 |
| 26 | Fixed costs | | | | =B7 |
| 27 |   Pretax income | | | | =E16-E26 |
| 28 | Income taxes | | | | =B9*E27 |
| 29 |   After-tax income | | | | =E27-E28 |
| 30 | | | | | |
| 31 | **Preliminary CVP Calculations** | | | | |
| 32 | Target pretax profit for CVP analysis | | | | =B8/(1-B9) |
| 33 | Fixed costs plus target pretax profit | | | | =B7+E32 |
| 34 | | | | | |
| 35 | **CVP analysis in units** | Youth Bikes | Road Bikes | Mtn. Bikes | Total Bikes |
| 36 | CVP calculation in units | =B21*$E$36 | =C21*$E$36 | =D21*$E$36 | =E33/E18 |
| 37 | Revenue | =B36*B4 | =C36*C4 | =D36*D4 | =SUM(B37:D37) |
| 38 | Variable costs | =B36*B5 | =C36*C5 | =D36*D5 | =SUM(B38:D38) |
| 39 | Contribution margin | =B37-B38 | =C37-C38 | =D37-D38 | =E37-E38 |
| 40 | Fixed costs | | | | =B7 |
| 41 | Pretax income | | | | =E39-E40 |
| 42 | Income taxes | | | | =E41*B9 |
| 43 | After-tax income | | | | =E41-E42 |
| 44 | | | | | |
| 45 | **CVP analysis in revenues** | Youth Bikes | Road Bikes | Mtn. Bikes | Total Bikes |
| 46 | CVP calculation in revenues | =$E$46*B22 | =$E$46*C22 | =$E$46*D22 | =E33/E19 |
| 47 | Variable costs | =B46*B5/B4 | =C46*C5/C4 | =D46*D5/D4 | =SUM(B47:D47) |
| 48 | Contribution margin | =B46-B47 | =C46-C47 | =D46-D47 | =E46-E47 |
| 49 | Fixed costs | | | | =B7 |
| 50 | Pretax income | | | | =E48-E49 |
| 51 | Income taxes | | | | =B9*E50 |
| 52 | After-tax income | | | | =E50-E51 |

# SUMMARY

 **What Is Cost–Volume–Profit (CVP) Analysis, and How Is It Used for Decision Making?**

### Cost-Volume-Profit (CVP) Analysis
A technique that examines changes in profits in response to changes in sales volumes, costs, and prices

### CVP Graph
Shows the relationship between total revenues and total costs; illustrates how an organization's profits are expected to change under different volumes of activity

### Uses

Describe volume, revenues, costs, and profits:

- Values at breakeven or target profit:
  - Units sold
  - Revenues
  - Variable, fixed, and total costs
- Sensitivity of results to changes in:
  - Levels of activity    – Selling price
  - Cost function    – Sales mix
- Indifference point between alternatives
- Feasibility of planned operations

Assist with plans and decisions such as:

- Budgets
- Product emphasis
- Selling price
- Production or activity levels
- Employee work schedules
- Raw material purchases

- Discretionary expenditures such as advertising
- Proportions of fixed versus variable costs

Monitor operations by comparing expected and actual:

- Volumes, revenues, costs, and profits
- Profitability risk

## Q2  How Are CVP Calculations Performed for a Single Product?

### CVP Formulas

**CVP analysis in units needed to attain target profit:**

$$Q = \frac{F + \text{Profit}}{\text{Contribution margin per unit}} = \frac{F + \text{Profit}}{P - V}$$

**CVP analysis in revenues needed to attain target profit:**

$$\text{Revenues} = \frac{F + \text{Profit}}{\text{Contribution margin ratio}} = \frac{F + \text{Profit}}{(P - V)/P} = \frac{F + \text{Profit}}{(\text{TR} - \text{TVC})/\text{TR}}$$

**Pretax profit needed to achieve a given level of after-tax profit:**

$$\text{Pretax profit} = \frac{\text{After-tax profit}}{(1 - \text{Tax rate})}$$

## Q3  How Are CVP Calculations Performed for Multiple Products?

### Use CVP Formulas for a Single Product, Except

$$\text{Weighted average contribution margin per unit} = \frac{\text{Total expected contribution margin}}{\text{Total expected number of units}}$$

$$\text{Weighted average contribution margin ratio} = \frac{\text{Total expected contribution margin}}{\text{Total expected revenue}}$$

## Q4  What Is the Breakeven Point?

### Breakeven Point

Level of operating activity at which revenues cover all fixed and variable costs, resulting in zero profit.

### Calculation

Set target profit equal to zero in the CVP formula.

## Q5  What Assumptions and Limitations Should Managers Consider When Using CVP Analysis?

### CVP Assumptions

- Operations within a relevant range of activity
- Linear cost function
  - Fixed costs remain fixed.
  - Variable cost per unit remains constant.
- Linear revenue function
  - Sales mix remains constant.
  - Prices remain constant.

### Uncertainties

- Actual future volumes, revenues, and costs are unknown.
- CVP assumptions might not hold.

### In Light of Assumptions and Uncertainties, Need to Evaluate:

- Quality of data used in CVP analyses
- Suitability of CVP analysis for the setting
- Sensitivity of CVP results to changes in data for important uncertainties

**How Are Margin of Safety and Operating Leverage Used to Assess Operational Risk?**

## Margin of Safety

$$\text{Margin of safety in units} = \text{Actual or estimated units of activity} - \text{Units at breakeven point}$$

$$\text{Margin of safety in revenues} = \text{Actual or estimated revenue} - \text{Revenue at breakeven point}$$

$$\text{Margin of safety percentage} = \frac{\text{Margin of safety in units}}{\text{Actual or estimated units}} = \frac{\text{Margin of safety in revenues}}{\text{Actual or estimated revenues}}$$

## Degree of Operating Leverage

**In terms of contribution margin:**

$$\text{Degree of operating leverage} = \frac{\text{Contribution margin}}{\text{Profit}} = \frac{TR - TVC}{\text{Profit}} = \frac{(P - V) \times Q}{\text{Profit}}$$

**In terms of fixed costs:**

$$\text{Degree of operating leverage} = \frac{F}{\text{Profit}} + 1$$

**Sensitivity of profits to changes in sales (units or revenues):**

$$\% \text{ change in profit} = \% \text{ change in sales} \times \text{Degree of operating leverage}$$

## Relationship Between Margin of Safety and Degree of Operating Leverage

$$\text{Margin of safety percentage} = \frac{1}{\text{Degree of operating leverage}}$$

## Higher Operating Leverage (Lower Margin of Safety) Leads to:

- Greater risk of loss
- Accelerated profits above the breakeven point

---

### KEY TO SYMBOLS

**e** This question requires students to extend knowledge beyond the applications shown in the textbook.

**1** This question requires Step 1 skills (**Identifying**) in Steps for Better Thinking (Exhibit 1.10).

**2** This question requires Step 2 skills (**Exploring**) in Steps for Better Thinking (Exhibit 1.10).

**3** This question requires Step 3 skills (**Prioritizing**) in Steps for Better Thinking (Exhibit 1.10).

**4** This question requires Step 4 skills (**Envisioning**) in Steps for Better Thinking (Exhibit 1.10).

---

## Self-Study Problems

**Self-Study Problem 1** **Cost Function, Target Profit, Margin of Safety, Operating Leverage**

Q1, Q3, Q5, Q6   Coffee Cart Supreme sells hot and iced coffee beverages and small snacks. The following is last month's income statement.

| | | |
|---|---:|---:|
| Revenue | | $5,000 |
| Cost of beverages and snacks | $2,000 | |
| Cost of napkins, straws, etc. | 500 | |
| Cost to rent cart | 500 | |
| Employee wages | 1,000 | 4,000 |
| Pretax profit | | 1,000 |
| Taxes | | 250 |
| After-tax profit | | $ 750 |

**REQUIRED:**

**②** **A.** What is the total cost function for Coffee Cart Supreme?

**ⓔ** **B.** What is the tax rate for Coffee Cart Supreme?

**C.** Calculate the amount of sales needed to reach a target after-tax profit of $1,500.

**D.** What was Coffee Cart Supreme's degree of operating leverage last month?

**E.** What was Coffee Cart Supreme's margin of safety in revenue last month?

**F.** What was Coffee Cart Supreme's margin of safety percentage last month?

**ⓔ** **G.** Suppose next month's actual revenues are $8,000 and pretax profit is $2,000. Would actual costs be higher or lower than expected?

**②** **H.** Coffee costs are volatile because worldwide coffee production varies from year to year. Explain how this volatility affects the quality of the cost function for Coffee Cart Supreme.

### Solution to Self–Study Problem 1

**A.** To estimate the cost function, we use judgment to classify costs as fixed, variable, or mixed. For a typical retail business, rent and wages are likely to be fixed. We estimate fixed costs as the sum of these two costs ($500 + $1,000 = $1,500). It seems reasonable that the costs of beverages and snacks ($2,000) and napkins, straws, etc. ($500) would vary with revenues. We use the revenues as the cost driver to estimate variable costs as $2,500 ÷ $5,000 = 0.50, or 50% of revenues. Thus, the cost function is

$$TC = \$1,500 + (50\% \times Revenue)$$

**B.** We use income tax expense and pretax profit from last month to estimate the tax rate:

$$Tax\ rate = Taxes \div Pretax\ profit = \$250 \div \$1,000 = 25\%$$

**C.** We first calculate the amount of pretax profit needed to achieve an after-tax profit of $1,500.

$$Targeted\ pretax\ profit = \$1,500 \div (1 - 0.25) = \$2,000$$

The contribution margin ratio is

$$(5,000 - 2,500) \div 5,000 = 0.50\ or\ 50\%$$

We then perform the CVP calculation for revenues.

$$Revenue = (\$1,500 + \$2,000) \div 0.50 = \$3,500 \div 0.50 = \$7,000$$

**D.** We use the results of our previous computations to calculate the contribution margin, and we then calculate the degree of operating leverage:

$$Contribution\ margin = \$5,000 - \$2,500 = \$2,500$$
$$Degree\ of\ operating\ leverage = Contribution\ margin \div Profit$$
$$Degree\ of\ operating\ leverage = \$2,500 \div \$1,000 = 2.50$$

**E.** Before calculating the margin of safety, we need to calculate the breakeven point. Note that the margin of safety must be calculated in revenue dollars. We do not have unit or product mix information. The breakeven point is calculated as

$$\$1,500 \div 0.50 = \$3,000\ in\ revenues$$

Current revenues are $5,000, so the margin of safety is calculated as

$$Margin\ of\ safety = \$5,000 - \$3,000 = \$2,000$$

**F.** We use the formula to calculate margin of safety percentage:

$$Margin\ of\ safety\ percentage = \$2,000 \div \$5,000 = 40\%$$

Note that we can check our previous degree of operating leverage computation as follows:

$$Degree\ of\ operating\ leverage = 1 \div Margin\ of\ safety\ percentage = 1 \div 0.40 = 2.50$$

**G.** The expected and actual costs at $8,000 revenue are

$$Expected\ Costs = \$1,500 + (50\% \times \$8,000) = \$5,500$$
$$Actual\ Costs = \$8,000 - \$2,000 = \$6,000$$

Actual costs are $500 higher than expected.

H. When any costs are volatile, predicting them is problematic. Worldwide coffee prices are uncertain for many reasons, such as weather conditions in coffee growing areas, the ability of farmers to increase crops, and coffee demand patterns. In addition, broader factors such as changes in economies and political upheaval influence costs. All of these factors reduce our ability to develop a cost function that accurately predicts future costs, which means that the quality of the cost function is diminished.

### Self-Study Problem 2   Sensitivity Analysis

**Q1, Q2, Q5**

**www.wiley.com/college/eldenburg**

**REQUIRED:**

The spreadsheet developed for the Magik Bicycles examples in this chapter is available on the Web at www.wiley.com/college/eldenburg. Download the template and use the spreadsheet to answer the following questions. A printout of the formulas used in the spreadsheet is available in Appendix 3A.

**②** A. Examine the spreadsheet so that you understand how the cells in the data input section are referenced. When all of the decision variables are located in one place in the spreadsheet, accountants and managers can easily perform sensitivity analysis by changing values in the data input section. Why is it important to be able to change the spreadsheet easily to reflect changes in assumptions?

B. Suppose that Magik adds a helmet to each youth bike sold. The helmets cost $25 each but incorporate new materials and an innovative design that has reduced injuries and deaths from children's bike accidents. Magik's managers believe that by advertising the new helmet as part of the youth bike package, sales will increase to 13,000. However, an advertising campaign will need to be undertaken to alert parents to the benefits of the new helmet. How much can Magik afford to spend on advertising and still expect to earn the original after-tax profit of $455,000? Assume the selling price remains at $200 per bike package.

**③** C. Identify CVP input factors that you believe are uncertain for this decision, and use your judgment to determine a new value for each factor. Reflect these changes in the spreadsheet to see how they affect the breakeven point and profitability. Choose a best-case and worst-case scenario to present to the managers of Magik Bicycles. Make a list of the points you would include in a memo explaining your sensitivity analysis to the managers.

### Solution to Self-Study Problem 2

A. Accountants and managers will explore changes in more assumptions and vary the values within the spreadsheet more readily if it is easy to do. When these changes are made and the results are analyzed, managers better understand how unplanned changes in future operations might affect profitability. This knowledge allows them to more readily evaluate results and adjust operating plans.

B. Exhibit 3.11 provides relevant parts of the spreadsheet with the changes. With increased sales of youth bikes from 10,000 to 13,000 and an increased variable cost from $75 to $100, expected pretax profits increase to $700,000. Comparing $700,000 to $650,000 (Exhibit 3.2), Magik can spend up to $50,000 on advertising to maintain its current level of profitability.

C. Many different scenarios could occur. No single answer is always correct. Your answer depends on the assumptions that you make. Following are some example assumptions for the best and worst cases. Your most likely case should be between these two values.

One best case is that the new strategy is very popular with customers. More than 13,000 of the bikes are sold. The managers discover that customers are willing to pay a higher price for the bike, so they raise the price. In addition, manufacturing efficiency improves with the greater volume, reducing variable cost per unit. Also, fixed costs are lower than expected because the managers found some costs that could be reduced.

One worst case is that the helmets fail to attract customers. In fact, sales fail to meet original expectations; fewer than 10,000 are sold. Because the company produced extra bikes expecting an increase in demand, the managers lower the selling price to encourage additional sales. In addition, the company hires extra workers to meet the expected demand, and other costs such as insurance and electricity are higher than expected. These changes caused both the variable and fixed costs to be higher than originally planned.

Your memo to the managers should include the following:
- Explain the assumptions for the best case and worst case scenarios.
- Explain the reasoning behind the most likely case.
- Ask managers to consider beforehand how they would respond to the best- and worst-case scenarios.
- Make suggestions for monitoring the results for the youth bike.
- Encourage the managers to evaluate the advertising and product results, and make suggestions for improving the operation or dropping the new helmet, if plans are unsuccessful.

**EXHIBIT 3.11**
Spreadsheet for Magik
Bicycles Youth Helmet
Decision

|  | A | B | C | D | E |
|---|---|---|---|---|---|
| 1 |  |  |  |  |  |
| 2 | **Input section** | Youth Bikes | Road Bikes | Mtn. Bikes |  |
| 3 | Expected sales volume-units | 13,000 | 18,000 | 12,000 |  |
| 4 | Price per unit | $200 | $700 | $800 |  |
| 5 | Variable cost per unit | $100 | $250 | $300 |  |
| 6 |  |  |  |  |  |
| 7 | Fixed costs | $14,700,000 |  |  |  |
| 8 | Desired after-tax profit | $100,000 | (enter zero for breakeven) |  |  |
| 9 | Income tax rate | 30% |  |  |  |
| 10 |  |  |  |  |  |
| 11 |  |  |  |  |  |
| 12 | **Contribution Margin** | Youth Bikes | Road Bikes | Mtn. Bikes | Total Bikes |
| 13 | Units | 13,000 | 18,000 | 12,000 | 43,000 |
| 14 | Revenue | $2,600,000 | $12,600,000 | $9,600,000 | $24,800,000 |
| 15 | Variable costs | 1,300,000 | 4,500,000 | 3,600,000 | 9,400,000 |
| 16 | Contribution margin | $1,300,000 | $8,100,000 | $6,000,000 | $15,400,000 |
| 17 |  |  |  |  |  |
| 18 | Contrib. margin per unit | $100.00 | $450.00 | $500.00 | $358.14 |
| 19 | Contrib. margin ratio | 50.00% | 64.29% | 62.50% | 62.10% |
| 20 |  |  |  |  |  |
| 21 | Expected sales mix in units | 30.23% | 41.86% | 27.91% | 100.00% |
| 22 | Expected sales mix in revenues | 10.48% | 50.81% | 38.71% | 100.00% |
| 23 |  |  |  |  |  |
| 24 | **Expected Income** |  |  |  |  |
| 25 | Contribution margin (above) |  |  |  | $15,400,000 |
| 26 | Fixed costs |  |  |  | 14,700,000 |
| 27 | Pretax income |  |  |  | 700,000 |
| 28 | Income taxes |  |  |  | 210,000 |
| 29 | After-tax income |  |  |  | $490,000 |

**REVIEW** Use the following boxes from the chapter to review key terms and key techniques, analyze chapter illustrations, improve your learning of new concepts, and practice ethical decision making:

Guide Your Learning 3.1: Key Terms (p. 91)

Guide Your Learning 3.2: The Spotted Cow Creamery (Part 1) (p. 93)

Guide Your Learning 3.3: The Spotted Cow Creamery (Part 2) (p. 98)

Guide Your Learning 3.4: Small Animal Clinic (p. 102)

Guide Your Learning 3.5: Key Terms (p. 106)

Focus on Ethical Decision Making: Temporary Labor (p. 107)

## QUESTIONS

**3.1** If a firm has a mixed cost function, a 10% increase in sales volume should increase income by more than 10%. Explain why.

**3.2** Explain how to calculate a weighted average contribution margin per unit.

**3.3** An organization experiences a 20% increase in pretax profits when revenues increase 20%. Assuming linearity, what do you know about the organization's cost function?

**3.4** What is the effect on a firm's breakeven point of a lower income tax rate?

**3.5** To estimate revenues, costs, and profits across a range of activity, we usually assume that the cost and revenue functions are linear. What are the specific underlying assumptions for linear cost and revenue functions, and how reasonable are these assumptions?

**3.6** Explain the relationship between margin of safety percentage and degree of operating leverage.

**3.7** How do volume discounts from suppliers affect our assumption that the cost function is linear? Explain how we incorporate this type of cost into a CVP analysis.

**3.8** Explain the term *sales mix* in your own words. How does sales mix affect the contribution margin?

**3.9** How are CVP analysis and breakeven analysis related?

**3.10** Can the margin of safety ever be negative? Explain your answer.

**3.11** Describe three uses for CVP analysis.

**3.12** Explain how CVP analysis can be used to make decisions about increases in advertising costs.

**3.13** Under what circumstances will managers want sensitivity analysis around results from a CVP analysis?

# EXERCISES

**3.14** **Target profit, not-for-profit breakeven**
Q2, Q4
    **A.** The variable cost per gift basket is $2, fixed costs are $5,000 per month, and the selling price of a basket is $7. How many baskets must be produced and sold in a month to earn a pretax profit of $1,000?

    ⓔ **B.** The Community Clinic (a not-for-profit medical clinic) received a lump-sum grant from the City of Tucson of $460,000 this year. The fixed costs of the clinic are expected to be $236,000. The average variable cost per patient visit is expected to be $7.64 and the average fee collected per patient visit is $4.64. What is the breakeven volume in patient visits?

**3.15** **CVP graph**
Q2, Q4
    **A.** Create a CVP graph using the information in Exercise 3.14, part (A). Explain the information in the graph.

    ⓔ **B.** Create a CVP graph using the information in Exercise 3.14, part (B). Explain the information in the graph.

**3.16** **Cost function, breakeven**
Q2, Q4
    ⓔ **A.** The average cost per unit was $234 at a volume of 1,200 units and $205 at a volume of 1,400 units. The profit was $24,000 at the lower volume. Estimate the variable cost per unit.

    ⓔ **B.** Sparkle Car Wash Supplier sells a hose washer for $0.25 that it buys from the manufacturer for $0.12. Variable selling costs are $0.02 per hose washer. Breakeven is currently at a sales volume of $10,600 per month. What are the monthly fixed costs associated with the washer?

    ⓔ **C.** Monthly fixed costs are $24,000 when volume is at or below 200 units and $36,000 when monthly volume is above 200 units. The variable cost per unit is $200 and the selling price is $300 per unit. What is the breakeven quantity?

**3.17** **Profit, price for target profit** The Martell Company has recently established operations in a competitive market. Management has been aggressive in its attempt to establish a market share. The price of the product was set at $5 per unit, well below that of the company's major competitors. Variable costs were $4.50 per unit, and total fixed costs were $600,000 during the first year.
Q2

REQUIRED:
    **A.** Assume that the firm was able to sell 1 million units in the first year. What was the pretax profit (loss) for the year?

    ⓔ **B.** Assume that the variable cost per unit and total fixed costs do not increase in the second year. Management has been successful in establishing its position in the market. What price must be set to achieve a pretax profit of $25,000? Assume that sales remain at 1 million units.

**3.18** **Cost function, breakeven** Data for the most recent three months of operations for the RainBeau Salon appear here:
Q4

|  | March | April | May |
|---|---|---|---|
| Number of appointments | 1,600 | 1,500 | 1,900 |
|  |  |  |  |
| Hair dresser salaries | $14,000 | $14,000 | $18,000 |
| Manicurist salaries | 12,000 | 12,000 | 16,000 |
| Supplies | 900 | 750 | 950 |
| Utilities | 600 | 480 | 400 |
| Rent | 1,000 | 1,000 | 1,000 |
| Miscellaneous | 3,500 | 3,450 | 3,580 |
| Total costs | $32,000 | $31,680 | $39,930 |

A general cost-of-living salary increase occurred at the beginning of May.

REQUIRED:
    ② **A.** What is the total cost function for RainBeau Salon?

    **B.** If the average fee per appointment is $25, estimate the appointments required in June to break even.

**3.19** **Breakeven, target profit, ROI target profit** Madden Company projected its income before taxes for next year as shown here. Madden is subject to a 40% income tax rate.
Ⓒ Q2, Q4

| Sales (160,000 units) | $8,000,000 |
|---|---|
| Cost of sales | |
| Variable costs | 2,000,000 |
| Fixed costs | 3,000,000 |
| Pretax profit | $3,000,000 |

**REQUIRED:**

**A.** What is Madden's breakeven point in units sold for the next year?

**B.** If Madden wants $4.5 million in pretax profit, what is the required level of sales in dollars?

 **C.** If Madden's net assets are $36 million, what amount of revenue must be achieved for Madden to earn a 10% after-tax return on assets?

**3.20**
**Q1, Q2, Q4**

**Breakeven, target profit, cost changes, selling price** Laraby Company produces a single product. It sold 25,000 units last year with the following results.

| Sales | $625,000 |
|---|---|
| Variable costs | 375,000 |
| Fixed costs | 150,000 |
| Income before taxes | 100,000 |
| Income taxes (45%) | 45,000 |
| After-tax profit | $ 55,000 |

In an attempt to improve its product, Laraby's managers are considering replacing a component part that costs $2.50 with a new and better part costing $4.50 per unit during the coming year. A new machine would also be needed to increase plant capacity. The machine would cost $18,000 and have a useful life of 6 years with no salvage value. The company uses straight-line depreciation on all plant assets.

**REQUIRED:**

**A.** What was Laraby Company's breakeven point in units last year?

**B.** How many units of product would Laraby Company have had to sell in the past year to earn $77,000 in after-tax profit?

 **C.** If Laraby Company holds the sales price constant and makes the suggested changes, how many units of product must be sold in the coming year to break even?

**D.** If Laraby Company holds the sales price constant and makes the suggested changes, how many units of product will the company have to sell to make the same after-tax profit as last year?

 **E.** If Laraby Company wishes to maintain the same contribution margin ratio, what selling price per unit of product must it charge next year to cover the increased materials costs?

**3.21**
**Q3**

**Target profit, progressive income tax rates, CVP graph** Dalton Brothers pay 15% in taxes on income between $1 and $40,000. All income above $40,000 is taxed at 40%. The firm's variable costs as a percent of revenues are 60%. Annual fixed costs are $250,000.

**REQUIRED:**

 **A.** What level of sales must the firm achieve to earn income after taxes of $150,000?

 **B.** Prepare a CVP graph for Dalton.

**3.22**
**Q1, Q3, Q4**

**Breakeven, selling price, target profit with price and cost changes** All-Day Candy Company is a wholesale distributor of candy. The company services grocery, convenience, and drug stores in a large metropolitan area. Small but steady growth in sales has been achieved by the All-Day Candy Company over the past few years, but candy prices also have been increasing. The company is reformulating its plans for the coming fiscal year. The following data were used to project the current year's after-tax income of $100,400.

| Average selling price | | $4.00 per box |
|---|---|---|
| Average variable costs | | |
| Cost of candy | | $2.00 per box |
| Selling costs | | 0.40 per box |
| Total | | $2.40 per box |
| Annual fixed costs | | |
| Selling | | $160,000 |
| Administrative | | 280,000 |
| Total | | $440,000 |

Expected annual sales (390,000 boxes) = $1,560,000
Tax rate = 40%

Candy manufacturers have announced that they will increase prices of their products an average of 15% in the coming year because of increases in raw material (sugar, cocoa, peanuts, and so on) and labor costs. All-Day Candy Company expects that all other costs will remain the same as during the current year.

**REQUIRED:**

**A.** What is All-Day Candy Company's breakeven point in boxes of candy for the current year?

**ⓔ B.** What average selling price per box must All-Day Candy Company charge to cover the 15% increase in the variable cost of candy and still maintain the current contribution margin ratio?

**ⓔ C.** What volume of sales in dollars must the All-Day Candy Company achieve in the coming year to maintain the same after-tax income as projected for the current year if the average selling price of candy remains at $4.00 per box and the cost of candy increases 15%?

**3.23**  **Breakeven, operating leverage, cost function decision** You are the advisor of a Junior Achievement group in a local high school. You need to help the group make a decision about fees that must
**Q1, Q2, Q4, Q6**  be paid to sell gardening tools at the Home and Garden Show. The group sells a set of tools for $20.00. The manufacturing cost (all variable) is $6 per set. The Home and Garden Show coordinator allows the following three payment options for groups exhibiting and selling at the show:

1. Pay a fixed booth fee of $5,600.
2. Pay a fee of $3,800 plus 10% of all revenue from tool sets sold at the show.
3. Pay 15% of all revenue from tool sets sold at the show.

**REQUIRED:**

**A.** Compute the breakeven number of tool sets for each option.
**B.** Which payment plan has the highest degree of operating leverage?
**ⓔ C.** Which payment plan has the lowest risk of loss for the organization? Explain.
**D.** At what level of revenue should the group be indifferent to options 1 and 2?
**E.** Which option should Junior Achievement choose, assuming sales are expected to be 1,000 sets of tools? Explain.

**3.24**  **ROI target profit, foreign exchange rates** Borg Controls has a net investment in its German sub-
**Q3**  sidiary of $2.68 million. The firm attempts to earn a 15% pretax return on its investment. Variable costs for the German subsidiary are 60% of revenues. Annual fixed costs are €321,000. For the current year, the manager of the German subsidiary anticipates revenues of €1.7 million. The exchange rate is expected to be €1.2 = $1.

**REQUIRED:**

**ⓔ A.** If operations meet expectations, what is the rate of return that Borg Controls will earn from its German subsidiary? (*Hint*: Calculate the rate of return by dividing pretax income by the net investment.)

**ⓔ B.** What level of revenue in euros would be required of the subsidiary for the parent to earn exactly a 15% rate of return in dollars, assuming no changes in the exchange rate?

**3.25**  **Target profit, margin of safety, operating leverage** The following budget data apply to Newberry's
**Q2, Q6**  Nutrition:

| | | |
|---|---|---|
| Sales (100,000 units) | | $1,000,000 |
| Costs | | |
|     Direct materials | $300,000 | |
|     Direct labor | 200,000 | |
|     Fixed factory overhead | 100,000 | |
|     Variable factory overhead | 150,000 | |
|     Marketing and administration | 160,000 | |
| Total costs | | 910,000 |
| Budgeted pretax income | | $ 90,000 |

Direct labor workers are paid hourly wages and go home when there is no work. The marketing and administration costs include $50,000 that varies proportionately with production volume. Assume that sales and production volumes are equal.

**REQUIRED:**
**A.** Compute the number of units that must be sold to achieve a target after-tax income of $120,000, assuming the tax rate is 40%.
**B.** Calculate the margin of safety in both revenues and units.
**C.** Calculate the degree of operating leverage.

**3.26**
**Q2, Q4, Q6**
**Breakeven, target profit, margin of safety, operating leverage** Pike Street Taffy makes and sells taffy in a variety of flavors in a shop located in the local public market. Data for a recent week are as follows:

| | | |
|---|---:|---:|
| Revenue (2,000 lbs. @ $4.80 per lb.) | | $9,600 |
| Cost of ingredients | $3,200 | |
| Rent | 800 | |
| Wages | 4,800 | 8,800 |
| Pretax income | | 800 |
| Taxes (20%) | | 160 |
| After-tax income | | $ 640 |

All employees work standard shifts, no matter how much taffy is produced or sold.

**REQUIRED:**
**A.** Calculate the breakeven point in units and in revenue.
**B.** Calculate the number of units and the amount of revenues that would be needed for after-tax income of $3,000.
**C.** Calculate the margin of safety in units and the margin of safety percentage.
**D.** Calculate the degree of operating leverage.

**3.27**
**Q2, Q4, Q6**
**Breakeven, target profit, margin of safety** Vines and Daughter manufactures and sells swimsuits for $40 each. The estimated income statement for 2005 is as follows:

| | |
|---|---:|
| Sales | $2,000,000 |
| Variable costs | 1,100,000 |
| Contribution margin | 900,000 |
| Fixed costs | 765,000 |
| Pretax profit | $ 135,000 |

**REQUIRED:**
**A.** Compute the contribution margin per swimsuit and the number of swimsuits that must be sold to break even.
**B.** What is the margin of safety in the number of swimsuits?
**C.** Suppose the margin of safety was 5,000 swimsuits in 2004. Are operations more or less risky in 2005 as compared to 2004? Explain.
**D.** Compute the contribution margin ratio and the breakeven point in revenues.
**E.** What is the margin of safety in revenues?
**F.** Suppose next year's revenue estimate is $200,000 higher. What would be the estimated pretax profit?
**G.** Assume a tax rate of 30%. How many swimsuits must be sold to earn an after-tax profit of $180,000?

# PROBLEMS

**3.28**
**Q2, Q4, Q5**
**Cost function, breakeven, quality of information, relevant range** Oysters Away picks, shucks, and packs oysters and then sells them wholesale to fine restaurants across the state. The income statement for last year follows:

| | | |
|---|---:|---:|
| Revenue (based on sales of 2,000 cases of oysters) | | $200,000 |
| Expenses: | | |
| Wages for pickers, shuckers, and packers | $100,000 | |
| Packing materials | 20,000 | |
| Rent and insurance | 25,000 | |
| Administrative and selling | 45,000 | 190,000 |
| Pretax income | | 10,000 |
| Taxes (20%) | | 2,000 |
| After-tax income | | $ 8,000 |

Pickers, shuckers, and packers are employed on an hourly basis and can be laid off whenever necessary. Salespeople mostly deliver the product and are paid on a salaried basis.

**REQUIRED:**

**A.** Estimate the cost function for Oysters Away.

**B.** What is the breakeven point in cases for Oysters Away?

**C.** The manager thinks that the company will harvest and sell 3,000 cases of oysters next year. Estimate the after-tax income.

**D.** Oysters Away harvested and sold 2,000 cases in each of the last several years. What does this suggest about the quality of the income information you calculated in part (C)?

**E.** Describe reasons why the cost function developed for the relevant range up to 2,000 cases might not hold for 2,001 to 3,000.

**3.29**
Q1, Q3, Q5

**Relevant information, breakeven, target profit, price, uncertainties** Francesca would like to lease a coffee cart in Aspen, Colorado. The lease is $800 per month and a city license to sell food and beverages costs $20 per month. The lessor of the stand has shown Francesca records indicating that gross revenues average $32 per hour. The out-of-pocket costs for ingredients are generally about 40% of gross revenues. Last year she paid 25% of her income in federal taxes.

Francesca pays $1,000 per month for her condominium. She could store the cart overnight in the condo's garage, which is currently unused. Real estate developers in Aspen estimate that about 20% of the cost of a residential building is for the garage.

At present, Francesca is earning $2,400 per month as a ski instructor for one of the big ski areas. In the summertime she earns about the same income as a kayaking instructor.

**REQUIRED:**

**A.** List each piece of quantitative information in this problem. For each item, indicate whether it is relevant to Francesca's decision and explain why.

**B.** If Francesca leases the cart and works 30 days in a month, how many hours will she have to work each day, on average, to be at least as well off financially as she is in her current job?

**C.** If Francesca wants to work only 25 days per month, how much will revenues have to increase for her to work 4 hours per day and be as financially well off as she is in her current job?

**D.** Can Francesca be certain that her revenues will average $32 per hour? Why or why not?

**E.** What other information might help Francesca with this decision?

**3.30**
Q3, Q4, Q5

**Sales mix, multiple product breakeven, uncertainties, quality of information** Keener produces two products: regular boomerangs and premium boomerangs. Last month 1,200 units of regular and 2,400 units of premium were produced and sold. Average prices and costs per unit for the month are displayed here.

|  | Regular | Premium |
|---|---|---|
| Selling price | $22.15 | $45.30 |
| Variable costs | 4.31 | 6.91 |
| Product line fixed costs | 8.17 | 24.92 |
| Corporate fixed costs | 5.62 | 5.62 |
| Operating Profit | $ 4.05 | $ 7.85 |

Product line fixed costs can be avoided if the product line is dropped. Corporate fixed costs can be avoided only if the firm goes out of business entirely. You may want to use a spreadsheet to perform calculations.

**REQUIRED:**

**A.** Assuming the sales mix remains constant, how many units of premium will be sold each time a unit of regular is sold?

**B.** What are the total fixed product line costs for each product?

**C.** What are the total corporate fixed costs?

**D.** What is the overall corporate breakeven in total revenue and for each product, assuming the sales mix is the same as last month's?

**E.** What is the breakeven in revenues for regular boomerangs, ignoring corporate fixed costs?

**F.** Why is the breakeven for regular boomerangs different when we calculate the individual product breakeven versus the combined product breakeven?

*(continued)*

**②** **G.** When managers monitor the profitability of regular boomerangs, are corporate fixed costs relevant? Explain.

**①** **H.** CVP analysis assumes that the sales mix will remain constant. Explain why managers generally cannot know for certain what their sales mix will be.

**②** **I.** What is the effect of uncertainty about the sales mix on the quality of the information obtained from CVP analyses?

**3.31**
Q1, Q2, Q4

**Cost function, marginal cost, opportunity cost, usefulness of CVP** A neighbor asked for your help preparing a grant for a not-for-profit after-school art program that would benefit elementary school children in the neighborhood. He wants to charge low fees for most children, but also offer some scholarships for low-income children. He needs to have one staff person for every six children to meet state regulations. He can use high school student volunteers for two of these positions, but is concerned about potential absences on their part if he relies on them for the state count. He would like the program to serve at least 30 children, and more, if possible.

He wants you to help him decide on the fees to charge and also to determine how many students could receive scholarships.

**REQUIRED:**

**A.** Think about the costs involved in an after-school program. Assume that your neighbor can use the local elementary school for free.

**②** **1.** List costs that will be incurred for the program, and categorize them as fixed, variable, or mixed.

**②** **2.** For each variable cost, choose a potential cost driver. Explain your choice.

**②** **B.** Do you think the cost structure would be primarily fixed or primarily variable? Explain. Remember, even though staff work only part time, they will have a regular schedule to meet the state regulations of six children per staff member.

**C.** Suppose one of the staff members has only one child to help. What is the marginal cost for three scholarships?

**e** **D.** Suppose the program is fully subscribed by fee-paying children. What is the opportunity cost per scholarship?

**②** **E.** Will CVP analysis help your neighbor choose a fee that would cover at least 10 scholarships? Explain how you would set up a spreadsheet so that your neighbor could perform sensitivity analysis to make more informed decisions.

**3.32**
Q1, Q2, Q4, Q5

**Breakeven, CVP, potential cost structure change, employee reaction** Ersatz manufactures a single product. The following income statement shows two different levels of activity, which are assumed to be within Ersatz's relevant range. You may want to use a spreadsheet to perform calculations.

**Ersatz, Inc.**
**Income Statement**

| | Activity Levels | |
|---|---|---|
| Volume | 1,000 units | 1,500 units |
| Sales @ $100 each | $100,000 | $150,000 |
| Less variable expenses | | |
| Manufacturing @ $40 each | 40,000 | 60,000 |
| Selling @ $10 each | 10,000 | 15,000 |
| Administration @ $6 each | 6,000 | 9,000 |
| Contribution margin | 44,000 | 66,000 |
| Less fixed expenses | | |
| Manufacturing | 10,000 | 10,000 |
| Selling | 11,000 | 11,000 |
| Administration | 20,000 | 20,000 |
| Pretax income | $ 3,000 | $ 25,000 |

**REQUIRED:**

**A.** What is Ersatz's breakeven point in units?

**B.** Draw a CVP chart showing the two levels of activity and the breakeven point.

**C.** If Ersatz plans to sell 1,300 units, what will pretax income be?

*(continued)*

③ **D.** Your boss asked you to draft an e-mail response to Ersatz's major stockholder, who wants to know why pretax income increases by more than 800% when sales increase by just 50%. Both your boss and the stockholder are busy people and expect short answers.

**E.** Management expects that variable costs and selling prices will rise by 3%, but fixed costs will not change. What will the new breakeven point be? Explain the result.

ⓔ **F.** Management wants to change the way that sales representatives are paid. At present, sales representatives are paid $11,000 + $10 per unit. Management will replace this formula with a payment of $20 per unit. At what level of sales will it make no difference in income which cost function is used?

**G.** Add the new cost function to the preceding CVP chart.

**H.** Which of the two cost functions will minimize selling expenses assuming that sales are above the indifference level calculated in part (F)?

② **I.** How would sales representatives be likely to respond to the new payment system?

② **J.** Discuss the pros and cons to the company of changing the way sales representatives are paid.

**3.33** **Breakeven, avoidable fixed costs, price, CVP assumptions, operating risk** Last year's income statement for King Salmon Sales follows.

Q1, Q2, Q4, Q5, Q6

| Revenue (100,000 lbs.) | | $800,000 |
|---|---|---|
| Expenses | | |
| Fish | $200,000 | |
| Smoking materials | 20,000 | |
| Packaging materials | 30,000 | |
| Labor (wages) | 300,000 | |
| Administrative | 150,000 | |
| Sales commissions | 10,000 | |
| Total expenses | | 710,000 |
| Income | | $ 90,000 |

The fishing season is only three to four months long, so labor costs (wages) are for employees who are college students and work in the summer. They are hired only as needed.

**REQUIRED:** ⓔ **A.** The state government curtailed fishing because of low fish counts. Because of this restriction, King Salmon Sales can only buy 50,000 pounds. Assume the administrative cost is incurred only if the company sells salmon. Assuming the managers will decide to operate if the company can at least break even, should they operate this year? (*Hint:* Calculate the breakeven quantity.) Provide calculations and explain your answer.

ⓔ **B.** Now assume that the administrative costs continue regardless of whether the company sells salmon. Assuming the managers will decide to operate if the company can at least break even, should they operate this year? Provide calculations and explain your answer.

ⓔ **C.** Because of the salmon shortage, suppose that retail salmon prices are increasing. What is the breakeven price for King Salmon? Assume that administrative costs continue regardless of whether the company sells salmon.

**D.** Suppose the managers rely on the preceding CVP analysis to decide whether to operate the business. What assumptions are they making?

② **E.** How reasonable are these CVP assumptions?

**F.** Suppose the owner of King Salmon Sales asked you about the company's cost structure. Because volumes of fish fluctuate a great deal from one year to the next, the owner is wondering if some way can be found to reduce the risk of an operating loss. Write a brief memo to explain how the proportion of fixed and variable costs affects the risk of loss when operations are close to the breakeven point.

☆ **3.34** **Cost function, breakeven, target profit, uncertainties and bias, interpretation** Joe Davies is thinking about starting a company to produce carved wooden clocks. He loves making the clocks. He sees it as an opportunity to be his own boss, making a living doing what he likes best.

Q1, Q2, Q4, Q5

Joe paid $300 for the plans for the first clock, and he has already purchased new equipment costing $2,000 to manufacture the clocks. He estimates that it will cost $30 in materials (wood, clock mechanism, and so on) to make each clock. If he decides to build clocks full time, he will need to rent office and manufacturing space, which he thinks would cost $2,500 per month for rent plus another $300 per month for various utility bills. Joe would perform all of the manufacturing and run the office, and he would like to pay himself a salary of $3,000 per month so that he would have enough money to live on. Because he does not want to take time away from manufacturing to sell the clocks, he plans to hire two salespeople at a base salary of $1,000 each per month plus a commission of $7 per clock.

Joe plans to sell each clock for $225. He believes that he can produce and sell 300 clocks in December for Christmas, but he is not sure what the sales will be during the rest of the year. However, he is fairly sure that the clocks will be popular because he has been selling similar items as a sideline for several years. Overall, he is confident that he can pay all of his business costs, pay himself the monthly salary of $3,000, and earn at least $4,000 more than that per month. (Ignore income taxes.)

**REQUIRED:
ANALYZE
INFORMATION**

The following questions will help you analyze the information for this problem. Do not turn in your answers to these questions unless your professor asks you to do so.

**A.** Perform analyses to estimate the number of clocks Joe would need to manufacture and sell each year for his business to be financially successful:
  1. List all of the costs described and indicate whether each cost is (a) a relevant fixed cost, (b) a relevant variable cost, or (c) NOT relevant to Joe's decision.
  2. Calculate the contribution margin per unit and the contribution margin ratio.
  3. Write down the total cost function for the clocks and calculate the annual breakeven point in units and in revenues.
  4. How many clocks would Joe need to sell annually to earn $4,000 per month more than his salary?

**①** **B.** Identify uncertainties about the CVP calculations:
  1. Explain why Joe cannot know for sure whether his actual costs will be the same dollar amounts that he estimated. In your explanation, identify as many uncertainties as you can. (*Hint:* For each of the costs Joe identified, think about reasons why the actual cost might be different than the amount he estimated.)
  2. Identify possible costs for Joe's business that he has not identified. List as many additional types of cost as you can.
  3. Explain why Joe cannot know for sure how many clocks he will sell each year. In your explanation, identify as many uncertainties as you can.

**②** **C.** Discuss whether Joe is likely to be biased in his revenue and cost estimates.

**②** **D.** Explain how uncertainties and Joe's potential biases might affect interpretation of the breakeven analysis results.

**REQUIRED:
WRITTEN ASSIGNMENT**

Suppose Joe has asked for your advice. Turn in your answers to the following.

**③** **E.** Use the information you learned from the preceding analyses to write a memo to Joe with your recommendations. Attach to the memo a schedule showing relevant information. As appropriate, refer to the schedule in the memo.

**3.35** **CVP sensitivity analysis, bias, quality of information** Jasmine Krishnan has been taking entrepreneurship courses as part of her business degree. She developed a plan to start a travel agency specializing in spring break trips for students.

**Q1, Q5**

**ETHICS**

She learned how to develop CVP analysis in her cost accounting class. Now she is preparing pro forma (i.e., forecasted) income statements for a brochure about her plans for the travel agency. She wants to use the information from the CVP as a basis for the statements. Her entrepreneurship professor criticized her business plan because Jasmine included too small an amount for liability insurance. However, when she included the amount suggested by her father's insurance agent, she had to set prices quite high, cut back on the amount she planned as her salary, find lower quality hotels for the students, or take some combination of these actions. She thought that hotel quality and prices would affect sales volumes negatively and did not want to risk incurring losses from low revenues during her first few years. She also needed a base level of salary to at least pay for her living expenses.

She decided to ask friends and relatives to invest in her travel agency to ensure she had enough capital for the first few years. Once her reputation was well established, she assumed that higher customer volumes would cover all of her expected costs. She was confident that her planned trips would attract enough students each year to cover most of her costs. From focus groups on campus, she learned which types of trips were most appealing to other students. Now she planned to use sensitivity analysis to solve for volumes that would make the pro forma statements look attractive to investors.

**REQUIRED:**   ❶ **A.** In general, what information do we hope to gain from performing sensitivity analyses? Explain.

❷ **B.** Explain how bias might enter into Jasmine's sensitivity analyses.

❷ **C.** How might Jasmine's bias affect the quality of the investment brochure information?

❶ **D.** Identify a potential ethical problem for Jasmine.

❸ **E.** When you consider the well-being of Jasmine's family and friends, how would you recommend that Jasmine use sensitivity analysis for her brochure? Explain.

**3.36**
**Q1, Q4, Q5**

**Small business owners, CVP research on the internet** The Internet provides many resources to help small business owners successfully manage their businesses. Resources include information about common techniques used for planning and managing operations.

**REQUIRED:**   ❷ **A.** Why are small business owners often unaware of common business techniques such as CVP analysis?

❷ **B.** Why might CVP analysis be even more useful to small business owners than to managers of large organizations? (*Hint:* Consider whether information about the margin of safety and size of potential losses might be especially important for people who own small businesses.)

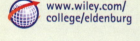
www.wiley.com/
college/eldenburg

❶ **C.** Use an Internet search engine to locate Web sites that provide information about the terms *breakeven analysis* and *cost-volume-profit analysis*. Also search for these terms on Web sites designed explicitly to help small business owners, such as the U.S. Small Business Administration (www.sba.gov). Summarize what your research tells you about the uses and usefulness of breakeven and CVP analysis.

❸ **D.** Suppose you are trying to help a small business owner learn to use breakeven and CVP analysis. Write a memo to the owner explaining what you think the owner should do and include appropriate references to Internet resources that would be useful to the owner. Assume that you have already had a brief conversation with the owner about breakeven and CVP analysis, and the owner expressed an interest in learning more. Focus on communicating effectively by avoiding unnecessarily technical language and concentrating on the most important points.

☆ **3.37**
**Q1, Q3, Q4, Q5, Q6**

**Cost function, operating leverage, keeping or dropping a business** The university's Wildcat Lair caters to students and serves sandwiches and beverages. It has been reporting losses in past months. In July, for example, the loss was $5,000.

| | | |
|---|---:|---:|
| Revenue | | $70,000 |
| Expenses | | |
| Purchases of prepared food | $21,000 | |
| Serving personnel | 30,000 | |
| Cashiers | 5,500 | |
| Administration | 10,000 | |
| University surcharge | 7,000 | |
| Utilities | 1,500 | 75,000 |
| Loss | | $ (5,000) |

The Lair purchases prepared food directly from University Food Services. This charge varies proportionately with the number and kind of meals served. Personnel paid by the Lair serve the food, tend the cash register, bus and clean tables, and wash dishes. The staffing levels rarely change; the existing staff can usually handle daily fluctuations in volume. Administrative costs are primarily the salaries of the manager and her office staff. Because the university provides support services for the

Lair, such as payroll, human resources, and other administrative support, the university charges a surcharge of 10% of its revenues. Utility costs are the costs of cooling, heating, and lighting during its normal operating hours.

The university's management is considering closing the Wildcat Lair because it has been operating at a loss.

**REQUIRED: ANALYZE INFORMATION**

The following questions will help you analyze the information for this problem. Do not turn in your answers to these questions unless your professor asks you to do so.

**A.** What is the breakeven point for Wildcat Lair from the university's perspective (including the university surcharge)? What is the breakeven point from Wildcat Lair's perspective (excluding the university surcharge)?

**B.** Define and calculate the degree of operating leverage for the Lair, ignoring the university surcharge.

**C.** From the perspective of university management, is the university surcharge a relevant cost in deciding whether to close the Lair? Why or why not?

**D.** Identify possible ways that operations could be modified so that some of the fixed costs become variable costs.

**E.** Given the Lair's cost function and operating leverage, describe possible benefits of modifying operations so that some of the fixed costs become variable costs.

**REQUIRED: WRITTEN ASSIGNMENT**

Turn in your answers to the following.

**F.** From the perspective of university management, describe the pros and cons of closing the Wildcat Lair.

**G.** Suppose you are the manager of the Wildcat Lair. Write a memo to persuade the university management to keep the club open.

**3.38**
Q1, Q2, Q4, Q5, Q6

**Not-for-profit breakeven price, budget alternatives** The Elder Clinic, a not-for-profit organization, provides limited medical services to low-income elderly patients. The manager's summary report for the past four months of operations is reproduced here.

| | March | April | May | June | Total |
|---|---|---|---|---|---|
| Patient visits | 849 | 821 | 778 | 842 | 3,290 |
| Patient fees | $ 4,230 | $ 4,180 | $ 3,875 | $ 4,260 | $ 16,545 |
| Medical staff salaries | 13,254 | 13,256 | 13,254 | 14,115 | 53,879 |
| Medical supplies used | 3,182 | 3,077 | 2,934 | 3,175 | 12,368 |
| Administrative salaries | 3,197 | 3,198 | 3,197 | 3,412 | 13,004 |
| Rent | 1,000 | 1,000 | 1,000 | 1,100 | 4,100 |
| Utilities | 532 | 378 | 321 | 226 | 1,457 |
| Other expenses | 2,854 | 2,776 | 2,671 | 2,828 | 11,129 |
| Total expenses | 24,019 | 23,685 | 23,377 | 24,856 | 95,937 |
| Operating surplus (loss) | $ (19,789) | $ (19,505) | $ (19,502) | $ (20,596) | $ (79,392) |

The clinic receives an operating subsidy from the city, but unfortunately, the operating loss incurred through June ($79,392) is larger than anticipated. Part of the problem is the salary increase that went into effect in June, which had been overlooked when the budget was submitted to the city last year. To compound the problem, the warm summer months traditionally bring with them an increase in heat-related health problems. Thus, the clinic is likely to experience an increase in patient visits during July.

The accountant made the following assumptions in developing the cost function:

- Salaries are fixed, and June values are used.
- Medical supplies vary with patient visits.
- Rent and utilities are fixed, and last period's costs are used.
- Other expenses are mixed and using regression, fixed cost is $702 and variable cost is $2.53 per patient visit.

Clinic management is considering an increase in patient fees to reduce losses.

**REQUIRED:**

**ⓔ A.** Develop a cost function for this data. You may have done this for Chapter 2, and in that case use that cost function. Solve for the average patient fee necessary to break even assuming there are 940 patient-visits using the cost function you developed. Compare this new fee with the average patient fee charged during March through June.

**❶ B.** Suppose the clinic raises its patient fees to break even. What problems do you see from the elderly patients' perspective if the fee is raised?

**❷ C.** In this setting, would an increase in fees be likely to affect patient volume? What problems do you see from the clinic's perspective if the fee is raised?

**❶ D.** Other than raising the fee, what ideas might the clinic consider to balance the budget?

**3.39**
Q1, Q3, Q4, Q5, Q6

**Cost function, target profit, operating leverage, CVP graph, owner goals** Elina Siljander owns Elina's Stained Glass in Helsinki, Finland. The business produces and sells three different types of stained glass windows: small, medium, and large. Elina has two full-time employees who work regular schedules to cut glass and assemble the windows. She borrowed money from the bank to start the business and pay living expenses. She is concerned that her cash flows might not be high enough either to pay herself or to repay the bank loan. She would like to generate approximately €10,000 (euros) in pretax profit each month to cover her living expenses and repay the loan.

The following revenue and cost information covers the past four months:

|  | June | July | August | September |
|---|---|---|---|---|
| Revenues | €9,050 | €10,531 | €12,946 | €16,116 |
| Raw materials and supplies | 1,745 | 2,433 | 3,074 | 4,029 |
| Labor | 3,880 | 4,041 | 4,246 | 4,282 |
| Rent | 2,000 | 2,000 | 2,000 | 2,200 |
| Miscellaneous | 525 | 701 | 747 | 793 |
| Profit | € 900 | € 1,356 | € 2,879 | € 4,812 |

**REQUIRED:**

**❷ A.** Develop a cost function for Elina's Stained Glass.

**B.** Determine the level of revenue Elina's Stained Glass must generate to achieve the targeted profit of €10,000 per month.

**C.** Calculate Elina's degree of operating leverage for September.

**❷ D.** Interpret Elina's degree of operating leverage.

**E.** Create a CVP graph showing the breakeven point, target profit, and margin of safety.

**❸ F.** Write a memo to Elina with recommendations about ways she might achieve her goals.

**3.40**
Q1, Q3, Q4, Q5

**Building and using a CVP financial model** Toddler Toy Company sells baby dolls, teddy bears, and toy cars. The managers established a preliminary budget using the following assumptions. They would now like to evaluate the sensitivity of budgeted results to different sets of assumptions.

**Toddler Toy Company**
**Assumptions for Coming Year**

|  | Baby Dolls | Teddy Bears | Toy Cars |
|---|---|---|---|
| Volume | 200,000 | 125,000 | 225,000 |
| Price | $ 3.50 | $ 2.75 | $ 3.15 |
| Variable costs | $ 2.05 | $ 1.75 | $ 2.45 |
| Fixed costs | $65,000 | $125,000 | $35,000 |

Target pretax income = $0
Investment = $2 million
Capacity = 1 million units

**REQUIRED:**

**A.** Create a spreadsheet that the managers can use for sensitivity analysis. (*Hint:* Use the Magik Bicycles spreadsheet in Exhibit 3.2 and Appendix 3A to help you set up a spreadsheet with a data input box.) Modify input data in the spreadsheet to answer the following parts of this problem. You may wish to add cell references for percentage changes in prices, volumes, and costs.

*(continued)*

**B.** Assume that the volume of dolls sold increases to 225,000 units with no change in fixed or variable costs. What is the new pretax income? Does the number produced by your financial model appear to be reasonable? (Manually estimate the increase in pretax income if volume increases and fixed costs remain constant. Compare this figure to your spreadsheet result.)

**C.** Based on the original assumptions, what is the effect on pretax income if variable costs increase by 5% for each of the three product lines? Assume that nothing else changes.

**D.** Return to the original assumptions. Assume that a sales manager proposed a new advertising campaign to boost sales volume. The campaign would cost $30,000 and is estimated to increase the volume of each product as follows:

Baby doll sales increase by 20,000 units.
Teddy bear sales increase by 7,500 units.
Toy car sales increase by 30,000 units.

What would be the effect on pretax income if this plan were adopted?

**E.** Return to the original assumptions. Now assume that due to competition, Toddler Toys must cut prices on each of its three products by 20%. In addition, a new advertising campaign costing $45,000 must be instituted to counteract bad publicity. Given these assumptions, what is the new breakeven point?

**F.** Return to the original assumptions. What would be the pretax income if Toddler Toys increases the price of all three products by 10% and the volume of each product line decreases by 5%?

**G.** Given the same assumptions as in part (F), how many units must Toddler Toys sell to earn a target pretax income of $100,000? A target pretax income of $150,000? A pretax return on investment (ROI) of 10%? (*Hint:* To determine the target pretax income, multiply 10% times amount invested.)

**H.** Spreadsheets for financial modeling allow sensitivity analysis of revenues, costs, and quantities such as estimated product volumes.

①   **1.** Explain why it is not possible to perfectly estimate revenues, costs, and quantities.
②   **2.** Explain how sensitivity analysis can help managers evaluate the pros and cons of alternatives.
②   **3.** Explain how manager bias might influence estimates of revenues, costs, and quantities.

**3.41**
**Q1, Q3, Q4, Q5**

**Building and using a CVP financial model** The following information for Pet Palace, a large retail store that sells pet-related merchandise, was recorded for the first quarter. The store tracks merchandise according to product type. The category "Other" includes accessories such as dog beds, leashes, kitty litter boxes, bird cages, and so on. The company is considering several different strategies to improve operations for the next quarter.

| Input Data | Food | Toys | Pets | Other | Total |
|---|---|---|---|---|---|
| Revenue | $500,000 | $150,000 | $75,000 | $200,000 | $925,000 |
| Variable cost | 200,000 | 50,000 | 60,000 | 50,000 | 360,000 |
| Fixed cost | | | | | 550,000 |
| Tax rate | | | | | 25% |

**REQUIRED:**

ⓔ **A.** Create a spreadsheet that Pet Palace managers can use for sensitivity analysis. Modify information in the data input section and answer the questions in the following parts.

**B.** What is Pet Palace's breakeven point? What total revenue is necessary for a target after-tax income of $100,000?

**C.** Pet Palace managers are considering their advertising campaign for the next period. They believe they could spend an additional $10,000 on advertising for a product line and increase sales by 10%. One manager wants to increase advertising on pets because that product line is currently the smallest. Another manager believes the ads should promote the most profitable products, but they are not sure which products those would be. What is the after-tax income if pets are promoted? What is the most profitable product? What is the after-tax income if that product is promoted?

① **D.** What factors, other than the quantitative results, might influence managers' decisions to increase advertising?

# BUILD YOUR PROFESSIONAL COMPETENCIES

**3.42**
Q1, Q2, Q3, Q4, Q5, Q6

**Focus on Professional Competency: Decision Modeling** *Model building for decision making, quality of analysis* Review the following definition and elements for the Decision Modeling competency.[9]

**DEFINITION:** *Individuals preparing to enter the accounting profession must be able to use strategic and critical approaches to decision-making. They must objectively consider issues, identify alternatives, and choose and implement solution approaches in order to deliver services and provide value.*

## ELEMENTS FOR THIS COMPETENCY INCLUDE

| Level 1 | Level 2 | Level 3 | Level 4 |
|---------|---------|---------|---------|
| 1. Identifies problems, potential solution approaches, and related uncertainties | 2. Objectively identifies strengths, weaknesses, opportunities, and threats associated with a specific scenario, case, or business activity<br><br>3. Uses quantitative techniques to explore the likelihood of alternative scenarios<br><br>4. Organizes and evaluates information, alternatives, cost/benefits, risks and rewards of alternative scenarios<br><br>5. Employs model-building techniques to quantify problems or test solutions | 6. Links data, knowledge, and insights together for decision-making purposes | 7. Engages in continuous improvement and constructs new models over time<br><br>8. Makes decisions over time as a result of engaging in continuous improvement and constructing new models |

**REQUIRED:**

**A.** Focus on the competency elements 1, 4, 6, and 8, which relate to the use of information in management decision making. Answer the following questions:

1. What types of management decisions were addressed in Chapter 3?
2. What types of quantitative analyses were used in Chapter 3 to address these decisions?
3. Were quantitative results the only information used by managers to make decisions? Why or why not?
4. Review the decision-making illustrations in Chapter 3. Provide an example where data, knowledge, and insights were linked together. Explain.
5. Review the decision-making illustrations in Chapter 3. Provide an example where an improvement in analysis led to improved decision making. Explain.

**B.** Focus on competency element 5, which addresses the use of model-building techniques. Explain how CVP analysis (a model-building technique) can be used to (1) quantify problems and (2) test solutions.

**C.** Focus on competency elements 2 and 3, which relate to the use of quantitative techniques to explore alternative scenarios. Answer the following questions:

1. What is CVP sensitivity analysis? How is it used to quantitatively explore the likelihood of alternative scenarios?
2. What is the degree of operating leverage? How is it used to quantitatively explore the likelihood of alternative scenarios?

**D.** Focus on competency element 6, which relates to the use of information in decision making. Suppose you plan to perform CVP analysis for an organization.

1. What types of data do you need to perform the CVP analysis?
2. Why is knowledge about the organization critical to your ability to perform a high-quality analysis? What do you need to know?

---

[9]The definition and elements are reprinted with permission from AICPA; copyright © 1978–2000 & 2003 by American Institute of Certified Public Accountants. The AICPA's Core Competency Framework can be accessed at eca.aicpaservices.org.

**3.43**  **Integrating Across the Curriculum: Economics and Marketing**  *Nonlinear revenue, maxi-*
**Q1, Q2, Q5**  *mize profits, CVP assumptions*  Hollis Company manufactures and markets a regulator used to

maintain high levels of accuracy in timing clocks. The market for these regulators is limited and highly dependent upon the selling price.

Based upon past relationships between the selling price and the resulting demand, as well as an informal survey of customers, management derived the following demand function, which is highly representative of the actual relationships.

$$D = 1,000 - 2P$$

where

$$D = \text{Annual demand in units}$$
$$P = \text{Price per unit}$$

The estimated manufacturing and selling costs for the coming year are as follows:

| | |
|---|---|
| Variable costs | |
| Manufacturing | $75 per unit |
| Selling | $25 per unit |
| Fixed costs | |
| Manufacturing | $24,000 per year |
| Selling | $6,000 per year |

**REQUIRED:**

ⓔ **A.** Write the function for total revenue. [*Hint:* Recall that total revenue equals price times quantity ($P \times Q$), and the demand function determines the quantity sold ($Q$).]

ⓔ **B.** Write the total cost function, substituting the demand function for $Q$.

ⓔ **C.** Perform a search on the Internet to find a quadratic equation calculator or go to www.wiley.com/college/eldenburg. Use the calculator to find the breakeven points. (*Hint:* Set the revenue function equal to the cost function and algebraically convert the equation to quadratic form: $AP^2 + BP + C = 0$.)

ⓔ **D.** Draw a graph with total revenue and total cost for $Q$ between zero and 1,000 units. Mark the breakeven points.

ⓔ **E.** Determine the selling price that Hollis Company should charge per regulator and the number of regulators the company should sell to maximize the company's profits for the coming year. (*Hint:* Recall that profit is maximized when marginal revenue equals marginal cost. You must be able to differentiate a simple function to answer this question.)

**F.** Which CVP assumption does this situation violate? Explain.

**G.** For the past several years, assume the company sold regulators at the price you calculated in part (E) and that volume varied between 375 and 425 units per year. In this situation, discuss whether it would be appropriate to use CVP analysis to estimate the company's profits.

www.wiley.com/
college/eldenburg

# Relevant Costs for Nonroutine Operating Decisions

## ▶In Brief

Managers make a variety of nonroutine operating decisions that include special orders, outsourcing, keeping or dropping a product line, and constrained resource management. Costs are an important part of making these decisions. However, qualitative factors are also important, sometimes overriding cost considerations. Managers weigh a variety of quantitative and qualitative factors in choosing the best course of action.

## This Chapter Addresses the Following Questions:

**Q1** What is the process for making nonroutine operating decisions?

**Q2** How are decisions made to accept, reject, and price special orders?

**Q3** How are decisions made to keep or drop products, segments, or whole businesses?

**Q4** How are decisions made to insource or outsource an activity (make or buy)?

**Q5** How are decisions made for product emphasis and constrained resources?

**Q6** What qualitative factors are important to nonroutine operating decisions?

**Q7** What limitations and uncertainties should be considered when making nonroutine operating decisions?

# CHARLESTON COUNTY: PUBLIC OPINION AND DECISION REVERSALS

For 19 years, the **Charleston (South Carolina) County Council** had awarded a contract for the county's administrative systems to a Dallas-based company. In early 2002, council members changed contractors. They awarded a new five-year contract to the U.S. unit of a company based in New Delhi, India. The new contractor's bid was $5.5 million lower than the existing contractor's bid. Thus, the county expected to save a substantial amount of money over the next five years.

The existing contractor responded with a lobbying campaign aimed at changing the decision. County council members heard that the new contractor would replace about 60 local workers with imported temporary workers earning less money. Given concerns about the loss of local jobs, the council canceled the new contract and rehired the prior contractor.

However, the story did not end there. Council members were told that some of the original contractor's employees were actually paid lower wages than the New Delhi-owned contractor's employees. Furthermore, about 10% of the existing workers had already been foreigners under work visas. After promising that it would try to retain 25% of the existing employees, the New Delhi-owned company was re-awarded the contract. ■

SOURCE: L. Vaas, "Where's Your Contractor's Work Force?" *eWeek*, May 13, 2002, p. 60.

**USING COST INFORMATION TO MAKE NONROUTINE OPERATING DECISIONS**

## ■ Key Decision Factors for the Charleston County Council

The Charleston County Council's difficulties began with a decision similar to those made by many management groups. It hired an outside contractor to run its administrative systems such as payroll, accounting, and information systems. Following is a summary of key aspects of the decisions made by the Charleston County Council.

**Knowing.** The choice among potential administrative system vendors required several types of knowledge, including: the contract bidding process, how contract costs would affect the county's finances, and how contractors vary in their pay scales and use of temporary foreign workers.

**Identifying.** When choosing among vendors, decision makers typically face numerous uncertainties. For the Charleston County decision, uncertainties included whether:

- The new contractor's performance would be satisfactory
- The information provided about the two contractors' pay and hiring practices was true
- The new contractor would honor its promise to try to retain 25% of the existing employees

The degree of uncertainty was also affected by prior experience. There was less uncertainty about the performance of the previous contractor, who had been hired by the county for 19 years, than for the new contractor.

**Exploring.** Before choosing a vendor, it was necessary to analyze a range of factors, including the cost and anticipated performance quality. Sometimes other factors, such as vendor employment practices, are significant and must also be explored. However, it can be difficult for decision makers to identify all of the important factors that should be analyzed. During the U.S. presidential campaign of 2004, the loss of jobs to foreign workers became a well-known issue. However, at the time of the Charleston County decision in 2002, this issue was not as widely considered. Contractor employment practices apparently did not become an issue in the decision until a consultant lobbied on behalf of local jobs.[1] Once questions were raised about the new contractor's employment practices, it became important to explore this factor for both contractors. It could not be assumed that a U.S.-owned contractor would necessarily hire only domestic workers, or that a foreign-owned contractor would necessarily hire only foreign workers.

**Prioritizing.** We cannot know what priorities the council members used when they originally awarded the contract, reversed their decision, and then reversed it again. However, their actions suggest a shift in priorities. Originally, the most important priority might have been a reduction in administrative cost. When the employment issue was raised, however, it might have become the most important issue. In its final agreement, Charleston County obtained a promise that the new contractor would try to retain 25% of the existing employees. The county ultimately achieved a balance of priorities—lower cost and at least some local employment.

**Envisioning.** This case illustrates that the important criteria for decision making can change, sometimes rapidly. Decision makers must continually reevaluate how they make decisions. In a governmental setting, this also requires consideration of changing public expectations.

## ■ Nonroutine Operating Decisions

This chapter focuses on nonroutine operating decisions. Routine operating decisions are made on a regular schedule. For example, budgeting is often done once a year, product prices are reviewed and set regularly, and ongoing purchases of raw materials and other resources are made. Nonroutine decisions occur less frequently than routine decisions. These types of decisions arise when we reevaluate operations because we want to improve processes, or because resource shortages occur or a customer wants special treatment. The following decisions are nonroutine, yet occur frequently in many organizations.

---

[1]L. Vaas, "Where's Your Contractor's Work Force?" *eWeek,* May 13, 2002, p. 60.

- Whether to commit resources for a special order
- Whether to use internal resources or to outsource some activities
- Whether to discontinue a product line or business subunit or segment
- How to manage limited resources

Most of these decisions help managers plan for the next period, typically a year or less in the future. In the Charleston County case, however, the decision involved a five-year contract.

## DECISION PROCESS FOR NONROUTINE OPERATING DECISIONS

> **Q1** What is the process for making nonroutine operating decisions?

Many management decisions are unique, making it impossible to create a "cookbook" to memorize and use. Instead, a decision-making process is needed. Exhibit 4.1 provides an overview of just such a process, one that can be applied to nonroutine operating decisions.

### Identify Type of Decision Managers Must Make

We do not know whether information is relevant to decision making until we know the type of decision to be made. We address problems more correctly and efficiently by clarifying the type of problem before jumping into an analysis. For example, if you need to make a decision about buying a new car or keeping the one you own, some costs are not relevant to the decision, such as parking fees at the university. To identify the relevant cash flows, however, you need to know the brand, year, and model of car you are considering. Even among similar types of cars, differences exist among brands and models in gasoline mileage, insurance rates, license fees, and so on. Until you choose a specific car to consider, you cannot accurately estimate these cash flows. If costs are an important consideration, you need to clarify your options before you can compare the cash flows to your current car.

### Identify and Apply Relevant Quantitative Analysis Techniques

In Chapters 2 and 3 we learned several analysis techniques, including regression and cost-volume-profit (CVP). In this chapter we will learn another, linear programming. All of these techniques generate information that can be relevant for decision making. We select techniques that provide the appropriate information needed for making a specific decision.

Once we have chosen a technique, we identify and gather the relevant information needed to apply it. **Quantitative information** is numerical information that is available for addressing a problem. We frequently must estimate future cash flows to produce the relevant information needed for nonroutine operating decisions. In Chapter 1 we learned about relevant and irrelevant cash flows. To be relevant, cash flows must (1) arise in the future and (2) vary with the action taken. We identify relevant cash flows by analyzing the decision alternatives and then selecting cash flows that are unique to each alternative. Then we estimate the incremental future cash flows under each decision alternative. We ignore irrelevant (unavoidable) cash

**EXHIBIT 4.1** Process for Addressing Nonroutine Operating Decisions

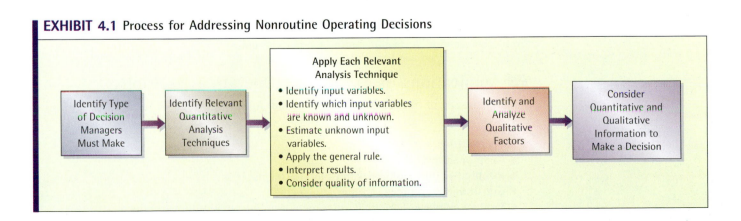

flows, those that do not differ among alternatives. Sunk costs (i.e., costs that were incurred in the past) are always irrelevant to decisions involving cash flows that arise in the future.

Some of the quantitative information we need for an analysis technique is known. These variables are either available as part of our information systems or can be calculated as a single correct value. If some of the quantitative information for an analysis technique is unknown, we can use a second technique to estimate it. For example, we often use regression analysis to estimate the fixed and variable portions of a mixed cost.

Where do we find quantitative information? We obtain some relevant information from the accounting system, such as past revenues and costs. In addition, each type of nonroutine decision requires specific kinds of information gathered from outside the accounting system. Such information could include bids from other companies to provide services such as payroll and telemarketing, or to manufacture parts prior to final assembly.

## ■ Identify and Analyze Qualitative Factors

 **Q6** What qualitative factors are important to nonroutine operating decisions?

Rarely in the business world do decisions rely solely on the results of quantitative analysis. **Qualitative information**—factors that are not valued in numerical terms—is vital to good decision making. Because qualitative factors cannot be numerically evaluated, they must be incorporated into our analysis using judgment. Qualitative factors that might be relevant to a nonroutine operating decision include the following:

- Whether the organization can increase or decrease capacity easily and quickly
- How important quality is for a product or service
- Whether timeliness of delivery is an important factor
- How easily customers might share price information
- Other potential uses for excess capacity or resources
- The effects of production practices on the environment
- Consistency of alternatives with the organization's vision and core competencies

Qualitative factors can be difficult to identify, because no set formula assures us that we have considered the important issues. In **Charleston County**, the contractor's employment policies were an important factor. It might have been possible to calculate numerical differences in pay rates or local employment levels. However, it would have been impossible to reliably calculate the value of each contractor's employment practices to the citizens of Charleston County.

## ■ Consider Quantitative and Qualitative Information to Make a Decision

Once the appropriate quantitative techniques have been applied, we identify the decision alternative with the highest dollar contribution to the organization. However, we do not always choose that option. Managers often make trade-offs among important issues when deciding on a course of action. Sometimes qualitative factors are more important than the quantitative analysis. In addition, we evaluate the quality of the information used. We rely more on higher-quality information than on lower-quality information. Sometimes qualitative factors are considered before performing quantitative analysis. For example, concerns about the reliability of a supplier's parts might lead managers to eliminate that vendor from consideration without any analysis. The managers would then explore alternatives such as purchasing from other vendors or manufacturing the parts in-house.

## ■ Applications of Nonroutine Operating Decisions

The remainder of the chapter illustrates the following types of nonroutine operating decisions:

- Special orders
- Keep or drop decisions
- Insource or outsource (make or buy) decisions
- Constrained resources
- Product emphasis—multiple resource constraints and multiple products

## SPECIAL ORDERS

 **Q2** How are decisions made to accept, reject, and price special orders?

**ALTERNATIVE TERMS**

Some people use the term *one-time-only order* instead of *special order*.

**CHAPTER REFERENCE**

Chapter 2 defined *opportunity costs* as the benefits we forgo when we choose one alternative over the next best alternative.

Managers need to determine whether to accept a customer's special order, one that is not part of the organization's normal operations. This type of decision has no long-term strategic impact because it involves a one-time sale of a specified quantity of goods or services, and often at a reduced price. For example, Right Print has been asked by the local Boys and Girls Club to print postcards inviting potential donors to a silent auction fundraiser. The club would like a discounted price for the printing. If Right Print has idle capacity—machine and labor time are not fully occupied with other orders—the incremental (relevant) cost of taking the order is only the variable costs of postcard paper and ink. Therefore, Right Print could accept the order as long as the price at least covers the cost of the paper and ink.

### ■ General Rule for Special Order Decisions

Each nonroutine operating decision introduced in this chapter employs a guideline—a general rule—to make a decision. The general rule for special orders is that we want to be as well off after accepting the order as we were before we accepted it. To make this decision, we need to know whether the order replaces regular business. If it does, the price should be at or above the usual price, because the opportunity cost of accepting this order is the loss of the usual contribution margin. On the other hand, if idle capacity is available, the special order is acceptable if the organization at least breaks even. In this case, the minimum acceptable price is equal to the incremental cost of the order. The incremental cost includes most of the variable costs and, at times, some fixed costs. The variable manufacturing costs are usually relevant. However, variable selling costs such as commissions are often irrelevant if the company requesting the special order places it directly with the manufacturer. Most fixed costs, such as rent and depreciation on plant and equipment, are unavoidable, making them irrelevant. Some fixed costs, such as the lease cost for a piece of equipment needed for the special order, are relevant because they are unique to the special order.

    The following Barkley Basketballs illustration provides an opportunity to practice making a special order decision.

### BARKLEY BASKETBALLS
#### SPECIAL ORDER

Barkley Basketballs manufactures high-quality basketballs at its plant, which has a production capacity of 50,000 basketballs per month. Current production is 35,000 per month. The manufacturing costs of $24 per basketball are categorized as follows:

| | Variable Cost per Unit | Fixed Cost per Unit (at 35,000 per month) | Total Cost per Unit |
|---|---|---|---|
| Manufacturing Costs: | | | |
|   Direct materials | $12.00 | $0.00 | $12.00 |
|   Direct labor | 2.00 | 0.00 | 2.00 |
|   Manufacturing overhead | 0.50 | 9.50 | 10.00 |
| Total cost to manufacture | $14.50 | $9.50 | $24.00 |
| Sales commission | $ 1.00 | $0.00 | $ 1.00 |

*(continued)*

Jack O'Neil operates not-for-profit basketball camps for disadvantaged youths on Indian reservations and throughout inner cities in large urban areas. Jack asks Billie Walton, CFO at Barkley Basketballs, to sell him 5,000 basketballs at $23.00 per ball, or $115,000 for the entire order.

Billie speaks to the cost accountant and then goes to the production floor to speak to several supervisors to gather information for this decision. She determines that the direct labor cost is variable. Workers are paid an hourly wage and are sent home when there are no balls to manufacture. These workers have no guaranteed salary, but demand is stable so they always work at least half-time, and often 40 hours a week.

Billie asks about the manufacturing overhead and finds that it consists of variable and fixed costs incurred to run the plant where the basketballs are manufactured. Overhead includes insurance, property taxes, depreciation, utilities, and various other plant-related costs. She finds that all of the fixed costs are related to a capacity level of 50,000 and will not change if she uses part of the idle capacity of 15,000 units. The foreman warns her, however, that once production exceeds 40,000 basketballs, bottlenecks occur and the production process will slow down and cause inventory levels to congest the plant, sometimes causing overtime to be paid.

## Quantitative Analysis

With the 5,000 basketballs produced for Jack, total production for the month would be 40,000 basketballs. Bottlenecks and slow downs do not occur until production exceeds 40,000. Therefore, the special order is within the relevant range of production; the fixed costs should remain fixed. The relevant revenues and costs per basketball are as follows:

| | |
|---|---|
| Selling price | $23.00 |
| Variable costs (materials, labor, and overhead) | $14.50 |

In deciding whether to accept this special order, fixed costs are irrelevant because they are unavoidable. They will be incurred whether 35,000 or 40,000 basketballs are produced. The variable cost of $1.00 sales commission per ball is also irrelevant because no sales representatives are involved in this particular transaction. Therefore, the contribution margin for each special order basketball would be $23.00 − $14.50 = $8.50. For 5,000 basketballs, the total contribution margin would be $42,500.

## Qualitative Factors

Based on the preceding quantitative analysis, Billie wants to accept the order. However, she first needs to consider the qualitative aspects of the decision. If she sells the basketballs at this lower price, other customers might demand lower prices too, causing Barkley Basketballs to get into a pricing war with itself. However, Jack's organization is not-for-profit; Billie doubts that other customers would object to giving it a discount.

Billie also believes that the company could enhance its reputation if Jack publicizes Barkley Basketballs' support of the basketball camps. To evaluate the value of such publicity, she meets with the marketing manager, Mark Jordan. Mark cannot quantify the value, but he suggests that the publicity would definitely help promote the Barkley Basketballs brand name. In addition, the company has funded basketball camps in the past, in keeping with its policy of supporting the community.

## Making the Decision

After considering all of these factors, Billie discusses the special order with Jack. She offers to lower the price even further than $23. Jack is pleasantly surprised and offers to publicize Barkley Basketballs' generosity. Billie and Jack settle on a price of $20 per ball. The contribution margin of the special order is reduced from $42,500 to $27,500 (5,000 balls at $20.00 − $14.50).

In this situation, Billie is willing to reduce the price of the special order even further for several reasons. In the past, the company donated money to not-for-profit basketball camps, so providing basketballs at a discount fits with management's desire to act in a socially responsible manner. She also believes the company will benefit from additional publicity. And, the company will still earn a profit from the special order. Although Billie has agreed to a lower price than usual, the special order meets the general rule: ample capacity is available, and the price is greater than the relevant costs (variable production costs).

## Evaluating the Decision Process

Later that week, Billie is reviewing the decision to sell Jack O'Neil basketballs at $20.00 each. She visits with Mark Jordan, who insists that the value of the publicity exceeds the reduction of $15,000 in contribution margin. Billie concludes that the decision to sell the balls at a discount was appropriate.

**EXHIBIT 4.2** Relevant Costs and Qualitative Factors for Barkley Basketballs

|  | Fixed Costs | Variable Costs | Qualitative |
|---|---|---|---|
| Relevant | May increase if $Q > 40,000$ per month (beyond the relevant range) | Direct material + direct labor + variable overhead = $12 + $2 + $0.50 as long as $Q < 40,000$ per month | Potential publicity for selling ball at a discount |
| Irrelevant | Manufacturing overhead | Sales commission per ball (not paid on this special order) | Price concerns of other customers |

Note the process used to make this decision. Billie first identified the type of decision (special order). She knew that she needed to know the relevant costs to make this decision. She determined whether enough capacity was available for the special order without causing fixed and variable costs to change. She categorized costs as fixed and variable to help her identify relevant information. Next she determined which costs were relevant and irrelevant to the special order. In this case, all of the variable production costs and none of the fixed costs or sales commissions were relevant. In manufacturing settings such as this one, where the same product is made repeatedly, manufacturing costs can be estimated with high accuracy. Billie had good reason to be confident in her quantitative analysis. She then weighed the quantitative factors and qualitative factors and decided that, overall, it was best for Barkley Basketballs to offer the special order at a price of $20 per ball.

Billie categorized costs and factors as shown in Exhibit 4.2.

## GUIDE YOUR LEARNING 4.2 Barkley Basketballs

Barkley Basketballs example illustrates special orders. For this illustration:

| Define It | Identify Problem and Information | Identify Uncertainties | Explore Pros and Cons | Prioritize Options |
|---|---|---|---|---|
| Which definitions, analysis techniques, and computations were used? | What decisions were being addressed? What information (quantitative and qualitative) was relevant to the decision? | What types of uncertainties were there? Consider uncertainties about:<br>• Revenue and cost estimates<br>• Interpreting quantitative results<br>• Relevant range of operations<br>• Qualitative factors | What were the pros and cons for each option available to the managers? | In your own words, describe how various quantitative and qualitative factors were weighed in reaching a decision. |

# PRODUCT LINE AND BUSINESS SEGMENT (KEEP OR DROP) DECISIONS

**Q3** How are decisions made to keep or drop products, segments, or whole businesses?

When organizations provide multiple products (goods or services), they periodically review operating results for each product, group of products (product line), or business segment and decide whether to keep or drop the product or segment. If financial statement data are used in these calculations, average costs are often mistakenly included as relevant information. However, managers need to separate relevant and irrelevant cash flows. Therefore, they may need to develop distinct cost functions for each product, product line, or segment.

## ■ General Rule for Keep or Drop Decisions

The general rule is that we discontinue a product, service, or business segment when its total contribution margin does not cover avoidable fixed costs (fixed costs that are eliminated

CURRENT PRACTICE

In 2003, DuPont announced a plan to sell its textile fibers businesses because of continuing operating losses.[2]

if the product is dropped). We first separate costs into fixed and variable. The variable costs are usually relevant. To identify relevant fixed costs, we consider how fixed costs would change if we drop the product, service, or segment. Thus, we categorize fixed costs as avoidable or unavoidable. To identify and estimate avoidable fixed costs, we analyze the nature of the fixed cost and its relation to the two alternatives (keep or drop). For example, dropping a product might mean that an employee in accounting or marketing could be laid off. The labor costs and fringe benefits for that employee are relevant to the keep or drop decision. They are fixed costs that can be directly associated with the product and are avoidable if the product is dropped. Alternatively, the lease cost for a manufacturing facility that produces a number of products is unavoidable if only one product is dropped. Therefore, the lease cost is irrelevant.

The following Home Aide Services illustration provides an opportunity to practice making a keep or drop decision.

## HOME AIDE SERVICES
### KEEP OR DROP

Home Aide Services is a not-for-profit organization that provides a variety of services for people who would prefer to live at home, but need assistance. The organization has several lines of service, including housekeeping, meals, and shopping and transportation services. Lately the organization has suffered a decline in surplus. The manager, Justin Bean, wants to drop one of the services to increase profitability. Following are the monthly cash flows for each service.

| Cash Flow | Housekeeping | Meals | Shopping | Total |
|---|---|---|---|---|
| Revenues | $30,000 | $15,000 | $10,000 | $55,000 |
| Variable costs | 15,000 | 3,000 | 1,000 | 19,000 |
| Contribution margin | 15,000 | 12,000 | 9,000 | 36,000 |
| Fixed costs | 20,000 | 6,000 | 5,000 | 31,000 |
| Surplus (deficit) | $ (5,000) | $ 6,000 | $ 4,000 | $ 5,000 |

### Quantitative Analysis

When Justin tells Elizabeth Klein, the accountant, that housekeeping services should be dropped to save the organization $5,000, Elizabeth says she needs to analyze costs further. The next day she reports to Justin that instead of having an overall surplus of $5,000, Home Aide Services would incur a deficit of $2,000 if housekeeping were dropped. She presents the following information about the remaining product lines if housekeeping were discontinued:

| Cash Flow | Meals | Shopping | Total |
|---|---|---|---|
| Revenues | $15,000 | $10,000 | $25,000 |
| Variable costs | 3,000 | 1,000 | 4,000 |
| Contribution margin | 12,000 | 9,000 | 21,000 |
| Fixed costs | 13,000 | 10,000 | 23,000 |
| Surplus (deficit) | $ (1,000) | $ (1,000) | $ (2,000) |

Justin asks how this could be. Elizabeth explains that when she analyzed the costs in more detail, she found that the fixed costs for housekeeping included benefits for the housekeepers. The cost of benefits would be avoided if housekeeping were dropped. These costs are $8,000. Total fixed costs are now $23,000 ($31,000 − $8,000). These fixed costs are unavoidable and are allocated to the remaining departments. They include the cost of depreciation on cars as well as administrative costs for the entire organization that had been allocated to housekeeping.

Labor costs are a small part of the meal department's total cost. Only $1,000 of fixed costs would be avoided if meals were dropped; the employees who prepare meals also help with administrative work. Shopping and transportation includes $4,000 in avoidable fixed costs. This

---

[2]See 2003 DuPont Form 10K, Financial statement Footnote 31 (Segment Information).

amount represents salary and benefits costs for drivers who are available all hours that the service is open.

| Cash Flow | Housekeeping | Meals | Shopping | Total |
|---|---|---|---|---|
| Revenues | $30,000 | $15,000 | $10,000 | $55,000 |
| Variable costs | 15,000 | 3,000 | 1,000 | 19,000 |
| Contribution margin | 15,000 | 12,000 | 9,000 | 36,000 |
| Avoidable fixed costs | 8,000 | 1,000 | 4,000 | 13,000 |
| Department surplus | $ 7,000 | $11,000 | $ 5,000 | 23,000 |
| Unavoidable fixed costs | | | | 18,000 |
| Overall surplus | | | | $ 5,000 |

Elizabeth prepares the following report for Justin.

| Relevant Benefits and Costs | Housekeeping | Meals | Shopping |
|---|---|---|---|
| Revenue forgone | $(30,000) | $(15,000) | $(10,000) |
| Savings in labor and overhead | 23,000 | 4,000 | 5,000 |
| Net benefit (cost) | $ (7,000) | $(11,000) | $ (5,000) |

With this new information, Justin analyzes the costs again. He realizes that all of the services are contributing to the unavoidable fixed costs and should be continued.

## Qualitative Factors

Elizabeth observes that competitors provide all three services. Therefore, dropping housekeeping could affect demand for the other services. Clients might not want to deal with two separate organizations, when one could provide all the different services they need. Even if housekeeping were just breaking even, it should not be eliminated if dropping it would alienate current customers and cause demand for the other services to decrease. In addition, employee morale could suffer if a number of workers were laid off.

## Making the Decision

Given this new cost analysis and the qualitative factors, Justin decides to retain all of the current services. However, he decides to investigate alternative ways that the organization could improve its surplus. First he considers any opportunity costs. If housekeeping were dropped, could Home Aide add nursing or other services instead? Would the surplus added from nursing be higher than housekeeping?

## GUIDE YOUR LEARNING 4.3 Home Aide Services

Home Aide Services example illustrates a product line keep or drop decision. For this illustration:

| Define It | Identify Problem and Information | Identify Uncertainties | Explore Pros and Cons | Prioritize Options |
|---|---|---|---|---|
| Which definitions, analysis techniques, and computations were used? | What decisions were being addressed? What information (quantitative and qualitative) was relevant to the decision? | What types of uncertainties were there? Consider uncertainties about:<br>• Revenue and cost estimates<br>• Interpreting quantitative results<br>• Dependence among product lines<br>• Alternative uses for capacity<br>• Qualitative factors | What are the pros and cons for each option available to the managers? | In your own words, describe how various quantitative and qualitative factors were weighed in reaching a decision. |

## INSOURCE OR OUTSOURCE (MAKE OR BUY) DECISIONS

 **Q4** How are decisions made to insource or outsource an activity (make or buy)?

The case about the **Charleston County Council** involved selecting an outside contractor to manage administrative systems rather than managing the systems internally. **Outsourcing,** the practice of finding outside vendors to supply products and services, has become an increasingly common practice. **Insourcing** is the practice of providing the good or service from internal resources. For manufacturers, outsourcing decisions are often called **make or buy** decisions: Does the company make the product or provide the service internally, or buy it from the outside? Potential cost savings as well as organizational strategies drive such decisions. Some managers outsource any activity they view as unrelated to the organization's core competencies.

### ■ General Rule for Make or Buy Decisions

The general rule for make or buy decisions is to choose the option with the lowest relevant cost. Managers compare the outsourcing costs with the incremental costs for insourcing. Existing fixed costs are relevant only if they can be avoided through outsourcing. The costs for insourcing also include opportunity costs. Sometimes extra space or capacity from outsourcing can be converted to other uses. Another product could be manufactured or the space rented out. The forgone benefits (contribution margin from the new product or rent payments) are an opportunity cost for insourcing.

The following Roadrunner Publishers (Part 1) illustration provides an opportunity to practice making an outsourcing decision.

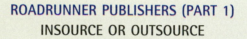

### ROADRUNNER PUBLISHERS (PART 1)
#### INSOURCE OR OUTSOURCE

Roadrunner Publishers produces the book covers for its hardbound books. Recently, Marliss Book Binders purchased new robotic equipment that cuts, trims, and prints book covers in one process. Marliss offered to provide book covers for Roadrunner at $2.00 per book. Mark Bonaray, the cost accountant for Roadrunner Publishers, analyzes the cost information for internally producing hardbound book covers as follows:

|  | Total Costs for 100,000 Book Covers | Cost per Unit |
|---|---|---|
| Direct materials | $ 75,000 | $0.75 |
| Direct labor | 50,000 | 0.50 |
| Manufacturing overhead | 100,000 | 1.00 |
| Foreman's salary | 50,000 | 0.50 |
| Total cost | $275,000 | $2.75 |

After summarizing the costs for producing the book covers in-house, Mark needs to identify costs that are relevant and irrelevant to the decision. First, he gathers more information. He learns from the production manager that the foreman could be laid off if the book covers are outsourced. As a cost accountant, Mark already knows that manufacturing overhead is an indirect cost. In this case, it is allocated to books based on the number of direct labor hours used in each production process. Overhead costs will be incurred even if the book covers are outsourced. However, after examining past utility bills, Mark estimates that closing off the part of the plant where book covers are produced would save about $30,000, or $0.30 per book cover.

#### Quantitative Analysis

Although outsourcing would save $30,000 of the manufacturing overhead, the remaining $70,000 (or $0.70 per book cover) will be incurred under each alternative and is therefore

[3]J.Swickard, "Safire will outsource as much of its component manufacturing as possible," *Business & Commercial Aviation,* June 2003, p. 12.
[4]P. Schneider Traylor, "Outsourcing: More Work Is Being Sent Packing, Often Far Away," *CFO.com* (online publication), November 17, 2003.

irrelevant to the decision. The relevant production and outsourcing costs for this decision are as follows:

|  | Cost per Unit | | Total Cost for 100,000 Book Covers | |
|---|---|---|---|---|
| Relevant Costs | Make | Buy | Make | Buy |
| Purchase book covers |  | $2.00 |  | $200,000 |
| Direct materials | $0.75 |  | $ 75,000 |  |
| Direct labor | 0.50 |  | 50,000 |  |
| Manufacturing overhead | 0.30 |  | 30,000 |  |
| Foreman's salary | 0.50 |  | 50,000 |  |
| Total relevant costs | $2.05 | $2.00 | $205,000 | $200,000 |

Based only on the preceding cost information, Roadrunner would save $5,000 by outsourcing the book covers. However, Mark has not yet considered potential opportunity costs of continuing to produce the book covers in-house. If Roadrunner Books has an alternative use for the space that houses the book cover operations, the contribution margin from the use of that space would be relevant to the decision. For simplicity, we assume that Roadrunner's management has no alternative use for the space and, therefore, no opportunity costs to consider for this decision.

## Qualitative Factors

Another factor Mark considers is the quality of the book covers, which is emphasized in Roadrunner's book production process. Roadrunner's sales managers believe that high-quality covers are important to sales. The quality of Marliss's sample covers appears to be high, possibly even higher than Roadrunner's current level of quality.

Mark is also concerned about the timeliness of delivery. He speaks with Roadrunner's book cover supervisor, who explains that the department is able to respond to changes in production volumes if given lead time. It has been relatively easy to have Roadrunner's employees work overtime or to hire part-time employees when a book appears to be a best seller, causing production levels to rise. When Mark asks Marliss about its ability to manage a very large order caused by unanticipated demand, the sales representative cannot guarantee that such an order could be produced quickly. This response concerns Mark, who is aware that when books are best sellers, large volumes must be produced quickly.

## Making the Decision

When Mark summarizes the relevant information for the decision, he concludes that the savings from outsourcing and the quality differences are relatively small. In addition, he decides that being able to meet demand is worth the additional cost. Based on his analysis, he recommends that the company continue producing its own book covers.

## GUIDE YOUR LEARNING 4.4  Roadrunner Publishers (Part 1)

Roadrunner Publishers (Part 1) illustrates an outsourcing decision. For this illustration:

| Define It | Identify Problem and Information | Identify Uncertainties | Explore Pros and Cons | Prioritize Options |
|---|---|---|---|---|
| Which definitions, analysis techniques, and computations were used? | What decisions were being addressed? What information (quantitative and qualitative) was relevant to the decision? | What types of uncertainties were there? Consider uncertainties about:<br>• Revenue and cost estimates<br>• Interpreting quantitative results<br>• Alternative uses for capacity<br>• Qualitative factors | What are the pros and cons for each option available to the managers? | In your own words, describe how various quantitative and qualitative factors were weighed in reaching a decision. |

## ■ Quality and Outsourcing Decisions

**Q6** What qualitative factors are important to nonroutine operating decisions?

Product or service quality is often a major factor in outsourcing decisions. To insure high quality, organizations typically negotiate outsource contracts that stipulate specific performance criteria, such as product specifications and timeliness. For example, the **American Institute of Certified Public Accountants** negotiated a contract with **Prometric Corporation** to provide computer testing centers for the CPA examination. The contract requires Prometric to accommodate test candidate appointments within a certain number of days and to report on its compliance with contract provisions. Some organizations use multiple outsource vendors to avoid overreliance on any one vendor. However, few outside vendors may be available for some activities, increasing the risk of quality problems.

On the other hand, organizations sometimes outsource because they find it difficult to or do not want to insure high-quality internally. Sometimes rapid growth prevents an organization from developing sufficient expertise in-house. Or the organization's managers do not consider an activity to be a core competency; they do not expend sufficient resources internally to achieve both cost effectiveness and high quality. For example, many e-commerce retailers outsource their warehouse operations to distribution companies that hold and deliver inventories for them. Unfortunately, many distribution companies are not equipped to fill many small orders. They might be unable to handle an increasingly large number of orders. Thus, some e-commerce retailers have been dissatisfied with the quality of distribution company performance.

As international outsourcing has become increasingly popular, organizations need to consider a variety of qualitative factors. Exhibit 4.3 presents a list of factors that financial institutions would consider in their decisions to outsource information technology.

**CURRENT PRACTICE**

In 2000, eToys Inc. increased its warehouse capacity so that it would no longer need to rely on distribution companies, which in 1999 had been unable to fill orders before Christmas.[5]

---

**EXHIBIT 4.3**
**Examples of Financial Institution Considerations for International IT Outsourcing**

- Corporate and cultural differences
- Potential language barriers
- Legal jurisdiction for contract disputes
- Political and economic stability
- Impact to existing employee morale
- Currency exchange rate risk

- Privacy, data protection, and security breach laws
- Intellectual property rights
- Employment laws
- Partner financial viability

SOURCE: "Section 9: Considerations for Cross-Border Outsourcing," *BITS Framework for Managing Technology Risk for IT Service Provider Relationships* Version II, November 2003, Washington, DC: BITS Financial Services Roundtable. Available at www.bitsinfo.org, click Publications.

---

# PRODUCT EMPHASIS DECISIONS

Instead of simply responding to demand and advertising products that sell well, managers may want to focus consumer attention on products that contribute more to profitability. Managers choose to emphasize particular products in their product mix through promotions and advertising campaigns, or by providing incentives for salespersons. Deciding which products to emphasize requires a short-term decision.

**Q5** How are decisions made for product emphasis and constrained resources?

## ■ General Rule for Product Emphasis Decisions

When no capacity constraints apply or alternative uses of fixed resources are available, the products with the highest contribution margins per unit are emphasized. The general rule is to rank products by contribution margin per unit and then emphasize products with higher contribution margins. This approach assumes that fixed costs are unaffected by product mix or customer requirements.

**ALTERNATIVE TERMS**

The following pairs of terms are synonymous: *product-mix decision* and *product emphasis decision; scarce resources* and *constrained resources.*

---

[5]L. Bannon and J. Pereira, "E-Business: Toy Wars II: Holiday Cyber Battle Begins—Two Big Online Toy Sellers Fight over Delivery Speed and Exclusive Products," *Wall Street Journal* (Eastern edition), September 25, 2000, p. B1.

## Constrained Resources

Sometimes managers face limits in capacity, materials, or labor. When these limits restrict an organization's ability to provide enough products (goods or services) to satisfy demand, the organization faces a **constraint.** For example, in the insource-outsource illustration, Roadrunner Publishers needs cardboard to make book covers. In the case of a shortage of cardboard, the company faces a shortage of direct materials, or a direct materials constraint. A shortage of labor to run machines or to load books into packing crates would be a labor constraint. Similarly, a shortage of machines to bind the covers onto the books would be a capacity constraint. With no internal constraints, demand becomes the constraint and the organization needs to focus on increasing demand.

When faced with one or more constrained resources, managers have several options. One option is to maximize the contribution margin within the constraint, that is, emphasize the product that contributes the most, in light of the constraint. A second option is to incur additional costs to relax the constraint. Two options are available to relax constraints.

1. Purchase goods or services from an outside supplier.
2. Add internal capacity or redesign products and processes to use existing capacity more efficiently.

Managers can also try both options, maximizing profit while simultaneously relaxing the constraint.

INTERNATIONAL

In a 2002 survey of Canadian manufacturers, the *Canadian HR Reporter* found that "lack of qualified personnel" was a major constraint on performance improvement.[6]

## General Rule for Choosing the Product Mix When Resources Are Constrained

When resources are constrained, we need to emphasize products and services that maximize the contribution margin per unit of constrained resource. For example, Fabulous Furniture produces teak tables and chairs for outdoor use. Normally the company sells about 100 tables and 800 chairs a month. Because of a strike at the local shipyards, it is unable to purchase enough lumber locally to meet current demand.

The sales manager wants to know which product to emphasize—the tables or the chairs—to maximize profits. The accountant calculates the contribution margin per board foot for tables and chairs to make this decision. The contribution margin per table is $400, and the contribution margin per chair is $150. Tables require 4 board feet of teak and chairs require 2 board feet. The contribution margin per board foot for tables is $100 ($400 ÷ 4 board feet) and for chairs is $75 ($150 ÷ 2 board feet). To maximize the contribution margin, the sales manager should emphasize tables and sell as many as possible. If the demand for tables is filled, then the sales manager should emphasize chairs.

## General Rule for Relaxing Constraints for One or Two Products

The general rule for relaxing a short-term constraint for direct materials, direct labor, or capacity is that managers would be willing to pay not only what they are already paying, but also some or the entire contribution margin per unit of constrained resource. Their goal would be to acquire added capacity, thereby eliminating the constraint.

In the furniture example, Fabulous Furniture is currently paying $50 per board foot for teak. Once the company has manufactured as many tables and chairs as possible with the limited supply of teak, it will still experience demand for chairs. Customers will buy elsewhere if they cannot purchase chairs from Fabulous. Fabulous forgoes $75 in contribution margin per board foot on each chair customers would have purchased had teak been available. Consequently, Fabulous can afford to pay what it currently pays ($50), plus up to the entire contribution margin per board foot ($75) to buy more teak. If Fabulous can find a source of teak for $125 ($50 + $75) or less per board foot, it can meet customer demand for chairs.

---

[6]Asha Tomlinson, "More training critical in manufacturing: Study," *Canadian HR Reporter* 15, no. 19 (November 4, 2002), p. 2.

**Q7** What limitations and uncertainties should be considered when making nonroutine operating decisions?

As the variable cost per unit (including the new cost of materials or labor) approaches the selling price of the product or service, managers become indifferent to purchasing more of the constrained resource for continued production. This general rule is valid under the following assumptions:

- The organization will forgo sales if the resource constraint is not relaxed.
- Fixed costs are unaffected by short-term decisions made to relax constraints.
- The managers want to maximize profits in the short term.
- Sales of one product do not affect sales of other products.

Capacity constraints are time constraints; that is, we have limited time available for processing products because one or more bottlenecks slow production. Any process, part, or machine that limits overall capacity is a **bottleneck.** To maximize use of bottleneck resources, we emphasize products that have the highest contribution margin per bottleneck hour. We calculate the relevant contribution margin in terms of time needed at the bottleneck resource.

For example, suppose Fabulous has only one three-axis milling machine (a computerized piece of equipment that cuts and routs unusual shapes). The milling machine processes all of the tables and chairs, but it can process only 4 tables per hour or 12 chairs per hour. The contribution margin per machine hour for tables is $1,600 (4 × $400) and for chairs is $1,800 ($150 × 12). Chairs should be emphasized because they have the highest contribution per hour at the bottleneck resource.

The following Roadrunner Publishers (Part 2) illustration provides an opportunity to practice making a constrained resource decision.

## ROADRUNNER PUBLISHERS (PART 2)
### CONSTRAINED RESOURCE

Suppose the managers of Roadrunner Publishers decide that the company should continue to make its own book covers. In performing his analysis, Mark assumes ample capacity and materials are available. However, one of Roadrunner's children's books, *Barry Plotter, Mathematical Wizard,* sells many more copies than expected. This increase in demand leads to a shortage of the special cardboard needed for the book covers. In turn, Roadrunner is unable to publish enough books to meet current demand. Customers—both children and their parents—are becoming quite frustrated.

### Qualitative Factors

Mark discusses the cardboard shortage with the sales manager, Dina Wilkinson, who thinks the company will in all likelihood forgo sales if demand cannot be met in a timely manner. In addition, the sales manager believes Roadrunner must continue to build positive brand name recognition for the Barry Plotter series, so that further books in the series will be well received. Given this information, Mark would like to find some way to produce enough books to meet customer demand.

### Quantitative Analysis

The books that have already been produced and sold covered all of the company's fixed costs related to developing, editing, and designing the books and their covers. The wholesale price of the books is $10.00 each. The direct materials ($0.75) and direct labor ($0.50) costs for the covers total $1.25. The remaining variable costs for each book are $1.50 for paper and $1.50 royalty to the author. Therefore, total variable costs per book are $4.25, and the contribution margin per book is $5.75.

At Mark's request, the purchasing agent, Bruce Maxwell, researches alternative cardboard suppliers. Although Bruce locates a supplier, he is concerned because the lowest-cost supplier is demanding a price of $4.00 per cover for timely delivery.

### Making the Decision

Mark decides that, in the short run, he is willing to give up some of the contribution margin for this title to build long-term customer satisfaction. Therefore, he is willing to pay as much as the original cost of the cardboard ($0.75 per book) and the original contribution margin ($5.75 per book), or $6.50 per book. He recommends that Bruce purchase additional cardboard at the asking price of $4.00 per book. The variable costs for this additional printing now include $4.00 (book cover materials), $0.50 (book cover labor), $1.50 (paper), and $1.50 (royalty), for a total of $7.50 per book. Thus, the contribution margin from each additional book that Roadrunner produces and sells will be $2.50 ($10.00 − $7.50). Even though this amount is lower than the original contribution margin of $5.75, Roadrunner continues to earn at least some contribution margin through its effort to relax the constrained resource of the book cover cardboard.

---

### GUIDE YOUR LEARNING 4.5 Roadrunner Publishers (Part 2)

Roadrunner Publishers (Part 2) illustrates a constrained resource. For this illustration:

| Define It | Identify Problem and Information | Identify Uncertainties | Explore Pros and Cons | Prioritize Options |
|---|---|---|---|---|
| Which definitions, analysis techniques, and computations were used? | What decisions were being addressed? What information (quantitative and qualitative) was relevant to the decision? | What types of uncertainties were there? Consider uncertainties about: <br>• Revenue and cost estimates <br>• Interpreting quantitative results <br>• Effect on brand name <br>• Other qualitative factors | What are the pros and cons for each option available to the managers? | In your own words, describe how various quantitative and qualitative factors were weighed in reaching a decision. |

---

## PRODUCT EMPHASIS: MULTIPLE RESOURCE CONSTRAINTS AND MULTIPLE PRODUCTS

**Q5** How are decisions made for product emphasis and constrained resources?

The preceding illustration is simplistic compared to most business environments. Most organizations have capacity constraints that affect more than one resource and more than one product.

### ◼ General Rule for Relaxing Constraints with Multiple Constraints and Multiple Products

The general rule is that managers want to maximize profits in the short term by selecting the product mix that achieves the highest contribution margin per set of constrained resources. When multiple resource constraints and multiple products are involved, managers must find the product mix that maximizes the contribution margin.

To find this mix, simultaneous equations are solved using **linear programming,** a mathematical technique that maximizes a linear objective function (such as the sum of contribution margins from multiple products) subject to linear constraints (such as the number of hours available for different manufacturing or services processes). Optimal solutions can be computed using linear programming software packages such as Excel® Solver and Vanguard DecisionPro™.

### ◼ Quantitative Analysis for Multiple Products and Multiple Constraints

When multiple products use different amounts of multiple resources, we set up the equations needed to solve the linear programming problem as follows:

1. Determine the contribution margin for each product and lay out the objective (target) function to be maximized.

2. List the amount of constrained resources required per product and the total amount of constrained resource available (often measured in hours).
3. Solve for the optimal product mix using Excel Solver or other software.
4. Interpret the output.

The output from Excel Solver and other programs provides information about binding constraints and slack resources. A **binding constraint** is a resource that limits production, such as the number of hours available for inspection. **Slack resources** do not limit production and could be used if no other constraints limit production. Slack resources reflect idle capacity.

Excel Solver output also provides a "shadow price" that tells us the contribution margin per constrained resource, given the other constraints in the problem. In addition, Excel Solver gives information about points at which the optimal product mix would change if changes occurred in contribution margins or constrained resources. The following Bertram Golf Carts illustration demonstrates these details.

## BERTRAM GOLF CARTS
## MULTIPLE CAPACITY CONSTRAINTS AND MULTIPLE PRODUCTS

Bertram Golf Carts manufactures regular and premium golf carts. The company's managers want to determine the mix of products that will maximize their contribution margin, so they will know which products should be emphasized.

Regular carts sell for $8,000, have a variable cost per unit of $5,600, and require 20 hours for assembly. Premium carts sell for $10,000, have a variable cost of $6,500, and require 50 hours for assembly. Because of the quality controls built into the assembly process, premium carts take only 2.5 hours to inspect and test, whereas regular carts take 5 hours to test and inspect. Bertram has 10,000 hours available for assembly and 1,200 hours for testing and inspection. In addition, a shortage of leather for seat covers limits production to only 150 premium carts. We next describe the output from Excel Solver for this problem. Instructions for using Excel Solver are presented in Appendix 4A.

The Excel Solver Answer Report gives the optimal solution (see Exhibit 4.4). For Bertram, the optimal product mix is 175 regular carts and 130 premium carts (under Final Value in the Adjustable Cells section). The total contribution margin for this product mix is $875,000 (under Final Value in the Target Cell section). The optimal product mix uses all of the available hours in both assembly and testing; these resources are binding because they limit further production. However, the amount of leather material available is not binding; only 130 premium carts are made. Enough leather is available for an additional 20 premium carts. The unused leather is considered a slack resource.

The Sensitivity Report provides sensitivity analysis around the product mix, contribution margins, and constrained resources (Exhibit 4.5). In the first section for adjustable cells, the objective coefficient represents the contribution margin per product: $2,400 for regular carts and $3,500 for premium carts. The "allowable increase" and "allowable decrease" values are the amount the contribution margin per unit could change before the product mix would change (holding

## EXHIBIT 4.4 Solver Output for Bertram Golf Carts: Answer Report

Target Cell (Max)

| Cell | Name | Original Value | Final Value |
|------|------|---------------|-------------|
| $B$8 | Target cell: contribution margin for product mix | $0 | $875,000 |

Adjustable Cells

| Cell | Name | Original Value | Final Value |
|------|------|---------------|-------------|
| $B$5 | Regular | 0 | 175 |
| $C$5 | Premium | 0 | 130 |

Constraints

| Cell | Name | Cell Value | Formula | Status | Slack |
|------|------|-----------|---------|--------|-------|
| $C$11 | Assembly hours used | 10000 | $C$11<=$D$11 | Binding | 0 |
| $C$12 | Testing hours used | 1200 | $C$12<=$D$12 | Binding | 0 |
| $C$13 | Leather seats used | 130 | $C$13<=$D$13 | Not Binding | 20 |

**EXHIBIT 4.5** Solver Output for Bertram Golf Carts: Sensitivity Report

Adjustable Cells

| Cell | Name | Final Value | Reduced Cost | Objective Coefficient | Allowable Increase | Allowable Decrease |
|------|------|-------------|--------------|----------------------|-------------------|-------------------|
| $B$5 | Regular | 175 | 0 | 2400 | 4600 | 1000 |
| $C$5 | Premium | 130 | 0 | 3500 | 2500 | 2300 |

Constraints

| Cell | Name | Final Value | Shadow Price | Constraint R.H. Side | Allowable Increase | Allowable Decrease |
|------|------|-------------|--------------|---------------------|-------------------|-------------------|
| $C$11 | Assembly hours used | 10000 | 57.5 | 10000 | 800 | 5200 |
| $C$12 | Testing hours used | 1200 | 250 | 1200 | 1300 | 200 |
| $C$13 | Leather seats used | 130 | 0 | 150 | 1E+30 | 20 |

everything else constant). For Bertram, the optimal product mix would change if the regular cart contribution margin increased to more than $7,000 ($2,400 + $4,600) or decreased to less than $1,400 ($2,400 − $1,000). Similarly, the contribution margin for premium carts could increase by $2,500 or decrease by $2,300 before affecting the optimal product mix.

The lower section of the Sensitivity Report gives similar information for the constraints. The optimal product mix would change if total assembly time increased by more than 800 hours to greater than 10,800 hours. The product mix would also change if total assembly time dropped by more than 5,200 hours to less than 4,800 hours. Similarly, the testing constraint could increase by 1,300 hours or decrease by 200 hours before changing the optimal product mix.

The shadow price provides the contribution margin per constrained resource. Following the general rule for constrained resources, Bertram's managers would be willing to pay up to $57.50 per hour in addition to what they are already paying to relax the constraint in assembly. Similarly, they would be willing to pay up to $250.00 per hour in addition to what they are already paying to relax the constraint in testing and inspection. The shadow price for leather is zero because the leather resource constraint is not binding.

| GUIDE YOUR LEARNING | 4.6 | Bertram Golf Carts |
|---|---|---|

Bertram Golf Carts illustrates linear programming to solve for constrained resources. For this illustration:

| Identify Problem | Identify Information Used | Identify Information Created | Describe Use |
|---|---|---|---|
| What decision was being addressed? | List the information that was used as inputs. Where would this information be obtained? | List the information that is created. | In your own words, write a description of how linear programming is used to make decisions about constrained resources. |

## METHODS FOR RELAXING CONSTRAINTS

**Q5** How are decisions made for product emphasis and constrained resources?

Managers analyze operations and make decisions about the use of resources. Scarce resources, such as capacity constraints, must be carefully managed. We can use quantitative techniques to choose the product mix that maximizes the contribution margin for bottleneck resources. Alternatively, we can relax or elevate the constraint. Because each setting is unique, managers choose among a number of different techniques.

### ■ Use Constrained Resources More Efficiently

In the Bertram Golf Carts illustration, managers could analyze the assembly and testing-inspection processes to find ways to use constrained resources most efficiently. One possibility would be to change when inspection takes place. If golf carts are inspected earlier and more often during assembly, spoiled units are removed from the line earlier in the assembly process. Fewer resources will then be needed in assembly and testing, helping to alleviate both assembly and testing constraints. Also, improvements in quality (lower defect rates) would ensure that only good units go through all processes.

In addition, workers from nonbottleneck resources can be reassigned to the bottleneck resources to increase the speed and constancy of the process. This reassignment is especially important during breaks and meals. To maximize output, bottleneck resources should be running as many hours as possible, regardless of the production team's schedule. Chapter 14 discusses increasing throughput, the rate at which product moves through the manufacturing process to the point of sale, or the rate at which services are produced.

Alternatively, efforts such as process reengineering (redesigning the manufacturing or service delivery process) can be undertaken to reduce use of the constrained resources. For example, Bertram could redesign its assembly process and outsource the assembly of the seats and seat covers to reduce the amount of time each cart spends in the assembly department.

## ■ Increase Available Resources

**CURRENT PRACTICE**

Eliahu Goldratt developed the Theory of Constraints, a formal method used to analyze organizational constraints and to improve operations. For more information, go to www.goldratt.com/.

Another possibility is to increase available resources. For example, managers can ask employees to work overtime. They can also increase capacity by buying new equipment or hiring new employees. Increasingly, companies use temporary labor or other outsourcing arrangements to increase available resources on an as-needed basis. Thus, resources might be increased either internally or externally.

## ■ Qualitative Factors for Constrained Resource Problems

As highlighted earlier in the Roadrunner Publishers illustration, managers might work to relax a constraint to protect customer loyalty or brand name recognition when the organization cannot deliver goods or services quickly. This factor, which has long-term effects, might outweigh cost considerations in some situations, especially if failure to deliver product would encourage new competition or customers to seek product substitutes. Another qualitative factor is the effect that any relaxation of the constrained resource could have on the price of that resource. A permanent increase in cost will decrease the contribution margin in the future. Product quality and timeliness of delivery from suppliers are also important if additional resources are used to relax a constraint.

---

### GUIDE YOUR LEARNING  4.7  Key Terms

Stop to confirm that you understand the new terms introduced in the last several pages:

| | |
|---|---|
| *Outsourcing (p. 138) | *Bottleneck (p. 142) |
| *Insourcing (p. 138) | Linear programming (p. 143) |
| *Make or buy (p. 138) | *Binding constraint (p. 144) |
| *Constraint (p. 141) | *Slack resources (p. 144) |

For each of these terms, write a definition in your own words. For starred terms, list at least one example that is different from the ones given in this textbook.

---

## UNCERTAINTIES AND LIMITATIONS FOR NONROUTINE OPERATING DECISIONS

Exhibit 4.6 summarizes the relevant information commonly used for making nonroutine operating decisions, as illustrated in this chapter.

Managers make higher-quality decisions when they use higher-quality information and higher-quality decision processes. It is not sufficient for managers to identify relevant information when making nonroutine operating decisions. They must also consider the quality of information, and they must evaluate alternatives objectively and thoroughly.

**EXHIBIT 4.6** Summary of Information Used in Nonroutine Operating Decisions

| Information | Type of Decision | | | | |
| --- | --- | --- | --- | --- | --- |
| | **Special Order** | **Product Line and Business Segment (Keep or Drop)** | **Insource or Outsource (Make or Buy)** | **Product Emphasis (under Constraints)** | **Relax Constrained Resource** |
| General decision rule | Accept if price is greater than or equal to the sum of variable cost, relevant fixed costs, and opportunity cost | Drop if contribution margin is less than the sum of relevant fixed costs and opportunity cost | Outsource if buy cost is less than or equal to the sum of variable cost and relevant fixed costs minus opportunity cost | Emphasize product with highest CM per unit unless resources are constrained, then emphasize product with highest CM per unit of constrained resource | Incur cost to relax constraint if cost is less than or equal to the sum of CM per unit of constrained resource and the current variable cost of the resource |
| Relevant fixed costs | Only new fixed costs associated with the special order | Only fixed costs that can be avoided if drop | Only fixed costs that can be avoided if buy | | Only new fixed costs to relax the constraint |
| Opportunity cost | Contribution margin of any regular business replaced | Benefits from using released capacity for other purposes | Benefits from using released capacity for other purposes | | |
| Examples of qualitative factors | • Will regular customers expect lower prices?<br>• Will this order lead to improved brand name recognition?<br>• Can we deliver without disrupting current schedules? | • Will dropping one product affect sales of other products?<br>• Will layoffs affect worker morale? | • Is it easier to ensure high quality via insourcing or outsourcing?<br>• Will delivery be timely?<br>• Are there uncertainties about the supplier's ability to meet contractual obligations?<br>• Is this activity a core competency? | • Does the product emphasis agree with strategic plans?<br>• Are sales of one product likely to affect sales of other products? | • Are there other ways to relax the constraint?<br>• How would brand recognition be affected by delivery delays?<br>• Will the decision affect future supply costs? |
| Examples of major uncertainties | • How accurate are the cost estimates?<br>• Are we operating in the relevant range?<br>• Will fixed costs increase at higher capacity levels? | • How accurate are the revenue and cost estimates?<br>• How will customers respond to the dropped product? | • How accurate are the cost estimates?<br>• Is our measure of quality appropriate?<br>• How reliable is the vendor or resource supplier? | • How accurate are the contribution margin estimates?<br>• How reliable are the product demand forecasts? | • How accurate are the contribution margin estimates?<br>• How accurate are the constraint use estimates? |

**Q7** What limitations and uncertainties should be considered when making nonroutine operating decisions?

**CHAPTER REFERENCE**

See Exhibit 1.9 for the path to higher quality decision.

# ■ Quality of Information

Three major factors affect the quality of information for nonroutine operating decisions: uncertainties, timeliness, and analysis technique assumptions.

**Uncertainties** Many uncertainties are involved in nonroutine operating decisions, as illustrated in the last row of Exhibit 4.6. Uncertainties about future revenues and costs affect all of these decisions. Future revenues and costs can vary depending on changes in the economic environment, customer demand, competition, government regulation, vendor quality, technology, and many other factors. However, the degree of uncertainty varies from decision to decision. For example, fewer uncertainties come with a special order from a long-time customer than from a new customer. Similarly, fewer uncertainties accompany outsourcing with a nearby company than with a company on another continent. In addition, decisions having a shorter time horizon, such as a special order that can be completed within one week, are less uncertain than decisions having a longer impact, such as dropping a product.

**Information Timeliness** Many nonroutine operating decisions must be made quickly and rely on up-to-date information. For example, a customer might require a prompt reply to a special order request, or managers may need to change production plans to emphasize different products as circumstances change. Access to timely information is particularly important in industries such as computer manufacturing, where technology, demand, and prices change rapidly. Cost information that is only one month old may be irrelevant. Thus, the accessibility and currency of the information system affect the quality of decisions.

**Analysis Technique Assumptions** The reasonableness of assumptions affects the quality of information generated from an analysis technique. For example, regression analysis is useful for estimating costs only within a relevant range of activity. CVP analysis assumes that the revenue and cost functions are linear and that operations remain in a relevant range of activity. Although the validity of assumptions cannot be known with certainty, the validity of assumptions in a rapidly changing business environment is more uncertain than in a stable environment.

The general decision rules we learned in this chapter assume that the organization's goal is to maximize short-term profits. This assumption ignores qualitative factors that might be more important than short-term profits for some decisions.

## ■ Quality of Decision Process

Three major aspects of the decision-making process affect the quality of nonroutine operating decisions: decision-maker bias, sensitivity analysis, and prioritization.

**Decision-Maker Bias** Sometimes decision makers are biased, which reduces their ability to objectively and thoroughly analyze relevant information. For example, fear of local job loss might have encouraged **Charleston County Council** members to become biased against the foreign contractor. When new information about the contractor's employment practices became available, the council reversed its outsourcing decision without adequately exploring information about the two contractors. Similarly, the **Motorola** case in Chapter 1 illustrated how bias in favor of one option can lead to poor business decisions.

Another type of bias involves a preference for either quantitative or qualitative information. Some people tend to rely primarily on quantitative analyses because they are more comfortable with what they view as precise answers. Others, recognizing the uncertainties in quantitative analyses, prefer to rely on qualitative factors to make decisions. The best approach is to weigh carefully both quantitative and qualitative factors, taking into account the strengths and weaknesses of information for a particular decision.

**Sensitivity Analysis** One way to improve decisions in light of low information quality and potential biases is to perform one or more sensitivity analyses. Sensitivity analysis helps managers evaluate how quantitative results would change with changes in various pieces of information. For example, estimates of incremental costs or of cost savings could be increased to evaluate risk. Sometimes the degree of risk in the quantitative estimates for one option might make that option less desirable than another option having less risk.

**CHAPTER REFERENCE**

Exhibit 1.1 in Chapter 1 provides more details about the relationships among vision, core competencies, and strategies.

**Prioritization** Operating plans are designed to help achieve an organization's long-term strategies. In turn, the strategies depend on an organization's vision and core competencies. When addressing any nonroutine operating decision, managers should consider whether each option is consistent with the organization's strategies, vision, and core competencies. For example, in the Charleston County case, contractor employment policies are important because the county's mission is to serve its citizens. Organizations such as **Toyota** have established a market position based on high product reliability, making that characteristic an important strategic issue. Some organizations, such as **Wal-Mart**, place strategic importance on low costs and prices. **Samsung Electronics'** strategy includes protecting the environment. By considering these types of qualitative issues, managers avoid taking actions that conflict with the organization's long-term interests.

# FOCUS ON ETHICAL DECISION MAKING
## Stewardship of Public Funds

Publicly elected officials are responsible for guarding taxpayers' money when making decisions about programs such as public education, roads, public transportation, and fire and police protection. Elected officials need to be extremely diligent in examining details when making decisions. If they fail to do so, poor decisions waste tax dollars as well as the time and effort involved in decision making. For example, the State of Arizona was threatened by sanctions from the Environmental Protection Agency because the air quality in Phoenix was very poor. To address this problem, the state legislature passed a bill in 2000 that refunded one-third of the cost of new vehicles that were equipped to run on gasoline and propane, which produces less pollution. In addition, the state would pay to convert vehicles to propane and waive sales tax and registration fees. For cars that run entirely on alternative fuels, the state would pay half the cost (Carlton 2000).

The new legislation failed to produce the desired result. Some of the vehicles purchased under the program were sport utility vehicles with propane tanks as small as three gallons. Many vehicles were capable of running on propane, but continued to rely on gasoline. The generous incentives, coupled with a typographical error that overstated the number of vehicles that could qualify for the program, caused costs to reach $420 million instead of the original estimate of $3 to $10 million. In September 2000, the governor announced that after October 11, refunds would be spread out over five years, instead of one year. Car buyers stormed showrooms to beat the deadline. About 20,000 people were due refunds of about $20,000 each when the governor signed a moratorium on the program.

SOURCE: J. Carlton, "If you paid half price for that new SUV, you must be in Arizona," *The Wall Street Journal*, October 26, 2000, p. A1.

### Practice Ethical Decision Making

In Chapter 1, we learned about a process for making ethical decisions (Exhibit 1.11). You can address the following questions for this ethical dilemma to improve your skills for making ethical decisions. Think about your answers to these questions and discuss them with others.

| Ethical Decision-Making Process | Questions to Consider about This Ethical Dilemma |
|---|---|
| Identify ethical problems as they arise. | Does passing legislation to provide incentives for drivers to use clean air vehicles appear to be an ethical dilemma? Why or why not? |
| Objectively consider the well-being of others and society when exploring alternatives. | What are the social costs and benefits of providing financial support to individuals for programs such as this one? Is misuse of taxpayer money a political issue, a business issue, a social issue, or all three? Explain. |
| Clarify and apply ethical values when choosing a course of action. | Identify the priorities and values you use to draw conclusions about the following questions:<br>• Should taxpayer funds ever be used to purchase or modify private vehicles?<br>• Should the legislators have anticipated that many of the program vehicles would be SUVs with propane tanks as small as three gallons?<br>• Should the legislation have been restricted to vehicles that burn only propane? |
| Work toward ongoing improvement of personal and organizational ethics. | How might the government monitor programs to ensure that they are meeting the public interest? |

## APPENDIX 4A

# Using Excel Solver for Product Emphasis and Constrained Resource Decisions

Linear programming problems can be solved using a spreadsheet application. This appendix provides detailed instructions for using Solver, a tool within Excel, to solve a product emphasis problem with resource constraints. We use data from the Bertram Golf Carts chapter illustration to demonstrate the instructions. These instructions and exhibits in this appendix were prepared using Excel 2003. Following is a summary of the steps we will learn in this appendix:

1. Determine the objective (target) function.
2. Create formulas for the resource constraints.
3. Set up an Excel spreadsheet.
4. Use Excel Solver to maximize the objective function.
5. Interpret the Solver output.

## ◼ 1. Determine the Objective (Target) Function

The general decision rule for a product emphasis problem when resources are constrained is to emphasize the product with highest contribution margin per unit of constrained resource. The goal is to maximize the organization's total contribution margin. Therefore, the objective function for the linear programming problem is to maximize the sum of contribution margins. In Excel Solver, the objective function is called the target function.

For Bertram Golf Carts, the objective (target) function is to maximize the total contribution margin from its two types of golf carts. Regular golf carts sell for $8,000 and have a variable cost per unit of $5,600. Premium carts sell for $10,000 and have a variable cost of $6,500.

> Objective (target) function
> = Total contribution margin
> = Regular carts × ($8,000 − $5,600) + Premium carts × ($10,000 − $6,500)
> = Regular carts × $2,400 + Premium carts × $3,500

## ◼ 2. Create Formulas for the Resource Constraints

The next step is to identify and write a function for each resource constraint. The function is the sum of the quantity of the resource used by each product, which must be less than or equal to the maximum available amount of the resource. In the Bertram Golf Cart illustration, three constrained resources are assembly hours, testing and inspection hours, and leather for seat covers. Bertram has 10,000 hours available for assembly. Regular carts require 20 assembly hours, while premium carts require 50 hours. For assembly, the constraint function is

> Regular carts × 20 hours + Premium carts × 50 hours ≤ 10,000 hours

Bertram has 1,200 hours for testing and inspection. Regular carts take 5 hours to test and inspect, while premium carts take only 2.5 hours. For testing and inspecting, the constraint function is

> Regular carts × 5 hours + Premium carts × 2.5 hours ≤ 1,200 hours

Bertram has only enough leather for 150 seat covers. Regular carts do not have leather seat covers, so this constraint relates to only premium carts.

> Premium carts × 1 seat cover ≤ 150 seat covers

## ◼ 3. Set Up an Excel Spreadsheet

Exhibit 4A.1(a) provides a general Excel spreadsheet format for a product emphasis problem with resource constraints. A spreadsheet using this format for Bertram Golf Carts is shown in Exhibit 4A.1(b). The following instructions describe how to create the spreadsheet.

Insert a title for the spreadsheet in cell B1. Then insert labels that will be useful later when using Solver: Type "Changing Cells:" in cell A5, "Target Cell:" in cell A8, and "Constraints:" in cell A11. Next insert headings for the product data: Type "Product Mix" in cell B3, and then type product names in cells B4 and C4. If more than two products are involved, enter product

**EXHIBIT 4A.1** Excel Spreadsheets for Product Emphasis with Constrained Resources

| | A | B | C | D |
|---|---|---|---|---|
| 1 | | Problem Name | | |
| 2 | | | | |
| 3 | | Product Mix | | |
| 4 | | Product 1 Units | Product 2 Units | Product 3 Units |
| 5 | Changing Cells: | 0 | 0 | 0 |
| 6 | | | | |
| 7 | | Contribution Margin for Product Mix | | |
| 8 | Target Cell: | Target Function Formula | | |
| 9 | | | | |
| 10 | | Constrained Resources | Used | Maximum |
| 11 | Constraints: | Resource A | Constraint Formula A | Max. Resource A |
| 12 | | Resource B | Constraint Formula B | Max. Resource B |
| 13 | | Etc. | Etc. | Etc. |

**(a) General Spreadsheet Format**

| | A | B | C | D |
|---|---|---|---|---|
| 1 | | Bertram Golf Carts | | |
| 2 | | | | |
| 3 | | Product Mix | | |
| 4 | | Regular Units | Premium Units | |
| 5 | Changing Cells: | 0 | 0 | |
| 6 | | | | |
| 7 | | Contribution Margin for Product Mix | | |
| 8 | Target Cell: | $0 | | |
| 9 | | | | |
| 10 | | Constrained Resources | Used | Maximum |
| 11 | Constraints: | Assembly hours | 0 | 10000 |
| 12 | | Testing hours | 0 | 1200 |
| 13 | | Leather seats | 0 | 150 |

**(b) Bertram Golf Carts**

Target cell formula:
=Regular*2400+Premium*3500

Constraint formulas:
=Regular*20+Premium*50
=Regular*5+Premium*2.5
=1*Premium

names in additional columns of row 4. If desired, enter the word "units" after the product name to indicate that Solver calculates the optimal number of units to be sold. Bertram Golf Carts produces only two products, so only cells B4 and C4 contain product names.

Rename the cells to the right of the Changing Cells and under the product names. Solver uses these cells to enter the number of units for the optimal product mix. These cells (B5, C5, and so on) must be given names that are used later in the spreadsheet for the target function formula and the constraint formulas. To assign a name to a given cell, first place the cursor in that cell. Next, find the cell number in the formula bar (if the formula bar is not visible, click on Formula Bar in the View menu). When you click on the cell number in the formula bar, the number will be highlighted. You can then replace the cell number with a name for the cell. This name will appear in Solver output reports, so you should choose a name that is recognizable. For Bertram Golf Carts, cell B5 is renamed "Regular" and cell C5 is renamed "Premium." Now enter a 0 in each of the renamed cells. For Bertram, a 0 is entered in cells B5 (renamed Regular) and C5 (renamed Premium). After Solver is run, Excel will replace these entries with the optimal number of units.

Insert a heading above the target cell: Type "Contribution Margin for Product Mix" in cell B7. In cell B8, enter an equal sign followed by the formula for the target function (i.e., the sum of the product contribution margins). When typing the formulas, use the names for cell references to the number of units for each product. If desired, format this cell as a dollar amount. For Bertram Golf Carts, the target function was determined in step 1. The formula is entered in cell B8 as:

$$=Regular*2400+Premium*3500$$

Because the initial units of regular and premium were entered as zeros in cells B5 and C5, Excel computes an initial value in cell B8 of $0.

Insert headings above the resource constraint cells: Type "Constrained Resources: in cell B10, "Used" in cell C10, and "Maximum" in cell D10. In column B, type a name for each constraint beginning in row 11. For Bertram Golf Carts, three constraints are named "Assembly hours" in cell B11, "Testing hours" in cell B12, and "Leather seats" in cell B13. The left- and right-hand sides of each resource constraint formula are entered in columns C and D, respectively. When typing the formulas, use the names for cell references to the renamed cells. For example, the formula for the Bertram assembly hours constraint was determined in step 2 as:

$$Regular\ carts*20\ hours+Premium\ carts*50\ hours \leq 10,000\ hours$$

Substituting the product cells names and omitting units of measurement, the formula becomes:

$$Regular*20+Premium*50 \leq 10000$$

Then, the left-hand side of the formula is entered in cell C11 as

$$=Regular*20+Premium*50$$

and the right-hand side of the formula (the maximum amount of the resource available) is entered in cell D11 as 10,000. Because the initial number of regular and premium units was entered as zero in cells B5 and C5, Excel computes an initial value of 0 for the number of constrained resources used in cell C11. Make similar entries for all of the constraints. Check to be sure the spreadsheet is similar to the ones in Exhibits 4A.1A and B.

## ■ 4. Use Excel Solver to Maximize the Objective Function

Once all information is entered in the spreadsheet, select Solver on the Tools menu in Excel. If Solver is not on the Tools menu, add it using the Add-Ins feature on the Tools menu. Once Solver is selected, a Solver Parameters dialog box like the first one shown in Exhibit 4A.2 will appear.

The Solver Parameters dialog box is used to select calculation options and to define the target function, product mix (i.e., change) variables, and the constraints. First, define the target function in Solver by entering a reference in the Set Target Cell area of the dialog box to the target function in the spreadsheet (cell B8). You can either (1) type "B8" in the Set Target Cell area of the dialog box, or (2) click in the Set Target Cell area of the dialog box and then click on the target function cell (B8) in the spreadsheet. (Excel will automatically convert "B8" to "$B$8.") Second, ensure that Solver will maximize the target function by verifying that the button next to Max is selected. Third, define the variables that Solver will change to maximize the target function by entering a reference to the cells that contain the number of units for each product (cells B5 and C5 for Bertram). You can either (1) type the cell range "B5:C5" in the By Changing Cells area of the dialog box, or (2) click in the By Changing Cells area of the dialog box and then highlight the range of cells (B5 through C5)

**EXHIBIT 4A.2** Solver Dialog Boxes

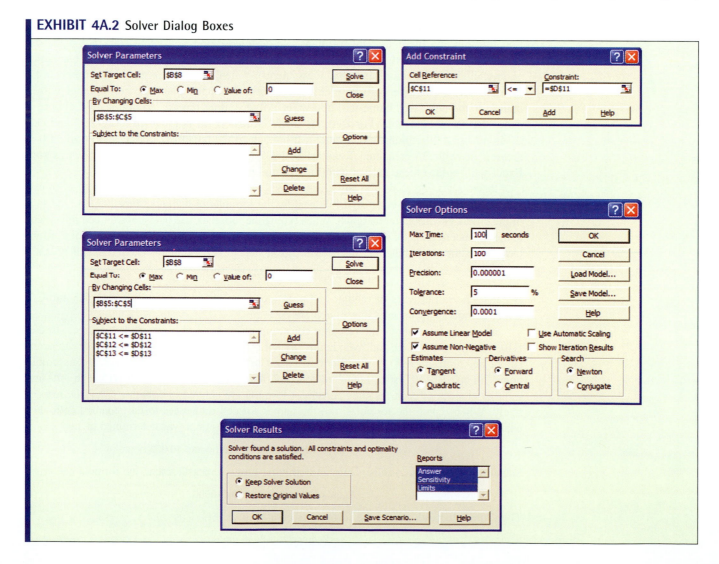

in the spreadsheet. Fourth, add constraints by clicking on the Add button, which will cause the Add Constraint dialog box shown in Exhibit 4A.2 to appear.

The constraints are defined one at a time in the Add Constraint dialog box. The Cell Reference area is used for the constraint formula, while the Constraint area is used for the maximum quantity available of each resource. The following instructions refer to the first constraint for Bertram. To set the Cell Reference, you can either (1) type "C11" in the Cell Reference area of the dialog box, or (2) click in the Cell Reference area of the dialog box and then click on constraint formula cell (C11) in the spreadsheet. Ensure that the constraint mathematical operation in the middle area shows as "<=". To set the Constraint, you can either (1) type "D11" in the Cell Reference area of the dialog box, or (2) click in the Cell Reference area of the dialog box and then click on constraint formula cell (D11) in the spreadsheet. Click on the Add button. The dialog box will then clear, and you can follow the preceding directions for the next constraint. After adding values for the last constraint, click OK. You will then return to the Solver Parameters dialog box (Exhibit 4A.2). Notice that all constraints appear in the Subject to the Constraints area of the dialog box.

Next, click on Options in the Solver Parameters dialog box and the Solver Options dialog box will appear (Exhibit 4A.2).

In the Solver Options dialog box, select Assume Linear Model and Assume Non-Negative. Then click OK. You will return to the Solver Parameters dialog box. Now click on Solve. Solver will perform its calculations and then open the Solver Results dialog box, (Exhibit 4A.2). An explanation will appear at the top of the dialogue box. If Solver ran successfully, the wording will appear.

When Solver runs successfully, the Solver Results dialog box contains three reports: Answer, Sensitivity, and Limits. Highlight the report names to save them as separate sheets in the spreadsheet file. Then click OK. Once Solver is finished, the spreadsheet for Bertram appears as shown in Exhibit 4A.3. The following results are shown in the spreadsheet:

- Number of units in the optimal product mix for each product
- Total contribution margin at the optimal product mix
- Quantity used for each constrained resource at the optimal product mix

If you use Solver again on the same spreadsheet, you must reset the Changing Cells (B5 and C5 for Bertram) to 0. Otherwise, the Solver solution may not be the optimum for the new variables.

## ■ 5. Interpret the Solver Output

Refer to the Bertram Golf Carts illustration in the chapter for discussions of the Answer Report (Exhibit 4.4 on page 144) and Sensitivity Report (Exhibit 4.5 on page 145).

**EXHIBIT 4A.3**
Spreadsheet after Solver Tool Is Run

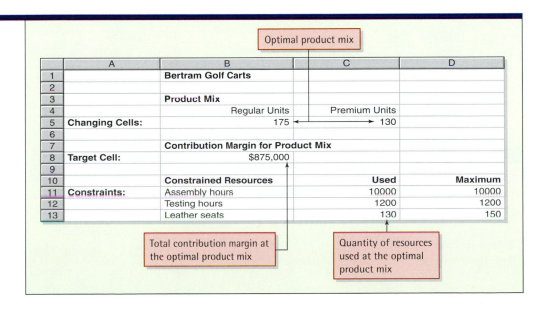

Optimal product mix

| | A | B | C | D |
|---|---|---|---|---|
| 1 | | Bertram Golf Carts | | |
| 2 | | | | |
| 3 | | Product Mix | | |
| 4 | | Regular Units | Premium Units | |
| 5 | Changing Cells: | 175 | 130 | |
| 6 | | | | |
| 7 | | Contribution Margin for Product Mix | | |
| 8 | Target Cell: | $875,000 | | |
| 9 | | | | |
| 10 | | Constrained Resources | Used | Maximum |
| 11 | Constraints: | Assembly hours | 10000 | 10000 |
| 12 | | Testing hours | 1200 | 1200 |
| 13 | | Leather seats | 130 | 150 |

Total contribution margin at the optimal product mix

Quantity of resources used at the optimal product mix

# SUMMARY

## Q1 What Is the Process for Making Nonroutine Operating Decisions?

### Decision Process

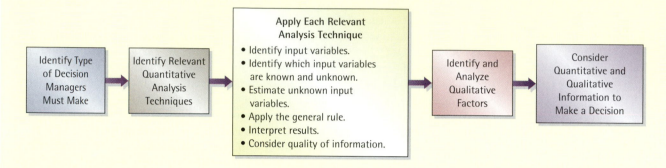

### General Decision Rule
Take the action that maximizes current period income (or minimizes current period losses).

### To Apply the General Decision Rule
Identify and calculate relevant revenues and costs:
- Contribution margin per unit
- Contribution margin per unit of constrained resource
- Fixed costs that differ across alternatives
- Opportunity costs

## Q2 How Are Decisions Made to Accept, Reject, and Price Special Orders?

### General Decision Rule
Accept if price is greater than or equal to the sum of variable cost, relevant fixed costs, and opportunity cost.

### Opportunity Cost
Contribution margin of any regular business replaced

### Relevant Fixed Costs
Only new fixed costs associated with the special order

## Q3 How Are Decisions Made to Keep or Drop Products, Segments, or Whole Businesses?

### General Decision Rule
Drop if contribution margin is less than the sum of relevant fixed costs and opportunity cost.

### Opportunity Cost
Benefits from using released capacity for other purposes

### Relevant Fixed Costs
Only fixed costs that can be avoided if drop

## Q4 How Are Decisions Made to Insource or Outsource an Activity (Make or Buy)?

### General Decision Rule
Outsource if buy cost is less than or equal to the sum of variable cost and relevant fixed costs minus opportunity cost.

### Opportunity Cost
Benefits from using released capacity for other purposes

### Relevant Fixed Costs
Only fixed costs that can be avoided if decision is to buy

## Q5 How Are Decisions Made for Product Emphasis and Constrained Resources?

### Types of Constrained Resource Problems
- Product emphasis
- Product mix when resources are constrained
- Relaxing constraints for two or fewer products
- Relaxing constraints for multiple products and multiple constraints

### General Decision Rule
Product Emphasis: Emphasize product with highest contribution margin per unit unless resources are constrained, then emphasize product with highest contribution margin per unit of constrained resource.

Constrained Resource: Incur cost to relax constraint if cost is less than or equal to the sum of contribution margin per unit of constrained resource and the current variable cost of the resource.

### Relevant Fixed Costs
Constrained Resource: Only new fixed costs to relax the constraint

## Q6 What Qualitative Factors Are Important to Nonroutine Operating Decisions?

### Examples of Qualitative Factors

| | Type of Decision | | | | |
|---|---|---|---|---|---|
| **Special Order** | **Product Line and Business Segment (keep or drop)** | **Insource or Outsource (make or buy)** | **Product Emphasis (under constraints)** | **Relax Constrained Resource** |
| • Will regular customers expect lower prices?<br>• Will this order lead to improved brand name recognition?<br>• Can we deliver without disrupting current schedules? | • Will dropping one product affect sales of other products?<br>• Will layoffs affect worker morale? | • Is it easier to ensure high quality via insourcing or outsourcing?<br>• Will delivery be timely?<br>• Are there uncertainties about the supplier's ability to meet contractual obligations?<br>• Is this activity a core competency? | • Does the product emphasis agree with strategic plans? | • Are there other ways to relax the constraint?<br>• How would brand recognition be affected by delivery delays?<br>• Will the decision affect future supply costs? |

## Q7 What Limitations and Uncertainties Should Be Considered When Making Nonroutine Operating Decisions?

### Quality of Information
- Uncertainties
- Information timeliness
- Analysis technique assumptions
  - Managers would like to maximize short-term profits
  - CVP assumptions (see Chapter 3)
  - Additional assumptions for constrained resource decisions:
    - The organization will forgo sales if the resource constraint is not relaxed.
    - Fixed costs are unaffected by short-term decisions made to relax constraints.
    - Sales of one product do not affect sales of other products.

### Quality of Decision Process
- Decision-maker bias
- Sensitivity analysis
- Prioritization

**Examples of Uncertainties**

| | Type of Decision | | | | |
|---|---|---|---|---|---|
| Special Order | Product Line and Business Segment (keep or drop) | Insource or Outsource (make or buy) | Product Emphasis (under constraints) | Relax (alleviate) Constrained Resource |
| • How accurate are the cost estimates?<br>• Are we operating in the relevant range?<br>• Will fixed costs increase at higher capacity levels? | • How accurate are the revenue and cost estimates?<br>• How will customers respond to the dropped product? | • How accurate are the cost estimates?<br>• Is our measure of quality appropriate?<br>• How reliable is the vendor or resource supplier? | • How accurate are the contribution margin estimates?<br>• How reliable are the product demand forecasts? | • How accurate are the contribution margin estimates?<br>• How accurate are the constraint use estimates? |

## KEY TO SYMBOLS

**e** This question requires students to extend knowledge beyond the applications shown in the textbook.

**1** This question requires Step 1 skills (**Identifying**) in Steps for Better Thinking (Exhibit 1.10).

**2** This question requires Step 2 skills (**Exploring**) in Steps for Better Thinking (Exhibit 1.10).

**3** This question requires Step 3 skills (**Prioritizing**) in Steps for Better Thinking (Exhibit 1.10).

**4** This question requires Step 4 skills (**Envisioning**) in Steps for Better Thinking (Exhibit 1.10).

## Self-Study Problems

### Self-Study Problem 1  Product Emphasis, Solver, Graph

**Q5**

Power Tool manufactures engines for a broad range of commercial and consumer products. At its plant in Cleveland, it assembles two engines—a rototiller engine and a riding lawn mower engine. Following is information for each product line:

| | Rototiller Engine | Riding Lawn Mower Engine |
|---|---|---|
| Selling price | $800 | $1,000 |
| Variable costs per unit | 560 | 625 |
| Contribution margin per unit | $240 | $ 375 |
| Contribution margin ratio | 30% | 37.5% |

Rototiller engines require 2 machine-hours each, and riding lawn mower engines require 5 machine hours each. Only 600 machine hours are available each day for assembling engines. Additional capacity cannot be obtained in the short run. Power Tools only has demand for 200 rototiller engines but can sell as many riding lawn mower engines as it produces.

**REQUIRED:**

**A.** Which product should Power Tools emphasize? Explain and support your answer with quantitative information.

**B.** Using the general decision rule, what premium per machine hour would the managers of Power Tools be willing to pay to increase the number of machine hours available?

**C.** Use Excel Solver or a similar program to determine the optimal product mix. From the sensitivity report, determine the amount per machine hour that Power Tools would be willing to spend to relax the constraint in assembly.

**e** **D.** Develop an answer by graphing the solution area.

**EXHIBIT 4.7**

Graphical Solution to
Power Tool Product
Emphasis Problem

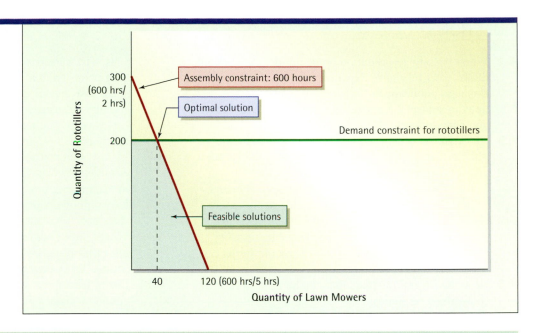

## Solution to Self-Study Problem 1

**A.** The contribution margin per unit of constrained resource for each engine is (MH = machine hour):

Rototiller: $240 ÷ 2 MH = $120 per MH
Lawn mower: $375 ÷ 5 MH = $75 per MH

For this constrained resource problem, Power Tools should emphasize the product having the highest contribution margin per unit of constrained resource. In this case, the company should emphasize the rototiller.

**B.** If Power Tools can sell more rototillers, it can spend up to $120 per machine hour plus whatever it spends now on variable production costs to increase machine hours. When the demand of rototiller engines has been met, it can spend up to $75 per machine hour plus what it spends now on variable production costs to increase machine hours for the production of lawn mower engines.

**C.** Using Excel Solver, the optimal product mix is 200 rototiller engines and 40 lawn mower engines. The shadow price is $75 for lawn mower engines, so Power would be willing to spend $75 per machine hour plus whatever it spends now on variable production costs. Notice this answer is the same as calculated in part (B).

**D.** The graphical solution for the problem is shown in Exhibit 4.7.
To create the graph:

- Each axis represents the volume of a product.
- Draw a line for each constraint.
- Find the feasible solution area, where all constraints are met.
- Calculate the total contribution margin at each corner point.
- Find the optimal sales mix by finding the corner with the highest contribution margin.

Notice that the optimal product mix in Exhibit 4.7 is the same as in Part (C): 200 rototiller engines and 40 lawn mower engines.

---

**REVIEW** Use the exercises in the following boxes in the chapter to review key terms and key techniques, analyze chapter illustrations, and improve your learning of new concepts, and practice ethical decision making:

Guide Your Learning 4.1: Key Terms (p. 133)

Guide Your Learning 4.2: Barkley Basketballs (p. 135)

Guide Your Learning 4.3: Home Aide Services (p. 137)

Guide Your Learning 4.4: Roadrunner Publishers (Part 1) (p. 139)

Guide Your Learning 4.5: Roadrunner Publishers (Part 2) (p. 143)

Guide Your Learning 4.6: Bertram Golf Carts (p. 145)

Guide Your Learning 4.7: Key Terms (p. 146)

Focus on Ethical Decision Making: Stewardship of Public Funds (p. 149)

## QUESTIONS

**4.1** When making a nonroutine operating decision, are all future costs relevant? Explain.

**4.2** Business publications frequently provide subscriptions to students at a substantial discount. Why do you suppose such offers are made?

**4.3** An organization is currently operating at capacity. Should it accept a request for a special order based on variable cost plus 40%? Explain.

**4.4** Refer to the general decision rule for special orders. Would this same general decision rule apply to a decision to sell afternoon theater tickets at a discounted price? Explain. Identify two other business pricing situations that are similar to the afternoon theater tickets.

**4.5** Describe several methods that can be used to relax constrained resources.

**4.6** In your own words, distinguish between quantitative and qualitative information.

**4.7** Grover Nursery is a large nursery in St. Charles, Illinois, that has always raised the bedding plants it sells. The managers recently decided to buy bedding plants from a wholesale nursery in another state. List several quantitative factors that might encourage the managers to buy from another grower. List several qualitative factors that might encourage the managers to grow their own plants.

**4.8** List two qualitative factors that often need to be considered when making a decision about whether to outsource a product or service.

**4.9** Explain how managers decide which products in a sales mix to emphasize.

**4.10** What kind of constraints would arise in an accounting firm during tax season? How could any constraints be relaxed?

**4.11** List at least three different types of nonroutine operating decisions and give an example of each one for a retail clothing factory outlet.

**4.12** List two qualitative factors that often need to be considered when making a decision about whether to accept a special order.

## EXERCISES

**4.13** **Make or buy, qualitative factors** Yoklic Corporation currently manufactures a subassembly for
**Q4, Q6** its main product. The costs per unit are as follows:

| | |
|---|---|
| Direct materials | $ 4.00 |
| Direct labor | 30.00 |
| Variable overhead | 15.00 |
| Fixed overhead | 25.00 |
| Total | $74.00 |

Regina Corp has contacted Yoklic with an offer to sell it 5,000 subassemblies for $55.00 each.

**REQUIRED:**
**A.** Should Yoklic make or buy the subassemblies? Create a schedule that shows the total quantitative differences between the two alternatives.
**B.** The accountant decided to investigate the fixed costs to see whether any incremental changes would occur if the subassembly were no longer manufactured. The accountant believes that Yoklic will eliminate $50,000 of fixed overhead if it accepts the proposal. Does this new information change the decision? Show your calculations.
**C.** What qualitative factors are important for accountants and managers to consider for Yoklic's make or buy decision?

**4.14** **Constrained resource, qualitative factors** Johnson and Sons, Inc., produces organic orange juice
**Q5, Q6** from oranges it raises. Unfortunately, it has been a bad year for oranges because of severe frosts. Johnson only has 10,000 gallons of juice. It usually sells 15,000 gallons at $3 per gallon. The variable costs of raising the oranges are $0.50 per gallon. Johnson has loyal customers, but its managers are worried the company will lose customers if it does not have juice available for sale when people stop by the farm. A neighbor is willing to sell 5,000 gallons of extra orange juice at $2.95 per gallon.

**REQUIRED:**
**A.** Which type of nonroutine operating decision is involved here? What are the managers' decision options?

**B.** Using the general decision rule, what is the most per gallon Johnson's managers would be willing to pay for additional juice?

**C.** Why would Johnson be willing to pay the amount calculated in part (B) for more juice?

**①  D.** Is the quality of the neighbor's juice a concern to Johnson's managers in making this decision? Why or why not?

**①  E.** List another qualitative factor that might affect the managers' decision.

**4.15**  **CVP, single constrained resource** Snowbird Snowboards converts regular snowboards by adding
**Q5**  outriggers and seats so that people who use wheelchairs can snowboard. The income statement for last year, in which 500 snowboards were produced and sold, appears here.

| Revenue | | $150,000 |
|---|---|---|
| Expenses: | | |
| Variable production costs | $60,000 | |
| Fixed production costs | 25,000 | |
| Variable selling and administration | 10,000 | |
| Fixed selling and administration | 35,000 | 130,000 |
| Income | | $ 20,000 |

**REQUIRED:**

**A.** What volume of snowboards must be sold to earn pretax profits of $30,000?

**B.** Snowbird's supplier of snowboards is unable to ship more than 500 boards for the upcoming season. Snowbird has been paying the supplier $85 for each snowboard. (The cost of the snowboards is included in variable production costs.) More expensive snowboards are available from other manufacturers for conversion. If Snowbird's managers expect to sell more than 500 converted snowboards in the upcoming season, what is the most they would be willing to pay outside suppliers for each additional snowboard?

**C.** Suppose Snowbird pays the price you calculated in part (B) and sells an additional 200 snowboards. What is the company's incremental profit on the 200 snowboards?

**4.16**  **Multiple products, multiple resource constraints, sensitivity** Mrs. Meadows sells two popular
**Q5**  brands of cookies, Chip Dip and Soft Chunk Chocolate Chip. Both cookies go through the mix-
**CMA**  ing and baking departments, but Chip Dip is also dipped in chocolate in the coating department.

Frank Roman, vice president for sales, believes that Mrs. Meadows can sell all of its daily production of Chip Dip and Soft Chunk. Both cookies are made in batches of 600 cookies. The batch times for producing each type of cookie and the minutes available per day are as follows.

| | Mixing | Baking | Dipping |
|---|---|---|---|
| Minutes required per batch | | | |
| Chip Dip | 20 | 40 | 15 |
| Soft Chunk | 30 | 20 | 0 |
| Minutes available per day | 4,000 | 6,000 | 2,000 |

Revenue per batch for Chip Dip is $150 and the variable costs per batch are $100. Fixed costs of $2,350 are allocated to Chip Dip. Revenue per batch for Soft Chunk Chocolate Chips is $175 and the variable costs per batch are $135. Allocated fixed costs are $1,500.

Set up the target function (contribution margin function) and the constraints for this problem. Enter these constraints and the target function into Excel Solver or another linear programming package and print out a formula sheet and all of the reports.

**REQUIRED:**

**A.** What is the optimal product mix?

**B.** What is the total contribution margin for that product mix?

**C.** Following the general decision rule, what would the managers of Mrs. Meadows be willing to pay to relax each constraint?

**D.** Which constraints are binding?

**E.** By how much could the contribution margin for Soft Chunk increase before the optimal product mix changes?

**4.17** **Keep or drop and constrained resource** The income statement for King Salmon Sales, which
Q3, Q5 produces smoked salmon, follows:

| | | |
|---|---:|---:|
| Revenue (100,000 lbs.) | | $800,000 |
| Expenses | | |
|     Fish | $200,000 | |
|     Smoking materials | 20,000 | |
|     Packaging materials | 30,000 | |
|     Labor (wages) | 300,000 | |
|     Administration | 150,000 | |
|     Sales commissions | 10,000 | |
| Total expenses | | 710,000 |
| Pretax income | | $ 90,000 |

Assume that the administrative costs are fixed and that all of the other costs are variable.

REQUIRED:
A. Suppose the state government curtails fishing because of low fish counts. As a result,
King Salmon Sales can buy only 50,000 pounds of salmon this year. Assume that the
selling price, the fixed costs, and the variable costs remain the same as last year. Using
only quantitative information, should King Salmon operate this year? Explain your answer, using calculations. (*Hint:* Before you begin, identify the type of nonroutine operating decision, the decision options, and the relevant information for this decision.)
B. Assume King Salmon can buy up to 70,000 pounds of fish at $2.00 per pound and that
the remainder of the fixed and variable costs remain the same as last year. Also assume
that the selling price remains the same as last year and that the market will purchase at
least another 30,000 pounds of fish. If the managers of King Salmon wish to sell more
salmon, what should they be willing to pay to purchase more fish? [*Hint:* This type of
decision is different from part (A). Before you begin, identify the type of nonroutine
decision, the decision options, and the relevant information.]

**4.18** **Product emphasis and constrained resource** Emily developed an innovative computer game,
Q5 called Home By Myself (HBM). It was so successful that she quickly followed up with two sequels: Home By Myself II (HBM2) and Home By Myself III (HBM3). The costs of developing
the games were $95,000 for HBM, $10,000 for HBM2, and $15,000 for HBM3.
    The production process consists of copying the games to blank DVDs using her computer and
then packing them with printed instructions in a display box. It takes longer to copy the original
game than the sequels. Emily can produce, ready for shipping, about 20 copies of HBM, 30 copies
of HBM2, or 45 copies of HBM3 in an hour.

| | HBM | HBM2 | HBM3 |
|---|---:|---:|---:|
| Selling price | $49.00 | $29.00 | $29.00 |
| Costs | | | |
|     Blank DVD | 1.00 | 0.50 | 0.50 |
|         Instructions and packaging | 4.00 | 2.00 | 2.00 |
|         Prorated development costs* | 19.00 | 1.00 | 3.00 |
| Margin | $25.00 | $25.50 | $23.50 |
| | | | |
| Daily demand | 120 games | 120 games | 90 games |

*The prorated development costs were determined for each game by dividing the game's development
costs by 5,000, the estimated minimum total demand for each game.

REQUIRED:
A. What is the contribution margin per hour of Emily's time for each game?
B. In what order should Emily produce the games?
C. Using the general decision rule for constrained capacity, what is the most Emily should
be willing to pay per hour for a worker to duplicate and pack diskettes after her normal
working hours? (Assume that the worker would work at the same pace as Emily.)

**4.19** **Multiple products and resource constraints, sensitivity analysis** Wildlife Foods prepares wild
Q5 birdseed mixes and sells them to local pet stores, grocery stores, and wild bird stores. Two types

of mixes have been most successful: Flight Fancy and Multigrain. Flight Fancy generates a contribution margin of $12 per 100 pound bag and Multigrain contributes $9 per 100 pounds. Because Wildlife Foods has been very thorough in its sterilization process, the birdseed never germinates and grows. Therefore, it is a top seller and the company can sell all of the birdseed it produces.

The seed is processed in three stages: mixing, sterilization, and packaging. The time requirements for each batch of 100 bags of Flight Fancy and 10,000 pounds of Multigrain (which is sold in bulk rather than bags) follow.

|  | Minutes Required | | |
|---|---|---|---|
|  | Mixing | Sterilization | Packaging |
| Flight Fancy | 200 | 200 | 100 |
| Multigrain | 100 | 300 | 0 (sold in bulk) |
| Minutes Available | 6,000 | 12,000 | 4,500 |

**REQUIRED:**

**A.** Using a spreadsheet program such as Excel Solver, find the optimal product mix given the current constraints and contribution margins.

**B.** Which constraints are binding?

**C.** What happens if minutes available for mixing are doubled? Does another constraint become binding? What is the optimal product mix now?

**4.20**
**Q2**

**Special order** The Cone Head House sells ice cream cones in a variety of flavors. Data for a recent week appear here:

| | |
|---|---|
| Revenue (1,000 cones @ $1.50 each) | $1,500 |
| Cost of ingredients | 530 |
| Rent | 300 |
| Store attendant | 600 |
| Income | $  70 |

The Cone Head's manager received a call from a university student club requesting a bid on 100 cones to be picked up in three days. The cones could be produced in advance by the store attendant during slack periods and then stored in the freezer. Each cone requires a special plastic cover that costs $0.05.

**REQUIRED:**

**A.** What are the managers' decision options?

**B.** What quantitative information is relevant for this decision?

**C.** Using the general decision rule, what is the minimum acceptable price per cone for this special order?

**D.** Explain why Cone Head's managers might be willing to sell cones at the price you calculated in part (C).

**4.21**
**Q2, Q6**

**Special order, qualitative factors** Cute Cookies (CC) sells cookies, brownies, and beverages to small local shops. The selling price per brownie is $1.25, the variable cost is $0.75, and the average cost is $1.00. The principal of an elementary school asked CC to provide 10 dozen brownies for its spring picnic. The principal wants to buy the brownies at CC's cost. Unlike regular sales, each special order brownie must be delivered in a plastic container to protect it from dust. The containers cost $0.05 each. The brownies can be prepared ahead of time when workers are not busy.

**REQUIRED:**

**A.** Under the general decision rule for special orders, what is the minimum price per brownie that CC's management should accept?

**B.** If the principal can pay no more than $0.80 per brownie, should CC take the order? Why or why not?

**❶ C.** List several qualitative factors that could affect CC's decision if the special order price for brownies is $0.80.

**4.22**    **Outsourcing computations, uncertainties** Saguaro Systems produces and sells speakers and CD
**Q4, Q7**   players. The following information has been collected about the costs related to the systems:

| | |
|---|---|
| Selling price per unit | $70 |
| Production costs per unit | |
|     Direct materials | $22 |
|     Direct labor | 16 |
|     Variable overhead | 2 |
| Total fixed overhead | $360,000 |

Saguaro normally produces 25,000 of these systems per year.

The managers have recently received an offer from a Mexican company to produce these systems
for $48 each. The managers estimate that $260,000 of Saguaro's fixed costs could be eliminated
if they accept the offer.

**REQUIRED:**      **A.** Which type of nonroutine operating decision is involved here? What are the managers'
decision options? What quantitative information is relevant to the decision?

       **B.** Perform a quantitative analysis for the decision, and present your results in a schedule.

       **C.** Under the general decision rule for this type of decision, what production level is re-
quired for Saguaro's managers to be indifferent?

       ❶ **D.** List as many uncertainties as you can for this decision.

**4.23**    **Special order computations, qualitative factors** The Feed Barn packages and distributes three
**Q2, Q6**   grades of animal feed. The material cost per ton and estimated annual sales for each of the products are listed.

| Product | Material Cost | Estimated Sales |
|---|---|---|
| Super Premium | $10.00 | 2,000 tons |
| Premium | 8.00 | 3,000 tons |
| Economy | 7.00 | 5,000 tons |

The fixed cost of operating the machinery used to package all three products is $10,000 per
year. In the past, prices have been set by allocating the fixed operating cost to products on the basis of estimated sales in tons. The resulting full costs (material costs plus allocated fixed operating cost) are then marked up 100%. The Feed Barn has received an offer from a foreign firm for
1,000 tons of the premium grade feed. Sales to the foreign firm would not affect domestic sales,
but would require an increase in fixed production costs of $2,000.

**REQUIRED:**      **A.** Which type of nonroutine operating decision is involved here? What are the managers'
decision options?

       **B.** What relevant quantitative information is required for this type of decision?

       **C.** Using only quantitative information, what is the minimum price that the Feed Barn's
managers should be willing to accept from the foreign firm?

       ❶ **D.** What types of qualitative factors would the Feed Barn's managers typically consider be-
fore agreeing to the sale? Explain.

**4.24**    **Keep or drop, multiple product breakeven, qualitative factors** Horton and Associates pro-
**Q3, Q6**   duces two products named the Big Winner and the Loser. Last month 1,000 units of the Loser and
4,000 units of the Big Winner were produced and sold. Average prices and costs for the two products for last month follow:

| | Loser | Big Winner |
|---|---|---|
| Selling price | $95 | $225 |
| Direct materials | 40 | 95 |
| Direct labor | 5 | 25 |
| Variable overhead | 5 | 15 |
| Product line fixed costs | 10 | 40 |
| Corporate fixed costs | 25 | 25 |
| Average margin per unit | $10 | $ 25 |

The production lines for both products are highly automated, so large changes in production cause
very little change in total direct labor costs. Workers who are classified as direct labor monitor the
production line and are permanent employees who regularly work 40 hours per week.

All costs other than corporate fixed costs listed under each product line could be avoided if the product line were dropped. Corporate fixed costs totaled $125,000, and the total sales amounted to 5,000 units, producing the average cost per unit of $25. About $10,000 of the corporate fixed costs could be avoided if the Loser were dropped, and about $15,000 of the corporate fixed costs could be avoided if the Big Winner were dropped. The remaining $100,000 could be avoided only by going out of business entirely.

**REQUIRED:**
   A. What is the overall corporate breakeven in total sales revenue, assuming the sales mix is the same as last month's?
   B. What is the breakeven sales volume (in units produced and sold) for the Loser? (In other words, what is the sales volume at which Horton should be financially indifferent between dropping and retaining the Loser?)
   ❶ C. List at least two qualitative factors that would affect the decision to keep or drop the Loser.

**4.25**
**Q3, Q5, Q6**
**Product emphasis and keep or drop, product breakeven, relevant information** The income statement information for Kallapur and Trombley Cotton Growers follows:

|  | Premium | Regular | Fancy | Total |
|---|---|---|---|---|
| Sales units | 100 bales | 100 bales | 100 bales | 300 bales |
| Sales | $2,200 | $1,600 | $1,800 | $5,600 |
| Variable costs | 1,400 | 1,000 | 1,080 | 3,480 |
| Contribution margin | 800 | 600 | 720 | 2,120 |
| Production line fixed costs* | 640 | 725 | 520 | 1,885 |
| Corporate costs (allocated)** | 90 | 80 | 105 | 275 |
| Total fixed costs | 730 | 805 | 625 | 2,160 |
| Operating income (loss) | $ 70 | $ (205) | $ 95 | $ (40) |

*If the company drops the product, these costs are no longer incurred.
**None of these corporate costs are expected to change if a product line is dropped.

**REQUIRED:**
   A. Using the general decision rule, which product should the corporation emphasize? Support your answer with calculations.
   B. Using the general decision rule, should the corporation drop Regular (assuming no changes in demand for other products)? Support your answer with calculations. Show how operating income would change if Regular were dropped.
   C. At what point (in bales) would the managers be indifferent to dropping Regular? In other words, what is the breakeven point for Regular?
   ❶ D. What other information would you want before you make a decision about whether to drop Regular?

# PROBLEMS

**4.26**
**Q2, Q5, Q6**
**Special order capacity constraint, relevant information, qualitative factors** Rightway Printers, a book printing shop, is operating at 95% capacity. The company has been offered a special order for book printing at $8.50 per book; the order requires 10% of capacity. No other use for the remaining 5% idle capacity can be found. The average cost per book is $8.00, and the contribution margin per book for regular sales is $1.50.

**REQUIRED:**
   A. Which type of nonroutine operating decision is involved here? What are the managers' decision options?
   ❶ B. What information is relevant for this decision? Does the problem give you all of the information the manager needs to make a decision? What other information is needed?
   C. Using the general decision rule, what premium is the manager willing to pay (per book) to relax the constrained capacity, assuming no qualitative factors are relevant?
   ❷ D. Explain how capacity affects the quantitative analysis for this decision.
   ❶ E. What qualitative factors could affect this decision?

**4.27**
 **Q4, Q6**
**Make or buy, qualitative factors** The Vernom Corporation produces and sells to wholesalers a highly successful line of summer lotion and insect repellents. Vernom has decided to diversify to

stabilize sales throughout the year. A natural area for the company to consider is the production of winter lotions and creams to prevent dry and chapped skin.

After considerable research, a winter products line has been developed. However, because of the conservative nature of company management, Vernom's president has decided to introduce only one of the new products for this coming winter. If the product is a success, further expansion in future years will be initiated.

The product selected is a lip balm to be sold in a lipstick-type tube. The product will be sold to wholesalers in boxes of 24 tubes for $8.00 per box. Because of available capacity, no additional fixed charges will be incurred to produce the product. However, a $200,000 fixed charge will be assigned to allocate a fair share of the company's fixed costs to the new product. The remaining overhead costs are variable.

Using estimated sales and production of 100,000 boxes of lip balm as the standard volume, the accounting department has developed the following costs per box of 24 tubes.

| | |
|---|---|
| Direct labor | $4.00 |
| Direct materials | 6.00 |
| Total overhead | 3.00 |
| Total | $13.00 |

Vernom approached a cosmetics manufacturer to discuss the possibility of purchasing the tubes for the new product. The purchase price of the empty tubes from the cosmetics manufacturer would be $1.80 per 24 tubes. If Vernom accepts the purchase proposal, it is estimated that direct labor and variable overhead costs would be reduced by 10% and direct materials costs would be reduced by 20%.

**REQUIRED:**

**A.** Should the Vernom Corporation make or buy the tubes? Show calculations to support your answer.

**B.** What would be the maximum purchase price acceptable to Vernom for the tubes? Explain.

**C.** Instead of sales of 100,000 boxes, revised estimates show sales volume at 125,000 boxes. At this new volume, additional equipment at an annual rental of $20,000 must be acquired to manufacture the tubes. However, this incremental cost would be the only additional fixed cost required, even if sales increased to 300,000 boxes. (The 300,000 level is the goal for the third year of production.) Under these circumstances should Vernom make or buy the tubes? Show calculations to support your answer.

**D.** The company has the option of making and buying at the same time. What is your answer to part (C) if this alternative is considered? Show calculations to support your answer.

**① E.** What qualitative factors should Vernom managers consider in determining whether they should make or buy the lipstick tubes?

☆ **4.28**
Q2, Q6, Q7

**Special order, qualitative factors, uncertainties, sensitivity** Jazzy Cases manufactures several different styles of jewelry cases. Management estimates that during the first quarter of this year the company will operate at about 80% of normal capacity. Two special orders have been received, and management is making a decision about whether to accept either or both orders.

The first order is from Penny-Wise Department Stores. The manager would like to market a jewelry case similar to one of Jazzy's current models. Penny-Wise wants its own label on the cases and is willing to pay $5.75 per case for 20,000 cases to be shipped by April 1. The cost data for Jazzy's case, which is similar to the requested case, follow:

| | |
|---|---|
| Selling price per unit | $9.00 |
| Cost per unit | |
| Raw materials | $2.50 |
| Direct labor (0.25 hrs. × $12) | 3.00 |
| Overhead (0.25 machine hrs. × $4) | 1.00 |
| Total cost per unit | $6.50 |

According to the specifications supplied by Penny-Wise, the special order case requires less expensive raw materials. Therefore, the raw materials for the special order will cost $2.25 per case. Management believes that the rest of the costs, labor time, and machine time will remain the same as for Jazzy's case.

The second order is from the Star-Mart Company. Its managers want 8,000 cases for $7.50 per case. These jewelry cases, to be marketed under the Star-Mart label, would also need to be shipped by April 1. However, these cases are somewhat different from any cases currently manufactured by Jazzy. Following are the estimated unit costs:

| Cost per unit | |
|---|---|
| Raw materials | $3.25 |
| Direct labor (0.25 hrs. × $12) | 3.00 |
| Overhead (0.5 machine hrs. × $4.00) | 2.00 |
| Total cost per unit | $8.25 |

In addition to these per-unit costs, Jazzy would incur $1,500 in setup costs and would need to purchase $2,500 in special equipment to manufacture these cases. Currently, Jazzy would have no other use for the equipment once this order was filled.

Jazzy's capacity constraint is total machine hours available. The plant capacity under normal operations is 90,000 machine hours per year, or 7,500 hours per month. Fixed manufacturing overhead costs are allocated to production on the basis of machine hours at $4.00 per hour and are budgeted at $360,000 per year.

Jazzy can work on the special orders throughout the entire first quarter, in addition to performing its normal production. Jazzy's managers do not expect any repeat sales to be generated from either special order.

**REQUIRED:**
**ANALYZE**
**INFORMATION**

The following questions will help you analyze the information for this problem. Do not turn in your answers to these questions unless your professor asks you to do so.

**A.** What is the excess capacity of machine hours available in the first quarter? Explain how machine hour capacity affects the special order decision.

**B.** Ignore the Star-Mart order. Using the general decision rule, what is the minimum acceptable price for the Penny-Wise order?

**C.** Ignore the Penny-Wise order. What is the contribution margin per case for the Star-Mart order? What would be the total expected profit (loss) incurred by accepting this order?

**D.** Using only quantitative information, decide which special orders Jazzy should accept.

**E.** What qualitative factors are likely to be important to this decision?

❶ **F.** Identify and explain uncertainties that affect Jazzy's decision.

❷ **G.** What might happen to costs if Jazzy's production exceeds 95% of its capacity? Discuss how increased use of capacity from a special order might affect the company's costs. (*Hint:* Think about whether bottlenecks could arise and how they might affect costs.)

**REQUIRED:**
**WRITTEN**
**ASSIGNMENT**

Suppose you are the cost accountant for Jazzy. Turn in your answers to the following.

❸ **H.** Write a memo to Jazzy's management recommending whether the company should accept each of the special orders. Attach to the memo a schedule showing your computations. As appropriate, refer to the schedule in the memo.

❸ **I.** Write one or two paragraphs explaining how you decided what information to include in your memo.

**4.29**
**Q2, Q6, Q7**
CMA

**Special order computations and decision** George Jackson operates a small machine shop. He manufactures one standard product available from many other similar businesses, and he also manufactures custom-ordered products. His accountant prepared the following annual income statement.

| | Custom Sales | Standard Sales | Total |
|---|---|---|---|
| Sales | $50,000 | $25,000 | $75,000 |
| Costs | | | |
| Material | 10,000 | 8,000 | 18,000 |
| Labor | 20,000 | 9,000 | 29,000 |
| Depreciation | 6,300 | 3,600 | 9,900 |
| Power | 700 | 400 | 1,100 |
| Rent | 6,000 | 1,000 | 7,000 |
| Heat and light | 600 | 100 | 700 |
| Other | 400 | 900 | 1,300 |
| Total costs | 44,000 | 23,000 | 67,000 |
| Income | $ 6,000 | $ 2,000 | $ 8,000 |

The depreciation charges are for machines used in the respective product lines. The power charge is apportioned on an estimate of power consumed. The rent is for the building space, which has been leased for 10 years at $7,000 per year. The rent and the heat and lights are apportioned to the product lines based on the amount of floor space occupied. All other costs are current expenses identified with the product line causing them.

A valued custom-parts customer has asked Jackson if he would manufacture 5,000 special units for her. Jackson is working at capacity and would have to give up some other business to take this order. He cannot renege on custom orders already agreed to, but he would have to reduce the output of his standard product by about one-half for a year while producing the specially requested customer part. The customer is willing to pay $7.00 for each part. The material cost will be about $2.00 per unit and the labor will be $3.60 per unit. Jackson will have to spend $2,000 for a special device that will be discarded when the job is done.

**REQUIRED:**

**A.** Calculate and present the following costs related to the 5,000-unit custom order.
  **1.** The incremental cost of the order
  **2.** The full cost of the order (incremental plus allocated fixed costs such as depreciation, rent, etc.)
  **3.** The opportunity cost of taking the order
  **4.** The sunk costs related to the order
**B.** Should Jackson take the order? Explain your answer.

---

**4.30**
Q3, Q4, Q5, Q6, Q7
ETHICS

**Foreign versus domestic production and comparative advantage** Scott Mills was originally a producer of fabrics, but several years ago intense foreign competition led management to restructure the firm as a vertically integrated cotton garment manufacturer. Scott purchased spinning firms that produce raw yarn and fabricators that produce the final garment. The firm has both domestic and international operations.

The domestic spinning and knitting operations are highly automated and use the latest technology. The domestic operations are able to produce cotton fabric for $1.52 per pound. The domestic fabricating operations are located exclusively in rural areas. Their locations keep total average labor costs to $16.40 per hour (including fringe benefits). The cost to ship products to the firm's distribution center is $0.10 per pound.

The firm's foreign subsidiary is a fabricating operation located in the Maldives, a group of islands near India. The average wage rate there is $0.70 per hour. The subsidiary purchases cotton fabric locally for $1.60 per pound. The finished products are shipped to Scott Mills' distribution center in New Orleans at a cost of $1.80 per pound. Both the domestic and foreign subsidiary use the same amount of fabric per product. Scott Mills has been producing three products for the private label market: sweatshirts, dress shirts, and lightweight jackets. In the past the firm processed a new order at whichever fabricating plant had the next available capacity. However, projections for the next few years indicate that orders will far exceed capacity. Management wants each plant to specialize in one of the products.

The plants are constrained by the amount of sewing time available in each. The domestic plant has 8,000 hours of sewing machine time available per week, while the foreign subsidiary has 10,000 hours available per week. The domestic plant's variable overhead is charged to products at $4.00 per machine hour, while the subsidiary's variable overhead averages $1.00 per machine hour.

The sweatshirts require 1 pound of cotton fabric to produce, the dress shirts use 4 ounces of fabric, and the jackets require 1 pound of fabric. The domestic plant has special-purpose equipment that allows workers to sew a sweatshirt in 6 minutes, a shirt in 15 minutes, and a jacket in one hour. The foreign plant's equipment constrains production to five sweatshirts per hour, three dress shirts per hour, or two jackets per hour. The wholesale prices are $8.76 each for the sweatshirts, $7.50 for the dress shirts, and $37.00 for the jackets.

**REQUIRED:**

**A.** Using only quantitative information, should the firm close its domestic operations and expand the foreign subsidiary?
**B.** Assuming that wages in the domestic operations remain constant, at what level of wages in the foreign subsidiary would the managers be indifferent between producing sweatshirts at one location versus the other?

❶ **C.** Discuss qualitative factors, including ethical issues, that might influence the decision in part (A).

❷ **D.** Discuss whether production quality is likely to be a bigger concern for products produced at the foreign subsidiary versus products produced in the domestic operation.

**E.** If demand for each product exceeds capacity, in which product should each plant specialize?

**F.** Management insists on manufacturing all three products to maintain good customer relations. If demand for each product exceeds capacity, management would prefer to specialize according to your answer to part (E). At which plant should management produce the third product?

**4.31**
Q4, Q6, Q7
ETHICS

**Outsource, relevant costs, qualitative factors, uncertainties, biases** Falco Services processes mortgage loan applications. The cost of home appraisals is included in its service fee, but Falco uses an outside appraisal service. The cost of appraisals has been increasing rapidly over the last several years, reaching $180 per appraisal last year. Falco's CFO asked one of the accountants to estimate the cost of doing the appraisals in-house. Several of Falco's mortgage brokers worked previously as real estate agents and have performed informal appraisals; however, none have professional appraisal experience. The accountant's son-in-law owns the firm that currently performs most of the appraisals.

The accountant prepares a report for the CFO that includes the following estimates for 1,000 appraisals. Appraisers would have to be hired, but no additional computer equipment, space, or supervision would be needed. The report states that the total costs for 1,000 appraisals would be $195,000 or $195.00 per appraisal. The current appraisal price is $180, so the report recommends that Falco continue to outsource the appraisal services.

| Costs: | |
|---|---|
| Supplies and paper | $ 5,000 |
| Professional labor | 100,000 |
| Overhead | 90,000 |
| Total costs | $195,000 |
| Cost per appraisal | $ 195 |

Professional labor is the cost to hire two appraisers. Overhead consists of fixed overhead, which is allocated at 50 percent of the cost of professional labor, and variable overhead (mostly fringe benefits), which is 40 percent of the cost of professional labor. Falco's CFO has to decide whether to continue to use the appraisal service or to hire appraisers and provide the service in-house.

**REQUIRED:**

ⓔ **A.** Which type of nonroutine operating decision is involved here? What are the managers' decision options?

**B.** What is the expected total incremental cost for 1,000 appraisals?

**C.** Which costs in the accountant's report are not relevant? Prepare a revised report that includes only relevant costs.

**D.** Using the general decision rule, should Falco outsource appraisal services or provide this service itself?

❶ **E.** List uncertainties about Falco's ability to begin a new appraisal service at or below the cost calculated. List as many uncertainties as you can.

❶ **F.** List possible qualitative factors that Falco's CFO should consider in making this decision. List as many as you can.

❷ **G.** Explain why the accountant might have been biased, and explain what effects that might have on the cost report.

❷ **H.** What are the costs to Falco of relying on the accountant's report for this decision? What are the costs to the accountant of admitting that he might be biased in preparing information for this decision?

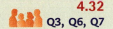

**4.32**
Q3, Q6, Q7

**Keep or drop uncertainties, relevant information, qualitative factors** Gourmet Fast Foods produces and sells many products in each of its 35 different product lines. Occasionally a product or an entire product line is dropped because it ceases to be profitable. The company does not have a formalized program for reviewing its products on a regular basis to identify products that should be eliminated.

At a recent meeting of Gourmet's top management, the head of operations stated that several products or possibly an entire product line were currently unprofitable. After considerable discussion, management decided that Gourmet should establish a formalized product discontinuance program. The purpose of the program would be to review the company's individual products and product lines on a regular and ongoing basis to identify problem areas.

The vice president of finance proposed that a person be assigned to the program on a full-time basis. This person would work closely with the marketing and accounting departments to determine the factors that indicate when a product's importance is declining and to gather the information that would be required to evaluate whether a product or product line should be discontinued.

**REQUIRED:**

**① A.** Explain why the managers of Gourmet Fast Foods cannot know for sure when a product or product line should be discontinued.

**① B.** What factors might indicate the diminishing importance of a product or product line? List as many factors as you can.

**① C.** If you were assigned to this position, what information would you want from the accounting system?

**① D.** If you were assigned to this position, would you want any information other than that produced by the accounting system? If so, what type of information would be useful, and where would you be likely to obtain it?

**② E.** List several benefits of assigning an employee full-time responsibility for a product discontinuance program.

**③ F.** If you were assigned to this position, describe the steps you would take as you analyze a given product.

---

**4.33**

Q4, Q6, Q7

**Outsource computations, qualitative factors, cost of quality** Mills and Vines just received a bid from a supplier for 6,000 motors per year used in the manufacture of electric lawn mowers. The supplier offered to sell the motors for $88 each. Mills and Vines' estimated costs of producing the motor follow.

| | |
|---|---|
| Direct materials | $40 |
| Direct labor | 20 |
| Variable overhead | 20 |
| Fixed overhead | 64 |

Prior to making a decision, the company's CEO commissioned a special study to see whether any decreases were possible in fixed overhead costs. The company would avoid two setups, which would reduce total spending by $10,000 per setup. One inspector would be laid off at a savings of $28,000. A person in materials handling could also be laid off at a savings of $20,000. Engineering work would be reduced by 500 hours at $15 per hour. Although the work decreases by 500 hours, the engineer assigned to the motor line also spends time on other products.

**REQUIRED:**

**A.** Ignore the information from the special study. Using the general decision rule, determine whether the motor should be produced internally or purchased from the supplier.

**B.** Repeat the analysis, using the information from the special study.

**② C.** Identify and discuss any qualitative factors that would affect the decision, including strategic implications.

**② D.** After reviewing the special study, the controller made the following remark: "This study ignores the additional activity demands that purchasing the motor would cause. For example, although the part would no longer be inspected on the production floor, we will need to inspect the incoming parts in the receiving area. Will we actually save any inspection costs?" Discuss whether you agree with the controller. Identify and explain other costs that might increase if the part is outsourced.

**4.34**
Q5, Q7

**Product emphasis with constrained resource, cost function, uncertainties** Riteway currently produces and sells five different products. Total demand for the products exceeds the firm's capacity to produce all of them. The constraint on production is the time available on a special machine. Data on the products and time required on the special machine are summarized in the following chart.

| | Product | | | | |
|---|---|---|---|---|---|
| | A | B | C | D | E |
| Selling price | $12 | $15 | $18 | $24 | $32 |
| Variable manufacturing cost | $8 | $9 | $11 | $12 | $18 |
| Variable marketing cost | $1 | $1 | $3 | $2 | $6 |
| Machine hours needed per unit | 0.2 | 0.3 | 0.25 | 0.5 | 0.4 |
| Maximum unit demand per period | 10,000 | 7,500 | 20,000 | 1,500 | 2,000 |

The firm has only 5,500 hours of time available on the special machine per period. Fixed costs are $110,000 per period.

**REQUIRED:**

**A.** How many units of each product should the firm produce and sell to maximize income?

**e B.** On further analysis, it was determined that while fixed costs do not vary as production volumes change, they do vary based on the number of different product lines. If only two types of products are produced, these costs are $60,000, but if all five types of products are produced, these costs will be $135,000. Using the two-point method, determine a linear cost function for the cost of product lines.

**② C.** Describe possible business reasons for the cost behavior described in part (B).

**e D.** Using the results from part (A) and the cost function you developed for part (B), prepare an income statement for the firm by product line and by total products.

**e E.** Review the results in part (D). Prepare a new product line income statement that reflects any changes that should be made in the production plans to maximize income.

**① F.** Identify reasons why the managers cannot be certain that they have accurately estimated the following for each product: selling price, variable costs, machine hours needed per unit, and maximum unit demand per period.

**② G.** Discuss how the uncertainties in part (F) might affect the managers' production decisions.

**4.35**
Q4, Q6, Q7

ETHICS

**International outsourcing of CPA services, service quality** During late 2003, the chair of the **Texas Society of CPAs**, Nita Clyde, wrote a letter to Scott Voynich, chair of the **American Institute of CPAs** (AICPA). The letter expressed concerns about the professional responsibilities of CPAs who outsource work internationally and asked the AICPA to study the issue. Specific concerns included whether clients should be informed that work is sent to foreign locations and whether client privacy was breached.

At the time, outsourcing was used increasingly for all types of goods and services. The accounting profession was no exception. Years earlier, CPAs had begun outsourcing by hiring part-time staff who sometimes worked at home. As staff shortage problems increased and CPAs looked for new ways to reduce costs, they entered into international outsourcing arrangements. Usually the type of work outsourced was routine, such as transaction processing or tax return preparation. Proponents argued that these arrangements reduced costs, improved efficiency, and freed CPAs to focus on more value-added client services.

Voynich responded that CPAs already had several professional standards relating to international outsourcing. In particular, AICPA ethics rulings required CPAs to insure that client confidentiality was maintained and that work was performed competently and with due professional care. Confidentiality included using encryption software and other controls when transmitting data. Voynich also asked the AICPA staff to provide additional guidance to CPAs.

SOURCES: Nita J. Clyde, Chairman, Texas Society of CPAs, letter to S. Scott Voynich, Chairman of Board of Directors, AICPA, November 11, 2003, available at www.tscpa.org/welcome/media/IntnlOutsourcingLtr.pdf and www.accountingweb.com/cgi-bin/item.cgi?id=98384; S. Scott Voynich, Chairman of Board of Directors, AICPA, letter to Nita J. Clyde, Chairman, Texas Society of CPAs, available in "Foreign Outsourcing Expected to Grow, but Tough Issues Abound," *AccountingWEB*, December 10, 2003, www.accountingweb.com/cgi-bin/item.cgi?id=98429; and "Foreign Outsourcing Expected to Grow, but Tough Issues Abound," *AccountingWEB*, December 10, 2003, available at www.accountingweb.com/cgi-bin/item.cgi?id=98459.

**REQUIRED:** Exhibit 4.3 provided examples of issues that financial institutions should consider when they engage in international outsourcing of information technology (IT). Refer to these issues as you answer the following questions. Suppose a CPA is thinking about outsourcing the preparation of routine income tax returns to an accounting firm in another country.

**②** **A.** Discuss whether the CPA can be sure that services are performed competently and with due professional care. Does it matter whether the services are performed by local staff or in another country? Why or why not?

**②** **B.** Discuss whether the CPA can be sure that client data will remain confidential. Does it matter whether the services are performed by local staff or in another country? Why or why not?

**❸** **C.** If the CPA decides to outsource, should clients be informed that their tax returns are prepared in another country? Why or why not?

**②** **D.** Describe the pros and cons of outsourcing to the CPA.

**4.36**
**Q3, Q6, Q7**

**Comprehensive problem** Elder Services is a not-for-profit organization that has three departments in three separate locations, in addition to the headquarters. The organization provides services for elderly clients who are still living at home. One department provides meals, one department provides cleaning services, and one department provides health care services. Elderly Services relies on client fees and a small grant from the county to provide services. Following are the results from last year's operations.

| Departments | Meals | Cleaning | Health | Total |
|---|---|---|---|---|
| Visits | 10,000 | 10,000 | 10,000 | 30,000 |
| Revenues | $50,000 | $100,000 | $150,000 | $300,000 |
| Variable cost (labor and supplies) | 30,000 | 50,000 | 120,000 | 200,000 |
| Fixed overhead costs | 4,000 | 8,000 | 10,000 | 22,000 |
| Transportation | | | | |
| ($4,000 fixed + $5,000 variable) | 9,000 | | | 9,000 |
| ($10,000 fixed + $2,000 variable) | | 12,000 | | 12,000 |
| $5,000 variable* | | | 5,000 | 5,000 |
| Headquarter costs allocated (based on revenues) | 10,000 | 20,000 | 30,000 | 60,000 |
| Total expenses | 53,000 | 90,000 | 165,000 | 308,000 |
| Surplus (deficit) | $ (3,000) | $ 10,000 | $ (15,000) | $ (8,000) |

*Nurses use their own cars.

In the past, the county provided small grants each year to cover losses for Elder Services. However, due to an economic downturn and decreased tax funds in the current year, the county will not be able to provide any support next year. In light of these changes, the managers of Elder Services are trying to decide how to balance the budget.

**REQUIRED:** **A.** What is the contribution margin per visit for each department?

Consider the next three situations independently.

**B.** To eliminate losses, the director of Elder Services would like to close the department that provides health services for clients. Assume no alternative uses are planned for the health services building and no change would occur in headquarters costs. Estimate the surplus (deficit) if the health services department is closed.

**C.** What would the estimated total surplus (deficit) be if cleaning services increase by 2,000 clients, assuming no changes in fixed costs?

**D.** What would the estimated total surplus (deficit) be if Elder closes the meals division and that space is leased to another organization for $2,000 per month?

Suppose you are hired to help Elder's managers decide what to do about the lack of funding from the county this year. Ignore parts (B), (C), and (D) and answer the following questions as part of your analysis.

**E.** Which type of nonroutine operating decision does Elder Services need to make? What are the managers' decision options?

**F.** Perform quantitative analyses to help you decide whether one or more of the options listed in parts (B), (C), and (D) would be beneficial to the finances of Elder Services.

**G.** Now assume that the options in parts (B), (C), and (D), above are available. List uncertainties about Elder Services' ability to achieve the quantitative results for each option: (B), (C), and (D). List as many uncertainties as you can.

**H.** List qualitative factors that the managers of Elder Services need to consider in making this decision. List as many factors as you can.

**I.** As a consultant to Elder Services, how might you go about acquiring qualitative information?

**J.** Suppose you decide to interview Elder Services employees to help you gather qualitative information. Identify possible reasons that information you obtain from employees might be biased. List as many reasons as you can.

**K.** Describe possible trade-offs the managers of Elder Services might need to make in deciding what to do.

# BUILD YOUR PROFESSIONAL COMPETENCIES

**4.37** **Q1, Q6, Q7** **Focus on Professional Competency: Problem Solving and Decision Making** *Relevant information, uncertainties, creativity, biases* Review the following definition and elements for the Problem Solving and Decision Making competency.[8]

**DEFINITION:** *Accounting professionals are often asked to discern the true nature of a situation and then determine the principles and techniques needed to solve problems or make judgments. Thus, individuals entering the accounting profession should display effective problem-solving and decision-making skills, good insight and judgment, as well as innovative and creative thinking.*

## ELEMENTS FOR THIS COMPETENCY INCLUDE

| Level 1 | Level 2 | Level 3 | Level 4 |
|---|---|---|---|
| 1. Lists information and evidence that is relevant for a problem | 3. Makes valid and reliable evaluations of information, including the significance of evidence or facts for problem definition and solution | 7. Synthesizes novel or original definitions of problems and solutions as circumstances dictate | 12. Strategically considers contingencies and future developments |
| 2. Identifies uncertainties about the interpretation or significance of information and evidence | 4. Considers unconventional approaches and solutions to problems | 8. Uses experience and comparison in forming opinions | 13. Adapts to new contexts and promotes constructive change |
| | 5. Analyzes the impact, pros, and cons of potential solutions or actions | 9. Seeks consensus where appropriate | |
| | 6. Analyzes the quality of information and evidence, including validity, reliability, and significance | 10. Reasons carefully and thinks effectively in abstract terms or generalizations | |
| | | 11. Knows when to follow directions, question plans, or seek help | |

[8]The definition and elements are reprinted with permission from AICPA; Copyright © 1978–2000 & 2003 by American Institute of Certified Public Accountants. The AICPA's Core Competency Framework can be accessed at eca.aicpaservices.org.

**REQUIRED:** ❶ **A.** Focus on competency element 1, which relates to the identification of relevant information. Explain why both quantitative and qualitative information are relevant for making nonroutine operating decisions.

**B.** Focus on competency elements 2, 6, and 12, which address uncertainties. Answer the following questions:

❶ 1. Explain why managers must consider contingencies and future developments as they make nonroutine operating decisions.

❶ 2. What types of uncertainties (including contingencies and future developments) affect nonroutine operating decisions? List as many as you can.

❷ 3. In your own words, explain what is meant by the quality of information. Then explain why it is important to analyze the quality of information when making nonroutine operating decisions.

**C.** Focus on competency elements 4 and 7, which relate to creativity in decision making. Answer the following questions:

❷ 1. Why is creativity useful when evaluating nonroutine operating decisions?

❷ 2. Explain how working in a group with other people helps you identify new approaches or ways of looking at a problem.

**D.** Focus on competency elements 3, 5, 10, and 13, which require accountants to fully explore problems and to avoid bias in decision making. Answer the following questions:

❷ 1. Explain why it is important to minimize bias and to objectively evaluate the pros and cons of more than one solution when making nonroutine operating decisions.

❷ 2. How do you know whether you are biased as you explore the information for a problem?

❷ 3. Think of a situation where you have resisted some type of change. What caused your resistance?

**4.38** **Integrating Across the Curriculum: Finance** *Special order, exchange rate options* General
**Q2, Q7** Robotic has received an order from an English firm to produce 10 robots that will perform welding tasks on the customer's assembly line. General Robotic's managers estimate that it will take four months to produce and deliver the robots. The total variable costs to produce the robots will be $600,000. The selling price to the customer is £64,000 each. Typically, payment is made at the time of delivery.

Currently the exchange rate between the British pound and the U.S. dollar is £1 = $1.25. Management is concerned about a potential adverse change in the exchange rate between now and four months from now. Three alternatives for dealing with this potential problem have been proposed:

1. Do nothing and hope for the best.
2. Offer the customer a $10,000 price reduction if the customer will pay one-half of the selling price now with the remainder due on delivery.
3. Buy a four-month option that gives the firm the right to sell £640,000 for $800,000. The cost of the option would be $30,000.

**REQUIRED:** ⓔ **A.** Write an equation for the pretax profit the company will earn under each option. Use "R" to represent the exchange rate four months from now. (Ignore any interest on the money.)

ⓔ **B.** What would the exchange rate need to be four months from now for the company to earn the same pretax profit on options 1 and 2?

ⓔ **C.** What would the exchange rate need to be four months from now for the company to earn the same pretax profit on options 2 and 3?

ⓔ **D.** What would the exchange rate need to be four months from now for the company to earn the same pretax profit on options 1 and 3?

**e** **E.** Prepare a schedule that shows the best action for every possible exchange rate that might occur four months from now.

**e** **F.** Assume that the managers chose option 3 and the actual exchange rate turns out to be £1 = $1.35 four months from now. How much profit did the company lose by choosing option 3 instead of option 1?

**2** **G.** Assume the same information as in part (F). Were the managers wrong to choose option 3? Why or why not?

# Job Costing

## ▶In Brief

Custom products and services, which are produced singly or in small batches, need to be valued for financial statements, tax reporting, and management monitoring. Job costing is an accounting method used to assign product costs to custom products or services. In job costing, direct costs are traced and overhead costs are allocated to individual jobs. Sometimes defects occur in custom products. Defective units can sometimes be reworked. The costs for both spoilage and rework need to be accounted for, as does the cost of scrap that arises from production.

## This Chapter Addresses the Following Questions:

**Q1** How are costs assigned to customized goods and services?

**Q2** How is overhead allocated to individual jobs?

**Q3** What is the difference between actual costing and normal costing?

**Q4** What are the uses and limitations of job cost information?

**Q5** How are spoilage, rework, and scrap handled in job costing?

**Q6** What are the quality and behavioral implications of spoilage?

# BOMBARDIER: CUSTOM MANUFACTURING

In 1942, the Canadian company **L'Auto-Neige Bombardier Limitée** began manufacturing tracked vehicles for snow-covered terrain. These vehicles were early models of what later became snowmobiles. In English, L'Auto-Neige means snow car. Over time, the company developed expertise in building engines and expanded into other markets such as personal watercraft, aircraft, subway cars, buses, and jet boats.

The company, eventually known as **Bombardier Inc.**, continued to expand, often by acquiring existing companies. For example, it acquired **Canadair** (the leading Canadian aircraft manufacturer), **Pullman Railcars** in the United States, and an Irish manufacturer of civil and military aircraft and defense systems.

In 1990, Bombardier acquired **Learjet Corporation**, a U.S. manufacturer of business aircraft. Learjet manufactures high-performance business jets. The jets, though relatively small, are well-appointed with interiors designed for personal comfort and convenience. They are often referred to as the limousines of the skies. These jets are built at Bombardier's plant in Wichita, Kansas. Models include the Learjet 31A (light jet), Learjet 45 (super-light jet), and Learjet 60 (midsize jet).

Bombardier operates Learjet completion centers in Wichita and Tucson, Arizona. The completion centers provide customized services such as exterior painting and installation of cabinetry and furniture. Corporate jet customers often order specialized interiors, including unique fabric, carpet, wood, and color; ergonomic seating; sound, video, and satellite communication systems; distinctive galleys; water systems; custom wiring; bulkhead reinforcements; and sound-proofing.

The center in Wichita completes approximately 120 Learjet 45 aircraft per year. Different types of work are performed in different areas of the facility. The facility includes two paint booths, two sand-and-strip areas, four preparation areas, and an interior mock-up room. ■

Sources: www.aerospace.bombardier.com/ and www.learjet.com.

## TRACKING COSTS FOR CUSTOMIZED PRODUCTS AND SERVICES

## ■ Key Accounting Design Issues for Bombardier

**Bombardier's** Learjet subsidiary produces corporate jets, and Learjet's completion centers provide services such as exterior painting and installation of cabinetry and furniture. When an organization produces customized products or services, specific accounting methods are required for measuring and monitoring both costs and profits. The following discussion summarizes key aspects of the issues Bombardier's accountants must consider as they design and use a cost system for Learjet completion services.

**Knowing.** Bombardier's Wichita completion center facility is divided into different areas where different types of work are performed. Each area uses different types of direct materials and requires employees to perform different types of work. To develop an appropriate accounting system, Bombardier's accountants need two major types of knowledge:

1. Types of completion costs and processes
   - The nature of work performed in each area
   - Costs that are common across all jets in a particular work area
   - Costs that vary with customization
   - Points in the completion process where cost information can be captured by the accounting system
2. Design of accounting systems and managers' information needs
   - Categorization of direct and indirect costs within each work area
   - Methods for tracing direct costs to each customized job
   - Methods for allocating indirect costs
   - Creation of meaningful cost and profit reports

**Identifying.** Accountants face many uncertainties in measuring costs for customized products. Suppose employees in the completion center need special training to properly install a particular type of bulkhead reinforcement. The training cost relates only to jets with this type of bulkhead reinforcement installed. How much of the training cost relates to a single jet with that feature, especially if the number of other orders requesting that feature is unknown? As another example, suppose a variety of supplies such as tool lubrication are used during production. It is generally not possible to measure the precise amount of supplies used for *each* jet; such measurements require estimation. Because of these uncertainties, Bombardier's accountants cannot measure with complete accuracy the costs for customized jet completion services. Instead, their goal is to provide a *reasonable* measure of each jet's cost.

**Exploring.** No single accounting system best measures costs for all customized products. Therefore, Bombardier's accountants must:

- Analyze alternative system design features
- Explore the pros and cons of alternative accounting methods, including costs and benefits
- Explore ways in which the company and its customization services affect the design of the accounting system
- Anticipate the needs of managers and others using the accounting information

**Prioritizing.** Bombardier's accountants weigh a variety of criteria as they choose among alternative designs for capturing and reporting cost information for customized products, including the following:

- Capturing significant direct costs and tracing them to individual products
- Logically allocating overhead costs
- Reporting relevant cost and profit information to managers and other users
- Motivating employees to use the organization's resources efficiently
- Ensuring that the costs of the accounting system do not exceed the benefits

**Envisioning.** Bombardier's accountants must continuously monitor and reconsider the design of accounting systems. Changes in the system might be triggered by changes in the business environment, technologies, the products themselves, or production processes.

## ■ Measuring and Monitoring Product Costs

Managers necessarily measure past costs when producing financial statements and other reports of an organization's profits. Outsiders, such as shareholders, use profitability to evaluate management performance and to make investment and other decisions. Past cost information is also used by managers to monitor operations, develop estimated costs for bids, and sometimes make long-term decisions such as whether to introduce a new product. To enable these various uses for cost information, we need to distinguish between product costs and other costs that are not directly related to production.

In this chapter, we focus on measuring and monitoring the product cost of customized goods and services. Customized products pose special problems because the nature and levels of costs vary from product to product. Therefore, the accounting systems must be designed to capture costs for individual units or batches of goods or services as the manufacturing or service delivery process unfolds.

---

## ASSIGNING PRODUCT COSTS TO INDIVIDUAL GOODS OR SERVICES

**Q1** How are costs assigned to customized goods and services?

**CHAPTER REFERENCE**

Chapter 2 defined *overhead costs* as all production costs except direct materials and direct labor.

---

**Product costs** are the direct and indirect costs of producing goods or services. For the production of a Bombardier Learjet, direct costs include materials such as metal, wiring, and cabinetry as well as labor directly involved in the production of an individual jet. In addition to direct materials and direct labor costs, product costs also include overhead costs related to production. At Bombardier, production overhead includes costs related to the manufacturing facility, such as depreciation of equipment and insurance costs. Product costs exclude the cost of operating activities that are not directly related to production, such as selling and administration.

The ease with which production costs are traced to individual products or services often depends on the degree of customization. As illustrated in Exhibit 5.1, some goods and services are one of a kind, and some are uniform. Other products require a hybrid process, in which most of the product is uniform but select features are customized. Bombardier's Learjet 45 model is a hybrid product. It has a single uniform aircraft design and manufacturing process, but the exterior paint and interior furnishings are customized at the completion center.

## ■ Process Costing

When goods or services are uniform and are mass-produced, tracing product costs to individual units is generally inefficient, if not impossible. For example, it would be impractical to trace the cost of food ingredients to a single box of breakfast cereal that is mass-produced. **Process costing** allocates both direct and overhead costs to continuous-flow processing lines;

---

**EXHIBIT 5.1** Products with Varying Degrees of Customization

| Product or Service | Customized | Hybrid | Uniform |
|---|---|---|---|
| Automobiles | One-of-a-kind vehicle (for example, a racing car) | Produced on an assembly line, but customer chooses colors, amenities | Produced on a continuous flow assembly line without customer specifications |
| Jewelry | Hand-designed and fabricated | Setting a specific diamond into a mass-produced gold ring | Uniform pieces of jewelry produced continuously |
| Accounting and tax services | Income tax research performed for a specific client | Tax services offered by the hour | Mass-produced tax returns such as 1040EZ |
| Health care | Hospitals: each patient receives treatment using different resources | Blood donation center | Flu vaccinations |

it is the approach generally used for mass-produced products. Direct and indirect costs are traced and allocated to production departments, and then allocated to units. Industries that use process costing include food and beverage manufacturers, petroleum refiners, and plastic and metal manufacturers. The details of process costing are found in Chapter 6.

## ■ Job Costing

When goods or services are customized, many costs are easily traced to individual products. For example, the interiors of Bombardier's Learjets are customized to suit each customer. Costs of direct materials such as carpeting or handcrafted cabinetry can easily be traced to an individual jet. It is also easy to trace the cost of direct labor to install the carpet and cabinetry. Other production costs, such as the completion facility manager's salary or building insurance are indirect and are allocated as part of overhead to an individual jet.

When a customer with specific product or service requirements places an order, we call the order a job. For example, suppose a famous diva orders a custom Learjet with a pink and white lace interior. Bombardier would consider this order a job. Orders are also placed for batches of product, such as a batch of a particular style and size of men's running shoes sold under the brand name of a retail shoe store. The shoe manufacturer would consider this order a job. Orders are also placed for services, such as the preparation of a tax return. When a client brings his tax records to an accountant, the accounting firm considers this order a job.

**Job costing** is the process of assigning costs to custom products or services. Direct materials and direct labor are traced to individual jobs, and production overhead is allocated. Manufacturers that use job costing include aircraft builders, custom motorcycle and automobile manufacturers, and custom designed jewelers, among others. Job costing is also frequently used in service industry organizations such as hospitals, accounting firms, and repair shops. We first learn about job costing in a manufacturing setting. Later in the chapter, we learn about job costing for services.

## JOB COSTING IN MANUFACTURING

 **Q1** How are costs assigned to customized goods and services?

One of the purposes of measuring current and past product costs is to provide information for financial statements. Under generally accepted accounting principles (GAAP), product costs must be assigned to inventory. Then, when products are sold, the cost is transferred to cost of goods sold. This practice allows inventory to be reported at cost on the balance sheet, and cost of goods sold to be matched against revenues on the income statement. Thus, job costing in a manufacturing organization assigns costs first to inventory and then to cost of goods sold when jobs are completed and sold, as shown in Exhibit 5.2.

**EXHIBIT 5.2** Cost Flows in a Manufacturing Job Costing System

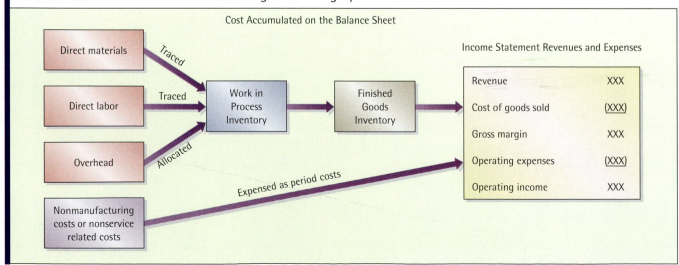

**EXHIBIT 5.3**
Tracing and Allocating
Product Costs to Jobs

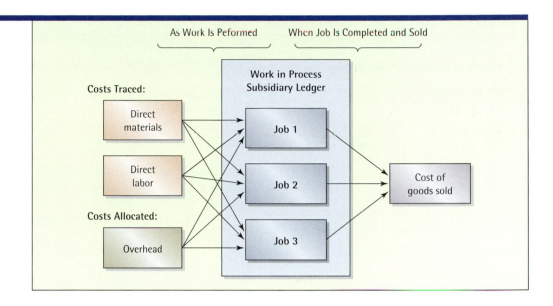

To measure the cost of individual jobs, job costing systems typically include a subsidiary ledger. As shown in Exhibit 5.3, direct costs are traced and overhead costs are allocated to each job. Total work in process (WIP) is equal to the sum of the accumulated costs for all jobs in the subsidiary ledger.

## Assigning Direct Costs

Accounting records are used to trace the costs of direct materials and direct labor to each job. For example, suppose that Aluminum Benders, Inc., produces aluminum vents for heating and cooling systems. The company works with contractors on large commercial buildings. Each job requires different styles and lengths of vents and joints. Therefore, the company uses job costing. Work is performed in two different departments: machining and assembly.

**Source documents** are manual or electronic records created to capture and provide information about transactions or events. For example, the direct labor employees at Aluminum Benders create daily time reports that show the time they spend on individual jobs. The accounting department uses the time reports to calculate employee pay and to trace direct labor hours to individual jobs. As shown in Exhibit 5.4, each time report may include several different jobs. Similarly, when materials such as sheet metal or metal joints are requisitioned for each job, they are tracked in the accounting system using the materials requisition form shown in Exhibit 5.4.

The cost and activity information gathered from source documents is used to record costs in a subsidiary ledger for each new job. This record is called a **job cost record** and contains all of the costs traced and assigned to a specific job, as shown in Exhibit 5.4. At Aluminum Benders, the cost per unit of direct materials is obtained from the company's raw materials inventory records. The hourly rate of pay for each employee is obtained from payroll records. Other companies may use an estimated, budgeted, or standard cost for direct materials and direct labor.

The sample job cost record shown in Exhibit 5.4 includes the direct costs of work performed on Job 482 in Aluminum Benders' Machining Department. The record is not yet complete; only some materials and labor have been recorded thus far, and the indirect costs have not yet been allocated. Aluminum Benders' job costing system calculates summary costs (totals for direct materials, direct labor, and manufacturing overhead by department) on each job cost record. The detailed information in the job cost record and the totals in work in process inventory are updated as new costs are incurred, until the job is completed.

## Computerized and Manual Job Costing Systems

Maintaining the detailed job cost records shown in Exhibit 5.4 can be time-consuming and prone to clerical error. Therefore, job cost records are often part of a software package.

**EXHIBIT 5.4** Job Cost Record for Aluminum Benders

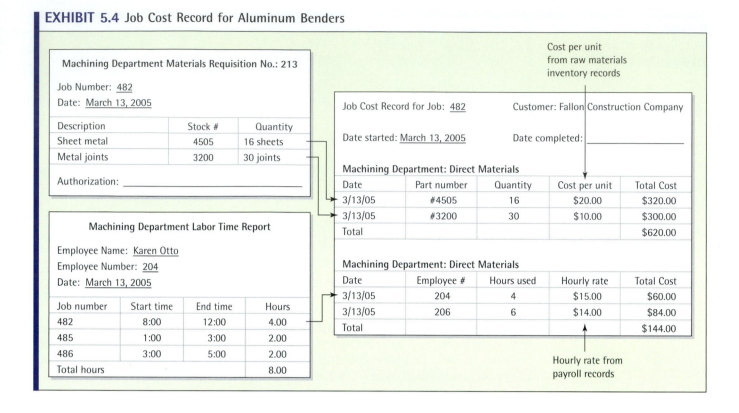

Cost per unit from raw materials inventory records

**Machining Department Materials Requisition No.: 213**

Job Number: 482

Date: March 13, 2005

| Description | Stock # | Quantity |
|---|---|---|
| Sheet metal | 4505 | 16 sheets |
| Metal joints | 3200 | 30 joints |

Authorization: _____

**Machining Department Labor Time Report**

Employee Name: Karen Otto

Employee Number: 204

Date: March 13, 2005

| Job number | Start time | End time | Hours |
|---|---|---|---|
| 482 | 8:00 | 12:00 | 4.00 |
| 485 | 1:00 | 3:00 | 2.00 |
| 486 | 3:00 | 5:00 | 2.00 |
| Total hours | | | 8.00 |

Job Cost Record for Job: 482          Customer: Fallon Construction Company

Date started: March 13, 2005          Date completed: _____

**Machining Department: Direct Materials**

| Date | Part number | Quantity | Cost per unit | Total Cost |
|---|---|---|---|---|
| 3/13/05 | #4505 | 16 | $20.00 | $320.00 |
| 3/13/05 | #3200 | 30 | $10.00 | $300.00 |
| Total | | | | $620.00 |

**Machining Department: Direct Materials**

| Date | Employee # | Hours used | Hourly rate | Total Cost |
|---|---|---|---|---|
| 3/13/05 | 204 | 4 | $15.00 | $60.00 |
| 3/13/05 | 206 | 6 | $14.00 | $84.00 |
| Total | | | | $144.00 |

Hourly rate from payroll records

Direct labor and direct material data are entered into electronic source documents (on-line time records and material requisitions). From there, the data are automatically posted into the job cost record and the general ledger system. This approach allows managers to immediately view job costs even before the job is completed. Specialized software packages are most likely to be used in large organizations or in businesses where jobs are complex or require many resources.

In small businesses, job cost records may be tied less formally to the general ledger system. Instead of using source documents to track direct costs, organizations may use a manual job cost record to track direct costs for individual jobs. The job sheet is physically attached to an individual job. As materials and direct labor hours are added to the job, the amounts are recorded on the sheet. An artist might use this method when producing crafts and art pieces. Carpenters and home contractors also frequently use this method to monitor direct costs. Amounts from the job cost sheet are recorded in the job cost record in the subsidiary ledger on a periodic basis, when the job is complete, or sometimes as resources are used.

## ALLOCATING OVERHEAD

 **Q2** How is overhead allocated to individual jobs?

Overhead includes all production costs except direct materials and direct labor. Allocating overhead to individual products is a two-stage process. In the first stage, a variety of overhead costs are collected in an overhead cost pool. A **cost pool** is a group of individual costs that are accumulated for a particular purpose. In the second stage, costs are allocated from the cost pool to individual jobs. Successful completion of the two stages requires four steps as follows.

1. Identify the relevant cost object.
2. Identify one or more overhead cost pools and allocation bases.
3. For each overhead cost pool, calculate an overhead allocation rate.
4. For each overhead cost pool, allocate costs to the cost object.

   **1. Identify the relevant cost object.** In a job costing system, the cost object is a job. Sometimes a job consists of an individual product, and sometimes it consists of a batch of products. For example, a job at a **Bombardier** completion center consists of the exterior and interior completion of one Learjet. A job at Aluminum Benders consists of a large number of aluminum vents required for a specific building.

**2. Identify one or more overhead cost pools and allocation bases.** Overhead costs are accumulated in one or more cost pools. Some organizations use a single company-wide or plantwide cost pool for all fixed and variable overhead costs. Other organizations use separate cost pools for fixed and variable overhead costs. Fixed overhead includes costs such as production management salaries and space rental. Variable overhead includes any cost that varies with activity levels, such as supplies and, sometimes, electricity. If work is performed in separate departments or work areas, separate overhead cost pools may be designated for each department or activity. Accountants use judgment in choosing the number and type of overhead cost pools for a given organization.

**HELPFUL HINT**

In process costing systems, overhead is allocated to departments and then to units. In ABC systems (Chapter 7), overhead is allocated to activities and then to units, batches, product lines, or other cost objects.

The choice of overhead cost pools depends on the organization of production, the nature of overhead costs, and the usefulness of different types of overhead information to management. For example, Bombardier's Wichita completion center has two paint booths, two sand-and-strip areas, four preparation areas, and an interior mock-up room. Each work area might be under the supervision of a different manager who is responsible for controlling costs. The use of separate overhead cost pools for each area would help top management monitor the performance of area managers. Alternatively, a single manager might oversee multiple work areas. If one manager is responsible for the exterior paint operation, overhead costs might be combined for the two paint booths. Organizations are also more likely to use different overhead cost pools for different types of work activities. For example, exterior painting is a different type of activity from preparation work such as installing carpeting, seating, and wiring. It is appropriate to use different cost pools when the nature or level of overhead costs differs across activities.

**CHAPTER REFERENCE**

In Chapter 2, a *cost driver* was defined as some input or activity that causes changes in total cost for a cost object.

For each overhead cost pool, an **allocation base** is chosen to assign overhead costs to cost objects. If some portion of an overhead cost pool varies with a cost driver, it can be used as the allocation base. For example, the cost of some employee benefits varies with labor hours and labor costs. Indirect costs such as supplies in a paint area may vary with machine use. For cost pools that consist only of variable costs or a mixture of fixed and variable costs, accountants use allocation bases that are likely to affect at least a portion of the costs. For a fixed overhead cost pool, accountants choose an allocation base that is related to activities even though fixed costs are not expected to vary with the allocation base. Manufacturing job costing systems frequently allocate overhead using one of the following bases:

**ALTERNATIVE TERMS**

The terms *cost application base* and *application base* mean the same as *allocation base*.

- Direct labor hours
- Direct labor costs
- Machine hours

**3. For each overhead cost pool, calculate an overhead allocation rate.** The allocation rate is the dollar amount per unit of allocation base used to allocate overhead to each cost object. (In a job costing system, each job is a cost object.) If we know the total amount of overhead cost and the total quantity of the allocation base, the **actual overhead allocation** rate is calculated as follows:

$$\text{Actual allocation rate} = \frac{\text{Actual overhead cost}}{\text{Actual quantity of allocation base}}$$

**ALTERNATIVE TERMS**

The *estimated allocation rate* is also called the *estimated application rate, standard overhead rate* (see Chapter 11), *budgeted application rate, predetermined application rate,* or simply an *allocation rate*.

Alternatively, overhead may be allocated using an **estimated allocation rate.** To compute an estimated rate for the next period, we estimate total overhead costs and the total quantity of the allocation base, and then calculate the rate as follows:

$$\text{Estimated allocation rate} = \frac{\text{Estimated overhead cost}}{\text{Estimated quantity of allocation base}}$$

Suppose we estimate overhead costs for Bombardier's exterior painting areas as $216,000 for the next three months and the hours paint employees will work as 5,400. If we use direct labor hours to allocate overhead costs, then the overhead allocation rate will be

$$\$216,000 \div 5,400 \text{ hours} = \$40 \text{ per direct labor hour}$$

**EXHIBIT 5.5**
Partial Job Cost Record
Showing Overhead
Allocation for Aluminum
Benders

| Job Cost Record for Job: _482_ | | Customer: Fallon Construction Company | | | |
|---|---|---|---|---|---|
| Date started: _March 13, 2005_ | | Date completed: _____ | | | |
| Machining Department: Overhead | | | | | |
| Date | Allocation Base | Hours Used | Allocation Rate per Hour | Allocated Overhead | |
| 3/13/05 | Machine hours | 3 | $56.00 | $168.00 | |
| Total | | | | $168.00 | |

**4. For each overhead cost pool, allocate costs to the cost object.** We allocate overhead costs by multiplying the overhead allocation rate times the quantity of the allocation base used by each job. In the previous example, we calculated the painting area's overhead allocation rate to be $40 per direct labor hour. When an exterior painting job requires 64 direct labor hours, the overhead cost allocation is

$$64 \text{ direct labor hours} \times \$40 \text{ per direct labor hour} = \$2,560$$

The overhead rate is also useful when completion center managers need to prepare bids for new jobs. Once the labor hours are estimated for a bid, the estimated allocation rate is used to estimate overhead cost for the job.

Software packages that trace direct costs to jobs can also automatically allocate overhead. Suppose labor cost is used to allocate overhead. As the software package records labor costs in specific job cost records, overhead is allocated to the job at the same time. However, the accounting department might need to create a source document to gather the allocation base information (such as machine hours) needed to allocate overhead costs. Data for direct labor hours and direct labor costs are automatically collected for payroll calculations, but specific details about each job's use of labor or machine hours need to be recorded by job in a job costing system. Appropriate data about machine hour usage might not be available unless special records are maintained.

For Aluminum Benders, suppose overhead in the machining department is allocated using machine hours. The company's accountants created an on-line system so that the machine operator records the machine hours used for each job. If three machine hours are recorded for Job 482 and the overhead is allocated based on an estimated allocation rate of $56.00 per machine hour, then the computer automatically allocates $168.00 in machining department overhead to Job 482, as shown in Exhibit 5.5.

## ■ Actual and Normal Costing

**Q3** What is the difference between actual costing and normal costing?

Under **actual costing,** overhead is allocated using the actual volume of the allocation base times the actual allocation rate. Because managers often need cost information before total actual cost and resource use information is available at the end of the period, estimates are typically used to allocate overhead. When the estimated allocation rate and actual quantity of the allocation base are used to allocate overhead, as in the preceding example, the method is called **normal costing.** Information from normal costing systems is used to prepare interim income statements, manage costs, and estimate costs for bids throughout a period. Exhibit 5.6 compares actual costing and normal costing. Under both methods, actual direct materials and direct labor are traced to each job.

Following is a more complete example of the normal costing method for Aluminum Benders.

**EXHIBIT 5.6** Similarities and Differences Between Actual and Normal Costing

| | Actual Costing | Normal Costing |
|---|---|---|
| **Direct Costs Recorded** | Actual cost of direct materials and direct labor | Actual cost of direct materials and direct labor |
| **Overhead Cost Allocation Rate** | $\dfrac{\text{Actual overhead cost}}{\text{Actual quantity of allocation base}}$ | $\dfrac{\text{Estimated overhead cost}}{\text{Estimated quantity of allocation base}}$ |
| **Overhead Allocation** | Actual allocation rate × Actual quantity of allocation base | Estimated allocation rate × Actual quantity of allocation base |

---

## GUIDE YOUR LEARNING 5.1 Key Terms

Stop to confirm that you understand the new terms introduced in the last several pages:

*Product costs (p. 177)              *Allocation base (p. 181)
 Process costing (p. 177)            Allocation rate (p. 181)
 Job costing (p. 178)               Actual allocation rate (p. 181)
*Source documents (p. 179)          Estimated allocation rate (p. 181)
 Job cost record (p. 179)           Actual costing (p. 182)
*Cost pool (p. 180)                 Normal costing (p. 182)

For each of these terms, write a definition in your own words. For starred terms, list at least one example that is different from the ones given in this textbook.

---

## ALUMINUM BENDERS (PART 1)
## ALLOCATING OVERHEAD COSTS IN JOB COSTING

Sean Hardy, recently hired as the accountant for Aluminum Benders, is responsible for producing annual financial statements for the owners, creditors, and employees. He knows that product costs must be allocated to each job for the financial statements and also for preparing the organization's income tax returns. Sean is also responsible for preparing cost reports to help management monitor direct and indirect job costs. Because he is new to the company, Sean needs to learn about the company's past job costing methods. He also plans to evaluate the quality of the methods to determine whether changes are needed.

### Evaluating Overhead Cost Pools and Allocation Bases

Sean learns that the company consists of two departments, machining and assembly. Separate overhead cost pools are used in each department, but fixed and variable costs are combined in each pool. In the machining department, overhead is allocated to production jobs using machine hours as the allocation base. In the assembly department, direct labor cost is used as the allocation base. In addition, the company uses a normal costing method to allocate an estimated overhead rate to each job.

Sean meets with the supervisor of each department to discuss the best allocation bases to use. In machining, he learns that the machines require little direct labor. A large portion of cost in the overhead pool relates to operating the machines, such as depreciation, maintenance, and replacement parts. Thus, Sean concludes that machine hours are a reasonable allocation base.

The assembly department has few machines, but labor is used heavily. The labor mix is varied, with both skilled and unskilled workers. Sean agrees that direct labor cost is a reasonable allocation base because some overhead expenses, such as vacation and sick leave pay, vary with labor cost.

### Understanding the Overhead Cost Allocation Method

The following estimates were developed by Sean's predecessor for all manufacturing during 2005:

| | Machining | Assembly |
|---|---|---|
| Production overhead | $1,400,000 | $2,400,000 |
| Direct labor cost | $ 700,000 | $1,000,000 |
| Direct labor hours | 35,000 | 100,000 |
| Machine hours | 25,000 | 10,000 |

*(continued)*

Sean uses this information to verify computations for the estimated overhead allocation rate for each department:

Machining: $1,400,000 ÷ 25,000 machine hours = $56.00 per machine hour

Assembly: $2,400,000 ÷ $1,000,000 direct labor cost = 240% of direct labor cost

Sean wants to be sure he understands how the company's job costing system allocates overhead cost, so he recalculates the allocations for Job 482. This job was completed this week and shipped to a large office building construction site. He obtains the following information from the job cost record for Job 482:

|  | Machining | Assembly |
|---|---|---|
| Direct materials requisitioned | $40,000 | $70,000 |
| Direct labor cost | $28,000 | $10,000 |
| Direct labor hours | 200 | 1,000 |
| Machine hours | 100 | 500 |

Using the allocation rates computed previously, Sean recalculates the amount of overhead for Job 482 as follows:

Machining: 100 machine hours × $56.00 per machine hour = $5,600

Assembly: $10,000 direct labor cost × 240% of direct labor cost = $24,000

Next, Sean queries the job costing system to create a report for management of the total costs for Job 482 as follows:

|  | Machining | Assembly | Total |
|---|---|---|---|
| Direct materials requisitioned | $40,000 | $ 70,000 | $110,000 |
| Direct labor cost | 28,000 | 10,000 | 38,000 |
| Overhead allocated | 5,600 | 24,000 | 29,600 |
| Total cost | $73,600 | $104,000 | $177,600 |

Sean believes it would be helpful to management if the report also included the revenue and profit, as well as the original job bid. However, the job costing system currently cannot access those pieces of information. Sean decides to investigate ways to link the job costing system with revenue and job bid data.

| GUIDE YOUR LEARNING  5.2  Aluminum Benders (Part 1) |
|---|

Aluminum Benders (Part 1) illustrates job costing entries. For this illustration:

| Define It | Identify Uncertainties | Explore Pros and Cons |
|---|---|---|
| In your own words, explain the purpose of allocating overhead to jobs. | What types of uncertainties were there? Consider uncertainties about:<br>• Choice of overhead cost pools<br>• Choice of overhead allocation bases<br>• Estimated overhead allocation rates | • In your own words, explain why Sean decided that each overhead allocation base was reasonable.<br>• Provide possible arguments that the overhead allocation bases were not appropriate.<br>• Provide possible reasons why fixed and variable costs were combined in the overhead cost pools. |

## GENERAL LEDGER ENTRIES FOR A MANUFACTURER

The general ledger in a manufacturer's job costing system typically includes separate inventory accounts for raw materials, work in process, and finished goods. These accounts are illustrated in Exhibit 5.7, which shows the entries that would be used by Aluminum Benders for Job 482.

Purchases of raw materials (not illustrated) are recorded in the raw materials inventory account. As direct materials are traced to a job, the cost of the materials is transferred to

**EXHIBIT 5.7** T-Accounts and Journal Entries for Job 482

| Raw Material Inventory | | Job 482 Work in Process Inventory | | Finished Goods Inventory | | Cost of Goods Sold | |
|---|---|---|---|---|---|---|---|
| 40,000 | 1 | 1 40,000 | | 7 177,600 | 177,600 8 | 8 177,600 | |
| 70,000 | 4 | 2 28,000 | | | | | |
| | | 3 5,600 | | | | | |
| | | 4 70,000 | | | | | |
| | | 5 10,000 | | | | | |
| | | 6 24,000 | 177,600 7 | | | | |
| | | 0 | | | | | |

| Wages Payable | | Machining Department Overhead Cost Control | | Assembly Department Overhead Cost Control | |
|---|---|---|---|---|---|
| 28,000 | 2 | | 5,600 3 | | 24,000 6 |
| 10,000 | 5 | | | | |

Journal Entries:

| | | | |
|---|---|---|---|
| 1 | Work in process (Job 482) | 40,000 | |
| |    Raw material inventory | | 40,000 |
| | To record direct materials requisitioned for Job 482 in machining | | |
| 2 | Work in process (Job 482) | 28,000 | |
| |    Wages payable | | 28,000 |
| | To record direct labor used for Job 482 in machining | | |
| 3 | Work in process (Job 482) | 5,600 | |
| |    Machining department overhead cost control | | 5,600 |
| | To record overhead allocated to Job 482 in machining | | |
| 4 | Work in process (Job 482) | 70,000 | |
| |    Raw material inventory | | 70,000 |
| | To record direct materials requisitioned for Job 482 in assembly | | |
| 5 | Work in process (Job 482) | 10,000 | |
| |    Wages payable | | 10,000 |
| | To record direct labor used for Job 482 in assembly | | |
| 6 | Work in process (Job 482) | 24,000 | |
| |    Assembly department overhead cost control | | 24,000 |
| | To record overhead allocated to Job 482 in assembly | | |
| 7 | Finished goods inventory (Job 482) | 177,600 | |
| |    Work in process (Job 482) | | 177,600 |
| | To record completion of Job 482 | | |
| 8 | Cost of goods sold | 177,600 | |
| |    Finished goods inventory (Job 482) | | 177,600 |
| | To record the delivery of Job 482 | | |

**Q1** How are costs assigned to customized goods and services?

**Q2** How is overhead allocated to individual jobs?

work in process inventory (entries 1 and 4). Some types of direct materials, such as supplies, are not traced to individual jobs when they are used; these costs are transferred into an overhead cost pool. However, this situation is not illustrated in Exhibit 5.7. As direct labor employees report their work time, the cost of their wages is debited to the jobs they work on and wages payable is credited for the wages earned (entries 2 and 5).[2]

Many organizations use overhead cost control accounts to monitor the costs for each overhead cost pool. As actual overhead costs are incurred, they are debited to the control account. For example, the assembly department supervisor's salary would be debited to the assembly

---

[2] The direct labor entries in Exhibit 5.7 show only the part of employee wages payable that relate to Job 482. The total amount of an individual employee's wages would be credited to wages payable, and debit entries would be made to all of the jobs the employee worked on during the pay period.

department overhead cost control and credited to wages payable. Overhead allocated to individual jobs is debited to work in process and credited to the control account (entries 3 and 6).

When a job is complete, the work in process account includes all of the direct material, direct labor, and overhead costs that have been assigned to the job. The total cost can then be transferred to finished goods inventory (entry 7). Finally, when revenue for the job is earned, the total cost is transferred from finished goods to cost of goods sold (entry 8).

## ■ Overapplied and Underapplied Overhead

> **Q3** What is the difference between actual costing and normal costing?

Under normal costing, periodic adjustments need to be made to reconcile the actual overhead cost with the amount of overhead that has been allocated to jobs. When we determine the overhead allocation rate, we estimate both the cost of overhead (numerator) and the volume of the allocation base (denominator). At the end of the period, the amounts of overhead in the inventory accounts (work in process, finished goods, and cost of goods sold) are either too little or too much, and so adjustments need to be made. **Overapplied overhead** occurs when actual costs are less than the total amount of overhead allocated to inventory accounts. In contrast, **underapplied overhead** occurs when actual costs are more than the amount of overhead allocated.

To correct for overapplied or underapplied overhead, we first compare the amount of overhead allocated to actual overhead cost. Suppose it is the end of the fiscal year at Aluminum Benders. Balances in the overhead cost control accounts for the machining department and assembly department cost pools are shown in Exhibit 5.8(a). Machining department overhead costs incurred totaled $1,600,000, while costs allocated to jobs totaled $1,120,000 (20,000 machine hours × $56). Assembly department overhead costs incurred totaled $2,700,000, while costs allocated to jobs totaled $2,880,000 ($1,200,000 direct labor cost × 240%). The combined amount of overapplied (underapplied) overhead is

|  | Overapplied or (Underapplied) Overhead |
|---|---|
| Machining | $(480,000) |
| Assembly | 180,000 |
| Net underapplied overhead | $(300,000) |

We then record an adjusting entry so that the total actual amount of overhead incurred is recorded as a product cost for the period. The balance of overapplied or underapplied overhead must be removed through an adjustment at the end of the accounting period. If the amount of the adjustment is material, it is prorated among work in process, finished goods (if any), and cost of goods sold. This proration is prescribed by generally accepted accounting principles, which require inventory to be recorded at actual cost. If the amount is immaterial, however, it is simply assigned to cost of goods sold.

---

**EXHIBIT 5.8**
Overhead Cost Control Accounts for Aluminum Benders

Machining Department Overhead Cost Control Account

| Total costs incurred | 1,600,000 | 1,120,000 | Total costs allocated |
|---|---|---|---|
| Underapplied overhead | 480,000 | | |

Assembly Department Overhead Cost Control Account

| Total costs incurred | 2,700,000 | 2,880,000 | Total costs allocated |
|---|---|---|---|
| | | 180,000 | Overapplied overhead |

**(a) Before Adjustment**

Machining Department Overhead Cost Control Account

| Total costs incurred | 1,600,000 | 1,120,000 | Total costs allocated |
|---|---|---|---|
| | | 480,000 | Adjustment |
| Balance | 0 | | |

Assembly Department Overhead Cost Control Account

| Total costs incurred | 2,700,000 | 2,880,000 | Total costs allocated |
|---|---|---|---|
| Adjustment | 180,000 | | |
| | | 0 | Balance |

**(b) After Adjustment**

Because the method of adjusting for overapplied or underapplied overhead depends on materiality, we need to decide whether the $300,000 amount for Aluminum Benders is material. One way to evaluate materiality is to calculate the net overapplied or underapplied overhead as a percent of actual overhead costs. For Aluminum Benders, this calculation follows:

$$\$300,000 \div (\$1,600,000 + \$2,700,000) = 7\%$$

Many accountants view amounts smaller than 10% to be immaterial. If we decide that the adjustment for Aluminum Benders is immaterial, we adjust the cost of goods sold total. Because overhead was underapplied, cost of goods sold would be increased, as follows:

**HELPFUL HINT**
Some accountants might use cost of goods sold to determine materiality.

| | | |
|---|---|---|
| Cost of goods sold | 300,000 | |
| Assembly department overhead cost control | 180,000 | |
| Machining department overhead cost control | | 480,000 |

If we decide that the adjustment for Aluminum Benders is material, it must be prorated among work in process, finished goods, and cost of goods sold. Suppose the balances in these accounts before the adjustment are:

| | |
|---|---|
| Ending work in process | $ 100,000 |
| Finished goods | 20,000 |
| Cost of goods sold | 10,000,000 |
| Total | $10,120,000 |

The adjustment of $300,000 would be prorated among these accounts based on each account's proportion of the total. The adjusting journal entry would be:

| | | |
|---|---|---|
| Ending work in process ($100,000 ÷ $10,120,000 × $300,000) | 2,964 | |
| Finished goods ($20,000 ÷ $10,120,000 × $300,000) | 593 | |
| Cost of goods sold ($10,000,000 ÷ $10,120,000 × $300,000) | 296,443 | |
| Assembly department overhead cost control | 180,000 | |
| Machining department overhead cost control | | 480,000 |

The balances before and after the adjustment would be:

| | Before Adjustment | Adjustment | After Adjustment |
|---|---|---|---|
| Ending work in process | $ 100,000 | $ 2,964 | $ 102,964 |
| Finished goods | 20,000 | 593 | 20,593 |
| Cost of goods sold | 10,000,000 | 296,443 | 10,296,443 |
| Total | $10,120,000 | $300,000 | $10,420,000 |

Whether the adjustment is considered material or immaterial, zero balances are left in both overhead cost control accounts after the adjustment, as shown in Exhibit 5.8(b).

---

## GUIDE YOUR LEARNING **5.3** Key Terms

Stop to confirm that you understand the new terms introduced in the last several pages:

Overapplied overhead (p. 186)
Underapplied overhead (p. 186)

For each of these terms, write a definition in your own words.

---

# SERVICE SECTOR JOB COSTING

**Q1** How are costs assigned to customized goods and services?

Many different kinds of organizations provide customized services for their clientele, for example hospitals, accounting firms, law firms, architects, and print shops. A major difference between job costing for service organizations and job costing for manufacturing organizations is that service companies typically do not carry product inventory on the balance sheet. Under generally accepted accounting principles, service revenues are usually earned as the services are performed. Therefore, both revenue and product costs are recorded on the income statement as

**Q2** How is overhead allocated to individual jobs?

services are performed. Although job costing information is not required for inventory record-keeping, many service organizations use job costing systems to help managers measure and monitor job costs and profits. In addition, the customer's price for a service is often calculated based on a percentage above cost. Costs in these contracts often include direct costs as well as allocated overhead costs. Thus, the allocation of overhead costs can directly affect revenues.

Jobs costing systems for service organizations are similar to the ones used by manufacturers. Source documents are used to trace direct costs to a specific job, and overhead costs are allocated. For example, in hospitals, physicians order treatments directly on computers at the nurses' stations. From these treatment orders, materials are requisitioned and costs and patient charges are recorded as part of each patient's stay. Charges and costs are also accumulated for resources such as the number of meals served, X-rays received, and minutes in the operating room. When the patient is sent home, the bill is sent to the payer and the costs (direct and allocated overhead) are recorded in a subsidiary ledger identified with the patient's medical number and a hospital episode number.

When allocating overhead, service organizations often use the labor hours of their professional employees as an allocation base. For example, accountants and lawyers record professional labor hours and other direct costs to specific jobs. Overhead cost is then allocated on the basis of the professional labor hours used for each specific job.

Service organizations often use information from their job costing systems to facilitate cost management, productivity measurement, and billing. Consulting firms and other organizations that manage large projects often track job costs in conjunction with their project management systems. Following is an example of job costing in a service organization.

## NIGHTHAWK LAW COMPANY
## JOB COSTING IN A LAW FIRM

Nighthawk Law Company specializes in copyright protection for authors. A client approached the law firm about handling his lawsuit against a large film company that he believes stole the plot from one of his novels for a made-for-TV movie.

### Estimated Job Costs and Price

The law partners estimated that the case would require 500 hours of professional labor. Nighthawk's accountant estimated the following direct costs:

| | |
|---|---:|
| Direct professional labor (500 hours) | $ 75,000 |
| Direct support labor | 20,000 |
| Fringe benefits for direct labor | 15,000 |
| Photocopying | 1,000 |
| Telephone calls | 1,000 |
| Total direct costs | $112,000 |

Last year, Nighthawk's overhead totaled $450,000. The two law partners worked about 5,000 professional labor hours. The accountant developed an estimated overhead allocation rate of $90 per direct labor hour ($450,000 ÷ 5,000). Therefore, the estimated overhead cost for this case is $90 × 500 hours = $45,000, and the total estimated cost is $157,000 ($45,000 + $112,000). The law firm's policy is to mark up cost by 20% for the estimated price. Using this markup, the estimated profit for the case is $31,400 ($157,000 × 20%). Using all of this information, the partners estimate the client's service price as follows:

| | |
|---|---:|
| Direct professional labor (500 hours) | $ 75,000 |
| Direct support labor | 20,000 |
| Fringe benefits for direct and professional labor | 15,000 |
| Photocopying | 1,000 |
| Telephone calls | 1,000 |
| Total direct costs | 112,000 |
| Overhead ($90 × 500 hours) | 45,000 |
| Total costs | 157,000 |
| Margin ($157,000 × 20%) | 31,400 |
| Total estimated service price | $188,400 |

### Competitor's Job Costs and Price

A competing law firm traces only the direct professional labor hours as a direct cost and considers all other costs to be indirect (overhead). These overhead costs are allocated at an estimated rate of $160 per professional labor hour. The accountant for this firm estimates this copyright case to cost $75,000 + $80,000 ($160 × 500) = $155,000. The competitor uses the same markup rate as Nighthawk: 20% of estimated total cost, or $31,000 ($155,000 × 20%). The partner in the competitor firm estimates the client's service price as follows:

| | |
|---|---:|
| Direct professional labor (500 hours) | $ 75,000 |
| Overhead ($160 × 500 hours) | 80,000 |
| Total costs | 155,000 |
| Margin ($155,000 × 20%) | 31,000 |
| Total estimated service price | $186,000 |

### Monitoring Job Costs

The prices estimated by the two law firms are very close in amount. However, the costs that are used to estimate the price are also used to monitor costs in the law firm. Nighthawk separately accounts for direct costs such as fringe benefits, photocopying, and telephone calls. The competitor includes these costs in overhead. Each approach has its pros and cons.

Nighthawk's accounting system incurs additional costs to separately accumulate and assign fringe benefits, photocopying, and telephone calls to individual jobs. Each of these costs is accumulated in a separate cost pool. Fringe benefits are allocated to jobs based on information that is already available about professional and support labor hours or costs. To allocate photocopying costs, the firm needs a system, such as the use of client codes, to record photocopying usage for each job. Telephone costs are traced using telephone logs. The accuracy of records for photocopying and telephone costs depends on the ability and desire of professional and support staff to maintain good records.

The benefit of separately accumulating and assigning fringe benefits, photocopying, and telephone call costs is improved monitoring of costs. The overhead cost pool is considerably smaller and includes fewer different types of costs. As the proportion of costs that can be directly traced to individual jobs increases, the accuracy of the costing system increases. Therefore systems with lower proportions of overhead more accurately capture the flow of resources to individual jobs.

## USES AND LIMITATIONS OF JOB COST INFORMATION

 **Q4** What are the uses and limitations of job cost information?

Job costing systems measure the cost of products, primarily for customized goods and services. The information from a job costing system can be used for several purposes, including the following:

- Reporting inventory and cost of goods sold values on financial statements and income tax returns
- Developing cost estimates to assist in bidding on potential future jobs
- Measuring actual costs to compare to estimated costs
- Developing cost estimates for short-term or long-term decisions

Because a job costing system accumulates and reports costs for individual jobs, the tendency is to mistakenly believe that job costs are measured accurately and that the costs assigned to a job are incremental, that is, would not be incurred if the job were not undertaken. However, job costing systems are subject to uncertainties and require judgment. In addition, analysis is required to identify the job costs that are relevant to a given decision.

### ■ Allocated Overhead Costs and Decision Making

Overhead costs are allocated to jobs to match revenues and product costs. However, allocated overhead costs are not relevant information for most short-term decisions, such as special orders or the use of constrained resources. Many overhead costs are fixed; they do not change with changes in the allocation base or any other measure of activity. Nevertheless, managers may mistakenly assume that these allocated costs are variable, particularly when the job costing system uses several cost pools and allocation bases. Another problem occurs if the allocation base used to allocate variable overhead costs is not a cost driver, which means it does not accurately reflect the use of variable cost resources.

Managers within an organization often do not understand how costs are allocated to individual jobs. They may misinterpret cost information and rely on irrelevant information. Accountants must not only produce relevant information for each decision, but also help educate managers about appropriate uses of cost information. The next illustration demonstrates the accountant's role in providing managers with relevant information for internal decision making.

**CHAPTER REFERENCE**

See Chapter 4 for more information on short-term decision making.

## ALUMINUM BENDERS (PART 2)
## JOB COSTS RELEVANT FOR DECISION MAKING

Suppose Aluminum Benders receives two new orders from two different contractors. Because of previous commitments, the company has only enough capacity during the next few weeks to accept one of the new orders. Sean estimates the direct costs for the new orders and the amount of overhead that will be allocated to each job. These figures allow him to estimate the contribution margin and operating income as follows:

|  | For Contractor A | For Contractor B |
|---|---|---|
| Estimated selling price | $150,000 | $230,000 |
| Less variable costs: |  |  |
|     Direct materials | 55,000 | 100,000 |
|     Direct labor |  |  |
|         Machining | 5,000 | 10,000 |
|         Assembly | 10,000 | 20,000 |
| Estimated contribution margin | 80,000 | 100,000 |
| Less allocated overhead: |  |  |
|     Machining: |  |  |
|         For Contractor A (85 hours × $56) | 4,760 |  |
|         For Contractor B (150 hours × $56) |  | 8,400 |
|     Assembly (direct labor cost × 240%) | 24,000 | 48,000 |
|     Estimated operating income | $ 51,240 | $ 43,600 |

Sean initially thinks that the company should accept the job from Contractor A because that job is expected to generate higher operating income. However, he realizes that operating income includes a reduction for allocated overhead. He knows that the contribution margin for each job is relevant to the decision; he is less sure whether overhead is relevant.

Sean studies the types of costs included in the overhead cost pools, and learns that most of the overhead costs are fixed. Direct labor employees are guaranteed a 40-hour work week, so the overhead costs of fringe benefits are likely fixed. The machine-related costs are also primarily fixed, although repair costs probably increase as volumes increase. He would like to break overhead into fixed and variable portions, but does not have time right now.

Given his quick analysis of the costs for each job, Sean believes he should only present the incremental costs in his report because managers may assume that allocated overhead costs actually vary with machine hours and labor cost and choose Contractor A's job with an estimated operating income of $51,240. Thus, Sean plans to recommend that the company accept the job from Contractor B. He expects the company to earn $20,000 more ($100,000 − $80,000) in incremental contribution margin from this job than from Contractor A's job.

### Qualitative Factors

Sean asks the controller for her advice. She agrees that only incremental costs should be presented. She tells Sean that he also needs to discuss some qualitative factors with the managers. For example, Contractor A is a profitable, ongoing customer who would become dissatisfied if the order were turned down. The job from Contractor B involves special machining that the company does not ordinarily perform, reducing the accountant's confidence in the job cost estimate. However, Contractor B is a new customer with whom Aluminum Benders would like to work in the future. These types of qualitative factors sometimes weigh more heavily than the estimated incremental contribution margin when managers make these types of decisions.

| GUIDE YOUR LEARNING | 5.4 | Aluminum Benders (Part 2) |

Aluminum Benders (Part 2) illustrates a decision between alternative customer orders. For this illustration:

| Identify Problem and Information | Identify Uncertainties | Explore Uncertainty |
|---|---|---|
| What decision was being addressed, and what information was relevant to the decision? In your own words, explain why allocated overhead costs were irrelevant to the decision. | What were the uncertainties? Consider uncertainties about: <br> • Revenues for each job <br> • Costs for each job <br> • Qualitative factors | How might the degree of uncertainty about job costs affect this decision? |

## ■ Uncertainties in Measuring Job Costs

Little uncertainty tends to surround the direct costs assigned to a job, because those costs are traced to each job. However, judgment is used to decide which direct costs will be traced. Occasionally direct costs are quite small, and the cost of creating a system to track them is greater than the benefit achieved. In these cases, costs that might potentially be traced are instead included with indirect costs in a pool of overhead costs. However, changes in technology sometimes allow accountants to trace costs that were previously too costly to trace. For example, most large photocopiers today include security systems that track the number of copies made to specific account codes. These systems minimize the cost of tracing photocopy costs to individual jobs. Without such a system, the cost of tracking individual copies could be overly expensive. Tracking the use of software and Internet services for networked computers or monitoring small supplies such as nails and tape during manufacturing is more difficult. These costs are treated as indirect costs and become part of overhead.

Accountants also choose the type and number of cost pools to use for overhead. For example, overhead costs were pooled at the department level in Aluminum Benders. However, overhead could have been pooled at the plant level. Alternatively, the overhead costs in each department could have been separated into fixed and variable pools. Accountants consider several factors when they choose the number and kind of cost pools to use. From a management control perspective, if costs are tracked to a department or a process, the managers of that department or process can be held responsible for controlling costs. When overhead costs from many departments are pooled, managers and employees within each department have little incentive to control costs. In addition, different departments usually perform different tasks, so their costs may be quite different. If costs are allocated on a department level and these costs more accurately reflect the flow of resources, products can be designed to spend less time in costly departments. When deciding whether to use department or plantwide cost pools, the benefit gained from gathering information about department costs and the use of department resources by other departments must be worth the cost of tracking them.

Ideally, we would prefer that the overhead allocation process reflect the flow of overhead resources to each product. Thus, an ideal overhead allocation base would be a cost driver. However, fixed overhead is not expected to vary with any allocation base, and it is not always possible to identify or to accurately measure a cost driver for variable overhead. Thus, allocated overhead generally does not accurately measure the overhead resources used by a job.

**CHAPTER REFERENCE**

Chapter 2 introduces several techniques for evaluating whether a potential cost driver explains the variation in a cost.

## ■ Uncertainties in Estimating Future Job Costs

Managers use job cost estimates to establish a bid for a job, decide whether to accept a job, or make other types of decisions. Managers then monitor operations by comparing actual job costs to the original estimate. Any time we estimate future events we face uncertainties about whether the estimates will be accurate. Thus, actual job costs will almost certainly be different from estimated job costs. Managers analyze the differences to evaluate the efficiency of operations and to improve future job cost estimates.

**CHAPTER REFERENCE**

Chapter 11 introduces variance analysis, which is used to evaluate differences between estimated and actual costs.

Under normal costing, overhead is allocated to jobs using an estimated overhead allocation rate. The estimated rate is based on estimates of the total overhead cost and the total volume of the allocation base. Actual costs and activity levels are affected by many unforeseen events. These include unanticipated cost inflation or deflation or an economic downturn that causes business activities to fall short of expectations. Actual costs also differ from expectations because of unexpected improvements or deterioration in production efficiency. Differences between estimates and actual amounts cause overhead to be overapplied or underapplied, and then adjustments are required at the end of an accounting period. However, judgment is necessary in the way that adjustments are made. The following ethical scenario illustrates a situation in which the method of adjusting costs affects an organization's revenues.

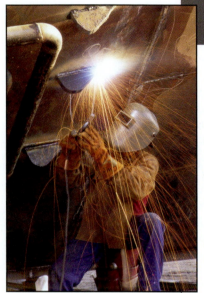

## FOCUS ON ETHICAL DECISION MAKING
## Inappropriate Prorating of Underapplied Overhead

The U.S. government contracts with defense industry firms to develop new military technology. These contracts are sometimes based on cost. Because these organizations also sell products to nongovernment businesses, incentives exist to shift overhead costs to the government, so that commercial operations become more competitive. Because cost allocations are private information, research provides only indirect evidence that this cost shifting occurs. For example, when the Cost Accounting Standards Board developed new standards for defense contractors during 1968–1970, the stock market price of these firms dropped, indicating that market analysts believed these firms would be hurt by more rigorous standards (Pownall, 1986). The following vignette is fictional, but it illustrates potential ethical problems that arise when governments use cost-based contracts for product development.

Deep Water Ship Building Company builds large ships and submarines for both commercial and government contracts. Because one of its commercial contracts fell through last year, the company had fewer jobs than anticipated. Consequently, the company's overhead costs were underapplied at the end of the year, so an adjustment was made to increase cost of goods sold.

Deep Water's policy is to allocate production overhead as a percentage of direct labor costs for each contract. One of the contracts completed last year was for a stealth watercraft for a branch of the military. The job contract was based on cost-plus-fixed-fee for a total cost of $245 million. The stealth project was Deep Water's only government contract last year. Commercial business completed was $105 million, so cost of goods sold (COGS) totaled $350 million.

### Disagreement about Underapplied Overhead Adjustment

The government official in charge of the contract complained to the federal contract auditor that Deep Water's underapplied overhead should not have been closed to COGS. Instead, he argued that it should have been prorated among the contracts in progress, finished goods, and COGS. The auditor asked to see the cost accounting records and financial statements for the period. Following is an analysis of the direct costs and cost allocations (in millions):

| | Contracts in Progress | Finished Goods Inventory | Cost of Goods Sold | Total Work on Jobs This Period |
|---|---|---|---|---|
| Direct materials used | $250 | $50 | $100 | $400 |
| Direct labor | 92 | 8 | 50 | 150 |
| Overhead allocated | 184 | 16 | 100 | 300 |
| Total before adjustment | 526 | 74 | 250 | 850 |
| Add: | | | | |
| Underapplied overhead | 0 | 0 | 100 | 100 |
| Total after adjustment | $526 | $74 | $350 | $950 |

The $350 million in COGS included $245 million for the government contract. When the underapplied overhead ($100 million) was closed to COGS, the government portion of underapplied overhead was $70 million [$100 × ($245 ÷ $350)]. Because the contract specified that the government would pay costs plus a fixed amount, the overhead adjustment effectively increased the revenue under the contract by $70 million.

Actual direct labor costs were $150 million, and the pre-adjustment allocated overhead was $300 million. Therefore, the original allocation rate was 200% ($300 ÷ $150) of direct labor cost.

Total actual overhead turned out to be $400 million (the $300 million plus the $100 million underapplied). If Deep Water accountants could have perfectly estimated overhead at $400 million and direct labor cost at $150 million, they would have used 267% ($400 ÷ $150) as the allocation rate.

The underapplied overhead amount was material ($100 million out of $400 million, or 25%). Therefore, the government auditor decided that it should have been prorated among the three accounts that reflected work done this period: contracts in progress, finished goods, and cost of goods sold. Had this method been used, the adjustment would have been prorated as follows:

| | |
|---|---|
| Contracts in progress ($526 million ÷ $850 million) × $100 million | $ 61.9 million |
| Finished goods ($74 million ÷ $850 million) × $100 million | 8.7 |
| Cost of goods sold ($250 million ÷ $850 million) × $100 million | 29.4 |
| Total adjustment | $100.0 million |

The government share of the COGS adjustment would be ($245 ÷ $350) × $29.4 million = $20.6 million. When the auditor compared this to the original adjustment of $70 million, she knew the government had been overcharged.

### Alternative Methods for Prorating Overapplied or Underapplied Overhead

The auditor offered Deep Water three alternatives for prorating the overhead adjustment. Under governmental contracts, underapplied overhead could be prorated based on direct materials cost, direct labor cost, or total direct costs. If Deep Water uses direct materials, COGS is increased by $25 million, of which the government portion is $17.5 million. If direct labor cost is used, COGS is increased by $33.3 million, of which the government portion is $23.3 million. If total direct cost is used, COGS is increased by $27.3 million, of which the government portion is $19.1 million.

The government and Deep Water must now negotiate to determine the most appropriate proration method.

SOURCE: G. Pownall, "An Empirical Analysis of the Regulation of the Defense Contracting Industry: The Cost Accounting Standards Board," *Journal of Accounting Research 24*, no. 2 (1986), pp. 291–316.

### Practice Ethical Decision Making

In Chapter 1, we learned a process for making ethical decisions (Exhibit 1.11). You can address the following questions for this ethical dilemma to improve your skills for making ethical decisions. Think about your answers to these questions and discuss them with others.

| Ethical Decision-Making Process | Questions to Consider about This Ethical Dilemma |
|---|---|
| Identify ethical problems as they arise. | Is allocating proportionately more cost to government contracts an ethical problem for Deep Water? Why or why not? |
| Objectively consider the well-being of others and society when exploring alternatives. | When the government pays more than commercial customers pay for work done, does this situation pose a business problem, a social problem, or both? Explain. Discuss the preferences of various stakeholders for this problem, including: <br> • Deep Water managers <br> • Deep Water shareholders <br> • Deep Water commercial customers <br> • Deep Water governmental customers <br> • Deep Water competitors <br> • U.S. taxpayers |
| Clarify and apply ethical values when choosing a course of action. | Identify the values you use as you answer the following questions: <br> • Is it fair for the government to pay more for products and services than commercial customers pay? <br> • Is it fair for taxes to subsidize the overhead costs for a private business? |
| Work toward ongoing improvement of personal and organizational ethics. | How can an organization monitor whether its accounting practices are ethical? |

# SPOILAGE, REWORK, AND SCRAP IN JOB COSTING

 **Q5** How are spoilage, rework, and scrap handled in job costing?

No matter how carefully goods are manufactured, occasionally some units do not meet quality standards; they are spoiled. **Spoilage** refers to units of product that are unacceptable and are discarded, reworked, or sold at a reduced price. Examples of spoilage in job costing include:

- Units in batches of clothing that have flaws in the material or sewing
- Several valves in a batch that do not function properly when tested at the end of production
- A custom-ordered birdhouse that has an off-center round hole

Different types of spoiled products are handled in different ways. For example, if the material flaws are not too noticeable, the clothing can be sold as irregular. Perhaps the birdhouse can be sold at a discount, but the valves probably cannot be sold and must be discarded or reworked.

Spoilage is typically identified through some type of inspection process. Sometimes inspection occurs at the end of the production process immediately before units are moved to finished goods inventory. Other times, inspection occurs at one or more intermediate stages during production. Inspection can also occur at the beginning of the process. For example, denim fabric can be checked for flaws before it is introduced into the production process for manufacturing jeans. Other practices, such as conducting preventive maintenance on equipment rather than waiting for machinery problems to develop, help minimize spoilage.

To determine the cost of a partially complete spoiled unit, we add up all direct materials and labor costs used and allocate overhead according to the amount of work completed before the unit was removed from production. The way spoilage cost is handled depends on whether the spoilage is considered normal or abnormal.

## ■ Normal and Abnormal Spoilage

**Normal spoilage** consists of defective units that arise as part of regular operations. If normal spoilage arises from the requirements of a specific job, the cost of the spoiled units is charged to the job. For example, suppose one of **Bombardier's** completion center customers wants leather interior walls. If the leather is more difficult to install than other materials and part of the leather is spoiled in the installation process, then the cost of the spoilage would be charged to that job.

Normal spoilage also occurs periodically as a regular part of all jobs. For example, suppose that the safety lighting system installed along the carpeting sometimes twists and breaks as it is being installed, no matter how carefully it is handled. This loss has nothing to do with any specific order; instead, it is a normal part of operations. The cost of normal spoilage common to all jobs is charged to overhead and is allocated with other overhead costs to all jobs.

**Abnormal spoilage** is spoilage that is not part of everyday operations. It occurs for reasons such as the following:

- Out-of-control manufacturing processes
- Unusual machine breakdowns
- Unexpected electrical outages that result in a number of spoiled units

Some abnormal spoilage is considered avoidable; that is, if managers monitor processes and maintain machinery appropriately, little spoilage will occur. To highlight these types of problems so that they can be monitored, abnormal spoilage is recorded in a Loss from Abnormal Spoilage Account in the general ledger and is not included in the job costing inventory accounts (work in process, finished goods, and cost of goods sold).

The following illustration demonstrates normal and abnormal spoilage for Aluminum Benders.

**HELPFUL HINT**

The accounting entries shown here for normal spoilage are based on current U.S. GAAP. Current international accounting standards do not permit the cost of spoilage to be included in inventory, and the FASB is considering a similar prohibition.

## ALUMINUM BENDERS (PART 3)
## ASSIGNING SPOILAGE COSTS

When Job 512 was being processed in the machining department, a piece of sheet metal was off center in the bending machine and two vents were spoiled. This problem occurs periodically, is considered normal spoilage, and is recorded as an overhead cost. Because this step comes first in the procedure for making the vents, the only costs incurred were for direct materials ($25). The following journal entry records normal spoilage as an overhead cost, assuming the sheet metal cannot be sold at a discount and its cost has been recorded in work in process inventory.

| | | |
|---|---|---|
| Overhead cost control (normal spoilage) | $25 | |
| Work in process inventory (cost of spoiled sheet metal) | | $25 |

If these costs had been abnormal spoilage, they would have been recorded to a loss from abnormal spoilage account instead of the overhead cost control account.

Job 489 required an especially thin sheet metal to reduce the weight of the vents. When two of the vents were being assembled, they were spoiled because the metal twisted and could not be joined properly. Because the thin metal was a specific requirement for this job, the costs for the spoiled units were recorded as a cost for Job 489. Direct materials cost $100 and direct labor cost $150 for the vents up to the time they were spoiled. The metal can be sold to a recycler at a discounted price of $50. The journal entries for the use of direct materials and labor are the same as if the direct materials and labor were not spoiled, because these are additional costs for this specific job. However, the following journal entries record the value of the sheet metal at the time it is spoiled and the subsequent sale of the metal.

| | | |
|---|---|---|
| Raw material inventory (metal to be sold to recycler) | $50 | |
| Work in process inventory (Job 489) | | $50 |
| Cash | $50 | |
| Raw material inventory | | $50 |

## ■ Rework

**Rework** consists of spoiled units that are repaired and sold as if they were originally produced correctly. For example, electronic equipment that is special ordered, such as computers or batches of cell phones, are reworked when defects are discovered during the manufacturing process or through inspection at the end of the process. If the cost of rework is tracked, it is recorded in the same manner as spoilage; normal rework is charged to overhead or to a specific job, and abnormal rework is recorded as a line item loss. Rework costs are often not tracked, however.

Units are sometimes reworked and then sold at a regular price through regular marketing channels. Other times reworked units remain flawed and must be sold at a reduced price. Costs and benefits are analyzed to decide whether to rework a spoiled unit. Suppose a clothing manufacturer discovers several jeans with back pockets sewn on upside down. If the pockets are carefully removed and then sewn on correctly, it may be difficult to tell that there was ever a problem. However, additional cost is added for the labor time to fix the pockets. Furthermore, the pockets might rip more easily because the material has been weakened. The managers need to evaluate whether the costs of reworking the pockets outweigh the benefits.

## ■ Scrap

**Scrap** consists of the bits of direct material left over from normal manufacturing processes. Sometimes it has value and can be sold, and sometimes it is discarded. New technology affects whether something is considered scrap. For example, for many years lumber mills burned sawdust, for which they had no alternative uses, in teepee-shaped silos that glowed red at night. As trees became a scarce resource, sawdust became more valuable. With improved glues and new manufacturing processes, products such as specialty logs for fireplaces and chipboard were developed. A process was developed to turn sawdust into pulp for

**CHAPTER REFERENCE**

Accounting for joint products and by-products is covered in Chapter 9.

paper mills. Sawdust is no longer scrap, but has become an important by-product of milling lumber.

Some manufacturers track scrap to measure whether resources are being used efficiently. Scrap is also tracked if it has value and could be stolen. Often it is recorded in physical terms. For example, gold scraps from jewelry manufacture are weighed, the weight is recorded, and the scraps are stored in a safe.

From an accounting standpoint, we need to plan for and sometimes guard scrap by setting up control systems. We also need to determine the effect of the value of scrap on inventory costing and the income statement. If scrap can be sold, the revenue is recorded either at the time it is produced or at the time it is sold. When the value of scrap is immaterial, it is simply recorded as part of other revenues in the income statement.

In job costing, scrap sometimes arises as part of specific jobs. If we can trace it to individual jobs, revenue from the scrap is credited to the specific job in work in process. Scrap revenue reduces the cost of the job with which it is associated. If scrap is common to all jobs, or if it is not worth tracing to individual jobs, the scrap revenue offsets overhead cost for the period. This entry reduces overhead cost for all jobs produced.

If scrap is held for a period of time before it is reused as direct material or sold, we need to estimate its net realizable value so that the value of the scrap can be used to offset overhead costs in the same period in which the overhead costs and associated revenues are recognized. When the price of scrap is volatile, such as gold in the previous example, estimating its value is more difficult.

Some organizations develop creative ways to use scrap to benefit employees and others. For example, print shops sometimes bind scrap paper into scratch pads and give them to employees, customers, or public schools. Employees working for a defense contractor near the Mexican border remove the nails and staples from lumber the company receives as packing crates for parts. The company then transports the lumber across the border for use by impoverished families living in homes made from cardboard. Such uses of scrap improve employee satisfaction, enhance the firm's reputation, and provide social value.

---

### GUIDE YOUR LEARNING 5.5 Key Terms

Stop to confirm that you understand the new terms introduced in the last several pages:

| | |
|---|---|
| Spoilage (p. 194) | Rework (p. 195) |
| Normal spoilage (p. 194) | Scrap (p. 195) |
| Abnormal spoilage (p. 194) | |

For each of these terms, write a definition in your own words. Also list at least one example that is different from the ones given in this textbook.

---

## PRODUCTION QUALITY AND BEHAVIOR IMPLICATIONS

**Q6** What are the quality and behavioral implications of spoilage?

In the preceding section, we learned about methods used to account for the direct costs of spoilage, rework, and scrap. Although the direct costs can be significant, managers need to consider several other issues related to the quality of their production processes.

### ■ Spoilage Opportunity Costs

The opportunity costs of spoilage and rework can be large. Opportunity costs include the following:

- Forgone profit
- Loss of reputation and market share

An organization forgoes the normal profit from resources that are used to produce spoiled units. Forgone profit is a bigger problem when capacity limits are involved, because the organization forgoes the profit on resources employed as well as the contribution margin from good units that might have been produced. In addition, some proportion of spoiled units is likely to mistakenly pass inspection. As the number of spoiled units increases, a larger number of spoiled units will inevitably be sold to customers. The sale of these defective units leads to loss of market share because consumers switch brands. The company eventually loses its reputation for quality products, leading to further erosion of market share, including customers who never had direct quality problems. These opportunity costs, which are often much greater than the cost of the spoiled units, are not tracked by the accounting system.

## ■ Investing in Quality

**CURRENT PRACTICE**

Organizations may voluntarily agree to comply with ISO 9000 standards, which are designed to improve quality management and facilitate business-to-business transactions.[3]

**CHAPTER REFERENCE**

To learn more about kaizen costing, see Chapter 13.

Some organizations position themselves as high-quality producers and work toward continuous improvement in quality. For example, **Bombardier's** Learjets have a reputation for high quality. In addition, customers may demand higher quality or may be willing to pay a premium price for quality. To improve quality, many organizations adopt a variety of business practices such as total quality management, Six Sigma®, lean manufacturing, and kaizen costing. Quality efforts can dramatically reduce spoilage, rework, and related opportunity costs.

However, measuring the costs and benefits of such improvements is difficult. Quality costs are often measured imprecisely. Employees often work on quality issues in addition to their other responsibilities, so time spent on quality is not tracked, but estimated. Measuring loss of market share due to quality problems is also difficult. Therefore, exactly identifying the costs and benefits of quality improvement measures is an uncertain process. Although managers may not be able to prove that their quality efforts are cost-effective, other qualitative benefits result from investments in quality.

---

**CURRENT PRACTICE**

### Quality as a Public Issue

The effects of quality go beyond the costs for individual organizations. Quality is often a public issue:

- In 1982, several bottles of Tylenol were contaminated with cyanide by a customer in Illinois retail stores. Although the manufacturer, **Johnson & Johnson**, did not cause the problem, the CEO, James Burke, pulled all Tylenol capsules off retail shelves at a cost of $100 million. Burke was responding to Johnson & Johnson's mission to a higher duty to "mothers and all others who use our products." For this and other similar actions, in 2003 Burke was awarded sixth place in *Fortune* 10 greatest CEOs of all time.
- The 2000 U.S. presidential election finished in a national controversy over the way that election ballots were counted in Florida. Antiquated and error-prone equipment caused a disproportionate number of ballots to be spoiled in poorer counties. Spoiled ballots are disqualified; they are not counted in the election results.

SOURCES: Jim Collins, "The 10 Greatest CEOS of All Time," *Fortune*, July 21, 2003, p. 62; and "Rights Commission's Report on Florida Election," executive summary by U.S. Commission on Civil Rights, June 5, 2001, available at www.washingtonpost.com.

---

## ■ Effect of Accounting on Manager Behavior

Accounting practices influence manager behavior, especially when managers are compensated based on accounting earnings. Only some types of spoilage and rework costs are reflected in the accounting records. These accounting procedures may not provide incentives that encourage managers to control spoilage, for example:

- Spoilage opportunity costs are not measured or recorded in the accounting records, which discourages management attention.
- Normal spoilage may seem insignificant because it is often a relatively small part of the total overhead cost pool.
- Judgment is used to determine normal spoilage, which influences the portion of spoilage costs included in the overhead cost pool versus the portion reported as a separate operating loss.

---

[3]Available at International Organization for Standardization (ISO) Web site: www.iso.org.

- Rework costs are not usually tracked, giving managers an incentive to inappropriately rework units to avoid recognizing abnormal spoilage.

To control for the potentially adverse effects of these accounting practices, some organizations institute systems to monitor defects and establish defect rates as part of management compensation criteria. Still other organizations prohibit rework to emphasize initial quality and to avoid the potential waste of additional resources.

## ◼ External Monitoring

External stakeholders such as shareholders typically do not have access to explicit information about an organization's spoilage rates or costs. Although abnormal spoilage is recorded in a separate loss account in the general ledger, it is typically combined with other financial statement items. Thus, spoilage rarely appears as a line item on published financial statements. Exceptions tend to be large catastrophes, such as damage caused by an earthquake, that are publicly known before financial statements are issued. Therefore, external stakeholders must use indirect ways to analyze the quality of an organization's production processes. An organization with a high spoilage rate might have a lower than average gross profit margin, higher than average warranty liabilities, or a poor reputation for product quality.

## SUMMARY

**Q1** How Are Costs Assigned to Customized Goods and Services?

### Cost Flows in Manufacturing Job Costing

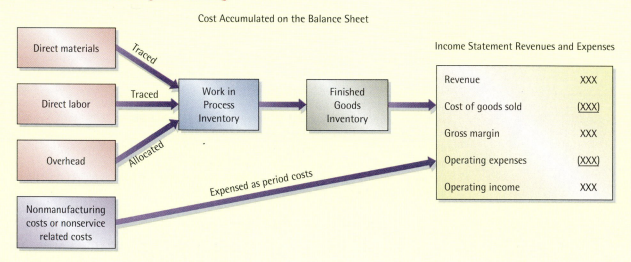

### Accounting System
- Source documents (e.g., employee time reports and material requisitions)
- Job cost record
- Job cost software

**Q2** How Is Overhead Allocated to Individual Jobs?

### Procedures for Allocating Overhead Costs to Jobs:
1. Identify the relevant cost object.
2. Identify one or more overhead cost pools and allocation bases.
3. For each overhead cost pool, calculate an overhead allocation rate.
4. For each overhead cost pool, allocate costs to the cost object.

### Types of Overhead Cost Pools
- Company-wide
- Plant-wide
- Separate departments
- Separate activities or processes
- Separate fixed and variable

## Q3 What Is the Difference Between Actual Costing and Normal Costing?

### Actual Costing
Actual quantity of allocation base for job × Actual allocation rate

### Normal Costing
Actual quantity of allocation base for job × Estimated allocation rate

### Adjustment for Overapplied or Underapplied Overhead
Overapplied (underapplied) overhead = Allocated overhead − Actual overhead

If material: Prorate among work in process, finished goods, and cost of goods sold

If not material: Apply to cost of goods sold

## Q4 What Are the Uses and Limitations of Job Cost Information?

### Uses of Job Cost Information
- Assign costs to work in process, finished goods, and cost of goods sold for financial statement and income tax returns
- Provide information to help managers:
  –Monitor operating costs
  –Develop job bids
  –Make short-term or long-term decisions

### Allocation of Overhead Costs
- Required for financial and tax accounting of manufactured goods
- Optional otherwise
- Fixed overhead allocation generally not relevant for short-term decisions

### Uncertainties
- Which estimated job costs are relevant for decision making
- Whether and how to trace direct costs
- Choice of overhead cost pools
- Choice of allocation bases
- Estimated overhead allocation rate (under normal costing)
- Method for adjusting overapplied or underapplied overhead (under normal costing)

## Q5 How Are Spoilage, Rework, and Scrap Handled in Job Costing?

| Type of Spoilage, Rework, or Scrap | Accounting Treatment |
|---|---|
| Normal spoilage arising from the requirements of a specific job | Charge to the individual job |
| Normal spoilage occurring periodically as a regular part of all jobs | Charge to overhead |
| Abnormal spoilage | Charge to separate loss account |
| Opportunity costs of spoilage | Not measured |
| Rework for defects arising from the requirements of a specific job | Charge to individual job |
| Rework for defects occurring periodically during normal production | Charge to overhead |
| Rework for abnormal defects | Charge to separate loss account |
| Sale of scrap | Record at time of production or at time sold<br>If not material: Record as other income |
| Scrap traced to individual jobs | Credit to individual job |
| Scrap common to all jobs or difficult to trace to jobs | Credit to overhead |

## Q6 What Are the Quality and Behavioral Implications of Spoilage?

### Spoilage Opportunity Costs
- Forgone profit
- Loss of reputation and market share

### Investing in Quality

### Effect of Accounting on Manager Behavior

### External Monitoring

## Self-Study Problems

### Self-Study Problem 1   Normal Costing with Two Overhead Cost Pools

**Q1, Q2, Q3, Q4**

William Felix & Sons uses an estimated overhead rate for allocating production overhead to job orders. The rate is on a machine hour basis for the machining department and on a direct labor cost basis for the finishing department. The company estimated the following for 2005:

|  | Machining | Finishing |
|---|---|---|
| Production overhead cost | $10,000,000 | $8,000,000 |
| Machine hours | 200,000 | 33,000 |
| Direct labor hours | 30,000 | 160,000 |
| Direct labor cost | $900,000 | $4,000,000 |

During the month of January, the cost record for job order No. 806 shows the following:

|  | Machining | Finishing |
|---|---|---|
| Direct materials requisitioned | $14,000 | $3,000 |
| Direct labor cost | $600 | $1,250 |
| Direct labor hours | 30 | 50 |
| Machine hours | 130 | 10 |

Total costs and machine hours were as follows for 2005:

|  | Machining | Finishing |
|---|---|---|
| Production overhead incurred | $10,200,000 | $7,900,000 |
| Direct labor cost | $950,000 | $3,900,000 |
| Machine hours | 220,000 | 32,000 |

**REQUIRED:**

**A.** What is the estimated overhead rate that should be used in the machining department? In the finishing department?

**B.** What is the total overhead allocated to Job 806?

**e C.** Assuming that Job 806 manufactured 200 units of product, what is the unit cost of Job 806?

**D.** What is the total amount of over- or underapplied overhead in each department at the end of 2005?

**2 E.** Provide reasons why Felix uses two different overhead application bases. Also discuss why Felix might use machine hours and labor costs to allocate overhead costs.

### Solution to Self-Study Problem 1

**A.** Overhead rates should be calculated using estimated costs and allocation bases:

Machining: $10,000,000 ÷ 200,000 = $50 per machine hour
Finishing: $8,000,000 ÷ $4,000,000 = 200% of direct labor cost

**B.** Using the overhead rates from part (A), the total overhead allocated to Job 806 should be as follows:

| | |
|---|---|
| Machining department: $50 × 130 machine hours | $6,500 |
| Finishing department: 200% × $1,250 direct labor cost | 2,500 |
| Total overhead allocated to Job 806 | $9,000 |

**C.** To calculate per-unit costs, first calculate the total cost for the batch and then divide by the number of units:

|  | Machining | Finishing |
|---|---|---|
| Direct materials | $14,000 | $3,000 |
| Direct labor | 600 | 1,250 |
| Overhead allocated | 6,500 | 2,500 |
| Total | $21,100 | $6,750 |

Total costs: $21,100 + $6,750 = $27,850

Cost per unit: $27,850 ÷ 200 units = $139.25 per unit

| D. Machining department overhead allocated (220,000 × $50) | $11,000,000 |
|---|---|
| Actual overhead in machining | 10,200,000 |
| Overapplied overhead | $ 800,000 |

| Finishing department overhead allocated ($3,900,000 × 200%) | $ 7,800,000 |
|---|---|
| Actual overhead in finishing | 7,900,000 |
| Underapplied overhead | $ 100,000 |

E. Felix must believe that the overhead costs in each department are related to different allocation bases. Machining is likely to have more overhead expense for buying, maintaining, and using machines. Therefore, machine hours are likely to reflect the activities involved in running machines. In the finishing department, more labor-related costs are incurred. Therefore, it is logical to use labor dollars as an allocation base. Although accountants attempt to pick allocation bases that are related to the activities in a cost center, the allocations are still arbitrary. Changes in volumes do not result in proportionate changes in costs. A portion of the costs are often fixed and unaffected by changes in the level of the allocation bases. In other words, allocation bases are not necessarily cost drivers. Instead, they are simply measures of activity used to allocate costs logically.

## Self-Study Problem 2 | Normal and Abnormal Spoilage

Q5, Q6

Flockhart Company produces custom-made garden sheds using recycled materials. Currently two jobs are in process, number 689 and 690. During production of Job 689, lightning hit the factory and caused an electricity surge followed by an outage. Lightning strikes are relatively unusual in the region where the factory is located. At the time of the strike, wood was being sawed to fit Job 689. The rip-saw malfunctioned and ruined a large piece of lumber that originally cost $175. During production of Job 690, two pieces of lumber had sawing errors and were scrapped. These pieces of lumber originally cost $80 and $75; they could be sold as scrap for $20 and $30. Sawing errors occur for many different jobs on a regular basis.

A. Consider the spoilage for Job 689. Should it be categorized as normal or abnormal spoilage? Explain.

B. Consider the spoilage for Job 690. Should it be categorized as normal or abnormal spoilage? Explain.

C. Prepare journal entries for the spoilage on both jobs. Assume that the scrap lumber has not yet been sold.

D. Describe the actual and opportunity costs of spoilage.

## Solution to Self-Study Problem 2

REQUIRED:

A. The spoilage for Job 689 is abnormal spoilage because it occurred from an unusual force of nature. Abnormal spoilage is not part of normal operations and occurs because systems are out of control or an unusual event occurs, such as loss of electricity from an unusual storm. Abnormal spoilage is recorded as a loss for the period.

B. The spoilage for Job 690 is normal spoilage because it arises as a part of ongoing operations. If it occurs because of the requirements of a specific job, it is recorded as a cost for that job. If it occurs as part of operations, it is recorded as an overhead cost.

C. Journal entry for abnormal spoilage (assuming the requisition of raw material was not recorded as a job cost):

| | | |
|---|---|---|
| Loss from abnormal spoilage | $175 | |
| Work in process inventory (Job 689—spoiled lumber at cost) | | $175 |

Journal entry for normal spoilage:

| | | |
|---|---|---|
| Overhead cost control | $105 | |
| Raw material inventory (scrap lumber) | $50 | |
| Work in process inventory (Job 690—spoiled lumber at cost) | | $155 |

D. The actual costs of spoilage include the dollar amounts for direct materials, direct labor, and overhead that have been incurred up to the point that the spoiled units are removed from production. The opportunity costs of spoilage include warranty and return costs, and potential loss of reputation and market share. It is difficult to estimate these costs, but they can be considerable.

REVIEW  Use the exercises in the following boxes in the chapter to review key terms and key techniques, analyze chapter illustrations, improve your learning of new concepts, and practice ethical decision making:

Guide Your Learning 5.1: Key Terms (p. 183)

Guide Your Learning 5.2: Aluminum Benders (Part 1) (p. 184)

Guide Your Learning 5.3: Key Terms (p. 187)

Guide Your Learning 5.4: Aluminum Benders (Part 2) (p. 191)

Guide Your Learning 5.5: Key Terms (p. 196)

Focus on Ethical Decision Making: Inappropriate Prorating of Underapplied Overhead (p. 192)

## QUESTIONS

**5.1** List three examples of job cost records you recently received for services provided to you. (*Hint:* Itemized bills made out to you are usually job cost records.)

**5.2** Will underapplied and overapplied overhead arise under both actual and normal costing? Explain your answer.

**5.3** Within the area where you live, work, or attend school, name three businesses that would likely use job costing and three that would likely use process costing.

**5.4** How does the point of inspection (and therefore completion) affect the cost of spoilage?

**5.5** Part of a contract between a union and a company guarantees that all manufacturing employees earn 5 hours of overtime each week. In the company's job costing system, should overtime be treated as a direct or indirect cost?

**5.6** Compare actual and normal cost systems. Discuss the ways in which they are similar and the ways they differ.

**5.7** Exquisite Furniture designs and manufactures custom furniture from exotic materials. Explain why spoilage is sometimes recorded as a cost for a specific job and other times as overhead for this company.

**5.8** Explain how manufacturing overhead cost pools and cost allocation are related.

**5.9** Describe the procedures used in job costing.

**5.10** List the most common allocation bases used in job costing and explain under what circumstances each base would be most appropriate.

**5.11** List several different sources of information used in job costing, and explain why this information is required.

## EXERCISES

**5.12** **Custom versus mass production** The following chart lists several different products.
Q1

| Custom | Mass | Product |
|--------|------|---------|
|  |  | Jewelry |
|  |  | Rolls Royce automobiles |
|  |  | Honda automobiles |
|  |  | Tax services in an accounting firm |
|  |  | Haircuts |
|  |  | Personal shopping services |
|  |  | Breakfast cereal production |

**REQUIRED:** Check the appropriate boxes to identify whether the products can be custom produced or mass produced. Some products, such as house construction, can be either mass manufactured or custom built. In such cases, both boxes would be checked.

**5.13** **Job costing in the service sector** Consider the following budgeted data for a client case of Bob
Q1, Q2, Q4  Crachit's accounting firm. The client wants a fixed price quotation.

| | |
|---|---:|
| Direct professional labor | $20,000 |
| Direct support labor | 10,000 |
| Fringe benefits for direct labor | 13,000 |
| Photocopying | 2,000 |
| Telephone calls | 2,000 |
| Computer lines | 6,000 |

Overhead is allocated at the rate of 100% of direct labor cost.

**REQUIRED:**  **A.** Prepare a schedule of the budgeted total costs for the client. Show subtotals for total direct labor costs and total costs as a basis for markup.

**B.** Assume that the partner's policy is to quote a fixed fee at 10% above the total costs. What fee would be quoted?

❶ **C.** Explain why the listed estimates for costs might not be similar to the actual costs for the job. What factors could affect the accuracy of these estimates? List as many factors as you can.

**5.14**
**Q1, Q2**
**Job costing for a hospital** Mercy Hospital uses a job costing system for all patients who have surgery. The hospital uses a budgeted overhead rate for allocating overhead to patient stays. In March, the operating room had a budgeted allocation base of 1,000 operating hours. The budgeted operating room overhead costs were $66,000.

Patient Dwight Schuller was in the operating room 4 hours during March. Other costs related to Schuller's 4-hour surgery include:

| | |
|---|---|
| Patient medicine | $ 250 |
| Cost of nurses | 3,500 |
| Cost of supplies | 800 |

Physician cost is not included because physicians bill patients separately from the hospital billing system.

**REQUIRED:**  **A.** Explain why the hospital uses a job costing system instead of a process costing system.

**B.** Determine the budgeted (i.e., estimated) overhead rate for the operating room.

**C.** Determine the total costs of Schuller's four-hour surgery.

**5.15**
**Q1, Q2, Q3**
**Job costing, over- and underapplied overhead, journal entries** Shane's Shovels produces small, custom earth-moving equipment for landscaping companies. Manufacturing overhead is allocated to work in process using an estimated overhead rate. During April, transactions for Shane's Shovels included the following:

| | |
|---|---|
| Direct materials issued to production | $180,000 |
| Indirect materials issued to production | 30,000 |
| Other manufacturing overhead incurred | 250,000 |
| Overhead allocated | 225,000 |
| Direct labor costs | 75,000 |

Beginning and ending work in process were both zero.

**REQUIRED:**  **A.** What was the cost of jobs completed in April?

**B.** Was manufacturing overhead underapplied or overapplied? By how much?

ⓔ **C.** Write out the journal entries for these transactions, including the adjustment.

**5.16**
**Q5**
**Normal and abnormal spoilage** Franklin Fabrication produces custom-made security doors and gates. Currently two jobs are in process, 359 and 360. During production of Job 359, the supervisor was on vacation and the employees made several errors in cutting the metal pieces for the two doors in the order. The spoiled metal pieces cost $20 each and had zero scrap value. In addition, an order of five gates that had been manufactured for Job 360 required a fine wire mesh that sometimes tore as it was being mounted. Because a similar wire could be used that was much easier to install, the customer had been warned that costs could run over the bid if any difficulty was encountered in installing the wire. One of the gates was spoiled during the process of installing the wire. The cost of the materials and direct labor for the gate was $150. The gate and metal were hauled to the dump and discarded.

**REQUIRED:**  **A.** Should the spoilage for Job 359 be categorized as normal or abnormal spoilage? Explain.

**B.** Should the spoilage for Job 360 be categorized as normal or abnormal spoilage? Explain.

**C.** Prepare spoilage journal entries for both jobs.

**5.17**
**Q1, Q2**
**Direct costs and overhead** Job 87M had direct material costs of $400 and a total cost of $2,100. Overhead is allocated at the rate of 75% of prime cost (direct material and direct labor).

**REQUIRED:**  ⓔ **A.** How much direct labor was used?

**B.** How much overhead was allocated?

**5.18** **Analysis of WIP T-account** Jeeter Company uses a job costing system. Overhead is allocated
Q1, Q2    based on 120% of direct labor cost. Last month's transactions in the work in process account are
shown here:

| Work in Process | | | |
|---|---|---|---|
| Beginning balance | 48,000 | | |
| Direct materials | 160,000 | To finished goods | 442,000 |
| Direct labor | 120,000 | | |
| Factory overhead | 150,000 | | |

Only one job, 850, was still in process at the end of the month. Job 850 was charged with $9,000
in overhead for the month.

**REQUIRED:**     **A.** What is the ending balance in the WIP account?
ⓔ **B.** How much direct labor cost was used for Job 850?
ⓔ **C.** What is the amount of direct materials used for Job 850?

**5.19** **Journal entries** Langley Ltd. uses a job costing system. At the beginning of the month of June,
Q1, Q2, Q3   two orders were in process as follows:

| | Order 88 | Order 105 |
|---|---|---|
| Direct materials | $1000 | $900 |
| Direct labor | 1,200 | 200 |
| Overhead allocated | 1,800 | 300 |

There was no inventory in finished goods on June 1. During the month of June, orders numbered
106 through 120, inclusive, were put into process.
Direct materials requirements amounted to $13,000, direct labor costs for the month were
$20,000, and actual manufacturing overhead recorded during the month amounted to $28,000.
The only order in process at the end of June was order 120, and the costs incurred for this
order were $1,150 of direct materials and $1,000 of direct labor. In addition, order 118, which
was 100% complete, was still on hand as of June 30. Total costs for this order were $3,300. The
firm's overhead allocation rate in June was the same as that used in May and is based on labor
cost.

**REQUIRED:** ⓔ **A.** Prepare journal entries, with supporting calculations, to record the cost of goods manufactured, the cost of goods sold, and the closing of the overapplied or underapplied overhead
to cost of goods sold.
**B.** Describe the two different approaches to closing overapplied or underapplied overhead at
the end of the period. How do you choose an appropriate method?

**5.20** **Cost of goods sold schedule** The Rebecca Corporation is a manufacturer of machines made to
Q1, Q2    customer specifications. All production costs are accumulated by means of a job order costing sys-
ⓒⱣᴬ      tem. The following information is available at the beginning of the month of October 20XX.

| | |
|---|---|
| Raw materials inventory, October 1 | $16,200 |
| Work in process, October 1 | 5,100 |

A review of the job order cost sheets revealed the composition of the work in process inventory on
October 1 as follows:

| | |
|---|---|
| Direct materials (assuming no indirect materials this month) | $1,320 |
| Direct labor (300 hours) | 3,000 |
| Factory overhead allocated | 780 |
| | $5,100 |

Activity during the month of October was as follows:

Raw materials costing $20,000 were purchased.

Direct labor for job orders totaled 3,300 hours at $10 per hour.

Factory overhead was allocated to production at the rate of $2.60 per direct labor hour.

On October 31, inventories consisted of the following:

| | |
|---|---|
| Raw materials inventory | $17,000 |
| Work in process: | |
| Direct labor (500 hours) | 5,000 |
| Factory overhead allocated | 1,300 |

**REQUIRED:** **e** Prepare in good form a detailed schedule showing the cost of goods manufactured for the month of October.

**5.21**
**Q1, Q2, Q3**
**Job costing journal entries** Vern's Van Service customizes light trucks according to customers' orders. This month the company worked on five jobs, numbered 207 through 211. Materials requisitions for the month were as follows:

| Ticket | Carpet | Paint | Electronics | Other | Total |
|---|---|---|---|---|---|
| 207 | $40 | $350 | $580 | — | $ 970 |
| 208 | 75 | 200 | 375 | — | 650 |
| 209 | 200 | 400 | 200 | — | 800 |
| 210 | 30 | 150 | 770 | — | 950 |
| 211 | 60 | — | 50 | — | 110 |
| Indirect | — | — | — | $750 | 750 |
| Total costs | | | | | $4,230 |

An analysis of the payroll records revealed the following distribution for labor costs:

| | Job | | | | | | |
|---|---|---|---|---|---|---|---|
| | 207 | 208 | 209 | 210 | 211 | Other | Total |
| Direct labor | $1,400 | $1,200 | $800 | $1,700 | $400 | — | $5,500 |
| Indirect labor | — | — | — | — | — | $2,200 | 2,200 |
| Total costs | | | | | | | $7,700 |

Other overhead costs (consisting of rent, depreciation, taxes, insurance, utilities, etc.) amounted to $3,600. At the beginning of the period, management anticipated that overhead cost would be $6,400 and total direct labor would amount to $5,000. Overhead is allocated on the basis of direct labor dollars.

Jobs 207 through 210 were finished during the month; Job 211 is still in process. Jobs 207 through 209 were picked up and paid for by customers. Job 210 is still on the lot waiting to be picked up.

**REQUIRED:** **e** **A.** Prepare the journal entries to reflect the incurrence of materials, labor, and overhead costs, the allocation of overhead, and the transfer of units to finished goods and cost of goods sold.
**B.** Close overapplied or underapplied overhead to cost of goods sold.

**5.22**
**Q2, Q3, Q5**
**Allocating overhead, over- and underapplied overhead, spoilage** The Futons for You Company sells batches of custom-made futons to customers and uses predetermined rates for fixed overhead, based on machine hours. The following data are available for last year:

| | |
|---|---|
| Budgeted and actual fixed factory overhead cost | $160,000 |
| Budgeted machine hours | 100,000 |
| Actual machine hours used | 110,000 |

| | Machine Hours Used |
|---|---|
| Job 20 | 11,000 |
| Job 21 | 16,000 |
| Job 22 | 14,000 |
| Job 23 | 9,000 |

**REQUIRED:** **A.** Compute the estimated overhead allocation rate to be used for the year.
**B.** Determine the overhead to be allocated to Job 21.
**C.** Determine total overapplied or underapplied overhead at the end of the year.

*(continued)*

**D.** Should cost of goods sold be increased or decreased at the end of the year? Why?

**E.** If the amount of overapplied or underapplied overhead is material, how is it assigned?

**F.** Suppose Job 21 required a special fabric cover for the futon pads. This type of fabric dulls the blades of the cutting machine, and a number of fabric covers were unusable. Should this spoilage be recorded for Job 21 or for all jobs processed this period? Explain your answer.

**5.23**
**Q1, Q2, Q3**

**Journal entries for job costing** At the beginning of the accounting period, the accountant for ABC Industries estimated that total overhead would be $80,000. Overhead is allocated to jobs on the basis of direct labor cost. Direct labor was budgeted to cost $200,000 this period. During the period only three jobs were worked on. The following summarizes the direct materials and labor costs for each:

|  | Job 1231 | Job 1232 | Job 1233 |
|---|---|---|---|
| Direct materials | $45,000 | $70,000 | $30,000 |
| Direct labor | 70,000 | 90,000 | 50,000 |

Job 1231 was finished and sold; job 1232 was finished but is waiting to be sold; and job 1233 is still in process. Actual overhead for the period was $82,000.

**REQUIRED:** Prepare the following journal entries.

**A.** Cost recorded during production

**B.** Cost of jobs completed

**C.** Cost of goods sold

**D.** Allocation of overapplied or underapplied overhead prorated to the ending balances in work in process, finished goods, and cost of goods sold

**5.24**
**Q5, Q6**

**Spoilage journal entries** Jones Company manufactures custom doors. When Job 186 (a batch of 14 custom doors) was being processed in the machining department, one of the wood panels on a door split. This problem occurs periodically and is considered normal spoilage. Direct materials and labor for the door, to the point of spoilage, were $35. In addition, a storm caused a surge in electricity, and a routing machine punctured the wood for Job 238. This incident occurred at the beginning of production, so spoilage amounted to only the cost of wood, at $200.

**REQUIRED:**

**A.** Prepare the journal entries for normal and abnormal spoilage.

**B.** Now suppose that the wood from abnormal spoilage can be sold for $25. Record the journal entries for the disposal value.

❷ **C.** Jones Company is considering hiring someone to inspect all wood after it arrives at the plant, but prior to production. Discuss the pros and cons of hiring an inspector.

# PROBLEMS

**5.25**
**Q1, Q2, Q4**

**Collecting overhead cost information** A family member asked you to review the accounting system used for Hanna's, a custom stained glass manufacturing business. The owner currently uses a software package to keep track of her checking account, but she does not produce financial statements. The owner seeks your help in setting up a costing system so that financial statements can be produced on a monthly basis.

**REQUIRED:**

**A.** What kind of costing system is needed for this setting?

❶ **B.** You plan to categorize the checkbook data for entry into the financial statement records. List the categories you might use for these entries. [List only broad categories here; see parts (C), (D), and (E) for more details.]

❶ **C.** List several costs that might be included in a fixed overhead category.

❶ **D.** List several costs that might be included in a variable overhead category.

❶ **E.** List several costs that might be included in direct materials.

❸ **F.** Write a memo to the owner discussing the alternative choices for the costing system. Include an explanation of the type of information that would need to be captured to support the costing system.

**5.26** **Cost of rework, control of scrap, accounting for scrap** Dapper Dan Draperies manufactures and
Q5, Q6 installs custom-ordered draperies.

REQUIRED:
A. For all drapes, occasionally the sewing equipment malfunctions and the drape must be reworked. Explain how to account for the cost of rework when it is needed.
B. Explain how to account for the cost of rework when customers choose a fabric that is
known to require rework.
❶ C. Explain why scrap will always arise in this business.
❶ D. Dapper Dan can sell scraps to quilting groups or just throw them away. List several factors that could affect this decision.
E. If Dapper Dan decides to sell scraps, explain the accounting choices for recording the
sales value.

**5.27** **Accounting for scrap** You are helping a friend, Jonah, set up a new accounting system for a small
Q5, Q6 start-up construction company. He specializes in custom, energy efficient homes that are built on
a cost-plus basis. Cost-plus means that his customers pay a fixed percentage above the sum of di-

ETHICS rect and overhead costs.
As he goes through the accounts, Jonah asks why you set up a separate account for scrap. He
does not believe that scrap should be recorded anywhere in his accounting system because it is
worth little, and theft is no problem. He makes weekly trips to a recycling plant where he receives
a small sum for the scrap. Most of the time Jonah is working on only one house and the scrap is
only for that house. However, once in a while he is working on several houses, and the scrap for
all of the houses is recycled at once.

REQUIRED:
A. Explain the two ways that scrap can be recorded in a job costing system.
ⓔ B. Choose the appropriate method for Jonah and explain your choice.
❷ C. Suppose you are a prospective homeowner. Explain to Jonah why you believe the revenue from scrap associated with your home should be recorded as a reduction in your
costs rather than his overall costs.
❸ D. Write a brief (and diplomatic) paragraph to convince Jonah that he needs to account for
the revenues from scrap.

**5.28** **Job costing, overhead rates** The Eastern Seaboard Company uses an estimated rate for allocat-
Q1, Q2, Q3, Q4 ing factory overhead to job orders based on machine hours for the machining department and on
a direct labor cost basis for the finishing department. The company budgeted the following for last
year:

|  | Machining | Finishing |
| --- | --- | --- |
| Factory overhead | $5,000,000 | $3,000,000 |
| Machine hours | 250,000 | 14,000 |
| Direct labor hours | 15,000 | 16,000 |
| Direct labor cost | $ 225,000 | $2,400,000 |

During the month of December, the cost record for Job 602 shows the following:

|  | Machining | Finishing |
| --- | --- | --- |
| Direct materials requisitioned | $7,000 | $2,000 |
| Direct labor cost | $ 300 | $6,750 |
| Direct labor hours | 20 | 300 |
| Machine hours | 35 | 5 |

REQUIRED:
A. What is the estimated overhead allocation rate that should be used in the machining department? In the finishing department?
B. What is the total overhead allocated to Job 602?
ⓔ C. Assuming that Job 602 consisted of 200 units of product, what is the unit cost for this
job?
❷ D. What factors affect the volume of production in a period? Can we know all of the factors
before the period begins? Why or why not?
❶ E. Explain why Seaboard would use two different overhead allocation bases.

**5.29**
**Q1, Q2, Q3, Q4**

**Job costing, service sector** Hawk and Eagle Co., a law firm, had the following costs last year:

| | |
|---|---|
| Direct professional labor | $15,000,000 |
| Overhead | 21,000,000 |
| Total costs | $36,000,000 |

The following costs were included in overhead:

| | |
|---|---|
| Fringe benefits for direct professional labor | $ 5,000,000 |
| Paralegal costs | 2,700,000 |
| Telephone call time with clients (estimated but not tabulated) | 600,000 |
| Computer time | 1,800,000 |
| Photocopying | 900,000 |
| Total overhead | $11,000,000 |

The firm recently improved its ability to document and trace costs to individual cases. Revised bookkeeping procedures now allow the firm to trace fringe benefit costs for direct professional labor, paralegal costs, telephone charges, computer time, and photocopying costs to each case individually. The managing partner needs to decide whether more costs than just direct professional labor should be traced directly to jobs to allow the firm to better justify billings to clients.

During the last year, more costs were traced to client engagements. Two of the case records showed the following:

| | Client Cases | |
|---|---|---|
| | 875 | 876 |
| Direct professional labor | $20,000 | $20,000 |
| Fringe benefits for direct labor | 3,000 | 3,000 |
| Secretarial costs | 2,000 | 6,000 |
| Telephone call time with clients | 1,000 | 2,000 |
| Computer time | 2,000 | 4,000 |
| Photocopying | 1,000 | 2,000 |
| Total costs | $29,000 | $37,000 |

Three methods are being considered for allocating overhead this year:

Method 1: Allocate overhead based on direct professional labor cost. Calculate the allocation rate using last year's direct professional labor costs of $15 million and overhead costs of $21 million.

Method 2: Allocate overhead based on direct professional labor cost. Calculate the allocation rate using last year's direct professional labor costs of $15 million and overhead costs of $10 million ($21 million less $11 million in direct costs that are traced this year).

Method 3: Allocate the $10 million overhead based on total direct costs. Calculate the allocation rate using last year's direct costs (professional labor of $15 million plus other direct costs of $11 million).

**REQUIRED:**

**A.** Compute the overhead allocation rate for method 1.
**B.** Compute the overhead allocation rate for method 2.
**C.** Compute the overhead allocation rate for method 3.
**D.** Using each of the three rates computed in parts (A), (B), and (C), compute the total costs of cases 875 and 876.
**e** **E.** Explain why the total costs allocated to cases 875 and 876 are not the same under the three methods.
**e** **F.** Explain why method 1 would be inappropriate.
**2** **G.** Would method 2 or method 3 be better? Explain.
**1** **H.** Explain how job costing in a service business is different from job costing in a manufacturing business.

**5.30**
**Q1, Q2, Q4**

**Plantwide versus production cost pools** Flexible Manufacturers, Inc., produces small batches of customized products. The accounting system is set up to allocate plant overhead to each job using the following production cost pools and overhead allocation rates:

| | |
|---|---|
| Labor-paced assembly | $25 per direct labor hour |
| Machine-paced assembly | $18 per machine hour |
| Quality testing | $2 per unit |

Actual resources used for Job 75:

| | |
|---|---|
| Direct labor hours | 3 hours |
| Machine hours | 1.25 hours |
| Number of units | 36 units |

The plant accountant wants to simplify the cost accounting system and use a plantwide rate. If the preceding costs are grouped into a single cost pool and allocated based on labor hours, the rate would be $35 per direct labor hour.

**REQUIRED:**

**A.** What cost should be allocated to Job 75 using the plantwide overhead rate?

**B.** What cost should be allocated to Job 75 using the production cost pool overhead rates?

**e** **C.** Why do the allocated amounts in parts (A) and (B) differ?

**3** **D.** Which method would you recommend? Explain your choice.

**5.31**

**Q1, Q2, Q4**

**Allocating variable and fixed overhead in the service sector** Prime Personal Trainers is a personal training service in Belgium for people who want to work out at home. Prime offers two different types of services: Setup and Continuous Improvement. Setup services consist of several home visits by a personal trainer who specializes in determining the proper equipment for each client and helping the client set up a home gym. Continuous Improvement services provide daily, weekly, or biweekly home visits by trainers.

Prime's accountant wants to create a job costing system for Setup services. She decides to use direct labor cost as the allocation base for variable overhead costs, and direct labor hours for fixed overhead cost. To estimate normal capacity, she calculates the average direct labor cost over the last several years. She estimates overhead by updating last year's overhead cost with expected increases in rent, supervisor's salaries, and so on. Following are her estimates (given in euros) for the current period.

| | |
|---|---|
| Direct labor hours (based on 250 normal hours per month) | 3,000 |
| Direct labor cost | € 75,000 |
| Indirect labor cost | 25,000 |
| Variable overhead (primarily fringe benefits) | 150,000 |
| Fixed overhead (office related costs) | 120,000 |

Inventories consist of exercise equipment and supplies that are used by Prime for new clients. The following information summarizes operations during the month of October. A number of new jobs were begun in October, but only two jobs were completed: Job 20 and Job 22.

Account balances on October 1:

| | |
|---|---|
| Equipment and supplies (raw materials) | €5,000 |
| Client contracts in process (Job 20) | 3,500 |
| Client contracts in process (Job 22) | 1,500 |

Purchases of equipment and supplies:

| | |
|---|---|
| Equipment | €54,000 |
| Supplies | 500 |
| Total | €54,500 |

Equipment and supplies requisitioned for clients:

| | |
|---|---|
| Job 20 | € 1,000 |
| Job 21 | 500 |
| Job 22 | 4,000 |
| Job 23 | 5,000 |
| Other jobs | 40,000 |
| Indirect supplies | 500 |
| Total | €51,000 |

Direct labor hours and cost:

| | Hours | Cost |
|---|---|---|
| Job 20 | 10 | € 250 |
| Job 21 | 18 | 450 |
| Job 22 | 15 | 375 |
| Job 23 | 6 | 150 |
| Other clients | 180 | 4,500 |
| Total | 229 | €5,725 |

Labor costs:

| | |
|---|---|
| Direct labor wages | € 5,725 |
| Indirect labor wages (160 hours) | 1,920 |
| Manager's salary | 6,250 |
| Total | €13,895 |

Office costs:

| | |
|---|---|
| Rent | €1,000 |
| Utilities | 100 |
| Insurance and taxes | 900 |
| Miscellaneous | 1,000 |
| Total | €3,000 |

**REQUIRED:**

**A.** What are the estimated allocation rates for fixed and variable overhead for the current period?

**B.** What is the total overhead cost allocated to Job 20 in October?

**C.** What is the total cost of Job 20?

**D.** Calculate the amounts of fixed and variable overhead allocated to jobs in October.

**❷ E.** Why would the accountant choose to use two cost pools instead of one? Will this method make a difference in client bills when the job includes more equipment and less labor than other jobs?

**5.32**

**Q1, Q2, Q4**

**Effects of robotic equipment on overhead rates** "Our costs are out of control, our accounting system is screwed up, or both!" screamed the sales manager. "We are simply noncompetitive on a great many of the jobs we bid on. Just last week we lost a customer when a competitor underbid us by 25%! And I bid the job at cost because the customer has been with us for years but has been complaining about our prices."

This problem, raised at the weekly management meeting, has been getting worse over the years. The Johnson Tool Company produces parts for specific customer orders. When the firm first became successful, it employed nearly 500 skilled machinists. Over the years the firm has become increasingly automated and now uses a number of different robotic machines. The firm currently employs only 75 production workers, but output has quadrupled.

The problems raised by the sales manager can be seen in the portions of two bid sheets brought to the meeting (as reproduced). The bids are from the cutting department, but the relative size of these three types of manufacturing costs is similar for other departments.

The cutting department charges overhead to products based on direct labor hours. For the current period, the department expects to use 4,000 direct labor hours. Departmental overhead, consisting mostly of depreciation on the robotic equipment, is expected to be $1,480,000.

An employee can typically set up any job on the appropriate equipment in about 15 minutes. Once machines are operating, an employee oversees five to eight machines simultaneously. All that is required is to load or unload materials and monitor calibrations. The department's robotic machines will log a total of 25,000 hours of run time in the current period.

For bid 74683 the firm was substantially underbid by a competitor. The firm did get the job for bid 74687, but the larger jobs are harder to find. Small jobs arise frequently, but the firm is rarely successful in obtaining them.

**CUTTING DEPARTMENT**

Bid # 74683        Machine Run Time 3 Hours

| | |
|---|---:|
| Materials | |
|     Steel sheeting | $280.25 |
| Direct labor | |
|     Equipment setup (0.25 hours @ $12.50) | 3.13 |
|     Equipment tending (1 hour @ $12.50) | 12.50 |
| Overhead (1.25 hours @ $370) | 462.50 |
|     Total costs | $758.38 |

**CUTTING DEPARTMENT**

Bid # 74687        Machine Run Time 11 Hours

| | |
|---|---:|
| Materials | |
|     Steel sheeting | $2,440.50 |
| Direct labor | |
|     Equipment setup (0.25 hours @ $12.50) | 3.13 |
|     Equipment tending (1.25 hours @ $12.50) | 15.63 |
| Overhead (1.5 hours @ $370) | 555.00 |
|     Total costs | $3,014.26 |

**REQUIRED:** ❷ **A.** Critique the cost allocation method used within the current cost accounting system.

**B.** Suggest a better approach for allocating overhead. Allocate costs using your approach and compare the costs of both jobs under the two systems.

❷ **C.** Discuss the pros and cons of using job costs to determine the price for a job order.

☆ **5.33**
**Q5, Q6**

**Classification of rework costs, uncertainties, critique of rework and scrap policy** Fran Markus is in the cost accounting group at Boats Galore, a large manufacturing company that produces customized boats and yachts. The company sometimes experiences quality problems with its fiberglass raw material, causing flawed areas in boat hulls. The problem is often fixed by reworking the flawed areas. Other times the hull is scrapped because it is too flawed, and a new hull is fabricated. The spoilage policy at Boats Galore is to charge the cost of rework and spoilage to overhead unless it arises because a hull design is particularly complicated. In those cases, the cost is assigned to the job.

Two boats currently under construction require triple the amount of materials and labor time to enhance boat security. The customer wants each hull to be able to withstand the explosion of a small bomb. It is the company's first order with this hull construction. Because of the new design and fiberglass process, the customer has agreed to a cost-plus contract and will pay cost plus a fixed percentage of cost. This contract assures that Boats Galore does not incur a loss from developing the enhanced security hull. This week, the third layer on one of the boat hulls had a flaw in the fiberglass. The area was reworked, after which it met the security requirements.

Fran receives weekly data on labor and materials for each boat under construction. For regular production, workers estimate the time and materials used to rework flawed fiberglass areas, and Fran adds those costs to overhead instead of recording them as a cost of the particular job. Now she needs to decide how to record the cost of rework for the enhanced security hulls. The production people are not sure whether the flaw was due to poor quality fiberglass or to the triple hull design. If Fran adds the cost to the job order, the customer will pay for the labor and supplies as part of the cost-plus price. If she adds the cost to overhead, the cost will be spread across all jobs and only part of it will be allocated to the job having the enhanced security hulls.

**REQUIRED:**
**ANALYZE**
**INFORMATION**

The following questions will help you analyze the information for this problem. Do not turn in your answers to these questions unless your professor asks you to do so.

❷ **A.** Critique the company's accounting policy for rework and scrap.

❶ **B.** Describe uncertainties about the accounting treatment for the rework costs on the enhanced security hull job.

❷ **C.** Discuss the pros and cons of alternative accounting treatments for the rework costs on this job.

**REQUIRED:**
**WRITTEN**
**ASSIGNMENT**

Suppose you are an accounting intern at Boats Galore. Fran asks you to recommend an accounting treatment for the rework costs on the enhanced security hull job. Turn in your answers to the following.

**❸ D.** Write a memo to Fran with your recommendation. As you write the memo, consider what information Fran will need from you to help her make a final decision.

**❸ E.** Write one or two paragraphs explaining how you decided what information to include in your memo.

# BUILD YOUR PROFESSIONAL COMPETENCIES

**5.34**
**Q1, Q2, Q4**

**Focus on Professional Competency: Project Management** *Job costing system, uncertainties, management of job costs* Review the following definition and elements for the Project Management competency.[4]

**DEFINITION:** *Accounting professionals must successfully manage a diversity of projects throughout their career. Individuals entering the accounting profession should demonstrate the ability to effectively control the course of a multi-dimensional, multi-step undertaking. This includes managing project assets, including human, financial, property, and technical resources.*

## ELEMENTS FOR THIS COMPETENCY INCLUDE

| Level 1 | Level 2 | Level 3 | Level 4 |
|---|---|---|---|
| 1. Lists information relevant to managing a project<br>2. Identifies uncertainties related to time and resource requirements for a project<br>3. Identifies project goals | 4. Develops alternative estimates of time and resource requirements for a project<br>5. Utilizes methods to measure project progress<br>6. Organizes the various aspects of a project in order to allocate resources for optimum results | 7. Prioritizes and delegates as needed<br>8. Recognizes situations where prompt and determined actions are needed and responds accordingly<br>9. Sees projects through to completion or orderly transition | 10. Effectively manages human resources that are committed to the project<br>11. Effectively facilitates and controls the project process and takes corrective action as needed |

**REQUIRED:** Chapter 5 does not directly address how to manage projects. However, the chapter provides methods for measuring costs associated with one type of project—a customized product or service. As you address the following questions, focus on how job costing information can assist in the management of projects.

**❶ A.** Focus on competency element 1, which addresses the need to identify relevant information. List the types of information that are measured using a job costing system. For each type, explain how the job costing information could potentially be relevant to managing a customized job.

**❶ B.** Focus on competency element 2, which relates to uncertainties. Identify uncertainties about (1) the expected costs for a job, and (2) how to measure costs in a job costing system.

**C.** Focus on competency elements 4, 5, 6, 8, and 11, which relate to measuring and monitoring the progress of projects. Answer the following questions:

**❷ 1.** Suppose a customized order is partially complete. The total estimated cost of the job is $100,000. So far, the job cost record indicates that direct costs and allocated overhead amount to $50,000. Does this accounting mean that the job is 50% complete? Why or why not?

**❷ 2.** Assume the same facts as in question 1. However, suppose the job is only 30% complete. Would you say that costs for the job are in control? Why or why not?

---

[4]The definition and elements are reprinted with permission from AICPA; copyright © 1978–2000 & 2003 by American Institute of Certified Public Accountants. The AICPA's Core Competency Framework can be accessed at eca.aicpaservices.org.

❷ **3.** Discuss things that managers might do if they learn that the costs for a job are significantly higher than expected.

❷ **4.** Discuss things that managers might do if they learn that the costs for a job are significantly lower than expected.

**5.35**

**Q1, Q2, Q3, Q4**

**Integrating Across the Curriculum: Financial Accounting and Auditing**   *Research financial accounting rules, evaluate overhead allocation policy* Refer to the information in Problem 5.30. Suppose you work for a CPA firm and are part of the team auditing the financial statements of Flexible Manufacturers. You have been assigned the responsibility for auditing the allocation of overhead costs.

**REQUIRED:**

**A.** Assume the company uses separate overhead allocation rates for labor-paced assembly, machine-paced assembly, and quality testing.

❷ **1.** Research financial accounting rules and determine whether the company's method for allocating overhead cost to inventory complies with U.S. generally accepted accounting principles (GAAP).

**2.** Use T-accounts to document your understanding of the company's overhead cost allocation method. (*Hint:* Prepare a schedule similar to Exhibit 5.7.)

**B.** Suppose you learn that the company plans to change its method of accounting for overhead to use a single plantwide overhead allocation rate. Research financial accounting rules and determine the following:

❶ **1.** Whether a plantwide overhead allocation rate complies with GAAP.

❶ **2.** The conditions under GAAP that must be met for the company to change its accounting method from using separate department overhead allocation rates to a single plantwide allocation rate.

❷ **C.** Suppose the company's policy is to include all overapplied or underapplied overhead as part of cost of goods sold on the income statement. As an auditor, would you consider this policy to be acceptable? Why or why not?

# 6

# Process Costing

## ▶In Brief

Some products are mass-produced, making it impractical to trace costs to individual units. Process costing provides a way to overcome this challenge by assigning costs to production departments and then allocating the costs from the department to individual units. The practice of process costing is complicated by the fact that some physical units are likely to be partially complete at the beginning and end of the accounting period. Furthermore, organizations typically produce some proportion of defective or spoiled units. To assign costs appropriately to all of the units processed (completed, partially complete, and spoiled), accountants must understand both the production process and the various methods for applying process costing.

### This Chapter Addresses the Following Questions:

**Q1** How are costs assigned to mass-produced products?

**Q2** What are equivalent units, and how do they relate to the production process?

**Q3** How is the weighted average method used in process costing?

**Q4** How is the FIFO method used in process costing?

**Q5** What alternative methods are used for mass production?

**Q6** How is process costing performed for multiple production departments?

**Q7** How are spoilage costs handled in process costing?

**Q8** What are the uses and limitations of process cost information?

# ELLIPTEC AG: MINI MOTOR MASS PRODUCTION

During 2002, the German company **Elliptec AG** was ready to launch a new type of miniature motor. Among their applications, mini motors are used to open and close air conditioning vents and CD-ROM trays, move parts in toys, and automate medical and industrial instruments. Elliptec's managers anticipated high demand for the new motor because it was smaller, quieter, more powerful, and more cost efficient than existing mini motors.

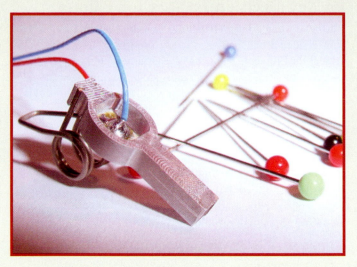

The size of a penny, Elliptec's new motor was smaller (one-twelfth the size) and lighter (one-fifth the weight) than the typical mini motor. In addition, it used only 3 to 6 volts and had only three parts. It operated without a gearbox, instead controlling speed with an electric signal. Elliptec claimed that the mini motor's speed and rotational motion were similar to current motors, but it was superior in applications calling for slow and well-controlled motion.

Elliptec's invention was a type of piezoelectric motor. Earlier piezoelectric motors cost hundreds of dollars and required high voltages, making them impractical. However, Elliptec's managers expected to sell the new motor for only $1 because it used less expensive materials and had only three parts.

Although patent approval was still pending, the company began sending prototypes to toymakers and electronics manufacturers in 2002. Its scientists announced that the first applications for the motor would be to improve products that currently used similar motors. Company managers hoped that the new motor would be seen as revolutionary, generating new inventions and a wide range of applications over time.

Elliptec's managers expected to begin production of the mini motor during the summer of 2002. To keep production costs down, the company initially accepted customer orders only for large quantities. This restriction enabled the company to achieve cost savings through mass production. The managers could assume that they would achieve even greater cost savings once demand increased and the company gained production efficiencies. ■

SOURCES: Christopher Boyce, "Mini Motor Sets Small Standard," *Research and Development, 44,* no. 7 (July 2002), p. 50; and www.elliptec.com.

## ■ Key Decision Factors for Elliptec

**Elliptec's** strategy was to sell the new mini motor for about $1. To achieve a profit, the company needed production costs to average less than $1 each. With such low profit margins, it was critical for Elliptec's managers to carefully estimate costs and to ensure that actual costs did not exceed estimates. The following discussion summarizes key decision factors that Elliptec's managers might have used in establishing and monitoring the mini motor's production costs.

**Knowing.** Elliptec developed the new mini motor and created a prototype. Thus, the company's managers knew at least one way to build the motor. This knowledge allowed them to design a production facility and to estimate production costs. Because fixed costs are usually high for setting up and operating a production facility, the managers knew that high production levels would be needed to achieve a low average cost per motor.

**Identifying.** Elliptec's managers could not be certain that they could produce the motor at a sufficiently low cost. They were faced with many uncertainties, leading to questions about how production should be organized and about their ability to succeed.

- What size facility should be built?
- What was the best way to minimize production costs?
- Will unforeseen technological problems arise in setting up the facility or achieving planned production levels?
- What competing products will appear on the market?
- Is $1 a sufficiently low price for toy and electronic manufacturers?
- What new uses for the motor will be developed?

**Exploring.** Elliptec's managers decided to initially sell the motor only in large quantities, most likely to help them achieve targeted costs. Before making this decision, they needed to explore pros and cons such as the following:

- Restricting sales to large orders allowed the company to mass produce the motors, reducing the average cost for each motor by spreading fixed costs across a large number of units.
- The company probably lost some sales by imposing a restriction on the order size. If the policy caused the company to sell fewer quantities overall, then the company's average costs per unit increased rather than decreased. The company may also have missed opportunities to combine several smaller, but sizable orders into a larger production run.

While exploring the various options for producing and selling the new motor, it was critical for Elliptec's managers to remain unbiased. Too often, managers lose objectivity when their company develops a new product or technology. Biases cause managers to ignore negative signals, relying instead on unrealistic revenue and cost forecasts. Because of biases, production costs for new products typically exceed forecasts.

**Prioritizing.** As Elliptec's managers developed and implemented plans for the new motor, each of their decisions had its own trade-offs. By explicitly weighing factors, the managers could make higher-quality decisions and be more likely to achieve profitability targets.

**Envisioning.** The uncertainties faced by Elliptec's managers obligated them to monitor production costs over time. Average product costs are driven by both cost levels and production volumes. Accordingly, the managers needed to develop and implement strategies for responding quickly to deviations from planned costs and production levels.

## ■ Role of Average Costs in Monitoring Profitability

Average costs include fixed costs such as the plant supervisor's salary and equipment depreciation. Within a relevant range of activity, fixed costs do not change with production levels. Accordingly, fixed costs are irrelevant for many types of short-term management decisions such as whether to accept a customer's special order. Nevertheless, average costs are important to managers. Companies such as Elliptec will not earn a profit unless the product selling price exceeds average cost. In addition, average costs are used in financial accounting to match revenue with expense when units are sold. In this chapter, we learn about the methods used to compute and allocate average costs to mass-produced goods and services. We also learn how managers monitor average costs for these types of products.

# ACCOUNTING FOR THE COST OF MASS-PRODUCED GOODS

 **Q1** How are costs assigned to mass-produced products?

**CURRENT PRACTICE**

During 2002, the U.S. Bureau of Engraving and Printing produced 2.88 billion $1 bills. The production process for printing U.S. paper currency includes 65 separate steps.[1]

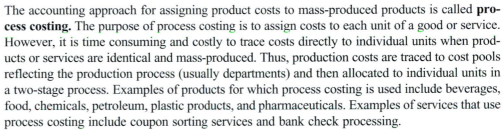

The accounting approach for assigning product costs to mass-produced products is called **process costing.** The purpose of process costing is to assign costs to each unit of a good or service. However, it is time consuming and costly to trace costs directly to individual units when products or services are identical and mass-produced. Thus, production costs are traced to cost pools reflecting the production process (usually departments) and then allocated to individual units in a two-stage process. Examples of products for which process costing is used include beverages, food, chemicals, petroleum, plastic products, and pharmaceuticals. Examples of services that use process costing include coupon sorting services and bank check processing.

In many organizations, the production process consists of work performed in a sequence of departments. Thus, costs are assigned to each production department and then allocated to all units that pass through the department. Consider the flow of work and costs for a cherry processor. Fresh cherries are received and washed in the first department. At this point in the process, some of the cherries are sold on the market as fresh cherries. Other cherries will be processed further. In the second department, the cherries are placed in vats and then covered with a syrup solution, brought to a boil, and then prepared for canning or drying. Most of the cherries are canned in the second department, but some are transferred to a third department where the syrup is drained and then they are dried and packaged. Notice that each department incurs a variety of costs. Costs in the first department include the purchase price of the cherries, labor, equipment depreciation and maintenance, water, electricity, and supplies. It would be impossible to directly measure the cost of water used to clean each pound (unit) of cherries. However, costs such as water are allocated to each pound of cherries by dividing the total cost of water by the total pounds of cherries processed.

## ■ Assigning Direct Materials and Conversion Costs

**HELPFUL HINT**

In both process and job costing, overhead costs are allocated using a two-stage approach (first allocated or traced to cost pools, then allocated to units). Direct costs are handled differently, though.

Similar to job costing, costs in a process costing system are assigned to products using a two-stage process. However, in process costing all costs are first assigned to departments. Costs are then allocated from departments to individual product units, as shown in Exhibit 6.1(a).

In a traditional process costing system, the two categories of product cost are direct materials and conversion costs. **Conversion costs** are direct labor and production overhead costs. Direct materials and conversion costs are allocated separately because they are usually incurred at different points in the production process. Exhibit 6.1(b) shows the cost flow within a department. Some costs, such as indirect materials and indirect labor, are traced to departments through materials and payroll records. However, a number of costs are allocated to departments, such as the cost of rent and insurance for a shared production facility.

Exhibit 6.2 illustrates how costs are incurred for the cherry production process. In the cleaning department, the direct materials (cherries) are added at the beginning of the process. In the cooking and canning department some direct materials (water and syrup) are added at the beginning of the process, and others (jars and lids) are added at the end of the process. In the drying department, packaging materials are used at the end of the process. The conversion costs are added throughout processing in all three departments.

## ■ Work in Process and Equivalent Units

**Q2** What are equivalent units, and how do they relate to the production process?

When the production process covers a span of time, organizations are likely to have partially complete units of goods or services at the beginning and end of an accounting

---

[1]See "Annual Production Figures" and "Money Facts," Bureau of Engraving and Printing, available at www. moneyfactory.com.

**EXHIBIT 6.1** A Traditional Process Costing System

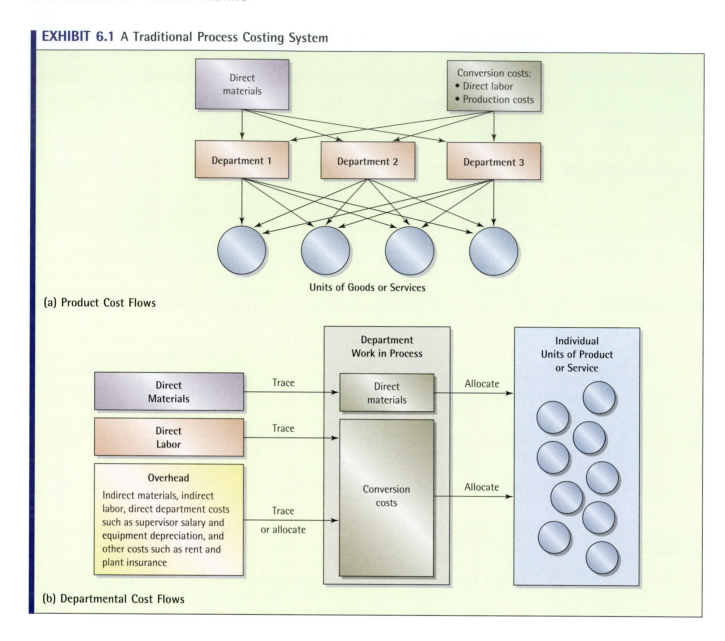

(a) Product Cost Flows

(b) Departmental Cost Flows

**EXHIBIT 6.2** Cost Flows for Producing Cherries

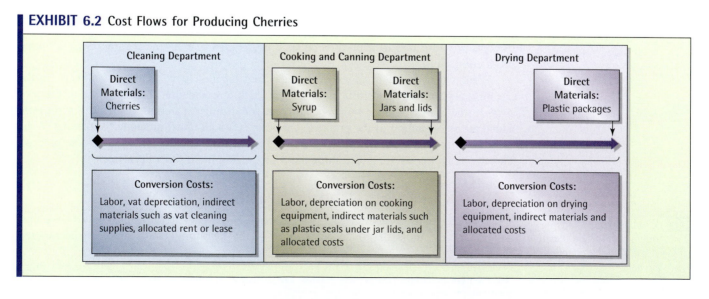

period. The cherry processing example would probably not have beginning or ending work in process (WIP) inventories for the cleaning and cooking and canning departments. The processing in these departments occurs quickly and is complete at the end of a day's operating activity. However, WIP inventory remains in the drying department for several days. Suppose at the end of an accounting period cherries in the drying department are in various stages of completion. Some are completely dried and waiting to be packaged. Others were just put into the drying equipment and will need to remain there for several days. We know the number of pounds the department is currently processing, and we know that we have cherries at many different stages of completion. We estimate the amount of completion for the entire volume of cherries in the department. For example, if a large amount of cherries have just begun the drying process, relative to all of the cherries in the department, we might estimate that the cherries are 20% complete, on average. However, if most of the cherries are waiting to be packaged, we might estimate that the cherries are 80% complete, on average.

To calculate the cost allocation for partially complete units, we take the percent of completion into account. **Equivalent units** measure the resources used in partially completed units relative to the resources needed to complete the units. For work in process inventory, equivalent units are the number of units that could have been completed if all resources had gone to complete whole units instead of to partially complete units. Suppose WIP in the drying department consists of 1,000 pounds of cherries estimated to be 20% complete. The conversion cost allocated to these cherries is equivalent to the cost needed to fully compete 200 pounds of cherries (1,000 lbs. × 20%). Thus, we estimate that WIP ending consists of 200 equivalent pounds with respect to conversion costs.

## PROCESS COSTING METHODS

**Q3** How is the weighted average method used in process costing?

**Q4** How is the FIFO method used in process costing?

Several methods are used to measure the costs that are allocated for process costing. In this chapter, we first learn the first-in, first-out (FIFO) and weighted average methods.

Under the **first-in, first-out (FIFO) method,** the current period's costs are used to allocate cost to work performed this period. In the **weighted average method,** costs from beginning WIP (performed last period) are averaged with costs incurred during the current period and then allocated to units completed and ending WIP. The following example is organized to point out their similarities and differences.

**GUIDE YOUR LEARNING** **6.1** Key Terms

Stop to confirm that you understand the new terms introduced in the last several pages:

Process costing (p. 217)
Conversion costs (p. 217)
Equivalent units (p. 219)

First-in, first-out (FIFO) method (p. 219)
Weighted average method (p. 219)

For each of these terms, write a definition in your own words.

## Detailed Example

Suppose a company called Premier Plastics mass-produces plastic products and small appliances designed by a famous Scandinavian architect. One manufacturing facility is dedicated to the production of a premier line of CD/DVD storage units. The plant has two production departments: the molding department and the assembly department.

In the molding department, plastic liquid is prepared and poured into molds. As shown in Exhibit 6.3, plastic mix ingredients are added at the beginning of the process. Conversion

**EXHIBIT 6.3**
Cost Flows for Producing Plastic CD/DVD Storage Units

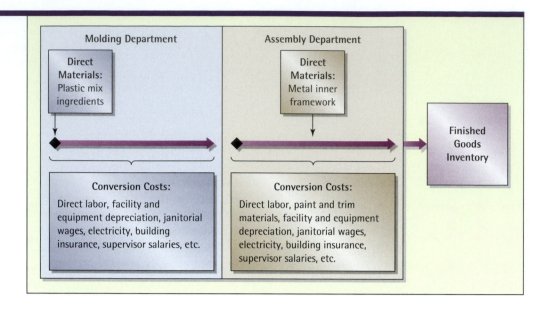

costs include direct labor, facility and equipment depreciation, janitorial wages, electricity, building insurance, supervisor salaries, and many other overhead costs. Although the conversion costs are incurred throughout the molding process, they are not incurred evenly. For example, the machines are periodically shut down for cleaning and maintenance. More labor is required to monitor certain parts of the process, such as when plastic mix ingredients are added. Nevertheless, we simplify the accounting by assuming that conversion costs are incurred evenly throughout the process. When the molding process is complete, the outer shells are transferred to the assembly department.

In the assembly department, machines remove any rough edges and then smooth the outer and inner surfaces. Next, a metal inner framework for holding CDs and DVDs is inserted. Thus, direct materials are added partway through this process. Finally, details are painted on each unit. Because the cost for paint and trim for each storage unit is small, those costs are considered indirect and included in conversion costs. The completed units are transferred to finished goods inventory. As orders are processed, the units are transferred to the shipping department for packing and delivery.

In the following calculations, we focus on process costing for the molding department over the course of three months of production activities. The first month portrays the simplest scenario, with no beginning or ending work in process. During the second month the computations become slightly more complex with the addition of ending WIP. The third month includes both beginning and ending WIP. For each month, we prepare cost reports to summarize and compare the results for the FIFO and weighted average methods.

**Process Cost Reports without Beginning or Ending WIP** Exhibit 6.4 presents the data and computations for the month of March with no beginning or ending WIP inventory in the molding department. During March, 10,000 units are started, completed, and transferred to the assembly department. The cost of direct materials used during March is $30,000, and conversion costs incurred are $70,000. When no work in process is involved, the equivalent unit cost is the average cost per unit for the period, calculated by dividing total cost for direct materials and conversion by the total units produced. Therefore, the cost per equivalent unit is the same under both the FIFO and weighted average methods.

---

[2]See Renewable Fuels Association, "How Ethanol Is Made," available at www.ethanolrfa.org.

**EXHIBIT 6.4** Process Cost Reports without Beginning and Ending WIP

Assumptions for March:
**Work performed:**
  10,000 units started, completed, and transferred out
**Costs added during the month:**
  Direct materials               $ 30,000
  Conversion costs                 70,000
    Total costs to account for   $100,000

**Summarize Physical and Equivalent Units**

|  | Beginning WIP | Complete Beginning WIP | Start and Complete | Start Ending WIP | Total Work Performed This Period | Total Units to Account For |
|---|---|---|---|---|---|---|
| | | | **Work This Period** | | | |
| Physical Units | 0 | 0 | 10,000 | 0 | 10,000 | 10,000 |
| Equivalent Units: | | | | | | **Total Work** |
| Direct materials | 0 | 0 | 10,000 | 0 | 10,000 | 10,000 |
| Conversion costs | 0 | 0 | 10,000 | 0 | 10,000 | 10,000 |

**Calculate Cost per Equivalent Unit**
  First-in, first-out:

Direct materials: $\dfrac{\text{Direct materials cost}}{\text{Equivalent units for total work performed this period}} = \dfrac{\$30,000}{10,000} = \$\ 3.00$

Conversion costs: $\dfrac{\text{Conversion costs}}{\text{Equivalent units for total work performed this period}} = \dfrac{\$70,000}{10,000} = \underline{\ 7.00}$

Total cost per equivalent unit: $\underline{\underline{\$10.00}}$

**Weighted average:** Computations are the same as for FIFO because there is no beginning WIP.

**Process Cost Reports for Molding Department: March**

| | First-In, First-Out | | | Weighted Average | | |
|---|---|---|---|---|---|---|
| | Computation | Units | Costs | Computation | Units | Costs |
| New units started, completed, and transferred out | 10,000 × $10.00 | 10,000 | $ 100,000 | | | |
| Total units completed and transferred out | | 10,000 | 100,000 | 10,000 × $10.00 | 10,000 | $ 100,000 |
| Total accounted for | | 10,000 | $100,000 | | 10,000 | $100,000 |

As shown in Exhibit 6.4 the summary of physical units and equivalent units manufactured during March is simple. Because no beginning or ending WIP need be accounted for, the number of physical units is equal to the number of equivalent units for both direct materials and conversion costs.

**FIFO and Weighted Average Costs.** Because no beginning WIP is involved, the costs per unit are the same under both the FIFO and weighted average methods. These methods differ only when beginning WIP must be taken into account. As shown in Exhibit 6.4, the direct material cost is $3.00 per unit and conversion cost is $7.00 per unit. Total cost per unit is $10.00. Thus, the cost for the 10,000 units produced is $100,000, which is equal to the total costs to account for.

**Comparison.** Without beginning WIP, no cost difference arises between the FIFO and weighted average methods.

**Process Cost Reports with Ending WIP** Exhibit 6.5 presents the data and computations for the month of April, which has ending WIP but no beginning WIP. During April, 10,000 units are started, completed, and transferred out. An additional 2,000 units are started, but are only 30% complete at the end of the month. The cost of direct materials used during April is $36,000, and conversion costs are $74,200.

The total work performed during April is the sum of the units that were started, completed, and transferred out and the equivalent units in ending WIP. Direct materials in the molding department are added at the beginning of production, so the 2,000 units in ending WIP are 100% complete with respect to direct materials, and equivalent units for direct materials equal 2,000. The total amount of work performed during April for direct materials is 12,000 equivalent units. However, we assume that conversion costs in the molding department are incurred evenly throughout production. Therefore, the 2,000 physical units in ending WIP are counted as 600 equivalent units (2,000 units × 30%) for conversion costs. The total amount of work performed during April for conversion costs is 10,600 equivalent units.

**FIFO and Weighted Average Costs.** Because Premier began April with no beginning WIP, the costs per unit are again the same under the FIFO and weighted average methods. However, because we have ending WIP that is partially complete, we now use equivalent units rather than

**EXHIBIT 6.5** Process Cost Reports with Ending WIP

**Assumptions for April:**
**Work performed:**

| | |
|---|---|
| Units started | 12,000 |
| Units completed and transferred out | 10,000 |
| Ending WIP | 2,000 |
| % complete direct materials | 100% |
| % complete conversion costs | 30% |

**Costs added during the month:**

| | |
|---|---|
| Direct materials | $ 36,000 |
| Conversion costs | 74,200 |
| Total costs to account for | $110,200 |

**Summarize Physical and Equivalent Units**

| | Beginning WIP | Complete Beginning WIP | Start and Complete | Start Ending WIP (30%) | Total Work Performed This Period | Total Units to Account For |
|---|---|---|---|---|---|---|
| | | | | | **Work This Period** | |
| Physical units | 0 | 0 | 10,000 | 2,000 | 12,000 | 12,000 |
| **Equivalent units:** | | | | | | **Total Work** |
| Direct materials | 0 | 0 | 10,000 | 2,000 | 12,000 | 12,000 |
| Conversion costs | 0 | 0 | 10,000 | 600 | 10,600 | 10,600 |

**Calculate Cost per Equivalent Unit**
**First-in, first-out:**

Direct materials: $\dfrac{\text{Direct materials cost}}{\text{Equivalent units for total work performed this period}} = \dfrac{\$36,000}{12,000} = \$\ 3.00$

Conversion costs: $\dfrac{\text{Conversion costs}}{\text{Equivalent units for total work performed this period}} = \dfrac{\$74,200}{10,600} = 7.00$

Total cost per equivalent unit: $\underline{\underline{\$10.00}}$

**Weighted average:** Computations are the same as for FIFO because there is no beginning WIP.

**Process Cost Reports for Molding Department: April**

| | First-In, First-Out | | | Weighted Average | | |
|---|---|---|---|---|---|---|
| | Computation | Units | Costs | Computation | Units | Costs |
| New units started, completed, and transferred out | 10,000 × $10.00 | 10,000 | $ 100,000 | | | |
| Total units completed and transferred out | | 10,000 | 100,000 | 10,000 × $10.00 | 10,000 | $100,000 |
| Ending WIP: | | 2,000 | | | 2,000 | |
| Direct materials | 2,000 × $3.00 | | 6,000 | 2,000 × $3.00 | | 6,000 |
| Conversion costs | 600 × $7.00 | | 4,200 | 600 × $7.00 | | 4,200 |
| Total ending WIP cost | | | 10,200 | | | 10,200 |
| Total accounts for | | 12,000 | $110,200 | | 12,000 | $110,200 |

**INTERNATIONAL**

Aracruz Celulose is the largest producer of bleached eucalyptus pulp, which is used in paper products. Its pulp production includes the following major processes: wood chipping, cooking, purifying/bleaching, drying, and packaging.[3]

actual units to calculate the per-unit cost. As shown in Exhibit 6.5, direct material cost remains $3.00 per unit and conversion cost is $7.00 per unit. So, the total equivalent unit cost remains $10.00. Thus, the cost allocated to the 10,000 units completed is $100,000. For ending WIP, the cost of direct materials is $6,000 and conversion cost is $4,200. We can double-check our computations by verifying that the sum of costs accounted for ($110,200) is equal to the sum of beginning WIP plus the costs incurred during April ($0 + $36,000 + $74,200 = $110,200).

**Comparison.** As before, with no beginning WIP, no cost difference occurs between the FIFO and weighted average methods.

**Process Cost Reports with Beginning and Ending WIP** Exhibit 6.6 presents the data and computations for the month of May, which has beginning WIP as well as ending WIP. For May, beginning WIP includes 2,000 units; 9,000 units are started, completed, and transferred to the assembly department; and another 1,000 units are started and 40% complete in ending WIP. The cost of direct materials used during May is $30,500, and conversion costs incurred are $76,680.

The total units to account for during May (12,000) include both beginning WIP and the units started during the month. In Exhibit 6.6, the total work performed during the month is the sum of work performed to complete beginning WIP units, the units both started and completed, and the work performed on units started but not yet completed. Because direct materials are added at the beginning of the process, no additional direct materials were needed to complete beginning WIP, meaning it is 100% complete with respect to direct materials. Conversion costs are added throughout the process, so part of the conversion costs for beginning WIP were incurred last period, and part were incurred this period. The beginning WIP consisted of 2,000 units that were 30% complete, or 600 equivalent units with respect to conversion costs. Conversion cost work performed during May consisted of completing the beginning WIP of 1,400 [2,000 units × (1 − 30%)] equivalent units, plus the 9,000 units started and completed, plus 400 equivalent units in ending WIP (1,000 units × 40%), for a total of 10,800 units.

**FIFO Costs.** To determine the equivalent unit cost under FIFO, current period costs are divided by the number of equivalent units for total work performed this period. During May, equivalent unit costs are calculated as shown in Exhibit 6.6: $3.05 for direct materials and $7.10 for

---

**EXHIBIT 6.6** Process Cost Reports with Beginning and Ending WIP

| Assumptions for May: | | | | |
|---|---|---|---|---|
| **Work performed:** | | | **Costs:** | |
| Beginning WIP | 2,000 | | Beginning WIP (FIFO and Weighted Average) | |
| % complete direct materials | 100% | | Direct materials | $ 6,000 |
| % complete conversion costs | 30% | | Conversion costs | 4,200 |
| Units started | 10,000 | | Total beginning WIP costs | 10,200 |
| Units completed and transferred out | 11,000 | | Costs added this month | |
| Ending WIP | 1,000 | | Direct materials | 30,500 |
| % complete direct materials | 100% | | Conversion costs | 76,680 |
| % complete conversion costs | 40% | | Total costs added | 107,180 |
| | | | Total costs to account for | $117,380 |

**Summarize Physical and Equivalent Units**

| | | | Work This Period | | | |
|---|---|---|---|---|---|---|
| | Beginning WIP (30%) | Complete Beginning WIP (70%) | Start and Complete | Start Ending WIP (40%) | Total Work Performed This Period | Total Units to Account For |
| Account for | | | | | | |
| Physical units | 2,000 | 0 | 9,000 | 1,000 | 10,000 | 12,000 |
| Equivalent units: | | | | | | Total Work |
| Direct materials | 2,000 | 0 | 9,000 | 1,000 | 10,000 | 12,000 |
| Conversion costs | 600 | 1,400 | 9,000 | 400 | 10,800 | 11,400 |

*(continued)*

---

[3]See Aracruz Celulose, "Pulp Production Process," available at www.aracruz.com.br/en/.

**EXHIBIT 6.6** (Continued)

Calculate Actual Cost per Equivalent Unit

First-in, first-out:

Direct materials: $\dfrac{\text{Direct materials cost}}{\text{Equivalent units for total work performed this period}} = \dfrac{\$30,500}{10,000} = \$\ 3.05$

Conversion costs: $\dfrac{\text{Conversion costs}}{\text{Equivalent units for total work performed this period}} = \dfrac{\$76,680}{10,800} = \underline{\phantom{0}7.10}$

Total cost per equivalent unit: $\underline{\underline{\$10.15}}$

Weighted average:

Direct materials: $\dfrac{\text{Beginning WIP + Direct materials cost}}{\text{Equivalent units for total work}} = \dfrac{\$6,000 + \$30,500}{12,000} = \$\ 3.0417$

Conversion costs: $\dfrac{\text{Beginning WIP + Conversion cost}}{\text{Equivalent units for total work}} = \dfrac{\$4,200 + \$76,680}{11,400} = \underline{\phantom{0}7.0947}$

Total cost per equivalent unit: $\underline{\underline{\$10.1364}}$

Process Cost Reports for Molding Department: May

| | First-In, First-Out | | | Weighted Average | | |
|---|---|---|---|---|---|---|
| | Computation | Units | Costs | Computation | Units | Costs |
| Beginning WIP | (from April cost report) | 2,000 | $ 10,200 | | | |
| Costs to complete beginning WIP: | | | | | | |
| Direct materials | 0 × $3.05 | | 0 | | | |
| Conversion costs | 1,400 × $7.10 | | 9,940 | | | |
| Total costs added this period | | | 9,940 | | | |
| Total cost of beginning WIP transferred out | | 2,000 | 20,140 | | | |
| New units started, completed, and transferred out | 9,000 × $10.15 | 9,000 | 91,350 | | | |
| Total units completed and transferred out | | 11,000 | 111,490 | (2,000 + 9,000) × $10.1364 | 11,000 | $111,500 |
| Ending WIP: | | 1,000 | | | 1,000 | |
| Direct materials | 1,000 × $3.05 | | 3,050 | 1,000 × $3.0417 | | 3,042 |
| Conversion costs | 400 × $7.10 | | 2,840 | 400 × $7.0947 | | 2,838 |
| Total ending WIP cost | | | 5,890 | | | 5,880 |
| Total accounted for | | 12,000 | $117,380 | | 12,000 | $117,380 |

conversion costs. These costs are allocated to the work performed to complete beginning WIP, to the units started and completed, and to the equivalent units in ending WIP. We can double-check our computations by verifying that the sum of costs accounted for ($117,380) is equal to the sum of beginning WIP plus costs incurred during May ($10,200 + $30,500 + $76,680 = $117,380).

**Weighted Average Costs.** Under the weighted average method, the costs from beginning WIP are averaged with the costs incurred during the period. Average costs—rather than current period costs alone—are then allocated to the units completed and in ending WIP. As shown in Exhibit 6.6, the weighted average cost per equivalent unit is $3.0417 for direct materials and $7.0947 for conversion costs. Because beginning WIP and current period costs are averaged under the weighted average method, average cost per unit is simply allocated to the total units completed and transferred out and to the equivalent units in ending WIP.

**Comparison.** During the month of May, the per-unit costs differ between FIFO and weighted average. FIFO reflects only the current period costs ($3.05 for direct materials and $7.10 for conversion), while weighted average blends last period's and this period's costs ($3.0417 for direct materials and $7.0947 for conversion). Most organizations experience at least some fluctuation in costs between accounting periods, leading to differences in the per-unit costs between weighted average and FIFO. The costs per unit under weighted average are lower than the FIFO costs, indicating that costs increased in May.

# GENERAL LEDGER ACCOUNTS FOR PROCESS COSTING

In process costing, separate WIP accounts are maintained for each production department. Pools of product costs are accumulated in WIP and are then allocated to the individual units. In a traditional system two cost pools are used for costs incurred within a department: direct material and conversion costs. As units are completed in the first department, their costs are transferred to WIP for the second department. The costs for transferred-in units are pooled separately from other costs in the second department. Then additional direct material (if any) and conversion costs are added. At the end of production in the second department, the three categories of cost (transferred-in costs, direct materials, and conversion costs) are assigned to units and the costs are transferred out. This process continues for each department until the products are transferred into finished goods.

Exhibit 6.7 shows the general ledger accounts and inventory cost flows for the two production departments at Premier Plastics. First, direct materials move from raw material inventory to the molding department. Conversion costs are accumulated in the WIP account for each department. The costs for the completed units in the molding department are transferred to the assembly department WIP account. In the assembly department, additional direct material and conversion costs are added. When assembly work is completed, costs are transferred from the assembly department WIP to finished goods inventory.

Journal entries for process costing are similar to those for job costing. The main difference is that materials, labor, and overhead costs are assigned to departments rather than to specific jobs. The costs are then allocated from each department to individual units. Exhibit 6.8 provides the general journal entries for FIFO process costing for the molding department of Premier Plastics during the month of May.

**EXHIBIT 6.7** Process Costing General Ledger Accounts for Producing Plastic CD/DVD Storage Units

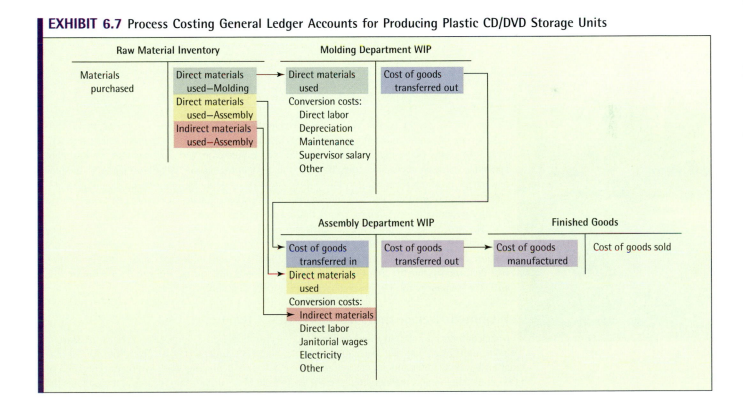

---

[4]See "Process Cost Accounting," *DoD Financial Management Regulation*, vol. 4, chap. 21, available at www.dod.mil/comptroller/fmr/04/04_21.pdf.

**EXHIBIT 6.8**
FIFO Process Costing
Journal Entries for
the Molding Department
for the Month of May

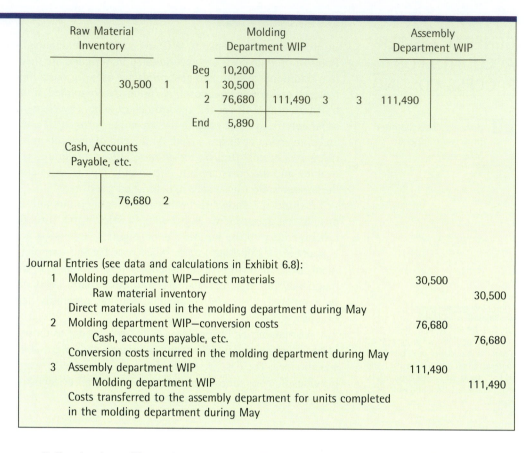

| | Raw Material Inventory | | | Molding Department WIP | | | Assembly Department WIP | |
|---|---|---|---|---|---|---|---|---|
| | 30,500 | 1 | Beg | 10,200 | | | | |
| | | | 1 | 30,500 | | | | |
| | | | 2 | 76,680 | 111,490 | 3 | 3 | 111,490 |
| | | | End | 5,890 | | | | |

Cash, Accounts Payable, etc.

76,680    2

Journal Entries (see data and calculations in Exhibit 6.8):

| | | | |
|---|---|---|---|
| 1 | Molding department WIP—direct materials | 30,500 | |
| | Raw material inventory | | 30,500 |
| | Direct materials used in the molding department during May | | |
| 2 | Molding department WIP—conversion costs | 76,680 | |
| | Cash, accounts payable, etc. | | 76,680 |
| | Conversion costs incurred in the molding department during May | | |
| 3 | Assembly department WIP | 111,490 | |
| | Molding department WIP | | 111,490 |
| | Costs transferred to the assembly department for units completed in the molding department during May | | |

Following is an illustration comparing FIFO and weighted average cost information for use in monitoring costs.

## CHOOSING A PROCESS COSTING METHOD

Nancy Redhouse is the cost accountant for Premier Plastics, a manufacturer of attractive CD/DVD racks. To reduce costs, the company's managers installed new machines in the molding department to reduce waste. Direct materials costs are expected to decrease, and the machines use less labor and time, reducing conversion costs. Nancy wants to help the managers monitor costs for the new equipment, so she is reconsidering the method used for process cost reports. The molding department head also wants to use cost information to motivate employees operating the machines to identify potential process improvements that could further reduce cost or increase quality.

The process cost reports are currently prepared using the weighted average method. Nancy is concerned that this method might not provide managers with the most current cost information. The FIFO method provides more current cost information. Nancy decides to prepare process cost reports for the month of June using both methods so that she can discuss the results with the managers and obtain feedback for the final decision.

### Weighted Average and FIFO Process Cost Reports

Nancy gathers information about June production and costs. During June, 12,000 units were started, 3,000 units in ending WIP were 50% complete, and 9,000 units were transferred out. Direct material cost was $33,600 and conversion costs were $74,925. Beginning work in process consisted of 1,000 units. She obtains the weighted average costs from May's accounting records and calculates the values that would have been used for FIFO. The costs for beginning WIP are as follows:

| | FIFO | Weighted Average |
|---|---|---|
| Direct materials: 1,000 equivalent units | $3,050 | $3,042 |
| Conversion costs: 400 equivalent units | 2,840 | 2,838 |
| Total beginning WIP | $5,890 | $5,880 |

Nancy uses a four-step process to prepare the process cost report under each method:

1. Summarize total costs to account for.
2. Summarize total physical and equivalent units.
3. Compute cost per equivalent unit.
4. Account for cost of units completed and cost of ending WIP.

The first step is to summarize total costs to account for, as shown in Exhibit 6.9. Nancy uses the beginning WIP costs and adds costs incurred during June. The total costs to account for are different under FIFO than under the weighted average method because the costs assigned to beginning WIP are different (see May computations in Exhibit 6.6).

The second step is to summarize the total physical and equivalent units. Nancy prepares only one schedule for FIFO and weighted average, as shown in Exhibit 6.9. However, she knows that under the FIFO method she needs only the equivalent units for work performed during June, whereas under weighted average she needs the equivalent units for total work during June and in beginning WIP. The equivalent units for work performed during June includes work to complete beginning WIP, work on units started and completed during June, and work on units started but not completed during June.

The third step is to compute the cost per equivalent unit for direct materials and conversion costs, as shown in Exhibit 6.9. The computations for FIFO use only the costs and equivalent units

**HELPFUL HINT**

Carry enough decimal places—typically four or more—or use a spreadsheet with cell references to avoid rounding errors.

**EXHIBIT 6.9** Premier Plastics Molding Department Process Cost Report for June

**1. Summarize Total Costs to Account For**
First-in, first-out:

| | Direct Materials | Conversion Costs | Total Cost |
|---|---|---|---|
| Beginning WIP | $ 3,050 | $ 2,840 | $ 5,890 |
| Current period costs | 33,600 | 74,925 | 108,525 |
| Total costs to account for | $36,650 | $77,765 | $114,415 |

Weighted average:

| | Direct Materials | Conversion Costs | Total Cost |
|---|---|---|---|
| Beginning WIP | $ 3,042 | $ 2,838 | $ 5,880 |
| Current period costs | 33,600 | 74,925 | 108,525 |
| Total costs to account for | $36,642 | $77,763 | $114,405 |

**2. Summarize Physical and Equivalent Units**

| | | | Work This Period | | | |
|---|---|---|---|---|---|---|
| | Beginning WIP (40%) | Complete Beginning WIP (60%) | Start and Complete | Start Ending WIP (50%) | Total Work Performed This Period | Total to Account For |
| Physical units | 1,000 | 0 | 9,000 | 3,000 | 12,000 | 13,000 |
| Equivalent units: | | | | | | **Total Work** |
| Direct materials | 1,000 | 0 | 9,000 | 3,000 | 12,000 | 13,000 |
| Conversion costs | 400 | 600 | 9,000 | 1,500 | 11,100 | 11,500 |

**3. Calculate Cost per Equivalent Unit**
First-in, first-out:

Direct materials: $\dfrac{\text{Direct materials cost}}{\text{Equivalent units for total work performed this period}} = \dfrac{\$33,600}{12,000} = \$2.80$

Conversion costs: $\dfrac{\text{Conversion costs}}{\text{Equivalent units for total work performed this period}} = \dfrac{\$74,925}{11,100} = \underline{6.75}$

Total cost per equivalent unit: $\underline{\underline{\$9.55}}$

Weighted average:

Direct materials: $\dfrac{\text{Beginning WIP} + \text{Direct materials cost}}{\text{Equivalent units for total work}} = \dfrac{\$36,642}{13,000} = \$2.8186$

Conversion costs: $\dfrac{\text{Beginning WIP} + \text{Conversion cost}}{\text{Equivalent units for total work}} = \dfrac{\$77,763}{11,500} = \underline{6.7620}$

Total cost per equivalent unit: $\underline{\underline{\$9.5806}}$

*(continued)*

**EXHIBIT 6.9** (Continued)

**4. Process Cost Reports for Molding Department: June**

| | | First-In, First-Out | | Weighted Average | | |
| | Computation | Units | Costs | Computation | Units | Costs |
|---|---|---|---|---|---|---|
| Beginning WIP | (from May cost report) | 1,000 | $ 5,890 | | | |
| Costs to complete beginning WIP: | | | | | | |
| Direct materials | 0 × $2.80 | | 0 | | | |
| Conversion costs | 600 × $6.75 | | 4,050 | | | |
| Total costs added this period | | | 4,050 | | | |
| Total cost of beginning WIP transferred out | | 1,000 | 9,940 | | | |
| New units started, completed, and transferred out | 9,000 × $9.55 | 9,000 | 85,950 | | | |
| Total units completed and transferred out | | 10,000 | 95,890 | (1,000 + 9,000) × $9.5806 | 10,000 | $ 95,806 |
| Ending WIP: | | 3,000 | | | 3,000 | |
| Direct materials | 3,000 × $2.80 | | 8,400 | 3,000 × $2.8186 | | 8,456 |
| Conversion costs | 1,500 × $6.75 | | 10,125 | 1,500 × $6.7620 | | 10,143 |
| Total ending WIP cost | | | 18,525 | | | 18,599 |
| **Total accounted for** | | 13,000 | $114,415 | | 13,000 | $114,405 |

for work performed during June, while the computations for weighted average use the costs and equivalent units in beginning WIP plus the work performed during June.

The fourth step is to prepare the process cost reports, as shown in Exhibit 6.9. Nancy prepares the FIFO and weighted average reports side-by-side to easily compare the results.

## Comparison of Weighted Average and FIFO

As Nancy reviews her work, she notices that the weighted average method requires fewer computations. However, she thinks the extra work for FIFO is not a problem because she plans to use a spreadsheet to create future reports. From a management perspective, she thinks that FIFO is probably a better method because it provides more precise information about any changes in per-unit cost between periods. During June, the difference in per-unit cost between weighted average and FIFO was small ($9.5806 versus $9.55). However, she believes it is large enough that managers will prefer the more current data provided by FIFO. When Nancy discusses the two methods with the managers, they agree that the FIFO method provides them with the best information for monitoring monthly costs.

| GUIDE YOUR LEARNING 6.2 | Premier Plastics (Part 1) |
|---|---|

Premier Plastics (Part 1) illustrates the creation of process cost reports using the weighted average and FIFO methods. For this illustration:

| Define It | Identify Problem and Information | Prioritize Options |
|---|---|---|
| How and why do computations differ between the FIFO and weighted average methods? | What types of decisions might be addressed using the information generated in a process cost report? | In your own words, explain why Nancy decided that the FIFO method provides better information than the weighted average method. |

# PROCESS COSTING UNDER DIFFERENT ASSUMPTIONS

 **Q5** What alternative methods are used for mass production?

In the preceding section, we performed process costing computations under the following assumptions:

- Direct materials added at the beginning of the process
- Conversion costs incurred evenly throughout the process
- Conversion costs accumulated in a single cost pool
- No costs transferred in from another department
- Fluctuations between beginning WIP and current period cost per unit

Now we consider the effects of different organizational settings on process costing.

## ■ Direct Materials Added During the Process

For manufactured products, the cost of direct materials is often a large proportion of the total cost per unit. If the point when direct materials are added is correctly identified, accuracy is increased in the equivalent unit calculations and cost for WIP inventories. In many processes, direct materials are added at the beginning and WIP is always 100% complete with respect to direct materials. However, direct materials are sometimes added later during the process, as shown in the assembly department in Exhibit 6.3. Direct materials may also be added at more than one point during the process as shown for the cooking and canning department in Exhibit 6.2. Alternatively, direct materials are not added in some processes. For example, if cherries were dried and packaged in separate departments, no direct materials would be added during the drying process. Because the process of adding direct materials varies, accountants must analyze the production process before performing process costing calculations.

## ■ Nonuniform Conversion Costs and Multiple Cost Pools

Accountants also analyze production processes to determine how conversion costs are incurred. We often assume that conversion costs are incurred evenly throughout the process in each department. However, conversion costs might be incurred unevenly. In addition, for some processes it might be easier to match costs to the work performed if conversion costs are separated into two or more cost pools.

For example, direct labor costs might be incurred in one pattern and other types of conversion costs might be incurred in a different pattern. In the cherry drying department portrayed in Exhibit 6.2, labor is used to load the cherries onto drying frames, and then the cherries sit for several days while drying. Few labor hours are needed to monitor the drying process. However, electricity and equipment are used evenly throughout the drying process. If it is relatively easy to separately track labor, the accountants may find it beneficial to allocate labor and overhead costs separately.

## ■ Costs Transferred from Another Department

**Q6** How is process costing performed for multiple production departments?

As illustrated in Exhibits 6.2 and 6.3, many processes are organized around multiple departments. Process costing for each department is performed separately, but costs for work done in one department are transferred to the next department as units are transferred. Completed units and costs are transferred from department to department until the last production department transfers completed units to finished goods inventory. After the first department, the number of units started consists of units transferred in from the preceding department. In addition, the total costs to account for includes a new cost category for costs transferred in.

In the following illustration, units and costs are transferred into Premier Plastic's assembly department. In addition, direct materials are added in the middle of the process. Both FIFO and weighted average methods are illustrated.

## PREMIER PLASTICS (PART 2)
### COSTS TRANSFERRED FROM ANOTHER DEPARTMENT AND DIRECT MATERIALS ADDED LATER IN THE PROCESS

After hearing that the managers in the molding department were pleased with their new FIFO process cost report, the managers in the assembly department asked Nancy to prepare a similar report for their department for the month of June.

Nancy first refers to the cost flows she previously developed for the assembly department, shown in Exhibit 6.3. The assembly department smoothes and finishes the plastic boxes and adds a metal framework for the CDs/DVDs. The metal frames are direct materials that are added when the storage units are about 50% complete. Nancy assumes that conversion costs are added evenly throughout the assembly process.

Next, Nancy gathers information about June's operations. Beginning WIP inventory (1,000 units) was 20% complete. The cost of beginning WIP includes the costs transferred in from the molding department in May under FIFO ($10.15 per unit) and weighted average ($10.1364 per unit). In addition, conversion costs in May were $10.00 per unit under FIFO (total cost of $10 × 200 = $2,000) and $9.95 per unit under weighted average (total cost of $9.95 × 200 = $1,990).

|  | FIFO | Weighted Average |
|---|---|---|
| Beginning WIP: |  |  |
| Transferred in: 1,000 equivalent units | $10,150 | $10,136 |
| Direct materials: 0 equivalent units | 0 | 0 |
| Conversion costs: 200 equivalent units | 2,000 | 1,990 |
| Total beginning WIP | $12,150 | $12,126 |

During June 10,000 units were transferred in from the molding department. The total cost of units transferred in under weighted average was $9.5806 per unit, or $95,806 total (Exhibit 6.9). Nancy calculates that the cost would have been $95,890 total under FIFO, or an average of $9.589 per unit. Of the 10,000 units transferred in, 8,000 units were completed and transferred out to finished goods inventory. The remaining 2,000 units in ending WIP inventory were 60% complete.

Nancy follows the same four steps she used for the molding department to create a cost report for the assembly department, as shown in Exhibit 6.10. The procedures to prepare the process cost reports for the assembly department are similar to those performed previously for the molding department except for the transferred-in costs and timing for the addition of direct materials.

Transferred-in costs are treated as a third category of cost, similar to the treatment of direct materials and conversion costs. However, as units are transferred from molding to assembly, they are always 100% complete.

Because direct materials are added when units are 50% complete and beginning WIP was only 20% complete, none of the units in beginning WIP included direct materials. Then, 100% of the direct materials were added to beginning WIP during June. Ending WIP was 60% complete, so 100% of the direct materials to those units were added during June.

After finishing the cost reports, Nancy compares the equivalent cost per unit in the assembly department using weighted average and FIFO. The weighted average equivalent unit cost is $21.434 and the FIFO cost is $21.389.

---

**EXHIBIT 6.10** Premier Plastics Assembly Department Process Cost Report for June

**1. Summarize Total Costs to Account For**
First-in, first-out:

|  | Transferred In | Direct Materials | Conversion Costs | Total Cost |
|---|---|---|---|---|
| Beginning WIP | $ 10,150 | $ 0 | $ 2,000 | $ 12,150 |
| Current period costs | 95,890 | 22,000 | 98,000 | 215,890 |
| Total costs to account for | $106,040 | $22,000 | $100,000 | $228,040 |

Weighted average:

|  | Transferred In | Direct Materials | Conversion Costs | Total Cost |
|---|---|---|---|---|
| Beginning WIP | $ 10,136 | $ 0 | $ 1,990 | $ 12,126 |
| Current period costs | 95,806 | 22,000 | 98,000 | 215,806 |
| Total costs to account for | $105,942 | $22,000 | $99,990 | $227,932 |

**EXHIBIT 6.10** (Continued)

### 2. Summarize Physical and Equivalent Units

| | Beginning WIP (20%) | Complete Beginning WIP (80%) | Start and Complete | Start Ending WIP (60%) | Total Work Performed This Period | Total Units to Account For |
|---|---|---|---|---|---|---|
| | | | | **Work This Period** | | |
| Physical units | 1,000 | 0 | 8,000 | 2,000 | 10,000 | 11,000 |
| Equivalent units: | | | | | | **Total Work** |
| Transferred in | 1,000 | 0 | 8,000 | 2,000 | 10,000 | 11,000 |
| Direct materials | 0 | 1,000 | 8,000 | 2,000 | 11,000 | 11,000 |
| Conversion costs | 200 | 800 | 8,000 | 1,200 | 10,000 | 10,200 |

### 3. Calculate Cost per Equivalent Unit

**First-in, first-out:**

Transferred in:
$$\frac{\text{Transferred-in costs}}{\text{Equivalent units for total work performed this period}} = \frac{\$95,890}{10,000} = \$\ 9.589$$

Direct materials:
$$\frac{\text{Direct materials cost}}{\text{Equivalent units for total work performed this period}} = \frac{\$22,000}{11,000} = 2.000$$

Conversion costs:
$$\frac{\text{Conversion costs}}{\text{Equivalent units for total work performed this period}} = \frac{\$98,000}{10,000} = 9.800$$

Total cost per equivalent unit:  $\$21.389$

**Weighted average:**

Transferred in:
$$\frac{\text{Beginning WIP} + \text{Transferred-in costs}}{\text{Equivalent units for total work}} = \frac{\$105,942}{11,000} = \$\ 9.6311$$

Direct materials:
$$\frac{\text{Beginning WIP} + \text{Direct materials cost}}{\text{Equivalent units for total work}} = \frac{\$22,000}{11,000} = 2.000$$

Conversion costs:
$$\frac{\text{Beginning WIP} + \text{Conversion cost}}{\text{Equivalent units for total work}} = \frac{\$99,990}{10,200} = 9.8029$$

Total cost per equivalent unit:  $\$21.4340$

### 4. Process Cost Reports for Assembly Department: June

| | **First-In, First-Out** | | | **Weighted Average** | | |
|---|---|---|---|---|---|---|
| | Computation | Units | Costs | Computation | Units | Costs |
| Beginning WIP | (from May cost report) | 1,000 | $ 12,150 | | | |
| Costs to complete beginning WIP: | | | | | | |
| Direct materials | 1,000 × $2 | | 2,000 | | | |
| Conversion costs | 800 × $9.8 | | 7,840 | | | |
| Total costs added | | | | | | |
| this period | | | 9,840 | | | |
| Total cost of beginning WIP | | | | | | |
| transferred out | | 1,000 | 21,990 | | | |
| New units started, completed, | | | | | | |
| and transferred out | 8,000 × $21.389 | 8,000 | 171,112 | | | |
| Total units completed and | | | | | | |
| transferred out | | 9,000 | 193,102 | (1,000 + 8,000) × $21.434 | 9,000 | $ 192,906 |
| Ending WIP: | | 2,000 | | | 2,000 | |
| Transferred in | 2,000 × $9.589 | | 19,178 | 2,000 × $9.6311 | | 19,262 |
| Direct materials | 2,000 × $2 | | 4,000 | 2,000 × $2 | | 4,000 |
| Conversion costs | 1,200 × $9.8 | | 11,760 | 1,200 × $9.8029 | | 11,764 |
| Total ending WIP cost | | | 34,938 | | | 35,026 |
| **Total accounted for** | | **11,000** | **$228,040** | | **11,000** | **$227,932** |

*(continued)*

Nancy notices that the cost per equivalent unit that is added in assembly is similar under both methods, which means that costs during June were similar to May's costs. She asks the managers whether costs in the assembly department fluctuate much from month to month. The managers tell her that a long-term contract with suppliers guarantees prices for at least a one-year period, and labor contracts are negotiated annually, so the costs do not fluctuate much from month to month. In addition, volumes do not fluctuate a great deal.

Because costs in the department rarely fluctuate and volumes are reasonably stable, the costs added will be similar under both methods, so either method would be appropriate. However, because molding is now using FIFO, units are transferred in at FIFO cost. To be consistent, Nancy decides that the assembly department should also use FIFO.

| GUIDE YOUR LEARNING **6.3** Premier Plastics (Part 2) |
| --- |

Premier Plastics (Part 2) illustrates costs transferred from another department and direct materials added at a point in the process other than the beginning. For this illustration:

| Compute It | Identify Uncertainties | Explore Information |
| --- | --- | --- |
| How and why are the computations affected by: <br> • Costs transferred in from another department <br> • Direct materials added other than at the beginning of the process | Why is the percent of completion uncertain for: <br> • Direct materials <br> • Conversion costs | Suppose the FIFO cost per unit had been higher than the weighted average cost per unit for each of the following. Provide possible explanations for each cost. <br> • Direct materials <br> • Conversion costs |

## ALTERNATIVE SYSTEMS FOR COSTING MASS PRODUCTION

**Q5** What alternative methods are used for mass production?

**CHAPTER REFERENCE**

Accounting entries in a standard process costing system are similar to the allocation of overhead using an estimated rate introduced in Chapter 5.

**CHAPTER REFERENCE**

Developing and using standard costs are discussed in more detail in Chapter 11.

The preceding sections of this chapter demonstrated traditional process costing methods for assigning product costs to mass-produced goods. In recent years several developments have affected the manufacturing environment and costing practices. Organizations have concentrated on reducing the amount of inventory in their systems and also on increasing their abilities to customize mass-produced goods. In addition, managers have sought better ways to monitor costs and motivate higher levels of performance. The costing systems used by organizations vary, depending on the information needs of the managers, the production processes used, and the nature of the organization's products or services. Next we learn about three types of alternative systems.

### ■ Standard Costing

A **standard cost** is the cost managers expect to incur for production of goods or services under operating plan assumptions. Under a standard costing system, accounting entries for direct materials, conversion costs, and transferred-in costs are recorded at standard, or expected, rather than actual costs. Actual costs are accumulated in a control account, and then costs are allocated to WIP using a standard rate per equivalent unit. At the end of the period, adjustments are made for the differences between actual and standard costs.

Standard costs are used for a variety of reasons. For example, they simplify the process of making accounting entries during the period; actual costs need not be compiled for product costs to be recorded. Standards also provide a benchmark against which actual costs can be compared. Managers and operating employees can then be rewarded based on whether the standards are achieved or exceeded. These rewards provide motivation for monitoring operations and maintaining higher productivity levels.

Standard costs are allocated to units in a manner similar to FIFO process costing. The difference is that no equivalent cost per unit is calculated. Instead, a standard cost is used to allocate costs to inventory. In Exhibit 6.11 the standard costs for the molding department of Premier Plastics in May are $3.00 for direct materials and $7.00 for conversion costs, or $10.00 per unit. Assuming no change from the prior month in the standard costs, the cost of beginning WIP is carried over from the previous month at the costs per equivalent unit. Therefore, beginning WIP includes direct materials cost of $6,000 (2,000 × $3.00) and conversion costs of $4,200 (600 × $7.00), for a total of $10,200. During May, standard costs are first allocated to the equivalent units of work performed to complete beginning WIP: $0 for direct materials and $9,800 for conversion costs. Next, standard costs of $90,000 ($10 × 9,000 units) are allocated to the units started, completed and transferred out. Finally, standard costs of $3,000 for direct materials and $2,800 for conversion costs are allocated to ending WIP. The total amount of standard cost to account for (beginning WIP plus costs allocated during May) is $115,800. Details of the cost report are presented in Exhibit 6.11.

**EXHIBIT 6.11** Premier Plastics Molding Department Standard Process Cost Report for May

**Assumptions for May:**
Direct materials standard cost = $3.00
Standard cost for conversion = $7.00

**Work performed:**

| | |
|---|---|
| Beginning WIP | 2,000 |
| % complete direct materials | 100% |
| % complete conversion costs | 30% |
| Units started | 10,000 |
| Units completed and transferred out | 11,000 |
| Ending WIP | 1,000 |
| % complete direct materials | 100% |
| % complete conversion costs | 40% |

**1. Summarize Total Costs to Account For**

| | |
|---|---|
| Direct materials: 12,000 equivalent units at standard cost of $3.00 per unit | $ 36,000 |
| Conversion costs: 11,400 equivalent units at standard cost of $7.00 per unit | 79,800 |
| Total standard costs to account for | $115,800 |

**2. Summarize Physical and Equivalent Units**

| | Beginning WIP (30%) | Complete Beginning WIP (70%) | Start and Complete | Start Ending WIP (40%) | Total Work Performed This Period | Total Units to Account For |
|---|---|---|---|---|---|---|
| | | | | | **Work This Period** | |
| Physical units | 2,000 | 0 | 9,000 | 1,000 | 10,000 | 12,000 |
| Equivalent units: | | | | | | **Total Work** |
| Direct materials | 2,000 | 0 | 9,000 | 1,000 | 10,000 | 12,000 |
| Conversion costs | 600 | 1,400 | 9,000 | 400 | 10,800 | 11,400 |

**3. Calculate Cost per Equivalent Unit** (This step is not needed for standard costs.)

**4. Process Cost Report for Molding Department: May**

| | Computation | Units | Cost |
|---|---|---|---|
| | | **Standard Cost** | |
| Beginning WIP | (from April cost report) | 2,000 | $ 10,200 |
| Costs to complete beginning WIP: | | | |
| Direct materials | 0 × $3.00 | | 0 |
| Conversion costs | 1,400 × $7.00 | | 9,800 |
| Total costs added this period | | | 20,000 |
| Total cost of beginning WIP transferred out | | 2,000 | 20,000 |
| New units started, completed, and transferred out | 9,000 × $10.00 | 9,000 | 90,000 |
| Total units completed and transferred out | | 11,000 | 110,000 |
| Ending WIP: | | 1,000 | |
| Direct materials | 1,000 × $3.00 | | 3,000 |
| Conversion costs | 400 × $7.00 | | 2,800 |
| Total ending WIP cost | | | 5,800 |
| **Total accounted for** | | **12,000** | **$115,800** |

When standard costs are used as benchmarks, they are compared to actual costs calculated using either weighted average or FIFO. In this example for Premier Plastics, Nancy could compare the standard cost of $10 per unit with the actual weighted average cost per equivalent unit in May of $10.1364 or to the FIFO cost of $10.15. From these comparisons, it appears that actual costs are higher than standard. When actual costs are higher than standard costs, managers investigate the causes and analyze ways to improve operations. If actual costs are lower, the causes may also be analyzed so that managers better understand the improvements that have taken place.

## ■ Just-in-Time and Long-Term Procurement Contracts

**CHAPTER REFERENCE**

For more information about JIT systems, see Chapter 13.

**HELPFUL HINT**

Just-in-time operations minimize inventory buildup during production. Raw materials and partially complete units are received just before they are needed for the next step in the manufacturing process.

Some organizations have few or no units in beginning or ending WIP inventories because the organization substantially completes processing at the end of each accounting period or because the organization uses just-in-time (JIT) production methods. With little or no WIP inventory, process costing is simple because beginning and ending inventories are small or nonexistent, making the computations similar to those shown in Exhibit 6.4. In essence, an average cost for the period is calculated by dividing total current costs incurred by total units completed. In addition, the choice between FIFO and weighted average method is unimportant because the dollar amounts in the two types of process cost reports are similar.

When organizations adopt just-in-time inventory practices, they often also alter their production processes so that work occurs in small teams rather than in departments. In such cases, the traditional cost pools for direct materials and conversions costs may no longer be appropriate.

Some organizations enter into long-term procurement contracts with suppliers, so the cost of raw materials is relatively stable over long periods of time. When few changes occur in costs between accounting periods, FIFO and weighted average process costing reports are similar.

## ■ Hybrid Costing Systems and Operation Costing

As manufacturing systems incorporate more technology, organizations become more flexible in meeting the diverse needs of their customers. Products that were once mass-produced are now customized. Although most of the manufacturing process might be performed identically for all units, at some point individual units are customized. For example, **Harley Davidson** customizes its motorcycles with special accessories and colors. Flexible manufacturing systems are used in many industries such as computers, cars, and bicycles. Customers order these products with specific features. The manufacturing process is a combination of mass-produced components, but during assembly the products are customized. **Hybrid costing** is the accounting approach used to assign product costs by applying a combination of both job and process costing. Often, process costing is used up to the point of customization, after which the direct costs are traced to each specific job.

**ALTERNATIVE TERMS**

In flexible manufacturing, batches are often called *production runs*.

**Operation costing** is a particular type of hybrid method used when similar batches of identical products are manufactured. Units in each batch are identical, but the processing of each batch is different and may not include the same steps. For example, consider the production of notebook computers having different configurations. Some batches go through the same processes but differ based on type of memory chip or size of hard drive installed. Some batches go through fewer processes than others. For example, some notebook computers are sold with only one installed battery, while others have both an installed battery and an extra battery.

Operation costing systems track costs using work orders for each batch. These work orders include detailed information about the direct materials required and the steps needed in the manufacturing operation. Direct materials are traced to each batch through the work orders and then allocated to units. In addition, all units within a batch are allocated uniform amounts of overhead. Unlike traditional process costing, operation costing usually includes more than two types of cost pools. The cost pools are designed to match the separate processes that may be allocated to batches of products. This matching of processes and cost pools improves the accuracy of cost assignment to individual products. Managers are better able to focus on the control of physical processes within a given production system because their financial information more accurately matches the flow of resources through specific processes.

**INTERNATIONAL**

In 2004, Hyundai Motor India announced plans to modify its production process so that three or more automobile models could be produced on the same production line.[5]

# ACCOUNTING FOR SPOILAGE IN PROCESS COSTING

 **Q7** How are spoilage costs handled in process costing?

**INTERNATIONAL**

Bridgestone Corporation incurred ¥162 billion (over $1.5 billion U.S.) in recall and litigation costs relating to claims that the tread on certain Firestone tires peeled off, causing numerous rollover accidents.[6]

**INTERNATIONAL**

Ball Packaging Europe uses a camera system on its beverage can production line to test for unit defects. A computer compares images from five cameras to image specifications.[7]

Production processes often create **spoilage**, which are units of product that are unacceptable and are either discarded or sold at a reduced price. Sometimes spoiled units are reworked, or repaired, and sold as if they were originally produced correctly. The costs of spoilage include the resources that are wasted due to spoilage, including the full amount of product costs for units that are discarded and the rework costs for units that are repaired. From an accounting perspective, decisions are made about how to record the costs of spoilage. Should they be included in the product cost of all good units sold, or should they be recognized as a separate loss? The accounting treatment depends on whether the spoilage is a normal part of the production process.

**Normal spoilage** consists of defective units that arise as part of regular operations. Because normal spoilage is considered an ordinary and inherent part of operations, the cost of normal spoilage is included in the costs of all good units produced. The cost of normal spoilage is considered necessary for producing good units. For example, if **Elliptec** finds that one out of every 1,000 mini motors fails to work properly when tested at the end of production, then that proportion of spoilage will be treated as normal. If the managers modify operations to reduce product failures, then a new lower rate of spoilage will become normal.

**Abnormal spoilage** is spoilage that is not part of everyday operations. Because abnormal spoilage is considered unusual and is not an inherent part of operations, the cost of abnormal spoilage is excluded from product costs and is recorded as a separate loss. Abnormal spoilage occurs because of events such as strikes and natural disasters, or it occurs because operations are out of control. For example, at Elliptec an equipment malfunction that ruins a large number of mini motors would be considered abnormal spoilage.

To properly account for spoilage in a process costing system, accountants need to identify the point in the production process where spoiled units are removed. Different organizations establish different procedures for inspection and removal of spoiled units. Spoilage caused by poor quality raw materials can sometimes be identified before materials are added to production. Inspection could also occur in the middle of production, at the end of the process in one department, or when processing in all departments is complete. If spoiled units are removed before they are 100% complete, the costs of direct materials and conversion need to be estimated at the point the units are removed from production.

The costs of spoilage are accounted for in a two-step process. First, all product costs are accumulated in the departmental WIP account as usual. The computation of cost per equivalent unit includes all work performed, regardless of whether the units are spoiled. If spoiled units are 100% complete at the time they are removed from production, they are treated the same as any other unit. If they are less than 100% complete, the calculation of equivalent units depends upon their completion percentage, similar to ending WIP. Second, the costs of normal spoilage are allocated to the good units produced, and the costs of abnormal spoilage are written off as a loss for the accounting period. Therefore, the cost of each good unit

[5]N. S. Gupta, "Hyundai to Move to New Production Process," *The Economic Times Online*, January 8, 2004, available at economictimes.indiatimes.com.

[6]Combined losses recorded during 2000 and 2001 on the income statement of Bridgestone Corporation and Subsidiaries Annual Report, December 31, 2002.

[7]Ball Packaging Europe, "Station: Testing for Internal Defects," under "Production Process," available at www.schmalbach.com/bpe_com_716_ENG_PHP.html.

includes an allocation for the cost of normal spoilage. The cost per good unit transferred out is computed as follows:

$$\text{Cost per good unit transferred out} = \frac{\text{Total cost of good units transferred out} + \text{Cost of normal spoilage}}{\text{Total good units transferred out}}$$

Following is a numerical illustration of spoilage using the FIFO method.

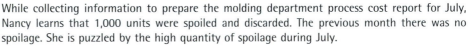

| GUIDE YOUR LEARNING | **6.4** | Key Terms |
|---|---|---|

Stop to confirm that you understand the new terms introduced in the last several pages:

Standard cost (p. 232)            *Spoilage (p. 235)
Hybrid costing (p. 234)            *Normal spoilage (p. 235)
Operation costing (p. 234)        *Abnormal spoilage (p. 235)

For each of these terms, write a definition in your own words. For starred terms, list at least one example that is different from the ones given in this textbook.

### PREMIER PLASTICS (PART 3)
### FIFO COST REPORT WITH NORMAL AND ABNORMAL SPOILAGE

While collecting information to prepare the molding department process cost report for July, Nancy learns that 1,000 units were spoiled and discarded. The previous month there was no spoilage. She is puzzled by the high quantity of spoilage during July.

Nancy discusses the spoilage with the molding department manager. He tells her that 300 units were spoiled because of a problem that occurs three or four times a year with the quality of the plastic raw material. The problem causes a slight discoloration in a number of units. In addition, a new employee accidentally programmed the molding machine incorrectly, spoiling 700 units during July. All spoilage is discovered when units are turned out of the molds, at the end of the molding processing (when they are 100% complete).

After further discussion with the molding department manager, Nancy learns that approximately 2% of units throughout the year are spoiled because of discoloration. Thus, she decides that for the raw material problem, up to 2% of units produced should be accounted for as normal spoilage. She decides that the spoilage caused by the incorrect equipment setting should be accounted for as abnormal spoilage because in a department with little employee turnover, the manager tells her, this problem rarely occurs.

Nancy finds that during July, 3,000 units in beginning WIP were completed, and 9,000 units were started and completed. Ending WIP consisted of 1,200 units that were 70% complete. Total costs added this period are $28,560 in direct materials and $86,184 in conversion costs.

### FIFO Process Cost Report and Journal Entries with Spoilage

Because a decision was made last month to adopt the FIFO method, Nancy prepares this month's cost report using only FIFO. She obtains the beginning WIP cost from the June FIFO cost report (Exhibit 6.9): $18,525 ($8,400 direct materials and $10,125 conversion costs). Given this information, she follows the same four steps as before to prepare the July cost report shown in Exhibit 6.12.

Nancy summarizes the total costs to account for as usual. However, the summary of physical and equivalent units takes into account the spoiled units. She first summarizes the work performed in terms of physical and equivalent units, and then adds a column showing the 1,000 spoiled units. Because spoiled units were identified and removed when they were 100% complete, they represent 1,000 equivalent units for both direct materials and conversion costs. Nancy next separates the spoilage between normal and abnormal. She calculates the maximum normal spoilage for July as 240 units (12,000 units completed during July × 2%), which is less than the 300 units spoiled due to discoloration. Therefore, she considers 240 units as normal spoilage. She classifies the remaining 60 discolored units plus the 700 units spoiled from the incorrect machine setting as abnormal spoilage (total 760 units).

**EXHIBIT 6.12** Premier Plastics Molding Department FIFO Cost Report with Spoilage for July

**1. Summarize Total Costs to Account For**
First-in, first-out:

| | Direct Materials | Conversion Costs | Total Cost |
|---|---|---|---|
| Beginning WIP | $ 8,400 | $10,125 | $ 18,525 |
| Current period costs | 28,560 | 86,184 | 114,744 |
| Total costs to account for | $36,960 | $96,309 | $133,269 |

**2. Summarize Physical and Equivalent Units**

| | Beginning WIP (50%) | Complete Beginning WIP (50%) | Start and Complete | Start Ending WIP (70%) | Total Work Performed This Period | Total Units to Account For | Spoiled Units (100%) |
|---|---|---|---|---|---|---|---|
| | | | **Work Performed This Period** | | | | |
| Physical units | 3,000 | 0 | 9,000 | 1,200 | 10,200 | 13,200 | (1,000) |
| Equivalent units: | | | | | | **Total Work** | |
| Direct materials | 3,000 | 0 | 9,000 | 1,200 | 10,200 | 13,200 | (1,000) |
| Conversion costs | 1,500 | 1,500 | 9,000 | 840 | 11,340 | 12,840 | (1,000) |
| Total spoilage | | | | | | | 1,000 |
| Less: Normal spoilage | | (3,000 + 9,000) × 2% | | | | | 240 |
| Abnormal spoilage | | | | | | | 760 |

**3. Calculate Cost per Equivalent Unit**
First-in, first-out:

Direct materials:
$$\frac{\text{Direct materials cost}}{\text{Equivalent units for total work performed this period}} = \frac{\$28,560}{10,200} = \$2.80$$

Conversion costs:
$$\frac{\text{Conversion costs}}{\text{Equivalent units for total work performed this period}} = \frac{\$86,184}{11,340} = 7.60$$

Total cost per equivalent unit: $10.40

**4. Process Cost Report for Molding Department: July**

First-In, First-Out

| | Computation | Units | Cost |
|---|---|---|---|
| Beginning WIP | (from June cost report) | 3,000 | $ 18,525 |
| Costs to complete beginning WIP: | | | |
| Direct materials | 0 × $2.80 | | 0 |
| Conversion costs | 1,500 × $7.60 | | 11,400 |
| Total costs added this period | | | 11,400 |
| Total cost of beginning WIP transferred out | | 3,000 | 29,925 |
| New units started, completed, and transferred out | (9,000 − 1,000) × $10.40 | 8,000 | 83,200 |
| Normal spoilage | 240 × $10.40 | | 2,496 |
| Total units completed and transferred out | | 11,000 | 115,621 |
| Abnormal spoilage | 760 × $10.40 | | 7,904 |
| Ending WIP: | | 1,200 | |
| Direct materials | 1,200 × $2.80 | | 3,360 |
| Conversion costs | 840 × $7.60 | | 6,384 |
| Total ending WIP cost | | | 9,744 |
| Total good units accounted for | 13,200 − 1,000 | 12,200 | |
| Total costs accounted for | | | $133,269 |

When Nancy prepares the cost report, she calculates the cost of good units started, completed, and transferred out. She then adds the cost of normal spoilage to arrive at the total cost transferred to the assembly department ($115,621). Abnormal spoilage is added below this subtotal to reconcile the total cost.

Nancy's journal entries are presented in Exhibit 6.13. Notice that normal spoilage costs are included in the cost of WIP transferred out. Abnormal spoilage costs are no longer associated with units, but are written off as a loss. *(continued)*

**EXHIBIT 6.13**
FIFO Process Costing Journal
Entries with Spoilage

| Raw Material Inventory | | Molding Department WIP | | Assembly Department WIP |
|---|---|---|---|---|
| | 28,560  1 | Beg  18,525 | | |
| | | 1  28,560 | 7,904  3 | |
| | | 2  86,184 | 115,621  4 | 4  115,621 |
| | | End  9,744 | | |

| Cash Accounts Payable, etc. | | Abnormal Spoilage Loss | |
|---|---|---|---|
| | 86,184  2 | 3  7,904 | |

Journal Entries:

| | | | |
|---|---|---|---|
| 1 | Molding department WIP–direct materials | 28,560 | |
| |    Raw material inventory | | 28,560 |
| | Cost of direct materials used in the molding department during July | | |
| 2 | Molding department WIP–conversion costs | 86,184 | |
| |    Cash, accounts payable, etc. | | 86,184 |
| | Conversion costs assigned to the molding department WIP during July | | |
| 3 | Abnormal spoilage loss | 7,904 | |
| |    Molding department WIP | | 7,904 |
| | To record abnormal spoilage costs for the molding department during July | | |
| 4 | Assembly department WIP | 115,621 | |
| |    Molding department WIP | | 115,621 |
| | Transfer costs for good units completed in the molding department during July | | |

## Using Spoilage Cost Information

Nancy is concerned about the total costs for spoilage this period. The 1,000 spoiled units cost $10,400 ($2,496 + $7,904). However, she is even more concerned about other problems that arise when spoilage is high. Sometimes inspectors miss some spoiled units, which are then sold as good units. When defective storage units are sold, return costs increase and customers are less satisfied. The designer storage units are expensive, and Premier's reputation suffers when units are less than perfect. Nancy knows that Japanese competitors have zero defect tolerance policies, so their customers rarely receive flawed storage units. She decides to meet with the Plastics department manager to emphasize the need for lower levels of spoilage.

---

### GUIDE YOUR LEARNING 6.5   Premier Plastics (Part 3)

Premier Plastics (Part 3) illustrates a FIFO process cost report with normal and abnormal spoilage. For this illustration:

| Define It | Compute It | Identify Uncertainties | Explore Information |
|---|---|---|---|
| In your own words, explain how abnormal spoilage is different from normal spoilage. | Explain how normal and abnormal spoilage affect:<br>• Computation of equivalent units<br>• Total costs to account for<br>• Process cost reports<br>• Cost per unit of good units transferred out | Explain why the amount of normal spoilage is likely to vary from month to month. | In your own words, explain why Nancy is concerned about the company's spoilage. How might the managers use information about normal and abnormal spoilage? |

**EXHIBIT 6.14**
Costs of Spoilage
and Quality

| Costs of Spoilage | Quality Costs to Prevent and Detect Spoilage |
| --- | --- |
| • Direct materials and conversion costs wasted<br>• Rework costs<br>• Loss of contribution margin for units that cannot be sold<br>• Disposal of spoiled units that cannot be reworked<br>• Warranty costs to repair or replace defective units sold<br>• Defective product return costs<br>• Loss of product quality reputation, leading to lower future revenues | • Labor and other resources to inspect:<br>　—Raw materials when purchased<br>　—Units during/after production<br>• Designing and implementing quality process improvements<br>• Preventive equipment maintenance<br>• Higher prices for raw materials and for ensuring high quality<br>• Higher labor costs for hiring and training qualified employees |

## ■ Quality-Related Costs

When manufactured products are spoiled, the organization loses the resources used to create the spoiled units as well as the potential contribution margin that might have been earned from selling a good product. To minimize spoilage losses, managers often expend additional resources to rework defective units. For example, if the metal racks are improperly installed in Premier Plastic's assembly department, the racks in the spoiled units could be taken out and then the unit could be sent back through the process for reworking. The cost of rework is usually not tracked separately. Because reworked units go through processes twice, they use more resources than good units. The costs for the extra use of resources is allocated to all of the units produced. Accordingly, rework costs cannot be easily tracked and monitored.

Managers also implement procedures to reduce or eliminate the occurrence of spoilage. Sometimes, however, spoiled units are not detected and are instead sold to customers. Sales of defective units lead to additional costs such as warranty expenditures and customer dissatisfaction.

Exhibit 6.14 provides a summary of the various types of spoilage and quality-related costs. Although some of these costs are impossible to measure, they could be large, making the difference between an organization's success or failure.

Managers make trade-offs between the costs spent to ensure quality and the costs of spoilage. Some managers adopt a strategy of achieving low or zero defect rates. **Motorola**, for example, developed a Six Sigma defect policy (limiting defects to no more than 3.4 defective parts per million). Motorola's managers believe that the costs to ensure high quality are lower than the costs of manufacturing and selling defective units.

CHAPTER REFERENCE

The opportunity costs of spoilage and other issues related to product quality are discussed in Chapter 5.

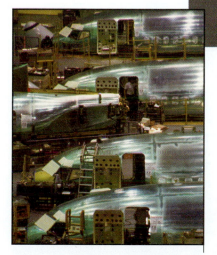

### FOCUS ON ETHICAL DECISION MAKING
### Cost Overruns at Boeing

During 2002, The Boeing Company settled, without admitting guilt, a securities fraud lawsuit. The lawsuit which was settled for $92.5 million, claimed that the company had improperly failed to report abnormal production losses on its income statement during the first half of 1997. The company's production had been out of control. The company's audit firm, Deloitte & Touche, notified the board of directors' audit committee that the company experienced negative trends during 1996 in "overtime, parts shortages, rework, defective parts, and out-of-sequence work" (Holmes and France, 2002, p. 213).

In most companies, production problems of this nature would have been reflected in inventory and then in cost of goods sold as units were sold. However, Boeing uses a practice called program accounting, a long-term standard costing system. Instead of assigning actual costs to each plane built, the company allocates an expected cost. Actual product costs are accumulated in a cost pool that is recorded as an asset. The asset is reduced for costs

*(continued)*

allocated to planes built. However, no adjustment is made each period for the amount of cost that has been underapplied or overapplied. Instead, the company depends on the reliability of its long-term cost estimates. Boeing uses this accounting method because it experiences a learning curve when it launches a new type of plane. The company expects higher production costs early in a program and lower production costs later. Thus, program accounting allows the company to allocate an average cost to planes throughout the life of a program.

As production problems grew, Boeing's managers estimated during May 1997 that total production costs would exceed estimates by $1 billion. The lawsuit claimed that the abnormal costs should have been recognized during the second quarter of 1997, similar to the treatment for abnormal spoilage presented in this chapter. However, Boeing's lawyer argued that the costs were typical for periods in which production levels were unusually high and that costs were expected to even out over the life of the project (Holmes and France 2002). The company ultimately announced an abnormal production loss in October 1997, when production on two product lines was temporarily halted.

Why should it matter whether the loss was reported in May versus October of 1997? In August 1997, Boeing completed its acquisition of McDonnell-Douglas and paid through a stock swap. According to Holmes and France (2002), "If investors had understood the scope of the problems, the stock would probably have tumbled and the McDonnell deal—a stock swap that hinged on Boeing's ability to maintain a lofty share price—would have been jeopardized."

Sources: S. Holmes and M. France, "Boeing's Secret: Did the Aircraft Giant Exploit Accounting Rules to Conceal a Huge Factory Snafu?" *Business Week*, May 20, 2002, pp. 110–120; and Boeing Company Annual Report for the year ended December 31, 2002, available under Investor Relations at www.boeing.com.

### Practice Ethical Decision Making

In Chapter 1, we learned about a process for making ethical decisions (Exhibit 1.11). You can address the following questions for this ethical dilemma to improve your skills for making ethical decisions. Think about your answers to these questions and discuss them with others.

| Ethical Decision-Making Process | Questions to Consider about This Ethical Dilemma |
| --- | --- |
| Identify ethical problems as they arise. | Was Boeing's delay in recognizing losses for its 777 program an ethical issue? Why or why not? |
| Objectively consider the well-being of others and society when exploring alternatives. | Describe a McDonnell-Douglas shareholder's viewpoint and a Boeing shareholder's viewpoint about whether Boeing should have recognized the losses earlier. What assumptions lie behind each viewpoint? |
| Clarify and apply ethical values when choosing a course of action. | When managers are faced with long-term uncertainties about their costs such as in this situation, what criteria should they use to decide how to report costs publicly? What values did you use to arrive at the solution? |
| Work toward ongoing improvement of personal and organizational ethics. | How might Boeing continuously improve its public reporting of product costs? |

## USES AND LIMITATIONS OF PROCESS COSTING INFORMATION

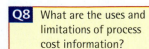

**Q8** What are the uses and limitations of process cost information?

Process costing systems measure the cost of products, primarily for mass-produced goods. The product costs are used to value inventory and cost of goods sold for external reports such as financial statements and income tax returns. They are also used by managers to monitor operations and develop estimates of future costs for decision making. When managers use process costing information, they need to be aware that it measures the costs of processes, which are then allocated to individual units. Thus, process costing is useful for measuring and monitoring processes. However, process costing is also subject to a number of limitations.

## ■ Monitoring Process Quality and Costs

An organization's profitability and long-term success often depend on the ability of managers to control processes and costs. Organizations frequently compete based on both product quality and cost. Managers use process cost information to help them evaluate whether production processes are operating as expected. They compare actual process costs to budgets, standards, or prior periods to identify potential production problems. For example, in Premier Plastics (Part 3), units were spoiled during July when an employee improperly programmed the molding equipment. This type of event causes actual costs to be higher than expected. If the managers had not already been aware of this production problem, the calculation of process costs at the end of the month would have alerted them to it.

Managers do not rely on process costing systems alone to monitor quality and cost. They also implement quality control systems, and they separately monitor resource use such as direct materials and direct labor. Quality systems can include inspection to identify spoiled units. Information about normal and abnormal spoilage can then be integrated into the process costing system to help managers measure and monitor the cost of resources wasted due to spoilage.

## ■ Process Costing Information and Decision Making

Product costs developed in a process costing system are average costs and might not adequately represent relevant costs for many types of decisions such as product pricing, outsourcing, product emphasis, or special orders. Sometimes process costing systems can be modified to do a better job of providing managers with estimates of relevant information, such as marginal (or incremental) cost per unit. For example, conversion costs could be divided into fixed and variable cost pools. Managers could then estimate marginal cost using the direct material cost per unit plus the variable conversion cost per unit. Production costing systems often include multiple cost pools representing different activities in the production process. More precise categorizations of cost improve the ability of managers to monitor operations as well as to estimate information for decisions.

## ■ Uncertainties and Mismeasurement of Cost Flows

It is rarely possible to determine exactly how costs are incurred during process costing. For example, in the molding department at Premier Plastics, more labor might be used during the beginning of the process when plastic ingredients are added and at the end of the process when units are turned out of the molds. Equipment and electricity use might be greater during the middle of the processing. However, it is difficult to exactly measure how and when costs such as labor, equipment depreciation, maintenance, and utilities are incurred. Accordingly, at least some mismeasurement typically occurs in the allocation of costs in a process costing system.

Also, mismeasurement occurs when accounting for spoilage. Normal spoilage is based on an estimate. Any errors in identifying normal spoilage quantities automatically cause mismeasurement in abnormal spoilage. Therefore, abnormal spoilage costs may be overestimated or underestimated, with an opposite mismeasurement in the cost of good units.

Mismeasurement is likely to be greatest in organizations that have little experience producing a product. Over time, greater knowledge is gained about production processes, and the cost allocations become more accurate. However, little benefit may come from developing an accounting system to more accurately allocate process costs. Often, the simple assumptions used throughout this chapter provide sufficiently accurate costs.

## ■ Work in Process Units at Different Stages of Completion

At the end of each period, the percentage of completion for work in process needs to be estimated. Depending on the process, all of the units in work in process inventories might be

---

[8]British Plastics Federation, "Comparative Production Costs for a Typical Component," available at www.bpf.co.uk/.
[9]Clay Roof Tile Council, "Interesting Facts—Did You Know?" under "Production Process," available at www.clayroof.co.uk.

at different stages of completion. For example, in the assembly department at Premier Plastics, some units of WIP will have the rough edges removed, but still be awaiting smoothing. Some will have been smoothed, but await the next step within assembly. Others will have the metal framework added, but await final paint and trim work.

When work is at many different stages of completion, estimating the average percentage of completion for ending inventories involves some guesswork. However, these estimates affect the equivalent unit costs for both the current and next period. If the percentage of completion is overestimated this period, the number of units in the denominator is too large, causing cost per equivalent unit to be too low this period. Because ending WIP is completed during the next period, an overestimate this period will cause an underestimate of the work performed next period. If ending inventories are a small part of the total costs allocated this period, inaccurate estimates are less of a problem. But if ending inventories are relatively large, inaccurate estimates could distort process cost reports this period and next period.

# SUMMARY

## Q1 How Are Costs Assigned to Mass-Produced Products?

### Cost Flow in Process Costing

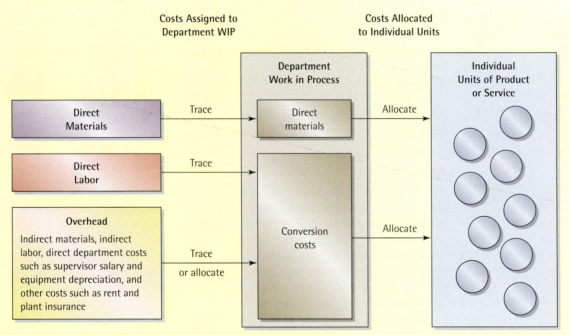

### Steps for Preparing a Process Cost Report

1. Summarize total costs to account for.
2. Summarize total physical and equivalent units.
3. Compute cost per equivalent unit.
4. Account for cost of units completed and cost of ending WIP.

## Q2 What Are Equivalent Units, and How Do They Relate to the Production Process?

### Equivalent Units
Measure of the resources used in partially completed units relative to the resources needed to complete the units.

### Equivalent Units and Pattern of Cost Flow
Direct Materials:
   –Added at the beginning of the process
   –Added during the process

Conversion Costs:
   –Incurred evenly throughout the process
   –Incurred unevenly

Identification of Spoiled Units:
   –Inspection at the end of the process
   –Inspection during the process

## Q3 How Is the Weighted Average Method Used in Process Costing?

### Weighted Average Method
Costs from beginning WIP (performed last period) are averaged with costs incurred during the current period and then allocated to units completed and ending WIP.

### Calculation of Cost per Equivalent Unit
$$\frac{\text{Beginning WIP} + \text{Current period costs}}{\text{Equivalent units for total work}}$$

## Q4 How Is the FIFO Method Used in Process Costing?

### First-in, First-out (FIFO) Method
The current period's costs are used to allocate cost to work performed this period.

### Calculation of Cost per Equivalent Unit
$$\frac{\text{Current period costs}}{\text{Equivalent units for work performed this period}}$$

## Q5 What Alternative Methods Are Used for Mass Production?

### Adaptations of Traditional Process Costing
Match equivalent units calculations to actual process.

Separate conversion costs into multiple pools.

### Standard Costing

### Alternative Production Systems
Just-in-time

Hybrid costing systems and operation costing

## Q6 How Is Process Costing Performed for Multiple Production Departments?

### Transferred-In Costs
Costs of processing performed in a previous department

Transferred-in costs are pooled separately from other costs.

## Q7 How Are Spoilage Costs Handled in Process Costing?

### Normal Spoilage
Definition: Defective units that arise as part of regular operations
Accounting: Cost of normal spoilage is allocated to good units produced

### Abnormal Spoilage
Definition: Spoilage that is not part of everyday operations
Accounting: Cost of abnormal spoilage is recorded as a loss for the period

## Q8 What Are the Uses and Limitations of Process Cost Information?

### Uses of Process Cost Information
- Measure costs of mass-produced products
- Assign costs to inventory and cost of goods sold for financial statements and income tax returns
- Monitor operations and costs
- Develop estimates of future costs for decision making
- Analyze the costs and benefits of quality improvements
- Identify potential areas for process improvements

### Uncertainties and Mismeasurement in Process Costing
- Actual cost flows might not be known:
  - When are direct materials added?
  - When are conversion costs incurred?
  - How complete are the units in ending work in process?
- What amount of spoilage is normal?
- How achievable are standard costs?

### KEY TO SYMBOLS
**e** This question requires students to extend knowledge beyond the applications shown in the textbook.

**1** This question requires Step 1 skills (**Identifying**) in Steps for Better Thinking (Exhibit 1.10).

**2** This question requires Step 2 skills (**Exploring**) in Steps for Better Thinking (Exhibit 1.10).

**3** This question requires Step 3 skills (**Prioritizing**) in Steps for Better Thinking (Exhibit 1.10).

**4** This question requires Step 4 skills (**Envisioning**) in Steps for Better Thinking (Exhibit 1.10).

# Self-Study Problems

## Self-Study Problem 1 Weighted Average and FIFO Process Cost Reports

**Q1, Q3, Q4**

Evergreen Kit Company produces kits for plastic airplanes and car models. The company uses process costing to assign costs to its inventory. The company always used the weighted average method. Jussi, the company's new accountant, is thinking about recommending a change to the first-in, first-out (FIFO) method. He plans to prepare inventory cost reports for March using both methods so that he can compare the results.

The company has only one production department. Direct materials are introduced at the beginning of the process, and conversion costs are incurred evenly throughout the manufacturing process. Once each unit is completed, it is transferred to finished goods inventory. Jussi collected the following data for the month of March:

| | | |
|---|---:|---:|
| Beginning inventory: | | |
| Work in process (40% complete) | | 10,000 units |
| Costs: | | |
| Direct material | $ 8,000 | |
| Conversion costs | 2,220 | |
| Total cost of beginning WIP | $10,220 | |
| Units completed and transferred out during March | | 48,000 units |
| Units started during March | | 40,000 units |
| Ending WIP inventory (50% complete) | | 2,000 units |
| Direct material cost used during March | $44,000 | |
| Conversion costs incurred during March | $36,000 | |

**REQUIRED:**

A. Using the weighted average method:
1. Summarize total costs to account for.
2. Summarize total physical units and equivalent units.
3. Compute costs per equivalent unit.
4. Prepare a process costing report.

B. Following the same procedures, prepare a process cost report using the FIFO method.

❶ C. Prepare a table to compare the total costs and cost per equivalent unit under weighted average and FIFO. Provide possible explanations for the difference between FIFO and weighted average costs.

## Solution to Self-Study Problem 1

### A. Weighted average
#### 1. Summarize total costs to account for

| | Direct Materials | Conversion Costs | Total Cost |
|---|---:|---:|---:|
| Beginning WIP | $ 8,000 | $ 2,220 | $10,220 |
| Current period costs | 44,000 | 36,000 | 80,000 |
| Total costs to account for | $52,000 | $38,220 | $90,220 |

#### 2. Summarize total physical units and equivalent units

Because direct materials are added at the beginning of the process, all 2,000 WIP units are 100% complete with respect to direct materials. However, these 2,000 units are only 50% complete with respect to conversion costs, which translates to 1,000 equivalent units in ending WIP for conversion costs (50% × 2,000).

| | | | Work This Period | | | |
|---|---:|---:|---:|---:|---:|---:|
| | Beginning WIP (40%) | Complete Beginning WIP (60%) | Start and Complete | Start Ending WIP (50%) | Total Work Performed | Total to Account for |
| Physical units | 10,000 | 0 | 38,000 | 2,000 | 40,000 | 50,000 |
| Equivalent units: | | | | | | Total Work |
| Direct materials | 10,000 | 0 | 38,000 | 2,000 | 40,000 | 50,000 |
| Conversion costs | 4,000 | 6,000 | 38,000 | 1,000 | 45,000 | 49,000 |

#### 3. Compute costs per equivalent unit

$$\text{Weighted average:} \quad \frac{\text{Beginning WIP + Current period costs}}{\text{Equivalent units for total work}}$$

| | | |
|---|---:|---:|
| Direct materials | $52,000 ÷ 50,000 | $1.04 |
| Conversion costs | $38,220 ÷ 49,000 | 0.78 |
| Total cost per equivalent unit | | $1.82 |

**4. Prepare a process cost report (i.e., account for cost of units completed and cost of ending WIP)**

| | Computations | Units | Costs |
|---|---|---|---|
| Completed and transferred out | (10,000 + 38,000) × $1.82 | 48,000 | $87,360 |
| Ending WIP | | 2,000 | |
|     Direct materials | 2,000 × $1.04 | | 2,080 |
|     Conversion costs | 1,000 × $0.78 | | 780 |
|         Total ending WIP | | | 2,860 |
| **Total accounted for** | | 50,000 | $90,220 |

## B. FIFO

Steps 1 and 2 are identical to the schedules presented in part (A). Because the problem did not provide separate beginning WIP costs for weighted average and FIFO, we use the same beginning WIP values for parts (A) and (B).

**3. Compute cost per equivalent unit**

$$\text{FIFO:} \quad \frac{\text{Current period costs}}{\text{Equivalent units for work performed this period}}$$

| | | |
|---|---|---|
| Direct materials | $44,000 ÷ 40,000 | $1.10 |
| Conversion costs | $36,000 ÷ 45,000 | 0.80 |
|     Total cost per equivalent unit | | $1.90 |

**4. Prepare a FIFO Cost Report (i.e., account for cost of units completed and cost of ending WIP)**

First-In, First-Out

| | Computation | Units | Costs |
|---|---|---|---|
| Beginning WIP | | 10,000 | $10,220 |
| Costs to complete beginning WIP: | | | |
|     Direct materials | 0 × $1.10 | | 0 |
|     Conversion costs | 6,000 × $0.80 | | 4,800 |
|         Total costs added this period | | | 4,800 |
| Total cost of beginning WIP transferred out | | 10,000 | 15,020 |
| New units started, completed, and transferred out | 38,000 × $1.90 | 38,000 | 72,200 |
| Total units completed and transferred out | | 48,000 | 87,220 |
| Ending WIP: | | 2,000 | |
|     Direct materials | 2,000 × $1.10 | | 2,200 |
|     Conversion costs | 1,000 × $0.80 | | 800 |
|         Total ending WIP cost | | | 3,000 |
| **Total accounted for** | | 50,000 | $90,220 |

## C. Compare weighted average and FIFO

The following table compares total costs and equivalent unit costs under weighted average and FIFO. Remember, the total costs accounted for are equal in this problem ONLY because we used the same beginning WIP costs for both methods.

| | Weighted Average | FIFO |
|---|---|---|
| Costs transferred out | $87,360 | $87,220 |
| Ending WIP | 2,860 | 3,000 |
|     Total costs accounted for | $90,220 | $90,220 |
| | | |
| Costs per equivalent unit: | | |
|     Direct materials | $1.04 | $1.10 |
|     Conversion costs | 0.78 | 0.80 |
|         Total | $1.82 | $1.90 |

The weighted average costs include both current period and prior period costs, while the FIFO costs include only current period costs. Because the costs per unit for FIFO are higher than for weighted average, average production costs during March were higher than during the previous month. An increase occurred in both direct materials and conversion costs. These increases might have been caused by inflation in the cost of resources, a decline in production volume, production inefficiencies, or other factors.

> **REVIEW** Use the exercises in the following boxes in the chapter to review key terms and key techniques, analyze chapter illustrations, improve your learning of new concepts, and practice ethical decision making:
>
> Guide Your Learning 6.1: Key Terms (p. 219)          Guide Your Learning 6.4: Key Terms (p. 236)
>
> Guide Your Learning 6.2: Premier Plastics (Part 1) (p. 228)          Guide Your Learning 6.5: Premier Plastics (Part 3) (p. 238)
>
> Guide Your Learning 6.3: Premier Plastics (Part 2) (p. 232)          Focus on Ethical Decision Making: Cost Overruns at Boeing (p. 239)

## QUESTIONS

**6.1** Under what conditions will weighted average and FIFO process costing consistently produce similar equivalent unit costs?

**6.2** Under what conditions could a process complete more units during the period than it started?

**6.3** "We treat spoiled units as fully completed regardless of when the spoiled units are detected. This method makes unit costing much simpler." What is wrong with this approach?

**6.4** In a continuous processing situation (such as an oil refinery), the beginning and ending WIP inventories are frequently the same. How does this simplify determination of equivalent units completed?

**6.5** Although process costing appears to use precise measurements, it requires several estimates. Discuss where judgment is needed in collecting information for process costing.

**6.6** Suppose the percent completion of ending WIP is overestimated at the end of year 1. How does this measurement error affect the process costing results in year 1 and year 2?

**6.7** Explain the difference between the weighted average and FIFO methods for process costing. Explain why an organization might choose one method over the other.

**6.8** Describe the differences between mass production and custom production of goods and services. Explain how these differences influence the costing method.

**6.9** A department within a processing operation has some finished units physically on hand. Should they be counted as completed units or as ending inventory in the department? Explain.

**6.10** In processes involving pipeline operations or assembly line operations, if the pipeline or assembly line is always full, then beginning and ending WIP inventories are always 50% complete with regard to conversion costs. Explain.

**6.11** When units are transferred from one department to another, how are normal spoilage costs recorded?

**6.12** A firm has one machine through which is drawn a standard type of wire to make nails. With minor adjustments, different sized nails are produced with different sized wire. Would you recommend that the firm employ job or process costing methods?

**6.13** List two factors that could affect managers' choices for the number of times and points in processing to inspect units.

**6.14** List three factors that managers might consider in deciding whether to expend resources to reduce spoilage.

## EXERCISES

**6.15** **Equivalent units under weighted average and FIFO** Francisco's mass-produces folding chairs in Mexico. All direct materials are added at the beginning of production, and conversion costs are incurred evenly throughout production. The following production information is for the month of May:

Q2, Q3, Q4

|  | Physical Units |
|---|---|
| Beginning WIP (40% complete) | 9,000 |
| Started in May | 50,000 |
| Completed in May | 47,000 |
| Ending WIP (30% complete) | 12,000 |

**REQUIRED:**

**A.** Calculate the equivalent units used to calculate cost per unit under the weighted average method.

**B.** Calculate the equivalent units used to calculate cost per unit under the FIFO method.

**6.16** **Equivalent unit cost under weighted average and FIFO** Fine Fans mass-produces small electric fans in Taiwan for home use. All direct materials are added at the beginning of production,

Q2, Q3, Q4

and conversion costs are incurred evenly throughout production. The following production information is for the month of October (currency is National Taiwan dollars):

|  | Physical Units |
|---|---|
| Started in October | 100,000 |
| Completed in October | 94,000 |
| Ending WIP (60% complete) | 15,000 |
| Beginning WIP (20% complete) | 9,000 |

|  | Costs |
|---|---|
| Beginning work in process costs: |  |
| Direct materials | NT$18,000 |
| Conversion costs | 36,000 |
| Costs added this period: |  |
| Direct materials | 100,000 |
| Conversion costs | 200,000 |

**REQUIRED:**   **A.** Calculate the equivalent cost per unit using the weighted average method.
**B.** Calculate the equivalent cost per unit using the FIFO method.

**6.17**
**Q7**
**Journal entry for abnormal spoilage** Rejected castings in a foundry are treated as spoilage. During the current period, 80 castings (costing $200 each to produce) were spoiled and sold at a net realizable value of $25 each.

**REQUIRED:** Prepare the journal entry, assuming that the spoilage was abnormal.

**6.18**
**Q7**
**Journal entry for normal and abnormal spoilage** A department started 10,000 units last month, and the total cost per equivalent unit was $5.00. The department completed and transferred 8,000 units to finished goods inventory. There were no beginning or ending WIP inventories.

**REQUIRED:** e **A.** Calculate the number and cost of spoiled units.
**B.** Prepare journal entries for the spoilage if it is all considered normal.
**C.** Prepare journal entries for the spoilage if it is all considered abnormal.

**6.19**
**Q2, Q3**
**Cost per equivalent unit under weighted average** Felix and Sons is a toy maker and produces Flying Flingbats, a soft foam rubber weapon. All direct materials are added at the beginning of production, and conversion costs are incurred evenly throughout production. Conversion was 75% complete for the 8,000 units in WIP on December 1 and 50% complete for the 6,000 units in WIP on December 31. During the month, 12,000 Flingbats were completed and transferred out as finished goods. Following is a summary of the costs for the period:

|  | Direct Materials | Conversion Costs |
|---|---|---|
| Work in process, December 1 | $19,200 | $ 7,200 |
| Costs added in December | 31,200 | 21,600 |

**REQUIRED:** Using the weighted average method, prepare a schedule calculating the total cost per equivalent unit for April.

**6.20**
**Q1, Q3**
**Account for costs under weighted average** Refer to the information presented in Exercise 6.19.

**REQUIRED:** Prepare a process cost report under the weighted average method.

**6.21**
**Q1, Q4**
**Cost per equivalent unit under FIFO** Refer to the information presented in Exercise 6.19.

**REQUIRED:** Using the FIFO method, prepare a schedule calculating the cost per equivalent unit for April.

**6.22**
**Q1, Q4**
**Account for costs under FIFO** Refer to the information presented in Exercise 6.19.

**REQUIRED:** Prepare a process cost report under the FIFO method.

**6.23**
Q1, Q3, Q4
**Costs and journal entries under weighted average and FIFO** Humphrey Manufacturing produces automobile parts and batteries. All direct materials are added at the beginning of production, and conversion costs are incurred evenly throughout production. The following production information is for the month of April:

Units:
    Work in process, March 31: 6,000 units, (40% complete)
    Units started in April: 42,000
    Units completed during April: 40,000
    Work in process April 30: 8,000 units, (25% complete)

| Costs in beginning WIP: | |
|---|---:|
| Direct materials | $ 7,500 |
| Conversion costs | 2,125 |
| Total | $ 9,625 |

| Costs added this period: | |
|---|---:|
| Direct materials added in April | $ 70,000 |
| Conversion costs added in April | 42,500 |
| Total | $112,500 |

REQUIRED:
**A.** Using the weighted average method, assign costs to production for this period.
**B.** Using the FIFO method, assign costs to production for this period.
**C.** Write out the journal entries for either the weighted average or FIFO methods.

**6.24**
Q1
**Process costing for a service** Your father is on the board of directors of a not-for-profit organization, For Seniors Only. One of its services is to prepare simple tax returns for senior citizens. Each return takes about the same amount of time and effort. Student volunteers from a local university help prepare returns. A small staff of part-time accountants is employed throughout the tax season. The busiest time is just before the returns are due in April, when student volunteers are busy with midterms. Because of this schedule conflict, additional help is hired for several weeks. To predict costs for the month of April, the board would like to know the average cost for a tax return prepared by paid employees. Some returns will be in process at the beginning and end of each month.

REQUIRED:
**A.** Is process costing appropriate in this situation? Explain your answer.
e **B.** What information do you need to determine the cost of preparing tax returns for the month of April?
**C.** List and explain the procedures you would use to determine the average cost per tax return prepared by paid employees.

# PROBLEMS

**6.25**
Q1, Q4, Q6
**FIFO process costing, transferred-in costs, direct materials added during process** Benton Industries began the year with 15,000 units in department 3 beginning WIP. These units were one-third complete, with $40,470 transferred-in cost for prior departments' work and $14,322 for department 3 conversion costs. During the year, 93,000 additional units were transferred into department 3 from department 2 at a cost of $224,130. Department 3 incurred materials costs of $166,840 and conversion costs of $315,228 during the year. Department 3 ended the year with 11,000 units in WIP ending. These units were 40% complete.

REQUIRED: Determine the cost of goods completed and the cost of ending WIP in department 3 using FIFO process costing. Assume that conversion costs are incurred evenly and materials are added in department 3 when units are 60% complete.

**6.26**
Q1, Q3, Q7
**Process costing under weighted average, spoilage, journal entries** Victoria's Closet massproduces luxurious sleepwear for women. Consider the following data for the Flannel Night Gown Department for the month of January. All direct materials are added at the beginning of production in the department, and conversion costs are incurred evenly throughout production. Inspection occurs when production is 100% completed. Normal spoilage is 6,600 units for the month.

|  | Physical Units |
|---|---|
| Beginning WIP (25% complete) | 11,000 |
| Started during January | 74,000 |
| Total to account for | 85,000 |
|  |  |
| Good units completed and transferred out during current period: |  |
| From beginning work in process | 11,000 |
| Started and completed | 50,000 |
| Spoiled units | 8,000 |
| Ending WIP (75% complete) | 16,000 |
| Total accounted for | 85,000 |

|  | Costs |
|---|---|
| Beginning WIP: |  |
| Direct materials | $ 220,000 |
| Conversion costs | 30,000 |
| Total beginning WIP | 250,000 |
| Costs added during current period: |  |
| Direct materials | 1,480,000 |
| Conversion costs | 942,000 |
| Costs to account for | $2,672,000 |

**REQUIRED:**
**A.** Prepare a process cost report using the weighted average method.
**B.** Write out the journal entries for this period's work.

**6.27** **Process costing under FIFO, spoilage, standard costing** Refer to the information provided in
**Q1, Q4, Q5, Q7** Problem 6.26.

**REQUIRED:**
**A.** Prepare a process cost report using the FIFO method.
**B.** Explain how a standard cost report would differ from the FIFO report you just produced.
❷ **C.** Under what circumstances would a standard cost report be preferable to a FIFO cost report? Explain your answer.

**6.28** **Abnormal spoilage, quality savings, opportunity costs** Kim Mills produces yardage for knitwear.
**Q7** The knit cloth is sold by the bolt. November data for its milling process follow. Beginning WIP was 20,000 units. Good units completed and transferred out during current period totaled 90,000. Ending WIP was 17,000 units. Inspection occurs at the 100% stage of completion regarding conversion costs, which are incurred evenly throughout the process. Total spoilage is 7,000 units. Normal spoilage is 3,600 units. Direct materials are added at the beginning of the process.

**REQUIRED:**
**A.** Compute abnormal spoilage in units.
ⓔ **B.** Assume that the manufacturing cost of a spoiled unit is $1,000. Compute the amount of potential savings if all spoilage were eliminated, assuming that all other costs would be unaffected.
❷ **C.** Discuss the opportunity costs of spoilage and why it might be important to require low defect rates in a manufacturing process.

**6.29** **Spoilage with inspection point other than 100%** Use the information for Kim Mills from Prob-
**Q7** lem 6.28. Now, assume that inspection occurs when units are 40% complete.

**REQUIRED:** ⓔ **A.** Calculate total spoilage for conversion cost calculations.
**B.** If normal spoilage is 1,800 units instead of 3,600, what is abnormal spoilage this period for conversion costs?
❷ **C.** List several costs and benefits from moving inspection to an earlier position in the manufacturing process.

**6.30** **Process costing under weighted average and FIFO, choice of method** Red Dog Products manu-
**Q1, Q3, Q4, Q8** factures toys for dogs and cats. The most popular toy is a small ball that dispenses tiny treats and is placed within a larger ball. To get the treats, dogs must roll the balls around until the treats fall out.

These balls are mass-produced from plastic. Direct materials are introduced at the beginning of the process, and conversion costs are incurred evenly throughout the manufacturing process. Once each unit is completed, it is transferred to finished goods. Data for the month of March are as follows:

| Beginning WIP (30% complete): | |
|---|---|
| Direct material | $25,000 |
| Conversion costs | 3,000 |
| Total | $28,000 |

| | |
|---|---|
| Units started during March | 80,000 units |
| Units completed and transferred out during March | 88,000 units |
| Ending WIP inventory (50% complete) | 12,000 units |
| Direct material cost added during March | $220,000 |
| Conversion costs added during March | $74,000 |

**REQUIRED:**
A. Prepare a process cost report using the weighted average method.
B. Prepare a process cost report using the FIFO method.
❷ C. What factors might affect the cost accountant's choice of process costing method? Explain.

**6.31**
**Q7**

**Normal and abnormal spoilage, quality improvements** Empire Forging produces small plumbing valves. January data for its valve-making process follow. Beginning WIP was 60,000 units. Good units completed and transferred out during the current period totaled 420,000. Ending WIP was 68,000 units. Inspection occurs at the 100% stage of completion with respect to conversion costs, which are incurred evenly throughout the process. Total spoilage is 36,000 units. Normal spoilage is 12,600 units. Direct materials are added at the beginning of the process.

**REQUIRED:**
A. Compute abnormal spoilage in units for January.
B. Compute the number of units started in January.
❶ C. Calculate the percentage of units produced that is considered normal spoilage, and calculate the total percentage of units spoiled this period. List several potential business risks when spoilage rates increase dramatically.
❸ D. Provide arguments for the manager of the valve department about the trade-offs between investing in quality improvements and incurring the costs of undetected spoiled units.

**6.32**
**Q1, Q3, Q4, Q7**

**Process costing under weighted average and FIFO, spoilage, journal entries** The Rally Company operates under a process cost system using the weighted average method. All direct materials are added at the beginning of production in the department, and conversion costs are incurred evenly throughout production. Inspection occurs when production is 100% completed.

Following are data for July. All unfinished work at the end of July is 25% completed. The beginning inventory is 80% completed.

| Beginning inventories | |
|---|---|
| Direct materials | $ 4,000 |
| Conversion costs | 3,200 |
| Costs added during current period | |
| Direct materials | $36,000 |
| Conversion costs | 32,000 |
| Physical units | |
| Units in beginning inventory | 2,000 |
| Units started this month | 18,000 |
| Total units completed and transferred out | 14,800 |
| Normal spoilage | 1,000 |
| Abnormal spoilage | 1,000 |

**REQUIRED:**
A. Prepare a spreadsheet that uses a data input box and calculates information necessary for a weighted average process cost report and presents the cost report in an easily understood format.
B. Write out the journal entries for this period's work.
C. Copy the spreadsheet into a new range or new worksheet. If you use a new worksheet, highlight the tab and rename the worksheet "FIFO." Now alter the weighted average

*(continued)*

calculations so that the spreadsheet uses data from the input box to calculate the information necessary for a FIFO process cost report and presents the cost report in an easily understood format.

**❸ D.** Describe factors that would affect an accountant's choice of process costing method, and make a recommendation for a process costing method for Rally. Explain your choice.

**6.33**
Q1, Q3, Q4, Q6, Q7, Q8

**Choice of costing method, process cost report, transferred-in units, spoilage** Toddler Toys produces toy construction vehicles for young children. Plastic pieces are molded in the plastics department. These pieces are transferred to the assembly department, where direct materials are added after some assembly has been done. For example, plastic pieces of road graders are put together, then the blades and wheel assemblies are added, and finally some details are painted on the sides and back. The direct materials are added in the assembly department when the process is 75% complete. Beginning inventory is 80% complete and ending inventory is 25% complete. Following are data for August.

Beginning inventory costs for the assembly department:

| | |
|---|---|
| Transferred in | $4,000 |
| Direct materials | 2,000 |
| Conversion costs | 1,600 |
| Total cost | $7,600 |

Costs incurred in the assembly department during current period:

| | |
|---|---|
| Transferred in | $36,000 |
| Direct materials | 18,000 |
| Conversion costs | 16,000 |
| Total cost | $70,000 |

Physical units in the assembly department:

| | |
|---|---|
| Units in beginning inventory | 2,000 |
| Units started this month | 18,000 |
| Total units completed and transferred out | 14,800 |
| Normal spoilage | 1,000 (100% complete) |
| Abnormal spoilage | 1,000 (100% complete) |

**REQUIRED:** **❸ A.** Choose a process costing method for the assembly department. Explain your choice and describe its pros and cons.

**B.** Prepare a cost report using the method you chose in part (A).

**C.** Write out journal entries for the cost report you prepared in part (B).

**6.34**
Q1, Q8
ETHICS

**Costs of workplace health and safety** Britain's **Health and Safety Commission** (HSC) provides information and proposes regulations to protect workers against health and safety risks. In its Strategic Statement issued in June 2000, HSC established the following national targets, to be achieved by 2010:

- Reduce the number of working days lost per 100,000 workers from work-related injury and ill health by 30%
- Reduce the incidence rate of fatal and major injury incidents by 10%
- Reduce the incidence rate of cases of work-related ill health by 20%

To achieve these targets, the HSC's Strategic Plan for 2001/2004 places priority on reducing incidents in the following areas that have historically high risks:

- Falls from height
- Workplace transport accidents
- Musculoskeletal disorders
- Work-related stress, anxiety, and depression
- Construction injuries and ill health
- Agriculture injuries
- Health services accidents, violence, and sickness
- Slips and trips

SOURCE: "Health and Safety Commission Strategic Plan 2001/2004—Summary," available at www.hse.gov.uk/aboutus/plans/index.htm.

**REQUIRED:** **❶** **A.** Employers incur many costs because of health and safety issues, including:
- Lost worker time
- Employer-paid medical costs
- Training to replace workers who are ill or injured
- Record-keeping to comply with governmental regulation

How would each of these costs be recognized in a process costing system?

**❷** **B.** Who is responsible for workplace health and safety? Discuss the responsibilities for each of the following groups:
- Governments
- Employers
- Managers
- Workers
- Customers

**❸** **C.** What goal should an individual company establish for workplace health and safety? Should the goal be to meet government regulations? Should the goal be to experience zero health and safety incidents? Or is some other goal appropriate? What values did you use to arrive at your answer?

**6.35**
Q1, Q3, Q4, Q7

**Process costing under weighted average and FIFO, spoilage, rework** The accountant at Cellular Advantage needs to close the books at the end of January using the following information. Direct materials are added at the start of production. Conversion costs are incurred evenly throughout production. Inspection occurs when production is 75% completed. Normal spoilage is 13,200 units per month.

**Physical Units**

| | |
|---|---:|
| Work in process, beginning (30% complete) | 22,000 |
| Started during the month | 148,000 |
| Total units to account for | 170,000 |
| Good units completed and transferred out during current period: | |
| From beginning work in process | 22,000 |
| Started and completed | 100,000 |
| Total good units completed | 122,000 |
| Spoiled units | 16,000 |
| Work in process, ending (60% complete) | 32,000 |
| Total units accounted for | 170,000 |

**Costs**

| | |
|---|---:|
| Beginning inventory: | |
| Direct materials | $ 440,000 |
| Conversion costs | 60,000 |
| Total beginning inventory | 500,000 |
| Costs added during current period: | |
| Direct materials | 2,960,000 |
| Conversion costs | 1,884,000 |
| Total costs to account for | $5,344,000 |

**REQUIRED:** **ⓔ** **A.** Prepare a process cost report using the weighted average method.
**ⓔ** **B.** Prepare a process cost report using the FIFO method.
**❶** **C.** Explain why an organization might specify limits for normal spoilage, after which spoilage is considered abnormal.
**ⓔ** **D.** To reduce spoilage, units are sometimes reworked. How are rework costs recorded?

**6.36**
Q1, Q3, Q4, Q5, Q8

**Two departments, two periods, FIFO and weighted average, estimate accuracy** Rausher Industries began a new product line this year. Management wants a cost report for the current year and a budget for next year. The product requires processing in two departments. Materials are added at the beginning of the process in department 1. Department 2 finishes the product but adds no direct materials.

During the year work was begun on 12,000 units in department 1, and 9,000 of these units were transferred to department 2. The remaining 3,000 units were 60% complete with regard to conversion costs in department 1, which incurred $36,000 in material costs and $14,040 in conversion costs.

Department 2 completed and sent 7,000 units to the finished goods warehouse. It ended the period with 2,000 units 40% complete with regard to department 2's conversion costs, which were $32,760 for the period.

The plan for next year is to begin an additional 15,000 units in department 1. Management expects to finish the year with 5,000 units one-half converted in department 1. Department 2 is expected to complete 14,000 units, and its ending inventory is expected to be 70% complete. Materials are expected to be $48,600, and conversion costs for departments 1 and 2 are expected to be $14,545 and $59,075, respectively.

**REQUIRED:** Prepare cost reports for the current year and a budgeted cost report for next year assuming the firm uses the following:

    **A.** FIFO process costing.

    **B.** Weighted average process costing.

    ❷ **C.** The employee responsible for estimating the percentage completion had experience estimating completion percentages for one of Rausher's other product lines. However, she is wondering whether she could improve the accuracy of her estimates. A colleague in another department suggested that she consider using techniques such as timing one unit through each department and identifying points in the production process where units appear to be 25% complete, 50% complete, and so on.

        **1.** Comment on whether the suggested method is likely to provide an accurate estimate of work in process.

        **2.** List two advantages of improving the accuracy of the estimate. What might be a disadvantage?

☆ **6.37** **Comparison of actual to standard processing costs, use in bonus decisions** Tiffany Campbell
**Q5, Q8** is the cost accountant in a small manufacturing company, Computer Components, Inc. (CC). CC produces components for one of the large computer manufacturers. Its strategy is to provide highly reliable components at the lowest possible price. To help maintain cost competitiveness, Tiffany produces two process cost reports each month, one based on the FIFO method and the other based on the standard cost method. When the reports are complete, costs from the two systems are compared. If actual costs are under control (i.e., within the standard costs) for a particular division, the manager receives a small bonus. If costs have been under control throughout the year, a larger bonus is given at the end of December.

    This month Tiffany investigates the results for Kevin Meledrez's division. Actual direct material costs are higher than standard cost, so the equivalent unit cost is higher than the standard. When she speaks to Kevin about the direct material costs in his division, he argues that the standard cost needs to be changed because the current supplier has increased the cost of a particular part. Kevin believes that he should not be held responsible for costs that are not under his control; when prices change, the standard should also change.

    Tiffany asks Kevin whether he had investigated other vendors who sell the same part to see whether the price change was across the board for all vendors. Kevin says that he has used this vendor for a number of years and is satisfied with the quality and timeliness of delivery. He does not believe that another vendor would provide the same quality and service, so he does not want to consider changing suppliers at this time.

**REQUIRED:** The following questions will help you analyze the information for this problem. Do not turn in
**ANALYZE** your answers to these questions unless your professor asks you to do so.
**INFORMATION**

    ❶ **A.** Identify a variety of reasons why actual costs are likely to be different from standard costs for CC.

    ❷ **B.** Discuss whether Kevin would be likely to make the same argument about changing the standard if the supplier's price had decreased.

    ❷ **C.** Describe the pros and cons of changing vendors.

    ❷ **D.** Explain the benefit to the company of giving managers bonuses based on comparisons of actual to standard costs.

    ❷ **E.** Discuss the advantages and disadvantages of adopting a policy of adjusting the standard cost for changes in vendor prices.

**REQUIRED:** Suppose Tiffany asks for your advice. Turn in your answers to the following.
**WRITTEN**
**ASSIGNMENT**   ❸ **F.** Use the information you learned from the preceding analyses to write a memo to Tiffany with your recommendation. As you write the memo, consider information that Tiffany needs from you to help her make a final decision.

# BUILD YOUR PROFESSIONAL COMPETENCIES

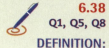

**6.38**
Q1, Q5, Q8

**DEFINITION:**

**Focus on Professional Competency: Reporting** *Process cost report content, preparation, and use; role of accountant* Review the following definition and elements for the Reporting competency.[10]

*Communicating the scope of work and findings or recommendations is an integral part of a professional service. An accounting professional in public practice might issue an audit or attestation report, recommendations for improved services, or tax or financial planning advice. An accounting professional in business, industry, or government might analyze operations or provide communications to the board of directors. Communicating clearly and objectively the work done and the resulting findings is critical to the value of the professional service. Some forms of communication are governed by professional standards (such as the form and content of the standard auditor's report or the required communications to audit committees) or law. Others are based on the service applied and the needs of those to whom the accounting professional reports.*

## ELEMENTS FOR THIS COMPETENCY INCLUDE

| Level 1 | Level 2 | Level 3 | Level 4 |
| --- | --- | --- | --- |
| 1. Lists types of information relevant to a given report | 2. Considers the pros and cons of alternative contents and formats in preparing written and oral presentations | 3. Using appropriate media, prepares reports with objectivity, conciseness, and clarity<br><br>4. Describes work performed and conclusions reached in a manner that enhances the reports' usefulness | 5. Serves as spokesperson for an organization<br><br>6 Continuously monitors and updates reports, as needed |

**REQUIRED:**

**❶ A.** Focus on competency element 1, which relates to relevant information for reports. Review the schedules used to create a process cost report. List the information used in this type of report. Also list information that is required to perform calculations needed for the report (e.g., the flow of costs in the production process).

**❷ B.** Focus on competency element 2, which addresses alternative ways to present reports. Which material in Chapter 6 addresses this competency element? Explain.

**❸ C.** Focus on competency element 3, which relates to report objectivity, conciseness, and clarity. Explain why these characteristics are important in preparing a process cost report.

**❸ D.** Focus on competency element 4, which relates to descriptions of work performed and conclusions reached. Suppose you are preparing a process cost report for the managers of a company. Describe how you would explain the work you performed to help non-accountant managers best use the information.

**❹ E.** Focus on competency element 5, which relates to serving as an organizational spokesperson. Refer to the Premier Plastics illustrations in Chapter 6. In what ways did the accountant serve as a spokesperson for her organization when preparing process cost reports and recommending accounting methods?

**F.** Focus on competency element 6, which addresses continuous improvement. Answer the following questions:

**❹ 1.** Explain ways in which the methods used to create process cost reports require monitoring and updating.

**❹ 2.** Explain how process cost reports can be used to monitor a company's operating performance.

**6.39**
Q1, Q5, Q8

**Integrating Across the Curriculum: Production Management** *Batch versus continuous processing, usefulness of process costing* Techtra makes electronic components used by other firms in a wide variety of end products. Initially the firm bid for any type of electronic assembly work that became available (mostly subcontract work from other firms experiencing temporary capacity problems). But over the years the firm narrowed its focus. It now produces essentially three products, although minor variations within each product line yield a large number of different models.

---

[10]The definition and elements are reprinted with permission from AICPA; copyright © 1978–2000 & 2003 by American Institute of Certified Public Accountants. The AICPA's Core Competency Framework can be accessed at eca.aicpaservices.org.

Each of the products goes through three separate operating departments: assembly, soldering, and testing. When an order is received, it goes to production scheduling. Personnel there schedule time in each of the three departments. The availability of parts usually determines when a job can be started in the assembly department. If parts are not in stock, they are usually received from suppliers within a week. On the appropriate day, the computerized scheduling program places the job on the assembly department's job list. Simultaneously, an electronic materials requisition goes to the stores department. Materials handling people then deliver the parts to the assembly department. The assembly operation is semiautomatic. When the department is ready to begin a new job, a worker inserts the appropriate guides into the equipment and adjusts the various settings. Parts are then loaded into the machines, which do the actual assembly. Because a worker keeps several machines running simultaneously, each order is processed using several (sometimes all) of the machines available in the department. Once the units for an order are assembled, an assembly department worker enters its completion in the computerized production system. The system then adds the job to the soldering department's job list. Materials handling personnel load assembled product onto racks and take them to the soldering department.

Soldering processes the jobs on a first-in, first-out basis unless production scheduling asks for priority treatment for a particular job. For each job the soldering machines must be set up for the appropriate product, but thereafter the operation is totally automatic. Once a job is completed, an entry is made in the production system, which adds it to the testing department's job list. The products are then reloaded onto racks and transported to the testing department.

By the time the products get to the testing department, many of the jobs are near or past their promised delivery date. Thus, the production scheduling system directs the testing department to work on jobs in the order of promised delivery date. Normally the firm expects 3% to 5% of the products to be defective and plans its lot size for each order accordingly. However, from time to time an entire order must be scrapped due to faulty assembly or soldering on every unit. When an order is scrapped, it is noted in the production system, and a rush replacement order is sent to the assembly department. Completed jobs that pass testing are immediately shipped to customers.

Workers in the assembly, soldering, and testing departments each enter information in the production system detailing the amount of time spent working on specific jobs. This information, plus the materials requisitions, are used by the cost accounting system to track the cost of each job. The cost accounting system allocates departmental overhead to each job using overhead allocation rates based on budgeted overhead costs and budgeted hours for each department. General factory overhead, which includes production scheduling, materials handling, property taxes, and so on, is charged to each job based on total materials costs. Within each of the three product types, the average cost per unit varies primarily with the size of each job order because of setup costs. The cost data are used to update the firm's pricing sheets and to determine the efficiency with which each order was produced.

Management is considering a change in the organization of the plant floor. Instead of being arranged in functional departments, they are considering arranging manufacturing "cells" for each product; that is, they would establish clusters of assembly machines, soldering machines, and test equipment. Each cluster would be dedicated to making only one type of product. Under this arrangement, when an order is processed, individual units would proceed one by one through the assembly, soldering, and test equipment in the appropriate cell. Most jobs would be completed within a day, but large jobs would sometimes take up to a week. Management is also considering a change in the way it orders parts from suppliers. The company would place orders for each job, requesting delivery of parts on the day production is scheduled to begin.

**REQUIRED:**
**A.** Describe how the proposed changes would likely affect each of the following:

❶ 1. Size of work in process and raw materials inventories
❶ 2. Material handling and machine setup costs
❷ 3. Cost of defective units
❷ 4. Ratio of units produced to units ordered
❶ 5. Production scheduling costs and machine utilization rates
❷ 6. Average cost per unit of product
❷ 7. Ability to fulfill a customer's rush order

**B.** Assuming the managers adopt the proposed manufacturing changes:

❷ 1. What would be the advantages of adopting a process costing system?
❷ 2. The company would no longer carry significant inventories. How would this change affect the cost accounting?

# Activity-Based Costing and Management

## ▶In Brief

Activity-based costing (ABC) is a system that assigns costs to the specific activities performed in a manufacturing or service delivery process. ABC attempts to trace costs more accurately to products or other cost objects than traditional costing methods. The costs of the various activities then become the building blocks used to compile costs for products or other cost objects. Activity-related costs are collected and cost drivers are chosen for each pool. Direct and indirect costs are then assigned to products or services using these activity-based cost pools and cost drivers. The information derived from ABC can be used with activity-based management (ABM) to improve operations and minimize activities that do not add value to the organization.

### This Chapter Addresses the Following Questions:

**Q1** How is activity-based costing (ABC) different from traditional costing?

**Q2** What are activities, and how are they identified?

**Q3** What process is used to assign costs in an ABC system?

**Q4** How are cost drivers selected for activities?

**Q5** What is activity-based management (ABM)?

**Q6** What are the benefits, costs, and limitations of ABC and ABM?

# REICHHOLD, INC.: COSTING PRODUCTION ACTIVITIES

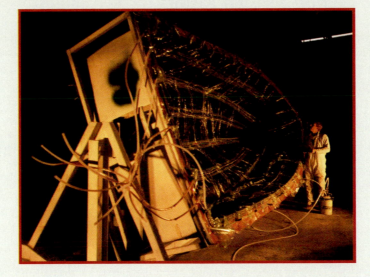

**R**eichhold, Inc., is the world's largest producer of polyester resins, selling more than a billion pounds of resins and gel coats annually. The company's products are used in architectural, industrial, and graphic arts applications. In 1997 Reichhold began a transformation from a company focused on product lines with a divisional structure into a customer-focused, team-based organization. Management's strategy was to position the firm as a high-value-added supplier. Reichhold could then improve its competitive position, increasing sales of specialty products and services that generate high gross margins.

To analyze the cost implications of this change in focus, Reichhold began implementing activity-based costing (ABC) in 1998. The desire to implement an ABC system originated with the accounting team, but was soon supported by other members of management. For example, those involved in waste management and pollution control saw an opportunity to link their goals with product cost; the methods for aggregating costs in an ABC system would make it easier to identify the costs of waste and pollution. Once production managers could see the effects of pollution on product costs, more effort would be spent reducing pollution.

The company formed a steering committee to oversee the design and implementation of the ABC system. The steering committee was composed of the senior management team, a business team leader, a member of the corporate manufacturing team, and several members of the financial team. In addition, a project team was assembled to handle implementation details for each plant site. Pilot projects were begun in three manufacturing sites, two in the United States and one in Canada. The company's managers wanted to produce reports that worked within the constraints of Reichhold's enterprise resource planning (ERP) system. An ERP system is the software that helps track and manage business activities and record and report accounting information.

The company's managers believed that ABC enabled them to comprehensively and accurately analyze the profitability of the company's different products. For example, the ABC system assigned greater costs to products that were heavy users of resources such as filtration and waste disposal. Before, the cost of these resources was spread more evenly across all products. In addition, the ABC system encouraged managers to analyze more carefully how resources were used. This analysis led to increased efficiency by changing the production batch size and resequencing plant activities.

When the three pilot projects were completed, members of the original pilot teams joined teams within the remaining 16 North America plants. As the implementation process continued, managers learned that frequent steering committee meetings were needed in each plant. In addition, continuous communication and sufficient training for the ABC teams were viewed as crucial to success. ■

SOURCE: E. Blocher, B. Wong and C. McKittrick, "Making Bottom-Up ABC Work at Reichhold, Inc.," *Strategic Finance,* April 2002.

## USING COSTS TO MEASURE, MONITOR, AND MOTIVATE

## ■ Key Decision Factors for Reichhold

The decision to implement activity-based costing (ABC) at **Reichhold** was driven by a shift in strategy. The company's accountants recommended an ABC system to help the managers become more focused on the most profitable products and to improve gross margins. The company's managers found that the ABC system improved their ability to measure and monitor product profitability; it also motivated better production decisions. Reichhold's managers needed to consider certain key factors as they implemented the ABC system.

**Knowing.** Before Reichhold could create an ABC system, the steering committee and project team needed knowledge about the company's production activities, the costs of activities, factors that drive costs, and ABC systems. A perceived benefit of the ABC system was that it further improved management's knowledge about the company's operating activities and product profitability.

**Identifying.** Reichhold's management faced many uncertainties, including the following:

- Which products created the highest value for the company
- How to optimize production activities, such as production batch sizes and sequence of plant activities
- How to design the ABC system, including how to define the company's activities, establish activity-based cost pools, and identify cost drivers
- Whether the ABC system would help managers achieve their goals

**Exploring.** The team approach adopted by Reichhold allowed the company to take advantage of a wide range of knowledge and perspectives as team members evaluated alternative ABC approaches. Team members likely considered: the types of information that might be useful to Reichhold managers for improving the company's operations and profitability, and alternative ways to define activities, assign costs to each activity, and establish cost drivers.

**Prioritizing.** The overall goal of Reichhold management in establishing the ABC system was to improve the company's focus on the most profitable products as well as to improve gross margins. Management also wanted to avoid excessive ABC implementation costs. Accordingly, the ABC teams needed to place high priority on the potential usefulness of ABC information in decision making while working within the ERP system's constraints.

**Envisioning.** Reichhold adopted ABC as part of an overall company transformation. The new system was designed to help the company improve over time in the following ways:

- Provide information to help managers improve operating decisions
- Identify inefficiencies and low-value-added activities
- Build on experience from the pilot projects for ABC implementation in other plants

ABC is sometimes seen as a cure-all for measuring an organization's costs. However, no accounting system provides managers with perfect information. For this reason, Reichhold accountants will need to monitor the costs and benefits of the new system and eventually decide whether the costs have been worth the benefits. Some companies abandon ABC systems because the costs outweigh the benefits or the systems do not meet their needs.[1]

## ■ Seeking Better Product Cost Information for Decision Making

The decision to implement activity-based costing (ABC) at Reichhold was driven by a shift in strategy. Managers wanted their cost accounting system to provide better information for decision making. They needed more accurate information about the costs of alternative products so that they could focus on the most profitable products and improve gross margins. As the business environment becomes increasingly competitive, managers of many organizations

[1]See C. Horngren, "Contribution Margin Analysis: No Longer Relevant. Strategic Cost Management: The New Paradigm," *Journal of Management Accounting Research 2* (1990), pp. 1–32; A. Nanni, R. Dixon, and T. Vollmann, "Integrated Performance Measurement: Management Accounting to Support the New Manufacturing Realities," *Journal of Management Accounting Research 4* (1992), pp. 1–19.

call for greater accuracy from their cost accounting systems. In their efforts to cut costs, they also need to identify activities that contribute the most and least value to the organization.

# ACTIVITY-BASED COSTING (ABC)

**Q1** How is activity-based costing (ABC) different from traditional costing?

**CHAPTER REFERENCE**

Chapters 5 and 6 provide details about traditional methods to allocate product costs. Chapter 8 addresses traditional methods for allocating nonmanufacturing overhead costs.

**CHAPTER REFERENCE**

A cost pool is a group of individual costs that are accumulated for a particular purpose (see Chapter 5).

Cost accounting systems were originally developed primarily to assign costs to products for financial reporting purposes. As seen in the Reichhold case, managers today want more from their cost accounting systems.

## ■ Traditional Cost Accounting Systems

Traditional cost accounting systems assign manufacturing production costs to individual products in inventory and cost of goods sold, while nonmanufacturing costs are recognized as period costs on the income statement. Traditional cost accounting methods are also used to allocate nonmanufacturing costs for some types of contractual reporting. For example, hospitals prepare cost reports for the government in which they allocate overhead to patient services. Also, defense contractors allocate nonmanufacturing overhead costs to products for cost reimbursement reports.

As illustrated in Exhibit 7.1, traditional cost accounting systems trace direct costs and allocate overhead costs to each individual product. Cost allocation is a two-stage process whereby overhead costs are grouped into one or more cost pools in the first stage and then allocated using an allocation base such as direct labor cost or hours, machine hours, or number of units in the second stage. Labor has been a common allocation base because it was historically a significant driver of manufacturing costs. As manufacturing has become less labor intensive, labor-related allocation bases are increasingly viewed as arbitrary. Allocation bases such as machine hours and number of units are also viewed as arbitrary because they may not reflect a product's use of resources. Some organizations attempt to increase cost allocation relevance by using more than one overhead cost pool. For example, fixed and variable overhead costs or overhead in different production departments might be pooled separately.

Even with multiple cost pools, traditional allocation bases rarely reflect the flow of resources to products of different complexity. Suppose that a computer manufacturer uses robotic equipment to assemble custom-ordered computers. Most of the manufacturing overhead costs (e.g., depreciation, insurance, maintenance, software maintenance) are related to the robotic equipment. If the company lacks an information system that tracks time on the robotic machines or number of new setups required, direct labor hours are likely to be used to allocate the fixed overhead related to the machines. However, direct labor might be used only to test and package the machines for shipping, and the times needed for these tasks are the same for every machine produced. As a result, fixed overhead costs are distributed equally among all of the computers regardless of the actual time spent by the robotic machines or the number of new machine setups required.

**EXHIBIT 7.1**
Traditional Overhead Cost Allocation System

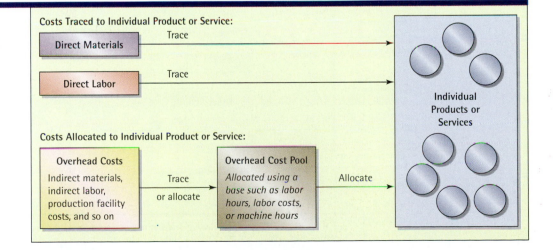

In this setting, the traditional system understates the cost of more complex computers that require more assembly time and machine setups in the robotic manufacturing process. At the same time, the system overstates the cost of simple computers requiring little robotic assembly time and few changes in setup. If the information generated by this traditional cost system is used for product decisions, the simple product could be deemphasized relative to more complex products. Yet it is highly unlikely that this emphasis reflects the optimal sales mix.

## ■ Activity-Based Costing Systems

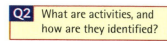

**Q2** What are activities, and how are they identified?

**Activity-based costing (ABC)** is a system that assigns overhead costs to the specific activities performed in a manufacturing or service delivery process. It attempts to trace costs more accurately to products or other cost objects. An **activity** is a type of task or function performed in an organization. The costs of the various activities become the building blocks used to compile total costs for products or other cost objects. The flow of costs in an ABC system is illustrated in Exhibit 7.2. Examples of the activities performed in a manufacturing setting include material handling (moving direct materials and supplies from one part of the plant to another), engineering, inspection, customer support, and information systems. Although the idea for ABC was proposed as long ago as 1949, a formalized version of activity analysis has been widely promoted and used only since the 1980s.[2]

Notice in Exhibit 7.2 that ABC is similar to traditional systems in that direct costs are traced to individual products or services. In addition, ABC overhead allocation is a two-stage process; costs are gathered into cost pools in the first stage, and then allocated to units in the second stage. However, under ABC, multiple cost pools are used to reflect the various

**EXHIBIT 7.2** ABC Cost Allocation System

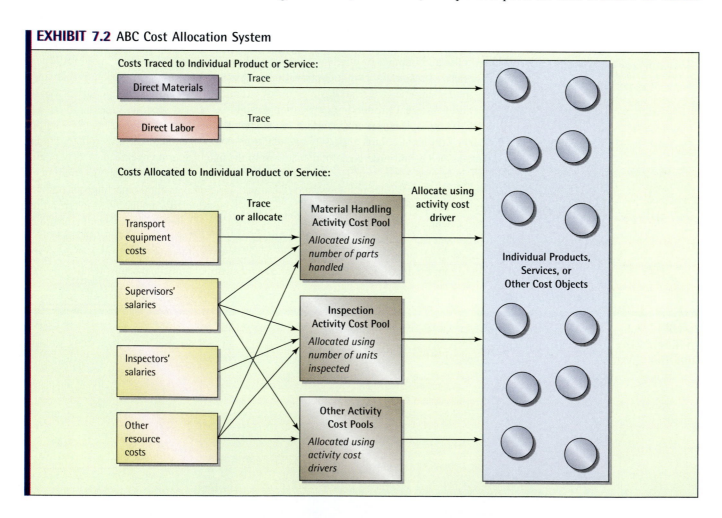

---

[2]See B. Goetz, *Management Planning and Control: A Managerial Approach to Industrial Accounting* (New York: McGraw-Hill, 1949), p. 142.

activities performed in manufacturing a good or providing a service. Accordingly, the costs of overhead resources are first assigned to activity cost pools, and then activity costs are allocated to individual products or services using cost drivers that are chosen to reflect the use of resources. Therefore, ABC differs from traditional systems because multiple activity cost pools and cost drivers are used to allocate overhead costs.

For example, if material handling is defined as an activity, the cost of buying and maintaining equipment for material handling, such as fork lifts or conveyor belts, is traced directly to an activity cost pool for material handling. Other costs, such as supervisors' salaries, may be allocated to a number of different activity cost pools, including material handling. A cost driver such as number of parts handled is used to allocate material handling costs to individual products. In this example, products that use more parts would be allocated a higher amount of material handling costs than products that use fewer parts.

# ABC COST HIERARCHY

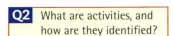

Q2 What are activities, and how are they identified?

Accountants often use a cost hierarchy to help them identify activities and then assign costs to these activities. ABC developers identified a number of general categories for the cost hierarchy based on different levels of operation. These categories include the following:

- Organization-sustaining
- Facility-sustaining
- Customer-sustaining
- Product-sustaining
- Batch-level
- Unit-level

A general description of each category with examples of costs and cost drivers is provided in Exhibit 7.3. Accountants are not restricted to these categories; others can also be used to analyze costs when organizations want to focus on different facets of their operations. For example, costs could be categorized by business segment or by strategic emphasis, such as quality or protection of the environment.

## ■ Organization-Sustaining Activities

**Organization-sustaining activities** are tasks or functions undertaken to oversee the entire entity. These activities occur no matter how many facilities are operated, customers are served, products are sold, batches are processed, or units are produced. For example, the world headquarters for **Reichhold** are located in Durham, North Carolina. Headquarters office activities and costs are considered organization-sustaining because they occur regardless of customer, product-line, batch, or unit volumes. The salaries and office costs of the chief executive officer and chief financial officer would be considered organization-sustaining costs. In addition, costs such as information technology services are organization-sustaining costs if they are performed for the entire organization.

Because many of these costs are fixed, such as administrative salaries, depreciation, and rent or lease costs, usually no cause-and-effect relationships exist between organization-sustaining costs and the activities performed at this level. Therefore, these activity costs are typically assigned to the entire organization and not allocated to specific product lines, batches, or units.

## ■ Facility-Sustaining Activities

**Facility-sustaining activities** are tasks or functions undertaken to provide and manage an area, location, or property. These activities occur no matter how many customers are served, products are sold, batches are processed, or units are produced. Therefore, they are assigned to the facility and not allocated to product lines, batches, or units. Reichhold operates 23 manufacturing facilities and four research facilities in 11 countries. Each of the manufacturing and research facilities incurs costs that do not vary with levels of activity in the facility, such as facility manager salary, building depreciation, insurance, and telephone services. These costs would be considered facility-sustaining costs. Occasionally managers want to know the full costs of production on a per-unit basis, in which case all manufacturing facility-sustaining costs are allocated.

**EXHIBIT 7.3** General Hierarchy of ABC Costs and Cost Drivers

| Level of Activities | Examples of Costs | Examples of Cost Drivers |
|---|---|---|
| **Organization-Sustaining** Activities are related to the overall organization and unaffected by number or types of facilities and customers or by volumes of products, batches, or units. | • Administrative salaries <br>• Headquarters housekeeping <br>• Information system salaries <br>• Accountant salaries and equipment | These costs are typically not allocated because they do not vary with activity volumes. |
| **Facility-Sustaining** Activities are related to the overall operations of a facility and unaffected by number of customers served or by quantities of products, batches, or units. | • Facility janitorial service <br>• Retail store insurance and heating <br>• Manufacturing plant manager's salary <br>• Depreciation and liability insurance for individual hospitals in a hospital system | These costs are typically not allocated except when the organization needs to allocate all product costs for a particular purpose. |
| **Customer-Sustaining** Activities are related to individual or groups of past, current, and future customers and are not driven by total sales volumes and mix. | • Customer sales representative salaries <br>• Technical support salaries and supplies <br>• Customer market research <br>• Special tools for a customer's order | • Number of sales calls <br>• Hours of technical suport (not tied to a specific product) <br>• Number of customers |
| **Product-Sustaining** Activities support the production and distribution of a single product or line of products. | • Production line supervisor salary <br>• Product advertising <br>• Product design engineer salaries <br>• Depreciation of equipment used to manufacture one type of product | • Number of engineering change orders <br>• Number of advertisements <br>• Machine hours |
| **Batch-Level** Activities performed for each batch of product and not related to the number of units in the batch. | • Labor cost for new setup at the beginning of a batch <br>• Utility costs for heating a kiln for batches of pottery <br>• Shipping costs for batches | • Setup hours <br>• Number of batches <br>• Weight of orders shipped |
| **Unit-Level** Activities to produce individual units of goods or services; resource cost is proportional to production volumes or sales volumes. | • Material handling wages <br>• Production workers paid based on quantity produced <br>• Supplies used to provide services | • Machine hours <br>• Units processed <br>• Materials quantity processed |

## ■ Customer-Sustaining Activities

**Customer-sustaining activities** are tasks or functions undertaken to service past, current, and future customers. These costs tend to vary with the needs of individual customers or groups of customers. The Coating and Performance Resins division of Reichhold operates sales offices located in the United States, Mexico, Austria, and Brazil. The division sells through distributors and agents in other parts of the world. The sales representatives most likely require technical training about possible uses for the company's products and their applications in various industries. For example, some of Reichhold's coating products are used on industrial machinery. The coatings are sold to some customers for application at the time equipment is manufactured and to other customers for equipment maintenance. Training aimed at particular customers would probably be considered customer-sustaining costs. Similarly, the commissions and fees paid to sales representatives and agents would be classified as customer-sustaining.

Customer-sustaining costs can be large. For example, large conglomerate manufacturers spend up to 25% of gross sales on incentives to acquire and maintain retail customers such as grocery chains.[3]

## ■ Product-Sustaining Activities

**Product-sustaining activities** are tasks or functions undertaken to support the production and distribution of a single product or line of products. These activities are not related to

[3]"Retailing: Trouble in Store," *The Economist*, May 17, 2003, pp. 55–56.

**ALTERNATIVE TERMS**

The term *product-sustaining* means the same as *product-level*. Similarly, the term *customer-sustaining* means the same as *customer-level, facility-sustaining* means the same as *facility-level*, and *organization-sustaining* means the same as *organization-level*.

units or batches, but to individual products or product lines. Reichhold is organized around two major divisions that represent its major product lines. The Coating and Performance Resins division manufactures powder coating resins, alkyds, acrylics, urethanes, epoxy resins, epoxy curing agents, and radiation-cured solutions. The Composites division manufactures mixtures including unsaturated polyester resins and gel coats. Some costs, such as division headquarters, research and development, and some types of marketing, are incurred exclusively for each product line and do not vary with levels of production or other activities. These costs would be classified as product-sustaining. Some of the product-sustaining costs apply to all of the products within a particular division, while other product-sustaining costs relate to only a single product such as a type of gel coat. Thus, numerous different ways can be used to define product-sustaining activities at a company such as Reichhold.

## ◼ Batch-Level Activities

**Batch-level activities** are tasks or functions undertaken for a collection of goods or services that are processed as a group. Batch-level costs do not relate to the number of units in the batch, but instead to the number of batches processed. Thus, batch costs increase as the number of batches increases. The manufacture of resins at Reichhold is performed in batches, similar to cooking a pot of stew. Workers measure and put specific quantities of powdered and liquid chemicals into a reactor vessel and then set the equipment to "cook" the mixture. Periodically, quality control personnel test the mixture to determine whether the appropriate chemical reactions have occurred. Once the resin is complete, it is transferred to a storage tank. The reactor vessel must then be cleaned before the next batch can be started. The batch-related costs include costs related to the reactor equipment and its maintenance and the supplies used to clean the reactor vessels.

**CURRENT PRACTICE**

To reduce batch-level costs,  Timken invested $150 million in a sophisticated new industrial bearings factory. Setup that had required half a day now takes only 15 to 30 minutes.[4]

## ◼ Unit-Level Activities

**Unit-level activities** are undertaken to produce individual units manufactured or services produced. Unit-level activities need to be performed for every unit of good or service, and therefore the cost should be proportional to the number of units produced. Reichhold probably sells resin in standard containers such as 55-gallon drums and railroad tanks. Unit-level costs include the costs to use and maintain the equipment for filling containers.

# ASSIGNING COSTS USING AN ABC SYSTEM

**Q3** What process is used to assign costs in an ABC system?

In an ABC system, the process of assigning costs is a two-stage process similar to other cost accounting methods we have studied: Overhead costs are gathered into cost pools in the first stage and then allocated to the cost objects, such as product line, batch, or units, in the second stage. ABC differs from other cost accounting methods in that overhead costs are assigned to a larger number of activity-based cost pools, and cost drivers are used as allocation bases. The following procedures are followed for the ABC method.

1. Identify the relevant cost object.
2. Identify activities.
3. Assign costs to activity-based cost pools.
4. For each ABC cost pool, choose a cost driver.
5. For each ABC cost pool, calculate an allocation rate.
6. For each ABC cost pool, allocate activity costs to the cost object.

## ◼ 1. Identify the Relevant Cost Object

Different managers have different purposes for implementing an ABC system. The design of the system begins with identification of one or more cost objects that are relevant to managers. For example, managers may wish to assign manufacturing costs to products when they

---

[4]A. Aston and M. Arndt, "The Flexible Factory," *Business Week*, May 5, 2003, pp. 90–91.

adopt an ABC system. In this case, direct manufacturing costs are traced to products and manufacturing overhead costs are allocated using ABC. However, the cost object could be customers, customer orders, a product line, batches, or any other aspect of operations in which managers are interested. In this part of the chapter, we focus on assigning manufacturing costs first to batches and then to units of product. Later in the chapter, we will learn about assigning costs to other cost objects and about assigning other types of costs, such as costs of quality, to cost objects.

Suppose the managers at Keener Doors and Windows want to improve their ability to measure the production costs of various types of windows. This information will help them identify potential improvements in the manufacturing process. In this case, the production costs of individual windows are the cost object. The accountant developing an ABC system would focus only on manufacturing activities and not on other activities such as marketing, distribution, or research and development.

**Q2** What are activities, and how are they identified?

## ■ 2. Identify Activities

To identify the activities performed within the production process, the use of resources must be tracked and, in many cases, additional information gathered from employees. For example, accountants may ask production managers about the types of tasks and functions performed in each production area. At this time, an accountant would categorize activities into unit, batch, product, customer, facility, and organization levels. This task might seem simple, but considerable judgment is needed to identify and choose the best set of cost pools for an ABC system. The goal is to account for separate activities in a way that provides managers useful information for decision making. In general, accountants try to identify activities so that the costs within each cost pool are homogeneous. **Homogeneous activities** are related in a logical manner and consume similar resources. Sometimes the cost driver helps establish whether activities should be combined or separated.

For Keener Doors and Windows, the accountant would identify all of the activities involved in window manufacturing, including handling and transporting the glass and framing materials, glass cutting, window framing, and preparation for distribution. The accountant must also decide whether to establish separate cost pools for each activity or whether to combine some activities into a single activity cost pool.

An appropriate cost driver for glass cutting might be the number of windows produced, especially if each window requires a similar amount of equipment and employee time. In this case, the window-cutting activities are homogenous, the window-cutting tasks are all related in a logical manner, and they require similar amounts of time and equipment per window. If, in turn, each window requires the same amount of time to frame, the accountant might conclude that the number of windows also drives the framing activity. In this case, both glass cutting and window framing have the same cost driver, and no benefit is likely to be gained by using separate cost pools for these two tasks. The accountant could combine the costs into one cost pool. Glass cutting and window framing are logically related, in that the glass is cut for a particular size frame and the activities take place sequentially, with glass cutting occurring first. In addition, the cost driver for both is number of windows produced because each window takes about the same amount of time and supplies to cut and frame. These activities could be considered homogeneous.

However, different windows might require different amounts of time and effort to cut. Each type of window would require the same amount of time to frame, but combining the activity costs in a single cost pool and using the same cost driver (number of windows processed) would not accurately reflect the cost of cutting resources. In this case, the two activities are not homogenous because they require different amounts of time and effort. Therefore, the accountant would probably separate glass cutting and window framing into two separate cost pools and choose time spent cutting as the cost driver for the cutting activity, and number of windows framed for framing activities.

## ■ 3. Assign Costs to Activity-Based Cost Pools

Costs related to each activity are identified and pooled. Some costs are directly traced to the cost pools. Indirect material costs are often traced directly to batch or unit cost pools, whereas costs such as property taxes, insurance, and lease or depreciation are directly traced to the facility. Similarly, costs such as depreciation on equipment used for only one product line are traced to a cost pool for that product line.

Suppose the accountant for Keener Doors and Windows identifies glass cutting as a separate activity. The supplies used to cut glass, such as blades and oil for the glass-cutting equipment, are traced directly to the cost pool for this activity. Depreciation on the glass-cutting equipment is also traced directly to the glass-cutting activity. However, other overhead costs, such as the salary of a supervisor who oversees several different activities in the window department, need to be allocated to the cost pools for these activities.

## ◼ 4. For Each ABC Cost Pool, Choose a Cost Driver

 **Q4** How are cost drivers selected for activities?

Ideally, activity costs are allocated to cost objects using a driver that explains changes in activity cost. Examples of cost drivers for various activities were listed in Exhibit 7.3. The terms *cost driver* and *allocation base* are sometimes used interchangeably. However, *cost driver* refers to some measure of activity that causes costs to fluctuate, whereas *allocation base* refers to the base used to allocate costs in an accounting system. Many allocation bases are not cost drivers. For example, in traditional costing systems square footage is often used as an allocation base for building-related costs such as property taxes and insurance, but no cause-and-effect relationship connects these costs with square footage in any specific work area or department. Therefore, the allocation base of square footage is not a cost driver. In contrast, the amount of time Keener employees spend cutting windows causes the cost of glass cutting to increase. Therefore, time spent cutting is a cost driver that can be used to allocate the cost pool for the glass cutting activity. Cost drivers are a special kind of allocation base.

A cost driver is the best allocation base choice for an ABC cost pool. In other words, a cause-and-effect relationship should be evident between the allocation base and activity costs. Often, information about potential cost drivers is elicited from employees involved in the activities. They may suggest several potential drivers, and accountants must choose the most appropriate cost driver.

**CHAPTER REFERENCE**
See Chapter 2 for details about choosing and evaluating potential cost drivers.

The accountant for Keener Doors and Windows needs to determine a cost driver for window-framing costs. The best choice depends on the accountant's analysis of the variation in cost (increases and decreases). If windows are framed in batches by robotic equipment, the number of batches is a likely choice for a cost driver. If windows are framed individually, time spent framing and number of windows are potential cost drivers. If each window takes a different amount of time, then time spent framing is a more accurate cost driver. However, if roughly the same amount of time and supplies are used per window, number of windows may be nearly as accurate and easier to track.

## ◼ 5. For Each ABC Cost Pool, Calculate an Allocation Rate

An allocation rate is calculated by dividing activity costs by some measure of volume for the cost driver. The choice of data for the activity costs and volume of the cost driver depend on the purpose of the ABC analysis. Sometimes managers are interested in measuring or analyzing past costs. In this case, the allocation rate is determined by dividing prior period cost by the prior period volume. Alternatively, managers may be interested in estimating future costs. In this case, estimated costs and estimated volumes could be used.

The accountant for Keener Doors and Windows might calculate an estimated allocation rate for window framing costs as follows:

$$\text{Estimated allocation rate} = \frac{\text{Estimated total cost of window framing}}{\text{Estimated number of batches}}$$

Suppose that the estimated total cost for framing windows is $5,000 this month, and the estimated number of batches of windows framed is 100. The estimated allocation rate for window framing is then $50 per batch ($5,000 ÷ 100 batches).

One of the potential benefits of ABC is that it can be used to measure the cost of an organization's capacity. **Practical capacity** is maximum capacity under typical operating conditions, assuming that some downtime is unavoidable for maintenance and holidays. If an estimated allocation rate is calculated using practical capacity in the denominator, then the allocation rate measures the cost of supplying the organization's production capacity. When this allocation rate is used to allocate costs, the ABC system will measure the cost of capacity used as well as the cost of unused capacity.

## ■ 6. For Each ABC Cost Pool, Allocate Activity Costs to the Cost Object

Costs are allocated to the cost object based on the actual volume of activity for the cost driver. In the Keener example, the cost object is individual window units. The cost of an individual window includes the unit-level costs as well as allocated batch-level costs. For the window-framing activity, suppose 95 batches are processed during the month. Using the estimated batch-level allocation rate of $50 per batch, the total batch costs for the month are estimated as $4,750 (95 batches × $50 per batch). Assuming each batch includes 10 windows, the total number of windows produced during the month is 950 (95 batches × 10 windows per batch). Thus, the allocated framing cost per window would be $5 ($4,750 ÷ 950). The total cost of an individual window would be estimated as the $5 cost for framing plus the per-unit cost of all other activities involved in producing the windows.

| GUIDE YOUR LEARNING 7.1 Key Terms |
| --- |

Stop to confirm that you understand the new terms introduced in the last several pages:

| | |
| --- | --- |
| Activity-based costing (p. 260) | *Product-sustaining activities (p. 262) |
| *Activity (p. 260) | *Batch-level activities (p. 263) |
| *Organization-sustaining activities (p. 261) | *Unit-level activities (p. 263) |
| *Facility-sustaining activities (p. 261) | Homogeneous activities (p. 264) |
| *Customer-sustaining activities (p. 262) | Practical capacity (p. 265) |

For each of these terms, write a definition in your own words. For starred terms, list at least one example that is different from the ones given in this textbook.

ABC provides a more accurate picture of the flow of overhead resources than traditional costing methods. This accuracy is useful when organizations need to determine which products to emphasize or whether their pricing schemes adequately reflect resources used. The illustration that follows compares costs assigned using a traditional system and an ABC system.

### KEENER DOORS AND WINDOWS (PART 1)
### COMPARISON OF ABC AND TRADITIONAL JOB COSTING

Keener Doors and Windows Company produces two types of wooden doors. Regular doors are high-volume and use standard parts and manufacturing processes. Premium doors are lower volume and are considered a customized, specialty item. Managers are considering the pricing policies for both doors because their major competitor recently lowered prices on regular doors. Premium doors have been selling well because they are priced lower than the competitor's specialty doors. The managers are concerned about the effects on profit margins if they reduce the price of regular doors to match the competition. Although they only consider variable costs in their pricing decisions, they would like to have more information about each product's use of overhead resources.

The cost accountant, Valerie Bradley, suggested that Keener consider implementing an ABC system to better understand the costs for all of the manufacturing activities needed to produce the doors. She believes that the regular doors use fewer overhead resources because all of the regular doors go through routine processes, whereas the premium doors require special processes. Both doors are produced in batches of 100. However, each premium door is processed further to add custom features, such as special routing effects in the wood or special window treatments. Currently overhead is allocated based on direct labor hours, but machines perform much of the work. Valerie believes that labor hours do not reflect the two products' different use of plant overhead resources.

An ABC team is assembled to analyze the manufacturing activities and costs for individual doors in both product lines. The team consists of Valerie, a product designer, and several employees from the manufacturing process. They want to compare costs under the current job costing system and a new ABC system. As they consider the task, they realize that ABC allocations typically ignore facility-related costs while job costing allocations include them. For purposes of comparison, they decide to ignore facility-sustaining costs in their calculations for job costing so that the results from both systems are comparable. From the general ledger, Valerie identifies overhead costs of $18,270,000 (not including any facility costs) that were assigned to regular and premium doors last period.

## Product Costs Using Job Costing

The team recreates the products' job costs using information from the general ledger. Each regular door requires $65 of direct materials and 2.5 hours of direct labor. Each premium door requires $100 of direct materials and 3 hours of direct labor. The job costing system allocates overhead using a factory-wide estimated allocation rate of $32.05 per direct labor hour based on a single cost pool for door production of $18,270,000 and direct labor hours of 570,000 for the year. The following schedule summarizes the cost of each type of door:

|  | Regular Doors | Premium Doors |
|---|---|---|
| Direct materials: |  |  |
| Regular | $ 65.00 |  |
| Premium |  | $100.00 |
| Direct labor: |  |  |
| Regular ($20 × 2.5 hours) | 50.00 |  |
| Premium ($20 × 3 hours) |  | 60.00 |
| Factory overhead: |  |  |
| Regular ($32.05 × 2.5 hours) | 80.13 |  |
| Premium ($32.05 × 3 hours) |  | 96.15 |
| Total cost | $195.13 | $256.15 |

The team members notice that the overhead allocation for premium doors is $16.02, or 20% greater than for regular doors under the job costing system. However, the shop supervisor believes that premium doors use two to three times more resources than regular doors because of extra processing the premium doors receive on the most expensive equipment.

## Product Costs Using ABC

The managers want to know whether their current pricing policy reflects any differences in resources used by regular doors compared to premium doors. Therefore, the ABC team decides that the relevant cost objects are individual doors and the activities involved in production must be analyzed.

When the team visits the production area, they ask about the activities performed for each type of door. They learn that the first activity is delivery of materials to work stations. They identify a material handling cost pool for this activity.

The next steps involve work done in batches, such as the initial cutting, sanding, and smoothing of doors. The team learns that two different activities are required: setting up machines for the next batch, and monitoring the machines as batches are processed. Some team members believe that these two activities could be combined into one cost pool allocated on the number of batches run. Valerie asks whether these activities differ between regular doors and premium doors. She learns that the setup for premium door batches is more complex and takes more time than for regular doors. The batches take the same amount of time, no matter what type of door is produced. Therefore the team identifies two activity pools, one for setup costs and one for batch monitoring costs because the activities in these pools are not homogeneous and cannot be allocated using a single cost driver.

After the doors are cut and sanded, they are processed through routing machines. The team discovers that premium doors require more routing machine hours because the designs are more complex. An activity pool for machining is identified.

The last activity is inspection. The inspectors explain that premium doors take longer to inspect because of their greater detail. The team identifies inspection as a cost pool.

Now that the cost pools are identified, costs need to be traced or allocated to each pool. Valerie uses annual accounting records and information from employees about supplies used and the

*(continued)*

amount of time they spend performing different tasks. Material handling costs are easy to trace because workers perform only material handling duties, so their wages are traced directly to the cost pool. Equipment depreciation accounts are analyzed, and the cost of material handling equipment is separated. Workers estimate fuel costs and some supply costs, because detailed records are not kept for these expenses. Employees who set up and monitor batches estimate the amount of time spent in each activity. The employees performing the machining estimate the time and indirect materials used on each type of door, as do the inspectors.

The team's next step is to select cost drivers. They decide to use number of parts as the cost driver for material handling because each part is handled separately. The setup for each batch varies with the complexity of the door design. Regular doors are processed using three simple designs. The machines automatically cut the doors to size and rout simple designs on the doors. Premium door setup requires more time because the door designs are more complex and usually include windows. The robotic machines cut holes for and insert windows. Setup for this process is more time intensive. The team decides to use setup time as the cost driver for this activity. Each batch requires about the same amount of monitoring, so the team selects number of batches as the cost driver for monitoring costs. Premium doors require more machine hours than regular doors because the routing designs are more complex, so machine hours are chosen as cost driver for machining costs. Each door requires a different amount of time to inspect, so the team selects inspection labor time as the cost driver for inspection.

Before calculating the allocation rates, the team estimates the volume for each cost driver. They have complete records for machine hours and labor hours, but are not sure about information for number of parts, because that statistic is not tracked. The material handling employees estimate the number of parts they handled last year. Records are maintained for the number of batches, so that information is readily available. Employees are asked to estimate time spent in setup. The number of doors inspected is available, as is total time spent inspecting. However, time per regular versus premium door has not been tracked, so inspectors estimate these figures.

Next, the team gathers information about the amount of each cost driver used by regular and premium doors last month as follows.

|  | Regular Doors | Premium Doors |
| --- | --- | --- |
| Number of doors per batch | 100 | 100 |
| Number of batches | 1,200 | 900 |
| Number of parts per door | 10 | 20 |
| Machine setup time | 1/2 hour per batch | 1 hour per batch |
| Machine hours per door | 1 | 3 |
| Inspection time per door | 1/2 hour | 1 hour |

Exhibit 7.4 summarizes the steps thus far, showing the activities, related cost drivers, overall costs, estimated volume for each cost driver, and estimated allocation rates.

Machine set-up time is $1/2$ hour per batch for regular doors. At $100 per hour, the cost is $50 per batch. Because each batch consists of 100 doors, the cost per regular door is $0.50. Similarly, the cost per premium door is $1.00.

The total ABC overhead cost for each type of door is calculated as follows:

|  |  | Regular Door |  | Premium Door |
| --- | --- | --- | --- | --- |
| Material handling | (10 × $1.00) | $10.00 | (20 × $1.00) | $ 20.00 |
| Machine setup | (1/2 × $100 ÷ 100) | 0.50 | (1 × $100 ÷ 100) | 1.00 |
| Monitoring batches | ($200 ÷ 100) | 2.00 | ($200 ÷ 100) | 2.00 |
| Machine hours | (1 × $30) | 30.00 | (3 × $30) | 90.00 |
| Inspections | (0.5 × $20) | 10.00 | (1 × $20) | 20.00 |
| Total overhead |  | $52.50 |  | $133.00 |

## Using ABC Product Cost Information

The team believes that the calculations under ABC costing confirm their intuition that the job costing system did not accurately reflect each product's use of resources. Under the job costing system, $80.13 in overhead was allocated to regular doors, and under ABC regular doors are allocated only $52.50. For the premium doors $96.15 in overhead cost was allocated by the job costing system compared to $133.00 under activity-based costing. These results suggest that the old system overstated the cost of regular doors and understated the cost of premium doors. The team believes that the ABC costs are more accurate because they better map the use of resources to each type of product.

**EXHIBIT 7.4** Estimated Volumes and Costs Developed by the ABC Team at Keener Doors and Windows

| Volume | Estimated Cost | Cost Driver | Cost Drivers: Estimated Volume | | | Estimated Allocation Rate |
| | | | Regular Doors | Premium Doors | Total | |
| --- | --- | --- | --- | --- | --- | --- |
| Number of doors | | | 120,000 | 90,000 | 210,000 | |
| Number of batches | | | 1,200 | 900 | 2,100 | |
| **Activity** | | | | | | |
| Material handling | $ 3,000,000 | Number of parts | 1,200,000 | 1,800,000 | 3,000,000 | $1.00 per part |
| Setting up machines | 150,000 | Time spent | 600 | 900 | 1,500 | $100 per setup hour |
| Monitoring batch operations | 420,000 | Number of batches | 1,200 | 900 | 2,100 | $200 per batch |
| Machining doors | 11,700,000 | Machine hours | 120,000 | 270,000 | 390,000 | $30 per machine hour |
| Inspecting doors | 3,000,000 | Time spent | 60,000 | 90,000 | 150,000 | $20 per inspection hour |
| Total cost | $18,270,000 | | | | | |

When the team presents its results to the company's managers, they decide that the regular door price can be reduced to match competitors' prices and the premium door price can be increased. Valerie reminds the managers that this ABC information contains some allocated fixed costs, such as salaries for supervisors and equipment depreciation, and that these costs probably will not change proportionately with changes in production volumes. Therefore, these ABC costs should only be used as a guide for pricing decisions. After any pricing changes are made, the managers need to monitor sales volumes to determine the effects of price changes on demand and determine whether profitability actually improves.

---

## GUIDE YOUR LEARNING 7.2 Keener Doors and Windows (Part 1)

Keener Doors and Windows (Part 1) illustrates the calculation of product costs under job and ABC costing. For this illustration:

| Define It | Identify Problem and Relevant Information | Identify Uncertainties | Explore Pros and Cons of Options |
| --- | --- | --- | --- |
| In your own words, define job costing and ABC costing. Explain the difference in product cost per unit under the two methods. | What decisions were being addressed? Why was product cost considered relevant to the decision? | What types of uncertainties were there? Consider uncertainties about:<br>• Identifying activities<br>• Identifying cost drivers<br>• Assigning costs to ABC cost pools<br>• Estimating the volumes of cost drivers<br>• Relevance of ABC product costs for the pricing decision | Why did the ABC team think that ABC cost information was better than job cost information? How was the quality of the ABC information different from information under traditional job costing? |

## ■ ABC for Nonmanufacturing Costs

In the Keener Doors illustration, ABC was used to allocate product manufacturing costs. ABC can also be used to allocate nonmanufacturing costs such as the costs of marketing and accounting. To allocate nonmanufacturing costs, the nonmanufacturing activities need to be analyzed and cost pools and cost drivers set up in the same manner as described for manufacturing costs.

For example, suppose the managers at **Reichhold** are interested in reevaluating some of their distributor relationships. An ABC analysis could be used to determine which distributor relationships are the most or least profitable. Similarly, the company could use ABC analysis to estimate the profitability of individual products, taking into account nonmanufacturing product-level costs such as research and development and marketing.

## ABC IN SERVICE ORGANIZATIONS

 **Q3** What process is used to assign costs using an ABC system?

ABC is used to assign costs not only to physical products, but also to services. Often, service organizations analyze cost performance by comparing their actual costs to budgeted costs each year. These types of comparisons do not provide information about cost per activity or service provided, which is needed to measure an organization's efficiency in providing services. To better understand the effects of activities on their costs, service organizations may benefit from developing ABC systems. By analyzing activities, these organizations may be able to improve efficiency or quality of service, and control or reduce costs. Service organizations follow the same process as manufacturing organizations for implementing an ABC system. Self-study problem 2 provides practice using ABC in a service setting.

## ACTIVITY-BASED MANAGEMENT

 **Q5** What is activity-based management (ABM)?

**Activity-based management (ABM)** is the process of using ABC information to evaluate the costs and benefits of production and internal support activities and to identify and implement opportunities for improvements in profitability, efficiency, and quality within an organization. ABM relies on accurate ABC information. Next we learn about five major uses of ABM:

- Managing customer profitability
- Managing product and process design
- Managing environmental costs
- Managing quality
- Managing constrained resources

## ■ Managing Customer Profitability

ABC can be used to identify characteristics that cause some customers to be more costly than others. Customer-sustaining activities include sales and technical support supplied to specific customers or groups of customers, costs of holding inventory for just-in-time deliveries, and costs of customizing orders. Exhibit 7.5 describes characteristics of customers having higher and lower costs.

As the costs of serving specific customers are determined, managers can choose different strategies for different types of customers. For example, some customers need very little service, but are quite price sensitive. Although margins for these customers are low, these customers are profitable when service costs are also kept low. Customers with high service costs are also profitable when their net margins are high enough to account for the extra service costs. Alternatively, the company can price its extra services and let customers pick the services they are willing to pay for.

---

[5]T. Holt, "Developing an Activity-Based Management System for the Army Medical Department," *Journal of Health Care Finance,* Spring 2001, pp. 41–46.
[6]"CIBC—Using Activity-Based Costing in Canada," *Financial World,* April 2002, p. xiv.

**EXHIBIT 7.5**
Characteristics of Customers with High and Low Service Costs

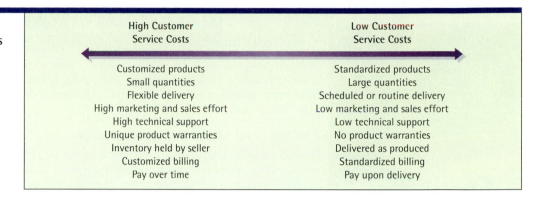

| High Customer Service Costs | Low Customer Service Costs |
| --- | --- |
| Customized products | Standardized products |
| Small quantities | Large quantities |
| Flexible delivery | Scheduled or routine delivery |
| High marketing and sales effort | Low marketing and sales effort |
| High technical support | Low technical support |
| Unique product warranties | No product warranties |
| Inventory held by seller | Delivered as produced |
| Customized billing | Standardized billing |
| Pay over time | Pay upon delivery |

The most valuable customers are those who order high-margin products, but have low service requirements. Managers can identify these customers using ABC information and then monitor their sales volumes. The organization can then compete for the best customers by offering discounts, special services, or other sales incentives when necessary.

Customers requiring the most creative approaches are those who order low-margin products, but require costly services. Customer-ordering patterns can be analyzed and information shared with these customers to improve predictability of orders, reduce engineering and delivery changes, reduce demand for technical or sales support, and increase standardization of product and delivery requirements. In addition, pricing arrangements can be modified to increase margins and to introduce a pricing system for specialized services.

## Managing Product and Process Design

**CHAPTER REFERENCE**

Chapter 13 provides more information about value-added and non-value-added activities and improvements to business processes.

An advantage of ABC is its focus on activities. As an organization's activities are analyzed more closely, managers improve their understanding of how resources are used. In turn, this analysis enables managers to improve operations and profits. They can focus resources on **value-added activities,** which increase the worth of an organization's goods or services to customers. Conversely, they can reduce or eliminate **non-value-added activities,** which are unnecessary and, therefore, waste resources.

**CURRENT PRACTICE**

During 2003, U.S. manufacturers spent an estimated $22 billion satisfying warranty claims.[7]

For example, Keener Doors and Windows incurs costs for warranty work on its doors. Sometimes warranty problems are addressed by rework that is performed during idle times. Although no incremental labor cost is incurred in this situation, the rework requires additional materials. In addition, some defective doors are replaced, and the company forgoes the cost of labor and materials in addition to the contribution margin on good doors that could be sold. Therefore, warranty costs are non-value-adding; that is, no real value is added for incurring these costs. If warranty activities could be reduced or eliminated, overall costs at Keener Doors and Windows would be reduced.

Under ABM, non-value-added activities are identified and eliminated when possible. As ABC systems are implemented, activities can be categorized as follows:

- Required to produce a good or service and cannot be improved at this time
- Required but the process could be improved or simplified
- Not required to produce a good or service and can eventually be eliminated
- Not required and can be eliminated by changing a process or procedure

The following illustration shows managers analyzing an activity to improve operations and reduce cost.

---

[7]S. Layne, "Warranty Chain Management Is Real," *Line56.com,* January 27, 2004.

## KEENER DOORS AND WINDOWS (PART 2)
## USING ABM TO REDUCE NONMANUFACTURING COSTS

The managers at Keener Doors and Windows are pleased with the ABC cost information for door production and ask for additional analysis of marketing and warranty costs for doors. They feel these costs could be reduced if they better understand marketing and warranty activities and their related costs.

### ABC Costs for Marketing and Warranty

Because marketing and warranty service is similar for regular and premium doors, the ABC team concludes that these costs can be analyzed using doors as a single product line and windows as the other product line. Thus, they plan to identify activities related to marketing and warranty costs and then separate the costs for doors from the costs for windows.

Product-sustaining marketing costs consist of advertising, marketing department employee costs, sales commissions, and marketing department supplies. The cost of advertising is relatively easy to assign because either doors or windows are featured in advertisements. Marketing department employees estimate the amount of time spent per product line, and any sales commissions are traced to each product line. Miscellaneous supplies are allocated according to employee time spent.

To analyze costs for product-sustaining warranty work, the ABC system needs to separate the costs for warranty work on doors from the warranty work on windows. Depending on the problem, sometimes doors are replaced. In these cases, detailed cost records are kept. Other times the doors are reworked. Tracking the costs of rework is difficult because employees take time from their regular tasks to rework and often complete rework tasks during idle times when batches are in process and do not need monitoring. Monthly rework costs rely on employee estimates of time and materials used for rework. The team concludes that the warranty work cost pool is probably measured with error. They decide to develop a tracking system for the time and materials used for rework to get better estimates of warranty costs in the future.

The final estimates of the per-door costs for marketing and warranty follow:

| | |
|---|---|
| Marketing | $20.00 per unit |
| Warranty work | $18.00 per unit |

### Applying Activity-Based Management

The team members are surprised that warranty costs are nearly as large as marketing costs. They invite the product design team to meet with customer service representatives to discuss possible product changes to reduce warranty costs. The data for last period indicate that more than half of the warranty costs—about $10 per door sold—resulted from hinge problems; the whole door must be replaced when a hinge fails. The team immediately begins to solve this problem.

The first suggestion is to reinforce the door around the hinge, but the team learns that this procedure costs $15 per door. One team member researches the newest technology in hinges and finds one that would eliminate 90% of the problem at a cost of $14.50 per door, whereas the current hinges cost $12 per door. After discussing a number of other alternatives, the team recommends the new hinges. Although this increases the cost of each door by $2.50, it is likely that overall warranty costs will be reduced by $9 per door ($10 × 90%). In addition, the team believes that Keener's reputation for high quality has been hurt by the hinge problem, resulting in a loss of market share. Management accepts the team's recommendation and issues engineering change orders for the new hinges to improve quality, reduce warranty work, and eventually increase market share.

## GUIDE YOUR LEARNING 7.3 Keener Doors and Windows (Part 2)

Keener Doors and Windows (Part 2) illustrates the use of ABC information for activity-based management. For this illustration:

| Identify Problem | Identify Uncertainties | Explore Pros and Cons | Prioritize Options |
|---|---|---|---|
| Why did the managers ask for additional analysis of marketing and warranty costs? | When managers use ABC information to improve operations, why is it impossible to be certain that the company will achieve benefits? | What benefits of ABM were illustrated? What costs did the company incur to generate these benefits? | In your own words, describe how various quantitative and qualitative factors were weighed in reaching a decision about the hinge problem. |

**CHAPTER REFERENCE**

Chapter 13 provides full discussions of target costing and Kaizen costing.

**Target and Kaizen Costing** ABC and ABM are often combined with other techniques as activities and processes are analyzed. Target costing is a cost control method by which products and their manufacturing processes are designed to meet specific target costs, based on expected product selling prices. ABC information helps the product and manufacturing process design teams within an organization understand the cost effects of their design choices. ABC improves the accuracy of product cost estimates, and ABM helps managers identify and remove non-value-added activities. Kaizen costing is a cost reduction and quality improvement process that occurs once a product has been manufactured for awhile. Once again, ABM helps managers identify non-value-added activities and redesign products and manufacturing processes to reduce cost and improve quality.

## ■ Managing Environmental Costs

Many managers are concerned with the effects of their organizations' manufacturing processes on the environment. In addition, many shareholders are concerned with the "green" reputation of companies in which they invest. Federal and state regulations may require organizations to reduce pollution levels. The direct costs of reducing pollution are often easily tracked, but identifying the costs and benefits of protecting the environment within traditional accounting systems is more difficult. ABC systems can be designed to identify the activities involved in environmental protection and to develop costs for those activities. Analyzing overhead activities also helps managers identify opportunities for improved environmental performance.

Suppose a high-quality printing company used inks that were detrimental to the environment. The cost of ink disposal was traditionally recorded as part of overhead cost. When management developed an ABC system, however, the disposal cost became part of an activity cost pool for the printing process that used these inks. As the activity was analyzed, the high cost of disposal became more noticeable. Managers realized that they could invest in an incinerator that used high temperatures to burn the ink so thoroughly that it left little airborne or solid residual. Thus, the ABC process motivated managers to consider alternative methods to reduce the cost of pollution. Once the cost effects of pollution, waste, and other environmental activities are identified, managers become more motivated to make investments that improve environmental performance. With these improvements, costs are reduced because organizations no longer incur the costs associated with pollution or waste. In addition, many non-value-added activities are eliminated, such as disposal or cleaning activities.

Although identifying the activities and costs related to environmental quality can be difficult, organizations are increasingly concerned with valuing the costs and benefits of developing environmentally friendly practices. The number of Japanese corporations that publish environmental reports listing environmental costs and benefits has been increasing rapidly. In February 2001, Japan's Ministry of the Environment published "Environmental Report Guidelines." Then in June 2001, the Ministry of Economy, Trade and Industry published the "Environmental Reporting Guideline for Stakeholders." According to the Ministry of Environment, environmental accounting procedures identify costs and benefits of environmental conservation activities (from "Understanding Environmental Accounting" published by Japan's Ministry of the Environment, September 2002). For examples of environmental accounting reports, go to the Web site of Pioneer (Japan) (www.pioneer.co.jp) or Panasonic (www.panasonic.co.jp/global), and click on the environmental activities buttons.

## ■ Managing Quality

Part of organizational strategy is the choice of product quality levels. Some organizations strive to maintain reputations for high-quality products, while other companies seek only to match the quality of their competitors. ABC can be used to determine the costs of quality and to help refine quality strategies. Exhibit 7.6 defines four categories of quality activities—prevention, appraisal, production, and postsales—and provides examples of activities performed within each category. These actions are taken to minimize the opportunity costs that arise when customers have problems with defective units or low-quality services. When quality failures occur, reputations suffer and market share is lost. These losses are difficult to value and are, therefore, often ignored when accountants and managers consider the costs and benefits of maintaining high-quality processes.

**CHAPTER REFERENCE**

Chapter 5 provides a more complete discussion of product quality opportunity costs.

**EXHIBIT 7.6**
Quality–Related Activities

| | Definition | Examples |
|---|---|---|
| **Prevention Activities** | Activities performed to insure defect-free production | Design and process engineering<br>Routine equipment maintenance<br>Inspection of incoming raw materials<br>Quality training and meetings |
| **Appraisal Activities** | Activities performed to identify defective units | Inspection of products<br>Inspection of manufacturing process<br>Monitoring of service delivery process<br>Testing |
| **Production Activities** | Activities undertaken in the production or rework of failed units | Producing spoiled units<br>Reworking spoiled units<br>Repairing machine and equipment<br>Reengineering and redesigning |
| **Postsales Activities** | Activities undertaken after the product has been sold to remedy problems caused by defects and failed units | Product recalls (replace both good and<br>    defective units)<br>Warranty repair work<br>Replacing defective units<br>Liability lawsuits |

Sometimes the costs of quality failures are extremely high, such as the loss of reputation and market share that occurs when a great deal of publicity is generated about defective goods or processes. The reputation and profitability of stores such as **Jack-in-the Box** suffer whenever a death from *E. coli* bacterial contamination occurs.[8] **Firestone** and **Ford** lost market share and experienced lower stock market prices when news was released about an increased rollover and fatality rate in Ford Explorers that was also associated with Firestone tires. One of Firestone's plants in which a strike had occurred and inexperienced workers had been hired to replace the striking employees has been implicated as a source of defective tires.[9] The cost of quality failures such as these catastrophes is nearly impossible to value, yet is extremely important to consider in measuring the costs and benefits of proposed quality improvement initiatives.

Managers make decisions about the trade-offs of investing in the different categories of quality activities. As organizations increasingly invest in prevention activities, competitors are forced to maintain equally high levels of quality. In the following illustration, ABC information and ABM practices are used to reduce cost and improve quality.

## SWISS WATCH
### ABM AND THE COST OF QUALITY

Swiss Watch, located in Switzerland, is a watch manufacturer with a reputation for producing high-quality watches. Lately, however, a competitor has advertised both quality improvements and price reductions in its line of watches. Pierre Borgeaud, the head of cost accounting at Swiss Watch, conducted a study to determine whether costs could be reduced. His initial focus was on activities related to quality. Although the managers want to maintain high quality, they also want to reduce costs and, in turn, prices. The study categorized quality costs into four activites: prevention, appraisal, production, and postsales.

### Estimating the Costs of Quality

Using information gathered from the general ledger, last year's quality activity costs were estimated as follows (amounts in Swiss Francs):

[8]See K. MacArthur, "Jack's Fighting at Fifty," *Advertising Age,* February 19, 2001, pp. 4–6; and C. Aldred, "E-coli Food Poisoning Leads to Lawsuits," *Business Insurance,* December 16, 1996, p. 23.
[9]See A. Merrick, "Bridgestone Tire Issue Clouds Labor Negotiations," *Wall Street Journal* (Eastern Edition), September 1, 2000, p. A4.

| | |
|---|---|
| Prevention costs (inspecting materials from suppliers) | SFr 10,000 |
| Appraisal costs (inspection) | 20,000 |
| Production costs (spoiled units) | 5,000 |
| Postsales costs (warranty) | 8,000 |
| Total costs of quality | SFr 43,000 |

When Pierre reviews these costs, he believes that they are too low. He decides to seek more information than is provided by the general ledger accounts. He speaks with employees both individually and in their work teams and finds that informal inspections occur frequently. He asks employees to estimate time spent on quality-related activities. He learns that when defect rates begin to increase, employees respond by spending more time on quality-related activities. He estimates that it cost an additional SFr 50,000 last year in prevention costs for the informal inspections that occurred when defect rates increased. In addition, employees would spend time analyzing and correcting the process to improve quality. He estimates this cost to be about SFr 2,000 and categorizes the cost as prevention-related. He also discovers additional production costs of SFr 6,000 incurred for rework that had not been included in the original estimates. Finally, he discovers an additional SFr 7,000 in postsales service costs for handling returns. He summarizes his revised estimate of the costs of quality as follows:

| | First Estimate | Additional Costs | Total Costs |
|---|---|---|---|
| Prevention costs | SFr 10,000 | SFr 50,000 + SFr 2,000 | SFr 62,000 |
| Appraisal costs | 20,000 | | 20,000 |
| Production costs | 5,000 | 6,000 | 11,000 |
| Postsales costs | 8,000 | 7,000 | 15,000 |
| Total costs of quality | SFr 43,000 | SFr 65,000 | SFr 108,000 |

## Using Quality Cost Information to Better Manage Operations

Pierre reports his revised cost estimate to managers who share the information with a team of production employees. The team members are surprised at the high cost, and they discuss ways to reduce it. The team believes that the company can reduce quality costs by identifying and removing defective units earlier in the production process. Therefore, they recommend tracking the number of defective units discovered by employees on the line versus those found by the inspectors.

Production employees also recommend analyzing the types of defects discovered by inspectors to help the employees identify and correct potential problems earlier in the production process. The team believes that some of the inspectors could be assigned to other activities, decreasing the overall costs of quality. In addition, the team recommends tracking the types of warranty problems that occur to determine changes in the design or manufacturing process that would minimize the cost of warranty work and, simultaneously, improve customer satisfaction.

| GUIDE YOUR LEARNING 7.4 Swiss Watch |
|---|

Swiss Watch illustrates the use of ABM to monitor and reduce the costs of quality. For this illustration:

| Define It | Identify Uncertainties | Explore Pros and Cons of Options |
|---|---|---|
| Describe the different costs of quality. | Why were there uncertainties about the total costs of quality? Why is this cost unknown? | What methods did the production team recommend for reducing the costs of quality? What are the likely costs and benefits of each recommendation? |

## ■ Managing Constrained Resources

If an organization faces capacity constraints, ABC can help identify each product's use of constrained resources. By analyzing the activities within the constraints, efficiency improvements can be proposed and tested. Thus, ABC information can help managers identify the best way to relax constraints. ABC information can also be used in designing products and manufacturing or service delivery processes that minimize use of constrained resources.

**CHAPTER REFERENCE**

For more details about maximizing constrained resources, see Chapter 4.

In addition, by developing an ABC system that separates committed from flexible costs, managers would have more accurate information to determine the contribution margin per constrained resource. When products with the highest contribution margin per constrained resource are emphasized, profits are maximized.

## BENEFITS, COSTS, AND LIMITATIONS OF ABC SYSTEMS

Accountants need to consider cost-benefit trade-offs when choosing activities and cost drivers for an ABC system. They must estimate the costs of alternative ABC systems and anticipate the potential benefits from alternative system designs. They also need to recognize that an ABC system might fail to meet expectations.

**Q6** What are the benefits, costs, and limitations of ABC and ABM?

### ■ Benefits of an ABC System

ABC systems enable managers to focus on measurement at the activity level. Once activities are identified and cost drivers are chosen, employees are more aware of cause-and-effect relationships. This awareness prompts employees to search for ways to improve performance simply because they have more information about the cost effects of an activity. By more carefully analyzing activity costs, the importance and materiality of some non-value-added costs become more apparent, and motivation to reduce those costs increases. In an ABC system, activities that do not add value to customers are more likely to be identified and eliminated from operations. Examples include holding excess levels of inventories, unnecessary motion and transportation, waste in the setup process, and inspection inefficiencies.

**HELPUL HINT**

Traditional costing is often referred to as peanut butter costing because it spreads overhead costs without regard to products' use of resources, and leads to product cost cross-subsidization.

More than other costing systems, ABC systems measure the flow of resources in an organization. They reduce the arbitrariness in cost measurement by more closely matching cost allocations to the actual use of resources by operating activities. Compared to the allocation bases used in a traditional costing system, the allocation bases used in an ABC system are more likely to be cost drivers and related to costs, rather than just used to allocate cost. For example, when the Keener ABC team used ABC to allocate overhead costs to regular and premium doors, the flow of resources was more accurately reflected and the allocated costs were different from the job costing system because more cost pools were used and each cost pool was allocated using a cost driver that better reflected the use of the resources in the activity cost pool.

### ■ Costs of an ABC System

Many costs are associated with designing and using an ABC system, including the following:

- System design costs such as employee time and consulting fees
- Accounting and information system modifications needed to gather and report activity and cost driver information
- Employee training to use the ABC system effectively

Sometimes the cost of developing ABC information is low, especially in cases where the activity cost is readily available and the number of times the activity is performed can easily be tracked. Suppose the activity is inspection of units. The cost consists of the salary and fringe benefits of the inspector, and all units are inspected. Identifying salary costs in an accounting system is easy, and fringe benefits costs can be estimated. The number of units produced should be readily available from production records, and the capacity of the inspection area can be easily estimated. Thus, developing an activity-based cost for inspection may be as simple as dividing the salary-related costs by a chosen measure of unit volume.

Other times, ABC information is more costly to develop. Suppose the activity is the setup process. This process often includes labor, supplies, and other resources. Because cost tracing is one of the components of cost assignment under ABC, it takes time and analysis to identify costs that can be traced and those that should be allocated. In addition, data for the cost driver, such as the number of setups, must be tracked.

In general, the costs of an ABC system are higher when more activities or more complex activities are involved. It is more difficult to accurately trace costs to activities as their complexity and number increase. In addition, increased employee training is often required. Also, the process of ABC system development bogs down if too much complexity is introduced at one time. However, a failure to sufficiently break down activities might prevent the system from providing useful information.

Accounting researchers questioned whether the costs of implementing ABC systems were worth the benefits received. They found that although ABC use was associated with higher quality and improved cycle time, for the average firm no significant association was found between ABC use and return on assets. However, ABC appeared to be related to profitability for firms using advanced manufacturing techniques that combine information technology with more flexible manufacturing practices.[10] Researchers who document successful implementations suggest that important factors include top management support and performance evaluations.[11] In addition, researchers have found that for small manufacturing firms, simple ABC systems with few activities and cost drivers are best. These systems are inexpensive yet efficient, and easier for managers to understand and implement.[12]

## ◼ Uncertainties in ABC and ABM Implementation

Managers face many uncertainties about how best to implement an ABC system as well as how useful an ABC system will be. Thus, they face uncertainties about the costs and benefits of using ABC and ABM systems.

Managers use judgment to decide which activities and cost drivers to include in an ABC system because of uncertainty about the set of activities and drivers that would provide the best information. As the number of activities increases, measurement error also tends to increase because a greater number of allocations are used to assign costs to activity cost pools. In addition, it is not always possible to determine the best cost driver. Information for some cost drivers may be readily available, whereas information for a potentially superior driver might be costly to accumulate. When designing an ABC system, accountants cannot foresee all of the various ways in which the new information could be used in ABM to reduce costs or improve decision making. For example, until activities and costs are evaluated, we may not be able to identify non-value-added activities. Accordingly, the ability to identify the most valuable activities to measure and track is uncertain.

Uncertainties are also part of choosing an appropriate denominator value to determine the allocation rate. The accuracy of estimates used in the denominator affect the allocation of cost. We overstate or understate cost when the denominator estimate is too large or small. Although ABC information is more detailed, measurement errors also increase because of estimates. Thus, the additional detail does not necessarily improve the quality of information.

Accountants also face uncertainties about how an organization's employees will respond to the design and implementation of an ABC system. In some cases, employees are afraid of major system changes, especially when their jobs might be viewed as non-value-added. As a result, some employees will fail to provide adequate information for designing the system; they might even provide misleading or incorrect information. If employees believe that their performance will be evaluated using ABC information, they may provide biased information to show better performance. Once the new system is designed, they may try to

[10]See C. Ittner, W. Lanen, and D. Larcker, "The Association Between Activity-Based Costing and Manufacturing Performance," *Journal of Accounting Research,* June 2002.

[11]See M. Shields, "An Empirical Analysis of Firms' Implementation Experiences with Activity-Based Costing," *Journal of Management Accounting Research 7* (1995), pp. 148–166; and G. Foster and D. Swenson, "Measuring the Success of Activity-Based Cost Management and Its Determinants," *Journal of Management Accounting Research 7* (1997), pp. 109–141.

[12]See Needy, Nachtmann, Roztocki, Warner, and Bidanda, "Implementing Activity-Based Costing Systems in Small Manufacturing Firms: A Field Study," *Engineering Management Journal,* March 2003, pp. 3–10.

undermine implementation and training efforts. Even when employees fully embrace the new ABC system, they might misunderstand it and make inappropriate decisions. Furthermore, if an ABC system is overly complex, even the most enthusiastic employees might not be able to take full advantage of it.

## ■ Mismeasurement of Costs Assigned to ABC Activities

As illustrated in Exhibit 7.2, costs must be assigned to each ABC cost pool. Errors may creep into the process of tracing or allocating individual costs, leading to mismeasurement in ABC costs. The allocation process often introduces a degree of measurement error. For example, costs such as supplies and employee benefits might be allocated to a number of activities such as setup, maintenance, and monitoring production. It is impossible to identify the exact amount of cost associated with each activity when we use allocated costs.

In addition, errors are sometimes made in assigning costs directly to ABC pools. In the case of Keener Doors and Windows, suppose a window is pulled periodically from the production line for quality testing and the direct cost of employee labor for this activity is traced to the inspection activity. If a defect is found, inspection activities probably increase, drawing labor resources temporarily away from other production activities. This type of event causes mismeasurement in the assignment of costs across ABC cost pools. The accounting system is unlikely to capture a temporary change in the type of work that employees perform. Because of the measurement error, allocations from the activity cost pools will not reflect the actual flow of resources. However, if the inspection activity is pooled with other production activities, then the temporary reassignment of employees within production will not cause mismeasurement.

In general, the risk of measurement error increases under the following circumstances:

- If uncertainties exist about the activity to which costs relate
- When costs are allocated to ABC cost pools instead of traced
- When the number of ABC cost pools increases

## ■ Relevant ABC Costs for Decision Making

When making decisions about short- or long-term use of resources, decision makers need to identify relevant costs. Therefore, they need to understand how alternative decisions will change costs. Managers sometimes use ABC cost allocation rates as if they are variable costs, that is, as if costs change proportionately as the activity increases or decreases. However, the activity pools often contain costs that do not vary with activity levels, such as fixed costs. Therefore, ABC cost information is often irrelevant or misleading for decision making.

To address this problem, the costs within an activity can be categorized as flexible or committed. **Flexible costs** vary with activity levels, and **committed costs** remain fixed regardless of activity levels. Committed costs are related to capacity and do not change in the short term. Therefore, they do not change proportionately with volume changes. When managers use ABC cost allocation rates for decision making without distinguishing between the flexible and committed costs, their estimates of relevant costs are biased upwards or downwards. The direction of bias depends on how the volume after alternative decisions are implemented compares to the volume upon which the current rates are based.

Suppose ABC cost rates were established at Keener Doors and Windows by estimating monthly ABC cost information. Machine setup costs for glass cutting in the window department were estimated to be $6,720 per month, and the practical capacity was estimated to be 320 batches. In other words, it costs $6,720 per month to supply enough capacity to handle 320 batches of windows. Given this information, the ABC cost allocation rate is set at $21 per batch ($6,720 ÷ 320 batches). If the $6,720 cost is committed, total costs will be $6,720 even when the number of actual batches run is less than 320 during the month. If the managers incorrectly assume that the $21 ABC cost per batch is a variable cost, they are likely to overestimate or underestimate actual costs. For example, if they plan for 200 batches, they would underestimate cost at $4,200 ($21 × 200 batches). If they plan for 400 batches, they would estimate cost at $8,400 ($21 × 400 batches). In this case, costs might be overestimated or underestimated depending on potential extra costs, such as employee overtime, that the company incurs when actual production exceeds practical capacity. ABC allocation rates do not provide accurate cost estimates when they include committed costs or when production levels move to a new relevant range of activity.

To provide managers with information that is more useful for decision making, the ABC system can be set up with separate activity pools and cost rates for:

- Different levels of the ABC cost hierarchy
- Committed and flexible costs within each hierarchy

---

### GUIDE YOUR LEARNING 7.5 Key Terms

Stop to confirm that you understand the new terms introduced in the last several pages.

Activity-based management (p. 270)
*Value-added activities (p. 271)
*Non-value-added activities (p. 271)

*Flexible costs (p. 278)
*Committed costs (p. 278)

For each of these terms, write a definition in your own words. For starred terms, list at least one example that is different from the ones given in this textbook.

---

**CHAPTER REFERENCE**

See Chapter 13 for more information on pricing and the death spiral.

## FOCUS ON ETHICAL DECISION MAKING
### Promoting Inappropriate Uses of ABC

When ABC was first developed, consultants sometimes promoted it for inappropriate uses. Many consulting services focused on using ABC information for short-term decisions such as pricing and product emphasis. Yet in the early stages of ABC and ABM development, both flexible and committed costs were included in ABC cost pools and were not tracked separately. As a result, ABC unit costs included both fixed and variable costs, even when the fixed costs were irrelevant for decision making. ABC promoters suggested that all costs were variable in the long run, and they ignored criticism of their methods.

If the ABC cost rates include fixed costs, their unquestioned use in setting prices is detrimental to operations. If demand falls, then production volumes may fall too, first causing cost per unit to increase and then prices to increase. This type of pricing policy can lead to a death spiral, in which prices increase inappropriately as volumes decline.

After ABC was developed, it was quickly added to cost accounting curriculums at many different universities. However, a few academics were highly critical of ABC and eventually provided evidence that overhead costs included a large portion of fixed costs, even in the long run (e.g., Noreen and Soderstrom, 1994). As research evidence accumulated, ABC consultants suggested that organizations not allocate facility level costs and categorize costs within each activity cost pool as flexible and committed. Then total costs could be used to analyze processes and improve operations, but flexible cost information could be retrieved for decision making.

Currently, "incremental ABC cost analysis" services are being promoted. These services are sometimes called predictive accounting. Because consulting services can be expensive and judging the outcome of new ideas can be difficult, managers need to incorporate healthy skepticism when considering the potential costs and benefits of products and services promoted by consultants.

SOURCE: E. Noreen and N. Soderstrom, "Are Overhead Costs Strictly Proportional to Activity? Evidence from Hospital Service Departments," *Journal of Accounting & Economics*, January 1994, pp. 255–279.

#### Practice Ethical Decision Making

Perform a Web search for articles about *activity-based costing* using one of your library's business search engines, such as ABI Inform and Lexis/Nexis. Also conduct a search for articles using the terms *incremental ABC* and *predictive accounting*. In Chapter 1, we learned about a process for making ethical decisions (Exhibit 1.11). You can address the following questions for this ethical dilemma to improve your skills for making ethical decisions. Think about your answers to these questions and discuss them with others.

*(continued)*

| Ethical Decision-Making Process | Questions to Consider about This Ethical Dilemma |
|---|---|
| Identify ethical problems as they arise. | Did you find articles promoting the use of:<br>• ABC for pricing and other short-term decisions?<br>• Incremental ABC or predictive accounting?<br>When consultants develop management techniques such as ABC, do uncertainties always remain about whether the technique will benefit clients? Does selling ABC consulting services create an ethical problem? Why or why not? |
| Objectively consider the well-being of others and society when exploring alternatives. | In light of uncertainties about whether consulting services will benefit clients:<br>• Why do consultants promote them?<br>• Why do clients purchase the services?<br>• What are the pros and cons to the clients?<br>Did your articles appear to promote appropriate or inappropriate uses of costs for decision making? How do you know? When consultants write articles about a technique such as ABC, are the articles likely to be biased? Why or why not? |
| Clarify and apply ethical values when choosing a course of action. | What are consultants' ethical obligations when selling consulting services that have uncertain outcomes? What values did you use to arrive at your conclusions? |
| Work toward ongoing improvement of personal and organizational ethics. | How can consultants increase the likelihood that clients will benefit from their consulting services? |

# SUMMARY

## Q1 How Is Activity-Based Costing (ABC) Different from Traditional Costing?

**Traditional Costing System**
Few cost pools allocated using traditional allocation bases.

**Activity-Based Costing System**
Multiple cost pools reflecting activities and cost drivers for allocation bases.

## Q2 What Are Activities, and How Are They Identified?

**Activity**
Type of task or function performed in an organization

**Activity Identification**
• Tracking the use of resources
• Using the cost hierarchy
• Grouping homogeneous costs

**Cost Hierarchy**
• Organization-sustaining activities
• Facility-sustaining activities
• Customer-sustaining activities
• Product-sustaining activities
• Batch-level activities
• Unit-level activities

## Q3  What Process Is Used to Assign Costs in an ABC System?

### ABC Procedures

1. Identify the relevant cost object.
2. Identify activities.
3. Assign (trace and allocate) costs to activity-based cost pools.
4. For each ABC cost pool, choose a cost driver.
5. For each ABC cost pool, calculate an allocation rate.

   Allocation rate = Activity cost ÷ Volume of cost driver

6. For each ABC cost pool, allocate activity costs to the cost object.

   Allocation = Allocation rate × Actual volume of activity

### Alternative Allocation Rates

- Past cost rate: Use past costs and past volumes.
- Estimated rate: Use estimated costs and estimated volumes.
- Supply-based rate: Use estimated costs and practical capacity.

## Q4  How Are Cost Drivers Selected for Activities?

### Selection of Cost Drivers

- Cause-and-effect relationship between cost driver and activity costs
- Judgment in choosing and evaluating potential cost drivers

## Q5  What Is Activity-Based Management (ABM)?

### Activity-Based Management

Process of using ABC information to evaluate the costs and benefits of production and internal support activities and to identify and implement opportunities for improvements in profitability, efficiency, and quality within an organization

### Applications of ABM

- Customer profitability
- Product and process design
  - Focus resources on value-added activities
  - Reduce or eliminate non-value-added activities
  - Target and kaizen costing
- Environmental costs
- Quality
  - Prevention activities
  - Appraisal activities
  - Production activities
  - Postsales activities
- Constrained resources

## Q6  What Are the Benefits, Costs, and Limitations of ABC and ABM?

### Benefits

- Increase awareness of cause-and-effect relationships
- Promote performance improvements
- Identify non-value-added activities
- Motivate cost reduction
- Reduce arbitrariness in cost measurement
- Optimize use of constrained resources

### Costs

- System design
- Accounting system modifications
- Employee training
- Higher costs when:
  - More activities are involved.
  - Activities are complex.
  - ABC system is complex.

### Uncertainties in ABC and ABM Implementation

- Choice of activities
- Choice of cost drivers
- Inability to foresee all possible uses of information
- Choice of denominator in allocation rate
- Employee response
- Mismeasurement of costs assigned to cost pools

### Misuse of ABC Information

- ABC costs incorrectly treated as variable costs
- To improve ABC design for decision making:
  - Use cost hierarchy.
  - Separate committed and flexible costs.
  - Choose enough cost pools, but not too many.

## Self-Study Problems

### Self-Study Problem 1  Compute Unit ABC Costs

**Q3**

The Fallon Company manufactures a variety of hand-crafted bed frames. The company's manufacturing activities and related data for the current year follow:

| Manufacturing Activity | Estimated Cost | Cost Driver Used as Allocation Base | Estimated Volume for Cost Driver |
|---|---|---|---|
| Material handling | $ 400,000 | Number of parts | 800,000 parts |
| Cutting | 1,200,000 | Machine hours | 800,000 hours |
| Assembly | 3,000,000 | Direct labor hours | 150,000 hours |
| Wood staining | 1,320,000 | Number of frames stained | 60,000 frames |

Two styles of bed frames were produced in July, a wood frame with fewer parts and a metal frame that required no staining activities. Direct labor is paid $25 per hour. Their quantities, direct material costs, and other data follow:

| | Units Produced | Direct Material | Machine Hours | Number of Parts | Direct Labor Hours |
|---|---|---|---|---|---|
| Wood frames | 5,000 | $600,000 | 5,000 | 100,000 | 6,000 |
| Metal frames | 1,000 | 200,000 | 500 | 10,000 | 3,000 |

**REQUIRED:**

**A.** Compute the ABC cost allocation rates and then calculate total manufacturing costs and unit costs of the wood and metal frames.

**B.** Suppose nonmanufacturing activities, such as product design, were analyzed and allocated to the wood frame at $10 each and the metal frame at $15 each. Moreover, similar analyses were conducted of other nonmanufacturing activities, such as distribution, marketing, and customer service. The support costs allocated were $50 per wood frame and $80 per metal frame. Compute the product cost per unit including the nonmanufacturing costs.

### Solution to Self-Study Problem 1

**A.**

| Resource or Activity | Wood Frames | | Metal Frames | |
|---|---|---|---|---|
| Direct materials | | $ 600,000 | | $200,000 |
| Direct labor | 6,000 × $25 | 150,000 | 3,000 × $25 | 75,000 |
| Material handling | 100,000 × $0.50 | 50,000 | 10,000 × $0.50 | 5,000 |
| Cutting | 5,000 × $30 | 150,000 | 500 × $30 | 15,000 |
| Assembly | 6,000 × $20 | 120,000 | 3,000 × $20 | 60,000 |
| Wood staining | 5,000 × $22 | 110,000 | 0 × $22 | 0 |
| Total | | $1,180,000 | | $355,000 |
| Per unit | $1,180,000 ÷ 5,000 | $236 per unit | $355,000 ÷ 1,000 | $355 per unit |

**B.** Product cost per unit including manufacturing and nonmanufacturing costs:

Wood frame = $236 + $10 + $50 = $296
Metal frame = $355 + $15 + $80 = $450

### Self-Study Problem 2  ABC Activities and Cost Drivers, Measurement Error, Usefulness

**Q2, Q4, Q5, Q6**

You have been asked to analyze your sister's preschool operation to determine in what ways she can improve quality and reduce costs. You decide to analyze the activities provided by the preschool and use an

ABC system to assign costs to the activities. The following list contains potential activities from which to choose.

- *Learning activities* At times during the day children are listening to stories, learning to sing simple songs, following simple directions as part of games or art activities, and playing interactively with special toys developed to enhance eye-hand coordination or understanding of spatial relations.
- *Resting* The children rest on mats during this activity while one teacher monitors and the other teachers prepare lesson plans.
- *Snack and meal activities* Snacks and meals are prepared by teachers and one food service employee. Sometimes the students prepare their own snacks and practice following directions.
- *Free play activities* While children play either inside or outside, a few teachers monitor their progress while others prepare learning activities to be used later.
- *Art and craft activities* These daily activities promote some of the same skills as the learning activities, but children are encouraged to be more creative.
- *Miscellaneous* These activities include greeting the children, helping them with their coats, helping them use the restroom, interacting with parents, and conferencing with parents.
- *Music activity* This weekly activity encourages the children's interest in music and dance.
- *Conferencing with parents* This quarterly activity consists of the head teacher (your sister) meeting with each child's parents for half an hour.

**REQUIRED:**

❸ A. Choose several activities to use for cost pools. Explain your choices.

❸ B. Choose cost drivers for these pools. Explain your choices.

❷ C. Identify possible reasons why measurement error might exist in the ABC costs.

❷ D. How would you estimate the increase in future costs if your sister plans to expand her operations?

## Solution to Self-Study Problem 2

**A.** First consider the activity hierarchy. Some costs can be allocated to the organization, such as rent, insurance, licenses, and so on. Greeting and helping children with coats may be considered part of the organization-sustaining costs, or they may be viewed as a separate activity cost pool. This reasoning is also true for interacting with parents. However, time greeting and interacting with parents varies on a daily basis but is not necessarily dependent on the number of children or number of classes. Therefore, these activities will most likely be considered part of the facility-sustaining costs.

No product-sustaining costs are evident because the organization has only one product.

In this organization, we can consider each class a batch when the children are all involved in a similar activity. Resting and free play could be combined into a single batch-level cost pool because no supplies are used in these activities and fewer teachers are interacting with the children. Learning, art, and music activities could be combined as a second batch-level cost pool because they require similar numbers of teachers and supplies.

Snacks and meals can be considered a unit-level cost pool, which varies with number of children. For this cost pool, flexible and committed costs could be tracked separately. Parent conferences could also be a unit-level cost pool because gathering information about each child and meeting with each child's parents would require about the same amount of time per child.

Notice that the choices of activities are somewhat arbitrary. As an alternative to the preceding set of activities, a separate pool could be established for each activity described in the problem.

**B.** The cost driver for resting and play could be measured in time or in days if the same times are used each day. Teacher time might be used as a cost driver for learning activities, because most of the teachers are involved in these activities. Number of meals served or number of children could drive the costs of snacks and meals. Number of children would be a likely cost driver for conferencing with parents.

**C.** We discuss only two possible types of measurement error in this solution; there are many other possible answers. Measurement error might occur if some of the teachers use unpaid time to prepare activities. These potential costs are not measured. The willingness to spend extra time on preparation varies among teachers. If a new teacher is hired who does not want to spend unpaid time then labor costs could increase or the quality of the program could decrease. Another type of measurement error occurs if different groups of children require different levels of monitoring for play time and nap time. For groups that require more time, labor costs could be understated if teachers require more preparation time, or the quality of the program could suffer if no more time is spent in preparation.

**D.** Because this organization relies heavily on labor, the best predictor for expansion costs is to determine the desired ratio of children to teachers. Facility-sustaining cost changes also need to be predicted. Meal and snack costs probably contain both flexible and committed components, taking into consideration the food service worker who is employed. The cost of raw materials, such as art supplies, would need to be separated from the activity cost pool to predict costs for more children.

---

**REVIEW** Use the exercises in the following boxes in the chapter to review key terms and key techniques, analyze chapter illustrations, improve your learning of new concepts, and practice ethical decision making:

Guide Your Learning 7.1: Key Terms (p. 266)

Guide Your Learning 7.2: Keener Doors and Windows (Part 1) (p. 269)

Guide Your Learning 7.3: Keener Doors and Windows (Part 2) (p. 272)

Guide Your Learning 7.4: Swiss Watch (p. 275)

Guide Your Learning 7.5: Key Terms (p. 279)

Focus on Ethical Decision Making: Promoting Inappropriate Uses of ABC (p. 279)

---

## QUESTIONS

**7.1** Mannon Company's accountant exclaimed, "Our cost accounting system allocates overhead based on direct labor hours, but our overhead costs appear to be more related to setup activities than to the use of direct labor. It seems as though our costing system allocates too much cost to large batches of product and not enough cost to small batches." Explain what she means.

**7.2** Describe the six ABC cost hierarchies.

**7.3** The results from allocations using ABC are usually different from the results using traditional cost systems. Explain why these differences arise.

**7.4** Does increasing the number of cost pools always increase the accuracy of allocations under an ABC system? Explain your answer.

**7.5** Is an ABC system appropriate for every industry and every type or organization? Explain your answer.

**7.6** Should ABC be used in service industries? Why or why not?

**7.7** Does measurement error increase or decrease when ABC systems are implemented? Explain your answer.

**7.8** List several costs and several benefits of implementing an ABC system.

**7.9** Suppose that you are part of a student consulting team working for your university. You need to analyze accounting department activities and set up cost pools for these activities. Explain how you would identify the activities and pools.

**7.10** Is ABC appropriate for an organization that sells a wide range of customized products manufactured using flexible manufacturing systems? Why or why not?

**7.11** Explain how traditional and ABC cost systems differ.

**7.12** Explain the difference between activity-based costing and activity-based management.

**7.13** Why might ABC and ABM be useful in reducing environmental costs?

**7.14** In your own words, describe the four types of quality-related activities.

---

## EXERCISES

**7.15**
**Q2**
**Mapping costs to the cost hierarchy** Each of the following is a cost incurred by Fairgood & Hernandez, a small CPA firm.

**REQUIRED:** ❶ Identify whether each of the following costs most likely relates to an (1) organization-sustaining activity, (2) customer-sustaining activity, (3) product-sustaining activity, (4) batch-level activity, or (5) unit-level activity. For each item, explain your choice.

___ A. Receptionist salary
___ B. Financial forecasting software
___ C. Photocopy machine rental
___ D. Janitorial service
___ E. Audit manager salary

___ F. Long-distance telephone charges
___ G. Meal costs for entertaining clients
___ H. Costs of annual employee golf party
___ I. Office supplies such as paperclips and tablets of paper
___ J. Annual subscription for income tax regulations

**7.16**
**Q2**

**Identifying costs using the ABC cost hierarchies** MicroBrew Northwest is a successful brewery engaged in the development and production of specialty micro brews. It uses an activity-based costing system. During the past year, it has incurred $1,250,000 of product development costs, $850,000 of materials handling costs, $2,500,000 of production line labor costs, $700,000 for production setup costs, $500,000 in power costs for cooling beer and running equipment, and $1,500,000 for manufacturing facility management.

**REQUIRED:** **①** In an ABC cost hierarchy, calculate the total cost that would be classified as:

A. Facility-sustaining.          C. Batch-level.

B. Product-sustaining.          D. Unit-level.

**7.17** **ABC cost hierarchy** In ABC systems, activities are often separated into a hierarchy of six
**Q2** categories.

**REQUIRED:** In your own words, define and give examples of the following types of activities and costs in an ABC system for a national car rental company such as **Hertz** or **Enterprise**:

A. Unit-level activities and costs.

B. Batch-level activities and costs.

C. Product-sustaining activities and costs.

D. Customer-sustaining activities and costs.

E. Facility-sustaining activities and costs.

F. Organization-sustaining activities and costs.

**7.18** **Cost pools and cost drivers** Following are lists of potential cost pools and cost drivers.
**Q4**

| Cost Pool | Cost Driver |
|---|---|
| _____ Machining | A. Number of employees |
| _____ Purchasing activities | B. Number of parts per unit |
| _____ Inspection | C. Pounds of laundry processed |
| _____ Assembly | D. Number of invoices |
| _____ Payroll | E. Number of batches |
| _____ A special quick-freezing process for food | F. Number of machine hours |
| _____ Laundry in a hospital | G. Number of units |

**REQUIRED:** Match each cost driver to the most appropriate cost pool. Use each cost driver only once. Explain your choice.

**7.19** **Traditional versus ABC costing** Kalder Products manufactures two component parts, AJ40 and
**Q1, Q3** AJ60. AJ40 components are being introduced currently, and AJ60 parts have been in production for several years. For the upcoming period, 1,000 units of each product are planned for manufacturing. Assume that the only relevant overhead cost is for engineering change orders (any requested changes in product design or the manufacturing process). AJ40 components are expected to require four change orders, and AJ60 only two. Each AJ40 requires 1 machine hour, and each AJ60 requires 1.5 machine hours. The cost of a change order is $300.

**REQUIRED:** A. Estimate the cost of engineering change orders for AJ40 and AJ60 components if Kalder uses a traditional costing method and machine hours as the allocation base.

B. Now suppose that Kalder uses an ABC system and allocates the cost of change orders using as cost driver the number of change orders. Estimate the cost for change orders for each unit of AJ40 and AJ60.

**ⓔ** C. Calculate the difference in overhead allocated to each product. This figure represents an amount that one product cross-subsidizes the other product. Explain what that means.

**7.20** **ABC costing, ABM** Applewood Electronics manufactures two large-screen television models, the
**Q1, Q3, Q5** Monarch, which has been produced since 2000 and sells for $900, and the Regal, a new model introduced in early 2005 that sells for $1,140. Applewood's CEO, Harry Hazelwood, suggested that
**CMA** the company should concentrate its marketing resources on the Regal model and begin to phase out the Monarch model.

Applewood currently uses a traditional costing system. The following cost information has been used as a basis for pricing decisions over the past year.

| Per-Unit Data | Monarch | Regal |
|---|---|---|
| Direct materials | $208 | $584 |
| Direct labor hours | 1.5 | 3.5 |
| Machine hours | 8.0 | 4.0 |
| Units produced | 22,000 | 4,000 |

Direct labor cost is $12 per hour, and the machine usage cost is $18 per hour. Manufacturing overhead costs were estimated at $4,800,000 and were allocated on the basis of machine hours.

Martin Alecks, the new company controller, suggested that an activity-based costing analysis first be run to get a better picture of the true manufacturing cost. The following data were collected:

| Activity Center | Cost Driver | Traceable Costs |
| --- | --- | --- |
| Soldering | Number of solder joints | $  942,000 |
| Shipments | Number of shipments | 860,000 |
| Quality control | Number of inspections | 1,240,000 |
| Purchase orders | Number of orders | 950,400 |
| Machining | Machine hours | 57,600 |
| Machine setups | Number of setups | 750,000 |
| Total traceable costs | | $4,800,000 |

| Activity | Number of Events | | |
| --- | --- | --- | --- |
| | Monarch | Regal | Total |
| Soldering | 1,185,000 | 385,000 | 1,570,000 |
| Shipments | 16,200 | 3,800 | 20,000 |
| Quality control | 56,200 | 21,300 | 77,500 |
| Purchase orders | 80,100 | 109,980 | 190,080 |
| Machining | 176,000 | 16,000 | 192,000 |
| Machine setups | 16,000 | 14,000 | 30,000 |

Selling, general, and administrative expenses per unit sold are $265.00 for Monarch and $244.50 for Regal.

**REQUIRED:**
**A.** Calculate the manufacturing cost per unit for Monarch and Regal under:
   **1.** A traditional costing system
   **2.** The ABC system
**B.** Explain the differences in manufacturing cost per unit calculated in part (A).
**C.** Calculate the operating profit per unit for Monarch and Regal under:
   **1.** A traditional costing system
   **2.** The ABC system
**② D.** Should Applewood concentrate its marketing efforts on Monarch or on Regal? Explain how the use of ABC affects your recommendation.

**7.21**
**Q3, Q5**
**CMA**
**ABC costing, ABM** Palmer Company uses an activity-based costing system. It has the following manufacturing activity areas, related drivers used as allocation bases, and cost allocation rates:

| Activity | Cost Driver | Cost Allocation Rate |
| --- | --- | --- |
| Machine setup | Number of setups | $50.00 |
| Material handling | Number of parts | 0.50 |
| Machining | Machine hours | 26.00 |
| Assembly | Direct labor hours | 22.00 |
| Inspection | Number of finished units | 12.00 |

During the month, 100 units were produced, requiring two setups. Each unit consisted of 19 parts, used 1.5 direct labor hours, and 1.25 machine hours. Direct materials cost $100 per finished unit. All other manufacturing costs are classified as conversion costs. ABC costs for research and marketing costs are $140. All other nonmanufacturing ABC costs are $320 per unit.

**REQUIRED:**
**A.** Calculate the manufacturing cost per unit for the period.
**B.** Calculate the total cost (manufacturing and nonmanufacturing costs) per unit for the period.
**ℯ C.** Suppose Palmer Company's managers want to implement target costing. Under target costing, the managers need to determine the amount of cost savings that must be achieved to earn a desired level of profit. If they must set a competitive price of $650 and require a 10% profit based on the total cost calculated in part (B), how much cost savings must they generate?

**7.22** **ABC in job costing, ABM, non-value-added activities** Kestral Manufacturing identified the following overhead costs and cost drivers for the current period. Kestral produces customized products that move through several different processes. Materials and intermediate products are moved among several different work stations. Custom features are designed by engineers.

Q3, Q5

| Activity | Cost Driver | Estimated Cost | Estimated Activity Level |
|---|---|---|---|
| Machine setup | Number of setups | $ 40,000 | 400 |
| Material handling | Number of times materials are moved | 160,000 | 16,000 |
| Product design | Design hours | 100,000 | 2,000 |
| Inspection | Number of inspections | 260,000 | 13,000 |
| Total cost | | $560,000 | |

Information for three of the jobs completed during the period follows.

| | Job 42 | Job 43 | Job 44 |
|---|---|---|---|
| Direct materials | $10,000 | $24,000 | $16,000 |
| Direct labor | $4,000 | $4,000 | $8,000 |
| Units completed | 200 | 100 | 400 |
| Number of setups | 2 | 4 | 8 |
| Number of materials moves | 60 | 20 | 100 |
| Number of inspections | 40 | 20 | 60 |
| Number of design hours | 20 | 100 | 20 |

**REQUIRED:**
A. If the company uses ABC, how much overhead cost should be assigned to Job 42?
B. If the company uses ABC, calculate the cost per unit for Job 43.
❶ C. Kestral would like to reduce the cost of its overhead activities. Describe non-value-added activities and explain why reducing these specific activities would also reduce cost.

**7.23** **Design ABC system, calculate per-unit ABC costs, uncertainties** Suppose that Elite Daycare provides two different services, full-time childcare for preschoolers, and after-school care for older children. The director would like to estimate an annual cost per child in each of the daycare programs, ignoring any facility-sustaining costs. She is considering expanding the services and wants to know whether full-time or after-school care is more profitable.

Q2, Q3, Q4, Q6

The following activities and annual costs apply to the daycare center. Salaries and wages are $100,000. Full-time children arrive between 8:00 and 9:00 A.M. Older children arrive about 3:00 P.M. All of the children are gone by 6:00 P.M. Employees estimate that they spend about 20% of their time on meal-related activities, 20% supervising naps or recreation, 10% in greeting or sending children home, and the rest of the time presenting educational experiences to the children. Meals and snacks cost about $20,000. Preschoolers receive two snacks and one meal per day, and the older children receive one snack per day. On average, snacks and meals do not differ in cost. Supplies cost $10,000 for the full-time childcare program and $8,000 for the after-school program.

Currently, 30 children participate in full-time care and 10 children in after-school care. Because Elite Daycare maintains a waiting list for openings in its programs, the number of children in each program remains steady.

**REQUIRED:**
🅔 A. Identify a cost object and then choose a set of activities and cost drivers for Elite Daycare's ABC system. Explain your choices.
🅔 B. Using the activities you chose in part (A), estimate the annual cost per child in each program.
❶ C. Do uncertainties exist about the proportion of salaries and wages that should be allocated to full-time care versus after-school care? Why or why not?

**7.24** **ABM, customer profitability** Suppose that you are asked for suggestions about increasing profitability for a customer that purchases low-margin products and requires costly services.

Q5

**REQUIRED:**
A. In your own words, define activity-based management (ABM).
B. In your own words, describe high-cost and low-cost customers.
❶ C. Prepare a brief paragraph suggesting methods to improve profitability for this customer.

**7.25**
Q1, Q3, Q5
CMA

**Quality costs using ABC versus traditional costing** New-Rage Cosmetics uses a traditional cost accounting system to allocate quality control costs uniformly to all products at a rate of 14.5% of direct labor cost. Monthly direct labor cost for Satin Sheen makeup is $27,500. In an attempt to more equitably distribute quality control costs, New-Rage is considering activity-based costing. The following monthly data have been gathered for Satin Sheen makeup.

> Incoming material inspection:
>     Cost driver—type of material
>     Cost allocation rate—$11.50 per type of material
>     Quantity—12 types of material
> In-process inspection:
>     Cost driver—number of units
>     Cost allocation rate—$0.14 per unit
>     Quantity—17,500 units
> Product certification:
>     Cost driver—per order
>     Cost allocation rate—$77 per order
>     Quantity—25 orders

REQUIRED: **ⓔ A.** Calculate the amount of quality control cost assigned to each order of Satin Sheen makeup using:
    **1.** Activity-based costing (*Hint:* Total all the ABC costs for one month and divide by the number of orders.)
    **2.** Traditional cost accounting
**B.** Explain the difference in quality control costs assigned under the two methods.

**7.26**
Q5

**Categorizing quality activities** Following is a list of quality-related activities:

| Type | Quality Activity |
|------|------------------|
| _____ | 1. Inspection of units when they are 100% complete to remove defective units |
| _____ | 2. Designing a process with as few parts as possible to reduce the chance of defects |
| _____ | 3. Warranty costs for defective products returned to the factory for rework |
| _____ | 4. Reworking spoiled units before they leave the factory |
| _____ | 5. Costs to defend the company against lawsuits for damages caused by defective products |
| _____ | 6. Tracking number of defects for each manufacturing team and posting daily defect rates on a plant-wide bulletin board |
| _____ | 7. Redesigning a manufacturing process to lower the rate of defects |

REQUIRED: **ⓔ** Mark each activity according to whether it pertains to the internal costs of prevention (P), appraisal (A), production (PR), or post sales (PS) costs.

# PROBLEMS

**7.27**
Q3, Q6

**Setting up an ABC system, uncertainties** Following is a list of steps that must be performed in setting up an ABC system:

> _____ Identify and sum the costs into activity-based cost pools.
> _____ Choose a cost driver for each activity.
> _____ For each ABC cost pool, allocate overhead costs to the product or service.
> _____ Identify the relevant cost object.
> _____ Identify the activities necessary for production or service delivery.
> _____ For each ABC cost pool, calculate a cost allocation rate.

REQUIRED: **A.** Number the steps from 1 through 6 to indicate the sequence in which they are performed.
**❶ B.** For each step, explain whether uncertainties are likely.
**❷ C.** Pick the step that you think would require the greatest use of judgment, that is, would include the most uncertainties. Explain your choice.

**7.28**
Q2, Q6

**ABC cost hierarchy, uncertainties** In ABC systems, activities are often separated into a hierarchy of categories.

REQUIRED: **A.** In your own words, explain what is meant by a cost hierarchy in ABC.
**❶ B.** Explain why uncertainty is possible in classifying costs within the cost hierarchy.
**❷ C.** Explain how categorizing costs into a hierarchy helps accountants determine how costs behave.

**7.29**
Q1, Q3, Q6

**ABC versus traditional job costing, uncertainties, advantages and disadvantages** Vines Corporation produces custom machine parts on a job order basis. The company has two direct product cost categories: direct materials and direct labor. In the past, indirect manufacturing costs were allocated to products using a single indirect cost pool, allocated based on direct labor hours. The indirect cost rate was $115 per direct labor hour.

The managers of Vines Corporation decided to switch from a manual system to software programs that release materials and signal machines when to begin working. Simultaneously, the company adopted an activity-based costing system. The manufacturing process has been organized into six activities, each with its own supervisor who is responsible for controlling costs. The following list indicates the activities, cost drivers, and cost allocation rates.

| Activity | Cost Driver | Cost per Unit of Cost Driver |
|---|---|---|
| Material handling | Number of parts | $ 0.40 |
| Milling | Machine hours | 20.00 |
| Grinding | Number of parts | 0.80 |
| Assembly | Hours spent in assembly | 5.00 |
| Inspection | Number of units produced | 25.00 |
| Shipping | Number of orders shipped | 1,500.00 |

The company's information system automatically collects the necessary data for these six activity areas. The data for two recent jobs follow:

| | Job Order 410 | Job Order 411 |
|---|---|---|
| Direct materials cost | $9,700 | $59,900 |
| Direct labor cost | $ 750 | $11,250 |
| Number of direct labor hours | 25 | 375 |
| Number of parts | 500 | 2,000 |
| Number of machine hours | 150 | 1,050 |
| Number of job orders shipped | 1 | 1 |
| Number of units | 10 | 200 |
| Number of hours in assembly | 2 | 30 |

**REQUIRED:**

**A.** Suppose the company had not adopted an ABC system. Compute the manufacturing cost per unit for Job Orders 410 and 411 under the old, traditional costing system.

**B.** Under the new ABC system, compute the manufacturing cost per unit for Job Orders 410 and 411.

**C.** Compare the costs per unit for Job Orders 410 and 411 as computed. Explain why the cost per unit under the traditional costing system is different from cost per unit under the ABC system.

**①D.** Explain why uncertainties may arise about the choice of cost drivers for each activity.

**②E.** Identify and explain to Vine Corporation's managers the possible advantages and disadvantages of adopting the ABC system.

**7.30**
Q1, Q3, Q5

**ABC and process costing** Kim Mills produces three different types of fabric using two departments. In department 1, machines weave the cloth. In department 2, the cloth is dyed a variety of colors. Information for the combined use of resources in both departments for the 3 types of fabric follows.

Bolts are 20 yards each. All fabric is inspected during production. Robotic equipment inspects the fabric for obvious flaws as the bolts are wound up. Each bolt spends about 5 minutes in the inspection process.

| | Denim | Lightweight Cotton | Heavyweight Cotton | Total |
|---|---|---|---|---|
| Monthly production in units (bolts of fabric) | 1,000 bolts | 4,000 bolts | 2,000 bolts | 7,000 bolts |
| Direct materials costs | $8,000 | $24,000 | $20,000 | $52,000 |
| Direct labor costs | $660 | $1,320 | $920 | $2,900 |
| Direct labor hours | 33 hours | 66 hours | 46 hours | 145 hours |
| Machine hours | 500 hours | 1,333.3 hours | 1,500 hours | 3,333.3 hours |
| Number of setups for dye color changes | 10 setups | 30 setups | 20 setups | 60 setups |
| Inspection time | 83.3 hours | 333.3 hours | 166.6 hours | 583.2 hours |

Combined overhead costs for the two departments follow:

| | |
|---|---:|
| Cost to operate and maintain machines | $40,000 |
| Setup costs | 11,000 |
| Inspection costs | 6,996 |
| Total | $57,996 |

Previously, Kim Mills used a process costing system that allocated direct materials to each product separately, but allocated direct labor and conversion costs as if they were incurred equally across the units produced. Under the process costing system, the overhead cost for department 1 is $19,332 and for department 2 it is $38,664. Direct labor hours and costs in department 1 are 55 hours at $1,100, and the remaining are in department 2. Direct materials for department 1 are $6,000 for denim, $16,000 for lightweight, and $15,000 for heavyweight. The remaining direct materials are added in department 2. No beginning or ending inventory or abnormal spoilage is recorded for Kim Mills this period.

**REQUIRED:**

**A.** Set up a spreadsheet to perform the following calculations. Use a data input section and cell referencing.

(e) **1.** Use traditional process costing to allocate the direct materials and conversion costs per department to total bolts produced. Develop a cost per bolt for each type of fabric. (*Hint:* You will need to first calculate the equivalent cost per bolt for conversion costs for each department.)

**2.** Using activity-based costing, develop a cost per bolt.

❶ **B.** Compare the process costing and ABC results. Identify the products with overstated costs and those with understated costs. Explain why the costs are misstated under traditional process costing.

❷ **C.** How could managers use the ABC information to improve operations?

**7.31** **ABC costs, uncertainties, ABM, non-value-added activities** The Pond Kit Company manufac-
**Q3, Q5** tures kits for fish ponds. The managers recently set up an ABC system to identify and reduce non-value-added activities. The ABC system includes the following cost pools, cost drivers, and estimated costs for manufacturing activities:

| Activity | Cost Driver | Cost Allocation Rate |
|---|---|---|
| Material handling | Number of parts | $ 1.00 per part |
| Forming | Molding hours | 40.00 per hour |
| Molding setup | Number of batches | 50.00 per batch |
| Packing and shipping | Weight | 1.30 per pound |
| Inspection | Finished kits | 10.00 per kit |
| Direct labor | Finished kits | 20.00 per kit |
| Direct materials | Finished kits | 100.00 per kit |

The company manufactures 10 kits per batch. Each kit requires 20 parts and two hours in molding, and weighs 30 pounds.

**REQUIRED:**

**A.** Calculate the total ABC manufacturing cost per batch.

**B.** Calculate the total ABC cost per finished kit.

**C.** Suppose that Pond Kit's managers also want to allocate marketing costs and customer service to each product. Total marketing costs for the period were $15,000, and customer service costs were $25,000. Number of batches produced was 1,000. Calculate the total ABC cost per unit and cost per kit, including the costs of marketing and customer services.

❶ **D.** Are the activities listed likely to be the only possible set of activities for Pond Kit Company? Why or why not?

❷ **E.** Describe how the managers and accountants of Pond Kit Company might use this new ABC system to identify non-value-added activities.

**7.32** **Uncertainties, actual versus estimated costs, practical capacity** Data Processors performs credit
**Q2, Q3, Q6** card services for banks. The company uses an ABC system. The following information applies to the past year:

| Activity | Estimated Cost | Actual Cost | Cost Driver |
|---|---|---|---|
| Processing transactions | $2,000,000 | $2,200,000 | Number of transactions |
| Issuing monthly statements | 1,000,000 | 1,300,000 | Number of statements |
| Issuing new credit cards | 500,000 | 400,000 | Number of new credit cards |
| Resolving billing disputes | 90,000 | 100,000 | Number of disputes |
| Total | $3,590,000 | $4,000,000 | |

| Cost Driver | Estimated Activity Level | Actual Activity Level |
|---|---|---|
| Number of transactions | 5,000,000 | 5,800,000 |
| Number of statements | 250,000 | 270,000 |
| Number of new credit cards | 100,000 | 110,000 |
| Number of disputes | 3,000 | 3,500 |

**REQUIRED:**

**❶ A.** Are the activities listed likely to be the only possible set of activities for the ABC system? Why or why not?

**B.** Using estimated values for costs and activity, calculate an ABC allocation rate for each activity.

**❶ C.** Explain why actual costs and activity levels are likely to be different from estimated amounts.

**ⓔ D.** Is practical capacity likely to be higher or lower than the estimated activity levels? Explain.

**7.33**

**Q3, Q6**

www.wiley.com/
college/eldenburg

**Government use of ABC, steps for performing ABC** Agencies of the federal government sometimes create handbooks on various business topics. The **Federal Aviation Administration** created the following handbook:

*Business Process Improvement (Reengineering): Handbook of Standards and Guidelines* November 30, 1995, version 1.0, published by Federal Aviation Administration (FAA) Office of Information Technology (AIT) Business Process Improvement (BPI) Program, available at www.faa.gov/ait/bpi/handbook/index.htm or go to www.wiley.com/college/eldenburg.

Chapter 5 of the handbook addresses activity-based costing. Skim the chapter and answer the following questions.

**REQUIRED:**

**❷ A.** Why are government agencies interested in improving their costing systems?

**❷ B.** List the five "Steps for Performing ABC" given in the handbook. Compare these steps to the steps given in this chapter. List their similarities and the differences.

**7.34**

**Q2, Q3, Q4, Q5**

**Design ABC cost system, usefulness for ABM** Jefferson County owns and operates an animal shelter that performs three services: housing and finding homes for stray and unwanted animals, providing health care and neutering services for the animals, and pet training services. One facility is dedicated to housing animals waiting to be adopted. A second facility houses veterinarian services. A third facility houses the director, his staff, and several dog trainers. This facility also has several large meeting rooms that are frequently used for classes given by the animal trainers. The trainers work with all of the animals to ensure that they are relatively easy to manage. They also provide dog obedience classes for adopting families.

Estimated annual costs for the animal shelter and its services are as follows:

| | |
|---|---|
| Director and staff salaries | $ 60,000 |
| Animal shelter employees' salaries | 100,000 |
| Veterinarians and technicians | 150,000 |
| Animal trainers | 40,000 |
| Food and supplies | 125,000 |
| Building-related costs | 200,000 |

On average, 75 animals per day are housed at the facility, or about 27,375 (75 × 365) animal days in total. The number of animals housed during the year totaled 4,500. In addition, the trainers offer about 125 classes during about 30 weeks throughout the year. On average, 10 families attend each class. Last year the veterinarian clinic experienced 5,000 animal visits.

One of the director's staff members just graduated from an accounting program and would like to set up an ABC system for the shelter so that the director can better understand the cost for each of the shelter's services.

He gathers the following information:

| Square footage for each facility: | |
|---|---|
| Animal shelter | 5,000 square feet |
| Director and training | 3,000 square feet |
| Veterinarian clinic | 2,000 square feet |
| Percentage of trainer time used in classes | 50% |
| Supplies used for veterinarian services | $75,000 |

**REQUIRED:**

**②  A.** Identify cost pools and assign costs to them, considering the three cost objects of interest.

**②  B.** Determine a cost driver for each cost pool and explain your choice.

**②  C.** Calculate the allocation rates for each cost pool and cost driver. Interpret the allocation rate for each cost pool (i.e., explain what it means).

**D.** Suppose that the director is concerned about an increase in number of adopted dogs returned to the shelter because of behavior problems. When dogs are returned, the shelter incurs extra animal intake and adoption costs, in addition to extra costs for board, room, and more training for the dogs. In addition, the director is concerned that adopting families may not want another dog because of their unhappy experience. The director views this as a quality problem and wants to improve quality in adoption services and reduce costs at the same time.

 **1.** List the four types of quality activities presented in the chapter. What type of quality problem is the shelter experiencing? Explain your answer.

**②**  **2.** Will the current ABC system help managers determine costs for their quality activities? Explain.

**②**  **3.** List one new cost pool and cost driver that could be used to improve the director's ability to analyze quality.

**7.35** **Benefits, costs, and uncertainties of ABC** In January 2003, CFO.com featured an article entitled, **Q6** "Where Are They Now? From corporate raiders to earnings management to activity-based costing, we take a look at some of finance's greatest hits." The author, David Katz, examined eight ideas that were big news in corporate finance and accounting practitioner journals over the last two decades. He rated these ideas using gold stars ("the idea is still peaking"), silver stars ("percolating along just fine"), and bronze stars (the idea is gone). Most of the ideas, including activity-based costing, were awarded silver stars. Activity-based costing was awarded a silver star because, although it has lost ground lately, Katz believed that interest may resurge if the recession continues.

When Robert Kaplan and other academics published their first papers explaining ABC in the late 1980s, business managers were highly interested. ABC involves identifying activities and cost drivers that should reflect a cause-and-effect relationship with cost for many of the resources used to produce goods. Kaplan and other consultants extolled the advantages of ABC for understanding product profitability. They suggested that managers did not really understand how products used resources in the manufacturing process.

By the mid-1990s, some business experts argued that ABC was being replaced with tools such as economic value-added (see Chapter 15) and the balanced scorecard (see Chapter 16). However, a large number of organizations continued to use ABC. For example, consulting firm **Bain & Company** found that 50 percent of the 708 companies they surveyed during 2002 use ABC. Bain & Company also found that companies are using multiple analytical tools—they are not relying on any single tool, such as ABC, to meet all of their needs.

"Some observers contend that ABC will come back in vogue—if the recession continues," says Katz. ABC provides information about customer profitability and could help companies develop ways to raise profits without raising prices.

SOURCES: D. M. Katz, "Where Are They Now?" *CFO.com*, January 5, 2003, available at www.cfo.com/Article?article=8473; and D. M. Katz, "Activity-Based Costing (ABC)," *CFO.com*, December 31, 2002, available at www.cfo.com/Article?article=8516. D. Rigby, "Management Tools Survey 2003: Usage Up as Companies Strive to Make Headway in Tough Times," *Strategy & Leadership* 31, no. 5 (2003), pp. 4–11.

**REQUIRED:**

    **A.** Why might accountants believe that ABC information would be useful?

**❶ B.** What uncertainties do managers face when they adopt ideas that are new and for which there is little data about effectiveness?

**❷ C.** Given uncertainties about whether a new method will be effective, why might managers consider adopting it?

**❷ D.** Discuss possible reasons for a method losing favor over time.

**❷ E.** How might a recession affect the popularity of ABC?

☆ **7.36**

Q1, Q2, Q4, Q6

**CASE:**
**COLOMBO**
**FROZEN YOGURT**

www.wiley.com/
college/eldenburg

**Traditional versus ABC system, activities and cost drivers, quality of information** Read the following case, which can be downloaded from the IMA Web site (IMA grants permission to copy this case for classroom use):

*J. Guy and J. Saly, "Colombo Frozen Yogurt: Activity-Based Costing Applied to Market-ing Costs," Case 6 (pp. 67–69) in* Cases from Management Accounting Practice, *vol. 15, Wayne Bremser and Jim Mackey (eds.) (Montvale, NJ: Institute of Management Accoun-tants, 2000), available online at www.imanet.org. (Click on* Interest Groups, *then* Aca-demics, *then* IMA Case e-Journal, *then* Volume 15, *then* Case 6) *or go to www.wiley.com/college/eldenburg.*

**REQUIRED:**
**ANALYZE**
**INFORMATION**

The following questions will help you analyze the information for this problem. Do not turn in your answers to these questions unless your professor asks you to do so.

    **A.** Using the ABC information in the case, prepare a new profit and loss statement for the yogurt segments.

**❶ B.** The first step in setting up an ABC system is to identify relevant cost objects. In this case, the cost objects are the two yogurt product segments. Were these likely to be the only possible cost objects for Colombo's yogurt business? Why or why not?

    **C.** The second step in setting up an ABC system is to identify activities. In this case, the managers identified activities that were identical to the categories of costs used in the old costing system.

**❷**     **1.** Why is the set of ABC activities usually different from the cost categories used in tra-ditional costing systems?

**❷**     **2.** Identify two possible reasons why Colombo's managers decided to establish ABC ac-tivities that were identical to the old cost categories.

**❷ D.** Briefly discuss whether each of the following cost pools for Colombo most likely relates to a facility-sustaining activity, customer-sustaining activity, product-sustaining activity, batch-level activity, or unit-level activity:

    **1.** Pick/pack and shipping costs

    **2.** Selling, general, and administrative costs

**❷ E.** The fourth step in setting up an ABC system is to choose a cost driver for each ABC cost pool. Discuss whether Colombo's ABC cost drivers for each of the following activities are reasonable:

    **1.** Pick/pack and shipping costs

    **2.** Selling, general, and administrative costs

**REQUIRED:**
**WRITTEN**
**ASSIGNMENT**

Suppose Colombo's accountants are thinking about making additional changes to the ABC sys-tem. You are an intern at Colombo and have been asked to critique the existing ABC system. Turn in your answer to the following.

**❸ F.** Use the information you learned from the preceding analyses to draft a memo to Colombo's controller presenting your evaluation of whether the profit and loss statement under ABC costing from part (A) provides a reasonable measure of the profit from the two yogurt segments. Provide the controller with appropriate information for understand-ing your evaluation.

# BUILD YOUR PROFESSIONAL COMPETENCIES

**7.37**
**Q3, Q6**

**Focus on Professional Competency: Research** *Uncertainties, research, guidelines, assumptions, and choices for ABC system* Review the following definition and elements for the Research competency.[13]

**DEFINITION:** *Although accounting professionals need a foundation in standards and other relevant rules, such guidance is constantly evolving. Many accounting profession functions depend on obtaining information from within and outside of an entity. Accordingly, the individual preparing to enter the accounting profession needs to have strong research skills to access relevant guidance or other information, understand it, and apply it.*

## ELEMENTS FOR THIS COMPETENCY INCLUDE

| Level 1 | Level 2 | Level 3 | Level 4 |
|---|---|---|---|
| 1. Employs relevant research skills for locating data<br><br>2. Identifies relevant information such as industry trends, internal performance history, benchmarks, and best practices<br><br>3. Accesses relevant standards, rules, and other information<br><br>4. Explains why there are uncertainties about the interpretation of information, including existing rules | 5. Articulates assumptions and reasoning associated with application of existing rules to a given problem<br><br>6. Qualitatively interprets research findings from a variety of viewpoints | 7. Articulates general concepts from existing rules and explains how those concepts apply across a range of problems, including problems not explicitly described<br><br>8. Develops and uses reasonable guidelines for drawing conclusions in light of conflicting or ambiguous data | 9. Employs relevant research skills over time to generate new information |

**REQUIRED:**

**❶ A.** Focus on competency element 4, which addresses uncertainty about interpretation of information. Which material in Chapter 7 addresses this competency element? Explain.

**B.** Focus on competency elements 1, 6, and 9, which describe the research skills accountants must use when implementing a method such as ABC. Answer the following questions:

**❶ 1.** Why is research needed when designing an ABC system? What kinds of research are used?

**❷ 2.** How does the use of an ABC team improve the quality of research when designing an ABC system?

**❹ 3.** Explain why the research process is not complete, even after an ABC system is implemented.

**C.** Focus on competency elements 3, 5, 7, and 8, which require accountants to appropriately identify and use information about accounting practices. There is no set of authoritative rules for most cost accounting practices, including ABC. However, some cost accounting practices are considered better than others. Answer the following questions:

**❶ 1.** What kinds of information are available about ABC and ABM practices?

**❷ 2.** When there are no authoritative rules, does that mean that it does not matter how accountants apply techniques such as ABC and ABM? Explain.

**❷ 3.** Why is it important to articulate the assumptions and reasoning association with implementation of ABC, such as choice of activities and cost drivers?

**❸ 4.** How can a cost accountant decide what to do when there are conflicting recommendations about how a technique such as ABC should be implemented?

**7.38**
**Q5, Q6**

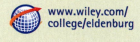

**Integrating Across the Curriculum: Corporate Social Responsibility** *Environmental accounting reports, ABC and ABM for environmental costs* Many countries provide motivation for businesses to produce environmental accounting reports. For example, the **Association of Chartered Certified Accountants (ACCA)** in the United Kingdom developed the European Environmental

---

[13]The definition and elements are reprinted with permission from AICPA; Copyright © 1978–2000 & 2003 by American Institute of Certified Public Accountants. The AICPA's Core Competency Framework can be accessed at eca.aicpaservices.org.

Reporting Awards program in 1997. Currently 12 countries, including the United Kingdom, Denmark, Netherlands, Belgium, France, and Germany, participate in this program. In Japan, the **Global Environmental Forum** and the **National Association for the Promotion of Environmental Conservation** have given "Environmental Report Awards" since 1997. In addition, **Toyo Keizai** and **Green Reporting Forum** have given a Green Reporting Award since 1998. These awards encourage businesses to take responsibility for environmental conditions that affect society's well-being.

Conduct research about corporate environmental disclosures. Choose one company located in Japan and a competitor located in the United States. Go to each company's Web site and search for information about environmental policies and procedures. Two possible companies are **Canon** (www.canon.com) and **Kodak** (www.kodak.com).

Also conduct research to find governmental guidelines for environmental accounting. Go to the Web site of the **U.S. Environmental Protection Agency** (www.epa.gov/) and search for information about environmental accounting. Now perform a similar search on the Web site of **Japan's Ministry of the Environment** (www.env.go.jp/en/). Skim through the information that you find on each Web site. These links are also available at www.wiley.com/college/eldenburg.

In its "Environmental Accounting Guidelines 2002," Japan's Ministry of the Environment identified the following environmental conservation cost categories:

| Category | Content |
| --- | --- |
| Business area cost | Environmental conservation cost to control environmental impacts which result from key business operations within the business area |
| Upstream/downstream cost | Environmental conservation cost to control environmental impacts which result from key business operations upstream or downstream |
| Administration cost | Environmental conservation cost stemming from administrative activities |
| R&D cost | Environmental conservation cost stemming from R&D activities |
| Social activity cost | Environmental conservation cost stemming from social activities |
| Environmental remediation cost | Cost incurred for dealing with environmental degradation |
| Other cost | Other costs related to environmental conservation |

**REQUIRED:**

**A.** Is environmental accounting an ethical issue? Why or why not?

**B.** Which company provides the easiest-to-find and most understandable information about environmental policies and procedures? Explain.

**C.** Discuss a company's responsibilities for reporting environmental information to various stakeholders, including shareholders, managers, employees, other companies, government regulators, product customers, and the general public.

**D.** If one company provides better reporting than a competitor of its environmental behavior, policies, and procedures, does that mean the company is more responsible than its competitor toward the environment? Why or why not?

**E.** What factors are likely to affect a company's willingness to publish an environmental accounting report?

**F.** Discuss possible reasons why the governments of different countries place different degrees of emphasis on environmental accounting reports.

**G.** Discuss ways in which ABC systems could be used to capture information for environmental accounting reports.

**H.** Discuss ways in which the process of preparing and publishing an environmental accounting report is likely to help a company reduce its environmental costs.

**I.** Should all governments require companies to publish environmental accounting reports? What values did you use to arrive at your conclusion?

# 8

# Measuring and Assigning Support Department Costs

## ▶In Brief

When managers and accountants consider the cost of their goods and services, they typically focus on operating costs. However, it is sometimes useful to measure and monitor the cost of all resources used to create a product or service. When all of an organization's costs are allocated, each unit's cost includes not only allocated operating costs, but also allocated costs of internal support such as accounting, purchasing, and marketing. These costs are particularly important when measuring and monitoring the cost of services provided by private and public not-for-profit organizations. They also help determine reimbursements under cost-based contracts, such as those in the defense industry. However, sometimes costs that include support department allocations are used inappropriately in decision making.

## This Chapter Addresses the Following Questions:

**Q1** What are support departments, and why are their costs allocated to other departments?

**Q2** What process is used to allocate support department costs?

**Q3** How is the direct method used to allocate support costs to operating departments?

**Q4** How is the step-down method used to allocate support costs to operating departments?

**Q5** How is the reciprocal method used to allocate support costs to operating departments?

**Q6** What is the difference between single- and dual-rate allocations?

**Q7** What are the limitations of support cost allocations, and how can the quality of information be improved?

# STANFORD UNIVERSITY: CLASSIFYING INDIRECT COSTS

In 1991, auditors from the **Department of Defense** and the **General Accounting Office (GAO)** told Congress that **Stanford University** had overcharged the government for research contract indirect costs. Among the indirect costs that the auditors questioned were $184,000 for physical education equipment including depreciation of a 72-foot luxury yacht, and $7,000 for linens in the university president's home (Stout, 1991; GAO, 1992, p. 17).

At issue is what research universities charge the U.S. government for overhead, that is, the indirect costs associated with research activities. When a university wins a research contract, it uses the grant to pay for direct costs of research, such as researchers' salaries and supplies. However, researchers also use support services such as accounting and administration, as well as other resources (e.g., utilities and building space). The government allows universities to add onto the contract a percentage to compensate for these indirect costs of research. Each university's indirect cost rate is negotiated periodically with a responsible governmental agency. In addition, universities submit annual reports of their actual indirect costs.

As a result of the accounting errors, Stanford returned $2.2 million to the government. (In the twelve years under dispute, Stanford received $2.4 billion in government research grants and contracts, of which $734 million was for indirect costs, or overhead (Casper, 1994). The university refunded this amount during 1991. The refund included the physical education equipment and other costs that were erroneously charged to indirect cost pools, plus $0.5 million for the costs of the university president's and two other res-idences (Stanford, 1991). Administrator residence costs were not specifically disallowed under federal indirect cost guidelines (GAO, 1992, p. 17). Nevertheless, Stanford officials stated that they voluntarily refunded the residence costs because they concluded it was improper to charge them to the government (*The Chronicle of Higher Education,* 1991).

Other universities varied in their treatment of administrator residence costs. Schools such as **Columbia, Harvard, Massachusetts Institute of Technology,** and **Cornell,** argued that the costs were part of administration and should be included in their indirect cost pools. Other schools, such as **Yale** and **Johns Hopkins,** decided that residence costs were not sufficiently material to expend effort in categorizing them as indirect. Some people argued that schools should not request federal reimbursement of residence costs because the public would view the practice as inappropriate (Tifft, 1991). ■

SOURCES: H. Stout, "Stanford Accused of Overcharging U.S. for Research," *The Wall Street Journal,* March 14, 1991 p. A5; General Accounting Office (GAO), "Federal Research: System for Reimbursing Universities' Indirect Costs Should Be Reevaluated," Resources, Community, and Economic Development Division RCED-92-203, Report to the Chairman, Subcommittee on Oversight and Investigations, Committee on Energy and Commerce, House of Representatives, August 1992, available at www.gao.gov; G. Casper, "Statement on the Resolution of Outstanding Disputes Between Stanford and the Government on Indirect Cost Issues," October 18, 1994, available online at www.stanford.edu/dept/pres-provost/president/speeches/941018indirect.html; Stanford University, "Stanford Gives Government Check, Report on Audit Cooperation," news release, May 8, 1991, available online at www.stanford.edu/dept/news/relaged/910508Arc1403.html; "How Stanford's Kennedy Responded to Revelations About His University's Charges to the Government," *The Chronicle of Higher Education, The Daily Report,* May 15, 1991; S. Tifft, "Scandal in the Laboratories," *Time Archive,* March 18, 1991.

## REQUESTING REIMBURSEMENT FOR OVERHEAD COSTS

### ■ Key Decision Factors for Stanford

Stanford University decided to refund administrator residence costs that it had previously included in indirect costs under federally funded research projects. The following discussion summarizes key issues that were likely relevant to this decision.

**Knowing.** Federal guidelines and the agreements Stanford had made with its supervisory governmental agency would have been the starting point for deciding which overhead costs could be reimbursed. Administrator residence costs were not specifically disallowed under federal indirect cost guidelines.

**Identifying.** There were uncertainties about how to classify administrator residence costs. Some people argued that such costs support research because they are part of general administration. However, others believed that it was inappropriate to include the costs in reimbursable indirect costs.

**Exploring.** In cases of uncertainty about how to classify various costs at a research institution, it is the natural tendency of accountants and managers to be biased in favor of classifying costs in overhead. By including more costs in the overhead calculation, they would receive a larger reimbursement from the government. However, another key issue is public perception. The news media criticized Stanford for costs such as the $7,000 in linens, even though the dollar amounts were insignificant in relation to the $734 million in government-funded indirect costs over the 12 years that were investigated. To avoid this type of criticism, accountants and managers may choose to be more conservative in their classification of indirect costs.

**Prioritizing.** In deciding how to classify questionable costs, accountants and managers must weigh the anticipated effects on the university and on various stakeholders. They must also consider university values. Stanford's president stated that the administrator residence costs were refunded to the government because the university's "obligation is not to do all the law permits, but to do what is right."[1]

**Envisioning.** In a 1992 report, the GAO concluded that indirect cost problems at universities were caused by three major factors: (1) inadequate governmental guidelines, (2) flaws in university internal controls, and (3) insufficient oversight by responsible governmental agencies. Since then, universities and the U.S. government have made progress to address these factors. For example, Stanford instituted new internal controls over its cost classifications. Governmental agencies instituted a variety of new rules to clarify which types of costs are reimbursable and to more closely monitor university costs.

### ■ Viewing Overhead as an Integral Part of Operations

Underlying the arguments about Stanford's overhead costs are questions concerning the best ways to meet the goals of the U.S. government and taxpayers in funding research projects. Overhead costs are considered necessary for universities to conduct research. However, much of a university's overhead costs would be incurred with or without a particular research project. Thus, it is possible to argue that only incremental overhead costs should be reimbursable as part of a research grant. However, the federal government's policy is to reimburse overhead costs for many different types of contracts, including university research grants, defense contracts, and Medicare reimbursements. Overhead is reimbursed under these contracts because overhead costs represent the common costs for a variety of activities necessary to produce goods and services, including the support services such as accounting, administration, human resources, and so on. In this chapter, we learn methods for allocating costs for these support services. In addition to reimbursements from outside parties, we learn that in some circumstances the allocation of such costs is useful for measuring, monitoring, and motivating performance within an organization.

---

[1]Stanford University, "Stanford Gives Government Check, Report on Audit Cooperation," news release, May 8, 1991, available online at www.stanford.eu/dept/news/relaged/910508Arc1403.html.

# SUPPORT DEPARTMENT COST ALLOCATION

**Q1** What are support departments, and why are their costs allocated to other departments?

**ALTERNATIVE TERMS**

*Common costs* are sometimes called *indirect, overhead,* or *joint costs. Operating departments* are often called *production* or *revenue-generating departments. Support departments* are also called *shared service* or *internal service departments.*

A **common cost** is the cost for a resource that is shared among two or more departments, activities, products, or other cost objects. In this chapter, we focus on methods for allocating the common costs of support departments to operating departments. **Operating departments** are the departments or divisions within an organization that manufacture goods or produce services for external customers or clients. In manufacturing businesses, operating departments produce goods for sale. In service organizations, these departments produce services for clients or customers. In a retail or distribution business, operating departments sell merchandise to customers. Government agencies produce services such as maintenance and repair of city streets, park and recreational facilities and classes, and police, fire, and emergency medical services. Other not-for-profit organizations provide services such as food banks, blood donation centers, and adult literacy courses.

**Support departments** provide services internal to the organization that support the operating departments. For example, a large bank headquarters may operate a cafeteria for its employees and have a human resources department that hires employees and keeps track of employee benefits for other departments. These services are provided as support for departments that interact with external customers to generate revenues for the bank. Typical support departments include accounting, information systems, human resources, marketing, research and development, and general administration.

Exhibit 8.1 provides examples of operating and support departments for various types of organizations.

## Objectives for Support Department Cost Allocation

Support department costs are generally treated as period expenses when preparing financial statements under generally accepted accounting principles. Therefore, support department costs are allocated for objectives other than financial statements reporting, as summarized in Exhibit 8.2.

**EXHIBIT 8.1**
Production and Support Departments

| Type of Organization | Operating Departments | Support Departments |
|---|---|---|
| Apparel manufacturer | Dresses<br>Suits | Customer services<br>Product design |
| Retail sales | Departments:<br>　Housewares, appliances<br>Individual stores | Janitorial<br>Purchasing |
| Breakfast cereal manufacturer | Processed cereals<br>Cereal bars | Maintenance and repair<br>Shipping |
| Electronic commerce and payment services | Electronic transaction processing<br>Credit card issuance | Transaction dispute resolution<br>Data processing |
| Certified public accounting firm | Accounting and auditing<br>Income taxes | Word processing<br>Reception |
| Not-for-profit organization for visually impaired persons | Audio book recordings<br>Community education | Accounting<br>Fund-raising |
| University | Academic departments<br>On-campus housing | Library<br>Buildings and grounds |
| Government bureau for fish and wildlife | Licenses<br>Wildlife management | Accounting<br>Research |
| Fitness center | Aerobics classes<br>Café | Advertising<br>General management |

**EXHIBIT 8.2**
Objectives for Allocating
Support Department Costs

| Objective | Example |
|---|---|
| External reporting | Cost reports for government contracts<br>Income tax returns<br>Reports prepared for reimbursement purposes |
| Motivation | Provide incentives for efficient production of support services<br>Provide incentives for appropriate use of support services<br>Monitor use and production of support services |
| Strategic or operating decisions | Insource or outsource<br>Pricing |

Some organizations must allocate support service costs when reporting to outsiders. For example, **Stanford University** allocates a portion of its overhead costs, including administration, to federally funded research projects. Hospitals prepare annual Medicare cost reports. These reports identify all of the costs incurred by hospitals to treat Medicare patients, including support costs such as housekeeping, patient billing, and food services. Government defense contractors are often paid based on cost, including support departments. Some support department costs, such as warehousing, must be allocated to inventory for U.S. income tax returns. Sometimes consulting firms are paid according to savings that result from their work. To fully value these savings, costs from support services may need to be allocated.

Some organizations allocate support department costs to motivate managers to improve cost control and efficiency. The managers of departments that provide support services are held responsible for their department costs, whereas managers of other departments are held responsible for their department's use of support services. An effective allocation system motivates both sets of managers to be efficient. Suppose an organization has a motor fleet department that manages all of the organization's vehicles. Each department using motor vehicles incurs a charge or cost allocation from the motor fleet department based on vehicle usage. Usage charges depend on the motor fleet department's budget. If the budget increases, charges also increase. The managers of departments that use the vehicles are responsible for monitoring and controlling their departmental cost budgets. Therefore, they have incentives to ensure that vehicle use is monitored and controlled. Meanwhile, the manager of the motor fleet department is motivated to provide cost-effective support. Otherwise, the other managers will argue in favor of outsourcing vehicle use to a lower-cost provider.

Sometimes allocated support department costs are used in making strategic or operating decisions, such as setting fees for services provided or deciding whether to outsource an activity. Support costs are relevant to such decisions only if they would be affected by the decision. For example, avoidable support costs would be relevant to an outsourcing decision. However, support department allocations often include fixed costs that are less likely to be relevant for decision making. Accountants need to help managers understand the uses and limitations of allocated cost information.

| GUIDE YOUR LEARNING **8.1** Key Terms |
|---|
| Stop to confirm that you understand the new terms introduced in the last several pages:<br><br>   *Common costs (p. 299)<br>   *Operating departments (p. 299)<br>   *Support departments (p. 299)<br><br>For each of these terms, write a definition in your own words. Also list at least one example that is different from the ones given in this textbook. |

[2] T. Hoffman, "IT's Role in Shared Services Remains Unclear," *ComputerWorld,* October 3, 2002 [on-line].

# PROCESS FOR ALLOCATING SUPPORT DEPARTMENT COSTS

**Q2** What process is used to allocate support department costs?

As shown in Exhibit 8.3, the process for allocating support department costs to operating departments is similar to the allocation methods discussed earlier in Chapters 5, 6, and 7. The process involves the following steps:

1. Clarify the purpose of the allocation.
2. Identify support and operating department cost pools.
3. Assign costs to cost pools.
4. For each support department cost pool, choose an allocation base.
5. Choose and apply a method for allocating support department costs to operating departments.
6. If relevant, allocate support costs from the operating departments to units of goods or services.

## ■ Clarifying the Purpose

Before we begin the allocation process, we need to know the purpose of the allocation. As shown in Exhibit 8.2, a variety of reasons prompts the allocation of support department costs to operating departments. The choices made in the following steps must be consistent with the purpose.

## ■ Identifying Support and Operating Department Cost Pools

We consider the purpose for allocating support department costs as we decide the type and number of support and operating department cost pools that will be used. For example, in the **Stanford University** case the purpose was to allocate overhead costs to federally funded grant programs. Stanford probably had at least one operating cost pool for the direct costs of each grant, and many indirect cost pools, with costs separated by functional area such as accounting, human resources, information technology, and general administration. The choice of support department cost pools to be allocated would depend on the types of indirect costs permitted under federal guidelines. Prior to 1991, Stanford did not use separate cost pools

**EXHIBIT 8.3**
Allocation of Support Department Costs

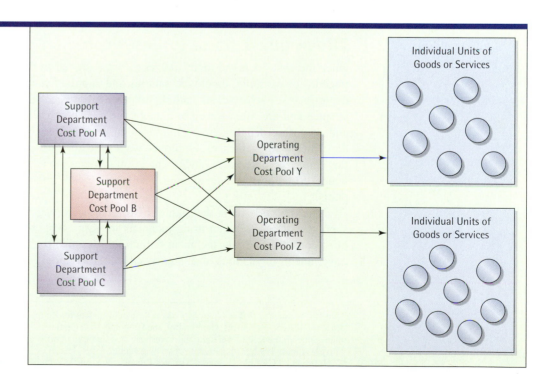

for allowable and unallowable indirect costs.[3] The Middletown Children's Clinic illustrations later in this chapter will provide additional examples.

Because many organizations already accumulate costs by department within their organizational structure, departments are often used as cost pools. Larger organizations usually have more support departments that provide specific services. For example, large organizations may have a purchasing department that is responsible for receiving materials requisitions and ordering everything required by other departments. In smaller organizations, the purchasing function may be performed by a single person in the administration department who may also be responsible for several other functions, such as preparing the paperwork for hiring a new employee, and making copies of reports for meetings.

The choice of cost pools is also influenced by the design of the accounting system. Some organizations have detailed accounting systems from which accountants can readily extract different kinds of costs for different purposes. However, it may be difficult and costly in some organizations to identify only specific types of support costs. Suppose accounting, purchasing, and human resources are aggregated with general administration into a single support cost pool in the general ledger. If an accountant wants to allocate only purchasing costs, the time and effort involved in isolating those costs might exceed the benefit. Sometimes fixed and variable support costs are allocated separately. If fixed and variable costs have not been assigned to separate cost pools in the accounting system, then it might be time-consuming and costly to separately allocate them.

Another factor influencing the number and type of support department cost pools is the ability to identify an appropriate allocation base. When too many different types of costs are pooled together, the allocation of costs becomes more arbitrary. Suppose the costs of purchasing and human resources are combined in one cost pool. The dollar amount of purchases might be an appropriate allocation base for purchasing department costs, whereas the number of employees might be an appropriate allocation base for human resources. However, neither of these allocation bases would appropriately reflect the activities of the combined cost pool.

In general, more accurate cost allocations can be achieved by separating support costs into a larger number of cost pools. However, as the number of support cost pools increases, the cost of collecting information also increases. Thus, we face trade-offs when choosing the number of support cost pools for an organization.

CURRENT PRACTICE

Armstrong World Industries manufactures floors, ceilings, and cabinets. The company's payroll, human resources, and finance services are combined into a single support operation.[4]

## ■ Assigning Costs to Cost Pools

Once the cost pools are identified, costs are assigned to them. Many costs can be directly traced. For example, employee salaries and supplies can be directly traced to individual departments. Facility costs include property insurance, utilities, property taxes, and maintenance and are often traced to a cost pool that is then allocated among all of the support and operating departments. Sometimes an employee provides services to more than one department. In such cases, employee wages are allocated to each department that receives the employee's services. Judgment is often required in deciding which costs belong to which cost pools and in making estimations when costs must be allocated among cost pools.

The central issue in the Stanford University case was the proper assignment of costs to support cost pools. When using judgment to assign costs to support cost pools, accountants must consider not only technical definitions, but also the perceived fairness. For example, government regulations did not specifically preclude reimbursement of administrators'

[3]General Accounting Office (GAO), "Federal Research: System for Reimbursing Universities' Indirect Costs Should Be Reevaluated," Resources, Community, and Economic Development Division RCED-92-203, Report to the Chairman, Subcommittee on Oversight and Investigations, Committee on Energy and Commerce, House of Representatives, August 1992, p. 4, available at www.gao.gov.
[4]T. Hoffman, "IT's Role in Shared Services Remains Unclear," ComputerWorld, October 3, 2002 [on-line].

housing costs. However, Stanford's managers decided to refund those costs for prior periods and to exclude them from future indirect cost allocations to government-funded research projects.

## ◼ Choosing Allocation Bases

A cause-and-effect relationship is desirable between the support costs and the allocation base that is used to allocate them. Thus, the best allocation base is a cost driver. In a hospital, pounds of laundry would be an appropriate cost driver for the laundry department because costs increase as the pounds of laundry increase. However, it may be difficult or impossible to find an appropriate cost driver if the department cost pool includes a number of different activities. In these cases, an allocation base is chosen to reflect some of the activities provided. Even though the number of employees does not reflect the use of accounting time, except perhaps payroll, it might be an appropriate choice for an allocation base for a department cost pool including both human resource and accounting activities. If accounting department employees track the time they spend on activities for all other departments, time spent would be an appropriate allocation base.

The cost of obtaining accurate allocation base information is an equally important consideration. Tracking time spent on different activities may cost more than the benefit gained from using it as an allocation base. As a result, accountants often use less accurate allocation bases for which data are available. Exhibit 8.4 presents a list of support departments and possible allocation bases.

## ◼ Allocation Methods

Three allocation methods can be used to allocate support department costs to operating departments:

- Direct method
- Step-down method
- Reciprocal method

Each method is formally introduced and illustrated in the following sections.

**CURRENT PRACTICE**

Medicare cost reports require allocation bases such as pounds of laundry for the laundry department, meals served for food services departments, and number of X-rays made for an X-ray laboratory.[5]

**EXHIBIT 8.4**
Support Departments and Possible Allocation Bases

| Support Departments | Possible Allocation Bases |
|---|---|
| Administration | Direct costs of other departments<br>Number of employees<br>Revenue of operating departments |
| Accounting | Direct costs of other departments<br>Number of accounting transactions<br>Time spent |
| Housekeeping | Time spent<br>Square feet cleaned |
| Purchasing | Number of requisitions<br>Number of items ordered<br>Total cost of items ordered |
| Employee training | Hours of training<br>Number of employees<br>Number of classes provided |

[5]L. Eldenburg and S. Kallapur, "Changes in Hospital Service Mix and Cost Allocations in Response to Changes in Medicare Reimbursement Schemes," *Journal of Accounting & Economics,* May 1997, pp. 31–52.

## DIRECT METHOD

**Q3** How is the direct method used to allocate support costs to operating departments?

The **direct method** allocates the costs of each support department only to the operating departments. Because no costs are allocated among support departments, none of the interactions among support departments are reflected under this method. In the following illustration we demonstrate the direct method using Middletown Children's Clinic (MCC). Suppose the accountants for MCC have identified two support departments, housekeeping and administration, and two operating departments, medical and dental. As shown in Exhibit 8.5, the direct method uses each support department's allocation base to allocate the costs for that department to each of the operating departments. Calculations for MCC are shown in the following illustration.

**EXHIBIT 8.5**
Direct Method

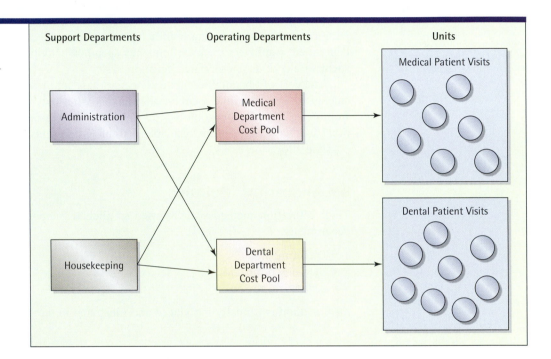

## MIDDLETOWN CHILDREN'S CLINIC (PART 1)
### DIRECT METHOD ALLOCATION

Middletown Children's Clinic, a not-for-profit organization, operates medical and dental clinics for children of low-income families. The organization receives private donations and state grants to help defray costs. The managers would like to set fees that are as low as possible, but at the same time cover costs. The state requires the clinic to submit an annual cost report showing total costs, including support department cost allocations. The state does not require particular methods or bases for the allocations.

The accounting department at the local college sponsors an intern program, in which accounting students develop their professional skills and contribute to the community by working as volunteers for not-for-profit organizations. This year, a team of accounting students has been assigned to the clinic. The students have been asked to help allocate all of the clinic's costs to patient visits. The clinic's managers plan to use this information to help them set fees. The students will also prepare the annual cost report for the state.

### Cost Object, Cost Pools, and Assigning Costs

The clinic provides two different types of services, medical and dental. Because costs probably differ by the type of service provided, the students decide to treat each type of patient visit as a cost object. Therefore, they calculate costs separately for each of the two operating departments and set up a cost pool for each. They learn from an interview with the accountant that the clinic has two support departments: administration and housekeeping. The students set up a cost pool for each of these departments.

The accountant helps the students trace the direct costs to each department cost pool. In addition, costs for the entire facility, such as rent and electricity are gathered into a cost pool and then allocated to all of the departments based on each department's square footage.

The students prepare a summary of the costs assigned to each department as follows.

| Cost | Administration | Housekeeping | Medical | Dental | Total |
|---|---|---|---|---|---|
| Salaries | $80,000 | $40,000 | $200,000 | $80,000 | $400,000 |
| Supplies | 15,000 | 20,000 | 35,000 | 10,000 | 80,000 |
| Facility costs | 3,240 | 360 | 28,800 | 3,600 | 36,000 |
| Total | $98,240 | $60,360 | $263,800 | $93,600 | $516,000 |

## Choosing Allocation Bases

Before the students allocate support department costs, they need to choose allocation bases for the services of the housekeeping and administration departments. One student suggests that square footage is a good base for allocating housekeeping costs. Another student thinks that hours spent in each department would provide a better basis because the departments have different kinds of equipment and different volumes of service. They agree that hours spent is a better choice, but then learn that housekeeping does not keep records of hours by department. Therefore, they return to their alternate choice and use square feet for allocating housekeeping costs.

For the administration allocation base, the accountant suggests using either the direct costs for each operating department or the number of employees. When the students study the administration department activities, they find that many services relate to employees, such as employee recruiting, training, benefits, and payroll. Other services include purchasing and maintenance. They decide that number of employees is more representative than direct costs for the overall activities in administration. Therefore, the students choose the number of employees in each department as the allocation base for administration.

The students gather the following information for the allocation bases.

| | Administration | Housekeeping | Medical | Dental | Total |
|---|---|---|---|---|---|
| Number of employees | 2 | 2 | 5 | 3 | 12 |
| Square feet | 900 | 100 | 8,000 | 1,000 | 10,000 |

Having calculated the total costs for each cost pool and chosen an allocation base for each support cost pool, the student interns are now ready to begin allocating support department costs to operating departments. The accountant tells the students that they can use any reasonable method for allocating support costs to operating departments. The students want to learn more about different methods and their effects on allocated costs. Therefore, they decide to perform calculations using the direct, step-down, and reciprocal methods.

## Direct Method Calculations

The students begin with the direct method, which is the easiest to perform. They first draw a diagram similar to the one in Exhibit 8.5 to clarify how they will perform calculations. They next calculate the percentage of each support department's costs allocated to each operating department. Costs for housekeeping are allocated based on square feet. One student observes that the square feet used by administration are not relevant to the direct method because housekeeping costs are not allocated to another support department. Of the 9,000 square feet used by the operating departments, the medical clinic uses 8,000 square feet, or 89%. Accordingly, 89% of the housekeeping costs will be allocated to medical, and the remaining 11% (1,000 square feet / 9,000 square feet) will be allocated to dental.

Costs for administration are allocated based on number of employees. The medical clinic employs five of the eight employees who work for operating departments, so 62.5% of the administration costs will be allocated to medical. The remaining 37.5% (3 employees / 8 employees) will be allocated to dental. *(continued)*

**EXHIBIT 8.6**
Direct Method Cost
Allocation Report for
Middletown Children's Clinic

| | Support | | Production | | |
| | Administration | Housekeeping | Medical | Dental | Total |
|---|---|---|---|---|---|
| Allocation Bases | | | | | |
| Square feet | | | 8,000 | 1,000 | 9,000 |
| | | | 89% | 11% | 100% |
| Number of employees | | | 5 | 3 | 8 |
| | | | 62.5% | 37.5% | 100% |
| | | | | | |
| Costs | | | | | |
| Department cost | $98,240 | $60,360 | $263,800 | $ 93,600 | $516,000 |
| Housekeeping | | (60,360) | 53,720 | 6,640 | 0 |
| Administration | (98,240) | | 61,400 | 36,840 | 0 |
| Total allocated cost | $ 0 | $ 0 | $378,920 | $137,080 | $516,000 |

The students prepare a report summarizing their allocations as shown in Exhibit 8.6. The line for department cost reflects the costs that the students had previously assigned to each department. Of the $60,360 housekeeping cost, 89% ($53,720) is allocated to medical and 11% ($6,640) is allocated to dental. Similarly, the administrative cost of $98,240 is allocated 62.5% ($61,400) to medical and 37.5% ($36,840) to dental. The costs allocated from the support departments are added to each oper-ating department's costs. Thus, the total allocated costs are $378,920 for the medical clinic and $137,080 for dental. Notice that the total costs of $516,000 have not been affected by the allocation.

**EXHIBIT 8.7**
Step-Down Method

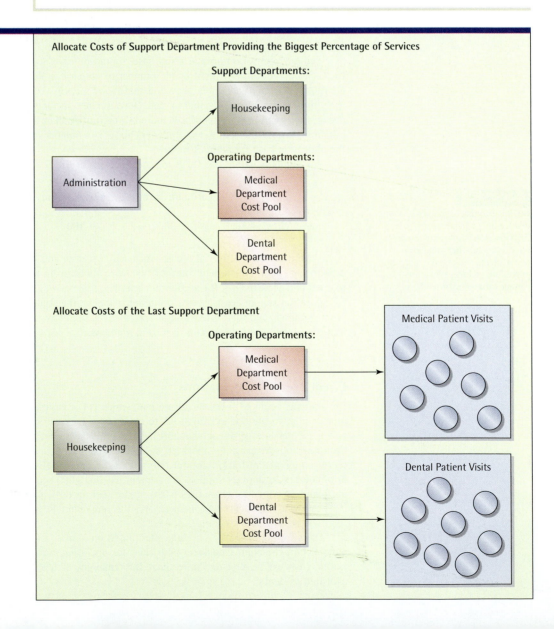

# STEP-DOWN METHOD

**Q4** How is the step-down method used to allocate support costs to operating departments?

**ALTERNATIVE TERMS**

The *step-down method* is sometimes called the *sequential method*.

The **step-down method** allocates support department costs one department at a time to remaining support and operating departments in a cascading manner until all support department costs have been allocated. This method goes beyond the direct method in recognizing that support departments provide support not only for the operating departments, but also for other support departments. As shown in Exhibit 8.7, the costs for the first support department chosen are allocated to the remaining departments, both support and operating. The process continues, and costs for the remaining support departments are allocated one at a time to the remaining departments until no support department costs remain. For example, in Exhibit 8.7 costs are allocated from administration to housekeeping, but not from housekeeping to administration.

The step-down method begins by ranking each support department according to the amount of service provided to other support departments. Then support department costs are allocated sequentially, beginning with the support department that provided the most service to other support departments and ending with the support department that provided the least service to other support departments. The ranking can be created using any reasonable criteria. Sometimes a qualitative judgment is made about the degree of services. Alternatively, departments can be ranked using a quantitative measure such as the dollar amount of services provided to other support departments. Calculations for the step-down method are illustrated in Middletown Children's Clinic (Part 2).

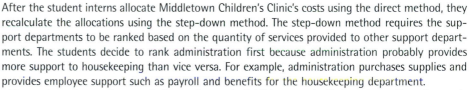

## MIDDLETOWN CHILDREN'S CLINIC (PART 2)
### STEP-DOWN METHOD ALLOCATION

After the student interns allocate Middletown Children's Clinic's costs using the direct method, they recalculate the allocations using the step-down method. The step-down method requires the support departments to be ranked based on the quantity of services provided to other support departments. The students decide to rank administration first because administration probably provides more support to housekeeping than vice versa. For example, administration purchases supplies and provides employee support such as payroll and benefits for the housekeeping department.

The students draw a diagram similar to the one in Exhibit 8.7 to clarify how they will perform calculations. They first allocate administration department costs to all the remaining departments—the other support department (housekeeping) and the two operating departments. Therefore, in determining the percentage of costs for each department, they factor in the two housekeeping employees with the operating department employees. Once the administrative costs are allocated, they next allocate housekeeping costs to the two operating departments. For this allocation, they use the same percentages used for the direct method, because only the two operating departments remain. The students summarize their calculations in the report shown in Exhibit 8.8.

In the first step, 20% of the administration department's $98,240 cost goes to housekeeping ($19,648), 50% to medical ($49,120), and 30% to dental ($29,472). In the second step, the housekeeping costs are now $80,008 ($60,360 + $19,648) because they include an allocation from administration. Therefore, 89% of $80,008 is allocated to medical ($71,207), and the remaining $8,801 is allocated to dental.

**EXHIBIT 8.8**
Step-Down Method Cost Allocation Report for Middletown Children's Clinic

| | Support | | Production | | |
| | Administration | Housekeeping | Medical | Dental | Total |
|---|---|---|---|---|---|
| **Allocation Bases** | | | | | |
| Number of employees | | 2 | 5 | 3 | 10 |
| | | 20% | 50% | 30% | 100% |
| Square feet | | | 8,000 | 1,000 | 9,000 |
| | | | 89% | 11% | 100% |
| **Costs** | | | | | |
| Total department cost | $ 98,240 | $ 60,360 | $263,800 | $ 93,600 | $516,000 |
| Step 1: Administration | (98,240) | 19,648 | 49,120 | 29,472 | 0 |
| Step 2: Housekeeping | 0 | (80,008) | 71,207 | 8,801 | 0 |
| Total Allocated Cost | $ 0 | $ 0 | $384,127 | $131,873 | $516,000 |

## RECIPROCAL METHOD

**Q5** How is the reciprocal method used to allocate support costs to operating departments?

ALTERNATIVE TERMS

The *reciprocal method* is sometimes called the *algebraic method*.

The **reciprocal method** simultaneously allocates costs among support departments and then from support departments to operating departments. Because the reciprocal method allows for all of the interactions among departments, it is widely used. This method reflects support department interactions more accurately than either the direct method, which does not address the interactions at all, or the step-down method, which addresses only part of the interactions.

The reciprocal method is performed in two phases. First, support department costs are allocated among each other. These interactions for Middletown Children's Clinic are shown in Exhibit 8.9(a). To capture the cost effects of these interactions, a set of equations is created and solved simultaneously. The exhibit shows the simple two-department case, which can easily be performed manually. However, when more than two support departments are involved, the reciprocal method becomes mathematically complex and is more easily performed using software programs such as spreadsheet functions that solve simultaneous equations. Thus, the computations for the reciprocal method are the most complex among the three methods introduced in this chapter.

After solving the simultaneous equations, the allocated cost for each support department includes costs allocated from the other support departments. Next this new total cost per support department is allocated to all of the other departments (support and operating) as shown in Exhibit 8.9(b). The reciprocal method is illustrated in Middletown Children's Clinic (Part 3).

**EXHIBIT 8.9**
Reciprocal Method

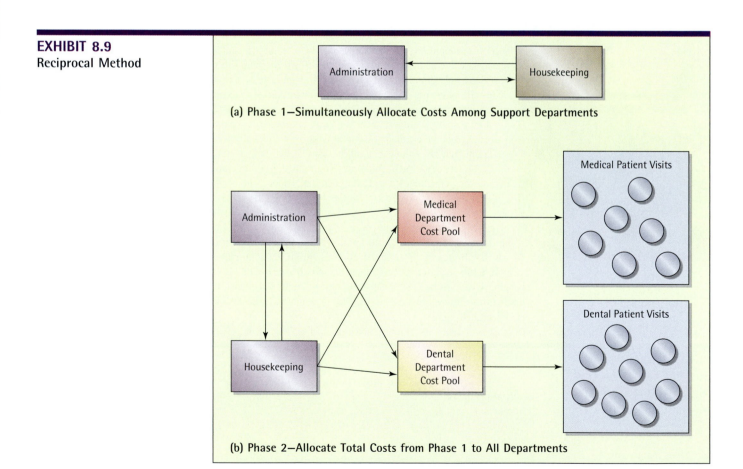

(a) Phase 1—Simultaneously Allocate Costs Among Support Departments

(b) Phase 2—Allocate Total Costs from Phase 1 to All Departments

## MIDDLETOWN CHILDREN'S CLINIC (PART 3)
## RECIPROCAL METHOD ALLOCATION

After completing the step-down method calculation, the student interns are ready to apply the reciprocal method to Middletown Children's Clinic's support costs. The students adopt the same allocation bases they used previously, and they draw diagrams similar to the ones in Exhibit 8.9(a) and 8.9(b) to clarify how they will perform calculations.

### Allocate Support Costs Among Support Departments

The students first allocate the support department costs to each other. To simultaneously compute costs between support departments, the students need to set up and solve simultaneous equations. The cost of each support department is written as a sum of directly assigned costs plus costs allocated from the other support department. Administration is allocated based on number of employees. The clinic has 10 employees outside of the administration department, with two of them working in housekeeping. For the purpose of allocating administration costs, housekeeping's portion of employees is 2/10, and

$$\text{Housekeeping} = \$60,360 + 0.2 \, (\text{Administration})$$

Similarly, housekeeping is allocated based on square feet. Of the 9,900 square feet that are not in housekeeping, 900 square feet are in administration. Thus, for the purpose of allocating housekeeping costs, administration's portion of square feet is $900 \div 9,900$, and

$$\text{Administration} = \$98,240 + 0.09 \, (\text{Housekeeping})$$

Because only two support departments are involved, only two equations need to be solved simultaneously. The students decide to use the substitution method to solve them. They substitute the administration equation into the housekeeping equation and solve for the total cost of housekeeping:

$$\text{Housekeeping} = \$60,360 + 0.2 \times (\$98,240 + 0.09 \times \text{Housekeeping})$$
$$\text{Housekeeping} = \$60,360 + \$19,648 + 0.018 \times \text{Housekeeping}$$
$$0.982 \times \text{Housekeeping} = \$80,008$$
$$\text{Housekeeping} = \$81,475$$

Next, they substitute the result for housekeeping into the administration equation and solve for the total cost of administration:

$$\text{Administration} = \$98,240 + 0.09 \times \$81,475$$
$$\text{Administration} = \$105,573$$

When an organization has three or more support departments, the simultaneous equations are set up in the same way. Each equation includes the total cost for the department plus a term for each of the other support departments. The simultaneous calculations become more complex, but can be easily solved with computer programs or repeated algebraic substitution.

### Allocate Support Costs to Operating Departments

The calculations performed using simultaneous equations provide a total cost for each support department that includes cost allocations from other support departments. These totals are the new amount that the students next allocate to all other departments (support and operating). The new total cost for housekeeping is $81,475, which includes the original department cost of $60,360 plus an allocation of $21,115 from administration. In Exhibit 8.10, the students allocate this new housekeeping cost based on square feet, with 9% to administration, 81% to medical, and 10% to dental.

Similarly, the new cost for administration of $105,573 includes the original cost of $98,240 plus an allocation of $7,333 from housekeeping. The students allocate this new administration amount based on number of employees, with 20% to housekeeping, 50% to medical, and 30% to dental. The students create a report to summarize their allocations and to demonstrate that zero cost remains in each support department after the allocations are complete, as shown in Exhibit 8.10.

*(continued)*

**EXHIBIT 8.10**
Reciprocal Method Cost Allocation Report for Middletown Children's Clinic

| | Support | | Operating | | |
|---|---|---|---|---|---|
| | Administration | Housekeeping | Medical | Dental | Total |
| **Cost Allocation Bases** | | | | | |
| Square feet | 900 | | 8,000 | 1,000 | 9,900 |
| | 9% | | 81% | 10% | 100% |
| Employees | | 2 | 5 | 3 | 10 |
| | | 20% | 50% | 30% | 100% |
| **Costs** | | | | | |
| Total department cost | $ 98,240 | $ 60,360 | $263,800 | $ 93,600 | $516,000 |
| Housekeeping | 7,333 | (81,475) | 65,995 | 8,147 | |
| Administration | (105,573) | 21,115 | 52,786 | 31,672 | |
| Total allocated cost | $ 0 | $ 0 | $382,581 | $133,419 | $516,000 |

## Comparing Results and Choosing an Allocation Method

When the students finish their calculations for the three allocation methods, they create the following schedule to compare their results.

| | Medical | Dental | Total |
|---|---|---|---|
| Direct method | $378,920 | $137,080 | $516,000 |
| Step-down method | 384,127 | 131,873 | 516,000 |
| Reciprocal method | 382,581 | 133,419 | 516,000 |

The managers want to know the cost for each patient visit. Therefore, the students also calculate the average allocated cost per visit. The accountant tells them that medical usually sees 12,000 patients, and dental sees 10,000 patients. Dividing the total allocated costs by these volumes, the total allocated cost per visit under each method is:

| | Medical | Dental |
|---|---|---|
| Direct method | $31.58 | $13.71 |
| Step-down method | 32.01 | 13.19 |
| Reciprocal method | 31.88 | 13.34 |

The students notice that the fully allocated costs do not vary significantly across methods. They ask their accounting professor whether this result is always true. He tells them that the variation depends on the data and number of departments for a given setting. With a larger number of support departments, the differences are usually greater. He also tells them that the step-down and reciprocal methods often yield similar results when only two support departments are involved. He adds that the reciprocal method is the most accurate because it takes into account all interactions.

The students discuss the effort that each method takes. They agree that the direct method requires the least amount of effort and that the reciprocal method requires the most. However, they also agree that they could easily set up a spreadsheet to calculate the clinic's allocations. After concluding that computational difficulty is not a major issue, they recommend the reciprocal method to the clinic.

---

**GUIDE YOUR LEARNING  8.2**  Middletown Children's Clinic (Parts 1, 2, and 3)

Middletown Children's Clinic (Parts 1, 2, and 3) illustrates the allocation of support costs using the direct, step-down, and reciprocal methods. For these illustrations:

| Define It | Identify Uncertainties | Prioritize Options |
|---|---|---|
| In your own words, define each allocation method. List the information that was used as inputs for the computations. Also list the information that was created. Explain why the allocated costs calculated under the three methods differ. | What types of uncertainties were there? Consider uncertainties about:<br>• Assigning costs to cost pools<br>• Allocation bases<br>• Degree of services provided among support departments<br>• Choice of allocation method | The students concluded that the reciprocal method provided the best measure of cost. What factors did the students weigh in drawing this conclusion? |

## ■ Comparing the Direct, Step-Down, and Reciprocal Methods

As shown in the Middletown Children's Clinic illustration, different allocation methods result in different values. Each method has its own pros and cons. The direct method is the easiest to calculate, but computer programs reduce the importance of this issue. An advantage of the direct and step-down methods is that the calculation methods are easier to explain to managers, yet the reciprocal method most accurately considers support department interactions.

## SINGLE- VERSUS DUAL-RATE ALLOCATIONS

 **Q6** What is the difference between single- and dual-rate allocations?

The practice of using only one base to allocate both fixed and variable costs is called **single-rate allocation.** For example, at Middletown Children's Clinic, square feet were used to allocate housekeeping costs. Square feet might be appropriate for allocating housekeeping fixed costs, such as depreciation on any cleaning equipment used, but some housekeeping costs vary with the type of work required in a given area. The time housekeepers spend in each area might be a more appropriate allocation base for the variable costs. Thus, single-rate allocation likely mismeasures resources used. In addition, managers may believe that all support costs are variable, even when they include a large proportion of fixed costs.

Under **dual-rate allocation,** support costs are separated into fixed and variable cost pools and cost drivers are identified for the variable cost pools to more accurately reflect the flow of resources. Exhibit 8.11 presents the dual-rate allocation process under the reciprocal method. Compared to the single-rate allocation, the variable cost allocations reflect a more accurate estimation of the incremental costs of providing support services. Some organizations use variable costs to measure use of a department's services and assign the fixed costs as part of a department's formally adopted budget.

The dual-rate system also has drawbacks. It costs more to develop and maintain. Furthermore, uncertainties about how to classify costs as fixed and variable can introduce additional mismeasurement.

The following illustration demonstrates the use of dual rates for Middletown Children's Clinic.

| GUIDE YOUR LEARNING 8.3 Key Terms |
| --- |

Stop to confirm that you understand the new terms introduced in the last several pages:

Direct method (p. 304)              Single-rate allocation (p. 311)
Step-down method (p. 307)       Dual-rate allocation (p. 311)
Reciprocal method (p. 308)

For each of these terms, write a definition in your own words.

**EXHIBIT 8.11**
Dual-Rate Allocation

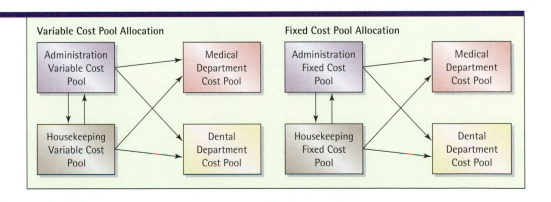

## MIDDLETOWN CHILDREN'S CLINIC (PART 4)
### DUAL RATES AND RECIPROCAL METHOD WITH THREE SUPPORT DEPARTMENTS

After the students allocated administration and housekeeping costs to the operating departments, the accountant asks them whether this information could be used to charge departments for their use of other departments' services. The accountant believes that by charging for support department services, the employees in the user departments would be motivated to manage their use of the support services more cost-consciously, and some support costs might be reduced. The charges would become part of the current budgeting system in which managers are held responsible for their budgets. Managers receive performance bonuses if costs are maintained at or under budgeted levels.

### Charges Based on Single-Rate Allocation

The students obtain the total allocated costs for each support department from their previous reciprocal method calculations: $105,573 for administration and $81,475 for housekeeping. Their goal is to calculate a charge representing the use of these services by other departments. Previously, they used number of employees as the allocation base for administration and square feet as the allocation base for housekeeping. They decide to use the allocation bases to calculate a charge for the use of each department's services. For administration services, other departments would be charged a cost per employee. The clinic has 12 employees, two of whom work in administration. The students calculate the charge for administration costs based on the 10 non-administration employees:

$$\$105,573 \text{ Administration costs} \div 10 \text{ employees} = \$10,557 \text{ per employee}$$

For housekeeping services, other departments would be charged a cost per square foot. The clinic has 10,000 total square feet, of which 100 are devoted to housekeeping. The students calculate the charge for housekeeping based on the 9,900 non-housekeeping square feet:

$$\$81,475 \text{ housekeeping costs} \div 9,900 \text{ square feet} = \$8.23 \text{ per square foot}$$

The students discuss whether the charges they calculated would be reasonable. They think that the administration charge seems high. They wonder whether other departments should be charged $10,557 for administrative costs for each employee in the department. The charge might encourage managers in the clinic departments to inappropriately reduce the number of employees. For example, the managers might replace an employee with services from a temporary labor agency that would cost the clinic more overall. When the students review the housekeeping charge, they believe that an average annual charge of $8.23 per square foot is reasonable. However, one student asks whether it is reasonable for the housekeeping cost rate for administration to be the same as the cost rate for medical and dental. The clinic areas require special cleaning supplies and greater effort than the administration area. In addition, employees in other departments might feel that they have no control over a fixed charge of $8.23 per square foot. A fixed charge might reduce their motivation to keep work areas clean, increasing the time required by housekeeping.

### Analysis of Cost Behavior and Revision of Cost Pools

The students had previously learned about dual rates for allocating costs, whereby fixed and variable costs are allocated separately. Some organizations use variable allocations as a charge rate for support services because the variable costs more closely represent the incremental costs that support departments incur to provide services. The students plan to analyze the behavior of costs in the administration and housekeeping cost pools to determine whether the cost pools should be broken down into separate fixed and variable cost pools. They had previously summarized the costs, as shown here.

| Cost | Administration | Housekeeping |
|---|---|---|
| Salaries | $80,000 | $40,000 |
| Supplies | 15,000 | 20,000 |
| Facility costs | 3,240 | 360 |
| Total | $98,240 | $60,360 |

The students focus first on administration costs. Most of them are for salaries of the manager and the accountant. The manager is responsible for general management of the clinic. The accountant is responsible for accounting and billing functions. The accountant says she spends much more time on billing functions for the operating clinics than on general functions for the whole organization. The billing functions include receiving information about each patient's charges from the operating departments and then billing patients or their insurance companies, receiving and depositing payments, and following up on denied insurance claims and bad debts. One student points out that the functions of the manager are different from the functions of the accountant. He argues that the costs for these two employees should not be combined in a single cost pool if other departments will be charged for the services. The other students agree that accuracy of the cost allocations will improve if they separate accounting costs from other administration costs, so they decide to establish a separate cost pool called accounting. The accountant helps the students identify the costs that should be assigned to the accounting cost pool, and she summarizes the time she usually spends on activities for each department.

When the students study the housekeeping department cost records, they find that housekeeping employees are paid according to an hourly wage, and part of the department's costs vary with time spent working in each area. Therefore, the students think that the variable part of housekeeping costs could be allocated to other departments based on the time spent cleaning each area. However, housekeeping employees do not currently keep track of their time by area. The students discuss this issue with the accountant, who agrees to establish a new record-keeping system for housekeeping employees to keep track of the hours they spend in each department.

Based on their discussions with the accountant and their investigation of the types of costs in each cost pool, the students conclude that costs for all three support departments could be broken down into fixed and variable components. The students and the accountant examine past accounting records and other information to identify fixed and variable costs. The accountant estimates the cost of supplies and postage for accounting and billing activities and the amount of her salary that should be considered a fixed cost of the accounting department. Variable costs in administration include payroll costs that vary by employee, such as fringe benefits, and supplies and record-keeping for employees. The costs are summarized as follows.

| Department | Administration | Accounting | Housekeeping | Total |
|---|---|---|---|---|
| Variable costs | $11,052 | $ 9,210 | $30,180 | $ 50,442 |
| Fixed costs | 50,348 | 27,630 | 30,180 | 108,158 |
| Total cost | $61,400 | $36,840 | $60,360 | $158,600 |

## Charges Based on Variable Cost Allocation

The students discuss with the accountant the effects of the new support cost pool on the calculation of charges to other departments. They conclude that other departments should be charged only for variable support costs. Thus, the cost object for each support department is the variable cost of support services provided to other departments.

They next discuss the allocation bases for the variable cost pools. They plan to use the accountant's time to allocate accounting costs. They decide to continue using number of employees for administration. They want to use the time spent in various departments for housekeeping, but they lack recorded information about the amount of time spent in each area. However, the housekeepers estimate that they spend 10% of their time cleaning the administration department, 5% in the accounting area, 55% in the medical clinic, and 30% in the dental clinic.

The new variable cost allocation base amounts for all departments are as follows:

| | Administration | Accounting | Housekeeping | Medical | Dental | Total |
|---|---|---|---|---|---|---|
| Employees | | 1 | 2 | 5 | 3 | 11 |
| Time spent accounting | 15% | | 10% | 50% | 25% | 100% |
| Time spent cleaning | 10% | 5% | | 55% | 30% | 100% |

To apply the reciprocal method, the students must first calculate the total support department variable costs including interactions. They set up simultaneous equations for the interactions among administration, accounting, and housekeeping. The equations are:

$$\text{Administration} = \$11,052 + 15\% \times \text{Accounting} + 10\% \times \text{Housekeeping}$$
$$\text{Accounting} = \$9,210 + (1/11) \times \text{Administration} + 5\% \times \text{Housekeeping}$$
$$\text{Housekeeping} = \$30,180 + (2/11) \times \text{Administration} + 10\% \times \text{Accounting}$$

*(continued)*

The students use Excel Solver to find the solutions to this set of simultaneous equations. Instructions for using Solver are presented in Appendix 8A. The Solver results for each department's total variable cost (including interactions) to be allocated are:

| | |
|---|---|
| Administration | $16,354 |
| Accounting | $12,416 |
| Housekeeping | $34,395 |

Given the total allocated variable cost for each support department, the students calculate the support charge per unit of allocation base. The charge for variable administration cost is based on the number of employees:

$$\$16,345 \div 11 \text{ employees} = \$1,486 \text{ per employee}$$

The charge for accounting is based on the time spent by the accountant. The accountant works full time. Allowing two weeks of vacation and eight holidays, her estimated work hours per year are:

$$[40 \text{ hours per week} \times (52 - 2) \text{ weeks}] - (8 \text{ days} \times 8 \text{ hours per day}) = 1,936 \text{ hours}$$

Thus, the charge for variable accounting cost is

$$\$12,416 \div 1,936 \text{ hours} = \$6.41 \text{ per hour}$$

The charge for housekeeping is based on time spent cleaning. The cleaning employees work full time, or an estimated 1,936 hours per year each. Based on the two housekeeping employees, the estimated total hours are 3,872 per year. The charge for variable housekeeping cost is

$$\$34,395 \div 3,872 \text{ hours} = \$8.88 \text{ per hour}$$

The students discuss these rates with the accountant. The administration charge per employee seems low, so department managers would probably not consider these charges in making decisions about employment levels. Many administrative costs are fixed, so the variable portion is small. The accounting charges also seem low, reflecting the high proportion of fixed costs in salary for the accountant. At the same time, charging each department for variable accounting costs helps the department managers recognize that they are using accounting resources.

The housekeeping charges are similar to costs that would be paid if an outside housekeeping service were used, so the managers of the user departments are likely to think that these charges are fair. At the same time, charging the departments for housekeeping based on time spent in each department provides the managers with incentives to keep work areas clean to reduce the number of hours that housecleaning spends in them. The accountant recommends that the fixed costs be assigned to other departments as part of their annual budgets. This way all costs will be allocated, but only variable costs will be charged based on some measure of usage.

## Dual-Rate Allocation

In addition, the accountant reminds the students that they need to allocate costs for the regulatory reports that are filed with the state. For these reports, all support costs must be allocated, not just the variable costs. The students can separately allocate the fixed support costs and then sum the fixed and variable allocations for state reporting.

The students discuss allocation bases for the fixed costs. They use number of employees as the allocation base for administration, time spent for accounting, and square footage for housekeeping. The fixed cost allocation base amounts for all departments are:

| | Administration | Accounting | Housekeeping | Medical | Dental | Total |
|---|---|---|---|---|---|---|
| Employees | | 1 | 2 | 5 | 3 | 11 |
| Accounting | 15% | | 10% | 50% | 25% | 100% |
| Square feet | 600 | 300 | | 8,000 | 1,000 | 9,900 |

Once again, the students use Excel Solver to simultaneously allocate the costs among the support departments. (The simultaneous equations and instructions for Excel Solver are found in Appendix 8A.)

The students prepare a schedule summarizing the variable and fixed cost allocations and calculating the total allocated costs for operating departments, as shown in Exhibit 8.12.

The students discuss how much they enjoyed helping the clinic and gaining experience using three different methods of allocating support department costs, including the use of Solver. They feel the internship was a worthwhile experience. The clinic accountant is glad that the student interns helped her with this task. She now knows how to use Solver and can revise the allocation scheme over time as the clinic's needs and cost estimates change.

**EXHIBIT 8.12** Dual-Rate Support Cost Allocations for Middletown Children's Clinic

| | Support Departments | | | Operating Departments | | |
| --- | --- | --- | --- | --- | --- | --- |
| | Administration | Accounting | Housekeeping | Medical | Dental | Total |
| Directly assigned costs | $ 61,400 | $ 36,840 | $ 60,360 | $263,800 | $ 93,600 | $516,000 |
| Variable Cost Allocation: | | | | | | |
| Administration | (16,354) | 1,486 | 2,973 | 7,434 | 4,460 | 0 |
| Accounting | 1,862 | (12,416) | 1,242 | 6,208 | 3,104 | 0 |
| Housekeeping | 3,440 | 1,720 | (34,395) | 18,917 | 10,319 | 0 |
| Fixed Cost Allocation: | | | | | | |
| Administration | (58,164) | 5,287 | 10,575 | 26,438 | 15,863 | 0 |
| Accounting | 5,138 | (34,256) | 3,426 | 17,128 | 8,564 | 0 |
| Housekeeping | 2,678 | 1,339 | (44,181) | 35,702 | 4,463 | 0 |
| Total allocated costs | $ 0 | $ 0 | $ 0 | $375,627 | $140,373 | $516,000 |

---

**GUIDE YOUR LEARNING 8.4** Middletown Children's Clinic (Part 4)

Middletown Children's Clinic (Part 4) illustrates the allocation of support costs using the reciprocal method with three support departments and using separate rates for variable and fixed costs. For this illustration:

| Define It | Identify Uncertainties | Explore Pros and Cons of Options | Prioritize Options |
| --- | --- | --- | --- |
| Explain how dual-rate allocation differs from single-rate allocation. What additional information was required to perform dual-rate allocation? | What types of uncertainties were there? Consider uncertainties about:<br>• Choice of cost pools<br>• Classifying costs as fixed and variable<br>• Allocation bases<br>• Reaction of managers to support charges | Explain the motivation for holding other departments responsible for the use of support services. How were other department managers expected to react to different ways of calculating the charges? | In your own words, describe how various factors were weighed when reaching decisions about the allocation methods. |

## SUPPORT COST INFORMATION QUALITY

 **Q7** What are the limitations of support cost allocations, and how can the quality of information be improved?

Support cost allocations are subject to the same uncertainties as other types of cost allocations. As discussed throughout this chapter, the process of allocating support costs involves many uncertainties, such as the following:

- Identifying appropriate cost pools for support and operating departments
- Whether to establish separate pools for fixed and variable costs
- How to assign costs to cost pools
- Identifying the most appropriate allocation bases for each cost pool
- Identifying the most appropriate allocation method
- Whether the benefits exceed the costs of establishing a more detailed support cost allocation system

Because the process of measuring and allocating support costs is uncertain and requires judgment, allocated support cost information can have low quality.

The quality of allocated support cost information can be improved many ways. Accountants, managers, and operational personnel can work together to identify more appropriate cost pools and allocation bases. Accounting systems can be redesigned to more accurately trace costs to activities and gather better allocation base data. In addition, accountants can adopt allocation methods to more closely match the purpose of the allocation. In the preceding section we learned about one type of improvement, dual-rate allocations. Other improvements can also be made.

## ■ Estimated Versus Actual Support Costs and Rates

If the goal is to measure the value of support resources actually used, then actual costs and actual allocation base volumes are appropriate. Sometimes, however, it is appropriate to use estimates rather than actual values. The use of estimated rates simplifies and expedites the calculation of allocated support costs. However, the appropriateness of using estimated versus actual costs depends on the purpose of the allocation (see Exhibit 8.2).

For external reporting, estimated support costs can be used only if permitted by the external party. For example, Medicare cost reports must be based on actual cost. On the other hand, the federal government allows educational institutions to negotiate a "predetermined" support cost allocation rate. The support cost allocation is calculated by multiplying either actual direct labor costs or actual total direct costs by a predetermined rate, which is based on estimates of support costs. The difference between actual and estimated support costs is typically included as an adjustment when negotiating future predetermined rates. Actual support costs are subject to audit even when a predetermined rate is negotiated, as demonstrated in the **Stanford University** case at the beginning of this chapter.[6]

When the purpose of support cost allocation is motivation, the goal is to charge other departments in a way that will encourage managers to use support services efficiently. Several possible ways can be used to measure support cost allocations within an organization. The general formula for charges to other departments is as follows:

$$\text{Allocation rate} = \frac{\text{Total support costs}}{\text{Total volume of allocation base}}$$

$$\text{Charge} = \text{Allocation rate} \times \text{Volume of support services used}$$

Each of the two components of the charge—the allocation rate and the volume of support services used—may be based on actual or estimated values. Estimated values are typically used only when an organization formally adopts a budget.

An advantage of using budgeted values for the entire calculation is that the support charge is known in advance by the managers of other departments and is not affected by the amount of support service actually used. However, this practice provides little incentive to use support services efficiently. An advantage of using actual values for the entire calculation is that managers of other departments are held responsible for the actual cost of the support services they use. However, this practice can lead to additional problems. For example, if one department uses much less of a support service than anticipated, the charge to the remaining departments increases to cover the total cost of the support department. Managers feel they have little control over the charges incurred by their departments under this system. One way to address this concern is to charge departments using a budgeted allocation rate and actual usage. These factors need to be considered when choosing budgeted or actual rates and usage.

For strategic or operating decisions, managers are interested in estimating future costs. Therefore, if they are relevant to a decision, support cost allocations should be based on future estimated costs and volumes of the allocation base. To simplify and expedite decision making, however, actual costs and volumes are often used to estimate future costs and volumes.

## ■ Additional Allocation Methods

The direct, step-down, and reciprocal methods introduced earlier in this chapter assume that all operating departments should be allocated costs based on their use of support services

**CURRENT PRACTICE**

The predetermined support cost rate for federally funded research during fiscal years 2002–2005 at Tennessee Tech University is 47% of direct salaries and wages.[7]

**CHAPTER REFERENCE**

Additional methods and issues related to charges between units within an organization, also called transfer prices, are discussed in Chapter 15.

---

[6]The federal government refers to the support cost rate as an F&A (facilities and administration) rate. For detailed regulations involving the negotiated rate, see *Circular A-21,* Office of Management and Budget, The Executive Office of the President, version August 8, 2000, available at www.whitehouse.gov/omb/circulars/a021/a021.html.
[7]*Indirect Costs on Contracts/Grants* Policy 3.0, Tennessee Tech University, available at www.tntech.edu/research/indirect.html.

and that no one operating department is inherently more responsible for support costs than any other operating department. These assumptions are not always appropriate. Sometimes other criteria, such as perceived fairness, are used to allocate common costs such as support department costs.

The perceived fairness of an allocation system depends on the circumstances and sometimes depends on the ability to bear costs. Suppose costs are being allocated from corporate headquarters to business segments, divisions, or departments. The organization's CEO and CFO want divisions to be aware that corporate costs must be covered for the organization to be profitable. In this case, they might choose revenues as an allocation base, because divisions with more revenues are likely to have increased ability to bear the headquarters supports costs. Division or department managers probably believe that revenues are a fair allocation base.

**CHAPTER REFERENCE**

Chapter 9 introduces several types of revenue-based allocation methods for the common costs of production.

Another way to address perceived fairness is to base common cost allocations on estimates of the costs that would be incurred if the services were not shared. Two methods rely on estimates of separately incurred costs: the stand-alone method and the incremental cost method.

Under the **stand-alone method,** common costs are allocated using weights based on information about the individual users of a cost object. Suppose a professor located in San Diego travels to present some new research at two different universities, one located in Denver and one located in Chicago. The total airfare for the trip from San Diego to Denver, on to Chicago, and then back to San Diego, is $600. If the professor were to travel only to each location and back, the round trip to Denver would cost $300 and the round trip to Chicago would cost $400. Under the stand-alone method, the university in Denver would pay its proportion of the total ticket cost of $600 based on its stand-alone airfare relative to the total stand-alone airfares. The amount allocated to Denver is [$300/($300 + $400)] × $600 = $257. The university in Chicago would pay the rest ($343).

Sometimes one user (cost object) is viewed as being more responsible for common costs than other users. Under the **incremental cost allocation method**, the most responsible user is allocated the cost that would have been incurred had the services not been shared with other users. Then the next most responsible user is allocated the incremental cost to use the shared resource. Suppose the professor had first been invited to Chicago. Under the incremental cost allocation method, Chicago would pay the equivalent of a full-fare ticket to Chicago, or $400, and Denver would pay the incremental cost to add the extra flight, or $200 ($600 − $400).

**CURRENT PRACTICE**

The U.S. Department of Health and Human Services requires the incremental cost method for allocating support costs to productivity improvement projects, which must be reported separately from other Medicare costs.[15]

## Cost-Based Contracting

Organizations typically conduct business with other organizations using a **fixed-price contract,** whereby the vendor provides products or services at a specific price. Alternatively, organizations sometimes use a **cost-based contract** where the vendor is reimbursed based on the costs incurred to produce the good or service. For example, the federal government awards cost-plus contracts for some defense equipment. The government allows support costs, such as administration and research and development, to be allocated to defense contracts.

Cost-based contracts have two major incentive problems. First, managers have little encouragement to control costs when they know that costs will be reimbursed. Second, when allocating costs, managers might be motivated to inappropriately shift costs from other types of contracts to cost-based contracts. Earlier, we learned that in its support cost calculations, Stanford University included costs that it later concluded were arguably inappropriate under its cost-based research grants.

---

[15]CMS Manual System Pub 100-06 Medicare Financial Management Transmittal 26, Department of Health and Human Services, Centers for Medicare and Medicaid Services (CMS), December 8, 2003, available at cms.hhs.gov/manuals/pm_trans/R26FM.pdf.

To reduce the likelihood that costs are inappropriately shifted to cost-based contracts, the government often requires contractors to follow specific rules for measuring costs. U.S. defense contractors must abide by rules established by the **Cost Accounting Standards Board (CASB)**. Nongovernmental agencies that award grants also establish their own detailed guidelines for cost measurement. Accountants must study and use judgment to apply the guidelines for a particular cost-based contract. However, as we have learned throughout this chapter, uncertainties arise in measuring and allocating support costs. Thus, no set of cost accounting rules completely eliminates discretion and bias.

**CURRENT PRACTICE**

You can find more information about CASB and the standard setting process at www.whitehouse.gov/omb/procurement/casb.html.

**Alternatives to Cost-Based Contracting** Some contract-granting organizations have developed ways to reduce incentive problems by moving away from cost-based contracting. For example, Medicare was established in 1965 as a federal cost-based reimbursement plan for elderly health care. Partly because the incentives under cost-based payment systems do not encourage cost containment, Medicare costs rose rapidly from 1965 until the 1980s. In 1983, Medicare changed its reimbursement policy for hospital inpatient services to a flat fee per diagnosis. This plan remains in place today. Congress periodically authorizes increases in Medicare fees. Hospitals report their costs through an annual Medicare Cost Report. The cost report includes allocations of support department costs, using either the step-down or the reciprocal method. Some health care insurers choose to reimburse hospitals using a per diem payment. Others pay a flat-fee per month for each of their insured clients.

---

## GUIDE YOUR LEARNING 8.5 Key Terms

Stop to confirm that you understand the new terms introduced in the last several pages:

Stand-alone method (p. 317)  Fixed-price contract (p. 317)
Incremental cost allocation method (p. 317)  Cost-based contract (p. 317)

For each of these terms, write a definition in your own words.

---

## FOCUS ON ETHICAL DECISION MAKING
### Quality of Accounting Estimates

During 2003, the U.S. Department of Health and Human Services (HHS) completed an audit of the 1999 Medicare organ acquisition costs at Tampa General Hospital. The auditors concluded that the hospital's $7 million in total organ acquisition costs were overstated by $1.5 million. The largest component of the overstatement was for overstatements in the costs directly traced to kidney, liver, and heart acquisitions and understatements in costs directly traced to heart acquisitions. In the executive summary of their report, the HHS auditors stated:

The hospital's accounting and cost reporting practices contributed to the excess Medicare reimbursement including:
- the use of improper methods for reporting the average costs of organ acquisitions;
- the improper allocation of employee benefits;
- the improper allocation of transplant office costs to the heart acquisition cost center; and
- the unsupported claim for provider-based physician compensation.
The [hospital's] procedures were not adequate to ensure that organ acquisition costs were properly assigned to all users and properly reported to Medicare.

As required by HHS, the chief financial officer (CFO) of Tampa General Hospital provided a written response to the audit. The CFO argued that the hospital's accounting practices were adequate and that most of the overstatement was caused by the use of accounting estimates. The hospital had used prior year data to accrue estimated costs when invoices were not received by the end of the fiscal year. This practice caused some costs to be overestimated and others to be underestimated. The CFO stated, "The errors they found are innocent errors." The hospital agreed to revise its procedures in the future to more accurately estimate costs when invoices are not yet received.

Because of uncertainties, accountants routinely use many types of estimates. They also weigh the costs and benefits in deciding whether to develop more precise accounting methods. Yet, outsiders often assume that accounting is an exact science and that any inaccuracies occur because of wrongdoing. Even for knowledgeable individuals, it is often difficult to evaluate the appropriateness of an organization's accounting procedures. Nonetheless, accountants are increasingly expected to improve the quality of accounting information. Organizations that are subject to public scrutiny, such as Tampa General Hospital, must consider not only the quality of information used internally, but also the public perception about accounting practices.

SOURCES: S. Snow, "HHS Audit: Tampa General Owes $1.46 million," *Tampa Bay Business Journal*, May 7, 2003, available at www.bizjournals.com/tampabay/stories/2003/05/05/daily26.html?t=printable; and "Audit of Medicare Costs for Organ Acquisitions at Tampa General Hospital," A-04-02-02017, Office of Inspector General, Department of Health and Human Services, April 17, 2003, available at oig.hhs.gov/oas/reports/region4/40202017.htm.

### Practice Ethical Decision Making

In Chapter 1, we learned about a process for making ethical decisions (Exhibit 1.11). You can address the following questions for this ethical dilemma to improve your skills for making ethical decisions. Think about your answers to these questions and discuss them with others.

| Ethical Decision-Making Process | Questions to Consider about This Ethical Dilemma |
|---|---|
| Identify ethical problems as they arise. | Does the accurate assignment of costs on a Medicare cost report create an ethical problem for accountants? Why or why not? How is it possible that an organization might not know its actual costs at the end of a fiscal year? |
| Objectively consider the well-being of others and society when exploring alternatives. | What are the costs and benefits of using estimates in accounting? Who are the various stakeholders affected by the use of estimates on a Medicare cost report? |
| Clarify and apply ethical values when choosing a course of action. | Recall that Tampa General Hospital's costs of $7 million were overstated by $1.5 million. Was it appropriate in this situation for the hospital to use estimates on its Medicare cost report? What values did you use to arrive at your conclusion? |
| Work toward ongoing improvement of personal and organizational ethics. | What is the role of the accounting system and procedures in helping an organization meet its responsibilities to various stakeholder groups? |

## APPENDIX 8A

## Using Solver to Calculate Simultaneous Equations for the Reciprocal Method

Solver, a tool within Excel, can be used to solve simultaneous equations. See Appendix 4A for an introduction to the use of Solver. In this appendix we learn to use Solver for allocating support costs under the reciprocal method.

In part 4 of the Middletown Children's illustration, the student interns increased the number of support department cost pools from two to three. Therefore, they decided to use Solver to calculate the support department allocations under the reciprocal method. Before using

Solver, it is necessary to specify the simultaneous equations. For the Middletown Children's Clinic fixed cost allocation, the simultaneous equations are as follows:

$$\text{Administration} = \$50,348 + 15\% \times \text{Accounting} + (600/9,900) \times \text{Housekeeping}$$
$$\text{Accounting} = \$27,630 + (1/11) \times \text{Administration} + (300/9,900) \times \text{Housekeeping}$$
$$\text{Housekeeping} = \$30,180 + (2/11) \times \text{Administration} + 10\% \times \text{Accounting}$$

Exhibits 8A.1 and 8A.2 provide results and formulas using Solver for this set of simultaneous equations. The change cells are given the names Admin, Acct, and Housekeep. Solver manipulates these cells to solve the simultaneous equations for each department's cost. The solution includes allocations from the other two support departments. The target function is the sum of the three change cells and is given the following formula:

$$=\text{Admin}+\text{Acct}+\text{Housekeep}$$

Notice in cells B15, B16, and B17 that the simultaneous equations are listed so that they can be entered into Solver as constraints. When adding each constraint in the Solver dialog box, set the simultaneous equation equal to (by selecting the equal sign in the pull-down menu) the change cell that represents the department for which cost you are solving. For example, the cell with the simultaneous equations for Administration should contain

$$=\text{B3}+\text{B7*Acct}+(\text{B8/G8})\text{*Housekeep}$$

Click Add next to the constraints box. The cell with this formula will be entered on the left-hand side under Cell Reference. Click on the box under Constraint and then highlight the department for the simultaneous equation in the cell reference, in this case Admin.

In the spreadsheet shown in Exhibits 8A.1 and 8A.2, solution values from Solver feed into the bottom part of the spreadsheet that performs the allocation process. You may need to go back and forth between these two spreadsheets to understand how to set up your own spreadsheet for this problem. Notice that the values for costs and allocation bases are at the top of the spreadsheet. If you change any of these values, you will need to run Solver again to determine the new amounts for the three support departments. Use the formula spreadsheet as a guide to set up this problem. If you have forgotten how to use Solver, go back to Appendix 4A for details.

**EXHIBIT 8A.1** Fixed Cost Allocation Spreadsheet for Using Solver

| | A | B | C | D | E | F | G |
|---|---|---|---|---|---|---|---|
| 1 | Middletown Clinic | | | | | | |
| 2 | Departments | Administration | Accounting | Housekeeping | Medical | Dental | Total |
| 3 | Costs | $50,348 | $27,630 | $30,180 | $263,800 | $93,600 | $465,558 |
| 4 | | | | | | | |
| 5 | Allocation Bases | | | | | | |
| 6 | Employees | 0 | 1 | 2 | 5 | 3 | 11 |
| 7 | Accounting time spent | 15% | 0% | 10% | 50% | 25% | 100% |
| 8 | Square footage | 600 | 300 | 0 | 8,000 | 1,000 | 9,900 |
| 9 | | | | | | | |
| 10 | Change cells for solver | | | | | | |
| 11 | Admin | Acct | Housekeep | | | | |
| 12 | $58,164 | $34,256 | $44,181 | | | | |
| 13 | | | | | | | |
| 14 | Simultaneous equations | | | | | | |
| 15 | Administration | $58,164 | | | | | |
| 16 | Accounting | $34,256 | | | | | |
| 17 | Housekeeping | $44,181 | | | | | |
| 18 | | | | | | | |
| 19 | Target function | | | | | | |
| 20 | 136601.5012 | | | | | | |
| 21 | | | | | | | |
| 22 | Allocation | Administration | Accounting | Housekeeping | Medical | Dental | Total |
| 23 | Department Cost | $50,348 | $27,630 | $30,180 | $263,800 | $93,600 | $465,558 |
| 24 | Administration Allocation | ($58,164) | $5,287 | $10,575 | $26,438 | $15,863 | $0 |
| 25 | Accounting Allocation | $5,138 | ($34,256) | $3,426 | $17,128 | $8,564 | $0 |
| 26 | Housekeep Allocation | $2,678 | $1,339 | ($44,181) | $35,702 | $4,463 | $0 |
| 27 | Total Allocated Cost | $0 | $0 | $0 | $343,068 | $122,490 | $456,558 |

**EXHIBIT 8A.2** Fixed Cost Allocation Spreadsheet for Using Solver with Formulas

| | A | B | C | D | E | F | G |
|---|---|---|---|---|---|---|---|
| 1 | Middletown Clinic | | | | | | |
| 2 | Departments | Administration | Accounting | Housekeeping | Medical | Dental | Total |
| 3 | Costs | 50348 | 27630 | 30180 | 263800 | 93600 | =SUM(B3:F3) |
| 4 | | | | | | | |
| 5 | Allocation Bases | | | | | | |
| 6 | Employees | 0 | 1 | 2 | 5 | 3 | =SUM(B6:F6) |
| 7 | Accounting time spent | 0.15 | 0 | 0.1 | .5 | 0.25 | =SUM(B7:F7) |
| 8 | Square footage | 600 | 300 | 0 | 8000 | 1000 | =SUM(B8:F8) |
| 9 | | | | | | | |
| 10 | Change cells for solver | | | | | | |
| 11 | Admin | Acct | Housekeep | | | | |
| 12 | 58164.1018577537 | 34256.4619090369 | 44180.9374373239 | | | | |
| 13 | | | | | | | |
| 14 | Simultaneous equations | | | | | | |
| 15 | Administration | =B3+B7*Acct+(B8/G8)*Housekeep | | | | | |
| 16 | Accounting | =C3+(C6/G6)*Admin+(C8/G8)*Housekeep | | | | | |
| 17 | Housekeeping | =D3+(D6/G6)*Admin+D7*Acct | | | | | |
| 18 | | | | | | | |
| 19 | Target function | | | | | | |
| 20 | =Admin+Acct+Housekeep | | | | | | |
| 21 | | | | | | | |
| 22 | Allocation | Administration | Accounting | Housekeeping | Medical | Dental | Total |
| 23 | Cost | =B3 | =C3 | =D3 | =E3 | =F3 | =SUM(B23:F23) |
| 24 | Administration Allocation | =-B15 | =(C6/$G$6)*$B$15 | =(D6/$G$6)*$B$15 | =(E6/$G$6)*$B$15 | =(F6/$G$6)*$B$15 | =SUM(B24:F24) |
| 25 | Accounting Allocation | =B7*B16 | =-B16 | =D7*$B$16 | =E7*$B$16 | =F7*$B$16 | =SUM(B25:F25) |
| 26 | Housekeep Allocation | =(B8/$G$8)*$B$17 | =(C8/$G$8)*$B$17 | =-B17 | =(E8/$G$8)*$B$17 | =(F8/$G$8)*$B$17 | =SUM(B26:F26) |
| 27 | Total Allocated Cost | =SUM(B23:B26) | =SUM(C23:C26) | =SUM(D23:D26) | =SUM(E23:E26) | =SUM(F23:F26) | =SUM(G23:G26) |

# SUMMARY

 **What Are Support Departments, and Why Are Their Costs Allocated to Other Departments?**

### Operating Departments

Operating departments are the departments or divisions within an organization that manufacture goods or produce services for external customers or clients.

### Support Departments

Support departments provide services internal to the organization that support the operating departments.

### Objectives for Allocating Support Department Costs

| Objective | Example |
|---|---|
| External reporting | Cost reports for government contracts<br>Income tax returns<br>Reports prepared for reimbursement purposes |
| Motivation | Provide incentives for efficient production of support services<br>Provide incentives for appropriate use of support services<br>Monitor use and production of support services |
| Strategic or operating decisions | Insource or outsource<br>Pricing |

## Q2 What Process Is Used to Allocate Support Department Costs?

### Process for Allocating Support Department Costs

1. Clarify the purpose of the allocation.
2. Identify support and operating department cost pools.
3. Assign costs to cost pools.
4. For each support department cost pool, choose an allocation base.

5. Choose and apply a method for allocating support department costs to operating departments.
6. If relevant, allocate support costs from the operating departments to units of goods or services.

## Q3 How Is the Direct Method Used to Allocate Support Costs to Operating Departments?

### Direct Method

Each support department's cost is allocated to only the operating departments.

### Pros and Cons

- Easiest method computationally, but computers make this factor less important
- Easy to explain to managers and others
- Ignores interactions among support departments

## Q4 How Is the Step-Down Method Used to Allocate Support Costs to Operating Departments?

### Step-Down Method

Support department costs are allocated one department at a time to remaining support and operating departments in a cascading manner until all support department costs have been allocated.

### Pros and Cons

- Requires ranking of support departments in terms of services provided to other support departments
- Moderately easy computations, depending on the number of support departments
- Moderately easy to explain to managers and others
- Takes into account some of the interactions among support departments

## Q5 How Is the Reciprocal Method Used to Allocate Support Costs to Operating Departments?

### Reciprocal Method

- First, support department costs are simultaneously allocated among support departments.
- Next, support department costs, including interactions, are allocated to operating departments.

### Pros and Cons

- Computationally the most complex, but computers simplify the process
- May be difficult to explain to managers and others
- Most accurate allocation method because it takes into account all of the interactions among support departments

## Q6 What Is the Difference Between Single- and Dual-Rate Allocations?

### Single-Rate Allocation

Uses only one base to allocate both fixed and variable costs

### Dual-Rate Allocation

Accumulates fixed and variable costs in separate cost pools and uses different allocation bases for these cost pools

### Pros and Cons

- Reduces mismeasurement of allocations
- Reduces misunderstandings about the behavior of support costs
- Costs more to develop and maintain
- May introduce additional mismeasurement from problems classifying costs as fixed and variable

## Q7 What Are the Limitations of Support Cost Allocations, and How Can the Quality of Information Be Improved?

### Uncertainties

- Identifying support and operating cost pools
- Assigning costs to cost pools
- Selecting allocation bases

- Choosing an allocation method
- Measuring the degree of services provided among support departments (step-down and reciprocal methods)

**Ways to Improve the Quality of Information**
- Dual rate allocations
- Redesign of accounting system for cost pools and allocation bases
- Choices regarding estimated versus actual support costs and rates
- Consideration of perceived fairness

- Use of alternative criteria for allocation:
  - Stand-alone method
  - Incremental cost allocation method
- Imposition of allocation rules by contracting parties
- Replacement of cost-based payments with fixed fee payments

## KEY TO SYMBOLS

**e** This question requires students to extend knowledge beyond the applications shown in the textbook.

**1** This question requires Step 1 skills (**Identifying**) in Steps for Better Thinking (Exhibit 1.10).

**2** This question requires Step 2 skills (**Exploring**) in Steps for Better Thinking (Exhibit 1.10).

**3** This question requires Step 3 skills (**Prioritizing**) in Steps for Better Thinking (Exhibit 1.10).

**4** This question requires Step 4 skills (**Envisioning**) in Steps for Better Thinking (Exhibit 1.10).

## Self-Study Problem

### Self-Study Problem 1 — Direct, Step-Down, and Reciprocal Methods; Use of Allocation Information

Q2, Q3, Q4, Q5, Q7

Pet Protection is a veterinary clinic that is subsidized by the local humane society. The not-for-profit organization was set up to encourage low-income pet owners to neuter and vaccinate their pets. The humane society would like to know the cost per animal visit to use in its fund-raising campaign literature.

The information for a recent period follows:

|  | Support Departments | | Operating Departments | | |
|---|---|---|---|---|---|
| Costs before allocation: | Janitorial | Administration | Neuter | Vaccinations | Total |
| Direct costs: | | | | | |
| Salaries | $25,000 | $40,000 | $100,000 | $ 75,000 | $240,000 |
| Supplies | 5,000 | 5,000 | 15,000 | 25,000 | 50,000 |
| Building-related costs | 2,400 | 3,600 | 12,000 | 6,000 | 24,000 |
| Total | $32,400 | $48,600 | $127,000 | $106,000 | $314,000 |
| Some possible allocation bases: | | | | | |
| Square feet | 200 | 300 | 1,000 | 500 | 2,000 |
| Employees | 1 | 1 | 5 | 3 | 10 |

**REQUIRED:**

A. Allocate the support department costs to the operating departments using the following:
  1. Direct method
  2. Step-down method
  3. Reciprocal method

B. Assume the neuter clinic handles 2,400 pet visits and vaccinations handles 5,000 pet visits. Calculate the cost per visit for each department under the three methods.

**2** C. A local TV station has contacted the head veterinarian at Pet Protection. The station will provide free advertising to encourage low-income pet owners to neuter their pets using Pet Protection's services. The veterinarian estimates the cost of a 10% increase in business volume using the total allocated costs developed in part (A) and becomes alarmed at the large total cost. Describe the calculation of total allocated costs and explain why these costs should not be used to estimate future costs.

### Solution to Self-Study Problem 1

A. Two assumptions are used in making these calculations: (1) the administration costs will be allocated using number of employees and janitorial costs will be allocated using square feet, and (2) the administration support department provides more services to the janitorial support department than the other way around.

1. Direct Method Allocation

| | Support Departments | | Operating Departments | | |
|---|---|---|---|---|---|
| | Janitorial | Administration | Neuter | Vaccinations | Total |
| Allocation base percentages: | | | | | |
| Administration | | | | | |
|   Employees | | | 5 | 3 | 8 |
|   Percent | | | 62.5% | 37.5% | 100% |
| Janitorial | | | | | |
|   Square feet | | | 1000 | 500 | 1500 |
|   Percent | | | 66.6667% | 33.3333% | 100% |
| Departmental costs | $ 32,400 | $ 48,600 | $127,000 | $106,000 | $314,000 |
| Allocations: | | | | | |
|   Administration | | (48,600) | 30,375 | 18,225 | |
|   Janitorial | (32,400) | | 21,600 | 10,800 | |
| Total allocated cost | $   0 | $   0 | $178,975 | $135,025 | $314,000 |

2. Step-Down Method Allocation

For the step-down allocation method, administrative costs are allocated first because they are largest.

| | Support Departments | | Operating Departments | | |
|---|---|---|---|---|---|
| | Janitorial | Administration | Neuter | Vaccinations | Total |
| Allocation base percentages: | | | | | |
| Administration | | | | | |
|   Employees | 1 | | 5 | 3 | 9 |
|   Percent | 11.1111% | | 55.5556% | 33.3333% | 100% |
| Janitorial | | | | | |
|   Square feet | | | 1,000 | 500 | 1,500 |
|   Percent | | | 66.6667% | 33.3333% | 100% |
| Departmental costs | $32,400 | $ 48,600 | $127,000 | $106,000 | $314,000 |
| Allocations: | | | | | |
|   Administration | 5,400 | (48,600) | 27,000 | 16,200 | |
|   Janitorial | (37,800) | | 25,200 | 12,600 | |
| Total allocated cost | $   0 | $   0 | $179,200 | $134,800 | $314,000 |

3. Reciprocal Method Allocation

The first task in the reciprocal method is to set up and solve simultaneous equations for the interactions among the support departments. The interactions are calculated using the allocation base percentages. When only two support departments are involved, the substitution method can be used to solve the simultaneous equations.

| | Support Departments | | Operating Departments | | |
|---|---|---|---|---|---|
| | Janitorial | Administration | Neuter | Vaccinations | Total |
| Allocation base percentages: | | | | | |
| Administration | | | | | |
|   Employees | 1 | | 5 | 3 | 9 |
|   Percent | 11.1111% | | 55.5556% | 33.3333% | 100% |
| Janitorial | | | | | |
|   Square feet | | 300 | 1,000 | 500 | 1,800 |
|   Percent | | 16.6667% | 55.5556% | 27.7777 | 100% |

**Simultaneous Equations:**

The equation for the total costs of each support department is equal to the costs assigned to the departmental cost pool plus an allocation of the costs from the other support department:

$$\text{Janitor} = \$32,400 + (1/9) \times \text{Administration}$$
$$\text{Administration} = \$48,600 + (300/1,800) \times \text{Janitor}$$

The cost for the janitorial department is calculated by substituting the administration equation into the janitor equation:

$$\text{Janitor} = \$32,400 + (1/9) \times (48,600 + (300/1,800) \times \text{Janitor})$$
$$0.98148148 \times \text{Janitor} = \$37,800$$
$$\text{Janitor} = \$38,513$$

The cost for the administration department is calculated by substituting the result for the janitorial cost into the administration equation:

$$\text{Administration} = \$48,600 + (300/1,800) \times \$38,513$$
$$\text{Administration} = \$55,019$$

Next, costs are allocated from each support department to the other support departments and to the operating departments. The amounts allocated are based on the computations from the simultaneous equations. The use of simultaneous equations ensures that zero cost remains in each support department after the allocations are complete. In other words, the total cost allocated from janitorial ($38,513) is equal to the costs assigned to the janitorial cost pool ($32,400) plus the costs allocated to janitorial from administration ($6,113). Similarly, the total cost allocated from administration ($55,019) is equal to the costs assigned to the administration cost pool ($48,600) plus the costs allocated to administration from janitorial ($6,419).

| | Support Departments | | Operating Departments | | |
| --- | --- | --- | --- | --- | --- |
| | Janitorial | Administration | Neuter | Vaccinations | Total |
| Departmental costs | $ 32,400 | $48,600 | $127,000 | $106,000 | $314,000 |
| Allocations: | | | | | |
| Administration | 6,113 | (55,019) | 30,566 | 18,340 | 0 |
| Janitorial | (38,513) | 6,419 | 21,396 | 10,698 | 0 |
| Total allocated cost | $        0 | $      0 | $178,962 | $135,038 | $314,000 |

**B.** The cost per visit is calculated by dividing each operating department's total direct and allocated costs by the number of pet visits per year.

| | Neuter | Vaccinations |
| --- | --- | --- |
| Direct method | $178,975 ÷ 2,400 = $74.57 per visit | $135,025 ÷ 5,000 = $27.01 per visit |
| Step-down method | $179,200 ÷ 2,400 = $74.67 per visit | $134,800 ÷ 5,000 = $26.96 per visit |
| Reciprocal method | $178,962 ÷ 2,400 = $74.57 per visit | $135,038 ÷ 5,000 = $27.01 per visit |

**C.** The costs per visit are calculated as follows. First, all clinic costs are assigned to departments. Some costs are traced directly to departments (salaries and supplies), and some (building-related costs) are gathered together in a general cost pool and distributed (allocated) among all of the departments. Then, the support department costs (administration and janitorial) are allocated to each other and then to the operating departments (neuter and vaccinations). Many of these costs are fixed and will not change as volumes increase, for example, salaries and building-related costs such as the lease.

Through the allocation process, all of the fixed costs become an average cost per unit. The cost per visit is accurate only at the level of visits used in the denominator. When the veterinarian multiplies the per-visit rate times a larger number of visits, the total cost is overestimated because the per-visit cost is an average cost that includes a portion of fixed cost. These fixed costs do not increase proportionately as volumes increase, but remain constant across a relevant range. To increase the accuracy of future cost estimates, past costs need to be separated into fixed and variable categories, and a cost function needs to be developed. In addition, some of the information used in the cost function should be updated to reflect any anticipated price changes.

---

| REVIEW | Use the exercises in the following boxes in the chapter to review key terms and key techniques, analyze chapter illustrations, improve your learning of new concepts, and practice ethical decision making. |
| --- | --- |

Guide Your Learning 8.1: Key Terms (p. 300)

Guide Your Learning 8.2: Middletown Children's Clinic (Parts 1, 2, and 3) (p. 310)

Guide Your Learning 8.3: Key Terms (p. 311)

Guide Your Learning 8.4: Middletown Children's Clinic (Part 4) (p. 315)

Guide Your Learning 8.5: Key Terms (p. 318)

Focus on Ethical Decision Making: Quality of Accounting Estimates (p. 318)

## QUESTIONS

**8.1** Explain the differences and similarities among the direct, step-down, and reciprocal methods.

**8.2** Explain the similarities and differences between support department costs and manufacturing overhead costs

**8.3** What should determine the choice of cost allocation method (direct, step-down, and reciprocal) discussed in this chapter?

**8.4** Sometimes costs that include support department allocations are used in short-term decision making. List several limitations of these costs when used in decision making and discuss ways to address the limitations.

**8.5** What factors should be considered when choosing allocation bases?

**8.6** A product is started in department 1 and completed in department 2. Is department 1 a support department or an operating department? Explain.

**8.7** Explain the difference between operating departments and support departments.

**8.8** List at least two advantages of the dual-rate method.

**8.9** Explain several problems that arise when allocated costs are used to charge for support services.

**8.10** Would better decisions be made with information from single-rate or dual-rate cost allocation systems? Explain your reasoning.

**8.11** What are the advantages and disadvantages of using estimated support cost allocation rates?

**8.12** List at least three possible allocation bases that could be used to allocate accounting department costs to other departments. Give one advantage and one disadvantage of using each allocation base.

**8.13** Describe GAAP as it applies to
a. Manufacturing overhead.
b. Support department costs.

## EXERCISES

**8.14**
**Q2, Q7**
**Allocation rates** A housekeeping support department budgets its costs at $40,000 per month plus $12 per hour. For November the following were the estimated and actual hours provided by the housekeeping support department to three operating departments.

|  | Estimated Hours Spent Cleaning | Actual Hours Spent Cleaning |
|---|---|---|
| Department A | 1,600 | 1,500 |
| Department B | 1,400 | 1,600 |
| Department C | 2,000 | 1,800 |
| Total | 5,000 | 4,900 |

**REQUIRED:**
**A.** What is the support department's allocation rate if estimated activity is the allocation base?
**B.** What is the support department's allocation rate if actual activity is the allocation base?
**C.** List one advantage and one disadvantage for each type of allocation rate.

**8.15**
**Q2**
**Allocating support costs to units** A local hospital is required to account for the total cost of patient care, including support costs. Patients are assigned all direct costs. Support costs are $240,000 per month plus $90 per patient day. This 120-bed hospital averages 80% occupancy.

**REQUIRED:** Calculate the average daily charge per patient for support costs, assuming 30 days in a month.

**8.16**
**Q1, Q3, Q7**
**Direct method using estimated costs, benchmarking** Devon allocates support department costs using the direct method and estimated costs. The support department costs are budgeted at $88,000 for department A, $63,000 for department B, and $40,000 for department C. These costs are allocated using the proportion of total cost the firm would pay to an outside service provider.

|  | Support | | | Operating | |
|---|---|---|---|---|---|
|  | Dept. A | Dept. B | Dept. C | Casting | Machine |
| Direct costs | $88,000 | $63,000 | $40,000 | – | – |
| Labor hours |  |  |  | 6,000 | 4,000 |
| Machine hours |  |  |  | 2,000 | 10,000 |
| Costs if support services were purchased outside: |  |  |  |  |  |
| Department A |  |  |  | $50,000 | $60,000 |
| Department B |  |  |  | $40,000 | $30,000 |
| Department C |  |  |  | $20,000 | $30,000 |

**REQUIRED:**    **A.** Allocate budgeted support department costs using the direct method, first using labor hours and then with the outside cost proportions as the allocation bases.

**2** **B.** Could Devon Inc. use the cost of purchasing outside as an efficiency benchmark for the cost of both the support departments and the user departments? List several advantages and disadvantages of this approach.

**8.17**    **Direct and step-down methods with dual rates** Petro-X uses the direct method for allocating
Q2, Q3, Q4, Q6    both fixed and variable costs from the physical plant and equipment maintenance support departments to operating departments X and Y. The bases for allocation are as follows:

| Physical plant: | Fixed costs on the basis of square feet occupied |
| | Variable costs on the basis of number of employees |
| Equipment maintenance: | Fixed costs on the basis of budgeted machine hours |
| | Variable costs on the basis of expected maintenance hours |

Costs for physical plant and equipment maintenance are:

| | Physical Plant | Equipment Maintenance |
|---|---|---|
| Fixed costs | $39,000 | $75,000 |
| Variable costs | $18,000 | $60,000 |

Allocation bases for all four departments are:

| | Support | | Operating | |
|---|---|---|---|---|
| | | Equipment | | |
| | Physical Plant | Maintenance | Department X | Department Y |
| Square feet | 1,600 | 3,900 | 5,000 | 8,000 |
| Number of employees | 10 | 12 | 40 | 50 |
| Budgeted machine hours | 0 | 100 | 10,000 | 15,000 |
| Budgeted maintenance hours | 10 | 20 | 200 | 400 |

**REQUIRED:**    **A.** Assign the support department costs to departments X and Y using the direct method.

**B.** Assign the support department costs to departments X and Y using the step-down method with the physical plant costs allocated first.

**C.** Assign the support department costs to departments X and Y using the step-down method with equipment maintenance costs allocated first.

**D.** Under the step-down method, what criterion should be used to decide which support department costs to allocate first?

**8.18**    **Reciprocal method** The Brown and Brinkley Brokerage firm is organized into two major sales di-
Q2, Q5    visions: institutional clients and retail clients. The firm also has two support departments: research and administration. The research department's costs are allocated to the other departments based on a log of hours spent on tasks for each user. The administration department's costs are allocated based on the number of employees in each department.

Records are available for last period as follows.

| | Support Departments | | Operating Departments | |
|---|---|---|---|---|
| | Research | Administration | Institutional | Retail |
| Payroll costs | $350,000 | $300,000 | $400,000 | $550,000 |
| Other costs | $230,000 | $150,000 | $120,000 | $240,000 |
| Research hours | 100 | 200 | 500 | 300 |
| Number of employees | 7 | 10 | 8 | 10 |

**REQUIRED:**    Using the reciprocal method, determine the total cost of operations for each sales division. Use either simultaneous equations or Excel Solver.

**8.19**    **Reciprocal method** Paul's Valley Protection Service has three support departments (S1, S2, and
Q2, Q5    S3) and three operating departments (P1, P2, and P3). The direct costs of each department are $30,000 for S1, $20,000 for S2, and $40,000 for S3. The proportions of service provided by each support department to the others are given in the following table.

| | | Support Departments | | | Operating Departments | | |
|---|---|---|---|---|---|---|---|
| | | S1 | S2 | S3 | P1 | P2 | P3 |
| | S1 | – | 0.4 | 0.1 | 0.2 | 0.2 | 0.1 |
| | S2 | 0.1 | – | 0.2 | 0.2 | – | 0.5 |
| | S3 | 0.2 | 0.2 | – | 0.1 | 0.4 | 0.1 |

**REQUIRED:** Using the reciprocal method, allocate the support department costs to the operating departments.

**8.20**
Q2, Q3, Q4, Q5, Q7

**Step-down, direct, and reciprocal methods, accuracy of allocation** Software Plus Corporation produces flight and driving simulations and games for personal computers. The president has a complaint about the accounting for support department costs. He points to the following table describing the use of various support departments in the company and says, "According to this table, every department receives services from all the support departments. But I understand that only some of the support departments are bearing costs from the other support departments. Why is that?"

| | | | | Percent Use of Services | | |
|---|---|---|---|---|---|---|
| Support Department | Cost | Administration | Maintenance | Information Systems | Games Manufacturing | Simulation Manufacturing |
| Administration | $40,000 | 0% | 10% | 50% | 10% | 30% |
| Maintenance | 20,000 | 20 | 0 | 10 | 40 | 30 |
| Information systems | 50,000 | 35 | 5 | 0 | 40 | 20 |

**REQUIRED:** ⓔ **A.** What method has Software Plus Corporation been using to allocate support costs? Explain how you know.

**B.** Which method would ignore all interactions among support departments? Explain.

**C.** Which method would consider all interactions among support departments? Explain.

❷ **D.** Allocate the support department costs to Games and Simulations using the step-down method. Explain how you decided which department's costs to allocate first.

**E.** Allocate the support department costs using the direct method.

**F.** Allocate the support department costs using the reciprocal method.

❶ **G.** In your own words, explain how the step-down method improves upon the direct method.

❶ **H.** In your own words, explain how the reciprocal method improves upon the step-down method.

**8.21**
Q2, Q3, Q4, Q5

**Direct, step-down, and reciprocal methods; assign costs to departments** Cost information for Lake County Library is as follows.

| | Support | | Operating | | |
|---|---|---|---|---|---|
| Direct Costs | Janitorial | Administration | Books | Other Media | Total |
| Salaries | $20,000 | $40,000 | $50,000 | $70,000 | $180,000 |
| Supplies | 5,000 | 5,000 | 15,000 | 25,000 | 50,000 |
| Allocation Base Volumes | | | | | |
| Square feet | 500 | 500 | 1,200 | 300 | 2,500 |
| Employees | 1 | 1 | 2 | 1 | 5 |

In addition to directly traceable costs, the library incurred $24,000 for a building lease.

**REQUIRED:** ⓔ **A.** Allocate to departments any costs that have not been traced, and then calculate total costs assigned to each department.

**B.** Allocate the support department costs to the operating departments using the direct method.

**C.** Allocate the support department costs to the operating departments using the step-down method. Allocate first the costs for the support department having the largest direct costs.

**D.** Allocate the support department costs to the operating departments using the reciprocal method. Use either simultaneous equations or Excel Solver.

**8.22** **Stand-alone and incremental cost allocation methods** Monty is the CFO of a large organization
**Q7** with fast-food outlets in London, Paris, and Frankfurt. When the manager at an outlet asks for his
help, he flies out and discusses matters such as the controls that are in place for each outlet and
any expected upcoming changes in costs or procedures that will affect productivity. The outlets
are charged for the airfare for these trips. Shortly after being contacted by the Frankfurt outlet, the
Paris outlet also called to set up a visit. Monty's airfare from London to Frankfurt to Paris to London is €300. If he travels round trip from London to Frankfurt, the cost would be €250, and if he
travels round trip from London to Paris the fare would be €200.

**REQUIRED:**      **A.** Calculate the charge for Monty's airfare to each outlet using the stand-alone allocation
method.
**B.** Calculate the charge for Monty's airfare to each outlet using the incremental cost allocation method.
**❸ C.** Which allocation method is most fair? Explain your reasoning.

**8.23** **Step-down and reciprocal methods, uncertainties, pricing** Kovacik manufactures two types of
**Q2, Q4, Q5, Q7** piggy banks in two different departments, a plain piggy bank and a javelina bank. The plant is
highly automated and contains only two other departments: (1) engineering and design and (2) information systems. Kovacik allocates support department costs according to estimated service use.
Estimated information for next year is as follows:

| | Support | | Operating | |
| --- | --- | --- | --- | --- |
| | Engineering and Design | Information Systems | Plain Bank | Javelina Bank |
| Direct costs | $2,700 | $8,000 | $10,000 | $20,000 |
| Services used | | | | |
|    Engineering and design | | 10% | 40% | 50% |
|    Information systems | 20% | | 30% | 50% |
| Production volume | | | 8,000 | 4,000 |

Total allocated costs are assigned to individual units using the production volume.

**REQUIRED:**      **A.** Determine the estimated total allocated costs for the operating departments using the step-
down method.
**B.** Determine the estimated total allocated cost per unit of the plain piggy bank and the
javelina piggy bank under the step-down method.
**❶ C.** Explain why actual total allocated costs will turn out to be different from the estimated
total allocated costs.
**D.** Determine the estimated total allocated costs for the operating departments using the reciprocal method. Use either simultaneous equations or Excel Solver.
**E.** Determine the estimated total allocated cost per unit of the plain piggy bank and the
javelina piggy bank under the reciprocal method

---

# PROBLEMS

**8.24** **Step-down and reciprocal methods, choosing methods, cost pools, uncertainties** Your brother
**Q2, Q4, Q5, Q7** is a physician and has decided to start a home health care agency. The state government will reimburse treatment costs for about half of the patients under a new state-sponsored health insurance
program for low-income residents. Your brother has asked you to explain the cost report that the
state government requires. He tells you that he can use either the step-down or the reciprocal allocation method. He has several choices in allocation bases, but has little choice in the type of cost
pools that are allowed.

**REQUIRED:**      **❷ A.** Explain to your brother the differences in the two allocation methods. Remember that
your brother is not familiar with accounting; use language he will understand.
**❶ B.** Your brother wants to know how to choose the best allocation method and bases for his
business. List some of the factors your brother should consider as he makes these decisions.
*(continued)*

**❷ C.** One of the cost pools allowed by the state is a pool for transportation-related costs. Your brother asked colleagues at other home health care agencies to list the costs they include in this pool. Each organization has some costs that are identical, such as depreciation on vehicles, gas, and repairs. However, other costs in the pool are different; some agencies include facilities-related costs, and others do not. Why would cost pools for the same activity include different types of cost?

**8.25**
**Q2**

**Cost pools and allocation bases** You are an accountant for a defense contractor. The federal government is considering a change of rules for the allocation of research and development costs. The government is asking contractors to submit a list of potential cost pools and allocation bases for activities within research and development. The government wants defense contractors to separate their research and development activities into several smaller cost pools with separate allocation bases.

Your research department performs a variety of different duties, including developing new designs for products, developing and testing new materials for use in these products, designing the manufacturing processes for new products, and redesigning old products and their manufacturing processes. In addition, the research and development department creates commercial uses for new technology that have been developed under government contracts.

**REQUIRED:**
**❶ A.** List at least four potential research and development activities that could be used as the basis for separate cost pools within the research and development department.
**❷ B.** List two or more potential cost allocation bases for each cost pool listed in part (A).
**❶ C.** List factors that you might consider in making a choice about the cost pools and the allocation bases.

**8.26**
**Q2, Q4, Q7**

**ETHICS**

**Step-down method, choosing allocation order and bases** Space Products manfactures commercial and military satellites. Under its defense contracts, the company is permitted to allocate administrative and other costs to its military division. These costs are then reimbursed by the Department of Defense (DOD). Under DOD guidelines, administrative costs can be allocated using either the direct costs incurred in the operating divisions or the number of employees as an allocation base. Management information systems (MIS) costs can be allocated either on the basis of direct costs incurred in the operating divisions or on the basis of CPUs (a measure of computer resources used). Data concerning the company's operations appear here.

|  | Support Departments | | Operating Departments | |
|---|---|---|---|---|
|  | Administrative | MIS | Commercial | Military |
| Direct costs | $600,000 | $200,000 | $2,000,000 | $4,000,000 |
| Employees | 20 | 10 | 40 | 50 |
| CPUs (millions) | 20 | 50 | 30 | 70 |

The MIS department is responsible for computer equipment and systems, and it maintains databases for the entire organization.

**REQUIRED:**
**A.** Suppose Space Products uses the step-down method for allocating support department costs. Administrative costs are allocated first on the basis of the number of employees, and then MIS costs are allocated on the basis of CPUs. How much support department cost will be allocated to the military division?
**B.** Space Products produced 100 military satellites in the period considered in this problem. Assuming the company uses the allocations calculated in part (A), what is the average cost per military satellite?
**ⓔ C.** Is the average cost that you calculated in part (B) most likely an underestimate, overestimate, or unbiased estimate of the incremental cost of producing one more military satellite? Explain.
**D.** Suppose Space Products uses the direct method of allocating support department costs. What is the maximum amount of support department cost that can be allocated to the military division under DOD rules?
**E.** Suppose the management of Space Products always calculates its support department cost allocations to maximize the amount of contribution received from the DOD. Management selects this policy because it allows the company to be more competitive in its commercial markets.
**❶ 1.** Discuss possible reasons why the DOD does not specify a single, unambiguous support cost allocation method.

**2.** From a taxpayer's point of view, discuss whether you would agree with Space Product's policy.

 **3.** From a competitor's point of view, discuss whether you would agree with Space Product's policy.

**8.27**
Q1, Q2, Q7

**Categorization of support costs** The **Better Business Bureau**, through its BBB Wise Giving Alliance, provides information on the Web about charitable organizations (see give.org/ or go to www.wiley.com/college/eldenburg). On the Web site, organizations are evaluated based on whether they meet the standards for charitable solicitations established by the Council of Better Business Bureaus. One of those standards states, "A reasonable percentage of total income from all sources shall be applied to programs and activities directly related to the purposes for which the organization exists." This standard reflects the desire of donors to be sure that an organization devotes its resources primarily to programs rather than to administration and fund-raising.

Suppose a charitable organization called Food on Wheels provides meals for low-income individuals who are unable to leave their homes. To support its services, it solicits contributions from individuals and businesses. The organization's director would like the organization to be listed on the BBB Wise Giving Alliance Web site. Food on Wheels needs to submit financial statements in which its expenses are assigned to the following cost pools: administrative, fund-raising, and programs.

The bookkeeper for Food on Wheels is a volunteer who is taking accounting classes at the local community college. He knows that all of the costs to prepare and deliver meals should be assigned to the program. However, he is not sure how to assign some of the costs. In particular, he is concerned about the following two items.

**Costs for printing and mailing a monthly newsletter.** The newsletter is sent out to donors and clients and asks for donations. It also describes the organization's activities, provides information for obtaining meal services, and provides recipes for some of the meals that are served. The director of the organization wants the cost of the newsletter to be classified as a program cost. She maintains that the program information and recipes should be considered educational material. Not-for-profit organizations typically classify educational materials as program expenses.

**Director's salary and benefits.** The director of Food on Wheels spends much of her time raising funds, meeting with the board of directors, and performing other administrative duties. She also manages the cooks and drivers, purchases food and delivery supplies, and schedules the food deliveries. The director has instructed the bookkeeper to allocate her salary and benefit costs as follows: 50% to the program, 25% to fund-raising, and 25% to administration.

**REQUIRED:**

**A.** Identify and discuss uncertainties about how each of the following costs should be classified:
   **1.** Costs to print and mail the newsletter
   **2.** Director's salary and benefits

**B.** Does this situation involve an ethical dilemma for the bookkeeper? Why or why not?

**C.** Explain why the director has a preference for costs to be assigned to program expenses.

**D.** Explain how you think donors would prefer for the costs in part (A) to be assigned.

**E.** Suppose you are reviewing cost information for another organization reported on the Better Business Bureau Web site. Would you expect the organization's program costs to be biased upward, biased downward, or to be unbiased? Explain.

**F.** How would you classify the costs in part (A) if you were the bookkeeper for Food on Wheels? Explain your reasoning.

**8.28**
Q2, Q3, Q4, Q5, Q6

**Direct, step-down, and reciprocal methods using dual rate and three departments** In Middletown Children's Clinic (Part 4), we did not perform direct or step-down methods for the dual-rate costs. Following are the allocation bases for these costs. The support cost data are on page 313.

| | Administration | Accounting | Housekeeping | Medical | Dental | Total |
|---|---|---|---|---|---|---|
| Number of employees | 1 | 1 | 2 | 5 | 3 | 12 |
| Square feet | 600 | 300 | 100 | 8,000 | 1,000 | 10,000 |
| Time spent accounting | 15% | | 10% | 50% | 25% | 100% |
| Time spent cleaning | 10% | 5% | | 55% | 30% | 100% |

**REQUIRED:**
**A.** Draw a diagram of the direct method for the Middletown Children's Clinic allocations using three support departments.

*(continued)*

**B.** Allocate the support department costs using dual rates and the direct method.

**❶ C.** Draw a diagram of the step-down method using the three support departments.

**D.** Allocate the support department costs using dual rates and the step-down method.

**E.** Write out the simultaneous equations for the reciprocal allocation.

**F.** Set up a spreadsheet that uses Excel Solver to solve the simultaneous equations and then allocates support costs using dual rates and the reciprocal method. Check to see that your solution matches the solution in the text.

☆ **8.29**
Q1, Q2, Q7

**Total cost under alternative allocation bases, special order price** Danish Hospital recently installed a RAP Scanner, which is a diagnostic tool used both in suspected cancer cases and for detecting certain birth defects while the fetus is still in the womb. The scanner is leased for $5,000 per month, and a full-time operator is paid $3,000 per month. Data concerning use of the scanner for a typical month follow.

|  | Cancer Detection | Birth Defect Detection |
|---|---|---|
| Revenue per scan | $600 | $400 |
| Direct costs per scan | $100 | $50 |
| Minutes required per scan | 30 | 10 |
| Number of scans performed | 20 | 40 |

The direct costs consist primarily of supplies that are consumed in the scanning process. Currently, less than 20% of the machine's capacity is used.

**REQUIRED:**
**ANALYZE**
**INFORMATION**

The following questions will help you analyze the information for this problem. Do not turn in your answers to these questions unless your professor asks you to do so.

**A.** If the lease cost and the operator salary are allocated on the basis of minutes on the scanner, what is the total cost of a cancer scan?

**B.** Suppose the cancer scans are experimental. Rather than charging $600 per scan, the hospital costs are reimbursed under a National Institutes of Health (NIH) contract. The NIH will reimburse direct costs as well as an allocated share of the lease cost and operator's salary. As an allocation base, the NIH allows either the number of scans or total minutes on the machine. What is the maximum reimbursable cost per cancer scan?

**❶ C.** The hospital is bidding on a state contract to supply birth defect scans to indigent pregnant women. The hospital would provide up to 14 scans a month for a fixed fee per scan. Assuming the hospital does not want to lose money on this contract, what is the minimum acceptable fee? Explain how you decided which costs are relevant.

**❶ D.** Identify uncertainties about which costs should be included in bidding for the contract described in part (C).

**❷ E.** Discuss the pros and cons of using total allocated costs, including administrative overhead, in bidding for the contract described in part (C).

**REQUIRED:**
**WRITTEN**
**ASSIGNMENT**

Suppose the hospital is bidding on the contract described in part (C). You have been asked to prepare a report of the hospital's expected costs for the contract. Turn in your answers to the following.

**❸ F.** Write a memo to the chief accountant recommending the costs you think should be included in the expected costs. Attach to the memo a schedule showing your computations. As appropriate, refer to the schedule in the memo.

**8.30**
Q1, Q2, Q4, Q7

**Step-down method, multiple versus single pool allocations, manager incentives** The Gleason Company, a U.S. division of a large international company, has prepared estimated costs for next year that can be traced to each department as follows:

| | |
|---|---|
| Building and grounds | $ 41,010 |
| Factory administration | 78,270 |
| Cafeteria—operating loss | 4,920 |
| Machining | 104,100 |
| Assembly | 146,700 |
| Total | $375,000 |

Management would like to know the estimated total allocated product cost per unit. These costs will be used as a benchmark for future period operations. The following information is available and can be used as possible allocation bases. The difference between direct labor hours and total labor hours represents hours of supervisory labor or labor hours that are used indirectly for manufacturing. The cost of these hours in machining and assembly is part of manufacturing overhead.

| Department | Direct Labor Hours | Number of Employees | Square Feet | Total Labor Hours | Number of Purchase Orders |
|---|---|---|---|---|---|
| Factory administration | | 2 | 500 | | 500 |
| Cafeteria | 1,000 | 2 | 1,000 | 1,000 | 4,000 |
| Machining | 3,000 | 4 | 3,500 | 8,000 | 2,000 |
| Assembly | 6,000 | 5 | 5,000 | 10,000 | 1,000 |
| Total | 12,000 | 14 | 10,000 | 21,000 | 8,000 |

**REQUIRED:**

**A.** Allocate the building and grounds costs to all other departments using square feet. Add the allocated costs to direct costs to arrive at the total costs assigned to each department.

**B.** Explain whether each remaining department is a support or operating department.

**C.** Select a reasonable allocation base for the costs of each support department. Justify your choices.

**D.** Compute allocated overhead costs for each operating department. Given the allocation bases you selected in part (B), allocate support department costs to each operating department using the step-down method. Then calculate an overhead rate per direct labor hour for each operating department.

**E.** Calculate overhead rates for the operating departments assuming that Gleason uses an average, plantwide factory overhead allocation rate based on direct labor hours. That is, aggregate the support department overhead costs into one cost pool and use direct labor hours as the allocation base to determine the overhead rate per direct labor hour.

**F.** What causes the difference between the rates you calculated in parts (D) and (E)?

**G.** Assume that factory administration costs are allocated based on total labor hours and that the total allocated cost is used to charge other departments for administrative services. List one advantage and one disadvantage of this charge system.

**H.** Suppose that you are the manager of the machining department at Gleason. You can outsource some of your department's work. Outsourcing would reduce direct labor hours and, therefore, reduce the amount of overhead allocated to your department. What factors should you consider in deciding whether to outsource?

**I.** Now suppose that you are the director of finance for Gleason. The manager of the machining department has decided to outsource some tasks. When you analyze the current period results, you notice that while direct labor costs decreased in machining, outsourcing costs are slightly higher this period than the prior period's direct labor costs. When you ask the manager about these costs, he replies that the outsourcing does cost more than using direct labor, but because the amount of overhead for the department decreases, it is more profitable. What happened to the overhead that is no longer allocated to machining? Is the manager's decision beneficial to Gleason Company as a whole? Explain.

**8.31** **Support cost allocation uncertainties and fairness** Andy Rich is an agent for Steve Kurl, a basketball player who has been on a number of championship professional teams over the last 10 years. Steve complained to Andy that his compensation does not seem to be what was promised. In addition to salary, Steve was promised a percentage of the gate receipts after deduction of expenses for each game. However, the organization's accountants told Steve that little profit is left after all of the expenses have been deducted.

Q1, Q2, Q7

Andy asks to review the financial reports from the last five games. As he reviews the reports, Andy notices that the expenses for each game include large amounts for administration and public relations. He asks the accountant about these expenses and is told that these costs are allocated using revenue as the allocation base. The rate is calculated by dividing estimated total administrative and public relations costs by estimated total revenue for all of the games played during the regular season.

Since Steve played in a number of championship games, Andy asks for the financial reports for those games, too. It appears that the same rate was used to allocate administration and public relations for postseason games. He brings this practice to the attention of the accountant, who responds that each game has to have a share of the expenses, and that it has always been done this way.

**REQUIRED:**

**① A.** Discuss uncertainties about how to measure the profit for each game. (Think about the following question: Why is there no single way to calculate profit for each game?)

**① B.** Is this scenario an ethical dilemma? Why or why not?

**② C.** The team allocates its administration and public relations costs using an estimated allocation rate. Is this method likely to be biased? In other words, are allocated costs likely to be higher or lower than actual costs for the year? Explain.

**② D.** Provide arguments in favor of allocating administration and public relations costs as an expense of each game.

**② E.** Provide arguments against allocating administration and public relations costs as an expense of each game.

**③ F.** Brainstorm ideas and recommend a method for calculating the profits for each game that you think would be fair to the owners and fair to the players. Explain how your conclusion addresses all important stakeholders.

☆ **8.32**
Q1, Q7

**Allowable costs under cost-based contract, accountant ethical responsibility** Review the **Stanford** case and the discussion presented in the textbook at the beginning of Chapter 8. During 1991 and 1992, the federal government also launched investigations into the overhead costs at numerous universities, including **Syracuse, Massachusetts Institute of Technology, Pennsylvania State, Harvard Medical School, Carnegie Mellon, Duke, Johns Hopkins,** and **Pittsburgh.** Government auditors claimed that universities had overcharged the government for indirect research costs.

Accountants often view it as part of their job to help their organizations succeed. Often, this assistance means developing strategies to maximize the organization's cash flows. For example, accountants promote income tax strategies to help companies minimize income tax payments. Similarly, accountants might promote strategies to maximize reimbursements under cost-based contracts. This type of strategy might encourage accountants to include a cost in an indirect cost pool when there is uncertainty about whether it is allowed.

**REQUIRED:**
**ANALYZE**
**INFORMATION**

The following questions will help you analyze the information for this problem. Do not turn in your answers to these questions unless your professor asks you to do so.

**① A.** Explain why accountants must often use judgment to decide whether a particular cost is reimbursable under a cost-based contract.

**① B.** Discuss whether maximizing reimbursements under cost-based contracts is an ethical issue for accountants.

**② C.** In the Stanford case, the total repayment of $2.2 million was small in relation to the total $734 million in indirect costs the university had received from the government. Is your answer to part (B) affected by the size of a potential overcharge? Why or why not?

**② D.** Identify the major groups of stakeholders for this problem. From the perspective of each major stakeholder group, discuss the pros and cons when accountants help their organizations maximize reimbursements under cost-based contracts.

**③ E.** What trade-offs must accountants make when deciding whether to help their organizations maximize reimbursements under cost-based contracts?

**REQUIRED:**
**WRITTEN**
**ASSIGNMENT**

Turn in your answer to the following.

**③ F.** Use the information you learned from the preceding analyses to help you write an essay in response to the following question: Is it ethical for accountants to help their organizations maximize reimbursements under cost-based contracts?

**8.33**
Q1, Q2, Q3, Q4, Q5,
Q6, Q7

**Comprehensive problem, dual versus single rates, purpose of allocation** Vines Company is a manufacturer of women's and men's swimsuits. The company uses a dual-rate system to allocate support costs. Last year's support departments' fixed and variable costs are as follows.

| Department | Accounting | Human Resources | Janitorial | Total |
|---|---|---|---|---|
| Variable costs | $18,420 | $ 22,104 | $ 60,360 | $100,884 |
| Fixed costs | 55,260 | 100,696 | 60,360 | 216,316 |
| Total cost | $73,680 | $122,800 | $120,720 | $317,200 |

Allocation base amounts for all of the departments are:

| Department | Accounting | Human Resources | Janitorial | Women's | Men's | Total |
|---|---|---|---|---|---|---|
| Employees | 2 | 2 | 4 | 10 | 6 | 24 |
| Time spent for accounting | 15% | 10% | 20% | 30% | 25% | 100% |
| Time spent cleaning | 5% | 10% | 15% | 30% | 40% | 100% |
| Square feet | 800 | 1,000 | 1,200 | 5,000 | 5,000 | 13,000 |
| Direct Costs | $73,680 | $122,800 | $120,720 | $800,000 | $500,000 | $1,617,200 |

**REQUIRED:**

**A.** Use the following allocation bases for fixed support costs: direct costs for accounting, number of employees for human resources, and square feet for janitorial.

    **1.** Allocate fixed support costs using the direct method.

    **2.** Allocate fixed support costs using the step-down method.

    **3.** Allocate fixed support costs using the reciprocal method.

**B.** Use the following allocation bases for variable support costs: time spent for accounting, number of employees for human resources, and time spent for janitorial.

    **1.** Allocate variable support costs using the direct method.

    **2.** Allocate variable support costs using the step-down method.

    **3.** Allocate variable support costs using the reciprocal method.

❶ **C.** Suppose support costs were not broken down into fixed and variable cost pools. What allocation base would you use to allocate the costs for each support department? Explain.

❶ **D.** Describe several possible reasons why the managers of Vines Company allocate support costs to operating departments.

❷ **E.** Discuss whether a dual-rate support cost allocation system is likely to be better for Vines Company than a single-rate system.

# BUILD YOUR PROFESSIONAL COMPETENCIES

**8.34** **Q1, Q2** **Focus on Professional Competency: Leverage Technology to Develop and Enhance Functional Competencies** *Information databases, use of technology, documenting work, adopting new technologies* Review the following definition and elements for Leverage Technology to Develop and Enhance Functional Competencies.[16]

**DEFINITION:** *Technology is pervasive in the accounting profession. Individuals entering the accounting profession must acquire the necessary skills to use technology tools effectively and efficiently. These technology tools can be used both to develop and apply other functional competencies.*

## ELEMENTS FOR THIS COMPETENCY INCLUDE

| Level 1 | Level 2 | Level 3 | Level 4 |
|---|---|---|---|
| 1. Accesses appropriate electronic databases to obtain decision-supporting information<br><br>2. Identifies risks associated with technology and automated business processes | 3. Uses technology-assisted tools to assess and control risk and document work performed<br><br>4. Appropriately uses electronic spreadsheets and other software to build models and simulations | 5. Assesses the degree of risk of technology and automated business processes | 6. Develops strategic uses of technology for enhancing work performance<br><br>7. Adopts new technology over time |

**REQUIRED:** Chapter 8 does not directly address how to leverage technology to develop and enhance functional competencies. However, the chapter introduces two major uses of technology that are related to accountants' functional competencies:

    **1.** Use of accounting information systems to accumulate cost and allocation base data.

    **2.** Use of Microsoft Solver for simultaneous equations.

---

[16]The definition and elements are reprinted with permission from AICPA; Copyright © 1978–2000 & 2003 by American Institute of Certified Public Accountants. The AICPA's Core Competency Framework can be accessed at eca.aicpaservices.org.

As you address the following questions, focus on how technology assists accountants in the process of allocating support department costs.

**A.** Focus on competency element 1, which links the use of technology to business decisions. Answer the following questions:

**①** **1.** What types of decisions are addressed in Chapter 8? List business decisions as well as decisions about accounting methods.

**①** **2.** For the decisions you identified above, list relevant information that might be stored in an electronic database.

**B.** Focus on competency elements 3 and 4, which address the use of technology by accountants to document their work. Perform the following:

**③** **1.** Create a spreadsheet for allocating costs from more than two support departments using the reciprocal method. Include in your spreadsheet information to document the work performed.

**②** **2.** Show the spreadsheet to someone else and ask him or her to explain the work documented in the spreadsheet. Make a list of items that the other person does and does not understand.

**③** **3.** Given the lists you created in part 2, modify the spreadsheet to improve its ability to document the work performed.

**④** **C.** Focus on competency element 7, which addresses the adoption of new technology over time. Think about situations where you have adopted new technologies. What strategies do you use to decide whether or when to adopt a new technology? Think about the following types of questions to help you identify strategies: Do you wait until you are required to use a new technology (such as in a course)? Do you seek information about new technologies on your own? How do you decide whether a new technology is worthwhile? How do you go about learning and adopting a new technology? Do you tend to be either reluctant or overly eager about new technologies? If so, how do you compensate for your tendencies?

**8.35** **Integrating Across the Curriculum: Governmental Accounting** *Types and uses of internal service funds in state and local governments* In governmental accounting, separate funds are created to keep track of revenues and costs for different activities. An internal service fund (ISF) accumulates the cost for services provided within the government. Common types of internal services include motor pools, central data processing, human resources, purchasing, accounting, duplicating and printing departments, and self-insurance pools. An ISF charges other funds for their share of service costs. Thus, ISF accounting is one way to allocate the cost of internal services to other governmental activities.

**Q1, Q7**

www.wiley.com/
college/eldenburg

The following table provides examples of internal service funds used by state and local governments in the United States:

| City of Laguna Beach, California | State of Michigan Department of Management and Budget | City of Arlington, Texas | Multnomah County, Oregon |
|---|---|---|---|
| Insurance and benefits | State-sponsored group insurance | General services | Risk management |
| Vehicle replacement | Information technology and energy | Communication services | Fleet management |
| | Motor transport | Fleet services | Telephone |
| | Office services revolving | Information technology services | Data processing |
| | Risk management | | Mail/distribution |
| | | | Facilities management |

In a 1993 survey of 237 city chief financial officers, researchers found that 28% of cities did not use ISF accounting. Even among cities that did use ISFs, many used them only for the motor pool and self-insurance and did not necessarily assign all relevant costs to those funds. Only 7 cities used a sophisticated cost accounting system that measured and allocated all internal service costs. When ISFs are not used, the costs of internal services are usually pooled with other administrative and general costs and are not allocated to other activities.

Survey respondents using ISFs reported that measuring and allocating service costs provided information to help them:

- Justify budget requests
- Price city services
- Decide whether to insource or outsource services
- Compare the costs of units performing similar services
- Analyze how costs vary with circumstances such as crew size, equipment condition, and weather

SOURCES: C. Coe and E. O'Sullivan, "Accounting for the Hidden Costs: A National Study of Internal Service Funds and Other Indirect Costing Methods in Municipal Governments" *Public Administration Review,* January/February 1993; Internal Service Funds, Adopted Budget—Fiscal Year 2003–04, City of Laguna Beach, California, available at 4.18.61.11/government/reference/budget; Executive Digest #0713701, Selected Internal Service Funds, Michigan Office of the Auditor General, June 2002, available at www.audgen.michigan.gov/digests/01_02/0713701.htm; Executive Summary, FY 2004 Annual Operating Budget, City of Arlington, Texas, available at www.ci.arlington.tx.us/budgets/; and Internal Service Funds (under Supplementary Information), Comprehensive Annual Financial Report, fiscal year ended June 30, 2002, available at www.co.multnomah.or.us/dbcs/finance/cafr2002/.

**REQUIRED:**

**A.** Conduct research on the Internet to locate information about the internal service funds used by a state or local government. What internal funds are used? What is the description for each fund?

**B.** How are the uses of internal service fund accounting in a government similar to the uses of support cost allocations in a business organization?

**C.** Proponents of ISF accounting argue that a failure to allocate internal service costs overstates the cost of general governmental management, making the government appear to be inefficient and understating the cost of other activities. Explain what these arguments mean.

**D.** As a citizen and taxpayer, do you think that state and local governments should use internal service fund accounting? Explain your reasoning.

# Joint Product and By-Product Costing

## ▶In Brief

Some products are produced jointly with other products. For example, when crude oil is processed, gasoline, diesel, and heating oil are produced. For external reports such as financial statements and tax returns, the common costs incurred to produce joint products are allocated to the resulting products. Accountants choose among several methods to allocate joint costs.

Managers and accountants also make decisions about when to sell joint products. Some goods and services are sold when joint production ends. Other goods and services are processed further and then sold. For example, managers of a food manufacturer must decide how much of the wheat they purchase to sell as flour and how much to process further into pasta or other food products. They must also identify relevant costs when making this type of decision.

## This Chapter Addresses the Following Questions:

**Q1** What is a joint process, and what is the difference between a by-product and a main product?

**Q2** How are joint costs allocated?

**Q3** What factors are considered in choosing a joint cost allocation method?

**Q4** What information is relevant for deciding whether to process a joint product beyond the split-off point?

**Q5** What methods are used to account for the sale of by-products?

**Q6** How does a sales mix affect joint cost allocation?

**Q7** What are the uses and limitations of joint cost information?

# HYPERION TREATMENT PLANT: GAINS FROM WASTE

In 1997, the **City of Los Angeles** Department of Airports (DOA) faced a statewide mandate to achieve 50% waste diversion by the year 2000. The goal was to dramatically decrease the amount of waste shipped to landfills. Despite a program launched with airport tenants to reduce, reuse, and recycle waste, the DOA was still short of its goals. After learning that food residuals from the airport's inflight catering, restaurants, bars, and employee commissaries accounted for more than 40% of the airport's waste, DOA managers decided to target food residuals for additional waste diversion efforts.

The Hyperion Wastewater Treatment Plant, also owned by the city, provided a possible solution. The Hyperion plant could be used to convert food residuals into two other products. The first was a methane-rich fuel gas called biogas, produced by the interaction of bacteria and organic waste matter. Biogas could be sold to an adjacent power plant owned by the city's Department of Water and Power. In turn, the power plant could use the biogas to produce electrical energy. The second product, biosolids, was the residue of biogas production sometimes referred to as "sludge," and would be disposed.

Hyperion and the DOA, together with other municipal agencies, launched a study to evaluate the economics of using airport food residuals to produce biogas. An important factor in the study was the cost of separating organic from nonorganic materials. The Hyperion plant could accept only organic materials, requiring organic food residuals to be separated from nonorganic materials such as cardboard and plastic. Airport tenants were already paying $30 to $32 per ton for landfill disposal of their waste. To induce them to separate the food residual from plastic and paper residual, Hyperion would need to charge a lower disposal price for picking up the food residual.

Hyperion's cash inflows for this arrangement would include revenues from airport tenants for disposing of their food residuals plus revenues from the sale of biogas to the power plant. Costs common to both sources of revenue would include plant operating costs, the cost of transporting the residual from the airport to Hyperion's plant, and the cost of disposing of the biosolids that would remain after biogas production.

The study concluded that Hyperion would profit from biogas production. Accordingly, Hyperion conducted a pilot production project. When it was completed satisfactorily, Hyperion agreed to launch a full-scale program. ■

SOURCES: R. T. Haug, G. Hernandez, T. Sarullo, and F. Gerringer, "Using Wastewater Digesters to Recycle Food Residuals into Energy," *BioCycle Emmaus 41,* no. 9 (September 2000), pp. 74–78; G. Hernandez, K. Redd, W. Wert, A. M. Liu, and T. Haug, "Los Angeles Digesters Produce Energy from Airport Food Residuals," *BioCycle Emmaus* 43, no. 1 (January 2002), pp. 53–55; R. T. Haug et al., "Two-Stage Thermophilic Process to Treat Biosolids in Los Angeles," *BioCycle Emmaus* 43, no. 6 (June 2002), pp. 22–25; and definition of biogas available at glossary.eea.eu.int/EEAGlossary/B/biogas.

## EVALUATING A JOINT PRODUCT DECISION

### ■ Key Decision Factors for the City of Los Angeles

Faced with a state mandate to divert more waste from landfills, several agencies of the **City of Los Angeles** cooperated in identifying an economically viable project to turn airport food residuals into biogas. Here is a summary of key aspects of this decision-making process.

**Knowing.** The success of the Hyperion project depended on the technical expertise of city engineers as well as operating experience at the Hyperion plant. In addition, the Department of Airports conducted research to learn about the type of waste generated at the airport. Without this information, city managers might not have focused on food residuals in their waste diversion efforts.

**Identifying.** Los Angeles city managers needed to identify different waste diversion projects for possible exploration. The idea for the Hyperion project was particularly creative because it combined two different products—waste disposal and biogas production. While evaluating the Hyperion project, city accountants made numerous estimates because of uncertainties such as the technical feasibility of the project and levels of future operating revenues and costs.

**Exploring.** Evaluating the technical and economic feasibility of the Hyperion project involved many different types of analysis, including:

- Conducting process experiments
- Interpreting technical data
- Estimating future revenues and costs
- Investigating incentives to encourage airport tenants to separate organic from nonorganic waste

**Prioritizing.** The ability of city managers to identify and pursue the Hyperion project demonstrates a commitment to achieving statewide goals to reduce landfill waste. At the same time, city accountants needed to ensure that the project was economically feasible—that incremental revenues would exceed incremental costs for the project.

**Envisioning.** The Hyperion project appeared to be both technically and economically feasible when the pilot study was completed. However, city accountants and managers needed to keep in mind that many estimates were used when evaluating the project. Actual future results could be better or worse than expected.

- Full-scale implementation of successful pilot projects could still exceed or fall short of estimated technical results.
- Future increases or decreases in costs and revenues could be significant.
- Unanticipated future regulations could restrict the disposal of biosolids.

The managers of the Hyperion plant, as well as managers of other affected city agencies, need to anticipate and plan for future technical and economic changes.

### ■ Decisions Involving More Than One Product

Success of the City of Los Angeles Hyperion project depended on the coordination of two separate products—waste disposal and biogas. When the production of two or more products is codependent, it becomes more difficult for managers to measure and monitor operations. In this chapter, we learn methods for measuring the cost of such products. We also learn the uses and limitations of costs that are allocated across interdependent products.

## JOINT PRODUCTS AND COSTS

Some industries simultaneously produce a group of products through a single process. Consider a fish farm where products include fresh fish, frozen fish, frozen fish entrees, and fish fertilizer. In the process of making one product, one or more other products or services are created, called **joint products.** As another example, the **City of Los Angeles** Hyperion plant's waste management process generates revenue from a product, biogas, as well as from a

**EXHIBIT 9.1** Examples of Industries That Manufacture Joint Products

| Industry | Main Products | By-Products | Example Company |
|---|---|---|---|
| Petroleum (crude oil) | Gasoline, diesel, jet fuel | Asphalt | Shell Oil |
| Copper mining | Copper, silver, lead, zinc | Malachite, azurite | BHP Mining |
| Cheese production | Fresh cheese, butter | Buttermilk | Tillamook Cheese |
| Lumber (logs) | Lumber, veneer, plywood | Bark dust, sawdust | Weyerhaeuser |
| Beef production | Cuts of meat, leather | Dog bones, bone meal for gardens | Hormel |

**Q1** What is a joint process, and what is the difference between a by-product and a main product?

service, the collection of food residuals. Other examples of joint products are readily found in many industries, such as oil and gas, chemicals, and foods.

Joint products fall into two categories. A **main product** has high sales value compared to other joint products. At the fish farm, fresh fish, frozen fish, and fish entrees are main products. A **by-product** has low sales value compared to the other joint products. Fish fertilizer is an example of a by-product. Exhibit 9.1 presents a list of industries that manufacture joint products and gives examples of main products and by-products.

**Joint costs** are all of the costs incurred to jointly produce a group of goods. These costs are common to all of the joint products and are incurred prior to the **split-off point,** the point at which individual products are identified. At the fish farm, the split-off point is the point at which the fish are caught and cleaned. The joint costs include the costs to maintain the fishponds such as labor, fish food, insurance, and property taxes, plus all of the costs to clean fish and prepare them for further processing.

**Separable costs** are the costs incurred after the split-off point. These incremental costs can be easily traced to each specific product. At the fish farm, separable costs are incurred for packaging fresh fish, freezing fish, preparing entrees, and pulverizing and emulsifying the waste and bottling it for fertilizer. Exhibit 9.2 shows the common and separable activities involved in raising fish and lists several of the costs for these activities.

**ALTERNATIVE TERMS**

The term *common costs* is similar to *joint costs*.

**EXHIBIT 9.2** Raising and Processing Fish at a Fish Farm

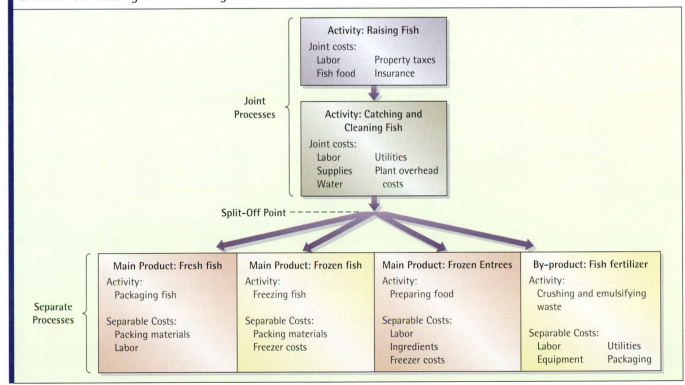

## ALLOCATING JOINT COSTS

**CHAPTER REFERENCE**

Transfer prices and policies are discussed further in Chapter 15.

An organization commits to joint costs when managers decide to produce joint products. Joint costs must be allocated to each product for reporting inventory and cost of goods sold on financial statements, income tax returns, and other types of reports. Joint costs must also be allocated for government regulatory reports when companies that sell to both government agencies and commercial organizations seek reimbursement of costs on government-funded projects. Occasionally legal processes scrutinize joint cost allocations, such as when an organization must support the transfer price used between divisions located in high-tax and low-tax countries. A tax audit by a government or corporate or government litigation may also require joint cost allocation information. In addition, joint costs are sometimes used internally for evaluating division or segment performance.

In the **City of Los Angeles** Hyperion case, joint costs are allocated between the collection of food residuals and the production of biogas and biosolids. The allocation of joint costs assists in matching revenues and costs. Therefore, the allocated costs of biogas would be expensed in the accounting period when biogas is sold, and the allocated costs of any unsold biogas would be included in inventory on the balance sheet. Similarly, the allocated cost of collecting food residuals would be recorded on the income statement in the same period in which the revenues are recorded.

Several different methods are used to allocate joint costs to main products. In this chapter we learn about the following methods:

- Physical output method
- Market-based methods:
  - Sales value at split-off point
  - Net realizable value (NRV)
  - Constant gross margin NRV

To illustrate these methods, we use a sawmill example. The Merritt Brothers own and operate a sawmill in northern Idaho. The brothers hire loggers who cut timber and bring it to the mill, where the logs are sawed into lumber. In addition, sawdust and wood chips from the sawmill operation are glued and pressed into chipboard. Exhibit 9.3 presents the costs and revenues from this operation. The joint costs of cutting trees, debarking logs, and sawing logs into lumber are $220 per log, which the Merritt Brothers commit to when a tree is cut down and sent to the sawmill. Revenue from lumber, the main product, is $400. The company could sell the sawdust and wood chips, a by-product, to a pulp mill for $40. However, Merritt Brothers currently process the sawdust and wood chips further by gluing and pressing them into chipboard, which is considered another main product. The cost of this additional processing is $46, and the chipboard sells for $146.

## ■ Physical Output Method

**Q2** How are joint costs allocated?

The **physical output method** allocates joint costs using the relative proportion of physical output for each main product. This method is only used when output for all main products can be expressed using the same physical measure, such as meters, pounds, or gallons. Each main product is allocated a proportion of joint costs based on that product's physical output divided by the total physical output of all main products.

For Merritt Brothers, either pounds or board feet could be used as an allocation base. Suppose the company uses pounds of final product as the physical volume allocation base. Each log processed results in 500 pounds of chipboard and 500 pounds of lumber. Thus, the relative weight of chipboard is 500 lbs/1,000 lbs. The joint costs of $220 are multiplied by this proportion to calculate the amount of joint costs allocated to chipboard:

$$(500 \text{ lbs}/1,000 \text{ lbs}) \times \$220 = \$110$$

**EXHIBIT 9.3** Merritt Brothers Revenues and Costs for Processing One Log

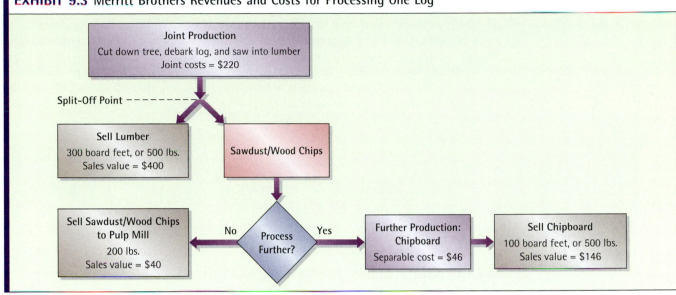

A similar set of calculations leads to allocation of $110 of joint costs to lumber as follows:

| | Main Products | | |
|---|---|---|---|
| | Chipboard | Lumber | Total |
| Base: Pounds of final product | 500 lbs | 500 lbs | 1,000 lbs |
| Proportion | 500 lb/1,000 lb | 500 lb/1,000 lb | |
| Allocated joint costs | $110 | $110 | $220 |

Suppose Merritt Brothers instead uses the number of board feet of final product as the allocation base. For each log processed, the company produces 100 board feet of chipboard and 300 board feet of lumber. In this case, the amount of joint costs allocated to each main product is calculated as follows:

| | Main Products | | |
|---|---|---|---|
| | Chipboard | Lumber | Total |
| Base: Board feet of final product | 100 bd ft | 300 bd ft | 400 bd ft |
| Proportion | 100 bd ft/400 bd ft | 300 bd ft/400 bd ft | |
| Allocated joint costs | $55 | $165 | $220 |

## ■ Sales Value at Split-Off Point Method

Market-based methods use some proportion of the profit contribution for each main product to determine the joint cost allocation rate. Under the **sales value at split-off point method,** joint costs are allocated based on the relative sales value of main products at the point where joint production ends. For Merritt Brothers, joint production of a log creates lumber that can be sold for $400 and sawdust and wood chips that can be sold without further processing for $40. The relative proportions of sales values at the split-off point are used to allocate the joint costs of each main product as follows:

| | Main Products | | |
|---|---|---|---|
| | Chipboard | Lumber | Total |
| Base: Sales value at split-off point | $40 | $400 | $440 |
| Proportion | $40/$440 | $400/$440 | |
| Allocated joint costs | $20 | $200 | $220 |

## ■ Net Realizable Value Method

The **net realizable value (NRV) method** allocates joint costs using the relative value of main products, taking into account both the additional sales value that is created and costs that are incurred after joint production ends. NRV for each main product is calculated as the final selling price minus separable costs. For Merritt Brothers, lumber is not processed further, so its net realizable value is equal to its sales value at the split-off point, or $400. The NRV for chipboard is expected to be $100 ($146 − $46) after further processing. The joint cost allocation calculations are as follows:

| | Main Products | | |
|---|---|---|---|
| | Chipboard | Lumber | Total |
| Base: Net realizable value | $100 | $400 | $500 |
| Proportion | $100/$500 | $400/$500 | |
| Allocated joint costs | $44 | $176 | $220 |

## ■ Constant Gross Margin NRV Method

The **constant gross margin NRV method** allocates joint costs so that the gross margin percentage for each main product is identical. This method involves two sets of computations. First, the combined gross margin percentage for main products is calculated. Second, joint costs are allocated to each main product to achieve a constant gross margin.

**1. Calculate the combined gross margin percentage.** To calculate the combined gross margin, create an income statement for the main products. The gross margin is determined by subtracting the joint and separable costs from the sales. Then the gross margin is divided by sales to determine the gross margin percentage. Continuing with the Merritt Brothers example,

| | | |
|---|---|---|
| Determine sales: | | |
| Sales: Lumber | | $400 |
| Chipboard | | 146 |
| Combined sales | | 546 |
| Determine costs: | | |
| Joint costs | $220 | |
| Separable costs: Lumber | 0 | |
| Chipboard | 46 | |
| Combined product costs | | 266 |
| Combined gross margin | | $280 |
| Combined gross margin percentage ($280 ÷ $546) | | 51.3% |

**2. Allocate joint costs to achieve a constant gross margin.** The desired gross margin, based on the preceding calculation, is first subtracted from the sales value to determine the desired amount of total product cost for each main product. Next, separable costs are subtracted from total product costs to determine the amount of joint costs to be allocated to each main product.

| | Main Products | | |
|---|---|---|---|
| | Chipboard | Lumber | Total |
| Sales | $146 | $400 | $546 |
| Less gross margin (51.3% × sales) | 75 | 205 | 280 |
| Total product costs | 71 | 195 | 266 |
| Less separable costs | 46 | 0 | 46 |
| Allocated joint costs | $ 25 | $195 | $220 |

# CHOOSING AN APPROPRIATE JOINT COST ALLOCATION METHOD

**Q3** What factors are considered in choosing a joint cost allocation method?

Although each of these joint cost allocation methods is logical, the allocation process itself is arbitrary. We cannot trace joint costs to each product because we always incur all of the joint costs to produce any one product. Therefore, no method for allocating joint costs develops a true cost per product.

Each method of joint cost allocation simply assigns a different proportion of cost to products and, therefore, results in a different allocated cost per product. In turn, different allocation methods result in different measures of profitability for each product. Consider the following comparison of the gross margin for Merritt Brothers under different allocation methods for each log processed and sold:

| Main Product | Physical Output (weight) | Sales Value at Split-Off Point | Net Realizable Value | Constant Gross Margin NRV |
| --- | --- | --- | --- | --- |
| Lumber: | | | | |
|   Sales value | $ 400 | $ 400 | $ 400 | $ 400 |
|   Allocated joint costs | (110) | (200) | (176) | (195) |
|   Separable costs | (0) | (0) | (0) | (0) |
|     Product gross margin | 290 | 200 | 224 | 205 |
| Chipboard: | | | | |
|   Sales value | 146 | 146 | 146 | 146 |
|   Allocated joint costs | (110) | (20) | (44) | (25) |
|   Separable costs | (46) | (46) | (46) | (46) |
|     Product gross margin | (10) | 80 | 56 | 75 |
|   Total gross margin | $ 280 | $ 280 | $ 280 | $ 280 |

Notice that the total gross margin per log is not affected by the joint cost allocation method. The cost allocation affects only the relative gross margins for the individual products. Accordingly, the joint cost allocation method used by a company affects the apparent profitability of different products. Sometimes a product can give the appearance that it is sold at a loss, when in fact the company profits from producing the joint product.

## ■ Pros and Cons of Alternative Allocation Methods

An allocation method should be chosen to avoid giving the mistaken impression that one or more products are sold at a loss. Under the physical output method, such distortions are likely to occur when the incremental contribution (incremental revenues less incremental costs) of some products is relatively high compared to other products. For example, if Merritt Brothers uses the physical output method using weight as the allocation base, the gross margin for chipboard is negative. If the managers make product-related decisions with this information, they might decide to quit producing chipboard. However, chipboard's incremental revenues exceed its incremental costs. If the company were to sell the sawdust and wood chips for $40 (the sales value at split-off point), it would forgo the $100 incremental contribution from producing and selling chipboard ($146 revenue less $46 in separable costs). Thus, if chipboard is dropped, profit drops by $60 per log ($100 − $40). To avoid this problem, market value methods are generally superior to the physical output method.

Nevertheless, the physical volume method is commonly used in some industries because all units are similar in size and have comparable net realizable values. Suppose a company grows tomatoes and then manufactures different products such as ketchup and salsa. The company incurs joint costs of raising, picking, cleaning, and chopping tomatoes. Possible physical output measures include weight, fluid ounces, or number of same-sized bottles. If the incremental contributions of the different products are similar, a physical output measure would provide approximately the same cost allocation as the other methods. In addition, the physical output method is the easiest to calculate.

If most or all products are sold at the split-off point, then the sales value at split-off point method is generally most appropriate. This method avoids the physical output method problem of negative contribution for some products. As long as the total gross margin at the split-off point is positive, expected revenues always exceed allocated costs under the sales value at split-off point method. However, some products may need further processing before they can be sold and have no value at the split-off point, or the net realizable value of each joint product may change greatly after further processing. In these cases, this method could distort the relative profitability of products. For example, at Merritt Brothers the net realizable value of the chipboard increases from $40 at the split-off point to $100 ($146 − $46) after processing.

The two NRV methods are generally preferred because they are based on the ability of each product to "pay" for its allocated cost. Using these methods, products appear profitable as long as their revenues are greater than their separable costs. Because the constant gross margin NRV method is more complicated, the NRV method is often chosen. However, the constant gross margin NRV method allocates joint costs so that all joint products appear to have equal profitability. This approach best reflects the inseparability of the joint production process.

Each of these allocation methods is illustrated in the following Merritt Brothers illustration.

## MERRITT BROTHERS (PART 1)
### CHOOSING AN APPROPRIATE ALLOCATION METHOD

Tim Nakamura, an accounting major at the local college, is working as an intern for Merritt Brothers. When Tim prepares financial statements for the company, he needs to choose an allocation base for assigning joint costs to products. First he examines the differences in the allocations and margins for chipboard under the different methods. The following table summarizes his findings:

| Allocation Method | Joint Cost Allocated to Chipboard | Chipboard Gross Margin |
| --- | --- | --- |
| Physical output (using weight) | $110 | $(10) |
| Sales value at split-off point | 20 | 80 |
| Net realizable value | 44 | 56 |
| Constant gross margin NRV | 25 | 75 |

Tim wants to find the simplest method that most fairly values the contribution of chipboard, since it is the joint product with least value. First, he eliminates the physical output method using weight as the allocation base. Weight distorts the profitability of chipboard because the allocated amount is higher than its revenue. With this allocation method, Merritt appears to lose money on each sale. Tim knows that the sale of chipboard contributes to overall profitability. Next he eliminates the constant gross margin NRV method because he thinks the calculations would be more difficult to explain to the mill owners and managers. Because the sales value at split-off point method does not reflect the increased value of separately producing chipboard, Tim decides that the NRV method would be the best choice. This method takes into account information about revenues and separable costs for the chipboard.

| GUIDE YOUR LEARNING | 9.2 | Merritt Brothers (Part 1) |
| --- | --- | --- |

Merritt Brothers (Part 1) demonstrates a choice of joint cost allocation method. For this illustration:

| Define It | Identify Uncertainties | Explore Use and Prioritize Options |
| --- | --- | --- |
| In your own words, describe each allocation method. Explain the differences in costs allocated under the various methods. | What uncertainties are involved in using the various joint cost allocation methods? Consider uncertainties about measuring:<br>• Physical output<br>• Revenues<br>• Separable costs | In your own words, describe the pros and cons of each method. Explain how the pros and cons were weighed in reaching the final decision. |

## PROCESSING A JOINT PRODUCT BEYOND THE SPLIT-OFF POINT

**Q4** What information is relevant for deciding whether to process a joint product beyond the split-off point?

**CHAPTER REFERENCE**

More details about product emphasis decisions are provided in Chapter 4.

Managers often have a choice about whether to sell a product at the split-off point or to process it further. For example, Merritt Brothers can sell the sawdust and wood chip scraps as a product, or they can use the scraps to produce and sell chipboard. When making decisions about whether to process a joint product beyond the split-off point, the joint costs are irrelevant because they are sunk costs. Once managers decide to produce a group of joint products, the joint costs are unavoidable and therefore irrelevant for making product emphasis decisions that identify the final products from a joint process. The product with the highest incremental contribution is the most profitable and should be emphasized. No allocation method is necessary for this type of decision because allocated joint costs represent sunk costs and are not included in the analysis. A decision-making example for Merritt Brothers follows.

### MERRITT BROTHERS (PART 2)
### JOINT PRODUCT DECISION MAKING

Merritt Brothers currently produces chipboard from its sawdust and wood chip scraps. A local pet store approached the Merritt Brothers and wants to buy sawdust and wood chip scraps. The pet store plans to use the scraps for pet bedding. The pet store is willing to pay $60 for 200 pounds (the quantity produced from one log) of sawdust and wood chips, which is more than the $40 the company would receive from a pulp mill. The managers of Merritt Brothers are deciding whether to accept this offer. If they sell sawdust and wood chips to the pet store, they will no longer produce chipboard.

The managers ask Tim to prepare an analysis for this decision. Tim begins his analysis by accessing sales, production, and cost records. Using this information, he creates a cost flowchart (Exhibit 9.4). Tim recalls learning in his cost accounting course that incremental revenues and costs are relevant for decision making. As Tim works on the flowchart, he realizes that the revenues from sale of the lumber of $400 and the joint costs of $220 are irrelevant to his analysis. Once a tree has been cut down and sawed into lumber, these revenues and costs occur whether sawdust and wood chip scrap is sold to the pet store or pulp mill or is converted into chipboard. Accordingly, only the incremental revenues and costs for the scraps and chipboard are relevant. Using this information, Tim presents the Merritt Brothers with the following analysis:

| | Sell Sawdust and Wood Chips | | Produce Chipboard |
| --- | --- | --- | --- |
| | To Pulp Mill | To Pet Store | |
| Incremental revenues | $40 | $60 | $146 |
| Incremental (separable) costs | 0 | 0 | 46 |
| Incremental contribution | $40 | $60 | $100 |

*(continued)*

**EXHIBIT 9.4**
Merritt Brothers Decision
for Use of Sawdust and
Wood Chips

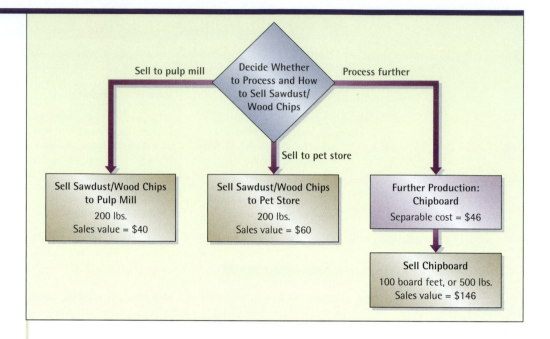

## Quantitative and Qualitative Factors

After Tim explains his analysis to the managers, they decide to continue producing chipboard. They expect to earn $40 ($100 − $60) more profit per log by producing chipboard than from selling scrap to the pet store. In addition, the brothers prefer this option because it avoids employee lay-offs that would be detrimental to individual employees and to the small town's economy.

| GUIDE YOUR LEARNING  9.3  Merritt Brothers (Part 2) | | |
|---|---|---|
| Merritt Brothers (Part 2) illustrates decision making for joint products. For this illustration: | | |
| **Identify Problem and Information** | **Identify Uncertainties** | **Prioritize Options** |
| What decision was being addressed and what alternatives were available? What information was relevant and irrelevant to the decision? Consider both quantitative and qualitative information. | What types of uncertainties were there? Consider uncertainties about:<br>• Future revenues<br>• Separable costs | In your own words, describe how various quantitative and qualitative factors were weighed in reaching a decision. Describe some factors that might cause managers to change their decision. |

## ■ Uncertainty and Bias in Incremental Revenue and Cost Estimates

Any estimate of future revenues and costs includes uncertainties about achievability. Changes are caused by many factors:

- Unforeseen economic trends
- Shifts in competition, demand, or supply
- Changes in technology

Managers need to consider the risk associated with these uncertainties when making decisions involving joint products. In addition, the degree of uncertainty might vary among alternatives. The overall degree of uncertainty is often greatest for options involving extra processing. For example, the Merritt Brothers decided to continue making chipboard. Their quantitative analysis required estimates of future revenues and costs under different alternatives. Fewer uncertainties overall were probably involved in the option to sell the sawdust and wood chips than for the option to produce chipboard. Thus, the managers might have been less confident in the data used to estimate their incremental profit under the chipboard option.

## JOINT PRODUCTS AND BY-PRODUCTS

> **Q5** What methods are used to account for the sale of by-products?

By definition, by-products have low sales values compared to the other products. In the Merritt Brothers' example, lumber is the main product, and scrap (sawdust and wood chips) is the by-product. If scrap is processed further into chipboard, it becomes a main product because the sales value of chipboard is relatively high. Deciding whether a product is a main product or by-product often requires judgment.

Sometimes products that were previously by-products become main products, or vice versa. A by-product can become valuable when new technologies or markets emerge. For example, when the Merritt Brothers first began their lumber mill, sawdust and wood chips were burned in large teepee-shaped metal incinerators. As the gluing and pressing processes improved and logs became a scarce natural resource, producing chipboard became technically and economically feasible. Lumber scraps are now used in a wide variety of products in addition to chipboard. For example, pulp mills pulverize the scraps and add liquid to make wood pulp that can be further processed into paper goods, cardboard, or building materials.

###  Accounting for By-Products

Sometimes by-products of a joint process are disposed of at a net cost, such as when metal scraps are hauled to a recycling center, or when a joint process results in hazardous material by-products that require special handling and disposal. In such cases, the costs of disposal are part of the joint costs of production. If the by-products have zero value, such as paper trimmings in a print shop, no accounting is needed for the by-product. However, if the by-product contributes to profits, a decision is made about accounting for the by-product.

By-products would not exist if the organization were not already producing one or more main products. Theoretically, then, it is reasonable to reduce joint costs by the net realizable value of by-products. The sale of a by-product reduces the cost of producing the main products. To achieve the best matching against the cost of main products, the value of by-products should be recorded at the time of production. However, by-products by definition have little value relative to main products, so they are typically immaterial to financial statements or other reports. Therefore, by-products may not be recorded in the most theoretically correct way; a great deal of variation occurs in practice.

In general, the selection of an accounting method depends on whether managers wish to establish control over by-products. Although they are not material relative to main products, they may have considerable absolute value. Managers may wish to establish controls to reduce the likelihood of theft or other loss. In this case, by-products are usually recorded at the time of production. When the value is so small that theft concerns are not a problem, by-products are often recorded at the time of sale.

The following income statements for Merritt Brothers use the two methods of accounting for by-products, assuming that sawdust and wood chips are sold to a pulp mill at the split-off point and are viewed as a by-product. The selling price is $40 for 200 pounds of scrap, or $0.20 per pound. We assume that 1,000 logs are processed during March, resulting in 300,000 (1,000 logs × 300 board feet per log) board feet of lumber and 200,000 (1,000 logs × 200 pounds per log) pounds of sawdust and wood chip scrap. Sales during the

> **CURRENT PRACTICE**
>
> Dakota Gasification previously considered carbon dioxide ($CO_2$) to be waste. It now sells $CO_2$ as a by-product that is injected into oil fields to release oil trapped in rock formations.[1]

---

[1]J. Fialka, "From Obsolete to Cutting Edge: Potential Power Plant of the Future Was Once Considered a Flop," *The Wall Street Journal*, October 15, 2003, p. A4.

month totaled 270,000 board feet of lumber and 190,000 pounds of scrap. Refer to Exhibit 9.3 for the per-log cost and sales value information.

| | Beginning Inventory | Production | Sales | Ending Inventory |
|---|---|---|---|---|
| Lumber (board feet) | 0 | 300,000 | 270,000 | 30,000 |
| Sawdust and wood chips (pounds) | 0 | 200,000 | 190,000 | 10,000 |

## ■ By-Product Value Recognized at the Time of Production

When by-product value is recognized at the time of production, the joint costs of the main product are reduced by the net realizable value of the by-product. Later, when the by-product is sold, no gain or loss is recorded. For Merritt Brothers, the net realizable value of the by-product is equal to its sales value at the split-off point ($0.20 per pound). This amount is subtracted from the joint cost and reduces the product cost of lumber. In turn, this computation reduces the per-unit cost of lumber in cost of goods sold and in ending inventory. Notice that ending inventory includes lumber at cost and by-product at net realizable value. This method allows managers to monitor both the quantity and value of by-products.

**ALTERNATIVE TERMS**

The terms *net realizable value approach* and *offset approach* mean the same as recognizing by-product value *at the time of production*.

| | |
|---|---|
| Production costs for the main product: | |
| Joint product costs incurred (1,000 logs × $220) | $220,000 |
| Less NRV of by-product (200,000 lbs × $0.20) | 40,000 |
| Net joint product cost | $180,000 |
| Product cost per log ($180,000 ÷ 1,000 logs) | $180 |
| Product cost per lumber board foot ($180 ÷ 300 bd ft) | $0.60 |
| Income statement: | |
| Revenue [270,000 bd ft × ($400 ÷ 300 bd ft)] | $360,000 |
| Cost of goods sold (270,000 bd ft × $0.60) | 162,000 |
| Gross margin | $198,000 |
| Ending inventory at March 31: | |
| Lumber (30,000 bd ft × $0.60) | $18,000 |
| By-product (10,000 lbs × $0.20) | 2,000 |
| Total inventory | $20,000 |

## ■ By-Product Value Recognized at the Time of Sale

When by-product value is recognized at the time of sale, the value may be recorded as sales revenue, other income, or as a reduction of cost of goods sold. Because by-products are viewed as immaterial, the choice of accounting treatment is considered unimportant. Until they are sold, by-products are not accounted for in the general ledger. For Merritt Brothers, this practice means that no inventory value is recorded for sawdust and wood chips. In the following example, we assume that the sales value of by-products is reported as part of revenue on the income statement.

**ALTERNATIVE TERMS**

The terms *realized value approach* and *income approach* mean the same as recognizing by-product value *at the time of sale*.

| | |
|---|---|
| Income statement: | |
| Revenue: | |
| Lumber [270,000 bd ft × ($400 ÷ 300 bd ft)] | $360,000 |
| Sawdust (190,000 lbs × $0.20) | 38,000 |
| Total revenue | 398,000 |
| Cost of goods sold [270,000 bd ft × ($220 ÷ 300 bd ft)] | 198,000 |
| Gross margin | $200,000 |
| Ending inventory at March 31: | |
| Lumber [30,000 bd ft × ($220 ÷ 300 bd ft)] | $22,000 |

For the Merritt Brothers example, the difference between gross margins under the two methods is $2,000 ($198,000 − $200,000). This amount is offset by the difference in the total values of ending inventory [$20,000 − $22,000 = $(2,000)], which is true only in cases where beginning inventory is zero. In general, the difference between gross margins under the two methods is equal to the difference in the change during the period in the values of total inventory. As long as by-product values are immaterial, the methods have little effect on the income statement and balance sheet.

| GUIDE YOUR LEARNING | 9.4 | By-Products for Merritt Brothers |
|---|---|---|

Merritt Brothers illustrated accounting for by-products (1) at the time of production, and (2) at the time of sale. For this illustration:

| Define It | Identify Uncertainties | Describe Use |
|---|---|---|
| Explain how each method is used to record the value of by-products. Write journal entries for each method. | Which method involved un–certainty? Explain. | Explain how recording by-product value at the time of production establishes control over by-products. |

## JOINT PRODUCT COSTING WITH A SALES MIX

**Q6** How does a sales mix affect joint cost allocation?

In the Merritt Brothers examples, the concepts and calculations for joint product costing were illustrated using simple products. However, in most settings, joint product costing is more complex. In this next illustration, we allocate costs when multiple products and multiple units are involved.

### PREMIUM PINEAPPLE COMPANY
### JOINT PRODUCT COSTING WITH A SALES MIX

Premium Pineapple Company, located in Taiwan, processes pineapples into pineapple syrup, pineapple juice, and canned pineapple. The company has three product managers, one for each of the three main products. The managers receive bonuses based on the profitability of their individual products. Lately some of the managers have been concerned about the allocations of joint costs and the effect these allocations have on the profitability of each of their product lines. They approached the accountant, Nancy Wu, about this problem. Nancy explained that several different allocation methods could be used, and that the gross margin of each product would change with each method. The managers wanted Nancy to prepare their usual reports using each of these methods. She agreed to provide the managers with information about product profitability using each of the acceptable joint product cost allocation methods. First she gathered data from the current period.

During the summer of 2004, the joint costs of processing pineapples were NT$8,000,000 (NT$ are New Taiwanese dollars). The company had no beginning or ending inventories for the summer. Production and sales value information for the growing season were as follows:

| Product | Cases | Sales Value at Split-Off Point | Separable Costs | Selling Price |
|---|---|---|---|---|
| Syrup | 400,000 | NT$16 per case | NT$4 per case | NT$22 per case |
| Juice | 400,000 | NT$18 per case | NT$5 per case | NT$25 per case |
| Canned | 800,000 | NT$6 per case | NT$3 per case | NT$14 per case |

Sales value at split-off for each product varies because the grade and pounds required for each option vary.

### Physical Output Method

The number of cases is used as the measure of physical output.

1. Determine the number of cases sold by product, and sum them.

| Number of Cases: | |
|---|---|
| Syrup | 400,000 cases |
| Juice | 400,000 |
| Canned | 800,000 |
| Total | 1,600,000 cases |

*(continued)*

2. Use each product's relative proportion of cases to allocate the joint costs.

Allocate joint costs:

| | |
|---|---:|
| Syrup [(400,000/1,600,000) × NT$8.0 mil.] | NT$2,000,000 |
| Juice [(400,000/1,600,000) × NT$8.0 mil.] | 2,000,000 |
| Canned [(800,000/1,600,000) × NT$8.0 mil.] | 4,000,000 |
| Total allocated joint costs | NT$8,000,000 |

## Sales Value at Split-Off Point Method

Each product's proportion of the total sales value at the split-off point is used.

1. Determine each product's total sales value at split-off, and calculate its relative proportion.

| | |
|---|---:|
| Syrup (400,000 × NT$16) | NT$ 6,400,000 |
| Juice (400,000 × NT$18) | 7,200,000 |
| Canned (800,000 × NT$6) | 4,800,000 |
| Total sales value at split-off point | NT$18,400,000 |

2. Use each product's relative proportion of sales value at split-off to allocate the joint cost.

Allocate joint costs:

| | |
|---|---:|
| To syrup [(NT$6.4 mil./NT$18.4 mil.) × NT$8 mil.] | NT$2,782,609 |
| To juice [(NT$7.2mil./NT$18.4 mil.) × NT$8 mil.] | 3,130,435 |
| To canned [(NT$4.8 mil./NT$18.4 mil.) × NT$8 mil.] | 2,086,956 |
| Total allocated joint costs | NT$8,000,000 |

## Net Realizable Value Method

The net realizable value (NRV) is the selling price minus separable costs.

1. Determine each product's net realizable value, and sum them.

| | |
|---|---:|
| Syrup [400,000 × (NT$22 − NT$4)] | NT$ 7,200,000 |
| Juice [400,000 × (NT$25 − NT$5)] | 8,000,000 |
| Canned [800,000 × (NT$14 − NT$3)] | 8,800,000 |
| Total net realizable value | NT$24,000,000 |

2. Use each product's relative proportion of net realizable value to allocate the joint costs.

Allocate joint costs:

| | |
|---|---:|
| To syrup [(NT$7.2 mil./NT$24.0 mil.) × NT$8.0 mil.] | NT$2,400,000 |
| To juice [(NT$8.0 mil./NT$24.0 mil.) × NT$8.0 mil.] | 2,666,667 |
| To canned [(NT$8.8 mil./NT$24.0 mil.) × NT$8.0 mil.] | 2,933,333 |
| Total allocated joint costs | NT$8,000,000 |

## Constant Gross Margin NRV Method

The constant gross margin NRV method uses the gross margin for all products in the joint cost allocation process.

1. Calculate the combined gross margin percentage:

| | |
|---|---:|
| Combined sales | |
| Syrup (NT$22 × 400,000) | NT$ 8,800,000 |
| Juice (NT$25 × 400,000) | 10,000,000 |
| Canned (NT$14 × 800,000) | 11,200,000 |
| Total combined sales | 30,000,000 |
| | |
| Less combined product costs: | |
| Joint costs | 8,000,000 |
| Syrup (NT$4 × 400,000) | 1,600,000 |
| Juice (NT$5 × 400,000) | 2,000,000 |
| Canned (NT$3 × 800,000) | 2,400,000 |
| Total combined product costs | 14,000,000 |
| Combined gross margin | NT$16,000,000 |
| Combined gross margin percentage (NT$16.0 mil./NT$30.0 mil.) | 53.3% |

2. Allocate joint costs to achieve a constant gross margin:

| | Syrup | Juice | Canned | Total |
|---|---|---|---|---|
| Sales | NT$8,800,000 | NT$10,000,000 | NT$11,200,000 | NT$30,000,000 |
| Less gross margin (16/30 × sales) | 4,693,333 | 5,333,333 | 5,973,334 | 16,000,000 |
| Total product costs | 4,106,667 | 4,666,667 | 5,226,666 | 14,000,000 |
| Less separable costs | 1,600,000 | 2,000,000 | 2,400,000 | 6,000,000 |
| Allocated joint costs | NT$2,506,667 | NT$ 2,666,667 | NT$ 2,826,666 | NT$ 8,000,000 |

## Comparing Methods

Nancy prepared the schedule shown in Exhibit 9.5 so that the managers could see the effects of the allocation system on their products' profitability. The syrup and juice managers prefer the physical measure method because it shows the greatest profit for their products. The manager of canned pineapple objects, because his profit was the smallest under this method. He wants to use the sales value at split-off point method, where his profits appear higher.

Nancy realizes that at least one manager will always be unhappy with the allocations and shows them that regardless of each product's profits, the overall benefit to the company is NT$16,000,000 (NRV − Joint costs = NT$24,000,000 − NT$8,000,000). The managers agree that all of these methods arbitrarily divide up the contribution and that for determining bonus amounts none of the methods are fair to every manager.

When they speak to the Director of Finance, he addresses the bonus issue from the perspective of responsibility. He points out that the managers are responsible for sales of their product lines and costs of further processing. He suggests that their bonuses should be based on each product's contribution to total profitability, before any allocations have been made. In addition, he believes that changes in the contribution over time should be as important as the total contribution, to provide incentives for them to increase sales and contain costs.

**EXHIBIT 9.5** Summary of Alternative Gross Margins for Premium Pineapple Company

| | Allocation Method | | | |
|---|---|---|---|---|
| | Physical Output | Sales Value at Split-Off Point | Net Realizable Value | Constant Gross Margin NRV |
| **Syrup:** | | | | |
| Sales | NT$ 8,800,000 | NT$ 8,800,000 | NT$ 8,800,000 | NT$ 8,800,000 |
| Separable costs | 1,600,000 | 1,600,000 | 1,600,000 | 1,600,000 |
| Incremental contribution | 7,200,000 | 7,200,000 | 7,200,000 | 7,200,000 |
| Allocated joint costs | (2,000,000) | (2,782,609) | (2,400,000) | (2,506,667) |
| Gross margin | 5,200,000 | 4,417,391 | 4,800,000 | 4,693,333 |
| **Juice:** | | | | |
| Sales | 10,000,000 | 10,000,000 | 10,000,000 | 10,000,000 |
| Separable costs | 2,000,000 | 2,000,000 | 2,000,000 | 2,000,000 |
| Incremental contribution | 8,000,000 | 8,000,000 | 8,000,000 | 8,000,000 |
| Allocated joint costs | (2,000,000) | (3,130,435) | (2,666,667) | (2,666,667) |
| Gross margin | 6,000,000 | 4,869,565 | 5,333,333 | 5,333,333 |
| **Canned:** | | | | |
| Sales | 11,200,000 | 11,200,000 | 11,200,000 | 11,200,000 |
| Separable costs | 2,400,000 | 2,400,000 | 2,400,000 | 2,400,000 |
| Incremental contribution | 8,800,000 | 8,800,000 | 8,800,000 | 8,800,000 |
| Allocated joint costs | (4,000,000) | (2,086,956) | (2,933,333) | (2,826,666) |
| Gross margin | 4,800,000 | 6,713,044 | 5,866,667 | 5,973,334 |
| **Combined gross margin** | NT$16,000,000 | NT$16,000,000 | NT$16,000,000 | NT$16,000,000 |

**GUIDE YOUR LEARNING** **9.5** Premium Pineapple Company

Premium Pineapple Company illustrates the allocation of joint costs with a sales mix. For this illustration:

| Define It | Identify Problem and Information | Identify Uncertainties | Explore Pros and Cons | Prioritize Options |
|---|---|---|---|---|
| Which definitions and computational methods were used? In your own words, explain how the sales mix affected the joint cost computations. | Why did the company need to allocate joint costs? How were the allocated costs used? Were allocated costs relevant to the managers? | What types of uncertainties were there? Consider uncertainties about: <br> • Estimates used in allocation computations <br> • Effect of allocation method on manager behavior | What were the pros and cons for each joint cost allocation method? How did manager incentives affect the pros and cons? | In your own words, describe how various quantitative and qualitative factors were weighed in reaching a decision. |

## ■ Uses and Limitations of Joint Cost Information

**Q7** What are the uses and limitations of joint cost information?

Joint costs are allocated to individual products primarily to meet requirements for financial accounting, income tax, government regulatory, or other external reporting. All product costs must be assigned to inventory and cost of goods sold. By definition, it is not possible to directly trace joint costs to individual products. Instead, an allocation method must be adopted. Several potential methods may be used, and most of the methods involve estimation of one or more of the following:

- Physical quantities
- Sales value at the split-off point
- Sales price if processed further
- Separable costs

Any time estimates are used, the potential arises for bias or other distortions caused by uncertainties.

Because joint costs are assigned to products, the tendency for managers is to use them in making decisions. However, allocated joint costs are irrelevant for most decisions. For example, joint cost allocations should not be used to decide whether to process a joint product beyond the split-off point or in evaluating individual product manager performance. Accountants assist managers by helping them understand whether joint costs are relevant to a particular decision.

### FOCUS ON ETHICAL DECISION MAKING: Hazardous Cement

Manufacturing and industrial processes often produce more than main products and by-products. They can also produce significant quantities of hazardous materials that must be disposed of, including the following:

- Acids and bases from chemical manufacturing
- Ink sludge containing heavy metals from the printing industry
- Wastewater containing benzene and other hydrocarbons from petroleum refining
- Paint waste and solvents from construction

The annual quantity of industrial hazardous waste produced in the United States is significant. In 1997, the Environmental Protection Agency (EPA) estimated the total amount at 41 million tons, excluding wastewaters.

U.S. environmental standards include extensive, costly requirements for the disposal of hazardous materials. To reduce costs, many companies began disposing of their hazardous waste by sending them to hazardous-waste-burning cement kilns. Part of the cement-making process requires high heat, so the cement ingredients are heated in kilns. In the mid-1980s, because cement companies were suffering losses, they began to charge for disposing of hazardous materials, and burned them to provide heat for the kilns. Because hazardous waste was simply viewed as a raw material in the production of cement, these companies were not required to meet the same standards as other forms of incineration. Therefore, their disposal prices were much cheaper.

Environmental groups claimed that cement kilns provided a loophole, allowing companies to improperly dispose of hazardous waste. They argued that the kilns released dangerous pollutants in the air, residual kiln dust contained hazardous materials requiring further treatment, and cement products were contaminated. During 1999, the EPA increased the air pollution standards for incinerators, including cement kilns. However, environmental groups continued to argue that regulations were inadequate.

Similar issues have arisen outside of the United States. For example, during 2003 an organization called Campaign Against the New Kiln battled against construction of a hazardous waste burning cement kiln planned for Padeswood, Flintshire, in the United Kingdom.

Cement Kiln Recycling Coalition, an industry trade association, argues that the cement industry has reduced its air pollutants more than any other industry, that kilns is subject to stringent governmental regulation, and that the quality of cement kiln products is not affected by the burning of hazardous wastes. In addition, it points out that the use of hazardous waste as a fuel conserves natural resources by reducing the consumption of non-renewable fossil fuels by 1 million tons per year. The kilns also burn scrap, including approximately 35 million tires per year.

SOURCES: Information about hazardous waste disposal in Texas, including descriptions of hazardous-waste-burning cement kilns: *Texas Environmental Profiles*, sponsored by joint project of Environmental Defense and the Texas Center for Policy Studies, available at www.texasep.org/html/wst/wst_4imn_incin.html; information provided by a Texas cement kiln opposition group, Downwinders at Risk, available at www.cementkiln.com/; information provided by an industry trade association, Cement Kiln Recycling Coalition, available at www.ckrc.org/; *Environmental Fact Sheet: Management Standards Proposed for Cement Kiln Dust Waste*, new rules proposed by the EPA, August 1999, available at www.epa.gov/epaoswer/other/ckd/ckd/ckdp-fs.pdf; and Information provided by a U.K. cement kiln opposition group, Campaign Against the New Kiln, available at www.cank.org.uk/.

### Practice Ethical Decision Making

In Chapter 1, we learned about a process for making ethical decisions (Exhibit 1.11). You can address the following questions for this ethical dilemma to improve your skills for making ethical decisions. Think about your answers to these questions and discuss them with others.

| Ethical Decision-Making Process | Questions to Consider about This Ethical Dilemma |
|---|---|
| Identify ethical problems as they arise. | Does the disposal of hazardous waste in cement kilns create an ethical problem for companies? Why or why not? |
| Objectively consider the well-being of others and society when exploring alternatives. | Describe different viewpoints about the safety and regulation of hazardous-waste-burning cement kilns. What assumptions lie behind each viewpoint? Consider the perspectives of: <br>• Managers of companies that produce hazardous waste <br>• Shareholders of companies that produce hazardous waste <br>• Operators of hazardous waste-burning cement kilns <br>• Government regulators <br>• Environmental groups <br>• Individuals who use products that create hazardous waste <br>• Individuals who live near cement kilns or near cement dust disposal sites <br>• Individuals who come in contact with cement products made from hazardous waste <br>What is the difference in ethical values for the different viewpoints? |
| Clarify and apply ethical values when choosing a course of action. | What is the best overall solution to this problem for society? What values did you use to arrive at the solution? |
| Work toward ongoing improvement of personal and organizational ethics. | How might manufacturers continuously improve their practices related to hazardous waste? |

# SUMMARY

**Q1** **What Is a Joint Process, and What Is the Difference Between a By-Product and a Main Product?**

### Joint Process

- Jointly produce more than one product.
- Joint costs cannot be traced to individual products.
- Joint production ends at the split-off point.
- Individual products might or might not be processed beyond the split-off point.

- Main product has high relative sales value.
- By-product has low relative sales value.

**Q2** **How Are Joint Costs Allocated?**

### Physical Output Method

- Allocate joint costs in proportion to the physical output for each main product
- Examples of physical measures: meters, pounds, gallons
- All main products must be expressed in the same physical measure

### Sales Value at Split-Off Point Method

- Allocate joint costs in proportion to the sales value for each main product at the point where joint production ends
- Not always possible to measure sales value at the split-off point

### Net Realizable Value (NRV) Method

- Allocate joint costs in proportion to the net realizable value for each main product, taking into account the final selling price and separable costs
- Same as the sales value at split-off method if no additional production occurs beyond the split-off point

### Constant Gross Margin NRV Method

- Allocate joint costs so that the gross margin percentage for all main products is the same.
  - First, calculate combined gross margin percentage for all main products.
  - Second, calculate joint cost allocation that will result in the same gross margin percentage for all main products, taking into account the final selling price and separable costs.

**Q3** **What Factors Are Considered in Choosing a Joint Cost Allocation Method?**

### Major Goal

Avoid distortion of individual main product values

### Physical Output Method

- May inappropriately give impression that a main product is unprofitable, even when it has a positive incremental value
- Appropriate when units of all main products are similar in size and have comparable NRVs

### Market-Based Methods

- Sales value at split-off point method:
  - Generally appropriate if most or all products are sold when joint production ends
  - Sales values must exist at the split-off point
- NRV methods generally preferred because allocation is based on the ability of each main product to "pay" for its allocated cost
- Constant gross margin NRV method best reflects the inseparability of the joint production process

## **Q4** What Information Is Relevant for Deciding Whether to Process a Joint Product Beyond the Split-Off Point?

### General Decision Rule (see Chapter 4)

Process further if the incremental revenue is greater than the incremental cost, including any relevant fixed costs and opportunity costs.
Assumptions:
- CVP assumptions
- Managers want to maximize profits in the short term
- Sales of one product do not affect sales of other products

### Uncertainty and Bias in Future Revenue and Separable Cost Estimates

### Consider Quantitative and Qualitative Factors to Reach Decision

## **Q5** What Methods Are Used to Account for the Sale of By-Products?

### Accounting for NRV of By-Products

- If net cost, include NRV in joint costs
- If net profit:
  – Method often considered unimportant because by-product values are immaterial
- Record at time of production
  – Subtract NRV from joint costs
  – By-product inventory carried at NRV
  – Establishes control over by-product inventory

- Record at time of sale
  – Sales revenue or other income, or
  – Subtract NRV from cost of goods sold

## **Q6** How Does a Sales Mix Affect Joint Cost Allocation?

### Effect of Sales Mix on Calculations

The sales mix is incorporated into the calculations for each allocation method.

## **Q7** What Are the Uses and Limitations of Joint Cost Information?

### Uses of Joint Cost Information

- Financial statements
- Income tax returns
- Government regulatory
- Other external reports

### Improper Use of Joint Cost Information

Joint costs are irrelevant for many types of decisions

### Estimates Used in Allocation Computations

- Physical quantities
- Sales value at split-off point
- Sales price if processed further
- Separable costs

## Self-Study Problem

### Self-Study Problem 1 — Four Allocation Methods, Further Processing Decision, Uncertainties

**Q2, Q3, Q4, Q7**

Atlantic Sand and Gravel Corp. produces two grades of sand: coarse and fine. Both grades are used to manufacture industrial abrasives. The results of operations in 2004 were as follows:

|  | Coarse | Fine | Total |
|---|---|---|---|
| Production | 4,000 tons | 6,000 tons | 10,000 tons |
| Sales value at split-off point | $40,000 | $50,000 | $90,000 |
| Revenue | $90,000 | $150,000 | $240,000 |
| Separable costs | $20,000 | $15,000 | $35,000 |

Joint product costs were $100,000. There were no beginning inventories.

**REQUIRED:**

A. Allocate the joint costs using the physical output method.

B. Allocate the joint costs using the sales value at split-off point method.

C. Allocate the joint costs using the net realizable value method.

D. Allocate the joint costs using the constant gross margin NRV method.

**2** E. Discuss the pros and cons of each method.

F. Suppose fine sand can be processed further by mixing in color. The cost of adding color is $15 per ton, and the sand can then be sold for $35 per ton. Should fine sand be processed further?

**1** G. What uncertainties do managers face in making the decision in part (F)?

**2** H. Which of the options in part (F) involves greater uncertainties and, therefore, greater risk for the company? Explain.

### Solution to Self-Study Problem 1

**A.** Allocate the joint costs using the physical output method.

| Joint costs allocated: | |
|---|---|
| To Coarse [(4,000 tons/10,000 tons) × $100,000] | $ 40,000 |
| To Fine [(6,000 tons/10,000 tons) × $100,000] | 60,000 |
| Total joint costs allocated | $100,000 |

**B.** Allocate the joint costs using the sales at split-off point method.

| Joint costs allocated: | |
|---|---|
| To coarse [($40,000/$90,000) × $100,000] | $ 44,444 |
| To fine [($50,000/$900,000) × $100,000] | 55,556 |
| Total joint costs allocated | $100,000 |

**C.** Allocate the joint costs using the net realizable value method.

| Total net realizable value: | |
|---|---|
| Coarse ($90,000 − $20,000) | $ 70,000 |
| Fine ($150,000 − $15,000) | 135,000 |
| Total NRV | $205,000 |

| Joint costs allocated: | |
|---|---|
| To Coarse [($70,000/$205,000) × $100,000] | $ 34,146 |
| To Fine [($135,000/$205,000) × $100,000] | 65,854 |
| Total joint costs allocated | $100,000 |

**D.** Allocate the joint costs using the constant gross margin NRV method.

Calculate the combined gross margin percentage:

| | |
|---|---:|
| Total revenue | $ 240,000 |
| Separable costs | (35,000) |
| Joint costs | (100,000) |
| Total combined gross margin | $ 105,000 |
| Combined gross margin percentage ($105,000/$240,000) | 43.75% |

Allocate joint costs to achieve a constant gross margin:

| | Coarse | Fine | Total |
|---|---:|---:|---:|
| Revenue | $ 90,000 | $150,000 | $ 240,000 |
| Less gross margin (Revenue × 0.4375) | (39,375) | (65,625) | (105,000) |
| Total product costs | 50,625 | 84,375 | 135,000 |
| Less separable costs | (20,000) | (15,000) | (35,000) |
| Allocated joint costs | $ 30,625 | $ 69,375 | $ 100,000 |

**E.** The physical output method is the simplest to calculate. It is usually easy to identify the information needed, because quantities of each product are often routinely measured during regular production and accounting activities. However, the contributions of different joint products are distorted unless all of the joint products have similar contributions. Some products could be allocated more joint cost than their contribution and would appear to be losers when actually a contribution can be realized by selling them. If all joint products have a similar physical output per unit and a similar contribution per unit, this method is the most simple and, therefore, would likely be preferred.

The sales value at split-off point method is relatively easy to calculate. If all joint products have a value at the time of split-off, this method requires less information and fewer calculations than the NRV methods. If all products are sold at split-off, this method is often the best. However, split-off values may not be available for some types of products.

The net realizable value method provides the least distortion of incremental contribution because the allocation is based on each product's incremental revenue and incremental cost. It requires a little more information and a few more calculations than the sales value at split-off point method. The allocations reflect each product's incremental contribution in the allocation scheme when products are processed after the split-off point.

The constant gross margin NRV method uses the contribution margin to allocate joint costs, so no product will be allocated more cost than its incremental revenue. It also considers the products' contributions after further processing. However, it is more complex to explain and requires more calculations than the net realizable value method. With spreadsheets and allocation software programs, the extra calculations are unlikely to be a problem.

**F.** This question involves a decision about additional processing beyond the split-off point. Joint costs are irrelevant for this decision, so no joint cost allocation is needed. Instead, we calculate the incremental contribution for each option. Currently, fine sand sells for $25 per ton and separable costs are $2.50 per ton, so the contribution per ton is $22.50. If the sand is processed further, it sells for $35 per ton, but costs an additional $15 to process. The contribution for this option is $17.50 ($35 − $15 − $2.50). Ignoring any possible qualitative factors, the managers should decide not to color the sand. They would rather receive $22.50 per ton than $17.50 per ton.

**G.** Many uncertainties are involved in this decision. The following list contains some of these.
- Future revenues are uncertain under both options; the managers cannot know with certainty that future prices will be equal to current prices.
- Additional costs for adding color are uncertain; the managers cannot know how much it will cost because they do not have experience creating this type of product. In addition, future costs might not be the same.
- The managers cannot know with certainty how their decision might affect sales of regular fine sand. Will the sale of colored sand replace the sale of regular fine sand? Is the demand for colored sand a short-term occurrence? Would the colored sand market create other opportunities for the company?

**H.** Two main reasons explain why uncertainties and risk for the colored sand option are probably greater than uncertainties and risk for selling regular fine sand. First, the company does not have experience creating colored sand. Accordingly, it faces greater uncertainty about production methods and customer markets. Second, products requiring more processing usually entail greater risk. The company must expend more resources before selling the product.

## QUESTIONS

**9.1** In your own words, explain what determines whether a product is a main product or by-product.

**9.2** One of the products from a joint process, Product A, can be sold at the split-off point for $10. The other products can all be sold at the split-off point for $200 or more. Would you categorize Product A as a main product or by-product? Explain.

**9.3** In your own words, explain the two methods for recognizing revenue from a by-product.

**9.4** Describe a group of main products and by-products for an industry located near your home or college.

**9.5** How are joint product costs and indirect costs similar? How are separable costs and direct costs similar?

**9.6** Describe the split-off point and explain its significance for joint product costing.

**9.7** Give an example of joint products in a service industry and describe the main products and by-products.

**9.8** A decision about processing a product further should not be influenced by joint cost allocation, but should be based on incremental costs and qualitative factors. Explain.

**9.9** The allocation of a joint cost among joint products is essentially an arbitrary process. If this statement is true, then why allocate?

**9.10** The owner of a business says, "I cannot uniquely determine the profitability of one of my joint products, but I can uniquely determine its contribution toward joint costs and profit." Explain.

**9.11** A specialty chemical company obtains 73 different products of relatively equal value from processing a single input. Should these products be treated as main products or by-products?

**9.12** What estimates are required to perform market-based joint cost allocations? Where would accountants obtain the information needed for these estimates?

**9.13** Provide three or more examples of qualitative factors that might influence a decision to process a joint product beyond the split-off point.

**9.14** Information about some by-products is not recorded in the accounting system. However, for other by-products, control systems are instituted and accounting records are kept. How do accountants identify by-products that need control systems and record-keeping and those that do not?

## EXERCISES

**9.15** **By-product further processing decision** For a given by-product, 100 units can be sold at the split-off point for $8 each, or processed further at a cost of $12 each and sold for $19.

**Q4**

**REQUIRED:** Should the by-product be processed further? Provide calculations and explain your answer.

**9.16** **Identifying joint products**

**Q1**

**REQUIRED:** ⓔ **A.** Which of the following related products would be considered joint products? Explain your choices.

    **1.** Sand produced with three levels of fineness

    **2.** Automobiles and trucks

    **3.** Milk, yogurt, butter, and cheese

    **4.** Motorcycles and mopeds

    **5.** Various lines of clothing manufactured for a discount department store

    **6.** An airline that provides first class, business class, and economy class service

ⓔ **B.** List two more additional product groups that could be considered joint products.

**9.17** **Identifying joint and separable costs** Cowboy Cattle Company raises cattle and sells beef products. Following is a list of costs for the operation.

**Q1**

**REQUIRED:** ❶ Identify whether each cost is most likely a (J) joint cost or a (S) separable cost. For each item, explain why.

1. Veterinary costs for the calves
2. The cost of grinding hamburger
3. The cost of feed for the cattle
4. The cost of labor to manage the cattle while they grow
5. The cost of labor to prepare the cowhide for sale as leather
6. The cost for packaging steaks and roasts
7. The depreciation on the loafing sheds that provide shelter for the cattle

**9.18**
**Q2, Q3, Q4**

**NRV method, contribution margin and further processing for a service** Deluxe Tours, a tour organizer, leased a cruise liner for a special round-the-world tour. The lease cost is $200,000. Two classes of passengers are booked on the tour: first class and economy class. The total revenue from the 100 first-class passengers is $200,000, and from the 200 economy-class passengers is $200,000. Other costs for the two classes of passengers amount to $30,000 for first class and $30,000 for economy class.

**REQUIRED:**

**A.** How much of the lease cost would be allocated to first-class passengers if the net realizable value method is used?
**B.** What is the contribution margin generated by first-class passengers?
**e C.** When the cruise liner managers are deciding whether to increase the number of first-class rooms, which joint cost allocation method is best to use? Explain.

**9.19**
**Q2, Q4, Q6**

**Four joint cost allocation methods with sales mix, further processing decision** The Palm Oil Company buys crude coconut and palm nut oil. Refining this oil results in four products at the split-off point: soap grade, cooking grade, light moisturizer, and heavy moisturizer. Light moisturizer is fully processed at the split-off point. Soap grade, cooking grade, and heavy moisturizer can individually be refined into fine soap, cooking oil, and premium moisturizer. In the most recent month (June), the output at the split-off point was:

| | |
|---|---|
| Soap grade | 100,000 gallons |
| Cooking grade | 300,000 gallons |
| Light moisturizer | 50,000 gallons |
| Heavy moisturizer | 50,000 gallons |

The joint costs of purchasing the crude coconut and palm nut oil and processing it were $100,000. There were no beginning or ending inventories. Sales of light moisturizer in June were $50,000. Total output of soap, cooking oil, and heavy moisturizer was further refined and then sold. Data relating to June are as follows:

| Product | Separable Costs | Sales |
|---|---|---|
| Fine soap | $200,000 | $300,000 |
| Superior cooking oil | 80,000 | 100,000 |
| Premium moisturizer | 90,000 | 120,000 |

Palm Oil Company had the option of selling the soap grade, cooking grade, and heavy moisturizer at the split-off point. This alternative would have yielded the following sales for the June production:

| | |
|---|---|
| Soap grade | $50,000 |
| Cooking grade | 30,000 |
| Heavy moisturizer | 70,000 |

**REQUIRED:**

**A.** Allocate the joint cost using each of the following methods: (1) sales value at split-off point, (2) physical output, (3) net realizable value, and (4) constant gross margin NRV.
**e B.** Could Palm Oil Company have increased its June operating income by making different decisions about further refining the soap grade, cooking grade, or heavy moisturizer palm nut oil? Show the effect on the contribution margin of any changes you recommend.

**9.20**
**Q2, Q4**

**Sales value at split-off, physical output, NRV methods; further processing decision** Flowering Friends is a small nursery. The company grows rhododendrons and azaleas. The plants are dug up and potted after three years of growth. Some of them are considered premium because they are taller and have more bloom buds than the rest. They are placed in a green house for several months, fertilized heavily, and then sold when they are in bloom. The others are sold at the time they are dug. Joint costs for raising the plants are $15,000. Following is information about potential allocation bases for the joint costs of growing the plants.

| Allocation Base | Premium | Regular |
|---|---|---|
| Number of pots | 2,000 pots | 8,000 pots |
| Sales value per pot at the time they are dug | $5 | $3 |
| Net realizable value (NRV) per pot | $25 | $10 |

**REQUIRED:**

A. Allocate the joint cost using the following methods:
1. Sales value at split-off point
2. Physical output
3. Net realizable value
B. If the premium plants are repotted in ceramic pots just before Mother's Day, they can be sold for $35. Labor (plus fringe benefits) for repotting costs $20 per hour and 4 plants can be repotted by an employee each hour. The ceramic pots cost $3 each. Should Flowering Friends process these plants further?

**9.21**
**Q2, Q4**
**NRV and physical output methods, further processing decision** Click and Clack Recyclers buys used motor oil for $0.75 per gallon from shops that specialize in oil changes and other minor services for cars. The cost of transporting and refining the motor oil is $1.25 per gallon. The refined oil becomes commercial-grade motor oil and a thick residual fuel oil. Each gallon of used motor oil yields 0.7 gallon of commercial-grade motor oil and 0.3 gallon of residual fuel oil. Commercial-grade motor oil is sold for $3 per gallon, and residual fuel oil is sold for $1.50 per gallon.

**REQUIRED:**

A. If the costs of purchasing and processing the used motor oil were allocated on the basis of their net realizable value, what would be the inventory cost per gallon of residual fuel oil?
B. If the costs of purchasing and processing the used motor oil were allocated on the basis of physical output, what would be the inventory cost of residual fuel oil?
ⓔ C. With additional processing, residual fuel oil can be converted into Special Fuel Oil. The additional processing costs $0.40 per gallon. What would be the minimum acceptable price for the Special Fuel Oil?

**9.22**
**Q5**
**By-product value recognized at time of production versus time of sale** Following is information about log production at Mile High Lumber Mill. Joint costs are $600,000.

| | Production | Sales | Inventory |
|---|---|---|---|
| Lumber (board feet) | 300,000 | 270,000 | 30,000 |
| Scraps (per log) | 1,000 logs | 900 logs | 100 logs |

The lumber can be sold for $3 per board foot. The scraps per log can be sold for $10 per log.

**REQUIRED:**

A. Create an income statement using the by-product value recognized at the time of sale method.
B. Create an income statement using the by-product value recognized at the time of production method.

**9.23**
**Q2, Q4**
**Physical output, NRV, and constant gross margin NRV methods; further processing decision** The Paint Palette Company produces two products, premium paint and regular paint, by a joint process. Joint costs amount to $10,000 per batch of output. Each batch totals 1,000 gallons, 30% premium and 70% regular. Both products are processed further.

| | |
|---|---|
| Separable processing costs: | |
| Premium | $4.00 per gallon |
| Regular | $1.00 per gallon |
| Selling price: | |
| Premium | $20.00 per gallon |
| Regular | $10.00 per gallon |

**REQUIRED:**

**A.** Allocate the joint costs according to the physical output method.

**B.** Allocate the joint costs according to the net realizable value method.

**C.** Allocate the joint costs according to the constant gross margin NRV method.

**D.** The company has discovered an additional process by which the regular paint can be made into paint that dries extremely quickly. The new selling price would be $22 per gallon. Additional processing would increase separable costs by $11 (in addition to the $1 separable cost required to yield regular). Assuming no other changes in cost, determine whether the company should begin producing quick-drying paint. Create a schedule that shows how you made the decision.

**9.24** **Calculate missing information for sales value at split-off point method** The Chile Salsa Com-
**Q2** pany manufactures three different types of salsa—mild, medium, and spicy hot—from a joint process. The following information is available:

|  | Mild | Medium | Spicy Hot | Total |
|---|---|---|---|---|
| Units produced | 24,000 | ? | ? | 48,000 |
| Joint costs | $24,000 | ? | ? | $60,000 |
| Sales value at split-off point | ? | ? | $25,000 | $100,000 |
| Additional cost if processed further | $9,000 | $7,000 | $5,000 | $21,000 |
| Sales value if processed further | $55,000 | $45,000 | $30,000 | $130,000 |

**REQUIRED:** **e** Assuming that joint product costs are allocated using the sales value at split-off point method, what was the sales value at the split-off for mild and medium salsa?

**9.25** **Further processing profit and decision** Conrad Miller owns a small sheet metal business. He
**Q2, Q4** produces three different types of sheet metal. Their sizes are similar, but they have different degrees of flexibility. Costs are allocated based on the sales value at split-off point method. Additional information for March production follows:

|  | Stiff | Flexible | Very Flexible | Total |
|---|---|---|---|---|
| Units produced | 100,000 | 80,000 | 20,000 | 200,000 |
| Joint costs | ? | ? | ? | $900,000 |
| Sales value at split-off point | $840,000 | $540,000 | $120,000 | $1,500,000 |
| Additional cost if processed further | $88,000 | $30,000 | $12,000 | $130,000 |
| Sales value if processed further | $948,000 | $565,000 | $135,000 | $1,648,000 |

**REQUIRED:**

**A.** Assuming that the 20,000 units of Very Flexible were processed further and sold, what is the gross margin on this sale?

**B.** Would you recommend that Miller process the Very Flexible sheet metal further? Show your calculations.

**9.26** **Accounting for main products and by-products** Georgette Rheingold owns and operates a fruit
**Q5** smoothie manufacturing operation, Nutri-smoothie. She processes fruit and adds it to yogurt and produces fruit smoothies, the main product. She sells the rinds and waste to a recycling organization that turns it into compost. Neither product requires processing after the split-off point. Information for last month's operations follows:

| | |
|---|---|
| Joint costs of smoothie production | $12,000 |
| Smoothie production (in pint bottles) | 20,000 |
| Price per bottle | $2 |
| Sales last month (bottles) | 18,000 |
| Compost production | 10,000 lbs. |
| Compost sales | 8,000 lbs. |
| Compost revenue | $2,000 |

**REQUIRED:**

**A.** What is Nutri-smoothie's gross margin for last month if the by-product value is recognized at the time of production?

*(continued)*

    **B.** What is Nutri-smoothie's gross margin for last month if the by-product value is recognized at the time of sale?

    **C.** Calculate the inventory value for both smoothies and compost on the balance sheet under the methods used in parts (A) and (B).

# PROBLEMS

**9.27**  **Q1, Q3**

**Identifying joint costs, choice of allocation method** Roses to Go is a flower farm that specializes in fragrant roses for florist shops.

**REQUIRED:**   **①** **A.** List five joint costs that are likely to be incurred by Roses to Go in raising roses.

    **①** **B.** The roses are sold by the dozen, with no difference in price for any of the bouquets. Which joint cost allocation method would be most appropriate? Explain your choice.

    **②** **C.** Now assume that Roses to Go raises two different types of roses, fragrant roses and regular roses. The growing requirements for the two types of roses do not differ. However, fragrant roses sell for twice as much as regular roses. Which joint cost allocation method would be most appropriate? Explain your choice.

**9.28**
**Q1, Q2, Q5, Q6**

**Separable and joint costs, NRV, operating income, by-product** Doe Corporation grows, processes, cans, and sells three main pineapple products: sliced pineapple, crushed pineapple, and pineapple juice. The outside skin, which is removed in the cutting department and processed as animal feed, is treated as a by-product.

Doe's production process is as follows: Pineapples are first processed in the cutting department. The pineapples are washed, and the outside skin is cut away. Then the pineapples are cored and trimmed for slicing. The three main products (sliced, crushed, juice) and the by-product (animal feed) are recognizable after processing in the cutting department. Each product is then transferred to a separate department for final processing.

The trimmed pineapples are forwarded to the slicing department where they are sliced and canned. Any juice generated during the slicing operation is packed in the cans with the slices. The pieces of pineapple trimmed from the fruit are diced and canned in the crushing department. Again, the juice generated during this operation is packed in the can with the crushed pineapple. The core and surplus pineapple generated from the cutting department are pulverized into a liquid in the juicing department. An evaporation loss equal to 8% of the weight of the good output produced in this department occurs as the juices are heated. The outside skin is chopped into animal feed in the feed department.

Doe Corporation uses the net realizable value method to assign costs of the joint process to its main products. The by-product is inventoried at its net realizable value. The NRV of the by-product reduces the joint costs of the main products.

A total of 270,000 pounds entered the cutting department in May. The schedule shows the costs incurred in each department, the proportion by weight transferred to the four final processing departments, and the selling price of each product.

### May Processing Data and Costs

| Department | Costs Incurred | Proportion of Product by Weight Transferred to Departments | Selling Price per Pound of Final Product |
|---|---|---|---|
| Cutting | $60,000 | – | None |
| Slicing | 4,700 | 35% | $0.60 |
| Crushing | 10,580 | 28 | 0.55 |
| Juicing | 3,250 | 27 | 0.30 |
| Animal Feed | 700 | 10 | 0.10 |
| Total | $79,230 | 100% | |

**REQUIRED:**   **ⓔ** **A.** How many pounds of pineapple result as output for pineapple slices, crushed pineapple, pineapple juice, and animal feed?

    **B.** What is the net realizable value of each of the main products?

    **C.** What is the amount of the cost of the cutting department (joint costs) assigned to each of the main products and the by-product using Doe's allocation method?

D. What is the gross margin for each of the three main products?

E. How valuable is the gross margin information for evaluating the profitability of each main product?

F. If no market exists for the outside skin as animal feed and, instead, it must be disposed of at a cost of $800, what effect will this cost have on the costs allocated to the main products?

**9.29**
**Q2, Q4, Q7**

**Physical output method, drop a product, special order** Jumping Juice Ltd. produces two grades of sparkling apple juice. A diagram of the production process appears in Exhibit 9.6. The process begins when the vat is loaded with apples. The incremental cost of raw materials and processing one load is $250. Each load produces one barrel of premium raw apple juice and two barrels of standard raw apple juice. The variable cost of carbonating and bottling the cider is $200 per barrel for premium cider and $100 per barrel for standard cider. Each barrel of raw juice produces 100 bottles of finished sparkling juice. The fixed costs for one month are: $5,000 for the plant, $2,000 for handling and bottling premium, and $1,000 for handling and bottling standard. Premium cider sells for $5 per bottle and standard cider for $3 per bottle, both wholesale. In a normal month, 100 loads are processed and converted into 20,000 bottles of standard cider and 10,000 bottles of premium cider.

**REQUIRED:**

A. In a normal month, what is the total allocated cost (fixed plus variable) per bottle of premium cider if the costs of the manufacturing operation are allocated on the basis of physical output measured by volume?

ⓔ B. In a normal month, what is the variable cost per bottle of premium cider if the joint variable costs of the juice company are allocated on the basis of physical output measured by volume?

ⓔ C. Assuming that the $1,000 in fixed costs for standard handling and bottling could be avoided, what would be the impact on the profit of the company in a normal month if the company discontinued the standard brand and treated all raw cider as premium grade?

① D. Explain to the CEO of the company why the variable cost per bottle of premium cider you calculated in part (B) should or should not be used in pricing special orders for the premium cider.

**EXHIBIT 9.6**
**Production Costs for Jumping Juice**

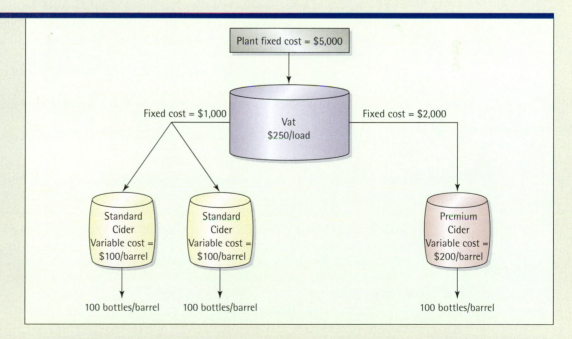

**9.30**
**Q2, Q4, Q6, Q7**

**Profit at split-off point and after further processing, manager incentives and decisions** The Champion Chip Company produces three grades of computer chips from a joint process: deluxe, superior, and good. Although the chips are manufactured in plants in several international locations, each grade is considered a separate product line and each product line manager earns a bonus based on the reported profit of his or her line. To calculate income upon which the bonuses are based, Champion allocates joint costs according to percentage of revenue. If all of the products are sold at the split-off point, this method would be the sales value at split-off point method. If products are processed further, each product's percentage of total revenues (without subtracting separable costs) is used as the allocation base.

The management office for the deluxe line is located outside of London. The management office for the superior line is located in San Francisco. The management office for the good line is located in Hong Kong. Assume that the exchange rates are as follows:

|  | U.S. Dollars |
| --- | --- |
| British pounds (£) | $2.00 |
| Hong Kong dollars (HK$) | $0.125 |

A batch of chips costing $1,000 yields chips with the following market values at the split-off point.

|  | Deluxe | Superior | Good |
| --- | --- | --- | --- |
| Sales value | £400 | HK$3,200 | US$200 |

Alternatively, each manager could process the chips further, in which case the new sales values and further processing costs would be as follows:

|  | Deluxe | Superior | Good |
| --- | --- | --- | --- |
| Sales value | £550 | HK$4,800 | US$800 |
| Separable costs | £200 | HK$800 | US$500 |

**REQUIRED:**

**A.** Determine product line and company-wide pretax income in U.S. dollars if each product is sold at the split-off point (use the sales value at split-off point method to allocate joint costs).

**e B.** Each product line manager decides whether to process chips further. In making that decision, each manager assumes that the other two managers will sell their products at the split-off point. Analyze each manager's decision choices and predict their decisions (translate all dollars to U.S. dollars first). Allocate the joint costs using each division's percentage of total revenues. Show your calculations.

**e C.** If optimal decisions were made for the entire firm (not just for each product line), what decision should each manager make about processing chips further?

**D.** Develop income statements by product line and for the entire organization assuming that managers make the decisions you predicted in part (B). Now develop income statements assuming that managers make the best decisions for the overall organization from part (C).

**E.** Now recast the income statements using the NRV method to determine the decisions managers would make.

**2 F.** Explain why the individual managers might make decisions that are not optimal for the company.

**3 G.** Recommend a bonus scheme that could reduce the problem of suboptimal decision making.

**9.31** **Joint product, by-products, weighted-average process costing** S-T, Inc., processes material in
Q2, Q5 1,000-gallon batches. Each batch results in 400 gallons of main product X, 500 gallons of main product Y, and 100 gallons of by-product Z. Material is added at the start of the process. The joint products emerge at the end of the process. By-product revenues are treated as a reduction of joint costs at the time of production. Joint costs are assigned to main products using the net realizable value method. Product X sells for $8 per gallon and has separable costs of $2 per gallon. Product Y sells for $11 per gallon and has separable costs of $3 per gallon. By-product Z sells for $1 per gallon.

The beginning inventory consists of two batches averaging 30% and 80% complete. Material costs are $8,550, and conversion costs are $3,007. The ending inventory consists of one batch, which is 50% complete. During the week 20 batches were completed and transferred out. Materials placed into production had a cost of $71,250 and conversion costs totaled $40,470.

**REQUIRED:** Using the weighted-average process costing method, what is the unit cost to be assigned to the completed products X, Y, and Z?

☆ **9.32**
**Q2, Q3, Q7**

ETHICS

**NRV method, division manager incentives, qualitative factors** Hudziak Industries has two separate profit centers: Chemicals and Cosmetics. The firm acquires its major ingredient for both divisions jointly. Currently this material is purchased in 1,000-pound lots for $2,000. The material is passed through an exclusive separator process. After separation, Chemicals receives 300 pounds of chemical J-52A and Cosmetics receives 200 gallons of quitoban. The Chemicals division must process chemical J-52A further before it can be sold. Additional processing costs $150 per lot, and the chemical is then sold for $5 per pound. The Cosmetics division bottles and packages quitoban as an antiperspirant at a cost of $250 per lot. The antiperspirant is sold for $7 per gallon.

**REQUIRED:**
**ANALYZE**
**INFORMATION**

The following questions will help you analyze the information for this problem. Do not turn in your answers to these questions unless your professor asks you to do so.

**A.** Determine the income per lot that each division would report if joint costs were allocated on a net realizable value basis.

**B.** Hudziak has the opportunity to buy higher-quality lots of raw materials for $3,000. Some questions have been raised about the health effects of certain ingredients in antiperspirants, and the higher-quality raw material does not contain any of these ingredients. If Hudziak buys the new material, Chemical's processing costs will increase to $400 per lot, but the selling price of its product will remain the same. Cosmetics' selling price will increase to $15 per gallon, and its separable costs will remain the same. Managers provide input to the decision-making process for such decisions, but the president of the firm makes the final decision.

    **1.** If you were the manager of Chemicals, would you want the firm to buy the higher-quality material? Show your calculations and explain your position.

    **2.** If you were the manager of Cosmetics, would you want the firm to buy the higher-quality material? Show your calculations and explain your position.

  ❷  **3.** Describe the pros and cons to the company as a whole from purchasing this material.

❶ **C.** Explain why top management faces uncertainties about how to handle situations such as the purchase described in part (B).

❶ **D.** What methods can be used to encourage managers who have conflicting interests to take actions that are in the best interests of the company as a whole?

❷ **E.** What are the advantages and disadvantages of the methods you identified in part (D)?

**REQUIRED:**
**WRITTEN**
**ASSIGNMENT**

Suppose you are the cost accountant for Hudziak Industries. Turn in your answers to the following.

❸ **F.** Write a memo to the president recommending a decision for the purchase described in part (B). Attach to the memo a schedule showing your computations. As appropriate, refer to the schedule in the memo.

❸ **G.** Include in your memo for part (F) your recommendations for avoiding potential conflicts for similar types of future decisions in a way that is fair to both managers.

# BUILD YOUR PROFESSIONAL COMPETENCIES

**9.33**
**Q7**

**Focus on Professional Competency: Marketing/Client Focus** *Internal and external customer relationships, accountant objectivity* Review the following definition and elements for the Marketing/Client Focus competency.[2]

**DEFINITION:**

*Individuals who are marketing- and client-focused are better able to anticipate and meet the changing needs of clients, employers, customers, and markets. This involves both the ability to recognize market needs and the ability to develop new markets.*

---

[2]The definition and elements are reprinted with permission from AICPA; Copyright © 1978–2000 & 2003 by American Institute of Certified Public Accountants. The AICPA's Core Competency Framework can be accessed at eca.aicpaservices.org.

**ELEMENTS FOR THIS COMPETENCY INCLUDE**

| Level 1 | Level 2 | Level 3 | Level 4 |
|---|---|---|---|
| 1. Identifies factors that motivate internal and external customers to enter into relationships or continue doing business with an organization<br><br>2. Articulates uncertainties about relationships with internal and external customers | 3. Recognizes and understands employer/client protocol and expectations | 4. Develops an effective plan for addressing a particular employer/client need | 5. Builds good working relationships over time<br><br>6. Generates new engagements for services over time |

**REQUIRED:**

**A.** An important goal for internal accountants is to enter into productive working relationships with internal customers—people they work with inside their organizations. Focus on competency elements 1, 2, 3, 4, and 5, which describe skills needed for effectively working with others. Answer the following questions:

❶ **1.** Why do accountants need to actively work on their relationships with internal customers? Why is relationship building an open-ended problem?

❶ **2.** List factors that might motivate internal customers to enter into productive working relationships with accounting personnel.

❷ **3.** What do internal customers typically expect from accounting personnel?

❷ **4.** How can accountants recognize whether they are developing good working relationships with internal customers?

❸ **5.** In this chapter, we learned that managers sometimes use joint cost accounting information inappropriately in making decisions. How can accountants help managers avoid this misuse of accounting information? Develop a strategy and describe how it could be implemented.

**B.** An important goal for public accountants is to enter into productive working relationships with their external customers. Consider competency elements 1, 2, 3, 4, and 5, and answer the following questions:

❷ **1.** How is working with internal customers the same as working with external customers? How is it different?

❷ **2.** Objectivity is a cornerstone of the accounting profession. Discuss the positive and negative aspects of how this affects the ability of auditors to develop good working relationships with their clients.

**9.34** **Integrating Across the Curriculum: Economics and Governmental Regulation** *Beef by-products in animal feed, by-product economics, regulator responsibilities* During early 2004, the

Q1

ETHICS

U.S. beef industry faced a crisis. A slaughtered dairy cow in Washington State was infected with bovine spongiform encephalopathy, more commonly known as "mad cow disease." Government regulators and consumer groups were alarmed because humans who eat contaminated beef may become ill with a fatal brain-wasting disease. The finding of mad cow disease caused domestic beef prices to drop considerably. It also triggered a potential loss of $3 billion in beef exports, as numerous countries immediately banned the import of U.S. beef. Mad cow disease destroyed the British beef industry during the 1990s, and industry groups wanted to avoid a similar fate in the United States.

The only known cause of mad cow disease was the ingestion of infected animal parts. For many years, cattle had routinely been fed by-products from the beef rendering industry. Before the 1990s, this practice was viewed as an economic and ecological success. Beef by-products from slaughterhouses, packing plants, butcher shops, and restaurants totaled approximately 44,000 tons per week in the United States. In the rendering process the remains were ground up and then cooked, which removed the water. The residue could be turned into fats, oils, or meat and bone meal. U.S. sales of meat and bone meal totaled approximately 3.2 billion tons per year. The rendering process provided beef by-product revenues, reduced the cost of protein in cattle feed, and avoided the need to dispose of the beef by-products.

Following an outbreak of mad cow disease in Britain, scientists determined the manner in which the disease spread. With this new information, regulators throughout the world banned the use of beef by-products in cattle feed. However, the 1997 U.S. ban did not prohibit the use of beef by-products in feed for other types of animals, such as poultry, pigs, and pets. The United States also allowed the use of by-products from other types of livestock to be used in cattle feed.

During early 2004, U.S. regulators were not sure how the Washington cow had acquired mad cow disease. The disease had an incubation period of many years, and the infected cow was 6.5 years old. Further complicating the investigation, the cow was purchased from a Canadian herd during 2001.

Some consumer activists called for a complete ban on the use of mammal by-products in animal feed. Others called for expanded testing of cattle, which presently could be done only on dead animals. Industry groups argued that these measures were not economical because they would dramatically increase the cost of beef, while consumers demanded low beef prices.

SOURCES: A. Tsao, "How Now, Mad Cow?" *Business Week Online*, January 14, 2004, available at www.businessweek.com/bwdaily/dnflash/jan2004/nf20040114_2848_db016.htm; J. T. Hallinan, "Cattle Feed Comes Under Scrutiny," *The Wall Street Journal*, December 31, 2003, p. B2; and E. Weise, "Consumers May Have a Beef with Cattle Feed," *USA Today*, June 9, 2003, available at www.usatoday.com/news/health/2003-06-09-beef-cover_x.htm.

**REQUIRED:** Conduct research on the Internet to find articles or other information that discuss both the pros and cons of using beef by-products in animal feed. Answer the following questions:

**A.** What is likely to happen to U.S. beef by-products if they are not sold for use in animal feed?

**B.** Suppose the U.S. government bans the use of all types of animal by-products in livestock feed.
   **1.** How would the ban most likely affect the cost of main products in the cattle industry? Explain.
   **2.** How would the ban most likely affect the cost of main products in other livestock industries, such as pigs and chicken? Explain.

**C.** Besides the effects in part (B), describe the likely economic effects on the U.S. cattle industry if the use of beef by-products is banned for all types of animal feed.

**D.** What responsibilities do U.S. regulators have to various stakeholders in this issue? Consider the following types of stakeholders:
   - U.S. cattle industry
   - Other U.S. livestock industries, such as pigs and chicken
   - Other U.S. food manufacturers
   - Consumers of U.S. beef

**E.** Industry representatives argue that consumers of U.S. beef face no serious risk from mad cow disease. How valid is this argument?

**F.** In your opinion, should the United States ban the use of all types of animal by-products in livestock feed? What values did you use to reach your conclusion?

# 10

# Static and Flexible Budgets

## ▶In Brief

An organization's long-term strategies are communicated and advanced through short-term and long-term budgets. In addition, budgets provide a mechanism for monitoring an organization's progress toward its goals. Comparisons of actual to budgeted revenues and costs help managers evaluate performance, leading to improved operations and more accurate planning. Some organizations provide employee incentives for meeting or exceeding budget-based benchmarks. Accordingly, budgets are used in planning, monitoring, and motivating performance.

## This Chapter Addresses the Following Questions:

**Q1** What are the relationships among budgets, long-term strategies, and short-term operating plans?

**Q2** What is a master budget, and how is it prepared?

**Q3** What are budget variances, and how are they calculated?

**Q4** What are the differences between static and flexible budgets?

**Q5** How are budgets used to monitor and motivate performance?

**Q6** What are other approaches to budgeting?

**Q7** How is the cash budget developed? (Appendix 10A)

# DUPONT: BACK TO BASICS

In 1998, Charles Holliday, Jr., was appointed chief executive officer of **E. I. du Pont de Nemours and Company (DuPont)**, a global scientific research and manufacturing company operating in more than 70 countries. When Holliday took over, he decided to reemphasize the company's scientific core competencies and increase its strategic focus on the development of new products.

DuPont was founded in 1802 as a producer of gunpowder. By 1820, it had become the major

supplier of gunpowder to the U.S. government. Over time, DuPont research created numerous highly popular products, including nylon, Teflon®, Lycra®, Stainmaster®, Corian®, and Coolmax®. DuPont now focuses on a wide range of products and services in polymer science and chemistry, math, physics, engineering, biology, and information science.

DuPont has always invested heavily in research and development; it currently owns more than 75 laboratories worldwide. However, when Holliday took over, he believed that the company was not sufficiently focused on its core strength of new product development. To address this problem, Holliday increased research and development expenditures from $990 million in 1996 to $1.6 billion in 2001. He also increased the proportion of budgeted research and development funds for new product development from one-third in the late 1990s to approximately one-half in 2003. He then announced plans to further increase the proportion to 65%.

Holliday also realigned DuPont's resources toward more profitable products. In early 2003, the company announced plans to focus its research and development activities on the 75 projects judged to have the highest revenue potential. In addition, DuPont would divest itself of business segments that had low profits and that diverted the company from its core competencies. For example, the company planned to spin off its textile fibers businesses, which included nylon, Lycra, and Stainmaster. Although the nylon and polyester segments were generating about 17% of total revenues, they both experienced operating losses in 1999 and 2001. Expected oil price increases would further reduce profits in these segments. To adopt more environmentally friendly products and reduce the company's reliance on oil prices, Holliday also pushed for development of products using renewable resources. For example, Dupont was developing a new synthetic fiber made from corn that would potentially compete with Dacron® and Lycra, which are both made from petroleum.

Some analysts were skeptical about Dupont's ability to generate growth and profits using Holliday's strategies. They argued that the company had not created a major new product in many years. They pointed out many uncertainties about the viability and future profitability of DuPont's current research and development projects. DuPont's managers countered that the company continuously generates new, profitable products. For example, in 2001 a DuPont team developed a more durable and eco-friendly clear spray coating for DaimlerChrysler's Dodge Durango, enabling the auto maker to meet stringent air pollution requirements. DuPont expected to achieve $30 million in annual sales from this new product, together with a new fabric for hospital operating rooms and a new generation of fuel-cell components. ■

SOURCES: Information available at heritage.dupont.com/ and www1.dupont.com/NASApp/dupontglobal/corp/index.jsp; C. R. Schoenberger, "Greenhouse Effect," *Forbes,* February 3, 2003; and H. Wee, "Does DuPont Have a Growth Catalyst?" *Business Week,* October 29, 2002.

BUSINESS
STRATEGIES AND
BUDGETS

## ■ Key Decision Factors for DuPont

The following discussion summarizes key aspects of the decision-making process used by Holliday as Chief Executive Officer of **DuPont** to focus the company's strategies on new product development.

**Knowing.** Holliday worked for DuPont for many years and gained experience in almost every branch of the company. He worked his way up from industrial engineer to analyst and then into management. He gained detailed technical knowledge about the company's products, people, and processes. This knowledge enhanced Holliday's ability to identify DuPont's core competencies and develop potentially successful strategies.

**Identifying.** Research and development are inherently risky. Scientific discoveries are often unpredictable, and potentially viable discoveries cannot always be converted into profitable products. Thus, Holliday would have faced many uncertainties about whether his strategy to focus on new product development would be successful.

**Exploring.** Holliday's decision to refocus the company on scientific discovery resulted from his analysis of the company's competitive strengths and weaknesses. In addition, the success of this strategy depends on the ability of DuPont's managers to choose the best research projects. While exploring their opportunities, the managers need to explore the viability of alternative research projects, their abilities to develop cost-effective products and production processes for new discoveries, and potential product demand. When evaluating alternative projects, the managers also need to consider the possibility that information generated by the personnel proposing or working on a project may be biased.

**Prioritizing.** Holliday believed that a strategy of focusing on new product development would lead to greater long-term growth and profitability than other potential strategies. When choosing specific projects for research and development, DuPont is likely to adopt a portfolio perspective. With such a perspective, managers recognize the uncertainties in research and development projects; they expect some projects to succeed and others to fail. Large companies such as DuPont can afford this type of portfolio approach; it allows the company to invest in projects that might be considered too risky for a smaller company. Nevertheless, the company's managers must still prioritize projects to decide which ones will be funded and the amount of funding for each.

**Envisioning.** DuPont's future performance depends on its managerial team's ability to anticipate and respond to change. The company is currently moving away from its reliance on petroleum-based products. In the future, the company may discover other threats or opportunities. Managers will need to reevaluate the company's vision and core competencies, which in turn could lead to changes in strategic direction.

## ■ Translating Strategies into Budgets

Given Holliday's strategic shift toward new product development, DuPont's spending pattern for research and development was altered. Overall, he significantly increased planned expenditures for research and development. In addition, he shifted the emphasis within research and development toward new products. As we learn in this chapter, these decisions are reflected in DuPont's budgets. Budgets communicate decisions to employees and are used to monitor operating performance and motivate employees to work toward the strategic goals envisioned by top management.

BUDGETING

College students routinely anticipate both school-related expenditures, such as tuition and books, and living expenses, such as rent and food. Before each term begins, they develop financial plans. These plans consider expenses and also incoming funds such as scholarships, loans, and wages.

At the end of each month or term, students might compare their actual expenditures to those they had planned. They use these comparisons to adjust their plans for future spending

**Q1** What are the relationships among budgets, long-term strategies, and short-term operating plans?

or financing. For example, if expenses are outpacing revenues, students have several choices. They can lower their living expenses. They might transfer to a less expensive college, switch from full-time to part-time status, or take fewer courses. They might also increase funds by applying for more scholarships or loans or by increasing their work hours.

Every organization faces the same budgetary problems that students face. In the upcoming fiscal period, plans must be developed to anticipate revenues, expenses, and cash flows. At the end of the period, actual results are compared to the plan to identify gaps, or variances, from the plan. A **budget** is a formalized financial plan for operations of an organization for a specified future period. This plan helps the organization coordinate the activities needed to carry out the plan. A budget is an organization's financial roadmap; it reflects management's forecast of the financial effects of an organization's plans for one or more future time periods. Several objectives are met through the use of budgets, as summarized in Exhibit 10.1.

**EXHIBIT 10.1**
Budget Objectives

- Developing and communicating organizational strategies and goals for the entire organization as well as for each segment, division, or department
- Assigning decision rights (authority to spend and responsibility for decision outcomes)
- Motivating managers to plan in advance
- Coordinating operating activities such as sales and production
- Establishing prices for the internal transfer of goods and services
- Measuring and comparing expected and actual outcomes
- Monitoring actual performance and investigating variances when necessary
- Motivating managers to provide appropriate estimates, meet expectations, and use resources efficiently
- Reevaluating and revising strategies and operating plans as conditions change

In preparing budgets, managers forecast a number of events such as the volume of goods or services they will sell. Using these estimates, plans are developed to determine the resources an organization needs, including employees, raw materials and supplies, cash, and anything else necessary to the future operations.

Budgets also provide a mechanism for defining the responsibilities and financial decision-making authority, or **decision rights,** of individual managers. For example, separate budgets are often developed for each department within an organization. The manager of each department is then given authority to spend the organization's resources in accordance with the budget, and is also responsible for meeting budgeted goals.

## ■ Budget Cycle

A **budget cycle** is a series of steps that organizations follow to develop and use budgets, as summarized in Exhibit 10.2. Managers typically begin the process by revisiting and possibly revising the organizational vision and core competencies. The opening case described this part of the process for DuPont; the managers decided to reemphasize the company's core competency of new product development. The next part of the budget cycle is to reconsider long-term strategies in light of the vision and core competencies. For example, DuPont's managers decided to increase emphasis on research and development and to divest low-profit business segments. Once long-term strategies are reviewed and revised, the current period's operating plans are developed. For DuPont, operating plans included major increases in planned research and development activities and greater emphasis on new products.

The rest of this chapter addresses the other steps in the budget cycle. We first learn to translate operating plans into a master budget and then learn how managers monitor actual results, investigate differences between actual and budget, and evaluate and reward performance.

**CURRENT PRACTICE**

During late 2003, Eastman Kodak reduced its shareholder dividend by 72% to help finance a management plan to shift the company's focus away from its traditional film photography products and toward digital technology products.[1]

---

[1]"Kodak Strategy Touches Off Battle with Investors," *USA Today,* October 21, 2003, available at www.usatoday.com/money/industries/manufacturing/2003-10-21-kodak-fight_x.htm.

**EXHIBIT 10.2**
Budget Cycle

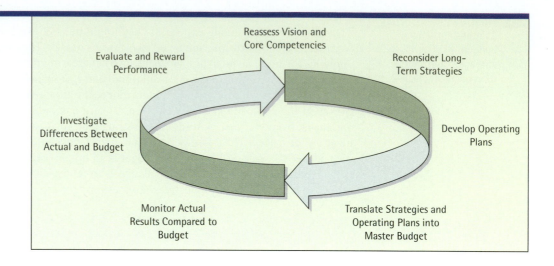

## ■ Master Budget

**Q2** What is a master budget, and how is it prepared?

A **master budget** is a comprehensive plan for an upcoming financial period, usually a year. Master budgets reflect an organization's future operating and financing decisions, and are often summarized in a set of **budgeted financial statements.** These statements are forecasts of the future income statement, balance sheet, and cash flows, given an organization's sales forecasts and expenditure plans for the next period.

Exhibit 10.3 shows the development of a master budget in a manufacturing organization. The master budget includes an **operating budget**—management's plan for revenues, production, and operating costs. Preparation of the operating budget begins with the organization's strategies, which in turn lead to a sales forecast and the revenue budget. The volume of production is next forecast using beginning inventory levels, sales forecasts, and desired ending inventory levels. The production budget leads to budgets for direct materials, direct labor, and manufacturing overhead. These budgets are used to create budgets for ending inventory and cost of goods sold. The operating budget also includes budgets for individual support department costs. All of the components of the operating budget are combined with any nonoperating items and income taxes in a budgeted income statement. Nonoperating items might include interest expenses, gains or losses on the sale of fixed assets, or earnings from investments.

The master budget also includes **financial budgets,** or management's plans for capital expenditures, long-term financing, and cash flows, leading to a budgeted balance sheet and budgeted statement of cash flows. The cash budget is part of the financial budgets. A **cash budget** reflects the effects of management's plans on cash and summarizes the information that accountants gather about the expected amounts and timing of cash receipts and disbursements. The cash budget is addressed in Appendix 10A. The capital budget reflects long-term investment. The long-term financing budget, budgeted balance sheet, and budgeted statement of cash flows are beyond the scope of this textbook.

**ALTERNATIVE TERMS**

Some people use the terms *pro forma financial statements, predicted financial statements,* or *forecasted financial statements* instead of *budgeted financial statements.*

**CHAPTER REFERENCE**

See Chapter 12 for details about capital budgeting.

## ■ Developing a Master Budget

Accountants develop a master budget in consultation with top management and every department within an organization. The master budget is developed using a set of **budget assumptions,** which are plans and predictions about next period's operating activities. Revenues are budgeted assuming a particular forecast of sales volumes and prices, or assuming an estimated percentage change from the prior year. Individual costs are budgeted assuming a fixed amount to be spent, as a percentage of revenues, as a percentage change from the prior year, or on some other basis. Accountants assist managers in the process of developing budget assumptions. They may analyze past revenue and cost trends and behavior, gather information about possible cost changes, and obtain estimates from engineers about the effects of planned production changes.

**EXHIBIT 10.3**

Developing a Manufacturer's Master Budget

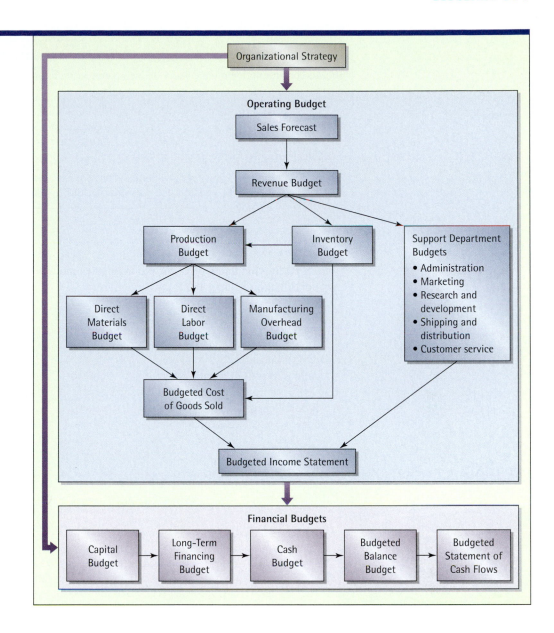

The master budget is usually developed in the sequence shown in Exhibit 10.3 for a manufacturing organization. Given the organization's strategy, the first step is to forecast sales volumes and revenues. However, some organizations develop the production and support department budgets simultaneously with the revenue budget. Also, some parts of the production and support department budgets might be developed independently of the revenue budget. For example, DuPont increased its research and development budget from $990 million in 1996 to $1.6 billion in 2001. This budget amount did not depend on the forecast of 2001 revenues.

The process of developing a master budget becomes increasingly complex as organizations become larger. It is often more complex for international organizations. Communication can be more time consuming because international business segments participate in the budgeting process. Cultural and legal differences influence both internal and external operations and need to be considered. The economies of different countries rarely move in tandem and forecasting sales is more difficult. In addition, currency translations and differences in inflation and deflation rates greatly increase uncertainty in the planning and budgeting process.

**INTERNATIONAL**

Budget factors vary internationally. For example, employees in Germany receive a legal minimum vacation of 20 working days per year, while vacation pay is not legally mandated in the United States.[2]

---

[2]"Wages, Salaries and Bonuses," available at www.invest-in-germany.de/en/, click "Business Guide" and then "Industrial Relations and Labor Legislation."

In the following budgeting illustration, the accountant develops a master budget by creating individual budgets in the following order:

- Revenue budget
- Production budget
- Direct materials budget
- Direct labor budget
- Manufacturing overhead budget
- Inventory and cost of goods sold budget
- Support department budgets
- Budgeted financial statements

## MOUNTAIN HIGH BIKES (PART 1)
### DEVELOPING A MASTER BUDGET

Sanjay Rajakrishnan is an accountant for Mountain High Bikes, a manufacturer of sturdy mountain bikes for intermediate-level bikers. The company's managers are forecasting an increase in sales because of the success of their current advertising campaign. They ask Sanjay to create a master budget for the upcoming year, given the forecasted sales increase.

To gather information needed for the budget, Sanjay first accesses relevant data about revenues, inventories, and production costs from last period's accounting records. Next, he obtains information from every department and meets with top management to identify changes in sales volumes and prices, production processes, manufacturing costs, and support department costs.

### Developing the Revenue Budget

Sanjay prepares the revenue budget first because he needs the volume of bike sales to develop the production and variable cost budgets. The managers forecasted that 100,000 bikes would be sold at a price of $800 each. Sanjay develops the revenue budget for Mountain High Bikes.

### REVENUE BUDGET

|  | Selling Price | Units Sold | Total Revenues |
|---|---|---|---|
| Bikes | $800 | 100,000 | $80,000,000 |

### Developing the Production Budget

Sanjay next develops the production budget. According to prior accounting records, beginning finished goods inventory consists of 2,500 bikes at a cost per unit of $454.75, or $1,136,875 total. Given the anticipated increase in sales volume, the managers want to increase finished goods inventory to 3,500 units. Sanjay calculates the number of bikes that will be manufactured this period, factoring in the sales forecast and both beginning and targeted ending inventory levels.

## PRODUCTION BUDGET (UNITS)

| | |
|---|---:|
| Sales | 100,000 |
| Target ending inventory | 3,500 |
| Total finished units needed | 103,500 |
| Less beginning inventory | (2,500) |
| Production | 101,000 |

## Developing the Direct Materials Budget

Now Sanjay can determine the amount of direct materials that must be purchased. The beginning inventory consists of:

| Beginning direct material inventories: | |
|---|---:|
| Wheels and tires | $ 20,000 |
| Components | 70,000 |
| Frames | 50,000 |
| Total | $140,000 |

The cost per unit of direct materials is expected to be:

| Direct materials (cost per unit): | |
|---|---:|
| Wheels and tires | $20 |
| Components | 70 |
| Frame | 50 |

The managers want ending inventories to be:

| Targeted ending direct material inventories: | |
|---|---:|
| Wheels and tires | $ 25,000 |
| Components | 87,500 |
| Frames | 62,500 |
| Total | $175,000 |

Given these assumptions, Sanjay prepares the following direct materials budget.

## DIRECT MATERIALS BUDGET

| Production of 101,000 bikes: | |
|---|---:|
| Wheels (101,000 × $20) | $ 2,020,000 |
| Components (101,000 × $70) | 7,070,000 |
| Frames (101,000 × $50) | 5,050,000 |
| Total direct materials used | 14,140,000 |
| Target ending inventory | 175,000 |
| Less beginning inventory | (140,000) |
| Total purchases | $14,175,000 |

## Developing the Direct Labor Budget

The quantity and cost of direct labor per unit is expected to be:

| Direct Labor | Hours | Cost per Hour |
|---|:---:|:---:|
| Assembly | 1.5 | $25 |
| Testing | 0.15 | 15 |

Sanjay prepares the direct labor budget, which forecasts the number of labor hours and the total direct labor costs for producing 101,000 bikes.

## DIRECT LABOR BUDGET

| Labor hours budget: | |
|---|---:|
| Assembly (101,000 units × 1.5 hours) | 151,500 hours |
| Testing (101,000 units × 0.15 hours) | 15,150 hours |
| Total labor hours | 166,650 hours |
| Labor cost budget: | |
| Assembly (151,500 × $25) | $3,787,500 |
| Testing (15,150 × $15) | 227,250 |
| Total labor cost | $4,014,750 |

*(continued)*

## Developing the Manufacturing Overhead Budget

In addition to the direct costs of production, overhead costs need to be included in the budgeting process. Sanjay uses information that he collected from last year's operations and updates it with current prices. The cost per unit of variable manufacturing overhead is expected to be as follows:

| Variable overhead (cost per unit): | |
|---|---|
| Supplies | $20.00 |
| Indirect labor | 37.50 |
| Maintenance | 10.00 |
| Miscellaneous | 7.50 |
| Total | $75.00 |

Sanjay expects $20,200,000 to be spent on fixed manufacturing overhead costs.

He calculates the fixed overhead allocation rate by dividing budgeted fixed overhead costs by the budgeted volume of production:

$$\$20,200,000 \div 101,000 \text{ units} = \$200 \text{ per unit}$$

Sanjay prepares the manufacturing overhead budget for producing 101,000 bikes.

### MANUFACTURING OVERHEAD BUDGET

| | |
|---|---|
| Variable manufacturing overhead costs: | |
| Supplies (101,000 units × $20.00) | $ 2,020,000 |
| Indirect labor (101,000 units × $37.50) | 3,787,500 |
| Maintenance (101,000 units × $10.00) | 1,010,000 |
| Miscellaneous (101,000 units × $7.50) | 757,500 |
| Total variable overhead (101,000 units × $75.00) | 7,575,000 |
| | |
| Fixed manufacturing overhead costs: | |
| Depreciation | 4,040,000 |
| Property taxes | 1,010,000 |
| Insurance | 1,414,000 |
| Plant supervision | 5,050,000 |
| Fringe benefits | 7,070,000 |
| Miscellaneous | 1,616,000 |
| Total fixed overhead | 20,200,000 |
| Total overhead | $27,775,000 |
| | |
| Manufacturing overhead allocation rates (cost per unit): | |
| Variable | $ 75 |
| Fixed | 200 |

## Developing the Inventory and Cost of Goods Sold Budgets

To prepare budgeted cost of goods sold, Sanjay needs forecasted costs for ending inventories. Using the fixed and variable production costs, he prepares the ending inventories budget, summarized as follows.

### ENDING INVENTORIES BUDGET

| | |
|---|---|
| Direct materials (cost per unit): | |
| Frame | $ 50.00 |
| Components | 70.00 |
| Wheels | 20.00 |
| Total direct materials | 140.00 |
| | |
| Direct labor: | |
| Assembly (1.5 hours × $25) | 37.50 |
| Testing (0.15 hours × $15) | 2.25 |
| Total direct labor | 39.75 |

| | | |
|---|---|---|
| Manufacturing overhead | | |
| Variable | | 75.00 |
| Fixed | | 200.00 |
| Total overhead | | 275.00 |
| Total cost per unit | | $454.75 |

Budgeted cost of ending inventory:

| | | |
|---|---|---|
| 3,500 units × $454.75 per unit | | $1,591,625 |

Using information from the preceding budgets, Sanjay prepares the cost of goods sold budget for the forecasted sale of 100,000 units.

### COST OF GOODS SOLD BUDGET

| | | |
|---|---|---|
| Beginning finished goods | | $ 1,136,875 |
| Direct materials used | $14,140,000 | |
| Direct labor | 4,014,750 | |
| Manufacturing overhead | 27,775,000 | |
| Cost of goods manufactured | | 45,929,750 |
| Total available | | 47,066,625 |
| Ending finished goods | | (1,591,625) |
| Cost of goods sold | | $45,475,000 |

## Developing the Support Department Budgets

Having completed the production cost budgets, Sanjay next estimates other operating costs, that is, the budgeted costs for all of the support departments. In this illustration, the support costs are all fixed. In other situations, support costs could contain a mixture of fixed and variable costs.

Support department information is gathered from each department manager. The support department budget is summarized as follows.

### SUPPORT DEPARTMENT BUDGET

| Department | Fixed Costs |
|---|---|
| Administration | $16,478,215 |
| Marketing | 9,886,929 |
| Distribution | 4,943,465 |
| Customer service | 1,647,821 |
| Total | $32,956,430 |

## Developing the Budgeted Income Statement

Finally, Sanjay combines the information from all of the individual operating budgets to prepare the budgeted income statement. The company's managers do not anticipate any nonoperating income statement items, so no additional items must be included in the budgeted income statement except for income taxes at the expected rate of 30%.

### BUDGETED INCOME STATEMENT

| | | |
|---|---|---|
| Revenues (Revenue budget) | | $80,000,000 |
| Cost of goods sold (Cost of goods sold budget) | | 45,475,000 |
| Gross margin | | 34,525,000 |
| Operating costs: (Support department budgets) | | |
| Administration | $16,478,215 | |
| Marketing | 9,886,929 | |
| Distribution | 4,943,465 | |
| Customer service | 1,647,821 | |
| Total operating costs | | 32,956,430 |
| Operating income | | 1,568,570 |
| Income taxes ($1,568,570 × 30%) | | 470,571 |
| Net income | | $ 1,097,999 |

Sanjay reviews the budgeted income statement information with the company's controller. The budgets are then presented at a meeting with the CEO and the various department heads.

Mountain High Bikes (Part 1) illustrates developing a master budget for a manufacturing organization. For this illustration:

| Identify Information Used | Identify Information Created | Describe Use |
| --- | --- | --- |
| List the information that is used as inputs for creating the master budget. How and where would the information be obtained? | Describe the information that is created. Explain the purpose for each of the individual budgets. | In your own words, explain how the managers of Mountain High Bikes might use the master budget. |

## ■ Budgeting in Nonmanufacturing Organizations

The individual budgets shown in Exhibit 10.3 are for a manufacturing organization. The specific types of budgets that comprise a master budget depend on the nature of an organization's goods or services and its accounting system. For example, some service organizations do not carry inventory; the direct costs of producing services are recognized as a period cost in the income statement. Thus, budgets for these organizations generally would not include inventory computations and might not include direct materials. Other service industries, such as retailers, would carry inventory. The categories chosen for individual budgets are based on the categories that managers use to plan and monitor operations.

In the not-for-profit sector, budgets are often a primary source of information about the operations of the organization. Although donors request financial statements, budgets provide much of the operating information used by managers. In governmental organizations, budgets must often be legally adopted, placing restrictions on spending authority.

**CURRENT PRACTICE**

The State of Tennessee publishes a citizens' guide to the state budget. It provides information about budgets for all state programs so that taxpayers receive an accounting of state expenditures.[3]

# BUDGETS AS PERFORMANCE BENCHMARKS

Managers and accountants use budgets to monitor operations by comparing actual results to the original budget forecasts. These comparisons serve as benchmarks for performance and help them evaluate whether strategies and operations are meeting expectations. For example, managers learn whether desired sales volumes are achieved or whether costs are under control. In addition, accountants monitor budgets to improve the quality of the budgeting process over time.

**Q3** What are budget variances, and how are they calculated?

**CHAPTER REFERENCE**

In Chapter 11, we learn more about the reasons for variances and the actions that managers take, if any, after analyzing variances.

**HELPFUL HINT**

Budget variances may be calculated based on either a static budget (static budget *variance*) or a flexible budget (flexible budget *variance*).

## ■ Budget Variances

Differences between budgeted and actual results are called **budget variances.** If actual revenues are larger than the budget, or actual costs are lower than the budget, the variance is categorized as a **favorable variance.** Conversely, an **unfavorable variance** occurs when actual costs are greater than budgeted or actual revenues are less than budgeted.

Budget variances occur for two general reasons. First, actual activities might not follow plans. For example, the Tickle Me Elmo doll produced by **Tyco Toys** was shown on national television by Rosie O'Donnell and then became a "hot item" during the 1996 Christmas season. It sold out at toy stores immediately.[4] Actual volumes of production might have increased greatly above budgeted amounts. Second, unanticipated increases or decreases in the purchase prices of direct materials or other input factors can cause the budget to be an inappropriate benchmark for performance. Accordingly, revision of the budget benchmark would take into account new information about costs.

Determining the underlying reasons for a variance is sometimes complicated. Suppose **DuPont** experiences a favorable research cost variance. This variance might be obtained by efficient use of research dollars. However, it could also occur because managers failed to follow budgeted plans and launched fewer research projects than expected.

---

[3]B. Connie and T. Poff, "Services Provided to the People of Tennessee: A Programmatic Accounting of Resource Investment," *Government Finance Review* 10(5), pp 15–18. The 2002 version of the citizen's guide can be found at www.state.tn.us/tacir/PDF_FILES/Taxes/CitznGuideBk.pdf.
[4]Kate Fitzgerald, "Tickle Me Elmo" *Advertising Age,* 68(26) (June 30, 1997), p. S38.

## ■ Variances and Budgeting Uncertainties

CURRENT PRACTICE

Following September 11, 2001, airline volume dropped dramatically and became more difficult to predict. The airlines then entered into cost reduction negotiations with labor unions, airport authorities, and other vendors.

Because budgets are based on forecasts about the future, it is impossible to prevent variances by exactly achieving budgeted revenues and costs. The degree of forecast uncertainty varies across organizations and across time. Some organizations have fairly predictable revenues and costs, especially organizations that purchase and sell under fixed price, long-term contracts. Other organizations have volatile or unpredictable revenues and costs. Budgets are likely to be less accurate—significant variances are more likely to occur—in highly competitive industries, when selling newly developed goods and services, or when subject to fluctuating raw material costs such as petroleum prices.

## ■ Static and Flexible Budgets

**Q4** What are the differences between static and flexible budgets?

The interpretation of budget variances is complicated by deviations from budgeted volume levels. Many costs are variable; they are expected to change proportionately with changes in production levels. Thus, we would expect total variable costs to deviate from budget if sales volumes—and, therefore, production volumes—deviate from budget. However, a **static budget** is based on forecasts of specific volumes of production or services. All variable costs are calculated for a specific volume of operations. If a static budget is compared to results for a different level of volume, budgeted variable costs are overstated when fewer units or services are produced than budgeted. Similarly, budgeted variable costs are understated if more units or services are produced. These volume effects hide any variances due to operational efficiencies or inefficiencies.

CHAPTER REFERENCE

See Chapter 3 for further discussion of CVP analysis.

CURRENT PRACTICE

Software vendors such as Hyperion, Great Plains, Soloman Software, and Computer Associates provide budgeting packages that allow changes in underlying assumptions.

A budget that reflects a range of operations is called a **flexible budget.** Cost-volume-profit analysis is a simple version of a flexible budget. Flexible budgets separate fixed and variable costs to more accurately reflect the effects of activity levels on cost. For planning purposes, flexible budgets are used to study the sensitivity of budgeted revenues and costs to different volume levels. A number of different software packages for flexible budgeting are available for large businesses. For small businesses, Excel and other spreadsheets provide similar analysis. These software packages and spreadsheets allow financial modeling of budgets under many different circumstances.

When evaluating actual results at the end of a period, the flexible budget is set at the actual sales or production volume and used as a benchmark for analyzing variances. Organizations that use a static budget transform it into a benchmark by adjusting its variable costs to reflect actual volume. However, because fixed costs are not expected to vary with volume, they are not adjusted for any differences between budgeted and actual volumes. Therefore, the flexible budget uses actual volume for variable costs and the budgeted fixed costs. Mountain High Bikes (Part 2) illustrates variances for static and flexible budgets.

### MOUNTAIN HIGH BIKES (PART 2)
### STATIC VERSUS FLEXIBLE BUDGET VARIANCES

At the end of the budget cycle, Sanjay compares actual results for the period to the budget. He plans to create a budget variance report for management.

### Static Budget Variances

Sanjay creates the summary in Exhibit 10.4, comparing revenues and costs under the static budget with the actual income statement. He uses the budgeted variable costs for this period. Variable costs per bike include:

| | |
|---|---|
| Direct materials: | |
| Wheels/tires | $ 20.00 |
| Components | 70.00 |
| Frame | 50.00 |
| Total direct materials | 140.00 |
| Direct labor | 39.75 |
| Variable overhead | 75.00 |
| Total cost per bike | $254.75 |

**EXHIBIT 10.4**
**Static Budget Variances at Mountain High Bikes**

| | Static Budget | Actual | Variance | |
|---|---|---|---|---|
| Bikes sold | 100,000 | 113,500 | 13,500 | Favorable |
| Revenue | $80,000,000 | $90,500,000 | $10,500,000 | Favorable |
| Production costs: | | | | |
|     Variable | 25,475,000[a] | 29,492,408 | (4,017,408) | Unfavorable |
|     Fixed overhead | 20,200,000 | 19,400,000 | 800,000 | Favorable |
| Support department costs | 32,956,430 | 37,565,337 | (4,608,907) | Unfavorable |
| Income | $ 1,368,570[b] | $ 4,042,255 | | |
| Total variance | | | $ 2,673,685 | Favorable |

[a]Budgeted variable costs × 100,000 = $254.75 × 100,000 = $25,475,000
[b]Differs from budgeted income statement total by $200,000 because some overhead costs are allocated to inventory on the budgeted balance sheet. An increase of 1,000 units in inventories was budgeted this period (beginning inventories = 2,500 and ending inventories = 3,500). These additional units give rise to a $200,000 (1,000 × $200 per unit overhead allocation) increase in income because this amount of fixed overhead is not included on the income statement.

Sanjay includes the budgeted fixed costs for manufacturing overhead ($20,200,000) and the budgeted support department costs ($32,956,430). He calculates variances for sales volume, revenue, and each of the cost categories. When Sanjay compares the actual results to the budget, he is pleased with the organization's performance during the period. The overall variance was favorable by nearly $2.7 million, and the revenue variance was positive and large—$10.5 million. However, he is concerned about the large unfavorable cost variances.

As Sanjay thinks more about the cost variances, he realizes that he would expect to see unfavorable variable production cost variances because the sales volume was higher than planned. Because he used a static budget in his schedule, the cost variances did not reflect the actual volume of sales. Therefore, the schedule gave him poor quality information for analyzing last period's costs.

## Flexible Budget Variances

Sanjay decides to create a new budget variance analysis that reflects the actual volume of sales. He first transforms the static budget into a flexible budget by recalculating budgeted revenues using actual sales volumes (113,500) and budgeted selling price ($800). He then recalculates budgeted variable production costs by multiplying the actual sales volume (113,500) times the budgeted variable cost per unit of $254.75. Because fixed costs are not expected to vary with changes in volume, no adjustments are made to either budgeted fixed production costs or support costs. Finally, Sanjay recalculates the variances. Exhibit 10.5 summarizes his revised variance schedule.

Based on the new schedule, Sanjay realizes that the company's performance was worse than he previously thought. After accounting for the higher sales volume, the total flexible budget variance is unfavorable by more than $4.6 million. These variances indicate the following:

- The average selling price per bike was lower than the budget.
- The average variable production cost per bike was higher than the budget.
- Total fixed production costs were lower than the budget.
- Total fixed support costs were significantly higher than the budget.

**EXHIBIT 10.5**
**Flexible Budget Variances at Mountain High Bikes**

| | Flexible Budget | Actual | Variance | |
|---|---|---|---|---|
| Bikes sold | 113,500 | 113,500 | | |
| Revenue | $90,800,000[a] | $90,500,000 | $ (300,000) | Unfavorable |
| Production costs: | | | | |
|     Variable | 28,914,125[b] | 29,492,408 | (578,283) | Unfavorable |
|     Fixed overhead | 20,200,000 | 19,400,000 | 800,000 | Favorable |
| Support department costs | 32,956,430 | 37,565,337 | (4,608,907) | Unfavorable |
| Income | $ 8,729,445 | $ 4,042,255 | | |
| Total variance | | | $(4,687,190) | Unfavorable |

[a]Actual quantity sold times budgeted selling price per bike of $800.
[b]Actual quantity sold times this period's budgeted variable cost per unit of $254.75.

Sanjay plans to investigate the reasons for the large unfavorable fixed support cost variance. However, he is unsure whether the other variances are significant enough to justify spending time investigating them. He decides to meet with the controller to discuss how to proceed. This discussion is presented later in the chapter, in Mountain High Bikes (Part 3).

| GUIDE YOUR LEARNING 10.3 Mountain High Bikes (Part 2) | | |
|---|---|---|

Mountain High Bikes (Part 2) illustrates static and flexible budget variances. For this illustration:

| Define It | Compare Information Created | Describe Use |
|---|---|---|
| Where did Sanjay obtain the actual revenues and costs? Explain how the static and flexible budget variances were calculated. | Explain what causes the variances to be different when calculated using the flexible budget instead of the static budget. Be specific. | In your own words, explain why the flexible budget provides better information about revenue and cost variances than the static budget. |

# BUDGETS, INCENTIVES, AND REWARDS

**Q5** How are budgets used to monitor and motivate performance?

Budgets are used to assign decision rights to individual managers within an organization. Managers are given authority over resources and then held responsible for meeting budget benchmarks, such as producing units at the budgeted cost per unit. Many organizations monitor individual manager performance by comparing actual results to the budget. Bonuses based on meeting or exceeding budget goals help motivate performance. Sometimes broader employee groups receive profit sharing, cash, or other bonuses based on achieving or exceeding budgeted income levels. For example, manufacturing plant workers who meet production volume, cost, and quality goals could be entitled to share in profits or receive cash bonuses. Sales representatives who meet target sales volumes may be rewarded with family trips to resort destinations or awards dinners to celebrate their good performance. These practices raise questions about how information is gathered for budgets and what levels of responsibility should be included.

Budget plans can be developed from the top down, using information that has been gathered from the bottom up. In other words, top management provides strategies and suggested organizational targets for the coming period. These strategies and targets are communicated "top-down" to division and department managers who incorporate them into the budgeted operating plans. Departmental budget requests are then communicated "bottom-up" to members of top management who are responsible for final budget approval. Although top managers approve the final budget, they rely on the knowledge and experience of individual managers to help them establish reasonable departmental budgets.

##  Participative Budgeting

When managers in the field have more knowledge about future operations than top management, budgets are often developed from the bottom-up. For example, sales representatives at Mountain High Bikes could submit their forecasts for next year to the marketing department. **Participative budgeting** occurs when managers who are responsible for meeting budgets also prepare the initial budget forecasts, setting targets for themselves. Theoretically, participative budgeting motivates employees to meet budget targets because they buy-in to the target-setting process. However, when employees set targets, incentives exist to set them low so that goals can be met easily. In contrast, when top management sets targets, incentives exist to raise targets to induce greater productivity. If targets are either too low or too high—easily met or unachievable—employees have little motivation to improve performance. Therefore, negotiations are often required over a period of time prior to setting the final budget.

[5]See B. D. Clinton and J. E. Hunton, "Linking Participative Budgeting Congruence to Organization Performance," *Behavioral Research in Accounting*, 13 (2001), pp. 127–152.

## ■ Zero-Based Budgeting

CURRENT PRACTICE

Zero-based budgeting has recently become more common for information technology budgets, as the weak economy forces managers to justify their spending decisions.[6]

Some managers simply add an adjustment increasing last year's budget to plan for the next period. This type of budgeting practice discourages them from seeking ways to use the organization's resources more efficiently. In addition, many organizations adopt policies so that departments lose authority over unspent budgeted costs and receive lower future budgets if actual costs are lower than the current budget. This policy encourages department managers to spend all of their budgeted funds to avoid future cutbacks. To reduce these types of problems, organizations may adopt **zero-based budgeting,** in which managers justify budget amounts as if no information about budgets or costs from prior budget cycles was available. This system encourages managers to cut costs and improve quality. A disadvantage is that it is time consuming, and the benefits may not be worth the extra time involved.

## ■ Budget Manipulation

If performance evaluations and bonuses are based on achieving budgeted results, managers have incentives to manipulate budget requests to meet targets more easily. **Budgetary slack** refers to the practice of intentionally setting revenue budgets too low and cost budgets too high. This practice hampers organizations when more precise information would result in better strategies and operating plans. For example, if sales targets are set too low, an organization could lose sales because it lacks the resources to increase production of goods or services over the short term.

Because uncertainties exist about future revenues and costs, top managers, shareholders, and others cannot easily identify and remedy budgets that have been manipulated. However, several methods are used to minimize budgetary slack. For example, independent sources such as consultants or market experts may prepare forecasts. These forecasts are compared to budgeted estimates so that employees providing budget information realize their estimates are being scrutinized. Also, bonuses can be given for accurate forecasts as well as for operating within the budget.

Incentives to manipulate budgets often increase in larger organizations where managers tend to focus only on the resources and performance of their own departments. As a result, they are less likely to consider the organization as a whole and to submit biased budget requests. These requests lead to misallocations of resources among competing departments or projects. To address this problem, some organizations give bonuses based on a combination of department results and overall organization profitability which reduces incentives to build in slack, while motivating managers to support each other by directing resources toward the best projects.

---

### GUIDE YOUR LEARNING  10.4  Key Terms

Stop to confirm that you understand the new terms introduced in the last several pages.

| | |
|---|---|
| Budget variance (p. 380) | Flexible budget (p. 381) |
| *Favorable variance (p. 380) | Participative budgeting (p. 383) |
| *Unfavorable variance (p. 380) | Zero-based budgeting (p. 384) |
| Static budget (p. 381) | Budgetary slack (p. 384) |

For each of these terms, write a definition in your own words. For starred terms, list at least one example that is different from the ones given in this textbook.

---

## ■ Budget Responsibility

CHAPTER REFERENCE

We will learn more about performance evaluation and manager responsibility in Chapter 15.

Budgets give managers authority over the use of an organization's resources. Accordingly, it seems reasonable to hold managers responsible for meeting budget benchmarks. However, when budget variances are used in performance evaluation, a number of challenges arise for managers being evaluated as well as managers conducting the evaluation. Exhibit 10.6 provides examples of these challenges. Notice that most of these problems relate to holding managers responsible for results when they lack control over factors that affect their variances.

---

[6]S. Deck, "Power of the Purse Strings," *Network World,* December 24–31, 2001, pp. 57–58.

**EXHIBIT 10.6**
Challenges in Appropriately
Assigning Decision Rights

| Challenges | Why They Arise | Specific Examples |
|---|---|---|
| Resentment | Department managers held responsible for costs over which they have no control | Allocated support department costs may be high because of poor management in support departments |
| Isolating the performance of individual managers | Interdependency among divisions and departments | Quality of customer services department affects ability of the sales department to meet future sales targets |
| Manager turnover | New manager is responsible for old manager's budget decisions | After the production manager is promoted to vice president, the new production manager faces unrealistic budget targets |
| Employee turnover | Employees are promoted, let go, or leave | Delays arise in hiring process or a hiring freeze occurs |
| Uncontrollable external factors | Unanticipated changes in volumes, costs, or prices | Oil price and availability changes because of broken pipelines |

## ■ Budget and Variance Adjustments

Because managers' budgets often include items not under their control, the following adjustments can be made when budgets are used to measure managers' performance.

- Use a flexible budget to determine expected revenues based on budgeted prices and actual volumes.
- Use a flexible budget to determine expected variable costs based on budgeted variable cost rates and actual volumes.
- Remove allocated costs that are not controllable by managers in the departments receiving allocations.
- Update costs for any anticipated price changes in direct materials, direct labor, and overhead-related resources.

An example of these adjustments follows.

### MOUNTAIN HIGH BIKES (PART 3)
### BUDGET ADJUSTMENTS FOR PERFORMANCE EVALUATION

Sanjay knows that the sales and production managers receive bonuses if their departmental performances exceed the budget. Before his planned meeting with the controller, Sanjay creates a performance schedule for each manager.

Sanjay reviews his flexible budget variance schedules (Exhibit 10.5). Because the sales department is responsible for the level of sales as well as prices, he decides that managers should be rewarded for the level of sales above the static budget, but any effects from sales discounts should also be included. Therefore, he prepares the following summary for the sales department.

### SALES VARIANCES

| | |
|---|---|
| Volume variance | |
| Budgeted sales | 100,000 bikes |
| Actual sales | 113,500 |
| Favorable variance | 13,500 bikes |
| | |
| Sales price variance | |
| Actual sales at budgeted prices | $90,800,000 |
| Actual sales at actual prices | 90,500,000 |
| Unfavorable variance | $ (300,000) |

*(continued)*

The production department sets manufacturing volumes according to information provided by the sales department. Therefore, the production department manager does not have control over production volumes. Sanjay decides that the flexible budget variances should reflect costs over which managers have control. The production manager is responsible for the fixed and variable costs in the manufacturing plant, so only those costs are included in his performance evaluation. Sanjay finds these details in the flexible budget he had earlier prepared and summarizes them for the controller. As he prepares the summary, he checks with the purchasing department to see if any price changes occurred this period. He finds that handlebars' price had increased by $10 per bike, but all other prices remained unchanged. He adds $1,135,000 to the adjusted flexible budget variable production costs to account for the additional $10 cost for each of the 113,500 bikes manufactured. The payroll department had no changes in budgeted labor rates. Sanjay also removed the support department costs because these were not under the production manager's control. Sanjay's summary is presented in Exhibit 10.7.

**EXHIBIT 10.7**
Adjusted Production Flexible Budget Variances at Mountain High Bikes

| | Flexible Budget, Adjusted for Price Changes | Actual | Variance | |
|---|---|---|---|---|
| Variable production costs | $30,049,125[a] | $29,492,408 | $ 556,717 | Favorable |
| Fixed production costs | 20,200,000 | 19,400,000 | 800,000 | Favorable |
| Total costs | $50,249,125 | $48,892,408 | | |
| Total variance | | | $1,356,717 | Favorable |

[a]Flexible budget at old price ($28,914,125) plus the effects of $10 price increase ($10 × 113,500 bikes), totaling $30,049,125.

### Evaluation of Department Manager Performance

Sanjay presents these variance summaries to the controller. He tells the controller that the sales manager probably should receive a bonus for an increased level of sales. However, some bikes were sold at a discount, and this fact needs to be investigated further because the discount resulted in $300,000 less in revenues than expected, given actual sales. Sanjay believes the production manager should receive a bonus for the total favorable production variance. In addition, he decides that the support department heads should meet to determine the reasons for the large unfavorable variance in their departments.

**CHAPTER REFERENCE**

In Chapter 11 we learn to calculate and analyze additional types of variances.

---

### GUIDE YOUR LEARNING  10.5  Mountain High Bikes (Part 3)

Mountain High Bikes (Part 3) illustrates the use of budget variances to evaluate department manager performance. For this illustration:

| Explore Information Relevance | Explore Incentives |
|---|---|
| Explain how the sales variance information relates to the performance of the sales manager. Explain how the adjusted production variance information relates to the performance of the production manager. | How are budget variances used to motivate department manager performance? Explain why the adjustments Sanjay made to the production department variances schedule could improve the production manager's incentives. |

## BEYOND TRADITIONAL BUDGETING

**Q6** What are other approaches to budgeting?

In addition to the more traditional methods, other approaches can be taken. Budgets are sometimes used for long- or short-term plans. As software systems have become increasingly complex, real-time information is more easily accessible and is used in updating budgets.

### ■ Long-Term Budgets

As illustrated in Exhibit 10.2, long-term strategies are an important consideration in the budget process. Therefore, budgets are often prepared for periods beyond one year. Frequently, organizations prepare budgets to forecast five or ten years into the future. Such budgets improve long-term planning and communication. They are also used to motivate performance consistent with long-term strategic goals. However, uncertainties increase when managers forecast further into future, making long-term budgets less reliable than short-term budgets. Accordingly, organizations often revise their long-term budgets each year.

## ■ Rolling Budgets

The business environment has become increasingly dynamic, requiring quick managerial response to change. A **rolling budget** is prepared monthly or quarterly and reflects planning changes going forward, often through the next 12 to 16 months. Many organizations use rolling budgets because they incorporate more current information than either static or flexible budgets. Rolling budgets reflect the most recent results and also incorporate significant changes in business strategy, operating plans, and the economy. For example, **General Bandwidth** manufactures equipment to provide voice services over broadband networks. As part of its rolling budget process, accountants compare actual monthly revenues and expenditures to their budgets. The results are circulated to managers within 8 days after the close of each month.[7] With current information at hand, the managers can quickly increase or decrease costs and inventory levels during economic upturns or downturns. In turn, production can probably be resumed or expanded quickly when the economy picks up.

**Cisco Systems** is a provider of hardware, software, and consulting services. It uses a budgeting system that combines traditional budgeting with a rolling budget that includes information from an Internet-based ordering system. The system provides real-time volume data to update forecasts. As a result, Cisco's managers can make quick changes in operations during downturns. Each year an annual plan is established based on a combination of top-down management guidance and bottom-up input from operational managers. This budget is then updated quarterly, and any changes are translated into budget targets for future periods.[9]

**CURRENT PRACTICE**

Enterprise resource planning (ERP) software includes integrated systems of financial, distribution, and production modules. These systems use actual operating data to create rolling budgets.[8]

## ■ Activity-Based Budgets

Traditional budget models are developed around a few cost drivers that are primarily output based. For example, in the Mountain High Bikes illustration, production costs were separated into direct materials, direct labor, and variable and fixed overhead. **Activity-based budgeting** uses activity cost pools and their related cost drivers to anticipate the costs for individual activities. A budget is developed for each activity in an organization's activity-based system.

Suppose that Mountain High Bikes used activity-based budgeting. Its key production cost drivers might then include frame assembly, wheel attachment, painting, accessory attachment, inspection, and packaging. In addition, activities would be developed for the support departments. For example, the marketing department might include personal customer contacts and Web site customer maintenance as well as other activities. The costs for each activity would be budgeted separately, as shown in Exhibit 10.8.

**CHAPTER REFERENCE**

ABC is presented in Chapter 7.

**EXHIBIT 10.8** ABC Budgeting for Marketing Department at Mountain High Bikes

| Activity | Budgeted Cost | Cost Driver | Budgeted Volume | Budgeted Cost per Unit of Cost Driver |
|---|---|---|---|---|
| **Customer-Related Costs:** | | | | |
| Personal customer contacts | $ 48,000 | Number of contacts | 2,400 contacts | $20 per customer contact |
| Web site customer maintenance | 30,000 | Web service hours | 2,000 hours | $15 per hour |
| Other activities | 9,808,929 | | | |
| Total marketing activities | $9,886,929 | | | |

---

[7]See Rick Whiting, "Number Crunch," *Information Week,* July 9, 2001, pp. 22–24.
[8]For more information about ERPs, see www.erp.ittoolbox.com.
[9]See Randy Myers, "Budgets on a Roll," *Journal of Accountancy,* December 2001, pp. 41–46.

**CHAPTER REFERENCE**

See Chapter 13 for more details about kaizen costing.

## ■ Kaizen Budgets

Kaizen costing is a system developed in Japan and used for products that tend to have decreasing prices or increasing quality across time, such as home entertainment centers, cell phones, and computers. **Kaizen budgets** set targeted cost reductions across time, anticipating market price reductions across the life of a product. In addition to cost reductions, quality improvements are also targeted. When kaizen budgeting is performed, cost reduction and quality improvement goals are explicitly embedded in the budgets. For example, Mountain High Bikes could budget for cost reductions of 15% for direct labor and 10% in assembly time to meet cost and production targets in anticipation of competitors' price decreases. In addition, the company could budget an increase in the quality of components. If the costs of quality improvements are less than the savings from reduced labor and cycle time, overall costs are reduced. Therefore, Mountain High Bike's kaizen budget would reduce the cost of each bike while improving quality.

## ■ Extreme Programming

Budgets are used for a variety of purposes beyond typical operating plans. For example, information technology (IT) projects are often managed using budgets developed with input from internal or external customers and from technical people who manage and perform the work. Communication is an important priority in these projects because customers often cannot fully articulate their needs. Furthermore, the scope of the project often faces technical limits or cost constraints. Traditionally, a relatively large amount of time and money is spent on up-front planning for IT projects to define the scope, specify the work to be performed, and establish the budget. IT personnel typically work in an isolated environment away from their customers. The resulting IT projects often fail to meet customer expectations and exceed budgeted costs. Accordingly, customers have become disillusioned and less willing to spend money on IT projects.

Recently, many organizations have moved away from traditional budgeting for IT projects. **Extreme programming** is a new type of IT project management in which customers and IT personnel communicate and collaborate actively throughout the life of a project. Little time is spent on up-front planning. Instead, the project proceeds in small steps, and decisions are made jointly as the work progresses. All parties share knowledge about the progress and design choices made, setting a tone of trust. Organizations benefit from accurate, up-to-date information through sources they believe to be reliable. In addition, IT project resources are used more efficiently because a larger proportion of time is spent on actual project development rather than on theoretical planning.

---

### GUIDE YOUR LEARNING 10.6 Key Terms

Stop to confirm that you understand the new terms introduced in the last several pages.

Rolling budget (p. 387)          Kaizen budgets (p. 388)
Activity-based budgeting (p. 387)     Extreme programming (p. 388)

For each of these terms, write a definition in your own words.

---

### FOCUS ON ETHICAL DECISION MAKING: Timely Reporting of Budget Problems

A dilemma that individuals face is whether to be truthful when it appears that a project is overbudget. Being overbudget typically means that actual costs exceed budgeted costs or that a planned time line will not be met. People often delay reporting an overbudget condition either because they believe they can catch up later or because they wish to delay negative repercussions. Unfortunately, information delays prevent managers from responding rapidly and decisively to delays in project timing and cost overruns, leading to additional dissatisfaction and inefficiencies.

Suppose a CPA firm establishes a budget of professional hours for a particular audit job. The hours are broken down by audit area, and one area is the valuation of inventory and cost of goods sold. During the last year, the audit client adopted new procedures for assigning product costs to individual units. The audit budget includes extra hours for the estimated time needed to document and assess the reasonableness of the new method. Many factors could cause this part of the audit to be overbudget. Consider the following two scenarios:

1. The client failed to establish appropriate records needed to easily audit the new method, and this part of the audit will require more than the budgeted time to complete.
2. The auditor assigned to this part of the audit is inexperienced and is unable to complete the work in the budgeted time.

Regardless of the reason for the overage, managers in charge of the audit need to be notified as soon as possible so that they can consider possible ways to realign staff and complete the total job on time. In addition, in the first scenario the audit firm might be able to bill the client for the extra work involved if the audit contract includes a provision for such price adjustments. However, this scenario would most likely require the client to be notified promptly, while the work is still being performed. In the second scenario, the overage may result in a poor performance evaluation, especially if the auditor has similar problems in other audit areas. Yet the overage may be considered reasonable in light of the auditor's inexperience. Even so, the auditor should be able to accomplish the following:[10]

- Develop alternative estimates of time and resource requirements for a project
- Effectively facilitate and control the project process and take corrective action as needed

Therefore, the auditor must quickly recognize an impending overage and formulate appropriate strategies for completing the task as efficiently as possible. The auditor also needs to keep her supervisor apprised of the situation and seek help, when needed.

### Practice Ethical Decision Making

In Chapter 1, we learned about a process for making ethical decisions (Exhibit 1.11). You can address the following questions for this ethical dilemma to improve your skills for making ethical decisions. First, *think about situations in which you worked with other people on a project*. Then think about your answers and discuss them with others.

| Ethical Decision-Making Process | Questions to Consider about This Ethical Dilemma |
|---|---|
| Identify ethical problems as they arise. | Have you ever failed to meet a deadline on a group project? If so, what were the reasons for the delay? When and how did you report the delay to your team members? Has someone else ever failed to meet a deadline? Does a failure to meet an agreed-upon deadline create an ethical problem? Why or why not? |
| Objectively consider the well-being of others and society when exploring alternatives. | Explore the responsibilities, expectations, assumptions, incentives, and consequences for this problem from different perspectives, including: <br> • The team member who is late <br> • Other team members <br> • The team's client |
| Clarify and apply ethical values when choosing a course of action. | Draft a policy statement that you could adopt with future team members to handle project delays. How might this policy lead to improved team performance? |
| Work toward ongoing improvement of personal and organizational ethics. | Think about your future career. How can you work toward developing your professional responsibility as a member of a work team? |

---

[10]These elements of Project Management (a personal competency) are defined in the AICPA Core Competency Framework (see eca.aicpaservices.org/).

## APPENDIX 10A

**Q7** How is the cash budget developed?

## Developing a Cash Budget

This appendix explains the preparation and use of a cash budget. The cash budget reflects the effects of management's plans on cash and summarizes information that accountants gather about the expected amounts and timing of cash receipts and disbursements. Cash budgets may be prepared quarterly, monthly, weekly, or even daily to help management plan the organization's short-term borrowing or investing.

### ■ Operating Cash Receipts and Disbursements

Operating cash receipts are estimated from budgeted revenues, taking into account the nature of customer transactions. For example, if sales are made on account, then forecasts must be made for bad debts and for the timing of customer payments. Mountain High Bikes (Part 4) includes a simple timing difference for accounts receivables. Several homework problems at the end of this chapter feature more variation in the timing of receivables and discounts and the effects of bad debts on the cash budget.

Operating cash disbursements are estimated from the budgets for direct materials, direct labor, manufacturing overhead, and support departments. The timing of cash disbursements for these items depends on the payment terms with employees and vendors. For example, the organization might pay employees on the fifteenth and last day of each month. Payments to vendors might be made in the month after the purchase of goods or services. Some expenses, such as depreciation, do not require a cash payment.

### ■ Other Planned Cash Flows

In addition to operating cash flows, organizations have many other types of cash flows, including the following:

- Purchasing or selling property, plant, and equipment
- Borrowing or repaying long-term debt
- Paying interest on debt[11]
- Issuing or redeeming capital stock
- Paying dividends to shareholders

Although the purchase or sale of property, plant, and equipment is planned in the capital budget, the cash effects of borrowing and repaying are reflected in annual cash budgets. Similarly, cash flows related to long-term debt and capital stock are planned in the long-term financing budget, but the changes in annual cash flows need to be reflected in the cash budget.

### ■ Short-Term Borrowing or Investing

Managers typically use short-term loans or investments to balance the cash budget, taking into account the desired cash balance. Short-term loans may be prearranged as a line of credit with a financial institution; the organization can borrow up to a specified amount as needed to cover cash shortages. Organizations often use excess cash to repay short-term debt, with any remainder placed in liquid investments.

The purpose of the cash budget is to ensure adequate levels of cash for day-to-day operations. If an organization lacks the necessary cash to fund its operations at any given moment, then it is insolvent. Successful new, fast-growing companies, especially franchise companies or companies growing by acquisition, sometimes fail because their assets are not liquid and they cannot pay their employees. At the same time, companies such as **United Airlines** are able to continue operating, even when they are legally bankrupt and are incurring losses, because their assets are liquid, they are able to sell nonliquid assets for the cash, or they are able to obtain the additional financing needed to stay in business while they restructure.[12]

---

[11]Financial accounting standards require interest expense to be classified under operations on the statement of cash flows. However, interest expense arises from financing rather than operating decisions.

[12]See, for example, H. Dicus, "United Airlines Lines up Exit Financing," *Pacific Business News*, December 17, 2003, available at www.bizjournals.com/pacific/stories/2003/12/15/daily35.html.

To prepare a cash budget, three types of cash transactions are planned:

1. Cash receipts
2. Cash disbursements
3. Short-term borrowings or investments

The following Mountain High Bikes illustration demonstrates the preparation of a cash budget.

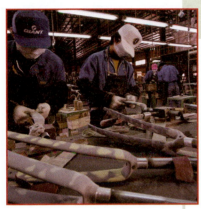

## MOUNTAIN HIGH BIKES (PART 4)
### DEVELOPING A CASH BUDGET

The managers tell Sanjay that they plan to invest $8 million in new equipment during the second quarter. This expenditure means that the company may not have enough cash and short-term investments to cover operating cash requirements. Sanjay decides to prepare a quarterly cash budget to estimate the company's borrowing needs.

### Cash Receipts

To develop the cash receipts portion of the budget, Sanjay creates a quarterly schedule showing the timing of cash receipts expected from customers during the year. Because the company sells merchandise to its customers on account, he needs to forecast the time it will take customers to pay their accounts. He analyzes prior accounting records to estimate the sales and collection patterns. He then asks the marketing and credit managers whether they anticipate any changes in sales or collection patterns.

Sanjay learns that about half of the company's $80 million sales occur in the fourth quarter because of holiday sales. Sales are fairly even throughout the other three quarters. Given this information, Sanjay forecasts sales revenues as follows:

| | |
|---|---:|
| First quarter (50% × $80,000,000 ÷ 3 quarters) | $13,333,333 |
| Second quarter | 13,333,333 |
| Third quarter | 13,333,334 |
| Fourth quarter (50% × $80,000,000) | 40,000,000 |
| Total budgeted revenue | $80,000,000 |

Customers usually pay in 30 days and sales are uniform within each quarter, so Sanjay forecasts that two-thirds of each quarter's sales will be received in cash during the quarter and one-third in the next quarter. Therefore, first quarter receipts will include collection of accounts receivable from the prior year. Fourth quarter revenues from the prior year were expected to be $30 million, so first quarter receipts should include $10 million (1/3 × $30,000,000). Mountain High sells to the same bicycle dealers every year and has eliminated those who do not pay on time. Therefore, bad debts are usually immaterial; he assumes that all accounts receivable will be collected. The managers do not anticipate any other receipts, such as new long-term borrowings, during the year. Sanjay's forecast of cash receipts is presented in Exhibit 10A.1. The total estimated amount received from customers ($76,666,667) is less than the budgeted amount of revenues ($80,000,000) because accounts receivable at the end of the year ($40,000,000 − $26,666,667 = $13,333,333) are greater than accounts receivable at the beginning of the year ($10,000,000).

*(continued)*

**EXHIBIT 10A.1** Cash Receipts from Customers at Mountain High Bikes

| | Quarter | | | | |
|---|---|---|---|---|---|
| | First | Second | Third | Fourth | Total |
| Beginning accounts receivable | $10,000,000 | | | | $10,000,000 |
| First quarter sales | 8,888,889 | $ 4,444,444 | | | 13,333,333 |
| Second quarter sales | | 8,888,889 | $ 4,444,444 | | 13,333,333 |
| Third quarter sales | | | 8,888,889 | $ 4,444,445 | 13,333,334 |
| Fourth quarter sales | | | | 26,666,667 | 26,666,667 |
| Total receipts | $18,888,889 | $13,333,333 | $13,333,333 | $31,111,112 | $76,666,667 |

## Cash Disbursements

Next, Sanjay analyzes prior accounting records and supplier contracts to identify the normal timing of cash payments to vendors, employees, and others. He also asks the production and other department managers whether they anticipate any changes in purchasing or payment patterns.

Sanjay forecasts that half of the production will take place during the fourth quarter, to match the pattern of sales. Therefore, half of the direct material purchases will occur during the fourth quarter, with the other half occurring during the first three quarters. Assuming that production is uniform across the first three quarters, Sanjay forecasts purchases as follows:

| | |
|---|---:|
| First quarter (50% × $14,175,000 ÷ 3 quarters) | $ 2,362,500 |
| Second quarter | 2,362,500 |
| Third quarter | 2,362,500 |
| Fourth quarter (50% × $14,175,000) | 7,087,500 |
| Total budgeted purchases | $14,175,000 |

Payments for direct materials are made a month after purchase. As a result, two-thirds of the purchases are paid during each quarter and one-third is paid during the following quarter. Fourth-quarter purchases for the prior year were expected to be $6 million, so payments for these purchases of $2 million (1/3 × $6,000,000) are expected in the first quarter. He uses this information to prepare the quarterly schedule for direct material disbursements in Exhibit 10A.2. The total amount paid ($13,812,500) is less than the budgeted amount of direct material purchases ($14,175,000) because accounts payable at the end of the year ($7,087,500 − $4,725,000 = $2,362,500) are greater than accounts payable at the beginning of the year ($2,000,000).

**EXHIBIT 10A.2** Disbursements for Direct Materials Purchases at Mountain High Bikes

| | Quarter | | | | |
|---|---|---|---|---|---|
| | First | Second | Third | Fourth | Total |
| Beginning accounts payable | $2,000,000 | | | | $ 2,000,000 |
| First quarter purchases | 1,575,000 | $ 787,500 | | | 2,362,500 |
| Second quarter purchases | | 1,575,000 | $ 787,500 | | 2,362,500 |
| Third quarter purchases | | | 1,575,000 | $ 787,500 | 2,362,500 |
| Fourth quarter purchases | | | | 4,725,000 | 4,725,000 |
| Total disbursements | $3,575,000 | $2,362,500 | $2,362,500 | $5,512,500 | $13,812,500 |

Sanjay forecasts that the remaining variable costs are incurred in the same pattern as direct material purchases—half over the first three quarters and half during the fourth quarter. He learns that property taxes are due in the second and fourth quarters and insurance payments are due in the first and third quarters. He also knows that depreciation will not be paid because it is a noncash expense, so he removes it from the list of expenses. Sanjay forecasts that the remaining fixed costs are incurred uniformly across the four quarters. He assumes that all costs other than direct material purchases are paid in the quarter in which they are incurred. In addition, he learns from management that the company will spend $8 million on new equipment during the second quarter. Given these forecasts and assumptions, Sanjay completes the cash disbursements section of the cash budget in Exhibit 10A.3.

## Short-Term Investments and Borrowings

Sanjay expects cash and short-term investments at the beginning of the period to total $9 million. The managers wish to maintain a minimum cash balance of $200,000. Any cash deficiencies are financed with the company's line of credit and require quarterly interest payments at an annual rate of 6%. The company's policy is to budget zero earnings on short-term investments.

Sanjay uses this information to complete the short-term financing portion of the cash budget. He realizes that the company will need to liquidate its short-term investments during the second quarter. It will also have to borrow $1,336,742 in the second quarter and an additional $3,360,951 in the third quarter. These short-term borrowings, totaling $4,697,693, can then be repaid during the fourth quarter when sales increase. Total interest costs on the line of credit are estimated to be $90,516. A summary of the short-term financing budget is shown in Exhibit 10A.4.

**EXHIBIT 10A.3** Summary of Cash Receipts and Disbursements for Mountain High Bikes

| | Quarter | | | | |
| --- | --- | --- | --- | --- | --- |
| | First | Second | Third | Fourth | Total |
| **Cash receipts:** | | | | | |
| Revenues (Exhibit 10A.1) | $18,888,889 | $ 13,333,333 | $13,333,333 | $31,111,112 | $76,666,667 |
| **Cash disbursements:** | | | | | |
| Direct materials purchases (Exhibit 10A.2) | 3,575,000 | 2,362,500 | 2,362,500 | 5,512,500 | 13,812,500 |
| Direct labor costs | 669,125 | 669,125 | 669,125 | 2,007,375 | 4,014,750 |
| Variable overhead costs: | | | | | |
|   Supplies | 336,666 | 336,667 | 336,667 | 1,010,000 | 2,020,000 |
|   Indirect labor | 631,250 | 631,250 | 631,250 | 1,893,750 | 3,787,500 |
|   Maintenance | 168,333 | 168,333 | 168,334 | 505,000 | 1,010,000 |
|   Miscellaneous | 126,250 | 126,250 | 126,250 | 378,750 | 757,500 |
| Fixed overhead costs: | | | | | |
|   Property taxes | | 505,000 | | 505,000 | 1,010,000 |
|   Insurance | 707,000 | | 707,000 | | 1,414,000 |
|   Plant supervision | 1,262,500 | 1,262,500 | 1,262,500 | 1,262,500 | 5,050,000 |
|   Fringe benefits | 1,767,500 | 1,767,500 | 1,767,500 | 1,767,500 | 7,070,000 |
|   Miscellaneous | 404,000 | 404,000 | 404,000 | 404,000 | 1,616,000 |
| Support department costs | 8,239,107 | 8,239,108 | 8,239,107 | 8,239,108 | 32,956,430 |
| Purchase of equipment | | 8,000,000 | | | 8,000,000 |
|     Total disbursements | 17,886,731 | 24,472,233 | 16,674,233 | 23,485,483 | 82,518,680 |
|     Excess receipts (disbursements) | $ 1,002,158 | $(11,138,900) | $ (3,340,900) | $ 7,625,629 | $ (5,852,013) |

**EXHIBIT 10A.4** Short-Term Financing Budget for Mountain High Bikes

| | Quarter | | | |
| --- | --- | --- | --- | --- |
| | First | Second | Third | Fourth |
| Beginning balance, cash and short-term investments | $ 9,000,000 | $ 10,002,158 | $ 200,000 | $ 200,000 |
| Excess receipts (disbursements) | 1,002,158 | (11,138,900) | (3,340,900) | 7,625,629 |
| Line of credit: | | | | |
|   Borrowings | | 1,336,742 | 3,360,951 | |
|   Interest on borrowings[a] | | | (20,051) | (70,465) |
|   Repayments | | | | (4,697,693) |
| Ending balance, cash and short-term investments | $10,002,158 | $ 200,000 | $ 200,000 | $ 3,057,471 |

[a]Interest is paid quarterly and is computed at an annual rate of 6%, assuming that borrowings and repayments take place at the end of each quarter.

---

**GUIDE YOUR LEARNING 10.7 Mountain High Bikes (Part 4)**

Mountain High Bikes (Part 4) illustrates developing a cash budget. For this illustration:

| Identify Information Used | Identify Information Created | Describe Use |
| --- | --- | --- |
| List the information that is used as inputs for creating the various parts of a cash budget. How and where would the information be obtained? | Explain the purpose for each of the individual cash budgets for Mountain High Bikes. | In your own words, explain how the managers of Mountain High Bikes might use the cash budget. |

# SUMMARY

**Q1** **What Are the Relationships Among Budgets, Long-Term Strategies, and Short-Term Operating Plans?**

**Budget Objectives**
See Exhibit 10.1.

**Budget Cycle**

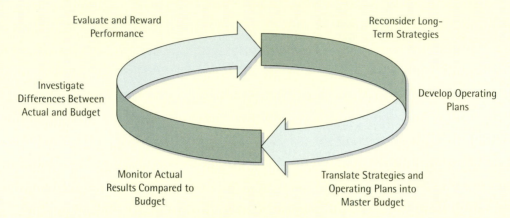

**Q2** **What Is a Master Budget, and How Is It Prepared?**

**Master Budget Overview**

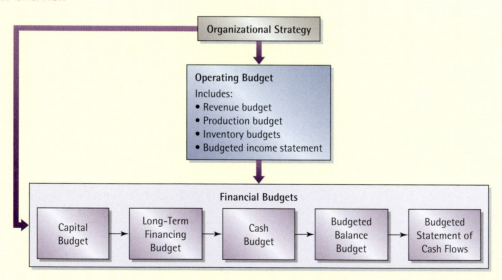

## Production and Inventory Budgets

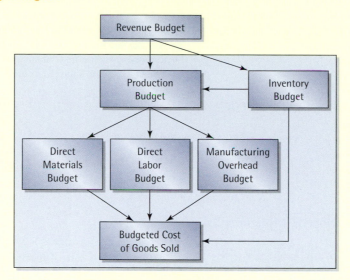

## Budgeted Income Statement

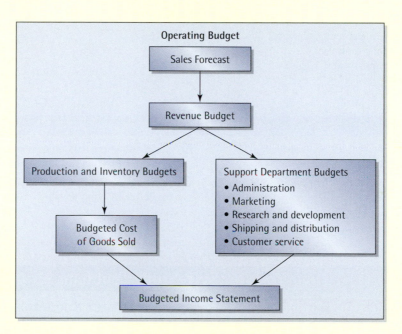

## Q3 What Are Budget Variances, and How Are They Calculated?

### Budget Variances
- Differences between budgeted and actual results
- May be favorable or unfavorable

### Major Reasons for Variances
- Actual activities do not follow plans
- Budget may be an inappropriate benchmark (i.e., budget assumptions may be incorrect)

## Q4 What Are the Differences Between Static and Flexible Budgets?

### Static Budget Variances
- Variances based on the budget for a specific volume of production or services
- Variable cost variances may be misleading
- Useful for measuring performance of individuals/departments responsible for achieving budgeted volume of activity

### Flexible Budget Variances
- Variances based on the budget adjusted for actual sales or production volume
- Variable costs are adjusted for actual volume of activity
- Useful for measuring performance of individuals/departments *not* responsible for achieving budgeted volume of activity

### Q5 How Are Budgets Used to Monitor and Motivate Performance?

- As benchmarks
- To reward performance

**Budget Adjustments for Performance Evaluation**
- Use flexible budget to adjust for actual volumes
- Remove costs not under managers' control
- Update costs for anticipated price changes

### Q6 What Are Other Approaches to Budgeting?

**Long-Term Budgets**

**Rolling Budgets**

**Activity-Based Budgets**

**Kaizen Budgets**

**Extreme Programming**

### Q7 How Is Cash Budget Developed? (Appendix 10A)

**Operating Cash Receipts and Disbursements**
- Forecast timing of cash receipts from customers
- Forecast timing of cash payments for direct materials, direct labor, variable and fixed overhead, and support department costs

**Other Planned Cash Flows**
- Purchase or sale of property, plant, and equipment
- Proceeds or repayments of long-term debt
- Proceeds or redemption of capital stock
- Dividends to shareholders

**Balancing the Cash Budget**
- Desired cash balance
- Purchase or liquidation of short-term investments
- Proceeds or repayments of short-term debt
- Interest on short-term debt

---

## KEY TO SYMBOLS

**e** This question requires students to extend knowledge beyond the applications shown in the textbook.

**1** This question requires Step 1 skills (**Identifying**) in Steps for Better Thinking (Exhibit 1.10).

**2** This question requires Step 2 skills (**Exploring**) in Steps for Better Thinking (Exhibit 1.10).

**3** This question requires Step 3 skills (**Prioritizing**) in Steps for Better Thinking (Exhibit 1.10).

**4** This question requires Step 4 skills (**Envisioning**) in Steps for Better Thinking (Exhibit 1.10).

---

## Self-Study Problems

### Self-Study Problem 1 Constructing a Master Budget

**Q2** Summer Select Patio Furniture is a manufacturer of patio furniture. The patio table department produces table sets. Each table set consists of four chairs, a table, and an umbrella. The accountant at Summer Select gathered the following information from all of the departments in the organization so that she can prepare next year's budget. No change occurred in costs from last period to this period. Support department costs are allocated between two separate production departments. Following is information about costs for the patio table department.

| MANUFACTURING COSTS | | |
|---|---|---|
| Direct materials | Chairs | $75 |
| | Table | $42 |
| | Umbrella | $20 |
| Direct labor | | |
| Hours | Assembly | 2 |
| | Packing | 0.2 |
| Cost per hour | Assembly | $20.00 |
| | Packing | $10.00 |
| Cost per unit | Assembly | $40.00 |
| | Packing | $2.00 |

## INVENTORIES

| | Beginning | Target Ending |
|---|---|---|
| Direct Materials | | |
| Chairs | $15,000 | $20,000 |
| Tables | $10,000 | $12,000 |
| Umbrellas | $5,000 | $7,000 |
| Finished goods | 1,000 units at $304 per unit | 1,200 units |

## REVENUE ASSUMPTIONS

| | |
|---|---|
| Selling price | $500 |
| Table sets sold | 50,000 |

## ESTIMATED VARIABLE MANUFACTURING OVERHEAD COSTS

| | |
|---|---|
| Supplies | $ 422,000 |
| Indirect labor | 627,500 |
| Maintenance | 80,000 |
| Miscellaneous | 125,500 |
| Total | $1,255,000 |

## ESTIMATED FIXED MANUFACTURING OVERHEAD COSTS

| | |
|---|---|
| Depreciation | $1,004,000 |
| Property taxes | 251,000 |
| Insurance | 351,400 |
| Plant supervision | 1,255,000 |
| Fringe benefits | 1,757,000 |
| Miscellaneous | 401,600 |
| Total | $5,020,000 |

## ESTIMATED SUPPORT DEPARTMENT COSTS

| Department | Fixed Costs |
|---|---|
| Administration | $4,819,200 |
| Marketing | 2,891,520 |
| Distribution | 1,445,760 |
| Customer service | 481,920 |
| Total | $9,638,400 |

**REQUIRED:** Prepare the following budgets: revenue, production, direct materials, direct manufacturing labor, manufacturing overhead, ending inventory, cost of goods sold, and support department. Then prepare a budgeted income statement, assuming an income tax rate of 35%.

## Solution to Self-Study Problem 1

### Revenue Budget

The revenue budget calculates forecasted revenues, given forecasted sales volume and price.

| | Selling Price | Units Sold | Total Revenues |
|---|---|---|---|
| Table sets | $500 | 50,000 | $25,000,000 |

### Production Budget (Units)

The production budget calculates the number of units that need to be produced, given current and targeted ending inventory levels and budgeted sales.

| | Table Sets |
|---|---|
| Sales | 50,000 |
| Target ending inventory | 1,200 |
| Total finished units needed | 51,200 |
| Less beginning inventory | 1,000 |
| Production | 50,200 |

### Direct Materials Budget

The direct materials budget calculates the budget for purchases of raw materials, given the beginning and targeted ending inventory levels and budgeted production volume.

| | |
|---|---:|
| Budgeted usage: | |
| Chairs (50,200 sets × $75 per set) | $3,765,000 |
| Tables (50,200 sets × $42 per set) | 2,108,400 |
| Umbrellas (50,200 sets × $20 per set) | 1,004,000 |
| Total direct materials used | 6,877,400 |
| Add target ending inventory | 39,000 |
| Deduct beginning inventory | (30,000) |
| Total purchases | $6,886,400 |

### Direct Manufacturing Labor Budget

The direct manufacturing labor budget calculates the amount of direct labor hours needed for budgeted production and then determines the cost.

| | |
|---|---:|
| Labor hours budget: | |
| Assembly (50,200 sets × 2 hours) | 100,400 |
| Packing (50,200 sets × 0.2 hours) | 10,040 |
| Total labor hours | 110,440 |
| Labor cost budget: | |
| Assembly (100,400 hours × $20 per hour) | $2,008,000 |
| Packing (10,040 hours × $10 per hour) | 100,400 |
| Total labor cost | $2,108,400 |

### Manufacturing Overhead Budget

The manufacturing overhead budget summarizes the expected fixed and variable overhead costs.

| | |
|---|---:|
| Variable manufacturing overhead costs: | |
| Supplies | $ 422,000 |
| Indirect labor | 627,500 |
| Maintenance | 80,000 |
| Miscellaneous | 125,500 |
| Total variable overhead | 1,255,000 |
| | |
| Fixed manufacturing overhead costs | |
| Depreciation | 1,004,000 |
| Property taxes | 251,000 |
| Insurance | 351,400 |
| Plant supervision | 1,255,000 |
| Fringe benefits | 1,757,000 |
| Miscellaneous | 401,600 |
| Total fixed overhead | 5,020,000 |
| Total overhead | $6,275,000 |

| | | Cost per Set |
|---|---|---:|
| Manufacturing overhead allocation rates | | |
| Variable | ($1,255,000 ÷ 50,200 sets) | $ 25 |
| Fixed | ($5,020,000 ÷ 50,200 sets) | $100 |

### Ending Inventories Budget

The ending inventories budget determines the unit costs and then forecasts the cost of ending inventory units.

| | Cost per Unit |
|---|---:|
| Unit costs (cost per table set): | |
| Direct materials: | |
| Chairs | $ 75.00 |
| Table | 42.00 |
| Umbrella | 20.00 |
| Total direct material | 137.00 |

*(continued)*

|  | Direct labor: | | |
|---|---|---|---|
|  | Assembly | | 40.00 |
|  | Packaging | | 2.00 |
|  | Total direct labor | | 42.00 |
|  | Overhead: | | |
|  | Variable | | 25.00 |
|  | Fixed | | 100.00 |
|  | Total overhead | | 125.00 |
|  | Total unit cost | | $304.00 |

## Cost of Goods Sold Budget

The cost of goods sold budget calculates the cost of inventory available for sale during the period and the cost of goods sold.

|  | | |
|---|---|---|
| Beginning finished goods (1,000 sets × $304 per set) | | $ 304,000 |
| Cost of goods manufactured: | | |
| Direct materials | $6,877,400 | |
| Direct labor | 2,108,400 | |
| Manufacturing overhead | 6,275,000 | |
| Total cost of goods manufactured | | 15,260,800 |
| Total goods available for sale | | 15,564,800 |
| Less ending finished goods (1,200 sets × $304 per set) | | (364,800) |
| Cost of goods sold | | $15,200,000 |

## Support Department Costs Budget

The support department costs budget forecasts the total nonmanufacturing-related costs for the period.

| Department | Fixed Costs |
|---|---|
| Administration | $4,819,200 |
| Marketing | 2,891,520 |
| Distribution | 1,445,760 |
| Customer service | 481,920 |
| Total | $9,638,400 |

## Budgeted Income Statement

Once all of the budget schedules have been prepared, the budgeted income statement is created. Revenue is drawn from the revenue budget, and COGS from the cost of goods sold budget. Then the operating costs from the support department costs budget are subtracted to determine operating income.

|  | | |
|---|---|---|
| Revenues | | $25,000,000 |
| Cost of goods sold | | 15,200,000 |
| Gross margin | | 9,800,000 |
| Operating costs: | | |
| Administration | $4,819,200 | |
| Marketing | 2,891,520 | |
| Distribution | 1,445,760 | |
| Customer service | 481,920 | 9,638,400 |
| Operating income | | 161,600 |
| Income tax expense ($161,600 × 35%) | | 56,560 |
| Net income | | $ 105,040 |

## Self-Study Problem 2 Comparing Actual Results to a Flexible Budget

Q3, Q4

Suppose that the manager of Summer Select Patio Furniture is evaluated based on budgeted expectations. She is responsible for both sales and production costs. This period the company produced and sold more units than budgeted, and she expects to get a bonus. Refer to Self-Study Problem 1 for Summer Select Patio Furniture's static budget. The company's actual results for the period were as follows:

| | |
|---|---|
| Sales volume | 54,000 table sets |
| Sales revenue | $25,500,000 |
| Variable production costs | 10,980,000 |
| Fixed production costs | 5,000,000 |
| Fixed support department costs | 9,415,300 |

**REQUIRED:**

A. Prepare a flexible budget based on actual sales volumes, and then calculate the flexible budget revenue and cost variances.

❷ B. Review the variances from part (A). For each variance, briefly describe the types of operating or budgeting problems that might have caused these variances.

❷ C. Compose at least three questions the accountant could ask the manager to better understand how the largest variances arose.

### Solution to Self-Study Problem 2

A. To create a flexible budget for evaluating the department manager's performance, we modify the static budget to reflect the actual volume of sales, and remove any costs not under the manager's control. It requires a recalculation of budgeted variable costs to reflect actual volume. Because fixed costs remain fixed within a relevant range, we assume that they will not change with the changes in volume. However, we remove the support department costs because they are allocated and not under control of the manager.

| | Static Budget | Flexible Budget | Actual | Variance<br>F = Favorable<br>U = Unfavorable |
|---|---|---|---|---|
| Sales volume | 50,000 | 54,000 | 54,000 | |
| Revenue | $25,000,000 | $ 27,000,000[a] | $25,500,000 | $1,500,000 U |
| Variable production costs | 10,200,000[b] | 11,016,000[c] | 10,980,000 | 36,000 F |
| Fixed production costs | 5,020,000[d] | 5,020,000 | 5,000,000 | 20,000 F |
| Fixed support costs | 9,638,400 | Not applicable | Not applicable | Not applicable |
| Forecasted operating income | $    141,600 | $ 10,964,000 | $ 9,520,000 | $1,444,000 U |

[a]54,000 × $500
[b]50,000 × ($137 + $42 + $25)
[c]54,000 × ($137 + $42 + $25)
[d]Total budgeted fixed costs

B. Following are possible explanations for each of the variances, you may have thought of others:

- The revenue variance is the biggest problem for Summer Select. Instead of selling the furniture for $500 a set, the average revenue was $472.22 ($25,500,000 ÷ 54,000). It is possible that weather or economic factors reduced demand, and so the furniture was discounted during the season. It is also possible that sales volumes were better than expected because of the discounted price. The volume is larger than budgeted, but with the reduced selling price, a large unfavorable revenue variance occurred.

- Variable production costs might be lower than the flexible budget because prices for direct materials, direct labor, or variable overhead costs were lower than budget. Or, the use of materials or labor might have been more efficient than in the budget. For example, less scrap might have occurred or employees might have been more productive than anticipated. Other types of variable production costs might also have been lower than budget. For example, machinery might have required fewer repairs than expected. Also economies of scale may have been introduced, such as fewer setup costs because production runs were longer, or direct materials costs may have been lower because of volume discounts. However, the favorable variance could possibly signal a reduction in quality, which could create a problem with future sales.

- Fixed production costs were slightly less than expected. The $20,000 variance is a small percentage of the budgeted fixed production costs, so it might be a random variation in cost.

- Fixed support costs might have been lower than the budget for many different reasons: unexpected decreases in the costs of fixed items such as computer software, better purchase prices for office supplies, or outsourcing of services.

It is important to keep in mind that the variances in part (A) are net amounts. Most likely, each cost category includes some favorable and some unfavorable variances. A relatively small net variance could consist of two or more large offsetting items.

C. The following list contains possible questions; you may think of others.
1. Why were prices discounted, and will the new price carry over to next period?
2. Is the favorable variance in variable production costs due to changes in the quality of materials? How did the savings arise?
3. Were any fixed production costs either much larger or much smaller than expected?

---

**REVIEW** Use the exercises in the following boxes in the chapter to review key terms and key techniques, analyze chapter illustrations, improve your learning of new concepts, and practice ethical decision making:

## QUESTIONS

**10.1** Explain how the following budgets relate to each other: the revenue budget, the production budget, and the direct materials budget.

**10.2** How can budgeting assist an organization to efficiently use its human resources?

**10.3** What are the objectives of participative budgeting?

**10.4** What distinguishes zero-based budgeting from other types of budgeting?

**10.5** How are the master budget and flexible budget related?

**10.6** What methods do organizations use to minimize budgetary slack?

**10.7** What adjustments should be made to static budgets before they are used for management performance evaluation?

**10.8** What are some of the challenges that organizations face when allocating budget authority and responsibility?

**10.9** (Appendix 10A) Snow Blowers produces and sells snowblowers. Production levels are high in the summer and beginning of fall and then taper off through the winter. Sales are high in the fall and early winter and then taper off in the spring. Explain why preparing a cash budget might be particularly important for Snow Blowers.

**10.10** Describe the types of information that managers use to develop budgets.

**10.11** Discuss the similarities and differences between annual budgets and rolling budgets.

**10.12** How are budgets related to organizational strategies?

## EXERCISES

**10.13** **Production, direct materials, and direct labor budgets** Seer Manufacturing has projected sales
**Q2** of its product for the next six months as follows:

| January | 40 units |
| February | 90 units |
| March | 100 units |
| April | 80 units |
| May | 30 units |
| June | 70 units |

The product sells for $100, variable expenses are $70 per unit, and fixed expenses are $1,500 per month. The finished product requires 3 units of raw material and 10 hours of direct labor. The company tries to maintain an ending inventory of finished goods equal to the next two months of sales and an ending inventory of raw materials equal to half of the current month's usage.

**REQUIRED:**
**A.** Prepare a production budget for February, March, and April.
**B.** Prepare a forecast of the units of direct materials required for February, March, and April.
**C.** Prepare a direct labor hours budget for February, March, and April.

**10.14**
**Q2, Q5**
**CMA**
**Production, labor, materials, and sales budgets** Bullen & Company makes and sells high-quality glare filters for microcomputer monitors. John Crane, controller, is responsible for preparing Bullen's master budget and has assembled the data below for 20X5.

The direct labor rate includes wages and all employee-related benefits and the employer's share of FICA. Labor saving machinery will be fully operational by March. Also, as of March 1, the company's union contract calls for an increase in direct labor wages that is included in the direct labor rate.

Bullen expects to have 10,000 glare filters in inventory at December 31, 20X4, and has a policy of carrying 50 percent of the following month's projected sales in inventory.

|  | 20X5 | | | |
| --- | --- | --- | --- | --- |
|  | January | February | March | April |
| Estimated unit sales | 20,000 | 24,000 | 16,000 | 18,000 |
| Sales price per unit | $80 | $80 | $75 | $75 |
| Direct labor hours per unit | 4.0 | 4.0 | 3.5 | 3.5 |
| Direct labor hourly rate | $15 | $15 | $16 | $16 |
| Direct materials cost per unit | $10 | $10 | $10 | $10 |

**REQUIRED:**
**A.** Prepare the following budgets for Bullen & Company for the first quarter of 20X5. Be sure to show supporting calculations: (1) production budget in units, (2) direct labor budget in hours, (3) direct materials budget, and (4) sales budget.
**e B.** Calculate the total budgeted contribution margin for Bullen & Company for the first quarter of 20X5. Be sure to show supporting calculations.
**2 C.** Discuss at least three behavorial considerations in the profit-planning and budgeting process.

**10.15**
**Q2, Q3, Q4**
**Flexible budget variances, profit effect of market share decline** Here are data for the Stove Division of Appliances Now, which produces and sells a complete line of kitchen stoves.

| (In thousands) | Budget | Actual |
| --- | --- | --- |
| Revenue | $16,491 | $17,480 |
| Variable production costs | 5,892 | 6,451 |
| Fixed manufacturing costs | 1,977 | 2,032 |
| Variable selling expenses | 456 | 550 |
| Fixed selling expenses | 1,275 | 1,268 |
| Administrative expenses | 4,773 | 5,550 |
| Operating income | $ 2,118 | $ 1,629 |

The budget, set at the beginning of the year, was based upon estimates of sales and costs. Administrative expenses include charges by corporate headquarters for providing strategic guidance. These fixed costs are allocated to divisions using revenues as the allocation base.

**REQUIRED:**
**e A.** Assume that a different volume of stoves was sold than was budgeted and prepare a flexible budget using the change in revenue to adjust the variable costs. Calculate budget variances.
**e B.** Due to a booming economy, the division's unit sales were higher than anticipated, even though the division's share of the home refrigerator market fell from 22% to 20% during the year. Using information from the flexible budget, estimate the impact on profits of the decline in market share. (*Hint:* First estimate what the total sales should have been.)

**10.16**
**Q2, Q7**
**CPA**
**Purchase, cost of goods sold, and cash collection budgets (Appendix 10A)** The Zel Company operates at local flea markets. It has budgeted the following sales for the indicated months.

|  | June | July | August |
|---|---|---|---|
| Sales on account | $1,500,000 | $1,600,000 | $1,700,000 |
| Cash sales | 200,000 | 210,000 | 220,000 |
| Total sales | $1,700,000 | $1,810,000 | $1,920,000 |

Zel's success in this specialty market is due in large part to the extension of credit terms and the budgeting techniques implemented by the firm's owner, Barbara Zel. Ms. Zel is a recycler; that is, she collects her merchandise daily at neighborhood garage sales and sells the merchandise weekly at regional flea markets. All merchandise is marked up to sell at its invoice cost (as purchased at garage sales) plus 25%. Stated differently, cost is 80% of selling price. Merchandise inventories at the beginning of each month are 30% of that month's forecasted cost of goods sold. With respect to sales on account, 40% of receivables are collected in the month of sale, 50% are collected in the month following, and 10% are never collected.

**REQUIRED:**  **e**  **A.** What is the anticipated cost of goods sold for June?

**B.** What is the beginning inventory for July expected to be?

**C.** What are the July purchases expected to be?

**e**  **D.** What are the forecasted July cash collections?

**10.17**  **Direct materials budgeted payments (Appendix 10A)** New Ventures intends to start business
**Q2, Q7**  on the first of January. Production plans for the first four months of operations are as follows:

| January | 20,000 units |
|---|---|
| February | 50,000 units |
| March | 70,000 units |
| April | 70,000 units |

Each unit requires 2 pounds of material. The firm would like to end each month with enough raw material inventory on hand to cover 25% of the following month's production needs. The material costs $7 per pound. Management anticipates being able to pay for 40% of its purchases in the month of purchase. They will receive a 10% discount for these early payments. They anticipate having to defer payment to the next month on 60% of their purchases. No discount will be taken on these late payments. The business starts with no inventories on January 1.

**REQUIRED:**  **e**  Determine the budgeted payments for purchases of materials for each of the first three months of operations.

**10.18**  **Cash budget for revenues and expenses (Appendix 10A)** Myrna Manufacturing is located in
**Q2, Q7**  France and has projected sales in units for four months of operations as follows:

| January | 25,000 |
|---|---|
| February | 30,000 |
| March | 32,000 |
| April | 35,000 |

The product sells for €18 per unit. Twenty-five percent of the customers are expected to pay in the month of sale and take a 3% discount; 70% are expected to pay in the month following sale. The remaining 5% will never pay.

It takes 2 pounds of materials to produce a unit of product. The materials cost €0.75 per pound. In January no raw materials are in beginning inventories, but managers want to end each month with enough materials for 20% of the next month's production. The firm pays for 60% of its materials purchases in the month of purchase and 40% in the following month.

It takes 0.5 hour of labor to produce each unit. Labor is paid €15.00 per hour and is paid in the same month as worked. Overhead is estimated to be €2.00 per unit plus €25,000 per month (including depreciation of €12,000). Overhead costs are paid as incurred.

Myrna will begin January with no finished goods or work in process inventory. The managers wish to end each month with 25% of the following month's sales in finished goods inventory. They will end each month with no work in process.

**REQUIRED:**  **e**  Prepare a cash budget listing cash receipts and disbursements for February. The firm will begin February with a cash balance of €80,000.

**10.19**

**Q1, Q4, Q5**

**Flexible budget and variances, performance measurement, reasons for variances** Play Time Toys is organized into two major divisions: marketing and production. The production division is further divided into three departments: puzzles, dolls, and video games. Each production department has its own manager.

The company's management believes that all costs must be covered by sales of the three product lines. Therefore, a portion of headquarters, marketing, and the production division costs are allocated to each product line.

The company's accountant prepared the following performance report for the manager of the dolls production department.

### PERFORMANCE REPORT DOLLS PRODUCTION DEPARTMENT
#### (Volumes and total dollar amounts are in thousands.)

|  | Cost Forecasts | Budget | Actual | Variance |
|---|---|---|---|---|
| Sales volume | 1,000 | 1,000 | 1,100 | 100 F |
| Revenue | $12.00/unit | $12,000 | $12,400 | $ 400 F |
| Direct materials | 2.00/unit | 2,000 | 2,100 | (100) U |
| Direct labor | 1.00/unit | 1,000 | 1,225 | (225) U |
| Variable factory overhead | 1.00/unit | 1,000 | 1,100 | (100) U |
| Fixed factory overhead | 0.80/unit | 800 | 1,020 | (220) U |
| Production division overhead | 0.10/unit | 100 | 105 | (5) U |
| Headquarters | 0.20/unit | 200 | 220 | (20) U |
| Marketing | 0.50/unit | 500 | 550 | (50) U |
| Operating income | $ 6.40/unit | $ 6,400 | $ 6,080 | $(320) U |

**REQUIRED:**

ⓔ **A.** Is Play Time using a static budget or a flexible budget to calculate variances? Explain. Do you agree with this approach? Why or why not?

ⓔ **B.** Develop an appropriate benchmark for evaluating the performance of the dolls production department. Decide whether to include or exclude each cost category, and explain your decisions.

**C.** Use the benchmark you created in part (B) to calculate variances.

ⓔ **D.** Review the variances from part (C). Briefly describe the types of operating or budgeting problems that might have caused these variances.

**10.20**

**Q7**

**Prepare cash budget (Appendix 10A)** A college student, Brad Worth, plans to sell atomic alarm clocks with CD players over the Internet and by mail order to help pay his expenses during the fall semester. He buys the clocks for $32 and sells them for $50. If payment by check accompanies the mail orders (estimated to be 40% of sales), he gives a 10% discount. If customers include a credit card number for either Internet or mail order sales (30% of sales), customers receive a 5% discount. The remaining collections are estimated to be:

| | |
|---|---|
| One month following | 15% |
| Two months following | 6% |
| Three months following | 4% |
| Uncollectible | 5% |

Sales forecasts are as follows:

| | |
|---|---|
| September | 120 units |
| October | 220 units |
| November | 320 units |
| December | 400 units |
| January | out of the business |

Brad plans to pay his supplier 50% in the month of purchase and 50% in the month following. A 6% discount is granted on payments made in the month of purchase; however, he will not be able to take any discounts on September purchases because of cash flow constraints. All September purchases will be paid for in October.

He has 50 clocks on hand (purchased in August and to be paid for in September) and plans to maintain enough end-of-month inventory to meet 70% of the next month's sales.

**REQUIRED:** ⓔ **A.** Prepare schedules for monthly budgeted cash receipts and cash disbursements for this venture. During which months will Brad need to finance purchases?

ⓔ **B.** Brad planned simply to write off the uncollectibles. However, his accounting professor suggested he turn them over to a collection agency. How much could Brad let the collection agency keep so that he would be no worse off?

---

## PROBLEMS

☆ **10.21** **Q1, Q3, Q5** **ETHICS**

**Time budget, uncertainties, performance evaluation, priorities** Patricia sighed and briefly closed her eyes. She was frustrated with the reconciliation she was working on. She was sure that she was missing something, but she could not determine what it was. And she felt the clock ticking. Patricia knew that the time budget for this assignment was only three hours, and she had already worked on it for two hours.

Patricia started with a CPA firm after graduation, three months ago. Her first few assignments had been stressful. She had been a good student in school, and she expected to do well at work, too. But she often felt inadequate here, as though she was supposed to know more than she did. Her supervisor, Ron, told her not to worry too much. He said that her job was to learn and that she would be performing well soon. "All new-hires are slow to begin with," he told her, "Just let me know if you have questions." However, Patricia felt that she had pestered him with enough questions. Most of the time, the answers to her questions seemed so obvious . . . after Ron had answered her.

She looked at the reconciliation again.

**REQUIRED: ANALYZE INFORMATION**

The following questions will help you analyze the information for this problem. Do not turn in your answers to these questions unless your professor asks you to do so.

① **A.** Explain why it might be difficult to establish accurate time budgets for accounting tasks.
① **B.** Provide possible reasons why Patricia's time on this assignment could exceed the budget.
② **C.** Explain why Patricia is reluctant to seek Ron's help on this assignment.
② **D.** Describe how Ron might evaluate Patricia's performance assuming:
    **1.** She seeks his help and completes the assignment in four hours.
    **2.** She does not seek his help and completes the assignment in eight hours.
③ **E.** Suppose Patricia does not seek Ron's help and completes the assignment in eight hours.
    **1.** What priorities has Patricia used in making this choice?
    **2.** Has Patricia behaved ethically? Why or why not?
④ **F.** What could Patricia learn from this experience that will improve her performance in the future?

**REQUIRED: WRITTEN ASSIGNMENT**

Suppose Patricia asked for your advice. Turn in your answers to the following.

③ **G.** Use the information you learned from the preceding analyses to write a memo to Patricia with your recommendation. Refer in your memo to the information that would be useful to Patricia.
③ **H.** Write one or two paragraphs explaining how you decided what information to include in your memo.

**10.22** **Q2, Q5, Q7**

**Budgeting for next semester, assumptions, monitoring (Appendix 10A)** Suppose a friend asks you to help her prepare a budget for the next semester.

**REQUIRED:** ① **A.** Assuming you followed a process similar to that presented in this chapter, which budgets would you help her prepare? Explain your choices.
① **B.** Create a list of information needed to complete the various budgets. Identify which pieces of information need to be estimated.
② **C.** Create a list of the assumptions your friend will need to make for estimating the necessary information.
③ **D.** How should your friend monitor her budget performance throughout the semester? Write an explanation that your friend, who is not familiar with accounting, will understand.

**10.23**

Q2, Q3, Q4, Q5

**Performance benchmark, variances, and analysis** Central County Public Clinic is a free outpa-tient clinic for public assistance patients. Among other services, the clinic provides visiting nurses for elderly patients in their homes. A homemaker who cleans and performs other household tasks accompanies each nurse. When the nurses are not visiting clients, they work at the office prepar-ing for visits. When the homemakers complete their visits, they go home.

Each year, the clinic receives a budget allotment from Central County. The county does not allow the clinic to spend more than this allotment. The clinic, in turn, allocates its budget among its various programs. The visiting nurse program was authorized (and spent) $250,396 in 2004 and $279,476 in 2005 as follows.

|  | 2004 | 2005 |
|---|---|---|
| Nurses | $135,378 | $145,019 |
| Homemakers | 60,046 | 71,500 |
| Medical supplies | 18,197 | 21,402 |
| Cleaning supplies | 6,894 | 9,216 |
| Transportation | 9,068 | 11,144 |
| Clinic general overhead | 20,813 | 21,195 |
| Total expenditures | $250,396 | $279,476 |
| Home visits | 4,312 | 5,101 |
| Average cost per home visit | $58.07 | $54.79 |

The nursing staff received a 5% increase in salary one-third of the way through 2005. The homemakers did not receive an increase in wages in 2004 or in 2005. The prices of medical sup-plies increased about 2% during 2005 compared to 2004. The prices of cleaning supplies were rel-atively constant across the two years.

Transportation is provided by the nurses, who are reimbursed $0.20 per mile. The clinic's gen-eral overhead is allocated to programs on the basis of budgeted program salaries.

**REQUIRED:**

**e A.** In this problem you are not given a budget for 2005. If you want to evaluate performance of the 2005 clinic, what can you use as the basis of a flexible budget to develop a benchmark?

**e B.** Prepare a schedule to evaluate the performance of this program in 2005 using the bench-mark suggested in part (A).

**2 C.** If you were the general manager of the clinic, what would you like to discuss with the head of the visiting nurse program concerning the 2005 results? Explain.

**e D.** How many patients should have been served in 2005 for $279,476 if costs had been un-der control?

**10.24**

PART 1:
SPREADSHEET
WITH INPUT BOX,
REVENUE AND
PRODUCTION
BUDGETS

Q2

**Comprehensive manufacturing master budget problem** The accountant at Fighting Kites has always prepared a budget that is calculated using only one estimated volume of sales. He has asked you to help him set up a spreadsheet that can be used for sensitivity analysis in the budg-eting process. This year it appears that the company may not meet expectations, which could result in a loss. He is concerned that the company will incur a loss again next year, and wants to develop a budget that will easily reflect changes in the assumptions. After gathering infor-mation about next year's operations, he will provide information using a what-if sensitivity analysis.

Following are the assumptions regarding revenues, direct materials and labor costs, and in-ventory levels.

| Direct materials per kite: | | |
|---|---|---|
| Nylon | $10 | |
| Ribs | $5 | |
| String | $2 | |
| **Direct labor:** | | |
| Hours | Assembly | 0.5 |
| | Packing | 0.1 |
| Cost per hour | Assembly | $30.00 |
| | Packing | $15.00 |
| Cost per kite | Assembly | $15.00 |
| | Packing | $1.50 |

Inventory information:

| Direct materials: | Beginning | Target Ending |
|---|---|---|
| Nylon | $5,000 | $7,000 |
| Ribs | $3,000 | $3,200 |
| String | $1,000 | $1,200 |
| Finished goods (units) | 2,000 kites | 2,200 kites |
| Finished goods (cost) | $97,850 | |

Revenue assumptions:

| Selling price | $75 |
|---|---|
| Volume of kite sales | 80,000 |

**REQUIRED:** ⓔ **A.** Create a spreadsheet with a data input box at the top. Into this box put all of the relevant assumption data. This box should be formatted with a border to separate the input data from the cell-referenced data. Set up each schedule with cell references to information in the data input box. Any changes made to information in this box should be reflected through all of the schedules that you set up. As you proceed through parts 2 and 3 of this problem, more information will be given that needs to be located in the assumptions box, such as next year's estimated variable and fixed manufacturing overhead, and support department costs. You will need to leave space in the data input box for this information, or add more rows as you develop the spreadsheet.

**B.** Prepare a revenue budget.

**C.** Prepare a production budget in units.

**D.** Prepare the direct materials usage budget and a direct materials purchases budget.

**E.** Prepare a direct labor budget (in hours and cost).

**PART 2: OVERHEAD, ENDING INVENTORY, AND COST OF GOODS SOLD BUDGETS**
**Q2**

Refer to the information for part 1. Following are estimated manufacturing overhead costs. Both fixed and variable overhead will be allocated based on the number of kites produced.

Estimated variable manufacturing overhead costs:

| Supplies | $160,250 |
|---|---|
| Indirect labor | 200,650 |
| Maintenance | 80,200 |
| Miscellaneous | 40,100 |
| Total variable overhead costs | $481,200 |

Estimated fixed manufacturing overhead costs:

| Depreciation | $211,728 |
|---|---|
| Property taxes | 28,872 |
| Insurance | 67,368 |
| Plant management | 240,600 |
| Fringe benefits | 336,840 |
| Miscellaneous | 76,992 |
| Total fixed overhead costs | $962,400 |

**REQUIRED:** **F.** Prepare a manufacturing overhead budget and determine variable and fixed overhead allocation rates by dividing the budgeted overhead by budgeted labor hours for the fixed overhead and units for the variable overhead.

**G.** Prepare a schedule that calculates the unit costs of ending inventory in finished goods, and then prepare the ending inventories budget.

**H.** Prepare a cost of goods sold budget.

**PART 3: BUDGETED INCOME STATEMENT**
**Q2**

Refer to the information for parts 1 and 2. Following is the information that the accountant collected about support department costs.

| Support Department: | Fixed Costs |
|---|---|
| Administration | $1,034,580 |
| Marketing | 620,748 |
| Distribution | 310,374 |
| Customer service | 103,458 |
| Total support department costs | $2,069,160 |

**REQUIRED:**

**I.** Prepare a support department costs budget.

**J.** Prepare a budgeted income statement. Assume an income tax rate of 25%.

**PART 4: CASH BUDGET WITH BAD DEBTS AND BORROWING (APPENDIX 10A)**
**Q7**

Refer to the information for parts 1, 2, and 3. The company's managers budget cash flows on a quarterly basis so that they can plan short-term investments and borrowings.

Kite sales are highest during the spring and summer. Sales are fairly even within each quarter, but sales vary across quarters as follows:

| | |
|---|---|
| January–March | 10% |
| April–June | 50% |
| July–September | 30% |
| October–December | 10% |

Accounts receivable at the end of the prior year, consisting of sales made during December, totaled $90,000. Payments from customers are usually received as follows:

| | |
|---|---|
| Pay during the month goods are received | 50% |
| Pay the next month | 47% |
| Bad debts | 3% |

The managers plan to maintain beginning inventory quantities during January and February, but to increase inventories to the targeted levels by the end of March and maintain those levels throughout the rest of the year. The company pays its vendors 10 days after raw materials are received, so approximately two-thirds of all purchases are paid in the month of production and one-third are paid the following month. Accounts payable at the end of the prior year totaled $13,000. Employee wages and other production costs are paid during the month incurred. Property taxes are paid in two equal installments on March 31 and September 30, and insurance is paid annually on June 30. Support costs are paid evenly throughout the year. Estimated income tax payments are made at the end of each quarter based on 25% of total estimated taxes for the year.

In addition to customer receipts, the company expects to receive $10,000 in proceeds from the sale of equipment during January. The company also plans to purchase and pay for new equipment costing $50,000 during January.

The company finances its short-term operations with a line of credit from the bank, which had a balance of $150,000 at the end of the prior year. The line of credit agreement requires the company to maintain a minimum cash balance of $100,000 (non-interest-bearing). The company's line of credit requires quarterly interest payments at an annual rate of 5.5%. (For simplicity, assume that all borrowings and repayments occur on the last day of each quarter.)

**REQUIRED:**

**K.** Prepare quarterly budgets for cash receipts, cash disbursements, and short-term financing.

**10.25**
**Q1, Q2**

**Budget planning sensitivity analysis** Refer to the information from Problem 10.24, parts 1, 2, and 3. The budget indicates that the company is likely to incur a loss during the next period. The accountant asks you to assist him in developing sensitivity analyses that will help the manager identify possible ways to avoid a loss. To perform sensitivity analysis, you will alter volume of production, volume of sales, selling prices, direct material prices, wage rates, and overhead and support department costs.

**REQUIRED:**

❷ **A.** Identify the assumptions that are relevant for sensitivity analysis. Relevant assumptions are ones that the manager could potentially influence by changing the company's operating plans.

❷ **B.** Identify possible changes in budget assumptions that might eliminate the forecasted loss (i.e., that would lead to a breakeven).

❸ **C.** Perform sensitivity analysis using the input section of your spreadsheet to determine a set of assumption changes that would cause budgeted income to break even. Explain your choices.

❷ **D.** Describe uncertainties and their effects on the assumptions you made in part (A).

**10.26**
**PART 1: REVENUES BUDGET, UNCERTAINTIES, REVENUE STRATEGIES**
**Q1, Q2**

**Comprehensive restaurant master budget problem** You are the accountant for Wok and Egg Roll Express. Following are assumptions about sales for the coming month. Wok offers three basic meals: noodle bowls, egg rolls, and rice bowls. Each meal can be prepared with several different meats or with vegetables only. Costs and prices are similar for all varieties of each meal. Prices for noodles bowls are $4.00 each, egg rolls are $3.00 each, and rice bowls are $3.50 each. Estimated sales for the next month are 200 noodle bowls, 100 egg roll meals, and 500 rice bowls per day.

**REQUIRED:**
A. Prepare a revenue budget for the next month assuming it is 30 days long.
**①** B. Discuss factors that affect the budgeted volumes of meals.
**②** C. Identify possible ways the owner could increase total revenues. Discuss the pros and cons for each of your ideas.

**PART 2: DIRECT MATERIALS BUDGET, UNCERTAINTIES, COST CONTROL STRATEGIES**
**Q1, Q2**

The owner of Wok and Egg Roll Express studied the cost of direct materials for each type of meal. He estimates that noodle bowls use about $1.00 in direct materials, egg rolls use about $0.75, and rice bowls use about $0.90. Food is purchased daily to ensure high quality. Beginning and ending inventory amounts are minimal.

**REQUIRED:**
**ⓔ** D. Explain why you would not need to prepare a production budget for Wok and Egg Roll Express.
E. Prepare a direct materials usage budget and a direct materials purchases budget.
**①** F. Discuss reasons why actual costs might be different from budgeted costs in part (E).
**②** G. Suppose the prices of food ingredients increase. Identify possible ways the owner could keep food costs within the budget. Discuss drawbacks for each of your ideas.

**PART 3: DIRECT LABOR BUDGET, UNCERTAINTIES, COST CONTROL STRATEGIES**
**Q1, Q2**

The owner of Wok and Egg Roll Express employs cooks and cashiers. The cashiers take orders and collect payment, transfer food from the cooks to customers, and clean tables. Cooks are paid $10 per hour, and cashiers are paid $8 per hour. Wok operates four shifts: 10 to 2, 11 to 2, 2 to 10, and 5 to 8. Weekdays and weekends are staffed similarly. Following are the shifts and required workers.

| Shift | Cooks | Cashiers |
|---|---|---|
| 10 a.m. to 2 p.m. | 2 | 2 |
| 11 a.m. to 2 p.m. | 3 | 3 |
| 2 p.m. to 10 p.m. | 2 | 2 |
| 5 p.m. to 8 p.m. | 3 | 3 |

**REQUIRED:**
H. Prepare a labor budget showing hours and costs for a month. (Assume 30 days per month.)
**①** I. Discuss reasons why actual labor costs might turn out to be different from budgeted costs in part (H).
**②** J. Identify possible ways the owner could reduce labor costs. Discuss possible drawbacks for each of your ideas.

**PART 4: OVERHEAD BUDGET, UNCERTAINTIES, COST CONTROL STRATEGIES**
**Q1, Q2**

Wok and Egg Roll Express does not separately account for production versus general overhead. Fixed overhead includes production overhead as well as support services and general administration. Variable overhead includes labor-related costs such as payroll taxes and employee benefits. Wok has estimated variable overhead costs as $2.50 per direct labor hour. Following are the estimated fixed overhead costs for one month:

| Fixed overhead costs: | |
|---|---|
| Utilities | $ 1,300 |
| Manager | 5,000 |
| Lease | 2,000 |
| Miscellaneous | 2,500 |
| Total | $10,800 |

**REQUIRED:**
K. Prepare an overhead costs budget for one month.
**①** L. Discuss reasons why actual overhead costs might turn out to be different from budgeted costs in part (K).
**②** M. Identify possible ways the owner could reduce overhead costs. Discuss possible drawbacks for each of your ideas.

**PART 5: BUDGETED INCOME STATEMENT, UNCERTAINTIES, PROFIT STRATEGIES**
**Q1, Q2**

Refer to the information from the preceding budgets. The income statement for Wok and Egg Roll Express consists of revenues less direct costs (direct materials and direct labor) to determine the gross margin. Then the overhead costs are deducted to determine operating income.

**REQUIRED:**
N. Prepare a budgeted income statement ignoring income taxes.
**②** O. What are the major uncertainties in Wok's budget? Explain.
**③** P. Wok's owner would like to increase profits from the store. Suggest several possible ways to accomplish this goal. Explain your reasoning.

**10.27** **Prepare cash budget from financial statements (Appendix 10A)** The Red Midget Company pro-
Q7 cesses and distributes beans. The beans are packed in 1-pound plastic bags and sold to grocery
chains for $0.50 each in boxes of 100 bags. During March the firm anticipates selling 16,000 boxes
(sales in February were 14,000 boxes). Typically, 80% of the firm's customers pay within the
month of sale, 18% of the customer pay the month after, and 2% of sales are never collected.

The firm buys beans from local farmers. The farmers are paid $0.20 per pound, cash. Most of
the processing is done automatically. Consequently, most ($80,000) of the firm's factory overhead
is depreciation expense.

The firm advertises heavily. For March managers expect to publish $75,000 worth of advertise-
ments in popular magazines. This amount is up from February's $60,000 of advertisements. The firm
pays for 10% of its advertising in the month the ads are run and 90% in the following month. March's
budgeted income statement and statement of cost of goods manufactured and sold follow. All costs
and expenses are paid for as incurred unless specifically indicated otherwise. The firm will begin March
with a cash balance of $25,000, and pays a monthly dividend of $15,000 to the owners.

### INCOME STATEMENT

| | |
|---|---:|
| Sales | $800,000 |
| Cost of goods sold | 540,000 |
| Gross margin | 260,000 |
| Administrative salaries | 80,000 |
| Sales commissions | 69,000 |
| Advertising | 75,000 |
| Bad debts expense | 16,000 |
| Operating income | $ 20,000 |

### STATEMENT OF COST OF GOODS MANUFACTURED AND SOLD

| | |
|---|---:|
| Beginning balance direct materials | $ 20,000 |
| Direct materials purchases | 330,000 |
| Materials available for use | 350,000 |
| Ending balance direct materials | 30,000 |
| Direct materials used | 320,000 |
| Labor costs incurred | 90,000 |
| Overhead costs | 115,000 |
| Cost of good manufactured | 525,000 |
| Beginning finished goods balance | 45,000 |
| Goods available for sale | 570,000 |
| Ending finished goods balance | 30,000 |
| Cost of good sold | $540,000 |

**REQUIRED:** From the information provided, prepare a cash budget for March.

**10.28** **Budgeting for a bequest in a not-for-profit organization, participative budgeting** During late 2003,
Q1, Q2, Q5 National Public Radio (NPR) announced a $200 million bequest from the estate of Joan B. Kroc.
Mrs. Kroc, widow of McDonald's founder Ray A. Kroc, was a longtime supporter of public radio.
NPR is a not-for-profit organization that produces and distributes news, talk, and entertainment pro-
gramming for a worldwide network of more than 770 independent public radio stations.

At the time of the announcement, NPR management stated that most of the bequest would be
placed in an endowment fund, and only the annual earnings would be spent. However, NPR's board
of directors had not yet made specific plans about how the funds would be used. The bequest would
significantly affect NPR's finances. The current endowment fund contained $35 million, and the
organization's annual budget was around $104 million. NPR and its affiliate stations were contin-
ually faced with tight operating budgets.

The announcement triggered speculations about how NPR would spend the money. Some people argued that NPR should reevaluate its strategies, with possible expansion into the Internet or
other platforms. A number of public radio station managers wanted part of the funds to support
their operations, perhaps through a reduction in NPR programming fees. Approximately half of
NPR's annual budget was financed through programming fees. An independent producer wanted

to see pay increases for the freelance workers who create NPR programming. Various groups voiced opinions about ways to improve the quality of NPR programming. Some observers were concerned that the large bequest might cause the organization's management to become overly conservative, reducing the likelihood of innovative new programming.

Some people were concerned that the bequest would discourage listener and other support to NPR and its affiliate stations. Others believed that the bequest would have the opposite effect.

SOURCES: "What Is NPR?" available at www.npr.org, click About NPR; NPR news release, "NPR Receives a Record Bequest of More Than $200 Million," November 6, 2003, available at www.npr.org/about/press/031106.kroc.html; M. Jurkowitz, "'Extraordinary' $200M Bequest Stuns, Elates NPR Staff," *The Boston Globe,* November 7, 2003; M. Janssen, "Kroc's $200 Million Gift Frees PubRadio's Dreams," *Current.org,* November 17, 2003, available at www.current.org/npr/npr0309kroc.shtml; and T. Lowry, J. Weber, and C. Yang, "Can NPR Bear the Burden of Wealth?" *Business Week,* December 15, 2003, p. 77.

**REQUIRED:**

**A.** Discuss why NPR's management should clarify the organization's vision, core competencies, and strategies (see Chapter 1 and Exhibit 1.1) before deciding how to budget the bequest funds.

**B.** Participative budgeting usually relates only to participation within an organization; however, it might apply also to NPR's negotiations with affiliate stations and freelance workers. Discuss the pros and cons of a participative budgeting approach for NPR's use of the bequest.

**C.** Suppose NPR decides to use the funds primarily to improve programming quality. Describe how this strategy might be translated into specific items in an annual master budget.

# BUILD YOUR PROFESSIONAL COMPETENCIES

**10.29**
Q1, Q2, Q3, Q5
www.wiley.com/
college/eldenburg

**Focus on Professional Competency: Resource Management** *Organizational resources, uncertainties, performance, government budget responsibility* Review the following definition and elements for the Resource Management competency.[13]

**DEFINITION:** *The ability to appreciate the importance of all resources (human, financial, physical, environmental, etc.) is critical for success. Individuals entering the accounting profession should be able to apply management and human resources development theories to human resource issues and organizational problems. Individuals preparing to enter the accounting profession should be able to identify sources of capital, and analyze the impact of participation in the global capital markets.*

## ELEMENTS FOR THIS COMPETENCY INCLUDE

| Level 1 | Level 2 | Level 3 | Level 4 |
|---|---|---|---|
| 1. Identifies resources available to an organization | 3. Articulates how organizations make decisions to allocate scarce resources, including recognition of both quantitative and qualitative constraints on these decisions (Specific examples include decisions regarding capacity and resource utilization.) | 6. Articulates how resource availability affects the organization's business functions, processes and administrative procedures | 9. Facilitates analysis of the organization and applies continuous improvement principles to the organization |
| 2. Explains why there are uncertainties about the availability and alternative uses of resources | 4. Identifies the effects of market forces on organizations' costs of capital, labor, commodities, etc. | 7. Identifies both traditional and nontraditional performance criteria and measurement methods by selecting appropriate success factors and measures of their achievement (see functional competencies) | |
| | 5. Analyzes the implications of an organization's lack of access to supply sources, financial markets, and intellectual capital (barriers to entry, expansion, or survival) | 8. Identifies and addresses the social costs and benefits of business decisions and evaluates the fiduciary performance of public sector and not-for-profit management | |

[13]The definition and elements are reprinted with permission from AICPA; Copyright © 1978–2000 & 2003 by American Institute of Certified Public Accountants. The AICPA's Core Competency Framework can be accessed at eca.aicpaservices.org.

**REQUIRED:**

**A.** Focus on competency elements 1 and 3, which address the identification and allocation of an organization's resources. Answer the following questions:

**①** **1.** Explain how the budgeting process helps top managers articulate decisions about the use of resources.

**①** **2.** Explain how a budget identifies the resources available to individual departments within an organization.

**B.** Focus on competency elements 2 and 4, which address uncertainties about and influences on resource costs. Answer the following questions:

**①** **1.** Explain why the cost of resources such as labor and direct materials is uncertain. Include the effects of market forces in your discussion.

**②** **2.** Explain how changes in the price of resources such as labor and direct materials might cause managers to change the way those resources are used.

**②** **3.** Explain how the issues you discussed in questions 1 and 2 can result in budget variances.

**C.** Focus on competency elements 7 and 9, which address skills for measuring performance and promoting improvement. Answer the following questions:

**①** **1.** Explain how budgets can be used to measure organizational performance.

**②** **2.** Explain how each of the following budget adjustments improves measurement of variances when evaluating the performance for individual managers within an organization:

  **a.** Using flexible budgets to adjust for actual volumes
  **b.** Removing allocated costs
  **c.** Updating costs for anticipated price changes

**④** **3.** How can the analysis of budget variances lead to continuous improvement in an organization?

**D.** Focus on competency element 8, which addresses social and fiduciary responsibilities. The federal government and many state and local governments publish a guide to help citizens understand the budgeting process. Perform a search on the Internet to find an example of a citizen's guide to the budget (consider using a search phrase such as "citizen's guide to _____ budget," filling the blank with "federal" or the name of a state, county, or city). Answer the following questions:

**②** **1.** Why would a government publish a citizen's guide to the budget?

**②** **2.** What are the components of the budgeting process described in the citizen's guide? Explain how the process compares to the budget cycle (Exhibit 10.2) in the textbook.

**②** **3.** As a citizen, explain how you can use a governmental budget to evaluate the fiduciary performance of the government's managers.

**10.30**
**Q1, Q2**

**Integrating Across the Curriculum: Financial Accounting and Attestation** *Prospective financial statements, types of attestation, assumptions* Delanna's, a privately owned, high-end women's clothing store, has been successful since it was opened five years ago. The owner, Delanna Ricci, wants to open a second store in a nearby city. She talked with her banker about a possible loan to cover the costs for opening the store. The banker wants Delanna to submit a business plan, including estimated income statements for the first three years for both stores. Delanna already has a line of credit agreement with the bank. During part of each year, she borrows money to finance inventory purchases. She has always paid the loans off by late December, which is the store's busiest time of year.

Last year's income statement for the existing store was as follows. The business is a sole proprietorship, so it does not include a salary expense for Delanna, who manages the store.

| | | |
|---|---:|---:|
| Revenues | | $632,000 |
| Cost of goods sold | | 350,000 |
| Gross margin | | 282,000 |
| Operating expenses | | |
| Employee wages and commissions | $82,000 | |
| Occupancy costs | 58,000 | |
| Store supplies | 6,000 | |
| Office and miscellaneous expenses | 18,000 | |
| Interest expense (line of credit loan) | 5,000 | |
| Total operating expenses | | 169,000 |
| Pretax income | | $113,000 |

Delanna has contacted her CPA firm to help her create estimated income statements that will be submitted to the bank. You have performed quarterly compilations of Delanna's financial statements, which are submitted to the bank under the line of credit agreement. Thus, you are assigned the job of helping Delanna develop financial statements for the new bank loan.

You have not helped a client develop estimated financial statements, but you find the following definitions in one of your old textbooks:

*Financial Forecast:* Prospective financial statements that present expected results based on assumptions about conditions expected to exist and the course of action the entity expects to take.

*Financial Projection:* Prospective financial statements that present expected results, given one or more hypothetical courses of action.

**REQUIRED:** Conduct research into financial accounting and attestation standards, as needed, to answer the following questions.

❶ **A.** Will Delanna's estimated income statements be considered financial forecasts or financial projections? Explain.

❶ **B.** What alternative types of attestation services can a CPA perform for prospective financial statements? Briefly describe the CPA's responsibilities for each type of attestation service.

❶ **C.** Suppose Delanna engaged your firm to perform a compilation. Write a list of questions to ask Delanna to help you gather the information necessary to create the estimated income statements.

❷ **D.** Discuss how you would use the prior year's income statement to help you prepare estimated future income statements for the two stores.

❷ **E.** The preparation of prospective financial statements requires a set of assumptions, similar to the assumptions needed when preparing a budget. Write a list of assumptions that will be needed to create the estimated income statements.

❷ **F.** Explain why Delanna is likely to be biased when she provides you with information for the estimated financial statements. Discuss whether you would be able to detect bias as you compile the estimated financial statements.

# 11

# Standard Costs and Variance Analysis

## ▶In Brief

Accountants produce information that managers use to monitor operations. Standard costs and variances from budgets are an important part of that information. Variances are calculated by comparing standard revenues and costs with actual revenues and costs. Through the analysis of these variances, managers identify operating processes that need investigation and possible improvements. They also learn whether planned improvements in operations have been achieved. Variance information helps managers create more accurate plans for future operations. In addition, variance analysis provides information for evaluating employee performance.

## This Chapter Addresses the Following Questions:

**Q1** How are standard costs established?

**Q2** What is variance analysis, and how is it performed?

**Q3** How are direct cost variances calculated?

**Q4** How is direct cost variance information analyzed and used?

**Q5** How are variable and fixed overhead variances calculated?

**Q6** How is overhead variance information analyzed and used?

**Q7** How are manufacturing cost variances closed?

**Q8** Which profit-related variances are commonly analyzed? (Appendix 11A)

# PROTECH: MONITORING LABOR PERFORMANCE

Protech (a pseudonym used to disguise its identity) is a division of a *Fortune* 500 company. The company manufactures control equipment, such as air conditioner controls, appliance thermostats, electric heat controls, and humidity controls. For many years, Protech maintained detailed information about the labor hours and costs used in production jobs at its 18 manufacturing plants. This information was used to create daily and weekly reports on individual employee and job productivity.

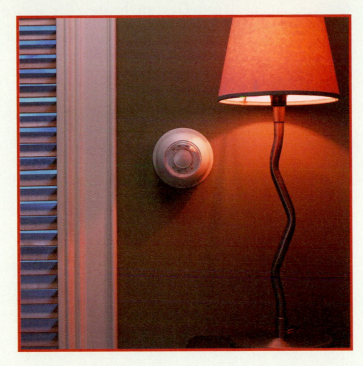

Protech's managers identified labor productivity and product quality as strategically important to the company's success. They established a system for evaluating production worker performance on those two factors. Productivity was measured using direct labor reports. Poor productivity resulted in counseling and potential dismissal. Highly productive workers were praised as "key players." Quality improvements and reductions in defects were also measured and rewarded.

During the early 1990s, Protech's managers decided to place greater emphasis on quality improvements. Detailed labor productivity record-keeping and reports were eliminated in an initial group of seven plants. The managers planned to eliminate similar reports at the remaining eleven plants as part of larger plans for changing the accounting system. The decision to eliminate the detailed labor reports was driven by two factors. First, the existing labor record-keeping system was costly; it required substantial computer resources as well as considerable time for workers, supervisors, and accounting staff. Second, Protech's managers doubted whether the labor productivity reports were sufficiently timely and whether they provided useful information. They knew that other companies were monitoring quality, lead time, and other types of strategically oriented performance measures. Yet, eliminating the labor reports would decrease supervisor information about individual worker efforts, making it more difficult to motivate employees to maintain high levels of productivity.

A team of academic accounting researchers conducted a study to determine the effects of Protech's decision to eliminate the detailed labor reports. The researchers collected data from all of the plants over a 36-month period. They studied the productivity and quality measures for the seven plants that dropped detailed labor reports and for the eleven plants that continued to use the reports. Compared to those plants that continued labor-reporting practices, the seven manufacturing plants experienced (1) significant costs caused by a decline in labor productivity and (2) substantial savings from a lower product reject rate. Overall, the researchers estimated that the cost savings from quality improvements were only one-sixth of the cost increase from decreased labor productivity. However, the researchers commented that they were unable to estimate the value of long-term benefits from quality improvements, such as increased sales.

When managers at Protech received the research results, they decided to reinstate the detailed labor record-keeping and reporting system. The managers believed that the reports were important for motivating manufacturing workers to achieve higher levels of productivity. ■

SOURCE: R. Banker, S. Devaraj, R. Schroeder, and K. Sinha, "Performance Impact of the Elimination of Direct Labor Reporting: A Field Study," *Journal of Accounting Research*, September 2002, pp. 1013–1036.

## MOTIVATING LABOR PRODUCTIVITY

### ■ Key Accounting Design Issues for Protech

The following discussion summarizes key aspects of the decision-making process at Protech for eliminating the detailed labor productivity record-keeping and reporting system and then for reinstating it.

**Knowing.** The managers at Protech had considerable knowledge about the accounting system and manufacturing processes. Prior to the change in the record-keeping requirements, the company's performance measures, such as production volume and product reject rates, were easily understood by managers, supervisors, and manufacturing workers.

**Identifying.** Protech's managers faced numerous uncertainties that prevented them from being absolutely certain how to best measure, monitor, and motivate production employee performance. For example:

- It was impossible to perfectly observe and measure employee performance.
- The effects of the previous system on worker performance were unknown.
- The managers could not perfectly predict the reactions of production supervisors or workers to the new system.
- Mismeasurement may have distorted the researchers' estimates of costs and benefits for the old and new systems.
- The research did not attempt to measure potential long-term quality benefits.
- Protech's managers could not know with certainty whether reverting to the old system would improve employee productivity—or by how much.

**Exploring.** Given the many uncertainties, Protech's managers faced a difficult task when exploring the pros and cons of the labor productivity reporting system. Arguments in favor of eliminating the old system included:

- The productivity record-keeping system was costly.
- The reports might have done little to motivate productivity.
- By focusing on productivity, the labor reports might have distracted employees from quality and other important initiatives.

Arguments in favor of keeping the old system included:

- Eliminating an easily understood performance measure might have increased employee uncertainty about how their performance would be measured.
- Employees might have misunderstood the change as a signal that productivity was no longer important.
- With less information about individual employee productivity, supervisors might have found it difficult to monitor and motivate higher levels of performance.

It is not clear whether Protech's managers considered alternative ways to motivate higher productivity besides reinstating the original system. They might have been biased toward readopting the old system because they already had the labor record-keeping system in place and knew how to use it.

**Prioritizing.** In the original decision to eliminate the labor productivity system, Protech's managers thought that the costs of the old system outweighed the benefits. When reversing their decision, they apparently believed the opposite. Implicitly, the reversal also suggested that the managers valued productivity over quality. In changing their position, Protech's managers probably relied heavily on the results of the research project. Because the research study focused on measuring short-term costs, reliance on the research results might have discouraged the managers from giving adequate attention to long-term effects or to qualitative factors such as employee attitudes and customer preferences.

**Envisioning.** The original decision of Protech's managers to drop the traditional monitoring system suggests a willingness to pursue innovative management techniques. The reversal of their decision might represent good management—an ability to quickly size up an error and avoid throwing good money after bad. Or, it might suggest an inability to give something new time to succeed. Were the managers unwilling to consider alternative ways to motivate worker productivity within the new system?

### ■ Monitoring and Motivating Performance

When managers create operating plans for the next period, they prepare a budget for revenues and costs. These plans include expectations about employee productivity and other factors that affect revenues and costs. Managers then monitor actual operations to determine whether operating targets are met. By studying differences between budgeted and actual results, managers also identify ways to improve future operations and to establish more realistic future budgets. In this chapter we learn the process that managers use to establish expectations and to analyze variances for major categories of revenues and costs.

**CHAPTER REFERENCE**

Chapter 10 defined a **budget variance** as a difference between budgeted and actual results.

## STANDARD COSTS

 **Q1** How are standard costs established?

To improve the ability of managers to plan operations and monitor performance, organizations often establish a set of standards for expected costs. We learned in Chapter 6 that a **standard cost** is the cost managers expect to incur to produce goods or services under operating plan assumptions. Key assumptions include the following:

- Volume of production activity
- Production processes and efficiency
- Prices and quality of inputs

As shown in Exhibit 11.1, the total standard cost for a unit of output is the sum of standard costs for the resources used in production. Typical resources include direct materials, direct labor, fixed overhead, and variable overhead. Standards are also established for the cost of each resource.

For example, the standards for direct costs include the price of the direct costs and the expected quantity of input for each unit of output. Suppose Benny's, a wholesale gourmet ice cream manufacturer, uses a standard cost system. Frozen blackberries are one of the direct materials used in Benny's Purple Madness ice cream. The company's managers determine that one pint of frozen blackberries should be included in each gallon of ice cream. They forecast that the cost of frozen blackberries this year will be $8.00 per gallon. Keeping in mind that 1 gallon = 8 pints, we can describe the standard cost of frozen blackberries as follows:

Standard price per unit of input:
    $8.00 per gallon = $8.00 per 8 pints = $1.00 per pint

Standard quantity of input per unit of output:
    1 pint of blackberries per gallon of ice cream

Standard cost of blackberries per unit of output:
    1 pint of blackberries per gallon of ice cream × $1.00 per pint of blackberries
    = $1.00 per gallon of ice cream

### EXHIBIT 11.1 Typical Cost Standards for Production

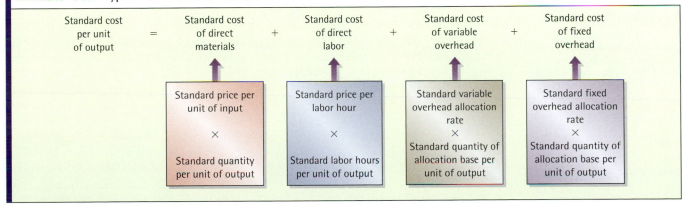

## ■ Standard Cost Categories

In this chapter, we focus on measuring and monitoring the standard costs for direct materials, direct labor, fixed overhead, and variable overhead. These cost categories are traditionally the ones used for manufactured goods. The cost categories that are measured and monitored in a given organization depend on the following:

- Nature of goods or services
- Cost accounting system used
- Costs that managers consider important
- Cost/benefit trade-off for monitoring individual costs

**CURRENT PRACTICE**

Hickory Farms monitors the following five cost categories for each of its products: direct materials, direct labor, product fixed costs, variable production expenses, and product distribution costs.[1]

For example, consider the cost of a clothing item sold by a retail store. The managers of the store might consider it unimportant to allocate and monitor labor and overhead costs for individual pieces of clothing sold. They might instead choose to focus only on the direct cost of the clothing. Professional service organizations, such as accounting firms, might track primarily direct labor costs. Organizations that use activity-based costing monitor overhead costs for individual activities. In the opening case in this chapter, Protech's managers decided to monitor not only overall labor production efficiency, but also production efficiency for individual employees.

In practice, many variations of specific costs are measured and monitored by accountants and managers. Although we focus in this chapter on traditional cost categories, the methods introduced here can be adapted to many different settings.

## ■ Developing Standard Costs

Standards are set for the price of direct materials, as well as for the amount of direct materials that should be used to produce each unit. Similarly, standards are set for the price per direct labor hour and for the amount of hours needed per unit of output. In addition, standards are set for overhead costs. No exact rules are prescribed for developing these standard costs. Sometimes managers simply use the most recent year's data, while at other times they evaluate and incorporate historical trends. To set a standard for the next period, they update historical data for expected changes in costs or processes. For new products, standards are often set with the assistance of industrial engineers, who estimate quantities and costs for direct materials, direct labor, and production overhead. Managers might also seek the periodic assistance of industrial engineers to find ways to improve efficiency, modify output quality, or identify cost reduction opportunities for existing products. Production plans include expected efficiency and quality, which means that the normal cost of waste and defects is included in standard costs.

Standard costs are reviewed periodically. Depending on organizational strategy, cost reduction goals may be incorporated into the standards, or quality improvements might require that standards be changed. Standards should serve as achievable targets. Working with current suppliers or investigating alternative suppliers for lower prices could lead to reduced direct materials price standards. As technology improves the productivity of robotic and labor processes, efficiency standards will also change.

**CHAPTER REFERENCE**

Chapter 15 addresses ways that organizations evaluate and compensate employees for meeting or exceeding budgets and standards.

Managers use standard costs not only to help plan future costs, but also to monitor and motivate employee performance. To encourage employees to achieve planned productivity, standards are often set at a level that is attainable, but without much slack. Sometimes tightening standards can promote productivity improvements.

The Cementos Juarez illustration that follows demonstrates the setting of standard costs for a manufacturer.

---

[1]T. W. Carey, "When Software Lets You Count Your Costs to the Penny," *CFO.com*, July 9, 2001.

## CEMENTOS JUAREZ (PART 1)
## SETTING STANDARD COSTS

Cementos Juarez manufactures concrete blocks at its plant in Mexico. When Carina Mendoza, the company's new accountant, started work last month, she learned that the company had never used standard costs. She decided to implement a standard cost system to help the managers monitor operating performance.

Carina toured the production facilities with Jorge, the labor supervisor. She learned that workers combine cement mix, sand, and water; and then they pour the mixture into block forms. The blocks are turned out of the forms and allowed to dry in the sun. Once the blocks are dry, they are stacked on pallets and loaded on trucks for shipment to customers. Workers can be sent home if no work is scheduled; therefore, direct labor cost is variable.

### Setting Cost Standards

Because the company had not previously used standard costs, Carina decided to set next month's standards based on past experience, adjusted for expected changes in activities or costs. To gather information for creating cost standards, Carina first studied the accounting and production records for the past year. Then she reviewed the next month's production schedule, which showed a planned volume of 90,000 blocks. After conducting interviews to learn about next month's production activities and costs, she did not expect any changes from prior costs.

Carina identified the following potential direct costs for producing the blocks: cement mix, sand, water, and direct labor. Sand and water are readily available on the company's land, so the company does not incur any costs for them.[2] Therefore, the only direct materials cost is the cement mix. Based on past accounting and production records, Carina set a standard cost for cement mix of 10 pesos per kilogram (kilo). She also estimated that it should take about 1 kilo of cement mix per block. In addition, Carina set the direct labor cost standard at 10 pesos per hour, and the standard for quantity of labor at 100 blocks per labor hour.

Carina next turned to the production overhead costs and determined that some costs were variable and others were fixed. Variable costs consisted of the cost of supervisors; as the number of direct labor hours increases, the number of supervisor hours also increases. Carina set the variable overhead standard at 2 pesos per labor hour. She then classified all remaining overhead costs as fixed, and estimated next month's spending at 180,000 pesos. After considering several allocation bases for the fixed overhead costs, Carina decided that volume of production would be appropriate. With planned production of 90,000 blocks, she set the standard fixed overhead allocation rate at 2 pesos (180,000 pesos ÷ 90,000 blocks) per block.

### Summary of Direct and Overhead Cost Standards

Following is a summary of the standards Carina established for the next month:

| | |
|---|---|
| Direct materials: | |
| Cost of cement mix | 10 pesos per kilo |
| Quantity of cement mix | 1 kilo per block |
| Standard cost per block (10 pesos per kilo × 1 kilo per block) | 10 pesos |
| Direct labor: | |
| Labor pay rate | 10 pesos per hour |
| Quantity of direct labor | 100 blocks per labor hour |
| Standard cost per block (10 pesos per hour × 1 hour per 100 blocks) | 0.10 pesos |
| Fixed overhead: | |
| Planned spending | 180,000 pesos |
| Volume of allocation base (blocks produced) | 90,000 blocks |
| Standard cost per block (180,000 pesos ÷ 90,000 blocks) | 2 pesos |
| Variable overhead: | |
| Spending per labor hour | 2 pesos |
| Standard cost per block (2 pesos ÷ 100 blocks) | 0.02 pesos |
| Total standard cost per block (10 + 0.10 + 2 + 0.02) | 12.12 pesos |

*(continued)*

---

[2]In reality, some costs would most likely be incurred for these resources; however, this illustration avoids complication by assuming no cost.

## Cost Budget

Based on these standards and the expected production volume of 90,000 blocks, Carina created the following budget for next month's production costs:

| | |
|---|---:|
| Direct materials (90,000 blocks × 10 pesos per block) | 900,000 pesos |
| Direct labor (90,000 blocks × 0.10 pesos per block) | 9,000 |
| Fixed overhead | 180,000 |
| Variable overhead (90,000 blocks × 0.02 pesos per block) | 1,800 |
| Total standard production costs (90,000 blocks × 12.12 pesos per block) | 1,090,800 pesos |

---

### GUIDE YOUR LEARNING 11.1  Cementos Juarez (Part 1)

Cementos Juarez (Part 1) demonstrates cost standard setting. For this illustration:

| Identify Problem and Information | Identify Uncertainties |
|---|---|
| What was the purpose of developing cost standards for Cementos Juarez? What information did Carina use to create the standards for direct materials, direct labor, variable overhead, and fixed overhead? | What were the uncertainties? Consider uncertainties about:<br>• Prices for materials, labor, and overhead<br>• Quantities used of materials, labor, and overhead resources |

---

## VARIANCE ANALYSIS

**Q2**  What is variance analysis, and how is it performed?

**CHAPTER REFERENCE**
Chapter 10 defined a **flexible budget** as a budget that reflects a range of operations.

Variances are calculated for two purposes: monitoring and bookkeeping. Variances calculated for bookkeeping purposes do not need to be analyzed, but variances used to monitor performance need to be analyzed. **Variance analysis** is the process of calculating variances and then investigating the reasons they occurred. This information is then used to improve future operating plans, as shown in Exhibit 11.2. We learned in Chapter 10 that a budget variance is a difference between budgeted and actual results. Similarly, a **standard cost variance** is a difference between a standard cost and an actual cost. Variance analysis can be used whether or not an organization uses a standard costing system. The process requires only the ability to compare actual results with some type of benchmark, which might be standard costs, budgeted costs, or some other measure of expectations. When organizations have a standard cost system in place, the standard costs are used in budgeting to develop flexible budgets.

### ■ Deciding Which Variances to Investigate

Simply calculating the dollar amount of the variance is not useful for decision making. The value of variance investigation is in identifying the reasons for the variance and then using that information to improve future decision making. However, variance investigation and decision making is time consuming. Therefore, managers perform detailed investigation only for variances they consider important.

Importance is decided in two ways. First, the variances that will be calculated and monitored need to be chosen. For example, in the opening case Protech's managers decided to stop measuring and analyzing individual employee productivity at several plants. However, when they learned that employee productivity declined, they decided to reinstate that analysis. Second, for those variances that are measured and monitored, managers decide whether a particular amount of variance is large enough to justify investigation. Managers may decide that a variance is important only if it is larger than a given dollar amount or a given percentage of the budget. Other factors also justify variance investigation. When variance trends are increasing, managers may want to know what causes the trend so that it can be eliminated if possible.

**INTERNATIONAL**
**Trimac**, a Canadian transportation and logistic services company, monitors the performance of individual truck hauls using standards such as mileage and loading time.[3]

---

[3] J. Caplan, "Applying a Little Business Intelligence," *CFO.com*, July 22, 2003.

**EXHIBIT 11.2** Variance Analysis

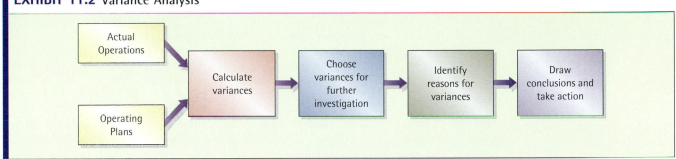

Suppose an unfavorable variance of $3,000 occurred last year in the cost of Benny's Purple Madness ice cream—actual cost exceeded standard cost by $3,000. Was it caused by an unanticipated increase in the cost of direct materials? Was labor less efficient than expected? If so, did an equipment failure create unexpected employee downtime? Was employee turnover higher than usual, reducing average worker productivity? Did total production levels decline, causing actual fixed overhead cost per unit to be higher than expected? Managers must evaluate these types of questions before deciding what actions to take, if any. Accountants assist in this process, acting as detectives who discover the reasons for cost variances.

## ■ Manager Conclusions and Actions

Once managers identify the reasons for variances, they draw conclusions about what has occurred and consider whether some type of corrective action is needed. Suppose the managers of Benny's find that the unfavorable variance was caused primarily by an unanticipated increase in the cost of ingredients. The managers would next want to know whether the cost increase was temporary or was expected to continue. If the higher cost is expected to continue, they might decide to bring costs back into control by switching to less expensive ingredients. Or, they might decide that their standard cost is no longer appropriate and should be increased to reflect the new cost. If the cost increase was temporary, they might decide that no action should be taken. Sometimes a variance investigation uncovers an error in the accounting records, causing the appearance of a variance when none exists. In this case, managers might take action to correct the accounting system to avoid similar future errors. Exhibit 11.3 provides a summary of the general conclusions about variances and related management actions.

## ■ Separating Variances into Components

Identifying the reasons for variances can be time consuming. However, by using categories in the accounting system to separate variances into component parts, the process becomes easier and the most useful information is produced. Suppose the unfavorable variance for

**EXHIBIT 11.3**

General Conclusions about Variances and Management Actions

| General Conclusion about Variance | General Management Action |
|---|---|
| Operations are out of control. | Take action to correct operations. |
| Operations are better than expected. | Monitor quality to ensure it is maintained. |
| Operations are better than expected and quality is maintained. | Modify future operating plans to take advantage of gains. |
| Benchmark is inappropriate. | Revise benchmark to improve the accuracy of future plans. |
| Error made is in accounting records. | Take action to correct accounting system. |
| Variance is random or is not expected to recur. | Do nothing. |

Benny's Purple Madness ice cream is separated into the following categories used in its standard costing system (F = Favorable and U = Unfavorable):

| | |
|---|---|
| Direct materials | $2,500 U |
| Direct labor | 700 F |
| Fixed overhead | 400 U |
| Variable overhead | 800 U |
| Total variance | $3,000 U |

This type of breakdown helps managers identify the sources of variances and also highlights possible offsetting of favorable and unfavorable variances between components. The aggregation of favorable and unfavorable variances could hide production problems that need to be investigated. In addition, this breakdown helps managers identify variances that are sufficiently large to justify further investigation.

## DIRECT COST VARIANCES

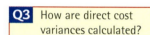

Q3 How are direct cost variances calculated?

Recall from Exhibit 11.1 that standard costs for direct materials and direct labor consist of a standard price times a standard quantity for each of the direct resources that should be used in production. As a result, as shown in Exhibit 11.4 the total variance for direct costs can be broken down into the following two components:

- Price variance
- Efficiency variance

### ■ Price Variances

A **price variance** is the difference between standard and actual prices paid for resources purchased and used in the production of goods or services. We informally calculate price variances frequently in our daily lives. For example, we may compare the advertised prices of groceries with a standard price (the price we usually pay), and then decide to purchase certain items. Suppose soda usually costs $5.00 for a 12-pack, but is on sale at $2.50. After comparing the sale price to the $5.00 standard, we may decide to purchase more than the usual amount. Our standard price for two 12-packs of soda would have been $10.00 ($5.00 per pack × 2 packs), and our actual cost would be $5.00 ($2.50 per pack × 2 packs). By taking advantage of the sale, we achieve a favorable price variance of $5.00 ($10.00 − $5.00).

**EXHIBIT 11.4**
Direct Cost Variances

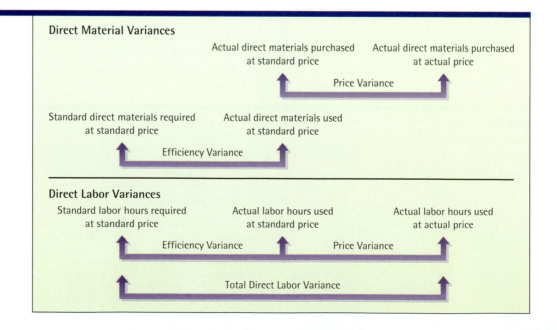

This example illustrates several limitations of a price variance. The price variance does not take into account whether sufficient cash flows, storage space, or usage requirements justify and accommodate purchasing resources in larger quantities. Perhaps our kitchen lacks sufficient space to store extra groceries if we purchase more than our weekly usage. If we purchase large quantities of perishable foods, they may spoil before they are needed. Also, the price variance does not reflect possible quality differences between resources purchased at higher or lower prices. Suppose the brand of soda that is on sale is not the brand we prefer. We may be willing to pay a higher price for our preferred brand. In a business organization, it might be inefficient to use lower-quality direct materials even when they are cheaper.

**Direct Materials Price Variance** A **direct materials price variance** compares the standard price for direct materials to the actual price for the amount of direct materials purchased. Direct materials price variances are calculated using the following formula:

**ALTERNATIVE TERMS**

Some people use the term *rate variance* instead of *price variance*, and *expected* or *budgeted price* instead of *standard price*.

$$\text{Direct materials price variance} = \left( \text{Standard price} - \text{Actual price} \right) \times \text{Quantity purchased}$$

Suppose that Benny's had purchased 110 pints of blackberries at $1.25 per pint. The standard cost is $1.00 per pint. Therefore, the price variance for these berries is

$$(1.00 \text{ per pint} - \$1.25 \text{ per pint}) \times 110 \text{ pints} = \$27.50 \text{ U}$$

This variance is unfavorable because the actual price paid for frozen blackberries is higher than the standard price. Similar calculations would be made for each of the direct materials used to produce Purple Madness ice cream.

The direct materials price variance is usually calculated at the time direct materials are purchased. Therefore, direct materials are recorded in raw material inventory at the standard cost rather than actual cost. Two advantages come with this practice. First, it reduces bookkeeping complexity. Because all units of direct material are recorded at the same standard cost, the actual cost of individual batches of direct material purchases need not be tracked. Second, this approach allows managers to identify the price variance during the period in which the variance occurred—at the time direct materials are purchased. Purchasing department personnel are often held accountable for price variances, so it is more appropriate to measure the variance at the time of purchase rather than at the time the direct materials are used. Depending on how quickly inventory is used, a delay in recognition could prevent managers from rapidly taking any needed action.

**Direct Labor Price Variance** A **direct labor price variance** compares the standard price with the actual price for labor. Direct labor price variances are calculated using the following formula:

$$\text{Direct labor price variance} = \left( \text{Standard labor price per hour} - \text{Actual labor price per hour} \right) \times \text{Actual hours used}$$

Suppose that Benny's paid $9 per hour for 9.5 hours of work in packing 100 gallons of Purple Madness ice cream (recall that the standard labor rate is $8 per hour). The direct labor price variance is calculated as

$$(\$8 \text{ per hour} - \$9 \text{ per hour}) \times 9.5 \text{ hours} = \$9.50 \text{ U}$$

This variance is unfavorable because Benny's paid more for labor per hour than the standard called for. Similar computations would be made for other types of direct labor used to produce Purple Madness ice cream.

## ■ Efficiency Variances

An **efficiency variance** provides information about how economically direct resources such as materials and labor were used. We informally assess our own efficiency frequently in our daily lives. For example, when we plan a bicycle ride on the weekend, we may believe that it will take two hours to ride 30 miles. Once we finish the ride we compare the actual length of time to our estimate. We might use this information to gauge our effort on the ride or to

**ALTERNATIVE TERMS**

Some people use the terms *usage variance* or *quantity variance* instead of *efficiency variance*.

change our estimate for future trips. The variance calculation does not consider any factors that might have affected efficiency; these factors must instead be considered by managers when investigating the variance. For example, suppose one of the tires on the bicycle is faulty and becomes flat during the ride. The time needed to fix the tire would cause us to take longer than expected to complete the trip.

**Direct Materials Efficiency Variance**  The **direct materials efficiency variance** compares the standard amount of materials that should have been used to the amount of materials actually used. This difference is valued at the standard price. The formula follows:

$$\frac{\text{Direct materials}}{\text{efficiency variance}} = \left( \frac{\text{Standard quantity}}{\text{for actual output}} - \frac{\text{Actual quantity}}{\text{for actual output}} \right) \times \frac{\text{Standard}}{\text{price}}$$

Assume Benny's produced a batch of 100 gallons of Purple Madness ice cream using 90 pints of blackberries (recall the standard quantity is 1 pint per gallon). Here are calculations for the variance:

$$[(1 \text{ pint per gallon} \times 100 \text{ gallons}) - 90 \text{ pints}] \times \$1.00 \text{ per pint}$$
$$= (100 \text{ pints} - 90 \text{ pints}) \times \$1.00 \text{ per pint} = \$10 \text{ F}$$

This variance is favorable because fewer direct materials were used than called for at standard. Although we call this variance favorable, using fewer blackberries likely affects the quality of Benny's ice cream, so this variance may be investigated. Similar efficiency variance computations would be performed for each of the direct materials used to produce Purple Madness ice cream.

**Direct Labor Efficiency Variance**  The **direct labor efficiency variance** compares the standard amount of labor hours that should have been used to the amount actually used; it values this difference at the standard labor price per hour.

$$\frac{\text{Direct labor}}{\text{efficiency}}_{\text{variance}} = \left( \frac{\text{Standard hours}}{\text{for actual output}} - \frac{\text{Actual hours for}}{\text{actual output}} \right) \times \frac{\text{Standard}}{\text{price}}$$

Suppose one group of employees at Benny's is responsible for hand-packing ice cream into 1-gallon containers. The standard amount of time to pack 1 gallon of ice cream is 0.1 hour, and 9.5 hours were used to pack 100 gallons. The direct labor efficiency variance is calculated as

$$[(100 \text{ gallons} \times 0.1 \text{ hour per gallon}) - 9.5 \text{ hours}] \times \$8 \text{ per hour}$$
$$= (10 \text{ hours} - 9.5 \text{ hours}) \times \$8 \text{ per hour} = \$4.00 \text{ F}$$

**CURRENT PRACTICE**

During the second quarter of 2003, productivity per labor hour in nonfarm U.S. businesses increased at an annual rate of 6.8%.[4]

This variance is favorable because actual hours were less than standard hours. Similar computations would be performed for other types of direct labor used to produce Purple Madness ice cream.

## ■ Journal Entries for Direct Costs and Variances

In a standard cost system for a manufacturer, inventory accounting entries are recorded using standard costs. Differences between actual and standard costs are recorded in variance accounts. Later in the chapter, we learn to close variance accounts at the end of an accounting period. Exhibit 11.5 summarizes the variances and journal entries used by Benny's for the frozen blackberries direct material and the direct labor for packing 100 gallons of Purple Madness ice cream.

When 110 pints of frozen blackberries are purchased, they are recorded in raw material inventory at standard cost ($110) and the price variance is recorded ($27.50 U). Then 90 pints are removed from raw materials inventory at standard cost ($90.00). The direct materials price and efficiency variances account for the difference between actual and standard costs.

The labor journal entry is also presented in Exhibit 11.5. The entry for work in process

---

[4]"The New 'New Economy,'" in "Special Report: American Productivity," *The Economist*, September 13, 2003, pp. 61–64.

**EXHIBIT 11.5**

Direct Cost Variances for Benny's Purple Madness Ice Cream

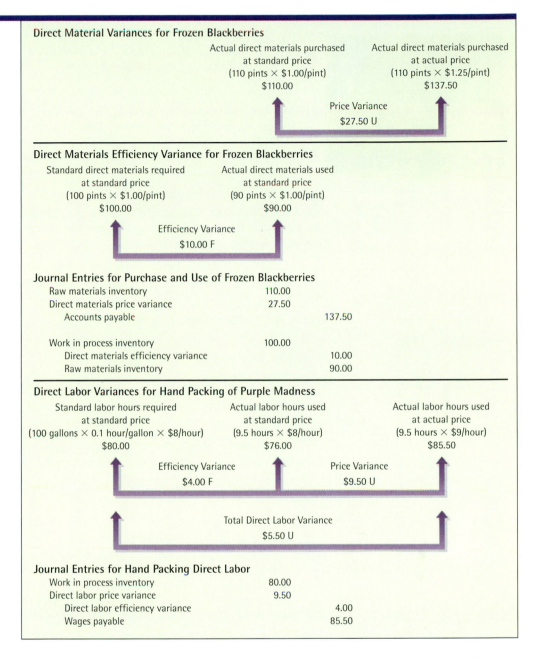

**Direct Material Variances for Frozen Blackberries**

| Actual direct materials purchased at standard price (110 pints × $1.00/pint) $110.00 | | Actual direct materials purchased at actual price (110 pints × $1.25/pint) $137.50 |
|---|---|---|
| | Price Variance $27.50 U | |

**Direct Materials Efficiency Variance for Frozen Blackberries**

| Standard direct materials required at standard price (100 pints × $1.00/pint) $100.00 | | Actual direct materials used at standard price (90 pints × $1.00/pint) $90.00 |
|---|---|---|
| | Efficiency Variance $10.00 F | |

**Journal Entries for Purchase and Use of Frozen Blackberries**

| | | |
|---|---|---|
| Raw materials inventory | 110.00 | |
| Direct materials price variance | 27.50 | |
| Accounts payable | | 137.50 |
| | | |
| Work in process inventory | 100.00 | |
| Direct materials efficiency variance | | 10.00 |
| Raw materials inventory | | 90.00 |

**Direct Labor Variances for Hand Packing of Purple Madness**

| Standard labor hours required at standard price (100 gallons × 0.1 hour/gallon × $8/hour) $80.00 | | Actual labor hours used at standard price (9.5 hours × $8/hour) $76.00 | | Actual labor hours used at actual price (9.5 hours × $9/hour) $85.50 |
|---|---|---|---|---|
| | Efficiency Variance $4.00 F | | Price Variance $9.50 U | |

Total Direct Labor Variance $5.50 U

**Journal Entries for Hand Packing Direct Labor**

| | | |
|---|---|---|
| Work in process inventory | 80.00 | |
| Direct labor price variance | 9.50 | |
| Direct labor efficiency variance | | 4.00 |
| Wages payable | | 85.50 |

inventory is made at the standard quantity and standard cost. Wages payable is credited for the actual wages owed to employees. The direct labor price and efficiency variances account for the difference between actual and standard costs.

Cementos Juarez (Part 2) demonstrates the calculation of direct cost variances and direct cost journal entries.

## CEMENTOS JUAREZ (PART 2)
## VARIANCES FOR DIRECT MATERIALS AND DIRECT LABOR

At the end of the first month of operations after Carina developed the cost standards, she collected the following data needed to perform a direct cost variance analysis:

- 100,000 cement blocks were produced.
- The company purchased 130,000 kilos of cement mix for 975,000 pesos.
- 120,000 kilos of cement mix were used.
- Direct labor employees were paid 16,500 pesos and worked 1,100 hours.

### Direct Materials Price Variance

Carina first calculates the direct materials price variance. The purchase price last month for the cement mix was 975,000 pesos for 130,000 kilos, or 7.5 pesos per kilo. The standard cost is 10 pesos per kilo. She calculates the direct materials price variance as follows:

$$(\text{Standard price} - \text{Actual price}) \times \text{Quantity purchased}$$
$$= (10 \text{ pesos} - 7.50 \text{ pesos}) \times 130,000 \text{ kilos} = 325,000 \text{ pesos F}$$

Because the price per kilo that Cementos Juarez paid last month is less than expected, the direct materials price variance is favorable.

### Direct Labor Price Variance

Next, Carina calculates the direct labor price variance. During the month, Cementos Juarez paid its employees 16,500 pesos for 1,100 hours of work. Thus, the actual price for labor was 15 pesos per hour (16,500 pesos/1,100 hours). The standard cost is 10 pesos per hour, so 11,000 pesos should have been paid for 1,100 hours of work. Therefore, the direct labor price variance is

$$(\text{Standard labor price per hour} - \text{Actual labor price per hour}) \times \text{Amount of labor hours used}$$
$$= (10 \text{ pesos} - 15 \text{ pesos}) \times 1,100 \text{ hours} = 5,500 \text{ pesos U}$$

Because the company paid more than the standard labor wage, the direct labor price variance is unfavorable.

### Direct Materials Efficiency Variance

After completing the direct cost price variances, Carina calculates the direct cost efficiency variances. Efficiency variances are calculated based on actual production volume (i.e., the quantity of concrete blocks produced). During the last month, the company produced 100,000 blocks, using 120,000 kilos of cement mix. The standard quantity of direct materials is 1 kilo per block for a total of 100,000 kilos of cement mix. Carina calculated the direct materials efficiency variance as follows:

$$(\text{Standard quantity for actual output} - \text{Actual quantity for actual output}) \times \text{Standard price}$$
$$= [(1 \text{ kilo per block} \times 100,000 \text{ blocks}) - 120,000 \text{ kilos}] \times 10 \text{ pesos per kilo}$$
$$= (100,000 \text{ kilos} - 120,000 \text{ kilos}) \times 10 \text{ pesos per kilo} = 200,000 \text{ pesos U}$$

The materials efficiency variance is unfavorable because more materials than the standard quantity were used.

### Direct Labor Efficiency Variance

To calculate the direct labor efficiency variance, Carina first determines the amount of labor that should have been used to produce 100,000 blocks and then compares it to the amount of labor actually used, 1,100 direct labor hours. The standard quantity of labor is 100 blocks per hour. The direct labor efficiency variance is calculated as follows:

$$(\text{Standard hours for actual output} - \text{Actual hours for actual output}) \times \text{Standard price}$$
$$= [(100,000 \text{ blocks} \times 1 \text{ hour per 100 blocks}) - 1,100 \text{ hours}] \times 10 \text{ pesos per hour}$$
$$= (1,000 \text{ hours} - 1,100 \text{ hours}) \times 10 \text{ pesos per hour} = 1,000 \text{ pesos U}$$

Because actual hours exceeded standard hours, the direct labor efficiency variance is unfavorable.

## Summary of Direct Cost Variances

After calculating the individual direct cost variances, Carina creates a summary showing all of the variances, as shown in Exhibit 11.6.

**EXHIBIT 11.6**
Direct Cost Variances for
Cementos Juarez

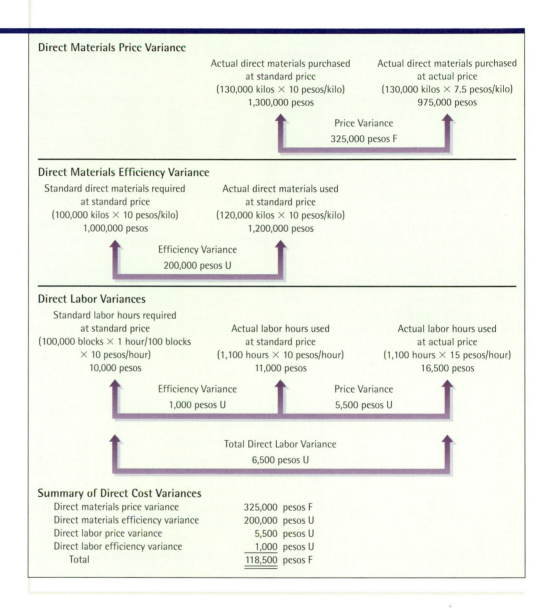

Direct Materials Price Variance

| Actual direct materials purchased at standard price (130,000 kilos × 10 pesos/kilo) 1,300,000 pesos | Actual direct materials purchased at actual price (130,000 kilos × 7.5 pesos/kilo) 975,000 pesos |

Price Variance
325,000 pesos F

Direct Materials Efficiency Variance

| Standard direct materials required at standard price (100,000 kilos × 10 pesos/kilo) 1,000,000 pesos | Actual direct materials used at standard price (120,000 kilos × 10 pesos/kilo) 1,200,000 pesos |

Efficiency Variance
200,000 pesos U

Direct Labor Variances

| Standard labor hours required at standard price (100,000 blocks × 1 hour/100 blocks × 10 pesos/hour) 10,000 pesos | Actual labor hours used at standard price (1,100 hours × 10 pesos/hour) 11,000 pesos | Actual labor hours used at actual price (1,100 hours × 15 pesos/hour) 16,500 pesos |

Efficiency Variance
1,000 pesos U

Price Variance
5,500 pesos U

Total Direct Labor Variance
6,500 pesos U

**Summary of Direct Cost Variances**

| | | |
|---|---:|---|
| Direct materials price variance | 325,000 | pesos F |
| Direct materials efficiency variance | 200,000 | pesos U |
| Direct labor price variance | 5,500 | pesos U |
| Direct labor efficiency variance | 1,000 | pesos U |
| Total | 118,500 | pesos F |

# ANALYZING DIRECT COST VARIANCE INFORMATION

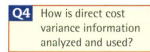

**Q4** How is direct cost variance information analyzed and used?

Direct cost variances are analyzed using the process introduced in Exhibit 11.2. The analysis begins with calculating the variances. For variances chosen for further investigation, the reasons for the variances are identified. Breaking the variances into price and efficiency components, as illustrated in Exhibit 11.4, helps to identify why actual direct costs differ from standard costs.

## ■ Identifying Reasons for Direct Cost Variances

In the Cementos Juarez example, a favorable direct materials price variance of 325,000 pesos arises for cement. The combined direct cost variances are 118,500 pesos favorable. Does this result mean that operations are performing better than expected? What about the unfavorable direct materials efficiency variance for cement of 200,000 pesos? Is some type of

**EXHIBIT 11.7** Examples of Reasons for Direct Cost Variances

| Direct Materials Variances | Direct Labor Variances |
|---|---|
| Price:<br>• Change in price paid for materials caused by:<br>—A change in the quality of materials purchased<br>—A change in quantity purchased, leading to a change in purchase discount<br>—A new supplier contract<br>• Unreasonable materials price standard<br>• Error in the accounting records for the actual price of materials | Price:<br>• Change in average wages paid to employees caused by:<br>—A new union contract<br>—A change in average experience or training of workers<br>—A change in the government-mandated minimum wage<br>• Unanticipated overtime hours<br>• Unreasonable labor price standard<br>• Error in the accounting records for the actual price of direct labor |
| Efficiency:<br>• Normal fluctuation in materials usage<br>• Change in production processes, causing a change in the quantity of materials used<br>• Change in proportion of materials spoiled caused by:<br>—A change in quality of materials<br>—A change in equipment, technology, or other aspect of production processes<br>—Equipment malfunction<br>—Intentional worker damage<br>• Theft of raw materials<br>• Unreasonable materials quantity standard<br>• Error in the accounting records for the quantity of materials used | Efficiency:<br>• Normal fluctuation in labor hours<br>• Change in average labor time caused by:<br>—A change in equipment, technology, or other aspect of production processes<br>—A change in average worker experience or training caused by:<br>  • Improved performance from effective training programs<br>  • Change in employee turnover<br>—Intentional work slowdown<br>• Intentional or unintentional over- or underreporting of labor hours<br>• Unreasonable labor hours standard<br>• Error in the accounting records for the quantity of labor hours |

corrective action needed? Before addressing these types of questions, it is necessary to discover the reasons for the direct cost variances.

Exhibit 11.7 lists examples of circumstances that can cause direct cost variances. Some types of variances are relatively easy to discover. For example, accountants would know whether the company negotiated a pay increase with a labor union, as well as the amount of the pay increase. To determine whether the pay increase explains an unfavorable direct labor price variance, they could simply compare the amount of the variance with the expected amount of the pay increase. Some types of variances are more difficult to discover. For example, it would not be easy to determine that workers intentionally worked slower than expected. Theft and fraud are hard to discover because the perpetrators deliberately try to hide them. Determining that a standard is incorrect, especially for price variances, may be relatively easy. For other types of variances, however, that process is more difficult because of uncertainties about the reasonableness of standard prices and quantities.

## ■ Recognizing Resource and Quality Trade-Offs

Sometimes trade-offs are made between price and efficiency or between different inputs. For example, it may be possible to hire more proficient workers at a higher wage per hour. Similarly, higher-quality direct materials with a higher price might produce less spoilage during production. Consider the cost of producing Purple Madness ice cream at Benny's. The company usually purchases frozen blackberries that have been cleaned and can be added directly to the ice cream. During fresh blackberry season, the company could pay a lower price for fresh blackberries that have not been cleaned. However, the company would incur greater direct labor time for cleaning the berries. Thus, the trade-off is made between the price paid for the blackberries and the labor time required. Quality differences also affect this decision. Suppose managers believe that fresh blackberries are better flavored than frozen blackberries. They may purchase fresh blackberries to achieve better flavor, even if they cost more overall.

When analyzing variances, it is necessary to consider possible trade-offs. A favorable variance in one area might be partially or completely offset by an unfavorable variance in another area. In the opening case in this chapter, Protech's managers eliminated monitoring of labor efficiency and focused on spoilage rates to increase quality at some plants. Researchers found that this change caused labor efficiency to decline and product defect rates to improve. However, they concluded that the variance caused by the decline in labor efficiency was larger than the gain from improved quality (lower product defect rates). This finding prompted the managers to resume monitoring practices to bring labor efficiency back into control.

# ■ Analyzing Interactions Between Incentives and Variances

Some organizations reward employees for meeting or exceeding benchmarks set as standard costs. However, such rewards create a new set of problems. Suppose employees in the cutting department of a clothing manufacturer are rewarded based on how quickly they cut fabric. The cut fabric is then transferred to the sewing department. If employees in the cutting department become less precise as they increase output, the sewing department could face a decrease in efficiency. That decrease could ripple through the rest of the production process. Or, the sewing department might pass along the quality problem into finished goods, contributing further to a long-term quality problem for the company. If the sewing department is also rewarded based on meeting efficiency standards, employees in that department would be penalized for fixing a problem created by the cutting department. Only when variances are analyzed can managers identify whether the incentives are working as expected to promote overall organizational success.

Cementos Juarez (Part 3) demonstrates the analysis of direct cost variances.

## CEMENTOS JUAREZ (PART 3)
### ANALYZING DIRECT COST VARIANCE INFORMATION

Carina examines the total favorable variance of 118,500 pesos (Exhibit 11.6). In some cases, an overall favorable variance means that the organization has no problems—operations performed better than expected. However, Carina is concerned about the large unfavorable efficiency variance for cement mix, and she is puzzled by its large favorable price variance. In addition, the unfavorable direct labor price variance seems high relative to total labor costs. However, Carina decides to focus her attention on only the two largest variances because these explain most of the total direct cost variance.

First, Carina considers the favorable price variance for cement mix. She speaks with Ricardo, who purchases direct materials. He has found a new supplier with better prices. Because he receives a bonus based on reducing the company's costs, he is looking forward to a sizeable bonus. Carina tentatively thinks that the future standard cost for cement mix should be reduced to reflect the new lower price.

Next, Carina investigates the unfavorable efficiency variance for cement mix. She speaks with Jorge, the labor supervisor. He is very upset about a decrease in the quality of the cement mix from the new supplier; the mix contains inadequate quantities of an ingredient that prevents the blocks from slumping, or losing shape, when they are turned out of the forms. Although 120,000 blocks were produced, 20,000 of them were rejected because of the slumping problem. In addition, more labor hours were needed, leading to overtime payments. These factors explain the unfavorable direct labor price variance. Jorge is concerned that some of the blocks shipped to customers are not the correct shape. Some customers might become dissatisfied and no longer purchase cement blocks from the company.

Carina plans to recommend to management that the company pay a higher price (the original standard) for the higher-quality cement mix. Although it appeared that the company saved money overall last month from the lower-priced mix, most of the savings were offset by unfavorable variances elsewhere caused by the lower quality. Furthermore, she believes that just the risk of lost sales in the future outweighs the cost savings. Carina also plans to work with management to design a better reward system that avoids any further adverse effects that result from the purchasing agent's bonus plan.

## OVERHEAD VARIANCES

**Q5** How are variable and fixed overhead variances calculated?

**CHAPTER REFERENCE**

To learn more about the accounting choices for estimated volumes of allocation bases, see Chapter 5.

Organizations use standard cost systems to monitor overhead costs in addition to direct costs. To monitor overhead costs, a **standard overhead allocation rate** is created at the beginning of each period. Overhead is typically allocated using an allocation base such as production units, direct labor costs, direct labor hours, or machine hours. Separate allocation bases and rates are often used for fixed and variable overhead costs.

The **standard variable overhead allocation rate** is determined by estimating the variable amount of overhead cost per unit of an allocation base as follows:

$$\text{Standard variable overhead allocation rate} = \frac{\text{Estimated variable overhead cost}}{\text{Estimated volume of an allocation base}}$$

For example, the accountant at Benny's estimated the variable overhead cost as $150,000 and the labor hours as 75,000, so the cost function for variable overhead costs is $2.00 per direct labor hour.

Accountants choose allocation bases for variable overhead that reflect the use of variable resources. Indirect labor costs, such as maintenance wages, might be related to direct labor costs; as the number of employees providing direct labor increases, the number of maintenance worker hours increases. When the proportion of labor-related costs in the variable overhead cost pool is high, direct labor hours or direct labor cost are appropriate allocation bases. Alternatively, indirect materials cost such as paint, plastic stripping, and decals applied to toy cars could be a large proportion of the variable overhead cost pool. In this case, the estimated volume of units would be the most appropriate allocation base.

Although fixed costs do not vary with volume, we need to develop an allocation rate to assign these costs to inventory and cost of goods sold. The **standard fixed overhead allocation rate** is determined as follows:

$$\text{Standard fixed overhead allocation rate} = \frac{\text{Estimated fixed overhead cost}}{\text{Estimated volume of an allocation base}}$$

For example, if the estimated fixed overhead cost for Benny's is $200,000 and the company allocates fixed overhead based on units produced using a normal volume of 500,000 gallons of ice cream during the year, the standard fixed overhead allocation rate is $200,000 ÷ 500,000 gallons, or $0.40 per gallon. Therefore, standard fixed overhead of $0.40 will be allocated to the cost of each gallon of ice cream.

At the end of the period, variances between standard allocated overhead costs and actual costs are analyzed. The **variable overhead budget variance** is the difference between allocated variable overhead cost and actual variable overhead cost. The **fixed overhead budget variance** is the difference between allocated fixed overhead cost and actual fixed

**EXHIBIT 11.8**
Overhead Cost Variances

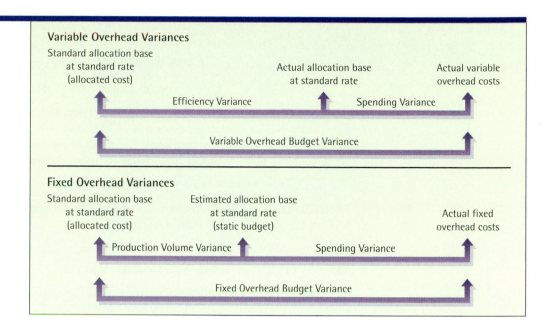

overhead cost. As shown in Exhibit 11.8, the overhead variances can be broken down into the following components:

Variable overhead budget variance:
- Spending variance
- Efficiency variance

Fixed overhead budget variance:
- Spending variance
- Volume variance

## ■ Variable Overhead Spending Variance

The **variable overhead spending variance** is the difference between the total expected variable overhead costs for the actual output and the actual variable overhead costs for that level of output. The variable overhead spending variance helps managers monitor whether the organization spent the planned amount on overhead. Because variable overhead costs are expected to vary with activity, the calculation for the spending variance takes into account the actual volume of activity.

For Benny's, the allocation base for variable overhead is direct labor hours. The normal volume of direct labor hours is 500,000 gallons × 0.15 hours per gallon, or 75,000 hours. The standard variable overhead allocation rate is $2.00 per direct labor hour. Suppose actual variable overhead costs total $147,000 and actual labor hours are 74,000. The variable overhead spending variance is calculated as:

$$\text{Variable overhead spending variance} = \left( \begin{array}{c} \text{Standard variable} \\ \text{overhead allocation rate} \end{array} \times \begin{array}{c} \text{Actual volume of} \\ \text{allocation base} \end{array} \right) - \begin{array}{c} \text{Actual variable} \\ \text{overhead cost} \end{array}$$

$$= (\$2.00 \text{ per hour} \times 74{,}000 \text{ hours}) - \$147{,}000 = \$148{,}000 - \$147{,}000 = \$1{,}000 \text{ F}$$

The variance is favorable because actual variable overhead costs were less than expected, given the actual volume of output.

## ■ Variable Overhead Efficiency Variance

The difference between the flexible budget for variable overhead cost and the standard amount of variable overhead for the actual volume of the allocation base is called the **variable overhead efficiency variance** (Exhibit 11.8). This variance is favorable if the actual volume of the allocation base is less than expected given actual production levels, and it will be unfavorable if the actual volume of the allocation base is more than expected. It is calculated as follows:

$$\text{Variable overhead}\atop\text{efficiency variance} = \left(\begin{array}{c}\text{Standard volume of}\\\text{allocation base}\\\text{for actual output}\end{array} - \begin{array}{c}\text{Actual volume}\\\text{of allocation}\\\text{base}\end{array}\right) \times \begin{array}{c}\text{Standard variable}\\\text{overhead}\\\text{allocation rate}\end{array}$$

For Benny's, assume that 498,000 gallons of ice cream were produced. The standard number of direct labor hours for actual production is 74,700 hours (498,000 gallons × 0.15 hours per gallon) and 74,000 actual hours were used. The standard variable overhead allocation rate is $2.00 per direct labor hour. Therefore the variable overhead efficiency variance calculation is:

$$(74{,}700 \text{ hours} - 74{,}000 \text{ hours}) \times \$2.00 \text{ per hour} = \$1{,}400 \text{ F}$$

The variance is favorable because actual direct labor hours are less than expected, given actual production of 498,000 pints of ice cream.

## ◼ Fixed Overhead Spending Variance

The **fixed overhead spending variance** is the difference between estimated fixed overhead costs and actual fixed overhead costs. Fixed overhead costs are not expected to fluctuate with levels of activity. Thus, the spending variance is not affected by the volume of activity; it reflects the amount by which the actual spending on fixed overhead differs from the estimated fixed overhead (the static budget), as shown in Exhibit 11.8. The spending variance helps managers monitor whether the organization spent the planned amount on overhead. We use the following formula:

**CHAPTER REFERENCE**

Chapter 10 defined a **static budget** as a budget that is not altered to reflect actual volume levels during the budget period.

$$\text{Fixed overhead}\atop\text{spending variance} = \text{Estimated fixed}\atop\text{overhead costs} - \text{Actual fixed}\atop\text{overhead costs}$$

The fixed overhead budget at Benny's was $200,000, and actual costs were $203,000. The fixed overhead spending variance is calculated as

$$\$200{,}000 - \$203{,}000 = \$3{,}000 \text{ U}$$

The variance is unfavorable because more was spent of fixed overhead than was estimated.

## ◼ Production Volume Variance

The difference between the standard amount of fixed overhead cost allocated to products and the estimated fixed overhead costs is called the **production volume variance** (Exhibit 11.8). If actual volumes of the allocation base exceed normal (i.e., estimated) volumes, fixed overhead will be overapplied and the variance will be favorable. Conversely, if actual volumes of the allocation base are less than normal volumes, fixed overhead will be underapplied and the variance will be unfavorable. The production volume variance is calculated only for fixed overhead. This variance is used for bookkeeping purposes. The actual overhead costs need to be allocated to inventory each period. This variance is used to adjust balances at the end of the period so that the total costs recorded in the financial statements are equal to the actual costs incurred. The variance is calculated as follows:

$$\text{Production}\atop\text{volume variance} = \left(\begin{array}{c}\text{Standard volume of}\\\text{allocation base}\\\text{for actual output}\end{array} - \begin{array}{c}\text{Estimated}\\\text{volume of}\\\text{allocation base}\end{array}\right) \times \begin{array}{c}\text{Standard fixed}\\\text{overhead}\\\text{allocation rate}\end{array}$$

For Benny's, suppose estimated fixed overhead was $200,000 and the estimated volume of the allocation base was 500,000 gallons (normal production). The standard allocation rate is $200,000 ÷ 500,000 gallons = $0.40 per gallon. Actual production was 498,000 gallons. The production volume variance is calculated as

$$(498{,}000 \text{ gallons} - 500{,}000 \text{ gallons}) \times \$0.40 \text{ per gallon} = \$800 \text{ U}$$

Because actual production was less than normal Benny's fixed overhead is underapplied, causing an unfavorable variance. These overhead variance computations are shown in Exhibit 11.9.

**EXHIBIT 11.9**
Overhead Variances
for Benny's

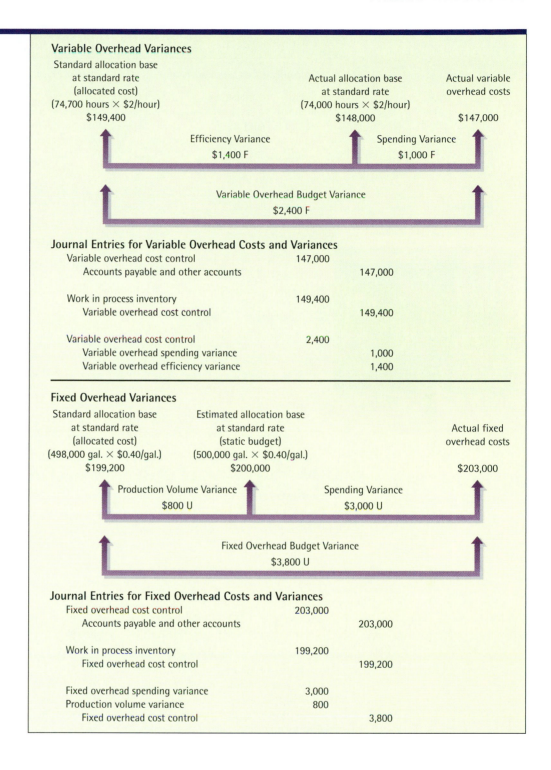

## ■ Journal Entries for Overhead Costs and Variances

Organizations often use an overhead cost control account to keep track of actual and allocated overhead costs. As actual overhead costs are incurred, they are debited to the account. The account is then credited for the standard amount of overhead costs allocated to inventory. The remaining balance in the overhead cost control account is the total variance. This balance for fixed overhead costs is closed to separate spending and volume variance accounts, while the balance for variable overhead costs is closed to separate spending and efficiency variance accounts. The journal entries for Benny's are shown in Exhibit 11.9.

Cementos Juarez (Part 4) demonstrates the calculation of fixed and variable overhead variances.

## GUIDE YOUR LEARNING  11.4  Key Terms

Stop to confirm that you understand the new terms introduced in the last several pages.

Standard overhead allocation rate (p. 430)
Standard variable overhead allocation rate (p. 430)
Standard fixed overhead allocation rate (p. 430)
Variable overhead budget variance (p. 430)

Fixed overhead budget variance (p. 430)
Variable overhead spending variance (p. 431)
Variable overhead efficiency variance (p. 431)
Fixed overhead spending variance (p. 432)
Production volume variance (p. 432)

For each of these terms, write a definition in your own words.

## CEMENTOS JUAREZ (PART 4)
## OVERHEAD VARIANCES

Carina had previously established the following standard costs for fixed and variable overhead:

Variable overhead (allocated based on direct labor hours):
| | |
|---|---|
| Standard cost per direct labor hour | 2 pesos |
| Standard quantity of allocation base per block | |
| (1 hour per 100 blocks) | 0.01 hours |
| Standard cost per block (0.01 hours per block × 2 pesos per hour) | 0.02 pesos |

Fixed overhead (allocated based on units):
| | |
|---|---|
| Estimated cost | 180,000 pesos |
| Estimated volume of allocation base (blocks produced) | 90,000 blocks |
| Standard cost per block (180,000 pesos ÷ 90,000 blocks) | 2 pesos |

At the end of the month, Carina determines that actual fixed overhead costs were 175,000 pesos. Actual variable overhead costs were 2,500 pesos, and 1,100 actual labor hours were used.

### Variable Overhead Spending and Efficiency Variances

Carina analyzes variable overhead costs, which are allocated based on direct labor hours. Actual variable overhead costs were 2,500 pesos, and actual direct labor hours were 1,100. She calculates the variable overhead spending variance as follows:

$$\left( \begin{array}{c} \text{Standard variable} \\ \text{overhead} \\ \text{allocation rate} \end{array} \times \begin{array}{c} \text{Actual} \\ \text{volume of} \\ \text{allocation base} \end{array} \right) - \begin{array}{c} \text{Actual} \\ \text{variable} \\ \text{overhead cost} \end{array}$$

= (2 pesos per labor hour × 1,100 hours) − 2,500 pesos
= 2,200 − 2,500 pesos = 300 pesos U

The variable overhead spending variance is unfavorable because more was actually spent than should have been spent, given actual labor hours.

Next she calculates the variable overhead efficiency variance. Based on actual production of 100,000 blocks, the standard volume of the allocation base is 1,000 direct labor hours (100,000 blocks × 0.01 hour per block). Given the standard cost of 2 pesos per hour, the variable overhead efficiency variance is calculated as follows:

$$\left( \begin{array}{c} \text{Standard volume of} \\ \text{allocation base for} \\ \text{actual output} \end{array} - \begin{array}{c} \text{Actual} \\ \text{volume of} \\ \text{allocation base} \end{array} \right) \times \begin{array}{c} \text{Standard} \\ \text{variable overhead} \\ \text{allocation rate} \end{array}$$

= (1,000 labor hours − 1,100 labor hours) × 2 pesos per hour
= 2,000 pesos − 2,200 pesos = 200 pesos U

The variance is unfavorable because actual labor hours used in production exceeded the standard number of labor hours (see Exhibit 11.10).

### Fixed Overhead Spending and Production Volume Variances

First Carina calculates the fixed overhead spending variance as follows:

Estimated fixed overhead costs − Actual fixed overhead costs
= 180,000 pesos − 175,000 pesos = 5,000 pesos F

**EXHIBIT 11.10**
Overhead Variances for
Cementos Juarez

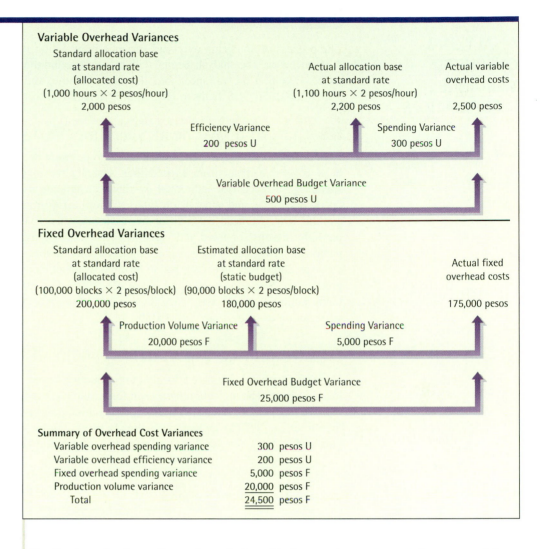

**Variable Overhead Variances**

Standard allocation base
at standard rate
(allocated cost)
(1,000 hours × 2 pesos/hour)
2,000 pesos

Actual allocation base
at standard rate
(1,100 hours × 2 pesos/hour)
2,200 pesos

Actual variable
overhead costs
2,500 pesos

Efficiency Variance
200 pesos U

Spending Variance
300 pesos U

Variable Overhead Budget Variance
500 pesos U

**Fixed Overhead Variances**

Standard allocation base
at standard rate
(allocated cost)
(100,000 blocks × 2 pesos/block)
200,000 pesos

Estimated allocation base
at standard rate
(static budget)
(90,000 blocks × 2 pesos/block)
180,000 pesos

Actual fixed
overhead costs
175,000 pesos

Production Volume Variance
20,000 pesos F

Spending Variance
5,000 pesos F

Fixed Overhead Budget Variance
25,000 pesos F

**Summary of Overhead Cost Variances**

| | |
|---|---|
| Variable overhead spending variance | 300 pesos U |
| Variable overhead efficiency variance | 200 pesos U |
| Fixed overhead spending variance | 5,000 pesos F |
| Production volume variance | 20,000 pesos F |
| Total | 24,500 pesos F |

The fixed overhead spending variance is favorable because less was spent than expected (see Exhibit 11.10).

Next Carina calculates the production volume variance as follows:

$$\left( \begin{array}{c} \text{Standard volume} \\ \text{of allocation base} \quad - \\ \text{for actual output} \end{array} \begin{array}{c} \text{Estimated} \\ \text{volume of} \\ \text{allocation base} \end{array} \right) \times \begin{array}{c} \text{Standard fixed} \\ \text{overhead} \\ \text{allocation rate} \end{array}$$

$$= (100{,}000 \text{ blocks} - 90{,}000 \text{ blocks}) \times 2 \text{ pesos per block} = 20{,}000 \text{ pesos F}$$

Estimated production volume was 90,000 blocks, but 100,000 blocks were actually produced. Therefore, 10,000 more blocks were produced than expected, resulting in a favorable production volume variance; that is, fixed overhead costs were overapplied by 20,000 pesos (2 pesos per block × 10,000 blocks).

## ANALYZING OVERHEAD VARIANCE INFORMATION

Q6 How is overhead variance information analyzed and used?

The process of analyzing overhead variance information is similar to the process for direct cost variances. The analysis begins with calculating and then identifying the reasons for variances. Breaking the variances into spending, volume, and efficiency components, as illustrated in Exhibit 11.8, helps to identify why actual overhead costs differ from standard costs.

### ■ Analyzing Overhead Spending Variances

Accountants investigate spending variances to pinpoint the specific fixed and variable overhead costs that differ from expectations. Usually the investigation includes analyzing the spending variances for individual overhead costs such as supplies, depreciation, property taxes, insurance, and supervision salaries. Similar to direct costs, many reasons potentially explain why overhead costs differ from expectations. Exhibit 11.11 provides examples of possible reasons for fixed and variable overhead spending variances. Sometimes unanticipated changes occur in costs. For example, an unfavorable spending variance might arise because an additional supervisor had to be hired when an increase in demand required increased production. Sometimes spending is out of control. For example, the staff may include too many janitorial employees. Once the reasons for variances are identified, managers decide what action to take, if any (see Exhibit 11.3).

### ■ Interpreting the Variable Overhead Efficiency Variance

Variable overhead costs are allocated to production based on an estimated volume of an allocation base. The allocation base used for variable costs is typically some type of resource input (such as labor hours, labor costs, or machine hours) or the volume of output. Because the direct cost efficiency variances already provide information about the efficiency of inputs and outputs, overhead efficiency variances provide no new information. For example,

**EXHIBIT 11.11** Examples of Reasons for Overhead Variances

| Variable Overhead Variances | Fixed Overhead Variances |
|---|---|
| **Spending:**<br>• Unanticipated change in prices paid for variable overhead resources caused by:<br>  —Variation in prices for supplies or indirect labor<br>  —New supplier or labor contract<br>• Out of control or improved efficiency in variable overhead cost spending<br>• Change in type or extent of variable overhead resources used, for example:<br>  —Change from in-house to outsourced equipment maintenance services<br>  —Increase or decrease in normal spoilage, rework, or scrap<br>• Unreasonable standard variable overhead allocation rate caused by:<br>  —Inappropriate allocation base<br>  —Poor estimate of variable overhead costs<br>  —Poor estimate of allocation base volume<br>• Error in the accounting records for actual variable overhead costs | **Spending:**<br>• Unanticipated change in prices for fixed overhead resources caused by:<br>  —Change in estimated asset life for depreciation<br>  —Change in electricity, other utility, insurance, or property tax rates<br>• Out-of-control or improved efficiency in fixed overhead cost spending<br>• Change in activity level to a new relevant range, requiring change in fixed resources such as:<br>  —Hire or lay off a supervisor<br>  —Increase or decrease fixed hours of janitorial staff<br>  —Depreciation change from purchase or disposal of property, plant, and equipment<br>• Unreasonable estimate for fixed overhead costs<br>• Error in the accounting records for actual fixed overhead costs |
| **Efficiency:**<br>• Fluctuation in efficiency of the allocation base (e.g., labor hours, labor costs, machine hours, units produced)—see efficiency examples in Exhibit 11.7 | **Production Volume:**<br>• Normal fluctuation in volume of allocation base (usually caused by changes in demand)<br>• Improved production processes<br>• Unreasonable estimate of volume of the allocation base<br>• Error in the accounting records for actual output |

consider the Cementos Juarez illustration. Recall that direct labor hours were used to calculate the standard variable overhead allocation rate. The variable overhead efficiency variance of 200 pesos was unfavorable because actual labor hours exceeded standard labor hours (see Exhibit 11.10). However, the inefficient use of labor hours was already reflected in the 1,000 pesos unfavorable direct labor efficiency variance (see Exhibit 11.6). Thus, the variable overhead efficiency variance provides no new information; for monitoring purposes it is meaningless. However, this variance must be calculated for bookkeeping reasons; it helps to explain why variable overhead costs allocated are different from actual variable overhead costs.

## ■ Interpreting the Production Volume Variance

By definition, fixed overhead costs are not expected to vary with volume of production. However, a production volume variance exists because fixed overhead costs are allocated to production based on an estimated level of an allocation base. In turn, the estimated level of the allocation base depends on the estimated level of production. We usually produce more or less than estimated, and so we allocate more or less of our estimated fixed cost than we expected. At the end of each accounting period, we adjust the accounting records for this difference. Exhibit 11.9 shows the adjusting journal entries for Benny's.

As shown in Exhibit 11.11, actual production volume (and volume of the allocation base) may differ from estimated volume because of normal fluctuations, production problems, improved production processes, unreasonable estimates, or accounting errors. Managers need to analyze the reasons for actual production volume differing from estimated volume to determine what type of action, if any, is needed. In general, we would expect production volume to vary with sales levels. Thus, the investigation of production volume variances tends to focus on the deviation between actual and estimated sales (see Appendix 11A). Although managers want to know why production volume deviates from the budget, the dollar amount of the production volume variance does not require investigation. The production volume variance also provides information about capacity utilization. Therefore, it may be monitored to achieve long-term goals of operating at optimal capacity levels. The relationship between capacity and demand may be monitored to find those optimum capacity levels where throughput (the rate at which products are manufactured) is equal to demand.

## COST VARIANCE ADJUSTMENTS

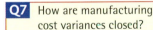
**Q7** How are manufacturing cost variances closed?

When all of the production entries and variances are recorded for an accounting period, an additional entry is made to eliminate the variance accounts. If the total variance is favorable, fewer resources were used than estimated, so we need to decrease the costs in inventory and cost of goods sold. If the total variance is unfavorable, more resources were used than estimated, so the costs in inventory and cost of goods sold need to be increased.

The type of adjustment made typically depends on whether variances are material, a decision that is a matter of judgment. Amounts are generally viewed as material if their treatment would affect the decisions of people who rely on reported values. If the net amount of variances is deemed immaterial, the adjustment is usually made only to cost of goods sold. However, the existence of material variances means that the standard costs assigned to product units do not fairly represent the actual cost of the units. Thus, if the net amount of variances is material, a more accurate adjustment procedure is needed. A proportionate share of the variance should be allocated to work in process, finished goods inventory, and cost of goods sold.

Consider the production cost variances for Cementos Juarez. The combined variances are as follows:

| | |
|---|---|
| Direct costs (see Exhibit 11.6) | 118,500 pesos F |
| Overhead costs (see Exhibit 11.10) | 24,500 pesos F |
| Total | 143,000 pesos F |

To evaluate materiality, we compare the combined variance amount to the total amount of actual production costs:

| | |
|---|---|
| Actual direct material costs (see Exhibit 11.6) | 975,000 pesos |
| Actual direct labor costs (see Exhibit 11.6) | 16,500 pesos |
| Actual variable overhead costs (see Exhibit 11.10) | 2,500 pesos |
| Actual fixed overhead costs (see Exhibit 11.10) | 175,000 pesos |
| Total | 1,169,000 pesos |

The combined variances amount to 143,000 pesos ÷ 1,169,000 pesos, or 12.2% of actual production costs. If we decide this amount is not material, the variances could simply be closed to cost of goods sold; that is, we decrease cost of goods sold by 143,000 pesos.

As a general guide, accountants often consider amounts larger than 10% to be material. Therefore, the combined variance for Cementos Juarez would most likely be considered material. In this case, the variances would be closed to the general ledger accounts that contain the current period's standard production costs. For Cementos Juarez, standard costs allocated to production during the period totaled 100,000 blocks × 12.12 pesos standard cost per block (see Cementos Juarez, Part 1), or 1,212,000 pesos. Assume that these costs are included in the following general ledger accounts at the end of the accounting period:

| | Pesos | Percent |
|---|---|---|
| Work in process inventory | 0 pesos | 0% |
| Finished goods inventory (5,000 blocks × 12.12 pesos per block) | 60,600 | 5 |
| Cost of goods sold (95,000 blocks × 12.12 pesos per block) | 1,151,400 | 95 |
| Total | 1,212,000 pesos | 100% |

Of the standard costs allocated during the accounting period, 5% remain in finished goods inventory and 95% is recognized in cost of goods sold. Therefore, we decrease each of these accounts; finished goods by 7,150 pesos (5% of 143,000), and cost of goods sold by 135,850 pesos (95% of 143,000). The journal entry to record the adjustment is:

| | | |
|---|---|---|
| Direct materials price variance | 325,000 pesos[5] | |
| Fixed overhead spending variance | 5,000 pesos | |
| Production volume variance | 20,000 pesos | |
|     Direct materials efficiency variance | | 200,000 pesos |
|     Direct labor price variance | | 5,500 pesos |
|     Direct labor efficiency variance | | 1,000 pesos |
|     Variable overhead spending variance | | 300 pesos |
|     Variable overhead efficiency variance | | 200 pesos |
|     Finished goods inventory | | 7,150 pesos |
|     Cost of goods sold | | 135,850 pesos |

After making this adjustment, the actual production costs are recorded in the inventory and cost of goods sold accounts, as required by generally accepted accounting principles for financial reporting.

## FOCUS ON ETHICAL DECISION MAKING
## Wasted Soup

While she was watching operations at a food processing plant, a consultant noticed a large amount of soup on the floor under a filling machine. An operator washed this soup away each day. When asked about the loss of soup, the production manager replied that no losses occurred. In this manager's view, no problem existed because the production line operating costs were below budgeted costs. Later, a productivity team analyzed the amount of soup wasted over a given

---

[5]This example is a simplified version of the adjustment for the direct materials price variance. Technically, if the variance were material, it would be prorated to direct materials and production, with the production amount added to the other production variances and closed in aggregate as shown in the full entry.

time period. The team estimated the cost of the leak to be $750,000 a year. To correct the problem, the company installed a set of valves costing $50,000. The new valves eliminated the loss of soup.

Instead of measuring performance against expected budget levels, managers could compare actual profits to ideal profits that could be earned if operations were to run at their true potential. By focusing on the gap between ideal and actual profits, managers are encouraged to identify lost profit potential and to reconsider critical processes. Once gaps are identified, managers rank them according to their value to the organization and correct them in priority order.

Source: I. Thompson and C. Rosen, "Accounting for Higher Profits," *Optimize*, January 2003, pp. 29–34.

### Practice Ethical Decision Making

In Chapter 1, we learned about a process for making ethical decisions (Exhibit 1.11). You can address the following questions for this ethical dilemma to improve your skills for making ethical decisions. Think about your answers to these questions and discuss them with others.

| Ethical Decision-Making Process | Questions to Consider about This Ethical Dilemma |
|---|---|
| Identify ethical problems as they arise. | Is it an ethical problem when employees observe inefficiencies in the workplace, such as the loss of soup in this case? Why or why not? |
| Objectively consider the well-being of others and society when exploring alternatives. | Why is it common for employees to do nothing when they observe inefficiencies? Compare the responsibility of operation workers to the responsibility of the operating manager with respect to identifying and correcting inefficiencies. In what ways are the responsibilities the same? In what ways are they different? |
| Clarify and apply ethical values when choosing a course of action. | Is it ethical for employees to ignore inefficiencies? Why or why not? What values did you use to arrive at the conclusion? |
| Work toward ongoing improvement of personal and organizational ethics. | People do not always seek to achieve their best performance. For example, students sometimes apply minimum effort to achieve a targeted grade. What does it mean for individuals to seek continuous improvement? |

## APPENDIX 11A

 **Q8** Which profit-related variances are commonly analyzed?

## Profit-Related Variances

This appendix introduces the analysis of variances that are used to monitor revenues and contribution margins. These variances help managers monitor factors other than cost that affect profitability.

### ■ Revenue Variances

Before managers estimate revenues for the next period, they assess market conditions, develop marketing strategies, and establish the type and quality of goods or services they wish to sell. Given assumptions and plans for these factors, they set the following standards for operating revenue performance:

$$\begin{array}{ccc} \text{Standard (or budgeted)} \\ \text{revenues} \end{array} = \begin{array}{c} \text{Standard (or budgeted)} \\ \text{selling price} \end{array} \times \begin{array}{c} \text{Standard (or budgeted)} \\ \text{sales volume} \end{array}$$

When actual revenues are compared to standard revenues, the difference is called a **revenue budget variance.** Revenue variances are caused by a number of different factors such as changes in demand, sales price, or discounting practices. In addition, because total revenue is based on a projected sales mix among products, changes in the mix cause changes in revenues. Managers are often concerned about variances between planned and actual revenues, therefore accountants produce and analyze several variances that reflect the success of marketing efforts.

## ■ Sales Price and Revenue Sales Quantity Variances

As shown in Exhibit 11A.1, the revenue budget variance can be broken down into two types of variances. The **sales price variance** reflects the difference between standard and actual selling prices for the volume of units actually sold. The sales price variance is calculated using the following formula:

Sales price variance = (Actual price − Standard price) × Actual volume sold

This variance is favorable if the actual selling price exceeds the standard price, and it is unfavorable if the reverse is true. When an organization sells more than one product or service, the combined variance is calculated as the sum of sales price variances for all products and services.

The **revenue sales quantity variance** reflects the difference between the standard and actual quantity of units sold at the standard selling price. The revenue sales quantity variance is calculated using the following formula:

Revenue sales quantity variance = (Actual volume sold − Standard volume sold) × Standard price

This variance is favorable when actual sales quantities exceed standard quantities, and it is unfavorable otherwise. When an organization sells more than one product or service, the combined variance is calculated as the sum of revenue sales quantity variances for all products and services.

Suppose that Benny's sells both blackberry and French vanilla ice cream. Following is information about the standard and actual sales for the period.

| Product | Standard Price | Standard Volume | Actual Price | Actual Volume |
|---|---|---|---|---|
| Blackberry | $7.00 per gallon | 1,000 gallons | $6.50 per gallon | 1,500 gallons |
| French vanilla | $6.00 per gallon | 2,000 gallons | $5.75 per gallon | 1,700 gallons |

Total standard revenues are $19,000: $7,000 (1,000 gallons × $7.00 per gallon) for blackberry ice cream and $12,000 (2,000 gallons × $6.00 per gallon) for French vanilla ice cream. Actual revenues are $19,525: $9,750 (1,500 gallons × $6.50 per gallon) for blackberry ice cream and $9,775 (1,700 gallons × $5.75 per gallon) for French vanilla ice cream. As shown in Exhibit 11A.2, the revenue budget variance is calculated as follows:

$$(1,000 \text{ gallons} \times \$7.00 \text{ per gallon} + 2,000 \text{ gallons} \times \$6.00 \text{ per gallon})$$
$$- (1,500 \text{ gallons} \times \$6.50 \text{ per gallon} + 1,700 \text{ gallons} \times \$5.75 \text{ per gallon})$$
$$= \$19,000 - \$19,525$$
$$= \$525 \text{ F}$$

This variance is favorable because revenues are higher than standard. However, sales prices for both products were less than expected. Benny's managers want to understand the influence of the price changes separately from the volume changes, so their accountant breaks this variance into the sales price variance and the revenue sales quantity variance.

The sales price variance for blackberry ice cream is $750 U [($6.50 per gallon − $7.00 per gallon) × 1,500 gallons], and the sales price variance for vanilla is $425 U [($5.75 per gallon − $6.00 per gallon) × 1,700 gallons]. The total sales price variance of $1,175 U ($750 U + $425 U) is unfavorable because both prices were lower than standard.

**EXHIBIT 11A.1**
**Revenue Budget Variances**

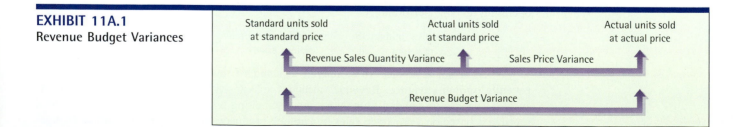

**EXHIBIT 11A.2**
Revenue Budget Variances
for Benny's (Two Products)

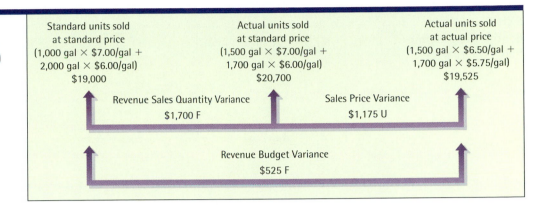

The revenue sales quantity variance for blackberry of $3,500 F [(1,500 gallons − 1,000 gallons) × $7.00 per gallon] is favorable because Benny's sold more than standard. The variance for vanilla of $1,800 U [(2,000 gallons − 1,700 gallons) × $6.00 per gallon] is unfavorable because Benny's sold less than standard. The total variance of $1,700 F ($3,500 F − $1,800 U) is favorable because the largest variance ($3,500) was favorable. The combined sales price and revenue sales quantity variance is $525 F ($1,700 F − $1,175 U), the same value as the revenue budget variance that we calculated earlier.

## ■ Contribution Margin–Related Variances

For organizations that sell more than one product, analysis of the total contribution margin is often useful, especially when a company's products are substitutes for each other. The **contribution margin budget variance** reflects the difference between standard and actual contribution margins. At Benny's, some ice cream flavors are more expensive than others because of the cost of special ingredients. For customers who are price sensitive, a cheaper flavor is probably a good substitute for a more expensive flavor. When the economy is down, Benny's probably sells more of the cheaper ice cream. When the economy recovers, expensive ice creams sell better. Because the contribution margin of each flavor affects profitability, plans are made for a specific sales mix with specific contribution margins. At the end of a period, managers analyze the contribution margin budget variance. This analysis helps them know which products to advertise and provides guidance for future budgeting tasks.

Suppose that Benny's has standard contribution margins for blackberry and vanilla ice cream as follows:

|  | Standard Contribution Margin | Actual Contribution Margin |
|---|---|---|
| Blackberry | $1.00 per gallon | $1.15 gallon |
| French vanilla | $1.25 per gallon | $1.00 gallon |

The standard contribution margin is $3,500 [(1,000 gallons × $1.00 per gallon) + (2,000 gallons × $1.25 per gallon)]. However, actual sales were 1,500 gallons of blackberry at a contribution margin of $1.15 each and 1,700 gallons of vanilla at a contribution margin of $1.00 each. The actual contribution margin for this sales mix and contribution margin per product is $3,425 (1,500 gallons × $1.15 per gallon + 1,700 gallons × $1.00 per gallon). The contribution margin budget variance is $75 U ($3,500 − $3,425), which is unfavorable because the total actual contribution margin is lower than the total standard contribution margin.

## ■ Contribution Margin Variance and Contribution Margin Sales Volume Variance

The contribution margin budget variance of $75 U can be broken into the contribution margin variance and the contribution margin sales volume variance, as shown in Exhibit 11A.3.

[6]See J. C. Stewart, "An Unwelcome Discount," *Quick Printing,* May 2003, pp. 20–21.

**EXHIBIT 11A.3**
Contribution Margin
Budget Variances

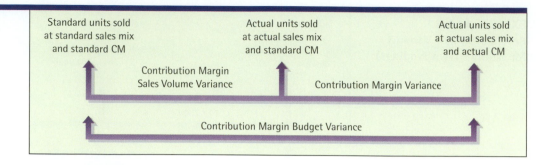

The **contribution margin variance** indicates the effects of changes in contribution margins, given the actual level of sales. This variance is calculated as follows:

$$\text{Contribution margin variance} = \left( \text{Actual contribution margin} - \text{Standard contribution margin} \right) \times \text{Actual volume sold}$$

This variance is favorable when the actual contribution margin is higher than the standard contribution margin, and it is unfavorable otherwise. When an organization sells more than one product or service, the combined variance is calculated as the sum of contribution margin variances for all products and services.

The **contribution margin sales volume variance** indicates the effects of changes in units sold, given the standard contribution margins. The variance is calculated as follows:

$$\text{Contribution margin sales volume variance} = \left( \text{Actual volume sold} - \text{Standard volume sold} \right) \times \text{Standard contribution margin}$$

This variance is favorable when actual sales quantities exceed standard quantities, and it is unfavorable otherwise. When an organization sells more than one product or service, the combined variance is calculated as the sum of contribution margin volume variances for all products and services.

For Benny's, the contribution margin variance for blackberry is $225 F [1,500 × ($1.00 − $1.15)] and for French vanilla is $425 U [1,700 × ($1.00 − $1.25)]. The total contribution margin variance is $200 U ($425 − $225), as shown in Exhibit 11A.4. In other words, the company achieved a lower average contribution margin per gallon than standard. Although the actual contribution margin per gallon for blackberry ice cream was higher than standard, it was more than offset by the reduction in contribution margin on French vanilla ice cream. The contribution margin sales variance for blackberry is $500 F [(1,500 gallons − 1,000 gallons) × $1.00 per gallon] and for French vanilla is $375 U [(1,700 gallons − 2,000 gallons) × $1.25 per gallon]. The total contribution margin sales volume variance is $125 F ($500 F + $375 U). Benny's sold more total units of ice cream than

**EXHIBIT 11A.4**
Contribution Margin
Budget Variances for
Benny's (Two Products)

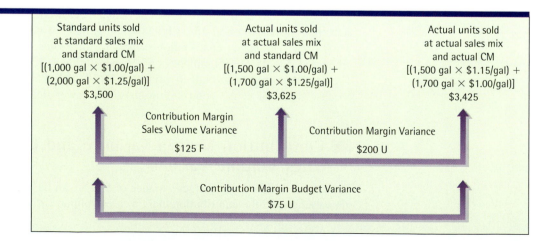

planned, resulting in a favorable contribution margin sales volume variance. The sum of the contribution margin variance of $200 U and the contribution margin sales volume variance of $125 F reflects the contribution margin budget variance of $75 U.

## ■ Contribution Margin Sales Mix Variance and Contribution Margin Sales Quantity Variance

When an organization sells more than one product or service, the contribution margin sales volume variance can be broken into two more variances, the contribution margin sales mix variance and the contribution margin sales quantity variance, as shown in Exhibit 11A.5. The **contribution margin sales mix variance** examines the effects of changes in the sales mix, given the standard contribution margin and actual quantity of units sold. The variance is calculated as follows, where total actual sales volume is the combined actual volume for all products:

$$
\begin{array}{l}
\text{Contribution} \\
\text{margin sales} \\
\text{mix variance}
\end{array}
=
\begin{array}{l}
\text{Sum} \\
\text{for all} \\
\text{products of}
\end{array}
\left\{
\left[
\begin{array}{l}
\text{Actual} \\
\text{sales} \\
\text{volume}
\end{array}
-
\left(
\begin{array}{l}
\text{Total} \\
\text{actual sales} \\
\text{volume}
\end{array}
\times
\begin{array}{l}
\text{Standard} \\
\text{sales mix} \\
\text{percentage}
\end{array}
\right)
\right]
\times
\begin{array}{l}
\text{Standard} \\
\text{contribution} \\
\text{margin}
\end{array}
\right\}
$$

The standard sales mix percentage is the standard number of units for the product as a percent of the total standard number of units for all products. This variance is favorable when a shift occurs in sales mix toward products having a higher standard contribution margin.

The **contribution margin sales quantity variance** examines the effects of changes in quantities sold, given the standard contribution margins and standard sales mix. The variance is calculated as:

$$
\begin{array}{l}
\text{Contribution} \\
\text{margin sales} \\
\text{quantity variance}
\end{array}
=
\begin{array}{l}
\text{Sum} \\
\text{for all} \\
\text{products of}
\end{array}
\left\{
\left[
\left(
\begin{array}{l}
\text{Total actual} \\
\text{sales} \\
\text{volume}
\end{array}
\times
\begin{array}{l}
\text{Standard} \\
\text{sales mix} \\
\text{percentage}
\end{array}
\right)
-
\begin{array}{l}
\text{Standard} \\
\text{sales} \\
\text{volume}
\end{array}
\right]
\times
\begin{array}{l}
\text{Standard} \\
\text{contribution} \\
\text{margin}
\end{array}
\right\}
$$

The standard sales mix percentage is the standard number of units for the product as a percent of the total standard number of units for all products. This variance is favorable if the total actual sales volume for the organization is greater than standard.

The calculations of these variances for Benny's are presented in Exhibit 11A.6. The standard proportion (i.e., sales mix) of gallons sold for blackberry is 33% [1,000 gallons ÷ (1,000 gallons + 2,000 gallons)], while the standard proportion for French vanilla is the remaining 67%. The contribution margin sales volume variance ($125 F) is broken into two other contribution margin variances. The contribution margin sales mix variance is $111 U [(1,500 gallons − (3,200 gallons × 0.33)) × $1.00 per gallon + (1,700 gallons − (3,200 gallons × 0.67)) × $1.25 per gallon]. The variance is unfavorable because a larger proportion of blackberry was sold than expected, and blackberry has a lower standard contribution margin than French vanilla. The sales quantity variance is $236 F [((3,200 gallons × 0.33) − 1,000 gallons) × $1.00 per gallon + ((3,200 gallons × 0.67) − 2,000 gallons) × $1.25 per gallon]. The favorable variance arose because Benny's expected to sell 3,000 gallons and actually sold 3,200 gallons.

**EXHIBIT 11A.5**
Contribution Margin Sales Volume Variances

---

[7]M. Herper, "Hassan Taps His Buddy List," *Forbes.com,* September 8, 2003. Net sales and profit by segment, *Annual Report to Shareholders* (Form 10-K), Schering-Plough Corporation, December 31, 2003, p. 7.

**EXHIBIT 11A.6**
Contribution Margin Sales Volume Variances for Benny's (Two Products)

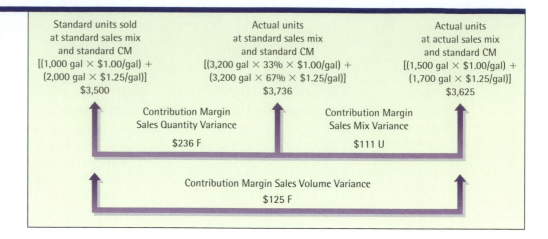

## ■ Analyzing Revenue and Contribution Margin Variance Information

The process of analyzing these variances is similar to the process used for cost variances. Once variances have been computed, the reasons for variances are investigated. For example, after analyzing the variances in Exhibits 11A.2, 11A.4, and 11A.6, Benny's managers might investigate the following questions.

- Why were ice cream selling prices different from standard prices? For example, does the price fluctuate from day to day based on the cost of cream or other ingredients? Are discounts sometimes offered?
- Why was the proportion of blackberry ice cream larger than standard? Did advertising emphasize the higher-priced blackberry ice cream?
- Why was the overall volume of sales higher than expected? Is this part of a trend? Are particular customers ordering more ice cream than usual? Is this event related to weather? Is the trend expected to continue?
- Will the increased contribution margin for blackberry ice cream continue? It appears that costs were reduced, because prices decreased and contribution margin increased. Will the cost reduction continue into the next period?
- Can cost reductions be found for French vanilla to compensate for the reduced price?
- Should advertising emphasize blackberry even more because it now has the largest contribution margin?
- What do the answers to all of the preceding questions suggest about ways to increase profits for Benny's?

After considering these types of questions, the managers would decide what action, if any, to take (see Exhibit 11.3).

| GUIDE YOUR LEARNING 11.6 Key Terms |
| --- |

Stop to confirm that you understand the new terms introduced in the last several pages:

Revenue budget variance (p. 439)
Sales price variance (p. 440)
Revenue sales quantity variance (p. 440)
Contribution margin budget variance (p. 441)
Contribution margin variance (p. 442)

Contribution margin sales volume variance (p. 442)
Contribution margin sales mix variance (p. 442)
Contribution margin sales quantity variance (p. 443)

For each of these terms, write a definition in your own words.

# SUMMARY

## Q1 How Are Standard Costs Established?

### Establishing Standard Costs

- Information used:
  - Historical costs and trends
  - Expected changes in costs or processes
  - Estimates from industrial engineers
- Key Assumptions:
  - Volume of production activity
  - Production processes and efficiency, including expected waste and defects
  - Prices and quality of inputs
- Attainability:
  - To motivate performance, set standards with little slack

### Standard Costs for Manufactured Products

$$\begin{array}{l} \text{Standard cost per} \\ \text{unit of output} \end{array} = \begin{array}{l} \text{Standard cost of} \\ \text{direct materials} \end{array} + \begin{array}{l} \text{Standard cost of} \\ \text{direct labor} \end{array}$$

$$+ \begin{array}{l} \text{Standard cost of} \\ \text{variable overhead} \end{array} + \begin{array}{l} \text{Standard cost of} \\ \text{fixed overhead} \end{array}$$

## Q2 What Is Variance Analysis, and How Is It Performed?

A *standard cost* variance is a difference between standard costs and actual costs.

### Variance Analysis Process

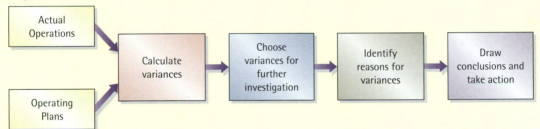

### Factors Influencing the Choice of Variances to Monitor

- Nature of goods or services
- Cost accounting system used
- Costs that managers consider important
- Cost/benefit trade-off for monitoring individual costs

### Factors Influencing Further Investigation of Variances

- Size of variance
- Trends in variances

### Management Conclusions and Actions
See Exhibit 11.3.

## Q3 How Are Direct Cost Variances Calculated?

### Direct Cost Variances

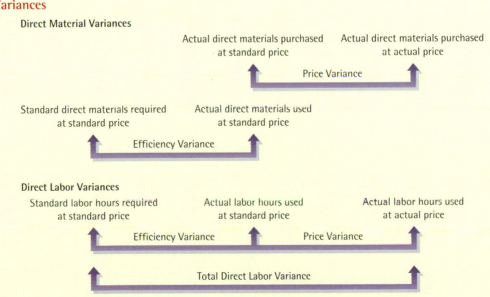

## Q4  How Is Direct Cost Variance Information Analyzed and Used?

For general process, see Q2.
For examples of reasons for direct cost variances, see
Exhibit 11.7.

**Resource and Quality Trade-Offs Reflected in Direct Cost Variances**
- Price and efficiency
- Different inputs

## Q5  How Are Variable and Fixed Overhead Variances Calculated?

### Overhead Variances

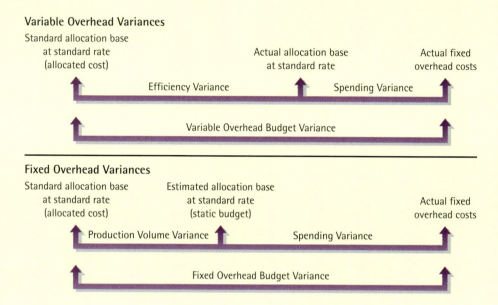

**Variable Overhead Variances**

| Standard allocation base at standard rate (allocated cost) | Actual allocation base at standard rate | Actual fixed overhead costs |
| --- | --- | --- |
| ← Efficiency Variance → | ← Spending Variance → | |
| ← Variable Overhead Budget Variance → | | |

**Fixed Overhead Variances**

| Standard allocation base at standard rate (allocated cost) | Estimated allocation base at standard rate (static budget) | Actual fixed overhead costs |
| --- | --- | --- |
| ← Production Volume Variance → | ← Spending Variance → | |
| ← Fixed Overhead Budget Variance → | | |

## Q6  How Is Overhead Variance Information Analyzed and Used?

For the general process, see Q2.
For examples of reasons for overhead variances, see Exhibit 11.11.

## Q7  How Are Manufacturing Cost Variances Closed?

### Immaterial Variances
- Amount would not affect information users' decisions
- Close to cost of goods sold

### Material Variances
- Standard costs do not fairly represent the actual cost of the units
- Prorate among:
  - Work in process
  - Finished goods
  - Cost of goods sold

## Q8  Which Profit-Related Variances Are Commonly Analyzed? (Appendix 11A)

### Revenue Variances

| Standard units sold at standard price | Actual units sold at standard price | Actual units sold at actual price |
| --- | --- | --- |
| ← Revenue Sales Quantity Variance → | ← Sales Price Variance → | |
| ← Revenue Budget Variance → | | |

## Contribution Margin Variances

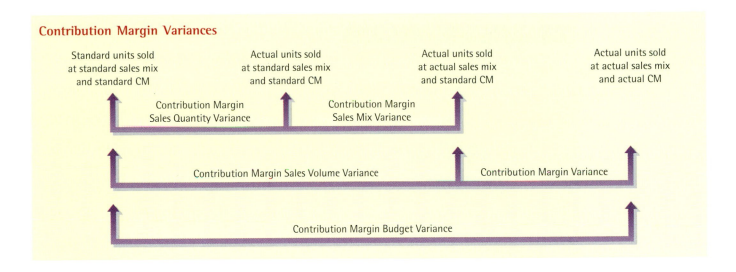

| | | | |
|---|---|---|---|
| Standard units sold at standard sales mix and standard CM | Actual units sold at standard sales mix and standard CM | Actual units sold at actual sales mix and standard CM | Actual units sold at actual sales mix and actual CM |

Contribution Margin Sales Quantity Variance

Contribution Margin Sales Mix Variance

Contribution Margin Sales Volume Variance

Contribution Margin Variance

Contribution Margin Budget Variance

---

### KEY TO SYMBOLS

**e** This question requires students to extend knowledge beyond the applications shown in the textbook.

**1** This question requires Step 1 skills (**Identifying**) in Steps for Better Thinking (Exhibit 1.10).

**2** This question requires Step 2 skills (**Exploring**) in Steps for Better Thinking (Exhibit 1.10).

**3** This question requires Step 3 skills (**Prioritizing**) in Steps for Better Thinking (Exhibit 1.10).

**4** This question requires Step 4 skills (**Envisioning**) in Steps for Better Thinking (Exhibit 1.10).

---

## Self-Study Problems

### Self-Study Problem 1   Direct Cost and Overhead Variances, Variance Analysis

**Q2, Q3, Q4, Q5, Q6**

Latiefa is the cost accountant at Hallet and Sons, manufacturer of exquisite glass serving bowls. The materials used for the bowls are inexpensive, but the process is labor intensive. The supervisor decided to use cheaper labor this period to see whether costs could be reduced. Latiefa needs to prepare a report for her supervisor about how effective operations had been during the month of January. She had set the following standards.

| | | Cost per Unit |
|---|---|---|
| Direct materials | 3 lbs @ $2.50 per lb | $ 7.50 |
| Direct labor | 5 hrs @ $15.00 per hour | 75.00 |
| Factory overhead: | | |
| Variable | $3.00 per direct labor hour | 15.00 |
| Fixed | $20.00 per unit | 20.00 |

Variable overhead is allocated by labor hours, and fixed overhead is allocated by unit. Estimated production per month is 40,000 standard direct labor hours.

Records for January based on production of 7,800 units indicated the following:

| | |
|---|---|
| Direct materials purchased | 25,000 lbs @ $2.60 |
| Direct materials used | 23,100 lbs |
| Direct labor | 40,100 hours @ $14.60 |
| Variable overhead | $119,000 |
| Fixed overhead | $180,000 |

The company's policy is to record direct material price variances at the time materials are purchased.

**REQUIRED:**

**A.** Prepare a simple, meaningful variance report for direct materials, direct labor, and variable and fixed overhead that Latiefa could present to her supervisor.

**2 B.** Attach to the variance report a discussion of the variances and a recommendation about whether some of them should be investigated further.

## Solution to Self-Study Problem 1

A. Latiefa could present the following variance report to her supervisor:

| | Favorable (F) or Unfavorable (U) Variance | | |
|---|---|---|---|
| | Price/Spending | Volume/Efficiency | Total |
| Direct materials | $ 2,500 U | $ 750 F | $ 1,750 U |
| Direct labor | 16,040 F | 16,500 U | 460 U |
| Total direct cost variance | | | 2,210 U |
| Variable overhead | 1,300 F | 3,300 U | 2,000 U |
| Fixed overhead | 20,000 U | 4,000 U | 24,000 U |
| Total overhead cost variance | | | 26,000 U |
| Total Variance | | | $28,210 U |

Computation check:

| | | |
|---|---|---|
| Standard costs allocated based on actual production | | |
| [7,800 units × ($7.50 + $75.00 + $20.00 + $15.00)] | | $916,500 |
| Less actual costs: | | |
| Direct materials: | | |
| Materials used at standard cost | | |
| (23,100 lbs × $2.50) | $ 57,750 | |
| Unfavorable price variance for material purchases | | |
| [25,000 lbs × ($2.60 − $2.50)] | 2,500 | |
| Total direct material cost | 60,250 | |
| Direct labor (40,100 hrs × $14.60) | 585,460 | |
| Variable overhead | 119,000 | |
| Fixed overhead | 180,000 | |
| Total actual costs | | 944,710 |
| Total variance | | $ 28,210 U |

Details of the calculations are shown in Exhibit 11.12.

B. Discussion of most significant variances:
- Because the supervisor hired less expensive labor this month, it is not surprising that the direct labor price variance is large and favorable ($16,040). However, this positive variance is more than offset by a large unfavorable direct labor efficiency variance ($16,500). It appears that more hours were required to compensate for less-skilled labor. This variance should be investigated to verify the conjectures.
- If less-skilled labor has a negative effect on quality, sales could be lost. Any potential change in the quality of output needs to be investigated.
- The fixed overhead spending variance was very large and unfavorable ($20,000). These costs might be out of control and need to be investigated.

Discussion of less significant variances:
- Given the unfavorable direct materials price variance ($2,500) and the favorable direct materials efficiency variance ($750), it is possible that the quality purchased this period has improved because less was used than expected. However, a price increase is also a possible explanation. These variances should be investigated to determine whether either or both of the standards should be changed.
- We need to determine whether a favorable variable overhead spending variance ($1,300) was due to improvements made in variable overhead costs and whether such improvements can be sustained (i.e., whether the standard should be changed).

## Self-Study Problem 2  Profit-Related Variances, Variance Analysis

Q2, Q8  Gift Baskets Galore (GBG) sells gift baskets at a small kiosk in a mall. Following is information about standard and actual sales for the first quarter. A competitor had changed its prices and GBG was forced to lower its price on the premium basket. The price for the regular basket was increased in an attempt to compensate for revenue that might be lost from the price decrease for premium baskets. The manager asked the accountant to help her determine how the price changes affected revenues.

**EXHIBIT 11.12** Calculations for Self-Study Problem 1

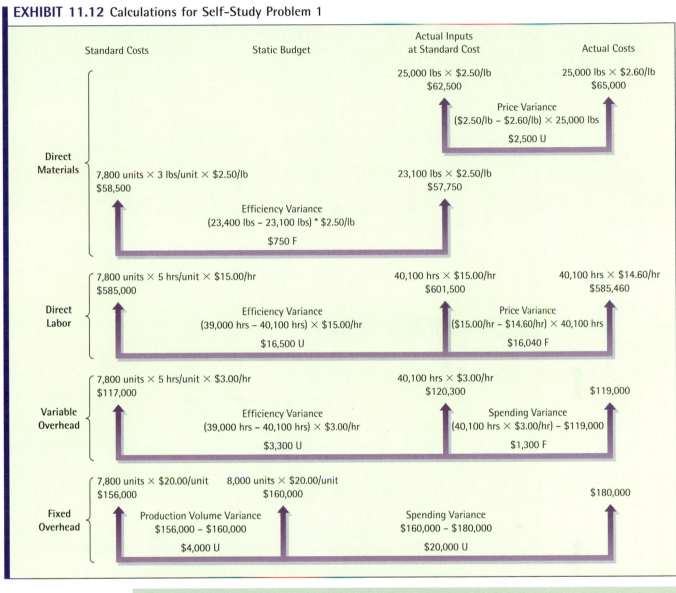

## Sales and Contribution Margin (CM) Forecasts for First Quarter

| Product | Standard Unit Price | Standard Unit CM | Standard Volume | Standard Revenue | Standard CM | Standard Volume Mix |
|---|---|---|---|---|---|---|
| Premium basket | $10.00 | $1.00 | 4,500 | $45,000 | $4,500 | 75% |
| Regular basket | 5.00 | 0.50 | 1,500 | 7,500 | 750 | 25% |
| Totals | | | 6,000 | $52,500 | $5,250 | 100% |

## Actual Sales and Contribution Margin (CM) for First Quarter

| Product | Actual Unit Price | Actual Unit CM | Actual Volume | Actual Revenue | Actual CM | Actual Volume Mix |
|---|---|---|---|---|---|---|
| Premium basket | $9.75 | $0.75 | 4,756 | $46,371 | $3,567 | 80% |
| Regular basket | 5.50 | 0.55 | 1,189 | 6,540 | 654 | 20% |
| Totals | | | 5,945 | $52,911 | $4,221 | 100% |

**REQUIRED:**   **A.** For the premium basket, calculate the two revenue budget variances: sales price variance and the revenue sales quantity variance.

**B.** Calculate all of the contribution margin variances: the contribution margin budget variance comprised of the contribution margin variance and contribution margin sales volume variance. Then

**EXHIBIT 11.13** Calculation of Premier Gift Basket Revenue Variances

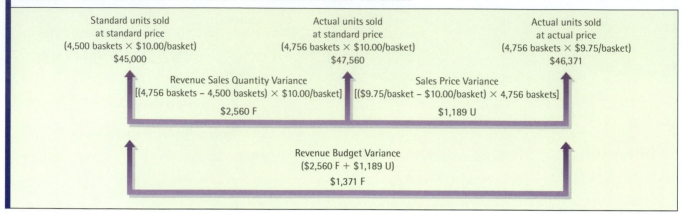

decompose the contribution margin sales volume variance into the contribution margin sales mix variance and the contribution margin sales quantity variance.

**C.** Write a paragraph discussing these variances. Examine the current pricing policy and explain any changes you think the manager should consider.

### Solution to Self-Study Problem 2

**A.** See Exhibit 11.13.

**B.** See Exhibit 11.14.

**C.** For the premium baskets, the price decrease is reflected in the unfavorable sales price variance ($1,189). However, the price variance is more than offset by a favorable revenue sales quantity variance ($2,560). The contribution margin budget variance for Gift Baskets Galore is $1,029 U. This variance is comprised of the contribution margin variance of $1,130 U (reflecting only the effect of the changes in contribution margin for each product), and the contribution margin sales volume variance of $101 F (reflecting the effects of the changes in number of units sold). The contribution margin sales volume variance ($101 F) can be broken into the contribution margin sales mix variance of $149 favorable (reflecting the effects of the change in sales mix on contribution margin) and the contribution margin sales quantity variance of $48 favorable (reflecting the effects of the changes in units sold).

More premium baskets were sold, and this variance favorably affected the revenue sales quantity variance. However, the contribution margin on premium baskets was lower than expected, resulting in an unfavorable contribution margin variance. Managers will want to investigate reasons for the price decrease of premium baskets and consider controlling costs to maintain the expected contribution margin.

**EXHIBIT 11.14** Calculation of Gift Baskets Galore Contribution Margin Variances

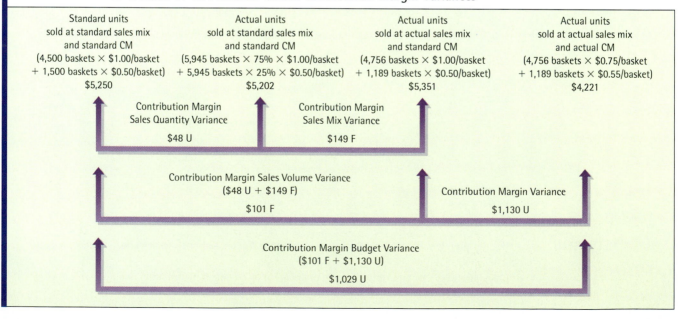

**REVIEW** Use the exercises in the following boxes in the chapter to review key terms and key techniques, analyze chapter illustrations, improve your learning of new concepts, and practice ethical decision making:

Guide Your Learning 11.1: Cementos Juarez (Part 1) (p. 420)

Guide Your Learning 11.2: Key Terms (p. 425)

Guide Your Learning 11.3: Cementos Juarez (Parts 2 and 3) (p. 430)

Guide Your Learning 11.4: Key Terms (p. 434)

Guide Your Learning 11.5: Cementos Juarez (Part 4) (p. 435)

Guide Your Learning 11.6: Key Terms (p. 444)

Focus on Ethical Decision Making: Wasted Soup (p. 438)

## QUESTIONS

**11.1** Explain why variances for direct material and direct labor are separated into price and efficiency variances.

**11.2** Suppose that utilities are considered a fixed cost for a retail clothing outlet. Why might we expect a variance to occur for the cost of utilities?

**11.3** Explain why the variance accounts need to be closed at the end of the period.

**11.4** Fly-a-Kite Company manufactures a variety of kite kits. You have been asked by the production manager to prepare a simple but meaningful variance report for product costs so that she can identify areas in need of improved cost control. List all of the variances you would present in the variance report for production costs and explain why each is useful.

**11.5** Identify the common variances that are needed to reconcile the accounting records at the end of the period for a manufacturing organization. How are these variances treated at the end of the period if the total variance is immaterial? How are they treated if the total variance is material?

**11.6** Discuss factors that affect accountants' decisions to investigate the reasons for variances.

**11.7** Explain how accountants and managers decide which cost variances to monitor.

**11.8** How are standard costs determined?

**11.9** List several ways that variances can be used to improve future operations.

**11.10** (Appendix 11A) Describe the contribution margin budget variances and explain why managers might monitor them.

**11.11** (Appendix 11A) Describe the revenue-related variances and explain why managers might monitor them.

**11.12** Suppose the direct materials price variance is large and favorable, and the direct materials efficiency variance is large and unfavorable. What questions would you be likely to ask when investigating these variances further?

**11.13** Why are direct materials price variances usually recorded at the time of purchase?

## EXERCISES

**11.14** **Direct labor variances and overhead spending variance** The following data for Kitchen Tile
Q3, Q5 Company relates to the production of 18,000 tiles during the past month. The company allocates fixed overhead costs at a standard rate of $19 per direct labor hour.

> Direct labor:
> Standard cost is 6 tiles per hour at $24.00 per hour
> Actual cost per hour was $24.50
> Labor efficiency variance was $6,720 F
> Fixed overhead costs:
> Estimated = $60,000
> Actual = $58,720

REQUIRED: A. How many actual labor hours were worked to produce the 18,000 tiles?
B. What is the price variance for direct labor?
C. What is the budget variance for fixed costs?

**11.15** **Direct materials and labor variances, variances to investigate** The managers of Nakatani
Q2, Q3, Q4 Enterprises established the following standards for Model 535:

| | Quantity Standard | Price Standard |
|---|---|---|
| Direct materials | 0.8 lb per unit | $2.00 per lb |
| Direct labor | 0.2 hours per unit | $17.00 per hour |

Last month, 15,342 units of Model 535 were produced at a cost of $26,870 for direct materials and $47,000 for direct labor. A total of 13,252 pounds of direct materials was used. Total direct labor hours amounted to 2,730 hours. During the same period, 11,000 pounds of direct material were purchased for $21,730. The company's policy is to record materials price variances at the time materials are purchased.

**REQUIRED:**

A. What is the total standard cost for direct materials and direct labor for the output this period?
B. What was the direct materials price variance?
C. What was the direct materials efficiency variance?
D. What was the direct labor price variance?
E. What was the direct labor efficiency variance?
 F. Identify any variances that are material (greater than 10% of total direct cost at standard). Discuss whether you would investigate these variances.

**11.16** **Direct materials and direct labor variances, journal entries** The following information pertains
**Q3** to Nell Company's production of one unit of its manufactured product during the month of June.
**CPA** The company recognizes the materials price variance when materials are purchased.

| | |
|---|---:|
| Standard quantity of materials | 5 lbs |
| Standard cost per pound | $0.20 |
| Standard direct labor hours | 0.4 |
| Standard wage rate per hour | $7.00 |
| Direct materials purchased | 100,000 lbs |
| Cost of direct materials purchased per pound | $0.17 |
| Direct materials consumed for manufacture of 10,000 units | 60,000 lbs |
| Actual direct labor hours required for 10,000 units | 3,900 |
| Actual direct labor cost per hour | $7.20 |

**REQUIRED:**

A. Calculate the price and efficiency (quantity) variances for materials and labor.
B. Record the journal entries for purchase and use of direct materials and the journal entries for direct labor.

**11.17** **Variable and fixed overhead variances, journal entries** Derf Company allocates overhead on
**Q5, Q7** the basis of direct labor hours. Two direct labor hours are required for each unit of product. Planned
**CMA** production for the period was set at 9,000 units. Manufacturing overhead is estimated at $135,000 for the period (20% of this cost is fixed). The 17,200 hours worked during the period resulted in the production of 8,500 units. Variable manufacturing overhead cost incurred was $108,500 and the fixed manufacturing overhead cost was $28,000.

**REQUIRED:**

A. Determine the variable overhead spending variance.
B. Determine the variable overhead efficiency (quantity) variance.
C. Determine the fixed overhead spending (budget) variance.
D. Determine the production volume (fixed overhead volume or denominator) variance.
E. Prepare journal entries to close these variances at the end of the period.

**11.18** **Profit-related variances (Appendix 11A)** Following is information for the Mitchellville Products
**Q8** Company for the month of July.
**CMA**

| | Master Budget | Actual |
|---|---:|---:|
| Units | 4,000 | 3,800 |
| Sales revenue | $60,000 | $53,200 |
| Variable manufacturing costs | 16,000 | 19,000 |
| Fixed manufacturing costs | 15,000 | 16,000 |
| Variable selling and administrative expense | 8,000 | 7,600 |
| Fixed selling and administrative expense | 9,000 | 10,000 |

**REQUIRED:**

A. Determine the revenue budget variance.
B. Determine the sales price variance.
C. Determine the revenue sales quantity variance.
D. Determine the contribution margin sales quantity variance.

**11.19** **Contribution margin variances, analysis (Appendix 11A)** Metropolitan Motors is an auto re-
**Q2, Q8** tailer. Salespeople have the authority to negotiate with customers for price, but are given target
profits. The firm classifies the cars it sells into one of three broad groups: economy, family, or
luxury. Target sales and average expected contribution margins per unit for March were estimated
as follows:

| Class | Unit Sales | Average Contribution Margin |
|---|---|---|
| Economy | 10 | $ 400 |
| Family | 20 | 800 |
| Luxury | 5 | 1,300 |

During March the auto manufacturer ran a special promotion to reduce an overstock of economy
cars. The manufacturer offered to pay directly to the salespeople a bonus of $75 for each econ-
omy car sold. Actual sales and total contribution margin earned by Metropolitan Motors for March
turned out to be as follows.

| Class | Unit Sales | Total Contribution Margin Earned |
|---|---|---|
| Economy | 25 | $5,625 |
| Family | 10 | $7,500 |
| Luxury | 3 | $4,200 |

**REQUIRED:**
    **A.** Calculate the contribution margin budget variance.
    **B.** Calculate the contribution margin variance and contribution margin sales volume variance.
    **C.** Calculate the contribution margin sales mix variance and the contribution margin sales
       quantity variance.
  ❷ **D.** Should the management of Metropolitan Motors be pleased or upset with the manufac-
       turer for running the special promotion? Why?

**11.20** **Direct cost and overhead variances, decision to automate** Plush pet toys are produced in a
**Q3, Q5** largely automated factory in standard lots of 100 toys each. A standard cost system is used to control costs and to assign cost to inventory.

| | Price Standard | Quantity Standard |
|---|---|---|
| Plush fabric | $2.00 per yard | 15 yards per lot |
| Direct labor | $10.00 per hour | 2 hours per lot |

Variable overhead, estimated at $5.00 per lot, consists of miscellaneous items such as thread,
a variety of plastic squeakers, and paints that are applied to create features such as eyes and whiskers.
Fixed overhead, estimated at $24,000 per month, consists largely of depreciation on the automated
machinery and rent for the building. Variable overhead is allocated based on lots produced. The
standard fixed overhead allocation rate is based on the estimated output of 1,000 lots per month.
    Actual data for last month follow.

| | |
|---|---|
| Production | 2,400 lots |
| Sales | 1,600 lots |
| Plush fabric purchased | 30,000 yards |
| Cost of fabric purchased | $62,000 |
| Fabric used | 34,000 yards |
| Direct labor | 4,200 hours |
| Direct labor cost | $39,000 |
| Variable overhead | $12,000 |
| Fixed overhead | $24,920 |

The company's policy is to record materials price variances at the time materials are purchased.

**REQUIRED:**
    **A.** Compute the commonly used direct cost and overhead variances.
    **B.** Management is considering further automation in the factory. Robotized forklifts could
       reduce the standard direct labor per lot to 1.5 hours.
  ⓔ    **1.** Estimate the savings per lot that would be realized from this additional automation.
  ⓔ    **2.** Assume the company would be able to generate the savings as calculated. Considering
       only quantitative factors, calculate the maximum price the managers would be willing
       to pay for the robotized forklifts. Assume the company's management requires equip-
       ment costs to be recovered in five years, ignoring the time value of money.

**11.21**    **Journal entries for closing variances** Following are the variances for Fine Products Manufac-
**Q7**    turing Company for the month of March. Assume that the price variance for direct materials is calculated at the time of purchase and that the amount of direct materials purchased is equal to the
amount of direct materials used, with no beginning or ending inventories for direct materials.

| | |
|---|---:|
| Direct materials price variance | $2,000 U |
| Direct materials efficiency variance | 1,500 F |
| Labor price variance | 5,000 U |
| Labor efficiency variance | 2,000 U |
| Fixed overhead spending variance | 200 U |
| Variable overhead spending variance | 1,000 F |
| Variable overhead efficiency variance | 1,200 U |

Fine Products considers anything greater than $5,000 as a material variance. Following are
end of period inventory balances.

| | |
|---|---:|
| Work in process | $ 2,000 |
| Finished goods | 6,000 |
| COGS | 24,000 |

**REQUIRED:**    **A.** Determine whether the total variance amount is material.
       **B.** Prepare a journal entry to close the variances at the end of March.

**11.22**    **Profit-related variances (Appendix 11A)** Pet Toys, Inc., expected to sell one plush toy for each
**Q8**    two Frisbees sold. Planned sales and variable costs for 2005 were as follows:

| | Frisbees | Plush Toys | Total |
|---|---:|---:|---:|
| Sales (100,000 frisbees) | $300,000 | $150,000 | $450,000 |
| Variable costs | 175,000 | 50,000 | 225,000 |
| Contribution margin | $125,000 | $100,000 | $225,000 |

During 2005 a competitor came out with a similar plush toy at a lower price. Management reacted by
dropping its selling price for plush toys, but the results were disappointing. Actual sales were as follows:

| | |
|---|---:|
| Frisbees (95,000 @ $3.30) | $313,500 |
| Plush toys (40,000 @ $2.40) | 96,000 |
| Total sales | $409,500 |

**REQUIRED:**    **A.** Determine the revenue budget variance, the sales price variance, and the revenue sales
       quantity variance.
       **B.** Determine the contribution margin budget variance, the contribution margin variance, and
       the contribution margin sales volume variance.
       **C.** Determine the contribution margin sales mix variance and the contribution margin sales
       quantity variance.

# PROBLEMS

**11.23**    **Cost variances, variance analysis, employee motivation** Raging Sage Coffee is a franchise that
**Q2, Q3, Q4, Q5, Q6**    sells cups of coffee from a cart in shopping centers. A computerized standard costing system is
provided as a part of the franchise package. A portion of the standard cost data follows.

| | Price | Quantity |
|---|---|---|
| Coffee beans | $6 per lb | 0.04 lbs per cup |
| Clerk/brewer | $10 per hour | 0.05 hours per cup |

In its first month of operation, the Philadelphia franchise recorded the following data:

| | |
|---|---:|
| Coffee sold | 8,260 cups |
| Coffee beans used | 224 lbs |
| Coffee beans purchased | 240 lbs |
| Cost of coffee beans purchased | $1,800 |
| Clerk/brewers' total hours | 600 hours |
| Clerk/brewers' total wages | $6,000 |

The company's policy is to record materials price variances at the time materials are purchased.

**REQUIRED:**
**1** **A.** Are direct labor hours for the cart most likely fixed or variable? Explain.
**e** **B.** Given your answer to part (A), should a direct labor efficiency variance be calculated? Why or why not?
  **C.** Calculate the direct materials price and efficiency variances.
**e** **D.** How many cups of coffee did the franchise owners expect to sell this period? Compare this estimate to the amount actually sold.
**1** **E.** Provide possible explanations for the drop in sales.
**2** **F.** Suppose the clerks/brewers currently receive a bonus based on their ability to control costs as measured using cost variances. Recommend a bonus system that might help the owners contain costs but also increase sales.

**11.24**
Q1, Q5, Q6
**Cost standards, cost variances, improving cost variance information** Sunglass Guys produces two types of wraparound sunglasses on one assembly line. The monthly fixed overhead is estimated at $235,707, and the variable overhead is estimated at $8.15 per Regular Wrap and $12.32 per Deluxe Wrap.

The company set up a standard costing system and follows the common practice of basing the overhead rate on the total standard direct labor hours required to produce the estimated volume. The company uses only one overhead rate for fixed and variable overhead costs. Data concerning these two products appear here:

|  | Regular | Deluxe |
|---|---|---|
| Estimated monthly volume | 4,300 units | 1,400 units |
| Standard direct labor | 0.2 hours per unit | 0.3 hours per unit |

Last month, actual production volume was 4,500 units of the Regular Wraps and 1,300 units of the Deluxe Wraps. Actual variable overhead was $54,238, and actual fixed overhead was $237,859. The 9 full-time employees who are classified as direct labor worked regular schedules for a total of 1,564 hours.

**REQUIRED:**
  **A.** Compute the standard overhead rate per direct labor hour.
**2** **B.** Explain why the company's overhead cost variances would provide poor information for monitoring and controlling costs.
  **C.** Using the information available to you in this problem, suggest a method of allocating overhead costs that would provide better variance information. Using this method, calculate relevant variances for monitoring and controlling overhead costs.
**e** **D.** For bookkeeping purposes, Sunglass Guys needs to calculate a production volume variance and a variable overhead efficiency variance. Calculate these variances, assuming that overhead costs are allocated using the method in part (C).
**2** **E.** Because employees work regular schedules, direct labor costs tend to be fixed. Also, variable overhead consists primarily of indirect materials and facility-level costs (such as building rent, assembly line equipment, and utilities). These costs do not differ between Regular Wraps and Deluxe Wraps. Given this information, recommend a better cost allocation base for variable overhead. Explain your choice.

**11.25**
Q1, Q2, Q3, Q4
**Developing direct cost standards, cost variances, use of variance analysis** The Mighty Morphs produces two popular games, "Powerful Puffs" (PP) and "Mini-Mite Morphs" (MMM). Following are standard costs:

|  | Powerful Puffs | | Mini-Mite Morphs | |
|---|---|---|---|---|
|  | Standard Quantity | Standard Price | Standard Quantity | Standard Price |
| DVDs | 1.08 DVD/unit | $0.35/DVD | 1.08 DVD/unit | $0.35/DVD |
| Documentation | 1.03 book/unit | $3.00/book | 1.03 book/unit | $5.00/book |
| Assembly labor | 0.01 hr/unit | $15.00/hr | 0.03 hr/unit | $15.00/hr |

The standards call for more than one disk and documentation book per unit because of normal waste due to faulty DVDs and poor binding.

Actual costs for last week follow:

| | |
|---|---:|
| DVDs purchased (@ $0.39) | $780 |
| DVDs used | 2,025 |
| Powerful Puffs games produced | 1,000 |
| Powerful Puffs documentation printed (@ $2.95) | $4,425 |
| Powerful Puffs documentation used | 1,005 |
| Mini-Mite Morphs games produced | 800 |
| Mini-Mite Morphs documentation printed (@ $4.75) | $4,750 |
| Mini-Mite Morphs documentation used | 825 |
| Assembly labor cost (55 hrs) | $795 |

Management decided that it would require too much effort to keep track of how many DVDs and hours are used for each of the games separately. Accordingly, the DVD materials and labor variances are combined rather than computed separately for each game. The price variances are recorded at the time of purchase.

**REQUIRED:**

**A.** What is the documentation price variance for MMM?

Ⓔ **B.** What is the efficiency variance for DVDs?

Ⓔ **C.** What is the sum of all variances for assembly labor for both games?

Ⓔ **D.** Calculate last week's estimated cost of waste for DVDs and documentation.

❷ **E.** Discuss the pros and cons of building waste into the standards.

**11.26** **Cost variance analysis, use of variance information** Baker Street Animal Clinic uses a par-
**Q2, Q3, Q4** ticular serum routinely in its vaccination program. Veterinarian technicians give the injections. The standard dose is 10cc per injection, and the cost has been $100 per 1,000cc. According to records, 2,000 injections were administered last month at a serum cost of $2,270. The veterinarian noted that the serum for the injections should have cost $2,000 [($0.10 per cc) × (10cc per injection) × (2,000 injections)]. Moreover, she noted some carelessness in handling the serum that could easily lead to unnecessary waste. When this issue was brought to the attention of the technicians, together with the $270 discrepancy in costs, they claimed that the $270 excess costs must be due to the inflated prices charged by the veterinarian supply company. Purchasing records reveal that the price for the serum used last month had indeed increased to $105 per 1,000cc.

**REQUIRED:**

❶ **A.** Provide variance calculations to help you evaluate the technicians' argument.

❷ **B.** Discuss whether a significant waste of serum occurred last month. Include quantitative and qualitative information in your discussion.

❷ **C.** If you were the manager for the Baker Street Animal Clinic, how would you use the results of your analyses in parts (A) and (B)? Explain.

**11.27** **Normal and abnormal waste, adjustment of variances** Damson Products prepares monthly fi-
**Q7** nancial statements. It closes its variance accounts at that time. For the month of May the firm's accounting records reveal the following variances (the comments were supplied by appropriate operating personnel).

| Variance | Amount | Percent of Standard | Comment |
|---|---|---|---|
| Direct material price | $ 658 U | 0.04% | Normal fluctuation |
| Direct material efficiency | 12,600 U | 11.38% | $13,000 lost in spring flood |
| Direct labor price | 376 F | 0.11% | Normal fluctuation |
| Direct labor efficiency | 9,700 U | 9.62% | $9,000 for days plant was closed during flood |
| Variable overhead spending | 507 F | 0.21% | Normal fluctuation |
| Variable overhead efficiency | 412 U | 0.18% | Normal fluctuation |
| Fixed overhead spending | 782 F | 0.07% | Normal fluctuation |
| Production volume | 10,400 U | 11.29% | $10,200 due to time lost in flood; the rest represents normal decreased spring operations |

The firm uses a standard fixed overhead allocation rate based on annual operations. The firm was closed several days when a nearby stream flooded after heavy rains. The firm does not have flood insurance, and the lost material and labor costs were charged to production. At the month end the firm has no raw material and no work in process inventories. The standard cost of finished goods inventory is $34,000, and the standard cost of goods sold is $305,000.

**REQUIRED:** **e** **A.** For each variance, explain whether the total amount of the variance should all be closed as a production variance or whether part of the amount should be closed to a separate flood loss account.

**B.** Prepare journal entries to close out the variances.

**C.** What is the cost of finished goods and cost of goods sold after the variance accounts are closed?

☆ **11.28**
Q1, Q2, Q5, Q6

**ABC costing, single versus dual rate spending variances, performance evaluation** Data Processors performs credit card services for banks. The company uses an ABC system. Following is information for the past year:

| Activity | Estimated Cost | Actual Cost | Cost Driver |
|---|---|---|---|
| Processing transactions | $2,000,000 | $2,200,000 | Number of transactions |
| Issuing monthly statements | 1,000,000 | 1,300,000 | Number of statements |
| Issuing new credit cards | 500,000 | 400,000 | Number of new credit cards |
| Resolving billing disputes | 90,000 | 100,000 | Number of disputes |
| Total | $3,590,000 | $4,000,000 | |

| Cost Driver | Estimated Activity Level | Actual Activity Level |
|---|---|---|
| Number of transactions | 5,000,000 | 5,800,000 |
| Number of statements | 250,000 | 270,000 |
| Number of new credit cards | 100,000 | 110,000 |
| Number of disputes | 3,000 | 3,500 |

**REQUIRED:**
**ANALYZE**
**INFORMATION**

The following questions will help you analyze the information for this problem. Do not turn in your answers to these questions unless your professor asks you to do so.

**A.** Using standard values for costs and activity, calculate an ABC allocation rate for each activity.

**e** **B.** Prepare an operating cost statement for Data Processors, Inc., that compares the static budget, the flexible budget, and actual costs.

**C.** Calculate the spending variance for the cost of processing transactions. (*Hint:* Treat this activity the same way you would treat variable overhead costs.)

**D.** Suppose the costs for processing transactions include some fixed and some variable costs, as shown:

| | Estimated Cost | Actual Cost |
|---|---|---|
| Fixed costs | $1,000,000 | $1,300,000 |
| Variable costs | 1,000,000 | 900,000 |
| Total | $2,000,000 | $2,200,000 |

Given this new information, calculate spending variances for the cost of processing transactions.

**1** **E.** Discuss possible reasons for the variances calculated in part (D).

**REQUIRED:**
**WRITTEN**
**ASSIGNMENT**

The CEO and CFO of Data Processors want your opinion about whether and how ABC variance information should be used in departmental manager performance evaluations. Turn in your answer to the following.

**3** **F.** Use the information you learned from the preceding analyses to write a memo to the CEO and CFO presenting your evaluation of (1) whether the use of ABC cost variances

(*continued*)

in departmental manager performance evaluations would likely improve organizational performance, and (2) which spending variance—the one from part (C) or part (D)—would provide better information for evaluating the credit card transaction processing manager's ability to control costs. As you write the memo, consider what information the CEO and CFO will need from you to help them make a final decision.

**11.29**
**Q3, Q4, Q5, Q6, Q8**

**Reconcile standard to actual income, performance evaluation, budget (Appendix 11A)** The Software Development Company produces computer programs on DVDs for home computers. This business is highly automated, causing fixed costs to be very high, but variable costs are minimal. The company is organized along three product lines: games, business programs, and educational programs. The average standard selling prices for each are $16 for games, $55 for business programs, and $20 for educational programs. The standard variable cost consists solely of one DVD per program at $2.00 per DVD, without regard to the type of program. Fixed costs for the period were estimated at $535,000. For the current period, standard sales are 40,000 games, 2,000 business programs, and 10,000 educational programs. Actual results are as follows.

| Sales: | | |
|---|---|---|
| Games | (35,000 DVDs) | $ 616,000 |
| Business | (4,000 DVDs) | 198,000 |
| Educational | (11,000 DVDs) | 220,000 |
| Total sales | | 1,034,000 |
| Variable costs | (50,750 DVDs) | 106,575 |
| Fixed costs | | 533,500 |
| Pretax income | | $ 393,925 |

**REQUIRED:**

**A.** Calculate standard pretax income and then reconcile it to actual pretax income by calculating the contribution margin sales mix variance, revenue sales quantity variance, sales price variance, materials price and quantity variances, and the fixed cost spending variance.

**B.** A new marketing manager was hired during the period. The manager changed prices and redirected sales efforts.

**1.** Discuss whether one or more of the preceding variances are relevant to evaluating the performance of the new marketing manager.

**2.** What do the variances suggest about the new manager's performance? Explain.

**C.** An analysis reveals that the company will have to pay $1.80 per DVD next period. Prepare next period's master budget. Assume a standard of one disk per program, total unit sales of 55,000, and the actual sales mix and sales prices from this period.

**D.** Discuss possible reasons why the company might not meet its budget for next period.

**11.30**
**Q1, Q2**

**Evaluate grading scheme, professional responsibilities** Variance analysis reflects information about actual performance relative to a standard. Variance analysis reports provide managers with information about the performance of employees, from direct labor to supervisors and managers. Grades provide similar information for recruiters who want to hire graduating students. Following is information about Professor E. Z. Grader's performance measurement system.

Professor Grader is popular; almost all of his students receive As. This phenomenon is widely attributed to Professor Grader's superior teaching skills. Grades for this professor's courses are determined as follows:

| Item | Points |
|---|---|
| Midterm exam | 200 |
| Attendance | 200 |
| Term paper | 200 |
| Final exam | 400 |

A student needs 700 points for an A, 600 points for a B, 500 for a C, and 400 for a D. From the 200 points given for perfect attendance, a student loses 5 points for every class missed (out of 40 class meetings); however, attendance is seldom taken.

If the term paper is 20 pages or longer, 200 points are earned; 10 points are lost for each page less than 20 (thus, a 12-page paper is worth 120 points).

Professor Grader has given the same midterm exam for the past 20 years. To reduce the number of exam copies in students' files, Professor Grader does not return the exams; grades are simply reported to individual students. A popular business fraternity obtained a copy of the exam 15 years ago. They have chosen not to share the exam with any person not a member of the fraternity; thus Professor Grader usually observes that grades on this exam are nearly normally distributed.

The final exam is a take-home exam that the students have two weeks to complete.

**REQUIRED:**

❶ **A.** Is it possible to develop a perfect system for measuring student performance in a course? Why or why not?

❷ **B.** How much variation is likely in student performance for each of the four graded items? Explain.

❷ **C.** Describe the weaknesses in Professor Grader's grading system as a performance measurement system.

❷ **D.** What are Professor Grader's professional responsibilities to various stakeholders in this situation?

❸ **E.** Discuss whether Professor Grader has acted ethically in this situation. Describe the ethical values you use to draw your conclusions.

❸ **F.** Is it ethical for students in this situation to access a copy of the prior midterm exam or to seek assistance in completing take-home assignments? Does Professor Grader's system affect the students' responsibilities? Describe the ethical values you use to draw your conclusions.

**11.31**
**Q1, Q2**

**Evaluating a proposal for measuring performance** Benerux Industries has been in business for 30 years. The firm's major product is a control unit for elevators. The firm has a reputation for manufacturing products of exceptionally high quality, resulting in higher prices for its units than competitors charge. Higher prices, in turn, have meant that the firm has been comfortably profitable. A major reason for the high product quality is a loyal and conscientious workforce. Production employees have been with the firm for an average of 18 years.

Recently the firm hired a cost accountant from the local university. After a few months at the firm, the new accountant proposed a performance measurement report consisting of two parts. The first part will report the actual number of units started during each month, the target number of units that should have been started, and a variance. The second part will calculate an actual cost per good unit completed during each month, the target cost per unit, and a variance.

The new accountant provided the following additional information concerning the performance report: The first part of the report concentrates on units started because many units are scrapped in the manufacturing process (to maintain high quality). Therefore, the best measure of effort expended is the number of units on which work was begun. The target number of units to be begun in a month is the number of units started in the corresponding month last year plus 5%. In the second part of the report, actual costs per unit will be calculated by dividing total production cost incurred during the month by the number of good units completed during the month. The target cost per unit is the average cost for manufacturing this kind of product as determined from industry newsletters.

The proposal concluded with the following comments: "This report should be prepared and distributed quarterly. For maximum benefit I suggest that a bonus be awarded whenever units started exceeds target and costs are below target. This system will result in substantially improved profits for the firm. It should be implemented immediately."

**REQUIRED:**

❶ **A.** Is it possible to develop a perfect system for monitoring and motivating worker performance? Why or why not?

❷ **B.** Explain what the managers might learn by monitoring each of the variances in the proposed performance measurement system.

❷ **C.** Discuss possible reasons why the company did not previously use a variance system to monitor and motivate worker performance.

❷ **D.** Describe weaknesses in the proposed performance measurement system.

❸ **E.** If you were the CFO of Benerux Industries, how would you respond to the new cost accountant's proposal? Discuss whether you agree with the proposal and explain how you would communicate your response.

**11.32**
**Q2, Q3, Q4, Q5, Q6, Q7**

**Direct and overhead cost variance analysis, closing accounts at end of period** Jennifer has just been promoted to manager of the piston division of Auto Parts Co. The division, which manufactures pistons for hydraulic drives, uses a standard cost system and calculates the standard cost of a completed piston as $85.00, as follows:

| | Quantity | Price | Cost per Piston |
|---|---|---|---|
| Piston shaft | 1 | $35/piston shaft | $35.00 |
| Shaft housing | 1 | $20/housing | 20.00 |
| Direct labor | 0.4 hours | $15/hour | 6.00 |
| Variable factory overhead | 0.4 hours | $10/hour | 4.00 |
| Fixed factory overhead | 0.4 hours | $50/hour | 20.00 |
| Total standard cost | | | $85.00 |

The fixed overhead rate is based on an estimated 1,000 units per month. Direct labor is nearly a fixed cost in this division. Selling and administrative costs are $50,000 per month plus $10 per piston sold.

The following information is for production during April:

| | |
|---|---|
| Number of pistons manufactured | 950 |
| Purchase of 1,000 piston shafts | $34,950 |
| Piston shafts used | 954 |
| Purchase of 1,000 shaft housings | $20,000 |
| Shaft housings used | 950 |
| Direct labor costs (397 hours) | $ 6,120 |
| Variable factory overhead costs | $ 3,677 |
| Fixed factory overhead costs | $18,325 |
| Selling and administrative costs | $59,101 |

The company's policy is to record materials price variances at the time materials are purchased. You may want to use a spreadsheet to perform calculations.

**REQUIRED:**

**A.** Prepare a flexible cost budget for the month of April.

**ⓔ B.** Calculate all of the common direct cost variances. (*Note:* There are no variances for shaft housings.)

**C.** Calculate all common factory overhead variances.

**D.** Calculate a total variance for the selling and administrative costs.

**❶ E.** Prepare a complete, yet concise, report that would be useful in evaluating control of production costs for April.

**F.** Prepare a report that sums all the variances necessary to prepare the reconciling journal entry at the end of the period. Explain how you would close the total variance; that is, identify the account or accounts that would be affected, and whether expenses in the accounts will be increased or decreased to adjust the records for the total variance.

**❷ G.** Suppose you are manager of the piston division and you are reviewing the report prepared in part (E). Use information in the report to identify questions you might have about April's production costs.

**11.33** **Cost-volume-profit pricing and standard cost variances** Bramlett Company has several divisions and just built a new plant with a capacity of 20,000 units of a new product. A standard costing system has been introduced to aid in evaluating managers' performance and for establishing a selling price for the new product. At the present time, Bramlett faces no competitors in this product market, and managers priced it at standard variable and fixed manufacturing cost, plus 60% markup. Managers hope this price will be maintained for several years.

**Q3, Q5, Q6**

During the first year of operations, 1,000 units per month will be produced. During the second year of operations, production is estimated to be 1,500 units per month. In the first month of operations, employees were learning the processes, so direct labor hours were estimated to be 20% greater than the standard hours allowed per unit. In subsequent months, employees were expected to meet the direct labor hours standards.

Experience in other plants and with similar products led managers to believe that variable manufacturing costs would vary in proportion to actual direct labor dollars. For the first several years, only one product will be manufactured in the new plant. Fixed overhead costs of the new plant per year are expected to be $1,920,000 incurred evenly throughout the year.

The standard variable manufacturing cost (after the break-in period) per unit of product has been set as follows:

| Direct materials (4 pieces @ $20 per piece) | $ 80 |
|---|---|
| Direct labor (10 hours @ $25 per hour) | 250 |
| Variable overhead (50% of direct labor cost) | 125 |
| Total | $455 |

At the end of the first month of operations, the actual costs incurred to make 950 units of product were as follows:

| Direct materials (3,850 pieces @ $19.80) | $ 76,230 |
|---|---|
| Direct labor (12,000 hours @ $26) | 312,000 |
| Variable overhead | 160,250 |
| Fixed overhead | 172,220 |

Bramlett managers want to compare actual costs to standard to analyze and investigate variances and take any corrective action.

**REQUIRED:**

**A.** What selling price should Bramlett set for the new product according to the new pricing policy? Explain.

**B.** Using long-term standard costs, compute all direct labor and manufacturing overhead variances.

**C.** Is it reasonable to use long-term standard costs to calculate variances for the first month of operations? Why or why not?

**D.** Revise the variance calculations in part (B), using the expected costs during the first month of operations as the standard costs.

**E.** Provide at least two possible explanations for each of the following variances:
   **1.** Direct labor price variance
   **2.** Direct labor efficiency variance
   **3.** Variable overhead spending variance
   **4.** Fixed overhead spending variance

**F.** As shown in Exhibit 11.2, the reasons for variances must be identified before conclusions and actions are decided upon. For two of the variance explanations you provided in part (E), explain what action(s) managers would most likely take.

**G.** Would it most likely be easier or more difficult to analyze the variances at the new plant compared to Bramlett's other plants? Explain.

# BUILD YOUR PROFESSIONAL COMPETENCIES

**11.34**
**Q1, Q2**

**DEFINITION:**

**Focus on Professional Competency: Interaction** *Team goals, standards, cooperation, and performance* Review the following definition and elements for the Interaction competency.[8]

*Accounting professionals must be able to work with others to accomplish objectives. This requires them to act as valuable business partners within organizations and markets and work in teams to provide business solutions. Thus, individuals entering the accounting profession should demonstrate an ability to work productively with individuals in a diversity of roles and with varying interests in the outcome.*

## ELEMENTS FOR THIS COMPETENCY INCLUDE

| Level 1 | Level 2 | Level 3 | Level 4 |
|---|---|---|---|
| 1. Accepts suggestions and guidance of team leaders and other members | 4. Recognizes and accommodates the protocols and expectations of teams | 7. Facilitates free expression and constructive activities of others | 8. Coaches or mentors in appropriate circumstances |
| 2. Commits to achievement of common goals when working on a team | 5. Recognizes the value of working within diverse, cross-functional teams | | |
| 3. Identifies uncertainties about interactions with others | 6. Interacts and cooperates productively and maturely with others | | |

[8]The definition and elements are reprinted with permission from AICPA; Copyright © 1978–2000 & 2003 by American Institute of Certified Public Accountants. The AICPA's Core Competency Framework can be accessed at eca.aicpaservices.org.

**REQUIRED:**

**A.** Focus on competency elements 2 and 5, which relate to the ability to address team goals and values. Answer the following questions:

① **1.** What role do accountants play in developing standards, analyzing variances, and recommending actions if needed?

② **2.** How does the material you learned in this chapter relate to teamwork? (*Hint:* Think about how the development of standard costs, the performance of variance analysis, the use of variance information, and the implementation of operating plans depend on teamwork.)

**B.** Focus on competency elements 1, 3, and 4, which relate to standards and protocols for team performance. Answer the following questions:

① **1.** Standards are often set so that they are attainable, but without much slack. Explain what this statement means, and explain why managers cannot know for sure whether standards are reasonable.

② **2.** When you participate as a team member, how do you recognize the team's protocols and expectations? Provide an example from your own experience.

② **3.** Discuss production employee incentives with respect to meeting cost standards. Be sure to address both positive and negative incentives.

**C.** Focus on competency elements 1, 3, 6, 7, and 8, which address cooperation and guidance within a team. Answer the following questions:

② **1.** Is it possible to engage in cooperation and at the same time allow free expression? Why or why not?

② **2.** Describe a situation where others have provided you with useful guidance and a situation where you have provided useful guidance to others. What was the role of coaching/mentoring in each situation?

**11.35**

Q1, Q2, Q4, Q6, Q7

**Integrating Across the Curriculum: Auditing** *Auditor evaluation of variances for error and fraud, accounting principles for variances* Statement on Auditing Standards (SAS) No. 99, "Consideration of Fraud in a Financial Statement Audit," requires auditors to plan and perform an audit to obtain reasonable assurance about whether the financial statements are free of material misstatements, which may be caused by either error or fraud. Errors are unintentional misstatements caused by factors such as mistakes in processing accounting data, misinterpretation of facts, and confusion about accounting principles. Fraudulent financial reporting and misappropriation of assets are the only two types of financial statement fraud. Fraudulent financial reporting consists of intentional misstatements caused by factors such as manipulation of accounting data, misrepresentation of facts, and intentional misapplication of accounting principles. Misappropriation of assets includes stealing assets such as inventory and causing an organization to pay for goods or services that were not received.

Auditors perform a variety of procedures to gather and evaluate information that will help them identify possible material misstatement. One potential audit procedure is to analyze a company's cost variances, which might be caused by error or fraud.

**REQUIRED:**

② **A.** For each of the following variances, describe *in detail* a possible error that could cause a variance even when no variance actually exists: Direct materials price, direct materials efficiency, direct labor price, direct labor efficiency, variable overhead spending, variable overhead efficiency, fixed overhead budget, and production volume.

② **B.** Suppose a material amount of raw materials inventory theft took place during the past year. Which of the variances in part (A) would most likely reflect this fraud? Explain.

② **C.** Discuss possible reasons why variance analysis might not uncover the theft described in part (B).

② **D.** Suppose a production manager fraudulently entered a fictitious employee into the payroll system during the past year. The fictitious employee's paychecks are deposited directly into a bank account that is then accessed by the production manager. Which of the variances in part (A) would most likely reflect this fraud? Explain.

② **E.** During the current year, suppose an accountant accidentally records a large equipment repair as an addition to property, plant, and equipment. Assume that equipment repairs and equipment depreciation are both recorded in variable overhead costs. Which of the variances in part (A) would most likely reflect this accounting error? Discuss how this error would affect the variance during the current year. Discuss how this error would affect the variance during the next year.

**②** **F.** Suppose a company's managers want to report higher earnings on the income statement. Describe in detail a possible way that the managers could improve reported earnings by intentionally misapplying accounting principles for variances.

# 12

# Strategic Investment Decisions

## ▶In Brief

Managers periodically make decisions about long-term investments for new projects or replacement of old assets. These decisions focus on creating long-term value consistent with organizational strategies. The outcomes from these decisions are generally more uncertain than shorter-term decisions because we forecast further into the future. In addition, the time value of money also becomes important.

## This Chapter Addresses the Following Questions:

**Q1** How are strategic investment decisions made?

**Q2** What cash flows are relevant for strategic investment decisions?

**Q3** How is net present value (NPV) analysis performed and interpreted?

**Q4** What are the uncertainties and limitations of NPV analysis?

**Q5** What alternative methods (IRR, payback, and accrual accounting rate of return) are used for strategic investment decisions?

**Q6** What additional issues should be considered for strategic investment decisions?

**Q7** How do income taxes affect strategic investment decision cash flows?

**Q8** How are the real and nominal methods used to address inflation in an NPV analysis? (Appendix 12A)

# TEXAS A&M: BULLISH FORECASTING

**T**exas A&M University developed the Net Present Value Sire Summary Program to help dairy producers better manage investments in genetic improvements. The Texas A&M software program, which applies the net present value technique you will learn in this chapter, helps farmers analyze data about their own farms and choose appropriate sires for their dairy herds.

Cows must have a calf before they can produce milk. Therefore, they must be fed and cared for until they are at least 27 months old before any cash flows from selling milk are recorded. Because the first cash flows are received several years in the future, the program incorporates the idea that dollars received in future years have lower values than dollars received today.

The Texas A&M program was developed because the most profitable sires of future cows for one dairy farm are not necessarily the most profitable ones for another farm with different objectives. The relevant cash flows used in the program are affected by several genetic characteristics that will be inherited by each bull's calves, including the amount of fat desired in the milk and the amount of milk produced per cow. Some farmers sell milk fat for butter and ice cream and want cows that produce a lot of fat per gallon of milk. Other farmers, who may prefer to sell milk that will be bottled and sold as a

beverage, want cows that produce as much milk as possible, regardless of the fat levels.

The program helps farmers evaluate relevant cash flows for their decisions. For example, future revenues in this program will vary depending on the prices of milk fat and milk. Other factors affecting relevant cash flows include the average reproduction rate by age of cow and the number of generations of a bull's descendants considered in the financial planning horizon. All such information is used to estimate the cash flows and profitability rankings for bulls. Profitability rankings are published twice a year in *Dairy* and *Dairy Herd Management* magazines.

Program reports also include the results of sensitivity analyses. Some factors affecting the cash flows are varied and then analyzed for assumptions about pounds of milk and amount of milk fat, the number of generations, and the discount rate. Other cash flow factors are not varied, such as the following assumptions: (1) feed costs will remain at 45 percent of milk income, (2) the average cow will be kept through a period where three calves are born, and (3) the replacement calf for the milking cow is the second calf born to that cow. ■

SOURCE: R. W. Blake, C. R. Shumway, and M. A. Tomaszewski, "Dairy Herd Improvement," 1986, available at www.agnr.umd.edu /Dairy Knowledge/dairy/NET_PRESENT_VALUE_SIRE _SUMMARIES.html.

## EVALUATING THE QUALITY OF A DECISION-MAKING AID

### ■ Key Decision Aid Issues for Dairy Producers

The purpose of the **Texas A&M** Sire Summary Program is to provide dairy farmers with relevant information for making better breeding decisions. In other words, the program is a type of decision aid. This particular decision aid involves an analysis technique called net present value, which is useful when evaluating decisions that affect profitability over many years. The following discussion summarizes the types of issues a dairy producer would probably consider when evaluating the quality of the Texas A&M program for decision making.

**Knowing.** A dairy producer would first consider the program creator's dairy breeding expertise. Texas A&M's reputation in this area would be likely to increase dairy producer interest in its program. Producers would also use their own knowledge to understand the design and usefulness of the program. This knowledge would include dairy product markets, theories and results from different breeding practices, and other decision aids that might be useful.

**Identifying.** After relevant information is input, the Texas A&M program creates information that is relevant for choosing bulls for breeding. A dairy producer wishing to use the program must gather information, including the following:

- Average age of breeding cows in the herd
- Decisions about planned milk and milk fat product mix
- Planning time horizon
- Cost per breeding

Given this information, the Texas A&M program creates reports that include the following:

- Rankings of expected profits for individual bulls
- Probable range (confidence interval) for expected profits by bull
- Alternative rankings based on factors such as product mix

Although the program provides dairy producers with relevant information for their breeding decisions, it does not guarantee profitable operations. Actual dairy producer profits are subject to many uncertainties.

- Amounts of the quantity of milk and percent of milk fat produced by a cow
- Future prices of milk and milk fat
- Conception rates
- Future dairy herd and production costs
- Future cost of financing

**Exploring.** Based on research and prior experience, the developers built a number of assumptions into the Texas A&M program.

- Average age of cows at first calving
- Number of times a cow is bred before being replaced
- Costs of feed relative to dairy prices
- Differences in profitability between average and top-performing bulls

Assumptions help to simplify computations by remaining constant while other inputs vary. When considering how much to rely on any analysis tool such as the Texas A&M program, dairy producers need to recognize and evaluate the reasonableness of that program's assumptions for their own operations. Assumptions that are appropriate for the specific circumstances of the decision lead to higher-quality information for decision making.

The Texas A&M program allows users to vary their inputs and obtain different outputs. As we learn in this chapter, the sensitivity of results to variations in input can help managers evaluate the risk of strategic investments. This feature of the Texas A&M program is especially useful to dairy producers.

**Prioritizing.** As with any analysis tool, the Texas A&M program does not tell dairy producers what decisions to make. Instead, farmers use the results of the program, along with other quantitative and qualitative factors, to make decisions that best meet their individual priorities.

**Envisioning.** Dairy producers must be prepared to modify their dairy herd strategies as conditions and their individual priorities change. The Texas A&M program encourages this process by providing updated profitability rankings twice per year.

## ■ Importance of Assumptions

No decision aid can remove the uncertainties of decision making. However, higher-quality decision aids make use of higher-quality techniques and help managers make better decisions in light of uncertainty. Evaluating assumptions is an important part of deciding whether a particular analysis method provides high-quality information. In this chapter we learn to identify and evaluate assumptions when making strategic investment decisions.

## STRATEGIC INVESTMENT DECISIONS

**Q1** How are strategic investment decisions made?

Compared to operating decisions that affect primarily the short term, strategic decisions have long-term effects. As we learned in Chapter 1, managers develop strategies from the organization's vision and core competencies. These strategies are aimed at the organization's overall purpose, which usually includes long-term profitability.

## ■ Capital Budgeting

Some strategic decisions involve choosing among potential long-term investment projects. **Capital budgeting** is a process that managers use when they choose among investment opportunities that have cash flows occurring over a number of years. These opportunities fall into two general categories:

- Developing or expanding products or services
- Replacing or reorganizing assets or services

For example, managers may wish to acquire another company to expand existing services. Or, they may wish to install new technology or reorganize operations to improve profitability. The objective of capital budgeting is to increase the long-term value of the organization.

Exhibit 12.1 summarizes the steps in the capital budgeting process. The process is similar to the process for nonroutine operating decisions (Chapter 4). The major difference is that capital budgeting decisions affect cash flows in future years. Therefore, the **time value of money,** which refers to the idea that a dollar received today is worth more than a dollar received in the future, is an important factor. Because of its importance, we will learn analysis techniques that allow managers to account for the time value of money when evaluating capital budget decisions.

## ■ Decision Alternatives

Organizations identify new projects, products, and services through a variety of methods. Individuals, teams, and whole departments are responsible for identifying future investment opportunities. Organizational strategies are reflected in long-term decisions about products, services, and acquiring new business segments. For example, organizations that maintain reputations for low-cost, high-quality products want to invest in new technology to improve quality while reducing cost. In the Texas A&M Sire Summary Program, farmers may choose

**EXHIBIT 12.1** Process for Addressing Capital Budgeting Decisions

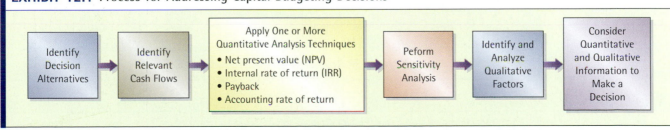

a strategy of developing herds that produce less milk with high fat, or herds that produce high quantities of milk with less fat. Bulls are then chosen to produce herds with the desired levels of milk fat and milk.

Sometimes organizational strategy requires consideration of new product lines or business segments to expand the organizational scope. For example, in Chapter 1 we learned that **Motorola** managers identified a need for global cellular phone service. In responding to this need, they expanded their product lines from manufacturing cellular phones to providing global cellular phone service. Similarly, **DuPont**, discussed in Chapter 10, revised its strategy to focus anew on developing new products. Once projects that align with company strategies are identified, capital budgeting analysis is performed to determine their financial viability.

When deciding whether to accept or reject proposals, managers analyze capital budgeting projects as if they were stand-alone projects. However, they may face capital constraints so that accepting one project would eliminate another. In these cases, alternative investments are analyzed simultaneously so that they can be compared.

**CURRENT PRACTICE**

Consistent with their strategy to sustain high levels of growth, the managers at Wendy's established a 2003 capital budget of $200 to $220 million for capital spending on new restaurant development.[1]

## ■ Relevant Cash Flows

**Q2** What cash flows are relevant for strategic investment decisions?

The process of identifying relevant cash flows for capital budgeting decisions is similar to the process for any other type of decision. We learned in Chapter 1 that relevant cash flows must arise in the future, and differ among decision alternatives (possible courses of action).

**EXHIBIT 12.2**
Common Cash Flows for Long-Term Decisions

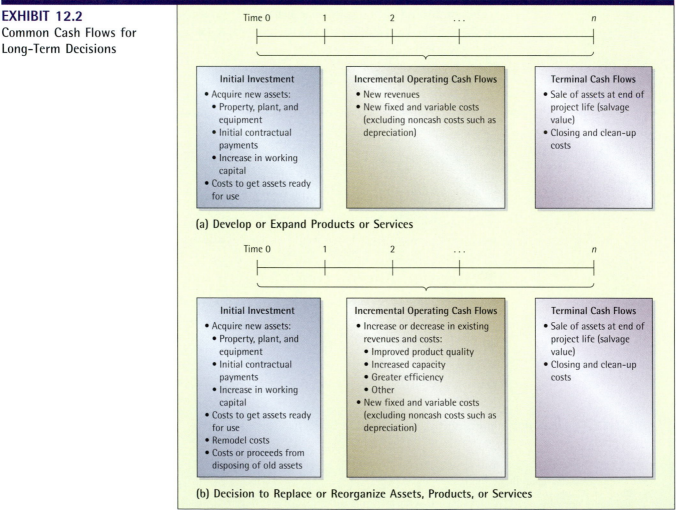

(a) Develop or Expand Products or Services

(b) Decision to Replace or Reorganize Assets, Products, or Services

---

[1]Wendy's International, Inc., "Investor Presentation," September 2003.

Exhibit 12.2a and b present timelines and lists of common types of cash flows for two different types of capital budgeting decisions, new product or process development, and asset replacement decisions. Cash flows must be estimated for all future periods affected by the potential investment. We usually begin by creating a timeline to help us think about the nature and timing of relevant cash flows.

At the beginning of the project, time 0, the company faces initial cash outflows such as the purchase of new property, plant, equipment, and other costs required to get assets ready for use in operations. Sometimes these outflows include initial contractual payments, such as signing bonuses, or additions to working capital, such as inventories. Initial cash inflows or outflows may also come from the disposal of old assets at the beginning of a project.

During years 1 through the life of the project (*n* years), the project has annual incremental operating cash flows. For a new or expanded product or service, these cash flows may include new revenues as well as new fixed and variable costs. When replacing or reorganizing assets, revenues and costs may increase or decrease because of improved product quality, increased capacity, or greater efficiency.

Any terminal cash flows appear at the end of the project's life (time *n*). Terminal cash flows typically include proceeds from the sale of assets at the end of the project (the salvage value). However, assets such as equipment may be obsolete and have zero salvage value. Some projects require terminal cash outflows, such as the costs to reinstate the quality of land (called land reclamation) at the end of a mining operation.

**ALTERNATIVE TERMS**

The terms *residual value, salvage value,* and *disposal value* mean the same as *terminal value.*

## ■ Quantitative Analysis Techniques

In this chapter, we learn the four methods listed in Exhibit 12.1 for quantitatively analyzing potential strategic investment projects. The first two methods, net present value (NPV) and internal rate of return (IRR), explicitly take into account the time value of money, making them preferred methods. However, many managers still use the other less-preferred methods: payback and accrual accounting rate of return. Therefore, we introduce all of these methods and present advantages and disadvantages of each.

# NET PRESENT VALUE METHOD

 **Q3** How is net present value (NPV) analysis performed and interpreted?

In business, we need to value a project today, but the cash flows occur in the future. Therefore, we discount the future dollars to determine their value in today's dollars. In Appendix 12B you will find tables with factors that you multiply by cash flows to determine either a **future value,** the amount received in the future for a given number of years at a given interest rate, for a given investment today, or a **present value,** the value in today's dollars of a sum received in the future.

Suppose you want to buy a $20,000 sports car two years from now. Assume you can invest money today and earn a rate of return of 10% per year. How much would you have to invest today so that in two years you will have $20,000? In other words, what present value is needed to create a future value of $20,000 at an annual interest rate of 10%? To calculate the present value, we multiply the future value ($20,000) by the present value factor for 10% and 2 time periods. Using the table Present Value of $1 in Appendix 12B, locate the 10% column and go down to the row representing two periods. The factor is 0.826. Multiply this factor by the future value of $20,000. You need $16,520 today to have enough money in two years to buy the car.

## ■ Present Value of a Series of Cash Flows

Managers are often involved in evaluating projects with different time horizons. One project might end in five years and another in ten years. The future values of such projects are not strictly comparable because a dollar received five years from now is not worth a dollar received ten years from now. For this and other reasons, the cash flows for projects are generally converted to their present values. The projects can then be compared on a common basis.

The **net present value method (NPV)** determines whether an organization would be better off investing in a project based on the net amount of discounted cash flows for the project. The net present value of a project is calculated as:

$$NPV = \sum_{t=0}^{n} \frac{\text{Expected cash flow}_t}{(1 + r)^t}$$

where

$t$ = time period (year)
$n$ = life of the project
$r$ = discount rate

The expected cash flows include the initial investment, incremental operating cash flows, and terminal cash flows. If the NPV is positive, the project is generally considered acceptable because it is expected to increase the organization's value. If investment resources are limited, invest in the project(s) having the highest NPV. Following is an example of the NPV method.

Suppose Gordon wants to convert a 30,000 square foot motel into apartments that he will rent to university students. The initial investment is $1,400,000. Gordon expects to rent the apartments for $1.00 per square foot per month and to pay a management company fees representing 15% of rents. He forecasts that property taxes and insurance will be about $30,000 per year. Therefore, the incremental cash flows are $276,000 = [$1 per sq ft × 30,000 sq ft × 12 months) × (1 − 0.15)] − $30,000. Gordon expects to be able to sell the building at the end of 10 years for $400,000. (We will ignore income taxes for these calculations.) Gordon's discount rate is 14%. The cash flows for this project are shown in Exhibit 12.3. The total discounted cash flow after the initial investment is the sum of individual present values, as follows:

| Period | Interest Rate | Present Value Factor (PVF) | Cash Flow | Discounted Cash Flow |
|---|---|---|---|---|
| 1 | 14% | 0.877 | $276,000 | $ 242,052 |
| 2 | 14 | 0.769 | 276,000 | 212,244 |
| 3 | 14 | 0.675 | 276,000 | 186,300 |
| 4 | 14 | 0.592 | 276,000 | 163,392 |
| 5 | 14 | 0.519 | 276,000 | 143,244 |
| 6 | 14 | 0.456 | 276,000 | 125,856 |
| 7 | 14 | 0.400 | 276,000 | 110,400 |
| 8 | 14 | 0.351 | 276,000 | 96,876 |
| 9 | 14 | 0.308 | 276,000 | 85,008 |
| 10 | 14 | 0.270 | 276,000 | 74,520 |
| 10 | 14 | 0.270 | 400,000 | 108,000 |
| | | | Total discounted cash flows | $1,547,892 |

Notice that the incremental operating cash flows during years 1 through 10 are identical. In other words, Gordon expects to receive an annual annuity of $276,000 per year for 10 years, and in year 10 he also receives the terminal value of $400,000. In the case of an annuity,

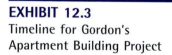

**EXHIBIT 12.3**
Timeline for Gordon's
Apartment Building Project

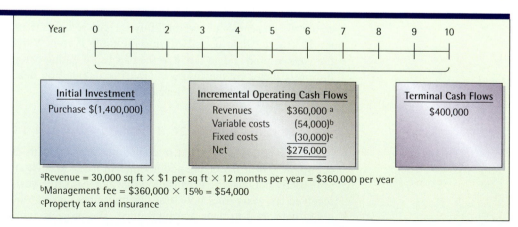

we can simplify the present value calculation using the Present Value of an Ordinary Annuity (PVFA) of $1 factor from Table 12B.2 in Appendix 12B as follows:

$$PV = \$276{,}000 \times (PVFA\ 10\ years,\ 14\%) + \$400{,}000 \times (PVF\ 10\ years,\ 14\%)$$
$$= \$276{,}000 \times 5.216 + \$400{,}000 \times 0.270$$
$$= \$1{,}439{,}616 + \$108{,}000$$
$$= \$1{,}547{,}616$$

Notice that we obtain the same present value for the project cash flows (the difference between $1,547,892 and $1,547,616 is due to rounding) regardless of the method we use. However, if we are performing these calculations manually, we can often save time by using the annuity table.

## ■ Net Present Value of a Project

Once we calculate the present value of a series of cash flows for Gordon's project, we can compare the net present value to the investment amount because both amounts are now valued in today's dollars. We use the following formula to calculate NPV for Gordon's apartment project:

$$NPV = Initial\ investment\ cash\ outflow + PV\ of\ cash\ inflows$$
$$= -\$1{,}400{,}000 + \$1{,}574{,}616$$
$$= \$174{,}616$$

At the end of 10 years, we estimate that Gordon will have realized $174,616 in today's dollars. Because this net present value amount is greater than zero, the general rule is that Gordon would want to invest in this project.

If Gordon were considering more than one investment, he could calculate the profitability index for each project. The **profitability index** is the ratio of the present value of the cash inflows to the present value of the investment cash outflows. The decision rule for a solitary investment is that the investment should be undertaken if the index is equal to or greater than 1. For example, Gordon's profitability index would be:

$$Profitability\ index = \frac{Present\ value\ of\ cash\ inflows}{Present\ value\ of\ investment\ cash\ outflows} = \frac{\$1{,}574{,}616}{\$1{,}400{,}000} = 1.125$$

If Gordon were comparing a number of different projects and could not undertake all of them, he would consider both today's dollar amount and the profitability index. The profitability index and the NPV method always accept and reject the same project, but the index allows managers to rank order projects. It provides a simple way to identify which projects are expected to earn a higher return.

## ■ Identifying a Reasonable Discount Rate

A discount rate, $r$, must be selected to apply the NPV formula. The **discount rate** is the interest rate that is used across time to reduce the value of future dollars to today's dollars. Many decision makers simply set the discount rate at the organization's **weighted average cost of capital,** which is the weighted average rate for the costs of the various sources of financing such as debt and stock. (Problem 12.36 provides practice at calculating the weighted average cost of capital.) However, this method ignores variations in risk among projects. If a project involves little risk, then a lower discount rate might be appropriate. Conversely, a higher discount rate is appropriate for projects having higher risk.

Judgment is required to incorporate an estimate of project risk. One way to think about project risk is to consider the return on other investment opportunities that appear to be of similar risk. For example, the stock market has returned, on average, about 11% across time. We can think about how the risk of a particular project compares with the risk of investing long term in the stock market. If the project seems more (less) risky than investing in the market, a discount rate greater (less) than 11% might be appropriate.

| GUIDE YOUR LEARNING | 12.1 | Key Terms |
|---|---|---|

Stop to confirm that you understand the new terms introduced in the last several pages.

| | |
|---|---|
| Capital budgeting (p. 467) | Net present value method (p. 470) |
| Time value of money (p. 467) | Profitability index (p. 471) |
| Future value (p. 469) | Discount rate (p. 471) |
| Present value (p. 469) | Weighted average cost of capital (p. 471) |

For each of these terms, write a definition in your own words.

| GUIDE YOUR LEARNING | 12.2 | Net Present Value |
|---|---|---|

Stop to confirm that you understand the net present value technique introduced in the last several pages. For this method:

| Identify Information Used | Identify Information Created | Describe Use |
|---|---|---|
| List the information that is used as inputs. | List the information that is created. | In your own words, describe how the technique is used to make a strategic investment decision. |

## UNCERTAINTIES AND SENSITIVITY ANALYSIS

 **Q4** What are the uncertainties and limitations of NPV analysis?

When we perform NPV analysis, the general rule is to accept the project if NPV is greater than zero. Many assumptions are built into this general rule. For example, we assume that we know each of the following:

- Cost of initial investment
- Timing and dollar amounts of incremental revenues and costs
- Terminal values
- Project life
- Appropriate discount rate

However, we cannot know any of these factors with absolute certainty. Also, uncertainties grow with the number of years being forecast; a 15-year project has more uncertainties than one completed in five years.

### ■ Cash Flow Uncertainties

The preceding illustration for Gordon's apartment building decision includes little uncertainty about the initial investment cash flows. Gordon knows for certain the purchase price of the motel and negotiates a final bid with a building contractor for converting the motel into apartments. Some uncertainty may be involved in the cost of renovation. As long as the specific nature of the renovations are known and can be completed fairly quickly before costs change, the cost estimate from the contractor should be reasonably close to the final cost. However, renovation of Gordon's motel could rise dramatically if contractors discover unforseen problems, such as asbestos that must be removed.

We always encounter uncertainty when estimating future revenues, costs, and terminal values. However, our ability to accurately estimate cash flows decreases as we forecast further into the future. Long time frames reduce our ability to anticipate customer tastes, changes in technology, productivity, competition, availability of resources, and changes in regulation. For example, certain organizations, such as health care providers that treat Medicare and Medicaid patients, rely heavily on reimbursement from the government. Changes in reimbursement rates or changes in the basis of reimbursement greatly affect the expected revenues of these organizations. As another example, unexpected spikes in gasoline and diesel prices affect transportation companies and the organizations that use them, such as produce haulers and grocery stores.

Estimating cash flows for projects involving new products or services is more difficult than for projects involving changes or expansions of existing products and services. Revenues must sometimes be based on a market that does not currently exist. It is nearly impossible to anticipate all potential costs. Substantial errors are likely in these types of predictions.

## ■ Project Life and Discount Rate Uncertainties

The expected life of a project is also uncertain. Difficulties in estimating the life of a project are often related to difficulties in estimating revenues and costs. For example, farmers using **Texas A&M's** Sire Summary Program may project a time period over which cows will produce specific amounts of milk, but an unexpected illness could cut these estimates short. Managers are likely to continue a project longer if it is profitable. The reverse is true if the project is unprofitable. Managers may also change how they define an organization's core competencies. Such changes increase or decrease the strategic importance of a project, leading to an extension or cancellation of the project.

Several factors affect the discount rate for NPV analysis including interest rates, inflation, and the riskiness of the project. However, none of these factors are known, and the length of time for capital projects increases the uncertainty.

## ■ Estimation Bias

Because of the many uncertainties involved, managers use considerable judgment in making capital project estimates. However, those responsible for forming the estimates are often the ones who originated the idea for the project. Intentionally or not, these managers are likely to form estimates that favor adoption of the project. In addition, they are more likely to fail to identify all possible project costs than to anticipate costs that will not occur—another estimation bias that favors project adoption.

---

**CURRENT PRACTICE**

### Amazon's Bold Bets

**Amazon's** founder and CEO, Jeff Bezos, established a long-term investment strategy that focused on market share growth, among other things. The company encountered many challenges along the way to achieving its goals. Jeff Bezos described one of the company's challenges in his Letter to Shareholders in Amazon's 2000 Annual Report:

*Many of you have heard me talk about the "bold bets" that we as a company have made and will continue to make—these bold bets have included everything from our investment in digital and wireless technologies, to our decision to invest in smaller e-commerce companies, including living.com and Pets.com, both of which shut down operations in 2000. We were significant shareholders in both and lost a significant amount of money on both.*

*We made these investments because we knew we wouldn't ourselves be entering these particular categories any time soon, and we believed passionately in the "land rush" metaphor for the Internet. Indeed, that metaphor was an extraordinarily useful decision aid for several years starting in 1994, but we now believe its usefulness largely faded away over the last couple of years. In retrospect, we significantly underestimated how much time would be available to enter these categories and underestimated how difficult it would be for single-category e-commerce companies to achieve the scale necessary to succeed.*

Source: Courtesy Amazon.com, Inc. All rights reserved. Amazon's 2000 Letter to Shareholders can be accessed under the Investor Relations section of Amazon's Web site at phx.corporate-ir.net/phoenix.zhtml?c=97664&p=irol-annualreports.

---

## ■ Sensitivity Analysis

Sensitivity analysis helps managers evaluate how their NPV results would change with variations in the input data. When spreadsheets are set up appropriately, the discount rate, cash

---

[2]See T. Reinsch and D. Larson, "Avoiding the Pitfalls Abroad," *Oil & Gas Investor,* April 2003, pp. 71–74.

flows, and any other underlying assumptions can be easily varied. Decision makers can then consider the results of alternative scenarios under different sets of assumptions. For example, what is the change in NPV if we reduce our revenue estimates by 10%? What if we increase the discount rate by 1%? What if the terminal value is zero? The sensitivity of results to variations in assumptions helps managers evaluate the risk of investments.

## GORDON'S HEALTH CLUB
## NET PRESENT VALUE AND SENSITIVITY ANALYSIS

Gordon has a basement space in the building that would not be suitable for living units because it has no windows. A friend offered to rent the space from Gordon for $60,000 per year, with an increase of $2,000 after three years. She will use the space to house an upscale health spa for women. However, Gordon would like to open a health club to serve the students at his building, people living in the neighborhood, and people who work nearby.

### Relevant Cash Flows and Timeline

Gordon hires a consultant to gather information about the project and to recommend a plan of action. The fee for this service is $5,000. The following list includes the relevant information the consulting firm estimates for the project.

1. The cost of renovation and new equipment that will be purchased is $650,000. The terminal value is estimated at $100,000 after five years.

2. Promotion costs to advertise the club will be $120,000 for the first year and $50,000 per year thereafter.

3. The revenues for the health club are estimated as $300,000 in the first year, $400,000 in the second, and $500,000 in the third through fifth years.

4. The operating costs for the health club are estimated as $200,000 for the first year and $130,000 for each of the following years.

Gordon sets up a time line as shown in Exhibit 12.4. Notice that he ignores sunk costs (the fee paid to the consulting firm), includes opportunity costs (foregone rent), and uses a 10% discount rate.

### NPV Analysis

Gordon sets up a spreadsheet as shown in Exhibit 12.5. He organizes the spreadsheet with an input section so that any of the assumptions made for the NPV analysis can be easily varied in performing a sensitivity analysis. He includes a cell reference for changes in revenues. Based on these NPV calculations, Gordon expects to realize $1,851 in today's dollars, over and above the investment amount of $650,000, if he invests in the health club.

When Gordon reviews his spreadsheet calculations with the consultants, they indicate some uncertainty about the assumptions. The consulting team is concerned that the revenue estimates

**EXHIBIT 12.4** Timeline for Gordon's Health Club Project

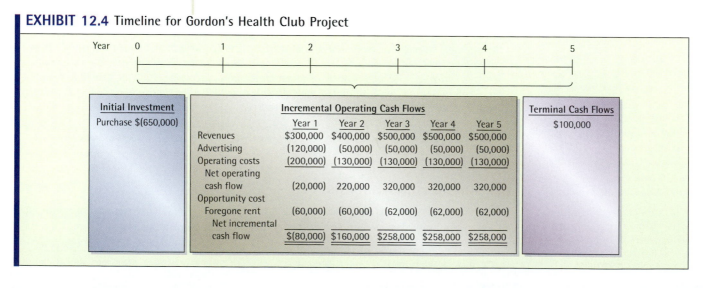

| | | Incremental Operating Cash Flows | | | | | |
|---|---|---|---|---|---|---|---|
| **Initial Investment** | | | Year 1 | Year 2 | Year 3 | Year 4 | Year 5 |
| Purchase $(650,000) | Revenues | | $300,000 | $400,000 | $500,000 | $500,000 | $500,000 |
| | Advertising | | (120,000) | (50,000) | (50,000) | (50,000) | (50,000) |
| | Operating costs | | (200,000) | (130,000) | (130,000) | (130,000) | (130,000) |
| | Net operating cash flow | | (20,000) | 220,000 | 320,000 | 320,000 | 320,000 |
| | Opportunity cost | | | | | | |
| | Foregone rent | | (60,000) | (60,000) | (62,000) | (62,000) | (62,000) |
| | Net incremental cash flow | | $(80,000) | $160,000 | $258,000 | $258,000 | $258,000 |

Terminal Cash Flows $100,000

**EXHIBIT 12.5**
NPV Calculations for
Gordon's Health Club

| | A | B | C | D | E |
|---|---|---|---|---|---|
| 1 | Gordon's Health Club Project | | | | |
| 2 | Assumptions | | | | |
| 3 | Discount rate | 10% | | Teminal value | $100,000 |
| 4 | Initial investment | $650,000 | | | |
| 5 | Cash Flows | | | | |
| 6 | Period | Revenues | Operating Costs | Advertising | Foregone Rent |
| 7 | 1 | $300,000 | $200,000 | $120,000 | $60,000 |
| 8 | 2 | $400,000 | $130,000 | $50,000 | $60,000 |
| 9 | 3 | $500,000 | $130,000 | $50,000 | $62,000 |
| 10 | 4 | $500,000 | $130,000 | $50,000 | $62,000 |
| 11 | 5 | $500,000 | $130,000 | $50,000 | $62,000 |
| 12 | Change to Assumptions for Sensitivity Analysis: | | | | |
| 13 | Change Revenues | 0% | | | |
| 14 | | | | | |
| 15 | | | | | |
| 16 | PV Calculations | | | | |
| 17 | | | Net Cash Flows | Discounted | | |
| 18 | | 1 | ($80,000) | ($72,727) | | |
| 19 | | 2 | $160,000 | $132,231 | | |
| 20 | | 3 | $258,000 | $193,839 | | |
| 21 | | 4 | $258,000 | $176,217 | | |
| 22 | | 5 | $258,000 | $160,198 | | |
| 23 | Total Discounted Operating CF | | $589,759 | | |
| 24 | Terminal value | | | | |
| 25 | | 5 | $100,000 | $62,092 | | |
| 26 | | | | | |
| 27 | NPV | | | | |
| 28 | Operating CF | $589,759 | | | |
| 29 | Terminal value | $62,092 | | | |
| 30 | Less | | | | |
| 31 | Investment | ($650,000) | | | |
| 32 | NPV | $1,851 | | | |

Examples of Excel formulas:
Net cash flow in cell B18: = (1+$B$13)*B7−(C7+D7+E7)
Discounted cash flow in cell C18: =−PV($B$3,A18,,B18)

might be too high. The building is located in an older part of town and people may not want to walk in the neighborhood at night to get to the club. They suggest that Gordon reduce the revenues by 5% for sensitivity analysis. He enters −5% in the appropriate input cell. With this drop in revenues, he would incur a $79,696 loss over the five-year life of the project. Gordon decides to develop a series of spreadsheets varying all of the assumptions to reflect possible changes in future economic conditions. He will then discuss this decision further with the consulting team.

## GUIDE YOUR LEARNING 12.3 Gordon's Health Club

Gordon's Health Club demonstrates the net present value method using a spreadsheet with sensitivity analysis. For this illustration:

| Calculate It | Identify Problem and Information | Identify Uncertainties | Explore Information |
|---|---|---|---|
| Manually recalculate some of the values in Exhibit 12.5 to be sure you understand how the computations were performed. | What decision was being addressed? Explain which cash flows were relevant and which were irrelevant. | What types of uncertainties were present? Consider uncertainties about:<br>• Initial investment<br>• Revenues<br>• Operating costs<br>• Advertising costs<br>• Terminal value<br>• Discount rate<br>• Interpreting results | Why did Gordon decide that additional sensitivity analyses were needed for this decision? What did he hope to learn? |

# INTERNAL RATE OF RETURN

**ALTERNATIVE TERMS**

Some people use the term *time-adjusted rate of return* to describe the method called *internal rate of return*.

The **internal rate of return (IRR)** method determines the discount rate necessary for the present value of the discounted cash flows to be equal to the investment. In other words, the method solves for the discount rate at which a project's NPV equals zero. The calculation of IRR is similar to NPV analysis in that it is based on discounted cash flows. In the NPV analysis, we assumed a discount rate and solved for the NPV. In the case of IRR, we search for the discount rate that results in an NPV of zero. This discount rate is the internal rate of return.

## ■ IRR Calculations

Earlier in the chapter, Gordon analyzed a decision to invest in the apartment building for students. Suppose he is now trying to decide whether to install coin-operated vending machines in the apartment building. He knows that students eat a lot of snack foods, but the closest 24-hour grocery is eight blocks away. Gordon thinks that the students will purchase beverages and food from vending machines if he installs them. The equipment will cost $5,000 and have a useful life of five years. He expects to net $1,500 in annual cash flows from operating the machines (revenues minus food and maintenance costs). The equipment will have no terminal value at the end of five years. Gordon thinks it could be a good investment, but he would like to know what his expected rate of return would be. The cash flows for this project are shown in Exhibit 12.6.

Gordon wants to find the discount rate at which the NPV equals zero. Recall that the NPV is calculated by subtracting the initial investment from the NPV of cash inflows. Because the cash inflows are uniform across time, Gordon can use the Present Value of an Ordinary Annuity of $1 table (see Appendix 12B). Then, the IRR is the interest rate (*X*%) at which:

$$\text{Initial investment} = \text{NPV of cash inflows}$$
$$\$5,000 = \$1,500 \times (\text{PVFA 5 years, } X\%)$$

Solving for the present value of an annuity factor:

$$(\text{PVFA 5 years, } X\%) = \$5,000 \div \$1,500 = 3.333$$

Gordon uses the table to locate the interest rate (*X*%) at which the present value of an annuity factor is approximately equal to 3.333 for a time period of five years. Finding the row for five time periods, he sees that the factor for 15% is 3.352. This factor is very close to 3.333, so he concludes that the IRR is close to 15%. This return is higher than the discount rate he used to calculate the net present value of the apartment complex, and this project is probably less risky, so Gordon decides it is a worthwhile investment.

The approach using the Present Value of an Ordinary Annuity of $1 table can be applied only when the cash flows from a project are uniform over time. For uneven cash inflows, such as for Gordon's apartment building project, a trial-and-error approach may be used along with the present value table. We first try a discount rate and calculate the NPV of the project using that discount rate. If the NPV is greater than zero, we try a larger discount rate; if it is less than zero, we decrease the discount rate.

We can easily calculate a more precise IRR using a spreadsheet. Using Excel's IRR function (see Exhibit 12.7), Gordon learns that the IRR for his coin-operated machine project is 15.24%. When he calculates the NPV using the IRR as the discount rate, the NPV is zero.

**EXHIBIT 12.6**
**Timeline for Gordon's Coin-Operated Equipment Project**

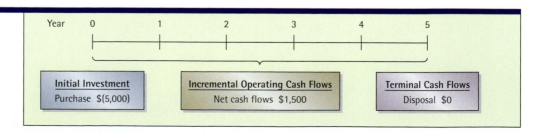

EXHIBIT 12.7
IRR for Gordon's
Coin-Operated
Equipment Project

**EXHIBIT 12.7**
IRR for Gordon's
Coin-Operated
Equipment Project

|    | A | B |
|----|---|---|
| 1  | Net Cash Flows: | |
| 2  | Time 0 | ($5,000) |
| 3  | Year 1 | $1,500 |
| 4  | Year 2 | $1,500 |
| 5  | Year 3 | $1,500 |
| 6  | Year 4 | $1,500 |
| 7  | Year 5 | $1,500 |
| 8  | | |
| 9  | IRR | 15.24% |
| 10 | NPV | $0 |

Excel formula to calculate internal rate of return in cell B9: =IRR(B2:B7)
Excel formula to calculate net present value in cell B10: =B2+NPV(B9,B3:B7)

## ◼ Comparison of NPV and IRR Methods

Certainly without spreadsheets, the net present value method is computationally simpler than the internal rate of return method. Determining IRR can be time consuming, particularly for projects returning uneven cash flows. The use of a spreadsheet reduces the effort considerably. However, if several projects are being analyzed, their NPVs can be summed to determine the NPV for that group, or portfolio, of projects, whereas IRR can be neither summed nor averaged.

An important difference between the two methods is that the IRR method assumes cash inflows can be reinvested to earn the same return that the project would generate. However, it may be difficult for an organization to identify other opportunities that could achieve the same rate when IRR is high. In contrast, the NPV method assumes that cash inflows can be reinvested and earn the discount rate—a more realistic assumption. If the discount rate is set equal to the organization's cost of capital, then alternative uses of cash would include paying off creditors or buying back stock. For the preceding reasons, the NPV method is preferable.

Both methods are used widely in business. One reason for the continued use of IRR is that many people find it intuitively easier to understand than NPV. In addition, managers may want to compare the IRR on prior projects to current project return rates as they consider new investment. For example, Gordon could compare the IRR for the health club with any new projects and decide whether to accept a project with a lower IRR.

CURRENT PRACTICE

Gaylord Entertainment compares an investment's IRR to a required rate of return slightly higher than its weighted average cost of capital. Subjective assessment of risk also influences managers' decisions.[3]

## PAYBACK METHOD

INTERNATIONAL

A survey of Swedish companies revealed that the payback method is used most often for capital budgets, with NPV use increasing. Tradition is the relevant explanation for choice of capital budgeting method.[4]

The **payback method** measures the amount of time required to recover the initial investment. Assuming that cash flows from the project are constant over future years, the payback period can be calculated by dividing the initial investment cash flow by the annual incremental operating cash flows. Consider Gordon's decision to install vending machines:

$$\text{Number of years to pay back the investment} = \frac{\text{Initial investment}}{\text{Annual incremental operating cash flow}} = \frac{\$5,000}{\$1,500} = 3.33$$

Thus, the payback period for this example is 3.33 years. If incremental annual cash flows are uneven, then the payback period can be found by calculating the cumulative incremental operating cash flows until the initial investment amount has been fully covered. The number of years needed to cover the initial investment is the payback period.

## ◼ Advantages and Disadvantages of the Payback Method

This method has some important disadvantages. First, it does not incorporate the time value of money. Future cash flows are not discounted to reflect the opportunity cost of using funds

---

[3]See G. Anthes, "Internal Rate of Return," *Computerworld,* February 17, 2003, p. 32.
[4]G. Sandahl and S. Sjogren, "Capital Budgeting Methods Among Sweden's Largest Groups of Companies," *International Journal of Production Economics,* April 11, 2003, p. 51.

for other projects. In addition, it does not value the cash flows that are received after the investment has been recovered. Because of these disadvantages, it cannot be used to choose among several projects. However, the payback method is used extensively outside the United States. In addition, payback is sometimes used with NPV or IRR when meaningful estimates of relevant cash flows are lacking because the project or product is so new that it provides no historical data for reference. Longer payback periods reflect higher risk; therefore, projects with shorter payback periods are preferable because cash is not committed over long periods.

## ACCRUAL ACCOUNTING RATE OF RETURN METHOD

**ALTERNATIVE TERMS**

The terms *return on investment (ROI)*, *average rate of return*, and *unadjusted rate of return* are often used to describe the method called *accrual accounting rate of return*.

The **accrual accounting rate of return** is the expected increase in average annual operating income as a percent of the initial increase in required investment. In Gordon's vending machine decision, the net increase in income needs to be adjusted so that it reflects accrual accounting income. For financial statements, suppose that Gordon uses straight-line depreciation. With a five-year life and no terminal value, annual financial statement depreciation is $1,000 per year ($5,000 ÷ 5 years). Assuming depreciation is the only difference between cash flows and financial statement income, accrual accounting income is $500 ($1,500 − $1,000). The accrual accounting rate of return of 10% is the expected incremental accounting income from the project divided by the initial investment ($500 ÷ $5,000).

### ■ Advantages and Disadvantages of the Accrual Accounting Rate of Return Method

This method presents several problems. First, it ignores the time value of money. In addition, depreciation is deducted from the numerator, but the full investment amount is the denominator, so the investment amount is essentially double counted. This method is frequently used to evaluate division or department performance because the financial information is readily available, but it is not an appropriate method for evaluating long-term investment decisions.

## OTHER CONSIDERATIONS FOR STRATEGIC INVESTMENT DECISIONS

 **Q6** What additional issues should be considered for strategic investment decisions?

**INTERNATIONAL**

For its new information system, Dominican Republic edible oil refiner La Fabril obtained several bids and then chose the system managers believed was best suited to its needs, without NPV analysis.[5]

Managers consider qualitative factors as well as quantitative analyses when making a strategic investment decision. In this section, we learn about a variety of factors that affect the final capital budgeting decision. We also discuss long-term monitoring of results.

### ■ Qualitative Factors

Qualitative factors often influence strategic investment decisions. Sometimes these factors cannot be quantified, and other times numerical estimates would be so uncertain that decision makers find them useless.

Estimating the future cash flows from implementing an enterprise-wide system such as those sold by **Oracle**, **PeopleSoft**, **SAP**, or **Baan** involves high uncertainty. The benefits of such systems include increased timeliness of information and increased availability of new information. Therefore, many organizations make these types of decisions based on the experience of other organizations as well as the information they receive from the enterprise-wide system developers and sales representatives.

The need for a timely decision sometimes overrides the use of a formal capital budgeting process such as NPV. Timeliness can be particularly important when new opportunities arise suddenly and an organization needs to take action before its competitors. Another related consideration is the ability of an organization to envision new products and services. Organizations often stumble when they concentrate solely on the improvement of existing products and services because they fail to recognize changes in customer preferences, technology, or other factors that call for shifts in products and services. Innovative organizations typically focus on combining formal quantitative analysis with exploration of future trends.

---

[5]See Marcam's Web site (www.marcam.com/) and click on Customers for more information about the decision.

# ■ Reputation, Environment, Quality, and Community

If a proposed capital project would affect the environment in a negative way, the project might harm an organization's reputation. Projects adversely affect the environment in a number of ways such as producing hazardous waste, emitting chemicals into the air, or polluting lakes, streams, or landfills. Sometimes the cost of environmental impact creates direct cash flow effects that are included in NPV analyses, such as permit fees for air emissions. However, many environmental costs are not borne by the emitting company, but by society as a whole. For example, real estate developers are not assessed for the degradation in neighborhood noise levels that result from increased traffic to a new shopping center. To encourage organizations to adopt environmentally friendly policies, several organizations index firms according to their pollution control practices. In addition, some mutual funds are comprised strictly of "green" investments.

Because reputation effects are difficult to value, managers typically incorporate these concerns qualitatively. An increasing number of companies are developing environmental policy statements to help guide their strategic decisions, and they may make environmental investments without formal quantitative analysis. To attract customers and investors who are concerned about the environment, some organizations advertise their "green" practices.

Investments spent to reduce pollution often result in financial benefit. For example, Anderson Lithograph publishes financial statements for large corporations. In 1997 the company decided to purchase equipment that would burn the particles emitted from its printing process. The decision was made in light of the values held by managers. However, the pollution-burning process also generated electricity for the firm. After the equipment had been installed and operated over a period of time, the company no longer relied on outside sources of electricity and was also able to sell electricity to the local power company. Anderson sold its pollution credits to other companies that could not curtail their emissions. The managers believed that their return on investment had far exceeded expectations.[6]

Many organizations invest a great deal of time and money to improve product or service quality. These decisions are often made without formal quantitative consideration of the long-term costs and benefits. For some organizations, quality requirements from markets such as the European Union must be met to sell products or services. Other firms hold high-quality standards as a part of their competitive strategies. Because measuring and predicting the costs and benefits of total quality management (TQM) practices are difficult, firms typically implement them without performing NPV analysis.

CURRENT PRACTICE

Some people are skeptical about benefits from implementing strategies promoted by the popular press and consultants. Research by economists and accountants fails to find increased financial performance for firms employing TQM.[7]

---

[6]To encourage organizations to reduce pollution, California issued pollution credits to firms in the late 1980s. These credits were given for current pollution levels. If pollution was reduced, the credits could be sold to other organizations that wanted to expand processes, but would produce pollution as a result. For more information, see Anderson's Web site at www.andlitho.com/home.html, then click on Plant Tour, then Environment and Safety.

[7]See, for example, Christopher Ittner and David Larcker, "Total Quality Management and the Choice of Information and Reward Systems," *Journal of Accounting Research,* 33 (Supplement 1995), pp. 1–34; J. Mathews and P. Katel, "The Cost of Quality," *Newsweek,* September 7, 1992, p. 48; and "The Cracks in Quality," *The Economist,* April 18, 1992, pp. 67–68.

In some cases, an investment under consideration would result in a potentially negative impact on employees. If new equipment or manufacturing processes replace employees, the impact needs to be evaluated for both displaced employees and also on the morale of remaining employees. If job responsibilities or perceptions of job stability change as a result of the project, the remaining employees may be negatively affected. Sometimes organizations forgo or modify projects to reduce negative impacts on employees.

Some projects result in a large impact on the community. Bringing a large new facility into a small community can change the dynamics of the entire community. Closing a plant or service upon which a community relies can result in a negative reputation for an organization. A negative corporate image can have far-reaching effects on the company as a whole, including loss of market share and morale problems with employees and management.

## ■ Making and Monitoring Strategic Investment Decisions

Managers consider a number of factors when making the final decision about a proposed capital budgeting project. The results of any quantitative analyses as well as the qualitative issues already discussed are taken into account. Accountants often prepare analyses of projects that align with organizations' strategic plans. Managers use these analyses to examine financial outcomes under a number of different scenarios. They often have a better grasp than accountants on certain business factors, such as competitors' product development and prices. In addition, managers may use their own informal estimates to determine an NPV.

After a project has been accepted, accountants and managers monitor its progress and compare actual performance to the capital budget expectations. Some projects are relatively simple to implement and require little monitoring (e.g., the replacement of equipment in a laundromat). Other projects are more complex, such as Gordon's new line of business through the health club. More complex projects that take longer to implement need more monitoring to reduce the probability of budget overruns.

Because these projects are long-lived, outcomes are always different from expected. A **post-investment audit** provides feedback about whether operations are meeting expectations. When results are below expectations, processes are investigated and improvements can be implemented. In addition, the process of reevaluating past decisions usually improves future decision making. The more we learn about factors that affect the accuracy of our forecasts and investigate unanticipated problems or benefits, the better we can predict these occurrences in future projects.

## FOCUS ON ETHICAL DECISION MAKING
### The Right Thing To Do

In the past, drug makers have been reluctant to invest in cures for diseases in developing countries such as Africa and South America. People in these countries cannot afford to pay for treatments, and managers have typically invested in other long-term projects having higher returns. However, a few pharmaceutical companies have chosen to invest in neglected diseases, including tuberculosis, malaria, and other tropical diseases. As an example, Glaxo-SmithKline formed a joint venture with the World Health Organization to develop a malaria drug that costs less than 50 cents for a three-day treatment.

This type of investment has several goals. From a reputation perspective, managers accused of keeping drug prices artificially high may believe that providing low-cost cures will alleviate pressure from regulators and consumers to lower prices for drugs sold in the United States and other developed countries. Furthermore, people from some less-developed countries will eventually have the ability to pay for cures. Finally, "it is the right thing to do," according to journalist Robert Langreth. Novartis's chairman Daniel Vasella says, "If you only look at maximizing short-term profit, you may not survive in the long term."

Source: Robert Langreth, "A Cure for Neglect," *Forbes*, March 18, 2002.

### Practice Ethical Decision Making

In Chapter 1, we learned about a process for making ethical decisions (Exhibit 1.11). You can address the following questions for this ethical dilemma to improve your skills for making ethical decisions. Think about your answers to these questions and discuss them with others.

| Ethical Decision-Making Process | Questions to Consider about This Ethical Dilemma |
|---|---|
| Identify ethical problems as they arise. | Does an ethical problem arise if pharmaceutical companies charge lower prices for drugs in developing countries than in developed countries? Why or why not? |
| Objectively consider the well-being of others and society when exploring alternatives. | Why might people argue that a drug company's investment in low-cost drugs is "the right thing to do"? Explore this problem from various perspectives, including:<br>• Patients in developing countries<br>• Patients in developed countries<br>• Pharmaceutical company managers<br>• Pharmaceutical company shareholders<br>• Competitor pharmaceutical companies |
| Clarify and apply ethical values when choosing a course of action. | How should ethical considerations affect managers' strategic investment decisions? What values did you use to arrive at the conclusion? |
| Work toward ongoing improvement of personal and organizational ethics. | Explain what Daniel Vasella of Novartis meant when he said, "If you only look at maximizing short-term profit, you may not survive in the long term." |

## INCOME TAXES AND THE NET PRESENT VALUE METHOD

 **Q7** How do income taxes affect strategic investment decision cash flows?

Income taxes affect an organization's cash flows and, in turn, capital budgeting decisions. Because individual states and countries have different income tax rules, the specific tax effects on a proposed project depend on the tax jurisdictions of the organization and the project. Even for small organizations that operate in only one state, tax laws can be complicated. Taxes become even more complex as an organization grows and expands domestically and internationally. In addition, income tax laws change periodically, and capital budgeting requires current knowledge of tax laws. Before developing NPV analyses in a complex business, accountants consult tax experts so that their analyses reflect the cash flows that would actually take place.

Exhibit 12.8 summarizes some of the major U.S. federal income tax effects for capital budgeting decisions. Most cash flows associated with capital budgeting projects either increase or decrease income taxes in the year of the cash flow. However, the initial investment generally cannot be deducted immediately from taxable income. Instead, depreciation can be deducted in future years for investments such as buildings, land improvements, equipment, and furnishings. This depreciation deduction is often referred to as a **tax shield;** the depreciation shields part of operating income from the payment of income taxes. In addition, operating cash flows and gains or losses on assets' terminal values affect the amount of income tax paid.

**EXHIBIT 12.8** U.S. Income Tax Provisions for Capital Budgeting Cash Flows

| Cash Flows | Major U.S. Income Tax Provisions |
|---|---|
| Initial Investment | • Property, plant, and equipment generally cannot be deducted from taxable income in the year of acquisition. <br> • Depreciation on buildings, land improvements, equipment, and furnishings can be deducted from taxable income over lives ranging from 3 to 39 years (see Appendix 12A). <br> • Costs for land cannot be depreciated. <br> • Costs to get an asset ready for use must generally be added to the cost of the asset. <br> • Costs such as employee training are generally deductible in the year incurred. <br> • Investments in other companies generally cannot be deducted from taxable income until the investment is sold. <br> • When an entire company is purchased, the purchase price is allocated among the assets acquired; tax treatment depends on the asset classifications. |
| Incremental Operating Cash Flows | • Positive incremental operating cash flows increase taxable income. <br> • Negative incremental operating cash flows decrease taxable income. |
| Terminal Cash Flows | • The gain or loss on sale of an asset is based on the difference between the sale proceeds and the taxable basis of the asset; taxable basis is cost less accumulated tax depreciation. <br> • If assets are abandoned, any remaining taxable basis can be taken as a deduction. |

---

## GUIDE YOUR LEARNING 12.4 Key Terms

Stop to confirm that you understand the new terms introduced in the last several pages.

Internal rate of return (IRR) (p. 476)     Post-investment audit (p. 480)
Payback (p. 477)                           Tax shield (p. 481)
Accrual accounting rate of return (p. 478)

For each of these terms, write a definition in your own words.

---

## ■ Calculating Incremental Tax Cash Flows

Once we forecast depreciation for the life of the project, we can calculate the incremental tax cash flow, the amount that will be paid or saved on taxes each year of the project. We combine the operating cash flow for each year with that year's depreciation, and then multiply the total by the marginal income tax rate.

We also need to calculate the tax cash flow based on the terminal value of the project. This calculation requires the following steps. First, find the total amount of tax depreciation that accumulated from the time of the initial investment to its disposal. Subtract the total depreciation from the initial investment; the remainder is the tax basis. In turn, subtract this amount from the disposal value. The remainder is a taxable gain or loss. Multiply this amount by the marginal income tax rate to find the incremental tax cash flow at the end of the project.

For Gordon's apartment building decision (Exhibit 12.3), the initial investment is $1,400,000 with estimated cash flows of $276,000 annually. Gordon expects to be able to sell the building at the end of 10 years for $400,000. Suppose for tax purposes Gordon uses straight-line depreciation with an annual deduction of $100,000 and has a 30% marginal income tax rate. His income tax expense each year will be $52,800 [($276,000 − $100,000) × 30%]. His incremental cash flow becomes $223,200 ($276,000 − $52,800). We discount these cash flows to compare them with the initial investment as follows:

$$PV = \$223,200 \times (PVFA\ 10\ years,\ 14\%) + \$400,000 \times (PVF\ 10\ years,\ 14\%)$$
$$= \$223,200 \times 5.216 + \$400,000 \times 0.270$$
$$= \$1,164,211 + \$108,000$$
$$= \$1,272,211$$

and the NPV = $1,272,211 − $1,400,000 = −$127,789. Before considering income taxes, our previous calculations resulted in an NPV of $174,616 ($1,574,616 − $1,400,000). When income taxes are factored in, the NPV becomes negative.

| GUIDE YOUR LEARNING | 12.5 | Net Present Value with Income Taxes |
| --- | --- | --- |

The preceding example for Gordon's apartment building project demonstrated the net present value method with income taxes. For this technique:

| Identify Problem | Identify Relevant Information | Use Information |
| --- | --- | --- |
| What decision was being addressed? | Why was depreciation—a non-cash expense—relevant to the calculations? | Explain how Gordon's decision would be affected by the income tax calculations. |

## APPENDIX 12A

 **Q8** How are the real and nominal methods used to address inflation in an NPV analysis?

# Inflation and the Net Present Value Method

The NPV computations in the chapter did not take into account the fact that many revenues and costs tend to inflate or deflate over time. When these changes occur, it is inappropriate to use today's revenue and cost values when forecasting future cash flows, particularly for projects spanning many years. Sometimes costs such as transportation fuel increase rapidly. Wages or supplies might increase at a slower rate over time. Still other costs, such as new technology, might actually decrease over time. Cash flows from projects in other countries sometimes have much higher inflation rates than in the United States. Managers need to incorporate these types of expected differences in their NPV analyses.

**Inflation** is the decline in the general purchasing power of the monetary unit, meaning that more monetary units, such as dollars, are needed to purchase goods or services. **Deflation** is the opposite, or an increase in the general purchasing power of the monetary unit. Because either can distort a NPV analysis, cash flows should be adjusted for anticipated levels of inflation or deflation.

## ■ Real and Nominal Methods for NPV Analysis

Two types of interest rates need to be considered when analyzing inflation, as shown in Exhibit 12A.1. The first type, the **real rate of interest,** is the rate of return required on investments when no inflation is a factor. It is calculated as the sum of the risk-free rate and a risk premium. The **risk-free rate** is the "pure" rate of interest paid on short-term government bonds (without considering inflation). The **risk premium** is an element above the risk-free rate that businesses demand for undertaking risks. The second type, the **nominal rate of interest,** is the rate of return required on investments when inflation is present. It is calculated by increasing the real rate of interest by the expected rate of inflation.

Cash flows and the discount rate should be measured using a consistent approach. In the **real method,** cash inflows and outflows are forecast in real dollars (no inflation) and discounted using a real rate. The examples we have used so far in the chapter used real cash flows.

In the **nominal method,** cash inflows and outflows are forecast in nominal dollars (inflated) and discounted using a nominal discount rate. Real cash flows can be converted to nominal cash flows using the following formula:

$$\text{Nominal cash flow} = \text{Real cash flow} \times (1 + i)^t$$

where
$i$ = rate of inflation
$t$ = number of time periods in the future

Suppose Gordon hires an accountant at $35,000 per year to help with his new businesses. If the accountant's salary is valued in a NPV analysis using the real method over a five-year period, the cash flows will be uniform across time. But if the salary inflates at 2% per year, the cash flows will increase across time. Exhibit 12A.2 compares the real and nominal cash flows.

**ALTERNATIVE TERMS**

The *real rate of interest* is also known as the *real discount rate.* Similarly, the *nominal rate of interest* is also known as the *nominal discount rate.*

**EXHIBIT 12A.1**
**Real and Nominal Interest Rates**

$$\frac{\text{Real rate}}{\text{of interest}} = \frac{\text{Risk-free}}{\text{rate}} + \frac{\text{Risk}}{\text{premium}}$$

$$\text{Nominal rate of interest} = (1 + \text{Real rate}) \times (1 + \text{Inflation rate}) - 1$$

**EXHIBIT 12A.2**
Real Versus Nominal Wages

| Period | Real Cash Flows | Nominal Cash Flows |
|---|---|---|
| 1 | $35,000 | $35,000 × 1.02 = $35,700 |
| 2 | $35,000 | $35,000 × $1.02^2$ = $36,414 |
| 3 | $35,000 | $35,000 × $1.02^3$ = $37,142 |
| 4 | $35,000 | $35,000 × $1.02^4$ = $37,885 |
| 5 | $35,000 | $35,000 × $1.02^5$ = $38,643 |

Unlike other types of U.S. income tax deductions, the amount of depreciation expense that can be deducted on an income tax return does not change over time. However, under inflation, the real amount of annual depreciation tax savings decreases over time. Nominal cash flows can be converted to real cash flows as follows:

$$\text{Real cash flow} = \frac{\text{Nominal cash flow}}{(1 + i)^t}$$

---

### GUIDE YOUR LEARNING 12.6 Key Terms

Stop to confirm that you understand the new terms introduced in the last several pages:

Inflation (p. 483)
Deflation (p. 483)
Real rate of interest (p. 483)
Risk-free rate (p. 483)

Risk premium (p. 483)
Nominal rate of interest (p. 483)
Real method (p. 483)
Nominal method (p. 483)

For each of these terms, write a definition in your own words.

---

## ■ Internal Consistency in NPV Analysis

If cash inflows and outflows are valued in real terms and then discounted using a nominal rate, or vice versa, the approach is internally inconsistent. Because nominal rates include inflation, they tend to be higher than real rates. Discounting real cash flows using a nominal rate creates a bias against the adoption of many worthwhile capital investment projects because the discounted present value of cash inflows is understated. Discounting nominal cash flows using a real rate overstates discounted cash flows and creates a bias toward accepting projects that may have a negative NPV.

**EXHIBIT 12A.3** Cash Flow Adjustments Required under the Real and Nominal Methods

| Cash Flow | Adjustments for Real Method | Adjustments for Nominal Method |
|---|---|---|
| Initial investment | No adjustment | No adjustment |
| Depreciation tax shield | Adjust from a nominal to a real amount for each year (deflate) | No adjustment |
| Remaining cash flows:<br>• Incremental operating cash flows<br>• Income taxes on incremental cash flows<br>• Terminal cash flows<br>• Income taxes on terminal gain or loss | If original cash flow estimates include inflation, then the cash flows must be adjusted from nominal to real amounts for each year; the tax cash flows must then be recalculated | If original cash flow estimates do not include inflation, then the cash flows must be adjusted from real to nominal amounts for each year; the tax cash flows must then be recalculated |

Adjustment Formulas:

$$\text{Nominal cash flow} = \text{Real cash flow} \times (1 + i)^t$$

$$\text{Real cash flow} = \frac{\text{Nominal cash flow}}{(1 + i)^t}$$

where  $i$ = rate of inflation
       $t$ = number of time periods in the future

When we expect relevant cash flows to be influenced by inflation or deflation, we must select a method (real or nominal) and then use that method consistently for all calculations. We perform the NPV analysis as before. The only differences are as follows:

- Cash flows must be adjusted so that they are internally consistent with the method used.
- Only a real discount rate should be used under the real method, and only a nominal discount rate should be used under the nominal method.

Exhibit 12A.3 summarizes the types of adjustments to cash flows that are required under the real and nominal methods.

## ■ Effects of U.S. Depreciation Rules

> **Q7** How do income taxes affect strategic investment decision cash flows?

Depreciation for income taxes is generally different from depreciation for financial reporting. In financial reporting, depreciation is calculated based on an asset's estimated useful life using a method that matches the cost of the asset against the benefits received. To encourage business investment, the U.S. government allows businesses to deduct depreciation using accelerated methods for most assets when computing taxable income. The current income tax depreciation scheme is called the *modified asset cost recovery system,* or *MACRS.* A summary of key MACRS provisions that affect cash flows for capital budgeting decisions is shown in Exhibit 12A.4.[8]

Every depreciable asset must be assigned to a classification, based on the type of property, as indicated in the left column of Exhibit 12A.4. The classification determines the methods of

**EXHIBIT 12A.4**
Major MACRS Property Classifications and Depreciation Methods

| Asset Classification | Depreciation Method |
|---|---|
| 3-year property<br>Examples:<br>• Materials handling devices such as pallets, baskets, and carts<br>• Special tools such as molds, jigs, gauges, and patterns | 200% declining balance method<br>3-year life<br>Half-year convention<br>No salvage value |
| 5-year property<br>Examples:<br>• Computers and peripheral equipment<br>• Automobiles and trucks<br>• Medical supply manufacturing equipment<br>• Logging equipment | 200% declining balance method<br>5-year life<br>Half-year convention<br>No salvage value |
| 7-year property<br>Examples:<br>• Office furniture, fixtures, and equipment<br>• Steel manufacturing equipment<br>• Toy manufacturing equipment<br>• Commercial aircraft | 200% declining balance method<br>7-year life<br>Half-year convention<br>No salvage value |
| 15-year property<br>Examples:<br>• Sidewalks, roads, fences, and landscaping<br>• Wharves and docks | 150% declining balance method<br>15-year life<br>Half-year convention<br>No salvage value |
| Residential rental property<br>Examples:<br>• Rental apartment building<br>• Rental mobile home | Straight-line method<br>27.5-year life<br>Mid-month convention<br>No salvage value |
| Nonresidential real property<br>Examples:<br>• Office building<br>• Hotel | Straight-line method<br>39-year life<br>Mid-month convention<br>No salvage value |

---

[8]These provisions were obtained from the IRS Publication 946: *How to Depreciate Property for Use in Preparing 2003 Returns*. You can obtain more detailed or current information about U.S. income tax depreciation methods from the most recent version of Publication 946 at www.irs.gov.

depreciation that may be used, as listed in the right column. The depreciation method includes a description of the depreciation pattern (declining balance or straight-line), the degree of acceleration for declining balance methods (200% or 150%), and the convention used to calculate depreciation in the first and last years. Under the half-year convention, assets are assumed to be purchased halfway through the year of acquisition. Under the mid-month convention, assets are assumed to be purchased halfway through the month of acquisition. The declining balance depreciation methods automatically switch to the straight-line method at the point in time when straight-line depreciation is higher than under the declining balance method.[9]

The **Internal Revenue Service** provides tables to simplify depreciation computations. Exhibit 12A.5 presents these tables for the asset classifications listed in Exhibit 12A.4.

**EXHIBIT 12A.5**

MACRS Depreciation Rate Schedules

| | Asset Classification | | | | | |
|---|---|---|---|---|---|---|
| | Declining Balance Half-Year Convention | | | | Straight-Line Mid-Month Convention[a] | |
| Year | 3-year | 5-year | 7-year | 15-year | 27.5-year | 39-year |
| 1 | 33.33% | 20.00% | 14.29% | 5.00% | 3.485% | 2.461% |
| 2 | 44.45 | 32.00 | 24.49 | 9.50 | 3.636 | 2.564 |
| 3 | 14.81 | 19.20 | 17.49 | 8.55 | 3.636 | 2.564 |
| 4 | 7.41 | 11.52 | 12.49 | 7.70 | 3.636 | 2.564 |
| 5 | | 11.52 | 8.93 | 6.93 | 3.636 | 2.564 |
| 6 | | 5.76 | 8.92 | 6.23 | 3.636 | 2.564 |
| 7 | | | 8.93 | 5.90 | 3.636 | 2.564 |
| 8 | | | 4.46 | 5.90 | 3.636 | 2.564 |
| 9 | | | | 5.91 | 3.636 | 2.564 |
| 10 | | | | 5.90 | 3.637 | 2.564 |
| 11 | | | | 5.91 | 3.636 | 2.564 |
| 12 | | | | 5.90 | 3.637 | 2.564 |
| 13 | | | | 5.91 | 3.636 | 2.564 |
| 14 | | | | 5.90 | 3.637 | 2.564 |
| 15 | | | | 5.91 | 3.636 | 2.564 |
| 16 | | | | 2.95 | 3.637 | 2.564 |
| 17 | | | | | 3.636 | 2.564 |
| 18 | | | | | 3.637 | 2.564 |
| 19 | | | | | 3.636 | 2.564 |
| 20 | | | | | 3.637 | 2.564 |
| 21 | | | | | 3.636 | 2.564 |
| 22 | | | | | 3.637 | 2.564 |
| 23 | | | | | 3.636 | 2.564 |
| 24 | | | | | 3.637 | 2.564 |
| 25 | | | | | 3.636 | 2.564 |
| 26 | | | | | 3.637 | 2.564 |
| 27 | | | | | 3.636 | 2.564 |
| 28 | | | | | 1.97 | 2.564 |
| 29 | | | | | | 2.564 |
| 30 | | | | | | 2.564 |
| 31 | | | | | | 2.564 |
| 32 | | | | | | 2.564 |
| 33 | | | | | | 2.564 |
| 34 | | | | | | 2.564 |
| 35 | | | | | | 2.564 |
| 36 | | | | | | 2.564 |
| 37 | | | | | | 2.564 |
| 38 | | | | | | 2.564 |
| 39 | | | | | | 2.564 |
| 40 | | | | | | 0.107 |

[a]Rates are shown only for assets acquired during the month of January.

---

[9]Tax laws provide for other methods in some circumstances. However, those issues are beyond the scope of this textbook.

Because of the half-year convention, depreciation is higher during the second year of an asset's life than during the first year. Depreciation is calculated by multiplying the cost of the asset by the table rate during each year of the asset's life. Salvage value is not taken into account; at the end of an asset's class life, the asset is fully depreciated.

The following illustration of an NPV analysis incorporates income taxes and inflation.

### CENTRAL IRRIGATION, INC. (PART 1)
### NPV ANALYSIS WITH INFLATION

Central Irrigation manufactures new and repairs old irrigation sprinkler systems for golf courses and agricultural uses. It produces metal pipes and fittings for large sprinkler systems. The company has been plagued with industrial accidents involving its old welding technology. A new, safer welding robot has been developed that will reduce labor costs, worker insurance costs, and direct material costs. The investment will be $10 million. The annual cash savings are estimated to be $5.75 million, but it will cost an additional $3 million per year to operate the machine. The old equipment will be disposed of, but its scrap price will equal the costs of removal, resulting in zero cash flow.

Sam Waters, CFO at Central Irrigation, believes that the robots would be used in production for six years and would then be sold for $1 million in today's dollars. He estimates inflation to be 5% per year and the risk-free rate to be 4% over the life of the project. He also estimates that a minimum risk premium of 6% is required for this project. Therefore, the real rate is 10% (4% + 6%), and the nominal rate is $[(1 + 0.10) \times (1 + 0.05) - 1] = 15.5\%$.

Sam asks the company's accountant, Georgia Taniwaki, to analyze the project. Georgia prepares the timeline in Exhibit 12A.6 to summarize the relevant nontax cash flows. The cash outflow for the initial investment is $10 million. The incremental operating cash flows in years 1 through 6 are $2.75 million ($5.75 − $3). The terminal value is $1 million.

Georgia knows that she also needs to consider income tax effects for the project. She determines that the robots would qualify for the 5-year MACRS class life for U.S. income tax depreciation. She also estimates that Central Irrigation's marginal income tax rate will be 25% over the next 6 years.

#### NPV Calculations: Real Method

Georgia's NPV calculations under the real method are presented in the spreadsheet shown in Exhibit 12A.7. The initial investment, incremental operating cash flows, and terminal cash flow are already estimated in real values, so no adjustment for inflation is needed for these amounts. The spreadsheet also provides the income tax cash flows. No tax cash flow occurs at time 0 because the initial investment is not immediately tax deductible, and the old equipment is expected to be sold at zero gain or loss.

The incremental operating cash flow is estimated to require an additional tax cash payment of $687,500 per year ($2,750,000 × 25% tax rate). The tax basis of the robots is expected to be zero at the end of year 6 ($10,000,000 cost − $10,000,000 total tax depreciation). If the robots are sold for $1,000,000, the full amount will be a taxable gain. Then, the income tax paid on the gain will be $250,000 ($1,000,000 gain × 25% tax rate).

The depreciation tax shield is calculated in three steps.

1. The annual depreciation is calculated by multiplying the initial investment by the MACRS rate (Exhibit 12A.5). For example, year 3 depreciation is $1,920,000 ($10,000,000 × 19.20%).

2. Because the depreciation is calculated based on the year 0 nominal cost, the next step is to convert the depreciation expense from nominal to real value. The real depreciation expense is calculated by dividing the nominal amount by $(1.05)^t$, where 5% is the inflation

*(continued)*

---

**EXHIBIT 12A.6**
Timeline for
Central Irrigation

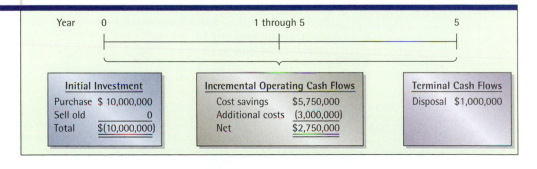

| Year | 0 | 1 through 5 | 5 |
|------|---|-------------|---|

| Initial Investment | | Incremental Operating Cash Flows | | Terminal Cash Flows | |
|---|---|---|---|---|---|
| Purchase | $ 10,000,000 | Cost savings | $5,750,000 | Disposal | $1,000,000 |
| Sell old | 0 | Additional costs | (3,000,000) | | |
| Total | $(10,000,000) | Net | $2,750,000 | | |

**EXHIBIT 12A.7** Real Method NPV for Central Irrigation

| | A | B | C | D | E | E | E | E |
|---|---|---|---|---|---|---|---|---|
| 1 | Real interest rate | 10% | | | | | | |
| 2 | Inflation rate | 5% | | | | | | |
| 3 | Income tax rate | 25% | | | | | | |
| 4 | Initial investment | $ 10,000,000 | | | | | | |
| 5 | Terminal cash flow | $ 1,000,000 | | | | | | |
| 6 | Incremental operating cash flow | $ 2,750,000 | | | | | | |
| 7 | | | | | | | | |
| 8 | Period | | 1 | 2 | 3 | 4 | 5 | 6 |
| 9 | Incremental operating cash flows | | $2,750,000 | $2,750,000 | $2,750,000 | $2,750,000 | $2,750,000 | $2,750,000 |
| 10 | Less income taxes | | $ (687,500) | $ (687,500) | $ (687,500) | $ (687,500) | $ (687,500) | $ (687,500) |
| 11 | | | | | | | | |
| 12 | Terminal cash flow | | | | | | | $1,000,000 |
| 13 | Income taxes on gain | | | | | | | $ (250,000) |
| 14 | | | | | | | | |
| 15 | Total | | $2,062,500 | $2,062,500 | $2,062,500 | $2,062,500 | $2,062,500 | $2,812,500 |
| 16 | | | | | | | | |
| 17 | Calculation of depreciation tax shield | | | | | | | |
| 18 | MACRS rate (5-year) | | 20.00% | 32.00% | 19.20% | 11.52% | 11.52% | 5.76% |
| 19 | Depreciation deduction (nominal) | | $2,000,000 | $3,200,000 | $1,920,000 | $1,152,000 | $1,152,000 | $ 576,000 |
| 20 | Depreciation deduction (real) | | $1,904,762 | $2,902,494 | $1,658,568 | $ 947,753 | $ 902,622 | $ 429,820 |
| 21 | Tax savings (tax shield) | | $ 476,190 | $ 725,624 | $ 414,642 | $ 236,938 | $ 225,656 | $ 107,455 |
| 22 | | | | | | | | |
| 23 | | | | | | | | |
| 24 | SUMMARY OF CASH FLOWS | | | | | | | |
| 25 | Incremental cash flows | | $2,062,500 | $2,062,500 | $2,062,500 | $2,062,500 | $2,062,500 | $2,062,500 |
| 26 | Tax savings from depreciation | | $ 476,190 | $ 725,624 | $ 414,642 | $ 236,938 | $ 225,656 | $ 107,455 |
| 27 | Total | | $2,538,690 | $2,788,124 | $2,477,142 | $2,299,438 | $2,288,156 | $2,919,955 |
| 28 | | | | | | | | |
| 29 | Present value | | $2,307,900 | $2,304,234 | $1,861,113 | $1,570,547 | $1,420,765 | $1,648,238 |
| 30 | | | | | | | | |
| 31 | PV of annual cash flows | $ 11,112,799 | | | | | | |
| 32 | Less initial investment | $ (10,000,000) | | | | | | |
| 33 | Net present value | $ 1,112,799 | | | | | | |

Excel formula to calculate the depreciation amount in real dollars in cell C20: =-PV($B$2,C8,,C19)
Excel formula to calculate net present value in cell D29: =-PV($B$1,D8,,D27)

rate and $t$ is the number of years in the future when the tax benefit will be received. For year 3 the real value of tax depreciation is $1,658,568 ($1,920,000 ÷ (1.05)³).

3. Finally, calculate the depreciation tax shield by multiplying the real value of the tax depreciation by the marginal tax rate. For year 3 it is $414,642 ($1,658,568 × 25% tax rate).

Georgia combines the incremental cash flows with the tax shield cash flows to determine the total incremental cash flow for each year. She then uses the real interest rate of 10% to calculate the present value for each year's incremental cash flows. Finally, she sums the present values for all years and subtracts the initial investment of $10 million to determine the NPV of $1,112,799. The NPV is positive, so she concludes that the robots would be a good investment for the company.

## NPV Calculations: Nominal Method

Georgia is not sure how inflation will affect her NPV calculations, so she decides to also compute the NPV using the nominal method. She prepares the spreadsheet shown in Exhibit 12A.8. Under the nominal method, real cash flows must be adjusted for inflation, which means that the incremental operating cash flows and terminal cash flows must be multiplied by $(1.05)^t$, where 5% is the inflation rate and $t$ is the number of years in the future when the cash flow will occur. For example, if the nominal amount of the incremental operating cash flow grows by the inflation rate of 5% each year, then they will increase in year 3 to $3,183,469 ($2,750,000 × (1.05)³). Then, the income tax that must be paid on the incremental operating income is $795,867 ($3,183,469 × 25% tax rate).

Inflation will also cause the terminal cash flows to increase from $1 million in today's dollars to $1,340,096 at the end of year 6. Once again, the taxable gain will equal the proceeds, because the robots will be fully depreciated in year 6. The amount of income tax payable on the nominal amount of the gain will be $335,024 ($1,340,096 × 25% tax rate).

Georgia uses the nominal interest rate of 15.5% to calculate the NPV, which is again positive and $1,112,799.

**EXHIBIT 12A.8** Nominal Method NPV for Central Irrigation

| | A | B | C | D | E | F | G | H |
|---|---|---|---|---|---|---|---|---|
| 1 | Real interest rate | 10% | | | | | | |
| 2 | Inflation rate | 5% | | | | | | |
| 3 | Nominal rate | 15.5% | | | | | | |
| 4 | Income tax rate | 25% | | | | | | |
| 5 | Initial investment | $ 10,000,000 | | | | | | |
| 6 | Terminal cash flow | $ 1,000,000 | | | | | | |
| 7 | Incremental operating cash flow | $ 2,750,000 | | | | | | |
| 8 | | | | | | | | |
| 9 | Period | | 1 | 2 | 3 | 4 | 5 | 6 |
| 10 | Incremental operating cash flows | | $2,750,000 | $2,750,000 | $2,750,000 | $2,750,000 | $2,750,000 | $2,750,000 |
| 11 | | | | | | | | |
| 12 | Inflated | | $2,887,500 | $3,031,875 | $3,183,469 | $3,342,642 | $3,509,774 | $3,685,263 |
| 13 | Less income taxes | | $ (721,875) | $ (757,969) | $ (795,867) | $ (835,661) | $ (877,444) | $ (921,316) |
| 14 | | | | | | | | |
| 15 | Terminal cash flow | | | | | | | $1,340,096 |
| 16 | Income taxes on gain | | | | | | | $ (335,024) |
| 17 | | | | | | | | |
| 18 | Total | | $2,165,625 | $2,273,906 | $2,387,602 | $2,506,982 | $2,632,331 | $3,769,019 |
| 19 | | | | | | | | |
| 20 | Calculation of depreciation tax shield | | | | | | | |
| 21 | MACRS rate (5-year) | | 20.00% | 32.00% | 19.20% | 11.52% | 11.52% | 5.76% |
| 22 | Depreciation deduction (nominal) | | $2,000,000 | $3,200,000 | $1,920,000 | $1,152,000 | $1,152,000 | $ 576,000 |
| 23 | Tax savings (tax shield) | | $ 500,000 | $ 800,000 | $ 480,000 | $ 288,000 | $ 288,000 | $ 144,000 |
| 24 | | | | | | | | |
| 25 | | | | | | | | |
| 26 | Summary of cash flows | | | | | | | |
| 27 | Incremental operating cash flows | | $2,165,625 | $2,273,906 | $2,387,602 | $2,506,982 | $2,632,331 | $3,769,019 |
| 28 | Tax savings from depreciation | | $ 500,000 | $ 800,000 | $ 480,000 | $ 288,000 | $ 288,000 | $ 144,000 |
| 29 | Total | | $2,655,625 | $3,073,906 | $2,867,602 | $2,794,982 | $2,920,331 | $3,913,019 |
| 30 | | | | | | | | |
| 31 | Present value | | $2,307,900 | $2,304,234 | $1,861,113 | $1,570,547 | $1,420,765 | $1,648,238 |
| 32 | | | | | | | | |
| 33 | PV of annual cash flows | $ 11,112,799 | | | | | | |
| 34 | Less initial investment | $ (10,000,000) | | | | | | |
| 35 | Net present value | $ 1,112,799 | | | | | | |

## Comparison of Nominal and Real Methods

Georgia notices that the NPV values under the nominal and real methods are the same. Then she remembers from her cost accounting class that these two methods give the same result when only one inflation rate is used for all cash flows.

## ■ Real and Nominal Methods under Varying Inflation Rates

Sometimes we expect different rates of inflation for different cash flows. Suppose the managers of Central Irrigation believe that salary costs will increase at a relatively low regional wage inflation rate, overhead costs such as utilities and property taxes will increase at a higher inflation rate, and the salvage value of the equipment will decrease over time as technology costs deflate. In these cases, we cannot use the real method because that method assumes all cash flows inflate at the same rate. Instead, the managers would need to use the nominal method to allow for different rates of inflation and deflation.

## GUIDE YOUR LEARNING 12.7 Central Irrigation

Central Irrigation illustrates NPV under the real and nominal methods. For this illustration:

| Define It | Identify Problem and Information | Explore Uncertainties | Prioritize Options |
|---|---|---|---|
| Describe how the real and nominal methods affect the NPV calculations. | What decision was being addressed? What additional quantitative information was relevant when using the real and nominal methods? | How can future inflation rates be estimated for NPV analysis? | If you were asked to perform an NPV analysis, would you use the real or the nominal method? Why? |

# APPENDIX 12B  Present and Future Value Tables

**TABLE 12B.1** Present Value of $1

| Periods | 4% | 5% | 6% | 7% | 8% | 9% | 10% | 11% | 12% | 13% | 14% | 15% | 16% | 17% | 18% |
|---|---|---|---|---|---|---|---|---|---|---|---|---|---|---|---|
| 1 | 0.962 | 0.952 | 0.943 | 0.935 | 0.926 | 0.917 | 0.909 | 0.901 | 0.893 | 0.885 | 0.877 | 0.870 | 0.862 | 0.855 | 0.847 |
| 2 | 0.925 | 0.907 | 0.890 | 0.873 | 0.857 | 0.842 | 0.826 | 0.812 | 0.797 | 0.783 | 0.769 | 0.756 | 0.743 | 0.731 | 0.718 |
| 3 | 0.889 | 0.864 | 0.840 | 0.816 | 0.794 | 0.772 | 0.751 | 0.731 | 0.712 | 0.693 | 0.675 | 0.658 | 0.641 | 0.624 | 0.609 |
| 4 | 0.855 | 0.823 | 0.792 | 0.763 | 0.735 | 0.708 | 0.683 | 0.659 | 0.636 | 0.613 | 0.592 | 0.572 | 0.552 | 0.534 | 0.516 |
| 5 | 0.822 | 0.784 | 0.747 | 0.713 | 0.681 | 0.650 | 0.621 | 0.593 | 0.567 | 0.543 | 0.519 | 0.497 | 0.476 | 0.456 | 0.437 |
| 6 | 0.790 | 0.746 | 0.705 | 0.666 | 0.630 | 0.596 | 0.564 | 0.535 | 0.507 | 0.480 | 0.456 | 0.432 | 0.410 | 0.390 | 0.370 |
| 7 | 0.760 | 0.711 | 0.665 | 0.623 | 0.583 | 0.547 | 0.513 | 0.482 | 0.452 | 0.425 | 0.400 | 0.376 | 0.354 | 0.333 | 0.314 |
| 8 | 0.731 | 0.677 | 0.627 | 0.582 | 0.540 | 0.502 | 0.467 | 0.434 | 0.404 | 0.376 | 0.351 | 0.327 | 0.305 | 0.285 | 0.266 |
| 9 | 0.703 | 0.645 | 0.592 | 0.544 | 0.500 | 0.460 | 0.424 | 0.391 | 0.361 | 0.333 | 0.308 | 0.284 | 0.263 | 0.243 | 0.225 |
| 10 | 0.676 | 0.614 | 0.558 | 0.508 | 0.463 | 0.422 | 0.386 | 0.352 | 0.322 | 0.295 | 0.270 | 0.247 | 0.227 | 0.208 | 0.191 |
| 11 | 0.650 | 0.585 | 0.527 | 0.475 | 0.429 | 0.388 | 0.350 | 0.317 | 0.287 | 0.261 | 0.237 | 0.215 | 0.195 | 0.178 | 0.162 |
| 12 | 0.625 | 0.557 | 0.497 | 0.444 | 0.397 | 0.356 | 0.319 | 0.286 | 0.257 | 0.231 | 0.208 | 0.187 | 0.168 | 0.152 | 0.137 |
| 13 | 0.601 | 0.530 | 0.469 | 0.415 | 0.368 | 0.326 | 0.290 | 0.258 | 0.229 | 0.204 | 0.182 | 0.163 | 0.145 | 0.130 | 0.116 |
| 14 | 0.577 | 0.505 | 0.442 | 0.388 | 0.340 | 0.299 | 0.263 | 0.232 | 0.205 | 0.181 | 0.160 | 0.141 | 0.125 | 0.111 | 0.099 |
| 15 | 0.555 | 0.481 | 0.417 | 0.362 | 0.315 | 0.275 | 0.239 | 0.209 | 0.183 | 0.160 | 0.140 | 0.123 | 0.108 | 0.095 | 0.084 |
| 16 | 0.534 | 0.458 | 0.394 | 0.339 | 0.292 | 0.252 | 0.218 | 0.188 | 0.163 | 0.141 | 0.123 | 0.107 | 0.093 | 0.081 | 0.071 |
| 17 | 0.513 | 0.436 | 0.371 | 0.317 | 0.270 | 0.231 | 0.198 | 0.170 | 0.146 | 0.125 | 0.108 | 0.093 | 0.080 | 0.069 | 0.060 |
| 18 | 0.494 | 0.416 | 0.350 | 0.296 | 0.250 | 0.212 | 0.180 | 0.153 | 0.130 | 0.111 | 0.095 | 0.081 | 0.069 | 0.059 | 0.051 |
| 19 | 0.475 | 0.396 | 0.331 | 0.277 | 0.232 | 0.194 | 0.164 | 0.138 | 0.116 | 0.098 | 0.083 | 0.070 | 0.060 | 0.051 | 0.043 |
| 20 | 0.456 | 0.377 | 0.312 | 0.258 | 0.215 | 0.178 | 0.149 | 0.124 | 0.104 | 0.087 | 0.073 | 0.061 | 0.051 | 0.043 | 0.037 |
| 21 | 0.439 | 0.359 | 0.294 | 0.242 | 0.199 | 0.164 | 0.135 | 0.112 | 0.093 | 0.077 | 0.064 | 0.053 | 0.044 | 0.037 | 0.031 |
| 22 | 0.422 | 0.342 | 0.278 | 0.226 | 0.184 | 0.150 | 0.123 | 0.101 | 0.083 | 0.068 | 0.056 | 0.046 | 0.038 | 0.032 | 0.026 |
| 23 | 0.406 | 0.326 | 0.262 | 0.211 | 0.170 | 0.138 | 0.112 | 0.091 | 0.074 | 0.060 | 0.049 | 0.040 | 0.033 | 0.027 | 0.022 |
| 24 | 0.390 | 0.310 | 0.247 | 0.197 | 0.158 | 0.126 | 0.102 | 0.082 | 0.066 | 0.053 | 0.043 | 0.035 | 0.028 | 0.023 | 0.019 |
| 25 | 0.375 | 0.295 | 0.233 | 0.184 | 0.146 | 0.116 | 0.092 | 0.074 | 0.059 | 0.047 | 0.038 | 0.030 | 0.024 | 0.020 | 0.016 |
| 26 | 0.361 | 0.281 | 0.220 | 0.172 | 0.135 | 0.106 | 0.084 | 0.066 | 0.053 | 0.042 | 0.033 | 0.026 | 0.021 | 0.017 | 0.014 |
| 27 | 0.347 | 0.268 | 0.207 | 0.161 | 0.125 | 0.098 | 0.076 | 0.060 | 0.047 | 0.037 | 0.029 | 0.023 | 0.018 | 0.014 | 0.011 |
| 28 | 0.333 | 0.255 | 0.196 | 0.150 | 0.116 | 0.090 | 0.069 | 0.054 | 0.042 | 0.033 | 0.026 | 0.020 | 0.016 | 0.012 | 0.010 |
| 29 | 0.321 | 0.243 | 0.185 | 0.141 | 0.107 | 0.082 | 0.063 | 0.048 | 0.037 | 0.029 | 0.022 | 0.017 | 0.014 | 0.011 | 0.008 |
| 30 | 0.308 | 0.231 | 0.174 | 0.131 | 0.099 | 0.075 | 0.057 | 0.044 | 0.033 | 0.026 | 0.020 | 0.015 | 0.012 | 0.009 | 0.007 |

**TABLE 12B.2** Present Value of an Ordinary Annuity of $1

| Periods | 4% | 5% | 6% | 7% | 8% | 9% | 10% | 11% | 12% | 13% | 14% | 15% | 16% | 17% | 18% |
|---|---|---|---|---|---|---|---|---|---|---|---|---|---|---|---|
| 1 | 0.962 | 0.952 | 0.943 | 0.935 | 0.926 | 0.917 | 0.909 | 0.901 | 0.893 | 0.885 | 0.877 | 0.870 | 0.862 | 0.855 | 0.847 |
| 2 | 1.886 | 1.859 | 1.833 | 1.808 | 1.783 | 1.759 | 1.736 | 1.713 | 1.690 | 1.668 | 1.647 | 1.626 | 1.605 | 1.585 | 1.566 |
| 3 | 2.775 | 2.723 | 2.673 | 2.624 | 2.577 | 2.531 | 2.487 | 2.444 | 2.402 | 2.361 | 2.322 | 2.283 | 2.246 | 2.210 | 2.174 |
| 4 | 3.630 | 3.546 | 3.465 | 3.387 | 3.312 | 3.240 | 3.170 | 3.102 | 3.037 | 2.974 | 2.914 | 2.855 | 2.798 | 2.743 | 2.690 |
| 5 | 4.452 | 4.329 | 4.212 | 4.100 | 3.993 | 3.890 | 3.791 | 3.696 | 3.605 | 3.517 | 3.433 | 3.352 | 3.274 | 3.199 | 3.127 |
| 6 | 5.242 | 5.076 | 4.917 | 4.767 | 4.623 | 4.486 | 4.355 | 4.231 | 4.111 | 3.998 | 3.889 | 3.784 | 3.685 | 3.589 | 3.498 |
| 7 | 6.002 | 5.786 | 5.582 | 5.389 | 5.206 | 5.033 | 4.868 | 4.712 | 4.564 | 4.423 | 4.288 | 4.160 | 4.039 | 3.922 | 3.812 |
| 8 | 6.733 | 6.463 | 6.210 | 5.971 | 5.747 | 5.535 | 5.335 | 5.146 | 4.968 | 4.799 | 4.639 | 4.487 | 4.344 | 4.207 | 4.078 |
| 9 | 7.435 | 7.108 | 6.802 | 6.515 | 6.247 | 5.995 | 5.759 | 5.537 | 5.328 | 5.132 | 4.946 | 4.772 | 4.607 | 4.451 | 4.303 |
| 10 | 8.111 | 7.722 | 7.360 | 7.024 | 6.710 | 6.418 | 6.145 | 5.889 | 5.650 | 5.426 | 5.216 | 5.019 | 4.833 | 4.659 | 4.494 |
| 11 | 8.760 | 8.306 | 7.887 | 7.499 | 7.139 | 6.805 | 6.495 | 6.207 | 5.938 | 5.687 | 5.453 | 5.234 | 5.029 | 4.836 | 4.656 |
| 12 | 9.385 | 8.863 | 8.384 | 7.943 | 7.536 | 7.161 | 6.814 | 6.492 | 6.194 | 5.918 | 5.660 | 5.421 | 5.197 | 4.988 | 4.793 |
| 13 | 9.986 | 9.394 | 8.853 | 8.358 | 7.904 | 7.487 | 7.103 | 6.750 | 6.424 | 6.122 | 5.842 | 5.583 | 5.342 | 5.118 | 4.910 |
| 14 | 10.563 | 9.899 | 9.295 | 8.745 | 8.244 | 7.786 | 7.367 | 6.982 | 6.628 | 6.302 | 6.002 | 5.724 | 5.468 | 5.229 | 5.008 |
| 15 | 11.118 | 10.380 | 9.712 | 9.108 | 8.559 | 8.061 | 7.606 | 7.191 | 6.811 | 6.462 | 6.142 | 5.847 | 5.575 | 5.324 | 5.092 |
| 16 | 11.652 | 10.838 | 10.106 | 9.447 | 8.851 | 8.313 | 7.824 | 7.379 | 6.974 | 6.604 | 6.265 | 5.954 | 5.668 | 5.405 | 5.162 |
| 17 | 12.166 | 11.274 | 10.477 | 9.763 | 9.122 | 8.544 | 8.022 | 7.549 | 7.120 | 6.729 | 6.373 | 6.047 | 5.749 | 5.475 | 5.222 |
| 18 | 12.659 | 11.690 | 10.828 | 10.059 | 9.372 | 8.756 | 8.201 | 7.702 | 7.250 | 6.840 | 6.467 | 6.128 | 5.818 | 5.534 | 5.273 |
| 19 | 13.134 | 12.085 | 11.158 | 10.336 | 9.604 | 8.950 | 8.365 | 7.839 | 7.366 | 6.938 | 6.550 | 6.198 | 5.877 | 5.584 | 5.316 |
| 20 | 13.590 | 12.462 | 11.470 | 10.594 | 9.818 | 9.129 | 8.514 | 7.963 | 7.469 | 7.025 | 6.623 | 6.259 | 5.929 | 5.628 | 5.353 |
| 21 | 14.029 | 12.821 | 11.764 | 10.836 | 10.017 | 9.292 | 8.649 | 8.075 | 7.562 | 7.102 | 6.687 | 6.312 | 5.973 | 5.665 | 5.384 |
| 22 | 14.451 | 13.163 | 12.042 | 11.061 | 10.201 | 9.442 | 8.772 | 8.176 | 7.645 | 7.170 | 6.743 | 6.359 | 6.011 | 5.696 | 5.410 |
| 23 | 14.857 | 13.489 | 12.303 | 11.272 | 10.371 | 9.580 | 8.883 | 8.266 | 7.718 | 7.230 | 6.792 | 6.399 | 6.044 | 5.723 | 5.432 |
| 24 | 15.247 | 13.799 | 12.550 | 11.469 | 10.529 | 9.707 | 8.985 | 8.348 | 7.784 | 7.283 | 6.835 | 6.434 | 6.073 | 5.746 | 5.451 |
| 25 | 15.622 | 14.094 | 12.783 | 11.654 | 10.675 | 9.823 | 9.077 | 8.422 | 7.843 | 7.330 | 6.873 | 6.464 | 6.097 | 5.766 | 5.467 |
| 26 | 15.983 | 14.375 | 13.003 | 11.826 | 10.810 | 9.929 | 9.161 | 8.488 | 7.896 | 7.372 | 6.906 | 6.491 | 6.118 | 5.783 | 5.480 |
| 27 | 16.330 | 14.643 | 13.211 | 11.987 | 10.935 | 10.027 | 9.237 | 8.548 | 7.943 | 7.409 | 6.935 | 6.514 | 6.136 | 5.798 | 5.492 |
| 28 | 16.663 | 14.898 | 13.406 | 12.137 | 11.051 | 10.116 | 9.307 | 8.602 | 7.984 | 7.441 | 6.961 | 6.534 | 6.152 | 5.810 | 5.502 |
| 29 | 16.984 | 15.141 | 13.591 | 12.278 | 11.158 | 10.198 | 9.370 | 8.650 | 8.022 | 7.470 | 6.983 | 6.551 | 6.166 | 5.820 | 5.510 |
| 30 | 17.292 | 15.372 | 13.765 | 12.409 | 11.258 | 10.274 | 9.427 | 8.694 | 8.055 | 7.496 | 7.003 | 6.566 | 6.177 | 5.829 | 5.517 |

**TABLE 12B.3** Future Value of $1

| Periods | 4% | 5% | 6% | 7% | 8% | 9% | 10% | 11% | 12% | 13% | 14% | 15% | 16% | 17% | 18% |
|---|---|---|---|---|---|---|---|---|---|---|---|---|---|---|---|
| 1 | 1.040 | 1.050 | 1.060 | 1.070 | 1.080 | 1.090 | 1.100 | 1.110 | 1.120 | 1.130 | 1.140 | 1.150 | 1.160 | 1.170 | 1.180 |
| 2 | 1.082 | 1.103 | 1.124 | 1.145 | 1.166 | 1.188 | 1.210 | 1.232 | 1.254 | 1.277 | 1.300 | 1.323 | 1.346 | 1.369 | 1.392 |
| 3 | 1.125 | 1.158 | 1.191 | 1.225 | 1.260 | 1.295 | 1.331 | 1.368 | 1.405 | 1.443 | 1.482 | 1.521 | 1.561 | 1.602 | 1.643 |
| 4 | 1.170 | 1.216 | 1.262 | 1.311 | 1.360 | 1.412 | 1.464 | 1.518 | 1.574 | 1.630 | 1.689 | 1.749 | 1.811 | 1.874 | 1.939 |
| 5 | 1.217 | 1.276 | 1.338 | 1.403 | 1.469 | 1.539 | 1.611 | 1.685 | 1.762 | 1.842 | 1.925 | 2.011 | 2.100 | 2.192 | 2.288 |
| 6 | 1.265 | 1.340 | 1.419 | 1.501 | 1.587 | 1.677 | 1.772 | 1.870 | 1.974 | 2.082 | 2.195 | 2.313 | 2.436 | 2.565 | 2.700 |
| 7 | 1.316 | 1.407 | 1.504 | 1.606 | 1.714 | 1.828 | 1.949 | 2.076 | 2.211 | 2.353 | 2.502 | 2.660 | 2.826 | 3.001 | 3.185 |
| 8 | 1.369 | 1.477 | 1.594 | 1.718 | 1.851 | 1.993 | 2.144 | 2.305 | 2.476 | 2.658 | 2.853 | 3.059 | 3.278 | 3.511 | 3.759 |
| 9 | 1.423 | 1.551 | 1.689 | 1.838 | 1.999 | 2.172 | 2.358 | 2.558 | 2.773 | 3.004 | 3.252 | 3.518 | 3.803 | 4.108 | 4.435 |
| 10 | 1.480 | 1.629 | 1.791 | 1.967 | 2.159 | 2.367 | 2.594 | 2.839 | 3.106 | 3.395 | 3.707 | 4.046 | 4.411 | 4.807 | 5.234 |
| 11 | 1.539 | 1.710 | 1.898 | 2.105 | 2.332 | 2.580 | 2.853 | 3.152 | 3.479 | 3.836 | 4.226 | 4.652 | 5.117 | 5.624 | 6.176 |
| 12 | 1.601 | 1.796 | 2.012 | 2.252 | 2.518 | 2.813 | 3.138 | 3.498 | 3.896 | 4.335 | 4.818 | 5.350 | 5.936 | 6.580 | 7.288 |
| 13 | 1.665 | 1.886 | 2.133 | 2.410 | 2.720 | 3.066 | 3.452 | 3.883 | 4.363 | 4.898 | 5.492 | 6.153 | 6.886 | 7.699 | 8.599 |
| 14 | 1.732 | 1.980 | 2.261 | 2.579 | 2.937 | 3.342 | 3.797 | 4.310 | 4.887 | 5.535 | 6.261 | 7.076 | 7.988 | 9.007 | 10.147 |
| 15 | 1.801 | 2.079 | 2.397 | 2.759 | 3.172 | 3.642 | 4.177 | 4.785 | 5.474 | 6.254 | 7.138 | 8.137 | 9.266 | 10.539 | 11.974 |
| 16 | 1.873 | 2.183 | 2.540 | 2.952 | 3.426 | 3.970 | 4.595 | 5.311 | 6.130 | 7.067 | 8.137 | 9.358 | 10.748 | 12.330 | 14.129 |
| 17 | 1.948 | 2.292 | 2.693 | 3.159 | 3.700 | 4.328 | 5.054 | 5.895 | 6.866 | 7.986 | 9.276 | 10.761 | 12.468 | 14.426 | 16.672 |
| 18 | 2.026 | 2.407 | 2.854 | 3.380 | 3.996 | 4.717 | 5.560 | 6.544 | 7.690 | 9.024 | 10.575 | 12.375 | 14.463 | 16.879 | 19.673 |
| 19 | 2.107 | 2.527 | 3.026 | 3.617 | 4.316 | 5.142 | 6.116 | 7.263 | 8.613 | 10.197 | 12.056 | 14.232 | 16.777 | 19.748 | 23.214 |
| 20 | 2.191 | 2.653 | 3.207 | 3.870 | 4.661 | 5.604 | 6.727 | 8.062 | 9.646 | 11.523 | 13.743 | 16.367 | 19.461 | 23.106 | 27.393 |
| 21 | 2.279 | 2.786 | 3.400 | 4.141 | 5.034 | 6.109 | 7.400 | 8.949 | 10.804 | 13.021 | 15.668 | 18.822 | 22.574 | 27.034 | 32.324 |
| 22 | 2.370 | 2.925 | 3.604 | 4.430 | 5.437 | 6.659 | 8.140 | 9.934 | 12.100 | 14.714 | 17.861 | 21.645 | 26.186 | 31.629 | 38.142 |
| 23 | 2.465 | 3.072 | 3.820 | 4.741 | 5.871 | 7.258 | 8.954 | 11.026 | 13.552 | 16.627 | 20.362 | 24.891 | 30.376 | 37.006 | 45.008 |
| 24 | 2.563 | 3.225 | 4.049 | 5.072 | 6.341 | 7.911 | 9.850 | 12.239 | 15.179 | 18.788 | 23.212 | 28.625 | 35.236 | 43.297 | 53.109 |
| 25 | 2.666 | 3.386 | 4.292 | 5.427 | 6.848 | 8.623 | 10.835 | 13.585 | 17.000 | 21.231 | 26.462 | 32.919 | 40.874 | 50.658 | 62.669 |
| 26 | 2.772 | 3.556 | 4.549 | 5.807 | 7.396 | 9.399 | 11.918 | 15.080 | 19.040 | 23.991 | 30.167 | 37.857 | 47.414 | 59.270 | 73.949 |
| 27 | 2.883 | 3.733 | 4.822 | 6.214 | 7.988 | 10.245 | 13.110 | 16.739 | 21.325 | 27.109 | 34.390 | 43.535 | 55.000 | 69.345 | 87.260 |
| 28 | 2.999 | 3.920 | 5.112 | 6.649 | 8.627 | 11.167 | 14.421 | 18.580 | 23.884 | 30.633 | 39.204 | 50.066 | 63.800 | 81.134 | 102.967 |
| 29 | 3.119 | 4.116 | 5.418 | 7.114 | 9.317 | 12.172 | 15.863 | 20.624 | 26.750 | 34.616 | 44.693 | 57.575 | 74.009 | 94.927 | 121.501 |
| 30 | 3.243 | 4.322 | 5.743 | 7.612 | 10.063 | 13.268 | 17.449 | 22.892 | 29.960 | 39.116 | 50.950 | 66.212 | 85.850 | 111.065 | 143.371 |

**TABLE 12B.4** Future Value of an Ordinary Annuity of $1

| Periods | 4% | 5% | 6% | 7% | 8% | 9% | 10% | 11% | 12% | 13% | 14% | 15% | 16% | 17% | 18% |
|---|---|---|---|---|---|---|---|---|---|---|---|---|---|---|---|
| 1 | 1.000 | 1.000 | 1.000 | 1.000 | 1.000 | 1.000 | 1.000 | 1.000 | 1.000 | 1.000 | 1.000 | 1.000 | 1.000 | 1.000 | 1.000 |
| 2 | 2.040 | 2.050 | 2.060 | 2.070 | 2.080 | 2.090 | 2.100 | 2.110 | 2.120 | 2.130 | 2.140 | 2.150 | 2.160 | 2.170 | 2.180 |
| 3 | 3.122 | 3.153 | 3.184 | 3.215 | 3.246 | 3.278 | 3.310 | 3.342 | 3.374 | 3.407 | 3.440 | 3.473 | 3.506 | 3.539 | 3.572 |
| 4 | 4.246 | 4.310 | 4.375 | 4.440 | 4.506 | 4.573 | 4.641 | 4.710 | 4.779 | 4.850 | 4.921 | 4.993 | 5.066 | 5.141 | 5.215 |
| 5 | 5.416 | 5.526 | 5.637 | 5.751 | 5.867 | 5.985 | 6.105 | 6.228 | 6.353 | 6.480 | 6.610 | 6.742 | 6.877 | 7.014 | 7.154 |
| 6 | 6.633 | 6.802 | 6.975 | 7.153 | 7.336 | 7.523 | 7.716 | 7.913 | 8.115 | 8.323 | 8.536 | 8.754 | 8.977 | 9.207 | 9.442 |
| 7 | 7.898 | 8.142 | 8.394 | 8.654 | 8.923 | 9.200 | 9.487 | 9.783 | 10.089 | 10.405 | 10.730 | 11.067 | 11.414 | 11.772 | 12.142 |
| 8 | 9.214 | 9.549 | 9.897 | 10.260 | 10.637 | 11.028 | 11.436 | 11.859 | 12.300 | 12.757 | 13.233 | 13.727 | 14.240 | 14.773 | 15.327 |
| 9 | 10.583 | 11.027 | 11.491 | 11.978 | 12.488 | 13.021 | 13.579 | 14.164 | 14.776 | 15.416 | 16.085 | 16.786 | 17.519 | 18.285 | 19.086 |
| 10 | 12.006 | 12.578 | 13.181 | 13.816 | 14.487 | 15.193 | 15.937 | 16.722 | 17.549 | 18.420 | 19.337 | 20.304 | 21.321 | 22.393 | 23.521 |
| 11 | 13.486 | 14.207 | 14.972 | 15.784 | 16.645 | 17.560 | 18.531 | 19.561 | 20.655 | 21.814 | 23.045 | 24.349 | 25.733 | 27.200 | 28.755 |
| 12 | 15.026 | 15.917 | 16.870 | 17.888 | 18.977 | 20.141 | 21.384 | 22.713 | 24.133 | 25.650 | 27.271 | 29.002 | 30.850 | 32.824 | 34.931 |
| 13 | 16.627 | 17.713 | 18.882 | 20.141 | 21.495 | 22.953 | 24.523 | 26.212 | 28.029 | 29.985 | 32.089 | 34.352 | 36.786 | 39.404 | 42.219 |
| 14 | 18.292 | 19.599 | 21.015 | 22.550 | 24.215 | 26.019 | 27.975 | 30.095 | 32.393 | 34.883 | 37.581 | 40.505 | 43.672 | 47.103 | 50.818 |
| 15 | 20.024 | 21.579 | 23.276 | 25.129 | 27.152 | 29.361 | 31.772 | 34.405 | 37.280 | 40.417 | 43.842 | 47.580 | 51.660 | 56.110 | 60.965 |
| 16 | 21.825 | 23.657 | 25.673 | 27.888 | 30.324 | 33.003 | 35.950 | 39.190 | 42.753 | 46.672 | 50.980 | 55.717 | 60.925 | 66.649 | 72.939 |
| 17 | 23.698 | 25.840 | 28.213 | 30.840 | 33.750 | 36.974 | 40.545 | 44.501 | 48.884 | 53.739 | 59.118 | 65.075 | 71.763 | 78.979 | 87.068 |
| 18 | 25.645 | 28.132 | 30.906 | 33.999 | 37.450 | 41.301 | 45.599 | 50.396 | 55.750 | 61.725 | 68.394 | 75.836 | 84.141 | 93.406 | 103.740 |
| 19 | 27.671 | 30.539 | 33.760 | 37.379 | 41.446 | 46.018 | 51.159 | 56.939 | 63.440 | 70.749 | 78.969 | 88.212 | 98.603 | 110.285 | 123.414 |
| 20 | 29.778 | 33.066 | 36.786 | 40.995 | 45.762 | 51.160 | 57.275 | 64.203 | 72.052 | 80.947 | 91.025 | 102.444 | 115.380 | 130.033 | 146.628 |
| 21 | 31.969 | 35.719 | 39.993 | 44.865 | 50.423 | 56.765 | 64.002 | 72.265 | 81.699 | 92.470 | 104.768 | 118.810 | 134.841 | 153.139 | 174.021 |
| 22 | 34.248 | 38.505 | 43.392 | 49.006 | 55.457 | 62.873 | 71.403 | 81.214 | 92.503 | 105.491 | 120.436 | 137.632 | 157.415 | 180.172 | 206.345 |
| 23 | 36.618 | 41.430 | 46.996 | 53.436 | 60.893 | 69.532 | 79.543 | 91.148 | 104.603 | 120.205 | 138.297 | 159.276 | 183.601 | 211.801 | 244.487 |
| 24 | 39.083 | 44.502 | 50.816 | 58.177 | 66.765 | 76.790 | 88.497 | 102.174 | 118.155 | 136.831 | 158.659 | 184.168 | 213.978 | 248.808 | 289.494 |
| 25 | 41.646 | 47.727 | 54.865 | 63.249 | 73.106 | 84.701 | 98.347 | 114.413 | 133.334 | 155.620 | 181.871 | 212.793 | 249.214 | 292.105 | 342.603 |
| 26 | 44.312 | 51.113 | 59.156 | 68.676 | 79.954 | 93.324 | 109.182 | 127.999 | 150.334 | 176.850 | 208.333 | 245.712 | 290.088 | 342.763 | 405.272 |
| 27 | 47.084 | 54.669 | 63.706 | 74.484 | 87.351 | 102.723 | 121.100 | 143.079 | 169.374 | 200.841 | 238.499 | 283.569 | 337.502 | 402.032 | 479.221 |
| 28 | 49.968 | 58.403 | 68.528 | 80.698 | 95.339 | 112.968 | 134.210 | 159.817 | 190.699 | 227.950 | 272.889 | 327.104 | 392.503 | 471.378 | 566.481 |
| 29 | 52.966 | 62.323 | 73.640 | 87.347 | 103.966 | 124.135 | 148.631 | 178.397 | 214.583 | 258.583 | 312.094 | 377.170 | 456.303 | 552.512 | 669.447 |
| 30 | 56.085 | 66.439 | 79.058 | 94.461 | 113.283 | 136.308 | 164.494 | 199.021 | 241.333 | 293.199 | 356.787 | 434.745 | 530.312 | 647.439 | 790.948 |

# SUMMARY

## Q1 How Are Strategic Investment Decisions Made?

### Capital Budgeting Process

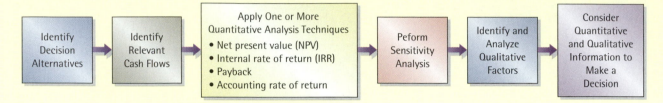

### Types of Long-Term Investment Decisions
- Developing or expanding products or services
- Replacing or reorganizing assets or services

## Q2 What Cash Flows Are Relevant for Strategic Investment Decisions?

### Common Types of Relevant Cash Flows

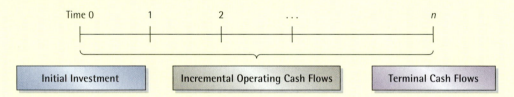

## Q3 How Is Net Present Value (NPV) Analysis Performed and Interpreted?

### Calculation of Net Present Value

$$NPV = \sum_{t=0}^{n} \frac{\text{Expected Cash Flow}_t}{(1 + r)^t}$$

$$= \sum_{t=0}^{n} \text{Expected Cash Flow}_t \times PVF_{r,t}$$

### Potential Discount Rates
- Weighted average cost of capital
- Rate reflecting project risk

### General Decision Rules
- Projects with a positive NPV are generally acceptable.
- If investment resources are limited, invest in the project(s) having the highest NPV.
- If profitability index is greater than 1, accept project.
- Projects can be rank-ordered on profitability index.

## Q4 What Are the Uncertainties and Limitations of NPV Analysis?

### Major Assumptions and Uncertainties
- Cost of initial investment
- Timing and dollar amounts of incremental revenues and costs
- Terminal values
- Project life
- Appropriate discount rate
- Marginal income tax rate
- Depreciation rules for income taxes

### Potential Manager Bias

### Sensitivity Analysis
Evaluate how NPV results change with variations in assumptions

## Q5 What Alternative Methods (IRR, Payback, and Accrual Accounting Rate of Return) Are Used for Strategic Investment Decisions?

### Internal Rate of Return (IRR)
Discount rate necessary for the present value of the discounted cash flows to be equal to the investment

### Payback
Measures the amount of time required to recover the initial investment

### Accrual Accounting Rate of Return
Expected increase in average annual operating income as a percent of the initial increase in required investment

## Q6 What Additional Issues Should Be Considered for Strategic Investment Decisions?

### Qualitative Issues
- Difficulty in estimating cash flows for new information technology
- Need for speedy decisions
- Encouraging innovation in new products and services
- Environmental effects
- Quality of product or service
- Employees
- Community
- Reputation

### Post-Investment Audit
Improve implementation, results, and accuracy of future capital budgets

## Q7 How Do Income Taxes Affect Strategic Investment Decision Cash Flows?

### Income Tax Cash Flows
- Tax on incremental operating cash flows
- Tax on terminal gain or loss
- Depreciation tax shield

### MACRS Depreciation (Appendix 12A)

## Q8 How Are the Real and Nominal Methods Used to Address Inflation in an NPV Analysis? (Appendix 12A)

### Real Method
Discount real cash flows at the real rate of interest

Real rate of interest = Risk-free rate + Risk premium

### Nominal Method
Discount nominal cash flows at the nominal rate of interest

$$\text{Nominal rate of interest} = (1 + \text{Real rate}) \times (1 + \text{Inflation rate}) - 1$$

### Internal Consistency in NPV Analysis
Cash flows and interest rate must be calculated using the same method (real or nominal)

### If Different Cash Flows Are Subject to Different Rates of Inflation (or Deflation)
Cannot use real method

---

### KEY TO SYMBOLS

**ⓔ** This question requires students to extend knowledge beyond the applications shown in the textbook.

**①** This question requires Step 1 skills (**Identifying**) in Steps for Better Thinking (Exhibit 1.10).

**②** This question requires Step 2 skills (**Exploring**) in Steps for Better Thinking (Exhibit 1.10).

**③** This question requires Step 3 skills (**Prioritizing**) in Steps for Better Thinking (Exhibit 1.10).

**④** This question requires Step 4 skills (**Envisioning**) in Steps for Better Thinking (Exhibit 1.10).

## Self-Study Problems

### Self-Study Problem 1 | Capital Budgeting Cash Flows, NPV, IRR, Payback, Sensitivity Analysis

**Q2, Q3, Q4, Q5**

Newberry and Mills Company is considering the purchase of new robotic manufacturing equipment. The purchase price is $85,000. The cost for shipping the machine to the plant is $2,000. Another $3,000 will be spent to remodel the area in which the machine is to be installed. The purchase price includes installation costs. The company has already spent $1,500 in travel costs and employee time on the search for this equipment. The machine is expected to save $30,000 a year in labor and insurance expenses over the next four years and is expected to be obsolete in four years. Newberry and Mills use a 10% discount rate as the required rate of return on capital budgeting projects. Ignore income taxes.

**REQUIRED:**

A. Calculate the net present value.
B. Calculate the profitability index.
C. Calculate the internal rate of return.
D. Calculate the payback period.
①E. List factors that you would vary to perform sensitivity analysis and explain why you would vary them.

### Solution to Self-Study Problem 1

A. First we summarize the cash flows across time. Notice that the $1,500 in travel and employee costs is a sunk cost and does not affect the NPV calculation. Also, no terminal cash flows occur for this project.

| Time 0 | Years 1–4 |
|---|---|
| Investment | $30,000 savings |
| $85,000 purchase | |
| 2,000 shipping | |
| 3,000 remodel | |
| $90,000 | |

Because cash flows are equal across time, we can treat the incremental cash flows in years 1 through 4 as an annuity to calculate NPV:

$$NPV = -\$90,000 + \$30,000 \times (PVFA\ 4\ years,\ 10\%)$$
$$= -\$90,000 + \$30,000 \times 3.170 = -\$90,000 + \$95,100$$
$$= \$5,100$$

B. Profitability index = $95,100 ÷ $90,000 = 1.057

C. IRR (calculated using the IRR function in an Excel spreadsheet) = 12.59%

D. Payback = $90,000 ÷ $30,000 = 3 years

E. Factors that could be varied for sensitivity analysis include all of the assumptions such as the initial investment amount, the labor and insurance savings, and the discount rate. Because we cannot know future economic conditions, and we cannot know whether technology developments will improve models more rapidly than we expect, we need to perform sensitivity analysis for all of the assumptions we make. Even the initial investment could change if remodeling is more substantial than expected.

### Self-Study Problem 2 | NPV, IRR, Payback with Inflation and Income Taxes (Appendix 12A)

**Q3, Q5, Q6, Q7, Q8**

Kestrel and Sons drills residential and commercial wells. The company is in the process of analyzing the purchase of a new drill that would cost $80,000 and have an expected useful life of 6 years. Several employees have spent $5,000 in travel expenses to locate the best drill. Operating the drill would increase revenue by $60,000 per year, but cost an additional $39,000 for labor, maintenance, and other related costs. The managers estimate the salvage value of the drill to be $8,000. Kestrel's marginal income tax rate is 25%. The state requires that each well be registered and that the location of the well meets certain health requirements, such as being at least 100 yards away from septic and sewage systems. An ongoing controversy over the last 15 years centers around whether individual homeowners should be allowed to drill wells, but so far no regulation has been proposed.

**REQUIRED:**

A. Using a 5-year MACRS schedule, an inflation rate of 4%, a risk-free rate of 5%, and a risk premium of 8%, calculate the net present value for the purchase of the drill using the nominal method.

**B.** Calculate the internal rate of return.

**C.** Calculate the payback period using nominal cash flows.

**1** **D.** What regulatory issues would Kestrel consider as qualitative factors?

**2** **E.** How would the issues you identified in part (D) affect your assessment of the project risk?

### Solution to Self-Study Problem 2

**A.** Exhibit 12.9 provides a spreadsheet with the NPV calculation using the nominal method for Kestrel and Sons. This spreadsheet demonstrates a different format than shown in the chapter examples.

**B.** Exhibit 12.10 provides a spreadsheet with the IRR calculation for Kestrel and Sons.

**C.** Because the net cash flows in this problem are not uniform (i.e., are not identical) across time, the payback period must be calculated by manually determining the years it takes to recover the investment. Payback does not include the time value of money, so we analyze the cash flows before they are discounted:

| | Net Nominal Cash Flow | Balance to Recover |
|---|---|---|
| Time 0 | | $80,000 |
| Year 1 | $16,380 + $4,000 = $20,380 | $80,000 − $20,380 = $59,620 |
| Year 2 | $17,035 + $6,400 = $23,435 | $59,620 − $23,435 = $36,185 |
| Year 3 | $17,717 + $3,840 = $21,557 | $36,185 − $21,557 = $14,628 |
| Year 4 | $18,425 + $2,304 = $20,729 | $14,628 − $14,628 = 0 |

**EXHIBIT 12.9**

NPV Calculation for Self-Study Problem 2

| | A | B | C | D | E |
|---|---|---|---|---|---|
| 1 | Cash Flows: | | | | |
| 2 | Increase in revenue | $60,000 | Discount rate information: | | |
| 3 | Increase in labor | ($39,000) | Risk free | 5.00% | |
| 4 | Total | $21,000 | Project risk | 8.00% | |
| 5 | Terminal value | $8,000 | Inflation | 4.00% | |
| 6 | Investment: | | | | |
| 7 | Purchase equipment | ($80,000) | Tax rate | 25.00% | |
| 8 | | | | | |
| 9 | Nominal discount rate | 17.52% | | | |
| 10 | | | | | |
| 11 | Incremental Cash Flows: | | | | |
| 12 | Period | Incremental CF | Inflated | Less Tax | Discounted |
| 13 | 1 | $21,000 | $21,840 | $16,380 | $13,938 |
| 14 | 2 | $21,000 | $22,714 | $17,035 | $12,335 |
| 15 | 3 | $21,000 | $23,622 | $17,717 | $10,916 |
| 16 | 4 | $21,000 | $24,567 | $18,425 | $9,660 |
| 17 | 5 | $21,000 | $25,550 | $19,162 | $8,548 |
| 18 | 6 | $21,000 | $26,572 | $19,929 | $7,565 |
| 19 | Total PV of Incremental Cash Flow | | | | $62,961 |
| 20 | | | | | |
| 21 | Depreciation Tax Savings: | | | | |
| 22 | Period | MACRS | Depreciation | Tax Savings | Discounted |
| 23 | 1 | 20.00% | $16,000 | $4,000 | $3,404 |
| 24 | 2 | 32.00% | $25,600 | $6,400 | $4,634 |
| 25 | 3 | 19.20% | $15,360 | $3,840 | $2,366 |
| 26 | 4 | 11.52% | $9,216 | $2,304 | $1,208 |
| 27 | 5 | 11.52% | $9,216 | $2,304 | $1,028 |
| 28 | 6 | 5.76% | $4,608 | $1,152 | $437 |
| 29 | Total PV of Tax Savings | | | | $13,077 |
| 30 | | | | | |
| 31 | | Today's Dollars | Inflated | After Tax | Discounted |
| 32 | Terminal value | $8,000 | $10,123 | $7,592 | $2,882 |
| 33 | | | | | |
| 34 | Net Present Value: | | | | |
| 35 | Incremental CF | $62,961 | | | |
| 36 | Tax savings | $13,077 | | | |
| 37 | Terminal value | $2,882 | | | |
| 38 | Less investment | ($80,000) | | | |
| 39 | NPV | ($1,080) | | | |

Examples of Excel formulas:

Nominal discount rate in cell B9: =(1+D3+D4)*(1+D5)−1

Inflated incremental cash flow in cell C15: =−FV($D$5,A15,,B15)

After-tax incremental cash flow in cell D15: =C15*(1−$D$7)

Present value of incremental cash flow in cell E15: =−PV($B$9,A15,,D15)

**EXHIBIT 12.10**
IRR Calculation for
Self–Study Problem 2

| | A | B | C | D | E | F |
|---|---|---|---|---|---|---|
| 41 | Combined Cash Flows: | | | | | |
| 42 | Period | Investment | Incremental CF | Tax Savings | Terminal | Total |
| 43 | 0 | ($80,000) | | | | ($80,000) |
| 44 | 1 | | $16,380 | $4,000 | | $20,380 |
| 45 | 2 | | $17,035 | $6,400 | | $23,435 |
| 46 | 3 | | $17,717 | $3,840 | | $21,557 |
| 47 | 4 | | $18,425 | $2,304 | | $20,729 |
| 48 | 5 | | $19,162 | $2,304 | | $21,466 |
| 49 | 6 | | $19,929 | $1,152 | $10,123 | $31,203 |
| 50 | | | | | | |
| 51 | Internal Rate of Return | 17.46% | | | | |

Excel formula to calculate internal rate of return in cell B51: =IRR(F43:F49)

The initial investment is expected to be fully recovered in more than three years, but less than four. We can estimate the proportion of the fourth year needed to complete the payback as:

$$\$14,628 \div \$20,729 = 0.7 \text{ of year } 4$$

Thus, the payback period is estimated as 3.7 years.

**D.** Kestrel would have to consider the possible upcoming change in regulation making it impossible for homeowners to drill wells. The percentage of wells drilled that are residential would decrease greatly. If this percentage is high, Kestrel may not be able to bring in the predicted revenue.

**E.** The risk premium should probably be increased if residential drilling is a large (say, greater than about 30%) proportion of Kestrel's business. Sensitivity analysis can be done around the discount rate by varying the risk premium to determine the risk rate that brings the net present value to zero.

---

**REVIEW**  Use the exercises in the following boxes in the chapter to review key terms and key techniques, analyze chapter illustrations, improve your learning of new concepts, and practice ethical decision making.

Guide Your Learning 12.1: Key Terms (p. 472)

Guide Your Learning 12.2: Net Present Value (p. 472)

Guide Your Learning 12.3: Gordon's Health Club (p. 475)

Guide Your Learning 12.4: Key Terms (p. 482)

Guide Your Learning 12.5: Net Present Value with Income Taxes (p. 483)

Guide Your Learning 12.6: Key Terms (p. 484)

Guide Your Learning 12.7: Central Irrigation (p. 489)

Focus on Ethical Decision Making: The Right Thing to Do (p. 480)

---

## QUESTIONS

**12.1** Forecasting the terminal value of equipment 20 years from now is difficult to do accurately, but errors in estimation probably have a small effect on the NPV. Explain.

**12.2** Suppose a company has five different capital budgeting projects from which to choose, but has constrained funds and cannot implement all of the projects. Explain why comparing the projects' NPVs is better than comparing their IRRs.

**12.3** Describe the pros and cons of each of the capital budgeting methods learned in this chapter: (a) net present value, (b) internal rate of return, (c) payback, and (d) accrual accounting rate of return.

**12.4** When projects have longer lives, it is more difficult to accurately estimate the cash flows and discount rates over the life of the project. Explain why this statement is true.

**12.5** (Appendix 12A) The present value of a given cash flow gets smaller as the number of periods gets larger, regardless of whether cash flow is discounted with a real rate or nominal rate. Explain why this relationship happens and what it means from an economic perspective.

**12.6** (Appendix 12A) Two methods can be used to incorporate the effects of inflation or deflation into an NPV analysis. In your own words, explain how a nominal discount rate is different from a real discount rate. Why are analyses using the nominal approach potentially more accurate than those using the real approach?

**12.7** (Appendix 12A) How might inflation influence a decision to acquire an asset now rather than later?

**12.8**  If a firm has unlimited funds, what criterion should be used to determine which projects to invest in?

**12.9**  An international firm requires a rate of return of 15% domestically and in developed countries, but 25% in less-developed countries. Does this requirement mean that the firm is exploiting the less-developed countries?

**12.10**  When we covered CPV analysis in Chapter 3, we calculated the amount of pretax profit needed to achieve a given level of after-tax profit. We could calculate a pretax rate of return given an after-tax rate of return. Why would it be inappropriate to use a pretax discount rate in capital budgeting? (For example, if a firm requires an after-tax return of 10% and has a marginal income tax rate of 50%, why not use a 20% pretax rate of return and ignore the separate income tax calculations?)

**12.11**  A well-known clinic in the Midwest operates as a not-for-profit organization. Typical capital expenditure decisions involve acquiring equipment that will perform medical tests beyond those currently possible at the clinic (hence, adding revenues) and/or perform tests more efficiently than currently (hence, decreasing expenses). To evaluate such expenditures, the clinic uses a discount rate equal to the return on its investment trust portfolio. Explain, briefly, why they do so.

# EXERCISES

**12.12**  **Time value of money**

A. What is the present value of $8,000 received in 7 years at 8% interest?

B. Bonnie Lee buys a savings bond for $125. The bond pays 6% and matures in 10 years. What amount will Bonnie receive when she redeems the bond?

C. Erik Peterson needs to have $10,000 at the end of 5 years to purchase a second car. His investment returns 6%. How much does he need to invest now?

D. Conan Bardwell will receive $1,000 in 6 years from an investment that returns 12%. How much did he invest?

**12.13**  **Capital budgeting process** Put the following 6 steps for capital budgeting in the most likely or-
**Q1**  der, numbering the first activity as number 1, the second as 2, and so on.

_____ Perform sensitivity analysis.

_____ Identify decision alternatives.

_____ Analyze qualitative factors.

_____ Identify relevant cash flows.

_____ Apply the relevant quantitative analysis technique.

_____ Consider quantitative and qualitative information to make a decision.

**12.14**  **NPV calculations with taxes** Overnight Laundry is considering the purchase of a new pressing
**Q3, Q7**  machine that would cost $96,000 and would produce incremental operating cash flows of $25,000 annually for 10 years. The machine has a terminal value of $6,000 and is depreciated for income tax purposes using straight-line depreciation over a 10-year life (ignore the half-year convention). Overnight Laundry's marginal tax rate is 33.3%. The company uses a discount rate of 18%.

**REQUIRED:**  What is the net present value of the project?

**12.15**  **NPV and IRR calculations** Axel Corporaton is planning to buy a new machine with the expec-
**Q3, Q5**  tation that this investment should earn a rate of return of at least 15%. This machine, which costs
**CPA**  $150,000, would yield an estimated net cash flow of $30,000 a year for 10 years.

**REQUIRED:**  A. What is the net present value for this proposal?

B. What is the internal rate of return for this proposal

**12.16**  **NPV, IRR, ARR, and payback methods** Amaro Hospital, a not-for-profit institution not subject
**Q3, Q5**  to income taxes, is considering the purchase of new equipment costing $20,000 to achieve cash
**CPA**  savings of $5,000 per year in operating costs. The estimated useful life is 10 years, with no salvage value. Amaro's minimum expected return is 14%.

**REQUIRED:**

  **A.** What is the net present value of this investment?

  **B.** What is the internal rate of return?

  **C.** What is the accrual accounting rate of return based on the initial investment?

  **D.** What is the payback period?

---

**12.17**
Q3
CMA

**Present value and future value calculations** Crown Corporation agreed to sell some used equipment to one of its employees. Alternative financing arrangements for the sale have been discussed, and the present and future values of each alternative have been determined.

**REQUIRED:**

  **A.** Crown offered to accept a $1,000 down payment and set up a note receivable that calls for four $1,000 payments at the end of each of the next four years. What is the net present value of this note if it is discounted at 6%?

  **B.** The employee agrees to the down payment but would like the note for $4,000 to be payable in full at the end of the fourth year. Because of the increased risk associated with the terms of this note, Crown would apply an 8% discount rate. What is the true selling price of the equipment?

  **C.** Suppose the employee borrows the $5,000 at 8% interest for four years from a bank so that he can pay Crown the full price of the equipment immediately. Also, suppose that Crown could invest the $5,000 for three years at 7%. What is the selling price of the equipment? What would be the future value of Crown's investment?

---

**12.18**
Q2, Q3, Q4, Q7, Q8

**Relevant cash flows, NPV analysis with taxes and inflation (Appendix 12A)** Clearwater Bottling Company sells bottled spring water for $12 per case, with variable costs of $7 per case. The company has been selling 200,000 cases per year and expects to continue at that rate unless it accepts a special order from Blue Danube Restaurant. Blue Danube has offered to buy 20,000 cases per year at $9 per case. Clearwater must agree to make the sales for a 5-year period. Blue Danube will not take fewer than 20,000 cases, but is willing to take more.

Clearwater's current capacity is 210,000 cases per year. Capacity could be increased to 260,000 per year if new equipment costing $100,000 were purchased. The equipment would have a useful life of 5 years and no salvage value. Maintenance on the new equipment would increase fixed costs by $20,000 each year. Variable costs per unit would be unchanged. Clearwater has a marginal income tax rate of 25%. Inflation is estimated to be 4% over each of the next 5 years. The risk-free rate is estimated to be 5%. Clearwater can earn a rate of 12% if it invests in an alternative investment having similar risk.

**REQUIRED:**

  **A.** Create a time line showing the relevant cash flows for this problem.

  **B.** Ignoring inflation, using straight-line depreciation over 5 years (ignore the half-year convention) and using a 12% discount rate, determine the NPV if 20,000 cases are sold.

  **C.** Ignoring inflation, using straight-line depreciation over 5 years (ignore the half-year convention), and using a 12% discount rate, determine the number of cases Blue Danube would need to purchase to bring the NPV to zero.

  **D.** (Appendix 12A) Set up a spreadsheet to do the following. Including inflation and using a three-year MACRS schedule, determine an appropriate discount rate and calculate the NPV of this project if Blue Danube purchases 20,000 cases per year.

---

**12.19**
Q3

**NPV analysis** The Parish County government supervisors are considering the purchase of a small, used plane to save on travel costs. The plane will cost $400,000 and can be sold in 5 years for 20% of the original cost.

**REQUIRED:**

  If 10% is the required rate of return, what minimum annual savings in transportation costs are needed for this plane to be a good investment? Ignore income taxes.

---

**12.20**
Q3, Q5, Q7

**NPV and payback with taxes** Equipment with a cost of $60,000 will, if acquired, generate annual savings of $30,000 for 6 years, at which time it will have no further use or value. The firm has a marginal tax rate of 40% and requires a 10% rate of return. It uses straight-line depreciation (ignore the half-year convention). Ignore inflation.

**REQUIRED:**

  **A.** What is the after-tax cash flow for each year?

  **B.** What is the NPV of this investment?

  **C.** What is the payback period?

**12.21**     **IRR** Ferris Industries has $50,000 available to invest in new equipment. Management is consid-
Q5, Q6    ering four different equipment investments, each of which requires $50,000. The expected after-
tax cash flow for each project has been estimated as follows:

| | Year | | | | | |
|---|---|---|---|---|---|---|
| | 1 | 2 | 3 | 4 | 5 | 6 |
| Project 1 | $10,000 | $12,000 | $14,000 | $16,000 | $16,000 | $16,000 |
| Project 2 | 40,000 | 5,000 | (3,000) | 40,000 | 5,000 | 1,000 |
| Project 3 | 18,000 | (16,000) | 50,000 | 50,000 | 3,000 | 3,000 |
| Project 4 | 30,000 | - | - | 30,000 | 30,000 | 30,000 |

REQUIRED:     **A.** Rank-order the projects in terms of desirability using the internal rate of return for each
project as the criterion. Use Excel or a similar spreadsheet to calculate the IRRs.
❶ **B.** What other factors should be considered in making the decision of which investment to
choose?

**12.22**     **Alternative technologies and capital budgeting with taxes** Lymbo Company, Inc., must install
Q3, Q7    safety devices throughout its plant or it will lose its insurance coverage. Two alternatives are acceptable to the insurer. The first costs $100,000 to install and $20,000 to maintain annually. The
second costs $150,000 to install and $10,000 to maintain annually. Each has a 5-year income tax
life and a 15-year useful life. Lymbo's discount rate is 12%, its marginal tax rate is 30% and it
uses straight-line depreciation (ignore the half-year convention).

REQUIRED:     **A.** Which system should be installed? Why?
**B.** If Lymbo were a not-for-profit organization that does not pay income taxes on its operations, which system would be installed?

**12.23**     **Equipment replacement, NPV, IRR, and payback** Garco is considering replacing an old ma-
Q3, Q5    chine that is currently being used. The old machine is fully depreciated, but it can be used for an-
CMA     other 5 years, at which time it would have no terminal value. Garco can sell the old machine for
$60,000 on the date that the new machine is purchased.

      If the purchase occurs, the new machine will be acquired for a cash payment of $1 million.
Because of the increased efficiency of the new machine, estimated annual cash savings of $300,000
would be generated during its useful life of 5 years. The new machine is not expected to have any
terminal value.

REQUIRED:     **A.** Garco requires investments to earn a 12% return. What is the net present value for re-
placing the old machine with the new machine?
**B.** What is the internal rate of return to replace the old machine?
**C.** What is the payback period for the new machine?

# PROBLEMS

**12.24**     **Capital budgeting methods, sensitivity analysis, spreadsheet development, uncertainties** Your
Q1, Q2, Q3, Q4, Q5, Q6    brother, Jackson, was laid off from his job with a large and famous software company. He would
like to sell his stock in the company and use the proceeds to start a restaurant. The stock is currently valued at $500,000. He received a job offer from a competitor that will pay $90,000 per year
plus benefits. He asked you to help him decide the best course of action.

REQUIRED:     **A.** What are the alternatives that Jackson faces?
❶ **B.** Choose the most appropriate analysis technique and explain your choice.
❶ **C.** If your brother chooses to open a restaurant, what are his opportunity costs?
❶ **D.** List the steps you would take to develop a spreadsheet that your brother could manipulate
to help with the quantitative aspects of this decision. Assume that you only have time to
set up a template and that your brother will fill in the specific information. However, you
need to tell him the general categories of information he will need to gather.
❶ **E.** List uncertainties about whether taking the job offer would turn out well for your brother.
List as many uncertainties as you can.
❶ **F.** List uncertainties about whether opening a restaurant would turn out well for your
brother. List as many uncertainties as you can.
❸ **G.** Explain why it is possible for your brother to make a good decision even though he cannot know for sure how well his alternatives would work out.

**12.25**
**Q3, Q4, Q5**

**IRR, developing a discount rate, evaluating risk** The local homeless shelter received a large donation from a wealthy benefactor and asked you to review its decision-making process for the proposed investment choice. The shelter's financial advisor suggested using the internal rate of return (IRR) to evaluate three different projects:

- A hotel that offers rooms based on the renter's ability to pay
- An apartment complex for elderly who receive rent subsidization from a federal agency
- A small cardboard box manufacturing company that will serve as a job training facility for homeless clients

**REQUIRED:**

**A.** In your own words, describe the advantages and disadvantages of IRR for this decision.

❷ **B.** This not-for-profit organization uses an IRR hurdle rate of 15% for most projects. Is it a good idea for an organization to use the same hurdle rate for most projects? Why or why not?

❶ **C.** List information that might help you develop a hurdle rate for each project.

❷ **D.** Which alternative do you believe is most financially risky for the homeless shelter? Explain your thinking.

**12.26**
**Q3, Q4, Q8**

**Real interest rates, uncertainties, effects of time (Appendix 12A)** Managers often use the real interest rate to help them decide whether to take on a new project.

**REQUIRED:**

**A.** What two factors are included in the real interest rate?

❶ **B.** What economic factors could affect the two aspects you identified in part (A)? List as many factors as you can.

❶ **C.** Discuss how certain you can be that interest rates will remain constant over the life of a project.

❶ **D.** Does the time length of a project affect your answer to part (C)? Why or why not?

**12.27**
**Q3, Q4, Q5, Q6**

**Choice of method, uncertainties, addressing company policy** Green Jade Resorts, a Singapore company that owns and operates golf resorts, has hired you to analyze its investment opportunities in the Southwest United States and Mexico. The company managers have always used the payback method and have asked you to prepare an analysis comparing three different resorts, one near the quaint mining town of Bisbee, Arizona; another at Puerta Penasco, a beach resort area on the Baja coast of Mexico; and a third golf resort near Taos, New Mexico.

**REQUIRED:**

**A.** List four methods that could be used to analyze this long-term decision. Describe each method in your own words.

❶ **B.** In your own words, describe the advantages and disadvantages of each method you identified in part (A).

❶ **C.** Explain why it is not possible to perfectly predict a project's cash flows.

❷ **D.** In using quantitative results for decision making, would you place equal reliance on the results of all four analysis techniques? Explain.

❷ **E.** Discuss how the managers of the Singapore company might respond to your advice if you recommend an analysis method other than the payback method.

❸ **F.** Write a brief memo to the CEO of the Singapore company, recommending your choice of analysis methods and explaining the most important issues for the CEO to consider when choosing an analysis method.

**12.28**
**Q2, Q3, Q4, Q5**

**Time line, relevant costs, NPV, payback, uncertainties** Irrigation Supply is negotiating with a major hardware chain to supply heavy-duty sprinkler heads at $18,000 each year for five years. Irrigation Supply would need to retool at a cost of $20,000 to fill this order. Incremental costs associated with the order (in addition to the retooling costs) would be $12,000 per year. In addition, existing fixed overhead costs would be reallocated among Irrigation Supply's products, which would result in a $1,000 overhead charge against the special order. For income taxes, the retooling costs would be depreciated using the straight-line method with no terminal value, ignoring the half-year convention. Irrigation Supply's marginal income tax rate is 25%. Assume that all cash flows (except the initial retooling costs) occur at year-end. The company's discount rate is 16%.

**REQUIRED:**

**A.** Create a time line showing the relevant cash flows for this problem.

**B.** What is the net present value of the special order?

**C.** What is the payback period for this project?

**❶ D.** For this problem, what do you learn from the NPV analysis, and what do you learn from the payback period?

**❶ E.** The managers of the hardware store (the customers in this problem) believe that demand will ensure their ability to purchase sprinkler heads from Irrigation Supply. Explain why the hardware chain's managers cannot be certain about the future demand for sprinkler heads.

**❷ F.** Discuss how uncertainties for the hardware store could lead to uncertainties for Irrigation Supply.

**12.29**
Q3, Q4, Q7, Q8

**NPV with and without inflation, tax effects (Appendix 12A)** Cy Keener, president of the Carbondale Architectural Design Group, is considering an investment to upgrade his current computer-aided design equipment. The new equipment would cost $110,000, have a 5-year useful life, and have a zero terminal value. The new equipment would generate annual cash operating savings of $36,000. The company's required rate of return is 18% per year.

**REQUIRED:**

**A.** Compute the net present value of the project. Assume a 25% marginal tax rate and straight-line depreciation, ignoring the half-year convention.

**B.** Keener is wondering whether the method in part (A) provides a correct analysis of the effects of inflation. The 18% required rate of return incorporates an element attributable to anticipated inflation. For purposes of his analysis, Keener assumes that the existing rate of inflation, 5% annually, will persist over the next 5 years. Recalculate the NPV, adjusting the cash flows, as appropriate, for the 5% inflation rate.

**ⓔ C.** Compare the quantitative results for parts (A) and (B). In general, how does inflation affect capital budgeting quantitative results?

**❶ D.** Explain why managers cannot predict future inflation rates with total accuracy.

**❷ E.** In your own words, explain how failure to consider the effects of inflation might bias managers' capital budgeting decisions.

**☆ 12.30**
Q1, Q2, Q3, Q4, Q6, Q7, Q8

**NPV with taxes and inflation, uncertainties, sensitivity analyses and interpretation (Appendix 12A)** Kelly Black is manager of the customer service division of a retail computer store, Quik Computers. Kelly would like to buy computer diagnostic equipment that costs $10,000. The equipment will last five years. Kelly estimates that the incremental operating cash savings from using the equipment will be $3,000 annually, measured at current prices. For income tax purposes, she will depreciate the equipment using the straight-line method ignoring the half-year convention. Kelly requires a 10% real rate of return. The annual inflation rate is 5%, and the marginal income tax rate is 30%.

**REQUIRED:**
**ANALYZE**
**INFORMATION**

The following questions will help you analyze the information for this problem. Do not turn in your answers to these questions unless your professor asks you to do so.

**A.** Create a spreadsheet schedule showing the net present value calculations for the equipment.

**❶ B.** Identify factors in your calculations that are uncertain, and explain why.

**❷ C.** Explain how changes in technology might influence the risk involved in this project.

**❷ D.** Decide which of the factors you identified in part (B) would likely have a significant impact on the net present value calculation. Use your spreadsheet to vary each of these factors, performing sensitivity analyses.

**❷ E.** Use the quantitative results and your judgment to interpret your sensitivity analyses. Which factors seem to have the largest and smallest effects on the NPV results?

**❷ F.** Describe the pros and cons of investing in the equipment.

**REQUIRED:**
**WRITTEN**
**ASSIGNMENT**

Suppose you are the cost accountant for Quik Computers. Turn in your answers to the following.

**❸ G.** Use the information you learned from the preceding analyses to write a memo to Kelly with your recommendation about whether to accept or reject this project. Refer in your memo to one or more attachments of spreadsheet schedules that would be useful to Kelly. In your memo, address the most important factors that Kelly should consider in making the decision.

**12.31**

Q2, Q3, Q4, Q6

**Time line, maximum payment for zero NPV, qualitative factors, uncertainties** The Hotshots are a professional basketball team with a long tradition of winning. However, over the last three years the team has not won a major championship, and attendance at games has dropped considerably. A large basketball manufacturer is the team's major corporate sponsor. Carl Cliff, president of the basketball company, is also the president of the Hotshots. Cliff proposes that the team purchase the services of a star player, Bob Jackson. Jackson would create great excitement for Hotshots fans and sponsors.

Jackson's agent notifies Cliff that terms for the superstar's signing with the Hotshots are a signing bonus of $8 million payable now and a house in the foothills near Sabino Canyon at a cost of $5 million. The annual salary and cost of living adjustments are under negotiation.

Cliff's initial reaction is one of shock. However, he decides to examine the cash inflows expected if Jackson is signed for a four-year contract. Net gate receipts would most likely increase by $2 million a year, corporate sponsorships would increase $2.5 million per year, television royalties would increase $0.5 million per year, and merchandise income (net of costs) would increase $1 million per year. Cliff believes that a 12% discount rate is appropriate for this investment. The Hotshots' marginal tax rate is 20%. The signing bonus can be amortized (depreciated) over the four-year period for income tax purposes, providing an annual tax deduction of $2 million.

REQUIRED:

**A.** Create a time line showing the relevant cash flows for this problem.

**e** **B.** Assuming that he is not willing to lose money on the contract, what is the maximum amount per year that Cliff would be willing to pay Jackson? You will need to set up a spreadsheet for this calculation and through trial and error find an amount that brings the NPV to zero, or use an algebraic approach and annuity factors.

**1** **C.** Identify possible additional factors that Cliff should consider when deciding whether to sign Jackson to the four-year contract. List as many factors as you can.

**1** **D.** For each of the relevant cash flows in this problem, discuss why Cliff cannot be certain about the dollar amount of the cash flow.

**12.32**

Q3, Q4, Q6, Q7, Q8

**NPV with taxes and inflation, qualitative factors, sensitivity analysis (Appendix 12A)** Wildcat Welders, Inc., manufactures new and repairs old irrigation sprinkler systems in the Okanogan Valley. The company has been plagued with industrial accidents involving its old welding technology. A new, safer welding robot has been developed that will reduce labor costs, worker insurance costs, and direct materials costs. The investment would be $10 million. The annual cash savings would be $7 million, but it would cost $2 million a year to operate the machine.

The robots have an 8-year useful life with a terminal value of $1 million. The robots qualify for the 7-year MACRS schedule. Inflation is estimated to be 5% per year. The risk-free rate is estimated to be 4%, and the company's managers require a minimum risk premium of 6%. Wildcat's marginal income tax rate is 25%.

REQUIRED:

**A.** Develop a spreadsheet to calculate the NPV of this project, using the nominal rate method. Be sure to include a data input box at the top of the spreadsheet to allow for sensitivity analysis.

**2** **B.** Identify a qualitative factor that could potentially override a negative NPV in making the decision to buy this equipment. Explain.

**C.** Alter the risk premium to perform sensitivity analyses, and answer the following questions:

**2** **1.** Explain how you decided which values of the risk premium were reasonable to investigate.

**2.** Describe how changing the risk premium affects the net present value for this project.

**2** **3.** The new equipment would most likely lower Wildcat's risk of future lawsuits because of the reduced accident rate. Explain how this factor affects your assessment of the appropriateness of the risk premium.

**D.** Because Wildcat is uncertain about whether the annual cash savings from the equipment would be $7 million, alter the cash savings to perform sensitivity analyses and answer the following questions:

**2** **1.** Explain how you decided which values of the cash savings were reasonable to investigate.

*(continued)*

**2.** Describe how changing the cash savings affects the net present value for this project.

**3.** Identify the level of cash savings that results in a NPV of zero.

**E.** Current inflation is 2%. Given this information, how reasonable is the inflation rate used by Wildcat? Perform sensitivity analysis around the inflation rate by changing the rate and observing the effects of the change on NPV. Explain how you made your choices.

**12.33**

Q1, Q2, Q4, Q6

**Cost/benefit analysis, qualitative factors, uncertainties** In 1977, public outcries arose when a memo written by **Ford Motor Company** executives was published. According to the memo, Ford continued to produce and market the Pinto automobile, even after company crash tests showed that its gas tank would burst into flames when rear-ended at low speeds. The memo indicated that Ford's managers used a cost/benefit analysis to make their decision. The analysis compared the expected benefit of avoiding future lawsuits filed on behalf of burn victims with the expected cost to recall and fix the defective gas tanks.

Beginning in 1977, automobiles sold in the United States were required to meet new federal standards requiring automobiles to withstand a rear-end collision at 30 miles per hour without causing fire. The Pinto met this standard. However, following publication of the Ford memo, the U.S. media became extremely critical of Ford's actions. This criticism led to an investigation by the **National Highway Transportation Safety Administration (NHTSA)**, which concluded that the Pinto gas tank represented a safety defect. Ford then recalled 1.4 million Pintos, including 1971–1976 models that were built before existence of the federal standard.

A few months before the recall, a civil jury in California awarded a burn victim a record $126 million. However, a judge later reduced the award to $6.6 million. Ford was indicted for reckless homicide and criminal recklessness by an Indiana grand jury after the burning death of three teenage girls. In this case, Ford was found not guilty (Lee, 1998, p. 391). Overall, Pintos were linked to more than 60 deaths (Winter, 2000).

Although Ford redesigned the fuel tank for the 1978 Pinto, sales of the model declined 45% from 1977. Ford ultimately dropped the Pinto brand. Over the next decade, sales of Japanese automobiles continued to increase, causing a long-term decline in the sale of automobiles by Ford and other U.S. manufacturers. Many consumers perceived Japanese automobiles as having higher quality. U.S. automobile companies were often viewed as callous and unconcerned about safety, reliability, and fuel efficiency.

In a 1998 analysis, University of Delaware Sociology and Criminal Justice professor Matthew T. Lee pointed out that the Pinto case occurred during a time of change in federal safety regulation and public expectation. He revealed that cost/benefit analyses had commonly been used by managers of automobile companies as well as NHTSA. His research indicated that NHTSA's conclusions in the Pinto case represented two important deviations from prior regulatory practice. First, during its investigation it held the Ford Pinto to a level of performance that was more stringent than existing federal safety guidelines. Second, NHTSA staff used the societal value of human life, rather than the commonly used average corporate payout, in their cost/benefit analysis. In addition, NHTSA staff had focused their investigation on Ford because of the public outcry over the Pinto. Other automobile companies were not held to the same safety standards.

SOURCES: M. Lee, "The Ford Pinto Case and the Development of Auto Safety Regulations, 1893–1978," *Business and Economic History*, Winter 1998, pp. 390–402; and D. Winter, "Together Again in the Headlines," *Ward's Auto World*, October 2000, pp. 57–58.

**REQUIRED:**

**A.** Had you previously heard about the gas tank problems of the Ford Pinto? If so:

**1.** Describe your previous impressions of the Pinto problem.

**2.** In what ways do these impressions create potential biases as you address this case?

**B.** Identify several ethical issues in this case—in other words, areas of conflicts of interest between stakeholders.

**C.** What were the opportunity costs (qualitative and quantitative) that were apparently overlooked by Ford's managers in valuing the cost of fixing the gas tanks during their cost/benefit analysis?

**D.** Ford's managers measured the potential benefit of eliminating the gas tank problems using the expected future cost of settling lawsuits filed on behalf of burn victims. NHTSA used the societal value of human life in its cost/benefit analysis. Explain how these measures are different,

*(continued)*

and describe the pros and cons of using each measure when analyzing the Pinto problem. Take into account the viewpoints of different stakeholders, including:

- Pinto crash victims and their families
- Ford's managers
- Pinto owners
- Ford's employees
- Potential Pinto owners
- Ford's shareholders
- Customers of other Ford vehicles
- Ford's domestic competitors
- General public
- Ford's Japanese competitors
- NHTSA staff members

**③ E.** What values did Ford's managers appear to use in reaching their decision to continue selling the Pinto with its existing gas tank design? Were these values reasonable under the circumstances? Why or why not?

**③ F.** What values did NHTSA staff appear to use in drawing their conclusions? Were these values reasonable under the circumstances? Why or why not?

**12.34**

Q2, Q3, Q4

www.wiley.com/
college/eldenburg

**NPV with taxes, sensitivity analysis, minimum volume, minimum selling price** The managers of Favorite Fish are considering a new project in which they would purchase equipment to produce canned sardines. You are to perform capital budgeting computations relating to this project.

A spreadsheet template developed to analyze the Favorite Fish decision is available at www. wiley.com/college.eldenburg. Notice that the first part of the spreadsheet computes the NPV of a project, given the information from the input box at the top of the spreadsheet. The lower portion of the spreadsheet computes the price necessary for the project to have an NPV of zero. You will manipulate the data in the data entry box as you alter the underlying assumptions of the analysis. For example, you can change the discount rate but leave all of the other information as it is in the original template. Each time you begin a new analysis, you should return to the original template values.

**REQUIRED:**

**A.** What is the NPV of the project if the discount rate is 15%?

**B.** What is the NPV of the project if the tax rate goes down to 30%?

**C.** What is the NPV if the cost of the equipment increases to $120,000?

**D.** What is the minimum price that must be charged to make this project acceptable given that 10,000 cases must be sold?

**E.** What is the NPV of the project if 12,000 cases are sold at $5.50 per case and variable costs remain unchanged?

**F.** What is the NPV of the project if variable costs increase to $2.75?

**G.** What is the NPV of the project if variable costs increase to $2.75 and the marginal tax rate declines to 30%?

**H.** What is the NPV of the project if variable costs increase to $2.75, the marginal tax rate declines to 30%, and the marginal discount rate is 24%?

**ⓔ I.** What is the minimum price that Favorite Fish must charge to make this project acceptable if the marginal tax rate becomes 50%?

**ⓔ J.** What is the minimum price to make the project acceptable if only 9,000 cases are sold?

**ⓔ K.** What is the minimum price if 8,000 cases are sold, the discount rate is 14%, and the tax rate is 30%?

**① L.** To help managers perform sensitivity analysis, it is useful to gather information about competitors' prices, current and future economic factors, and any other relevant information. Where could you find information that would help you or a manager decide on the values to use for this type of sensitivity analysis?

# BUILD YOUR PROFESSIONAL COMPETENCIES

**12.35**

Q1, Q2, Q4, Q6

**DEFINITION:**

**Focus on Professional Competency: Industry/Sector Perspective** *Team goals, standards, cooperation, and performance* Review the following definition and elements for the Industry/ Sector Perspective competency.[10]

*Individuals entering the accounting profession should be able to identify (through research and analysis) the economics and broad business financial risks and opportunities of the industry and economic sector in which a given organization operates. Identification of these risks and opportunities should include both issues specific to the enterprise, as well as those pervasive throughout the industry/sector.*

---

[10] The definition and elements are reprinted with permission from AICPA; Copyright © 1978–2000 & 2003 by American Institute of Certified Public Accountants. The AICPA's Core Competency Framework can be accessed at eca.aicpaservices.org.

## ELEMENTS FOR THIS COMPETENCY INCLUDE

| Level 1 | Level 2 | Level 3 | Level 4 |
|---|---|---|---|
| 1. Identifies the economic, broad business, and financial risks of the industry/sector | 2. Describes market forces that make a given organization a candidate for merger, acquisition, and/or strategic alliance<br><br>3. Identifies and describes competitive advantages and disadvantages | 4. Recommends courses of action that take advantage of an organization's key competitive advantages and disadvantages<br><br>5. Communicates the financial and nonfinancial performance of an organization's operational processes | 6. Effectively addresses changes in the economic, broad business, and financial risks of the industry/sector over time |

**REQUIRED:**

**A.** Focus on competency elements 1, 3, and 4, which require accountants to have knowledge about the business environment and competitive advantage. Answer the following questions:

❷ **1.** Explain how industry/sector risks lead to uncertainties in making the types of long-term investment decisions addressed in this chapter.

❷ **2.** Explain how competitive advantages can lead to a positive NPV for a proposed long-term investment project.

❷ **3.** Explain how competitive disadvantages can lead to failure of a long-term investment project after it has been accepted.

❷ **4.** Explain why the managers who propose a project might not fully recognize relevant competitive disadvantages.

❹ **B.** Focus on competency element 6, which addresses change in the business environment over time. How can an organization monitor long-term investment projects to effectively address changes in risks over time?

❷ **C.** Focus on competency element 2, which addresses knowledge of the synergies between businesses. Refer to the scenario presented in the chapter, "Focus on Ethical Decision Making: The Right Thing to Do." What market forces might have encouraged **Glaxo-SmithKline** to enter into a strategic alliance with the **World Health Organization** to develop a low-cost malaria drug?

**12.36**
**Q4, Q7**

**Integrating Across the Curriculum: Finance** *Weighted average cost of capital, estimation problems* The weighted average cost of capital is the weighted average rate for the costs of the various sources of financing in an organization. These sources for Tudor Industries are as follows:

| Source of Capital | Market Value | Cost |
|---|---|---|
| Short-term debt | $300,000 | 8% |
| Bonds | 900,000 | 6% |
| Leases | 200,000 | 7% |
| Common stock | 900,000 | 10% |

The short-term debt represents revolving credit, which is periodically renewed. Income taxes average 25%.

**REQUIRED:**

🄴 **A.** Calculate the weighted average cost of capital (WACC) for Tudor Industries. If you need a formula, use a finance textbook or conduct an Internet search for "weighted average cost of capital." One Web site providing a formula is: www.investopedia.com/terms/w/wacc.asp.

🄴 **B.** Explain how and why income taxes affect the calculation of WACC.

❶ **C.** Discuss uncertainties about the best measure to use for the discount rate in a capital budgeting problem.

❷ **D.** Discuss the pros and cons of using WACC as a discount rate in capital budgeting.

❷ **E.** The market value for each source of capital is used when calculating WACC. Suppose you work for Tudor and need to calculate its WACC, but you do not know the market values. Describe possible ways that you could estimate the market value for each of Tudor's sources of capital.

❷ **F.** Some people use financial statement book values to calculate WACC. Discuss reasons why this approach might result in an inappropriate value for WACC.

# 13

# Joint Management of Revenues and Costs

## ▶In Brief

Managers and accountants make decisions about long-term organizational strategies as well as short-term operating plans. These strategies and plans include mutually dependent decisions about how to control costs and price products. Managers increasingly adopt practices such as target costing and just-in-time inventory management to help them improve efficiency and achieve profitability goals. Cost measurements help managers make these types of decisions.

## This Chapter Addresses the Following Questions:

**Q1** How is value chain analysis used to improve operations?

**Q2** What is target costing, and how is it performed?

**Q3** What is kaizen costing, and how does it compare to target costing?

**Q4** What is life cycle costing?

**Q5** How are cost-based prices established?

**Q6** How are market-based prices established?

**Q7** What are the uses and limitations of cost-based and market-based pricing?

**Q8** What additional factors affect prices?

# MICROSOFT: XBOX STRATEGIC LOSSES

In May 2002 **Microsoft** reduced the price of its Xbox game console from $299 to $199 in the United States. This news followed an announcement by **Sony** that it would reduce the price of its game console, PlayStation 2, to $199. Microsoft also announced plans to invest an additional $2 billion in the Xbox.

During 2001 when Microsoft began selling its new Xbox game console, analysts predicted that the product would sell at a loss for three years or more. Outside contractors manufactured the Xbox, and production costs were expected to total about $375 per box. This was on top of huge investments in research, product development, and advertising to launch the Xbox. However, the price Microsoft could charge its customers was limited by competition.

Such losses represent a standard practice in the videogame console industry. Manufacturers rely on income from software sales and licensing to subsidize their hardware costs. Managers plan for losses immediately after launching a new console design, but expect to generate profits over the console's life. Historically, a particular console design lasts about five years before being replaced by a new design. Thus, managers expect repeated cycles of loss followed by profit.

It can be difficult for managers to decide whether to continue investing in a product that is currently unprofitable. Microsoft's May 2002 announcements made it clear that its managers intended to continue investing in Xbox. However, in 1991, after many years of losses, **Sega's** managers decided to drop their Dreamcast console product line. ■

SOURCES: D. Becker and J. Wilcox, "Will Xbox Drain Microsoft?" *CNET News.com,* March 6, 2001; and K. T. L. Tran, "Microsoft Vows to Spend $2 Billion to Restore Xbox Game's Momentum," *The Wall Street Journal Online,* May 21, 2002.

## SIMULTANEOUSLY MANAGING REVENUES AND COSTS

## ■ Key Decision Issues for Microsoft

**Microsoft's** managers made a major commitment when they launched the Xbox. Not only had the company already spent enormous sums in researching and developing the initial product, but it would continue to lose money in the near future. Why were Microsoft's managers willing to sell a product below cost, reduce the selling price even further, and continue to spend money on the product? The following discussion summarizes key aspects of Microsoft's May 2002 decisions to reduce its Xbox price and to commit $2 billion of additional investments.

**Knowing.** Microsoft's managers needed in-depth knowledge of the videogame business, including console design and production, software, and licensing. From its other products, Microsoft knew software and licensing well. However, prior to launching Xbox, the company had little experience with hardware design and production. By outsourcing Xbox production, the managers could reduce the need for production expertise.

**Identifying.** Microsoft's managers first needed to identify pricing and investment options. The managers most likely restricted their attention to what they saw as a relevant set of price and investment alternatives. For example, in May 2002 they might have explored the following pricing options:

- Maintain the current price
- Increase the price
- Reduce the price to some amount other than $199
- Match or beat Sony's PlayStation 2 or Nintendo's GameCube price

They might have explored the following investment options:

- Drop the product
- Budget investments at low, moderate, or high amounts

The decision was full of uncertainties, such as the following:

- Demand for Xbox
- Number, type, timing, and popularity of Xbox game software
- Software and licensing revenues
- Competitors' product designs, prices, and promotions
- Production costs
- Xbox quality and performance

**Exploring.** As always, managers make better decisions when they recognize and control for potential biases. For the Microsoft Xbox project, the managers might have been unwilling to consider dropping a product that had only recently been launched at great cost. Or, they might have believed that the company's other software successes would automatically lead to success in the game industry.

It was also important for Microsoft's managers to consider how outsiders would view their decisions and announcements. For example, the company's announcement that it would invest $2 billion most likely had several effects:

- It reassured game software developers who were deciding whether to invest in games for the Xbox platform.
- It put potential customers at ease about the long-term availability of games should they choose to purchase the console.
- It let competitors know that Microsoft planned to compete aggressively.

**Prioritizing.** This case demonstrates that decisions do not always follow the general decision rule introduced in Chapters 3 and 4, that a product's contribution margin must cover its fixed cost to be produced. Microsoft matched Sony's price reduction and planned substantial additional investments. These decisions would clearly reduce Xbox short-term profits. Thus, Microsoft's managers must have decided that other factors were more important than short-term profits. The following priorities are consistent with Microsoft's May 2002 announcements:

- Maintaining competitive prices
- Investing sufficient sums to further develop the product and promote sales growth
- Signaling long-term intent to compete
- Gaining long-term profitability

**Envisioning.** To charge competitive prices and still earn a reasonable profit, companies must continuously improve their products and reduce costs. Therefore, Microsoft's managers must visualize and develop beyond the current Xbox technology. Because of the highly competitive environment, Microsoft must also anticipate future competitor actions and develop strategies for long-term success.

## ◼ Simultaneous Management of Costs and Revenues

The link between costs and prices has become increasingly important with global competition. Managers and accountants must simultaneously manage both. Successful companies continuously improve their cost efficiency, charge competitive prices, and focus on long-term organizational strategies. We begin this chapter by learning several specific methods used to reduce costs, and then we explore pricing methods.

## SECTION 1

## Continuous Cost Improvement

## VALUE CHAIN ANALYSIS

> **Q1** How is value chain analysis used to improve operations?

Over the long term, profitable organizations continuously seek ways to become more efficient, reduce costs, and improve interactions with suppliers and customers. A variety of methods are available for analyzing and improving the systems used to produce and deliver goods and services.

A **value chain** is the sequence of business processes in which value is added to a product or service. In 1985 Harvard Professor Michael Porter introduced a generic value chain and suggested that the details of these models varied by industry.[1] In Exhibit 13.1 we present a diagram of a generic manufacturer's value chain similar to Porter's chain of primary activities. The value chain for a service organization is similar, but focuses on the process for providing services rather than manufactured goods.

An organization's value chain encompasses not only customers and suppliers, but even incorporates, in some cases, the customers' customers and the suppliers' suppliers. Analysis of the value chain leads to improved relationships between the organization and others in the value chain, creating an extended organization that can respond flexibly to dynamic and competitive environments. In other words, value chains explicitly recognize that no organization operates in isolation from suppliers and customers.

## ◼ Value-Added and Non-Value-Added Activities

Value chain analysis involves studying each step in the business process to determine whether some activities can be eliminated because they do not add value. This analysis extends to suppliers and customers, and includes shared planning, inventory, human resources, information technology systems, and even corporate cultures. Eventually, the analysis leads to business decisions for improving value.

For example, **United Parcel Service (UPS)** implemented one of the world's largest wireless networks because its managers wanted to reduce paperwork and improve inventory tracking. They believed that the traditional paperwork did not add value, even though the information was necessary. With this new system, package sorters use wireless ring scanners (a bar code scanner worn as a ring) to monitor inventory in warehouses and in transit. The wireless system eliminates paper-based processes and improves the flow of information throughout the

---

[1]M. Porter, *Competitive Advantage* (New York: The Free Press, 1985).

**EXHIBIT 13.1**
Value Chain for
a Manufacturer

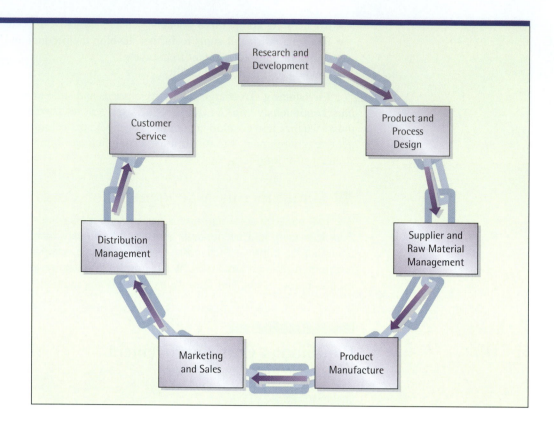

delivery process.[2] The system enables UPS to give customers updated information about their packages. Meanwhile, managers have more planning information about capacity levels across locations. The new system allowed UPS to eliminate a non-value-added activity and also to add value by producing more timely information both for internal purposes and for customers.

Before activities in the value chain can be improved or eliminated, they must be identified and then categorized as **value-added** or **non-value-added.** Some organizations use four categories, recognizing both that it may be possible to improve value-added activities and that time may be needed to eliminate non-value-added activities.[3] Exhibit 13.2 presents these four categories with examples of actions that managers could take to improve value. The process of analyzing and categorizing activities also improves communication, as individuals in each part of the process begin to share their abilities, needs, and requirements with others in the value chain.

Value chain analysis encourages managers to consider whether they should outsource some of their value-added activities. Sometimes outsourcing is less costly than performing the activity internally. Managers often choose to outsource an activity because it is not a core competency of the organization. For example, **Microsoft's** managers probably decided to outsource Xbox manufacturing because the production of hardware components is not one of Microsoft's core competencies. Ultimately, the decision of whether to outsource an activity depends on both quantitative and qualitative factors.

**CHAPTER REFERENCE**

For more details about making nonroutine decisions, such as whether to insource or outsource a service or product, see Chapter 4.

### ■ Supply Chain Analysis

As organizations work to increase profitability, improving their relationships with suppliers becomes a priority. Improvements can be identified through supply chain analysis. The **supply chain** is the flow of resources from the initial suppliers through the delivery of goods and services to customers and clients. The initial suppliers may be inside or outside the organization. Negotiating lower costs with suppliers is a straightforward way to reduce costs.

[2]P. K. Tam, "Going Mobile," *Transportation and Distribution,* July 2003, p 23.
[3]R. Kaplan and R. Cooper, *Cost and Effect* (Cambridge, MA: Harvard Business School Press, 1998).

**EXHIBIT 13.2** Classification of Value-Added and Non-Value-Added Activities

| Activity Classification | Action to Improve Value |
|---|---|
| A necessary activity that cannot be improved upon at this time | None |
| A necessary activity that could be changed to improve the process | Modify the process to improve value<br><br>*Example:* Plant layout could be changed so that materials handling activities are reduced. |
| An unnecessary activity that can eventually be eliminated by changing the process | Eventually eliminate the unnecessary activity<br><br>*Example:* Eliminate manual recording of employee hours using time cards. A new payroll system is eventually implemented. Plastic identity cards with magnetic strips are swiped through time clocks. The system electronically tracks hours worked and processes paychecks. |
| An unnecessary activity that can quickly be eliminated by changing the process | Immediately eliminate the unnecessary activity<br><br>*Example:* In team manufacturing, inspection of units completed can be eliminated if each team member inspects each unit before it passes to the next team member. |

**CURRENT PRACTICE**

In 2003, IBM reduced annual operating costs by $5.6 billion by overhauling its supply chains. Savings resulted from falling component prices, cheaper production locations, and cutting suppliers by half (to 33,000).[4]

Suppliers may be willing to reduce prices, particularly for organizations willing to sign long-term purchase commitments. Occasionally organizations work with suppliers to help them reduce their costs, so that the savings can be passed along. Suppose MagikBikes, a mountain bike manufacturer, sends a team of employees to its handlebar supplier to help redesign the component to be lighter weight, sturdier, and require fewer parts and labor. If successful, both the cost of handlebars and their shipping costs would decrease.

Accountants analyze supply chains by determining inventory level requirements, starting with customer demand for products or services. Opportunities to reduce cost and improve quality are identified through tracking and analyzing use patterns of raw materials, supplies, finished goods, and shipped goods. Vendors are included in inventory management decisions as part of this process. With close cooperation, inventory levels can be managed to reduce the quantitative costs of insurance and storage and the qualitative costs of quality changes and timeliness of delivery.

## ■ Using the Internet to Improve Inventory Supply

The Internet increasingly provides suppliers with access to their customers' inventory level information. Suppliers use this information to time deliveries so that their customers maintain desired inventory levels. Suppliers also use this information to improve their own production planning.

The cooperation between retailer **Costco** and its supplier **Kimberly-Clark** is a good example of supply chain efficiency. Kimberly-Clark uses an automated Internet system to monitor disposable diaper quantities in each Costco store. The system manages the reordering and delivery of goods as needed to maintain inventory levels.[5] This type of system reduces Costco's inventory costs, while also enabling Kimberly-Clark to anticipate production needs and work with its own suppliers to receive raw materials in a timely manner.

Providing Internet access to product or service information can be risky, however. Organizations need adequate security measures such as firewalls to protect sensitive information that might have competitive value.

**CURRENT PRACTICE**

Cisco Systems has a private information hub on the Internet that links manufacturers, distributors, and component suppliers. Cisco can immediately notify its suppliers of any changes in requirements.[6]

---

[4]See D. Lyons, "Back on the Chain Gang," *Forbes,* September 25, 2003, on-line edition.
[5] E. Melson and A. Zimmerman, "Minding the Store: Kimberly-Clark Keeps Costco in Diapers . . . ," *The Wall Street Journal,* September 7, 2000, p. A1.
[6]P. K. Tam, "Going Mobile," *Transportation and Distribution,* July 2003, p 23.

## ■ Just-in-Time Production

With **just-in-time (JIT) production and inventory control systems,** materials are purchased and units are produced at the time customers demand them. JIT is considered a *demand-pull system* because products and their parts are manufactured just as they are needed for each step in the manufacturing process. In JIT inventory control systems, organizations work with suppliers so that goods or materials are delivered just as they are needed for production or for sale. Suppliers make frequent deliveries of small lots of goods directly to the production floor or to sales areas in merchandising organizations.

In JIT manufacturing systems, the production process is often broken into steps that are performed in *manufacturing cells*. A cell is an area where all of the equipment and labor is grouped for a particular part of the manufacturing process as shown in Exhibit 13.3. Parts and supplies arrive just in time to be used for each specific manufacturing task. When one cell finishes its set of tasks, the product is either complete or moves to the next cell where more work is performed. Production is continuous; as soon as team members finish their production tasks on one unit, another unit is begun. The product moves through all of the cells until the manufacturing process is complete. The manufacturing sequence is organized not only to minimize handling and storage, but also to minimize defect rates.

Successful implementation of JIT systems requires that organizations

- Find high quality suppliers.
- Choose a manageable number of suppliers.
- Locate suppliers with short transit times for materials being delivered.
- Develop efficient and reliable materials handling processes.
- Develop management commitment to the JIT process.

JIT systems reduce costs by maximizing the use of space, reducing defect rates, and increasing manufacturing flexibility. Each team member is responsible for product inspection so that defects are identified quickly and quality problems can be remedied immediately. When manufacturers produce a number of different product models under a JIT system, changeover to the next model occurs almost immediately. This approach enhances manufacturing flexibility. Experts in operations management believe that the JIT approach may be one of the most significant developments in management innovation in the last century.[7]

**ALTERNATIVE TERMS**

Some people use the terms *lean production* or *kanban* to describe a *just-in-time* production system. The term *JIT* is also used broadly, in conjunction with services such as "JIT education."

**CURRENT PRACTICE**

In the United States, efficiencies gained under JIT systems have accelerated productivity. Between 1990 and 2000, manufacturer inventory levels dropped from an average of 50 days down to 40 days.[8]

**EXHIBIT 13.3**
Cellular Manufacturing System at Master Lock Factory in Nogales, Mexico

[7]R. J. Schonberger, *World Class Manufacturing: The Next Decade* (New York: The Free Press, 1996).
[8]G. Ip, "Risky Business," *The Wall Street Journal,* October 24, 2001, p. A1.

One drawback of JIT systems is that production halts when suppliers are unable to deliver supplies as needed. Sometimes unforeseen events interrupt the delivery schedule. For example, shortly after the terrorist attacks of September 11, 2001, **Toyota** came within 15 hours of halting production of the Sequoia SUV in its Princeton, Indiana, plant. One of Toyota's suppliers was waiting for steering sensors that were usually imported from Germany by plane, but air travel to the United States was prohibited for several days. To avoid this type of problem in the future, the supplier now ships the part by ocean rather than air and stores enough steering sensors in the United States to provide a supply for two weeks rather than one. Although Toyota preserved its JIT system, its supplier is now required to maintain higher inventory levels than before.[9]

## ■ Other Benefits of Analyzing Production and Service Systems

**CHAPTER REFERENCE**

Chapter 14 further discusses production cycle time when throughput accounting is introduced.

Value chain analysis, supply chain analysis, and just-in-time systems provide benefits beyond reducing non-value-added activities and costs such as inventory storage and insurance. These methods lead to further cost reductions by focusing management attention on minimizing rework, scrap, and waste. In addition, managers often identify opportunities to reduce production cycle time.

Sometimes the use of one method leads to another method. For example, value chain analysis might encourage accountants to analyze their supply chain and adopt JIT to reduce non-value-added activities. Value chain analysis might help accountants identify bottlenecks or other process constraints. Then Theory of Constraints analysis could be used to improve the system, while balancing the flow of production with demand. Managers use a wide range of tools to analyze production and delivery systems, with the goal of improving cost and quality. Accountants help managers by bringing these tools to their attention and providing the analysis.

**CHAPTER REFERENCE**

See Chapter 4 for more information about the Theory of Constraints.

| GUIDE YOUR LEARNING **13.1** Key Terms |
| --- |

Stop to confirm that you understand the new terms introduced in the last several pages.

Value chain (p. 511)  
*Value-added activity (p. 512)  
*Non-value-added activity (p. 512)  

Supply chain (p. 512)  
Just-in-time production and inventory control systems (p. 514)

For each of these terms, write a definition in your own words. For starred terms, list at least one example that is different from the ones given in this textbook.

## BUILDING DESIRED PROFIT INTO DECISIONS

Accountants use estimates of revenues and costs to provide information for a range of operating decisions. In the short term, the general rule is to sell goods or services as long as estimated revenues exceed estimated variable costs. However, in the long term, organizations need to earn a reasonable return on investment. Next, we will discuss the following techniques used to plan for long-term profitability:

- Target costing
- Kaizen costing
- Life cycle costing

Although these methods alone do not result in increased profitability, they help accountants become more deliberate about profit planning. When costs appear to be too high, these methods also encourage accountants and managers to identify and implement cost management techniques.

**CHAPTER REFERENCE**

For more information on short-term decisions, see Chapters 3 and 4.

[9]G. Ip, "Risky Business," *The Wall Street Journal,* October 24, 2001, p. A1.

## TARGET COSTING

 **Q2** What is target costing, and how is it performed?

Toyota is credited with inventing target costing and has been using it since the 1960s.[10]

When launching a new product, managers traditionally determined the cost of the product and then used the cost to help them set a price that would achieve a desired profit margin. Given this information, the managers evaluated the feasibility of the new product. An alternative decision-making approach is **target costing,** which uses market-based prices to determine whether products and services can be delivered at costs low enough for an acceptable profit. Competitors' products are *reverse engineered* (taken apart and put back together again) to better understand the manufacturing process and the product design. In turn, the product and manufacturing process are redesigned so that the product meets a prespecified target cost. Organizations can then sell products at competitive prices and still earn profits.

In the late 1970s and early 1980s **Komatsu**, a heavy equipment company, used target costing to develop products similar in quality and functionality to those of **Caterpillar**. Komatsu was able to set its prices lower than Caterpillar. Prior to the mid-1980s, Caterpillar was financially stable. But in the late 1980s, the company struggled against a weak global economy and the competition from Komatsu, losing $1 billion over a three-year period. Mark Thompson, a business analysis manager with Caterpillar's wheel-loader and excavator division, recalled, "We had to do something drastic. The viability of the company depended on it."[11] Caterpillar's managers turned to target costing, the same method that enabled Komatsu to become so competitive. Caterpillar accountants and analysts studied publicly available financial statements to identify Komatsu's costs. They learned that Caterpillar's production costs were 30% higher than Komatsu's.

Next, Caterpillar's engineers purchased, tore apart, and reverse-engineered Komatsu's products to determine the processes and designs Komatsu used in manufacturing. Caterpillar managers then invested $1.8 billion in plant modernization. They eliminated non-value-added processes, examined their procedures to purchase raw materials and supplies, moved to a just-in-time inventory system, and reduced the number of parts used in Caterpillar products. Using target costing techniques, Caterpillar produced record-setting profits. Although the company's profits declined during a downturn in the heavy equipment industry during 2001 and 2002, profits rebounded with a 38% increase during 2003.[12] Analysts recommended the company as an investment as of February 2004.[13]

### ■ Target Costing Process

As highlighted in the Caterpillar example, target costing helps organizations improve production processes and profits. Target costing is the process of researching consumer markets to estimate an appropriate market price, then subtracting the desired return to determine a maximum allowable cost. This target cost is the maximum cost at which the company can produce a good or service to generate the desired profit margin. The organization then determines whether the good or service can be designed and produced to meet the target cost. This step involves managing both product design and manufacturing phases. If expected costs exceed the target, managers will choose not to provide a good or service. To date, target costing has been used primarily for products that have already been manufactured by other companies; however, it is increasingly used for new goods and services.

The key value of target costing is that it focuses managers' attention on the design phase where most cost savings potentially occur because 70% to 80% of product costs are typically committed at this point. Costs that occur both when the manufacturing process is set up and during manufacturing are locked in during the design phase. For example, new equipment is chosen and direct materials are specified that will be used in production. Although the actual costs occur over a product's life cycle, the decisions made in the

---

[10]For more information, see "On Target . . . Time after Time," *The Journal of Product and Brand Management,* 5(5), (1996), pp. 8–10.
[11]K. Kroll, "On Target," *Industry Week,* June 9, 1997, pp. 14–22.
[12]"Quarterly Financial Results," news release, January 2004, available at www.caterpillar.com, click Investor Information.
[13]M. Kahn, "Consumer Non-Cyclicals May Cycle Higher," *Barron's Online,* February 9, 2004.

**EXHIBIT 13.4** Steps in a Target Costing Design Cycle

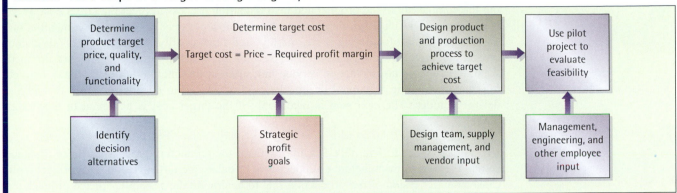

planning phase have the greatest influence over those costs. Under target costing, the decision to produce a good or service depends on expected costs developed in the design phase. The steps in a target costing design cycle are summarized in Exhibit 13.4. The description of each step follows.

**Determine the Product Target Price, Quality, and Functionality** Accountants and managers use studies such as consumer surveys, focus groups, and market research of competitors' prices to determine a competitive price for a specific product. Researchers collect information about consumer preferences, including trade-offs customers are willing to make among price, quality, and functionality for a product or service. A competitive price *for a given level of product quality and functionality* can then be estimated. In industries where customers are willing to pay higher prices for higher quality or more functionality, managers strategically differentiate their products and establish market positions. The same is true when customers are willing to give up a certain amount of quality or functionality to obtain lower prices.

The automobile industry provides a good example of product differentiation. Some manufacturers emphasize a low price for lower levels of quality and functionality. Other manufacturers emphasize quality and are able to charge higher prices. Some manufacturers emphasize functionality such as four-wheel-drive capability or trucks with four-door cabs. Increases in functionality are usually accompanied by increases in product prices. When cars are being designed, the marketing department analyzes consumer preferences to determine the optimal levels of quality and functionality for a particular price.

Customers in some industries are unwilling to pay for higher quality or functionality. In Caterpillar's industry (heavy machinery), the products are used in construction. Purchasing decisions tend to revolve around price and only one quality factor—reliability. Extra functions such as air-conditioned cabs are unlikely to increase a product's marketability.

**Determine Target Cost** After a competitive price is determined for specific levels of product quality and functionality, the required profit margin is subtracted from the price to arrive at the target cost:

$$\text{Target cost} = \text{Price} - \text{Required profit margin}$$

The required profit margin is usually a function of the organization's long-term strategic goals. Managers who use this method assume that producers cannot set the price, but instead must take the market's price. Accordingly, the production decision focuses on the organization's ability to produce goods or services at the specified target cost.

**Design Product and Production Process to Achieve the Target Cost** A product design team is assembled from personnel in product engineering, marketing, and accounting. This team designs the product at the specified levels of quality and functionality and then

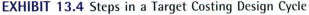

**INTERNATIONAL**

Toyota took market share from U.S. manfacturers in the early 1990s by introducing a four-wheel-drive vehicle at lower cost and higher quality.[14]

[14]T. Tananka, "Target Costing at Toyota," *Journal of Cost Management,* Spring 1993, pp. 4–11.

develops the manufacturing process. During the design phase, the team focuses on reducing the complexity of the product and manufacturing process to meet the target cost. If the team is unable to meet the target cost, the design process is reiterated with negotiations on possible trade-offs among price, quality, and functionality. If the product still cannot be manufactured at the target cost after several iterations, production plans are dropped. A similar process takes place in service industries; teams including professional, marketing, and accounting personnel design the type of service to be provided and the service delivery modes. The next step is taken only if the target cost is achieved in the design phase.

**Use Pilot Project to Evaluate Feasibility** Once the production process has been designed so that the cost to manufacture a product is at or below the target cost, a pilot project replicates a small version of the production line to determine the feasibility of the product and process design and cost. If the pilot project is successful, full production begins. If it is unsuccessful, the team returns to the design phase. Similar pilot projects are used in service organizations to evaluate feasibility.

## ■ Factors That Affect the Success of Target Costing

Target costing performs best in the following situations:

- Product development and design phases are long and complex.
- The production process is complex.
- The market is willing to pay for differences in quality or function.
- The manufacturer can push some cost reductions onto suppliers and subcontractors.
- The manufacturer can influence the design of subparts.

Target costing is inappropriate in industries with simple production processes, such as food products and beverages, which are typically unable to differentiate their products based on quality and functionality. In the food industry, advertising campaigns and brand name recognition influence price the most.

The following example describes the target costing process for a bike manufacturer.

### MOUNT RAINIER BIKES (PART 1)
### TARGET COSTING

Mount Rainier Bikes (MRB) is a start-up company that manufactures high-quality mountain bikes that compete with products from companies such as Trek and Bianchi. One of MRB's employees developed a new braking system that allows bikers to descend steep slopes using a consistent braking pattern that pumps both front and back brakes at regular, preset intervals, depending on the brake setting that the biker chooses. The marketing department surveyed current customers and found they would be willing to pay more for this option. Because MRB's brand name is not yet well-established, prices for its bikes need to be kept below those of its major competitors. MRB's owner, Michelle Miles, wants the company to launch a line of bikes with the new braking system. Her accountant recommended that the company use target costing to develop the new product to ensure that the design is feasible.

#### Determine Product Target Price, Quality, and Functionality

After conducting customer surveys and a number of focus groups, MRB's marketing staff identified five features that are highly important to prospective customers: the weight of the bike, the bike's ability to withstand hard riding in difficult terrain for long periods of time, appearance, ease of handling, and riding comfort over rough terrain. Depending on the brand name of the bike and its components, the market price for competing models with these features ranges between $800 and $1,200. The model with the highest market share in that price range is priced at $949. From the survey and focus group information gathered, Michelle believes that a bike with the new braking system and the same levels of quality and functionality as the competitors' models should be priced at $950 to achieve a 25% market share. She decides to call the new model the Mountain Braker.

## Determine Target Cost

Michelle sets a minimum profit margin of 10% on new products. Given this information, Michelle's accountant sets the new product's target cost:

| | |
|---|---|
| Price | $950 |
| Less profit margin | 95 |
| Target cost | $855 |

## Design Product and Production Process to Achieve Target Cost

Michelle establishes a team to handle the product and manufacturing process design. The team consists of one person from each of the following areas: marketing, engineering, purchasing, accounting, and administration.

First, the team identifies an initial cost for the Mountain Braker. The engineer alters MRB's basic bike design to incorporate the new braking system. The cost estimate of $905 is higher than the target cost of $855, so the team considers ways to reduce the cost. The team assembles information about current costs and necessary cost reductions, assuming sales of 50,000 bikes. They identify areas with the most potential for cost reduction, and then establish the following estimates for these reductions.

| Cost Category | Current Cost per Bike | Target Cost | Cost Reduction Needed |
|---|---|---|---|
| New brake development | $ 50 | $ 50 | $ 0 |
| Manufacturing | 710 | 680 | 30 |
| Total manufacturing costs | 760 | 730 | 30 |
| Selling and distribution | 55 | 50 | 5 |
| Warranty and support | 35 | 30 | 5 |
| Administration | 55 | 45 | 10 |
| Total cost | $905 | $855 | $50 |

### Product Design Changes

The team decides to use value chain analysis (Exhibit 13.1) to seek opportunities for cost reduction. They focus on the product design phase of the value chain. The engineer analyzes the current design, searching for steps in the manufacturing process and components that can be eliminated. The accountant provides cost information for prospective changes. The marketing person provides information about customer reactions to proposed changes.

**Reflectors.** The team suggests elimination of the reflectors mounted on the spokes. Because the Mountain Braker would be used primarily in very rough terrain, any reflectors are likely to break. Furthermore, the relatively few riders who use the bike on roads do not rely on reflectors, but use battery-operated head and taillights instead. The accountant estimates that $15 per bike can be saved by eliminating both the reflectors and the process of mounting them. After sending e-mails to prospective customers, the marketing team member confirms that eliminating reflectors will not affect consumer demand for the product or expected price.

**Bike Seats.** When the engineer suggests a cheaper bike seat that is easier to mount, the marketing representative organizes a focus group with prospective customers to determine the effect on sales. Feedback from the focus group indicates that the price would have to be reduced if a lower-quality seat is installed, so this idea is dropped.

### Supplier Negotiations

The team next focuses on the direct materials purchasing function in their value chain analysis. They investigate cost reductions from current suppliers and search for similar quality components at reduced prices from new suppliers. Purchasing personnel meet with all of the components suppliers to negotiate cost reductions.

**Handlebars.** The handlebars supplier suggests a new product with comparable quality to the current handlebars and at a cost reduction of $10 per bike. Marketing determines that the new handlebars would not affect customers' perceptions of quality.

**Tires.** Purchasing works with the company that supplies tires. Buying tires in larger lots can save the supplier delivery and storage costs, and MRB currently has storage space available. The new purchase agreement reduces costs by $5 per bike.

**Tire Tubes.** Purchasing finds a new tire tube vendor that can supply tubes at a cost reduction of $5 per bike.

Combined, the changes recommended by the team are expected to reduce manufacturing costs by $35 ($15 + $10 + $5 + $5), rather than the needed $30. Thus, the target cost for manufacturing costs is met. The team now focuses on the remaining costs that need to be reduced. *(continued)*

## Nonmanufacturing Costs

The target costing team meets with the marketing department and the director of finance to identify reductions in selling and distribution, warranty and support, and administration costs.

**Selling and Distribution.** Marketing is concerned that reducing commissions or advertising will affect total sales and potential market share gains for MRB. Marketing wants no cost reduction on advertising or commissions for this new product. The successful introduction of the new braking system relies in part on individual sales representatives highlighting the feature and in part on an advertisement campaign featuring the braking system. However, the shipping company has agreed to a reduction in shipping costs of $5 per bike because MRB's volumes have been increasing rapidly; it is cheaper for the shipping company to ship large lots.

**Warranty and Support.** MRB's managers are concerned that reducing customer warranty and support costs—both areas in which MRB currently has a strong reputation—would be risky with a new product. If the company reduces these costs and then is unable to provide its current level of service, a loss of reputation could result. Fortunately manufacturing costs were reduced by $5 more than originally planned. Therefore, the team decides not to reduce warranty and support costs at this time.

**Administration.** Some administrative functions, such as payroll, have recently been outsourced. It appears that the administrative cost reduction of $10 per bike will be easily met.

## Total Planned Cost Reduction

The following summary shows the cost reduction estimates achieved by the design team.

| Cost Category | Reduction Needed (Revised) | Reduction Achieved |
|---|---|---|
| New brake development | $ 0 | $ 0 |
| Manufacturing: | 35 | |
|    Reflectors | | 15 |
|    Handlebars | | 10 |
|    Tires | | 5 |
|    Tubes | | 5 |
| Selling and distribution (reduced shipping charges) | 5 | 5 |
| Warranty and support (no reduction necessary) | 0 | 0 |
| Administration (outsourcing services) | 10 | 10 |
| Total | $50 | $50 |

## Pilot Project to Evaluate Feasibility

Once the team reconfigures the bike, a pilot manufacturing line is set up and 100 bikes are produced. The first 50 bikes cost $780 to produce, but the manufacturing line employees learned how to install the new braking system more quickly, so the last 50 bikes cost $730, as projected.

The managers decide to begin full production of the new product. This decision turns out well for the company; the bike sells faster and in larger numbers than anticipated.

---

## GUIDE YOUR LEARNING 13.2   Mount Rainier Bikes (Part 1)

Mount Rainier Bikes (Part 1) illustrates target costing. For this illustration:

| Define It | Identify Problem and Information | Identify Uncertainties | Explore Biases | Prioritize Options |
|---|---|---|---|---|
| Which definitions, analysis techniques, and computations were used? | What decision was being addressed, and what information was relevant to the decision? | What types of uncertainties were there? Consider uncertainties about:<br>• Price and cost estimates<br>• Potential cost reduction opportunities<br>• Ability to achieve cost reductions | Why and how might bias influence the target costing process? | In your own words, describe how each decision was reached for targeted cost reduction. |

# KAIZEN COSTING

**Q3** What is kaizen costing, and how does it compare to target costing?

**INTERNATIONAL**

To meet strategic objectives, Daihatsu, a Japanese manufacturer of compact cars, uses kaizen costing as part of its annual budgeting cycle, building in cost reduction and quality improvement goals.[15]

**Kaizen costing** is continuous improvement in product cost, quality, and functionality. It is similar to target costing in that cost targets (goals) are set based on price predictions. However, kaizen costing occurs after the product has been designed and the first production cycle is complete. Market prices tend to decrease over many products' life cycles. Under kaizen costing, accountants forecast declining prices and establish cost reduction goals to maintain a desired level of profit margin. Therefore, the objectives of kaizen costing include not only continuous improvement, but also continuous cost reduction.

Because kaizen costing relies on sales forecasts, the kaizen plan is similar to a budget, except that kaizen costing provides for explicit cost reductions. Exhibit 13.5 summarizes the kaizen planning process for revenues and costs.

## Planned Cost Reductions

In manufacturing organizations, estimated variable costs are the sum of estimates for direct material and direct labor costs, and variable manufacturing overhead. Accountants and managers develop plans to estimate reductions for these variable costs. Estimated reductions in fixed costs are developed from human resource plans for fixed labor and service department personnel, combined with facility investment plans and the fixed expense plans (design, maintenance, advertising, sales promotions, and general and administrative expenses). These estimated costs are based on the prior period's actual costs, adjusted for any anticipated price changes.

In service organizations, the estimated variable costs are developed from projections of supplies and direct labor that vary with the amount of services provided, variable overhead, and any variable merchandising costs in retail industries. The estimated fixed costs are developed in the same manner used for manufacturing organizations.

## Achieving Planned Cost Reductions

After the targeted cost reduction goals are set, each department is assigned responsibility for specific cost reduction amounts. These goals are met in several ways. One option is to use value chain analysis to redesign the production or service process to increase overall productivity and efficiency. Meetings may be held with manufacturing or service personnel to brainstorm ideas for cost reduction. To encourage idea generation, some companies even share any initial gains in cost reduction with the employees who suggest the cost-reducing changes. Another option is to use supply chain analysis, working with suppliers and issuing target cost reductions for intermediate manufacturing parts or service supplies. Some companies work with suppliers to develop new product and process designs needed to achieve cost reductions.

**EXHIBIT 13.5**
Kaizen Planning Process for Revenues and Costs

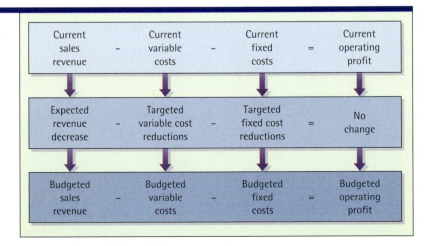

[15]Y. Monden and J. Lee, "How a Japanese Auto Maker Reduces Costs," *Management Accounting,* August 1993, pp. 22–27.

## MOUNT RAINIER BIKES (PART 2)
## KAIZEN COSTING

Mount Rainier Bikes has now been producing Mountain Brakers for two years, and sales are beginning to drop because competitors are producing similar braking systems. MRB's marketing manager believes that if the company wants sales and market share to increase, prices will have to decrease. The accountant recommends that the company use kaizen costing to reduce the price and cost of the Mountain Braker.

### Cost Reductions

The marketing manager estimates that the bike's price should be reduced by 10% to be competitive with other manufacturers. Therefore, costs also need to be reduced by 10% to maintain the same percentage margin, although the dollar value of the margin will decrease. The bike's current price is $950 with a cost of $855. The new price will be $855, and the corresponding cost reduction needed is $85.50. The current margin is $95, and the new margin will be $85.50. The following summary assumes that reductions will be made proportionately across all cost categories:

| Cost Category | Current Cost per Bike | Needed Cost Reduction (10% goal) |
|---|---|---|
| New brake development | $ 50 | $ 5.00 |
| Manufacturing | 675 | 67.50 |
| Selling and distribution | 50 | 5.00 |
| Warranty and support | 35 | 3.50 |
| Administration | 45 | 4.50 |
| Total | $855 | $85.50 |

The same team that developed the Mountain Braker at target cost in the design phase meets again to suggest further cost reduction plans. After careful analysis, they find no way to reduce costs for the new braking system at this time. Therefore, the $5 needed cost reduction for the brakes will have to come from another process or component.

**Process Design Changes.** Using value chain analysis, the team reviews both the manufacturing processes and the bike design, searching for non-value-added activities or components that can be eliminated. A new gear system has been developed by one of the vendors that eliminates two steps in the manufacturing process. As a result, the engineer estimates that one laborer could be moved to another bike production line to replace a retiring worker, reducing total labor costs. This reduction amounts to $10 per bike.

**Supply Chain Analysis.** The MRB team meets with suppliers to determine whether cost reductions or product improvements are possible from the components used in manufacturing. The wheel and spoke vendor has improved the quality of its product and dropped the price, saving $13 per bike. A new bike frame that is just as solid as the current frame has been developed from an innovative new alloy and will save MRB $35.

At the end of the last quarter, the supplier of tubes and tires asked for a small price increase. The purchasing department surveys vendor Web sites for tubes and tires. After contacting several different vendors, a price reduction is negotiated with a new supplier of tires. An additional vendor is added to supply tubes at a reduced price. These two cost savings amount to $10 per bike.

Overall, the team is able to achieve total cost reduction for manufacturing of $68 ($10 + $13 + $35 + $10). This amount is $0.50 more than is needed from manufacturing, but leaves a $4.50 required reduction because the cost of brakes could not be reduced.

**Nonmanufacturing Costs.** The team now turns its attention to achieving the remaining cost reductions. The marketing representative points out that several top mountain bike race competitors currently using the new bike generate sales efficiently. Relying on their efforts costs less than the current advertising campaign. Therefore, the team decides to reduce advertising costs by $5 per bike, which meets the selling and distribution cost target. Warranty and support costs are significantly lower than anticipated, primarily because the new braking system is so reliable. A reduction of $8 is easily attainable at this time. This amount is $4.50 ahead of target, making up for the lack of cost reduction from the brakes.

The team member from administration mentions that a new information system was installed last quarter. The department dropped some non-value-added activities, such as manual entry of production data. One staff member resigned and will not be replaced. The savings will be at least the needed $4.50 per bike.

The overall cost reduction targets and estimates are as follows:

| Cost Category | Kaizen Cost Reduction | Actual Cost Reduction |
|---|---|---|
| New brake development | $ 5.00 | $ 0.00 |
| Manufacturing: | 67.50 | |
|     Process change | | 10.00 |
|     Wheel and spoke system | | 13.00 |
|     Frame | | 35.00 |
|     Tires and tubes | | 10.00 |
| Selling and distribution | 5.00 | 5.00 |
| Warranty and support | 3.50 | 8.00 |
| Administration | 4.50 | 4.50 |
| Total | $85.50 | $85.50 |

### Continuous Monitoring of Costs

The team reports back to the accounting department that the overall cost reduction targets can be met. Once the changes have been made, the marketing department decides to cut costs even further. However, a problem arises with the braking system. To maintain the current quality, MRB will have to pay $4 more for components because several vendors raised their prices. With these two changes, MRB is still below the kaizen cost reduction target.

---

**GUIDE YOUR LEARNING** `13.3` **Mount Rainier Bikes (Part 2)**

Mount Rainier Bike (Part 2) illustrates kaizen costing. For this illustration:

| Define It | Identify Problem and Information | Identify Uncertainties | Explore Biases | Prioritize Options |
|---|---|---|---|---|
| Which definitions, analysis techniques, and computations were used? In your own words, explain how kaizen costing is different from target costing. | What decision was being addressed, and what information was relevant to the decision? | What types of uncertainties were there? Consider uncertainties about: <br>• Price and cost estimates <br>• Potential cost reduction opportunities <br>• Ability to achieve cost reductions | Why and how might bias influence the kaizen costing process? | In your own words, describe how each decision was reached for kaizen cost reduction. |

---

## ■ Using Target and Kaizen Costing over Time

Target and kaizen costing are used together in organizations facing declining prices across time. Exhibit 13.6 provides a generic time line showing the use of these two methods across a product's life cycle. Some organizations may lower margins before dropping the product, but at some point the product is discontinued because cost is equal to price and no further cost reductions are possible.

Exhibit 13.7 compares target costing and kaizen costing, listing their similarities, differences, and common advantages and disadvantages.

## LIFE CYCLE COSTING

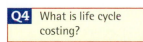

**Q4** What is life cycle costing?

**Life cycle costing** is a decision-making method that considers changes in price and costs over the entire life cycle of a good or service, from the time the product is introduced through a number of years. Some products have high up-front costs such as research and development; other products may incur large costs when the product is abandoned, such as environmental cleanup costs. Sometimes products cannot achieve high revenues at the beginning

**EXHIBIT 13.6**
Target and Kaizen
Costing over Time for
a Product

| | Time | | |
|---|---|---|---|
| Before production | First production period | Continuous production | Drop product |
| Target costing | Cost is maintained | Kaizen costing | |
| Product and manufacturing process design | Manufacturing at target cost | Periodic cost reduction goals set and met | No further cost reductions available |

of their life, but generate increasing revenues over the product's life cycle. Under target costing, such products might be rejected even though they have good long-term potential. Under life cycle costing, managers consider the profitability of the product over a number of years. If forecasts predict that sales, over time, will cover all product costs and eventually add to profits, a life cycle budget is developed for both manufacturing and environmental costs, so that decision makers can evaluate their decision and identify possible areas for cost reductions across time.

Life cycle costing is used when the initial product is produced and sold at a loss, but accountants and managers anticipate that a combination of continued sales volumes and cost reductions over time will lead to profits in the long term. It is also used to identify products that may not be profitable when the costs of decommissioning the operation are included as part of total product costs, for example, environmental cleanup costs when mines are shut down. In addition, life cycle costing is used to focus managers' attention on the high development or decommissioning costs during the product and manufacturing design phase to encourage them to manage all of these costs as they develop new products.

The opening vignette about the **Microsoft** Xbox is an example of a product decision that considered the product's life cycle. Microsoft's managers decided to sell Xbox at a loss, but they expected continuing sales of games to eventually create profits for the entire product line. In addition, Microsoft probably anticipates manufacturing cost reductions for the Xbox over time. Another example of life cycle costing is the manufacture of printers and ink cartridges. Printers are often sold at a loss, but the revenue streams from ink cartridges more than make up for these initial losses.

**CURRENT PRACTICE**

CPA firms sometimes forgo profits on initial audit engagements, when considerable time is spent to learn a new client's business. Later, audits are completed more quickly, so profits increase.

**EXHIBIT 13.7**
Target Costing Compared to
Kaizen Costing

**Similarities**
- Rely on goal setting to achieve cost reduction
- Focus on product design and the manufacturing process to find ways to reduce costs
- Encourage organizations to work with suppliers to reduce costs
- Use functional teams to determine where costs can be cut
- Encourage employees to take an active part in the cost-cutting decision-making process
- Take advantage of the trade-offs among price, functionality, and quality
- Focus on continuous improvements in products and processes

**Differences**
- Target costing occurs at beginning of the product life cycle and kaizen after that
- Target costing sets a single goal for cost; kaizen sets cost-reduction goals

**Common Advantage**
- Use of goal setting encourages better performance

**Common Disadvantages**
- Stress of cost reduction environment can impair employee well-being
- Encourages organizations to forgo some products having long-term profit potential

## SECTION 2  Price Management

## PRICING METHODS

**Q5** How are cost-based prices established?

Determining appropriate prices for an organization's products or services is an important activity because pricing decisions have both short- and long-term consequences. The Microsoft Xbox case indicates that, even in markets with few competitors, prices are often based on competitor's prices, not just production costs.

### ■ Cost-Based Pricing

**Cost-based prices** are determined by adding a markup to some calculation of the product's cost. To apply this method, both a cost base and a markup rate are selected. The cost base can be calculated in several ways. Some organizations use variable cost as the base, whereas others use an average cost that includes both variable and fixed costs. Organizations frequently rely on markups they have used for many years. Such markups often originate from general industry practice and may be found in trade journals. For example, clothing retailers typically price using a 100% markup on their variable costs. If a retailer pays $10 per blouse to the wholesaler, the variable cost per blouse is $10, and the blouse would be priced at $20. Markup percentages are also chosen so that the organization earns a target rate of return on investment. Given differences in calculation methods and cost structures, cost-based prices vary a great deal across organizations.

Suppose Jackson Jets is a small company that customizes Learjets for wealthy clients. At present, the company's managers are negotiating with three potential customers for next year's sales. The company's accountants summarized cost information for each plane as follows:

**ALTERNATIVE TERMS**

We learned in Chapter 1 that *avoidable (incremental) cash flows* are relevant because they can be avoided depending on the course of action taken. Conversely, *unavoidable cash flows* are not relevant.

|  | Potential Customer | | | |
| --- | --- | --- | --- | --- |
| (In Thousands) | Rock Star | CEO | Sports Figure | Total |
| Avoidable costs | | | | |
| Basic jet plane | $ 800 | $ 800 | $ 800 | $2,400 |
| Production | 200 | 1,200 | 600 | 2,000 |
| Selling costs | 100 | 200 | 100 | 400 |
| Total avoidable costs | $1,100 | $2,200 | $1,500 | $4,800 |
| Unavoidable costs | | | | |
| Production | | | | $3,000 |
| Administration | | | | 600 |
| Total unavoidable costs | | | | $3,600 |

The unavoidable costs are the overhead costs to customize the jets, such as facility costs (rent or depreciation, etc.) and equipment-related costs. These costs are primarily fixed.

The company has a policy of calculating price by applying a 50% markup on cost. Two potential cost-based pricing schemes follow.

**Alternative A.** Under this alternative, unavoidable costs are allocated to the three contracts equally ($3,600 ÷ 3 jets = $1,200 per jet). Then a markup of 50% is added to total costs as follows:

|  | Potential Customer | | | |
| --- | --- | --- | --- | --- |
| (In Thousands) | Rock Star | CEO | Sports Figure | Total |
| Total avoidable costs | $1,100 | $2,200 | $1,500 | $ 4,800 |
| Allocated unavoidable costs | 1,200 | 1,200 | 1,200 | 3,600 |
| Total cost | $2,300 | $3,400 | $2,700 | $ 8,400 |
| Price (150% of total cost) | $3,450 | $5,100 | $4,050 | $12,600 |

**Alternative B.** Under this alternative, unavoidable costs are allocated to each contract based on its proportion of avoidable costs. For example, the rock star's allocated cost is ($1,100 ÷ $4,800) × $3,600 = $825. A markup of 50% is then added to total costs to arrive at the price as follows:

|  | Potential Customer | | | |
| --- | --- | --- | --- | --- |
| (In Thousands) | Rock Star | CEO | Sports Figure | Total |
| Total avoidable costs | $1,100 | $2,200 | $1,500 | $ 4,800 |
| Allocated unavoidable costs | 825 | 1,650 | 1,125 | 3,600 |
| Total cost | $1,925 | $3,850 | $2,625 | $ 8,400 |
| Price (150% of total cost) | $2,887 | $5,775 | $3,938 | $12,600 |

Which alternative would you recommend? Would you want any additional information before making this decision? As illustrated by these two price alternatives, determining product cost is not straightforward. Decision makers always face uncertainty in determining an appropriate cost base. The price differences under alternatives A and B are caused by arbitrary allocations for overhead costs that cannot be attributed directly to the product. Should such allocations influence prices? To avoid this problem, some companies use only avoidable costs in their price calculations. However, they also face uncertainty in determining an appropriate markup percentage. Why is the markup 50% and not 20%, 30%, or some other amount? What should the markup be if only avoidable costs are included in the calculation? Most important, what are customers willing to pay?

# ■ Market-Based Pricing

**Q6** How are market-based prices established?

High quality and brand name for a company such as Jackson Jets are likely to be as important, if not more important, than price. Accordingly, a cost-based pricing scheme might not maximize profits. As the company's managers make pricing decisions, they need to understand competitors' prices; however, they should also consider each buyer's ability and willingness to pay for the product. To maximize profits, Jackson Jets should charge the highest price possible, but not such a high price that the customer buys from a competitor or decides not to buy a jet.

**Market-based prices** are determined using some measure of customer demand. Under market-based pricing, managers strive to identify what customers are willing to pay for a good or service. As illustrated in Exhibit 13.8, market prices are influenced by the degree of product differentiation and competition.

At one extreme, organizations face many competitors and cannot differentiate their products. In this case, the market price is the commodity price that customers would pay to any organization offering the good or service. For example, farmers typically sell agricultural products at a quoted market price. The same is true for mining companies selling gold or silver. In such cases, managers estimate prices by referring to published rates.

At the other extreme are monopolies selling unique goods or services and having no competition. Monopolies such as residential water services are often owned or regulated by the government. In these cases, the organization is not allowed to establish a free market price, but must charge the regulated price. Occasionally short-term monopolies arise. For example, the only store in town with snow shovels after a blizzard can theoretically charge as much as the market will bear, until competitors receive shovel shipments. Most goods and services fall between these two extremes. Organizations can typically differentiate their product in the

**EXHIBIT 13.8**
Market Prices, Product
Differentiation, and Degree
of Competition

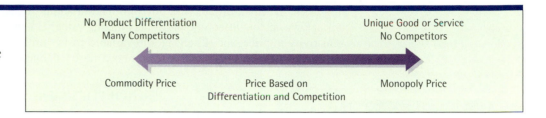

No Product Differentiation
Many Competitors

Unique Good or Service
No Competitors

Commodity Price

Price Based on
Differentiation and Competition

Monopoly Price

market because features and brand names are important. However, these organizations are subject to competition, which must be considered when setting prices. To set prices, they estimate consumer demand for product characteristics such as quality and functionality.

## PROFIT-MAXIMIZING MARKET-BASED PRICE

**Q6** How are market-based prices established?

**CURRENT PRACTICE**

Some states increased cigarette taxes to discourage teenage cigarette sales. When cigarette prices jumped 70% from 1997 to 2000, the proportion of teens who smoked dropped from 36% to 29%.[16]

Organizations with differentiated products can formally or informally incorporate consumer demand into their pricing policies. For example, contractors who build expensive houses often negotiate prices with individual buyers. The negotiations continue throughout the construction period when unforeseen costs arise or when the home buyer makes choices such as carpeting and wall coverings that are more expensive than anticipated. A more formal way to incorporate demand into prices is through the price elasticity of demand.

### ■ Price Elasticity of Demand

As prices increase, demand usually falls. This sensitivity of sales to price increases is called the **price elasticity of demand.** Cigarettes are an example of a product where changes in price have a substantial effect on sales; that is, demand is elastic. In contrast, customized planes such as Jackson Jets are a product with relatively inelastic demand. Price changes have little effect on demand, and factors such as quality and the ability to customize are more important, within limits, than price.

To develop a price that maximizes profit, we follow the steps shown in Exhibit 13.9. The first step is to calculate the price elasticity of demand. To perform this calculation, data must be available to calculate the percentage change in quantity that occurs for a percentage change in price. The second step is to determine the profit-maximizing price, a calculation that is based on the strong assumption that changes in volume result *only* from changes in price. This assumption is never completely true, however, so the markup amount needs to be interpreted with caution. It only provides guidance about pricing decisions.

**EXHIBIT 13.9**
Computing the
Profit-Maximizing
Price

**Step 1: Calculate the price elasticity of demand.**

$$\text{Elasticity} = \frac{\ln(1 + \% \text{ change in quantity sold})}{\ln(1 + \% \text{ change in price})}$$

where ln is the mathematical function for natural logarithm

**Step 2: Calculate the profit-maximizing price.[a]**

$$\text{Profit-maximizing price} = \left[\frac{\text{Elasticity}}{(\text{Elasticity} + 1)}\right] \times \text{Variable cost}$$

[a]The profit-maximizing markup formula is $\left[\frac{\text{Elasticity}}{(\text{Elasticity} + 1)} - 1\right]$. We add 1 to the markup before we multiply it by variable cost to determine the profit-maximizing price.

---

[16]Sources: Centers for Disease Control, available at www.cdc.gov; H. Ross and F. Chaloupka, "The Effect of Cigarette Prices on Youth Smoking," *Health Economics,* 12(3), (March 2003), p. 217; and "Tobacco and Taxes: Smoke Alarm," *The Economist,* March 2, 2002, p. 71.

These calculations are based on information about prices, sales volumes, and variable costs. Two factors affect the profit-maximizing price: (1) changes in the product's demand sensitivity to price, and (2) changes in variable costs. Information about fixed costs is irrelevant. The following illustration shows how these calculations help a company set prices.

## FRENCH PERFUMERY
### USING PRICE ELASTICITY TO CALCULATE PRODUCT PRICES

French Perfumery produces two perfumes: Breezy and Exotique. Breezy is a well-known inexpensive perfume, and its customers are sensitive to price. Several competitors market similar products, and close substitutes are available at discount drug and department stores. Exotique is a customized perfume sold only in small boutique stores where few substitutes are available and where customers are less sensitive to price. French's accountant, Mimi, needs to develop pricing guidelines for management. She performs the following analysis.

### Profit-Maximizing Prices for Breezy and Exotique

Mimi calculates the variable cost of Breezy as $2 per ounce and $10 per ounce for Exotique. Based on information from historical accounting records, she believes that every 10% increase in price for Breezy results in a decrease in sales of 20% because customers for this product are so price sensitive. She calculates the price elasticity for Breezy as −2.34 [ln(1 − 0.2) ÷ ln(1 + 0.1)]. In turn, she uses the elasticity to calculate a profit-maximizing price of $3.50 {[−2.34 ÷ (−2.34 + 1)] × $2}.

Mimi estimates that for every 10% increase in price, sales of Exotique would decrease only 12%. She calculates the price elasticity of demand for Exotique as −1.34 [ln(1 − 0.12) ÷ ln(1 + 0.1)]. The profit-maximizing price is then $39.40 {[−1.34 ÷ (−1.34 + 1)] × $10}. According to these calculations, the markup for Breezy is 75% and the markup for Exotique is 294%. Exotique's demand is less sensitive to price changes than Breezy's, so Mimi knows that Exotique's demand is more inelastic. Products or services with inelastic demand have higher optimal markups than products or services with more elastic demand.

### Market Price Guidelines

When Mimi presents her calculations to managers, she cautions them about this information. Although the calculations seem precise, they should be interpreted only as guidelines for price setting, not absolute determinants of price. She warns them that similar to other decisions, the managers need to consider uncertainties when making pricing decisions. For example, measurement error may occur in collecting information about how price changes affect sales. She explains to the managers that these formulas are extremely sensitive to errors, and small changes in assumptions create a large effect on the calculations. Also, price elasticity can vary over time due to changes in competitor prices and customer preferences. Managers need to anticipate and monitor for changes in product demand.

Mimi also explains the following assumptions underlying her calculations:

- The price elasticity of demand is constant.
- The variable cost is constant.
- The product price has no effect on other product costs or sales.

The managers know that these assumptions may not always hold, so they decide to make small incremental changes to prices and then track profitability to determine the profit-maximizing price.

## GUIDE YOUR LEARNING  13.5  French Perfumery

French Perfumery illustrates profit-maximizing prices. For this illustration:

| Define It | Identify Uncertainties | Compare Alternatives | Explore Assumptions |
|---|---|---|---|
| In your own words, describe how a profit-maximizing price is calculated. | Is it possible to know the change in quantity sold for a given change in price? Explain. | Compare the process of developing a profit-maximizing price with the process of developing a cost-based price. Given the input information required, is one method more "certain" than the other? Explain. | Are the assumptions for a profit-maximizing price likely to be reasonable for French Perfumery? |

## ■ Estimating the Effect of Prices on Demand

Accountants use historical information to estimate the effects of price changes on sales volume. Some organizations might rely on price elasticity information published by their industries. Other organizations use optical scanners to capture historical price and volume data. The quality of this type of information improves as sales volumes increase. Companies can rapidly gather data and monitor relationships between price and volume. They can also analyze how sales behave for groups of products. For example, grocery stores often sell some products as "loss leaders," lowering the price on a specific product to bring customers into the store. In these cases, managers assume that increases in sales of other products will more than make up for the forgone profit from the loss leader.

The quality of product demand estimates using historical data depends in part on sales volumes. Large retailers collect large amounts of sales data and conduct price experiments to learn more about how volumes respond to price changes. Organizations with lower sales volumes also collect sales and price data, but they are likely to face more error in their estimates of product demand.

## OTHER MARKET-BASED PRICING METHODS

**Q6** How are market-based prices established?

As illustrated with the **Microsoft** Xbox, companies sometimes use competitors' prices to establish their own market prices. For common products in retail settings, competitors' prices are easily observed. However, it may be difficult to learn about competitors' prices when fewer transactions occur or are made in nonretail settings.

The Internet makes it possible to learn about market prices for items that were previously difficult to value. Auction Web sites such as **e-Bay**, **Bidz**, **Yahoo!**, and **Amazon** provide information on prices. Given the large range of products and prices that are readily available, these sites increase the consistency of prices, even for objects such as antiques. Because increasing numbers of organizations include product and service price information on their Web sites, the Internet also makes it easier for managers to monitor competitors' prices.

The Internet is likely to cause prices to become more elastic because close substitutes are more easily found and priced. The Internet also increases the global reach of many companies. Together, the Internet and global competition have forced an increasingly large number of organizations to use market-based pricing.

## COST-BASED VERSUS MARKET-BASED PRICING

**Q7** What are the uses and limitations of cost-based and market-based pricing?

A major drawback of cost-based pricing is that it ignores customer demand. Prices are likely to be higher or lower than what customers are willing to pay for goods or services. For example, **Motorola** based the price of its global cellular phones on costs, rather than surveying the market for a competitive price. This decision resulted first in prices for the phone and calling rates that were higher than customers would pay, and eventually contributed to the bankruptcy of the entire project. In other situations, cost-based prices are too low, and organizations forgo potential profits.

With cost-based prices, sales volumes inappropriately influence the price, causing a downward demand spiral, known as the **death spiral.** If production decreases because demand has decreased, then the average product cost increases and the price based on that average cost increases. When the product has an elastic demand curve, price increases cause sales to decline even more. This decline, in turn, causes average cost to increase even further, producing more price increases and more sales deterioration. This pattern persists until the product is discontinued because it cannot cover its costs.

[17]A. Cortese, "The Power of Optimal Pricing," *Business 2.0,* September 2002, pp. 68–70, available at www.business2.com/b2/.

Despite these disadvantages, cost-based pricing is the most commonly used method in the United States.[18] Surveys of manufacturers consistently report that they prefer to mark up an average cost that includes a portion of fixed cost, using a markup system based on desired return.[19] This preference might reflect the fact that it was difficult in the past for companies' information systems to gather the data needed to calculate profit-maximizing sales prices. The major benefit of using cost-based pricing is its simplicity. Prices are calculated from readily available cost data.

Using market-based prices to estimate revenues, managers make better decisions about sales volumes or whether to sell goods or services, leading to more success in organizational strategies. The disadvantage is that estimating market demand and prices is often difficult. However, more sophisticated information systems make it easier for managers to estimate demand, marginal costs, and revenues, leading to an increasing trend in the use of market-based pricing.

## OTHER INFLUENCES ON PRICE

**Q8** What additional factors affect prices?

**CURRENT PRACTICE**

During a recent recession (2001), two reporters from *The Wall Street Journal* visited 50 retail stores and negotiated prices at 18 of them, including Nordic Track, Sunglass Hut, and Eddie Bauer.[20]

Regardless of the general technique used, a number of other factors influence prices for individual organizations or in specific circumstances.

Some industries charge different prices at different times to reduce capacity constraints, a practice called **peak load pricing.** For example, movie theatres charge less for movies shown early in the day. Telephone companies often charge less for calls made at night or on the weekend. In the airline industry, a variety of prices are offered to customers based on factors such as advanced ticket purchase, whether the customer is traveling for business or leisure, and whether the customer wants preferential seating and other services. During economic downturns, even organizations with set prices may negotiate with customers.

**Price skimming** occurs when a higher price is charged for a product or service when it is first introduced. The term refers to the practice of skimming the cream off the market. When new technology is introduced, such as notepads that transcribe handwriting to word processing, high prices are charged to cover the initial research and development. Prices are then reduced as competitors enter the market.

**Penetration pricing** is the practice of setting low prices when new products are introduced to increase market share. This practice describes Microsoft's willingness to reduce the price of Xbox to match its competition. Penetration pricing is legal if its intent is to reduce customer uncertainty about product or service value. However, if the purpose is to eliminate competition, then it could be considered predatory pricing, which is illegal in the United States.

Sometimes managers take advantage of unusual circumstances to increase prices. **Price gouging** is the practice of charging a price viewed by consumers as too high. If managers can convince consumers that prices are based on costs, they avoid being labeled as price gougers. After deregulation, energy brokers in California and New York were considered to have price gouged.

**Transfer prices** are the prices charged for transactions that take place within an organization. Prices are set for the use of support departments such as human resources and accounting. In a manufacturing setting, intermediate products are often transferred to other departments where further assembly takes place before the final product is sold to external markets. These intermediate products need to be priced so that appropriate decisions can be made about the value of selling products internally or externally. Transfer price policies also have incentive and tax effects; they are discussed in more detail in Chapter 15.

---

[18]*Survey of American Manufacturers* (New York: Grant Thornton, 1992); and K. Mochtar and D. Arditi, "Pricing Strategy in the US Construction Industry," *Construction Management and Economics,* July 2001, pp. 405–415.
[19]E. Shim and E. Sudit, "How Manufacturers Price Products," *Management Accounting,* February 1995.
[20]T. Agins and S. Collins, "A Haggler's Christmas," *The Wall Street Journal,* November 16, 2001, p. W1.

## FOCUS ON ETHICAL DECISION MAKING
### Price Gouging after Tragedy

The terrorist events of September 11, 2001, disrupted commerce throughout the United States. Some managers immediately raised their prices. For example, prices doubled or tripled at many gasoline stations. Such price increases caused public anger, and government officials in several states took action against the gasoline station owners for charging prices so far over market levels.

Managers of other businesses refrained from increasing their prices, even though product demand increased. For example, the suspension of air traffic increased the demand for rental cars. Most rental car companies extended customers' rental periods without increasing rental rates. They also waived the charges customers are usually required to pay for dropping cars off at a location different from where the car was rented.

SOURCE: T. Egan, "After the Attacks: The Profiteers," *The New York Times*, September 15, 2001.

### Practice Ethical Decision Making

In Chapter 1, we learned about a process for making ethical decisions (Exhibit 1.11). You can address the following questions for this ethical dilemma to improve your skills for making ethical decisions. Think about your answers to these questions and discuss them with others.

| Ethical Decision-Making Process | Questions to Consider about This Ethical Dilemma |
| --- | --- |
| Identify ethical problems as they arise. | Following the events of September 11, 2001, did increased demand create an ethical problem for setting prices? Why or why not? |
| Objectively consider the well-being of others and society when exploring alternatives. | What might have motivated the gasoline station managers to increase their prices? What might have motivated rental car managers to forgo extra charges? What might have been the assumptions of each group of managers? What might have been the ethical values of each group? |
| Clarify and apply ethical values when choosing a course of action. | Identify the values you use as you answer the following questions:<br>• Is it wrong for managers to increase their prices when customers are willing to pay a higher price?<br>• At what point does an organization's price increase become inappropriate? |
| Work toward ongoing improvement of personal and organizational ethics. | How can managers ensure that the prices they charge are ethical? |

## PRICING IN NOT-FOR-PROFIT ORGANIZATIONS

 **Q8** What additional factors affect prices?

Not-for-profit organizations are concerned with many objectives other than profit maximization. Their pricing methods tend to be more complex than those used by for-profit organizations. Grants, donations, and interest from endowed funds often help defray the cost of products and services. Because of these sources of funds, not-for-profits do not always expect to recover all of their costs from prices or fees they charge.

Some not-for-profit organizations charge a fee based on the client's income. This fee is called a sliding scale fee; as client income decreases, the fee decreases. Clients who can afford to pay more are charged more. Other not-for-profits charge high prices to everyone, but then provide charity services for low-income clients or discount the charges to selected clients. For example, hospitals might set prices for services high enough that revenues from insured patients cover the costs of providing services to uninsured patients. In addition, Medicaid often pays for only a portion of the costs incurred by Medicaid patients. Therefore, hospital managers attempt to use pricing policies to shift some of these costs to other patients. The result is that charity care and treatment of Medicaid patients tend to inflate hospital prices for other patients.

Some not-for-profit organizations use price-setting policies to achieve organizational goals. For example, many universities discount tuition or offer grants and scholarships to students with high SAT scores and GPAs. Their goal is to improve the quality of incoming students. A stronger student body enhances these schools' reputations and may in turn increase the number of applicants.

## GOVERNMENT REGULATIONS AND PRICING

**Q8** What additional factors affect prices?

Organizations are not free to establish any price they wish; some pricing practices are illegal. In the United States, illegal practices include price discrimination, predatory pricing, collusive pricing, and dumping. Courts often use costs to determine whether an organization has violated laws.

**Price discrimination** is the practice of setting different prices for different customers. Although not-for-profit organizations charge prices according to ability to pay, U.S. regulations forbid for-profit organizations from charging some customers higher prices for the same product if the intent is to lessen or prevent competition for customers. Organizations can use cost differences as a defense against price discrimination charges.

It is also illegal for organizations to practice **predatory pricing,** which is the deliberate act of setting prices low to drive competitors out of the market and then raising prices. However, low prices are not considered predatory if they can be justified by cost differences.

Many governments also forbid **collusive pricing,** which occurs when two or more organizations conspire to set prices above a competitive price. Consumer welfare is harmed by such practices. In 2001, the **Federal Trade Commission (FTC)** investigated differences in gasoline prices in western states, looking for evidence of collusion. They found that the gasoline companies were employing "zone pricing," with different prices set within different small geographic areas. Although they found the gasoline companies' pricing practices "reprehensible" and "oligopolistic," they concluded that current laws were not violated.[22]

Under U.S. laws, **dumping** occurs when a foreign-based company sells products in the United States at prices below the market value in the country where the product is produced and the price could harm a U.S. industry. The U.S. government imposes an antidumping tariff. The tariff is set so that the new price will be equivalent to the prices charged by U.S. companies. These rules have been applied in a number of industries, most recently in the computer chip industry. Other countries enact similar laws to protect home country manufacturers from unfair competition from foreign businesses. For example, from 1999 through 2000, steel exports from India grew by 53%. Because prices for Indian steel were much lower than domestic prices in the United States, Canada, and Europe, these governments levied antidumping duties on certain steel products to protect the domestic industry.[23]

---

**GUIDE YOUR LEARNING** `13.6` Key Terms

Stop to confirm that you understand the new terms introduced in the last several pages.

Cost-based prices (p. 525)
Market-based prices (p. 526)
Price elasticity of demand (p. 527)
Death spiral (p. 529)
*Peak load pricing (p. 530)
*Price skimming (p. 530)
*Penetration pricing (p. 530)

*Price gouging (p. 530)
Transfer prices (p. 530)
*Price discrimination (p. 532)
*Predatory pricing (p. 532)
Collusive pricing (p. 532)
Dumping (p. 532)

For each of these terms, write a definition in your own words. For starred terms, list at least one example that is different from the ones given in this textbook.

---

[21]J. Kronholz, "On Sale Now: College Tuition," *The Wall Street Journal,* May 16, 2002, p. D1.
[22]J. Wilke, "FTC Drops Probe of Gas Pricing in West, Says Refiners Didn't Violate Antitrust Law," *The Wall Street Journal,* May 8, 2001, p. A14.
[23]R. Krishnan, "Anti-dumping Action: Steel Industry's Bane," *Hindu Business Line* (Internet publication), January 20, 2002.

# SUMMARY

**Q1** How Is Value Chain Analysis Used to Improve Operations?

### Goal
Continuously improve costs over the long term by:
- Enhancing efficiency
- Reducing costs
- Improving interactions with suppliers and customers
- Identifying and eliminating non-value-added activities
- Minimizing rework, scrap, and waste
- Reducing production cycle time
- Negotiating lower prices with suppliers

### Supply Chain Analysis

### Just-in-Time Production or Inventory Control Systems
Systems in which materials are purchased and units are produced as customers demand them

### Manufacturer Value Chain

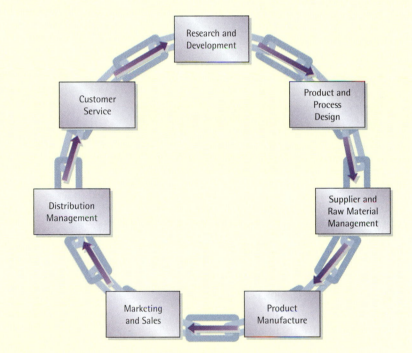

**Q2** What Is Target Costing, and How Is It Performed?

### Target Costing
Decision-making method that considers prices as given and then determines whether products and services can be provided at costs low enough for an acceptable profit

### Target Costing Design Cycle

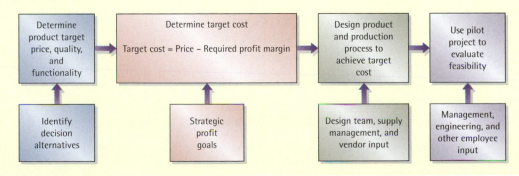

**Q3** What Is Kaizen Costing, and How Does It Compare to Target Costing?

## Kaizen Costing

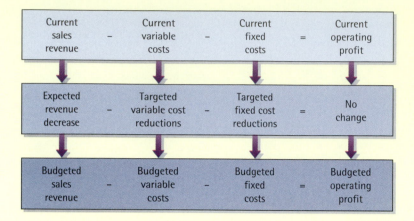

## Comparison of Kaizen and Target Costing

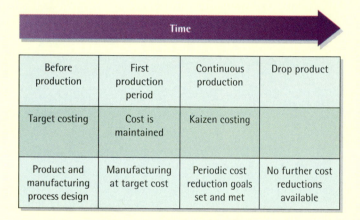

**Q4** What Is Life Cycle Costing?

### Life Cycle Costing

Consider changes in price and costs over the entire life cycle of a good or service, from the time the product is introduced through a number of years

- Allow initial losses or large decommissioning costs
- Expect a combination of sales volume increases and cost reductions over time

**Q5** How Are Cost-Based Prices Established?

### Cost-Based Price

$$\text{Price} = \text{Cost} \times (1 + \text{Markup \%})$$

### Must Choose:

- Measure of cost (variable, fixed and variable, etc.)
- Markup %

**Q6** How Are Market-Based Prices Established?

### Factors Affecting Market Prices

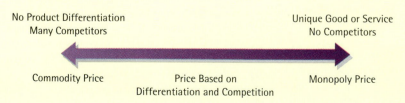

## Computations for Profit-Maximizing Price

Step 1: Calculate the price elasticity of demand.

$$\text{Elasticity} = \frac{\ln(1 + \% \text{ change in quantity sold})}{\ln(1 + \% \text{ change in price})}$$

Step 2: Calculate the profit-maximizing price.

$$\text{Profit-maximizing price} = \left[ \frac{\text{Elasticity}}{(\text{Elasticity} + 1)} \right] \times \text{Variable cost}$$

## Other Market-Based Pricing Methods

Match competitors' prices using information from
- Competitor retail stores
- Competitor Web sites
- Internet auction sites

## Q7 What Are the Uses and Limitations of Cost-Based and Market-Based Pricing?

### Advantages and Disadvantages

|  | Cost-Based Pricing | Market-Based Pricing |
|---|---|---|
| Advantages | • Most commonly used method<br>• Simple<br>• Calculated from readily available cost data | • Offers better decisions about how much or whether to sell a product<br>• Provides better success with strategies |
| Disadvantages | • Ignores customer demand<br>• Prices may be too high or too low<br>• Sales volumes inappropriately influence price if fixed costs are included | • Difficult to estimate market demand and prices<br>• Method not commonly used |

## Q8 What Additional Factors Affect Prices?

### Other Influences on Price
- Peak load pricing
- Price skimming
- Penetration pricing
- Price gouging
- Transfer prices
- Prices are often based on ability to pay
- Organizational goals influence prices

### Pricing in Not-for-Profit Organizations
- Prices need not cover costs
- Different prices can be set for different customers

### Governmental Regulations
- Price discrimination
- Predatory pricing
- Collusive pricing
- Dumping

---

### KEY TO SYMBOLS

**e** This question requires students to extend knowledge beyond the applications shown in the textbook.

**1** This question requires Step 1 skills (**Identifying**) in Steps for Better Thinking (Exhibit 1.10).

**2** This question requires Step 2 skills (**Exploring**) in Steps for Better Thinking (Exhibit 1.10).

**3** This question requires Step 3 skills (**Prioritizing**) in Steps for Better Thinking (Exhibit 1.10).

**4** This question requires Step 4 skills (**Envisioning**) in Steps for Better Thinking (Exhibit 1.10).

## Self-Study Problems

### Self-Study Problem 1   Target and Kaizen Costing

**Q2, Q3**

You have recently been hired as an accountant for a start-up firm in the computer peripherals industry. The owners have developed and are manufacturing several wireless devices to enhance user mobility, such as a small electronic notebook. They want to become more competitive in this market and also develop several other products. They have asked you for ideas about ways to control costs and determine whether proposed new products will be profitable.

**REQUIRED:**

❷ Write a memo to the owners describing how they could use target costing and kaizen costing.

### Solution to Self-Study Problem 1

Many possible approaches may be taken to write a memo on these topics. The body of one possible memo follows. Note that the memo is written to inform and help the managers of the company make a decision.

> You asked for my recommendations about ways to control costs and to determine whether proposed new products will be profitable. In this memo I briefly describe two techniques—target costing and kaizen costing—that could be implemented to achieve these goals.
>
> **Target Costing.** Target costing helps determine whether a proposed new product will be profitable. This technique involves the following steps:
>
> - Estimate the market price of the proposed product.
> - Given the market price, determine what the cost must be to achieve our desired profitability.
> - Estimate the costs of producing the product. If the estimated cost exceeds the target cost, search for ways to reduce costs. Drop the product idea if it is not feasible to achieve the target cost.
> - For potentially feasible new products, conduct pilot production projects to further evaluate estimated costs.
>
> The biggest advantage of target costing is that it would help us focus on ways to design products and manufacturing processes to meet our profitability goals. If costs are too high, we will be forced to look for ways to reduce them, which might also lead us to make changes to the proposed features of a new product.
>
> The target costing process would also help us involve everyone in the company in making product decisions and setting cost goals. This involvement would encourage employees to "buy in" to the target costs, which will help us achieve them.
>
> **Kaizen Costing.** Kaizen costing helps control costs over the life of a product, taking into account the fact that selling prices decline over some product's life. The process for kaizen costing is similar to the process described for target costing. We would estimate the future selling prices of our existing products and determine the cost we need to achieve for our desired profit.
>
> Kaizen costing would help us make decisions about products we wish to continue. If we cannot find ways to reduce costs to achieve desired profitability, then we should consider dropping it.
>
> **Risks.** I believe that both of these methods would help us meet our goals. However, you should be aware of three major risks:
>
> - Both methods involve a great deal of estimation for prices and costs. The rapid change in our industry presents a high risk of errors in our estimates that might prevent us from achieving our profitability goals.
> - Teams of personnel from marketing, engineering, production, and accounting would be needed for implementation. It will be critical for everyone to work toward common goals rather than to focus only on their own work areas. Thus, the team members should be chosen carefully and would need to understand that the teams have high priority.
> - These techniques might discourage us from adopting new products or continuing existing products that have long-term value. The teams need to consider long-term as well as short-term factors in making final recommendations.
>
> I will be happy to discuss these ideas with you further.

## Self-Study Problem 2  Cost-Based and Market-Based Prices, Minimum Acceptable Price

**Q5, Q6**

The OK Feed Store packages and distributes three grades of animal feed. The material cost per ton and estimated annual sales for each of the products are listed here:

| Product | Material Cost | Estimated Sales |
|---|---|---|
| Super Premium | $16.00 | 1,000 tons |
| Premium | $12.00 | 1,500 tons |
| Economy | $10.00 | 2,500 tons |

The fixed cost of operating the machinery used to package all three products is $20,000 per year. In the past, prices have been set by allocating the fixed overhead to products on the basis of estimated sales in tons. The resulting total costs (material costs plus allocated fixed overhead) are then marked up by 100%.

**REQUIRED:**

A. Determine the price per ton for each grade of feed using the method described for setting prices.

B. Does the price in part (A) take into account how much customers are willing to pay for the product? Explain.

C. Suppose a 10% increase in price would result in about a 40% decrease in the amount of the economy grade feed sold. Estimate the price that would maximize profits on the economy grade feed.

D. Explain how the price for economy grade feed calculated in part (C) should be used.

E. Suppose a Canadian distributor would like to buy 200 tons of economy grade feed and has offered to pay $2,400 for the special order.
  1. What is the relevant cost to OK feeds for this order?
  2. Considering only quantitative factors, what is the minimum acceptable price per ton?

## Solution to Self-Study Problem 2

A.

| | Economy | Premium | Super Premium |
|---|---|---|---|
| Materials cost | $10.00 | $12.00 | $16.00 |
| Allocated fixed overhead | | | |
| $20,000 ÷ 5,000 = $4 per ton | 4.00 | 4.00 | 4.00 |
| Total cost | 14.00 | 16.00 | 20.00 |
| Markup (100% of total cost) | 14.00 | 16.00 | 20.00 |
| Price | $28.00 | $32.00 | $40.00 |

B. No. A cost-based price *assumes* that customers are willing to pay a set markup above cost. However, a price based on cost might be higher or lower than customers are willing to pay.

C. The price for Economy can be computed in two steps:

$$\text{Elasticity of demand} = -\ln(1 - 0.40) \div \ln(1 + 0.10) = -5.36$$
$$\text{Profit-maximizing price} = [-5.36 \div (-5.36 + 1)] \times \$10 = \$12.30$$

D. The price in part (C) is only a guideline for pricing. The elasticity formulas are sensitive to error, so the profit-maximizing prices are used only as guidelines. OK Feeds could reduce the price of economy grade feed slowly and see how volumes and profits change.

E. 1. This problem requires a special order calculation (see Chapter 4). The relevant cost of filling the special order is the variable cost, which in this problem is the cost of materials: $10 per ton × 200 tons = $2,000.

  2. Under the general quantitative decision rule for special orders, the minimum acceptable price is the variable cost. The minimum acceptable price would be $10 per ton.

---

**REVIEW**  Use the exercises in the following boxes in the chapter to review key terms and key techniques, analyze chapter illustrations, improve your learning of new concepts, and practice ethical decision making:

Guide Your Learning 13.1: Key Terms (p. 515)

Guide Your Learning 13.2: Mount Rainier Bikes (Part 1) (p. 520)

Guide Your Learning 13.3: Mount Rainier Bikes (Part 2) (p. 523)

Guide Your Learning 13.4: Key Terms (p. 525)

Guide Your Learning 13.5: French Perfumery (p. 528)

Guide Your Learning 13.6: Key Terms (p. 532)

Focus on Ethical Decision Making: Price Gouging after Tragedy (p. 531)

## QUESTIONS

**13.1** What is a just-in-time manufacturing system? Why would organizations choose to adopt it?

**13.2** Explain the similarities and differences among target costing, kaizen costing, and life cycle costing.

**13.3** Identify three products for which target costing and kaizen costing could be used. Identify three products for which target costing and kaizen costing would be inappropriate.

**13.4** Explain the value chain and list the ways that value chain analysis benefits organizations.

**13.5** Explain the target costing cycle, and discuss the decision criteria used to determine whether a product will be manufactured using a target costing approach.

**13.6** Explain cost-based pricing and give an example that shows how prices would be determined using this method.

**13.7** Explain market-based pricing and explain where managers and accountants can find information that would help them set prices using this type of approach.

**13.8** Supply chain analysis focuses particularly on one aspect of value chain analysis. Explain how supply chain analysis is performed and how it relates to value chain analysis.

**13.9** List some common advantages and disadvantages for target and kaizen costing.

**13.10** If fixed costs are included in the marked up costs used in setting cost-based prices, a problem may occur when demand declines. Describe this problem.

**13.11** Explain why not-for-profit organizations do not always set prices so that their operating costs are recovered.

## EXERCISES

**13.12**
**Q1**

**Value-added and non-value-added activities** Some activities add value to an organization, while others do not.

**REQUIRED:** ❷ Determine whether each of the following activities is likely to be value-added or non-value-added and explain your choice.

    **A.** Inspection activities
    **B.** Moving materials to work stations
    **C.** Manufacturing extra inventory to keep employees busy

**13.13**
**Q6**

**Market-based price (elasticity formula)** Lickety Split sells ice cream cones in a variety of flavors. Data for a recent week appear here:

| | | |
|---|---:|---:|
| Revenue (1,000 cones @ $1.75 each) | | $1,750 |
| Cost of ingredients | $640 | |
| Rent | 500 | |
| Store attendant | 600 | 1,740 |
| Pretax income | | $ 10 |

The manager estimates that if she were to increase the price of cones from $1.75 to $1.93 each, weekly volume would be cut to 850 cones due to competition from other nearby ice cream shops.

**REQUIRED:** Estimate the profit-maximizing price per cone.

**13.14**
**Q6**

**Market-based prices (elasticity formula)** Harold's Flowers is a small neighborhood florist shop. Harold sells flowers for bouquets, and he also prepares and delivers flower arrangements.

**REQUIRED:**
    **A.** Harold is trying to decide how much to charge for a new type of rose that wholesales for $0.40 per bud. He ran a special on a similar rose last month and discovered that a 20% discount on the usual price increased sales by about 35%. What would you suggest as a starting price for the rose? Explain.

    ❸ **B.** Harold has been wondering whether he has been charging the right prices on some of his specialty bouquets. He has been using a markup for all specialty items of 200% (i.e., he charges three times wholesale cost). Harold estimates that a 10% increase in price on such items would decrease his unit sales by about 12%. Perform calculations to estimate a profit-maximizing markup. Based on your calculation, do you think he should increase or decrease his markup? Explain.

**13.15** **JIT production** Big Bertram uses the just-in-time method to manufacture golf clubs. The manu-
**Q1** facturing schedule for the clubs is developed as customers place orders. Each club is made within
a cell where five workers have production stations. The raw materials are delivered to the cell as
needed. Each worker in the cell performs one step in the manufacturing process and then inspects
the club before giving it to the next person. When a club is finished, it is set on a finished goods
rack, which is sent to the packaging department at regular intervals.

**REQUIRED:**
    **A.** What do we call a manufacturing system such as the one used by Big Bertram?
    **B.** Describe general advantages of this type of system.
    ❶ **C.** The supplier that manufactures the weights that are inserted in each club head would like
    to monitor Big Bertram's inventory levels through the Internet so that its new software
    program could release deliveries at appropriate times. List qualitative factors that might
    affect Big Bertram's decision about this proposal.

**13.16** **Target costing** Suppose that Chrysler used target costing to decide whether to produce a new ve-
**Q2** hicle, such as the PT Cruiser.

**REQUIRED:**
    **A.** Describe the steps Chrysler's design team would have taken.
    ❶ **B.** Explain why managers cannot easily predict demand for a new product such as
    Chrysler's PT Cruiser.

**13.17** **Market-based price (elasticity formula), uncertainties, other pricing factors** Sea Breeze Taffy
**Q6, Q7, Q8** is a shop located in Atlantic City along the boardwalk. It makes and sells taffy in a variety of flavors. Revenue and cost data for a recent week appear here:

| | | |
|---|---:|---:|
| Revenue (1,500 lbs @ $6.00 per lb) | | $9,000 |
| Cost of ingredients | $2,400 | |
| Rent | 800 | |
| Wages | 3,200 | 6,400 |
| Pretax income | | $2,600 |

All employees work standard shifts, regardless of how much fudge is produced or sold. Jasmine,
the shop's manager, estimates that if she were to decrease the price of taffy by $0.60 per lb. to a
new price of $5.40 per lb., weekly volume would increase by 20%.

**REQUIRED:**
    **A.** Calculate the price elasticity of demand.
    ⓔ **B.** Calculate the profit-maximizing price
    **C.** Based on the profit-maximizing price, does it appear that Jasmine should drop the price
    of the taffy? Why or why not?
    ❶ **D.** List possible relevant factors that could influence Jasmine's price decision. List as many
    factors as you can.

**13.18** **Market-based (elasticity formula) and cost-based prices, special order decision** Oysters Away
**Q5, Q6, Q8** shucks and packs oysters and sells them wholesale to fine restaurants across the state. The income
statement for last year follows:

| | | |
|---|---:|---:|
| Revenue (2,000 cases) | | $200,000 |
| Expenses: | | |
|   Wages for pickers, shuckers, and packers | $100,000 | |
|   Packing materials | 20,000 | |
|   Rent and insurance | 25,000 | |
|   Administration and selling | 45,000 | |
| | | 190,000 |
| Pretax Income | | $ 10,000 |

Pickers, shuckers, and packers are employed on an hourly basis and can be laid off whenever necessary. Salespeople merely deliver the product, and so are paid on a salaried basis.
    Linda Hanson, manager of Oysters Away, believes that a price increase of 10% would result
in a 15% decrease in sales.

The King Krab Restaurant is providing dinner for a meeting of the Pickers, Shuckers, and Packers Union in Seattle. King Krab offered to pay Oysters Away $65 a case for 300 cases of oysters. This sale would not affect Oysters Away's regular sales.

**REQUIRED:**

**A.** Ignoring the King Krab offer, estimate the profit-maximizing price for Oysters Away.

**B.** Assuming Linda is not willing to lose money on the King Krab order, what is the minimum price that she should accept for the special order (Chapter 4)?

**①** **C.** What other relevant factors might Linda consider before she makes a decision about the King Krab order? List as many factors as you can.

**13.19** **Kaizen costing** Blade Runner produces regular scooters and motorized scooters. Blade Runner
**Q3** scooters are considered the most reliable in the marketplace. Demand has been volatile, with huge increases in demand during Christmas and Hanukah and just before university classes begin in the fall. In the past, the company filled demand by anticipating demand increases and manufacturing inventories ahead of time.

Recently, competition in the motorized scooter line has escalated, and Blade Runner needs to reduce prices and, therefore, cut costs. The motorized scooter's current cost is $150. To be competitive, the marketing department says the price should be 10% lower than the current price. Management currently achieves a pretax return of 10% on sales of the scooters and wants to continue this rate of return.

The following per-unit costs for motorized scooters are based on production of 700,000 per year.

| | |
|---|---:|
| Direct materials (variable) | $ 45 |
| Direct labor (variable) | 15 |
| Machining costs (fixed depreciation and maintenance) | 10 |
| Inspection costs (variable) | 10 |
| Engineering costs (fixed) | 20 |
| Marketing costs (fixed) | 25 |
| Administrative costs (fixed) | 25 |
| Total cost | $150 |

**REQUIRED:**

**ⓔ** **A.** Calculate the price recommended by the marketing department.

**B.** Given the price you calculated in part (A), calculate the new contribution margin and the target cost.

**C.** Calculate the planned cost reduction for each cost category, assuming proportional cost reduction across categories.

**13.20** **Kaizen costing, proposed cost reductions, uncertainties** Refer to the information in Exercise
**Q1, Q3** 13.19. The following cost reduction suggestions were made by the kaizen costing team.

Direct materials:
   Suppliers agreed to cost reductions of $4.50 for direct materials.

Direct labor:
   An engineer suggested that the scooters could be manufactured more quickly if production batches were cut in half. The engineer believes that a labor savings of $1.50 per scooter could be attained.

Machining costs:
   The team has been unable to identify ways to reduce machining costs in the manufacturing process, but suggests that some of the machining tasks could be outsourced to suppliers so that some parts are preassembled, reducing the need for machine hours. This outsourcing would increase the cost of direct materials by $0.50 per unit, but cut machining costs by $1.30 per unit. The supplier has been very reliable, but does not currently have the machining expertise and would have to purchase equipment and hire several workers to fill these orders.

Marketing:
   Marketing has agreed to combine ad campaigns for both products and believes they will save $2.50 per unit without losing sales.

> Administration and Engineering:
> > No cost containment appears possible in administration because a new enterprise re-source program was recently acquired. However, the head of engineering believes that his costs can be cut by $4.00 per unit. He believes that some employees are no longer needed because part of the new program was designed especially to provide information for product and manufacturing process design that had been hand collected in the past.

**REQUIRED:**  **A.** Calculate the new cost per category. Compare the total cost with the kaizen cost. Determine whether further cost containment efforts need to be made.

**B.** In your own words, describe the next step in the kaizen process.

❶ **C.** List qualitative factors that might be relevant to Blade Runner's managers as they decide on any product or process changes. List as many factors as you can.

❶ **D.** For each of the planned cost reductions, discuss uncertainties about whether the company will achieve the planned cost reduction.

# PROBLEMS

**13.21**
**Q1**

**Cost reduction, JIT, value chain analysis** Budget Cupboards produces kitchen and bathroom cupboards that incorporate unusual functions, such as specialty drawers for knives and kitchen tools, and kitchen appliance holders that pop up from under the counter top. Competition in this industry has recently increased. Budget's management wants to cut costs for its basic cupboard models and then cut prices.

**REQUIRED:**  ❶ **A.** The following table lists potential areas for cost reduction. Two potential cost reductions are provided for the first area listed (design phase). For each of the remaining areas, identify two potential ways that Budget Cupboard's management could reduce costs.

| Potential Area for Cost Reduction | Potential Cost Reductions | |
|---|---|---|
| | (1) | (2) |
| EXAMPLE: Design phase | Work with suppliers to reduce direct materials costs | Redesign cupboards to use fewer parts |
| Manufacturing process | | |
| Administration | | |
| Changes in quality or functionality | | |

❶ **B.** Budget does not currently use just-in-time production or value chain analysis. Describe several advantages of using these methods when price competition increases.

**13.22**
**Q2, Q3**

**Target and kaizen costing, uncertainties, manager incentives** Suppose you are having a conversation with Sandy, another student in this course. Sandy is confused about the differences and similarities between target costing and kaizen costing.

Another student, Kevin, overhears your conversation with Sandy and insists that neither of these methods is beneficial. Kevin argues that some companies run into financial problems using these methods because their managers manipulated the cost estimates to appear however they wanted. If the managers wanted to launch a new product or keep an old one, they made sure their cost estimates supported their decision.

**REQUIRED:**  **A.** In your own words, explain how target costing and kaizen costing are the same and how they are different.

❶ **B.** Compare the information needed to apply the target costing and kaizen costing methods:
**1.** List the types of relevant information needed for each method.
**2.** List the uncertainties in the relevant information for each method.

❷ **C.** Discuss ways in which managers might be able to create biased estimates under a target or kaizen costing system.

❷ **D.** Kevin argues that the types of issues you described in part (C) mean that target and kaizen costing are not beneficial. Discuss the validity of this argument.

**13.23** **Cost-based and market-based pricing, elasticity, uncertainties, economy effects** John Gold has
Q5, Q6, Q7, Q8 owned and operated Heritage Jewelry Store for a number of years. He uses the standard markup
of 300% (known as a triple key in this industry) and uses an average cost that includes an allocation of overhead as the cost base. Lately, jewelry sales at the store have faltered as the country
faces a recession. John's son is taking a cost accounting course and suggests that his father should
use a pricing formula based on the price elasticity of demand.

REQUIRED:
 **A.** In your own words, provide a plausible explanation for John's current use of cost-based
  pricing.
 **B.** Explain elasticity to John in simple terms.
 **C.** In your own words, explain how price changes affect demand for products that are highly
  elastic.
 **❶ D.** Explain why John's price elasticity of demand cannot be predicted with certainty.
 **❶ E.** List possible reasons why a product's price elasticity of demand would change. List as
  many reasons as you can.
 **❷ F.** Explain how changes in the economy affect prices. Give examples from the current business environment.

**13.24** **Cost-based pricing, death spiral, uncertainties, customer reaction** Suppose the owner of Hay-
Q8 wood Ceramics needs to raise prices to stay in business, but is concerned that raising prices would
result in a death spiral. To avoid a decline in sales, the owner is considering sending letters to her
customers explaining why the price increase is necessary. The letter would inform customers about
the cost increases that necessitated the price increase, explain what the company is doing to keep
costs as low as possible, and allow customers to place orders for a given time period at the current price.

REQUIRED:
 **A.** Describe the death spiral in your own words.
 **❶ B.** Explain why the owner cannot be sure how customers will respond to a price increase.
 **❷ C.** Suppose the owner decides to send letters to her customers. From a customer's point of
  view, discuss possible pros and cons of this strategy.
 **❸ D.** Would you recommend that the owner send letters to her customers? Why or why not?

**13.25** **Market-based pricing, relevant information** Java Alive, a small boutique coffee shop, has asked
Q6, Q8 your advice in setting pricing policies. Java has information about prices and sales over the last
4 years.

REQUIRED:
 **A.** Explain how you would use the prices and sales information to suggest a possible pricing
  strategy.
 **❶ B.** What other information would you gather before you complete your recommendation?
  List as many types of information as you can.

**13.26** **Market-based pricing, customer preferences** Transrapid is a new magnetically levitated train
Q5, Q6, Q7, Q8 being developed to run between major cities in Germany at a speed of 300 miles per hour. Engineers developed a system with trains departing every 10 minutes. Suppose Transrapid asked you
to research customer preferences and to recommend a pricing policy. It costs considerably more
to have trains depart as frequently as 10 minutes apart, so a cost-based pricing schedule will result in ticket prices that are considerably higher than alternative modes of transportation.

REQUIRED:
 **❶ A.** In addition to customer preferences, what information would you like to gather before
  recommending a pricing policy? Explain why each item you list is relevant.
 **❷ B.** Explain why it is important to understand customer preferences before building the
  system.
 **❷ C.** Is the need to consider customer preferences different for this organization than for another type of organization? Why or why not?

**13.27** **Market-based price (elasticity formula), uncertainties** Hanson & Daughters produces a premium
Q6, Q7 label apple juice to wholesalers at a current price of $7.00 per 5-gallon container. Costs for a recent
month, in which 100,000 5-gallon containers were produced and sold, appear on following page:

|  | Variable | Fixed |
|---|---|---|
| Materials | $10,000 | $ 0 |
| Labor | 20,000 | 40,000 |
| Factory overhead | 10,000 | 80,000 |
| Selling and administration | 10,000 | 100,000 |
| Total | $50,000 | $220,000 |

Hanson & Daughters' customers are loyal. Recently, a 10% increase in wholesale price resulted in only a 10% decrease in gallons sold.

**REQUIRED:**

**A.** Calculate the price elasticity of demand.

**B.** Calculate the profit-maximizing price.

❶ **C.** Explain why the management of Hanson & Daughters cannot be certain that another 10% price increase would cause only another 10% decrease in gallons sold.

❷ **D.** Provide possible reasons why so many customers were willing to continue purchasing the apple juice when prices increased by 10%. List as many reasons as you can.

❷ **E.** Describe the assumptions underlying the profit-maximizing price you calculated in part (B). How realistic are these assumptions for Hanson & Daughters? What might occur if these assumptions are not met for Hanson & Daughters?

❸ **F.** What would you recommend to Hanson & Daughters concerning its price for apple juice? Explain your reasoning.

**13.28**

**Q1, Q3, Q6, Q8**

**Cost reduction and market-based prices at a university** Bainbridge University offers an MBA degree that is widely respected around the world. The tuition for the program has always covered the costs of the program until a recent recession increased the sensitivity of students to the cost of tuition. The business school managers decided to freeze the tuition cost for the past few years. The director of the MBA program asked a cost accounting class to act as consultants for the program and to make recommendations on possible ways to reduce costs or to increase tuition. You are part of a student team assigned to this project.

**REQUIRED:**

❶ **A.** Is this problem open-ended? Why or why not?

❶ **B.** List relevant types of analyses that your team might perform.

❷ **C.** Describe the steps you will take as you analyze the program, including the types of information you would like to use.

❸ **D.** Explain how you would decide on an appropriate level of tuition.

**13.29**

**Q1, Q2, Q3, Q4, Q5**

**Life cycle costing** Fancy Fleece developed a new outdoor wear fleece fabric that is both wind and water resistant, but retains a soft and fuzzy feel. The research and development process was more expensive than Fancy's managers anticipated, and the materials in the fabric are also more expensive than anticipated. The managers believe that if Fancy prices the fleece to cover total costs, no one will buy it. The marketing department held several focus groups with manufacturers who produce and sell winter jackets and pants to determine an appropriate price. The marketing department also surveyed customers who recently purchased fleece jackets to determine the amount of premium they would be willing to pay for a jacket that is both wind and water resistant. The marketing department concluded that the new fleece fabric would sell at a price that covers variable costs, but does not cover the total costs of production and development. You have been asked to help the managers decide whether to produce the fleece and how to price it if they do produce it.

**REQUIRED:**

**A.** What kind(s) of analysis would you perform for this decision?

**B.** Explain whether it would generally be better for Fancy Fleece to use cost-based or market-based pricing.

❶ **C.** Identify uncertainties about how much it will cost to produce the fleece. List as many uncertainties as you can.

❶ **D.** Explain why the managers of Fancy Fleece cannot be certain that they would be able to sell the polar fleece to cover variable costs.

☆ **13.30**
Q5, Q6, Q7, Q8

**For-profit versus not-for-profit pricing, setting a market price** Suppose the State of Arizona decided to preserve some beautiful caves in the southwestern part of the state. To defray the cost of preservation, state managers decided to open the caves to guided tours. To prepare the caves for visitors, vapor locks were built so that the moisture content of the caves would remain stable. The state spent $10 million on the facilities. Now the managers need to decide on a price for the tours.

**REQUIRED:**
**ANALYZE**
**INFORMATION**

The following questions will help you analyze the information for this problem. Do not turn in your answers to these questions unless your professor asks you to do so.

  **A.** Describe how pricing policies in not-for-profit organizations are different from pricing policies in for-profit organizations.

❶ **B.** Use the Internet or other sources to identify current prices for other similar attractions.

❶ **C.** What additional information would you gather to evaluate the price?

❷ **D.** Do you believe that the volume of tours is likely to be sensitive to the price charged for tours? Why or why not?

**REQUIRED:**
**WRITTEN**
**ASSIGNMENT**

The managers of the park department need your price recommendation. Turn in your answer to the following.

❸ **E.** Use the information you learned from the preceding analyses to write a memo to the park department recommending a price for the tour. Provide appropriate information for park department managers to understand your methodology and evaluate the risks associated with your price recommendation.

**13.31**
Q5, Q6, Q7, Q8

ETHICS

**Cost-based and market-based pricing, collusion** Burton Turner and Short Whittum live in a small town in northern Idaho. They both own gas stations and provide gasoline and engine repair services for the area. The town is somewhat isolated, and during the winter it is sometimes difficult to travel to other cities in the surrounding area. While having coffee one morning, Turner and Whittum discuss the prices they charge for gasoline and for repair services. They decide that it would be a good policy if they both set the same prices, because then customers would choose between the two businesses based on the quality of service and the brand name of the gasoline.

**REQUIRED:**

❶ **A.** What pricing alternatives are available to Turner and Whittum for setting prices? List as many alternatives as you can.

❶ **B.** Is this an open-ended problem? Why or why not?

❷ **C.** Explore this problem from different perspectives:
  **1.** Turner and Whittum
  **2.** Customers
  **3.** Government officials

❷ **D.** Compare and contrast the legal and ethical issues in this situation. How are they the same? How are they different?

❸ **E.** Ignoring possible legal issues, is the proposed pricing policy of Turner and Whittum ethical? Why or why not?

❹ **F.** Suppose you are a government official, and you receive an anonymous phone call telling you that Turner and Whittum are charging the same prices for gasoline and repair services. How might you monitor the two businesses to determine whether their actions are illegal?

**13.32**
Q5, Q7, Q8

**Cost-based pricing in a not-for-profit organization** Mountain County Legal Services is part of a larger not-for-profit organization (Mountain County Resource Center) that provides free legal and job placement services and houses a food bank for qualified clients. Last year's costs for 5,000 visits to legal services are presented here.

| | |
|---|---:|
| Lawyer's salary | $ 90,000 |
| Part-time secretary | 12,000 |
| Miscellaneous supplies | 6,000 |
| Paralegals' salaries | 70,000 |
| Administrative costs[a] | 34,000 |
| Rent[b] | 10,000 |
| | $222,000 |

[a]A portion of the administrative costs of the Mountain County Services. These costs have been allocated to programs based upon the salary costs of the program.
[b]A portion of the rent for the Mountain County Resource Center. Total rent is allocated on the basis of the space occupied by each program.

Expected grants for the next year from **United Way** and the county have been reduced due to an economic downturn. The organization's executive director is considering dropping legal services. Eliminating the legal services program will result in a savings of about $4,000 in administrative costs. The space vacated by legal services could be used by the food bank, which is presently renting quarters in another building for $8,000 a year.

The executive director decided that individuals receiving legal services from the resource center are to pay for their services, with exceptions based upon need determined on a case-by-case basis. It is not clear what the director means when he says that clients are to pay for their services.

**REQUIRED:**

**A.** If the executive director means that each person using legal services should pay for his or her own avoidable costs, what minimum fee should be charged on average for a legal service visit?

**B.** If the executive director means that all of the people using legal services should collectively pay for the avoidable costs of the legal services program, what minimum fee should be charged on average for a visit?

**C.** If the executive director wants the fee to cover the total costs of the Mountain County Legal Services including avoidable and allocated costs, what minimum fee should be charged for a visit?

**D.** Suppose the Center begins charging the price you calculated in part (B). What problems might arise if these fees are implemented? Consider whether the price change would affect the client's behavior, and then how that behavior change might affect Legal Services.

**E.** Suppose the Center begins charging the price you calculated in part (C). Considering that the price is based on allocated costs, explain why this price might be viewed as arbitrary.

**F.** Discuss why a county executive might issue an edict about having clients pay for their services, but not provide guidance about what the edict means.

**13.33** **Profit effect of price change** The accountants at French Perfumery decided to increase the price
**Q7** of a scent called Breezy by 10%, from $6.00 per bottle to $6.60. French's accountants expect the 10% price increase to reduce unit sales by 20%. Current sales are 200,000 bottles, and total variable costs are $800,000.

**REQUIRED:**

**A.** Estimate the pretax profit effect of the price change, assuming no effect on the variable cost rate, on total fixed costs, or on sales of other products. (*Hint:* Calculate the contribution margin at the old and new prices and volumes.)

**B.** How certain can the accountant be that volume will decline 20% if the selling price increases to $6.60? What effect does this uncertainty have on the managers' decision to increase the selling price?

# BUILD YOUR PROFESSIONAL COMPETENCIES

**13.34** **Focus on Professional Competency: International/Global Perspective** *Global economic effects,*
**Q1, Q2, Q8** *social issues, communication* Review the following definition and elements for the International/
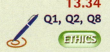 Global Perspective competency.[24]

**DEFINITION:** *Individuals entering the accounting profession should be able to identify and communicate the variety of threats and opportunities of doing business in a borderless world. The accounting professional of the future must provide services to support and facilitate commerce in the global marketplace.*

---

[24]The definition and elements are reprinted with permission from AICPA; Copyright © 1978–2000 & 2003 by American Institute of Certified Public Accountants. The AICPA's Core Competency Framework can be accessed at eca.aicpaservices.org.

## ELEMENTS FOR THIS COMPETENCY INCLUDE

| Level 1 | Level 2 | Level 3 | Level 4 |
|---|---|---|---|
| 1. Identifies global issues relevant to a business decision<br><br>2. Describes uncertainties about the cultural and financial impacts of moving into new markets, and expanding existing markets | 3. Identifies and analyzes the social costs and benefits of relevant decisions, including human and financial resource management, in the global marketplace/environment<br><br>4. Analyzes global customer and supplier demographics<br><br>5. Analyzes the cultural and financial impacts of moving into new markets, and expanding existing markets | 6. Modifies communications as appropriate for global settings<br><br>7. Objectively considers and prioritizes global issues in reaching business decisions | 8. Develops, implements, and monitors global business strategies |

**REQUIRED:**

**A.** Focus on elements 1, 2, 7, and 8 which address knowledge of the effects of global competition and answer the following questions:

   ❷   **1.** Why does global competition increase managers' focus on cost management?

   ❷   **2.** How does global competition affect market prices for goods and services?

**B.** Focus on element 3, which requires accountants to consider social issues in global business. Reread the **Caterpillar** case presented in the chapter. **Komatsu** reverse-engineered Caterpillar's products during the late 1970s and early 1980s. Komatsu's management used this information to design its products to compete effectively against Caterpillar. During the late 1980s, Caterpillar used this same method of reverse-engineering to redesign its products and manufacturing processes. Answer the following questions:

   ❷   **1.** Does reverse-engineering create an ethical problem? In other words, is reverse-engineering a form of business espionage?

   ❷   **2.** What are the social costs and benefits from reverse-engineering a competitor's product?

   ❷   **3.** When companies redesign their products and manufacturing processes for cost efficiency, they often reduce their reliance on manufacturing labor. What are the social costs and benefits of this practice?

**C.** Focus on element 4, which addresses global customer and supplier relationships and answer the following questions.

   ❶   **1.** What is meant by "global supplier demographics"?

   ❷   **2.** How might global supplier demographics affect the prices a company pays when it acquires resources (goods or services)?

   ❶   **3.** What is meant by "global customer demographics"?

   ❷   **4.** How might global customer demographics affect the market price for a product or service?

**D.** Focus on element 6, which addresses communication skills in a global environment and answer the following questions.

   ❶   **1.** Where might a manager obtain information about how to communicate effectively in a given global setting?

   ❷   **2.** How are communications in global settings different from communications in domestic settings?

**13.35**    **Integrating Across the Curriculum: Information Technology**    *Inventory management system,*
**Q1**    *data accuracy, internal controls, estimating benefits* During 2000, automobile parts company
**Mopar** implemented a new inventory management system costing $1.5 million. Mopar, a unit of **Daimler-Chrysler,** distributed parts from 3 central and 11 regional warehouses to hundreds of parts dealers. The company filled orders for approximately 1 million line items per week from an inventory of 280,000 parts for Chrysler, Dodge, and Jeep brand vehicles.

Mopar implemented the new system to improve its management of inventory levels. The company previously maintained inventories based on forecasted demand, but often ran out of some parts and carried inventory levels that were too high for other parts. When a customer ordered a part that was out of stock at a particular warehouse, the company incurred extra costs to search for the part at other warehouses. If the part was not found, Mopar placed a rush order to have it shipped directly to the customer from one of its 3,000 suppliers. When inventory of a part was too high, valuable warehouse space was wasted and the company incurred unnecessary inventory carrying costs. To reduce these types of problems, the company had manually tracked data for 100 of the highest-cost and best-selling parts. The managers used measures such as how often a part was out of stock to adjust inventory purchases.

The new inventory system included a database that would track parts at all warehouses as well as suppliers, customers, and forecast levels. The system helped managers identify $3.5 million in overstocked inventory. They expected an additional $10 million in annual savings from reduced backorders and rush orders.

SOURCES: Mopar's Web site at www.mopar.com and J. Xenakis, "How to Slash Inventory Costs," *CFO.com*, December 13, 2000.

**REQUIRED:**

❶ **A.** Is Mopar's new inventory system likely to completely eliminate out-of-stock occurrences? Why or why not?

❷ **B.** Discuss whether it would be beneficial for Mopar to institute a JIT inventory management system.

❶ **C.** Benefits from Mopar's new system depend on the accuracy of data in its inventory database. Identify possible reasons why the data may be inaccurate.

❷ **D.** Describe possible internal controls that could prevent or detect and correct inaccuracies in Mopar's inventory database.

❷ **E.** Mopar's managers expected to achieve $10 million in annual savings from reduced backorders and rush orders. Suppose you are asked to develop an estimate of these savings. How might you go about making the estimate? Why types of data would you use? What types of assumptions would you need to make?

# 14

# Measuring and Assigning Costs for Income Statements

## ▶In Brief

Accountants use absorption costing for inventory and cost of goods sold when preparing financial statements according to generally accepted accounting principles (GAAP). Under absorption costing, all production costs, including allocated overhead, are assigned to units manufactured. This accounting method provides useful information by matching production costs against revenues. However, managers often need information about incremental costs when making short-term operating decisions. Variable costing and throughput costing are two methods that accountants use to provide managers with incremental cost information.

## This Chapter Addresses the Following Questions:

**Q1** How are absorption costing income statements constructed?

**Q2** What factors affect the choice of production volume measures for allocating fixed overhead?

**Q3** How are variable costing income statements constructed?

**Q4** How are throughput costing income statements constructed?

**Q5** What are the uses and limitations of absorption, variable, and throughput costing income statements?

# HARLEY-DAVIDSON: SCARCITY OR ABUNDANCE?

As of February 2002, **Harley-Davidson**'s sales had grown steadily for several years; the company's stock price was up 31% over the previous 12 months. However, the company's dealers reported that they were now carrying inventories, whereas they had previously waited one to two years to fill customer orders. These reports led analysts to conclude that sales for Harley-Davidson's motorcycles were slowing. The analysts argued that the company was trying to hide the slowdown by engaging in channel stuffing—pushing dealers to buy bikes they did not need (Brown, 2002).

The analysts' arguments seemed plausible because channel stuffing had been used by managers of other companies to artificially boost sales and profits during sales downturns. This tactic works best in situations such as Harley-Davidson's; dealers are willing to buy excess inventories because their future allocations of hot models depend on past purchases. Furthermore, the company's financing arm provides loans to finance dealer purchases. Harley-Davidson recognizes revenue from its dealers even if the dealers have not yet sold the bikes to their customers (Brown, 2002).

Harley-Davidson's managers stated that demand for the company's products had not slowed down. They argued instead that they had boosted inventories to meet customer demand. For a number of years prior to 2002, production had increased by 15% annually. Harley's managers said that they wanted to keep frustrated biker "wannabes" from buying competing brands instead of waiting for a backordered Harley. They also claimed that they had increased inventories of bikes and accessories in anticipation of the company's 100-year anniversary in 2003 (Brown, 2002).

Under generally accepted accounting principles (GAAP), inventories and cost of goods sold must be accounted for using full absorption costing in which both variable and fixed production costs are assigned to all units produced. When production increases, as it did for Harley-Davidson, the cost per unit usually decreases because the fixed cost per unit generally decreases. Lower per-unit costs then result in a higher gross margin for each unit sold, leading to the appearance of higher profitability on the income statement. In addition, under absorption costing, when inventory levels increase during a time period, the cost of goods sold (COGS) *expense* on the income statement is smaller than the production *costs* incurred because some units (and their allocated fixed costs) are held in inventory.

These effects of full absorption accounting are not a problem, as long as sales levels do not decline. However, if sales slow and inventory from prior periods is sold, COGS expense will be higher than the production costs incurred during the period. In this case, declining sales have an especially negative effect on profits because of both declining revenue and higher COGS.

Harley-Davidson's financial statements may not have resolved investors' concerns when evaluating the arguments made by analysts and by company managers. If sales were artificially high, then absorption costing would delay recognition of costs on the income statement. The main question was whether Harley's sales would continue to grow. As long as sales increased each year and its variable and fixed costs did not increase, profits would continue to increase. However, if sales were to drop off, then the company's financial performance would deteriorate rapidly.

Fortunately for Harley-Davidson, its sales continued to increase during 2002. Although the U.S. economy suffered, sales in some sectors increased. Americans began purchasing expensive toys such as all-terrain vehicles and motorcycles, even though they were cutting back on other expensive items such as costly dinners and clothing (Hallinan, 2002). ■

Sources: K. Brown, "Heard on the Street," *The Wall Street Journal*, February 12, 2002, p. C1; and J. Hallinan, "Serious Fun," *The Wall Street Journal*, August 27, 2002, p. A1.

## MONITORING INVENTORY AND PRODUCTION COSTS

### ■ Key Analysis Issues for Harley-Davidson's Investors

Data and inferences about **Harley-Davidson's** inventories and production costs are important to the company's managers and accountants, as well as to external financial statement users. Managers are interested in monitoring operations, whereas the accountants are responsible for anticipating and providing the types of information that managers need. External users such as investors are interested in monitoring an organization's management and performance. The following discussion summarizes the skills that investors needed to analyze Harley-Davidson's inventory and production costs during 2002.

**Knowing.** Most investors had little specific knowledge about Harley-Davidson's manufacturing processes, although they needed to have at least general knowledge about the following:

- Nature of costs and production processes
- Types of operating decisions made by managers
- Industry and competition
- Economic trends

Informed users of financial statement information knew that GAAP requires fixed costs to be allocated to units produced and, therefore, to inventory on the balance sheet. They also understood the effects various trends in sales and inventory levels would have on reported profits.

**Identifying.** The idea of monitoring inventory and production costs presumes some type of uncertainty. Otherwise, monitoring would be unnecessary. Harley-Davidson's investors faced many uncertainties, such as whether

- Inventory and production levels were out of control.
- Harley-Davidson's managers had engaged in channel stuffing.
- Increasing motorcycle availability would have a positive or negative effect on sales in the long term.

**Exploring.** For manufacturing companies such as Harley-Davidson, investors routinely analyze the portions of financial statements covering inventory and cost of goods sold. Investors use this information to infer information about the company's future prospects. Harley-Davidson's investors would analyze this information to address questions such as the following:

- What are the trends in Harley-Davidson's profits?
- Are inventory levels too high? If so, what does this factor suggest about future profits?
- Have the managers engaged in channel stuffing—dumping inventory on retailers? If so, what does this activity suggest about other possible biases in the managers' actions and reported financial results?
- How reputable are the company's managers?
- Are the financial statements a reliable measure of Harley-Davidson's profitability?

Harley-Davidson's investors would use a variety of analysis techniques to address these questions. For example, investors probably analyze the gross profit margin percentage and inventory turnover rates for Harley-Davidson over time and in comparison with competitors.[1] The investors would also include information from other sources in their analyses. The analysts' reports might have been an important source of information during 2002. Analysts' questions about Harley-Davidson's inventory practices would increase investor concerns about the company's future prospects.

**Prioritizing.** In general, investors analyze information about a company to help them decide whether to buy, hold, or sell an investment. For Harley-Davidson during 2002, investors needed to weigh analysts' concerns against management's statements and other information to conclude whether the company's inventory management was out of control.

**Envisioning.** Although Harley-Davidson's investors were monitoring information about past inventories and costs, the goal was to make decisions about the future. Therefore, the

---

[1]Refer to financial accounting or finance textbooks for explanations about using these ratios to analyze financial statements. The gross profit margin percentage is calculated as (Sales revenue − Cost of goods sold) ÷ Sales revenue × 100%. Inventory turnover is usually calculated as Cost of goods sold ÷ Average inventory.

investors would look for any changes from past patterns. Their goal was to anticipate future trends for Harley-Davidson.

## ■ Different Measures of Cost for Different Purposes

No single measure of inventory and cost of goods sold is best for all situations. Financial statement reporting requires average costs, but short-term internal decision making requires only incremental costs. Managers use both variable and fixed cost information for monitoring operations. Meanwhile, GAAP determines how costs should be measured for reporting to external parties such as investors. As we learn in this chapter, different types of information are useful in different settings.

## ABSORPTION COSTING AND VARIABLE COSTING

**Q1** How are absorption costing income statements constructed?

**CHAPTER REFERENCE**

In Chapters 5 and 6 we learned two methods of product costing: job costing and process costing.

**ALTERNATIVE TERMS**

In financial accounting, *product costs* are the fixed and variable costs assigned to products. These costs remain in inventory until products sell and are also known as *inventoriable costs* or *capitalized costs*.

With computerized accounting systems, accountants can easily calculate costs in a variety of ways; reports for outside distribution can be different from reports for inside management. In this section we compare absorption costing, which is intended for outside distribution, with variable costing, which is often used for managerial decision making.

## ■ Absorption Costing

When accountants prepare financial statements according to GAAP, they use absorption costing. Under **absorption costing,** all production costs are recorded on the balance sheet as part of the cost of inventory and are then expensed as part of the cost of goods sold (COGS) when units are sold (Exhibit 14.1). Both fixed and variable production costs are assumed to have future value to the organization, and are accordingly treated as **product costs.** They include direct materials, direct labor, and production overhead.

Under absorption costing, direct costs are traced to products and manufacturing overhead is allocated to products. Fixed overhead may be allocated to units using either an actual or budgeted allocation rate. If production volume is used as the allocation base, fixed overhead cost can be allocated to units using either an actual or an estimated allocation rate as follows:

$$\text{Actual fixed overhead allocation rate} = \frac{\text{Actual fixed overhead cost}}{\text{Actual production volume}}$$

$$\text{Estimated fixed overhead allocation rate} = \frac{\text{Estimated fixed overhead cost}}{\text{Estimated production volume}}$$

**EXHIBIT 14.1**
Absorption Costing

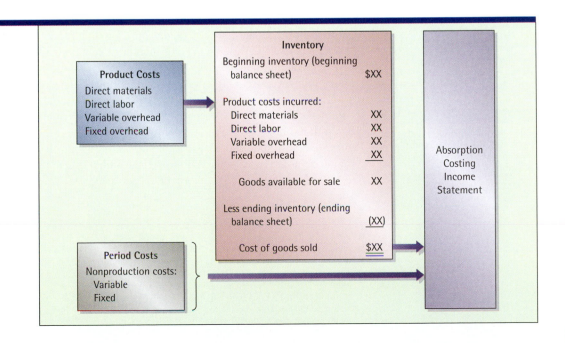

**EXHIBIT 14.2**
Absorption Cost
Income Statement

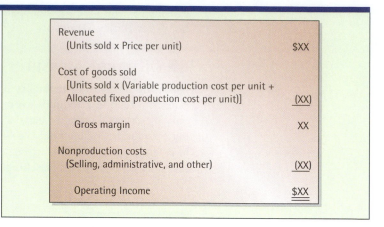

| | |
|---|---|
| Revenue (Units sold x Price per unit) | $XX |
| Cost of goods sold [Units sold x (Variable production cost per unit + Allocated fixed production cost per unit)] | (XX) |
| Gross margin | XX |
| Nonproduction costs (Selling, administrative, and other) | (XX) |
| Operating Income | $XX |

When using an estimated fixed overhead allocation rate, several alternative choices are available for the estimated production volume; we learn about these later in the chapter.

Given the treatment of fixed overhead costs under absorption costing, both production and sales volumes affect the timing of when fixed overhead is recognized as an expense. If units are produced and sold this period, overhead costs incurred to produce these units are expensed this period. If units from last period are sold, some overhead costs from last period are expensed in this period. If units produced this period are not yet sold, the overhead allocated to those units will not be expensed until a future date when the units are sold.[2] The overhead cost associated with those units is included in inventory on the balance sheet.

The absorption costing income statement (Exhibit 14.2) reflects the focus in GAAP on distinguishing between production and nonproduction costs. All production costs are expensed as COGS to match them against revenues when units are sold. Nonproduction costs such as administration, marketing, and distribution are treated as **period costs.** GAAP requires that period costs be expensed when incurred because these costs are assumed to have no future benefit.

## Variable Costing

Under **variable costing,** all variable costs are matched against revenues and fixed costs are treated as period costs. Therefore, product costs consist of only variable production costs such as direct materials, direct labor, and variable production overhead (Exhibit 14.3). Then, inventory on the balance sheet includes only variable production costs under variable costing.

Expenses in a variable costing income statement are organized differently from an absorption costing income statement. In a variable costing income statement, all costs are separated into variable and fixed categories (Exhibit 14.4); variable production costs are reported separately from fixed production costs. Similarly, variable nonproduction costs, such as sales commissions, are reported separately from fixed nonproduction costs. All variable costs, production and nonproduction, are subtracted from revenues to arrive at the contribution margin. Then all fixed costs, production and nonproduction, are subtracted to determine operating income. This presentation improves the ability of managers to identify cash flows relevant to a product or service for internal decision making.[4]

---

**HELPFUL HINT**

A cost is not the same as an expense. A *cost* is the value of resources given up to obtain an economic benefit. An *expense* is an income statement category that reduces net income.

**INTERNATIONAL**

International Accounting Standard (IAS) No. 2 requires inventory to include "all costs to bring the inventories to their present condition and location." Thus, all countries adopting IAS require absorption costing.[3]

 **Q3** How are variable costing income statements constructed?

**ALTERNATIVE TERMS**

Some people use the terms *direct costing* or *marginal costing* to describe the method called *variable costing.*

**CHAPTER REFERENCE**

We learned in Chapter 4 that managers often use the contribution margin when making nonroutine operating decisions.

---

[2]For simplicity, we ignore the income statement effects of possible inventory writedowns under financial accounting rules for lower of cost or market.

[3]For more information about IAS, see the Web site of the International Accounting Standards Board at www.iasb.org.

[4]Several authors argue that variable costing income statements are not strictly prohibited by GAAP. See, for example, M. Schiff, "Variable Costing: A Closer Look," *Management Accounting,* February 1987, pp. 36–39. Absorption costing is conventionally used for GAAP reporting, and auditors may require organizations to use it. It is also required for U.S. income tax accounting; however, more period costs must be absorbed into inventories for income tax purposes than for GAAP.

**EXHIBIT 14.3**
Variable Costing

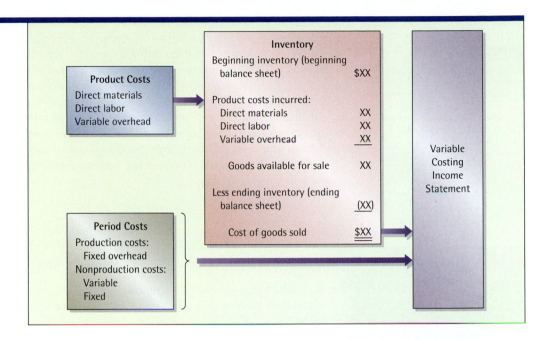

**EXHIBIT 14.4**
Variable Costing
Income Statement

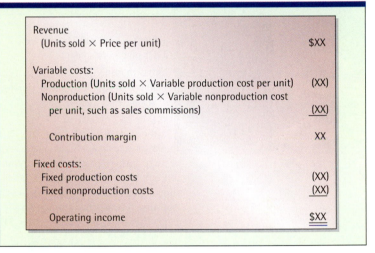

| | |
|---|---|
| Revenue | |
| (Units sold × Price per unit) | $XX |
| | |
| Variable costs: | |
| Production (Units sold × Variable production cost per unit) | (XX) |
| Nonproduction (Units sold × Variable nonproduction cost per unit, such as sales commissions) | (XX) |
| | |
| Contribution margin | XX |
| | |
| Fixed costs: | |
| Fixed production costs | (XX) |
| Fixed nonproduction costs | (XX) |
| | |
| Operating income | $XX |

---

**GUIDE YOUR LEARNING** **14.1** **Key Terms**

Stop to confirm that you understand the new terms introduced in the last several pages.

Absorption costing (p. 551)     *Period costs (p. 552)
*Product costs (p. 551)          Variable costing (p. 552)

For each of these terms, write a definition in your own words. For starred terms, list at least one example that is different from the ones given in this textbook.

---

## Absorption Costing Compared to Variable Costing

**Q5** What are the uses and limitations of absorption, variable, and throughput costing income statements?

Managers and other employees regularly make decisions about short-term resource allocations within an organization. To do so, they estimate the effects of alternative decisions on cash flows (incremental revenues and costs). Because fixed costs are constant within a relevant range of activity, total fixed costs generally do not change under alternative short-term decisions. Thus, income statements based on absorption costing do not provide managers or other users with the relevant information needed for short-term operating decisions because they factor in costs that are not relevant to those decisions. Therefore, variable costing income statements are often preferred for internal reporting.

Although the use of variable costing for internal reports has many advantages, many organizations use absorption costing for both internal and external reporting. Often, managers traditionally used absorption costing because it was expensive and inconvenient to use two different reporting formats. Also, advocates of absorption costing for internal reporting believe that matching revenue and costs provides better information about opportunity costs for the organization. They believe that fixed costs are essentially capacity costs and, therefore, absorption costs reflect different products' use of capacity.

The following illustration compares income statements across time under absorption costing and variable costing.

## BOATS AFLOAT YACHT COMPANY (PART 1)
### ABSORPTION COSTING AND VARIABLE COSTING INCOME STATEMENTS

Boats Afloat Yacht Company recently organized to produce recreational yachts. The accountant, Joan Ardmore, prepared the second quarter income statements using absorption costing as follows.

### BOATS AFLOAT YACHT COMPANY
### SECOND QUARTER INCOME STATEMENTS

|  | April | May | June | Quarter Total |
|---|---|---|---|---|
| Revenue @ $100,000 per unit | $100,000 | $100,000 | $300,000 | $500,000 |
| Cost of goods sold | 100,000 | 70,000 | 210,000 | 380,000 |
| Gross margin | 0 | 30,000 | 90,000 | 120,000 |
| Administrative and selling expenses | 20,000 | 20,000 | 40,000 | 80,000 |
| Operating income (loss) | $(20,000) | $ 10,000 | $ 50,000 | $ 40,000 |

The sales manager, Stephanie Reynolds, analyzes these results and asks Joan to explain why a loss was posted in April but not in May, given that one boat was sold each month. The income statement was prepared using absorption costing, with fixed overhead allocated based on actual costs and actual production volumes. Joan decides to prepare variable costing income statements for the same period so that she can more easily explain the absorption costing income statement to Stephanie. Joan first reviews the information she gathered and her calculations for the absorption income statement. The selling price per yacht is $100,000, and the company incurred the following costs.

| Variable Costs per Yacht | |
|---|---|
| Direct materials | $20,000 |
| Direct labor | $15,000 |
| Variable production overhead | $ 5,000 |
| Variable selling | $10,000 |

| Fixed Costs per Month | |
|---|---|
| Fixed production overhead | $60,000 |
| Fixed administrative and selling | $10,000 |

Production and Sales Quantities

|  | April | May | June |
|---|---|---|---|
| Production | 1 | 2 | 2 |
| Sales | 1 | 1 | 3 |

### Absorption Costing

When absorption costing is used, all production overhead (fixed as well as variable) is allocated to inventory. When the company produces only one product, fixed production overhead costs can be easily prorated among the actual units produced. The absorption cost per unit is the sum of the variable production cost per unit plus the actual fixed overhead allocation rate per unit.

## ABSORPTION COST PER UNIT

|  | April | May | June |
|---|---|---|---|
| Fixed production overhead | $ 60,000 | $60,000 | $60,000 |
| Divided by number of units produced | 1 | 2 | 2 |
| Actual fixed overhead per unit | 60,000 | 30,000 | 30,000 |
| Variable production costs per unit: |  |  |  |
|   Direct materials | 20,000 | 20,000 | 20,000 |
|   Direct labor | 15,000 | 15,000 | 15,000 |
|   Variable production overhead | 5,000 | 5,000 | 5,000 |
|     Total variable cost per unit | 40,000 | 40,000 | 40,000 |
| Total absorption cost per unit | $100,000 | $70,000 | $70,000 |

## ABSORPTION COST OF GOODS SOLD

|  | April | May | June |
|---|---|---|---|
| Number of units sold | 1 | 1 | 3 |
| Absorption cost of unit(s) sold: |  |  |  |
|   Produced during April | $100,000 |  |  |
|   Produced during May |  | $70,000 | $ 70,000 |
|   Produced during June |  |  |  |
|   (2 @ $70,000 each) |  |  | 140,000 |
|     Total cost of goods sold | $100,000 | $70,000 | $210,000 |

During April, Boats Afloat produced and sold the same quantity of yachts, resulting in no ending inventory. In May, however, Boats Afloat produced two units and sold only one. Thus, one unit remained in inventory at a cost of $70,000. Then in June, two units were produced and three were sold. June's cost of goods sold reflected sales of three units; two produced in June and one drawn from inventory. Inventory at the end of June was zero.

Joan now separates administrative and selling expenses into variable and fixed categories and prepares variable costing income statements. Notice that under variable costing, income for the months when one boat was sold (April and May) is the same.

## ADMINISTRATIVE AND SELLING COSTS

|  | April | May | June |
|---|---|---|---|
| Variable selling cost per unit | $10,000 | $10,000 | $10,000 |
| Times number of units sold | 1 | 1 | 3 |
|   Total variable selling cost | 10,000 | 10,000 | 30,000 |
| Fixed administrative and selling expenses | 10,000 | 10,000 | 10,000 |
|   Total administrative and selling expenses | $20,000 | $20,000 | $40,000 |

## VARIABLE COSTING INCOME STATEMENTS

|  | April | May | June | Quarter Total |
|---|---|---|---|---|
| Revenue @ $100,000 per unit | $100,000 | $100,000 | $300,000 | $500,000 |
| Variable production expenses (for units sold) | 40,000 | 40,000 | 120,000 | 200,000 |
| Variable selling expenses | 10,000 | 10,000 | 30,000 | 50,000 |
|   Contribution margin | 50,000 | 50,000 | 150,000 | 250,000 |
| Fixed production expenses | 60,000 | 60,000 | 60,000 | 180,000 |
| Fixed administrative and selling expenses | 10,000 | 10,000 | 10,000 | 30,000 |
|   Operating income (loss) | $ (20,000) | $ (20,000) | $ 80,000 | $ 40,000 |

## ■ Reconciling Absorption and Variable Costing Incomes

Notice in the preceding illustration that when production levels are the same as sales levels, income is the same under absorption and variable costing. When production is greater than sales, absorption income is greater than variable income. In turn, when production is less than sales, absorption income is less than variable income. Reconciling the two incomes involves calculating the difference in overhead cost that is either added to or subtracted from inventory because sales volumes do not equal production volumes. Exhibit 14.5 presents reconciliation calculations that are then illustrated using Boats Afloat.

**EXHIBIT 14.5** Reconciling Absorption Cost and Variable Costing Income

| | Absorption Versus Variable Costing[a] | | |
| --- | --- | --- | --- |
| | **Operating Income** | **Inventory on the Balance Sheet** | **Reconciliation Calculations** |
| Production = Sales | Absorption costing income = Variable costing income | No change in inventory quantity on the balance sheet | No reconciliation needed because no difference in income |
| Production > Sales | Absorption costing income > Variable costing income | Inventory quantities on the balance sheet increase | Difference in income is equal to: (1) Increase in absorption costing inventory minus increase in variable costing inventory (2) Fixed overhead allocated during the current period to units added to inventory |
| Production < Sales | Absorption costing income < Variable costing income | Inventory quantities on the balance sheet decrease | Difference in income is equal to: (1) Decrease in absorption costing inventory minus decrease in variable costing inventory (2) Fixed overhead allocated to units in prior period to units removed from inventory |

[a]All comparisons assume either zero cost inflation/deflation or use of the LIFO cost flow assumption.

## BOATS AFLOAT YACHT COMPANY (PART 2)
### RECONCILING ABSORPTION COSTING AND VARIABLE COSTING INCOME STATEMENTS

Working from the two income statements, Joan prepares the following reconciliation report. Next she shows Stephanie the two income statements, explaining the preparation of each one. When Stephanie observes that the quarterly incomes under the two methods are the same, Joan points out that this occurred because the quarter had no beginning or ending inventories. Joan then shows Stephanie the reconciliation report and explains her calculations.

| | April | May | June |
| --- | --- | --- | --- |
| Difference in income: | | | |
| Absorption costing income (loss) | $(20,000) | $ 10,000 | $ 50,000 |
| Variable costing income (loss) | (20,000) | (20,000) | 80,000 |
| Difference | $    0 | $ 30,000 | $(30,000) |
| Difference in change in inventory: | | | |
| Absorption costing: | | | |
| Ending inventory | $    0 | $ 70,000 | $    0 |
| Beginning inventory | 0 | 0 | 70,000 |
| Increase (decrease) | 0 | 70,000 | (70,000) |
| Variable costing: | | | |
| Ending inventory | $    0 | $ 40,000 | $    0 |
| Beginning inventory | 0 | 0 | 40,000 |
| Increase (decrease) | 0 | 40,000 | (40,000) |
| Difference | $    0 | $ 30,000 | $(30,000) |

The only difference in inventory cost between absorption costing and variable costing is the amount of fixed overhead allocated to inventory under absorption costing. Therefore, the change in inventory difference can be presented by calculating the change in fixed costs included in absorption costing inventory. Ending inventory in May consists of one unit produced during May, when

$30,000 in fixed overhead was allocated to each unit. This unit was then sold during June. The difference in operating income between absorption and variable costing is summarized as follows:

|  | April | May | June |
|---|---|---|---|
| Change in fixed costs included in absorption costing inventory: | | | |
| Fixed costs in ending inventory | $ 0 | $30,000 | $ 0 |
| Fixed costs in beginning inventory | 0 | 0 | 30,000 |
| Increase (decrease) | $ 0 | $30,000 | $(30,000) |

After examining the two different income statements and the reconciling report, Stephanie decides that she wants to receive monthly income statements using both methods. She wants the same financial statement information that is shared with banks and other external stakeholders, in case someone calls and has questions about the organization's financial performance measured under GAAP. But she also wants to use the variable costing income statement to analyze the operating performance of the organization and its managers.

Stephanie also wants to set up a profit-sharing plan for all employees, rewarding employees when the amounts received from sales cover the costs for the period. She realizes that the variable costing income statement provides this information by more accurately measuring substantive economic changes across time.

---

## GUIDE YOUR LEARNING 14.2 Boats Afloat Yacht Company (Parts 1 and 2)

Boats Afloat Yacht Company illustrates absorption and variable costing income statements. For this illustration:

| Define It | Identify Problem | Explore Pros and Cons | Explore Use of Information |
|---|---|---|---|
| Describe how the computations were performed for absorption costing and for variable costing. How were the computations the same? How were they different? | Why was a variable costing income statement prepared? What was the problem? | What are the pros and cons of absorption costing and variable costing income statements? | What did the manager learn from the variable costing income statement? How did the manager plan to use the variable costing information? |

---

## ABSORPTION COSTING USING NORMAL COSTING

**Q1** How are absorption costing income statements constructed?

CHAPTER REFERENCE

In Chapter 5, *normal costing* was described as a costing method that allocates overhead using an estimated overhead allocation rate and the actual quantity of the allocation base.

CHAPTER REFERENCE

The methods being used in this section with normal costing can also be used with standard costing. We learn about standard costing in Chapters 6 and 11.

Under absorption costing in the Boats Afloat illustration, fixed production overhead was allocated to each yacht based on the actual cost incurred and the actual number of yachts produced each month. An alternative method under absorption costing is to allocate fixed overhead costs using normal costing. Normal costing uses actual direct costs and actual production volumes with an estimated fixed overhead allocation rate.

Suppose the accountant for Boats Afloat calculates an estimated fixed overhead allocation rate based on annual budget data. Assuming that budgeted fixed overhead is $720,000 and annual production is budgeted to be 24 units, the rate used for allocation would be estimated as follows:

$$\text{Estimated fixed overhead allocation rate} = \text{Estimated fixed overhead cost} \div \text{Estimated production volume}$$

$$= \$720,000 \div 24 \text{ units}$$
$$= \$30,000 \text{ per unit}$$

The fixed overhead allocation for the month of April would be:

$$\text{Fixed overhead allocation} = \text{Actual units produced} \times \text{Estimated fixed overhead allocation rate}$$
$$= 1 \text{ unit} \times \$30,000 \text{ per unit}$$
$$= \$30,000$$

### ◼ Motivation for Normal Costing

Using an estimated fixed overhead allocation rate is often preferred to the use of rates based on actual costs for three reasons: denominator, numerator, and information timeliness.

**Actual production volumes fluctuate (denominator reason).** If overhead is allocated based on actual volume, then the fixed cost per unit could be artificially high or low in different time periods. In the Boats Afloat illustration, total cost per yacht varied from $70,000 to $100,000 because of differences in fixed production overhead per unit. These differences were caused by variations in production volume across individual months. If production volumes fluctuate randomly or seasonally, then an estimated fixed production overhead rate could be used to avoid distorting costs for individual units.

**Fixed production overhead costs fluctuate (numerator reason).** Fixed overhead costs often fluctuate throughout a time period. Suppose an organization is located in a region with cold winters. Utility costs for production facilities might be high during winter months and low during summer months. If fixed overhead is allocated based on actual costs incurred each month, units produced during the winter would be allocated higher overhead costs than units produced during summer months. When an estimated fixed production overhead rate is used, this type of per-unit cost distortion would be avoided.

**Actual volume and fixed overhead costs are not known until after accounting for the period is completed (information timeliness).** Normal costing allows managers to assign costs to inventory when the accounting cycle has not been completed. Managers often need to cost inventory during each month or shortly after a month's end. It might not be possible to gather and report complete cost and volume data quickly enough to use actual costs for fixed overhead allocation. As long as normal costs are reasonable estimates, they can be used for faster-paced valuations.

### ◼ Allocation Rate Denominator Considerations

**Q2** What factors affect the choice of production volume measures for allocating fixed overhead?

When calculating an estimated fixed overhead allocation rate, accountants choose the allocation base to use as the denominator. Allocation bases such as direct labor hours, direct labor costs, machine hours, or number of units are often used. In this chapter we focus on allocating fixed overhead based on production volumes or different measures of capacity to present the most general case. Capacity is a measure of the constraints within an organization. It can be measured in a number of ways.

Four different levels of capacity could be used as the estimated volume of production under absorption costing. Two of these measures are *supply-based capacity levels;* they measure the amount of capacity that is available for production:

- **Theoretical capacity** is the upper capacity limit; it assumes continuous, uninterrupted production 365 days per year. Theoretical capacity is the maximum volume of goods or services that an organization could hypothetically produce.
- **Practical capacity** is the upper capacity limit that takes into account the organization's regularly scheduled times for production. Practical capacity excludes potential production that could take place during anticipated and scheduled maintenance downtimes, holidays, or other times in which production would normally be interrupted. In other words, practical capacity is theoretical capacity reduced for expected downtimes. Practical capacity is estimated using engineering studies and labor use patterns. The **Internal Revenue Service (IRS)** requires the use of practical capacity for U.S. income tax accounting because this level does not rely on demand. It is, therefore, more stable across time and less subject to manipulation.

**CURRENT PRACTICE**

Absorption costing is often used to value inventory for state and local property tax reports. The State of Ohio uses modified absorption costing, with depreciation excluded from inventory for property tax assessments.[6]

Two additional measures are *demand-based capacity levels;* they measure the amount of capacity needed to meet sales volumes:

---

[6]J. Belinfante and T. Carolson, "Reporting Inventory in Ohio," *Journal of Property Valuation and Taxation,* Summer 2002, pp. 4–10.

- **Normal capacity** is an average use of capacity over time. Normal capacity is the typical volume of goods or services an organization produces to meet customer demand.
- **Budgeted or expected capacity** is the anticipated use of capacity over the next period. Budgeted or expected capacity is based on management's planned operations in which customer demand is forecast.

## ◼ Volume Variance with Normal Costing

The **volume variance** is the difference between the amount of estimated fixed overhead costs used to calculate the allocation rate and the amount of fixed overhead costs actually allocated to inventory during the period. If allocated volume is greater than estimated volume, then too much fixed overhead is allocated to inventory and the inventory amounts need to be reduced by the variance amount. If allocated volume is less than estimated volume; too little fixed overhead cost is allocated to inventory and inventory values need to be increased by the variance amount. For example, suppose Boats Afloat estimates that fixed overhead costs will be $60,000 per month and fixed overhead is allocated to units using normal capacity of two units per month, or $30,000 per unit. In a month when only one yacht is produced, the volume variance would be:

$$\text{Volume variance} = \text{Expected fixed overhead cost} - \text{Allocated fixed overhead cost}$$
$$= \$60,000 - \$30,000$$
$$= \$30,000$$

In this example, allocated overhead was less than estimated overhead, so inventory accounts on the financial statements need to be increased by $30,000 to ensure that the expense recorded this period is equal to estimated fixed overhead.

When preparing financial statements under GAAP, this variance would be closed to cost of goods sold if it were immaterial. If material, it would be prorated among cost of goods sold, finished goods, and work in process (if any). In this example, the volume variance would be considered material because it is large compared to estimated fixed overhead costs, so cost of goods sold, finished goods, and work in process would all be increased.

## ◼ Evaluating Denominator Choices

Because volume variances must be adjusted at the end of an accounting period, the inventory and cost of goods sold values on the financial statements are not affected by the choice of denominator when calculating the estimated fixed overhead allocation rate. Therefore, no income effects need to be considered when choosing the denominator value.

However, managers sometimes use information from the normal costing system for pricing and product emphasis decisions. In addition, the denominator choice often affects budgets. To provide the highest-quality cost information for planning and decision making, inventory values should reflect realistic estimates of the use of resources. The quality of information for decision making and planning decreases when absorption cost information is based on unrealistic capacity levels.

Another factor to consider in choosing the denominator is how the choice affects the management of an organization's capacity. The largest costs in fixed production overhead are often related to capacity, such as building rent, depreciation, utilities, and maintenance. Thus, we can think of the estimated fixed overhead allocation rate as an estimated cost of capacity per unit that could be used to motivate managers to use capacity efficiently. The best choice would allocate a cost to each unit produced, not only to emphasize the need to cover fixed costs, but also to provide information about the opportunity cost of unused capacity.

If theoretical capacity is used as the allocation base, the fixed overhead allocation rate is unrealistically small. Therefore, theoretical capacity is rarely used in practice. If normal or budgeted capacity is used, inventory values simply reflect the current use of capacity, which may not be the most efficient use of capacity. In contrast, practical capacity reflects an attainable target for production. When practical capacity is used in the denominator, the fixed overhead allocation rate reflects the cost of supplying capacity. Internal reports can be developed to highlight the capacity available versus the capacity used. These reports focus managers' attention on unused capacity. Thus, the use of practical capacity motivates managers to find new ways to use available capacity. They may be encouraged to increase demand, develop new products, or consider leasing out or eliminating unused capacity.

**CHAPTER REFERENCE**

GAAP requires adjustments for all variances, not just volume variance. Other variances that must be adjusted include the fixed overhead spending variance. Chapter 11 explains calculations for this and other variances.

**HELPFUL HINT**

GAAP permits managers to defer closing variance accounts for interim financial statements if they expect any material variances to be absorbed by fiscal year end.

## SKI DOODLE

### COMPARING RESULTS USING ACTUAL PRODUCTION VOLUMES AND NORMAL CAPACITY

Ski Doodle is a small family-owned business that manufactures snowmobiles. Abel, the co-owner's son, has performed the company's accounting functions for several years. He always prepares variable costing income statements because the family makes product-related decisions on a regular basis and prefers using incremental costs for those decisions. Recently the family decided to apply for a loan to expand operations. The bank asked for this month's financial statements and wants them to conform to GAAP.

### Variable Costing

The information for the current period reports along with Ski Doodle's variable costing income statement follow.

Ordinarily, Ski Doodle's prices and costs are:

| | |
|---|---|
| Price | $10,000 per snowmobile |
| Variable production costs: | |
|     Raw materials | $2,000 per snowmobile |
|     Direct labor and variable overhead | $2,000 per snowmobile |
| Fixed production costs | $60,000 per month |
| Selling and administrative costs: | |
|     Variable | $500 per snowmobile |
|     Fixed | $30,000 per month |

Beginning finished goods inventory for the year was zero. Average production is about 12 snowmobiles per month. Sales are seasonal, so in some months no snowmobiles are produced or sold, while production and sales are high in other months.

This month beginning inventory was zero, 20 snowmobiles were manufactured, and 18 snowmobiles were sold.

### VARIABLE COSTING INCOME STATEMENT

| | | |
|---|---:|---:|
| Revenue (18 × $10,000) | | $180,000 |
| Variable costs | | |
|     Production (18 × $4,000) | $72,000 | |
|     Selling (18 × $500) | 9,000 | 81,000 |
|         Contribution margin | | 99,000 |
| Fixed costs | | |
|     Production | $60,000 | |
|     Administrative and selling | 30,000 | 90,000 |
|         Operating Income | | $  9,000 |

Ending inventory is valued at $8,000 (2 units × $4,000 variable production cost per unit).

### Absorption Costing with Actual Volume

When Abel develops the absorption costing income statement, he realizes that he needs to choose either actual volume or some estimate of volume to calculate the fixed overhead allocation rate. He decides to produce this month's statement both ways to see how they differ from each other and from the variable costing income statement information with which he is familiar.

First Abel produces an absorption costing income statement using actual production levels. The actual fixed overhead allocation rate is $60,000 ÷ 20 units = $3,000 per unit. Accordingly, the absorption cost per unit is $7,000 ($4,000 variable cost plus $3,000 allocated fixed overhead), and COGS is $126,000 (18 units sold × $7,000 per unit).

### ABSORPTION COSTING INCOME STATEMENT
#### (ACTUAL VOLUME)

| | |
|---|---:|
| Revenue (18 × $10,000) | $180,000 |
| Cost of goods sold (18 × $7,000) | 126,000 |
| Gross margin | 54,000 |
| Administrative and selling ($30,000 + 18 × $500) | 39,000 |
| Operating income | $ 15,000 |

Ending inventory is valued at $14,000 [2 units × ($4,000 + $3,000)].

The difference in incomes between variable costing and absorption costing arises because allocated fixed overhead costs increase the value of the absorption costing inventory on the balance sheet. With no beginning inventory, the change in this illustration equals the fixed overhead costs that are included in ending inventory. The two units in ending inventory were each allocated $3,000 in fixed overhead. Therefore, total fixed overhead in ending inventory is $6,000. Abel prepares a formal reconciliation of the two incomes as follows:

| | |
|---|---:|
| Variable costing income | $ 9,000 |
| Increase in fixed overhead costs in absorption inventory | |
| ($6,000 ending − $0 beginning) | 6,000 |
| Absorption costing income | $15,000 |

Another way to reconcile the two incomes is to calculate the difference in the change in inventory cost between the two costing methods:

| | |
|---|---:|
| Increase in absorption costing inventory | |
| ($14,000 ending − $0 beginning) | $14,000 |
| Increase in variable costing inventory | |
| ($8,000 ending − $0 beginning) | 8,000 |
| Difference | $ 6,000 |

## Absorption Costing with Normal Capacity

Next, Abel allocates fixed overhead using an estimated allocation rate based on a normal capacity level of 12 snowmobiles per month. In this case, the estimated fixed overhead allocation rate is $5,000 per unit ($60,000 ÷ 12 units). The cost of each unit produced under absorption costing is now $9,000 ($4,000 variable cost + $5,000 allocated fixed overhead).

### ABSORPTION COSTING INCOME STATEMENT
#### (NORMAL CAPACITY)

| | |
|---|---:|
| Revenue (18 × $10,000) | $180,000 |
| Cost of goods sold (18 × $9,000) | 162,000 |
| Gross margin | 18,000 |
| Administrative and selling ($30,000 + 18 × $500) | 39,000 |
| Operating income (loss) | $ (21,000) |

## Choice of Fixed Overhead Allocation Rate Denominator and Volume Variance Adjustment

After he completes the preceding calculations, Abel realizes that his choice of denominator level for the fixed overhead allocation rate affects the operating income, which in turn affects the bank's appraisal of Ski Doodle's creditworthiness. Based on his analyses, he thinks the bank will view the company more favorably if fixed overhead is allocated using the actual production level. Income for the current period appears higher than when using normal capacity.

Although Abel does accounting for the family business, he is not formally trained as an accountant. Therefore, he is unsure whether his calculations and conclusions are accurate. He suspects that too much overhead has been allocated under the normal capacity version of the absorption costing income statement. He decides to meet with Matt Goodings, the company's CPA.

Matt tells Abel, "I'm very impressed with what you've done here. I have only one comment about your calculations. When using an estimated volume to allocate fixed costs, there is always a volume variance—the difference between estimated and allocated fixed overhead cost. You estimated a normal capacity of 12 units per month, but said that sales increased more than expected this year. You now expect that production will average more than 12 units per month. You estimated fixed overhead costs to be $60,000. However, under your estimated normal capacity, $100,000 (20 units × $5,000) of fixed overhead costs is allocated to units produced last month. Thus, you have a volume variance of $40,000—you allocated more overhead to snowmobiles than the estimated cost. Generally accepted accounting principles require you to make an adjustment for this variance in your calculations to insure that only actual costs are recorded in inventory and cost of goods sold. I'll show you how." Matt shows Abel the following calculations.

$$\text{Volume variance} = \text{Estimated fixed overhead} - \text{Allocated fixed overhead}$$
$$= \$60,000 - (20 \text{ units} \times \$5,000 \text{ per unit})$$
$$= \$40,000$$

The volume variance of $40,000 is far more than 10% of the estimated fixed overhead cost of $60,000. Matt concludes that the variance is material and should be prorated among the 20 units produced that are in cost of goods sold and ending inventory. The adjustment is $2,000 per unit ($40,000 ÷ 20 units):

| Adjustment for the volume variance: | |
|---|---|
| Cost of goods sold ($2,000 × 18 units) | $36,000 |
| Ending inventory ($2,000 × 2 units) | 4,000 |
| Total volume variance | $40,000 |

Because more fixed overhead was allocated than estimated, the absorption cost per unit should be reduced by $2,000 per unit. Abel recasts the income statement with the volume variance adjustment as follows

### ABSORPTION COSTING INCOME STATEMENT
### (NORMAL CAPACITY WITH VOLUME VARIANCE ADJUSTMENT)

| | | |
|---|---|---|
| Revenue (18 × $10,000) | | $ 180,000 |
| Cost of goods sold: | | |
| Normal costing (18 × $9,000) | $(162,000) | |
| Volume variance (18 × $2,000) | 36,000 | (126,000) |
| Gross margin | | 54,000 |
| Administrative and selling [$30,000 + (18 × $500)] | | (39,000) |
| Operating income (loss) | | $  15,000 |

Abel observes that the operating income using normal capacity with the volume variance adjustment is now identical to the operating income when actual volume was used to allocate fixed overhead. Therefore, the financial statements are not affected by the choice of denominator used for the estimated fixed overhead allocation rate.

---

### GUIDE YOUR LEARNING  14.4  Ski Doodle

Ski Doodle illustrates income statements under variable costing, absorption costing using actual volume, and absorption costing using normal capacity. For this illustration:

| Define It | Identify Problem and Information | Identify Uncertainties | Explore Alternatives |
|---|---|---|---|
| In your own words, explain how and why the computations differ for each of the income statements presented in the illustration. | What decision was being addressed? What information (quantitative and qualitative) was relevant to the decision? | What types of uncertainties were there? Consider uncertainties about:<br>• How the bank will evaluate the income statement<br>• Estimating normal capacity | Discuss the pros and cons of each type of income statement:<br>• Variable costing<br>• Absorption costing with actual volume<br>• Absorption costing with normal capacity (including the volume variance adjustment)<br>What factors not discussed in the illustration might affect the best choice of a denominator to use in estimating the fixed overhead allocation rate? |

**Q1** How are absorption costing income statements constructed?

**Q3** How are variable costing income statements constructed?

# The Effects of Beginning Inventory Balances on Income Reconciliation

So far in this chapter, we prepared income statements that assumed no beginning inventories. However, most organizations have units in inventory. To simplify our calculations, we assume either zero cost inflation/deflation or use of the last-in, first-out (LIFO) inventory cost flow assumption in this chapter. Under zero cost inflation/deflation, current period and prior period costs per unit are the same. Under LIFO, any increase in inventory quantity on the balance sheet is valued using the current period costs. Any decrease in inventory quantity on the balance sheet is valued using the prior period costs.

To reconcile absorption cost and variable costing incomes under LIFO, we first need to determine whether inventory quantity increased or decreased during the period (i.e., whether production was higher or lower than sales). We then reconcile the incomes using the general formulas shown in Exhibit 14.5. If inventory quantities increased during the period, the simplest way to reconcile incomes is to multiply the fixed overhead cost rate for the current period (adjusted for any volume variance) times the number of units added to inventory. If inventory quantities decreased, it is first necessary to determine the allocation rate that was originally used to allocate fixed overhead cost to each unit in beginning inventory. (For simplicity, we will assume that there is only one LIFO cost layer in beginning inventory.) Income is reconciled by multiplying this rate times the number of units that were removed from inventory during the current period.

## FLYING FORTRESS
### ABSORPTION AND VARIABLE INCOME STATEMENTS WITH BEGINNING INVENTORIES

Your brother owns Flying Fortress, a company producing kits for model airplanes that actually fly. Your brother has an MBA and has always prepared a simple spreadsheet showing the difference between the cash that comes in and cash that goes out during a period and uses this information for planning and monitoring purposes. His tax accountant prepares tax reports. You have been asked to prepare financial statements for the business because your brother may want to ask others to invest in his company. You decide to prepare both variable and absorption income statements and explain to your brother the differences and uses of both.

During 2005, the company produced 10,000 kits and sold 9,000 of them. The kits sell for $200 each. Costs incurred in 2005 are listed here.

| | |
|---|---|
| Materials purchased | $500,000 |
| Materials used | $400,000 |
| Other variable production costs | $800,000 |
| Fixed overhead costs | $150,000 |
| Variable selling costs | $135,000 |
| Fixed selling and administrative costs | $200,000 |

In January 2005, 2,000 kits were in beginning inventory. Assume that the value of this inventory was $220,000 under variable costing and $250,000 under absorption costing. Ending inventory contains 3,000 kits because production exceeded sales by 1,000 kits during 2005.

### Variable Costing

You first perform the calculations needed to prepare the variable costing income statement. These calculations include determining the production variable cost per unit:

$$\text{Total variable production cost} = \text{Materials used} + \text{Other variable production costs}$$
$$= \$400,000 + \$800,000 = \$1,200,000$$
$$\text{Variable cost per unit} = \$1,200,000 \div 10,000 \text{ units}$$
$$= \$120 \text{ per unit}$$

You also calculate the variable selling cost per unit:

$$\text{Variable selling cost per unit} = \text{Total variable selling cost} \div \text{Units sold}$$
$$= \$135,000 \div 9,000 \text{ units}$$
$$= \$15 \text{ per unit}$$

*(continued)*

Using these calculations and other information provided, you create the following variable costing income statement:

### VARIABLE COSTING INCOME STATEMENT

| | | |
|---|---:|---:|
| Revenue (9,000 units × $200) | | $1,800,000 |
| Less variable costs: | | |
|     Production (9,000 units × $120) | $1,080,000 | |
|     Selling (9,000 units × $15) | 135,000 | 1,215,000 |
|         Contribution margin | | 585,000 |
| Fixed costs: | | |
|     Production overhead | $ 150,000 | |
|     Selling and administrative | 200,000 | 350,000 |
|         Variable costing operating income | | $ 235,000 |

You also determine the ending inventory:

| | |
|---|---:|
| Variable costing finished goods inventory: | |
|     Beginning inventory (2,000 units × $110) | $ 220,000 |
|     Add variable production costs (10,000 units × $120) | 1,200,000 |
|         Goods available for sale | 1,420,000 |
|     Less cost of goods sold (9,000 units × $120) | 1,080,000 |
|         Ending inventory ($220,000 + 1,000 units × $120) | $ 340,000 |

You notice that variable cost per unit changed between last period and this period. Last period's inventory was valued at $110 each, and this period's production is valued at $120 each.

## Absorption Costing

You now perform the calculations needed to prepare the absorption costing income statement. You decide to use practical capacity of 15,000 units per year to estimate a fixed overhead allocation rate because your brother may want to use this information to examine his use of existing capacity.

Estimated fixed overhead allocation rate = Estimated fixed overhead cost ÷ Practical capacity
= $150,000 ÷ 15,000 units
= $10 per unit

You then determine the volume variance:

Volume variance = Estimated fixed overhead cost − Allocated fixed overhead cost
= $150,000 − ($10 per unit × 10,000 units)
= $50,000

You decide that the volume variance is material because it amounts to one-third ($50,000 ÷ $150,000) of the estimated fixed overhead cost. Thus, you prorate the volume variance among the 10,000 units produced during 2005 at $50,000 ÷ 10,000 units = $5 per unit. You will increase the cost of goods sold and inventory by $5 per unit because less overhead was allocated to units than the estimated total fixed overhead cost for 2005. (*Note:* This illustration has no work in process inventory.)

| | |
|---|---:|
| Prorated volume variance: | |
|     Cost of goods sold (9,000 units × $5 per unit) | $45,000 |
|     Inventory (1,000 units × $5 per unit) | 5,000 |
|         Total volume variance | $50,000 |

Now you prepare the absorption costing income statement. The absorption cost per unit sold is $135 ($120 variable cost + $10 fixed overhead allocation rate + $5 volume variance adjustment).

### ABSORPTION COSTING INCOME STATEMENT

| | |
|---|---:|
| Revenue (9,000 units × $200) | $1,800,000 |
| Cost of goods sold (9,000 units × $135) | 1,215,000 |
|     Gross margin | 585,000 |
| Selling and administrative costs ($135,000 + $200,000) | 335,000 |
|     Absorption costing operating income | $ 250,000 |

Finally, you calculate the ending absorption costing inventory amount:

| | |
|---|---:|
| Beginning inventory (2,000 units × $125) | $ 250,000 |
| Add variable production costs (10,000 units × $120) | 1,200,000 |
| Add fixed overhead costs (10,000 units × $10) | 100,000 |
| Add volume variance adjustment (10,000 units × $5) | 50,000 |
| Goods available for sale (12,000 units × $135) | 1,600,000 |
| Less cost of goods sold (9,000 units sold × $135) | 1,215,000 |
| Ending inventory (2,000 units × $125 + 1,000 units × $135) | $ 385,000 |

You also produce an alternative format for the absorption income statement with more detail because it may be easier for your brother to understand.

### ABSORPTION COSTING INCOME STATEMENT
### (WITH ADDITIONAL DETAIL)

| | | |
|---|---:|---:|
| Revenue | | $1,800,000 |
| Cost of goods sold: | | |
| Beginning inventory | $ 250,000 | |
| Variable production costs | 1,200,000 | |
| Fixed overhead costs allocated | 100,000 | |
| Adjustment for volume variance | 50,000 | |
| Cost of goods available for sale | 1,600,000 | |
| Ending inventory (2,000 × $125 + 1,000 × $135) | (385,000) | |
| Cost of goods sold | | 1,215,000 |
| Gross margin | | 585,000 |
| Operating costs: | | |
| Variable selling | 135,000 | |
| Fixed selling and administrative expenses | 200,000 | 335,000 |
| Absorption costing operating income | | $ 250,000 |

## Reconciliation of Variable and Absorption Costing Income

You prepare a reconciliation to help your brother understand the difference between the variable costing and absorption costing income statements. Because inventory increased during the year, you calculate the increase in fixed overhead costs added to inventory this year to explain why absorption costing income was higher than variable costing income.

| | |
|---|---:|
| Variable costing income | $235,000 |
| Increase in fixed overhead costs in absorption inventory | |
| [1,000 units added to inventory × ($10 + $5) per unit fixed overhead cost] | 15,000 |
| Absorption costing income | $250,000 |

The reconciliation could also be calculated by determining the change during the year in the total amount of fixed overhead cost including in inventory. You notice that last period's inventory was $220,000 under variable costing and $250,000 under absorption costing. Because the only difference between the two methods is the allocation of fixed overhead cost, the $30,000 difference must consist only of fixed overhead cost allocated to units during one or more prior periods. Because beginning inventory held 2,000 units, the average fixed overhead cost in inventory was $15 per unit ($30,000 ÷ 2,000 units). This period, fixed production overhead is also $15 per unit, made up of $10 in the fixed overhead allocation rate plus the $5 volume variance adjustment. Therefore, the change in fixed costs included in inventory during 2005 is:

| | |
|---|---:|
| Fixed cost in ending inventory (3,000 × $15) | $45,000 |
| Fixed cost in beginning inventory (2,000 × $15) | 30,000 |
| Difference between absorption and variable costing income | $15,000 |

## Using Variable and Absorption Costing Information

After you discuss these statements with your brother, he decides to prepare both statements on a monthly basis instead of using the spreadsheet that he previously developed. He wants the

*(continued)*

absorption costing income statement so that he can monitor the information that people outside his company, such as bankers and any other creditors, will be using. He believes this statement will also help him focus on the use of capacity. Each month when he calculates the volume variance, he will know how close to practical capacity that month's operations were. He also wants variable costing income statements because he believes this method represents a more accurate economic picture of his operations.

---

### GUIDE YOUR LEARNING  14.5  Flying Fortress

Flying Fortress illustrates variable and absorption costing income statements with beginning inventories. For this illustration:

| Define It | Anticipate Computational Changes | Prioritize Options |
|---|---|---|
| In your own words, explain how beginning inventories affected the computations. | Explain how the computations would be the same and how they would be different if inventory quantity decreased during 2005. | In your own words, explain why the owner decided to use both types of income statements in the future. |

---

## INCENTIVES TO BUILD UP INVENTORIES

**Q5** What are the uses and limitations of absorption, variable, and throughput costing income statements?

In this chapter's examples, absorption costing operating income is higher than variable costing operating income in periods when the inventory quantities increase. Under absorption costing, part of an organization's fixed overhead cost is recorded as inventory on the balance sheet. As inventory quantity increases, the amount of fixed cost included in inventory increases. Because that portion of fixed cost is not expensed until later, operating income also increases. As a result, managers using absorption costing have incentives to inappropriately build up inventory quantities, especially when sales during the current period decrease. Managers may be motivated by many factors:

- Managers' reputations often increase with reported operating income.
- Managers frequently receive bonus payments based on their ability to meet or exceed targeted operating income levels.
- Managers may be biased in their sales forecasts, preventing them from promptly recognizing a decline in sales.

### ■ Disincentives to Build Up Inventories

Managers might avoid inventory buildups for several reasons. If managers become aware of a sales decline, they could be unwilling to use an inventory buildup that, while strengthening short-term earnings, would negatively affect future earnings when those units are either sold or written off. If bonuses are based on variable costing income, managers will not be rewarded for inventory buildups. The **Harley-Davidson** case that opened this chapter shows another disincentive; analysts routinely monitor companies' inventory levels. Excessive inventory levels are often viewed as evidence of poor management or deteriorating sales. In addition, some organizations use just-in-time (JIT) inventory management. Under JIT, the potential buildup of inventory is unlikely; therefore, income differences under absorption and variable costing are small.

**CURRENT PRACTICE**

When organizations adopt JIT systems (see Chapter 13 for more details), the first year of the change often decreases financial statement profitability (under absorption costing) because inventory levels are greatly reduced.[7]

---

[7]D. Boyd, L. Kronk, and R. Skinner, "The Effects of Just-in-Time Systems on Financial Accounting Metrics," *Industrial Management + Data Systems,* 102(3/4), (2002), pp. 153–165.

## ■ Uncertainties about Desirable Inventory Levels

In the Harley-Davidson case, managers stated that they intentionally wanted dealers to carry higher inventories to better meet customer demand. Analysts responded that sales were in decline and that dealer inventory increases signaled a forthcoming decline in the company's financial health. Because of uncertainties about factors influencing future sales, it was not possible for outsiders such as investors to determine whether Harley-Davidson's inventories were too high. These uncertainties included the following:

- The extent to which long wait times would cause customers to buy from competitors
- The increase in sales to individuals who would not have waited
- Whether an increase in inventories and corresponding decrease in customer wait times would reduce the mystique of the Harley-Davidson brand, causing a decrease in future product demand
- The most desirable production and inventory levels

To further complicate matters, outsiders could not know whether the managers were completely candid in explaining their production policies or whether their production decisions were biased.

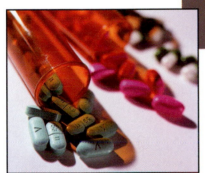

## FOCUS ON ETHICAL DECISION MAKING
### Channel Stuffing at Bristol-Myers Squibb

In August of 2002, the Securities and Exchange Commission (SEC) launched a formal investigation into Bristol-Myers Squibb's accounting and operations practices centered around inventories. Later in the year, the U.S. Attorney began an inquiry into the company's inventory practices. Share prices for Bristol-Myers dropped 50% during the six months prior to the SEC's inquiry because of suspicions about the reliability of its accounting numbers (*Wall Street Journal*, August 30, 2002; Harris, Oct. 10, 2002).

In previous years, Bristol-Myers used sales incentives to encourage wholesalers to buy more drugs than necessary to meet patients' needs. This overstocking made the company's pharmaceutical products appear more popular than they actually were, but reduced sales in later periods. As the problem unfolded, Barbara Ryan, an analyst with Deutsche Bank Securities exclaimed, "Do wholesalers keep finding boxes of product in the basement? This is laughable" (Harris, July 24, 2002).

Facing a public controversy about its sales, the managers of Bristol-Myers admitted that excessive wholesaler buying amounted to at least $1.5 billion in sales during 2000 and 2001. The company adopted its practice of channel stuffing because sales were falling as patent protections expired and its products began to compete with cheaper generic drugs (*Wall Street Journal*, Aug. 30, 2002; Harris, July 24, 2002). In a report released in early March 2003, Bristol-Myers conceded that it had used "inappropriate" accounting between 1999 and 2002, resulting in earnings that were inflated by as much as $2.75 billion (Harris, March 11, 2003).

In the opening case in this chapter, analysts accused Harley-Davidson of channel stuffing. However, those excess inventories were sold in the next period. Had motorcycle sales decreased the next period, company officials might have been subject to the same regulatory actions as Bristol-Myers. A fine line separates managing inventories for valid business purposes and managing inventories for earnings manipulation.

SOURCES: G. Harris, "U.S. Attorney Starts Bristol Inquiry," *The Wall Street Journal*, October 10, 2002, p. B4; R.C. Altman, "The Market Punishes Its Own," *The Wall Street Journal*, July 23, 2002, p. A14; "Bristol-Myers Says SEC Inquiry Is Now Formal Investigation," *The Wall Street Journal*, August 30, 2002, p. B2; G. Harris, "Big Drug Firms Report Divergent Results," *The Wall Street Journal*, July 24, 2002, p. B3; G. Harris, "The Economy: Bristol-Myers Says Accounting Was 'Inappropriate,' Inflated Sales," *The Wall Street Journal*, March 11, 2003, p. A2.

#### Practice Ethical Decision Making

In Chapter 1, we learned about a process for making ethical decisions (Exhibit 1.11). You can address the following questions for this ethical dilemma to improve your skills for making ethical decisions. Think about your answers to these questions and discuss them with others.

*(continued)*

| Ethical Decision-Making Process | Questions to Consider about This Ethical Dilemma |
|---|---|
| Identify ethical problems as they arise. | Is channel stuffing an ethical problem? Why or why not? |
| Objectively consider the well-being of others and society when exploring alternatives. | Compare managers who accidentally over-produce inventory because they overestimate future sales levels with managers who deliberately overproduce inventory to report higher earnings. What assumptions lie behind these managers' decisions? Do you see a difference in ethical values? From the viewpoint of investors, discuss whether it matters why inventories are overproduced. |
| Clarify and apply ethical values when choosing a course of action. | Recommend two or more company policies that might prevent channel stuffing. What values did you use to arrive at your solution? |
| Work toward ongoing improvement of personal and organizational ethics. | Discuss limitations of the policies you recommended. In light of these limitations, how can companies prevent behaviors such as channel stuffing? |

# THROUGHPUT COSTING

 **Q4** How are throughput costing income statements constructed?

**CHAPTER REFERENCE**

Operating decisions involving constrained resources, part of the Theory of Constraints, are discussed in more detail in Chapter 4.

**Throughput costing** is a modified form of variable costing that treats direct labor and variable overhead as period expenses. Developed in the 1980s as part of the Theory of Constraints, throughput costing has become popular for internal reporting purposes in the United States and Europe. It was developed when some managers realized that product costs under both absorption and variable costing are excessive because they include more than direct materials.

In many organizations, conversion costs such as direct labor and overhead do not vary proportionately with volume of production. Under throughput costing, inventory is valued using only direct material costs (Exhibit 14.6). All other costs are treated as period costs. The throughput contribution is defined as revenue less direct materials costs for the units sold. Accountants and managers in companies using Theory of Constraints methods believe that throughput costing helps them make better short-term decisions because costs other than direct materials tend to be

**EXHIBIT 14.6**
**Throughput Costing**

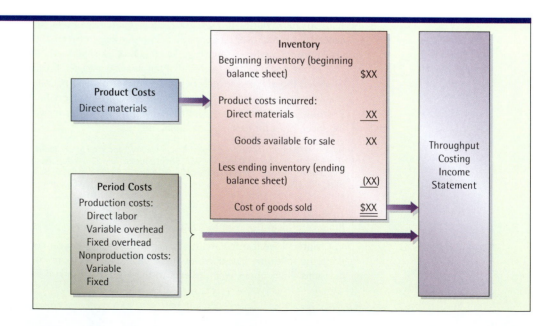

**EXHIBIT 14.7**
**Throughput Costing Income Statement**

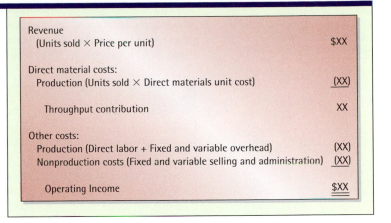

| | |
|---|---|
| Revenue (Units sold × Price per unit) | $XX |
| Direct material costs: | |
| Production (Units sold × Direct materials unit cost) | (XX) |
| Throughput contribution | XX |
| Other costs: | |
| Production (Direct labor + Fixed and variable overhead) | (XX) |
| Nonproduction costs (Fixed and variable selling and administration) | (XX) |
| Operating Income | $XX |

relatively fixed in the short run. For example, direct labor may be a fixed cost if workers are guaranteed a work schedule such as a 40-hour week. When direct labor is fixed and little or no variable overhead cost is involved, the variable income statement is similar to the throughput costing income statement. Exhibit 14.7 shows an income statement format for throughput costing.

Following is a throughput income statement using data from the Flying Fortress illustration.

| | |
|---|---|
| Revenue (9,000 units × $200 per unit) | $1,800,000 |
| Direct materials (9,000 units × $40 per unit) | 360,000 |
| Throughput contribution | 1,440,000 |
| Other costs: | |
| Operating expenses | 1,285,000 |
| Throughput costing operating income | $ 155,000 |

Throughput contribution is revenue less the cost of direct materials for the units sold. The operating expenses of $1,285,000 include the costs of direct labor and variable overhead for the entire period (10,000 units × $80 per unit = $800,000), variable selling costs ($135,000), fixed production cost ($150,000), and fixed selling costs ($200,000). As an alternative format, totals for production- and nonproduction-related costs may also be presented separately. Ending inventory increased under throughput costing only by the amount of direct materials: 1,000 units × $40 per unit = $40,000.

Variable costing income was $235,000. Throughput costing operating income is $80,000 less than operating income under variable costing. This difference arises because $80,000 (1,000 units × $80 per unit) of variable overhead and direct labor costs are included in inventory under variable costing, but expensed as a period cost under throughput costing.

ALTERNATIVE TERMS

Some people refer to *throughput costing* as *super-variable costing*.

### GUIDE YOUR LEARNING 14.6 Key Terms

Stop to confirm that you understand the new term introduced in the last several pages.

Throughput costing (p. 568)

Write a definition of this term in your own words.

**Q5** What are the uses and limitations of absorption, variable, and throughput costing income statements?

## ■ Advantages of Throughput Costing

Throughput costing can be thought of as an extreme version of variable costing. Only direct material costs are assigned to inventory and cost of goods sold. When costs such as direct labor and production overhead are categorized and treated as operating costs rather than product costs (inventory), managers' attitudes about these costs tend to change. They are encouraged to reduce operating costs when needed, such as when sales decline. Under throughput costing, managers are more likely to consider reducing costs such as direct labor. Conversely, under absorption costing many production costs are initially categorized as assets (inventory) until goods are sold. As a result, managers may perceive less need to reduce direct labor and overhead cost. Compared to absorption and variable costing, throughput costing also reduces the incentives for managers to build up inventory to inappropriate levels.

## GUIDE YOUR LEARNING 14.7 Throughput Costing

The Flying Fortress example demonstrates throughput costing. For this example:

| Define It | Compare It | Extend It |
|---|---|---|
| Describe how computations are performed for throughput costing. | How are the computations the same and how are they different from the computations for variable costing and absorption costing? | Compare the operating income for Ski Doodle under throughput costing and absorption costing. How would you reconcile the difference between incomes under these two methods? (*Hint:* Think about how the calculations shown in Exhibit 14.5 would change.) |

## COMPARISON OF ABSORPTION, VARIABLE, AND THROUGHPUT COSTING

Exhibit 14.8 compares the assumptions used in absorption costing, variable costing, and throughput costing. These accounting methods differ based on the costs that are considered product costs. Under absorption costing, all production costs are product costs. Under variable costing, only variable production costs are product costs. Under throughput costing, only direct materials costs are product costs. These methods affect how quickly production overhead and other costs are expensed on the income statement. Because managers monitor

**EXHIBIT 14.8** Comparison of Absorption, Variable, and Throughput Costing

| Absorption Costing | Variable Costing | Throughput Costing |
|---|---|---|
| GAAP | Not GAAP | Not GAAP |
| Useful for external reporting purposes | Useful for performance evaluation and internal decision making | Useful for short-term capacity decision making, focuses managers attention on reducing labor and overhead costs because they are considered operating costs instead of product costs (inventory) |
| Direct material and direct labor are inventory costs | Direct material and direct labor are inventory costs | Only direct materials are inventory costs |
| Fixed and variable production overhead allocated to inventory | Fixed production overhead expensed as a period cost. Variable production overhead allocated to inventory | Direct labor, fixed and variable overhead, and all other costs expensed as operational expense, a period cost |
| Administrative and selling costs (both fixed and variable) expensed as period costs | Administrative and selling costs separated into fixed and variable costs and expensed as period costs | Administrative and selling costs expensed as operational expense, a period cost |
| Inventory costs (including per unit fixed and variable production costs) not expensed until the units are sold | Inventory costs (only production variable costs) not expensed until the units are sold | Inventory costs (only direct materials) not expensed until the units are sold |

---

[8]"Offshoot of TOC—Throughput Accounting—Overcomes Localized Constraint Optimization," *MSI,* September 2003, p. 34.

**Q5** What are the uses and limitations of absorption, variable, and throughput costing income statements?

operating income, these methods affect how quickly they are motivated to consider changing production plans related to these costs.

## ■ Different Methods for Different Purposes

Before technology made it relatively easy to draw many different reports from one database, most organizations established an accounting system designed primarily to meet financial and tax accounting requirements. Because absorption costing is required by GAAP and income tax rules, it tended to be the only method used. With improved technology, organizations are now able to produce information reports for many different purposes.

Absorption costing income statements focus on matching production costs to revenues on the income statement. This information is important for external users, such as investors, who monitor the trends in product costs for an organization over time and for comparison with competitors. Variable costing income statements are often used to evaluate the performance of a division or manager, or as a source for information for decision making. Throughput costing statements help managers determine the most efficient use of resources in the short term.

**CURRENT PRACTICE**

Master Industries, an injection molding company, displays charts of throughput costing and quality control data in the workplace. Managers use the throughput costing data in day-to-day business decisions.[9]

## SUMMARY

**Q1** How Are Absorption Costing Income Statements Constructed?

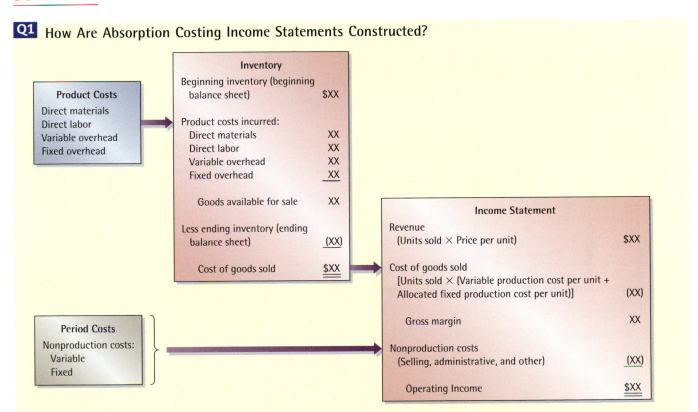

**Q2** What Factors Affect the Choice of Production Volume Measures for Allocating Fixed Overhead?

### Actual Costing

$$\text{Actual fixed overhead allocation rate} = \frac{\text{Actual fixed overhead cost}}{\text{Actual production volume}}$$

### Normal Costing

$$\text{Estimated fixed overhead allocation rate} = \frac{\text{Estimated fixed overhead cost}}{\text{Estimated production volume}}$$

---

[9]J. Long , J. Castellano, and H. Roehm, "A User Friendly Financial Reporting System," *Quality Progress,* January 2002, pp. 60–66.

**Alternative Measures of Production Volume for Normal Costing**
- Theoretical capacity (p. 548)
- Practical capacity (p. 548)
- Normal capacity (p. 549)
- Budgeted or expected capacity (p. 549)

**Volume Variance under Normal Costing**

Volume variance = Expected fixed overhead cost − Allocated fixed overhead cost

If material: Prorate among all production during the period (units in work in process, finished goods, and cost of goods sold)

If immaterial: Allocate to cost of goods sold

## Q3 How Are Variable Costing Income Statements Constructed?

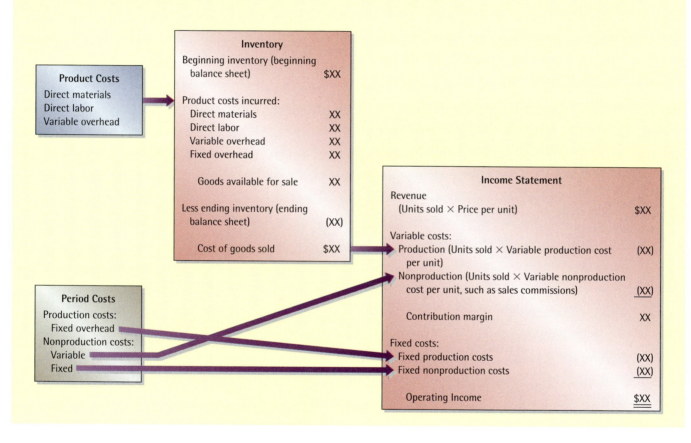

**Q4** How Are Throughput Costing Income Statements Constructed?

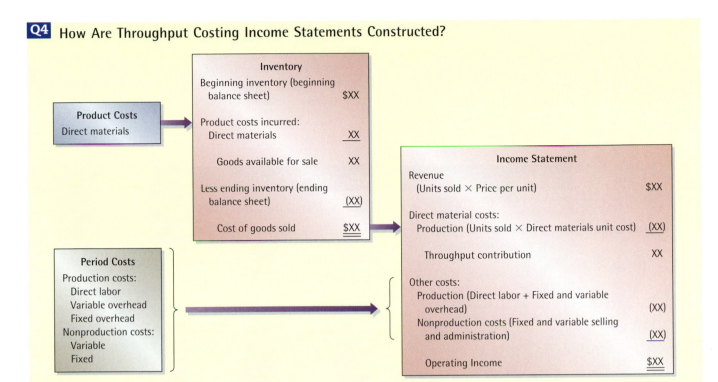

**Q5** What Are the Uses and Limitations of Absorption, Variable, and Throughput Costing Income Statements?

| Absorption Costing | Variable Costing | Throughput Costing |
|---|---|---|
| GAAP | Not GAAP | Not GAAP |
| Useful for external reporting purposes | Useful for performance evaluation and internal decision making | Useful for short-term capacity decision making, focuses managers attention on reducing labor and overhead costs because they are considered operating costs instead of product costs (inventory) |
| Direct material and direct labor are inventory costs | Direct material and direct labor are inventory costs | Only direct materials are inventory costs |
| Fixed and variable production overhead allocated to inventory | Fixed production overhead expensed as a period cost. Variable production overhead allocated to inventory | Direct labor, fixed and variable overhead, and all other costs expensed as operational expense, a period cost |
| Administrative and selling costs (both fixed and variable) expensed as period costs | Administrative and selling costs separated into fixed and variable costs and expensed as period costs | Administrative and selling costs expensed as operational expense, a period cost |
| Inventory costs (including per unit fixed and variable production costs) not expensed until the units are sold | Inventory costs (only production variable costs) not expensed until the units are sold | Inventory costs (only direct materials) not expensed until the units are sold |

## KEY TO SYMBOLS

**e** This question requires students to extend knowledge beyond the applications shown in the textbook.

**1** This question requires Step 1 skills (**Identifying**) in Steps for Better Thinking (Exhibit 1.10).

**2** This question requires Step 2 skills (**Exploring**) in Steps for Better Thinking (Exhibit 1.10).

**3** This question requires Step 3 skills (**Prioritizing**) in Steps for Better Thinking (Exhibit 1.10).

**4** This question requires Step 4 skills (**Envisioning**) in Steps for Better Thinking (Exhibit 1.10).

## Self-Study Problem

### Self-Study Problem 1  Absorption, Variable, and Throughput Costing

**Q1, Q3, Q4**

During its second year of operations, Grilling Machines, a company that manufactures and sells electric table-top grills, produced 275,000 units and sold 250,000 units at $60 per unit. The beginning inventory balance was 5,000 units. No changes in fixed or variable costs occurred in the second year. The managers expected to sell 220,000 units, the same volume of production as last year. They set that amount as the normal capacity for allocating fixed overhead costs during the second year. For simplicity, assume that the budgeted fixed production overhead cost equals the actual cost this period. Also, assume that the company uses the LIFO cost flow assumption. The following costs were incurred during the year:

| | |
|---|---|
| Variable cost per unit: | |
| Direct materials | $15.00 |
| Direct labor | 10.00 |
| Manufacturing overhead | 12.50 |
| Selling and administrative | 2.50 |
| Total fixed costs: | |
| Production overhead | $2,200,000 |
| Selling and administrative | 1,375,000 |

**REQUIRED:**

**A.** Prepare income statements using absorption costing, variable costing, and throughput costing. Provide the details of your calculations in a schedule for each income statement.

**B.** Reconcile the difference between operating incomes based on absorption costing and variable costing. Create a schedule to show your work.

**e C.** Reconcile the difference between operating incomes based on variable costing and throughput costing. Create a schedule to show your work.

**D.** Suppose the accountant for Grilling Machines used an actual fixed overhead allocation rate rather than an estimated rate. Using this method, calculate the cost of goods sold and ending inventory under absorption costing. Compare the results to those calculated in part (A).

**E.** If the volume variance is not material, how is it closed at the end of the period? Explain the reasoning behind this treatment.

### Solution to Self-Study Problem 1

**A. Calculations for the Absorption Costing Income Statement**

Before calculating the product cost per unit, it is necessary to compute the fixed overhead cost allocation and the volume variance adjustment:

The company's policy is to allocate fixed overhead using normal capacity, which was estimated at 220,000 units.

$$\text{Estimated fixed overhead allocation rate} = \$2,200,000 \text{ estimated fixed overhead} \div 220,000 \text{ normal volume of units}$$

$$= \$10.00 \text{ per unit}$$

At the end of the year, the company must make an adjustment for its volume variance, which is the difference between total fixed overhead allocated to production and the original estimate of fixed overhead costs.

| | |
|---|---|
| Estimated fixed overhead ($10 per unit × 220,000 units) | $2,200,000 |
| Allocated overhead ($10 per unit × 275,000 units) | 2,750,000 |
| Volume variance | $ 550,000 |

The volume variance is considered material, because it is greater than 10% of the estimated fixed overhead cost.

$$\$550,000 \div \$2,200,000 = 25\%$$

Material volume variances are adjusted to all units produced. For this problem, 250,000 of the units are in cost of goods sold, and 25,000 units are added to inventory. Because more fixed overhead cost was allocated than estimated, the absorption cost per unit must be reduced by the volume variance.

$$\text{Volume variance per unit produced} = \$550,000 \div 275,000 \text{ units}$$
$$= \$2.00 \text{ per unit}$$

Given the preceding calculations, the absorption product cost per unit is:

| | |
|---|---:|
| Direct materials | $15.00 |
| Direct labor | 10.00 |
| Variable overhead | 12.50 |
| Fixed overhead allocation rate | 10.00 |
| Subtotal before volume variance adjustment | 47.50 |
| Volume variance adjustment per unit | (2.00) |
| Total absorption cost per unit | $45.50 |

We can now calculate the value of ending inventory. 275,000 units were produced this year, and 250,000 were sold, causing inventory to increase by 25,000 units. Beginning inventory was 5,000 units, so ending inventory is 30,000 units. Also, recall that the costs in year 1 were the same as the costs in year 2. Because actual volume during year 1 was 220,000 units (rather than 275,000), no volume variance adjustment was needed in year 1. Therefore, beginning inventory was valued at an absorption cost of $47.50 per unit. Under the LIFO cost flow assumption, those costs remain in ending inventory, and the units added this year are valued at $45.50 per unit.

| | |
|---|---:|
| Beginning inventory (5,000 units × $47.50 per unit) | $ 237,500 |
| Units added to inventory (25,000 units × $45.50 per unit) | 1,137,500 |
| Ending inventory | $1,375,000 |

Because inventory increased during year 2, cost of goods sold under LIFO is calculated as the current year cost per unit times the number of units sold:

| | |
|---|---:|
| Cost of goods sold (250,000 units × $45.50 per unit) | $11,375,000 |

Exhibit 14.9 shows the three income statements.

**EXHIBIT 14.9** Absorption, Variable, and Throughput Costing Income Statements for Grilling Machines

| Absorption Costing | | Variable Costing | | Throughput Costing | |
|---|---|---|---|---|---|
| **Income Statement** | | **Income Statement** | | **Income Statement** | |
| Revenue ($60 × 250,000) | $ 15,000,000 | Revenue ($60 × 250,000) | $15,000,000 | Revenue ($60 × 250,000) | $15,000,000 |
| Cost of goods sold | (11,375,000) | Variable costs: | | Cost of goods sold | (3,750,000) |
| Gross margin | 3,625,000 | Cost of goods sold | (9,375,000) | Throughput contribution | 11,250,000 |
| Selling and administrative | (2,000,000) | Selling and administrative | (625,000) | Other costs: | |
| Operating income | $ 1,625,000 | Contribution margin | 5,000,000 | Production conversion | (8,387,500) |
| | | Fixed costs: | | costs | |
| | | Fixed production overhead | (2,200,000) | Selling and administrative | (2,000,000) |
| | | Fixed selling and | (1,375,000) | Operating income | $ 862,500 |
| | | administrative | | | |
| | | Operating income | $ 1,425,000 | | |
| **Reconciliation of Product Costs** | | **Reconciliation of Product Costs** | | **Reconciliation of Product Costs** | |
| Beginning inventory | $ 237,500 | Beginning inventory | $ 187,500 | Beginning inventory | $ 75,000 |
| Product costs incurred: | | Product costs incurred: | | Produce costs incurred: | |
| Direct materials | 4,125,000 | Direct materials | 4,125,000 | Direct materials | 4,125,000 |
| Direct labor | 2,750,000 | Direct labor | 2,750,000 | Goods available for sale | 4,200,000 |
| Variable overhead | 3,437,500 | Variable overhead | 3,437,500 | Less ending inventory | (450,000) |
| Fixed overhead allocated | 2,750,000 | Goods available for sale | 10,500,000 | Cost of goods sold | $3,750,000 |
| Volume variance | (550,000) | Less ending inventory | (1,125,000) | | |
| adjustment | | Cost of goods sold | $ 9,375,000 | | |
| Goods available for sale | 12,750,000 | | | | |
| Less ending inventory | (1,375,000) | | | | |
| Cost of goods sold | $ 11,375,000 | | | | |

To prepare the reconciliation of total product costs in Exhibit 14.9, calculate the total amounts for each of the variable production costs, based on actual production of 275,000 units:

| | |
|---|---:|
| Direct materials (275,000 units produced × $15.00 per unit) | $ 4,125,000 |
| Direct labor (275,000 units produced × $10.00 per unit) | 2,750,000 |
| Variable overhead (275,000 units produced × $12.50 per unit) | 3,437,500 |
| Total variable production costs | $10,312,500 |

The reconciliation of product costs shown in Exhibit 14.9 provides a double-check on the accuracy of the cost of goods sold and inventory calculations.

Fixed and variable selling and administrative costs are combined on the absorption costing income statement:

| | |
|---|---:|
| Fixed selling and administrative | $1,375,000 |
| Variable selling and administrative (250,000 units sold × $2.50) | 625,000 |
| Total selling and administrative | $2,000,000 |

### Calculations for the Variable Costing Income Statement

The calculations for the variable costing income statement are similar to those for the absorption costing income statement, except fixed overhead is not allocated as a product cost. Therefore, the variable production cost per unit used in calculating cost of goods sold and inventory is:

| | |
|---|---:|
| Direct materials | $15.00 |
| Direct labor | 10.00 |
| Variable overhead | 12.50 |
| Total variable cost per unit | $37.50 |

Because last year's variable cost per unit is the same as this year's, the units in beginning inventory and the units added to inventory are each valued at $37.50 per unit:

| | |
|---|---:|
| Beginning inventory (5,000 units × $37.50 per unit) | $ 187,500 |
| Units added to inventory (25,000 units × $37.50 per unit) | 937,500 |
| Ending inventory | $1,125,000 |

Cost of goods sold is also valued at $37.50 per unit:

| | |
|---|---:|
| Cost of goods sold (250,000 units × $37.50 per unit) | $9,375,000 |

The reconciliation of product costs shown in Exhibit 14.9 provides a double-check on the accuracy of the cost of goods sold and inventory calculations.

When preparing the income statement, variable selling and administrative costs are separated from fixed selling and administrative costs.

### Calculations for the Throughput Costing Income Statement

The calculations for the throughput costing income statement are similar to those for the variable costing income statement, except that the only product cost is direct materials. Therefore, the cost per unit used in calculating cost of goods sold and inventory is:

| | |
|---|---:|
| Direct materials | $15.00 |

Because last year's direct material cost per unit is the same as this year's direct material cost per unit, the units in beginning inventory and the units added to inventory are each valued at $15.00 per unit:

| | |
|---|---:|
| Beginning inventory (5,000 units × $15.00 per unit) | $ 75,000 |
| Units added to inventory (25,000 units × $15.00 per unit) | 375,000 |
| Ending inventory | $450,000 |

Cost of goods sold is also valued at $15.00 per unit:

| | |
|---|---:|
| Cost of goods sold (250,000 units × $15.00 per unit) | $3,750,000 |

The reconciliation of product costs shown in Exhibit 14.9 provides a double-check on the accuracy of the cost of goods sold and inventory calculations.

All of the production conversion costs are combined into a single line item on the throughput costing income statement:

| | |
|---|---:|
| Direct labor (275,000 units produced × $10.00 per unit) | $2,750,000 |
| Variable overhead (275,000 units produced × $12.50 per unit) | 3,437,500 |
| Fixed overhead | 2,200,000 |
| Total conversion costs | $8,387,500 |

The fixed and variable selling and administrative costs are combined as previously calculated for the absorption costing income statement.

**B.** Reconciliation of absorption costing and variable costing income:

| | |
|---|---:|
| Variable costing income | $1,425,000 |
| Increase in fixed overhead costs in absorption inventory: | |
| Units added to inventory × Fixed overhead cost per unit | |
| [25,000 units × ($10.00 per unit − $2.00 per unit)] | 200,000 |
| Absorption costing income | $1,625,000 |

Under absorption costing, $200,000 of this year's fixed overhead cost is held as ending inventory. Therefore, absorption costing income is $200,000 higher than variable costing income.

The difference in income also could have been calculated using the difference between costing methods in the change in inventory during the year:

| | | |
|---|---:|---:|
| Change in absorption costing inventory: | | |
| Ending inventory | $1,375,000 | |
| Beginning inventory | 237,500 | |
| Change | | $1,137,500 |
| Change in variable costing inventory: | | |
| Ending inventory | $1,125,000 | |
| Beginning inventory | 187,500 | |
| Change | | 937,500 |
| Difference between methods | | $ 200,000 |

**C.** Reconciliation of variable and throughput costing income:

| | |
|---|---:|
| Throughput costing income | $ 862,500 |
| Increase in variable conversion costs in absorption inventory: | |
| Units added to inventory × Variable conversion cost per unit | |
| [25,000 units × ($10.00 + $12.50)] | 562,500 |
| Variable costing income | $1,425,000 |

Under variable costing, the direct labor of $10.00 per unit and the variable production costs of $12.50 per unit are held as ending inventory. Therefore, variable costing income is $562,500 higher than throughput costing income.

The difference in income also could have been calculated using the difference between costing methods in the change in inventory during the year:

| | | |
|---|---:|---:|
| Change in variable costing inventory: | | |
| Ending inventory | $1,125,000 | |
| Beginning inventory | 187,500 | |
| Change | | $937,500 |
| Change in throughput costing inventory: | | |
| Ending inventory | $ 450,000 | |
| Beginning inventory | 75,000 | |
| Change | | 375,000 |
| Difference between methods | | $562,500 |

**D.** Using actual fixed overhead costs and actual production, the fixed overhead allocation rate would have been:

$2,200,000 ÷ 275,000 units produced = $8.00 per unit

This rate is equal to the net amount allocated in part (A) under the normal costing method:

| | |
|---|---|
| Estimated fixed overhead allocation rate | $10.00 |
| Volume variance adjustment per unit | (2.00) |
| Net fixed overhead allocation | $ 8.00 |

This calculation demonstrates that it does not matter which volume measure is used to allocate fixed overhead during the year. Under absorption costing, any material volume variance is adjusted to all units produced, so that actual fixed overhead cost is reflected on the financial statements.

E. When the volume variance is not material, accountants simplify the adjustment by allocating the entire amount to cost of goods sold. This simplification eliminates the need to revalue units in inventory. Although revaluing the inventory was not difficult for this self-study problem, the computations and accounting entries can become cumbersome when an organization has many products. By definition, an immaterial volume variance would not affect the decisions of people who rely on the financial statements. Therefore, it does not matter how the volume variance is adjusted. It is simpler to allocate the entire amount to cost of goods sold.

---

**REVIEW** Use the exercises in the following boxes in the chapter to review key terms and key techniques, analyze chapter illustrations, improve your learning of new concepts, and practice ethical decision making:

Guide Your Learning 14.1: Key Terms (p. 553)

Guide Your Learning 14.2: Boats Afloat Yacht Company (Parts 1 and 2) (p. 557)

Guide Your Learning 14.3: Key Terms (p. 560)

Guide Your Learning 14.4: Ski Doodle (p. 562)

Guide Your Learning 14.5: Flying Fortress (p. 566)

Guide Your Learning 14.6: Key Terms (p. 569)

Guide Your Learning 14.7: Throughput Costing (p. 570)

Focus on Ethical Decision Making: Channel Stuffing at Bristol-Myers Squibb (p. 567)

---

# QUESTIONS

**14.1** Explain the similarities and differences among absorption, variable, and throughput costing.

**14.2** Explain how variable costing income statements can be reconciled to absorption costing income statements.

**14.3** Explain why no volume variance occurs when variable costing is used.

**14.4** The volume of production in a period has an effect on income calculated using absorption costing but has no effect on income calculated using variable costing. Explain.

**14.5** The basic issue in variable and absorption costing could be said to be one of timing rather than amount. Explain.

**14.6** What is the difference between a cost that is variable and variable costing?

**14.7** What is the relationship between the quantity required to break even and the quantity used for denominator volume to determine the fixed overhead allocation rate?

**14.8** If inventory physically increases during the period, income under absorption costing will be higher than income using variable costing. Explain.

**14.9** Why does GAAP require absorption costing?

**14.10** A firm uses variable costing for internal reports and updates these reports daily. It must convert the variable costing results to absorption costing results for external reports. How can this conversion be accomplished?

**14.11** How are joint costs allocated under variable costing? (*Hint:* This question assumes knowledge of Chapter 9.)

---

# EXERCISES

**14.12** **Absorption and variable income** Famous Desk Company manufactures desks for office use. The
Q1, Q3    variable cost of 100 units in beginning inventory is $80 each. The absorption cost is $146.67 each. Following is information about this period's production.

| Selling price | $300 per desk |
|---|---|
| Variable production cost | $80 per desk |
| Fixed production costs | $10,000 per month |
| Variable selling and administrative | $30 per desk |
| Fixed selling and administrative | $6,000 per month |

**REQUIRED:**

A. Estimate operating income for a month in which 200 desks are manufactured and 220 are sold if the company uses variable costing.

B. Estimate operating income for a month in which 200 desks are manufactured and 220 are sold if the company uses absorption costing and allocates fixed production costs to inventory using a rate based on normal capacity of 150 desks per month.

**14.13**
**Q1, Q3**

**Absorption and variable income, reconcile incomes** Rock Crusher Corp. produces two grades of sand, A100 and A300, used in the manufacture of industrial abrasives. The results of operations last year were as follows:

| | A100 | A300 | Total |
|---|---|---|---|
| Production | 4,000 tons | 6,000 tons | 10,000 tons |
| Sales | 3,000 tons | 4,000 tons | 7,000 tons |
| Revenue | $90,000 | $150,000 | $240,000 |
| Variable production costs | $20,000 | $15,000 | $35,000 |
| Variable selling costs | $15,000 | $20,000 | $35,000 |

Fixed production costs were $100,000 and fixed selling and administrative costs were $60,000. The company held no beginning inventories.

**REQUIRED:** Prepare a spreadsheet that can be used to answer all of the following questions.

A. If Rock Crusher uses a variable costing system, what was the operating income?

B. If Rock Crusher uses absorption costing and allocates actual fixed production costs to inventory on the basis of actual tons produced, what was the operating income?

C. Reconcile and explain the difference between your answers to parts (A) and (B).

**14.14**
**Q1, Q3**

**Absorption and variable inventory and income** Plains Irrigation uses absorption costing for its external reports and variable costing for its internal reports. Data concerning inventories appear here:

| Valuation Basis | September | October | November |
|---|---|---|---|
| Absorption cost | $1,346 | $2,598 | $2,136 |
| Variable cost | $ 854 | $1,647 | $1,329 |

**REQUIRED:**

A. Why is the value of inventory for Plains Irrigation higher when absorption costing is used than when variable costing is used? Is this result always the case? Why or why not?

B. What is the relationship between absorption costing and variable costing operating income in October? (State which valuation basis will yield the higher operating income and by how much the two operating incomes will differ.)

**14.15**
**Q1, Q3, Q4**

**Absorption, variable, and throughput inventory and income** Asian Iron began last year with no inventories. During the year, 10,500 units were produced, of which 9,400 were sold. Data concerning last year's operations appear here (in New Taiwanese dollars, NT$):

| Revenue | NT$32,900 |
|---|---|
| Variable direct materials costs | 2,300 |
| Variable direct labor costs | 3,300 |
| Variable manufacturing overhead | 2,800 |
| Variable selling | 940 |
| Fixed manufacturing overhead | 8,250 |
| Fixed selling and administrative costs | 14,560 |

Variable manufacturing costs reflect the variable cost to produce the number of units manufactured. However, variable selling costs are not incurred until the units are sold, so they reflect the cost for the number of units sold. Asian Iron allocates actual manufacturing overhead costs to inventory based on actual units produced.

**REQUIRED:**

**A.** Calculate the value of ending inventory on the balance sheet under the following:
1. Variable costing
2. Absorption costing
3. Throughput costing

**B.** Calculate operating income under each of the following methods:
1. Variable costing
2. Absorption costing
3. Throughput costing

**C.** Estimate the variable costing operating income if 12,110 units were produced and sold in a year.

**14.16**
**Q1, Q3**
**CMA**

**Absorption and variable inventory and income, reconcile incomes** Wild Bird Feeders produces deluxe bird feeders for distribution to catalog companies and wild bird stores. The company uses an absorption costing system for internal reporting purposes, but is considering using variable costing. Data regarding Wild Bird's planned and actual operations for 2004 are presented here.

| | Beginning finished goods inventory in units | | 30,000 |
|---|---|---|---|

| | Planned Activity | Actual Activity |
|---|---|---|
| Sales in units | 140,000 | 125,000 |
| Production in units | 140,000 | 130,000 |

The planned per-unit cost figures shown in the schedule were based on production and sale of 140,000 units in 2004. Wild Bird uses an estimated manufacturing overhead rate for allocating manufacturing overhead to its product; thus, a combined manufacturing overhead rate of $9 per unit was employed for absorption costing purposes in 2004. Any overapplied or underapplied manufacturing overhead is closed to cost of goods sold at the end of the reporting year.

| | Planned Costs | | Incurred |
|---|---|---|---|
| | Per Unit | Total | Costs |
| Direct materials | $24.00 | $ 3,360,000 | $ 3,120,000 |
| Direct labor | 18.00 | 2,520,000 | 2,340,000 |
| Variable manufacturing overhead | 4.00 | 560,000 | 520,000 |
| Fixed manufacturing overhead | 5.00 | 700,000 | 710,000 |
| Variable selling expenses | 14.00 | 1,960,000 | 1,750,000 |
| Fixed selling expenses | 7.00 | 980,000 | 980,000 |
| Variable administrative expenses | 1.00 | 140,000 | 125,000 |
| Fixed administrative expenses | 6.00 | 840,000 | 850,000 |
| Total | $79.00 | $11,060,000 | $10,395,000 |

The 2004 beginning finished goods inventory for absorption costing purposes was valued at the 2003 planned unit manufacturing cost, which was the same as the 2004 planned unit manufacturing cost. No work in process inventories were recorded either at the beginning or end of the year. The planned and actual unit selling price was $99.00 per unit for 2004. You may want to use a spreadsheet to perform calculations.

**REQUIRED:**

**A.** What was the value of Wild Bird's actual ending finished goods inventory on the absorption costing basis?

**B.** What was the 2004 actual ending finished goods inventory on the variable costing basis?

**C.** What were the manufacturing contribution margin and the total contribution margin under variable costing for Wild Bird's actual results for 2004?

**D.** Under absorption costing, what were the total fixed costs on the income statement?
1. What were the fixed selling and administrative costs?
2. What was the amount of overhead allocated to COGS at standard?
3. Do we need to consider sales of units from last period?
4. What was the amount of underapplied or overapplied overhead closed to COGS?
5. Sum these amounts for the total fixed costs.

**E.** What was the total variable cost expensed in 2004 on the variable costing income statement?

*(continued)*

F. Was absorption costing income higher or lower than variable costing income for 2004? Why?

G. What is the amount of difference in income using absorption costing versus variable costing? How did it arise?

**14.17**

**Q1, Q3, Q4**

**Absorption, variable, and throughput income, reconcile incomes** The following price and operating cost information applies to Happy Bikers Motorcycle Company.

| | |
|---|---|
| Price | $10,000 per motorcycle |
| Variable production costs: | |
|     Raw materials | $2,000 per motorcycle |
|     Direct labor and variable overhead | $1,000 per motorcycle |
| Fixed production costs | $40,000 per month |
| Variable selling and administrative | $250 per motorcycle |
| Fixed selling and administrative | $40,000 per month |

No beginning balance in finished goods is evident because the beginning inventory account on the balance sheet is zero. Average production is 10 motorcycles per month. Sales are seasonal, so in some months no motorcycles are produced, while in other months production is high.

During the most recent month, the company produced 18 and sold 15 motorcycles.

**REQUIRED:**

A. Prepare an income statement for the most recent month using the variable costing method.

B. Prepare an income statement for the most recent month using the absorption costing method and choose a denominator level that represents "normal" capacity.

C. Prepare an income statement for the most recent month using the throughput costing method.

D. Prepare a schedule that reconciles the incomes among the three income statements.

# PROBLEMS

**14.18**

**Q1, Q3, Q5**

**Differences in income, choice of absorption and variable costing** Maine Lobster Company is a privately held company that buys lobsters from local fishermen and then delivers them to restaurants in several of Maine's larger cities. The owners use variable costing income statements, but one owner's daughter, who just started taking accounting classes at the local university, suggested that absorption income statements meet GAAP and, therefore, should be used.

**REQUIRED:**

A. Explain the difference between absorption and variable income statements.

❷ B. Provide possible reasons why the company uses variable costing income statements.

❷ C. Provide possible benefits to the company from using an absorption costing income statement.

❸ D. What type of statement would you recommend for Maine Lobster Company? Why?

❹ E. What additional information about Maine Lobster Company would you like to have to improve your recommendation in part (D)?

**14.19**

**Q1, Q2, Q3, Q4**

**Absorption, variable, and throughput income; normal capacity; choice of denominator** Giant Jets is a French company that produces jet airplanes for commercial cargo companies. The selling price (in euros) per jet is €1,000,000. Currently the company uses actual volumes to allocate fixed production overhead to units. However, Giant Jets' accountant is considering the use of standard costs to produce the absorption income statements. The company anticipates the following.

| | |
|---|---|
| Variable costs per jet: | |
|     Direct materials | €200,000 |
|     Direct labor | 150,000 |
|     Variable production overhead | 50,000 |
|     Variable selling | 100,000 |
| | |
| Fixed costs per month: | |
|     Fixed production overhead | €600,000 |
|     Fixed administrative and selling | 100,000 |

| Sales and production quantities: | 2004 | 2005 | 2006 |
|---|---|---|---|
| Production | 10 | 6 | 8 |
| Sales | 10 | 4 | 10 |

**REQUIRED:**
    **A.** Prepare income statements using the variable costing method.
    **B.** Prepare income statements using the throughput costing method.
    **C.** Prepare income statements using the absorption costing method. Allocate fixed overhead using actual units produced in the denominator.
    **D.** In your own words, define *normal capacity.*
    ❸ **E.** Prepare an income statement using the absorption cost method and choose a denominator level that represents normal capacity. Explain your choice for normal capacity.
    **F.** Prepare a brief summary that reconciles the incomes among the three income statements for each year.

**14.20** **Absorption, variable, and throughput income and inventory; method for manager bonus**
Q1, Q2, Q3, Q4, Q5 Fighting Kites produces several different kite kits. Last year, the company produced 20,000 kits and sold all but 2,000 kits. The kits sell for $30 each. Costs incurred are listed here.

| | |
|---|---:|
| Materials purchased | $ 50,000 |
| Materials used | 40,000 |
| Other variable production costs | 60,000 |
| Fixed production costs | 100,000 |
| Variable selling costs | 18,000 |
| Fixed selling and administrative costs | 100,000 |

    Beginning inventory last year held 2,000 kits. Assume that under variable costing, the value of this inventory would have been $10,000. Assume that under absorption costing, the value of this inventory would have been $15,000.

**REQUIRED:**
    **A.** If Fighting Kites uses variable costing, what was its operating income? What was the ending balance in finished goods inventory?
    **B.** If Fighting Kites uses throughput costing, what was its operating income? What was the ending balance in finished goods inventory?
    **C.** If Fighting Kites uses absorption costing and a denominator level of 25,000, what was its operating income?
    ❸ **D.** If you were asked to make a recommendation for the absorption costing denominator level for next period's operations, what would you suggest? Explain your choice.
    ❸ **E.** If the manager of Fighting Kites is given a bonus based on income, which type of income statement would you recommend to evaluate manager performance? Explain your choice.

**14.21** **Absorption and variable income and uses, reconcile incomes** Security Vehicles converts Hummers into luxury, high-security vehicles by adding a computerized alarm and radar system and various luxury components. The finished vehicles are sold for $100,000 each. Variable production costs (including the cost of the basic Hummer) are about $60,000 per vehicle. Fixed production costs are $60,000 per month. The fixed costs for administrative and selling expenses are $20,000 per month plus $5,000 per vehicle sold.
    At the beginning of last year Security had no inventories of finished vehicles. In January it produced four vehicles and sold three. In February it produced five and sold six.

**REQUIRED:**
    **A.** What is the operating income for January if Security uses a variable costing system?
    **B.** What is the operating income for January if Security uses an absorption costing system?
    **C.** Reconcile the difference between the absorption and variable costing operating incomes in February.
    ❷ **D.** Explain why Security Vehicles might produce both variable and absorption income statements for the same time period.

**14.22** **Over/underapplied overhead, units versus machine hours as allocation base** Northcoast Man-
Q1, Q2, Q5 ufacturing Company, a small manufacturer of parts used in appliances, just completed its first year
 of operations. The company's controller, Vic Trainor, has been reviewing the actual results for the
 year and is concerned about the allocation of production overhead. Trainor uses the following information to assess operations.

    • Northcoast's equipment consists of several machines with a combined cost of $2,200,000 and no residual value. Each machine has an output of five units of product per hour and a useful life of 20,000 hours.

- Selected actual data of Northcoast's operations for the year just ended is presented here.

| | |
|---|---|
| Product manufactured | 500,000 units |
| Machine utilization | 130,000 hours |
| Direct labor usage | 35,000 hours |
| Labor rate | $15 per hour |
| Total production overhead | $1,130,000 |
| Cost of goods sold | $1,720,960 |
| Finished goods inventory (at year-end) | $430,240 |
| Work in process inventory (at year-end) | $0 |

- Total production overhead is allocated to each unit using an estimated plantwide rate.
- The budgeted activity for the year included 20 employees, each working 1,800 productive hours per year to produce 540,000 units of product. The machines are highly automated, and each employee can operate two to four machines simultaneously. Normal activity is for each employee to operate three machines. Machine operators are paid $15 per hour.
- Budgeted production overhead costs for the past year for various levels of activity are shown here.

| | | | |
|---|---|---|---|
| Units of product | 360,000 | 540,000 | 720,000 |
| Labor hours | 30,000 | 36,000 | 42,000 |
| Machine hours | 72,000 | 108,000 | 144,000 |
| | | | |
| Production overhead costs: | | | |
| Plant supervision | $ 70,000 | $ 70,000 | $   70,000 |
| Plant rent | 40,000 | 40,000 | 40,000 |
| Equipment depreciation | 288,000 | 432,000 | 576,000 |
| Maintenance | 42,000 | 51,000 | 60,000 |
| Utilities | 144,600 | 216,600 | 288,600 |
| Indirect material | 90,000 | 135,000 | 180,000 |
| Other costs | 11,200 | 16,600 | 22,000 |
| Total | $685,800 | $961,200 | $1,236,600 |

You may want to use a spreadsheet to perform calculations.

**REQUIRED:**

**A.** Choose the budgeted level of activity (in units) closest to actual activity for the period and determine the dollar amount of total over/underapplied production overhead. Explain why this amount is material.

**B.** Vic Trainor believes that Northcoast Manufacturing Company should be using machine hours to allocate production overhead. Using the data given, determine the amount of total over/underapplied production overhead if machine hours had been used as the allocation base.

**C.** Explain why machine hours might be a more appropriate allocation base than number of units.

**D.** Explain why using units as denominator volume might cause managers to build up inventories under absorption costing in periods when sales were slumping.

**14.23** **Recommend income format** Your brother started a small business, GameZ, that produces a software game he developed. It is his first year in business, and he kept detailed records of the business. However, his business records consist primarily of entries in his checkbook plus information using a simple method of adding and subtracting cash on a spreadsheet.

**Q5**

Your brother has asked your advice about the kind of financial statements that would be helpful to his business. He would like you to prepare information for two different uses. First, he needs a small bank loan to provide cash during the low season at the end of summer. Most of his sales are made in December. He has a steady, low volume of sales most of the rest of the year, but sales drop to near zero in August when school is beginning for many children. He wants to approach his bank about a line of credit upon which he could draw in August and then pay off in January. In addition, he would like to be able to analyze information from his operations to make decisions about whether to develop a new game, what price to set, and how much he could devote to advertising. He also recently hired an assistant to whom he assigned a great deal of responsibility for general operations. He would like to be able to monitor and reward her performance in some way.

**REQUIRED:** Write a memo to your brother in response to his request. Include the following aspects in your memo.

**①** **A.** Outline his possible choices for income statement formats.
**②** **B.** List the advantages and disadvantages of each format.
**③** **C.** Recommend and explain which type of statement should be used for each of his desired purposes.

☆ **14.24**
Q1, Q3, Q5

**Bonuses and production decisions, profit variances, income statement format** Palm Producers (PP) is expecting sales growth, and so it built nearly identical automated plants in San Jose, California, and in Singapore to produce its new Palm Powerhouse.

Each plant manager is responsible for producing adequate inventories to meet sales orders and for maintaining quality while producing the Palm Powerhouse at the lowest possible cost. Under PP's decentralized organization, each plant maintains its own accounting records. Quarterly reports are filed with the corporate controller's office and are then reviewed by corporate management. The following reports were filed for the third and fourth quarter by the two plants.

SAN JOSE, CALIFORNIA, PLANT
INCOME STATEMENT FOR THIRD AND FOURTH QUARTERS
(IN THOUSANDS OF DOLLARS)

|  | Third Quarter | Fourth Quarter |
|---|---|---|
| Revenue | $97,452 | $110,951 |
| Cost of goods sold | 77,165 | 74,613 |
| Selling and administration expenses | 12,378 | 12,632 |
| Interest expense | 4,312 | 4,251 |
| Tax expense | 1,259 | 6,809 |
| Net income | $ 2,338 | $ 12,646 |

SAN JOSE, CALIFORNIA, PLANT
STATEMENT OF FINANCIAL POSITION FOR THIRD AND FOURTH QUARTERS
(IN THOUSANDS OF DOLLARS)

|  | Third Quarter | Fourth Quarter |
|---|---|---|
| Assets |  |  |
| Cash | $ 2,346 | $ 322 |
| Inventory | 12,872 | 30,972 |
| Plant (net of depreciation) | 152,456 | 148,635 |
| Total assets | $167,674 | $179,929 |
| Liabilities and Owners' Equities |  |  |
| Accounts payable | $ 214 | $ 1,782 |
| Construction bond payable | 140,385 | 138,426 |
| Owners' equity | 27,075 | 39,721 |
| Total liabilities & OE | $167,674 | $179,929 |

SINGAPORE PLANT
INCOME STATEMENT FOR THIRD AND FOURTH QUARTERS
(TRANSLATED TO U.S. CURRENCY, IN THOUSANDS OF DOLLARS)

|  | Third Quarter | Fourth Quarter |
|---|---|---|
| Revenue | $101,832 | $111,085 |
| Cost of goods sold | 82,127 | 87,990 |
| Selling and administration expenses | 10,943 | 10,453 |
| Interest expense | 3,854 | 3,733 |
| Tax expense | 1,718 | 3,118 |
| Net income | $ 3,190 | $ 5,791 |

## SINGAPORE PLANT
### STATEMENT OF FINANCIAL POSITION FOR THIRD AND FOURTH QUARTERS
### (TRANSLATED TO U.S. CURRENCY, IN THOUSANDS OF DOLLARS)

| | Third Quarter | Fourth Quarter |
|---|---|---|
| **Assets** | | |
| Cash | $ 1,564 | $ 3,642 |
| Inventory | 11,324 | 13,832 |
| Plant (net of depreciation) | 142,342 | 138,580 |
| Total assets | $155,230 | $156,054 |
| **Liabilities and Owners' Equities** | | |
| Accounts payable | $ 347 | $ 221 |
| Bond payable | 135,762 | 130,921 |
| Owners' equity | 19,121 | 24,912 |
| Total liabilities & OE | $155,230 | $156,054 |

**REQUIRED: ANALYZE INFORMATION**

The following questions will help you analyze the information for this problem. Do not turn in your answers to these questions unless your professor asks you to do so.

**❷ A.** Suppose each plant manager receives a bonus based on absorption costing operating income that is 5% of operating income. Calculate the bonus for each manager. Explain how this bonus plan might affect the managers' production decisions.

**❷ B.** Examine changes in sales relative to cost of goods sold between the two quarters. What are two possible explanations for the San Jose plant's profit increase during the fourth quarter?

**❸ C.** Assume that variable costs in this industry are an immaterial part of cost of goods sold. Recast the financial statements using the variable costing approach.

**❷ D.** What would you conclude about the relative performances of the two plant managers in the fourth quarter?

**REQUIRED: WRITTEN ASSIGNMENT**

Suppose you are the cost accountant for Palm Producers. Turn in your answers to the following.

**❸ E.** Write a memo to the CFO recommending the type of income statement that would be best for monitoring divisional performance. Attach to the memo a schedule showing any computations that might be useful to the CFO. As appropiate, refer to the schedule in the memo.

---

# BUILD YOUR PROFESSIONAL COMPETENCIES

**14.25**
**Q5**

**Focus on Professional Competency: Communication**   *Communication strategies, communication provided by accounting reports* Review the following definition and elements for the Communication competency.[10]

**DEFINITION:**   *Accounting professionals are called upon to communicate financial and non-financial information so that it is understood by individuals with diverse capabilities and interests. Individuals entering the accounting profession should have the skills necessary to give and exchange information within a meaningful context and with appropriate delivery. They should have the ability to listen, deliver powerful presentations and produce examples of effective business writing.*

---

[10]The definition and elements are reprinted with permission from AICPA; Copyright © 1978–2000 & 2003 by American Institute of Certified Public Accountants. The AICPA's Core Competency Framework can be accessed at eca.aicpaservices.org.

**ELEMENTS FOR THIS COMPETENCY INCLUDE**

| Level 1 | Level 2 | Level 3 | Level 4 |
|---------|---------|---------|---------|
| 1. Expresses information and concepts with conciseness and clarity when writing and speaking<br>2. Identifies uncertainties about the best way to communicate | 3. Places information in appropriate context when listening, reading, writing and speaking<br>4. Selects appropriate media for dissemination or accumulation of information | 5. Organizes and effectively displays information so that it is meaningful to the receiving party<br>6. Receives and originates direct and indirect messages as appropriate when listening, reading, writing and speaking | 7. Uses interpersonal skills to facilitate effective interaction over time<br>8. Communicates decisions appropriately over time |

**REQUIRED:**

**A.** Focus on competency element 1, which addresses the need for accountants to communicate concisely and clearly. Identify ways that you can work toward improving the conciseness and clarity of your written and spoken communications.

**B.** Focus on competency elements 2, 4, and 5, which describe skills for choosing appropriate methods of communication. Answer the following questions:

  **1.** Why do uncertainties exist about the best way to communicate?

  **2.** After brainstorming with other people, create a list of strategies you could use to do a better job of adapting your communications for the setting and audience.

  **3.** Identify three different types of situations where you needed to communicate information to others. For each situation, explain how you modified your communication for the setting and audience.

  **4.** In this chapter, you learned three ways to present cost information in an income statement. Discuss how each of these methods communicates different information about an organization's operations.

**C.** Focus on competency elements 6, 7, and 8, which address the interpersonal nature of communication. Answer the following questions:

  **1.** What are indirect messages? Give examples of indirect messages when listening, writing, and speaking.

  **2.** Discuss ways in which indirect messages can help and hinder communication.

  **3.** What does it mean to engage in effective communication over time? Provide an example where you have communicated over time with one or more other people.

  **4.** Provide examples where you have modified your communications over time to improve interactions with others.

**D.** Focus on competency element 4, which addresses the selection of communication media. List at least four types of media that you can use to communicate accounting information to other people. For each medium, discuss the pros and cons and the situations where that medium might be the best choice.

**14.26**
**Q5**

**Integrating Across the Curriculum: Financial Accounting and Auditing** *Channel stuffing, uncertainties, error versus fraud, fraud incentives and costs* Auditors are responsible for verifying that public company financial statements are presented in accordance with generally accepted accounting principles (GAAP). This responsibility includes proper revenue recognition as well as proper absorption costing for inventories and cost of goods sold.

In this chapter, two real cases of channel stuffing were presented. For **Harley-Davidson**, analysts were concerned about channel stuffing because stock was building up at dealerships, and Harley's stock price declined. However, sales in the next period picked up, reassuring analysts and investors that Harley's product sales were continuing to grow.

**Bristol-Myers Squibb** tried a similar practice, but was hit with several rounds of income restatements and inquiries from both the **Securities and Exchange Commission (SEC)** and the U.S. Attorney's office. In the Bristol-Myers case, sales did not increase in the next period. In fact, sales slowed down for a number of periods, but managers kept pushing inventory onto drug store customers.

When the SEC investigates and asks companies to restate income, it alleges fraudulent behavior on the part of managers. When companies restate income, they often explain that they were not behaving fraudulently, but rather they are restating income to appease the SEC. When auditors discover a misstatement (a situation where the financial statements do not comply with GAAP), they must determine whether it is caused by an error or by fraud. An error is defined as an unintentional mistake, while fraud is intentional.

**REQUIRED:**

**A.** In your own words, define *channel stuffing*.

❶ **B.** Explain why the managers of companies such as Bristol-Myers and Harley-Davidson cannot know for sure what their sales will be next period or how much inventory to produce.

❷ **C.** Explain why the customers of companies such as Bristol-Myers and Harley-Davidson might be willing to purchase excess inventories.

❷ **D.** Assume that you are a manager at Harley-Davidson and are defending the decision to encourage dealers to stock up on inventory. Write a brief paragraph defending Harley's behavior. (Refer back to the case for arguments that Harley provided, but interpret the situation in your own words as you believe a manager might respond.)

❷ **E.** In both the Harley-Davidson and Bristol-Myers cases, the companies shipped merchandise to their customers and recognized the shipments as revenue. How could the SEC claim that Bristol-Myers had improperly recognized revenue? In other words, does channel stuffing violate revenue recognition under GAAP? In your answer, discuss and provide references to relevant financial accounting standards and concepts.

❷ **F.** From an auditor's perspective, discuss the likelihood that the Bristol-Myers restatement of $1.5 billion in sales resulted from error versus fraud.

❸ **G.** Explain why it might be considered so important to continue showing sales and earnings growth that managers might behave in an allegedly fraudulent manner.

❷ **H.** Describe the costs for this kind of behavior, in addition to negative reputation effects for the company.

# 15

# Performance Evaluation and Compensation

## ▶In Brief

When owners give managers authority to make decisions and guide operations, problems arise because owners' and managers' interests often conflict. Owners use accounting information to measure performance, monitor managers' actions, and motivate decisions that are in the owners' interest. Similarly, managers use accounting information to measure, monitor, and motivate the actions of employees. Before managers or other employees can be held accountable for the results of their decisions and actions, their rights and responsibilities need to be defined. Then return on investment, residual income, economic value added, or other measures can be used to gauge and reward performance. In large organizations, resources may be transferred internally from one department to another. The prices set for these transfers affect financial measures of performance. When these transfer prices are set appropriately, managers have incentives to increase the value of the overall organization. However, transfer prices can encourage suboptimal decisions that may be beneficial at the local level, but are not in the best interest of the global organization.

## This Chapter Addresses the Following Questions:

**Q1** What is agency theory?

**Q2** How are decision-making responsibility and authority related to performance evaluation?

**Q3** How are responsibility centers used to measure, monitor, and motivate performance?

**Q4** What are the uses and limitations of return on investment, residual income, and economic value added for monitoring performance?

**Q5** How is compensation used to motivate performance?

**Q6** What prices are used for transferring goods and services within an organization?

**Q7** What are the uses and limitations of transfer pricing?

# HEDGEWOOD PROPERTIES: EMPOWERING TEAMS FOR SUCCESS

Pam Sessions started **Hedgewood Properties** in 1985 after she built a customized home for a friend. At that time, little customization occurred in the housing market. Hedgewood started on a small scale, focusing on design and custom features. By 1989 Sessions' husband, Don Donnelly, joined the business.

As Hedgewood's volume grew, operating procedures were adopted to ensure consistent design, quality, and cost. The company became a centralized organization in which most operating decisions were made at headquarters. As a result, little decision making occurred on the job sites.

Faced by intense competition and concerns that Hedgewood had become too inflexible, Sessions and Donnelly reevaluated their strategy. In 2000, they decided to return to the company's roots, focusing on what they saw as their core competency—design. With this renewed focus, Sessions and Donnelly reorganized the company. They changed the organizational structure, giving decision-making authority to employees in the field. They eliminated nearly all middle managers and information technology professionals.

Hedgewood now uses field project teams of sales

agents and builders. Team members, who meet with shoppers and buyers every day, pick plans and set **specification** levels for the homes in each project. They also choose vendors and assemble the materials and subcontractors. Revenues and costs are jointly measured and monitored on a project-by-project basis. Because sales agents and builders share responsibility for each project, they also share greater ownership of overall results.

Sessions says the company receives many calls from people who want to work for them, suggesting that their new organizational structure has increased their reputation as a desirable workplace. Employees are excited by the company's opportunities to work flexibly and to innovate.

Some types of decisions are still made centrally. For example, headquarters monitors architectural styles and detailing because Hedgewood's brand niche is home designs based on historical architecture. However, project teams still work with customers to customize the features of each home. ■

SOURCES: M. Stromberg and B. Lurz, "Success by Design," *Professional Builder,* December 2002, pp. 52–55; and B. Lurz, "Decentralized Structure Empowers Site Teams," *Professional Builder,* December 2002, pp. 50–51.

## GIVING DECISION RESPONSIBILITY TO EMPLOYEES

### ■ Key Decision Factors for Hedgewood Properties

Because the company began on a small scale, the owners of **Hedgewood Properties** originally made all key decisions. For many years, they could personally monitor operations. As the business grew, information systems and specific procedures were instituted to ensure their continued control over operations. The increased size of the business, combined with the strategic focus on customization, eventually led the owners to give greater decision responsibility to employees in the field. The following discussion summarizes key aspects of the decision-making process that led to the change in organizational structure at Hedgewood Properties.

**Knowing.** Hedgewood's owners had many years of experience designing and building homes. Their employees also had considerable experience. The level of knowledge among employees made it possible for the owners to shift project-level decision making to the project teams. By combining the expertise of the sales agents and the builders, each team had the knowledge and skills needed for project success. The owners no longer needed to make all key decisions.

**Identifying.** Hedgewood's owners could not know how well the project team structure would work. They saw a number of pros and cons with each type of organizational structure. In addition, the owners made the switch as part of an overall plan to emphasize customization over volume. The owners could not know with certainty whether the new project teams could adequately implement the new strategic emphasis.

**Exploring.** The new organizational structure presented several potential drawbacks.

- Hedgewood's owners might have been reluctant to give up a major part of their decision-making authority.
- The project teams might make poor decisions, leading to project losses and deteriorating company performance.
- The sales agents and builders might be unable to work well together.
- The new approach would require greater expertise among team members, increasing hiring and training costs.
- If team members disliked the new approach, employee turnover might increase.

At the same time, the new organizational structure offered several potential benefits:

- The owners and other headquarters personnel would be freed from day-to-day decision making, enabling them to do a better job of establishing, implementing, and monitoring the company's long-term strategies.
- The field team approach might lead to better customer service and better cost management, increasing company profitability.
- The new level of responsibility might help the company retain its best employees.
- The field team approach might be the only way the company can operate at a fairly large size and make the types of flexible decisions required for a strategic focus on customization.

**Prioritizing.** In choosing to give significant decision-making responsibility to employees, Hedgewood's owners most likely prioritized speed and flexibility in the field over their own control of day-to-day operations. Consistent with their new strategic focus, they also prioritized customization over mass production of homes. To address concerns about employee performance under the new system, the owners instituted procedures for measuring and monitoring the performance of individual projects. This system ensures that project teams are held accountable for performance.

**Envisioning.** The owners' decision resulted from reevaluation of Hedgewood's core competencies and strategies. They recognized that their existing organizational structure hindered operations, which in turn hampered the new strategic focus. They were willing to envision a new way of organizing day-to-day operating decisions. In the future, the owners will need to continuously monitor the new approach and consider additional changes to strategies and organizational structure.

## ◼ Importance of Measuring, Monitoring, and Motivating Decision Making

As organizations grow in size, top managers have an increasingly difficult time maintaining control over decision making. In addition, many organizations benefit from the wide range of expertise among employees. However, as decision making is dispersed, mechanisms must be established for measuring, monitoring, and motivating decisions throughout the organization. Because it is generally inefficient or impossible to monitor individual decisions, top managers and owners typically use broad measures of results to monitor performance. For example, shareholders of public companies often focus on earnings and stock returns. In the case of Hedgewood Properties, the owners evaluate project profitability. Their system also motivates employees to make good decisions because they are held responsible for project results.

## AGENCY THEORY

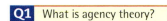
**Q1** What is agency theory?

**Agency theory** is an analytical framework that examines potential conflicts between owners and managers and between managers and employees; it suggests solutions to align the incentives. Agency problems arise when managers do not own firms. In for-profit firms, owners often sell off part of the firm at some point in time, as the organization grows. Not-for-profit firms are often owned by organizations, such as churches or governments. Within agency theory, the two types of information consumers are **principals** and **agents.** Principals hire agents to make decisions for them and to act in their behalf. As shown in Exhibit 15.1, shareholders of a corporation are principals, and the chief executive officer (CEO) is their agent. In not-for-profit organizations, stakeholders such as donors own the organization and hire the CEO. As the top manager of an organization owned by shareholders or other stakeholders, the CEO makes decisions, plans strategies, and protects the interests of the owners. At the same time, the CEO is a principal and the lower-level managers and employees are agents for both the CEO and, in turn, the owners.

## ◼ Agency Costs

Problems arise when the goals of principals are not completely shared by their agents. For example, employees may exert insufficient effort, or managers may waste organizational resources. The costs that arise when agents fail to act in the interest of principals are **agency costs.** Exhibit 15.2 shows several types of agency costs, including the direct costs that occur when agents do not work in the principals' best interests, as well as costs incurred to monitor and motivate agent performance.

When organizations are small, principals minimize agency costs by personally overseeing agent behavior and performance. However, as organizations grow larger, agent behavior is more difficult to observe, and agency costs tend to increase. To reduce agency costs, organizations establish accounting systems to monitor and influence agent behavior. For example, public companies publish audited financial statements, and employees are often paid

**EXHIBIT 15.1**
Principals and Agents
in a Corporation

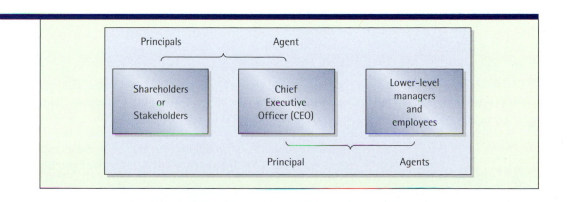

**EXHIBIT 15.2** Agency Costs

| General Agency Cost | Explanation | Specific Examples |
|---|---|---|
| Losses from poor decisions | Agents may not expend the effort needed to gather appropriate information and make make good decisions | • Purchasing poor-quality raw materials<br>• Investing in an unprofitable project<br>• Not prioritizing projects by attributes that would benefit the organization |
| Losses from incongruent goals | Agents do not value the same goals and objectives as principals | • Consumption of perquisites such as expensive offices and travel<br>• Excessive executive pay<br>• Underinvestment in projects that are in the principal's best interests |
| Monitoring costs | Costs to monitor agents' behavior and to provide information about agent effort | Costs for producing and auditing:<br>• Financial statements<br>• Internal performance reports |
| Goal alignment costs | Payments to encourage agents to act in the best interests of the principals | • Bonuses, stock options, and other types of incentives<br>• Sales commissions |
| Contracting costs | Transaction costs incurred to write and enforce employment contracts | Legal fees to:<br>• Negotiate contracts between organizations and employees<br>• Sue employees when they do not meet contractual obligations |

**CURRENT PRACTICE**
During 2003, the reputation of the *New York Times* was called into question when their agent (a reporter named Jayson Blair) was found to have written falsified and pasted-together stories.[1]

bonuses for achieving profit goals. Thus, accounting information is used not only to measure and monitor an organization's activities, but also to measure, monitor, and motivate the performance of agents.

It is impossible to completely eliminate agency costs because agent behavior and decision making cannot be perfectly observed or measured. Poor results might be caused by poor agent performance or by circumstances outside of the agent's control. Similarly, favorable results cannot be attributed to the agent's performance alone. For example, the sales generated by a salesperson are partly a function of the effort and skills of the salesperson and partly a function of the price and quality of the product, economic conditions, competition, customer tastes, and so on.

In this chapter, we learn about a variety of mechanisms used in business organizations to measure, monitor, and motivate agent performance, including the following:

• Assigning responsibility for decision making
• Linking decision-making authority to performance measurement
• Using income-based measures to assess performance
• Motivating performance with compensation schemes
• Establishing prices for the transfer of goods and services within an organization

## DECISION-MAKING AUTHORITY AND RESPONSIBILITY

One way to reduce agency costs is to give specific decision-making authority to agents and then hold them responsible for the results of their decisions. This idea lies behind the corporate form of business organization. Shareholders give managers authority to decide how corporations' resources are used. Then shareholders hold the managers responsible for creating shareholder value. Similarly, the authority for decisions can be dispersed throughout an organization. To reduce agency costs, individual employees are held responsible for their

[1]"Unfit to Print," *The Economist,* May 17, 2003, p. 56.

Q2 How are decision-making responsibility and authority related to performance evaluation?

decisions, and limits are placed on their decision-making authority. For example, the maitre d' in a restaurant is responsible for seating people and has the authority to choose where customers sit. However, the maitre d' has no responsibility for the menu items; the chef has the authority to purchase food and to choose the items to be offered on the menu.

Many different approaches can be taken in assigning decision-making authority. Managers can also periodically restructure authority within organizations. For example, the owners of **Hedgewood Properties** decided that some decisions are best made at headquarters, whereas others are best made out in the field. As the business environment becomes increasingly technical and competitive, the timeliness of decision making becomes increasingly important to economic success. The need for more timely decision making often encourages managers to reconsider how decision-making authority is assigned.

## Centralized and Decentralized Organizations

When managers make choices about locating decision-making authority, they are also making choices about organizational structure. When decision making is *centralized,* the right to make or authorize decisions lies within top levels of management. When decision making is *decentralized,* the rights and responsibilities for decision making permeate all levels of the organization.

In the current dynamic business environment, many factors influence organizational structures, and changes in these structures are made over time. The type of knowledge needed for successful operations influences the location of authority and responsibility. When Hedgewood Properties was a small organization, top managers were sufficiently knowledgeable about operations, but as the company grew, it became more difficult and costly to transfer knowledge about customer needs to top management and then back down to construction crews. The owners then changed the organizational structure to reflect the changing knowledge needs.

## General Versus Specific Knowledge

Knowledge is an important resource within organizations. The type of knowledge needed to make high-quality decisions affects the location of authority within organizations. **General knowledge,** such as information about volume of sales or product prices when organizations sell few products, is usually easy to transfer from one person to the next. Decisions based on general knowledge are likely to be centralized, made primarily by the chief executive officer (CEO) and other top managers. Transferring the general knowledge needed for decision making to an organization's headquarters is relatively easy and, therefore, not very costly. Examples of centralized organizations include small businesses where the owner makes most of the operating decisions and relies on a few employees to carry out those decisions. Large businesses that produce few products, such as steel companies, are often centralized.

Some decisions require **specific knowledge,** that is, detailed information about particular processes, customers, or products—information that is costly to transfer within the organization. Examples of specific knowledge are the technical details of the manufacturing or service delivery processes and information gained over time from working with individual customers. When decision makers need specific knowledge, they must either have the knowledge themselves or seek ways to obtain it. At Hedgewood Properties, specific knowledge of customer preferences is important to organizational success. When project teams work directly with customers and make decisions in the field, customer service improves as do timeliness and accuracy of decision making.

## Technology and Globalization

Technology has enhanced global communications and reduced the costs of business transactions so that organizations can more easily locate units in other countries. Accordingly, organizations have become increasingly multinational. When organizations expand to other

[2]S. Leibs, "Technology Throws Another Curve," *CFO.com,* September 15, 2003.
[3]J. Karaian, "Corralling Costs: Marketing's Reputation as the Free-Spending Cowboy Department Is Being Reined in by the Growing Use of an Ambitious Suite of Software," *CFO.com,* November 11, 2003.

countries, managers within each country are likely to have specific knowledge of cultural and customer preferences. Decisions made at the unit level are likely to be more timely and of higher quality because local decision makers best understand how to gather information relevant to operations in that country.

## ■ Choosing a Centralized Versus Decentralized Organizational Structure

Advantages and disadvantages for each type of organizational form are listed in Exhibit 15.3. Whether decision making within an organization should be centralized or decentralized is not always a straightforward decision. Organizations often begin with centralized decision making, then adopt a decentralized structure as they grow large. However, some large organizations find that a centralized approach is best because it leads to greater alignment of decisions with the organizational vision and strategies.

For example, when Soichiro Honda founded **Honda Motor Company** in 1948, he personally made most of the product-related decisions, while his partner made the finance and marketing decisions. The firm was much larger in 1973 when Honda retired. A new decision-making process involving 30 senior executives was adopted. Research and design engineers were given more control over new model development. With this process, it was difficult for the company to respond to a more dynamic consumer market, and Honda began to lose market share. In the early 1990s, however, a new CEO reestablished centralized decision making. Although employees resisted the change, decision making rested in the hands of a few powerful executives. This strategy produced the 1994 Accord, named one of the top 10 cars of 1994 by *Car and Driver* magazine.

During the time period that Honda centralized decision making, many other organizations such as **Fiat**, **General Electric**, and **Motorola** decentralized theirs. With increased technology and access to information, timeliness of decision making becomes a competitive strategy. To increase the speed of decisions, organizations are increasingly giving decision-making authority to employees who have the most knowledge about the organization's production processes and customer characteristics. Leaner organizations with fewer middle managers more easily move decision authority up and down the hierarchy.

**CURRENT PRACTICE**

Professor William Bielby suggests that Wal-Mart lacks workforce diversity because of decentralized hiring practices. Fewer than 35% of Wal-Mart store managers are women, compared to 57% at 20 comparable retailers.[4]

**EXHIBIT 15.3** Advantages and Disadvantages of Centralized and Decentralized Organizations

| Centralized Organizations | | Decentralized Organizations | |
|---|---|---|---|
| **Advantages** | **Disadvantages** | **Advantages** | **Disadvantages** |
| • Less monitoring of decisions<br>• Decisions are intended to benefit the overall organization<br>• If decision makers have complete information, timely and efficient decisions are made<br>• Good for stable operations and economic conditions | • More monitoring of employee effort because employees may be less motivated<br>• Decision makers may not have complete information, resulting in poorer quality decisions<br>• When knowledge from subunits is required, the decision-making process slows down<br>• Not appropriate for dynamic processes and volatile economic conditions | • Timely decision making; appropriate for dynamic processes and unstable economic conditions<br>• Decisions are made by individuals having the most knowledge and expertise<br>• Upper management has time to focus on organizational strategies<br>• Decision-making authority combined with reward systems provide more motivation to exert optimal effort at the subunit level | • Decisions may meet objectives of the decision maker's subunit, but not meet organizational goals<br>• Decisions may not be coordinated among subunits, resulting in less effective decision making for the organization as a whole<br>• Decision makers may not understand or agree with organizational strategies<br>• Lack of coordination among subunits may lead to duplication of products, services, and effort |

---

[4]See the Diversity topic under Careers at the Wal-Mart Stores Web site (www.walmartstores.com/wmstore/wmstores/HomePage.jsp); and W. Zellner, "No Way to Treat a Lady?" *Business Week Online,* March 3, 2003.

# RESPONSIBILITY ACCOUNTING

Accounting information is used in both centralized and decentralized organizations to measure, monitor, and reward performance. In centralized organizations, information produced by the accounting system for decision making is used primarily by top managers who are held responsible for both their effort and the quality of their decisions. Employees carry out tasks that result from these decisions and are held responsible for their effort and compliance with top-down decisions. Therefore, individual and team efforts require close monitoring to determine their contributions toward success. Managers use variance and productivity reports to gauge employee (individual and team) efforts.

In decentralized organizations, decision making occurs throughout management levels and in the field. Employees in lower levels are held responsible for their efforts and the quality of their decisions. Therefore, accounting systems are used to provide decision-making information for all levels, from management to front-line employees. Broader accounting measures related to overall financial performance are then used to measure and monitor performance.

**Responsibility accounting** is the process of assigning authority and responsibility to managers of subunits and then measuring and evaluating their performance. Under responsibility accounting, managers are held responsible only for factors over which they have control. **Responsibility centers** are subunits (e.g., segments, divisions, departments) in which managers are accountable for specific types of operating activities. Four common types of responsibility centers are cost centers, revenue centers, profit centers, and investment centers. Exhibit 15.4 provides specific examples of each responsibility center and examples of performance measures that are likely to be used in these centers.

## ■ Cost Centers

In **cost centers,** managers are held responsible only for the costs under their control. Some cost centers provide support services that are relatively easy to monitor because their outputs are measurable. Cost centers are also used for subunits that produce goods or services eventually sold by others. Managers in these cost centers are responsible for producing their goods or services efficiently. In **discretionary cost centers,** the output is not easily measurable in dollars or activities. Cost centers are found in for-profit, not-for-profit, and government organizations.

**EXHIBIT 15.4** Examples of Responsibility Centers and Performance Measures

| Responsibility Centers | Examples | Performance Measures Used |
|---|---|---|
| Cost centers | Manufacturing departments<br>Service production departments, such as road maintenance for a city<br>Support departments, such as accounting and billing departments in a hospital<br>Discretionary cost centers, such as marketing and research and development | Cost budgets and variances<br>Comparisons to benchmark cost per unit or service<br>Efficiency measures (days to close, number of new products)<br>Industry benchmarks (e.g., R&D as a percentage of sales) |
| Revenue centers | Travel agencies<br>Sales departments for manufacturers | Revenue budgets and variances<br>Growth in revenues<br>Customer satisfaction |
| Profit centers | Retail sales outlets for clothing, books, or restaurants<br>Corporate divisions and departments responsible for revenues and costs | Revenue and cost budgets and variances<br>Accounting earnings such as operating income or earnings before or after taxes |
| Investment centers | Corporate divisions and business segments responsible for investment decisions | Return on investment (ROI)<br>Residual income<br>Economic value added (EVA) |

**CHAPTER REFERENCE**
Budgets are addressed in Chapter 10, and revenue and cost variances are addressed in Chapter 11.

Cost center managers are expected either to minimize costs for a certain level of output or to maximize output for a certain level of cost. Cost center performance is measured and monitored several ways. Some organizations rely on cost budgets and variances. Measures of other factors such as quality and timeliness of delivery are also relevant.

## Revenue Centers

In **revenue centers,** managers are held responsible for the revenues under their control. Revenue centers frequently sell products from manufacturing subunits. Managers are expected to maximize sales. If the manager in a revenue center is responsible for setting prices, gross revenues can be used as a performance measure. If corporate headquarters, rather than the manager, sets prices, then managers' performance can be evaluated using a combination of sales volumes measured in units and sales mix. Many organizations treat their sales departments as revenue centers and reward employees based on sales generated. In not-for-profit organizations, fundraising activities might be treated as a revenue center.

## Profit Centers

Managers in **profit centers** are held responsible for both revenues and costs under their control. Profit centers produce and sell goods or services, and may include one or several cost centers. Profit center managers are responsible for decisions about inputs, product mix, pricing, and volume of goods or services produced. Because profit centers include both revenues and costs, performance is typically measured using some combination of revenue and cost measures. Not-for-profit organizations tend to use revenue and cost budgets and variances as performance measures, although some focus managers' attention on operating margins when performance is poor. For-profit organizations use some measure of profits such as accounting earnings.

## Investment Centers

Managers of **investment centers** are held responsible for the revenues, costs, and investments under their control. Investments include any assets related to the investment center, such as fixed assets, inventory, intangible assets, and accounts receivable. Investment centers resemble profit centers, where profitability is related to the assets used to generate the profits.

Because investment centers include revenues, costs, and investment, performance measures need to address all of these factors. Later in this chapter we will learn about three commonly used measures: return on investment (ROI), residual income, and economic value added (EVA).

## Responsibility Centers and Suboptimal Decision Making

Top managers use judgment to decide the best types of responsibility centers for the organization. The choices depend on the size of the organization, the nature of operations, and the organizational structure. Ideally, responsibility centers should reduce agency costs by holding managers responsible for decisions over which they have authority. For example, accounting departments are often viewed as cost centers because their managers have authority primarily for the expenditure of resources. Similarly, business segments are generally treated as investment centers because segment managers have authority over revenues, costs, and investment.

Nevertheless, responsibility center accounting sometimes leads to suboptimal decision making. Too often managers make decisions that are in the best interests of their own responsibility centers, but suboptimal for the organization as a whole. Each type of responsibility center has a specific set of agency problems. Managers in cost centers focus on minimizing costs and maximizing efficiency, which can lead to declines in quality and delivery timeliness. In turn, sales could drop and the overall organization suffers. Similarly, revenue center managers, who are typically rewarded for increasing revenues, may fail to consider product contribution margins and inappropriately emphasize less-profitable products. These managers have incentives to offer discounts and generous payment terms that reduce overall profitability. In profit centers, managers are encouraged to stress short-run profits by cutting maintenance, research and development, and advertising costs that benefit long-term performance. Similarly in investment centers, managers may reduce investment to increase short-term results. Or, they may invest in projects that are more or less risky than is appropriate for the organization. To address these agency problems, appropriate performance measures and reward systems need to be implemented.

---

### GUIDE YOUR LEARNING 15.1 Key Terms

Stop to confirm that you understand the new terms introduced in the last several pages.

Agency theory (p. 591)
*Principals (p. 591)
*Agents (p. 591)
Agency costs (p. 591)
*General knowledge (p. 593)
*Specific knowledge (p. 593)
Responsibility accounting (p. 595)

Responsibility centers (p. 595)
Cost centers (p. 595)
Discretionary cost centers (p. 595)
Revenue centers (p. 596)
Profit centers (p. 596)
Investment centers (p. 596)

For each of these terms, write a definition in your own words. For starred terms, list at least one example that is different from the ones given in this textbook.

---

## INCOME-BASED PERFORMANCE EVALUATION

 **Q4** What are the uses and limitations of return on investment, residual income, and economic value added for monitoring performance?

Investment centers are common in large decentralized organizations. Because managers are responsible for costs and revenues, as well as for investments, the measures used for monitoring and motivating purposes typically include the return and the size of investment. Three measures commonly used to evaluate investment center performance are:

- Return on investment
- Residual income
- Economic value added

### Return on Investment

**Return on investment (ROI)** is the ratio of operating income to average operating assets. Operating income is calculated as earnings before interest and taxes (EBIT). Operating assets include all assets used in the production of goods or services, such as cash, accounts receivable, inventory, and plant and equipment. Nonoperating assets, such as investments in other companies or property and equipment currently rented to other companies, are excluded from this calculation. When evaluating the entire company's performance, all assets would be included because owners want to evaluate their return based on the entire investment. But when evaluating the performance of a subunit, judgment is used to determine which assets should be included. Any assets included should be under the control of the managers being evaluated. The average of beginning and ending operating assets is calculated for this component for several reasons. First, the measure is intended to capture operations over a period of time, not just at the end of the time period. Second, the measure could be manipulated by temporarily decreasing investment at the time performance is measured.

ROI is used to evaluate investment center performance. It can be compared across subunits within a single organization, among a group of firms within an industry, and within a single organization across time.[5] In addition, ROI can be decomposed into two components

---

[5]Another measure similar to ROI is return on total assets (ROA). This measure also shows how well assets are employed, and it is measured as follows:

$$\text{Return on total assets} = \frac{\text{Net income} + [\text{Interest expense} \times (1 - \text{Tax rate})]}{\text{Average total assets}}$$

Because after-tax interest expense is added back in the numerator, ROA is not influenced by how the assets were financed. This approach allows comparison across divisions or companies with differing amounts of debt, or for a single company that has changed its level of debt over time.

that provide additional information about performance. ROI is decomposed by multiplying both the numerator and denominator by revenue and then rearranging terms:

$$\text{ROI} = \text{Operating income} \div \text{Average operating assets}$$
$$= (\text{Operating income} \div \text{Average operating assets}) \times (\text{Revenue} \div \text{Revenue})$$
$$= (\text{Revenue} \div \text{Average operating assets}) \times (\text{Operating income} \div \text{Revenue})$$

Because revenue divided by average operating assets represents investment turnover, and operating income divided by revenue represents the return on sales, we can now rewrite the ROI formula as:

$$\text{ROI} = \text{Investment turnover} \times \text{Return on sales}$$

The decomposition of ROI into investment turnover and return on sales is often referred to as DuPont analysis. The method originated at the **DuPont Company** in the early 1900s so that results from a wider range of business activities could be compared. Investment turnover is a measure of the sales generated by each dollar invested in operating assets. Return on sales measures managers' abilities to control the operating expenses related to sales during a period. This decomposition focuses attention on the role that assets play in generating revenues and the role that increased revenues and decreased costs play in generating profits. Improvement in ROI occurs when sales increase and costs do not increase proportionately (some cost is fixed), when costs are reduced for a given level of sales, or when investment decreases for a given level of income. In this manner, ROI provides managers guidance about factors that improve performance.

**ALTERNATIVE TERMS**

The term *asset turnover* means the same as *investment turnover*. Similarly, the term *profit margin ratio* means the same as *return on sales*.

## COMPUTER WIZARDS (PART 1)
### RETURN ON INVESTMENT

Computer Wizards produces and sells computer monitors nationally and internationally. Jason Black is responsible for Canadian operations and Cecilia Earnhart manages the New Jersey division. Following is information about two divisions.

|  | Canada | New Jersey |
| --- | --- | --- |
| Average operating assets | $2,000,000 | $200,000 |
| Operating income | $500,000 | $60,000 |

The top managers of Computer Wizards measure the performance of its divisions using ROI. Following are the calculations for each division.

$$\text{Canada's ROI} = \$500,000 \div \$2,000,000 = 25\%$$
$$\text{New Jersey's ROI} = \$60,000 \div \$200,000 = 30\%$$

Jason was recently hired from outside of the company to improve operations in the Canadian division. One of his objectives is to achieve an ROI at least as high as the New Jersey division. Given the Canadian division's sales of $5,000,000, Jason decomposes the ROI as follows.

$$\text{Return on sales} = \$500,000 \div \$5,000,000 = 10\%$$
$$\text{Investment turnover} = \$5,000,000 \div \$2,000,000 = 2.5 \text{ times}$$
$$\text{ROI} = 10\% \times 2.5 = 25\%$$

This decomposition highlights three general ways he can increase ROI; increase sales, decrease costs, or decrease investment in operating assets. Jason decides to investigate these alternatives.

### Increasing ROI

One alternative is to focus primarily on increased sales. The Canadian division currently has idle capacity, and Jason would like to emphasize a new group of products. He believes that current capacity can support an increase in sales of $600,000, without requiring additional investment. The increased sales would increase operating income by $116,000. The expected return on sales would then be

$$\$616,000 \div \$5,600,000 = 11\%$$

and investment turnover would be

$$\$5,600,000 \div \$2,000,000 = 2.8 \text{ times}$$

leading to an improved ROI slightly higher than that of the New Jersey division:

$$\$616,000 \div \$2,000,000 = 30.8\% = 11\% \times 2.8$$

Alternatively, Jason could focus on reducing expenses. He believes that manufacturing costs could be reduced by as much as $100,000. He would implement this plan using kaizen costing, that is, by organizing a team with members from marketing, accounting, and engineering to analyze production activities and identify non-value-added activities that could be eliminated. Also, the products and manufacturing processes could be redesigned to reduce the number of parts or processes. If the team is successful and expenses are reduced by $100,000, operating income would be $600,000 instead of $500,000. This plan alone could increase return on sales to

$$\$600,000 \div \$5,000,000 = 12\%$$

and ROI would equal that of the New Jersey division:

$$12\% \times 2.5 = 30\%$$

Jason considers one more approach to increase ROI. He can reduce the Canadian division's investment in operating assets. He knows that internal processes are inefficient; inventory and work in process are built up throughout different manufacturing areas. He would like to implement cellular production and just-in-time inventory practices. These modifications would allow the division to sell a small building currently in use. He believes that these actions would reduce operating assets to $1,667,000. The investment turnover would then be

$$\$5,000,000 \div \$1,667,000 = 3 \text{ times}$$

and ROI would be

$$10\% \times 3 = 30\%$$

Jason knows that increasing sales, reducing costs, and changing production processes are all worthy long-term goals, but it will take a year or longer to see the results of any of these plans. He would prefer to increase ROI within a shorter time frame. Recently a competitor made an offer to sell the Canadian division a component that is currently manufactured in-house. If Jason purchases the component, operating earnings would decrease, but he could easily sell the small building because most of it houses the production facility for the component. Investment turnover would still be 3 times, but return on sales would drop to 9% ($450,000 ÷ $5,000,000), which would increase ROI to 27%.

### Choosing a Plan of Action

Jason decides to discuss his options with Renee Forsyth, the Director of Finance for Computer Wizards. All of the plans he is considering require a great deal of time and effort. He believes that the strategies are sound, but is uncertain whether his expectations can be met. An increase in sales depends in part on the continuing upswing of the economy. Cost reductions take time and concentrated effort on the part of employees. Changing the manufacturing process could take several years because a new floor plan would have to be laid out, teams would have to be established, and work would be disrupted while implementing the new lines. Furthermore, the employees might need several months to work efficiently under the new system. The easiest choice is to outsource, and Jason knows that outsourcing would improve his ROI in the short run. However, he believes that focusing on in-house manufacturing cost reductions would be a better strategy for Computer Wizards in the long run. The company's use of ROI to measure performance discourages this type of strategy, so Jason wonders whether a different performance measure could be adopted that would better reward behavior to benefit the overall organization.

## ■ Advantages and Disadvantages of ROI

A division's ROI is easily compared with internal and external benchmarks and with other divisions' returns on investment. Holding managers responsible for some level of ROI reduces the tendency of managers to overinvest in projects. Another advantage of ROI is that its components motivate managers to increase sales, decrease costs, and minimize asset investments.

However, ROI also discourages managers from investing in projects that reduce the division's ROI, even though they improve the ROI for the overall organization. Suppose Jason had an opportunity to invest $1,750,000 in a project that would generate sales of

$2,500,000 and a return on sales of 10% (same as the original assumptions), or $250,000 operating income per year. The division's ROI including this investment would be

$$\text{Investment turnover} = \$7,500,000 \div 3,750,000 = 2 \text{ times}$$
$$\text{ROI} = 10\% \times 2 = 20\%$$

Even though the investment reduces the division's ROI, Computer Wizards forgoes $250,000 if the project is not undertaken. If the level of risk and the return are comparable to projects from other divisions, Computer Wizards would prefer the benefits from this investment.

Another disadvantage of ROI is that it does not incorporate measures of risk. Managers can potentially increase ROI by investing in riskier projects, which often have higher returns than less risky projects. If they are rewarded solely for increasing ROI, managers may undertake risky projects, without considering the added risk to the organization. This problem arises more often when managers' time horizons are short, for example, when they are planning to retire or move to another company. In such cases, managers often prefer immediate improvements in performance measures.

Furthermore, when managers with short-time horizons evaluate projects based on ROI, they might inappropriately cut costs that provide long-term benefit for the organization. For example, they might cut research and development, maintenance, or employee training.

ROI is typically calculated using financial accounting assets and income. Under financial accounting rules, assets are recorded at their original cost, and some intangible assets, such as brand name, are not recognized. These rules cause the investment in assets to be understated, particularly when the value of assets, such as property, has increased or when a company has significant intangible assets. Understatements in assets cause ROI and investment turnover to be overstated. In addition, financial accounting rules measure revenues and costs in ways that can distort ROI. For example, overhead or support department costs might be allocated to a division using a method that does not reflect the division's use of resources. If the division's costs are understated or overstated, ROI will be distorted.

**CURRENT PRACTICE**

Companies often use nontraditional ways to measure ROI. For its retail Web site, Mikasa measures ROI in terms of customer loyalty in addition to revenues and cost-cutting.[6]

## ■ Residual Income

Because of the disadvantages of ROI just described, some organizations prefer to use residual income to measure performance of subunits. **Residual income** measures the dollar amount of profits in excess of a required rate of return. It is calculated as follows:

$$\text{Residual income} = \text{Operating income} - (\text{Required rate of return} \times \text{Average operating assets})$$

Many organizations set a minimum return expectation for operations and new investments. Residual income takes this expectation into consideration; it is the difference between actual operating income and the required income, given the organization's investment in operating assets and its required rate of return. The size of investment affects residual income less than ROI because it is used only to value the dollar amount of expected return, not as a denominator. Compared to ROI, residual income is less influenced by changes in investment.

**CHAPTER REFERENCE**

See Chapter 12 for a more complete discussion about determining the required rate of return.

### COMPUTER WIZARDS (PART 2)
#### RESIDUAL INCOME

Jason consults with Renee, and they decide to investigate other performance measures. The first option they consider is residual income. The required rate of return for the company is 10%. Given the investment in operating assets, the required dollar amount of return for each division is as follows:

|  | Canada | New Jersey |
| --- | --- | --- |
| Average operating assets | $2,000,000 | $200,000 |
| Times required rate of return | 10% | 10% |
| Required return | $ 200,000 | $ 20,000 |

[6]R. Banham and H. Rosenberg, "ROI: Mad to Measure," *CFO.com*, September 15, 2001.

Residual income is calculated as follows:

|  | Canada | New Jersey |
|---|---|---|
| Operating income | $500,000 | $60,000 |
| Required return | 200,000 | 20,000 |
| Residual income | $300,000 | $40,000 |

Renee explains that the Canadian division provides Computer Wizards with $300,000 in income above and beyond the required return. However, as they discuss the value of residual income as a performance measure, Jason suggests that it has some of the same problems as ROI because it is still based on operating income. In addition, Renee cannot compare results in the Canadian division to New Jersey's because of the size difference in the two divisions. Therefore, they decide to consider other alternatives.

## Advantages and Disadvantages of Residual Income

The use of residual income does not penalize investment in projects with lower returns than current project returns. Suppose the Canadian division invests $1,750,000 in new assets that generate annual sales of $2,500,000 and operating income of 10% ($250,000). If this project is undertaken, the Canadian division residual income will be

| Operating income ($500,000 + $250,000) | $750,000 |
|---|---|
| Required return [($2,000,000 + $1,750,000) × 10%] | 375,000 |
| Residual income | $375,000 |

Because the project is expected to increase residual income by $75,000 ($375,000 − $300,000), managers would be motivated to invest in it. In general, when residual income is used as a performance measure, managers are willing to invest in any projects with returns equal to or greater than the required rate of return.

However, residual income has its own problems. Because it is an absolute dollar value, larger subunits are more likely to have larger residual incomes. For Computer Wizards, the Canadian division's residual income is much greater than that of the New Jersey division. As a result, managers find it difficult to compare performance across units.

A disadvantage it shares with ROI is that residual income increases as investment and costs decrease (holding sales constant). Therefore, managers may cut costs such as research and development, maintenance, or employee training that likely have long-term benefits for the organization.

Another problem with residual income occurs if senior managers from each subunit estimate their own required rate of return; they have incentives to set a required rate of return that is too low. In turn, a low required rate of return encourages managers to invest in less profitable projects. They may also invest in less risky projects and forego riskier projects that would be profitable for the overall organization. Because operating income is measured using financial accounting information, residual income suffers from the same earnings-related problems as ROI.

## Economic Value Added

**Economic value added** (EVA®) is a type of residual income that incorporates a number of adjustments to reduce the disadvantages produced by residual income.[7] Many different organizations use EVA, such as **AT&T**, **Coca-Cola**, **Quaker Oats**, and **General Electric**.[8] The basic EVA calculation follows:

$$\text{EVA} = \frac{\text{Adjusted after-tax}}{\text{operating income}} - \left[ \frac{\text{Weighted average}}{\text{cost of capital}} \times \left( \frac{\text{Adjusted}}{\text{total assets}} - \frac{\text{Current}}{\text{liabilities}} \right) \right]$$

---

[7]EVA® is a registered trademark of **Stern Stewart & Co**.
[8]See D. McConville, "All About EVA," *Industry Week*, 243(8) (April 18, 1994), pp. 55–57.

The weighted average cost of capital (WACC) is calculated by analyzing all sources of invested funds, including both debt and equity financing (valued as the opportunity cost to investors). It is the after-tax cost of all long-term financing for the company or division. With EVA, each division can use its actual cost of capital, taking into consideration the industry and risk characteristics.

The adjustments made to develop the EVA calculation include substituting after-tax operating income for EBIT, which is consistent with using the (after-tax) weighted average cost of capital and also gives managers incentives to reduce taxes. Analysts and consultants recommend that organizations choose among 160 other adjustments to provide managers with incentives specific to the firm. One purpose of adjusting financial accounting income and assets is to minimize suboptimal decision making.

Measures used for internal purposes need not follow generally accepted accounting principles (GAAP), but are created to reflect economic costs and benefits over time. For example, research and development costs, which must be recognized immediately as an expense under GAAP, are often capitalized for EVA calculations. This adjustment encourages managers to invest in research and development projects that have long-term value for the organization. Similarly, long-term leases accounted for as operating leases under GAAP are often treated as capital leases for EVA calculations. This adjustment reduces managers' incentives to use operating leases to artificially understate the organization's investment in assets. They are then encouraged to make long-term asset acquisition decisions based on the best alternative for the organization, rather than on their financial accounting treatment.

## COMPUTER WIZARDS (PART 3)
### ECONOMIC VALUE ADDED

Jason and Renee next consider the use of EVA at Computer Wizards, and calculate EVA for each division. Jason develops the following information:

|  | Canada | New Jersey |
| --- | --- | --- |
| Total assets | $2,000,000 | $200,000 |
| Operating income | $500,000 | $60,000 |
| Weighted average cost of capital | 7.2% | 10% |
| Current liabilities | $20,000 | $5,000 |
| After-tax operating income | $300,000 | $40,000 |
| Tax rate | 40% | 33.33% |

Jason and Renee first calculate EVA without any adjustments beyond income taxes:

$$\text{EVA} = \begin{matrix}\text{Adjusted after-tax} \\ \text{operating income}\end{matrix} - \left[ \begin{matrix}\text{Weighted average} \\ \text{cost of capital}\end{matrix} \times \left( \begin{matrix}\text{Total} \\ \text{assets}\end{matrix} - \begin{matrix}\text{Current} \\ \text{liabilities}\end{matrix} \right) \right]$$

EVA Canada:
| | |
| --- | --- |
| After-tax operating income | $300,000 |
| WACC × (Total assets − Current liabilities) | |
| [7.2% × ($2,000,000 − $20,000)] | 142,560 |
| | $157,440 |

EVA New Jersey:
| | |
| --- | --- |
| After-tax operating income | $40,000 |
| WACC × (Total assets − Current liabilities) | |
| [10% × ($200,000 − $5,000)] | 19,500 |
| | $20,500 |

Because EVA incorporates income taxes, incentive is provided to minimize taxes paid. In addition, the weighted average cost of capital is a more realistic capital charge than managers' subjective choices of required rates of return. The New Jersey division operates in a riskier business environment than the Canadian division, which is reflected in its higher WACC.

### Comparison of ROI, Residual Income, and EVA

After completing these computations, Jason and Renee decide to examine the rankings of the two divisions using these three measures. Under ROI, the New Jersey division (30%) appears to perform better than the Canadian division (25%). But under residual income and EVA the Canadian division outperforms the New Jersey division. They recognize that size has an effect on both residual income and EVA. Renee decides to use both ROI and EVA as performance measures. Jason suggests that Renee also consider the use of nonfinancial performance measures. He believes that increasing customer satisfaction should increase financial performance because repeat and new customers will increase revenues. Renee agrees that by focusing on customer satisfaction, any potential customer-related problems are likely to be discovered sooner, and agrees to give the measure further consideration.

---

### GUIDE YOUR LEARNING 15.2 Computer Wizards (Parts 1, 2, and 3)

Computer Wizards (Parts 1, 2, and 3) illustrates ROI, residual income, and EVA. For these illustrations:

| Define It | Identify Problem and Information | Identify Uncertainties | Explore Pros and Cons of Options | Prioritize Options |
|---|---|---|---|---|
| In your own words, define and describe the computations used for ROI, residual income, and EVA. | What decisions were being addressed? In other words, what was the goal of investigating alternative performance measures? | What types of uncertainties were involved? Consider uncertainties about:<br>• Estimates used in computing ROI, residual income, and EVA<br>• Ability to increase revenues, decrease costs, and reduce investment<br>• Effects of measures on manager performance | Describe the advantages and disadvantages of ROI, residual income, and EVA. | Explain why more than one measure was chosen. What factors influenced the decision? |

---

## ■ Advantages and Disadvantages of EVA

Several advantages of EVA result from the various adjustments made to personalize the measure to each organization. These adjustments provide specific incentives that align the goals of managers with owners. However, some disadvantages need to be considered as well. For example, the appropriateness of the specific cost of capital for a division or organization is a matter of judgment, as is the level of risk that has been incorporated. The adjustments are also a matter of judgment. We do not know how to perfectly measure economic revenues, costs, or assets, and a variety of acceptable ways provide different incentives. Because EVA is so complex, consulting firms often must be used to determine the appropriate adjustments. This process can be expensive and time-consuming.

## MOTIVATING PERFORMANCE WITH COMPENSATION

 **Q5** How is compensation used to motivate performance?

To reduce agency costs, organizations use compensation contracts that provide incentives for agents to increase the value of the organization. These contracts include cash-based bonuses, stock options, and other types of bonuses based on stock prices. Earnings and growth targets are often set as goals in these compensation packages.

## ■ Bonus System Incentives

As organizations increase in size, more sophisticated incentive packages are required to align the goals of employees and owners. Compensation contracts can be based on accounting

**EXHIBIT 15.5** Financial Measures and Examples of Targets and Rewards

| Financial Measure | Example of Benchmark or Target | Example of Reward |
|---|---|---|
| ROI | 20% | Cash bonus or stock-related reward |
| EVA | Dollar target or percentage change | Cash bonus or stock-related reward |
| Operating income or growth in income | Dollar target or percentage growth target | Cash bonus or profit sharing |
| Cost savings | Cost reduction of 5% | Gain sharing—employees receive a percentage of the savings |
| Revenue growth | 10% | Cash bonus plus paid family vacation to award ceremony at resort destination |

earnings; other financial measures such as ROI, residual income, and EVA; and nonfinancial measures such as customer satisfaction or defects rates. Examples of financial performance measures are shown in Exhibit 15.5, along with examples of benchmarks or targets and the rewards that could be used to motivate behavior.

**CURRENT PRACTICE**

The pay package of a Menards store manager included penalties of a 60% pay cut if store employees unionized and a $5 fine for not inspecting lunchboxes as employees left the premises.[10]

Compensation contracts often include a base salary and bonuses. In the largest U.S. corporations, bonuses typically make up 50% or more of the total compensation for top executives. Bonuses may be a combination of cash, stock, stock options (options to buy stock in the future at a set price), and deferred compensation (salary or bonuses paid in the future, often after retirement). For professional, technical, and managerial employees, incentive pay and bonuses represent as much as 10% of salary.[9]

A wide variation exists in compensation packages among executives. For example, in 2003 CEO John Finnegan at **Chubb**, a large New Jersey based property-casualty insurer, received $1.2 million in salary, $3.2 million in stock options and restricted shares of stock, and annual bonuses worth $3 million. In contrast, John Chambers, CEO of **Cisco Systems,** received an annual salary of $1 from 2001 to 2003, and turned down bonuses in those years because he had not met his individual or corporate goals. However, he was granted $4 million in stock options that could be worth as much as $85.7 million, depending on the future stock value. In July 2003, he held stock options worth $196.5 million.[11]

**CURRENT PRACTICE**

Soon after American Airlines employees accepted major cutbacks in salaries to prevent bankruptcy, news was released that top managers received bonuses in the form of large contributions to their pension plans.[12]

To protect shareholders, executive compensation is usually set by a committee of the board of directors. Ideally, the compensation committee consists of directors who are considered outsiders, with no formal connections to the management team. Bonuses are sometimes limited to some fraction of accounting earnings. In addition, shareholders may have the ability to vote periodically on compensation contracts. However, considerable evidence suggests that management compensation is not in fact independently determined, but rather that top managers influence the decisions made by the compensation committee.

## ■ Long-Term Versus Short-Term Incentives

**CHAPTER REFERENCE**

Chapter 14 describes the relationship between inventories and income, and presents alternative income calculations that reduce suboptimal incentives.

For many years, U.S. compensation practices were criticized because they were based on accounting earnings. In addition to the problems already described, managers could also reduce the level of investment in assets such as equipment, thereby reducing depreciation expense and, in turn, increasing accounting earnings. However, the reduced investment negatively affects future earnings if sales are forgone because of either limited capacity or increases in maintenance and downtime costs for old equipment that should have been

---

[9]P. Kennedy "Redefining Compensation in Challenging Times," *Employee Benefits Journal,* September 2003, p. 63.
[10]J. Novack, "The Do-It-Yourself Billionaire," *Forbes.com,* October 6, 2003.
[11]J. Lublin, "Executive Pay Keeps Rising, Despite Outcry," *The Wall Street Journal,* October 3, 2003, p. B1.
[12]L. Yoon, "Former CFO Now CEO at American Airlines, Union Leader Praises Arpey Appointment. Will Creditors, Shareholders Feel the Same Way?" *CFO.com,* April 28, 2003.

replaced. In addition, manufacturers sometimes increase revenues by forcing their customers to carry large inventories. These types of actions may increase short-term earnings, but often have negative effects on long-term earnings potential.

To focus managers more on the long term, many companies in the United States increased the use of stock-based compensation. Stock options, in particular, became popular during the 1980s and 1990s. Compensation tied to the value of stock was viewed as a way to encourage managers and other employees to focus on increasing the long-term value of the company. However, company stock prices are sensitive to changes in earnings. Some managers engaged in unethical or illegal activities to boost reported income so that stock prices would remain stable or increase. Earnings manipulation was a significant problem during the early 2000s; many large U.S. corporations and their accounting firms came under scrutiny from the **Securities Exchange Commission**.

## ■ International Compensation

In the past, compensation practices outside of the United States often focused on factors other than stock price. In France and Germany, for example, CEO and top management rewards were sometimes tied to the average salary of all employees because the board of directors included labor union representation. These types of contracts provide incentives to increase the wages of all employees. However, in the early 2000s European companies, which were struggling to attract and retain highly skilled and talented people, began using stock options for top and mid-level managers.

For example, a new law was passed in Germany in 1998, making it easier for companies to use stock options. About 50% of companies listed in Frankfurt's DAX 100 stock index now have stock option plans. European companies tend to link the options to specific performance hurdles, such as increases in share price relative to competitors. Recently, shareholders in Europe have begun to actively examine top executives' compensation packages. Shareholders in the United Kingdom have criticized several large companies, including telecommunications giant **Vodafone Group** and insurer **Prudential** for paying excessive executive compensation, or even for considering executive pay packages perceived as being too large.[13]

Some countries still discourage options. In Belgium and Switzerland, managers are required to pay taxes on the potential gain at the time stock options are granted. If stock prices fall, managers are not allowed to receive a refund of taxes previously paid. In France the capital gains tax rate is 50%, greatly reducing the value of stock options.[15]

**INTERNATIONAL**

According to *Forbes*, the most detailed information about executive pay and benefits during 2002 was provided by U.K. and Scandinavian companies. Asian companies provided little or no information about executive pay.[14]

## FOCUS ON ETHICAL DECISION MAKING
### Level of Executive Pay

The **New York Stock Exchange (NYSE)** is a not-for-profit corporation that operates a board of exchange. The NYSE is owned by more than 1,300 members (memberships are often referred to as "seats") and is managed by corporate officers and a board of directors. The NYSE is a private organization that assumes responsibility for regulating the activities on its exchange. It is also subject to federal regulation by the Securities and Exchange Commission (SEC).

During March 2004, as many as 65 former members of the NYSE board of directors received subpoenas from the SEC. The former directors were expected to provide details about how they established pay for former NYSE chairman Richard (Dick) Grasso (Associated Press, 2004).

*(continued)*

---

[13]D. Bilefsky, "Mad about Money," *The Wall Street Journal,* April 14, 2003, p. R3.

[14]S. Kitchens, "The Top of the Heap," *Forbes.com,* September 2, 2002.

[15]D. Woodruff, "Europe, a Latecomer, Embraces Options," *The Wall Street Journal,* May 15, 2001, p. A18; and D. Bilefsky, "Mad about Money," *The Wall Street Journal,* April 14, 2003, p. R3.

Two months earlier, the SEC announced a formal investigation into whether the NYSE's compensation process for Grasso had violated any laws or NYSE rules (SEC, 2004).

Controversy over Dick Grasso's pay began during August 2003, when the NYSE for the first time ever publicly released information about the pay of its top executives. Grasso's annual pay was disclosed to include $1.4 million in salary plus a nonguaranteed bonus of approximately $1 million. Nonsalary compensation for the preceding four years had ranged from $9.9 million to $24.2 million per year (McCall, 2003). Grasso received a 2003 payout of approximately $140 million through withdrawals from a retirement plan, a savings plan, and prior bonus awards. The $140 million was characterized in the news media as "outlandish," "excessive," "outsized," and "unseemly." The disclosures caused a public outcry, followed by Grasso's resignation in September 2003 (Weiss, 2003; Weiss et al., 2003).

Considerable disagreement arose about whether the level of pay was too high. Arguments in support of Grasso's pay included the following (Weiss, 2003; McCall, 2003):

- Positive NYSE performance during Grasso's tenure:
  —NYSE seat prices tripled.
  —NYSE invested $2 billion in technology and trading upgrades.
  —NYSE handled record volumes and maintained business in the face of increased competition.
  —Grasso was viewed as a good manager.
- NYSE's use of compensation consultants and a separate board of directors' compensation committee to help set the pay levels.
- Comparability of Grasso's pay to that of public company executives.
- NYSE goal to "attract and retain superior 'world class' executives" (McCall, p. 2).
- Reasonableness of $140 million in light of Grasso's long tenure at NYSE; he had been hired as a clerk in 1968, rose to president in 1988, and became chairman in 1994.

Arguments against Grasso's pay included the following (Weiss, 2003; Parker et al., 2004; Associated Press, 2004):

- Concerns that NYSE board of directors was not sufficiently independent and exercised poor governance.
- Claims that the NYSE board of directors was "hand-picked" by Grasso and that the compensation committee was headed by a close Grasso friend.
- Charges that under Grasso the NYSE had not adequately regulated floor traders or member firms.
- Comparison of Grasso's pay to that of regulators such as SEC chairman William Donaldson, who earned about $140,000 per year.
- Findings from an internal NYSE investigation that reportedly concluded Grasso had been cumulatively overpaid $100 million in pension accounts and $40 million in deferred compensation.
- The uncommon nature of lump-sum withdrawals from pension and savings plans.

Some observers, such as financial author Roger Lowenstein, pointed out that it is not clear how to determine an appropriate level of pay for executives. However, he also argued that the board of directors serves as an agent on behalf of NYSE members. Board members who lack independence may be unable to design compensation packages that adequately reflect free-market incentives (Lowenstein, 2003). In the NYSE case, the SEC stated that the approval of Grasso's pay package "raised serious questions regarding the effectiveness of NYSE's current governance structure" (SEC, 2004).

Sources: Associated Press, "Ex-NYSE Directors Subpoenaed," MSNBC, March 5, 2004, available at www.msnbc.msn.com/id/4455963; "SEC Authorizes Formal Investigation of Matters Raised in Webb Report," press release 2004-3, Securities and Exchange Commission, January 8, 2004; G. Weiss, P. Dwyer, and M. Der Hovanesian, "Big Changes for the Big Board," *BusinessWeek online*, September 29, 2003; G. Weiss, "The $140,000,000 Man," *BusinessWeek online*, September 15, 2003; H. Carl McCall, Chairman, NYSE Human Resources and Compensation Committee, letter to William H. Donaldson, Chairman, U.S. Securities and Exchange Commission, September 9, 2003, available at www.nyse.com/pdfs/donaldsonletter.pdf; J. Parker, C. P. Gallagher, and J. Landry, "Former NYSE Chair Richard Grasso's Pay Included $8.4 Million Pension, Reports *Fortune* Magazine," press release, *Fortune.com*, February 2, 2004; and R. Lowenstein, "Excess Unlimited: Can Corporate America Curb the Monster?" *WashingtonPost.com*, October 12, 2003, p. B01.

### Practice Ethical Decision Making

In Chapter 1, we learned about a process for making ethical decisions (Exhibit 1.11). You can address the following questions for this ethical dilemma to improve your skills for making ethical decisions. Think about your answers to these questions and discuss them with others.

| Ethical Decision-Making Process | Questions to Consider about This Ethical Dilemma |
|---|---|
| Identify ethical problems as they arise. | Is the level of executive pay an ethical issue for boards of directors? Why or why not? Why is it impossible to determine with certainty what Grasso's pay should have been? |
| Objectively consider the well-being of others and society when exploring alternatives. | From the viewpoint of a member of the board of directors, discuss the pros and cons of Grasso's $140 million payout. Consider the effects on stakeholders such as:<br>• Other NYSE employees<br>• Shareholders (NYSE members)<br>• Competitors (other stock exchanges)<br>• Companies listed on the NYSE<br>• External auditors<br>• Regulators such as the SEC<br>• Society |
| Clarify and apply ethical values when choosing a course of action. | What should the NYSE board of directors do to achieve better corporate governance over executive pay? Clarify the values you use in drawing your conclusions. |
| Work toward ongoing improvement of personal and organizational ethics. | It is possible to argue that the NYSE board of directors failed to recognize a change from the "old days" when high executive pay was acceptable, to a new environment in which executive pay must be justified. How can a board of directors continuously reevaluate and improve its approach to issues such as this one? |

# TRANSFER PRICE POLICIES

 **Q6** What prices are used for transferring goods and services within an organization?

 **Q7** What are the uses and limitations of transfer pricing?

When one unit relies on other units within an organization for goods or services, a problem arises that affects the measurement of financial performance. Suppose Porcelain & More, a kitchen and bath fixtures manufacturer, operates with three profit centers: fixtures, sinks, and tubs. Sinks and tubs are sold as kits that include fixtures. In their kits, the sink and tub profit centers use the faucets and handles produced by the fixture profit center. Thus, these fixtures are transferred from one department to the other two departments, and the fixtures need to be priced appropriately. A **transfer price** is the price used to record revenue and cost when goods or services are transferred between responsibility centers in an organization.

## ■ Transfer Prices and Conflicts Among Managers

When compensation is tied to the financial performance of subunits, managers tend to overlook their contribution to the entire organization and focus instead on how decisions affect their subunit's financial performance. Conflicts arise among managers, leading to suboptimal operating decisions.

Suppose that the fixtures department at Porcelain & More sells fixtures for a market price of $20 to external customers. When sold externally, the fixtures department receives credit in its operating income for the entire contribution margin. How should the fixtures be priced, however, when fixtures are transferred internally to the sink and tub departments? The manager of the fixtures department would like to recognize the same revenue that is recorded for external sales. However, managers from the sink and tub departments would like to record in their books only the variable cost for the fixtures that are internally transferred.

They have legitimate claims, because their departments are responsible for selling kits that include fixtures. The managers from the three departments are in conflict with each other. All of them would prefer to show high profits and, therefore, would prefer to recognize most of the contribution for each product sold.

The following chart shows prices and sales for last year. Assume that the fixtures department has plenty of capacity and sells 37,000 sets of fixtures. Of these, 20,000 sets go to the external market, 12,000 to the sinks department, and 5,000 to the tubs department.

|  | Fixtures | Sinks | Tubs | Total |
|---|---|---|---|---|
| Units sold | 37,000 | 12,000 | 5,000 | 54,000 |
| Market price | $20 | $75 | $150 | |
| Variable cost | $10 | $30 | $75 | |

Each department's contribution margin, assuming that fixtures are transferred at market price, is summarized as follows:

|  | Fixtures | Sinks | Tubs | Total |
|---|---|---|---|---|
| External revenue | $ 400,000 | $ 900,000 | $ 750,000 | $ 2,050,000 |
| Transfer price | 340,000 | (240,000) | (100,000) | 0 |
| Other variable costs | (370,000) | (360,000) | (375,000) | (1,105,000) |
| Contribution margin | $ 370,000 | $ 300,000 | $ 275,000 | $ 945,000 |

The external market demand is for only 20,000 sets of fixtures. Suppose the sink and tub department managers insist on using the variable cost of $10 for the transfer price. The following calculations summarize each department's contribution margin if all departments record variable cost as the transfer price for fixtures.

|  | Fixtures | Sinks | Tubs | Total |
|---|---|---|---|---|
| Revenue | $ 400,000 | $ 900,000 | $ 750,000 | $ 2,050,000 |
| Transfer price | 170,000 | (120,000) | (50,000) | 0 |
| Other variable costs | (370,000) | (360,000) | (375,000) | (1,105,000) |
| Contribution margin | $ 200,000 | $ 420,000 | $ 325,000 | $ 945,000 |

Notice that the total contribution margin to Porcelain & More does not change under either alternative—it is $945,000 regardless of the transfer price policy. If the fixtures department always has excess capacity, its managers may be willing to sell at variable cost because they have no other outlets for their fixtures. However, they would prefer a transfer price that includes some portion of fixed costs, because fixture production requires the use of resources such as equipment and supervisor time. If the fixtures department has no excess capacity, that is, if every set of fixtures produced can be sold on the open market, its managers will be unwilling to sell internally when the transfer price is below market price.

Now assume that the transfer price is set at the market price of $20. The fixtures department has excess capacity, but sinks and tubs can buy fixtures from a supplier who sells them for $18 a set, although the quality is slightly lower than those manufactured by the fixtures department. The fixtures department continues to sell 20,000 units externally. Sinks and tubs purchase from the outside supplier. Following is the contribution margin for each department.

|  | Fixtures | Sinks | Tubs | Total |
|---|---|---|---|---|
| Revenue | $ 400,000 | $ 900,000 | $ 750,000 | $2,050,000 |
| Fixtures purchase cost | 0 | (216,000) | (90,000) | (306,000) |
| Other variable costs | (200,000) | (360,000) | (375,000) | (935,000) |
| Contribution margin | $ 200,000 | $ 324,000 | $ 285,000 | $ 809,000 |

Compared to the results with fixtures transferred internally, the overall contribution margin for Porcelain & More is lower by $136,000 ($945,000 − $809,000). The difference is equal to the incremental cost to the company of purchasing the fixtures externally versus manufacturing them internally: 17,000 units × ($18 − $10) = $136,000. In addition, the sinks and tubs are sold with lower-quality fixtures. Yet, when fixtures are purchased externally, managers in both the sink and tub departments appear to be better off when they are evaluated on the performance of their individual departments. A transfer price policy based on market price encourages the managers to make suboptimal decisions for the company as a whole.

# ■ Setting an Appropriate Transfer Price

The perfect transfer price would be the opportunity cost of transferring goods and services internally. If external demand is zero and the selling division has excess capacity, the transfer price would be the variable cost. This price is the minimum price the selling division would typically be willing to accept from an outside buyer when it has excess capacity. However, if capacity is limited and goods or services can be sold externally, then the opportunity cost would be the market price. To sell internally, the department forgoes an external sale and, therefore, should charge the market price.

Although the opportunity cost is the best transfer price policy, it is rarely used because the price would vary with capacity. Most managers prefer stable transfer prices across time. In addition, selling managers may regard a price equal to variable cost as unfair when excess capacity exists, because the purchasing department receives credit for the entire contribution margin for products that are essentially manufactured by both departments. Therefore, other transfer price polices are typically used.

The following methods are often used for setting transfer price policies in manufacturing and service organizations.

- Cost based
- Activity based
- Market based
- Dual rate
- Negotiated

### Cost-Based Transfer Prices

**Cost-based transfer prices** are based on the cost of the good or service transferred. Cost can be computed in different ways, ranging from variable costs to fully allocated costs. If a product has no external market because it is a subcomponent of another product, some type of cost-based transfer price is commonly used.

Suppose that the fixtures department of Porcelain & More usually produces about 40,000 sets of fixtures and incurs about $200,000 in manufacturing overhead cost during an accounting period. The average fixed cost per unit would be $5 ($200,000 ÷ 40,000 units). Under a full production cost transfer price policy, Porcelain & More could set a transfer price of $15 ($10 variable cost + $5 fixed cost). This transfer price allows each department to split the contribution margin that arises when fixtures are sold as part of sink and tub kits.

Cost-based transfer prices present several disadvantages. When products have an external market and departments are profit centers, the transfer price affects decisions about transferring internally or purchasing externally. This situation can lead to suboptimal decisions, such as the purchase of units from external providers shown in the earlier Porcelain & More example. In addition, when transfer prices include allocated fixed costs, managers in selling departments do not have as much incentive to reduce fixed costs. They can pass the responsibility for allocated fixed costs to another department through the transfer pricing policy.

### Activity-Based Transfer Prices

A variation of cost-based transfer prices is the use of **activity-based transfer prices.** Here, the purchasing unit is charged for the unit-level, batch-level, and possibly some product-level costs for products transferred, plus an annual fixed fee that is a portion of the facility-level costs. Suppose the tubs department at Porcelain & More plans to buy enough fixtures internally so that it uses 20% of fixture's capacity. Under activity-based transfer pricing, the tubs department could pay for the unit and batch costs of each fixture and also pay 20% of the fixtures department facility-level costs. By making this lump sum payment, the tubs department essentially reserves some of the fixture department's capacity for units it will purchase internally.

An advantage of activity-based transfer pricing is that the purchasing department has an incentive to accurately project the number of units it will purchase internally. This accuracy enhances an organization's planning abilities. Suppose managers in the fixtures department believe that external sales will be forgone by selling 20% of their fixtures to the tub department. Because they receive a fixed price from the tub department, they know ahead of time that they need to increase capacity to accommodate external sales. They can more easily plan for these changes.

However, because of uncertainty in demand, organizations may sometimes need to re-allocate capacity to attain the highest contribution. In a changing business environment, departments should be allowed to subcontract with each other so that the departments with the best opportunities are using most of the capacity.

**Market-Based Transfer Prices** **Market-based transfer prices** are based on competitors' prices or on the supply-and-demand relationship. They are appropriate under a restrictive set of conditions. These conditions include the presence of a highly competitive market for the intermediate product so that the selling department can sell as much as it wants to outside customers, and the purchasing department can buy as much as it wants from outside suppliers, all without affecting the price. These conditions are rarely met. However, when they are, the market price provides an objective value for intermediate products. The problem with market-based transfer prices is that information about underlying costs is not revealed, and this lack of information encourages suboptimal decision making, as illustrated in the Porcelain and More example.

**Dual Rate Transfer Prices** **Dual rate transfer prices** allow the selling department to be credited for the market price and the purchasing department to be charged the variable cost. When financial statements are consolidated at the end of the accounting period, adjustments are made so that overall organizational profit is accurately reported. This method provides appropriate information and incentives when the selling department has excess capacity. Also, it is most similar to a policy that uses an opportunity cost for the transfer price. A disadvantage of the method is that it overstates profitability at the subunit level, and managers may believe that the organization as a whole is more profitable than it actually is.

**Negotiated Transfer Prices** **Negotiated transfer prices** are based on an agreement reached between the managers of the selling and purchasing departments. This method ensures that both managers have full information about costs and market prices and that the transfer price provides appropriate incentives. A disadvantage of this method is that it usually requires more time because both managers prefer more contribution margin. Managers' time is valuable to the organization for other responsibilities, and negotiation time may not be a high priority for the organization as a whole.

## COMPUTER WIZARDS (PART 4)
### NEGOTIATED TRANSFER PRICES

The Canadian division of Computer Wizards produces computer monitors. These monitors are sold on the open market for $110 each or the New Jersey division uses them as part of a complete computer package. When the monitor is transferred internally, the entire computer package has a contribution margin of $415 each. The organization currently uses market price plus shipping as a transfer price. Jason is happy with this transfer price, but Cecelia has asked Renee to consider changing the policy, because her division shows lower earnings than it should. She would prefer to purchase monitors from Jason, but often purchases less-expensive and lower-quality monitors from an external vendor to improve her division's earnings.

The Canadian division has capacity to produce 10,000 monitors per month and usually operates at 70% of capacity. The following data pertain to production at this level.

|  | Average Cost |
|---|---|
| Direct materials | $25 |
| Direct labor | 15 |
| Supplies | 5 |
| Total variable cost per monitor | 45 |
| Allocated fixed costs | 50 |
| Total average cost per monitor | $95 |

If a monitor is sold on the open market, the customer pays the shipping cost. The cost of shipping a monitor from Canada to New Jersey is about $10 each.

The Canadian division is currently operating at 50% of its capacity, substantially below normal. Jason would like to sell more monitors internally to help cover fixed costs. Both managers contact Renee, who tells them to negotiate a policy that is fair to both divisions. Jason would like to set a transfer price that is below the market price but above the variable cost, so that some of the fixed costs are covered by internal transfers. Cecelia would prefer to pay only the variable cost plus the shipping charge, because the Canadian division's fixed costs will not change if production increases, and workers would be idle part of the time without the internal transfers.

After negotiating for several weeks, the two managers go back to Renee for help. Renee has laid out the following information based on a selling price for the computer package of $950.

|  | Average Cost |
|---|---|
| Direct materials | $240 |
| Direct labor | 75 |
| Supplies | 175 |
| Total variable costs excluding monitor | 490 |
| Cost of monitor | 110 |
| Allocated fixed costs | 200 |
| Total average cost per computer package | $800 |

Renee explains that, from Computer Wizard's perspective, the contribution margin on monitors sold externally is $65 ($110 − $45). When the monitor is transferred internally, the relevant cost to Computer Wizards is $45, the variable cost. The relevant contribution margin for the computer package is $415 ($950 − $490 − $45). When Cecelia purchases a monitor externally for $110, the contribution margin is $350 ($950 − $490 − $110). Therefore, corporate headquarters would prefer internal transfers over purchases from outside vendors.

Renee suggests that Cecelia pay Jason a flat amount to help cover fixed costs and also pay the variable cost for each monitor transferred. Jason agrees to this policy as long as the division operates with excess capacity. However, he points out that when the division lacks enough capacity to fill both external and internal orders, he will sell externally and forgo internal transfers to increase profits for the Canadian division.

Renee calculates the difference in the company-wide contribution margin when transferring monitors internally versus purchasing them externally at $65 ($415 − $350). This difference happens to be the same as the contribution margin for the Canadian division when monitors are sold externally. Therefore, Jason and Cecelia are indifferent to whether sales take place internally or externally *when the Canadian division is at capacity.* Meanwhile, both managers agree that developing a transfer price policy that suits not only both divisions but also the overall organization is more difficult than it first appeared.

## GUIDE YOUR LEARNING  15.3  Computer Wizards (Part 4)

Computer Wizards (Part 4) illustrates transfer prices. For this illustration:

| Identify Problem and Information | Explore Incentives | Explore Pros and Cons of Options |
|---|---|---|
| What decisions were being addressed? What alternative transfer prices could have been used? | Describe the incentives of the managers of the two divisions. Why might these managers make decisions that are not in the best interests of the organization as a whole? | What were the pros and cons of different transfer prices for this scenario? |

## ADDITIONAL TRANSFER PRICE CONSIDERATIONS

 **Q7** What are the uses and limitations of transfer pricing?

**INTERNATIONAL**

In the Ernst & Young *Transfer Pricing 2003 Global Survey,* multinational parents and subsidiaries cited transfer pricing as their most important international tax issue.[16] Multinational companies are frequently audited, and tax authorities often require taxable income adjustments that result in double taxation.

**CHAPTER REFERENCE**

See Chapter 11 for more details about allocating service department costs.

The preceding section addressed the incentives of managers for transfer prices between operating units. The following additional factors affect the choice of transfer prices.

### ■ International Income Taxes

For organizations that do business internationally, the taxable location of profit is affected by transfer price policies. An organization with subsidiaries located in high-tax and low-tax countries could potentially charge a high transfer price in the low-tax countries so that most of the contribution margin arises where taxes are lowest. To restrict firms' abilities to shift income in this manner, income tax regulations typically stipulate the use of market-based transfer prices. The details of international tax regulation are complex and beyond the scope of this textbook.

### ■ Transfer Prices for Support Services

Many organizations set transfer prices for support services. Their objective is to motivate efficient use and cost-effective production of internal support services such as accounting, printing, human resources, and purchasing. When support departments provide services without charge to user departments, the user departments tend to use the support services inefficiently. In turn, inefficient use tends to encourage support departments to grow unnecessarily large. Transfer prices can encourage more efficient use of support services.

Transfer prices are often based on fully allocated costs and therefore include allocations of fixed support department costs and allocations from other support departments. As a result, the transfer prices can be high. High transfer prices can encourage user departments to outsource the support services. As we learned in the Porcelain & More example, outsourcing is not always beneficial to the organization as a whole. Outsourcing can cause internal services to be duplicated, resulting in excess capacity and inefficient use of resources.

### ■ Setting Transfer Prices for Internal Services

Because top managers prefer to have support services used efficiently, they want to set transfer prices that motivate this behavior. The best transfer price policy is an opportunity cost approach. Each department is charged an amount that reflects the value of any opportunities forgone by not using the service for its next best alternative use.

Suppose that Computer Wizards' production and assembly equipment needs routine maintenance to prevent downtime during regular hours of operation. The maintenance department schedules its repair and maintenance time during lunch hours and at the end of each production shift. Currently, the maintenance department is operating close to capacity. Other departments need to schedule nonroutine tasks, such as painting walls and repairing damaged flooring, well in advance. If a department wants maintenance personnel to hang pictures in an office, the value of the opportunity forgone might be the cost of hiring a contractor to provide routine maintenance on equipment or to paint walls. However, if the maintenance department has extra capacity and workers are idle part of the time, the opportunity cost of hanging pictures would be zero.

Implementing a transfer price policy based on opportunity costs is problematic because opportunities change over time with changes in demand and capacity. In addition, finding and valuing alternative uses for some services can be difficult. Therefore, organizations use transfer price policies for internal services similar to those used for transferring goods. Cost-based transfer prices range from variable costs to fully allocated costs. Market-based transfer prices are set at amounts that would be paid if the service were outsourced.

Some organizations establish a price per job for each task, keep prices low on jobs they want to have performed internally, and set prices high on jobs that are considered unnecessary

[16]"Transfer Pricing: Most Important International Tax Issue, Says Ernst & Young Survey," press release, Ernst & Young, November 5, 2003.

or inappropriate. Suppose the managers of Computer Wizards believe that the maintenance personnel should not be hanging pictures. They could set the transfer price for hanging pictures high enough to discourage other departments from asking the maintenance department to perform this service.

## ■ Transfer of Corporate Overhead Costs

Another type of transfer price occurs when corporate overhead costs are allocated to other responsibility centers. Managerial performance rewarded based on accounting profits can stimulate much discussion between corporate headquarters and profit center managers about whether allocating overhead costs is appropriate, and whether the allocation plan and allocation bases are appropriate. Under responsibility accounting, managers should be held accountable only for costs that they control. Because they have little or no control over corporate costs, they should not be held responsible for those costs in performance evaluations.

Many organizations do allocate corporate headquarters costs, however. Sometimes these are considered a corporate tax and are allocated based on revenues or profitability. In this manner, subunits operating under optimal circumstances absorb more overhead than subunits with poor results because of economic or industry conditions that are not under managers' control.

**CHAPTER REFERENCE**
See Chapter 10 for information about the use of flexible budgets to evaluate performance.

---

### GUIDE YOUR LEARNING 15.4 Key Terms

Stop to confirm that you understand the new terms introduced in the last several pages.

Return on investment (ROI) (p. 597)
Residual income (p. 600)
Economic value added (EVA) (p. 601)
Transfer price (p. 607)
Cost-based transfer prices (p. 609)

Activity-based transfer prices (p. 609)
Market-based transfer prices (p. 610)
Dual rate transfer prices (p. 610)
Negotiated transfer prices (p. 610)

For each of these terms, write a definition in your own words.

---

# SUMMARY

### Q1 What Is Agency Theory?

**Principals and Agents**
Principals hire agents to make decisions for them and to act in their behalf.

**Agency Costs**
Costs that arise when agents fail to act in the interest of principals:

- Losses from poor decisions
- Losses from incongruent goals
- Monitoring costs
- Goal alignment costs
- Contracting costs

**Reducing Agency Costs**
To measure, monitor, and motivate performance:

- Assign responsibility for decision making
- Link decision-making authority to performance measurement
- Use income-based measures to assess performance
- Motivate performance with compensation schemes
- Establish prices for the transfer of goods and services within an organization

### Q2 How Are Decision-Making Responsibility and Authority Related to Performance Evaluation?

**Centralized and Decentralized Organizations**
Advantages and disadvantages: See Exhibit 15.3.

**General Versus Specific Knowledge**
Decision authority is related to the type of knowledge within an organization.

**Q3** How Are Responsibility Centers Used to Measure, Monitor, and Motivate Performance?

### Types of Responsibility Centers
- Cost centers
  - Discretionary cost centers
- Revenue centers
- Profit centers
- Investment centers

### Issues
- Reduce agency costs by holding managers responsible for the decisions over which they have authority
- Measuring performance at the responsibility center level can lead to suboptimal decisions

**Q4** What Are the Uses and Limitations of Return on Investment, Residual Income, and Economic Value Added for Monitoring Performance?

### Return on Investment (ROI)

$$ROI = \frac{\text{Operating income}}{\text{Average operating assets}}$$

DuPont Analysis:

$$ROI = \left(\frac{\text{Sales}}{\text{Average operating assets}}\right) \times \left(\frac{\text{Operating income}}{\text{Sales}}\right)$$

$$ROI = \text{Investment turnover} \times \text{Return on sales}$$

### Residual Income

$$\frac{\text{Residual}}{\text{income}} = \frac{\text{Operating}}{\text{income}} - \left(\frac{\text{Required rate}}{\text{of return}} \times \frac{\text{Average}}{\text{operating assets}}\right)$$

### Economic Value Added (EVA)

$$EVA = \frac{\text{Adjusted}}{\text{after-tax}} \frac{}{\text{operating}} \frac{}{\text{income}} - \left[\frac{\text{Weighted}}{\text{average}} \frac{}{\text{cost of}} \frac{}{\text{capital}} \times \left(\frac{\text{Adjusted}}{\text{total}} \frac{}{\text{assets}} - \frac{\text{Current}}{\text{liabilities}}\right)\right]$$

### Advantages and Disadvantages
ROI is easier to compare across subunits, but motivates suboptimal decisions, both in long-term investment and short-term cost cutting

Residual Income provides more appropriate investment incentives than ROI, but is not comparable across subunits

EVA minimizes suboptimal decision-making incentives, but is complex to calculate and not comparable across subunits.

**Q5** How Is Compensation Used to Motivate Performance?

### Bonus System Incentives
Examples of performance measures:

- ROI
- Residual income
- EVA
- Operating income or growth in income

- Cost savings
- Revenue growth

### Motivating Long-Term Versus Short-Term Performance

**Q6** What Prices Are Used for Transferring Goods and Services Within an Organization?

### Ideal Transfer Price
- Opportunity cost

### Alternatives
- Cost-based transfer price
- Activity-based transfer price
- Market-based transfer price
- Dual rate transfer price
- Negotiated transfer price

**Q7** What Are the Uses and Limitations of Transfer Pricing?

### Uses
- Assign cost to goods and services transferred internally for financial reporting and income taxes
- Motivate efficient use of support services
- Allocate corporate overhead costs

### Incentive Issues
- Conflicts among managers
- Suboptimal decision making
- Managers should not be held responsible for costs over which they have no control
- International income taxes

## KEY TO SYMBOLS

**e** This question requires students to extend knowledge beyond the applications shown in the textbook.

**1** This question requires Step 1 skills (**Identifying**) in Steps for Better Thinking (Exhibit 1.10).

**2** This question requires Step 2 skills (**Exploring**) in Steps for Better Thinking (Exhibit 1.10).

**3** This question requires Step 3 skills (**Prioritizing**) in Steps for Better Thinking (Exhibit 1.10).

**4** This question requires Step 4 skills (**Envisioning**) in Steps for Better Thinking (Exhibit 1.10).

## Self-Study Problems

**Q4** | **Self-Study Problem 1** | **ROI, Residual Income, EVA**

Outdoor Express is a large manufacturer of recreational equipment. Performance of the Camping division is measured as an investment center because the managers make all the decisions about investments in operating equipment and space. Following is financial information for the Camping division:

| | |
|---|---|
| Average operating assets | $2,000,000 |
| Current liabilities | 500,000 |
| Operating income | 300,000 |

Camping division's required rate of return is 12%, but Outdoor Express's weighted average cost of capital is 9%, and the tax rate is 30%.

**REQUIRED:**

A. Calculate return on investment for the Camping division.

B. Calculate residual income for the Camping division.

C. Calculate EVA for the Camping division.

**2** D. Briefly discuss the advantages and disadvantages of each method.

### Solution to Self-Study Problem 1

A.

$$\text{ROI} = \frac{\text{Net operating income}}{\text{Average operating assets}} = \frac{\$300,000}{\$2,000,000} = 15\%$$

B. Residual income = Net operating income − (Required rate of return × Investment)

= $300,000 − (12% × $2,000,000) = $300,000 − $240,000 = $60,000

C. EVA = After-tax operating income − [Weighted average cost of capital × (Total assets − Current liabilities)]

= [$300,000 × (1 − 0.30)] − [9% × ($2,000,000 − $500,000)] = $210,000 − $135,000 = $75,000

D. ROI and residual income motivate managers to reduce costs and investment, whereas EVA provides incentives to invest as long as the return is equal to or greater than the required rate of return. In addition, ROI and residual income do not include taxes, so no incentive is provided for managers to minimize taxes. EVA can be adjusted for intangibles such as leases and R&D spending. Therefore, it can be designed to minimize managers' abilities to artificially improve the performance measure. Also, see page 614.

**Q6, Q7** | **Self-Study Problem 2** | **Transfer Price, Excess versus Full Capacity, Outsourcing**

The Kansas division of Aeronautic Controls (AC) produces a digital thermometer. The thermometer can be sold on the open market for $180 each, or it can be used by the Texas division in the production of a temperature control gauge that has a unit contribution margin of $140 (given that the digital thermometer is transferred at variable cost plus shipping).

The Kansas division is currently operating at 70% of its capacity of 2,000 digital thermometers per month. Following are average costs per unit at this level of capacity:

| | Average Cost |
|---|---|
| Direct materials | $ 50 |
| Variable supplies | 10 |
| Fixed costs | 100 |
| Total average cost per thermometer | $160 |

If a digital thermometer is sold on the open market, the customer pays the shipping cost. The cost of shipping a digital thermometer from Kansas to Texas is $15.

**REQUIRED:**

A. What is the best transfer price for AC overall if a digital thermometer is transferred to Texas and the Kansas division is operating at 70% of capacity?

B. What is the best transfer price for AC overall if a digital thermometer is transferred to Texas, but the Kansas division is operating at full capacity and the digital thermometer could have been sold on the open market?

**e** C. Suppose the Texas division can purchase a substitute for the digital thermometer from an outside supplier for $100 (including shipping costs). Under ordinary circumstances, what single transfer price would motivate the managers of both divisions to act in AC's interests at either excess or full capacity?

**2** D. What are the potential problems with the transfer price identified in part (C)? Explain.

### Solution to Self-Study Problem 2

A. When the Kansas division has excess capacity (30% in the problem), the transfer price should be the variable cost of $75 (direct materials of $50 plus supplies of $10 and shipping of $15).

B. If the Kansas division could sell all of its thermometers on the open market, the transfer price should be the market price of $180 plus $15 shipping = $195.

C. First consider the contribution margin for each division from the perspective of the entire organization. Selling the temperature control gauge results in a contribution margin of $140 per unit. Selling the digital thermometers results in a contribution margin of $105 ($180 − $75 thermometer variable cost). When Kansas has excess capacity, the total contribution margin is $245 ($140 + $105).

For each unit produced with a digital thermometer from an outside supplier, the Texas division's contribution margin is reduced by $25 ($100 − $75) from $140 to $115. However, from the perspective of the entire organization, the contribution margin is $115 from Texas plus $105 from Kansas, or $220 in total. If the internal transfer takes place, the contribution margin is only $140. Therefore, transfers should take place only when Kansas has excess capacity. To motivate this behavior, the transfer price should be equal to or greater than $75 and equal to or less than $100. Setting the transfer price at $90 + $10 shipping would give Texas incentive to purchase inside if Kansas had capacity, but purchase outside if Kansas had no capacity because the transfer price would be the same with either purchase. In addition, Kansas would have incentive to sell to the external market when possible because the contribution margin of $105 on external sales is greater than the $35 ($90 − $65) contribution margin for internal sales.

D. The Texas division might find an external vendor that could produce the digital thermometer at a cost less than the transfer price, but that would decrease AC's overall contribution margin. In addition, the Texas division could forgo special orders that would have a positive contribution margin for AC if the division uses the internal transfer price to determine whether to accept the order.

---

**REVIEW** Use the exercises in the following boxes in the chapter to review key terms and key techniques, analyze chapter illustrations, improve your learning of new concepts, and practice ethical decision making:

Guide Your Learning 15.1: Key Terms (p. 597)

Guide Your Learning 15.2: Computer Wizards (Parts 1, 2, and 3) (p. 603)

Guide Your Learning 15.3: Computer Wizards (Part 4) (p. 611)

Guide Your Learning 15.4: Key Terms (p. 613)

Focus on Ethical Decision Making: Level of Executive Pay (p. 605)

---

## QUESTIONS

**15.1** Explain how return on investment (ROI) is calculated and how it can be decomposed into two financial measures.

**15.2** Explain how and why the use of ROI for performance evaluation can cause managers to make decisions that could be harmful to an organization in the long run.

**15.3** Explain how residual income is calculated, and define required rate of return in your own words.

**15.4** Explain why the use of residual income for performance evaluation provides better incentives, in some ways, than ROI, but still causes managers to make some decisions that could be harmful to an organization in the long run.

**15.5** Explain the differences between general and specific knowledge. Give an example of an industry where knowledge is quite general and an example of an industry that requires specific knowledge.

**15.6** Explain why organizational form may vary if specific knowledge versus general knowledge is needed for decision making.

**15.7** Describe agency costs and give several examples of them.

**15.8** Explain how EVA differs from residual income.

**15.9** Identify the four different types of responsibility centers and explain the general objectives of each.

**15.10** An organization's plant in Tennessee manufactures a product that is shipped to a branch in Oregon for sale. Does it make any difference which branch (each is a profit center) is charged for the cost of transportation? Explain.

**15.11** A national corporation, Fast Print, decided to expand into several developing countries. The corporation has been managed under a centralized organizational form, but is considering changing to a decentralized form. List the advantages and disadvantages of making this change.

**15.12** Suppose transfer prices are set at market prices and a manager who previously purchased internally begins to purchase externally. Explain what it means to say that the outsourcing decision might have been suboptimal.

**15.13** Describe as many different methods for setting transfer prices as you can.

# EXERCISES

**15.14**
Q1, Q2, Q3, Q4, Q5

**Responsibility centers, agency theory, and performance measures** Your brother recently bought a small business with several coffee carts located around the city. Two workers share responsibility for each cart. All beverages are prepared using identical recipes and ingredients, but the baked goods and other items sold by each cart are chosen by the employees who operate the carts each day. Your brother asked your advice in determining how best to compensate the employees. He thinks he should give them bonuses when costs are contained, and pay them a flat salary otherwise.

REQUIRED:
**A.** What type of responsibility center is each cart?
**B.** Explain how agency theory relates to your brother's situation.
**C.** List several financial performance measures that might be relevant for measuring employee performance.
**e D.** List one nonfinancial measure that might be important to the success of this business.

**15.15**
Q4

**Residual income, ROI, and EVA** The following selected data pertain to Brannard Company's Construction Division for last year.

| | |
|---|---|
| Sales | $2,000,000 |
| Variable costs | $1,200,000 |
| Traceable fixed costs | $200,000 |
| Average invested capital (assets) | $3,000,000 |
| Current liabilities | $200,000 |
| Required rate of return | 15% |
| Marginal tax rate | 36% |
| Weighted average cost of capital | 12% |

REQUIRED:
**A.** Calculate the residual income.
**B.** Calculate the return on investment.
**C.** Calculate the economic value added.

**15.16**
Q4
CPA

**ROI, residual income, breakeven point, contribution margin** Oslo Company's industrial photo-finishing division, Rho, incurred the following costs and expenses in the last period.

| | Variable | Fixed |
|---|---|---|
| Direct materials | $200,000 | |
| Direct labor | 150,000 | |
| Factory overhead | 70,000 | $42,000 |
| General, selling, and administrative | 30,000 | 48,000 |
| Totals | $450,000 | $90,000 |

During the period, Rho produced 300,000 units of industrial photo prints, which were sold for $2.00 each. Oslo's investment in Rho was $500,000 and $700,000 at the beginning and ending of the year, respectively. Oslo's weighted average cost of capital is 15%.

**REQUIRED:**
A. Determine Rho's return on investment for the year.
B. Compute Rho's residual income (loss) for the year.
C. How many industrial photo print units did Rho have to sell during the year to break even?
D. What was Rho's contribution margin for the year?

**15.17**
**Q4**
**EVA for segments** Following is information for the Fulcrum Company's three business segments located in Europe.

|  | Segment A | Segment B | Segment C |
|---|---|---|---|
| Pretax operating income | € 8,000,000 | € 4,000,000 | € 6,000,000 |
| Current assets | 8,000,000 | 6,000,000 | 8,000,000 |
| Long-term assets | 32,000,000 | 26,000,000 | 16,000,000 |
| Current liabilities | 4,000,000 | 2,000,000 | 3,000,000 |

Fulcrum's applicable tax rate for the segments is 30%, and its weighted average cost of capital for each segment is 10%.

**REQUIRED:** Determine the segment with the highest EVA.

**15.18**
**Q4, Q6, Q7**
**ROI, transfer prices, taxes, employee motivation** Fowler Electronics produces color plasma screens in its Windsor, Ontario, plant. The screens are then shipped to the company's plant in Detroit, Michigan, where they are incorporated into finished televisions. Although the Windsor plant never sells plasma screens to any other assembler, the market for them is competitive. The market price is $750 per screen.

Variable costs to manufacture the screens are $350. Fixed costs at the Windsor plant are $2,000,000 per period. The plant typically manufactures and ships 10,000 screens per period to the Detroit plant. Taxes in Canada amount to 30%, of pretax income. The Canadian plant has total assets of $20,000,000.

The Detroit plant incurs variable costs to complete the televisions of $110 per set (in addition to the cost of the screens). The Detroit plant's fixed costs amount to $4,000,000 per period. The 10,000 sets produced each period are sold for an average of $2,500 each. The U.S. tax rate is 45% of pretax income. The U.S. plant has total assets of $30,000,000.

**REQUIRED:**
A. Determine the return on investment for each plant if the screens are transferred at variable cost.
B. Determine the return on investment for each plant if the screens are transferred at market price.
C. To reduce taxes, will Fowler prefer a transfer price based on cost or market price? Explain.
D. Will the top managers in each plant prefer to use cost or market price as the transfer price? Explain.
❶ E. How would you resolve potential conflict over the transfer price policy?

**15.19**
**Q6, Q7**
**Choice of transfer price** The following information relates to a new computer chip that Hand Held has developed for its new cell phone that contains a personal organizer:

| CHIP DIVISION | |
|---|---|
| Market price of finished chip to outsiders | $24 |
| Variable cost per unit | 12 |
| Contribution margin | $12 |
|  |  |
| Total contribution for 30,000 units | $360,000 |

## CELL PHONE DIVISION

| | |
|---|---:|
| Market price of finished products | $128 |
| Variable costs: | |
| From Chip Division | 12 |
| Other direct materials | 50 |
| Cell Phone Division | |
| Assembly | 38 |
| Packaging | 20 |
| Contribution margin | $ 8 |
| | |
| Total contribution for 20,000 units | $160,000 |

The variable costs of the Cell Phone Division will be incurred whether it buys from the Chip Division or from an outside supplier.

**REQUIRED:**

**A.** What is the highest price that the managers of the Cell Phone Division would want to pay the Chip Division for the chip? Explain.

**B.** If the Chip Division is working at full capacity and cannot produce additional units, what transfer price for the chip would be best for the company as a whole? Explain.

**C.** If the Chip Division is not operating at capacity and has no prospect of reaching capacity, what is the lowest price its managers would typically be willing to sell chips to the Cell Phone Division?

**15.20** **Choice of transfer price, fairness to managers** [*Note:* This problem is based on transfer prices
**Q6, Q7** and incentives for a real company. However, the name of the company and the data are fictional.]

Prem International has two large subsidiaries, Oil and Chemical. Oil is an oil-refining business, and its main product is gasoline. Chemical produces and sells a variety of chemical products.

Chemical owns a polystyrene processing plant next to Oil's refinery. The polystyrene plant was built at the same time that Oil built a benzene plant at the refinery. Benzene is the raw material needed by Chemical to produce polystyrene. Chemical's managers believe they can sell 100 million pounds of polystyrene per year, which is less than full capacity. Following are Chemical's expected revenues and costs for the polystyrene plant (volume is measured using weight in pounds rather than using a liquid measure such as gallons because weight is not affected by temperature):

| | Per Pound |
|---|---:|
| Selling price | $0.30 |
| Costs: Benzene (to be purchased from Oil) | $ ? |
| Variable production costs | 0.03 |
| Fixed production costs | 0.05 |

Oil can operate at full capacity and sell all of the gasoline it produces. Following are Oil's expected revenues and costs for the production of gasoline:

| | Per Pound |
|---|---:|
| Selling price | $0.16 |
| Costs: Crude oil | $0.06 |
| Variable production costs | 0.02 |
| Fixed production costs | 0.07 |

For every pound of benzene that Oil produces, it will forgo selling a pound of gasoline. However, 100 million pounds per year would be only a small portion of total volume at the refinery. Following are Oil's expected revenues and costs for the production of benzene (these costs include the costs of refining the crude oil):

| | Per Pound |
|---|---:|
| Selling price (to Chemical) | $ ? |
| Costs: Crude oil | $0.06 |
| Variable production costs | 0.04 |
| Fixed production costs | 0.09 |

**REQUIRED:**

**A.** On a company-wide basis, should Prem International produce polystyrene this year? Why or why not?

**B.** Using the usual quantitative rules for short-term decisions (Chapter 4), what is the maximum price that Chemical's managers would be willing to pay for benzene?

**ⓔ C.** Would Chemical's managers be willing to pay the maximum transfer price calculated in part (B)? Why or why not?

**D.** Using the usual quantitative rules for short-term decisions (Chapter 4), what is the minimum price that Oil's managers would be willing to receive for benzene?

**ⓔ E.** Would Oil's managers be willing to receive the minimum transfer price calculated in part (D)? Why or why not?

**ⓔ F.** What transfer price might be fair to the managers of both subsidiaries? Explain.

**15.21**
**Q6, Q7**
**CPA**

**Transfer price, sale to outside versus inside customer** Ajax division of Carlyle Corporation produces electric motors, 20% of which are sold to the Bradley division of Carlyle and the remainder to outside customers. Carlyle treats its divisions as profit centers and allows division managers to choose their sources of sale and supply. Corporate policy requires that all interdivisional sales and purchases be recorded at variable cost as transfer price. Ajax division's estimated sales and standard cost data for 2005, based on its full capacity of 100,000 units are as follows:

|  | Bradley | Outsiders |
|---|---|---|
| Sales | $ 900,000 | $ 8,000,000 |
| Variable costs | (900,000) | (3,600,000) |
| Fixed costs | (300,000) | (1,200,000) |
| Gross margin | $(300,000) | $ 3,200,000 |
|  |  |  |
| Unit sales | 20,000 | 80,000 |

Ajax has an opportunity to sell the 20,000 units to an outside customer at a price of $75 per unit on a continuing basis. Bradley can purchase its requirements from an outside supplier for $85 per unit.

**REQUIRED:** Assuming that Ajax division desires to maximize its gross margin, should Ajax accept the new customer and drop its sales to Bradley for 2005? Why or why not?

# PROBLEMS

**15.22**
**Q4**

**ROI, residual income, explaining the better measure** The following financial data are for the evaluation of performance for Midwest Mining:

| | |
|---|---|
| Average operating assets | $500,000 |
| Net operating income | $65,000 |
| Minimum required rate of return | 10% |

Midwest Mining currently uses return on investment to evaluate investment center managers. An accounting intern from the local university suggested to the controller that residual income may be a better performance measure.

**REQUIRED:**

**A.** Calculate ROI for Midwest Mining.

**B.** Calculate residual income for Midwest Mining.

**③ C.** Write a brief memo to the controller explaining why residual income is a better performance measure.

**15.23**
**Q3, Q4**

**Lease versus buy decision, ROI, residual income, EVA, manager incentives** Refer to the information in Problem 15.22. The manager of Midwest Mining is considering a new project. She can buy or lease equipment that will reprocess tailings from old mines to remove any traces of gold left behind by the original separating processes. The purchase price of the equipment is $150,000. The cost to lease is $2,000 per month. She estimates the return (incremental revenues minus incremental expenses, including lease cost) to be $40,000 per year. She knows that purchasing the equipment will increase the value of average operating assets. If she leases the equipment, expenses will increase, but not assets. (In other words, the lease will be accounted for as an operating lease.) Although it is more cost effective to purchase the equipment, she has decided to lease it.

**REQUIRED:**

**A.** Calculate the new ROI if the equipment is (1) purchased or (2) leased.

**B.** Calculate the new residual income if the equipment is (1) purchased, or (2) leased.

**❷ C.** One of the adjustments that can be made using EVA is to treat all operating lease costs as if they were purchases—in other words, to capitalize the lease. If Midwest Mining used EVA with this adjustment, how might the manager's incentives and behavior change? Explain.

**15.24**
**Q6, Q7**

**Transfer price, company versus division profit, idle capacity** The Furniture Division of International Woodworking purchases lumber and makes tables, chairs, and other wood furniture. Most of the lumber is purchased from the Port Angeles Mill, also a division of International Woodworking. The Furniture Division and the Port Angeles Mill are profit centers.

The Furniture Division manager proposed a new Danish-designed chair that will sell for $150. The manager wants to purchase the lumber from the Port Angeles Mill. Production of 800 chairs is planned, using capacity in the Furniture Division that is currently idle.

The Furniture Division can purchase the lumber for each chair from an outside supplier for $60. International Woodworkers has a policy that internal transfers are priced at variable cost plus allocated fixed costs.

Assume the following costs for the production of one chair:

| Port Angeles Mill | | Furniture Division | |
|---|---|---|---|
| Variable cost | $40 | Variable costs: | |
| Allocated fixed cost | 30 | Lumber: Port Angeles Mill | $ 70 |
| Fully absorbed cost | $70 | Furniture Division variable costs: | |
| | | Manufacturing | 75 |
| | | Selling | 10 |
| | | Total variable cost | $155 |

**REQUIRED:**

**A.** Assume that the Port Angeles Mill has idle capacity and would incur no additional fixed costs to produce the required lumber. Would the Furniture Division manager buy the lumber for the chair from the Port Angeles Mill, given the existing transfer price policy? Why or why not?

**B.** Calculate the contribution margin for the company as a whole if the manager decides to buy from the Port Angeles Mill and is able to sell 800 chairs.

**❷ C.** What transfer price policy would you recommend if the Port Angeles Mill always has idle (excess) capacity? Explain why this transfer price policy provides incentives for the managers to act in the best interests of the company as a whole.

**❷ D.** Explain how the idle capacity affects the recommendation in part (C).

**15.25**
**Q6, Q7**

**Transfer price, incentives for internal services** Avra Valley Services has two divisions, Computer Services and Management Advisory Services. Both divisions work for external customers and, in addition, work for each other. Fees earned by Computer Services from external customers were $400,000 in 2004. Fees earned by Management Advisory Services from external customers were $700,000 in 2004. Computer Services worked 3,000 hours for Management Advisory Services last year, and Management Advisory Services worked 1,200 hours for Computer Services. The total costs of external services performed by Computer Services were $220,000, and for Management Advisory Services costs were $480,000.

**REQUIRED:**

**A.** Determine the operating income for each division and for the company as a whole if the transfer price from Computer Services to Management Advisory Services is $50 per hour

*(continued)*

and the transfer price from Management Advisory Services to Computer Services is $60 per hour.

**ⓒ B.** The manager of Computer Services has found another company willing to provide the same services as Management Advisory Services at $50 per hour. All of the employees in both units are guaranteed 40-hour work weeks. Currently, Management Advisory Services has idle capacity because of an economic downturn. Calculate the change in operating income for the company as a whole if Computer Services uses outsourced services instead of using Management Advisory Services.

**❸ C.** Recommend a transfer price policy that would provide incentives to use the internal services. Explain your recommendation.

**❷ D.** Discuss possible qualitative factors that might affect the attractiveness of the outsourcing option.

---

**15.26**  **ROI, residual income, EVA, effect on investment decision, performance evaluation** Strong
**Q4**  Welding Equipment Company produces and sells welding equipment nationally and internationally. Following is information about two divisions.

|  | Brazil | U.S. |
|---|---|---|
| Invested capital (total assets) | $4,000,000 | $400,000 |
| Net operating income | $1,000,000 | $120,000 |
| Required rate of return | 10% | 10% |
| Weighted average cost of capital | 9% | 9% |
| Current liabilities | $80,000 | $10,000 |
| After-tax income | $600,000 | $80,000 |

**REQUIRED:**
**A.** Calculate each division's ROI.
**B.** Calculate each division's residual income.
**C.** Calculate each division's EVA.
**❶ D.** Suppose the Brazilian division had an opportunity to invest $3,500,000 in a project that would generate sales of $5,000,000 and return on sales of 10%, or $500,000. Would the division manager be likely to undertake this project if he or she is evaluated using ROI? Explain.
**❸ E.** Recommend a performance evaluation measure that would increase the managers' incentives to make decisions that would be in the best interests of the owners.

---

**15.27**  **Choosing type of responsibility center, support cost allocation, ROI** The ATCO Company pur-
**Q2, Q3, Q4**  chased the Dexter Company three years ago. Prior to the acquisition, Dexter manufactured and
  sold plastic products to a wide variety of customers. Since becoming a division of ATCO, Dexter only manufactures plastic components for products made by ATCO's Macon division. Macon sells its products to hardware wholesalers.

ATCO's corporate management gives the Dexter division management a considerable amount of authority in running the division's operation. However, corporate management retains the authority for decisions regarding capital investments, price setting of all products, and the quantity of each product to be produced by the Dexter division.

ATCO has a formal performance evaluation program for the management of all of its divisions. The performance evaluation program relies heavily on each division's return on investment. The accompanying income statement of Dexter division provides the basis for the evaluation of Dexter's divisional management.

The corporate accounting staff prepares all of the divisions' financial statements. The corporate general services costs are allocated on the basis of sales dollars, and the computer department's actual costs are apportioned among the divisions on the basis of use. The net division investment includes division fixed assets at net book value (cost less depreciation), division inventory, and corporate working capital apportioned to the division on the basis of sales dollars.

**DEXTER DIVISION OF ATCO COMPANY**
**INCOME STATEMENT**
**FOR THE YEAR ENDED OCTOBER 31, 20XX**
**(IN THOUSANDS OF DOLLARS)**

| | | |
|---|---:|---:|
| Sales | | $4,000 |
| Costs and expenses: | | |
| Direct materials | $ 500 | |
| Direct labor | 1,100 | |
| Factory overhead | 1,300 | |
| Total | 2,900 | |
| Less: Increase in inventory | 350 | |
| Cost of goods sold | | 2,550 |
| Engineering and research | | 120 |
| Shipping and receiving | | 240 |
| Division administration: | | |
| Manager's office | 210 | |
| Cost accounting | 40 | |
| Personnel | 82 | |
| Total division administration | | 332 |
| Corporate headquarters costs: | | |
| Computer | 48 | |
| General services | 230 | |
| Total corporate headquarter costs | | 278 |
| Total costs and expenses | | 3,520 |
| Divisional operating income | | $ 480 |
| | | |
| Net plant investment | | $1,600 |
| Return on investment | | 30% |

**REQUIRED:**  ❷ **A.** Discuss the financial reporting and performance evaluation program of ATCO Company as it relates to the responsibilities of the Dexter division.

❸ **B.** Based upon your response to part (A), recommend appropriate revisions of the financial information and reports used to evaluate the performance of Dexter's divisional management. If you conclude that revisions are not necessary, explain why they are not needed.

☆ **15.28**  **Agency costs, indemnification of corporate officers** During 2001, **Xerox** restated its prior year earn-
**Q1, Q5**  ings. The original earnings for the years 1997–2000 had been overstated by approximately $3 billion
**ETHICS**  before-tax. According to Securities and Exchange Commission (SEC) allegations, earnings had been
overstated to help the company meet internal earnings targets as well as financial analyst estimates. Fur-

thermore, according to the SEC, the overstatements were allegedly performed with the knowledge of
top management and included the cooperation of managers in the United States, Europe, and Brazil.

During 2003, the SEC charged six senior executives with securities fraud. These officers later
reached a settlement with the SEC, without admitting or denying the allegations. According to SEC
regulations, wrongdoers pay a civil penalty and are also required to "disgorge" or repay any ill-
gotten gains. For the Xerox managers, these regulations meant they were required to repay the $14
million in bonuses and other benefits that were based on the overstated earnings. In addition, the
SEC requires wrongdoers to pay interest on disgorgements to ensure that they do not benefit from
an interest-free loan. Overall, the six officers were required to pay the following amounts:

| | |
|---|---|
| Disgorgement | $14 million |
| Interest on disgorgement | 5 |
| Civil penalties | 3 |
| Total | $22 million |

However, the only cash actually paid by the six officers was for the civil penalties of $3 million.
Xerox paid $19 million for the disgorgement, interest, and officers' legal fees. According to Note
15 (Litigation, Regulatory Matters, and Other Contingencies) in the 2003 Xerox annual report:

*"Our corporate by-laws require that, except to the extent expressly prohibited by law, we
must indemnify Xerox Corporation's officers and directors against judgments, fines, penalties*

*and amounts paid in settlement, including legal fees and all appeals, incurred in connection with civil or criminal action or proceedings, as it relates to their services to Xerox Corporation and our subsidiaries."*

SOURCES: "Six Former Senior Executives of Xerox Settle SEC Enforcement Action Charging Them with Fraud," SEC press release 2003-70, available at www.sec.gov/news/press/2003-70.htm; L. Lavelle, "Making CEOs Pay for Bogus Books," *Business Week online,* October 16, 2003; J. Bookman, "Cultural Shift Gives Executives License to Steal," *The Atlanta Journal-Constitution,* June 12, 2003, available at ajc.com; and Xerox 2003 Annual Report, available at xerox.com.

**REQUIRED: ANALYZE INFORMATION**

The following questions will help you analyze the information for this problem. Do not turn in your answers to these questions unless your professor asks you to do so.

**❶ A.** In this chapter, we learned about different types of agency costs. Do agency costs always involve an ethical problem? Why or why not?

**❶ B.** Describe a hypothetical situation where a company officer incurs settlement and legal costs, but has done nothing wrong.

**❷ C.** Discuss pros and cons of Xerox's bylaw to indemnify officers and directors.

**❸ D.** Does it matter whether the payments were made by an insurance company versus by Xerox? Why or why not? Clarify the values you use in drawing your conclusions.

**REQUIRED: WRITTEN ASSIGNMENT**

Turn in your answer to the following.

**❸ E.** Use the information you learned from the preceding analyses to write an essay in response to the following question: Was it ethical for the officers to allow costs to be paid by Xerox and its insurance companies?

**15.29**
**Q2, Q3**

**Responsibility centers, performance measures** Harry Klein, inventor, formed Peerless Load Levelers Company in 1955 to produce a simple three-piece device for automatically leveling loads on industrial conveyor belts. As the business grew and prospered, Klein expanded the factory and added employees, but he continued to control every aspect of the enterprise himself. Klein only hired individuals who would follow his orders unquestioningly. Over the years, the product mix was expanded to include several products, all variants of the original design.

Klein had no need to develop a human resources function, accounting systems, or computerized business systems. He also felt that he did not need a budget process. "I know exactly how well we are doing," he would repeatedly assert. "Why do I need some new budgeting idea to tell me what I already know?"

In 1995, Peerless reached a level of 180 production employees, 3 managers (who reported directly to Klein), and 20 clerical people. The three managers are John Richards, Shaping and Forming Department; Karl Willis, Assembly Department; and Susan Lyle, Finishing Department. Each manager is responsible for all aspects of his or her department's product manufacturing including purchasing, production, inspection, and customer complaints.

In 2005, Klein passed away unexpectedly. The situation at Peerless turned to chaos because only Klein had the complete view of the company. Eileen Klein-Robb, Klein's daughter and current president, had never been involved in the business and needed help quickly. She engaged Robert Snider, consultant, to determine what Peerless needs to do to bring sense and structure to the operation.

Snider, after studying the operation, suggested that Peerless needs a method of evaluating, monitoring, and controlling performance, especially at the production level. Snider's recommendation does not change the reporting relationship of Richards, Willis, and Lyle. However, the functions of the three managers change in the following ways:

• Richards will be the purchasing manager and handle all vendor relationships and raw materials inventories.
• Willis will be the production manager and oversee three newly promoted supervisors of the Shaping and Forming Department, the Assembly Department, and the Finishing Department.
• Lyle will be the quality manager and oversee product quality, inspection, customer relations, and engineering changes.

Snider also suggested installing a responsibility accounting and budgeting system to control performance at the various levels of production and management. Klein-Robb, although interested in this system, is uncertain and wants more information about responsibility accounting.

**REQUIRED:**
- **A.** List four characteristics and requirements for a responsibility accounting system.
- **B.** Describe the following centers and define their missions when used with a responsibility accounting system.
  - **1.** Cost centers
  - **2.** Profit centers
  - **3.** Investment centers
- **C. 1.** Identify at least three advantages that may be gained from a responsibility accounting system.
  - **2.** Identify at least one major risk of using a responsibility accounting system.
- **D.** If Eileen Klein-Robb were to incorporate Robert Snider's functional recommendations at Peerless Load Levelers company, identify and explain at least two specific operational performance measures that Klein-Robb should implement for these roles:
  - John Richards, purchasing manager
  - Karl Willis, production manager
  - Susan Lyle, quality manager

---

# BUILD YOUR PROFESSIONAL COMPETENCIES

**15.30**
**Q1, Q2, Q3, Q5**

**Focus on Professional Competency: Risk Analysis** *Agency costs, incentive compensation, responsibility centers, risk management* Review the following definition and elements for the Risk Analysis competency.[17]

**DEFINITION:** *Risk analysis and control is fundamental to professional service delivery. The identification and management of audit risk (that is, the risk that the auditor will fail to detect a misstatement, caused by inadvertent error or fraud, that is material to financial statements) is the basis for the conduct of a GAAS audit. The understanding of business risk (that is, the risk that an entity—either a client or the prospective accounting professional's employer—will fail to achieve its objectives) affects how business strategy is created and implemented.*

### ELEMENTS FOR THIS COMPETENCY INCLUDE

| Level 1 | Level 2 | Level 3 | Level 4 |
|---|---|---|---|
| 1. Explains why controls cannot completely eliminate risk of negative outcomes | 2. Identifies risks of negative outcomes (including fraud) for particular scenarios<br><br>3. Describes the pros and cons of controls that mitigate risk of negative outcomes through prevention or detection and correction | 4. Assesses and controls unmitigated risks through, for example, designing, applying, and drawing conclusions from tests<br><br>5. Communicates the impact of identified risks and recommends corrective action | 6. Develops and monitors strategies for managing risk over time<br><br>7. Implements appropriate corrective action over time |

**REQUIRED:**
- **A.** Focus on competency elements 1, 3, and 7, which address actions taken to control risk. Answer the following questions:
  - **1.** Describe how the risks addressed by these competency elements relate to agency theory.
  - **2.** Explain why responsibility accounting and performance-based compensation cannot completely eliminate agency costs.
  - **3.** Discuss the pros and cons of bonuses based on reported earnings of a responsibility center.

*(continued)*

---

[17]The definition and elements are reprinted with permission from AICPA; Copyright © 1978–2000 & 2003 by American Institute of Certified Public Accountants. The AICPA's Core Competency Framework can be accessed at eca.aicpaservices.org.

④     **4.** Even with their imperfections, explain how responsibility accounting and performance-based compensation can help an organization identify appropriate corrective actions over time.

    **B.** Focus on competency elements 1, 2, and 6, which address risk and reward. Answer the following questions:

①     **1.** Describe several types of risk *other than* agency costs that might affect an organization's outcomes.

②     **2.** What is meant by a trade-off between risk and reward? Provide an example.

③     **3.** Should managers always try to eliminate risk? Explain.

④     **4.** What does it mean to manage risk over time? Provide an example.

    **C.** Focus on competency element 4, which addresses the accountant's responsibility for using tests and evidence to control risk. Answer the following questions:

②     **1.** What is meant by the term *unmitigated risks* in the context of performance evaluation? Use a dictionary, as needed, and relate the meaning of this term to material in the chapter.

②     **2.** Accountants typically think of auditing when they perform tests. However, it is possible to think of performance evaluation as a type of test. The accountant chooses one or more performance measures (i.e., tests), collects information for the measures, and then draws conclusions from the results. How does this testing process help to assess and control unmitigated risks?

**15.31**    Q5    **Integrating Across the Curriculum: Business Law**    *Executive compensation for public companies, SEC disclosures* The **Securities and Exchange Commission (SEC)** requires specific disclosures about executive compensation for public companies. The following Web pages contain information about SEC executive compensation regulations:

www.wiley.com/college/eldenburg

Executive Compensation: A Guide for Investors:
    www.sec.gov/investor/pubs/execomp0803.htm or go to www.wiley.com/college/eldenburg

Federal regulations over disclosure of information about executive compensation (Regulation S-K, Item 402):
    www.sec.gov/divisions/corpfin/forms/regsk.htm or go to www.wiley.com/college/eldenburg

**REQUIRED:**

②  **A.** Discuss why the SEC requires special disclosures for executive compensation.

    **B.** Conduct research to locate the annual CEO compensation report contained in a business publication such as *Business Week* or *Forbes*. Pick a company in the report, and answer the following questions:

①     **1.** What types of information does the report provide?

①     **2.** What rating was given for the CEO compensation of your company? How was the rating determined?

    **C.** For the company you selected in part (B), conduct research to identify the company's disclosures about executive compensation. Answer the following questions:

①     **1.** Discuss the ease with which you located the executive compensation information.

②     **2.** The SEC requires companies to provide a "clear, concise and understandable disclosure" for executive compensation. Discuss whether the information you found met this requirement.

①     **3.** Summarize the major types of pay received by the company's CEO.

①     **4.** Does the company appear to use performance-based pay in compensating its top executives? Explain.

②  **D.** Describe uncertainties about whether the CEO pay for your company was reasonable.

③  **E.** Draw your own conclusion about whether the CEO pay for your company was reasonable. Explain.

**15.32**    Q4    **Integrating Across the Curriculum: Finance**    *Calculation of weighted average cost of capital* The weighted average cost of capital (WACC) is the weighted average after-tax cost of an organization's various sources of financing such as debt and stock. In this chapter, we learned that the WACC is used when calculating economic value added. The WACC is also used in capital budgeting (Chapter 12).

Calculations for the weighted average cost of capital are usually found in finance textbooks. The formula is simple; we determine how much financing comes from various sources, and then calculate the weighted average. For example, suppose a company has $600,000 financing from debt at a pretax interest rate of 7% and $400,000 financing from equity having a cost of 9%. The company's tax rate is 30%, and only the interest is tax deductible. The WACC is 6.54%, calculated as follows:

| Source | Market Value | Proportion | After–Tax Cost | Weighted Cost |
|--------|--------------|------------|----------------|---------------|
| Debt | $ 600,000 | 60% | 4.9% | 2.94% |
| Equity | 400,000 | 40 | 9.0% | 3.60 |
| Total | $1,000,000 | 100% | | 6.54% |

Although the computations are simple, it is not always easy to find the information needed for the computations. For example, consider the following balance sheet for **Amazon.com** as of December 31, 2002 (amounts in $ thousands):

**Excerpts from Balance Sheet:**

| | | |
|--|--|--|
| Current liabilities | | $ 1,065,958 |
| Long-term debt and other | | 2,277,305 |
| Common stock—$0.01 par value | | |
| Authorized shares—5,000,000 | | |
| Issued and outstanding shares—387,906 shares | $  3,879 | |
| Additional paid-in capital | 1,649,946 | |
| Deferred stock-based compensation | (6,591) | |
| Accumulated other comprehensive income (loss) | 9,662 | |
| Accumulated deficit | (3,009,710) | |
| Total stockholders' deficit | | (1,352,814) |
| Total liabilities and stockholders' deficit | | $ 1,990,449 |

**Excerpts from Note 6: Long-Term Debt and Other**
The Company's long-term debt and other long-term liabilities are summarized as follows:

| | |
|--|--|
| 4.75% Convertible Subordinated Notes | $1,249,807 |
| 6.875% PEACS | 724,500 |
| 10% Senior Discount Notes | 255,597 |
| Long-term restructuring liabilities | 31,614 |
| Euro currency swap | 12,159 |
| Capital lease obligations | 8,491 |
| Other long-term debt | 8,456 |
| | 2,290,624 |
| Less current portion of capital lease obligations | (7,506) |
| Less current portion of other long-term debt | (5,813) |
| | $2,277,305 |

**REQUIRED:**

**②** **A.** Explain why book values might be poor estimates of market values for Amazon's debt and stock.

**③** **B.** Which liabilities do you think should be included in the WACC computation? Explain your choices.

**①** **C.** Identify possible sources of information for the following:

1. Market value of common stock
2. Cost of equity capital
3. Market value for each type of debt
4. Pretax interest rates
5. Income tax rate

# 16

# Strategic Performance Measurement

## ▶In Brief

Successful organizations adopt a strategic decision-making process to ensure that strategies and operating activities are aligned with the organization's vision and core competencies. They also engage in continuous improvement by monitoring and learning from the results of their strategies and operations. Accountants develop and track a variety of financial and nonfinancial measures to monitor results. The balanced scorecard is a formal approach for identifying and measuring an organization's performance from four perspectives: financial, customer, internal business process, and learning and growth. Approaches such as the balanced scorecard motivate individuals and units throughout an organization to work toward a common vision and improve strategic and operating success.

## This Chapter Addresses the Following Questions:

**Q1** What is strategic decision making?

**Q2** How are financial and nonfinancial measures used to evaluate organizational performance?

**Q3** What is a balanced scorecard?

**Q4** How is a balanced scorecard implemented?

**Q5** What are the strengths and weaknesses of the balanced scorecard?

**Q6** What is the future direction of cost accounting?

# WAL-MART STORES: MAINTAINING A LOW-COST STRATEGY

In 2003, **Wal-Mart Stores** was not just the largest retail company in the world; it was three times the size of the next-largest retailer, France's **Carrefour**. The company operated 4,750 stores and employed more than 1.2 million people. It was the largest retailer in the United States, Mexico, and Canada. It also operated in Argentina, Brazil, China, Germany, Korea, Puerto Rico, and the United Kingdom. The company's managers planned to move into additional countries.

Wal-Mart's founder, Sam Walton, began operations during 1950 with a five-and-dime store in Bentonville, Arkansas. He opened the first Wal-Mart Store in 1962. The company originally grew through its Wal-Mart general merchandise discount stores. It later expanded into the sale of groceries and other consumer goods with large super centers and membership warehouse clubs. Recently, the company began to focus on smaller neighborhood stores and the Internet.

Throughout its history, Wal-Mart had been highly focused on Sam Walton's vision. He established the customer as the company's key focal point. The company's major strategies included:

- Providing customers with the best possible service
- Earning a profit through high volume rather than high markup
- Passing cost savings on to customers through price reductions
- Working with suppliers to reduce costs
- Continuously improving supply chain efficiency
- Developing and adopting the forefront of retail technology
- Identifying and moving into new growth markets

In 2003, many financial analysts believed Wal-Mart was a well-run company with excellent long-term growth potential. Although its stock price declined during the retail slump of 2002, the company fared considerably better than other retailers. Its stock price then increased by 6% during 2003. Its success during the economic downturn was attributed to its ability to offer low prices and good service and a lower level of reliance on discretionary goods compared to retailers such as **Home Depot** and **Toys "R" Us**. The company could offer lower prices than other retailers because of its size and innovative use of technology. It was able to negotiate the lowest wholesale prices, efficiently manage inventories, and analyze point-of sale data to predict which products would sell. In addition, Wal-Mart's labor costs were about 20% to 30% less than grocery store competitors because its workers were nonunion.

At the same time, some analysts were skeptical about Wal-Mart's long-term prospects. The company faced pressures on its cost structure as it moved into new markets. It also faced frequent unionization attempts that promised to grow fiercer as unions lost membership due to the decline of Wal-Mart's competitors. Wal-Mart was also expected to pay higher prices for land, labor, and other resources as it moved increasingly into urban areas. Some suppliers had stopped doing business with Wal-Mart because of concerns that the company was sacrificing quality to achieve low cost.

Furthermore, Wal-Mart faced potential problems with public opinion. The company was a defendant in the country's largest class-action sex discrimination lawsuit, and it was often blamed for low pay levels throughout the retail sector. According to reporter Marcelo Prince, the largest environmental organization in the United States, Sierra Club, excluded Wal-Mart from its investment portfolios because of the company's labor practices. Wal-Mart increasingly imported merchandise and was blamed for contributing to the loss of U.S. manufacturing jobs. In addition, Wal-Mart was successfully banned by 164 towns that passed ordinances prohibiting large stores. The company's large size and aggressive business practices might eventually lead to federal backlash. It could potentially lose favorable import terms through the imposition of tariffs or quotas, or its Third World trading partners could lose favorable trading rights. Also, the U.S. Justice Department could potentially argue that its pricing policies constitute price discrimination under the Robinson-Patman Act.

Wal-Mart's managers face continual challenges as they guide the company into the future. According to Babson College history professor James Hoopes, "The history of the last 150 years in retailing would say that if you don't like Wal-Mart, be patient. There will be new models eventually that will do Wal-Mart in, and Wal-Mart won't see it coming" (Bianco and Zellner, 2003). ∎

SOURCES: Wal-Mart's Web site at www.walmartstores.com; A. Bianco and W. Zellner, "Is Wal-Mart Too Powerful?" *Business Week,* October 5, 2003, pp. 100–110; A. Tsao, "How Wal-Mart Keeps Getting It Right," *Business Week online,* April 16, 2003; and M. Prince, "Tip Sheet: Sierra Club Jumps into the Mutual Fund Fray," *The Wall Street Journal Online,* October 14, 2003.

## LONG-TERM STRATEGIC PERFORMANCE

### ■ Key Strategic Decision Issues for Wal-Mart

Managers are often focused on organizations' day-to-day operations. Although monitoring short-term performance is important, long-term performance depends on the success of organizational long-term strategies. The following discussion summarizes key aspects of decision making for **Wal-Mart's** long-term strategies.

**Knowing.** Wal-Mart's managers clearly need thorough knowledge about the company's own resources and operations. To develop viable long-term strategies, they also need significant knowledge beyond the organization itself—about customers, suppliers, competitors, regulators, economic trends, potential new store locations, and so on. In addition, one of Wal-Mart's key strategies is the innovative use of technology. This strategy requires the company to conduct research and development to gain knowledge about the application and effectiveness of new and emerging technologies.

**Identifying.** Because of their time frame, long-term strategies are subject to a greater degree of uncertainty than short-term operating plans. Some of the major long-term uncertainties for Wal-Mart include the following:

- Success of unionization attempts
- Ability to keep costs low in new urban locations
- Potential repercussions from negative pubic opinion
- Future actions by competitors
- Shifts in customer tastes
- Successful implementation of new technologies
- Ability to maintain long-term growth

Historically, Wal-Mart has grown and prospered because its managers identified new business models and new technologies for reducing costs. The company's long-term strategies depend on the ability of the managers to continue identifying successful new growth and technological opportunities.

**Exploring.** Wal-Mart's managers must consider many pros and cons as they select and pursue long-term strategies. For example, the company's ability to achieve low costs and offer low prices depends in part on its nonunion stance. However, the company's low pay exposes it to potential political backlash. Similarly, the company's low costs depend on its size—both the size of individual stores and the overall size of the company. Greater size allows Wal-Mart to achieve lower purchasing and inventory handling costs. Yet, its size and aggressive business tactics prompt some towns to pass laws banning large stores.

**Prioritizing.** The selection of long-term strategies requires Wal-Mart's managers to weigh the potential benefits and costs of alternatives. The decision process also requires them to choose and apply corporate values in making trade-offs. For example, Sam Walton originally established the customer as the company's key focal point. This focus meant that offering low prices to customers was valued more than paying higher wages to employees.

**Envisioning.** The prediction by Professor Hoopes—"There will be new models eventually that will do Wal-Mart in, and Wal-Mart won't see it coming"—describes the most important long-term challenge for Wal-Mart's managers. How can they ensure that their strategies will be successful not only today, but also in the future? Professor Hoopes identified the fatal flaw of once-successful retail organizations that ultimately failed. They did not recognize new forms of competition, and they continued to use outdated and ultimately ineffective strategies. Wal-Mart's managers need to actively seek and consider new strategies, even though this focus could require fundamental shifts in their business model and priorities.

### ■ Monitoring Long-Term Performance

How can managers determine whether an organization is headed for long-term success, failure, or mediocrity? How can they make the most of positive trends and learn about potentially negative ones? Traditionally, managers relied heavily on measures such as sales and profits to monitor an organization's performance. However, these types of measures suffer from several weaknesses. For example, they focus on current and past performance rather than the future. Also, they do not capture potentially important information such as product market share or employee satisfaction. To overcome these weaknesses, organizations may decide to adopt a broader set of measures. In this chapter, we learn about a particular approach—the balanced scorecard—for measuring an organization's performance.

## STRATEGIC DECISION MAKING

**Q1** What is strategic decision making?

This textbook began with an overview of management decision making in Chapter 1. The process summarized in Exhibit 16.1 assumes that managers make decisions in a strategic way. Periodically they clarify the organization's vision and core competencies. The vision is the core purpose and ideology of the organization, while the core competencies are the organization's strengths relative to competitors. Strategies are the tactics managers use to take advantage of core competencies while working toward the organization's vision. Strategies guide long-term decisions such as the types of goods and services offered and the long-term methods of competition. Strategies also lead to operating plans, including an annual budget. In turn, operating plans guide short-term decisions such as launching advertising campaigns, hiring employees, or purchasing inventory. As organizations' actual operations unfold, results are measured and monitored against both short-term operating plans and long-term strategies. The feedback loops in Exhibit 16.1 lead to revisions at any of the levels of management decision making.

The nature of the organization's strategies and operating plans influences the types of performance objectives that are used. **Performance objectives,** the specific goals that managers choose to measure and monitor, help motivate employees to carry out strategies and plans. For example, being the market leader for a specific product might be a long-term goal.

**EXHIBIT 16.1** Overview of Management Decision Making

**Organizational Vision**
Core Purpose and Ideology
Create Value for Stakeholders:
 –Owner (for-profit)
 –Donors (not-for-profit)
 –Constituents (governmental)
 –Employees
 –Customers/clients
 –Suppliers
 –Community
 –Society
 –Others

**Core Competencies**
Strengths Relative to
Competitors:
 –Productivity
 –Skills
 –Knowledge
 –Technologies
 –Physical resources
 –Customer/supplier
  relationships
 –Reputation
 –Growth opportunities
 –Legal rights
 –Regulatory advantages
 –Financial resources

**Organizational Strategies**
Long-Term Goals
Organizational Structure
Financial Structure
Long-Term Resource Allocation
 –Investments/divestments
 –Nature of operations
 –Products or services and
  markets

**Operating Plans**
Specific Performance Objectives
Short-Term Financing
Short-Term Resource Allocation
 –Production of goods/services
 –Inbound and outbound
  logistics
 –Marketing and sales
 –Service
 –Technology
 –Human resources
 –Cash flows

**Actual Operations**

Measure Performance, Monitor Progress, and Motivate Employees

This goal could be tied to the performance objective of achieving a 35% market share within a five-year time horizon.

Successful organizations communicate to all employees their organizational vision, strategies, goals, and objectives. This communication helps align employee goals with organizational goals. Accountants develop and track financial and nonfinancial performance measures to evaluate the efforts of individual employees, teams, departments, divisions, and subunits. When performance measures are monitored throughout the organization, progress toward the vision is more easily evaluated and rewarded.

## ■ Communicating the Organization's Vision

The concept of organizational vision—core purpose and ideology—is broad. Managers sometimes divide the vision into separate statements. The definitions of these statements vary from organization to organization. In general, a vision statement is a theoretical description of what the organization should become. A mission statement is a high-level declaration of the organization's purpose. A core values statement is a summary of the beliefs that define the organization's culture. Together, these statements convey the organization's overall direction and approaches toward its various stakeholder groups.

The vision and mission statements and the list of core values for **Wendy's International** are shown in Exhibit 16.2. Wendy's statements are closely aligned; all highlight the importance of quality. The mission statement for Wendy's is more specific than the vision statement about products and customers. The core values establish the company's philosophy and provide guidance for the principles that managers and other employees use in decision making.

Managers do not always define and communicate their vision using vision, mission, and core values statements. For example, none of these statements are presented explicitly on Wal-Mart's Web site.[2] However, Wal-Mart's Web site provides information about its vision in the form of "3 Basic Beliefs," "Sam's Rules for Building a Business," "Pricing Philosophy," and other guidelines for Wal-Mart's culture.[3]

## ■ Clarifying Core Competencies and Developing Strategies

How an organization clarifies its core competencies and develops its strategies are closely related. Organizations are likely to be more successful when their core competencies and strategies are well aligned. For example, Wal-Mart's core competencies include its technological

**CURRENT PRACTICE**

Management researcher and best-selling author Jim Collins argues that holding consistently to a set of core values is one of the distinguishing characteristics of companies that achieve and maintain greatness.[1]

---

**EXHIBIT 16.2**
Vision, Mission, and Core Values of Wendy's International, Inc.

**Vision Statement:**

Our vision is to be the quality leader in everything we do.

**Mission Statement:**

Our guiding mission is to deliver superior quality products and services for our customers and communities through leadership, innovation and partnerships.

**Core Values:[a]**

- Quality
- Integrity
- Leadership
- People focus
- Customer satisfaction
- Continuous improvement
- Community involvement
- Commitment to stakeholders

SOURCE: www.wendys-invest.com. Used with permission of Wendy's.
[a]Descriptions of the core values are omitted here.

---

[1]Jim Collins, *Good to Great: Why Some Companies Make the Leap . . . and Others Don't* (New York: Harper-Business, 2001), pp. 193–196.
[2]Based on searches of www.walmartstores.com and www.walmart.com (accessed July 28, 2004).
[3]See "About Wal-Mart" and "The Wal-Mart Culture" available at www.walmartstores.com.

systems for predicting sales and managing inventories efficiently. These core competencies were developed because Wal-Mart managers devote long-term resources to them.

When identifying and choosing strategies, managers anticipate responses from customers, suppliers, competitors, and others. Managers must also continually visualize new ways to gain competitive advantage. Frequently, strategies that worked in the past must be modified or replaced. However, managers consider a few general types of strategies in their decision-making processes, as described next.

**Cost Leadership** One way to compete effectively is to maintain lower costs than competitors, which is one of Wal-Mart's main strategies. The company continuously reduces costs and then passes the savings on to customers in the form of lower prices. Lower costs are achieved through techniques such as supply chain analysis, just-in-time production and purchasing, reengineering, target costing, kaizen costing, and life cycle costing. Investments in new technologies or other long-term resources can also reduce costs.

**CHAPTER REFERENCE**

Supply chain analysis, just-in-time production and purchasing, reengineering, target costing, Kaizen costing, and life cycle costing are discussed in detail in Chapter 13.

**Product Differentiation: Quality and Functionality** In industries with customers willing to pay higher prices for higher quality or more functionality, managers strategically differentiate their products and establish market positions. For example, during 2002 Wendy's did not join the price war started by other competitors such as **McDonald's**. Wendy's managers believed that their customers would pay higher prices for higher quality and for a greater diversity of products.[4] The company has also differentiated itself by offering a variety of salads, which can be customized with separate toppings. McDonald's and others later followed Wendy's salad strategy.

**Other Pricing Strategies** Sometimes managers engage in pricing strategies that take advantage of special circumstances through practices such as price skimming, penetration pricing, and peak load pricing. Some of these strategies work only for certain time periods, such as before competitors enter a market. Others, such as peak load pricing, can be used over long periods of time.

**CHAPTER REFERENCE**

Definitions for and examples of price skimming, penetration pricing, and peak load pricing are presented in Chapter 13.

## ■ Developing Operating Plans

Once strategies are developed, they should lead to the organization's operating plans. Operating plans typically include specific performance objectives and action plans for achieving the objectives. Budgets are often used to define performance objectives for revenues, costs, cash flows, and so on. Action plans describe specific operating activities. For example, Wendy's action plans for 2002 included new advertising campaigns for its Garden Sensations salad line, its line of Classic Hamburgers, and its late night hours.[5] For 2003, Wendy's planned to open 560–605 new restaurants, consisting of the following brands: 285–300 Wendy's in North America, 10–15 international Wendy's, 170–175 Tim Horton's in Canada, 25–35 Tim Horton's in the United States, and 70–80 Baja Fresh. The company planned $325 to $365 million in capital expenditures.[6]

## ■ Management Decision Making Throughout an Organization

The decision-making process portrayed in Exhibit 16.1 applies to organizations as a whole. It also applies to subsets of an organization, such as business units, product lines, and functions (e.g., human resources or inventory management). As an example, the Baja Fresh Mexican Grill product line of Wendy's has its own vision and mission statements as shown in Exhibit 16.3. These vision and mission statements are consistent with Wendy's overall statements, but they are more detailed in describing the business focus and purpose for one product line.

---

[4]G. Marcial, "How Wendy's Stayed Out of the Fire," *Business Week online,* December 9, 2002.
[5]"Strategic Plan Highlights," excerpt from 2001 annual report, available at www.wendys-invest.com.
[6]"Investor Presentation," Wendy's International, September 2003, available at www.wendys-invest.com.

**EXHIBIT 16.3**
Vision and Mission of Baja Fresh Mexican Grill (a Division of Wendy's International, Inc.)

**Vision Statement:**

To become the leading national restaurant brand known as the defining standard for the highest quality and convenience in *fresh* Mexican food.

**Mission Statement:**

To proudly prepare the most flavorful and fresh Mexican food, conveniently offered for eat-in or take-out in a clean and upbeat environment, serviced with a genuine smile and concern for our Customers' Absolute Satisfaction.

SOURCE: "Strategic Overview" from 2003 Analyst and Investor Meeting, September 18, 2003, available at www.wendys-invest.com. Used with the permission of Wendy's.

**CHAPTER REFERENCE**

To learn more about assigning decision authority and responsibility centers, see Chapter 14.

Even when no statements of individual vision, mission, and core values are established, managers often establish performance objectives for individual divisions, product lines, and departments. These objectives help organizations assign decision authority and responsibilities to individual managers and other employees. When performance objectives are well-aligned throughout the organization, managers can more easily monitor the progress toward meeting overall goals within various parts of the organization.

# MEASURING ORGANIZATIONAL PERFORMANCE

**Q2** How are financial and nonfinancial measures used to evaluate organizational performance?

**CURRENT PRACTICE**

When costs such as storage, distribution, handling, damage, labor, and rent were measured, the managers at Staples learned that furniture was less profitable than other items such as office supplies.[7]

Exhibit 16.4 illustrates a process that accountants and managers use to evaluate the organization's progress toward its vision. First, actual results are compared to plans. Then any differences are analyzed. Finally, employees are rewarded and improvements are identified for future planning. Reevaluation of the vision is also often undertaken at this time. Both financial and nonfinancial measures are used to monitor performance and to provide information for this process.

## ■ Financial Measures

Managers traditionally relied on **financial measures** that provide information measured in dollars or ratios of dollars. Sales, costs, or operating income are among those measures usually obtained from the financial accounting system, which is designed to report financial measures for the overall organization, divisions, product lines, and departments. Financial measures also compare budget to actual results.

In a 2003 presentation to investors, Wendy's managers reported several financial measures including company-wide revenues, pretax income, net income, earnings per share, long-term debt to equity, debt to total capitalization, and cash balances. They also reported sales and sales growth by product line.[8] In all likelihood, more detailed information was used to evaluate performance inside the company, but that information is not made publicly available.

**EXHIBIT 16.4** Monitoring Measurable Performance Objectives

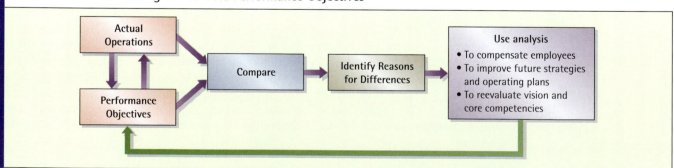

[7]J. Caplan, "Applying a Little Business Intelligence," *CFO.com,* July 22, 2003.
[8]See "Investor Presentation" of Wendy's International, September 2003, available at www.wendys-invest.com.

# ■ Nonfinancial Measures

**Nonfinancial measures** provide performance information that cannot be measured in dollars. Defect rates, customer satisfaction, throughput time, and employee retention are among the nonfinancial measures used more frequently in recent years to reflect performance that promotes long-term financial success.

In 2003, Wendy's managers reported many nonfinancial measures, including those shown in Exhibit 16.5. The number of Wendy's restaurants and their market share focus on long-term growth and size relative to competitors. Wendy's ranking among competitors on speed of service provides information about the company's progress toward its strategy of fast delivery. Employee turnover measures a range of employee-related factors such as employee satisfaction. The customer preference measures reflect the company's relative success in satisfying customers compared to its two major competitors. Two of the customer preference measures address relatively new strategies for Wendy's: its expanded salad menu and late night hours.

# ■ Using a Combination of Measures

A combination of measures is often used to monitor and motivate performance within an organization. No single measure provides a complete picture of performance. In addition, a combination of financial and nonfinancial measures is usually more consistent with an organization's long-term goals than financial measures alone.

One of Wendy's major strategies is to provide customers with fast service. As shown in Exhibit 16.5, Wendy's managers monitor the seconds it takes to complete a customer order at the drive-through window and at the pick-up counter. If Wendy's managers were to use only this measure to monitor and motivate performance, employees might be encouraged to prepare food in advance so that it could be delivered more quickly to customers. However, this practice would conflict with another strategy that requires food to be freshly prepared. Customer sales might ultimately decline if the quality were lowered. In addition, advance preparation would probably increase waste, increasing costs and lowering profits. To address all of these goals simultaneously, Wendy's managers monitor customer delivery time, customer satisfaction, sales trends, and the cost of food products sold.

Once a set of performance measures is chosen, the information system is designed to collect data and produce periodic reports for these measures and their trends. For example, Wendy's service delivery time and customer preference measures might be obtained from data reported by outsiders such as industry analysts or from internal research. Sometimes competitors agree to collect and report specific data to an association that publishes comparative data in an industry publication.

---

**EXHIBIT 16.5**
Nonfinancial Measures Used in Investor Presentation by Wendy's International, Inc.

**Selected Information about Wendy's Restaurants:**

- Total number of restaurants, 1969 through 2002
- Quick-service restaurant market share, compared to five competitors
- Quick-service hamburger market share, compared to four competitors
- Drive-through average service time in seconds, compared to four competitors
- Pick-up window average service time in seconds, 1999 through second quarter 2003
- Employee turnover rates, 1998 through second quarter 2003:
  - Crew
  - Co/Assistant Managers
  - General Managers
- Customer preferences, 1998 through second quarter of 2003 data compared to McDonald's and Burger King:
  - Percent of people choosing Wendy's as the best tasting salads
  - Percent of people citing Wendy's as their personal favorite
  - Percent of people choosing Wendy's to satisfy their late-night hunger

Source: "Investor Presentation," Wendy's International, September 2003, available at www.wendys-invest.com.

---

[9]C. Lazere, "All Together Now: Why You Must Link Budgeting and Forecasting to Planning and Performance," *CFO Magazine*, February 1, 1998, available at www.cfo.com.

# BALANCED SCORECARD

**Q3** What is a balanced scorecard?

Traditionally, organizations focused on financial outcomes such as sales and profits. When evaluating business processes, they tended to focus on ways to maintain control over product costs. Although financial outcomes are important, this limited focus does not automatically provide guidance in achieving desired results. Nor does it encourage improvements when current financial results are satisfactory. Some organizations focused on long-term strategies, but their approaches were often informal and piecemeal. For example, organizations collect data about customer satisfaction, but then only use the data to find areas that need immediate improvement, not as part of an overall strategic approach.

In the early 1990s, **Harvard University** professor Robert Kaplan and consultant David Norton developed the **balanced scorecard,** a formal method to incorporate both financial and nonfinancial performance measures into organizational management systems. The aim of the balanced scorecard is to translate organizational visions and strategies into performance objectives and related measures that can be monitored over time. The balanced scorecard approach helps managers more fully integrate strategies throughout the organization, anticipate and prevent possible future problems, and identify and take advantage of opportunities.

At the heart of the balanced scorecard is a continuous, strategic analysis of the organization from multiple perspectives. The most common approach is to use the four perspectives shown in Exhibit 16.6: financial, customer, internal business process, and learning and growth. Within each perspective, managers and other employees study the organization and identify linkages with other perspectives. For example, if employees are better trained (under learning and growth), they are more likely to make suggestions that improve customer-related business

**EXHIBIT 16.6**
Four Perspectives in a Balanced Scorecard

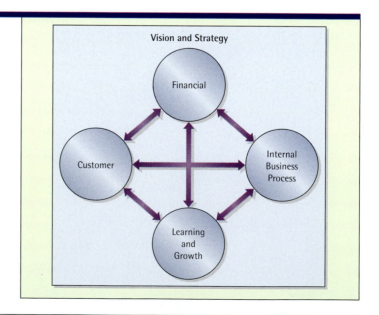

[10]C. Lazere, "All Together Now: Why You Must Link Budgeting and Forecasting to Planning and Performance," *CFO Magazine,* February 1, 1998, available at www.cfo.com.

processes, such as reducing the time between receipt of a customer order and product delivery. As customer satisfaction increases, financial performance is also more likely to increase. These analyses help accountants and managers identify the most important performance objectives—the aspects of operations that must be successful for the organization to achieve its vision. Measures are then developed for the performance objectives within each perspective to help managers and employees monitor and work toward long-term goals.

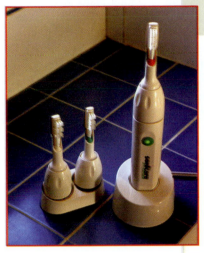

## ROYAL PHILIPS ELECTRONICS
### ADOPTING A BALANCED SCORECARD

In 2002, Royal Philips Electronics was a global conglomerate with 250,000 employees in 150 countries. Philips specialized in electronics, such as lighting, consumer electronics, domestic appliances, semiconductors, and medical systems. In the early 2000s, the Board of Management in Europe responded to a perceived need to streamline management of such a large and complex organization with a diverse group of product lines and divisions. They decided that the balanced scorecard could be used both to align the organization around the company's vision and to help employees better understand the business and their respective contributions to the overall organization.

Since 2002, Philip's organizational vision has been "Let's make things better." This vision includes making better products, better systems, and better services. The strategy at Philips is to find new ways to improve products and to offer innovative products to consumers. The company's quality program encompasses all employees. The overall strategy is to strive to be one of the best companies in the world: the best to trade with, work for, and invest in.

Several balanced scorecard measures developed for Philips are listed in Exhibit 16.7. We discuss these measures next, as we learn about each perspective.

SOURCES: Royal Philips Electronics Web site at www.philips.com; and A. Gumbus and B. Lyons, "The Balanced Scorecard at Philips Electronics," *Strategic Finance*, November 2002, pp. 45–49.

**EXHIBIT 16.7**
Balanced Scorecard
Measures at Royal Philips
Electronics

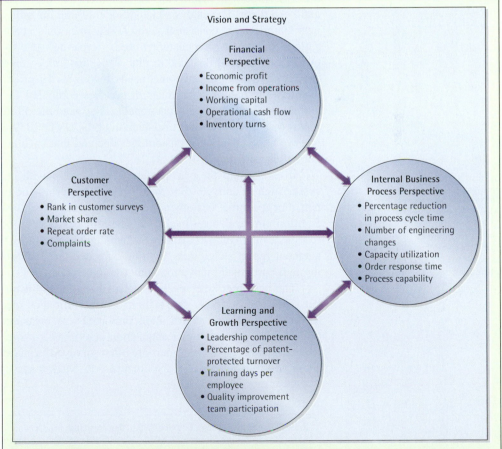

SOURCE: Copyright 2002, *Strategic Finance*, published by the Institute of Management Accountants (IMA), Montvale, N.J., www.imanet.org. Used with permission.

# ■ Financial Perspective and Related Measures

When accountants and managers analyze their organizations from a **financial perspective,** they identify desired financial results, given the organization's vision. For-profit organizations usually have goals of providing owners with some level of return on investment. Not-for-profit organizations typically have financial goals of maintaining a certain level of financial liquidity and stability, accumulating sufficient resources for some long-term purpose, or gaining maximum efficiency from resources. Financial goals and objectives encourage managers to evaluate the effectiveness of their strategies and operating plans based on the economic well-being of the organization. They also help employees relate the activities they perform to the organization's financial outcomes.

**CHAPTER REFERENCE**

For more information about return on investment, residual income, and economic value-added, see Chapter 15. For budgets and their variances, see Chapter 10.

Financial perspective measures are designed to determine an organization's progress toward desired financial results. In for-profit organizations, these measures are usually related to profitability, growth, and owner value. Common measures include operating income, return on investment, residual income, and economic value-added. In not-for-profit organizations, financial measures often include operating income, cost per service provided, and variances from budgets.

Some of the financial perspective measures adopted by Philips are shown in Exhibit 16.7. Similar measures are used by other large conglomerate for-profit organizations. Economic profit implies measuring long-term profitability, whereas income from operations measures short-term results. Focusing managers' attention on inventory turns, working capital, and operational cash flows should increase operating income and add to long-term economic profits.

# ■ Customer Perspective and Related Measures

When accountants and managers analyze the organization from a **customer perspective,** they are concerned with identifying the customers that they want, and developing strategies to get and keep them. The analysis includes identifying the targeted customers, markets, and products that are most consistent with the organization's vision and core competencies. Organizations that better meet customer needs—creating value for customers—are also more likely to generate desired financial results. Thus, this link connects the financial and customer perspectives. In assessing customer needs, managers consider their organizational strategies, and examine the nature of products or services compared to consumer views about trade-offs among price, quality, and functionality. For example, Philips states in its 2002 management report that "the successful introduction of the DVD+RW and the PixelPlus TV range shows that we understand what customers value and that such an understanding can lead to strong market share gains."[11]

**CURRENT PRACTICE**

Many golf courses built during the 1990s performed poorly because they were designed by and for professional golfers and were too difficult for most customers, who came from the local area.[13]

In evaluating the organization's relationship with customers, managers consider processes such as delivery time and accuracy. Ordering and payment processes are also important. For example, customers increasingly demand sophisticated e-business capabilities. In addition, future changes in customer preferences and competition must be considered. Philips recognizes the value of customer-related innovation in its Lighting Division. The 2002 management report stated that "lighting outpaced the competition, maintaining strong margins through continued innovation and customer focus."[12]

The customer's perspective is usually evaluated using outcome measures such as market share and customer satisfaction. The performance measures used in for-profit and not-for-profit organizations are often similar. These measures include customer retention and profitability, new customer acquisition, and market share in a targeted market segment or geographical region. Customers are often surveyed to gather information on their perceptions about and interactions with the organization. Market surveys and focus groups are also used to measure image and reputation.

---

[11]"Range" means the different models within that particular product line. Management Report, 2002 financial statements, Royal Philips Electronics N.V., p. 7, available at www.philips.com.
[12]Management Report, 2002 financial statements, Royal Philips Electronics N.V., p. 4, available at www.philips.com.
[13]"Course Corrections," an interview by P. Cooke with golf course appraiser B. Hanley, *Forbes FYI,* Winter 2003, pp. 45–47.

Some of the customer perspective measures adopted by Philips are shown in Exhibit 16.7. Philips's focus on reducing customer complaints should increase both its rank in customer surveys and its repeat order rate. Increases in these measures should lead to increased market share and increased profitability.

## ◼ Internal Business Process Perspective and Related Measures

When accountants and managers analyze the organization from an **internal business process perspective,** they are concerned with the methods and practices used inside the organization to produce and deliver goods and services. One goal of this analysis is to improve processes that will increase customer satisfaction. Another goal is to improve the efficiency of operations, which contributes directly to the organization's financial results. Internal business processes can be analyzed using a value chain approach. A value chain is the sequence of business processes through which value is added to goods and services. Analysis of the value chain leads to the identification of processes that are critical to the organization's success. Often, customer-related processes are emphasized in balanced scorecards because these processes have the greatest impact on customer satisfaction and financial success. Exhibit 16.8 presents a generic customer-oriented value chain including three principal internal business processes: the innovation cycle, the operations cycle, and the post-sales service cycle.

An alternative to the value chain approach is an operational audit conducted by internal auditors. An operational audit is an objective and systematic examination of evidence to provide an independent assessment of the performance of an organization, program, activity, or function. Operational audits provide information to improve accountability and to facilitate decision making.

**CHAPTER REFERENCE**

For more information about value-chain analysis, see Chapter 13.

**CURRENT PRACTICE**

Arm & Hammer's baking soda is advertised for many uses, among them to absorb odors in refrigerators. Recently the product added new packaging specifically designed for use in refrigerators.

**CURRENT PRACTICE**

Apple Computer's iTunes Music Store was the digital music market leader in 2003, but analysts warned that the company needed to develop new delivery systems beyond computers to satisfy customers and compete effectively.[14]

**Innovation Cycle and Related Measures**  The first step in the value chain, the **innovation cycle,** is concerned with processes to identify customer needs and to design goods and services that meet those needs. Many organizations mistakenly focus their efforts primarily on more efficient production of existing products. Yet goods and services must meet customer needs. The balanced scorecard encourages managers to establish internal processes that identify customer preferences for quality, functionality, and price, and also predict the potential market size. Organizations often use market and customer research to identify and nurture new markets, new customers, and new needs of current customers. Managers brainstorm completely new products, and also develop new opportunities and markets for existing products. For example, in September 2002, Philips and **Nike** collaborated on a variety of portable sports audio products. Another example of innovative changes to existing products is repackaging soups so that consumers can heat a single serving in the microwave without pouring the soup from a can into a different container.

The innovation process also ensures that proposed goods and services are produced efficiently, given the organization's core competencies. For example, organizations use target costing and kaizen costing to reduce product prices and improve quality.

**EXHIBIT 16.8** Customer-Oriented Value Chain Analysis

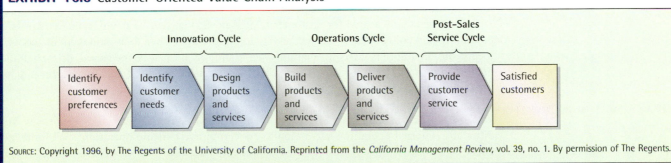

SOURCE: Copyright 1996, by The Regents of the University of California. Reprinted from the *California Management Review*, vol. 39, no. 1. By permission of The Regents.

---

[14]A. Hesseldahl, "Digital Music Without a PC," *Forbes.com,* October 22, 2003.

**Operations Cycle and Related Measures** The second step in the value chain, the **operations cycle,** is concerned with production and delivery of goods or services that are identified and designed in the innovation cycle. The operations cycle addresses the short-term well-being of the organization. It begins with the systems used to accept and process customer orders and is complete with delivery of the good or service. Quality, efficiency, consistency, and on-time delivery are emphasized in this part of the value chain.

Historically, many organizations focused on the operations process. Cost containment goals and cost monitoring methods were often in place at the commencement of operations. Traditional financial measures such as standard costs, budgets, and variances were often used to monitor operational performance. This focus sometimes led to suboptimal behavior. For example, efficiency measures create incentives to build inventories so that labor and machines are kept busy. Quality is sacrificed to increase efficiency. Excessive inventory levels and poor quality are costly to organizations over time. As a result, traditional measures of operations may be only a small part of a balanced scorecard approach.

Over the last several decades, organizations have increasingly competed on quality and timely delivery, in addition to price. For example, **Dell Computers** advertises the quality and reliability of its systems as well as its ability to deliver computers within days of an order. Measurements of quality, cycle time, and cost are developed to monitor and enhance performance in these areas. With the growth of Internet sales, competition on price and product customization has intensified. For example, price information about computers and peripherals is widely available on the Internet, both by manufacturers such as Dell and Apple Computer and by retail sellers such as **Bigclearance.com**. To be competitive, organizations must improve their operations processes to meet or beat their competitors' prices, quality, and reliability.

Organizations that specialize in custom products often measure the accuracy with which orders are completed and speed of delivery. The specific operating characteristics identified and monitored as performance objectives depend on the organization's vision, core competencies, and strategies. Managers choose performance measures to monitor organizational progress, rewarding positive trends in areas that lead to customer satisfaction and financial success.

**Post-Sales Service Cycle and Related Measures** The final step in the value chain, the **post-sales service cycle,** considers the service provided to customers after product delivery. Post-sales services include providing warranty work, handling returns, correcting defects, and collecting and processing payments. In addition, when products are highly sophisticated, organizations often train the employees who will be using them. Another aspect of the post-sales service cycle is the safe disposal of hazardous wastes and by-products.

For some organizations, post-sales service is part of a product differentiation strategy. For example, Saturn, a **General Motors** subsidiary, builds customer goodwill by providing fast and friendly warranty work, and salespeople often deliver cars personally to new owners. Hospitals have recently focused on the billing and collection processes of post-sales service. By emphasizing accurate coding on patient bills, hospitals have fewer claims denied by insurers and increase their operating revenues. To achieve greater accuracy in coding, many hospitals provide in-depth employee training and hire better-educated employees in their billing and collections departments.

Performance measures for customer-related post-sales service could include aspects of the billing and collections cycle such as the dollar amount of bad debts and days in accounts receivable. In addition, costs for warranty work and rework can be measured, or the number of defective products returned or reworked can be tracked. Measures for waste and by-product disposal could include number of pounds of waste and clean-up costs.

**Traditional Versus Balanced Scorecard Approaches to Internal Business Processes** Traditionally, internal operations were monitored to improve existing operations. With the balanced scorecard approach, the emphasis is on identifying *new* processes and eliminating non-value-added processes. In addition, the balanced scorecard approach strives to incorporate

[15]G. H. Anthes, "ROI Guide: Balanced Scorecard," *ComputerWorld,* February 17, 2003.

---

CURRENT PRACTICE

Web sites such as Price.com provide price and vendor information about a wide variety of electronic and high-tech products.

CURRENT PRACTICE

A balanced scorecard helped Southwest Airlines managers see the link between financial performance and the operational measures previously collected, such as the time aircraft spent on the ground.[15]

innovative processes into operations, whereas traditional measurement systems emphasize delivery of today's products to current customers.

Some of the internal business process perspective measures adopted by Philips are shown in Exhibit 16.7. Reductions in cycle time free resources for alternative uses. Philips continually improves current products and develops new products and, therefore, benefits from reduced cycle times for current products. As the number of engineering changes increases, disruption of the manufacturing cycle increases because new designs are being implemented or different components are required in the manufacturing processes. Optimal response time keeps inventory levels low, but also reduces potential stock-outs.

## ■ Learning and Growth Perspective and Related Measures

When accountants and managers analyze the organization from a **learning and growth perspective,** they are concerned with achieving future success by discovering new and better strategies. They also want to improve customer satisfaction and internal business processes, ensure that employees have sufficient knowledge and expertise, and check that internal processes support existing strategies. The learning and growth perspective is naturally linked to the internal business process perspective. As managers focus on improving internal business processes, they also identify opportunities for enhancing the capabilities of employees, information systems, and operating procedures. To take advantage of these opportunities, employee training and education is emphasized, as is the development of information technology and systems. For example, Wal-Mart developed innovative uses of technology to identify potentially profitable products and to improve efficiency of its supply chain. By analyzing and improving procedures, organizations also work toward aligning the goals and objectives of all stakeholders, including employees, suppliers, customers, and shareholders. Implementation of a balanced scorecard system is an example of this type of process; it is a formal method for engaging in learning and growth throughout an organization.

Employee learning and growth measures include satisfaction, retention, training, and skill development. These measures are tailored for the type of organization and industry. To assist in decision making, information systems must produce timely, reliable, and accurate information about customers, competitors, and operations. Measures of information timeliness and accuracy include number of days to close (the amount of time that elapses before financial statements are available to managers) and errors per report. Over time, company policies become outdated. Periodically, these policies need to be analyzed to determine whether they are current or should be changed in response to new knowledge or technologies. A performance measure could be the number of times that policies and procedures are reviewed over a five-year period. To monitor learning and growth measures, current performance of operations is usually used as a baseline, and improvements are evaluated over time.

Some of the learning and growth perspective measures adopted by Philips are shown in Exhibit 16.7. Because research and development is such a large part of Philips's strategy, the percentage of patent-protected turnover (sales to value of patent assets) is measured and monitored to determine returns on investments in research and development. In addition, employee training needs to be current and appropriate. Setting benchmarks for an optimal amount of employee training helps managers provide funds and time for employee training.

| GUIDE YOUR LEARNING 16.2 Key Terms |
|---|

Stop to confirm that you understand the new terms introduced in the last several pages.

*Performance objective (p. 631)  
*Financial measures (p. 634)  
*Nonfinancial measures (p. 635)  
Balanced scorecard (p. 636)  
Financial perspective (p. 638)  
Customer perspective (p. 638)

Internal business process perspective (p. 639)  
*Innovation cycle (p. 639)  
*Operations cycle (p. 640)  
*Post-sales service cycle (p. 640)  
Learning and growth perspective (p. 641)

For each of these terms, write a definition in your own words. For starred terms, list at least one example that is different from the ones given in this textbook.

| GUIDE YOUR LEARNING 16.3 Royal Philips Electronics |||
|---|---|---|
| Royal Philips Electronics illustrates perspectives and measures in a balanced scorecard. For this illustration: |||
| **Identify Problem and Information** | **Identify Uncertainties** | **Explore Alternatives** |
| Why did the managers decide to adopt a balanced scorecard? What decisions did they want to address? | What types of uncertainties existed? Consider uncertainties about:<br>• Important performance objectives<br>• Best measures for the performance objectives<br>• Links between perspectives | For each measure in Exhibit 16.7:<br>• In your own words, explain how the measure might provide managers with useful information<br>• Describe weaknesses in the measure (e.g., uncertainties about what it measures or questions about the quality of information) |

## IMPLEMENTING A BALANCED SCORECARD

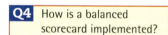

Q4  How is a balanced scorecard implemented?

**CURRENT PRACTICE**

Consulting firm The Hackett Group found that only 40% of companies gain internal consensus on definitions of goods and services, and only 32% define customers in the same way.[16]

The process of implementing a balanced scorecard is summarized in Exhibit 16.9. These general steps are customized for each organization.

### ■ Clarify Vision, Core Competencies, and Strategies

Clarifying the organization's vision, core competencies, and strategies is central to the balanced scorecard approach. The vision provides an overall direction for the organization. The core competencies and strategies provide guidance for achieving the organizational vision over the long term. To clarify the vision, statements are developed at the organizational level and for divisions, product lines, or departments. This process leads to discussion and consensus, which further clarify an organization's purpose. Similarly, the process of clarifying core competencies and strategies helps others understand how to achieve the organization's vision.

### ■ Analyze Perspectives to Develop Performance Objectives and Measures

The next step is to analyze the organization from the four perspectives. This step translates the organization's vision and strategies into a set of performance objectives within each perspective. The analyses identify what the organization must do well to attain its vision, focusing on the linkages between perspectives. The performance objectives should be limited to factors that achieve the organization's vision and strategies.

**EXHIBIT 16.9** Steps in Implementing a Balanced Scorecard

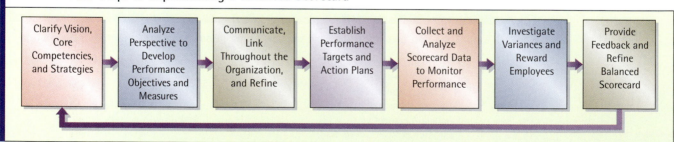

---

[16]C. Lazere, "All Together Now: Why You Must Link Budgeting and Forecasting to Planning and Performance," *CFO Magazine,* February 1, 1998, available at www.cfo.com.

**EXHIBIT 16.10** Alternative Sets of Balanced Scorecard Perspectives

| | | |
|---|---|---|
| EDUCAUSE | Not-for-profit association | • Member satisfaction<br>• Impact/outreach/innovation<br>• Internal processes<br>• Financial outcomes |
| Rohm and Haas | Specialty materials manufacturing | • Voice of the customer<br>• Voice of the owner<br>• Voice of the employee<br>• Voice of the community<br>• Voice of the process |
| Hilton Hotels | Hotels and resorts | • Operational effectiveness<br>• Revenue maximization<br>• Brand management<br>• Loyalty, learning, and growth |
| Business and Administrative Services, University of California, Berkeley | Not-for-profit state university | • People<br>• Processes<br>• Resources<br>• Service |
| Siemens | Electronics manufacturing | • Employee development and growth<br>• Processes<br>• Clients<br>• Financial |
| Office of Acquisition Management, U.S. Department of Commerce | U.S. government | • Customer<br>• Finance<br>• Internal business processes<br>• Learning and growth |
| Customer Relationship Management System, United Parcel Service | Express carrier and package delivery | • Customer relationship management<br>• Package management<br>• Product management<br>• Customer information management |

SOURCES: EDUCAUSE, available at www.educause.edu/about/membership.asp; Rohm and Haas, available under Career Opportunities at www.rohmhaas.com; Hilton Hotels: Hilton and Doubletree Hotels Recognized for Their 'Million Dollar' Performance; Hilton Hotels Corporation Awards Top Honors to Nine Hotels," news release, May 12, 2003; Business and Administrative Services, University of California, Berkeley; Siemens, available under Human Capital at www.siemens.com.br; Office of Acquisition Management, U.S. Department of Commerce, available at oamweb.osec.doc.gov/bsc/; and Customer Relationship Management System, UPS, "UPS Receives 'Partners in Alignment Award'," press release, UPS, September 20, 2002.

The four perspectives introduced earlier are most commonly used for balanced scorecards. However, different organizations define their perspectives differently, as illustrated in Exhibit 16.10. These perspectives differ by ownership type (for-profit versus not-for-profit), by industry, by organization, and by subunit within organizations.

For each performance objective, one or more measures are identified to monitor the organization's progress. Corrective action is then taken, as needed. The measures are financial and nonfinancial, covering both quantitative and qualitative data. Accountants are often more comfortable with quantitative measures, such as the average time to complete a customer's order or the number of new customers obtained. However, qualitative data, such as the results of customer and employee satisfaction surveys, are useful for some performance objectives.

Input measures capture activity or effort whereas outcome measures capture results. For example, Philips's balanced scorecard in Exhibit 16.10 includes both order response time (an input measure) and market share (an outcome measure). Philips's managers likely believe that decreasing order response time should lead to increased market share. Balanced scorecards focus on these types of expected links. Overall, balanced scorecards usually contain a range of measures, with four to seven performance measures used for each of the perspectives.

**CURRENT PRACTICE**

KPMG Peat Marwick partner Robert Hershey questions the amount of data that organizations can absorb and recommends no more than 20 balanced scorecard measures—five for each of the four perspectives.[17]

---

[17]C. Lazere, "All Together Now," *CFO Magazine,* February 1, 1998, available at www.cfo.com.

## ■ Communicate, Link Throughout the Organization, and Refine

The balanced scorecard is usually presented as a top-down plan. High-level executives define the vision, core competencies, and strategies of the organization, then communicate them to divisions and departments. Yet, success of the balanced scorecard approach depends on the efforts of individuals throughout the organization. To succeed, the balanced scorecard must be communicated both up and down the organization. Links must be developed between organizational, divisional, departmental, and individual objectives. Aligning goals increases the likelihood that all employees work together.

Sometimes the results of multiple units are formally combined with the results of another unit. For example, the results of individual departments might be combined into the results of a division. In Exhibit 16.11, data for the director's office, safety office, and human resources office are combined into a single balanced scorecard within the physical plant department at **University of California at Berkeley**. Part of this balanced scorecard combines data for all offices within the physical plant department. For instance, the safety office is responsible for all lost time from work-related injuries and for ensuring that all physical plant employees receive peer review safety training. Similarly, the human resources office is responsible for hiring employees within a desired timeframe.

Sometimes a common set of balanced scorecard measures is used across departments. For example, several of the measures in Exhibit 16.11 are identical for the physical plant director's office and the cashier's office. These measures are common because some of the performance objectives are the same. Common measures help ensure consensus throughout the organization, minimizing the need to develop separate systems for data collection. Measures that differ across offices relate to operating activities that are unique to individual offices.

Organization-wide implementation of a balanced scorecard, such as occurred at the University of California, Berkeley, requires significant amounts of communication and time. The process often begins with pilot projects, then expands across the organization as experience is gained and additional buy-in takes place. Refinements are often made to the original balanced scorecard after organizations have implemented it at the lowest levels.

## ■ Establish Performance Targets and Action Plans

It is not sufficient for an organization to create a balanced scorecard to measure progress toward its long-term vision and strategies. The organization must also establish specific performance targets and related action plans, all of which are usually tied directly to each performance objective in the balanced scorecard. Performance targets are set for three- to five-year periods with interim milestones, increasing the organization's focus on long-term results. Some organizations formally reward individuals or groups of employees for attaining performance targets. The action plans give employees specific guidance about their efforts towards targets.

For example, **Futura Industries** is a Utah-based international company that provides extruded aluminum products used as trims in electronics, transportation, shower doors, and marine fixtures. Futura's balanced scorecard has several measures of employee satisfaction. During their birthday months, employees are interviewed about the work climate. The interview questions cover topics such as whether employees feel they get enough support and information from the company to be successful. On a rating scale of 1 to 4, the company's target is an average of 3.2 for the interview questions. Another measure used in the learning and growth perspective is the average level of employee certification. As employees complete additional training, they receive certificates enabling them to move up a level on an internally developed training matrix. The goal is for 80% of employees to move to the next level when they are reviewed annually.[18]

When the balanced scorecard is used to compensate employees, different weights are placed on various measures in employee bonus packages. For example, if customer satisfaction ratings are inadequate, bonuses are made more dependent on improved satisfaction

**CURRENT PRACTICE**

Consultants argue that linking compensation to tools such as the balanced scorecards increases effectiveness. However, studying 50 companies, The Hackett Group found that only 58% tie compensation to strategic plans.[19]

---

[18]A. Gumbus and S. Johnson, "The Balanced Scorecard at Futura Industries," *Strategic Finance,* July 2003, p. 36.
[19]C. Lazere, "All Together Now," *CFO Magazine,* February 1, 1998, available at www.cfo.com.

**EXHIBIT 16.11** Balanced Scorecards at University of California, Berkeley

| Physical Plant Director's Office, Safety Office, and Human Resources Office | Cashier's Office |
|---|---|
| **People** | **People** |
| Objective: Excellent Workplace Climate<br>  Measure: Staff climate survey<br>Objective: Promote Learning and Employee Development<br>  Measure: Staff individual learning plans<br>Objective: Improve Employee Health and Safety<br>  Measures:<br>    Injury/illness prevention plan<br>    Injury/illness rate | Objective: Excellent Workplace Climate<br>  Measure: Staff climate survey<br>Objective: Promote Learning and Employee Development<br>  Measure: Staff individual learning plans<br>Objective: Improve Employee Health and Safety<br>  Measures:<br>    Injury/illness prevention plan<br>    Injury/illness rate |
| **Resources** | **Resources** |
| Objective: Sound Financial Performance<br>  Measure: Expenditures as a percent of budget<br>Objective (Safety Office): Reduce Lost Time Caused by Work-Related Injuries<br>  Measure: Lost time from work-related injuries[a]<br>Objective (Human Resources Office): Meet and Maintain Staffing Needs<br>  Measures:<br>    Hirings achieved within 45 days[a]<br>    Turnover rate | Objective: Sound Financial Performance<br>  Measure: Expenditures as a percent of budget |
| **Processes** | **Processes** |
| Objective (Safety Office): Improve Employee Safety<br>  Measures:<br>    Percent of staff receiving a safety peer review[a]<br>    Percent of VDT assessments completed | Objective: High Level of Accuracy<br>  Measure: Percent of days that the office balanced within $1<br>Objective: Reengineer Noncore Processes<br>  Measure: Percent of special services identified for conversion/reengineering |
| **Service** | **Service** |
| Objective: Satisfied Customers<br>  Measure: Customer satisfaction survey<br>Objective: Effective Training Programs<br>  Measure: Evaluation of training sessions | Objective: Satisfied Customers<br>  Measure: Customer satisfaction survey |

[a]Data are for the entire Physical Plant-Campus Services Department.
SOURCE: Available at 128.32.241.181/BalancedScorecards/Home.htm (accessed October 11, 2003). © The University of California. Permission for the publication or other use of the Balanced ScoreCard name and Diagram thereof may be granted only by The University of California.

ratings. However, finding the optimal weighting among measures is difficult. If too much weight is put on customer satisfaction and not enough on financial measures, employees may spend a great deal of time in activities that increase satisfaction but do not improve profits.

## ■ Collect and Analyze Scorecard Data

Balanced scorecard measures are captured periodically, which might mean monthly, quarterly, annually, or other time frames. Scorecard data are collected and analyzed for different measures using different time frames. For example, all of the measures for the cashier's office in Exhibit 16.11 are collected and monitored quarterly except the staff individual learning plans, which are analyzed semiannually, and the two surveys, which are analyzed annually.

Before calculations and comparisons to targets can be performed, systems for data collection must be established. In some cases, accounting systems are developed to capture relevant data. Nonfinancial measurement instruments may need to be developed. Survey instruments are either acquired or developed. Methods then need to be established for collecting samples and summarizing results. Trends in balanced scorecard measures are analyzed.

## ■ Investigate Variances and Reward Employees

Actual results are compared to performance targets to determine whether the results are better or worse than desired. Then significant variances are analyzed to identify their causes, leading to modifications in future plans. If the balanced scorecard is also used for employee compensation, rewards are computed and distributed.

## ■ Provide Feedback and Refine Balanced Scorecard

An important part of the balanced scorecard method is the feedback loop that uses results and experience to refine the process. Managers use their analysis of balanced scorecard results to evaluate the success of their strategies and operating plans. This evaluation leads to revisions in organizations' visions, core competencies, strategies, and operating plans. For example, Holly Snyder, **Nationwide Financial Services** director of planning and management reporting, suggests that the balanced scorecard helps managers decide what to do if the company's growth in premium revenue is 4% below expectations. "Maybe we hire more wholesalers; maybe we change our brand image. Whatever it is, the scorecard model is the tool we use to outline necessary changes."[20]

The effectiveness of the balanced scorecard is also gauged. Accountants and managers modify the set of measures to adapt to changes in the organization and to provide better information over time. Some measures may be dropped or changed, and new measures may be added.

Following is an example of the implementation of a balanced scorecard in a hospital setting.

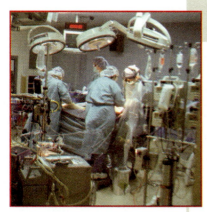

### COMMUNITY HOSPITAL
### IMPLEMENTING A BALANCED SCORECARD

Two hospitals in a city near the Mexican border have trauma centers, but neither trauma center is financially successful. Because the town needs at least one trauma center, the state and local governments meet with hospital officials to determine the best course of action. Both hospitals had spent considerable time reviewing their visions, core competencies, and current business strategies. They agree that only the teaching hospital should continue operating a trauma center. The teaching hospital's mission is to provide both high-quality patient care and a learning center for medical students. The teaching hospital needs a trauma center so that medical students can prepare more thoroughly for careers as physicians and specialists. Teaching hospitals also have a mission to provide care to patients who are unable to pay,[21] and the trauma center provides treatment for a large number of uninsured patients every year. Therefore, the decision to continue treating patients at the trauma center fits well with the teaching hospital's mission.

Top managers at the teaching hospital decide to institute a balanced scorecard. They focus first on service in the trauma center because many more patients will be admitted when the other hospital closes its trauma center. These managers believe that new measures of efficiency could help ease the transition.

The managers are also concerned about the current losses incurred by the trauma center. Care is provided for a number of patients who are unable to pay, including undocumented immigrants who, in attempting to cross the border desert in the heat of summer, suffer from dehydration and heat exhaustion. Uninsured car accident and gunshot wound victims also require care. Clinical processes in the trauma center need to be both cost-effective and high quality to maintain the hospital's reputation.

#### Clarify Vision, Core Competencies, and Strategies

A team of hospital administrators and trauma center employees meet to discuss the balanced scorecard implementation. The team decides that the hospital's vision, core competencies, and strategies also apply to the trauma center. The hospital and trauma center's patient care goals are to provide high-quality care in a timely manner and at a low cost for all patients, and also to provide care for those patients unable to pay. The hospital and trauma center's teaching goals are to provide a high-quality education for medical students, focusing on technological developments and innovative patient care treatment.

---

[20]C. Lazere, "All Together Now," *CFO Magazine,* February 1, 1998, available at www.cfo.com.
[21]"A Shared Responsibility: Academic Health Centers and the Provision of Care to the Poor and Uninsured," The Commonwealth Fund Task Force on Academic Health Centers, April 2001, available at www.cmwf.org.

### Analyze Perspectives to Develop Performance Objectives and Measures

The team decides that the standard four perspectives (financial, customer, internal business process, and learning and growth) are appropriate for analyzing the trauma center strategies and operations.

From a financial perspective, the hospital needs to at least break even to guarantee ongoing operations. The controller analyzes historical records for the department and finds that it has always operated at a loss. Until last year, research grants and government subsidies were usually enough so that the center broke even. The financial perspective is important because the center needs financial resources to continuously update the equipment and technology needed to provide high-quality patient care. After discussing performance measures, three are chosen that are identical to those used by the hospital as a whole (see Exhibit 16.12). Two of the measures are profit margin ratios, which address the trauma center's ability to control costs relative to revenues. The operating margin ratio includes only operating costs and revenues, while the excess income margin ratio includes nonoperating revenue in the form of donations and grants, which typically supply the needed funds for expansion or new technology. The third measure addresses reimbursement levels for the trauma center.

Next, the team analyzes the customer perspective. The hospital outsources patient satisfaction surveying, and it monitors average satisfaction by department to focus on patients' perceived quality of care. However, the survey results are only available quarterly. The department wants measures that predict patient satisfaction and that can be monitored daily. With timely feedback, problems will be identified and corrected quickly, before too many patients are unhappy with some aspect of service. The team decides that most patients would care about the average time they wait for a nurse to respond to their call buttons. In addition, several quality-of-care measures could be monitored, such as the error rate in medication delivery and patient satisfaction with meals. The final list is included in Exhibit 16.12.

(continued)

**EXHIBIT 16.12** Balanced Scorecard Measures for Community Hospital Trauma Center

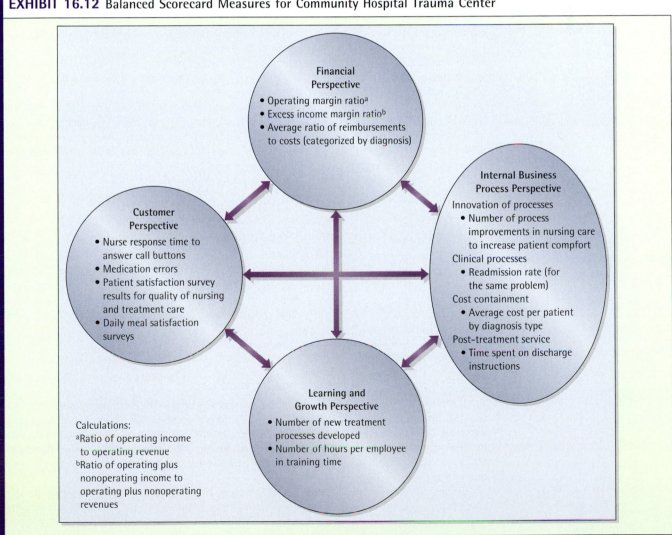

The team then analyzes the internal business process perspective. The hospital's long-term goals include managing patient care and clinical processes efficiently to maintain high quality and contain costs. The team decides that four aspects of internal business processes are critical to the trauma center's success. It then focuses on identifying measures for those four aspects.

For innovation processes, the team would like to motivate improvements in routine care such as delivering medications, changing wound dressings, and answering call buttons. Process improvements include innovative ways to streamline daily routines and to increase patient comfort. The number of process improvements in routine care will be tracked.

Clinical processes involve the technical aspects of care giving, such as setting up monitoring equipment and then using the information provided. The team decides to focus on the readmission rate as a performance measure for clinical processes. Sometimes patients are readmitted because complications arise at home. Some insurance companies will not pay for readmissions, and patients are unhappy to be readmitted. In addition to focusing on the decision to discharge patients at an appropriate time, tracking this measure will also encourage nurses to focus on the discharge process. The team believes that time spent on discharge instructions is linked to the readmission rate. For example, patients are sometimes readmitted because they become dehydrated at home. Some medications require patients to drink extra amounts of water; if this requirement is not carefully explained during the discharge instruction process, patients do not recover as quickly and may require readmission. The team considered using length of stay as a measure, but this factor varies a great deal with patients' severity of illness and is not under the nurses' control.

The team considers several possible ways to measure cost containment, but decides to focus initially on a general measure of cost—the average cost per patient by diagnosis type. This measure can be monitored as frequently as desired, allowing trauma center managers to quickly identify any adverse trends in cost. It also provides a way for managers to monitor cost effects when new procedures are implemented.

The trauma center's managers consider post-treatment service to be very important. Service after a patient leaves the center contributes to the quality of the patient's care. The team decides to measure this aspect using the time spent on discharge instructions. With more time spent on discharge instructions, patients should receive better home care, reducing the probability that they will be readmitted. The team considers measuring the number of phone calls made and e-mails sent with follow-up questions about patient home care, but decides that it is more important to focus on instructions before the patient goes home.

Finally the team focuses on the learning and growth perspective. To maintain and improve the trauma center's reputation for innovative patient treatment, the team decides to track the number of new treatment processes developed. Because new technologies and care-giving practices are developed continually, the hospital provides a variety of medical education classes for nurses and other department staff. To encourage employees to take advantage of these classes, the team chooses number of hours of training per employee as performance measure.

## Communicate, Link Throughout the Organization, and Refine

Once the team develops a tentative balanced scorecard for the trauma center, the plan is presented to top hospital administrators and to employees in the center. The administrators consider whether the trauma center objectives align with the overall hospital mission, strategies, and objectives. They believe that this scorecard appropriately addresses the hospital mission and praises the team. Employees and medical students also feel that the scorecard helps them understand how the trauma center's objectives should be carried out.

## Establish Performance Targets and Action Plans

The balanced scorecard team believes that the measures in Exhibit 16.12 are appropriate for analysis. They ask the accounting department to collect information about last year's operations so they will have baseline information for comparison with future results. The team recommends that management and employees review the trends each month. After three months, the usefulness of this list of performance measures will be reassessed and the balanced scorecard can be changed accordingly.

Exhibit 16.13 summarizes the information developed by the accounting department for last year's operations. The hospital's accounting system tracks patient charges for supplies and services

**EXHIBIT 16.13**
Balanced Scorecard Data for Community Hospital Trauma Center

| | |
|---|---:|
| Overall department financial information: | |
| Patient revenue | $5,040,000 |
| Operating costs (cost of patient care) | 6,300,000 |
| Nonoperating revenues | 1,500,000 |
| Nonoperating costs | 300,000 |
| Information on trauma center operations | |
| Number of patient admissions | 252 |
| Total nurse response time to call button (200 patient calls) | 1,000 minutes |
| Number of medication errors | 10 |
| Patient satisfaction survey results for quality of nursing and treatment care | |
| Number surveyed | 130 |
| Average satisfaction rating (1 to 5=very satisfied) | 3.8 |
| Other patient-related data | |
| Average satisfaction rating on daily meal satisfaction surveys (1 to 5=very satisfied) | 2.9 |
| Total patient days | 2,142 |
| Readmissions | 5 |
| Minutes spent on discharge instructions | 5,040 |
| Employee-related information | |
| Total time spent in training (hours) | 875 |
| Number of employees | 35 |
| Process improvement | |
| Number of process improvements in nursing care | 3 |
| Number of process improvements in treatment | 2 |

by department; however, reimbursement is tracked at the hospital level because different payers pay different portions of charges, and some patients do not pay. Therefore, the patient revenue is assigned to the trauma center based on its average mix of care for nonpaying patients, Medicare, HMO, and other patients. As a result, revenue is measured with error, and the information may not be of quality high enough for a performance measure.

The cost data about patient care in the trauma center is quite accurate, although patient costs include fixed cost allocations. Any change in the allocation bases or methods reduces comparability of patient cost information over time. Patient survey information is gathered by the Quality and Utilization Department. Although the team would like daily information about customer satisfaction measures, surveys about meals and nurse response time to call buttons are given randomly to 20% of the trauma center patients during the first three days of each month. The survey response information is forwarded to the accounting department on the third day. The accounting department does not have time to track this measure more frequently. Employees estimate their time in training each month. Because they do not always fill out the reports, they are contacted by accounting each month to update any missing estimates. Time spent on discharge instructions for each patient will be reported by discharge nurses using a new form developed by the accounting department. Once a month, accountants will meet with physicians and nurses to determine the number and type of improvements and innovations in treatment and care-giving processes.

The balanced scorecard team uses the information in Exhibit 16.13 to calculate last year's performance as shown in Exhibit 16.14. Team members review this information and then meet with personnel at the other hospital to collect information about its trauma center. They then determine appropriate benchmarks and action plans for Community Hospital's trauma center during the transition period.

Because measures for the combined trauma centers are likely to be different from the current center, a transition period will be needed to determine appropriate benchmarks. During the transition time, trauma center staff hired from the other hospital will be introduced to the scorecard. Within several months, targets can be set for every performance measure, and monitoring will begin. Information from the scorecard will be evaluated to determine areas in need of improvement. In addition, the current balanced scorecard will be reevaluated and changed as appropriate. *(continued)*

**EXHIBIT 16.14**
Baseline Balanced Scorecard
Results for Community
Hospital Trauma Center

**Financial Perspective Performance Measures**

Operating margin ratio:

$$\frac{\text{Operating margin}}{\text{Patient revenue}} = \frac{5,040,000 - 6,300,000}{5,040,000} \qquad (25)\%$$

Excess income margin ratio:

$$\frac{\text{Operating plus nonoperating income}}{\text{Operating plus nonoperating revenue}} = \frac{\$(60,000)}{\$6,540,000} \qquad (1)\%$$

Ratio of reimbursement to cost

$$\frac{\text{Patient revenue}}{\text{Operating costs}} = \frac{\$5,040,000}{\$6,300,000} \qquad 0.8$$

**Customer Perspective Performance Measures**

| | |
|---|---|
| Average nurse response time to answer call buttons (in minutes) | 5 |
| Medication errors | 10 |
| Average satisfaction with quality of nursing and treatment care | 3.8 |
| Average satisfaction with daily meals | 2.9 |

**Internal Business Process Perspective**

Innovation of processes

| | |
|---|---|
| Number of process improvements in routine care | 3 |

Clinical processes

| | |
|---|---|
| Readmission rate (readmissions ÷ total admissions) | 2% |

Cost containment

| | |
|---|---|
| Average cost per patient (operating costs ÷ #admissions) | $25,000 |

Post-treatment service

| | |
|---|---|
| Time spent on discharge instructions (minutes) | 20 |

**Learning and Growth**

| | |
|---|---|
| Number of new treatment processes developed | 2 |
| Average training hours per employee | 25 |

---

## GUIDE YOUR LEARNING  16.4  Community Hospital

Community Hospital illustrates the implementation of a balanced scorecard. For this illustration:

| Identify Problem and Information | Identify Uncertainties | Explore Alternatives | Explore Perspectives |
|---|---|---|---|
| What decisions were being addressed? Why did the managers think that a balanced scorecard would be a useful management tool? | What types of uncertainties were there? Consider uncertainties about: <br> • Usefulness of a balanced scorecard <br> • Definition of four perspectives <br> • Best set of performance objectives <br> • Best set of performance measures | In your own words, explain what managers would learn from evaluating each of the performance measures. Describe one or more weaknesses in each measure. | Identify the stakeholders for this problem. Discuss how implementation of the balanced scorecard is likely to affect each group of stakeholders. Address both positive and negative effects. |

---

## STRENGTHS AND WEAKNESSES OF THE BALANCED SCORECARD

Similar to other new accounting techniques, the balanced scorecard has both strengths and weaknesses.

### ■ Strengths

Organizations are under increasing pressure to meet customer needs, use resources efficiently, compete effectively under changing conditions, employ new technologies and

**EXHIBIT 16.15** Strengths and Weaknesses of Balanced Scorecard

| Strengths | Weaknesses |
|---|---|
| Communication and linkages<br>• Encourages clarification and updating of vision and strategies<br>• Improves communication and consensus throughout the organization<br>• Links short-term and long-term performance objectives to the vision and strategies<br><br>Guidance for improvements<br>• Enables periodic performance reviews of progress toward vision and strategies<br>• Leads to improved financial performance<br>• Helps managers use operational data for decision making<br><br>Motivation<br>• Aligns unit and individual goals with the organizational vision and strategies<br>• Motivates employee effort<br>• Reduces optimization of subunits at the expense of the organization as a whole<br>• Promotes action toward achieving strategies | Implementation is expensive and time-consuming<br>Uncertainties<br>• Appropriateness of vision and strategies<br>• Accuracy of identified core competencies<br>• Best set of performance objectives and measures<br>• Reliability of scorecard data<br>• Reasonableness of targets<br>• Doubt about links among perspectives<br><br>Mistakes in implementation<br>• Ambiguous or generally defined objectives<br>• Information systems not integrated<br>• Insufficient resources<br>• Lack of senior management support<br>• Focusing on inappropriate objectives<br><br>Biases<br>• Manager selection of familiar or easily attainable objectives and measures<br>• Resistance from units and individuals<br>• Process viewed as a temporary fad<br><br>May be inappropriate for compensation<br>Vision may not adequately capture core values including relations with regulators, approach toward the environment, etc. |

| Q5 | What are the strengths and weaknesses of the balanced scorecard? |
|---|---|

**CURRENT PRACTICE**

In 1997, Harvard Business Review named the balanced scorecard one of the most influential management ideas of the previous 75 years.

operating methods, and provide a good return to shareholders. These demands require more effective implementation of vision and strategies. The proponents of the balanced scorecard method argue that it improves performance by helping organizations integrate their visions and strategies into operations more completely. Many of the advantages of this approach, already described, are summarized in Exhibit 16.15.

## ■ Weaknesses

Any method designed to help organizations improve management decision making involves weaknesses because the process of management decision making is inherently uncertain. No perfect solutions have yet been discovered. Major weaknesses of the balanced scorecard approach are summarized in Exhibit 16.15. First, the balanced scorecard faces questions about its costs and benefits. Considerable time and effort are needed to develop and use the balanced scorecard. Outside consultants are often employed, and the time involved for key managers can be considerable.

**Uncertainties**   Uncertainty is part of any balanced scorecard. The underlying assumptions are that the vision and core competencies have been properly identified and that implementation of the organization's strategies leads to success. However, the best choices for a vision and set of strategies are ambiguous; managers might incorrectly identify the organization's strengths relative to competitors.

Furthermore, the process of identifying appropriate performance objectives and measures is not straightforward. The balanced scorecard methodology requires managers to identify the most important aspects of operations, yet they cannot be known with certainty. Once performance objectives are selected, additional uncertainty about the best set of measures arises. Some measures are more reliable than others, although less reliable measures can at times address a more relevant aspect of operations.

Uncertainties about choices of information for a balanced scorecard challenge managers and accountants. For example, potential customer satisfaction measures include market share, number of return customers, number of new customers, and ratings on satisfaction surveys. Although the number of return customers and number of new customers can be measured with a high degree of accuracy, this information may not be as relevant for gauging customer satisfaction as other measures. Market share may or may not be reliable, depending on the accuracy of information about total industry sales. Many factors influence the reliability of survey ratings, including the survey design, methods for collecting samples, and the types of customers surveyed. To decide on the best measure, managers and accountants need to weigh the quality and relevance of information across potential measures.

Another uncertainty is the best choice for performance targets, including how quickly an organization should be able to achieve its performance objectives. Low targets may fail to motivate sufficient effort. High targets discourage performance when employees perceive them as unrealistic.

The balanced scorecard also assumes specific linkages among the four perspectives. In particular, it assumes that improved performance in internal business processes and in learning and growth lead to improved customer-related measures. In turn, improved customer-related measures are assumed to lead to improved financial performance. These assumptions, however, might not hold because of uncertainties about the measures and about the interrelationships among aspects of an organization's activities. Researchers found cause-and-effect relationships only between the customer perspective measures and financial performance measures.[22] Although research studies do not prove the absence of links, they raise doubts about the linkage that managers and accountants need to consider.

**Mistakes in Implementation** Analysts and consultants point out a number of areas where mistakes are often made in balanced scorecard implementations, leading to poor results. Sometimes performance objectives are ambiguous or defined too generally, reducing the balanced scorecard's effectiveness in communicating the actions needed to achieve the organization's vision and strategies. Sometimes the organization's information systems are not designed adequately to capture information needed. The balanced scorecard can be expensive to implement, and may face inadequate resources for designing, implementing, communicating, following through on results, and refining the methodology over time. Although senior managers are generally involved in the initial adoption of a balanced scorecard, they may give the process inadequate support.

Another mistake relates to the selection of inappropriate objectives and related measures. Author Jim Collins argues that many companies focus on the wrong financial measures. His research suggests that managers of the best-performing companies often succeed because they adopt more insightful measures to monitor their businesses. For example, **Gillette** shifted its focus from profit per division to profit per customer. This shift helped the company recognize the importance of repeatable purchases of high margin products such as Mach3 razor cartridges. Companies where managers failed to adopt similarly insightful measures were not as successful.[23]

**Biases** Several types of biases reduce the effectiveness of a balanced scorecard. Recent research suggests that managers select performance measures with which they are most familiar—measures that may not induce behavior that leads to financial success.[24] In addition, managers have incentives to choose performance objectives and measures that highlight areas that are strengths, instead of areas that need improvement. Any organizational change is likely to encounter resistance. For example, employees may view the balanced scorecard as a temporary management whim that does not deserve their attention. These types of resistance can prevent the organization-wide commitment and effort required for balanced scorecard success.

**Other Factors** Some questions surround whether or how the balanced scorecard should be used to compensate employees. Because of the uncertainties already discussed, many employees perceive balanced scorecard measures to be unfair for use in compensation calculations. In addition, weights or other formulaic approaches for using balanced scorecard results lead to game-playing and suboptimization, contrary to the purpose of a balanced scorecard.

Another criticism of the balanced scorecard approach is that it does not adequately capture core values including relations with regulators or approaches toward the environment.

---

[22]C. Ittner and D. Larcker, "Are Nonfinancial Measures Leading Indicators of Financial Performance? An Analysis of Customer Satisfaction," *Journal of Accounting Research,* 36 (1998), pp. 1–35.

[23]J. Collins, *Good to Great: Why Some Companies Make the Leap . . . and Others Don't* (New York: HarperBusiness, 2001), pp. 106–107.

[24]M. Lipe and S. Salterio, "The Balanced Scorecard: Judgmental Effects of Common and Unique Performance Measures," *The Accounting Review,* 75(3), July 2000, pp. 283–296.

**EXHIBIT 16.16**
Path to Higher-Quality Management Decisions

An organization's core values are theoretically embedded in its vision and strategies. However, current literature on the balanced scorecard places little emphasis on values.

## ■ How Valuable Is the Balanced Scorecard?

Given these perceived weaknesses in the balanced scorecard, some people are inclined to dismiss this methodology; they want greater certainty about benefits. However, any method that managers use to help them develop and implement business strategies is subject to significant uncertainty. We learned in Chapter 1 about the path to higher-quality management decisions, presented again in Exhibit 16.16. Higher-quality decisions occur from use of the following:

- Higher-quality information
- Higher-quality reports
- Higher-quality decision-making processes

The best questions to ask about the balanced scorecard methodology are whether it helps managers and employees throughout the organization make higher-quality decisions and whether the benefits from improved decision making exceed the costs of implementing and maintaining a balanced scorecard. Is the information in a balanced scorecard of higher-quality than the information managers previously used? Are balanced scorecard reports more relevant, understandable, and available on a timely basis? Does use of the balanced scorecard encourage managers and other employees to be more thorough, less biased, more focused, and more strategic, creative, and visionary? Proponents of the balanced scorecard methodology argue that the answer to each of these questions is "yes." They also point out that the balanced scorecard should not be viewed as a static formulaic approach. Instead, it must be reevaluated and refined periodically to provide better information for monitoring and motivating performance. Periodic reevaluation allows managers to eliminate or alter measures that do not fit well and to identify potential new measures that offset unintended negative effects. As the organization learns, it can do a better job of designing and using a balanced scorecard. Organizations that fail to engage in continuous improvement are less likely to achieve high-quality results.

### FOCUS ON ETHICAL DECISION MAKING
### Accountable Volunteer Organizations

Chartered Management Accountants (CMAs) in Canada have helped volunteer sector organizations develop accountability frameworks that measure progress toward their missions. The number and size of volunteer organizations is significant. Canada has 177,000 volunteer organizations with revenues of $90.5 billion (Canadian dollars), amounting to 12% of the Canadian gross domestic product. These organizations provide community and social services; organize cultural, educational, and recreational activities; and lobby for social, political, and economic change.

Some of these volunteer organizations have had serious problems, eroding public faith. For example, the Multiple Sclerosis Society of Canada fired members of its Calgary board because they had allegedly exceeded their power. The Canadian Society of Association Executives invested in technology projects that failed to meet their original financial projections, resulting in a

*(continued)*

$550,000 deficit for the fiscal year 2001–2002. In 1996, 71% of survey respondents saw a need for greater accountability in this sector (Markham, 2002–2003). Similar problems have arisen in the United States. For example, the American Red Cross has been criticized by some for its management of donations to the Liberty Disaster Relief Fund for the victims of September 11 (Chaker, 2002; Brill 2002).

Problems such as these prompted federal, provincial, and municipal governments to review existing volunteer sector codes, laws, and regulations. In addition, some volunteer organizations enlisted the help of CMAs to develop comprehensive performance measurement systems to gauge progress toward their missions. The organizations themselves are concerned that failing to meet public expectations in terms of quality and value will increase the opportunities of for-profit organizations to perform the same services.

The CMAs encouraged a balanced scorecard approach for volunteer organizations. One organization adopting this approach is the Ontario Physical and Health Education Association that helps children and youth live active, healthy lives. The organization set the following goals for measurement in its balanced scorecard:

- Improvement of performance, coordination, and productivity
- Greater focus on business objectives and clients' expectations
- Achievement and maintenance of high-quality goods and services to meet clients' stated and implied needs

An advantage of the balanced scorecard approach for voluntary organizations is the documentation it requires of financial and nonfinancial performance. When these organizations seek donations and grants from the local community and from state and federal governments, they produce evidence of their progress toward missions. Balanced scorecard reports reassure donors and grant selection committees that resources are used effectively and efficiently. A disadvantage is that the costs to the organization may exceed the benefits, particularly because resources allocated to the implementation process are no longer available for an organization's program.

SOURCES: C. Markham, "Charity's Changed Environment," *CMA Management*, December 2002/January 2003, pp. 24–28; A. M. Chaker, "Red Cross Gives Disaster Relief to Tony Enclave," *The Wall Street Journal*, February 7, 2002, p. B1; and S. Brill "An Excess of Riches," *Newsweek*, February 11, 2002, p. 40.

### Practice Ethical Decision Making

In Chapter 1, we learned about a process for making ethical decisions (Exhibit 1.11). You can address the following questions for this ethical dilemma to improve your skills for making ethical decisions. Think about your answers to these questions and discuss them with others.

| Ethical Decision-Making Process | Questions to Consider about This Ethical Dilemma |
|---|---|
| Identify ethical problems as they arise. | Is the efficient and effective use of resources an ethical issue for the managers of not-for-profit organizations? Why or why not? |
| Objectively consider the well-being of others and society when exploring alternatives. | How is the well-being of society affected when not-for-profit organizations fail to use resources in an efficient and effective way? Why might the managers of not-for-profit organizations fail to use resources efficiently and effectively? Identify both intentional and unintentional problems. Discuss whether these issues are different between not-for-profit and for-profit organizations. |
| Clarify and apply ethical values when choosing a course of action. | Suppose you were to write a memo to the managers of a not-for-profit organization to help them decide whether to adopt a balanced scorecard approach. What ethical values would you use in presenting the pros and cons of a balanced scorecard? |
| Work toward ongoing improvement of personal and organizational ethics. | Explain how use of a strategy management system such as the balanced scorecard could potentially help a not-for-profit organization's managers meet their ethical responsibilities over time. |

## ENVISIONING THE FUTURE OF COST ACCOUNTING

 **Q6** What is the future direction of cost accounting?

Throughout this textbook, we learned that cost accounting information is increasingly defined to include both financial and nonfinancial information and also to include things that do not relate strictly to the allocation of costs. The demand for new and expanded information results from increased pressure for accountants to provide more relevant and useful information for internal decision making. Accountants promote better decision making in their organizations by providing better information, and also by recommending and helping their organizations adopt appropriate management techniques. For example, we learned about the balanced scorecard in this chapter. As experts on measurement, accountants play critical roles in helping their organizations successfully implement balanced scorecards.

A huge array of new management tools and techniques has been introduced in recent years, and this trend will likely continue. In addition to the balanced scorecard, several other prominent techniques are introduced throughout this textbook, including activity-based management (Chapter 7), outsourcing (Chapter 4), supply chain management (Chapter 13), and economic value-added (Chapter 15). As new tools and techniques are introduced, accountants add value by learning about them and evaluating whether they are appropriate for their organizations. Sometimes it is difficult to know whether a given technique is useful until a significant number of organizations has implemented and gained experience in its use. Over time, the best techniques are increasingly used, while the less-useful techniques become less prevalent. One way to gauge the potential usefulness of a management technique is to gather data about its implementation among other organizations. For example, Exhibit 16.17

**EXHIBIT 16.17**

Use of Management Tools and Techniques in 2002

| | Percent Usage | Satisfaction Rating |
| --- | --- | --- |
| Strategic planning | 89% | 4.04 |
| Benchmarking | 84 | 3.96 |
| Mission and vision statements | 84 | 3.74 |
| Customer segmentation | 79 | 4.01 |
| Outsourcing | 78 | 3.84 |
| Customer surveys | 78 | 3.99 |
| Customer relationship management | 78 | 3.81 |
| Corporate code of ethics | 78 | 4.05 |
| Growth strategies | 76 | 3.82 |
| Pay-for-performance | 76 | 3.90 |
| Core competencies | 75 | 4.01 |
| Contingency planning | 70 | 3.81 |
| Strategic alliances | 69 | 3.80 |
| Change management programs | 64 | 3.80 |
| Knowledge management | 62 | 3.63 |
| Balanced scorecard | 62 | 3.88 |
| Downsizing | 59 | 3.49 |
| Total quality management | 57 | 3.80 |
| Reengineering | 54 | 3.75 |
| Supply chain integration | 52 | 3.80 |
| Economic value-added analysis | 52 | 3.85 |
| Activity-based management | 50 | 3.76 |
| Merger integration teams | 37 | 3.83 |
| Corporate venturing | 32 | 3.45 |
| Stock buybacks | 18 | 3.74 |
| Average satisfaction rating | | 3.85 |
| Average number of tools used | | |
| North America | 15.8 tools | |
| Europe | 16.2 | |
| Asia | 17.5 | |
| South America | 14.3 | |

*Note:* Based on a survey of senior executives from 708 companies about their tool usage and satisfaction during year 2002 conducted by consulting firm Bain & Company. Bain has conducted similar surveys since 1993.
SOURCE: D. Rigby, "Management Tools Survey 2003: Usage Up as Companies Strive to Make Headway in Tough Times," *Strategy & Leadership,* 31(5), 2003, pp. 4–11. Published with permission of Emerald Group Publishing Limited, www.emeraldinsight.com.

[25]C. Lazere, "All Together Now," *CFO Magazine,* February 1, 1998, available at www.cfo.com.

presents data about the use of and satisfaction with 25 top management tools during the year 2002.

Although the approaches in Exhibit 16.17 are widely used, they are likely to work best for specific types of organizations. For example, activity-based management is less useful for companies with simple processes and few overhead activities. It is more useful for organizations with multiple and complex products that use advanced manufacturing systems. Accountants add value by understanding the strengths and weaknesses of each approach and determining whether an approach would be a good fit for their organizations.

In the past, accountants spent most of their time recording events and preparing reports based upon prior period results. Over the last several decades, technology has created less need for accountants to spend time on bookkeeping activities. Instead, they spend more time helping their organizations respond to current conditions in the business environment and preparing for anticipated and unanticipated changes over time.

Organizations expect their accountants to continuously learn. As new tools and techniques are developed, accountants need to evaluate the appropriateness of these techniques for their respective organizations. Cost/benefit analyses should be prepared to help managers make high-quality decisions. Mathematical modeling may become a more important part of accountants' skill sets. Creative, innovative, and thoughtful analyses will be crucial to the success of individual accountants and their organizations.

# SUMMARY

**Q1** What Is Strategic Decision Making?

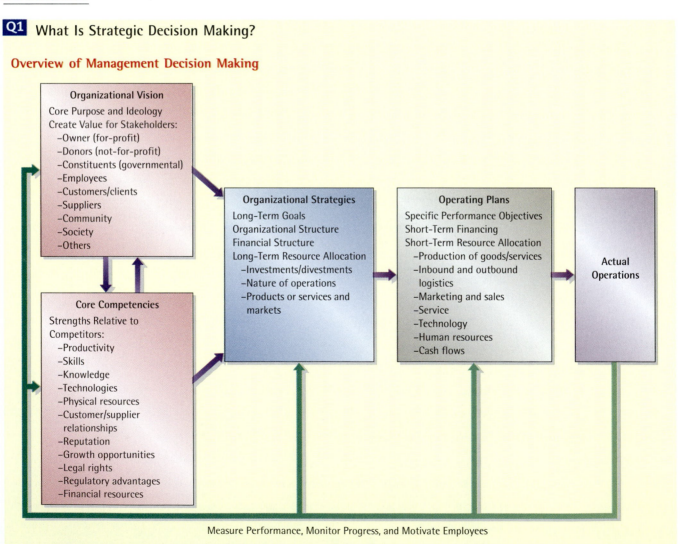

**Overview of Management Decision Making**

**Organizational Vision**
Core Purpose and Ideology
Create Value for Stakeholders:
  –Owner (for-profit)
  –Donors (not-for-profit)
  –Constituents (governmental)
  –Employees
  –Customers/clients
  –Suppliers
  –Community
  –Society
  –Others

**Core Competencies**
Strengths Relative to
Competitors:
  –Productivity
  –Skills
  –Knowledge
  –Technologies
  –Physical resources
  –Customer/supplier
   relationships
  –Reputation
  –Growth opportunities
  –Legal rights
  –Regulatory advantages
  –Financial resources

**Organizational Strategies**
Long-Term Goals
Organizational Structure
Financial Structure
Long-Term Resource Allocation
  –Investments/divestments
  –Nature of operations
  –Products or services and
   markets

**Operating Plans**
Specific Performance Objectives
Short-Term Financing
Short-Term Resource Allocation
  –Production of goods/services
  –Inbound and outbound
   logistics
  –Marketing and sales
  –Service
  –Technology
  –Human resources
  –Cash flows

**Actual Operations**

Measure Performance, Monitor Progress, and Motivate Employees

## Q2 How Are Financial and Nonfinancial Measures Used to Evaluate Organizational Performance?

### Financial Measures

Information measured in dollars or ratios of dollars

### Nonfinancial Measures

Information that cannot be measured in dollars

### Monitoring Measurable Performance Objectives

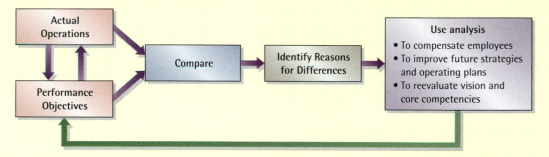

## Q3 What Is a Balanced Scorecard?

### Balanced Scorecard

Formal method to incorporate both financial and nonfinancial performance measures into organizational management systems. Translates organizational vision and strategies into performance objectives and related performance measures that can be monitored over time.

### Four Perspectives

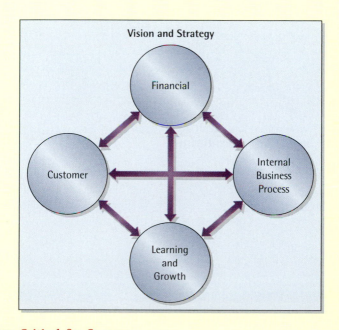

### Identifying Internal Processes Critical for Success

- Innovation cycle
- Operations cycle
- Post-sales service cycle

**Q4** How Is a Balanced Scorecard Implemented?

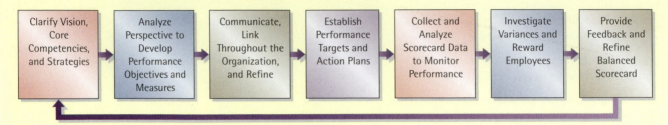

| Clarify Vision, Core Competencies, and Strategies | → | Analyze Perspective to Develop Performance Objectives and Measures | → | Communicate, Link Throughout the Organization, and Refine | → | Establish Performance Targets and Action Plans | → | Collect and Analyze Scorecard Data to Monitor Performance | → | Investigate Variances and Reward Employees | → | Provide Feedback and Refine Balanced Scorecard |

**Q5** What Are the Strengths and Weaknesses of the Balanced Scorecard?

| Strengths | Weaknesses |
|---|---|
| Communication and linkages<br>• Encourages clarification and updating of vision and strategies<br>• Improves communication and consensus throughout the organization<br>• Links short-term and long-term performance objectives to the vision and strategies<br><br>Guidance for improvements<br>• Enables periodic performance reviews of progress toward vision and strategies<br>• Leads to improved financial performance<br>• Helps managers use operational data for decision making<br><br>Motivation<br>• Aligns unit and individual goals with the organizational vision and strategies<br>• Motivates employee effort<br>• Reduces optimization of subunits at the expense of the organization as a whole<br>• Promotes action toward achieving strategies | Implementation is expensive and time-consuming<br>Uncertainties<br>• Appropriateness of vision and strategies<br>• Accuracy of identified core competencies<br>• Best set of performance objectives and measures<br>• Reliability of scorecard data<br>• Reasonableness of targets<br>• Doubt about links among perspectives<br><br>Mistakes in implementation<br>• Ambiguous or generally defined objectives<br>• Information systems not integrated<br>• Insufficient resources<br>• Lack of senior management support<br>• Focusing on inappropriate objectives<br><br>Biases<br>• Manager selection of familiar or easily attainable objectives and measures<br>• Resistance from units and individuals<br>• Process viewed as a temporary fad<br><br>May be inappropriate for compensation<br>Vision may not adequately capture core values including relations with regulators, approach toward the environment, etc. |

**Q6** What Is the Future Direction of Cost Accounting?

**Increasing Focus**
• Both financial and nonfinancial information
• More relevant and useful information

• Information to predict future operations
• Continuous learning of new techniques
• Creativity, innovation, and thoughtful analysis

## Self-Study Problem 1 Balanced Scorecard Implementation, Pros and Cons

**Q3, Q4, Q5**

Mountain High Bikes (MHB) wants to implement a balanced scorecard. Its mission statement reads, "We build high-quality, reliable bikes at competitive prices." The company's competitive strategy is to continuously improve the functionality, reliability, and quality of its bikes, while holding prices at levels similar to competitors. The company operates three subunits organized around the product lines for the three types of mountain bikes it currently produces. A fourth bike line in development includes a finished design, with engineers currently working on the plans for the manufacturing process. MHB sells directly to bike shops and operates an Internet site that allows bike shops to place orders for customized products.

**REQUIRED:**

A. Describe the implementation cycle for the balanced scorecard at MHB.

**①** B. Describe the four perspectives of the balanced scorecard and list one or more performance objectives for each perspective that are likely to be important for MHB.

**②** C. Pick one performance objective for each perspective in part (B) and identify two or more potential measures. Explain how each measure would link to improved financial performance.

**②** D. Describe the pros and cons of implementing a balanced scorecard for MHB.

### Solution to Self-Study Problem 1

A. Steps for implementing a balanced scorecard for MHB (see Exhibit 16.9):

1. *Clarify Vision, Core Competencies, and Strategies.* MHB already developed its mission statement. The company's managers should also consider writing a vision statement and core values statement. In addition, the managers need to clarify the company's core competencies. Even though the company already specified its strategies, the managers should review them and revise them as necessary.

2. *Analyze Perspectives to Develop Performance Objectives and Measures.* The managers need to analyze the company's vision and strategies from each of the four perspectives for the balanced scorecard: financial, customer, internal business process, and learning and growth. Within each perspective, they need to identify performance objectives and related measures. To identify performance objectives, the managers must determine the critical actions that the organization must take to achieve its strategies. They need to define what they mean by high quality from a customer's perspective. They also need to analyze competitors' prices and quality to determine the amount of cost containment and levels of quality needed.

3. *Communicate, Link Throughout the Organization, and Refine.* The managers will develop a communication plan and obtain assistance from personnel throughout the organization in clarifying and refining the decisions made in steps 1 and 2. The managers would then decide whether the different subunits should develop their own balanced scorecards. The final set of performance objectives and measures must be communicated effectively to align employee efforts with the company's objectives.

4. *Establish Performance Targets and Action Plans.* Through discussions among management and employees at different levels in the company and analysis of previous results, performance targets and action plans are developed for each performance objective. The managers must also decide whether to use the balanced scorecard data for employee compensation. For employees whose compensation depends on the results, managers need to prioritize the objectives that relate to that employee's performance and establish a weighting scheme for linking rewards to performance. For example, production line employees could receive bonuses when production quantity and quality reach target levels.

5. *Collect and Analyze Scorecard Data to Monitor Performance.* The managers need to ensure that information systems are in place to collect and report scorecard data. Trends can be noted. As data are collected, actual results can be compared to targets.

6. *Investigate Variances and Reward Employees.* The managers need to analyze reasons for variance from targets. They also need to consider what the results mean for future strategies, operating plans, and performance objectives.

7. *Provide Feedback and Refine Balanced Scorecard.* The managers need to establish a feedback loop so that the information they learn is used to make adjustments as they go through the balanced scorecard process in the future. It means a reevaluation of the process, beginning at step 1, as necessary.

B. Four perspectives and possible performance objectives:

The *financial perspective* analyzes the economic consequences of MHB's operations and decisions. A possible performance objective is a profitability level that is in the top quartile within the industry.

The *customer perspective* analyzes the role of customers in MHB's success. Possible performance objectives are:
- Provision of goods and services that satisfy customers so that they remain loyal.
- An increase in the size of the loyal customer base.

*(continued)*

The *internal business process perspective* analyzes the role of the company's internal methods and practices in MHB's success. Possible performance objectives are:

- Continuous improvements in functionality and quality that are important to customers (innovation cycle).
- Production of each bike as cost effectively as possible in a timely manner (operations cycle).
- Reliable products, with few returns and little warranty work (operations and post-sales service cycle).
- Customer satisfaction with interactions that occur after purchase (post-sales service cycle).

The *learning and growth perspective* analyzes the role of continuous improvement efforts in MHB's success. Possible performance objectives are:

- Productive and well-trained employees.
- Systems that support operations in a cost-effective manner.

C.

| Performance Objective | Measures and Links to Financial Performance |
|---|---|
| **Financial Perspective**<br>A profitability level in top quartile within the industry | • Operating margin. A higher operating margin leads to higher profits, which is a common indicator of financial success.<br>• Economic value-added. EVA takes into account the level of profits as well as the cost of capital.<br>• Average price per bike. The average price feeds into both operating margin and EVA. As prices go up, if costs and volumes are held constant, operating margins and EVA should increase. |
| **Customer Perspective**<br>Provision of goods and services that satisfy customers so that they remain loyal | • Customer satisfaction ratings (with emphasis on quality and price satisfaction). If customer satisfaction ratings are high, MHB is likely to keep its current customers and add new ones, which would lead to higher market share, higher sales volumes, better operating margins, and higher EVA.<br>• Market share. Higher market share would lead to higher sales volumes, better operating margins, and higher EVA.<br>• Number of return customers and number of new customers. If the number of return and new customers increases, then sales volumes should also increase, leading to better operating margins and higher EVA. |
| **Internal Business Process Perspective**<br>Reliable products with few returns and little warranty work | • Number of bikes returned. If return rates and warranty work are low, customers are more satisfied and sales increase, leading to higher profits. In addition, MHB spends less on post-sales service, which also increases profits.<br>• Dollar value of warranty work. Same as above. |
| **Learning and Growth Perspective**<br>Productive and well-trained employees | • Employee retention. Satisfied and well-trained employees are less likely to leave the company. They also will monitor quality and efficiency of the production lines and make suggestions for improvements, leading to better cost efficiency and higher-quality products, in turn leading to higher profits. More satisfied employees are also more likely to have positive interactions with customers, leading to improved sales and higher profitability.<br>• Employee hours of training. Better training improves performance of work and interactions with customers, leading to higher sales and lower costs, increasing profits. |

**D. Pros:** MHB begins the process of clarifying and updating its vision. Communication improves throughout the organization as the vision and strategies are refined. Long-term and short-term performance objectives are linked to the vision and strategies. This linkage enables employees to understand their contribution to the overall organization and aligns employee goals with those of MHB. Individual employees use their scorecards to guide their efforts toward reaching MHB's goals and objectives. MHB managers will periodically review their vision and core competencies and their progress toward achieving them. Managers also have better information for decision making. These actions should lead to improved financial performance.

**Cons:** Implementing a balanced scorecard is expensive and time consuming. If MHB is already operating efficiently, the benefits from implementing the scoreboard may not be as large as the costs. If the vision or understanding of core competencies is inappropriate or inadequate, goals and objectives in the balanced scorecard may not relate to improved financial performance. If targets are unreasonably high or low, employees have no motivation to meet them. If the objectives are not well thought-out and communicated clearly, employees may not understand the objectives or how they relate to overall organizational performance. Measures could be chosen for which no data are available, or the data available are measured incorrectly or with error. Managers may choose performance measures that represent their strengths, rather than making unbiased choices.

---

**REVIEW** Use the exercises in the following boxes in the chapter to review key terms and key techniques, analyze chapter illustrations, improve your learning of new concepts, and practice ethical decision making:

Guide Your Learning 16.1: Wendy's International (p. 636)

Guide Your Learning 16.2: Key Terms (p. 641)

Guide Your Learning 16.3: Royal Philips Electronics (p. 642)

Guide Your Learning 16.4: Community Hospital (p. 650)

Focus on Ethical Decision Making: Accountable Volunteer Organizations (p. 653)

---

## QUESTIONS

**16.1** Explain the differences between financial and nonfinancial performance measures and give two examples of each.

**16.2** Identify four potential perspectives for a balanced scorecard and explain how they are related.

**16.3** Allied Trucking moves produce from farms to markets. Its managers decided to implement a balanced scorecard around the company's vision statement: "We aim to be the industry leader in cost-effective and timely delivery of produce." Provide two potential performance measures for each of the four perspectives for the balanced scorecard for Allied Trucking.

**16.4** Explain what core competencies are. How do they relate to organizational strategies?

**16.5** Suppose that a car dealership decided it would no longer compensate employees with sales commissions, but instead pay a salary with a bonus for high customer satisfaction ratings. What problems would you foresee from the dealership's financial perspective?

**16.6** Describe the implementation process for the balanced scorecard.

**16.7** What is strategic decision making? What role does it play in the balanced scorecard?

**16.8** Search the Web to locate current information about the vision, mission, core values, or similar attributes of **McDonald's** and **Wendy's**. (For hints about where to find this information, go to www.wiley.com/college/eldenburg.) List the similarities and differences between McDonald's and Wendy's vision, mission, and core values.

**16.9** Pick two public companies, go to their Web sites, and identify their major strategies. Pick one of these companies and go to the Web site of a competitor in the same industry. For example, if you chose **Best Buy**, you might go to the Web site of **Circuit City**. Now compare the strategies of both companies listing any similarities and differences. (For hints about where to find this type of information, go to www.wiley.com/college/eldenburg.)

**16.10** Explain why demand may increase for relevant and useful information in the future. What professional skills will help you meet that need?

**16.11** Explain why you will need to continuously learn new accounting techniques, as well as develop in-depth knowledge about industries within which you work.

## EXERCISES

**16.12**
**Q2, Q3**

**Balanced scorecard measures for financial perspective** Following is financial information for last period about China Express, a regional company with a number of fast-food stores:

| | |
|---|---|
| Revenue from operations | $10,450,200 |
| Operating costs | 9,927,690 |
| After-tax profits | 391,883 |
| Cost of capital | 12% |
| Required rate of return | 15% |
| Average assets | $4,180,080 |

**REQUIRED:**  ❶ Describe and calculate several measures that could be used for the financial perspective.

**16.13**
**Q2**

**Financial and nonfinancial measures** Managers increasingly use a mixture of financial and nonfinancial measures for organizational performance.

**REQUIRED:**  In the following list of performance measures, identify those that are financial (F) and those that are nonfinancial (N).

___ **A.** Customer satisfaction ratings
___ **B.** Market share
___ **C.** Operating margin
___ **D.** Return on sales
___ **E.** Annual average purchase amount per customer
___ **F.** Defect rate
___ **G.** Normal spoilage
___ **H.** Labor efficiency variance
___ **I.** Number of new products developed annually
___ **J.** Revenues from new products introduced this year

**16.14**
**Q2, Q3, Q4**

**Balanced scorecard measures for customer perspective** Flowing Wells High School is in the process of developing a balanced scorecard. The administrators decided that their customers are parents and future employers of their students. They believe the students are their products.

**REQUIRED:**  ❷ Discuss whether each of the following potential measures would be useful for the customer perspective in the balanced scorecard.

**A.** Parent ratings of satisfaction with the high school curriculum
**B.** Graduation rate
**C.** Percentage of students employed during the summer after graduation
**D.** Employer satisfaction ratings for Flowing Wells High School graduates
**E.** Monthly earnings of graduates
**F.** Number of graduates attending classes beyond high school
**G.** Cost per student per year
**H.** Number of classes per student per semester
**I.** Average number of college credit hours completed per teacher

**16.15**
**Q2, Q3**

**Learning and growth perspective** Suppose Markman Corporation, a large pharmaceutical company, is concerned about the ability of its research and development department to develop profitable new prescription drugs. Once a drug has been developed and patented, it takes 9 to 12 years to meet all of the **Food and Drug Administration (FDA)** requirements. According to the **U.S. Congressional Budget Office**, the company can then market the drug for about 11.5 years, on average, before the patent expires.[26] Then competitors produce generic drugs. Employees currently participate in profit-sharing plans, but the company wants to give additional bonuses to improve performance. Markman decided to implement a balanced scorecard approach.

**REQUIRED:**  ❶ **A.** Explain why monitoring and rewarding nonfinancial performance might be particularly important for Markman.
❶ **B.** List one objective for Markman's learning and growth perspective.
❶ **C.** List two performance measures for the objective you picked in part (B).

---

[26]"How Increased Competition from Generic Drugs Has Affected Prices and Returns in the Pharmaceutical Industry," Congressional Budget Office (1998).

**16.16** **Balanced scorecard measures for four perspectives** Part of the process for developing a balanced scorecard is to identify one or more measures for each perspective.

Q2, Q3, Q4

REQUIRED: Categorize each of the following potential balanced scorecard measures according to the following perspectives:

F   Financial

C   Customer

I    Internal business process

L   Learning and growth

___ A. Percentage of customer orders delivered on time
___ B. Ratio of research and development cost to number of new products developed
___ C. Economic value added (EVA)
___ D. Number of hours of employee training
___ E. Direct labor price variance
___ F. Market share
___ G. Percentage of customer orders delivered without error
___ H. Days in accounts receivables
___ I. Throughput time
___ J. Direct materials efficiency variance
___ K. Asset turnover
___ L. Employee retention rate
___ M. Percentage of bad debts collected
___ N. Customer satisfaction ratings
___ O. Number of degrees and certificates held per employee or department
___ P. Percentage of purchase orders that are error free

**16.17** **Strategic plans, balanced scorecard measures for not-for-profit organization** Suppose you have been invited by a classmate to help found a new not-for-profit organization named Students Care. The organization's purpose is to provide scholarship money for children in Africa who have become orphans because of the AIDS epidemic. The organization will operate only on campus, and the target donors are students. Suppose Oprah Winfrey has offered to coordinate distribution of the scholarship funds to needy students, but wants to see a business plan for the organization that describes the organizational vision and lists the core competencies, strategies, and operating plans.

Q1, Q2, Q3, Q4

REQUIRED: 
① A. Explain what each item on Oprah's list means. For each item, provide a possible example for Students Care.
② B. Consider the perspective of internal business processes. Your classmate wants to measure the number of hours per week that volunteers spend collecting donations, but you believe it should be dollars collected per volunteer hour spent in collection, measured on a weekly basis. Give one advantage and one disadvantage for each measure.
② C. You have had difficulty determining a measure of learning and growth, but a campus association recently organized a series of short workshops on improving student fundraising activities, as well as other aspects of governing student organizations. Discuss the advantages and disadvantages of using the number of Students Care volunteers attending workshops as a measure for this perspective.

**16.18** **Balanced scorecard measures for cashier's office** Refer to the **University of California, Berkeley**, cashier's office balanced scorecard in Exhibit 16.11.

Q2, Q3, Q4

REQUIRED: 
① A. Describe how each of the following measures might be calculated (be specific about the data used):
   **1.** Injury/illness rate
   **2.** Expenditures as a percent of budget
   **3.** Percent of days that the office balanced within $1
   **4.** Customer satisfaction survey
② B. Assuming the type of data and calculation you described in part (A), provide one advantage and one disadvantage for each measure.

**16.19**
Q2, Q3, Q4

**Balanced scorecard measures for physical plant office** Refer to the **University of California, Berkeley**, physical plant director's office (and others) balanced scorecard in Exhibit 16.11.

REQUIRED:   ① **A.** Describe how each of the following measures might be calculated (be specific about the data used):
   **1.** Injury/illness rate
   **2.** Turnover rate
   **3.** Evaluation of training sessions
② **B.** Assuming the type of data and calculation you described in part (A), discuss how well each measure relates to the stated objective.

**16.20**
Q2, Q3

**Balanced scorecard perspectives, performance objectives, and measures** Perspectives, performance objectives, and potential performance measures for the balanced scorecard at Holiday Resorts are as follows:

Perspectives
   I. Financial
   II. Customer
   III. Internal business
   IV. Learning and growth

Performance objectives
   a. Reduce housekeeping costs
   b. Improve the quality of and results from advertising campaigns
   c. Decrease vacancy rate during the off-season
   d. Increase number of return customers
   e. Increase overall profits
   f. Increase the use of Web-based reservations
   g. Retain high-quality employees
   h. Increase the number of activities available to customers
   i. Improve the quality of stay for vacationers
   j. Provide employee training in quality customer service
   k. Reduce error rate in reservations

Potential performance measures
   1. Operating margin
   2. Customer complaint rate
   3. Survey customers at check-in about how they first heard about the resorts
   4. Housekeeping cost per room
   5. Number of employee hours spent in training
   6. Error rate in reservation process
   7. Percentage of reservations made using the Web site
   8. Customer surveys about satisfaction and quality
   9. Employee turnover rates
   10. Number of activities per resort that are available to customers
   11. Percentage and number of return customers
   12. Number of hours of employee training offered
   13. Vacancy rates
   14. Customer focus groups inquiring about quality and potential success of advertising
   15. Number of suggestions that improve quality of service

REQUIRED:   ① **A.** For each perspective (I–IV), identify at least one appropriate performance objective (a–k).
① **B.** For each performance objective (a–k), identify at least one appropriate performance measure (1–15).

**16.21**
Q6

**Future direction of accounting information** Think about the type of work you will perform in your future career.

REQUIRED:

**①A.** Give examples of the types of financial and nonfinancial information you will probably use in your work.

**①B.** List several methods you could use to produce information that will help predict future operations for your employer or for clients.

**②C.** What types of continuous learning do you foresee in your career?

**②D.** Explain why you may need to use creative or innovative ideas in your career.

# PROBLEMS

**16.22**
Q3, Q4

**Balanced scorecard and implementation** Mark Moreland, a dentist, decided to join a small group of dentists so that he no longer has to be on call every night. Practice members share the responsibility of emergencies with other members of the group. In the past, Mark differentiated his practice by specializing in the treatment of families with children. None of the other dentists specialize in families, but all of them treat some children. Mark's son just finished an accounting degree and recommended that the dental group consider implementing a balanced scorecard as they develop the policies and practices for the new group.

REQUIRED:

**②A.** Explain what each of the four perspectives of the balanced scorecard mean in the context of a dental group.

**②B.** Recommend several methods the group could use to assess a performance objective of patient satisfaction.

**②C.** Recommend two measures for each of the four perspectives for the dental group. Explain your recommendations.

**16.23**
Q2, Q3, Q4

**Balanced scorecard, financial and nonfinancial measures** Dyggur Equipment manufactures and sells heavy equipment used in construction and mining. Customers are contractors who want reliable equipment at a low cost. The firm's strategy is to provide reliable products at a price lower than its competitors. Management wants to emphasize quick delivery and quick turnaround when equipment needs repair or service so that contractors are not without their equipment often or for long. Dyggur is considering the following performance measures for use in its balanced scorecard.

REQUIRED:

Categorize each of the following potential balanced scorecard measures as follows:

F  Financial

C  Customer

I  Internal business process

L  Learning and growth

___ **A.** Manufacturing cycle time per product
___ **B.** Market share
___ **C.** Average ratings on customer satisfaction surveys
___ **D.** Average cost per unit
___ **E.** Economic value added
___ **F.** Percent of receivables collected
___ **G.** Dollar value of warranty work
___ **H.** Time between order and delivery
___ **I.** Time it takes to repair returned equipment
___ **J.** Number of focus groups for new products
___ **K.** Number of new uses for current products
___ **L.** Number of times new technology is applied to current products
___ **M.** Number of product change suggestions from sales
___ **N.** Number of engineering change orders to improve manufacturing cycle
___ **O.** Revenue growth
___ **P.** Employee training hours
___ **Q.** Number of quality improvement suggestions from employees

*(continued)*

____ **R.** Number of new customers
____ **S.** Number of repeat customers
____ **T.** Employee turnover rate
____ **U.** Defect rates for manufacturing production
____ **V.** Percentage of error free-rates in:
    ____ **1.** Purchasing
    ____ **2.** Billing
    ____ **3.** Customer record-keeping

**16.24**
Q1, Q2, Q4

**Strategy, balanced scorecard measures and process** Refer to the information in Problem 16.23. Dyggur Equipment wants to offer weekend servicing of heavy equipment. None of its competitors offer this service, and management believes this service will bring in new business and help retain current customers.

REQUIRED:

**A.** List several advantages and disadvantages of this strategy.

**B.** List one financial and two nonfinancial performance measures that could be used to monitor the success of this plan.

**C.** Suppose the managers decide to launch this new service. At the end of the first year of operating weekend service, performance is evaluated by gathering and analyzing measures such as those identified in part (B). How can this information be used to improve performance for the next period?

**16.25**
Q1, Q2, Q3, Q4

**Mission statement, strategy, balanced scorecard implementation** Squeezers Juice and Tea Company manufactures organic juices and chai teas that are sold at whole foods stores. Several of its products have been featured in movies because the company's products are popular with celebrities. The owners and employees value organic products and innovative combinations of juices and teas with outstanding taste. Several employees have found sources of unusual ingredients from organic farmers around the world. The ingredients are more expensive than those used by other juice manufacturers. Although Squeezers cannot set unrealistically high prices, it focuses on high quality. Demand for the company's products is stable, even though it sets the highest prices for juices in its market.

Recently, the costs of several unusual ingredients increased because of weather conditions. The owner is concerned that increasing prices any more could reduce demand. She has taken a business workshop and learned about the balanced scorecard. She wants to incorporate a balanced scorecard at Squeezers.

REQUIRED:

**A.** Draft a potential mission statement for Squeezers. Explain how you decided what should be included in the statement and how it should be worded.

**B.** Explain the company's business strategy and core competencies.

**C.** Identify several performance objectives for each of the four perspectives.

**D.** Select two performance objectives for each of the four perspectives, and identify a potential performance measure for each. Explain your choices.

**E.** Describe possible methods to collect the data needed for each of the performance measures in part (D). For example, what existing information might be available? What new record-keeping might be required? Would the company need to develop surveys?

**16.26**
Q2, Q3, Q4

**Balanced scorecard measures** China Express owns a number of stores that sell fast food. As part of its compensation packages, China Express provides employees with bonuses based on customer satisfaction surveys. Recent analysis of the data shows a positive correlation between survey ratings and sales; that is, as customer satisfaction increases, sales increase. However, at a certain point in this trend, sales plateau even though the ratings continue to increase. In addition, increasing customer satisfaction causes costs to also increase because more time is spent with each customer and more employees are on hand to help with food preparation and cashiering to reduce the time that customers wait for their food to be prepared. Other factors that appear to affect customer satisfaction are the general cleanliness of the store and the attitudes of the cashiers as they provide customer service. A factor that strongly affects sales at each store is its county health department rating. These ratings are published in the local daily newspaper. When a store has a low rating, sales at that outlet drop off until publication of an improved rating occurs. The owner wants to add one or more financial performance measures to the bonus package so that employees will earn more money when customer satisfaction increases at the same time that financial performance is also increasing.

REQUIRED:

**❷ A.** Describe advantages and disadvantages of using a combination of performance measures reflecting the customer and financial perspectives.

**❷ B.** Management would like to add other customer-related measures and is considering replacing survey satisfaction with some other measure. List one potential measure and list at least one advantage and one disadvantage for it.

**❷ C.** List one additional performance measure that could be included in the compensation package. Explain what it is and what it would contribute.

**16.27**
Q1, Q4, Q5
CMA

**Participative strategic planning process and benefits, manager behavior** (Assumes knowledge from management classes) Quantum Computers produces and sells laptop computers. The company is currently deciding whether to continue concentrating on the laptop computer market or to expand by entering the highly competitive computer desktop workstation market.

Most of the management staff has been with Quantum for a long time. Michael Mitchem, Quantum's president, wants his management staff to assist him in Quantum's strategic planning process. Mitchem has scheduled a three-day offsite meeting for the management staff to join together for the company's strategic planning process.

REQUIRED:

**❸ A.** What functional areas should be discussed during the strategic planning process?

**❸ B.** Identify at least six factors to be considered in a thorough strategic planning process that will move a company such as Quantum to another level of product development.

**❶ C.** Identify at least three benefits that Quantum can derive from a participatory strategic planning process.

**❷ D.** Discuss the expected behavior of the managers at Quantum who participate in the three-day offsite strategic planning meeting.

**16.28**
Q3, Q4, Q5

**Balanced scorecard, strengths and weaknesses** Brewster House is a not-for-profit shelter for the homeless. Lately funding has decreased, but the demand for overnight shelter has increased. In cold weather, clients are turned away because the shelter is full. The director believes that the current capacity could be used more efficiently. No one has taken time to analyze the physical layout of the shelter and current use of space. Several rooms are used for storage that could probably be used for temporary housing. The stored boxes need to be sorted and moved. Volunteers currently assign beds and manage overnight housing, because the director is busy with fund-raising. Volunteers work just a few shifts each week, so no one has taken responsibility for coordinating improvements in the services offered. The director is considering whether to implement a balanced scorecard to focus the attention of all volunteers on areas that need improvement.

Brewster receives funds from several sources including a set annual budget from the county and direct donations from supporters. The director develops a budget each year based on expected funding, but she cannot precisely predict donations. The budget is used primarily to justify funding requests submitted to the county.

The director has asked a group of accounting students from the local university to evaluate operations and recommend whether the organization should develop a balanced scorecard. She cannot give bonuses based on the measures, but she wonders whether developing and monitoring performance measures would encourage the volunteers to increase the use of capacity. She also wonders whether some information from the balanced scorecard could be used to show donors the effectiveness of operations.

REQUIRED:

**❷ A.** Describe several potential costs and benefits of the balanced scorecard for this organization.

**❷ B.** Describe one potential measure for each scorecard perspective appropriate for Brewster House. Explain how information for each measure will be collected.

**❸ C.** Prepare a memo to the director that recommends whether Brewster House should adopt a balanced scorecard. In writing the memo, consider what information the director needs from you to help her make a decision.

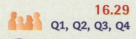

**16.29**
Q1, Q2, Q3, Q4

www.wiley.com/
college/eldenburg

**Strategies and balanced scorecard measures for a country** Brian Henshall, foundation emeritus professor of management at **The University of Auckland**, suggests a number of potential performance measures that could be used to monitor performance for the country of **New Zealand**. Henshall recommends that the country publish measures monthly to gauge progress. He also argues that a discussion of potential performance measures would help citizens define what they want. Ultimately, the measures could be used to monitor the performance of elected officials. Following are some of Henshall's suggestions.

Tangible wealth:

- Gross domestic product (GDP) percent change as a measure of growth
- The ratio of government wealth creation to business wealth creation as a measure of government economic performance
- GDP per person employed and per total number of people in New Zealand as efficiency measures
- New Zealand dollar exchange rate (percentage change for last quarter or last year) as a measure of economic stability
- Number of bankrupt firms to all trading entities as a measure of business stability

Environmental intangible wealth:

- A pollution index that measures degradation of the environment from pollution
- A ratio of protected land relative to total government-owned land
- A ratio of alternative energy resources relative to total energy produced

Physical and social infrastructure:

- Educational expense as a percent of GDP
- Health care expense as a percent of GDP
- Accidents index
- Serious crimes index

Demographics:

- Changes in population growth, year to year
- Growth in education levels
- A demographic index that monitors innovations by diversity of peoples
- Unemployment rates

SOURCE: B. D. Henshall, "Kiwi Scorecard," *New Zealand Management,* 49(6), (July 2002), pp. 15 ff.

REQUIRED:

**A.** Suppose government officials developed an objective to increase the number of college graduates because they believe increased education will lead to increased GDP. Brainstorm and identify several ideas for action plans to carry out this strategy.

**B.** Pick one of your ideas from part (A) and discuss its pros and cons.

**C.** Brainstorm ideas for action plans to increase the number of high school graduates.

**D.** Pick one of your ideas from part (C) and discuss its pros and cons.

**E.** Research information on the Internet to determine appropriate target graduation rates for high school and college levels. (For hints about where to find this information, go to www.wiley/com/college/eldenburg.) Use your research findings to recommend targets for New Zealand. Explain.

**16.30**
Q2, Q3, Q5

**Strategy, balanced scorecard for organization and employee** Mark Hopper owns Dane Champions, a dog kennel that raises champion Great Danes for showing and breeding. His vision is to be the best-known breeder of Great Danes globally. His strategy is to breed and sell dogs from outstanding lineage from the standpoint of both physical health and good-natured temperaments. Following is information about operations over the last year.

| | |
|---|---|
| Number of breedings | 10 |
| Number of puppies | 45 |
| Number of puppies sold | 40 |

| | |
|---|---:|
| Number of puppies returned | 2 |
| Revenue from puppies | $24,000 |
| Kennel operating costs (not including Mark's salary) | $35,000 |
| Travel expenditures | $55,000 |
| Number of trips to dog shows | 20 |
| Winnings from dog shows | $110,000 |
| Number of championships | 17 |
| Number of dogs shown | 4 |
| Puppy owners' average satisfaction rating on a scale of 1 to 5, with 5 as most satisfied | 4.5 |
| Training time to prepare puppies for new homes (total hours) | 14 |
| Training time to prepare dogs for shows (hours per week per dog) | 2 |

**REQUIRED:**

**A.** Is the company's strategy one of cost leadership or product differentiation? Explain.

**② B.** Prepare a simple balanced scorecard with one performance measure for each of the four perspectives for Dane Champions using only the data presented. Explain your choices.

**② C.** Kennel operating costs include the cost of a local high school student who cleans out the kennels every afternoon after school. Mark is considering whether to set up an individual scorecard for the student. He only pays minimum wage, and although the student is fairly slow, the kennels are kept reasonably clean. Mark wonders whether the student would resent being monitored more closely. Describe one reason for using a scorecard with the student and one reason against using it.

**16.31**
**Q2, Q3, Q4**

**Balanced scorecard variances** A large hardware store has used a balanced scorecard for several years. The store's vision is to provide customers with low-cost goods and a high-quality shopping experience. The company's strategy has been to focus on reducing wait time for help on the floor and at the checkout counter. Information for the last two years follows.

| | 2004 | 2005 |
|---|---:|---:|
| Average sale (total revenue/total invoices) | $15 | $12 |
| Average variable cost per sale | $7 | $7 |
| Average customer wait time at counter | 1.5 minutes | 1.5 minutes |
| Average customer wait time for help on the sales floor | 3 minutes | 2 minutes |
| Shipping cost per order | $18 | $15 |
| Total returns | $57,000 | $60,000 |
| Total revenue | $800,000 | $748,000 |
| Total labor cost | $200,000 | $220,000 |
| Utilities cost (electricity and phone) | $2,100 | $2,400 |
| Number of items out of stock | 120 | 180 |
| Employee turnover | 2 | 3 |

**REQUIRED:**

**❶ A.** Classify each performance measure according to one of the four balanced scorecard perspectives.

**② B.** Analyze the change in each performance measure from 2004 to 2005. Give one possible reason for the change.

**② C.** Which performance measures need further investigation? Explain.

**❸ D.** What do the balanced scorecard results suggest about the success of the company's strategy to reduce wait time? Explain.

**❸ E.** When an organization focuses on one strategy, problems sometimes arise in other areas. Do the balanced scorecard results provide evidence of possible deterioration in any operational areas? Explain.

**☆ 16.32**
**Q2, Q3, Q4, Q5**

**Evaluate balanced scorecard design** Frieda's Fizz brews specialty soft drinks, including root beer and other flavors. Its vision is "To proudly produce and sell extraordinarily smooth, rich, and delicious soft drinks to satisfy kids of all ages." The company has a reputation for high quality and unique flavor, enabling it to sell soft drinks at a premium price to gourmet grocery stores in the New York area. The company's managers plan to expand the business to other geographic regions, but they want to ensure that they maintain high quality as the company grows. They have decided to implement a balanced scorecard, and they have chosen the following balanced scorecard measures:

**Financial Perspective**
1. Breakdown of manufacturing cost per case: ingredients, direct labor, packaging materials, and overhead
2. Operating profit per case
3. Return on investment

**Customer Perspective**
4. Number of customer complaints relating to taste, freshness, package integrity, appearance, and foreign objects
5. Quality index (an internal measure of manufacturing quality, including microbiology and chemistry)
6. Percentage sales growth

**Internal Business Process Perspective**
7. Ratio of plant production hours to total available time
8. Throughput (number of cases packaged)
9. Waste and scrap as a percent of total production cost

**Learning and Growth Perspective**
10. Number of work-related injuries
11. Number of training hours per employee
12. Number of community volunteer hours per employee

**REQUIRED:**
**ANALYZE**
**INFORMATION**

The following questions will help you analyze the information for this problem. Do not turn in your answers to these questions unless your professor asks you to do so.

**A.** Explain why uncertainties exist about the best balanced scorecard measures for Frieda's Fizz. (Do NOT discuss any of the measures already listed. Instead, focus on why any set of measures might not provide ideal information and on why the managers cannot know with certainty which set of measures is best.)

**B.** For the balanced scorecard perspective:
   **1.** Describe the strengths and weaknesses of the measures chosen for that category.
   **2.** Reach a conclusion about the reasonableness of the set of balanced scorecard measures for that category.

**C.** What are the pros and cons of implementing a balanced scorecard?

**D.** How valuable do you think the balanced scorecard will be in helping the managers of Frieda's Fizz meet its vision? Explain.

**REQUIRED:**
**WRITTEN**
**ASSIGNMENT**

The managers of Frieda's Fizz want your evaluation of their proposed balanced scorecard. Turn in your answer to the following.

**E.** Use the information you learned from the preceding analyses to write a memo to the managers presenting your evaluation of (1) whether they should adopt a balanced scorecard, and (2) the proposed balanced scorecard design. As you write the memo, consider what information the managers will need from you to help them make a final decision.

**16.33**
**Q1, Q2**
ETHICS

**Corporate social responsibility, outsourcing, monitoring measures** To reduce costs and focus on core competencies, U.S. companies increasingly outsource manufacturing activities to vendors in countries having low labor costs such as China, India, Thailand, Indonesia, and Mexico.

Certain activists claim that this practice is socially irresponsible. They claim that numerous factory problems in low-cost countries include excessive work hours, poverty wages, toxic gas releases, and harassment of union organizers (e.g., Connor, 2001; The NikeWatch Campaign). Such conditions have prompted individuals and organizations to reconsider their purchasing habits and policies. For example, during 2002 the **Minneapolis Board of Education** adopted a "sweat-free" purchasing policy that was promoted by student activists (Plimpton, 2003).

Activist groups sometimes target individual companies to publicize outsourcer working conditions. Since 1995, **Nike** has been criticized for human rights abuses, labor exploitation, and environmental damage by companies that manufacture its athletic shoes and apparel. Nike outsources manufacturing to more than 900 factories in more than 50 countries (www.nike.com/nikebiz), but most of its manufacturing is done in a handful of low-cost countries. Several groups recommend that consumers should boycott Nike products until its outsource factories meet acceptable standards (Connor, 2001; The NikeWatch Campaign).

Nike has actively worked to address concerns about worker conditions in its outsource factories. Its manufacturing code of conduct has been in place since 1992, and the following mission statement for its workers and factories is posted on its Web site:

*Mission: To make responsible sourcing\* a business reality that enhances workers' lives.*
\*Through compliance, partnerships and outreach

The company established a set of goals to improve working conditions and instituted monitoring practices to evaluate factory compliance. Nike now considers compliance issues before placing production orders, and it includes compliance monitoring costs in its purchasing decision process. It conducts audits of the manufacturing facilities and implements action plans to resolve issues related to health and safety, pay and benefits, terms of work, and management–worker relations (www.nike.com/nikebiz).

During 2004, controversy remained about whether Nike had done enough to improve worker conditions. Nike's managers asserted that they had resolved problems with conditions in outsource factories. However, activists contended that the problems persisted. Nike had been targeted by these groups partly because it operated in an industry that had widespread labor abuse, it was the largest sportswear maker in the world, and it had high profits. They argued that Nike could afford to pay more to its outsource partners to improve worker pay and factory conditions. They hoped that Nike would change its policies, placing greater pressure on other companies to take similar actions (The NikeWatch Campaign, 2004). On the other hand, some people argued that boycotts against companies such as Nike caused more harm than good; workers who were already poor often lost their jobs, and unionization efforts and other improvements were hindered (Connor, 2001). It was also difficult for companies to adequately monitor working conditions at outsource locations. Workers were often afraid to talk with inspectors, and they sometimes provided inaccurate information. For example, they sometimes erroneously said that they were not paid overtime because they did not understand how their pay was calculated (*Economist.com,* 1999).

SOURCES: "Just Stop It," The NikeWatch Campaign, available at www.caa.org.au/campaigns/nike; T. Connor, "Still Waiting for Nike to Respect the Right to Organize," *Global Exchange,* June 28, 2001, available at www.corpwatch.org/campaigns/PRT.jsp?articleid=619; B. Plimpton, "Sweat-Free School Purchasing Resolutions: A New Trend?" *Special to CorpWatch,* February 6, 2003, available at www.corpwatch.org/issues/PRT.jsp?articleid=5488; "Responsibility" and "Workers & Factories" available at www.nike.com/nikebiz; and "Sweatshop Wars," *Economist.com,* February 25, 1999.

**REQUIRED:**

❶ **A.** Describe whether and how corporate social responsibility (i.e., business practices related to human rights, labor standards, and the environment) affects your decisions as a consumer.

❶ **B.** Is it possible for you to know the conditions under which the products you purchase are produced? Why or why not?

❶ **C.** Is it possible for managers of companies such as Nike to know with certainty that their outsource partners comply with agreed-upon working conditions? Why or why not?

❷ **D.** What does it mean for Nike to include compliance monitoring costs in its purchasing decision process?

❷ **E.** Identify and explain four measures that a company such as Nike could use to monitor worker conditions in outsource partners. For each measure, describe how the company might collect reliable data.

❸ **F.** How should companies such as Nike weigh corporate social responsibility and profits when deciding whether or how to outsource manufacturing? Describe the values you use in drawing your conclusions.

# BUILD YOUR PROFESSIONAL COMPETENCIES

**16.34**
Q1, Q2, Q3, Q4, Q5, Q6

**Focus on Professional Competency: Strategic/Critical Thinking** *Strategic planning, SWOT analysis, continuous improvement* Review the following definition and elements for the Strategic/Critical Thinking competency.[27]

**DEFINITION:** *Critical thinking encompasses the ability to link data, knowledge, and insight together from various disciplines to provide information for decision-making. Being in tune with the "big picture" perspective is a necessary component for success. Individuals entering the accounting profession should be able to communicate to others the vision, strategy, goals, and culture of organizations.*

## ELEMENTS FOR THIS COMPETENCY INCLUDE

| Level 1 | Level 2 | Level 3 | Level 4 |
|---|---|---|---|
| 1. Articulates the principles of the strategic planning process<br><br>2. Identifies and gathers data from a wide variety of sources for decision-making<br><br>3. Identifies uncertainties about an organization's strengths, weaknesses, opportunities, and threats | 4. Transfers knowledge from one situation to another<br><br>5. Analyzes strategic information (e.g., market share, customer satisfaction, competitor actions, product innovation, etc.) | 6. Considers strengths, weaknesses, opportunities, and threats in reaching conclusions | 7. Develops, monitors, implements, and transforms business strategies over time |

**REQUIRED:**

**❶ A.** Focus on competency element 1, which requires accountants to understand the process of strategic planning. Refer to Exhibit 16.1. Explain the purpose of each of the steps in the management decision process.

**B.** Focus on competency elements 3, 5, and 6, which address the ability to analyze an organization's strengths, weaknesses, opportunities, and threats. Answer the following questions:

**❷ 1.** Explain why uncertainties about an organization's strengths, weaknesses, opportunities, and threats lead to uncertainties about the organization's core competencies and strategies.

**❷ 2.** Explain the role of strategic information in:
  **a.** Identifying an organization's core competencies.
  **b.** Choosing strategies.
  **c.** Choosing measures for a balanced scorecard.

**❷ C.** Focus on competency element 2, which addresses the use of data in strategic decision making. Explain why the use of both financial and nonfinancial measures is important for evaluating an organization's performance.

**D.** Focus on competency elements 4 and 7, which relate to improvement of organizational performance over time. Answer the following questions:

**❹ 1.** Explain the purpose and importance of the feedback loops in Exhibit 16.1, Exhibit 16.4, and Exhibit 16.9.

**❹ 2.** Explain why the process of developing a balanced scorecard is never complete.

**16.35**
Q1, Q3, Q5

**Integrating Across the Curriculum: Management and Marketing** *SWOT analysis* A common business analysis technique is a SWOT analysis, or analysis of an organization's **S**trengths, **W**eaknesses, **O**pportunities, and **T**hreats. In marketing, a SWOT analysis is often used to decide whether to launch a new product or to identify ways to improve an existing product. In management, SWOT analyses might be used to assist managers in identifying viable strategies.

Review the information about **Wal-Mart** provided at the beginning of Chapter 16.

---

[27]The definition and elements are reprinted with permission from AICPA; Copyright © 1978–2000 & 2003 by American Institute of Certified Public Accountants. The AICPA's Core Competency Framework can be accessed at eca.aicpaservices.org.

**REQUIRED:**  ❷ **A.** What appear to be Wal-Mart's strengths relative to competitors (i.e., its core competencies)?

❷ **B.** One of the reasons Wal-Mart is successful is that it takes advantage of its competitors' weaknesses. Suppose you work for a family-owned variety store in a town where Wal-Mart is currently building a store. What are your company's weaknesses relative to Wal-Mart?

❷ **C.** An organization's opportunities are identified by looking at the external environment and discovering potential new markets, technologies, or other prospects. What types of opportunities does Wal-Mart currently appear to be taking advantage of?

❷ **D.** What appear to be major threats to Wal-Mart's future success?

❷ **E.** Discuss how a balanced scorecard can assist an organization in addressing its strengths, weaknesses, opportunities, and threats.

# Glossary

Note: Numbers in parentheses refer to the page on which the term is found. **Bolded** page numbers refer to key terms.

**Abnormal spoilage.** Spoilage that is not part of normal operations. (**194, 235**)

**Absorption costing.** All production costs, including direct materials, direct labor, and manufacturing overhead, are assigned to inventory as product costs. (**551**)

**Accounting system.** Computerized or manual structure of procedures and records that document organizational performance.

**Accrual accounting rate of return.** Capital budgeting method that measures the expected increase in average annual operating income as a percent of the initial increase in investment. (**478**)

**Activity.** A type of task or function performed in an organization. (**260**)

**Activity-based budgeting.** Uses activity cost pools and their related cost drivers to anticipate the costs for individual activities. (**387**)

**Activity-based costing (ABC).** Process of assigning overhead costs to specific activities in a manufacturing or service delivery process. (**260**)

**Activity-based management.** Process of using ABC information to evaluate the costs and benefits of production and internal support activities and to identify and implement opportunities for improvements in profitability, efficiency, and quality within an organization. (**270**)

**Activity-based transfer prices.** Cost-based transfer price based on unit-level, batch-level, and possibly some product-level costs for products transferred, plus an annual fixed fee that is a portion of the facility-level costs. (**609**)

**Actual allocation rate.** Allocation rate calculated by dividing actual overhead cost by the actual quantity of the allocation base. (**181, 316, 551**)

**Actual costing.** Method for allocating overhead costs using the actual allocation rate and actual quantity of the allocation base. (**182**)

**Actual operations.** The various actions taken and results achieved over a period of time, including customer orders received, revenues earned, number of employees hired, costs incurred, units of goods or services produced, cash received and paid, etc. Data about actual operations are collected and measured by the organization's information system and then used to monitor and motivate performance. (**7, 631**)

**Adjusted coefficient of determination.** See *adjusted R-square.*

**Adjusted R-square.** Reflects an estimate of the percent of variation in the dependent variable that is explained by the independent variable(s) in regression analysis. When estimating a cost function, the percent of cost that is explained by the cost driver(s). (**57**)

**After-tax profit (loss).** In general, revenues minus expenses and income taxes. Under GAAP, all revenues and gains minus all expenses, losses, and income taxes. (88)

**Agency costs.** Costs that arise when *agents* fail to act in the interest of *principals*. (**591**)

**Agency theory.** Analytical framework that examines potential conflicts and suggests solutions for incentive problems between *principals* and *agents*. (**591**)

**Agent.** In agency theory, a person who acts on behalf of others (called principals). For example, managers are agents for shareholders, and employees are agents for managers. (**591**)

**AICPA Core Competency Framework.** Published list of core competencies with their definitions and elements, considered critical for success of entry-level accountants. (23)

**Algebraic method.** See *reciprocal method.*

**Allocated overhead.** Amount of overhead cost allocated to a cost object. May be based on an actual or estimated allocation rate times an actual or estimated volume of the allocation base. Also see *normal costing* and *actual costing.* (180)

**Allocating costs.** Assigning indirect costs to a cost object. Costs are allocated if they cannot be traced to a cost object. (61, 178, 217, 259, 301, 345)

**Allocation base.** Measure of activity, preferably a cost driver, used to allocate costs to a cost object. Examples include number of units, labor hours, labor costs, machine hours, number of parts, and sales. (**181**, 259, 303)

**Allocation rate.** Dollar amount per unit of allocation base used to allocate overhead to each cost object. (181)

**Alpha coefficient.** See *intercept.*

**American Institute of Certified Public Accountants (AICPA).** Professional organization for CPAs in the United States. (23)

**Analysis at the account level.** Method for estimating a cost function by reviewing the pattern of past costs in the accounting system and using knowledge of operations to classify the cost as variable, fixed, or mixed. (**50**)

**Application base.** See *allocation base.*

**Applied overhead.** See *allocated overhead.*

**Applying costs.** See *allocating costs.*

**Appraisal activities.** Quality-related tasks or functions undertaken to identify defective units of goods or services. (274)

**Appraisal costs.** Costs of quality for *appraisal activities.*

**Asset turnover.** See *investment turnover.*

**Assigning costs.** Practice of measuring costs for a cost object; includes tracing direct costs and allocating indirect costs. (178, 217, 259, 301, 345)

**Assumption.** Hypothesis, belief, or conjecture made when something is not known with certainty. In cost accounting, assumptions exist for the various quantitative analysis techniques (e.g., CVP or regression analysis) and general decision rules (e.g., for product emphasis decisions). People also make assumptions to create cost accounting information (e.g., linear cost function). Poor quality assumptions lead to poor quality information and decisions. Failure to objectively analyze assumptions can lead to biases. (17, 49, 99, 148)

**Attainable standards.** Standards that are set at achievable levels, but without much slack. Contrast with *ideal standards*. (418)

**Average cost.** Arithmetic mean cost, computed as total costs (TC) divided by the quantity (Q) of activity or production. (62)

**Average rate of return.** See *accrual accounting rate of return*.

**Avoidable cash flows.** See *relevant cash flows*.

**Balanced scorecard.** A formal approach used to help organizations translate their vision into objectives that can be measured and monitored using both financial and non-financial performance measures. (**9**, **636**)

**Batch-level activities.** Tasks or functions undertaken for a collection of goods or services that are processed as a group. Batch-level costs do not relate to the number of units in the batch, but instead to the number of batches processed. (**263**)

**Benchmark.** A measurement or standard that serves as a reference for evaluating performance. (380, 604)

**Best-case scenario or case.** Sensitivity analysis using the most positive (but still reasonable) set of assumptions. Contrast with *worst-case scenario*. (60)

**Beta coefficient.** See *slope coefficient*.

**Biased information.** Unfair or distorted data that inhibit high-quality decision making. (15)

**Biases.** Preconceived notions that are adopted without careful thought; cause decision makers to ignore weaknesses in their preferred course of action and prevent them from adequately exploring alternatives. (**4**)

**Binding constraint.** A resource, such as the number of hours available for inspection, which limits production at the optimal solution of a linear programming problem. (**144**)

**Bottleneck.** Any process, part, or machine that limits overall capacity. (**142**)

**Bottom-up budgeting.** See *participative budgeting*.

**Breakeven point.** Level of operating activity at which revenues cover all fixed and variable costs and there is no profit. (**91**)

**Budget.** A formalized financial plan for operations of an organization for a specified future period. Used to assign decision rights to individual managers within an organization. (373)

**Budget adjustments for performance evaluation.** Modifications made when budgets are used to measure managers' performance. (385)

**Budget assumptions.** Plans and predictions about next period's operating activities used to develop a master budget. (374)

**Budget cycle.** Series of steps used to develop and use budgets. (373)

**Budget variance.** Difference between budgeted and actual results (e.g., revenues, expenses, or cash flows). (**380**, 417)

**Budgetary slack.** Practice of intentionally setting revenue budgets too low and cost budgets too high. (**384**)

**Budgeted application rate.** See *estimated allocation rate*.

**Budgeted capacity.** Anticipated use of capacity over the next period based on management's planned operations. (**559**)

**Budgeted financial statements.** Forecasts of the future income statement, balance sheet, and cash flows, given an organization's master budget. (374)

**Budgeted indirect cost rate.** See *estimated allocation rate*.

**Business intelligence (BI).** Refers to an information system that supports management efforts to save costs and improve profitability through the use and communication of information within an organization and with external parties such as customers and suppliers. (11)

**Business segment decision.** See *keep or drop decision*.

**By-product.** Joint product that has low sales value compared to other joint products. Contrast with *main product*. (**341**)

**Capacity.** In cost accounting, usually refers to the volume of goods or services possible, given existing investments in production assets. (558)

**Capacity utilization.** Relative amount of productive capacity used. (437)

**Capital budget.** Budget for long-term investment. (374)

**Capital budgeting.** Process for choosing among investment opportunities that have cash flows occurring over a number of years. (**467**)

**Cash budget.** Budget for cash receipts, cash disbursements, and short-term financing, including the expected amounts and timing of cash flows. (**374**)

**Cause-and-effect relationship.** Refers to the influence of an activity on cost; considered when classifying a cost as direct or indirect and when evaluating potential cost drivers. (39, 44, 276, 303)

**Centralized decision making.** Decision-making authority lies within the top levels of management. Contrast with *decentralized decision making*. (593)

**Certified Management Accountant (CMA).** Internationally recognized designation offered by the IMA to individuals who meet educational and work experience requirements and pass a four-part examination covering business analysis, management accounting and reporting, strategic management, and business applications. (9)

**Choice criterion.** See *objective function*.

**Collusive pricing.** Illegal practice by two or more organizations that conspire to set prices above a competitive price. (**532**)

**Committed cost.** Cost that remains fixed regardless of activity levels. (41, **278**)

**Commodity price.** Product selling price under conditions of no product differentiation and many competitors. Contrast with *monopoly price*. (526)

**Common cost.** Cost for a resource that is shared among two or more departments, activities, products, or other cost objects. Also called *indirect cost, overhead cost,* or *joint cost.* (299)

**Competitive advantage.** See *organizational core competencies.*

**Constant (in dollar amount) cost.** See *fixed cost.*

**Constant gross margin NRV method.** Allocates joint costs so that the gross margin percentage for each main product is identical. (344)

**Constrained resource.** See *constraint.*

**Constraint.** Limit that restricts an organization's ability to provide enough products (goods or services) to satisfy demand. Also called *constrained* or *scarce resource.* (141)

**Continuous budgets.** See *rolling budget.*

**Contribution margin.** Total revenues minus total variable costs. (89)

**Contribution margin budget variance.** Difference between standard contribution margin based on static budget and actual contribution margin. (441)

**Contribution margin per unit.** Selling price per unit minus variable cost per unit. (89)

**Contribution margin percentage.** See *contribution margin ratio.*

**Contribution margin ratio.** Percent by which the selling price (or revenue) per unit exceeds the variable cost per unit, or contribution margin as a percent of revenue. (90)

**Contribution margin sales mix variance.** Difference in contribution margin caused by a difference between standard and actual sales mix, given the standard contribution margin and actual quantity of units sold. (442)

**Contribution margin sales quantity variance.** Difference in contribution margin caused by a difference between standard and actual quantities sold, given the standard contribution margins and standard sales mix. (443)

**Contribution margin sales volume variance.** Difference in contribution margin caused by differences between standard and actual sales volumes, times the standard contribution margins. (442)

**Contribution margin variance.** Difference in contribution margin caused by differences in contribution margin per unit, given the actual volume of sales. (442)

**Conversion costs.** Direct labor and production overhead costs. (217)

**Core competencies.** See *organizational core competencies.*

**Core values statement.** Summary of the beliefs that define the organization's culture. (5, 622)

**Cost accounting.** According to IMA Statement on Management Accounting No. 2, "a technique or method for determining the cost of a project, process, or thing," with costs determined through "direct measurement, arbitrary assignment, or systematic and rational allocation." (8)

**Cost Accounting Standards Board (CASB).** Independent board within the Office of Management and Budget's Office of Federal Procurement Policy with authority to establish cost accounting standards for U.S. government contractors. (318)

**Cost allocation.** See *allocating costs.*

**Cost allocation base.** See *allocation base.*

**Cost application base.** See *allocation base.*

**Cost assignment.** See *assigning costs.*

**Cost-based contract.** Contract in which the vendor is reimbursed based on the costs incurred to produce the good or service. Contrast with *fixed-price contract.* (317)

**Cost-based price.** Product selling price determined by adding a markup to some calculation of the product's cost. Requires selection of a cost base and a markup rate. (525)

**Cost-based transfer price.** Transfer price based on the cost of the goods or services transferred. (609)

**Cost behavior.** The variation in costs relative to the variation in an organization's activities. (41)

**Cost-benefit analysis or cost-benefit trade-offs.** Investigation to determine whether the benefits exceed the costs for a proposed course of action. Often used to evaluate whether to add features or complexity to a cost accounting system. (12, 63, 191, 241, 276, 302, 418, 656)

**Cost center.** Responsibility center in which managers are accountable for producing goods or services efficiently (minimizing costs for a certain level of output, or maximizing output for a certain level of cost). (595)

**Cost driver.** Some input or activity that causes changes in total cost for a cost object. (44, 265)

**Cost function.** Algebraic representation of the total cost of a cost object over a relevant range of activity, represented as $TC = F + V \times Q$. (44)

**Cost hierarchy.** General categories of activities based on different levels of operations. Used to identify activities and assign costs in an ABC system. (261)

**Cost leadership.** Strategy to gain competitive advantage by maintaining lower costs than competitors. (633)

**Cost management.** See *strategic cost management.*

**Cost object.** A thing or activity for which we measure costs, such as a particular production activity, an individual product, a product line, a project, an individual or group of customers, a department, and even the entire company. (39)

**Cost of capital.** See *weighted average cost of capital.*

**Cost of quality.** Costs incurred to insure high quality and/or the actual and opportunity costs from problems with poor quality. Also see *quality-related activities.* (194, 239, 273)

**Cost pool.** Group of individual costs that are accumulated in the accounting system for a particular purpose. Examples include overhead costs or department-level process costs. (180, 259)

**Cost tracing.** See *tracing costs.*

**Cost-volume-profit (CVP) analysis.** Technique that examines changes in profits in response to changes in sales volumes, costs, and prices. Used to identify the levels of operating activity needed to avoid losses, achieve targeted profits, plan future operations, and monitor organizational performance. (89, 381)

**Cost-volume-profit (CVP) graph.** Diagram of the relationship between total revenues and total costs; illustrates expected changes in an organization's profits under different volumes of activity. **(91)**

**Cumulative average-time learning curve.** Learning curve approach in which the cumulative average time to produce a unit declines by a constant percentage each time the cumulative quantity of units produced doubles. (46)

**Custom (or customized) product or service.** One-of-a-kind product or service that is produced according to the needs of an individual customer. (177)

**Customer-level activities.** See *customer-sustaining activities.*

**Customer perspective.** Translation of organizational vision and strategies in terms of creating value for customers; part of a balanced scorecard. **(638)**

**Customer profitability analysis.** Evaluation of customer service costs and profitability, often using activity-based management. (270)

**Customer-sustaining activities.** Tasks or functions undertaken to service past, current, and future customers. These costs tend to vary with the needs of individual customers or groups of customers. **(262)**

**CVP analysis.** See *cost-volume-profit analysis.*

**Death spiral.** Deterioration in profitability caused by the use of cost-based pricing for a product with elastic demand. When sales volumes drop, fixed costs are spread over fewer units, leading to higher cost-based prices and further decline in sales. **(529)**

**Decentralized decision making.** Decision-making authority permeates all levels of the organization. Contrast with *centralized decision making.* (593)

**Decision-making authority.** Refers to the decisions that *agents* are authorized to make on behalf of *principals.* (592)

**Decision model.** Systematic method using quantitative and/or qualitative information to choose between alternatives.

**Decision quality.** Refers to the characteristics of a decision that affect the likelihood of achieving a positive outcome. Also see *higher quality management decisions.* (4)

**Decision rights.** Responsibilities and financial decision-making authority of individual managers. **(373, 383)**

**Declining balance depreciation.** Accelerated method of calculating depreciation, in which depreciation is higher in the early years of the estimated useful life than in the later years. (486)

**Deflation.** Increase in the general purchasing power of the monetary unit, meaning that fewer monetary units, such as dollars, are needed to purchase goods or services. Opposite of *inflation.* (483)

**Degree of operating leverage.** Index of the extent to which the cost function consists of fixed costs. **(104)**

**Demand-based capacity levels.** Measure the amount of capacity needed to meet sales volumes. Include *normal capacity* and *budgeted* or *expected capacity.* (558)

**Demand-pull system.** See *just-in-time production and inventory control systems.*

**Dependent variable.** In regression analysis, the variable whose values are explained by changes in one or more independent variables. When estimating a cost function, the dependent variable is the cost. (55)

**Differential cost.** See *marginal cost.*

**Direct cost.** Cost that is easily traced to a cost object; a clear cause-and-effect relationship generally exists between the cost object and the cost. **(39)**

**Direct costing.** Another term for *variable costing.*

**Direct labor efficiency variance.** Difference between standard and actual quantity of direct labor used for the actual amount of goods or services produced valued at the standard labor price. **(424)**

**Direct labor price variance.** Difference between standard and actual price times the actual amount of direct labor hours worked. **(423)**

**Direct materials efficiency variance.** Difference between standard and actual quantity of direct materials used for the actual amount of goods or services produced valued at the standard materials price. **(424)**

**Direct materials price variance.** Difference between standard and actual price times the actual amount of direct materials purchased or used. **(423)**

**Direct method.** Allocates support department costs only to the operating departments. Reflects none of the interactions among support departments. **(304)**

**Discount rate.** Interest rate that is used across time to reduce the value of future dollars to today's dollars. **(471)**

**Discounted cash flow.** See *present value.*

**Discretionary cost.** Reflects periodic (usually annual) decisions about the maximum amount that will be spent on costs for activities such as advertising, executive travel, or research and development. Amount spent can easily be altered during the period. **(46)**

**Discretionary cost center.** Cost center for which output is not easily measurable in dollars or activities. **(595)**

**Disposal value.** See *terminal value.*

**Downward demand spiral.** See *death spiral.*

**Driver.** See *cost driver.*

**Dual-rate allocation.** Practice of allocating fixed and variable support department costs separately, using different allocation bases to more accurately reflect the flow of resources. Contrast with *single-rate allocation.* **(311)**

**Dual-rate transfer price.** Transfer price in which the selling department is credited for the market price and the purchasing department is charged the variable cost. **(610)**

**Dumping.** Illegal practice in which a company sells products in a different country at prices below the market value in its own country. **(532)**

**DuPont analysis.** Decomposition of return on investment (ROI) into investment turnover and return on sales. (598)

**Dysfunctional decision.** See *suboptimal decision.*

**Economic plausibility.** When estimating a cost function, refers to the likelihood that a potential cost driver causes changes in the cost being estimated. (64)

**Economic value added (EVA).** Type of residual income

that incorporates a number of adjustments to operating income and operating assets. (**601**)

**Economies of scale.** Refers to a reduction in cost per unit due to operational efficiencies as the volume of activity increases. (46)

**Efficiency variance.** Difference between standard and actual quantity of resources used in the production of goods or services, valued at the standard price. (**423**)

**Elastic demand.** Price changes have a substantial effect on the quantity demanded. Contrast with *inelastic demand*. (527)

**Engineered estimate of cost.** Method for estimating a cost function by analyzing and assigning costs to the labor time, materials, and other resources used in each activity. (**49**)

**Enterprise resource program (ERP).** Software program system that supports databases and automates business processes such as production, distribution, human resources, and financial accounting; often includes both financial and nonfinancial information. (45)

**Environmental cost analysis.** Evaluation of the costs and benefits associated with environmental performance, often using activity-based management. (273)

**Envisioning.** Step 4 in *Steps for Better Thinking*; acting strategically to recognize change and new threats and also to visualize new opportunities. Homework problems requiring these skills are denoted with the ④ symbol. (17)

**Epsilon.** See *error term*.

**Equivalent units.** Resources used in partially completed units relative to the resources needed to complete the units. (**219**)

**Error term.** In simple regression analysis, the distance between each observation and the regression line. When estimating a cost function, the difference between the actual and estimated cost for a data point. Also called *epsilon* or *residual*.

**Estimated allocation rate.** Allocation rate calculated by dividing estimated overhead cost by the estimated quantity of the allocation base. (**181**, 265, 316, 551)

**Estimated application rate.** See *estimated allocation rate*.

**Ethical decision making.** Process for making ethical decisions that involves identifying ethical problems as they arise, objectively considering the well-being of others and society when exploring alternatives, clarifying and applying ethical values when choosing a course of action, and working toward ongoing improvement of personal and organizational ethics. (**17**)

**Expected capacity.** See *budgeted capacity*.

**Exploring.** Step 2 in *Steps for Better Thinking;* involves thorough analysis of the strengths and weaknesses of different alternatives by acknowledging and controlling biases, considering uncertainties, interpreting information from different viewpoints, recognizing and evaluating assumptions, and gauging the quality of information. Homework problems requiring these skills are denoted with the ② symbol. (17)

**External failure costs.** Costs of activities undertaken after the product has been sold to remedy problems caused by defects and failed units. Also see *quality-related post-sales activities*.

**External report.** Document that presents information for use outside an organization, such as financial statements, news releases, inventory reports for suppliers, tax returns, and regulatory reports. (**10**)

**Extreme programming.** Project management system in which customers and IT personnel communicate and collaborate actively throughout the life of a project. (**388**)

**Facility-level activities.** See *facility-sustaining activities*.

**Facility-sustaining activities.** Tasks or functions undertaken to provide and manage an area, location, or property. These activities occur no matter how many customers are served, products are sold, batches are processed, or units are produced. (**261**)

**Factory burden or factory overhead cost.** See *overhead cost*.

**Favorable variance.** Budget variance in which actual results are better than budgeted results (e.g., actual revenues are larger than the budget, or actual costs are lower than the budget). (**380**)

**Financial budget.** Budget for capital expenditures, long-term financing, and cash flows. (**374**)

**Financial information.** Knowledge, facts, data, or factors that can be measured in dollars or ratios of dollars. (8)

**Financial measure.** Performance measure that provides information in dollars or ratios of dollars. (**634**)

**Financial perspective.** Translation of organizational vision and strategies in terms of desired financial results; part of a balanced scorecard. (**638**)

**Finished goods.** Usually refers to the general ledger account used to account for the cost of inventory that is available for delivery or sale to customers. (178)

**First-in, first-out (FIFO) method.** In process costing, a method in which the current period's costs are used to allocate cost to work performed this period. (**219**)

**Fixed cost.** Cost that does not change with small changes in activity levels of a cost object. (**41**)

**Fixed overhead budget variance.** Difference between allocated fixed overhead cost and actual fixed overhead cost. (**430**)

**Fixed overhead cost pool.** Cost pool used to accumulate only fixed overhead costs. (181, 311)

**Fixed overhead spending variance.** Difference between estimated fixed overhead costs (i.e., static budget) and actual fixed overhead costs. (**432**)

**Fixed overhead volume variance.** See *production volume variance*.

**Fixed-price contract.** Contract in which the vendor provides products or services at a specific price. Contrast with *cost-based contract*. (**317**)

**Flexible budget.** Budget that reflects a range of operations. When evaluating actual results at the end of a period, the flexible budget is set at the actual sales or production volume and used as a benchmark for analyzing variances. (97, **381**, 420)

**Flexible budget variance.** Budget variance (difference between budgeted and actual results) calculated using a flexible budget. (380)

**Flexible cost.** Cost that varies proportionately with activity levels; a variable cost of an activity. (**278**)

**Forecasted financial statements.** See *budgeted financial statements.*

**Full costing.** See *absorption costing.*

**Future value.** Amount to be received in the future, calculated for a given number of years at a given interest. (**469**)

**General decision rule.** See *general rule.*

**General knowledge.** Information that is easy to transfer from one person to another within an organization. Contrast with *specific knowledge.* (**593**)

**Generally Accepted Accounting Principles (GAAP).** The set of accounting methods and disclosures typically used to prepare financial statements for distribution to external parties; not always ideal for management decision making. (11)

**General rule.** Guideline for making a decision, often based only on quantitative information. (132)

**Goal congruence.** In agency theory, condition in which goals of *agents* and *principals* are the same.

**Goals.** See *long-term goals* and *performance objective.*

**Goodness of fit statistic.** See *adjusted R-square.*

**Half-year convention.** Convention for calculating depreciation under the modified asset cost recovery system (MACRS) system, in which assets are assumed to be purchased halfway through the year of acquisition. (486)

**Higher quality management decisions.** Refer to the use of higher quality information, higher quality reports, and a higher quality decision-making process to increase the likelihood of achieving positive outcomes; involve fewer deficiencies such as uncertainties and biases. (12, 653)

**High-low method.** Specific application of the two-point method for estimating cost functions using the highest and lowest data points of the cost driver. (**51**)

**Homogeneous activities.** Tasks or functions that are related in a logical manner and consume similar resources. (**264**)

**Hurdle rate.** See *required rate of return.*

**Hybrid costing.** Accounting approach for assigning product costs using a combination of both job and process costing. (**234**)

**Hybrid product or service.** Mostly uniform product or service that is partially customized according to the needs of an individual customer. (177)

**Ideal standards.** Standards that are achievable under ideal operating conditions. Contrast with *attainable standards.*

**Identifying.** Step 1 in *Steps for Better Thinking;* involves recognizing an open-ended problem, obtaining relevant information, and acknowledging uncertainties. Homework problems requiring these skills are denoted with the ❶ symbol. (17)

**Idle capacity.** See *slack resource.*

**IMA knowledge, skills, and abilities (KSAs).** Published reports on important professional for management accounting professionals. (23)

**Incentives.** Factors that motivate and influence behavior. In agency theory, compensation incentives such as bonuses or stock options may be used to encourage desired actions or behavior. (19, 603)

**Income (loss) before income taxes.** See *pretax profit (loss).*

**Incongruent goals.** In agency theory, conflicts of interest that encourage *agents* to take actions that are not in the best interests of *principals.* (592)

**Incremental cash flows.** See *relevant cash flows.*

**Incremental cost.** See *marginal cost.*

**Incremental cost allocation method.** Allocates common costs to the most responsible user based on the cost that would have been incurred had the services not been shared. Then the next most responsible user is allocated the incremental cost to use the shared resource. (**317**)

**Independent variable.** In regression analysis, a variable used to explain changes in the dependent variable. When estimating a cost function, an independent variable is a potential cost driver. (55)

**Indifference point.** The level of activity where costs or profits are equal across multiple alternatives. (**105**)

**Indirect cost.** Cost that is not easily traced to a cost object; no clear cause-and-effect relationship exists between the cost object and the cost, or the cost of tracing the cost to the cost object exceeds the benefit. Also called *common cost.* (**39**)

**Indirect cost rate.** See *allocation rate.*

**Indirect manufacturing cost.** See *manufacturing overhead cost.*

**Industrial engineering method.** See *engineered estimate of cost.*

**Inelastic demand.** Price changes have little effect on the quantity demanded, and factors such as quality and the ability to customize are more important, within limits, than price. Contrast with *elastic demand.* (527)

**Inflation.** Decline in the general purchasing power of the monetary unit, meaning that more monetary units, such as dollars, are needed to purchase goods or services. (**483**)

**Information.** See *relevant information.*

**Information system.** Computerized or manual structure of procedures and records.

**Innovation cycle.** Internal business processes concerned with identifying customer needs and designing goods and services to meet those needs. (**639**)

**Input measures.** Performance measures that capture activity or effort. (643)

**Insourcing.** The practice of providing goods or services from internal resources. The opposite of outsourcing. (**138**)

**Institute of Management Accountants (IMA).** International organization of financial management executives and accountants that provides a wide variety of information and activities for its members, including local meetings with informative speakers, continuing professional education, and Web-based and printed information about current management and cost accounting practices. (9)

**Intellectual capital.** Information held in the minds of employees; generally not formally captured by the information system, preventing it from being readily accessible by managers. (10)

**Intercept.** Fixed cost when estimating a cost function using regression analysis. Also called *alpha coefficient* or *intercept parameter*. (55)

**Intermediate product.** Product transferred from one department to another, where further assembly takes place before final sale to an external customer. Product transfers are recorded using a *transfer price*. (530, 610)

**Internal business process perspective.** Translation of organizational vision and strategies in terms of the efficiency and effectiveness of practices used inside organizations to produce and deliver goods and services; part of a balanced scorecard. (**639**)

**Internal consistency.** In net present value calculations involving inflation, refers to the consistent use of either the real method or the nominal method. (484)

**Internal failure costs.** Costs of activities undertaken in the production or rework of defective units. Also see *quality-related production activities*.

**Internal rate of return (IRR).** Capital budgeting method that determines the discount rate necessary for the present value of the discounted cash flows to be equal to the investment (i.e., the discount rate at which the project's net present value equals zero). (**476**)

**Internal report.** Document that presents information for use only inside an organization, such as a capital budget, analysis of a potential acquisition, operating and other budgets, bonus computations, and analysis of supplier quality. (**10**)

**Internal service department.** See *support department*.

**Inventoriable costs.** See *product costs*.

**Investment center.** Responsibility center in which managers are accountable for revenues, costs, and investments. (**596**)

**Investment turnover.** Revenue divided by average operating assets. Measures sales generated by each dollar invested in operating assets. (598)

**Irrelevant cash flows.** Cash flows that occur regardless of which course of action or decision alternative is chosen. Also called *unavoidable cash flows*. (**13**)

**Irrelevant information.** Knowledge, facts, data, factors, or issues that do not help the decision maker evaluate and choose among alternative courses of action; does not vary with the action taken. (**13**)

**ISO 9000.** Standards designed to improve quality management and facilitate business-to-business transactions. (197)

**Job.** Customized production of one unit or multiple units in a group for an individual customer. (178)

**Job cost record.** Manual or electronic record that contains all of the costs traced and allocated to a specific job. (**179**)

**Job costing.** Process of assigning costs to custom products or services. (**178**)

**Job order costing.** See *job costing*.

**Job record.** See *job cost record*.

**Job sheet.** See *job cost record*.

**Joint costs.** Common costs to produce a group of goods or services, incurred prior to the split-off point. Cannot be traced to individual joint products. (**341**)

**Joint products.** Goods or services that are created simultaneously with other goods or services, using common resources. (**340**)

**Just-in-time (JIT) production and inventory control systems.** Systems in which materials are purchased and units are produced at the time customers demand them. In JIT inventory control systems, organizations work with suppliers so that goods or materials are delivered just as they are needed for production or for sale. In JIT manufacturing systems, the production process is often broken into steps that are performed in manufacturing cells. (234, **514**)

**Kaizen budget.** Sets targeted cost reductions across time, anticipating market price reductions across the life of a product. (**388**)

**Kaizen costing.** Planning process for achieving continuous improvement in product cost, quality, and functionality. Similar to target costing, but occurs after the product has been designed and the first production cycle is complete. (197, 273, **521**)

**Kanban cellular manufacturing.** Also see *just-in-time production and inventory control systems*.

**Keep or drop decision.** Nonroutine decision to continue or to stop operations for a product, group of products (product line), or business segment. Also called *product line decision* or *business segment decision*. (135)

**Knowing.** Knowledge and basic skills needed to deal with a problem. The foundation of *Steps for Better Thinking*. (16)

**Lean production.** See *just-in-time production and inventory control systems*.

**Learning and growth perspective.** Translation of organizational vision and strategies in terms of discovery and human capital; part of a balanced scorecard. (**641**)

**Learning curve.** Rate at which labor hours decrease as the volume of production or services increases. Also see *cumulative average-time learning curve*. (**46**)

**Least-squares regression.** See *simple regression analysis* and *multiple regression analysis*.

**Life cycle costing.** Decision-making method that considers changes in price and costs over the entire life cycle of a good or service, from the time the product is introduced through a number of years. (**523**)

**Linear programming.** A mathematical technique that maximizes a linear objective function (such as the sum of contribution margins from multiple products) subject to linear constraints (such as the number of hours available for different manufacturing or services processes). (**143**)

**Linear regression.** See *simple regression analysis* and *multiple regression analysis*.

**Long-term goals.** Strategic targets that managers plan to achieve over a long time period (longer than one year);

used to monitor long-term organizational performance. Sometimes called *objectives*. (7)

**Main product.** Joint product that has high sales value compared to other joint products. Contrast with *by-product*. (**341**)

**Make or buy.** See *outsourcing*.

**Management accounting.** Process of gathering, summarizing, and reporting information used internally by managers to make decisions; includes measurement of costs as well as other financial and non-financial information. (**8**)

**Management by exception.** Management emphasis on variances to control operations.

**Management decision making.** Methodical process for making decisions that begins with organizational vision and organizational core competencies, which lead to organizational strategies, then to operating plans, and finally to actual operations. Actual operations are measured and monitored against strategies and plans to motivate performance throughout the organization and to guide revisions to the entire process. (4, 631)

**Manufacturing cell.** Area where all of the equipment and labor is grouped for a particular part of the manufacturing process. See *kanban*. (**514**)

**Manufacturing overhead cost.** Overhead cost related to manufacturing activities. (179)

**Margin of safety.** Excess of an organization's expected future sales (in either revenue or units) above the breakeven point. (**103**)

**Margin of safety percentage.** Margin of safety as a percentage of actual or estimated sales (units or revenues). (**103**)

**Marginal cost.** Incremental cost of an activity, such as producing the next unit of goods or services. (**43**)

**Marginal costing.** See *variable costing*.

**Market-based price.** Product selling price determined using some measure of customer demand. (**526**)

**Market-based transfer price.** Transfer price based on competitors' prices or on the supply and demand relationship. (**610**)

**Markup.** Increase in cost to arrive at a product's selling price, expressed in dollars or as a percentage of cost or selling price. (525)

**Mass-produced product or service.** Uniform product or service that is produced in large quantities. (177)

**Master budget.** Comprehensive plan for an upcoming financial period, usually a year. (**374**)

**Materiality.** Significance of an amount (e.g., cost, variance, or adjustment). Amounts are generally viewed as material if their treatment would affect the decisions of people who rely on reported values. (187, 438)

**Measure.** Value assigned (noun) or the process of assigning a value (verb) to an object through calculation, appraisal, estimation, or some other method. See also *financial measure* and *nonfinancial measure*. (39)

**Measuring performance.** In cost management, a process of capturing and assigning values to financial or nonfinancial

information about actual operations; used to monitor and motivate organizational performance. (7, 591, 631)

**Method of least squares.** See *multiple regression analysis* and *simple regression analysis*.

**Mid-month convention.** Convention for calculating depreciation for real property under the modified asset cost recovery system (MACRS) system, in which assets are assumed to be purchased halfway through the month of acquisition. (486)

**Mission statement.** High-level declaration of the organization's purpose. (5, 622)

**Mixed cost.** Cost that is partly fixed and partly variable. (**42**)

**Modified asset cost recovery system (MACRS).** Current scheme for calculating depreciation deductions under the U.S. income tax code. (485)

**Monitoring costs.** In agency theory, costs incurred by *principals* to measure and analyze *agent* behavior. (592)

**Monitoring progress.** In cost management, a process of measuring and comparing actual operations to plans such as budgets and long-term goals to evaluate the success of decisions and motivate employees. (7, 380, 417, 480, 551, 591, 631)

**Monopoly price.** Product selling price for a unique good or service with no competitors. Contrast with *commodity price*. (527)

**Most-likely scenario or case.** Sensitivity analysis using the set of assumptions that is expected to occur. Contrast with *best-case* and *worst-case scenario*.

**Motivating Employees.** In cost management, a process of measuring organizational performance and monitoring the results to encourage employees to work toward the organizational vision; often involves the use of incentives tied to pay or other employee benefits. (7, 417, 591, 631)

**Multicollinearity.** High correlation among independent variables in a regression analysis, causing coefficients to be inaccurate. (66)

**Multiple regression analysis.** Statistical technique that measures the average change in a dependent variable for every unit change in two or more independent variables. When used to estimate a mixed cost function, the independent variables are potential cost drivers. (**55**)

**Negotiated transfer price.** Transfer price based on an agreement reached between the managers of the selling and purchasing departments. (**610**)

**Net income (loss).** See *after-tax profit (loss)*.

**Net present value.** Capital budgeting method that determines whether an organization would be better off investing in a project based on the net amount of discounted cash flows for the project. (**470**)

**Net realizable value (NRV) method.** Allocates joint costs using the relative value of main products, taking into account both the additional sales value that is created and costs that are incurred after joint production ends. (**344**)

**Nominal discount rate.** See *nominal rate of interest*.

**Nominal method.** Approach for calculating discounted cash flows in which cash inflows and outflows are forecast in nominal dollars (inflated) and discounted using a nominal discount rate. (**483**)

**Nominal rate of interest.** Rate of return required on investments when inflation is present. Calculated by increasing the real rate of interest by the expected rate of inflation. (**483**)

**Nonfinancial information.** Knowledge, facts, data, or factors that cannot be measured in dollars or ratios of dollars. (8)

**Nonfinancial measure.** Performance measure of information that cannot be measured in dollars. (**635**)

**Noninventoriable costs.** See *period costs.*

**Nonroutine operating decision.** Operating decision that is not made on a regular schedule and occurs less frequently than other types of operating decisions. Examples include: special orders, keep or drop, outsourcing (make or buy), product emphasis, and constrained resource. (130)

**Non-value-added activities.** Tasks or functions that are unnecessary and waste resources because they do not increase the worth of an organization's goods or services to customers. (**271**, **511**)

**Normal capacity.** Average use of capacity over time; typical volume of goods or services produced. (**559**)

**Normal costing.** Method for allocating overhead costs using an estimated allocation rate and actual quantity of the allocation base. (**182**, **557**)

**Normal spoilage.** Spoilage that arises as part of regular operations. (**194**, **235**)

**Objective function.** In linear programming, the mathematical function to be optimized. Also called *target function.* (143)

**One-time-only special order.** See *special order.*

**Open-ended problem.** A problem with no single "correct" solution, often due to significant uncertainties. The decision maker's task is to find the best—not the only— possible solution. (**15**)

**Operating budget.** Budget for revenues, production, and operating costs. (**374**)

**Operating department.** Department or division within an organization that manufactures goods or produces services for external customers or clients. (**299**)

**Operating income (loss).** Operating revenues minus operating expenses. Also see *pretax profit (loss).* (92)

**Operating plans.** Specific short-term decisions that shape the organization's day-to-day activities such as drawing cash from a bank line of credit, hiring an employee, or ordering materials; often include specific performance objectives, such as budgeted revenues and costs. (7, 633)

**Operation costing.** Type of hybrid costing used when similar batches of identical products are manufactured. Units in each batch are identical, but the processing varies across batches. (**234**)

**Operational audit.** Objective and systematic examination of evidence to provide an independent assessment of the performance of an organization, program, activity, or function. (639)

**Operations cycle.** Internal business processes concerned with the production and delivery of goods or services. (**640**)

**Opportunity cost.** Benefit forgone when one alternative is chosen over the next best alternative. (**40**, 133)

**Opportunity costs of spoilage.** Benefit forgone from the production of spoiled units. (196, 239, 273)

**Optimal solution.** In linear programming, a solution that maximizes the objective function. (143)

**Organization-level activities.** *See organization-sustaining activities.*

**Organization-sustaining activities.** Tasks or functions undertaken to oversee the entire entity. These activities occur no matter how many facilities are operated, customers are served, products are sold, batches are processed, or units are produced. (**261**)

**Organizational core competencies.** The organization's strengths relative to competitors; closely related to *organizational vision.* (**6**, 622)

**Organizational strategies.** Tactics that managers use to take advantage of core competencies while working toward the organizational vision; guide long-term decisions such as the proportion of financing through debt and equity, types of goods and services offered, and investments in property, plant, and equipment. (**6**, 622)

**Organizational vision.** Core purpose and ideology of an organization, which guides the organization's overall direction and approaches toward various stakeholder groups. (**5**, 622)

**Outcome measures.** Performance measures that capture results. (643)

**Outlier.** In regression analysis, a data observation that is much larger or much smaller than usual, unduly influencing the results. (68)

**Outsourcing.** The practice of hiring outside vendors to supply products and services. Outsourcing decisions are also called *make or buy* decisions (138, 512)

**Overabsorbed overhead or indirect costs.** See *overapplied overhead.*

**Overallocated overhead or indirect costs.** See *overapplied overhead.*

**Overapplied overhead.** Occurs when actual costs are less than the total amount of overhead allocated to inventory accounts. (**186**)

**Overhead allocation rate.** See *allocation rate.*

**Overhead cost.** Often refers to a pool of production costs other than direct materials and direct labor. May also refer to other types of *common costs,* such as general and administrative costs. (**40**, 177)

**Overhead cost pool.** Cost pool used to accumulate overhead costs. (180)

**Overhead variance adjustment.** General ledger entry to eliminate overapplied or underapplied overhead at the end of an accounting period. (186, 559)

**Participative budgeting.** Budget requests that are communicated "bottom up" from departments to members in top management who are responsible for final budget approval. (**383**)

**Payback.** Capital budgeting method that measures the

amount of time required to recover the initial investment. (**477**)

**Peak load pricing.** Practice of charging different prices at different times to reduce capacity constraints. (**530**)

**Peanut butter costing.** Practice of spreading overhead costs to products without regard to their use of resources. (**276**)

**Penetration pricing.** Practice of setting low prices when new products are introduced to increase market share. (**530**)

**Performance measure.** An indicator, usually calculated quantitatively, that is used to monitor performance of an organization, subunit, process, manager, or other object. (597)

**Performance objective.** Specific goal that managers measure and monitor to help move the organization toward its vision. (7, **631**)

**Period costs.** All costs other than production costs that are assigned to the cost of inventory. Includes nonproduction costs such as administration, marketing, and distribution. (**552**)

**Physical output method.** Allocates joint costs using the relative proportion of physical output for each main product. (**342**)

**Piecewise linear cost function.** Cost function in which the variable cost per unit changes across relevant ranges of activity. (**44**)

**Post-investment audit.** Provides feedback about whether operations are meeting expectations for a capital budgeting project. (**480**)

**Post-sales activities.** See *quality-related post-sales activities.*

**Post-sales service cycle.** Internal business processes concerned with the service provided to customers after product delivery. (**640**)

**Practical capacity.** Upper capacity limit under typical operating conditions, assuming that some downtime is unavoidable for maintenance and holidays. *Theoretical capacity* reduced for expected downtimes. (**265, 558**)

**Predatory pricing.** Illegal practice of setting prices low to drive competitors out of the market and then raising prices. (**532**)

**Predetermined application or overhead rate.** See *estimated allocation rate.*

**Predicted financial statements.** See *budgeted financial statements.*

**Present value.** Value in today's dollars of an amount to be received in the future, calculated for a given number of years at a given interest. (**469**)

**Pretax profit (loss).** In general, revenues minus expenses. Under GAAP, all revenues and gains minus all expenses (other than income taxes) and losses. (92)

**Prevention activities.** Quality-related tasks or functions undertaken to produce defect-free units of goods or services. (274)

**Price discrimination.** Illegal practice of setting different prices for different customers if the intent is to lessen or prevent competition. (**532**)

**Price elasticity of demand.** Sensitivity of sales to price increases. (**527**)

**Price gouging.** Practice of charging a price viewed by consumers as too high. (**530**)

**Price skimming.** Practice of setting a higher price for a product or service when it is first introduced. (**530**)

**Price variance.** Difference between standard and actual prices paid for resources purchased and used in the production of goods or services. (**422**)

**Prime costs.** Direct material and direct labor costs. (178)

**Principal.** In agency theory, a person or entity represented by an agent. (**591**)

**Prioritizing.** Step 3 in *Steps for Better Thinking;* making trade-offs and choosing the best possible alternative for an open-ended problem, and then efficiently implementing it. For managers, includes ensuring that the organization's values, core competencies, and strategies are adequately considered; and motivating performance within the organization. Homework problems requiring these skills are denoted with the ❸ symbol. (17)

**Process costing.** Method for allocating both direct and overhead costs to continuous-flow processing lines; it is the approach generally used for mass-produced products. Direct and indirect costs are traced and allocated to production departments, and then allocated to units. (**177, 217**)

**Product cost cross-subsidization.** Cost allocations that do not represent the use of resources, resulting in the overallocation of costs to some products and the underallocation of costs to others. (276)

**Product costs.** Direct and indirect production costs that are assigned to the cost of inventory on the balance sheet and then expensed as part of cost of goods sold when units are sold. (**177, 551**)

**Product differentiation.** Practice of strategically positioning a product based on its quality or functionality. (517, 633)

**Product emphasis decision.** Deciding which products to emphasize (140)

**Product-level activities.** See *product-sustaining activities.*

**Product line decision.** See *keep or drop decision.*

**Product-mix decision.** See *product emphasis decision.*

**Product-sustaining activities.** Tasks or functions undertaken to support the production and distribution of a single product or line of products. These activities are not related to units or batches, but to individual products or product lines. (**262**)

**Production department.** See *operating department.*

**Production volume variance.** Difference between the standard amount of fixed overhead costs for the actual amount of goods or services produced and the estimated fixed overhead costs (i.e., static budget). (**432**)

**Profit center.** Responsibility center in which managers are accountable for both revenues and costs (i.e., profits). (**596**)

**Profit margin ratio.** See *return on sales.*

**Profit-maximizing price.** Product selling price calculated using variable costs and an estimate of the product's price elasticity of demand. (527)

**Profitability index.** Ratio of the present value of the benefits to the present value of the costs of a capital budgeting opportunity. (**471**)

**Pro forma financial statements.** See *budgeted financial statements.*

**p-value.** Statistical probability that an alpha or beta coefficient is significantly different from zero in a regression analysis. Used to assess whether fixed and variable costs are greater than zero when estimating a cost function. (57)

**Qualitative information.** Factors that are not valued in numerical terms. (**132**)

**Quality cost.** See *cost of quality.*

**Quality-related activities.** Tasks or functions undertaken to minimize the opportunity costs that arise when customers have problems with defective units or low-quality services. Include four types of activities: prevention, appraisal, quality-related production, and quality-related post-sales. (273)

**Quality-related post-sales activities.** Quality-related tasks or functions undertaken after the product has been sold to remedy problems caused by defects and failed units of goods or services. (274)

**Quality-related production activities.** Quality-related tasks or functions undertaken to produce or rework defective units of goods or services. (274)

**Quantitative analysis.** Computation and interpretation of numerical information when addressing a problem. (131)

**Quantitative information.** Numerical information that is available for addressing a problem. (**131**)

**Quantity variance.** See *efficiency variance.*

**Radio frequency identification (RFID) tags.** Attached to inventory to allow tracking via active or passive radio signals. (34)

**Rate variance.** See *price variance.*

**Real discount rate.** See *real rate of interest.*

**Real method.** Approach for calculating discounted cash flows in which cash inflows and outflows are forecast in real dollars (no inflation) and discounted using a real rate. (**483**)

**Real rate of interest.** Rate of return required on investments when no inflation is a factor. Sum of the risk-free rate and a risk premium. (**483**)

**Reciprocal method.** Simultaneously allocates costs among support departments and then from support departments to operating departments. Allows for all of the interactions among departments. (308)

**Regression analysis.** See *simple regression analysis* and *multiple regression analysis.*

**Relax a constraint.** One or more changes in operations to reduce or eliminate a constraint. (141)

**Relevant cash flows.** Cash flows that occur under one course of action or decision alternative, but not under another. Also called *incremental* or *avoidable cash flows.* (13, 131)

**Relevant costs.** Costs that occur under one course of action or decision alternative, but not under another. See also *relevant cash flows.* (39)

**Relevant information.** Knowledge, facts, data, or factors that help the decision maker evaluate and choose among alternative courses of action; concerns the future and varies with the action taken. (13)

**Relevant range.** Span of activity for a given cost object where total fixed costs remain constant and the variable cost per unit of activity remains constant. (**43**, 99)

**Required rate of return.** Minimum acceptable discount rate established by management for a capital budgeting project. (471, 600)

**Residual.** See *error term.*

**Residual income.** Performance measure calculated as the dollar amount of actual profits in excess of a required rate of return on average operating assets. (**600**)

**Residual value.** See *terminal value.*

**Responsibility accounting.** Process of assigning decision-making authority and responsibility to managers of subunits and then monitoring their performance. (**595**)

**Responsibility center.** Subunit (e.g., segment, division, or department) over which managers are accountable for specific types of operating activities. (**595**)

**Return on investment (ROI).** Performance measure calculated as the ratio of operating income to average operating assets. Measures profitability relative to asset investment. (**597**)

**Return on sales.** Operating income divided by revenues. Measures managers' abilities to control operating expenses relative to sales. (598)

**Revenue budget variance.** Difference between actual and standard (or budgeted) revenues. (**439**)

**Revenue center.** Responsibility center in which managers are accountable for revenues. (**596**)

**Revenue-generating department.** See *operating department.*

**Revenue sales quantity variance.** Difference between standard and actual quantity of units sold times the standard selling price. (440)

**Reverse engineering.** The process of taking a competitor's product apart and putting it back together again to better understand the manufacturing process and the product design. (516)

**Rework.** Spoiled units that are repaired and sold as if they were originally produced correctly. (**195**)

**Risk-free rate.** "Pure" rate of interest paid on short-term government bonds (without considering inflation). (**483**)

**Risk premium.** Rate of return above the risk-free rate that businesses demand for undertaking risks. (**483**)

**Rolling budget.** Budget prepared monthly or quarterly that reflects planning changes going forward, often through the next 12 to 16 months. Planning changes include the most recent results as well as changes in business strategy, operating plans, and the economy. (**387**)

**Sales mix.** Proportion of different products or services that an organization sells. (**90**)

**Sales price variance.** Difference between standard and actual selling price times the actual volume of goods or services sold. (**440**)

**Sales value at split-off point method.** Allocates joint

costs based on the relative sales value of main products at the point where joint production ends. **(343)**

**Salvage value.** See *terminal value*.

**Sarbanes-Oxley Act.** Requires U.S. public company managers and boards of directors to assume greater legal responsibility, such as self-assessing internal controls and financial reporting risk, and increasing the oversight of managers and auditors by the board of directors and its audit committee. (20)

**Scarce resource.** See *constraint*.

**Scatter plot.** Graphical technique in which data points for past costs are plotted against a potential cost driver. Visual analysis of a scatter plot is used to study the relationship between a cost and potential cost driver and to decide whether a cost might be completely fixed, completely variable, or mixed. **(50)**

**Scattergraph technique.** See *two-point method*.

**Scrap.** Bits of direct material left over from normal manufacturing processes. Scrap sometimes has value and can be sold, and sometimes it is discarded. **(195)**

**Semifixed.** See *stepwise linear cost function*.

**Semivariable cost.** See *mixed cost*.

**Sensitivity analysis.** Use of quantitative and qualitative information to study changes in results with changes in various assumptions. Also see *best-case* and *worst-case scenario*. (96, 148, 381, 473)

**Separable costs.** Incremental production costs for a joint product incurred after the *split-off point*. **(341)**

**Sequential method.** See *step-down method*.

**Service department.** See *support department*.

**Shadow price.** Contribution margin per constrained resource, given the other constraints in the problem, at the optimal solution of a linear programming problem. (144)

**Shared service department.** See *support department*.

**Simple regression analysis.** Statistical technique that measures the average change in a dependent variable for every unit change in one independent variable. When used to estimate a mixed cost function, the independent variable is a potential cost driver. **(55)**

**Single-rate allocation.** Practice of using only one base to allocate both fixed and variable costs. Contrast with *dual-rate allocation*. **(311)**

**Six Sigma®.** Quality program developed by Motorola that focuses on achieving a defect rate of fewer than 3.4 defects per million items. (197)

**Slack resource.** A resource such as capacity or direct materials that is not binding and could be used if there were no other binding constraints. **(144)**

**Slope coefficient.** Variable cost per unit of a cost driver when estimating a cost function using regression analysis. Also called *beta coefficient* or *slope parameter*. **(55)**

**Source documents.** Manual or electronic records created to capture and provide information about transactions or events. Examples include employee time records and raw material requisitions. **(179)**

**Special order.** Customer order that is not part of the organization's normal operations. (133)

**Special order decision.** Decision about whether to accept or reject a customer order that is not part of the organization's normal operations. (133)

**Specific knowledge.** Detailed information about particular processes, customers, or products; information that is costly to transfer within the organization. Contrast with *general knowledge*. **(593)**

**Split-off point.** Point during production at which individual joint products can be identified. **(341)**

**Spoilage.** Units of product that are unacceptable and are discarded, reworked, or sold at a reduced price. **(194, 235)**

**Squared error.** In simple regression analysis, the square of the distance from each observation to the regression line. When estimating a cost function, the squared difference between the actual and estimated cost for a data point. (55)

**Stand-alone method.** Allocates common costs using weights based on information about the individual users of a cost object. **(317)**

**Standard cost.** Cost that managers expect to incur for production of goods or services under operating plan assumptions. **(232, 417)**

**Standard cost variance.** Difference between a standard cost and an actual cost. **(420)**

**Standard cost variance adjustment.** General ledger entry to close standard cost variance accounts at the end of an accounting period. (232, 437)

**Standard error.** In regression analysis, provides an estimate of the expected amount of variation in a coefficient. (56)

**Standard fixed overhead allocation rate.** Standard dollar amount per unit of allocation base used to allocate fixed overhead to products. **(430)**

**Standard overhead allocation rate.** Standard dollar amount per unit of allocation base used to allocate overhead to products. Also see *estimated allocation rate*. (181, **430**)

**Standard variable overhead allocation rate.** Standard dollar amount per unit of allocation base used to allocate variable overhead to products. **(430)**

**Static budget.** Budget based on forecasts of specific volumes of production or services. **(381, 432)**

**Static budget variance.** Budget variance (difference between budgeted and actual results) calculated using a static budget. (380)

**Step-down method.** Allocates support department costs one department at a time to the remaining support and operating departments in a cascading manner until all support department costs have been allocated. Recognizes that support departments provide support for operating departments as well as other support departments, but addresses only part of the interactions. **(307)**

**Steps for Better Thinking.** Decision-making process that leads to higher-quality decisions. Also a cognitive development model that was used to define levels of complexity within the *AICPA Core Competency Framework*. (15)

**Steps in ethical decision making.** See *ethical decision making*.

**Stepwise linear cost function.** Cost function in which fixed cost changes across relevant ranges of activity. (**44**)

**Straight-line depreciation.** Method of calculating depreciation, in which the asset cost is spread uniformly over the estimated useful life of the asset. (486)

**Strategic cost management.** Expansion of *management accounting* to simultaneous focus on reducing costs and strengthening an organization's strategic position. (**9**)

**Strategic decision making.** See *management decision making*.

**Strategies.** See *organizational strategies*.

**Suboptimal decision.** Decision that is not in the best interests of the organization as a whole. (596)

**Sunk cost.** Expenditures made in the past, which cannot be changed by any future decisions; unavoidable and therefore not relevant to decision making. (**40**)

**Super-variable costing.** See *throughput costing*.

**Supply-based allocation rate.** Overhead cost allocation rate based on estimated costs and practical capacity. Allows measurement of the cost of capacity used as well as the cost of unused capacity. (266)

**Supply-based capacity levels.** Measure the amount of capacity that is available for production. Include *theoretical capacity* and *practical capacity*. (265, 558)

**Supply chain.** Flow of resources from the initial suppliers (internal or external) through the delivery of goods and services to customers and clients. (**512**)

**Support department.** Department or division within an organization that provides services used internally and that supports the operating departments. (**299**)

**Tactics.** See *organizational strategies*.

**Target cost.** Target price less required profit margin. (507)

**Target costing.** Product decision-making approach that uses market-based prices to determine whether products and services can be delivered at low enough costs for an acceptable profit. Product and manufacturing processes are redesigned so that the product meets a prespecified target cost. (273, **516**)

**Target function.** See *objective function*.

**Target price.** Competitive product selling price for a given level of product quality and functionality (517)

**Tax shield.** Depreciation deduction for the initial investment cost of a capital budgeting project, taken on future years' income tax returns. (**481**)

**Terminal value (or terminal cash flow).** Cash flows that occur at the end of a project's life. (**469**)

**Theoretical capacity.** Upper capacity limit assuming continuous, uninterrupted production 365 days per year. Maximum volume of goods or services that an organization could hypothetically produce. (**558**)

**Theory of constraints.** Formal method used to analyze organizational constraints and improve operations. (146, 505, 568)

**Throughput.** Rate at which products are manufactured and sold. (437)

**Throughput costing.** Extreme version of variable costing, in which only direct material costs are assigned to inventory as product costs. Assumes that direct labor and overhead do not vary proportionately with volume of production. (**568**)

**Time-adjusted rate of return.** See *internal rate of return*.

**Time value of money.** Concept that a dollar received today is worth more than a dollar received in the future. (**467**)

**Top-down budgeting.** Strategies and targets that are communicated from top management to division and department managers who incorporate them into the budgeted operating plans. (383)

**Total quality management.** Procedures and policies aimed at organization-wide continuous improvement. (197, 479)

**Tracing costs.** Assigning direct costs to a cost object. To be traced, a cost must be easily linked or attached to the cost object. (39, 177, 217, 259, 303, 341)

**Traditional costing systems.** Refers to the practice of accumulating overhead costs in a small number of cost pools and allocating costs using bases that do not necessarily drive costs, such as labor hours, labor costs, and machine hours. (259)

**Transfer price.** Price used to record revenue and cost when goods or services are transferred between responsibility centers in an organization. (**530, 607**)

**Transferred-in costs.** In process costing, costs transferred from one processing department to the next. (225)

**t-statistic.** Alpha or beta coefficient relative to its standard error in a regression analysis. Used to assess whether fixed and variable costs are greater than zero when estimating a cost function. (56)

**Two-point method.** Algebraic method for estimating a mixed cost function using any two data points of the cost and cost driver, preferably using two representative points. (**50**)

**Unadjusted rate of return.** See *accrual accounting rate of return*.

**Unavoidable cash flows.** See *irrelevant cash flows*.

**Uncertainties.** Issues and information about which we have doubt; prevent managers from accurately describing a problem, identifying all possible options, knowing the outcomes of various options, or anticipating all future conditions. (4, 11)

**Underabsorbed overhead or indirect costs.** See *underapplied overhead*.

**Underallocated overhead or indirect costs.** See *underapplied overhead*.

**Underapplied overhead.** Occurs when actual costs are greater than the total amount of overhead allocated to inventory accounts. (**186**)

**Unfavorable variance.** Budget variance in which actual results are worse than budgeted results (e.g., actual costs are greater than budgeted or actual revenues are less than budgeted). (**380**)

**Uniform product or service.** Product or service that is produced identically for all customers. (177)

**Unit-level activities.** Tasks or functions undertaken to produce individual units manufactured or services produced. Unit-level activities need to be performed for every unit of good or service, and therefore the cost should be proportional to the number of units produced. (**263**)

**Usage variance.** *See efficiency variance.*

**Value-added activities.** Tasks or functions that increase the worth of an organization's goods or services to customers. (**271, 511**)

**Value chain.** Sequence of business processes in which value is added to a product or service. Encompasses customers and suppliers as well as, in some cases, the customers' customers and the suppliers' suppliers. (**511, 639**)

**Value chain analysis.** Process of studying each step in the business process to determine whether some activities can be eliminated because they do not add value. (**511, 639**)

**Variable cost.** Cost that changes proportionately with changes in volumes or activity levels. (**41**)

**Variable cost ratio.** Total variable costs divided by total revenue.

**Variable costing.** Only variable production costs, such as direct materials, direct labor, and variable manufacturing overhead, are assigned to inventory as product costs. (**552**)

**Variable overhead budget variance.** Difference between allocated variable overhead cost and actual variable overhead cost. (**430**)

**Variable overhead cost pool.** Cost pool used to accumulate only variable overhead costs. (181, 311)

**Variable overhead efficiency variance.** Difference between the total expected variable overhead costs for the actual amount of goods or services produced (i.e., the flexible budget) and the standard amount of variable overhead for the actual volume of the allocation base. (**431**)

**Variable overhead spending variance.** Difference between the total expected variable overhead costs for the actual amount of goods or services produced (i.e., the flexible budget) and actual variable overhead costs. (**431**)

**Variance analysis.** The process of calculating variances and then investigating the reasons they occurred. (**420**)

**Vision Statement.** Theoretical description of what the organization should become. (5, 622)

**Volume discount.** Price reduction or refund received from suppliers of goods or services based on exceeding a specified volume of activity. (46)

**Volume of activity.** The quantity of a task or function (such as number of product units produced, facilities operated, or customer sales calls made) performed in an organization over a period of time. Also called *level of activity* or *volume of cost driver; Q* in the cost function. (44)

**Volume variance.** Difference between the estimated fixed overhead costs used to calculate the estimated allocation rate and the amount of fixed overhead costs actually allocated to inventory during the period. Also see *production volume variance.* (**559**)

**Weighted average contribution margin per unit.** Average contribution margin per unit for multiple products, weighted by the sales mix. (94)

**Weighted average contribution margin ratio.** Average contribution margin ratio for multiple products, weighted by the sales mix. (94)

**Weighted average cost of capital.** Weighted average after-tax rate for the costs of the various sources of long-term financing such as debt and stock. Sometimes used as the *discount rate* in capital budgeting. (**471**, 602)

**Weighted average method.** In process costing, a method in which costs from beginning WIP (performed last period) are averaged with costs incurred during the current period and then allocated to all units completed and ending WIP. (**219**)

**What-if analysis.** See *sensitivity analysis.*

**Work in process (WIP).** Usually refers to the general ledger inventory account used to accumulate costs for partially-complete manufactured goods. Also used generically to refer to any good or service that is partially complete. (170)

**Work in progress.** See *work in process.*

**Work-measurement method.** See *engineered estimate of cost.*

**Worst-case scenario or case.** Sensitivity analysis using the most negative (but still reasonable) set of assumptions. Contrast with *best-case scenario.* (60)

**Yield variance.** See *efficiency variance.*

**Zero-based budgeting.** Budgets developed as if there were no information about budgets or costs from prior budget cycles available. (**384**)

**Zero defect policy.** Operating practice that does not allow for any normal spoilage. (198)

# Credits

## Chapter 1

Opener: PhotoDisc, Inc./Getty Images. Page 5: Syracuse Newspapers/Michelle Gabel/The Image Works. Page 14: Jeffrey W. Myers/Corbis Images. Page 19: PhotoDisc, Inc./Getty Images.

## Chapter 2

Opener: Reuters NewMedia/Corbis Images. Page 39: Joe Sohm/Alamy Images. Page 47: Maximilian Stock LTD/Phototake. Pages 52 & 58: Richard Hutchings/PhotoEdit.

## Chapter 3

Opener: Jacques M. Chenet/Corbis Images. Pages 92 & 98: PhotoDisc, Inc./Getty Images. Page 101: Richard Hutchings/PhotoEdit. Page 106: Spencer Grant/PhotoEdit.

## Chapter 4

Opener: ©AP/Wide World Photos. Page 133: Corbis Digital Stock. Page 136: Don Smetzer/Stone/Getty Images. Pages 138, 142 & 149: Michael Newman/PhotoEdit. Page 144: Paul A. Souders/Corbis Images.

## Chapter 5

Opener: George Hall/Corbis Images. Page 183: Royalty-Free/Corbis Images. Page 188: Michael Newman/PhotoEdit. Page 190: Royalty-Free/Corbis Images. Page 192: Kevin Fleming/Corbis Images. Page 195: Royalty-Free/Corbis Images.

## Chapter 6

Opener: Courtesy Elliptec, Dortmund, Germany. Page 226: Tom Carroll/Phototake. Page 230: Mark Richards/PhotoEdit. Page 236: Tom Carroll/Phototake. Page 239: Ed Kashi/Phototake.

## Chapter 7

Opener: Onne van der Wal/Corbis Images. Pages 266 & 272: Layne Kennedy/Corbis Images. Page 274: Dean Conger/Corbis Images. Page 279: Jose Luis Pelaez, Inc./Corbis Images.

## Chapter 8

Opener: Kit Kittle/Corbis Images. Pages 304, 307, 309 & 312: Michael Newman/PhotoEdit. Page 318: Getty Images News and Sport Services.

## Chapter 9

Opener: Tom Carroll/Phototake. Pages 342 & 346: PhotoDisc, Inc./Getty Images. Page 347: Topham/The Image Works. Page 351: James L. Amos/Corbis Images. Page 354: Raymond Gehman/Corbis Images.

## Chapter 10

Opener: Cindy Charles/PhotoEdit. Pages 376, 381, 385 & 391: Bojan Brecelj/Corbis Images. Page 388: Bill Lai/The Image Works.

## Chapter 11

Opener: George B. Diebold/Corbis Images. Pages 419, 426, 429 & 434: Keith Dannemiller/Corbis Images. Page 438: Thor Swift/The Image Works.

## Chapter 12

Opener: Richard Hutchings/PhotoEdit. Page 474: Image Source/Alamy Images. Page 480: Malcolm Linton/Liaison/Getty Images News and Sport Services. Page 487: Lester Lefkowitz/Corbis Images.

## Chapter 13

Opener: Reuters/Corbis Images. Page 514: Courtesy Masterlock, Nogales Mexico. Page 516: Tom Wagner/Corbis SABA. Pages 518 & 522: Peter Endig/dpa/Landov LLC. Page 528: Paul Almasy/Corbis Images. Page 531: David Young-Wolff/Stone/Getty Images.

## Chapter 14

Opener: Rick Friedman/Corbis Images. Pages 554 & 556: Chung Sung-Ju/Getty Images News and Sport Services. Page 560: Christopher J. Morris/Corbis Images. Page 563: Jim Sugar/Corbis Images. Page 567: Corbis Digital Stock.

## Chapter 15

Opener: Sean Cayton/The Image Works. Page 594: Peter Parks/AFP/Getty Images News and Sport Services. Pages 598, 600, 602 & 610: Claro Cortes IV/Corbis Images. Page 605: Stephen Chernin/Getty Images News and Sport Services.

## Chapter 16

Opener: Alan Schein Photography/Corbis Images. Page 632: Wally McNamee/Corbis Images. Page 637: David Young-Wolff/PhotoEdit. Page 646: Tom Stewart/Corbis Images. Page 653: Ariel Skelley/Corbis Images.

## We wish to thank the following for giving us permission to reproduce and/or adapt material in the following exercises and problems.

3.19, 3.20, 3.22, 4.16, 4.27, 4.29, 7.16, 7.20, 7.21, 7.25, 9.28, 10.14, 11.17, 11.18, 12.17, 12.23, 14.16, 14.22, 15.27, 15.29, 16.27—Materials from the Certified Management Accountant Examination, Copyright 1987-1997, by the Institute of Certified Management Accountants, are reprinted and/or adapted with permission.

5.20, 10.16, 11.16, 12.15, 12.16, 15.16, 15.21—Material from the Uniform CPA Examination Questions and Unofficial Answers, Copyright © 1978 through 2000; 1991; 2004 by the American Institute of Certified Public Accountants, Inc., is reprinted (or adapted) with permission.

# Organization and
# People Index

# Subject Index

# ☆ COMPETENCY ASSESSMENT PROBLEMS

One or more problems in each chapter are designed specifically for *assessment of competencies* such as decision making, risk analysis, and strategic/critical thinking. Designated by a star ☆, each problem is open-ended and requires students to use judgment and to communicate their thinking. Instructor resources include a detailed assessment rubric, student examples, and a discussion of typical student approaches.

| Problem | Student Task |
|---------|--------------|
| Pre-Course | Recommend classification of hourly labor costs in budget for retail coffee stores |
| 1.23 | Identify and analyze relevant costs; recommend choice of college living arrangement |
| 2.36 | Estimate future costs for not-for-profit medical clinic; communicate methodology and results to director |
| 3.34 | Analyze quality of data and CVP results; recommendations about potential start-up of clock manufacturing business |
| 3.37 | Estimate cost function for university café operation; analyze breakeven and degree of operating leverage; write persuasive memorandum about continuing operations |
| 4.28 | Analyze quantitative and qualitative information for two special orders of jewelry case manufacturer; provide management with recommendation |
| 5.33 | Recommend accounting for rework costs under cost-plus job contract for boat manufacturer |
| 6.37 | Recommend whether to modify cost standard for bonus computation for a division of a computer component manufacturer |
| 7.36 | Critique profit and loss statement under new ABC system at **Colombo Frozen Yogurt**. |
| 8.29 | Prepare expected cost report for hospital bid on state contract to supply birth defect scans |
| 8.32 | Evaluate accountant responsibilities to employers and others; write essay about whether it is ethical for accountants to help their organizations maximize reimbursements under cost-based contracts |
| 9.32 | Evaluate cost and quality of joint product ingredients; recommend method for resolving conflict of interest between managers of chemical and cosmetics divisions |
| 10.21 | Recommend whether new staff accountant in CPA firm should seek help from supervisor |
| 11.28 | Recommend whether and how ABC variance information should be used in credit card transaction processing manager's performance evaluation |
| 12.30 | Perform NPV analysis; recommend whether retail computer store should purchase computer diagnostic equipment |
| 13.30 | Conduct research on market prices; recommend park department price for tour of caves |
| 14.24 | Convert division financial statements from absorption costing to variable costing; recommend type of income statement for monitoring divisional performance |
| 15.28 | Write essay about whether it was ethical for officers to allow SEC settlement costs to be paid by **Xerox** and its insurance companies |
| 16.32 | Evaluate proposed balanced scorecard design; recommend whether a balanced scorecard should be adopted |

# INTEGRATING ACROSS THE CURRICULUM HOMEWORK PROBLEMS

One or two *Integrating Across the Curriculum* problems in each chapter ask students to integrate cost accounting material with the content of other accounting and business core courses.

| Problem | Subjects | Topics |
|---|---|---|
| 1.29 | Auditing | Measuring and interpreting product defect information |
| 1.30 | Technology Information Systems | RFID technology information and internal reports |
| 2.41 | Statistics | Improve cost function estimate using multiple regression with cost inflation and lagged cost driver |
| 3.43 | Economics Marketing | Create demand and cost functions and perform CVP analysis with nonlinear revenue |
| 4.38 | Finance | Currency exchange rate uncertainty and special order decision |
| 5.35 | Financial Accounting Auditing | Research financial accounting rules; audit overhead allocation policy |
| 6.39 | Production Management | Batch versus continuous processing, usefulness of process costing |
| 7.38 | Corporate Social Responsibility | Corporate responsibilities and use of ABC for environmental accounting reports; U.S. and Japanese governmental guidelines |
| 8.35 | Governmental Accounting | Types and uses of internal service funds in state and local governments |
| 9.34 | Economics Governmental Regulation | Beef by-products in animal feed, by-product economics, regulator responsibilities |
| 10.30 | Financial Accounting Attestation | Prospective financial statements, types of attestation, assumptions |
| 11.35 | Auditing | Auditor evaluation of variances for error and fraud; accounting principles for variances |
| 12.36 | Finance | Weighted average cost of capital, estimation problems |
| 13.35 | Information Technology | Inventory management system adopted by **Mopar**, data accuracy, internal controls, estimating benefits |
| 14.26 | Financial Accounting Auditing | Channel stuffing, uncertainties, error versus fraud, fraud incentives and cost |
| 15.31 | Business Law | Executive compensation for public companies, SEC disclosures |
| 15.32 | Finance | Weighted average cost of capital for **Amazon.com** |
| 16.35 | Management Marketing | SWOT analysis for **Wal-Mart** |